THE OXFORD HANDBOOK OF
THOMAS MORE'S *UTOPIA*

THE OXFORD HANDBOOK OF

THOMAS

MORE'S *UTOPIA*

Edited by
CATHY SHRANK
and
PHIL WITHINGTON

OXFORD
UNIVERSITY PRESS

Great Clarendon Street, Oxford, OX2 6DP,
United Kingdom

Oxford University Press is a department of the University of Oxford.
It furthers the University's objective of excellence in research, scholarship,
and education by publishing worldwide. Oxford is a registered trade mark of
Oxford University Press in the UK and in certain other countries

© The several contributors 2024

The moral rights of the authors have been asserted

First Edition published in 2024

All rights reserved. No part of this publication may be reproduced, stored in
a retrieval system, or transmitted, in any form or by any means, without the
prior permission in writing of Oxford University Press, or as expressly permitted
by law, by licence or under terms agreed with the appropriate reprographics
rights organization. Enquiries concerning reproduction outside the scope of the
above should be sent to the Rights Department, Oxford University Press, at the
address above

You must not circulate this work in any other form
and you must impose this same condition on any acquirer

Published in the United States of America by Oxford University Press
198 Madison Avenue, New York, NY 10016, United States of America

British Library Cataloguing in Publication Data
Data available

Library of Congress Control Number: 2023937473

ISBN 978–0–19–888101–8

DOI: 10.1093/oxfordhb/9780198881018.001.0001

Printed and bound by
CPI Group (UK) Ltd, Croydon, CR0 4YY

Links to third party websites are provided by Oxford in good faith and
for information only. Oxford disclaims any responsibility for the materials
contained in any third party website referenced in this work.

To Ellen and Meg

Acknowledgements

This book has accrued many debts along the way. We are grateful to the Faculty of Arts and Humanities, University of Sheffield for 'seedcorn' funding, and to the British Academy and Leverhulme Trust for a small grant which funded two workshops on translating and appropriating *Utopia*: these papers became the core of the present handbook. In addition to the speakers at those events, we would like to extend particular thanks to Gregory Claeys, Derek Offord, Richard Steadman-Jones, and Bob Stern for their input at those workshops. We are also very grateful to Terence Cave and Quentin Skinner for encouraging the project from the outset, and to Jacqueline Baker from Oxford University Press for her consistent support. Gavin Schwartz-Leeper did invaluable bibliographical work in the early stages, tracking down editions and translations from 1516 to the mid-twentieth century. We would also like to thank Oxford University Press' anonymous readers, who helped shaped the project at the proposal stage, as well as the libraries and collections which supplied images and the copyright holders who have allowed us to use them: the Bayerische Staatsbibliothek München; The British Library; The Bodleian Libraries, Oxford; Collection Van Abbemuseum, Findhoven; Huntington Library, San Marino; King Baudouin Foundation; Michel Wuyts & Bart Huysmans; Staatliche Bibliothek Regensburg; and Stephen Walter. Thanks are also due to Alfred Hiatt and Gabriela Schmidt who helped us secure a number of these images and permission to use them, and to all the librarians worldwide who helped colleagues keep working during the various lockdowns in 2019–20. The production team did a heroic job on a complex project: particular thanks our due to our eagle-eyed copy-editor. Finally, we are extremely grateful to all our authors without whom—quite obviously—the book would not exist at all.

Contents

List of Figures   xiii
List of Tables   xv
Abbreviations and Conventions   xvii
List of Contributors   xix

Introduction to Thomas More's *Utopia*   1
PHIL WITHINGTON AND CATHY SHRANK

PART ONE: ORIGINS AND CONTEXTS

1. More and the Republics of Plato   19
   ANGELA HOBBS

2. Hythloday's Books: *Utopia*, Humanism, and the Republic of Letters   36
   CARLA SUTHREN

3. *Nec minus salutaris quam festivus*: Wit, Style, and the Body in More's *Utopia*   53
   ANDREW ZURCHER

4. The Religions of the Utopians: Sin and Salvation in Thomas More's *Utopia*   72
   DAVID HARRIS SACKS

5. 'Nothing is private anywhere': *Utopia* in the Context of More's Thought   89
   JOANNE PAUL

6. *Utopia* and Travel Writing   105
   ANDREW HADFIELD

7. *Utopia*'s Empire: Thomas More's Text and the Early British Atlantic World, *c.*1510–1625   120
   JESSICA S. HOWER

8. The Urban Context for *Utopia*: The English Urban System,
   1450–1516   135
   Eliza Hartrich

9. *Utopia* Unbound: The Fabrication of the First Latin Editions,
   1516–1519   149
   Andrew W. Taylor

PART TWO: TRANSLATIONS AND EDITIONS, 1524–1799

10. *Ad fontes et ad futurum*: A Survey of Latin *Utopias*   175
    Lucy Nicholas

11. From Prototype to Genre: Translations and Imitations of *Utopia*
    in Early Modern Germany (1524–1753)   195
    Gabriela Schmidt

12. Receiving More: *Utopia* in Spain and New Spain   215
    Darcy Kern

13. *Utopia* in Sixteenth-Century Italy   231
    Cathy Shrank

14. Inventing *Utopia*: The Case of Early Modern France   248
    Richard Scholar

15. *Utopia* in Tudor London: Ralph Robinson's Translations and
    Their Civic, Personal, and Political Contexts   265
    Jennifer Bishop

16. Dialogue, Debate, and Orality in Ralph Robinson's *Utopias*   278
    Dermot Cavanagh

17. 'Het onbekent en wonderlijk Eyland': Frans van Hoogstraten's
    Translation of *Utopia* (1677)   295
    Wiep van Bunge

18. *Utopia* and Gilbert Burnet in 1684   307
    Phil Withington

19. From Humanism to Enlightenment: Nicolas Gueudeville and His
    Translation of Thomas More's *Utopia* 324
    FLORIS VERHAART

20. Thomas Rousseau, Translator of an Enlightened *Utopia* 341
    KATHERINE ASTBURY

PART THREE: TRANSLATIONS AND EDITIONS AFTER 1800

21. False Friends (and Their Uses): Thomas More's *Utopia* Among
    the Victorians 361
    MARCUS WAITHE

22. The Cultural Politics of Translation: Translating Thomas More's
    Utopia into German in the Late Nineteenth Century 378
    JANET STEWART

23. Not Just a Light-Hearted Joke: Russian Moreana from the Age of
    Karamzin to the Rise of Social Democracy and Lenin's 'Stele of
    Freedom' 394
    FRANCES NETHERCOTT

24. *Utopia* in East Central Europe: The Hungarian Scene 411
    ZSOLT CZIGÁNYIK

25. A Catalan in Search of Humanists: Josep Pin i Soler's Translation
    of More's *Utopia* (1912) 428
    P. LOUISE JOHNSON

26. The Historical Fallacy: *Utopia* and the Problem of Fiction in
    Weimar Germany 444
    CAT MOIR

27. Japanese Translations of More's *Utopia* 461
    TERUHITO SAKO

28. The Multiple Lives of *Utopia* in Modern China 476
    TEHYUN MA

29. *Utopia* and Utopian Writing in Arabic 492
    PETER HILL

PART FOUR: BEYOND *UTOPIA*

30. Early Modern Utopian Fiction: *Utopia* and *The Isle of Pines*   509
    CHLOË HOUSTON

31. Of Survival and Living Together: The Eighteenth-Century Utopian Novel   522
    NICOLE POHL

32. Conversation, Formation, and Forms of Utopia in Fin-de-Siècle Socialist Journals   537
    INGRID HANSON

33. *Utopia*, the Imperial Settler Utopia, and Imperial Settler Science Fiction   553
    REBECCA WEAVER-HIGHTOWER AND MUSAB BAJABER

34. Away from the Ancestral Home: Utopia and Philosophy in Bloch and Beyond   567
    JOHAN SIEBERS

35. Human Rights and/in Utopia?   579
    MIGUEL ANGEL RAMIRO AVILÉS

36. Utopia and Moral Economy   596
    MARTIN LUTZ

37. Utopia and Architecture   614
    DIANE MORGAN

38. Mapping Utopia   634
    ALFRED HIATT

39. Contemporary Utopianism: An Island Renaissance   652
    RHYS WILLIAMS

Appendix: Outline of More's Utopia   663
Bibliography   669
Index   757

Figures

0.1. Portrait of 'Tomas Mor', in Thomas More, *Utopiia*, trans. Aleksandr G. Genkel' (Kharkov: Proletariat Press, 1923), Historical Library, Moscow. xxiv

1.1. Utopian alphabet and tetrastichon, in Thomas More, *De optimo reip. Statu, deque nova insula utopia* (Basel: Johann Froben, November-December 1518), The Bodleian Libraries, University of Oxford, Wood 639, p. 13. 34

5.1. Ambrosius Holbein, map of *Utopia*, in Thomas More, *De optimo reip. Statu, deque nova insula utopia* (Basel: Johann Froben, November-December 1518), The Bodleian Libraries, University of Oxford, Wood 639, p. 12. 103

9.1. Map of *Utopia*, in Thomas More, *Libellus vere aureus nec minus salutaris quam festivus de optimo rei[publicae] statu deq[ue] nova insula Utopia* (Louvain: Thierry Martens, 1516), The Bodleian Libraries, University of Oxford, Arch. B.e.44, sig. A1v. 153

9.2. Title page, Thomas More, *De optimo reip. Statu, deque nova insula utopia* (Basel: Johann Froben, November-December 1518), The Bodleian Libraries, University of Oxford, Wood 639. 164

9.3. Opening page of More's letter to Giles, including the 'Triton Struggle' border by Hans Holbein the Younger, in Thomas More, *De optimo reip. Statu, deque nova insula utopia* (Basel: Johann Froben, November-December 1518), 17. The Bodleian Libraries, University of Oxford. 166

11.1. Utopian alphabet and poem, in Thomas More, *Von der wunderbarlichen Innsel Utopia genant das ander Buch*, trans. Claudius Cantiuncula [Claude Chasonette] (Basel: Johann Bebel, 1524), sig. A2r. Bayerische Staatsbibliothek München, 4 Pol.g. 162 d, urn:nbn:de:bvb:12-bsb10166830-0. 203

11.2. Map of Utopia, in Thomas More, *De optimo Reipublicae Statu, Libellus vere aureus: Ordentliche vnd Außführliche Beschreibung Der vberaus herrlichen und gantz wunderbarlichen / doch wenigen bißhero bekandten Insel UTOPIA*, trans. Gregor Wintermonat (Leipzig: Henning Grosse, 1612), Bayerische Staatsbibliothek München, Pol.g. 670 f. 207

11.3. Title page, Thomas More, *De optimo Reipublicae Statu, Libellus vere aureus. Ordentliche vnd Außführliche Beschreibung Der vberaus*

	herrlichen und gantz wunderbarlichen / doch wenigen bißhero bekandten Insel Utopia, trans. Gregor Wintermonat (Leipzig: Henning Grosse, 1612), Bayerische Staatsbibliothek München, Pol.g. 670 f, urn:nbn:de:bvb:12-bsb10770043-4.	208
11.4.	Title page, Joseph Hall (attrib. Alberico Gentili), *Utopiae Pars II: Mundus alter & idem*, trans. Gregor Wintermonat (Leipzig: Henning Grosse, 1613), Staatliche Bibliothek Regensburg; 999/Philos.1049, urn:nbn:de:bvb:12-bsb11109903-0.	209
16.1.	Thomas More, *A frutefull, pleasaunt and wittie worke, of the beste state of a publique weale, and of the new yle, called Utopia*, trans. Ralph Robinson (London: [Richard Tottel] for Abraham Veale, 1556), The Huntington Library, San Marino, California, call number 12572, sigs L4v-L5r.	281
21.1.	Thomas More, *Utopia*, trans. Ralph Robinson, ed. F. S. Ellis (Hammersmith: Kelmscott Press, 1893), The Bodleian Libraries, University of Oxford, Kelmscott Press e.12, p. 44.	367
37.1.	Ambrosius Holbein, woodcut of the garden scene, in Thomas More, *De optimo reip. Statu, deque nova insula utopia* (Basel: Johann Froben, November-December 1518), The Bodleian Libraries, University of Oxford, Wood 639, p. 25.	628
38.1.	Abraham Ortelius, 'Utopiae typus' (Antwerp, 1596), Coll. Charles Vreeken Fund, King Baudouin Foundation, entrusted to the Plantin-Moretus Museum, Antwerp, © Michel Wuyts & Bart Huysmans.	639
38.2.	Qiu Zhijie, 'Map of Utopia' (2012). Collection Van Abbemuseum, Eindhoven, The Netherlands. Photo: Peter Cox.	644
38.3.	Stephen Walter, 'Nova Utopia' (2013), British Library, Maps CC 6.a.91, © Stephen Walter, published by TAG Fine Arts.	646
38.4.	Detail from Stephen Walter, 'Nova Utopia' (2013), British Library, Maps CC 6.a.91, © Stephen Walter, published by TAG Fine Arts.	647

Tables

18.1.	Comparative Uses of 'Slave' and Synonyms in Early English Translations of *Utopia*	319
27.1.	Books and Translations Printed in Meiji Japan	463
27.2.	Genres of Translations Printed in Meiji Japan	464
27.3.	Names of Public Bathhouses in Japan (2016) by Popularity	473

Abbreviations and Conventions

AN	Archives nationales (de France)
BC	Biblioteca de Catalunya
BL	British Library
BnF	Bibliothèque nationale, France
CP	Cecil Papers, Hatfield House
CPR	*Calendar of Patent Rolls*
CSPD	*Calendar of State Papers, Domestic*
CSPF	*Calendar of State Papers, Foreign*
CWE	*The Collected Works of Erasmus*
CWM	*The Complete Works of St Thomas More*
EEBO-TCP	Early English Books Online, Text Creation Partnership
HP	Hartlib Papers
KJV	Bible, King James Version
LP	*Letters and Papers, Foreign and Domestic*, ed. Brewer et al.
MS	Manuscript
n.d.	no date given
n.p.	no place of publication given
n.pub.	no publisher given
ns	new series
OED	*Oxford English Dictionary*
os	original series
RB	Real Biblioteca
SP	State Papers
TNA	The National Archives, Kew, UK

Throughout the volume, 'Morus' is used to distinguish More-the-speaker within *Utopia* from More-the-author.

Utopia (italicized) refers to More's book; Utopia (capitalized, but not italicized) refers to the island described in that work; utopia (no capital or italics) refers to the concept/ a work written in the genre of utopian fiction. Similarly, Utopian (capitalized) refers to the inhabitants of More's island and/or to its features and customs; utopian (without a capital) is the adjective deriving from the genre or concept. (Note, quotations follow the form used in the work cited and do not necessarily adhere to this system.)

Arabic, Classical Greek, Chinese, and Japanese have been transliterated except where necessary to retain the original.

'Early modern' refers to the period *c.*1500–1700.

When citing from texts before 1700, the original punctuation and spelling have been retained, although i/j and u/v are standardized, and brevigraphs (e.g. the y-thorn, tilde) have been silently expanded.

Books before the later seventeenth century are rarely paginated; the same applies to manuscripts (i.e. handwritten documents). References to such works are therefore either to 'folio' or 'signature'. Folio numbers refer to the leaf on which the cited passage appears (r = recto; v = verso), i.e. 70r indicates the recto of leaf 70; 70v indicates the verso (reverse) of the same leaf. Signatures (an alphabetic character + number) indicate which leaf of a quire (or gathering) a cited passage appears on, i.e. A4r indicates the recto of the fourth leaf of quire A; B1v indicates the verso of the first leaf of quire B.

As editors, we did not prescribe which edition or translation of *Utopia* our contributors used: in a volume about its multiple afterlives, to prioritize one version in this way risked inscribing it as the 'correct' text. In the event, this flexibility was fortuitous, since our contributors were writing or revising their chapters whilst libraries across the globe were closed due to COVID-19. They therefore needed to work with what was to hand, or available online. The multiplicity of copies cited thus retains the traces of the particular historical context in which this work was produced.

Contributors

Katherine Astbury is Professor of French Studies at the University of Warwick. Her works include *Narrative Responses to the Trauma of the French Revolution* (Oxford University Press, 2012) and *Napoleon's One Hundred Days and the Politics of Legitimacy* (Palgrave, 2018), co-edited with Mark Philp.

Musab Bajaber is Assistant Professor in English Literature, King Saud University and works on utopian science fiction and fantasy.

Jennifer Bishop works at the Cambridge Group for the History of Population and Social Structure. She has published on the English translation of *Utopia*, and on other aspects of civic culture and political discourse in sixteenth-century England. Her current research focuses on record-keeping practices in early modern London.

Dermot Cavanagh is Senior Lecturer in English Literature at the University of Edinburgh. He has published widely on early modern political drama and ideas of commonwealth.

Zsolt Czigányik is Associate Professor in the Department of English Studies at Eötvös Loránd University (ELTE), Hungary and a Gerda Henkel Scholar at the Central European University's Democracy Institute. He has published extensively on utopian topics in both Hungarian and English. His most recent book is *Utopia Between East and West in Hungarian Literature* (Palgrave, 2023).

Andrew Hadfield FBA is Professor of English at the University of Sussex. Major works include *Literature and Class* (Manchester University Press, 2021), *Lying in Early Modern English Culture* (Oxford University Press, 2017), *Edmund Spenser: A Life* (Oxford University Press, 2012), and *The Oxford Handbook of English Prose* (Oxford University Press, 2016).

Ingrid Hanson is Lecturer in English Literature at the University of Manchester. She is the author of *William Morris and the Uses of Violence, 1856–1890* (Anthem Press, 2013) and co-editor of *Poetry, Politics, and Pictures: Culture and Identity, 1840–1914* (Peter Lang, 2013).

Eliza Hartrich is Lecturer in Late Medieval History at the University of York. Her first monograph *Politics and the Urban Sector in Fifteenth-Century England, 1413–1471* was published by Oxford University Press in 2019.

Alfred Hiatt is Professor of Medieval Studies at Queen Mary University of London. Major publications include *Dislocations: Maps, Classical Tradition, and Spatial Play in the European Middle Ages* (Pontifical Institute of Mediaeval Studies, 2020), *Terra Incognita: Mapping the Antipodes before 1600* (British Library, 2008), and *The Making of Medieval Forgeries* (British Library, 2004).

Peter Hill is Assistant Professor of History at Northumbria University and specializes in the history of the Arab world in the long nineteenth century. His publications include *Utopia and Civilisation in the Arab Nahda* (Cambridge University Press, 2020) and articles on translation and political thought in the Middle East.

Angela Hobbs is Professor of the Public Understanding of Philosophy at the University of Sheffield. She has published widely on ancient Greek philosophy, ethics (ancient and modern), and ideas of heroism. She contributes regularly to radio and TV programmes and other media. Recent publications include *Plato's Republic* (Michael Joseph, 2019).

Chloë Houston is Associate Professor in English Literature at the University of Reading. She has published widely on the portrayal of the Persian Empire in Renaissance drama and on sixteenth- and seventeenth-century utopias, including the monographs *The Renaissance Utopia* (Ashgate, 2013) and *Persia in Early Modern English Drama, 1530-1699* (Palgrave Macmillan, 2023), and the edited collection *New Worlds Reflected* (Ashgate, 2010).

Jessica S. Hower is Associate Professor of History at Southwestern University, Texas. Her monograph *Tudor Empire: The Making of Early Modern Britain and the British Atlantic World, 1485–1603* was published by Palgrave Macmillan in 2020.

P. Louise Johnson is Director of Catalan Studies at the University of Sheffield and has published on major twentieth-century Catalan writers including Llorenç Villalonga, Manuel de Pedrolo, and Maria Aurèlia Capmany. Her translation of Villalonga's dystopian *Andrea Víctrix* was published by Fum D'Estampa in 2021.

Darcy Kern is Associate Professor of History at Southern Connecticut State University. She has published on topics including Jean Gerson's conciliarism in late medieval Spain, fifteenth-century Castilian histories, and Spanish narratives of Mary I.

Martin Lutz is a Postdoctoral Researcher and Lecturer in Social and Economic History at Humboldt University of Berlin. His research focuses on the influence of religion in modern economic history. Publications include a monograph on the entrepreneur Carl von Siemens (C. H. Beck, 2013; English translation by Bill Chilcot, 2016).

Tehyun Ma is Lecturer in International History at the University of Sheffield. Her research focuses on the history of state- and nation-building in twentieth-century China and Taiwan. She has published on topics including the reconstruction of China after the Second World War II, and the Chinese empire from the Manchus to Mao.

Cat Moir is an independent scholar who was previously Senior Lecturer in the Faculty of Arts and Social Sciences, University of Sydney. She is the author of *Ernst Bloch's Speculative Materialism: Ontology, Epistemology, Politics* (Brill, 2020).

Diane Morgan is Lecturer in Cultural Studies at the University of Leeds. She has published widely on Enlightenment culture, and on nineteenth-century French utopian socialism. Publications include *Kant for Architects* (Routledge, 2018) and the co-edited collection *Cosmopolitics and the Emergence of Future* (Palgrave Macmillan, 2007).

Frances Nethercott is Reader in the School of History, University of St Andrews. She works on Russian intellectual and cultural history from the eighteenth to the late twentieth century. Publications include *Writing History in Late Imperial Russia* (Bloomsbury, 2020) and *Russian Legal Culture Before and After Communism* (Routledge, 2007).

Lucy Nicholas is Lecturer in Latin and Greek Language and Culture, The Warburg Institute, London. Publications include the co-edited collection *Roger Ascham and His Sixteenth-Century World* (Brill, 2020), *An Anthology of European Neo-Latin Literature* (Bloomsbury, 2020), and a parallel text edition (in Latin and English) of Ascham's *Defence of the Lord's Supper* (Brill, 2017).

Joanne Paul is Honorary Senior Lecturer in Intellectual History at the University of Sussex. Publications include *The House of Dudley* (Penguin, 2022), *Counsel and Command in Early Modern England* (Cambridge University Press, 2020), and *Thomas More* (Polity, 2016). She is currently working on a biography of Thomas More for Penguin and a new edition of *Utopia* for Oxford World Classics.

Nicole Pohl is Professor in Early Modern Literature and Critical Theory at Oxford Brookes University. She has published widely on seventeenth- and eighteenth-century women's utopian writings and on epistolarity, including *Women, Space, and Utopia, 1600–1800* (Ashgate, 2006) and an edition of *The Letters of Sarah Scott* (Pickering & Chatto, 2013). She is editor of the journal *Utopian Studies*.

Miguel Angel Ramiro Avilés is Associate Professor (Profesor Titular) in the School of Law at the University of Alcalá, Madrid. His publications include *Utopía y Derecho* (Marcial Pons, 2002), and edited collections *Anatomía de la utopía* (Dykinson, 2008), *Los derechos humanos: La utopía de los excluidos* (Dykinson, 2010), and *Utopian Moments* (Bloomsbury, 2012).

David Harris Sacks is Richard F. Scholz Professor of History and Humanities, Emeritus at Reed College, Oregon. He has published widely on topics including the early English Atlantic, urban and national citizenship, travel writing, and religion, and edited Ralph Robinson's translation of *Utopia* (St Martin's Press, 1999).

Teruhito Sako is Professor in the Department of Sociology at Tokyo Metropolitan University. His publication include *Japanese Family and Society* (Routledge, 2007), and articles, in Japanese and English, on topics such as Confucianism and sociology, and the language of citizenship and civil society.

Gabriela Schmidt is Senior Lecturer in the Department of British and American Studies at the University of Munich (LMU). Her publications include *Thomas More und die Sprachenfrage* (Universitätsverlag Winter, 2009) and the edited collection *Elizabethan Translation and Literary Culture* (De Gruyter, 2013). She serves on the editorial board of *Moreana*.

Richard Scholar is Professor of French at Durham University. His major publications include *Émigrés: French Words that Turned English* (Princeton University Press, 2020), *Montaigne and the Art of Free-Thinking* (Peter Lang, 2010), and *The* Je-Ne-Sais-Quoi *in Early Modern Europe* (Oxford University Press, 2005).

Cathy Shrank is Professor of Tudor and Renaissance Literature, University of Sheffield. Publications include *Writing the Nation in Reformation England* (Oxford University Press, 2004), the co-edited collection *The Oxford Handbook of Tudor Literature* (Oxford University Press, 2009), and—with Raphael Lyne—an edition of *Shakespeare's Poems* (Routledge, 2017).

Johan Siebers is Director of the Ernst Bloch Centre for German Thought at the School of Advanced Study, University of London, and Professor of Philosophy of Language and Communication at Middlesex University. He has published widely on Bloch, and on the philosophical, theoretical, and practical dimensions of human communication.

Janet Stewart is Professor of Visual Culture and German and Executive Dean (Arts and Humanities) at Durham University. Key publications include *Fashioning Vienna: Adolf Loos's Cultural Criticism* (Routledge, 2000) and *Public Speaking in the City: Debating and Shaping the Urban Experience* (Palgrave Macmillan, 2009).

Carla Suthren is a Stipendiary Lecturer in English at St Catherine's College, Oxford. She works on classical reception and translation (especially of Greek) and is working on her first monograph, on Shakespeare and the Renaissance reception of Euripides.

Andrew W. Taylor is Senior Lecturer, Fellow, and Director of Studies in English at Churchill College, Cambridge. He has published widely on humanism, neo-Latin, and the transmission of Greek and Latin learning in early modern Europe.

Wiep van Bunge is Professor of the History of Philosophy at Erasmus University, Rotterdam. His publications include *Spinoza Past and Present* (Brill, 2012) and *From Bayle to the Batavian Revolution* (Brill, 2019). He was also part of the team editing the correspondence of Pierre Bayle (Voltaire Foundation, 1999–2017).

Floris Verhaart is a Postdoctoral Fellow at the University of Warwick. His publications include *Classical Learning in Britain, France, and the Dutch Republic, 1690–1750* (Oxford University Press, 2020) and the co-edited anthology *Protestant Politics beyond Calvin: Reformed Theologians on War in the Sixteenth and Seventeenth Centuries* (Routledge, 2022).

Marcus Waithe is Professor of Literature and the Applied Arts at the University of Cambridge, and a Fellow of Magdalene College. His books include *The Work of Words* (2023), *Words Made Stone* (co-written with Lida Cardozo Kindersley) (2022), *Thinking through Style* (co-edited with Michael Hurley) (2018), *The Labour of Literature in Britain and France, 1830-1910* (co-edited with Claire White) (2018), and *William Morris's Utopia of Strangers* (2016).

Rebecca Weaver-Hightower is Professor and Chair of the Department of English at Virginia Tech. Her publications include *Frontier Fictions* (Palgrave Macmillan, 2018) and *Empire Islands* (University of Minnesota Press, 2007), and the co-edited collections *Cinematic Settlers* (Routledge, 2020), *Archiving Settler Colonialism* (Routledge, 2019), and *Postcolonial Film* (Routledge, 2014).

Rhys Williams is Lecturer in Energy and Environmental Humanities at the University of Glasgow. He has published on topics including solarpunk, New Food, science fiction, utopia, and radical politics in journals including *South Atlantic Quarterly* and *Science Fiction Studies*.

Phil Withington is Professor of Social and Cultural History at the University of Sheffield. Publications include *The Politics of Commonwealth* (Cambridge University Press, 2005), *Society in Early Modern England* (Polity, 2010), and the co-edited collection *Cultures of Intoxication* (*Past & Present*, supplement 9, 2014).

Andrew Zurcher is Senior Lecturer and Fellow of Queens' College, Cambridge. His publications include *Edmund Spenser, The Faerie Queene: A Reading Guide* (Edinburgh University Press, 2011), *Shakespeare and Law* (Methuen, 2010), and *Edmund Spenser: Selected Letters and Other Papers* (Oxford University Press, 2009).

FIG. 0.1. Portrait of 'Tomas Mor', in Thomas More, *Utopiia*, trans. Aleksandr G. Genkel' (Kharkov: Proletariat Press, 1923), Historical Library, Moscow.

INTRODUCTION TO THOMAS MORE'S *UTOPIA*

PHIL WITHINGTON AND CATHY SHRANK

Thomas More and His *Utopia*

Thomas More was born on 6 February 1478 on Milk Street, Cheapside in London, the son of a successful barrister, John More, and Agnes Graunger, daughter of a London citizen and tallow chandler. He was educated in turn at London's leading grammar school, St Anthony's; the household of the cleric John Morton (see below); Canterbury College, Oxford; New Inn, London, where he began to learn law; and Lincoln's Inn, into which he was admitted in February 1496.[1] More became part of an influential network of humanists based in London, becoming friends with the Dutchman Desiderius Erasmus in 1499: a friendship that was crucial to the development of *Utopia* (see chapter by Taylor). More also developed strong links with the English Carthusians, an enclosed religious order which emphasized contemplation and asceticism. However, in 1505 he married Jane Colt, from a landed family in Royden in Essex, and set up household in the parish of St Stephen Walbrook, a year after sitting in the House of Commons for the first time. Jane died in 1511 and a month later More married Alice, widow of the merchant John Middleton. While maintaining an energetic literary life—for example, translating Lucian from Greek with Erasmus (see chapters by Suthren and Zurcher)—and developing his interest in learned piety with the Carthusians, More also forged a busy professional and civic career. In 1509 he became a citizen of the Mercers' Company and magistrate for Middlesex; a year later he was made one of the two undersheriffs of London; he was elected to parliament again in 1512, became Reader at Lincoln's Inn in 1514, and was also elected to the Doctors' Commons, the governing body of civil lawyers (as opposed to common lawyers) in England. In the meantime, his friendship with Erasmus introduced him to a European

---

[1] For short, accessible introductions to More's life see Baker House 2008; Baker-Smith 2014b.

network of like-minded humanists, enabling More to exchange letters with men like Jerome Busleyden (who contributed paratexts to *Utopia*) about shared scholarly and antiquarian interests, not least collecting Roman coins (Weil Baker 2003).

This balancing of business, learning, piety, and friendship continued throughout the 1510s. More's burgeoning reputation as a legal expert in international trade caught the attention of the royal court and in 1515 he was commissioned to join Cuthbert Tunstall to negotiate a commercial treaty with the Flemish in Bruges. It was on this trip and just after that he wrote Book Two and then Book One of *Utopia*, drafting most of the second book in the summer of 1515 on that sojourn in the Low Countries and composing most of Book One on his return to London later that year.[2] The work, with additional paratexts, was first published in Louvain, back in the Low Countries, in 1516 (Hexter 1952: 21–30; Adams and Logan in More 2016: xvi–xvii).

More formally entered the service of Henry VIII in 1518 under the patronage of Thomas Wolsey, Henry's chief minister. Thereafter, however, the tenor and purpose of his literary and political activities changed, More becoming a polemicist for his monarch against the confessional writings of Martin Luther; a fixer for the Crown in urban, parliamentary, and international politics; and an opponent—and prosecutor—of religious heretics. When Wolsey fell in 1529 (having failed to secure Henry's divorce from his first wife Catherine of Aragon), More took over Wolsey's role as Lord Chancellor; but while he maintained his patron's resolute defence of orthodox religion, he was unable to develop a safe or at least unthreatening position on the question of the king's divorce and, by extension, the powers and autonomy of the Church in relation to the Crown. More was imprisoned in 1534 for refusing to swear to the Act of Succession and put on trial in July 1535 for allegedly refuting Henry VIII's claim to be Supreme Head of the Church of England. The author of *Utopia* was beheaded on 6 July 1535 and canonized 400 years later by Pope Pius XI.

Utopia was first published, then, at an important juncture in both More's life and the religious and political history of Europe. This Oxford Handbook is about More's *Utopia*, but by way of introduction it is helpful to note a few points of comparison with Niccolò Machiavelli's *Il Principe* (*The Prince*), which Machiavelli began drafting in 1513 (two years before More's *Utopia*) just outside his home city of Florence in northern Italy, about 800 miles south of Bruges. Completed by August 1516, *The Prince* circulated extensively in manuscript before it was first published in Rome in 1532 (Black 2013: 84–96; Skinner and Price 2019: xi).

A Tale of Two Texts

Finished the same year, *Utopia* and *The Prince* are two of the most famous and influential books, if not *the* most famous and influential books, of that complicated historical

---

[2] For an overview of the contents of More's *Utopia*, see Appendix.

process now known as the European Renaissance. The similarities are obvious enough. Both texts quickly became celebrated and notorious across much of Europe and were firmly established in the public imaginary by 1700. Both books also transcended the time and place of their initial production and reception, becoming significant works of fictional and political literature in the eighteenth, nineteenth, and twentieth centuries, and on a global as well as European scale. And both *Utopia* and *The Prince* quite quickly morphed into terminologies and genres that were, and remain, recognizable to people who have never encountered the texts themselves. The labels 'Machiavel' and 'Machiavellian', for example, were prominent in England as shorthand for the tenets and values associated with *The Prince* long before the work was translated into English in 1640; and it remains a recognizable and powerful vocabulary today (Raab 1965: 30–101). From the sixteenth century, the language of 'utopia' and 'utopian' began to be affixed to an enormous range of activities and practices—from ways of thinking, to forms of writing, to modes of politics, to ideas for living—that invoke More's text even if, in substance, they carry little resemblance to it (see, for example, chapters by Schmidt, Houston, and Sako in this volume).

If there are similarities between *Utopia* and *The Prince* going forward from 1515 then so, too, do they resemble each other in terms of their relationship to the past. This is because both More and Machiavelli engaged intensely with 'ancient' culture—with the Romans and, especially in the case of More, the Greeks—to contribute to and inform the culture of their respective presents and futures (see chapters by Hobbs, Suthren, and Zurcher in this volume). This dialectic between antiquity and the 'early modern' contemporary was one of the defining features of Renaissance humanism; and in the case of both *The Prince* and *Utopia* it resulted in texts that did not simply repeat or imitate classical wisdom—about politics, for instance, or the nature of the good life—so much as challenge, emulate, critique, and supersede received wisdom (Adams and Logan in More 2016: xviii–xxix; Skinner and Price 2019: xix–xxvi; Black 2013: xxiii–xxv). But in neither case was this learning for learning's sake: rather, both writers used their texts to address immediate challenges and issues. For Machiavelli, an exile of Florence after more than a decade working at the centre of its government, these lay in the treacherous politics of the Italian city state and how to effectively maintain and use political power (Black 2013: 73–126). For More, a London lawyer and citizen recently seconded as a diplomat for the English Crown, they were to be found in the social and economic problems perceived to be facing England and the worrying dissonance between political philosophy and practice (Wrightson 2000: 3–10; Hexter 1952: 99–155; Bradshaw 1981: 23–27). The results in both cases were texts at once deeply informed by Graeco-Roman learning, shrewdly observant of contemporary customs and practices, and perennially fascinating—and influential—in their methods, style, and content.

For all their similarities, there are equally obvious differences between these two epitomes of Renaissance literature. One is the nature of their generic qualities and the kinds of thinking with which they have subsequently been associated. *The Prince* marked an important development in the genre of political advice literature and helped define 'the political' as a sphere of activity distinct from the social (and some might say ethical) worlds, coming to signify a 'reason of state' mentality in which, most famously, ends justify means. *Utopia*, in contrast, merged the literary and the political to create a new genre of social imagining and dialogue. Rather than learning to exploit the realities of current circumstances and peccadillos of human nature—as Machiavelli recommended—More established the possibility of envisaging and discussing alternative or ideal worlds and behaviours. This utopian discourse might conjure aspirations for the future, serve as contemporary critique, or provide timeless distraction: either way, it was as much the commitment to imagining as the world so imagined that mattered.

A second difference between *The Prince* and *Utopia* is the language in which they were originally written and shared. Machiavelli wrote his treatise in the Tuscan form of Italian, probably to contribute to a Florentine political discussion group and to advertise his know-how to the Medici regime in a bid to return to public office (Skinner and Price 2019: xxviii–ix). It was only printed posthumously, and by a Roman rather than Florentine publisher. More, in contrast, wrote in Latin, the lingua franca of the European intelligentsia, for a network of humanist 'friends' and contacts spread across the cities of north-western Europe. The locations and frequently civic duties of these correspondents—as inhabitants, citizens, or natives of cities from London to Paris, Aalst to Nuremberg—are carefully recorded in the work's parerga, so that the work preserves the sense of a transnational republic of letters: these are citizens of somewhere, even as they discuss and delight in a concept of 'nowhere' (*ou-topia*).

Besides contributing letters and other paratexts to the textual artefact, these humanist networks also ensured that it was published in five different Latin editions in rapid succession (see Taylor in this volume). Or to put that slightly differently: Machiavelli wrote *The Prince* in the Italian vernacular after decades of intense political conflict within Florence: conflict, it should be noted, that included the militant evangelism inspired by Girolamo Savonarola (executed in 1498 for his civic disturbances and challenges to ecclesiastical authority). More, in contrast, wrote *Utopia* as part of a transnational elite in what we can see retrospectively to be the relative quiet before the confessional storm of the European Reformation. This difference in part reflects how Renaissance vernacularization was more advanced in Italy, with Italian acknowledged by the 1510s to be equivalent to Latin as a language of complex communication and eloquence in a way that the languages of north-western Europe in general, and English in particular, were not. But it also highlights the transformations that *Utopia* was to go through in the decades after 1518, when it proliferated from being the product of a cosmopolitan and broadly consensual culture of Christian humanism into numerous vernacular—national—editions and versions. These vernacular editions were translated in circumstances often radically different from those experienced by More in 1515–16 and for audiences much more localized, socially diverse, and ideologically variegated and conflicted than *Utopia*'s original and intended readership. And this only became more so over time.

The similarities and differences between More's *Utopia* and Machiavelli's *The Prince*—and, indeed, between utopianism and Machiavellianism—help to indicate the kind of text this Handbook is about and the range of factors and issues it raises. *Utopia* is one of the major works of the European Renaissance that drew cleverly and knowingly on the Graeco-Roman past to contribute to an emergent sense of European modernity. It encouraged readers to look elsewhere—at once geographically, temporally, and imaginatively—in search of the good life and how to live it; and it spawned an adjective for alternative, idealistic, and progressive thinking. But although the attractions of utopianism may seem timeless, the text itself began a remarkable journey almost as soon as it was published. While Latin versions continued to be printed (see Nicholas in this volume), it was increasingly translated or taken into new and different vernaculars and contexts—in Europe, the Americas, the Middle East and Northern Africa, Russia, Asia. This was not a passive process, equating with straightforward reproduction, but rather creative and dynamic. Just as translation from one language to another inevitably impacts on the organization, language, and meanings of a text, so the circumstances and contexts that encouraged translation informed how *Utopia* was read, interpreted, and appropriated. This Handbook is interested in the genesis and legacies of *Utopia*; but it is also interested in the vernacular histories of the book itself.

There are extensive historiographies and critical literatures on these different aspects of *Utopia* and its adjective, albeit with certain aspects more extensively studied than others. Much scholarship has been devoted to the contexts informing the initial authorship of *Utopia* in the 1510s: about the language, style, format, and ideas used by More and his friends; about what the text or may not have 'meant'; and about what these can tell us about the culture and society of the time (Hexter 1952; McCutcheon 1971; Skinner 1978, 2002a; Bradshaw 1981; Baker-Smith 1991). There is likewise plenty of work on both the modern emergence of 'utopianism' as an intellectual enterprise and examples of 'utopian' ways of thinking, doing, and saying things across a range of academic, cultural, and practical fields of expertise (Manuel and Manuel 1979; Schaer et al. 2000). However, less is known about the vernacularization of *Utopia* across Europe during the early modern era (but see Lydia Hunt 1991; Golec 2017); still less about the appropriation of the text globally after 1850. Certainly, the pioneering volume of essays in this area, edited by Terence Cave in 2008, focuses on translations of *Utopia*'s paratexts and limits its purview to 1650. As strikingly, these different approaches to *Utopia* and utopianism rarely, if ever, talk to each other.

There is no single and definitive version of *Utopia*. The first Latin editions, published between 1516 and 1519, were different in various ways (primarily through the addition of paratexts) and vernacular translations thereafter only compounded this textual heterogeneity. As the chapters in Part Two and Three of this volume show, translators elided sections or added their own; they sometimes translated Book Two without Book One; they included the text, or parts of it, in anthologies of writings; they had political agendas that implicitly or explicitly inflected their respective texts; and they inevitably translated with the linguistic tools, literary conventions, and repositories of knowledge available to them. For example, perusing the first English versions of *Utopia*, by Ralph Robinson in 1551 and 1556, alongside Gilbert Burnet's 1684 translation is in many respects like reading different books. This Handbook has therefore been developed to allow readers to consider in one place these different facets of *Utopia* and, as importantly, to provide fresh and original contributions to our understanding of the book's creation, vernacularization, and afterlives. In so doing, it provides an integrated overview of More's text, as well as new contributions to the range of scholarship and debates that *Utopia* continues to attract. Faced with a text of such richness and complexity, this Handbook divides into four parts: on the origins and contexts of Utopia in the 1510s; on histories of its translation into different vernaculars during the early modern and then the modern eras; and on various manifestations of utopianism up to the present day.

Part One: Origins and Contexts

We begin with three chapters on More's indebtedness to classical learning in general and his Hellenism in particular. Angela Hobbs reconstructs More's unusually deep and knowing engagement with Plato and shows that by drawing on a rich Hellenistic tradition of social imaginary, he and his network adeptly crafted a serio-comic dialogue between contrasting elements within Platonic thought. In similar vein, Carla Suthren (Chapter 2) persuasively demonstrates that just as it is Greek books that dominate Utopian interactions with Europe, so More and his humanist collaborators deliberately used their Latin to promulgate the contemporary—European—learning and understanding of ancient Greek. And in Chapter 3 on the epigrammatic style favoured by More, Andrew Zurcher corroborates this Hellenic imperative while also demonstrating how literary form and tropes are fundamental to the meaning and substantive preoccupations of the text. The next two chapters point to More's Christian faith as the key to two of the great puzzles surrounding *Utopia*. David Harris Sacks (Chapter 4) argues that the religious and philosophical beliefs of the Utopians are key to understanding whether Utopia really represents, for More, not simply the 'best' or realizable of commonwealths, but one that Christian readers should *want* to realize. Joanne Paul (Chapter 5) then revisits the longer trajectory of More's thought, and the puzzle of why More the humanist writer of the 1510s should morph into the Catholic polemicist, persecutor, and martyr of the 1520s and 1530s. She suggests that there are continuities in More's thinking, especially his views about true and ultimate commonalty, that help explain his reactions to rapidly changing circumstances.

While the first five chapters of Part One focus primarily on the humanist and confessional contexts of the early *Utopias*, attention then shifts to spatial and institutional matters. Andrew Hadfield (Chapter 6) situates *Utopia* in the burgeoning traditions of cosmographical and travel writing, pointing out that these popular genres not only leant *Utopia* its essential ambiguity—is it fact or fiction?—but also link the work to an accelerating process of European expansion and colonization. The point is nicely developed by Jessica S. Hower (Chapter 7), who observes that just as the publication of *Utopia* coincides with attempts to consolidate Henrician imperium over the Flemish city of Tournai (which was held by the English between 1513 and 1519), so *Utopia* was a regular point of justification for English and Welsh colonists—successful and unsuccessful—over the next century. This complements Eliza Hartrich's focus in Chapter 8 on the 'urban systems' found in both the topography of Utopia (which Hythloday depicts as an island federation of fifty-four cities) and the late medieval network of boroughs and cities linking London to provincial England and Ireland. Hartrich explores how Utopian urbanism in part develops and perfects the urban realities with which More would have been all too familiar. Other urban networks are invoked by Andrew Taylor in Chapter 9 in his fascinating story of the publication of the first Latin editions of *Utopia*: those of urbane humanist elites based in Louvain, Basel, Paris, and Florence. But while the first four editions of the book reflect the collaborative, paratextual, and witty preoccupations of the friends of More and Erasmus, the fifth edition, published amidst the same political tensions that inspired Machiavelli's *The Prince*, bears few traces of the parodic communalism that characterized the genesis of *Utopia*. In many respects, it is the shape of things to come.

PART TWO: TRANSLATIONS AND EDITIONS, 1524–1799

The chapters in Part Two turn to vernacular editions of *Utopia* between its first translation (into German) in 1524 and the second edition of a new French translation in the fateful year of 1789. Building on the approach of Cave's 2008 collection, these chapters reveal at once the variety of forms *Utopia* began to take and the diverse sets of circumstances informing its publication, and to which it contributed, during this era of Reformations and revolutions. In the first instance, however, Lucy Nicholas provides an important reminder that new Latin editions of *Utopia* also flourished over the same period. As a counter-narrative to the cultural distancing and appropriation enabled by vernacularization, she finds that, well into the eighteenth century, Latin copies often retained the ethos of collaborative and 'playful profundity' of the original editions. The same is partially true, argues Gabriela Schmidt (in Chapter 11), of the first German translation, penned by the eminent civil lawyer Claudius Cantiuncula (aka Claude Chansonette) in 1524 in Basel: the location for the authoritative Latin editions of 1518. But although Cantiuncula was connected to More's wider humanist circle and sympathetic to their intellectual agenda, changes to the text were afoot: he only translated Book Two (replacing Book One with a new preface reflecting his legal interest in classical notions of equity) and presented the text as a parting gift to a city government facing unprecedented confessional conflict. Schmidt also notes the German affinity with *Utopia* and utopianism thereafter, with 'what we might call the first anthology of early modern utopias' appearing in German in 1643.

Whilst German is rightly recognized as the first target language for the translation of *Utopia* (and the only vernacular version of *Utopia* to appear in More's lifetime), received wisdom is that *Utopia* comes late to Spain. Darcy Kern (Chapter 12) shows that—despite its tardy appearance in print (thanks to the region's religious politics)—there is actually remarkably early engagement with *Utopia* in Spain and its colonies in the New World: although it was not until 1637 that a Spanish edition appeared in print, Spanish versions were circulating in manuscript by the 1530s and Franciscan colonists were annotating More's book in the Americas a decade earlier. As Kern shows, in the process, the text underwent manifold changes that elided, for example, the imperatives of religious diversity and common weal.

Where early Spanish engagement with *Utopia* left few printed traces, its Italian history, explored by Cathy Shrank (Chapter 13), was very different. The site of the first posthumous translation—and the first vernacular translation of both Books One and Two—to appear in print was by Ortensio Lando in Venice in 1548. Book Two of Lando's version—appropriated by Francesco Sansovino as the final part of an influential anthology of 'ancient and modern' polities—then appeared in print a further six times before 1607. Lando's and Sansovino's versions also reflect divergent traditions for the reception of More's work. Lando, a lapsed monk of heterodox views, shared a love of the absurd and of Erasmian satire with the writer Anton Francesco Doni, who ushered the work into print. Sansovino's volume re-presented Lando's version in a work that revered More as a martyr and defender of religious orthodoxy.

Turning to sixteenth-century France, Richard Scholar (Chapter 14) corroborates translation as an intensive and fundamentally inventive process which, in the case of *Utopia*, contributed to various traditions of French literary culture—from satire to political philosophy—and provided an opportunity for translators like Jean Le Blond to purposefully enhance the French language. As importantly, from the 1550s different and competing versions of the text (in Paris and Lyons) became available to French readers that were based on previous translations, including Sansovino's, rather than Latin originals. The 1550s was also an important moment for English translations of *Utopia*. However, in contrast to France it was the same author producing different editions of the text in the same city. Jennifer Bishop (Chapter 15) contextualizes the 1551 and 1556 translations by Ralph Robinson, linking them to two overlapping readerships within Edwardian and Marian London. Her analysis is complemented by Dermot Cavanagh (Chapter 16), who explores Robinson's use of language and form to convert More's Latin into quintessentially colloquial, conversational, and inclusive English.

The focus of the Handbook then shifts to translations made in the later seventeenth and eighteenth centuries. The remaining four chapters in Part Two demonstrate that *Utopia* appealed to a range of Enlightenment writers and polemicists capable of translating its serio-comic and neo-Latin text into contemporary satire and critique. Wiep van Bunge (Chapter 17) notes that the first Dutch *Utopia* was published anonymously in 1553 (in the same decade as the earliest French and English versions) before unpacking the circumstances behind the second translation, by Frans van Hoogstraten, in Rotterdam in 1677. He shows this text to be part of a larger initiative in civic pride—to help memorialize Erasmus, Rotterdam's most famous son—and an argument for toleration in a city wracked by confessional divisions. Religious and political conflict was also the context for Gilbert Burnet's self-consciously 'modern' English translation seven years later, in London in 1684. Phil Withington (Chapter 18) argues that in the light of the so-called Rye House Plot and the execution of his Whig friends for treason, Burnet turned to More's text as a way of obliquely critiquing the absolutist and self-interested tendencies of the Stuart monarchy. Floris Verhaart (Chapter 19) identifies similar impulses behind the Huguenot Nicolas Gueudeville's French translation of 1715. A vehement opponent of Louis XIV of France, Gueudeville worked with the Amsterdam printer Pieter van der Aa to turn More's Renaissance Latin into a popular and commercially successful satire of French politics and society. Katherine Astbury (Chapter 20) then argues that although leading French thinkers of the Enlightenment tended to ignore *Utopia*, regarding it as an act of fiction rather than political philosophy, the reformer and revolutionary Thomas Rousseau proved adept at using it to promulgate a reformatory agenda. She shows, moreover, that while Rousseau's translation of 1780 appealed for social reform within the parameters of the French monarchy, his re-edition of 1789 deployed additional glosses and asides to link his text to a rapidly developing revolutionary context.

PART THREE: TRANSLATIONS AND EDITIONS AFTER 1800

Part Three looks at translations and editions of *Utopia* in the nineteenth and twentieth centuries, with chapters on versions of the book and their reception in Europe, the Arabic-speaking world, the USA, and East Asia. Marcus Waithe (Chapter 21) demonstrates how *Utopia* was a popular and polyvalent text in Victorian England, the very different editions by Robinson (1556) and Burnet (1684) (discussed in earlier chapters) repeatedly re-edited for different readerships. Waithe memorably shows that while Victorians had little time for More's literary 'tricksiness', the book's 'archaic futurism' appealed not only to working class autodidacts and Marxists like William Morris, but also Eton headmasters and paternalist Tories like Benjamin Disraeli. Also interested in *Utopia*'s fin-de-siècle (and socialist) appeal, Janet Stewart focuses on a single text (Chapter 22). This is the German translation by Ignaz Wessely, published in Munich by Max Ernst under the editorship of the future cultural historian Edward Fuchs in 1895. Stewart situates the text in its broader political and social contexts and forensically unpacks the contemporary 'cultures of translation' and interpretation informing its production and meanings. Taking us further east, Frances Nethercott (Chapter 23) then outlines a tradition of 'Russian Moreana' spanning from the French Revolution, when Rousseau's edition was translated into Russian, to the wholesale ideological appropriation of More by the Bolsheviks after 1917. In between, Nethercott tells a fascinating story of interpretative and academic politics—involving various kinds of political and intellectual censorship—hinging on the 1901 translation by the historian and left-wing thinker Evgeny Terle.

These chapters on Britain, Germany, and Russia indicate the political significance and urgency of translations of *Utopia* at the start of the twentieth century: how it was a text revered by socialist reformers and distrusted by the authorities, and how translation in general was very much an ideological as well as intellectual and commercial enterprise. Zsolt Czigányik argues, in turn, that in Hungary the complicated and fluid geopolitics of central Europe was key to explaining the conflicting and mutable appropriations of More's text (Chapter 24). He explains how Latin editions of *Utopia* were influential long before the first translation in 1910 by Ferenc Kelen (a professional translator who also vernacularized the works of Oscar Wilde); how these stimulated a powerful indigenous tradition of utopianism, often tending to the dystopian; and how, over time, religious as well as socialist activists were drawn to different aspects of More's text. A different politics informed the Catalan translation of *Utopia* in 1912 by Josep Pin i Soler, the first Iberian version since 1637 and the first to include Books One and Two. P. Louise Johnson (Chapter 25) notes that Pin was a 'literary regionalist' rather than 'political nationalist' whose scholarly version of the text highlighted not so much More's incipient socialism as his imperial prescience: the archetypally English attitude towards colonialism, war, and foreign relations that turned Britain into a global power. These aspects are also discussed by Cat Moir in Chapter 26 in her contextualization of the 1922 German edition by Gerhard Ritter, a protégé of the historian Hermann Oncken. Moir argues that this controversial contribution to Weimar's academic and political culture did not so much justify National Socialism, as has sometimes been argued, as foreground the historical origins of British imperial hypocrisy and the danger that it might now be emulated in the name of German socialism and nationalism.

A further three chapters in Part Three examine the appropriation of *Utopia* beyond Europe and Russia. Teruhito Sako (Chapter 27) charts the remarkable popularity of More's text in Japan following the decision to implement a programme of Western modernization in the 1860s. First translated by the entrepreneurial translator Tsutomu Inoue in 1882, *Utopia* was published ten times between the Meiji era (1868–1912) and end of the twentieth century, making it the most vernacularized text after Adam Smith's *Wealth of Nations* (fifteen editions) and Shakespeare's *Hamlet* (thirteen editions). He charts the changing uses of the text, as it evolved from a covert critique of society to a work for academic study, and the way in which it simultaneously became established as a cultural concept to appropriate, be it to sell real estate or a visit to a public bath. Tehyun Ma (Chapter 28) notes that while the translation of *Utopia* into Chinese was comparatively tardy, utopianism (as both a genre and idea) preceded More's text through Japanese and European influences. When it was translated, it was for political purposes. In 1935 the commercial translator Liu Lingsheng appropriated it as part of a general programme of vernacularization and public enlightenment delivered through print capitalism. Twenty years later, *Utopia* was selected by the centralized National Compilation and Translation Bureau of the General Publication Administration (NCTBA) to be presented by the Maoist academic Dai Liuling as a template for Chinese urbanization and collectivization. In contrast to China, Peter Hill (Chapter 29) explains that there was a long, autonomous, and often conservative Arabic tradition of Platonic social imagining that *Utopia* had the potential to disrupt in the early twentieth century, albeit in vernacularized fragments: in encyclopedia entries and abridged anthologized versions.

Part Four: Beyond *Utopia*

The final section of the Handbook turns from the appropriation of *Utopia* across time and place to the genres and traditions of social imagining inspired, directly or indirectly, by More's book and the adjective derived from it. Contributors consider forms of literary—and filmic—utopianism in the seventeenth, eighteenth, nineteenth, and twentieth centuries; utopianism in relation to philosophy, law, and economics; and utopian architecture, cartography, and curation and environmental practices past and present.

Part Four starts with Chloë Houston (Chapter 30) showing that by the early seventeenth century 'utopia' and 'utopian' had become free-standing and semantically autonomous English words. Houston argues that despite the words' fanciful and witty connotations, utopian writing nevertheless emerged as an important and distinctive literary practice that combined the comedic and serious and which intersected with numerous literary genres. Nicole Pohl (Chapter 31) picks up the baton with a panoramic examination of the origins and characteristics of the 'utopian novel' in the eighteenth century. Noting a diverse set of literary antecedents that ranged from 'knowledge for living' literature (*Lebenswissenschaft*) to Renaissance satire, romance, and prose, Pohl shows that in the eighteenth century these utopian and novelistic elements crystallized into a 'polymodal literary genre' that encouraged reflection about both how to live and how the world in which we live should be changed. Ingrid Hanson (Chapter 32) then examines the prevalence of utopias and utopianism—what she terms a 'utopian moment'—in the socialist movement of 1890s Britain. Focusing on two rival newspapers, the revolutionary *Commonweal* and the reformist *Clarion*, she demonstrates the shared editorial commitment to utopias and utopian thinking and the contrasting modes of dialogic and conversational discourse with which the writers for each journal sought to engage the attention, imagination, and support of readers. Rebecca Weaver-Hightower and Musab Bajaber (Chapter 33) suggest that *Utopia* serves as an important source for what they term the 'imperial settler' ideology of the United States. This is the sense of cultural superiority and civilizing mission that has justified state interventions across the North American landmass and beyond, and which is never better dramatized than by the hugely popular *Star Trek* franchise.

Johan Siebers (Chapter 34) turns our attention to utopianism in Continental philosophy and social thought. He affirms a point made by several contributors about the importance of Ernst Bloch in turning 'utopian' from a 'swear word' into a respectable and creative mode of philosophical method, before picking out some examples of its influence: for example, in the utopian sociology of Ruth Levitas and Siebers' own exercise in utopian self-ethnography. Miguel Angel Ramiro Avilés (Chapter 35) then seeks to revise some of the more negative lessons that modern legal and political scholars sometimes take from *Utopia*. Whilst acknowledging that the Utopian 'state' and its imperialist tendencies can appear menacing to liberal readers, Avilés nevertheless highlights various aspects of the Utopian polity that are potentially resonant with modern notions of human rights. Key in this respect is that institutions create a culture in which all citizens are protected from the domineering will of others and that law is not only simple and understandable, but also functions according to principles of equity and fairness. Martin Lutz (Chapter 36) in turn outlines the foundational role of *Utopia* for modern concepts of 'moral economy'. Lutz argues that not only does More provided a normative vision of how economies should function morally, in the interests of the individual and commonwealth, but that he also intimates a method of academic analysis, increasingly popular among social scientists, that is committed to identifying the moral dimensions of any economic context.

The volume closes with three perhaps less optimistic chapters that focus on some of the material and visual aspects of Utopia and utopianism. Diane Morgan (Chapter 37) considers Utopia and architecture. Eschewing the usual generalizations about the standardizing tendencies of utopian buildings in Book Two, she turns instead to Book One, combining a close reading of architectural detail within the text with a deep knowledge of utopian scholarship. In so doing, she seeks both to deconstruct and recreate the playfully dialogic (and fundamentally utopian) format created by More and his friends. Alfred Hiatt veers, in turn, between historical and contemporary moments of 'Mapping Utopia' (Chapter 38). Hiatt contextualizes the relatively few maps of Utopia commissioned in the premodern era before turning to the plethora produced since the 1990s. He concludes with Stephen Walter's powerful 'Nova Utopia' (2013), which depicts the island after a capitalist and military revolution in which the entirety of the environment is commodified, venal, and exploitative. Rhys Williams begins from a similarly bleak point (Chapter 39). Arguing that 'utopianism' has been partly responsible for bringing the earth and its inhabitants to the brink, his prognosis is twofold. One is that we recognize that a global apocalypse is not so much imminent as ongoing, having commenced four hundred years ago with transatlantic colonization and the slave trade. The second is that a very different kind of island utopianism to that envisaged by More might well be the 'Seeds of Good Anthropocenes': this is the everyday practices and 'micro-cultures' of eco- and ethically friendly island communities.

Some Themes

The range and richness of these chapters is testimony to the complexity, charm, and impact of More's little book, as well as the extensive and multidisciplinary scholarship it has attracted. To expect a single interpretation or even overarching argument from a volume that brings together so many new analyses and approaches is clearly fool's gold; it is also antithetical to the ambivalence and mutability of *Utopia* over the past five centuries. Taken together the chapters nevertheless reveal some general themes and insights that are nicely intimated by the image of Thomas More ('Tomas Mor') and the 1923 reprint of Aleksandr G. Genkel''s 1903 Russian translation of *Utopia* that it adorns (Fig. 0.1). Produced by the publishing house Proletariat based in the Ukrainian city of Kharkov, according to Frances Nethercott in this volume, this fourth edition of Genkel's translation was both a timely reminder of the Bolshevik 'goal of revolution and a vindication of the heady optimism accompanying the belief that a golden age of communism was, at last, well within reach'.

The first theme suggested by the image is authorship. Genkel' and his collaborator N. A. Maksheeva were not simply passive transmitters of More's *Utopia*. Like the scores of other translators discussed in this Handbook and elsewhere, they were authors involved in what Scholar characterizes as a fundamentally inventive process. Be they Latin or vernacular, the re-production of texts involved innumerable decisions—about language, phrasing, and typography; about which sections to include or exclude; about paratexts, digressions, and points of interpretation—that impacted on the meanings and significations of specific editions. As importantly, translators worked within what Stewart styles a 'translating culture' specific to time and place, whereby in any given context many others had the potential to contribute directly or indirectly to the process of textual production: as publishers, patrons, friends, censors, employers, referees of academic publishing presses, or in the case of the Maoist literary scholar Dai Liuling, the Chinese state's National Compilation and Translation Bureau. Thereafter, a translation could become the authoritative template for new editions not only within vernaculars, but also across them: from Italian into French, German into Russian, English into Japanese (see, for example, the chapters by Scholar, Nethercott, Sako).

But this Handbook also shows that it is not simply translation that complicates our understanding of authorship. First, a recurring point of the chapters in Part One is that, in writing *Utopia*, More was involved in a deeply collaborative process (so much so that he was not even responsible for coining the name of his island) at a specific moment in his intellectual and political career. He created the text—or rather different versions of it—with Erasmus and Giles, with a wider network of humanist writers and publishers, and in dialogue with Greek and neo-Latin authors like Plato, Lucian, and Augustine whom they so admired and emulated. Second, in so doing, More's circle engaged in translation through authorship: of the texts of their Greek heroes as well as the contemporary travel and other treatises informing the text (see Lydia Hunt 1991). The subsequent transformation in More's writing in the 1520s, discussed in this volume by Paul, can be explained at least in part by the loss of his literary sociability. Third, lurking in the analyses of many of the chapters is another type of figure with significant agency over how *Utopia* and utopianism has been appropriated over time and space: the influential interpreter, who translates the meaning—rather than the words—of the text. Genkel', for example, was just one of many modern translators influenced by Karl Kautsky's *Thomas More and His Utopia* (1888), a historical materialist analysis which did more than any other to establish More as both an acute observer of incipient capitalist development and the prescient proponent, and patron saint, of state-organized communism.

Chapters by Waithe, Hanson, Moir, and Siebert likewise point to the long interpretative shadows of William Morris and Ernst Bloch.

It is striking, secondly, that while 'Tomas Mor' certainly resembles the Thomas More painted by Hans Holbein the Younger, he has also been endowed with a fine moustache that gives him a distinctly Russian—perhaps Stalinesque—resemblance. If this visually captures the process of cultural assimilation that vernacularization of the text inevitably entailed, then it also suggests a humorous touch that, as numerous chapters remind us, also characterizes *Utopia*. Indeed, the 'Mor' portrait invokes the essential dualism of the work: that it is a serious and philosophically demanding dialogue that is nevertheless delivered with wit and 'tricksiness'. This volume's chapters confirm that the serio-comic quality of *Utopia* is integral to its meaning: as Hobbs and Sacks demonstrate, even the most venerable philosophical and spiritual subjects are the vehicle of jokes. Combined with More's conversational and observational style—which as Cavanagh, Veerhart, and Astbury each show could be amplified and adapted by translators—it creates a teasingly ironic and discursive moment in which ideas are shared, and imaginations provoked, rather than a manifesto with a singular message delivered.

But what the chapters collected here also show is that this tonal and stylistic complexity can be lost in translation, deliberately or otherwise. Translators seized on the programmatic or literariness of the text, but not necessarily both together: Book Two is often translated without Book One, altering the entire context and problematic for Hythloday's monologue; provocative sections—about religious toleration, or living in common, or the abolition of money, or the problems with kings—are either excised from the text or endowed with immense ideological certainty. The context of Genkel' 's translation, as a justification for the Bolshevik seizure of power, is a reminder that adaptations of form and content and the creation of interpretative frameworks really mattered. It is in this way that *Utopia* became a handbook for European colonists (Hower) and a spark for Arab nationalism (Hill); a critique of Catholic orthodoxies and defence of Catholic orthodoxies (Shrank, Kern); a vehicle for revolutionaries as disparate as English Whigs and American separatists (Withington) or French Jacobins (Astbury); a template for Meiji Westernization (Sako) and Maoist collectivization (Ma). As More well knew, and as the chapters in this volume testify, the vernacular *Utopia* can be a powerful and dangerous book, its discussion at political meetings a police concern (Sako).

Nethercott reminds us, finally, that the Proletariat imprint of Genkel' 's *Utopia* was this translation's fourth edition. Its third edition was in 1918: the same year More was memorialized by the Bolsheviks on an obelisk close to the walls of the Kremlin and 400 years since the publication of Johann Froben's two Basel Latin editions. *Utopia*'s significance in revolutionary Russia stemmed, as noted, from the claims of Kautsky and others that More was the first to observe the nature of incipient modern capitalism and its eventual cure. This reflects, however, a more general and extremely powerful feature of the book: the way it integrates observational and ethnographic detail alongside classical ideas and cosmographical conventions to create a text that seems to talk directly to social relationships, practices, and processes both in time and across time: a kind of *Lebenswissenschaft*, as Pohl puts it, with recommendations for the future. For nineteenth- and twentieth-century socialists, the most striking praxeological feature of the text was its descriptions of social and economic 'realities' in Book One and their amelioration in Book Two through 'institutions and customs' (in More's language) that were communist, democratic, equitable, and productive. The chapters by Siebers, Avilés, Lutz, and Sako demonstrate that, even in the twenty-first century, *Utopia*—and utopianism—can be an intellectual resource for thinking about subjects as diverse and important as philosophical 'becoming', legal rights and obligations, moral economies, and spiritual and material bliss.

Other chapters reveal more unfamiliar themes that nevertheless characterize the content of the text and its changing resonance across space and time. One is *Utopia*'s urbanism. The book was created by a London citizen for his best friend from Rotterdam along with a wider network of collaborators based in some of the major cities of northwestern Europe (Taylor). The island they depict is a confederated system of fifty-four city states combining classical and early modern characteristics: a perfected version of England's urban system in which Platonic notions of urban and rustic are placed in seriocomic dialogue (Hartrich, Hobbs), and in which the very possibility of utopian discourse is facilitated by a particular kind of urban environment (Morgan). Contextualizing the early translations likewise suggests that the vernacular and urban were synonymous, and not simply because publishers were based in cities. Shrank reminds us that the first vernacular translation of Books One and Two (in Italian) was indebted to a network of bankers based in Lucca and nine other European cities; Schmidt, Bishop, and van Bunge point to the localized civic politics behind early translations in Basel, London, and Rotterdam; and Hiatt shows that the innovation of Ortelius' map of Utopia in 1595 was to draw in the fifty-four cities and give them classical, modern, or familial names. The wider dissemination of the text was also dependent on networks of urban intelligentsia: as Ma notes, it was entirely predictable that the first Chinese version of the text should be published in Shanghai, 'the Paris of the East'. But here, also, the dissonance between what urbanism was in the premodern world and what industrialization and modernization made it become is palpable. Waithe notes that by the Victorian era Ruskin was dismissing More as a 'farmer'. And as the chapters by Hiatt and Williams vividly testify, urbanization today is perceived not so much as the source of the good life as the antithesis of utopianism.

This pessimism likewise haunts a second set of 'institutions and customs': namely, the imperialism and slavery ensconcing the civil and communal prosperity of the Utopian citizenry. Just as Hadfield and Hower emphasize the prospect of global colonization and imperium as formative contexts for the genesis of *Utopia*, so Lutz and Avilés recognize that the pleasurable, moneyless, and equitable lives enjoyed by Utopians depends on their domination of the regional economy (and so a very positive balance of trade) and the labour of enslaved peoples. It seems that in each of these respects More and his humanist collaborators were historically prescient, even preternatural. Kern and Withington show that Spanish and English versions of *Utopia* in the sixteenth century used the vocabulary of feudal and household relations (for example, 'bondsman' and 'servant') to translate More's sometimes ambiguous designation of *servus*.

A century later, with the Atlantic slave trade fully established, this language had changed to 'esclavos' and 'slave' respectively. The chapters by Johnson and Moir demonstrate that just as Austrian and Russian revolutionaries were eulogizing More for his socialism, so Catalan and Weimar translators looked to the realities of British imperialism to highlight what they regarded as the most prophetic sections of the book. This was the justification of belligerence and Machiavellian cunning beyond Utopia's borders to secure peace and prosperity within: a kind of civilizing jingoism that, as Hanson shows, was adopted by English proponents of utopianism in the years before the 1914, and which Weaver-Hightower and Bajaber find to be perpetuated in Hollywood by Captain James T. Kirk and the USS *Enterprise*. That the best of possible commonwealths should also be a remorseless and arrogant imperial power is a reminder, if one is needed, that *Utopia* and *The Prince* really were products of the same cultural moment.

None of which is to discount the historical importance of *Utopia* across the premodern and modern eras. On the contrary, tracing and connecting the history of its genesis and vernacular translations is to illuminate moments of hope and idealism, and conflict and tragedy, on a truly global scale. It is also to show how a historically minded and philosophically jokey Renaissance text can exert enormous influence on how modern societies view themselves and their futures. *Utopia* remains required reading today and tomorrow, too. It reveals utopianism as a way of thinking rather than a set of thoughts. And it depicts futures lost, as well as what might be found.

PART ONE

ORIGINS AND CONTEXTS

CHAPTER 1

MORE AND THE REPUBLICS OF PLATO

ANGELA HOBBS

'But now with Plato's state I can compare,
Perhaps outdo her (for what he only drew
In empty words I have made live anew
In men and wealth, as well as splendid laws):
"The Good Place"[1] they should call me, with good cause.'

('Six Lines on the Island of Utopia Written by Anemolius,
Poet Laureate, and Nephew to Hythloday by his Sister')[2]

'So let us first consider how our citizens ... will live ... In the summer they will for the most part work unclothed and unshod, in the winter they will be clothed and shod suitably. For food they will prepare wheat-meal or barley-meal for baking or kneading. They will serve splendid cakes and loaves on rushes or fresh leaves, and will sit down to feast with their children on couches of myrtle and bryony; and they will have wine to drink too, and pray to the gods with garlands on their heads, and enjoy each other's company. And fear of poverty and war will make them keep the numbers of their families within their means.'

'I say,' interrupted Glaucon, 'that's pretty plain fare for a feast, isn't it?'

'You're quite right,' I said. 'I had forgotten; they will have a few luxuries. Salt, of course, and olive oil and cheese, and different kinds of vegetables from which to make country dishes. And we must give them some dessert, figs and peas and beans, and myrtle-berries and acorns to roast at the fire as they sip their wine. So they will live a peaceful and healthy life, and probably die at a ripe old age, bequeathing a similar way of life to their children.'

---

[1] *Utopia* is a coinage from the Greek adverb *ou* ('not') and the noun *topos* ('place'); it puns with another Greek compound in which *topos* is conjoined with the adverb *eu* ('well', although in compounds it translates as 'happy', 'fortunate').

[2] More 1995: 19. Unless I am specifically citing the Latin, I reference the page numbers of the English translation in this edition throughout. The actual author of this poem is unknown (More? Erasmus? Giles?). Baker-Smith (1994: 95) favours Giles.

> 'Really, Socrates,' Glaucon commented,' that's just the fodder you would provide if you were founding a community of pigs!'
> ... 'All right ... For though the society we have described seems to me the true one, like a man in health, there's nothing to prevent us, if you wish, studying one in a fever.'
> (Plato, *Republic* 372a–d)[3]

There is no doubt that Thomas More (aided by his humanist friends Peter Giles and Desiderius Erasmus who assisted with its publication) situates both *Utopia* and the Utopia it describes at least partly in relation to, and in playful competition with, Plato's *Republic*. In addition to the opening poem by 'Anemolius' (from the Greek *anemolios*, meaning 'windy'), Giles writes in a letter to Jerome Busleyden in 1516: 'It is a place known so far to only a few men, but which should be known by everyone, as going far beyond Plato's Republic' (More 1995: 25). The 'Giles' who appears as a character in the text also compares Raphael Hythloday to both Ulysses and Plato (all three are explorers, whether geographically or intellectually), and 'Morus'—More's persona in the text—when speaking to Hythloday, refers to Plato as 'your friend'. In this chapter we shall have cause to note plenty of features of the Utopian way of life—not just the communal living—which plainly both derive from, and play with, the *Republic*.

However, it is my main contention that More's knowledge of Greek, and understanding of Greek thought and methodologies, allows him to engage much more deeply with the *Republic*—and Plato's corpus overall—than is immediately obvious from the surface resemblances, and that in consequence it richly repays us to consider afresh Plato's not one but *two* imagined communities in the *Republic*—which I shall outline shortly—and reflect on what he is trying to do with them, in order better to understand More's own deliberately elliptical approach and intentions. And an understanding of Plato's idealized communities in general (particularly the two in the *Republic* but also touching on those in the *Timaeus*, *Critias*, *Politicus* (*Statesman*), and *Laws*) will in turn require us to locate them within the broader context of Greek thinking on imaginary communities from Homer and Hesiod in the eighth and seventh centuries BCE to Lucian in the second century CE.

I argue that such a perspective enables us better to appreciate More's serio-comic tone, and see that its purpose is more complicated than simply to sweeten the medicine of the message with honey (as More suggests in his second letter to Giles in the 1517 edition). It will also help us better understand More's complex deployment of the dialogue form and, above all, see how the uses of serio-comedy and dialogue *interconnect* in *Utopia* to form an exploratory pedagogic work which, I argue, is More's deepest debt to Plato. *Utopia* is a work in which the description of Utopia in Book Two is consciously framed in dialogue both with Book One and with all those, Greek and otherwise, who have speculated and will continue to speculate on the nature of the ideally structured and organized community, and the extent to which such communities either can or should

---

[3] Throughout, I have modified the translation of the *Republic* by Lee (Plato 2007).

be put into practice. Central to these discourses is an examination of how ideals relate to the daily exigencies of practical politics which More understood so well.

To substantiate my case, I first need to show both that More's knowledge of Greek was good enough for such a deeper engagement and that he had sufficient access to Plato and other Greek writers in the Greek original as well as in Latin translation. As excellent scholarship already exists on both questions, I can be reasonably brief.[4] But the case still needs to be clearly made. I then outline the main similarities between Utopia and the ideally just, tripartite state constructed by Socrates in the *Republic*, a state composed of Philosopher Rulers (both Kings and Queens), their Auxiliary helpers (who live with the Rulers in communes and combine with them as Guardians of the State), and the Producers who provide food, clothing, and housing for them all. As this is also fairly well-explored territory, I can be succinct; but again, the case still needs to be made. At this point, however, I diverge from any standard comparison between Utopia and the tripartite state, arguing that there are also important *differences*, and in addition that More makes use of many other Greek sources, Platonic and otherwise. Central to my argument is the claim that Utopia is in important respects similar not only to the tripartite state of the *Republic* but also to the original, apolitical, pastoral community described above in the quote from 372a–d, and that this bucolic vision in *Republic* II has been overlooked as an influence on More. This matters, because an understanding of the interrelation between the two idealized communities of the *Republic* helps us appreciate the complex ways in which Plato employs the dialogue form and ambivalence of tone for philosophical ends, and this in turn enables us better to understand More's own deployment of tone and dialogue in *Utopia*.

In 1439 the library bequest of Humphrey, Duke of Gloucester arrived in Oxford, the main introduction of the university to the new humanist learning from the Continent. The bequest included Pier Candido Decembrio's Latin translation of Plato's *Republic*. During More's two years of study at Oxford between c.1492 and 1494 he would thus certainly have had access to Plato in Latin (and he may also have seen Marsilio Ficino's Latin translation of Plato, first published in 1484). His stay also coincided with the lectures on the new learning given by William Grocyn; More may well have heard his lectures—Grocyn gave the first public lecture on Greek literature in Oxford in 1491 (McConica 2011: 25)—and he may even have studied with him. He may also have studied Greek with the scribe John Serbopoulos, who was producing Greek manuscripts in Oxford between 1484 and 1500 (McConica 2011: 26; Catto and Evans 1992: 2.781; Weiss 1957: 173–174). But by whatever means he acquired some Greek while at Oxford, acquire it he did: according to Nicholas Harpsfield, 'he wonderfully profited in the knowledge of the latin and greeke tonges' (Harpsfield 1932: 12; cf. Roper 1962: 198).

More's classical studies (of Greek in particular) continued when in 1496 Grocyn was appointed vicar of St Lawrence Jewry in London, in the parish of More's family (an

---

[4] See e.g. C. Barron 2011: 3–21; McConica 2011: 22–45; Baker-Smith 1994: 86–99; Suthren in this volume.

appointment which in itself may suggest that More and Grocyn had indeed met during More's stay in Oxford). In a letter to the grammarian and pioneering humanist teacher John Holt in 1501, More says that he is studying Greek with Grocyn very seriously, and indeed has put Latin aside for it (More et al. 1947: 2; cf. McConica 2011: 26). (More may have got to know Holt while he was at Oxford, when Holt was usher of Magdalen College School. Another connection was John Morton, Archbishop of Canterbury: Holt was schoolmaster to the boys in Morton's household in 1495, while More had been a page for Morton c.1490 –2.) In addition to learning from Grocyn himself, More now had easy access to his large library of Greek and Latin texts.

During this period More also became friends with a humanist circle centred around Grocyn and dedicated to Greek studies, including Thomas Linacre, William Lily, William Latimer, and John Colet. Linacre had travelled in Italy and acquired an extensive library of Greek books, while Lily had studied Greek and Latin in Rhodes. Latimer and Colet had also both travelled in Italy, and Colet in addition corresponded with Ficino.[5] Linacre was older than More and acted as teacher as well as friend: More says he read Aristotle's *Meteorologica* under his guidance. Lily was his closest companion (they both lodged with the Carthusian monks in the London Charterhouse in the late 1490s) and they competed with each other in translating poems from the *Greek Anthology* into Latin. More's view of the members of this close circle is nicely illustrated in a letter of his to Colet in 1504: 'while you are away, [Grocyn] is the only master of my life, [Linacre] the director of my studies, [Lily] the dearest companion of my affairs' (More et al. 1947: 8–9).

This humanist circle was in its turn responsible for More's introduction to Erasmus when he first visited England in 1499, an introduction assisted by the fact that Erasmus' pupil William Blount, Lord Mountjoy, knew More's family. More and Erasmus became close friends and in 1505 they translated into Latin some of the dialogues of the Greek satirist Lucian, both relishing his incisive exposure of humanity's capacity for self-deception and hypocrisy cloaked by cultural convention. More was responsible for *Menippus*, *Philopseudēs*, and (probably) *Cynicus*. We shall be returning to Lucian later, but it is worth noting immediately that in the introduction to his translations (published in 1506) More commends Lucian for his serio-comic tone, saying that he perfectly exemplifies Horace's injunction 'to combine delight with instruction', an allusion to Horace, *Satires* 1.1.24, 'ridentem dicere verum', 'to tell the truth while laughing' (*CWM* 3/1.3). It is also interesting that in this 1506 introduction More approves of Lucian's critique of the 'fruitless contentions of philosophers' (*CWM* 3/1.3–9). Some particularly notable examples of this critique occur in the *True History*: when Lucian's travellers arrive at the Isle of the Blest, they find many of the old Greek heroes, poets, and philosophers; Plato, however, is absent: 'allegedly he was living in his imaginary city under the constitution and laws that he drew up himself' (Lucian 2005: 223). On the Isle of the Blest, too, all the women are held in common and no man objects, 'in which respect they are absolutely the best Platonists in the world' adds the narrator drily. However, while More is happy

---

[5] C. Barron 2011: 11. For Colet's correspondence with Ficino, see Baker-Smith 1994: 88 and Jayne 1963.

to concur with this (fairly) gentle mockery in 1506, it is a view that he will have revised considerably—although not entirely—when he comes to write *Utopia* in 1515.

More's Greek, then, is very good. Just as importantly, he has access to a wide range of Greek texts, first at Oxford and later in the personal libraries of Grocyn and Linacre. And from 1495 these libraries would have been hugely enriched by the heroic endeavours of the humanist scholar Aldus Manutius, who was the first to publish a very substantial part of the extant Greek corpus, and whom Linacre helped in preparing the first printed edition of Aristotle. As Carla Suthren notes in this volume, *all* the texts that Hythloday introduces to the highly receptive Utopians appear in the Aldine Greek collection, and Hythloday explicitly specifies that the Sophocles is in 'the small typeface of the Aldine edition' ('tum Sophoclem minusculis Aldi formulis') (More 1995: 182). He later says that he showed the Utopians the books printed in Aldine letters ('Nam quum ostenderemus eis libris chartaceis impressas ab Aldo literas') (182). This is a deliberate anachronism as Hythloday's final voyage to Utopia was in May 1503, and not all the Aldine editions of the texts that Hythloday mentions had appeared by then. But the salient point is that they *had* been published by 1515; More is acknowledging his great debt to the Aldine enterprise. For our purposes the most relevant Aldine publications are Aristotle (1495–8); Hesiod (1496); Aristophanes (1498); Lucian (1503); Homer (1504); Plutarch (1509); and of course Plato (1513).

By 1515, then, More was not only highly proficient in Greek but also had considerable access not just to Greek texts in general but, specifically, to Plato's *Republic* in both the Aldine Greek edition and in the Latin translations of Ficino and Decembrio; and lectures that he gave in St Lawrence Jewry on Augustine's *City of God c*.1501 would also have directed him to ponder the *Republic* (see C. Barron 2011: 15; McConica 2011: 27). It is no surprise, therefore, that in depicting the Utopians' way of life More is able to call upon many precise details from the *Republic*, and particularly—though certainly not only—from the second 'fevered' polis that Socrates describes from 372e, which in the interests of clarity I shall refer to as the 'tripartite state' to distinguish it from the first, simple, pastoral community described at the start of this chapter. As mentioned, as this is also reasonably well-covered ground (e.g. Baker-Smith 1994: 86–99; T. I. White 1982: 329–354), I will again only provide the evidence necessary to build my main case. I am certainly not claiming that the *Republic* is More's only Greek source, or even his only Platonic one, and we shall be considering some of the other sources below. However, I want to focus on the *Republic* as I believe that More's relation to it is much richer than is usually understood.

The most obvious similarity between the tripartite state of the *Republic* and Utopia is the communal way of life, although we should note at once that in the former this is only practised by the two Guardian classes, the Philosopher-Rulers and the Auxiliaries, whereas in Utopia all the citizens participate (the slaves to a far lesser extent). Nevertheless, it is the communism that Hythloday emphasizes in Book One of *Utopia*, explicitly praising the communal way of life in the *Republic* (More 1995: 99). In both Utopia and the Guardian classes there are shared belongings and shared meals, and the shared living quarters of the Guardians are partly replicated in the large rural dwellings in Utopia in which at least forty adult men and women (plus two slaves) reside for two-year stints to work the land (and although in towns Utopians live in separate houses in family units, these houses are kept unlocked and the citizens are free to come and go between them as they please).[6] In this and several other respects, Plato is influenced by Spartan practices (Schoeck 1956: 366–375). (It is also probable that the communism of the Utopians owes something to Vespucci's *New World* (first printed in Paris, about 1503, describing a voyage begun in 1501): Hythloday is said to have accompanied Vespucci on three of his four voyages. However, as stated, my focus here is on the clear and deliberate echoes of the *Republic*.)

Furthermore, the principal aim of these communal practices in both works is to create a deep sense of unity and harmony. In *Republic* 462b–c Socrates claims that social cohesion results from 'the common feelings of pleasure and pain which you get when all members of a society are glad or sorry at the same successes and failures' (see also 464d), and that 'the best ordered state is one in which as many people as possible use the words "mine" and "not mine" in the same sense of the same things.' In Utopia, too, all the citizens will feel equally at home everywhere (More 1995: 145), and 'the whole island is like a single family' (147; cf. Baker-Smith 2011: 153). Here too Plato is influenced by Spartan ideals: when the Spartan lawgiver Lycurgus returned from his travels, he is said to have remarked that 'All Laconia looks like a family estate divided among many brothers' (Plutarch, *Lycurgus* 8.4; Plato's source, of course, cannot have been Plutarch (from first to second century CE), but the story appears to be an old one). And the absence of a private life for both the Guardians and the Utopians means there will be no divided loyalties and no distractions: 'here, where there is no private business, every man zealously pursues the public business', enthuses Hythloday (241); compare *Republic* 417a, 420a, and 463d–e.

This communal way of life is one of simplicity: in both states greed is seen as the root of most evil (More 1995: 253–255); *Republic* 373e). The Guardians are not even allowed to touch gold and silver (*Republic* 417a), and in Utopia the authorities deliberately devise a system for ensuring that gold is utterly despised, employing it for chamber pots and prisoners' chains; jewels are similarly set aside as the playthings of very young children (More 1995: 149–151). More's disparagement of gold and precious stones is also influenced by Lucian's *Nigrinus* which satirizes a rich man 'conspicuous for his vulgarity'; another source is Vespucci, who reports meeting inhabitants of the New World who prefer feathers to gold or pearls (Markham 2010: 9; Baker-Smith 2011: 147 n.). Intriguingly, the low status of gold in Utopia—compounded by Hythloday's attack on useless goldsmiths (More 1995: 243)—throws a mocking light on the description of the work on the title page as a 'truly golden handbook'—a key point and one to which we shall be returning.

---

[6] Shared belongings and shared living quarters: More 1995: 137, 241; *Republic* 416d, 458c, 464b–c; shared meals: More 1995: 27, 139; *Republic* 416e, 464c; free movement between houses: More 1995: 119.

It is also a way of life in which women are far more prominent than they were in Plato's Athens or More's England. Girls in Utopia and the Guardian classes both receive the same good education as the boys (More 1995: 155; *Republic* 451c–452a, 466c–d), and we also learn that adult women in Utopia are encouraged to attend public lectures as well as the men (More 1995: 127). Guardian women and women in Utopia both work outside the home (*Republic* 451e, 466c–d; More 1995: 125), and both groups of women are trained for and participate in war (*Republic* 452a, 466d, 471d; More 1995: 201, 211). Indeed, in both the Guardian classes and Utopia war is undertaken by family units, one of the most precise resemblances of detail between the two (*Republic* 466e; More 1995: 211–213). There are differences: women do not participate in ruling in Utopia as the Philosopher-Queens do in the tripartite state (*Republic* 540c), and there do not appear to be any female priests in the latter as there are in the former, although More qualifies this by noting that only elderly widows are eligible, and not often chosen (1995: 231). Nevertheless, the proposals outlined by Socrates in the *Republic* for the education of (Guardian) women and the utilization of their potential would appear to be a profound influence on More.

The similarities do not only exist between Utopia and the way of life of the Guardians; there are also links between Utopia and the tripartite state as a whole. The emphasis on both communality and frugality, for example, results in strictures in both works on the size of the state (More 1995: 135; *Republic* 460a). In both communities there is job specialization (More 1995: 125; *Republic*, passim, especially 369d–370c), although Utopia does not follow the strict 'one person, one job' principle deployed throughout the tripartite state: in addition to their particular jobs, all citizens in Utopia are also trained in farming, and as adults farm for at least two years. Class mobility is also possible in both states: in Utopia, a craftsman who devotes his leisure to study may be promoted to the class of scholars, while a disappointing scholar can be required to become a workman (More 1995: 131); and Socrates makes it clear that those born into the class of Producers, Auxiliaries, or Rulers may be moved up or down as their potential and disposition develop (*Republic* 415a–c). More and the character of Socrates also share an intense dislike of both 'drones'—the idle rich and their hangers-on—and tyrants, and More agrees with Socrates' claim that no one who actually *wants* power should be allowed to have it (More 1995: 129, 243, 123, 195; *Republic* 564b–c, 562a–576b, 347b). Both utterly despise convention for convention's sake (More 1995: 155; *Republic* 457a–b).

There are also broader connections between Utopia and the tripartite state in respect of some of their most fundamental values and ideals. Although at first glance the Utopians' view that happiness is to be equated with pleasure owes most to Epicurus, the fact that happiness (*felicitas*) is identified specifically with the *higher* types of pleasure (More 1995: 163) is in fact precisely what Socrates says of flourishing (*eudaimonia*: there is no precise equivalent of 'happiness' in Greek) in *Republic* IX (580d–583a). Another key link is the rational religion of the Utopians, which has a family resemblance to Socrates' quest to apprehend the divine and purely rational Forms—the perfect, unchanging, and non-sensible paradigms of, for example, Beauty, Justice, and the Good which account for and connect all the inevitably imperfect instances of beauty, justice, and goodness that we meet in our daily lives (though see below for the Utopians' attitude to the notion of Forms themselves). When discussing the religious principles of the Utopians, Hythloday states clearly: 'Though these are indeed religious principles, they think that reason leads us to believe and accept them' (More 1995: 161). Ficino is almost certainly a mediating factor here. Throughout his works, and particularly in the *Theologia Platonica* (1482) and *De christiana religione* (1474), he seeks to reveal and refresh a 'docta religio' informed by 'pia philosophia' (Hobbs 2019: 253–254). The rationality of Utopian religion is especially highlighted by Ernst Cassirer in his discussion of the debt to Plato in Renaissance thought (Cassirer 1953: 23, 108–110).

Highly significantly, in both the tripartite state and Utopia education is given much greater prominence than law (More 1995: 195; *Republic* 427a). Hythloday also stresses that it is only good to obey laws *if* they have been made by a wise ruler (More 1995: 165), and he attacks the unjust laws of contemporary European states with great force (245). In Book One he criticizes the tendency of such states to over-regulate in general (101). Moral education is central to both works, and Hythloday's emphasis on the pliability of young minds and their capacity to be moulded seems a deliberate echo of key passages in *Republic* III. Here is Hythloday:

> The priests do the teaching of children and young people. Instruction in morality and virtue is considered no less important than learning proper. They make every effort to instil in the pupils' minds, while they are still young and pliable, principles useful to the commonwealth. What is planted in the minds of children lives on in the minds of grown men and serves greatly to strengthen the commonwealth; its decline can always be traced to vices that arise from wrong attitudes. (231)

Compare Socrates at *Republic* 377a–b, discussing the primary education of the young Guardians:

> And the first step, as you know, is always what matters most, particularly when we are dealing with those who are young and tender. That is the time when they are easily moulded and when any impression we choose to make leaves a permanent mark.

Hythloday also agrees with Socrates that this moral education is not just instilled by dedicated teachers and priests but is absorbed by the young from their entire social environment. He explicitly states that sound principles result from a combination of 'teaching' and 'the good institutions of the commonwealth' ('quibus et doctrina et bonis reipublicae institutis imbuti a pueris sunt') (More 1995: 212); while at *Republic* 400c–402a Socrates expands on the importance of environment with lyrical force, although his emphasis is not so much on institutions as on young children growing up surrounded by beautiful and noble works of art. The Utopians' dismissal of gold, silver, and jewels is also said to arise from the combined influence of their institutions, education, and reading (More 1995: 155).

However, while Utopia clearly shares many features with the tripartite state of the *Republic*, its relation to it is highly complex: as the ambitious opening poem suggests, it is anything but a carbon copy. Plenty is simply made up (see Logan 1983: 10–11; McConica 2011: 39, 45 n.). And there are also specific *differences*. Apart from the fact that in the tripartite state the communal way of life is only practised by the two Guardian classes, the communism of Utopia is less radical: there is no community, for instance, of wives and children. It is true that there are communal nurseries in Utopia (More 1995: 141), but mothers feed and look after their own children within them; in the *Republic*, the children of Guardian women are taken away at birth and raised in state nurseries (460c–d). (It is possible that More may have vacillated on this issue: Erasmus writes of a lost dialogue in which More defended the community of wives put forward by Socrates in the *Republic* (More 2016: xvi)—but of course this may be one of Erasmus' jokes.)

Another key divergence is that Utopians devotedly care for their sick and frail (e.g. More 1995: 139–141, 241–243), whereas Socrates takes a much tougher line with those who are no longer able to serve the state (*Republic* 405c–408b). Utopians are also more open than the reclusive tripartite state both to new ideas (such as the introduction of ancient Greek texts) and also—within limits—to trade: the Utopians import iron, gold, and silver, the last two for bribing foreign states and paying mercenaries (More 1995: 185). And their resistance to the whole notion of universals—mind-independent entities, such as 'blueness', in which (blue) particulars are grounded—would tellingly put them at odds not just with medieval scholasticism, but also with the key metaphysical principle of the *Republic*, namely the perfect, unchanging, non-sensible Forms, knowledge of which both legitimizes and necessitates rule by philosophers. More (in this instance specifically More rather than Hythloday) has some fun mocking late medieval logic in general and its universals in particular (157), but as these universals have their roots in Platonic Forms, he is inevitably mocking these, too.

Also, as we have touched on, there are plenty of other Greek and Roman sources in addition to Plato: Aristotle, the Stoics and Epicureans, Tacitus; Plutarch.[7] And, as we have also seen, these ancient sources are often filtered through Ficino. Cassirer (1953: 111) emphasizes that Ficino's *De amore* is 'a source book of English poetics throughout the whole of the sixteenth century', but his influence extends far beyond poets, deep into the intellectual hinterland (Hobbs 2019). There are other Platonic sources too, apart from the *Republic*: in particular, the *Gorgias*, *Philebus*, and *Laws*. To take just a few examples, the Utopians' identification of the Good with the higher pleasures (More 1995: 163–179) is not only indebted to *Republic* 580d–583a—as we saw above—but also to *Gorgias* 494c and the *Philebus* (particularly 46 and 51) as well as to Epicurus (see Cassirer 1953: 110). The *Laws* is an even more important source. See *Laws* 739c–d, for example, for a strong defence of communism: the ideal is that 'friends have all things in common' (a motto taken up by Erasmus in his 1508 *Adages*) and that citizens be unified by praising and blaming, and rejoicing in and being pained by, the same things; the laws should aim at creating this unity of feeling. Utopia also resembles the state envisaged in the *Laws*

---

[7] These other sources are well referenced in the notes in More 1995, and in the notes accompanying Paul Turner's translation for Penguin Classics (More 2003). The Stoics are the main sources for the Utopian ideal of living in accordance with nature (see Sacks in this volume).

in the great respect paid to the elderly, as well as the stipulations regarding the size of households. Although the general point about concern to limit the size of the state appears in the *Republic*, the very precise restrictions specified in Utopia—ten to sixteen adults per household and 6,000 households per city—are in fact closer to *Laws* 740a–741a, which limits the polis to 5,040 households. Plato's resonant myth of the island of Atlantis, depicted so vividly in the *Timaeus* and *Critias*, also strikes me as a powerful influence, in details as well as in general fantasy: Utopia is not dissimilar to Atlantis in shape, and the Utopians' fondness for communal gardens and gardening (More 1995: 119) also has echoes of Atlantis (*Critias* 117c) as well as the Garden of Epicurus, given to a young Epicurus by his supporters, and where he established a community known as the Garden.[8]

At least as important, however (and to the best of my knowledge overlooked in the secondary literature) is the fact that in three key respects Utopia resembles not the second, fevered, tripartite state of the *Republic*, but the *original* idealized community, the one compared in our opening quote to a 'man in health' (369b–372e). The first key similarity is that in the original pastoral community the simple and communal way of life applies to *all* the citizens, just as it does in in Utopia, whereas in the fevered tripartite state, as we have seen, it only applies to the two Guardian classes, the Philosopher-Rulers and their Auxiliaries. Also critical is the fact that the *reason* the original rural community in the *Republic* is compared to a man in health is because in this community only the healthy desires that are necessary for contented survival are satisfied (or even apparently felt); there is no mention of the 'unnecessary' desires (373b) of the bloated tripartite state, which demand more sophisticated goods and diverse pleasures. (This is another respect in which Plato may well have been influenced by Spartan culture: Plutarch says that Lycurgus, the renowned lawgiver of Sparta, 'banished the unnecessary and superfluous arts' (*Lycurgus* ix.3).) In Utopia, too, it is strongly emphasized that the only goods produced are those which satisfy natural and healthy needs and pleasures (More 1995: 129–131). The third way in which Utopia is deeply in sympathy with this first rustic community is that, although there are fifty-four city states (*civitas*, rendering the Greek *polis*) in Utopia, all the citizens are, as we have seen, trained in agriculture and spend at least two years working on the farms. More than this, there is throughout the island deep respect for rural life.

So there is clearly no straightforward correlation between Utopia and the second, tripartite state of the *Republic* (the state usually referred to as the Republic). Furthermore, the deliberate echoes of the *Republic* do not just occur in Book Two of *Utopia*, but apply to the work as a whole: the entire conversation, including that of Book One, begins with a chance meeting after a religious ceremony, just as the conversation of the *Republic* opens with Socrates and Glaucon walking up from the Piraeus, where they had been attending a religious festival to welcome the introduction into Athens of a new goddess

---

[8] More seems to have felt gardens to be an ideal location for philosophic reflection and debate: a garden in Antwerp is of course the setting for the conversation between Morus, Giles, and Hythloday. For more on gardens and *Utopia*, see Zurcher and Morgan in this volume.

(Bendis, a Thracian deity similar to Artemis, goddess of the moon, hunt, and forest), and coming upon Polemarchus, Adeimantus, and others. In Book One Hythloday also deploys a number of features of Utopia to critique current practices in England and other European states, in particular the profoundly unequal distribution of goods and labour, and the unnecessary suffering that results.

To work out what is going on, we need, I think, to take a step back and delve more deeply into what Plato—as opposed to the character of Socrates—is doing overall in the *Republic*: as we have seen, by 1515 More has acquired the deep knowledge of both Greek in general and the text of the *Republic* in particular to undertake such an exploration for himself. So let us return to the first, pastoral community of 369b–372d.[9] In the attempt to define justice and decide whether it is helpful or harmful to the individual, Socrates has proposed that they first consider justice on the larger canvas of the state, and argues that this can most effectively be achieved by constructing a community from scratch, in order to see precisely why, and how, political justice comes into being. He begins by constructing a simple classless community based on economic need and exchange. Each individual is to specialize and devote their time and energies to a particular job, such as weaving, and exchange the products of their craft with those of, for example, the farmer. There is no political structure: there is just this one class of producers and consumers; there are also, as far as we can tell, no arts and no philosophy. It is a community at peace with itself and its neighbours: there is no poverty and no war.

The tone of the passage is very difficult to gauge. Is Socrates' account supposed to be a serious analysis, either of the actual historical development of human communities, or at least of their economic and psychological origins? Or is it intended simply as a joke, perhaps a satire on the contemporary fashion for fantasies of a distant Golden Age or Reign of Cronos?[10] Such legends of former halcyon idylls had been popular at least from the time of Hesiod in around the late eighth century BCE. In *Works and Days*, Hesiod specifically calls the men who lived in the blessed Reign of Cronos 'golden' (108–10), in bleak contrast to the degenerates of the current age: for Hesiod, we have lost the gold from our natures and the idyll can never be recreated. The philosopher, poet, and (self-styled) magician Empedocles may also have described a golden age in his *Purifications* (see Barnes 1987: 198–201). And it is highly likely that of these More had at least read Hesiod, not simply because he was one of the most revered Greek poets and had been published by the Aldine Press in 1496, but also because he is mentioned very favourably by Lucian, one of More's (and indeed the Utopians') favourite authors: in Lucian's fantastical *True History*, the intrepid travellers arrive at the Isle of the Blest and see Hesiod crowned winning poet at the games—even though Homer was still said to be 'too good for them all' (2.22).

Depending on both writer and immediate context, the tone of such legends can range 'from wistful nostalgia through critique of contemporary mores to absurdist parody'

---

[9] For a more detailed discussion of this section, see Hobbs 2007: esp. 180–185.

[10] For a general discussion of the tradition of a Golden Age in Greek literature, see Baldry 1952: 83–92 and Guthrie 1957: 69–79.

(Hobbs 2007: 183).[11] Burnyeat (1999: 215–324), for example, focuses on Socrates' 'teasing' tone in this passage and his liberal use of irony, while Malcolm Schofield (2000: 190–232) calls Socrates' account 'tongue-in-cheek' and 'a comic explosion'. A third option is that Socrates is combining satire with making a serious point: he could be genuinely attracted to this first, austere community—he does, after all, liken it to a 'man in health'—while at the same time enjoying making fun of some literary treatments of similar rustic scenes. Witness R. Barney (2001: 216–217) who emphasizes the 'parodic' nature of the passage, and J. M. Dillon (1992: 26) who writes that 'Plato appears to go out of his way to make fun of the simple society he has postulated'. Yet both these writers maintain that the picture has a serious import as well, or at least fulfils a serious role within the dialogue as a whole.

The question of tone is made even more intricate when we consider Glaucon's contemptuous response, dismissing it as a 'community of pigs' (probably a sly reference to the dessert of roasted acorns). It has sometimes been assumed that this derisive snort is firm proof that the pastoral community is intended solely as a parody, but this does not necessarily follow: Glaucon is no mouthpiece for Plato (nor, as we shall see, is the character of Socrates). The historical Glaucon was one of Plato's brothers, and his character in the *Republic* often challenges Socrates' proposals (sometimes as devil's advocate to clarify the argument, as he admits at 358c), and he is always portrayed as a forceful supporter of a culturally sophisticated way of life: at *Republic* 399e he is tellingly called *mousikos*, 'cultured', a follower of the Muses. So while Glaucon intends his 'community of pigs' retort to satirize the rural community, Plato may also be gently teasing his urbane brother.

Socrates' response to Glaucon's challenge also requires careful appraisal and suggests that the pastoral community is not simply to be dismissed as a parody. He is adamant that it is this community that is the healthy one but says that if Glaucon wants him to construct a more bloated and 'feverish' state, then he can indeed oblige. And he does oblige, lavishly providing gastronomic delicacies and confectionery, perfumes and cosmetics, couches and tables, gold and ivory, and a wide variety of the fine arts. Life will thus be more luxurious and comfortable, and indeed intellectually and aesthetically stimulating, but the increased size of the state will lead to encroaching on the territory of others, thereby provoking jealousy and resentment, and war will result. The state which aims to satisfy the unnecessary as well as the necessary desires will no longer be at peace.

I believe that Plato (not just the character of Socrates) sees genuine strengths and weaknesses in both these imagined communities: the simple apolitical rustic community and the complex tripartite state that follows. And I submit that one of the very many

---

[11] For nostalgic treatments, see Aristotle, *Athenian Constitution* 16.7; Athenaeus, *Deipnosophists* VI, 267e–270a (although some of the texts that Athenaeus mentions are satirical). See also the vegetarian Peripatetic Dicaearchus appealing to the myth in support of his views in Guthrie 1957: 74 and Vidal-Naquet 1986: 285–287. Aristophanes mocks characters trying to restore the Reign of Cronos at *Clouds* 398, 1070 and *Wealth* 581. Vidal-Naquet 1986: 285–301 contains a general discussion of ambivalent responses to the Golden Age; cf. Brisson 1970: 402–438; J. M. Dillon 1992: 21–36.

things that Plato is trying to do with these two imagined communities is to set them in *dialogue* with each other. This would fit in with the dialogue form of the work as a whole, in which Socrates is challenged not only rigorously by Glaucon and Adeimantus (another brother of Plato), but also ferociously by the sophist Thrasymachus. It is absolutely fundamental to Plato's project that he never writes in his own voice: he always wants to open up discussion, not close it down, and thus always leaves space for future readers to enter the debate and think for themselves. Humour, such as that to be found in 372, plays a vital part in this open-ended dialogue form, as humour and wit also require interpreting. (It is worth noting that a fair amount of the humorous interjections in the *Republic*, as in 372d, come from Glaucon: witness his sardonic response to Socrates' lyrical description of the Form of the Good at 509a.) The similes and myths too require hermeneutic effort from us, such as the similes of the Sun, Divided Line, and Cave which illustrate the relation between this imperfect and transitory world of the senses and the perfect, eternal, intelligible Forms (*Republic* 507a–518b), or the Myth of Er (613e–621c), which portrays the rewards and punishments of the afterlife, and how it is our individual human choices in this life which bring them about, not some arbitrary divine will. In short, the account of the first rural community of 369b–372d and the responses both of Glaucon to it and of Socrates to Glaucon are in keeping with Plato's entire corpus: the tone is deliberately ambivalent and we are to be given no comforting authorial voice to settle the matter once and for all. There is no doubt that Plato wants us to think hard for ourselves in this section. The question is: what does he particularly want us to think about?

The elusive tone and the often sceptical responses of Glaucon (and indeed Adeimantus) strongly suggest that not only is Plato prompting us to ask what the best form of human community might be; he also wants us to ask to what degree it is either possible, or even desirable, to seek to attain it, starting from where we are now. In addition, we are also being urged to consider how contemporary Athens fares against such an ideal community: witness the vivid account in *Republic* 487b–497a of the prejudice against philosophy in contemporary society and how naturally philosophic natures become perverted within it; also the incisive portrait—simultaneously witty, affectionate, and devastating—of the extreme variety of direct democracy practised in Athens (555b–558c). And throughout the *Republic* we are further impelled to reflect on how far the contemplative philosopher—who imagines the ideal—should get involved in the imperfect, practical business of trying to work towards that ideal: at 473d we have the famous proclamation by Socrates that there will be no end to the ills of humankind until philosophers become kings or kings become philosophers (as we have seen, it is later made clear in 540c that there are to be Philosopher-Queens too), and at 501a Socrates adds that the first thing the ruling philosopher-artist must do is wipe the slate clean. However, by 592a–b this optimistic mood has waned considerably, and Socrates and Glaucon now agree that philosophers can only usefully get involved in politics if the state is *already* perfected.

In all this, Plato is making his indelible mark on a debate regarding the ideal community—whether past or future—which, as we have seen, was a vibrant theme in

Greek literature and thought since at least the time of Hesiod around 700 BCE, and—I would argue—from the written version of the *Odyssey* a little before that, where Odysseus' travels to the Land of the Phaeacians (Books VII–VIII) and the Isle of the Lotus-Eaters (Book IX) can be seen as the first written contributions to this tradition. It is not a coincidence that it was during this period that Greek colonization and trade expanded considerably: Greeks were coming into contact with an increasing number of different ways of living and organizing states. (Hebrew tales of the Garden of Eden are emerging at around the same time.) Plato explores the theme of the ideal society and its surrounding questions not only in the *Republic*, but also in *Politicus* (269c–274e), describing the idyllic and mythical Reign of Cronos, and *Timaeus* (17a–27b), where there are two idealized states: although Atlantis in its early stages (before it is corrupted by greed and lust for power) is depicted as very enticing, the main object of Socrates' praise is (the fantasy of) prehistorical Athens, which is ironically said to anticipate the tripartite state of the *Republic* that Socrates had outlined the day before 'by some miraculous stroke of luck' (25e).[12] The island state of Atlantis is further described in luscious detail in *Critias* 106a–121c. The whole of the *Laws*, meanwhile, constructs a semi-ideal 'second-best' state governed by allegedly perfect laws which we must strive towards if no ideal philosopher-ruler (or rulers) emerges; *Laws* 731 also paints an alluring picture of the mythical Reign of Cronos as a pattern to emulate. And the exploration continues after Plato: the semi-ideal state envisioned by Aristotle in *Politics* VII–VIII, the Stoic notion of the ideal cosmopolis of rational beings, Epicurus' garden community of friends, Ovid's *Metamorphoses* 15.75–152—where meat-eating precipitates humanity's fall from grace—and Lucian's *True History* are all important contributions to the genre. For our present purposes, the key point is that this topic takes the form of an open and ongoing *conversation*, and Plato's treatment of the topic is part of that conversation—a debate that he conducts with his predecessors and contemporaries within a number of his dialogues, especially the *Republic*, and which he also conducts *between* dialogues.

It is to the rebirth and development of this ancient conversation that More dedicates himself in *Utopia*. The point I wish to emphasize is that More's deep engagement with the *Republic* (as well as the Platonic corpus in general) *strengthens the case* for a reading of *Utopia* which positions it as an open-ended, questioning, and ambivalent work. Although in 1506 we saw More happy to join Lucian in mocking Plato, by 1515 he has come to understand him much more profoundly, and has imbued the lessons of the offstage author, inviting readers into the dialogue and requiring them to think and interpret for themselves. It is true that Hythloday seems to assume that Socrates in the *Republic* speaks for Plato (e.g. More 1995: 99, 101), but this does not necessarily mean that More concurs; and even if he does, he has still taken on board the basic lesson of inviting readers into a complex dialogue of ambivalent tone which requires active interpretation and encourages the reader to contribute their own views. It is not just that *Utopia* takes

---

[12] As the Timaeus opens, Socrates reminds his interlocutors that the previous day they had been discussing certain features of the ideally just state; these features roughly correspond to Republic II-V.

the form of a dialogue between the characters of Morus, Hythloday, and Giles (in which Books One and Two are further placed by More in dialogue with each other), or that the work contains within it accounts of other dialogues and debates, such as the ones in Cardinal Morton's house, or the French and Macarian Councils (see Shrank 2013; C. Houston 2014: 15). Nor is it simply that these dialogues within the text are extended beyond it by the marginal notes of the real Giles (or perhaps Erasmus).[13] It is also, and crucially, that in *Utopia* More is in dialogue with the ancient world, conversing with the imagined communities in the *Republic*, and indeed with the *Republic* as a whole, as well as with much else of the Platonic corpus and with many of the other Greek and Latin philosophical and literary works known to him. And just as Morus says of Utopia that he recommends selective adoption of its best features rather than wholesale imitation, so More adopts certain features of the two idealized communities both of the *Republic*, and of other Greek imagined states, for the creation of his own Utopia.

More also inherits and modifies from Plato other specific issues: like Plato, he not only interrogates the imaginary ideal itself, but also raises the question of how the ideal should best relate to the actual. And, also like Plato, he supplies at least a partial answer to this question when he uses the ideal to critique contemporary Europe, and England above all. Another key Platonic inheritance is the linked question of whether to try to balance the contemplative and the practical life, and, if so, how. There is also an echo of the *Republic* in the sceptical, pragmatic voice of Morus, which is suggestive of the down-to-earth scepticism of Adeimantus.

Yet Morus is not More, and it is the elusiveness of More—which is at the heart of the ambivalent tone of the entire work—which is I suggest More's deepest debt to Plato of all. 'Morus' is at most only half of More: in the Utopian language 'he' means 'I',[14] so whenever More writes of Hythloday 'he said', he is also writing 'I said'. Morus and Hythloday both represent different aspects and approaches of More and show how he is wrestling with such thorny issues as the question of how far one should keep one's own hands clean, free from the messy compromises of politics. And to add yet another layer of complexity, Morus cannot even be simply associated with the pragmatic side of the argument: *morus* is also the Latin for 'fool', a happy coincidence which Erasmus had played with in the title of *Praise of Folly* (*Moriae Encomium*, in Latin). More the offstage author indeed combines features of both Morus and Hythloday, but he is more multivalent than either. Like Plato, he hides behind many mirrors. When Morus recommends taking the 'indirect approach' in counsel, More is giving us a strong indication of how to approach *Utopia* as a whole.

And the wit—of both Plato and More—plays a key role in their indirect approaches. Let us conclude by returning to More's second letter to Giles. In it More writes teasingly

---

[13] In his letter to Busleyden which appears in all the early editions, Giles appears to claim that he wrote all the marginal glosses; on the title page of the 1517 edition, however, the glosses are attributed to Erasmus. See More 1995: 27 n. and Taylor in this volume.

[14] See the Utopian tetrastichon in the paratext (Fig. 1.1), with its interlinear transliteration and Latin translation.

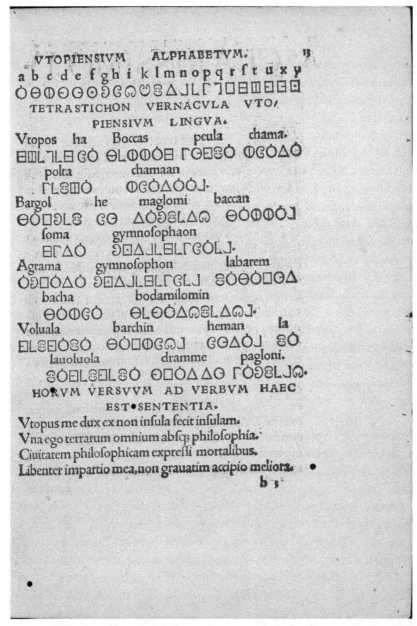

FIG. 1.1. Utopian alphabet and tetrastichon, in Thomas More, *De optimo reip. Statu, deque nova insula utopia* (Basel: Johann Froben, November-December 1518), The Bodleian Libraries, University of Oxford, Wood 639, p. 13.

that *of course Utopia* is a factual account of a real place, but *had* he wanted to write a fiction, he might well have chosen a pleasing style in which the truth, 'like medicine smeared with honey', entered the mind a little more agreeably (More 1995: 269). At the heart of this ironical jest lies the implication that jesting is simply honey. But this is only part of the story. Jokes and wit also act as a mask behind which the author and their true views can hide: jokes, like the dialogue form, require interpreting. More, writes his biographer John Guy, 'was most witty when least amused' (Guy 1980: 23). In the *Republic*, both Glaucon and Adeimantus poke—mostly affectionate—fun at Socrates, so that we do not quite know how to respond to what Socrates is saying, and the character of Socrates is not even Plato. Ironic wit underpins the entire dialogue: the work which we call the *Republic*—*politeia* in the Greek—would be banned in the tripartite state that it depicts, as it does not meet the censorship criteria. Morus, the fool, agrees in part with what Hythloday—he, I—says, and finds other parts absurd, but we are not told precisely *which* parts. *Utopia* proclaims itself on its title page to be a 'golden book', but we learn within it that gold is despised in Utopia and is used for chamber pots and prisoners' chains. One of the main reasons the *Republic* is still debated is that, through the intricately interwoven devices of the dialogue form, myth, fantasy, and wit, Plato requires hermeneutic engagement from his readers, and, crucially, he allows space for them to enter the discussion and put forward their own views. I submit that in respect of this most fundamental lesson of all, More has learnt well from his main source, and in consequence his longevity is likely to be as durable.

CHAPTER 2

HYTHLODAY'S BOOKS
Utopia, *Humanism, and the Republic of Letters*

CARLA SUTHREN

On board a ship headed to Utopia, a monkey mutilates a copy of Theophrastus. The unfortunate book forms part of the capsule library which Hythloday packs in preparation for his final visit to the Utopians. This library has been selected with care: it represents a substantial proportion of the Aldine Greek collection, printed by the great humanist scholar and publisher Aldus Manutius in Venice, and it covers the range of materials recommended for students in early sixteenth-century educational manuals. The Utopians are to receive an exemplary humanist education. In spite of the remoteness of their island home, they can peruse exactly the same texts as were available to Thomas More's readers, both in England and on the Continent. England was regularly characterized as a remote intellectual backwater, but Aldus' innovative Greek type allowed English humanists to participate in a trans-European academic conversation by standardizing Greek texts and greatly increasing their availability. Thus, the establishment of a humanist Republic of Letters was fed by the Greek letters of Aldus' type as well as the exchange of epistolary communications between men (and occasionally women) of letters across Europe, which was its lifeblood. Through its prefatory materials and other devices, *Utopia* consciously positions itself as a forum for exchange within the Republic of Letters. However, the disruptive monkey refuses to be ignored. Interrupting the smooth transmission of Greek knowledge to Utopia, it offers a figure for the incompetent reader, unable to digest the leaves of the book it covets. In doing so, it raises questions about the place of Utopia—and indeed *Utopia*—in the Republic of Letters, in a way that is typical of the Lucianic games that More plays with his readers.

In 1963, Peter Allen complained that 'the letters and verses written for the early editions of *Utopia* by Sir Thomas More and his fellow humanists have had remarkably little influence on More's critics and in later editions have been reprinted (if at all) more as literary curiosities than as significant contributions to our understanding of the work' (P. R. Allen 1963: 91). These letters and verses, of course, signal *Utopia*'s participation in the Republic of Letters, or *respublica litteraria*. Since Allen was writing, there have been many useful studies of the various communities of scholars which made up the Republic of Letters in the early sixteenth century.[1] Alongside this work on the historical players and their interactions, others—notably Peter Burke (1999) and Anthony Grafton (2009a, 2009b)—have engaged with the idea of the Republic of Letters on a more conceptual level, as an 'imagined community'. Others have placed *Utopia* specifically within the context of the early Erasmian Republic of Letters: Constance Furey (2006) from the perspective of its religious dimensions, and Hanan Yoran (2010) in relation to the unresolvable contradictions which he finds in More's text and in Erasmian humanism. Nonetheless, modern editions of *Utopia* rarely choose to restore to it the paraphernalia of the Republic of Letters in the way that Allen's approach invited. The widely used edition in the Cambridge Texts in the History of Political Thought series, for instance, relegates all of the epistolary contributions except for More's own preface to the end of the volume, which reflects a privileging of 'Utopia'-as-thought-experiment, over *Utopia*-as-book (More 2016b). Taking my cue from David Scott Kastan's reminder that 'literature exists, in any useful sense, only and always in its materializations, and that these are the conditions of its meaning rather than merely the containers of it' (Kastan 2001: 4), my approach draws on the 'material turn' in literary criticism to suggest that engaging with the intellectual content while ignoring its material premises fails to engage with exactly the tension between reality and imagination which the book itself deliberately sets up. Reading Hythoday's Greek books not only situates English humanism within a wider European context; it also offers an opportunity to uncover some of *Utopia*'s characteristic ironies in action.

Educating Utopia

On his final voyage to Utopia, Hythloday reports, he brought with him 'a good-sized packet of books' (*librorum sarcinam mediocrem*), containing works by Plato, Aristotle, Theophrastus, Lascaris, Hesychius, Dioscorides, Plutarch, Lucian, Aristophanes, Homer, Euripides, Sophocles, Thucydides, Herodotus, and Herodian (More 1995: 180–181).[2] They are all Greek works, as we might expect from Hythloday, who is introduced to us at the beginning of Book One as a keen Hellenist, and who considers Greek authors to be superior in general to Latin ones. On this subject, Hythloday's opinions are strongly expressed: he considers that 'except for the historians and poets, there was nothing in Latin that [the Utopians] would value', and that in the field of philosophy 'the Romans have left us nothing very valuable except certain works of Seneca and Cicero'

---

[1] e.g. M. Lowry 1979 on the Aldine circle; Bietenholz and Deutscher 1985–7 on contemporaries of Erasmus; Taylor in this volume. For a recent view of the English context, see Lazarus 2015. The research leading to these results has received funding from the European Research Council under the European Union's Seventh Framework Programme (FP7/2007–2013) / ERC grant agreement n° 617849.

[2] Throughout, I quote the Latin text only where particularly relevant.

(181, 45). At first glance, such statements seem rather extreme (though counting the historians, poets, Seneca, and Cicero, this actually adds up to quite a lot of Latin), and we might be tempted to conclude that Hythloday is living up to his Greek name, commonly construed as 'distributer of nonsense' (from *huthlos*, 'nonsense' + *daiein*, 'to distribute').[3] But in a letter to Oxford in 1518, two years after the publication of *Utopia*, More says the much the same thing: 'apart from the works left by Cicero and Seneca, the schools of the Latins have nothing to offer that is not either Greek or translated from Greek' (*CWM* 15.142–143). More, taking up his pen to defend the study of Greek, may have found a little Hythlodaic exaggeration useful. But an enthusiasm for Greek is something that Hythloday and his author both certainly shared.

Hythloday is prompted to bring his Greek books to Utopia by the enthusiasm of the Utopians themselves, who, having heard about 'the literature and learning of the Greeks' (*de literis et disciplina Graecorum*) from the travellers, demanded to be taught the language (More 1995: 180). Hythloday confesses that he and his companions began to teach them so as not to seem lazy, but were swiftly impressed by the dedication and abilities of their students:

> They picked up the forms of the letters so easily, pronounced the language so aptly, memorised it so quickly, and began to recite so accurately, that it seemed a miracle [...]. Thus in less than three years they had perfect control over the language, and could recite the best authors fluently, unless the text was corrupt. (181)

The books, then, represent not merely a personal collection, but a careful selection of 'the best authors' (*boni auctores*) based on the humanist Greek curriculum. Compare, for instance, the instructions for learning Greek set out by More's close friend, the great Dutch humanist Desiderius Erasmus, in *De ratione studii* ('On the Foundations of Study', 1512). Students who (like the Utopians) do not have access to the best teachers, must rely on 'the best authors' (*optimi auctores*) (*CWE* 24.667). These, Erasmus advises, should be 'limited in number but carefully chosen'. He declares that for grammar, 'everyone assigns first place to Theodorus Gaza; Constantine Lascaris, in my opinon, rightly lays claim to second place'. Hythloday's statement that 'of the grammarians they have only Lascaris, for I did not take Theodorus with me' evidently reflects a similar hierarchy (More 1995: 181). For prose, Erasmus recommends Lucian, Demosthenes, and Herodotus, and for poetry Aristophanes, Homer, and Euripides; these, he considers, are sufficient for knowledge of the language (*CWE* 24.669).[4] For more advanced study, Erasmus recommends Plato, Aristotle, and Theophrastus as 'the best teachers of philosophy' (673). Elsewhere (in *The Education of a Christian Prince*, 1516) Erasmus adds Plutarch's *Apophthegms*, *Moralia*, and *Lives*, 'for you can find nothing sounder than these' in terms of moral content (*CWE* 27.251). Hythloday supplements this catalogue with Hesychius, Dioscorides,

---

[3] For a discussion of Hythloday's name, see N. G. Wilson 1992. Halpern 1991: 142 offers an alternative view.

[4] The only one of these missing from Hythloday's list is Demosthenes, for some reason.

Thucydides, and Herodian. These further works are all recommended in a later treatise, *De tradendis disciplinis* (1531), by the Spanish humanist Juan Luis Vives, another associate of Erasmus (Vives 1964: 6.335–336, 49).

Clearly, the Utopians are to receive a textbook humanist education. It is an education, moreover, which More himself was involved in establishing in England, in the face of some resistance. More probably began to learn Greek at Oxford, which he attended between about 1492 and 1494. William Grocyn, who was 'at this time [...] the best-trained Grecian in the kingdom, having studied for two years in Florence', was lecturing on Greek there between 1491 and 1493, at exactly the right time for More to have learnt from him (McConica 2011: 25–26). Back in London, More had the opportunity to study with Grocyn again, and reported in a letter to his friend John Holt (another humanist teacher) in 1501: 'I have set aside Latin, and am pursuing Greek' ('Ita enim sepositis Latinis litteris, Grecas sequor', More 1947: 4; my translation). Through Grocyn, More was introduced into 'the very heart of an eminently distinguished humanist circle' (McConica 2011: 27). In a letter to John Colet in 1504, More reports that he is spending his time with Grocyn, Linacre, and Lily: 'the first (as you know) is, while you are away, the only master of my life; the second the director of my studies; the third the dearest companion of my affairs' ('altero (ut tu scis) solo (dum to abes) vitae meae magistro; altero studiorum praeceptore; tertio charissimo rerum mearum socio', More 1947: 8–9; my translation). Like Grocyn, Colet and Thomas Linacre had also studied Greek in Italy, while William Lily had made it as far as Rhodes. These men, along with others such as Richard Pace, came to form the core of a 'Graecophile coterie (whom More dubbed *Graecistes*)' (E. Nelson 2001: 897).[5] Colet founded St Paul's School with a humanist curriculum, and Lily was appointed as the first headmaster. When Erasmus visited England for the first time in 1499, he inevitably fell in with this circle, and as a result his influence on English educational reform was very great.[6] In fact, his educational publications of 1512 (*De ratione studii* and *De copia*) were produced for St Paul's at Colet's request, directly shaping the curriculum. Lisa Jardine has suggested that Colet was also the intended recipient, via Cuthbert Tunstall, of a first edition of *Utopia* which is bound with 'a collection of elementary texts for teaching Greek' (now at Yale University). This composite volume actively promotes engagement with the programme of education espoused by Hythloday and his books: it 'offer[s] the reader the means to access Greek learning, handily packaged together with the encouraging work of fiction' (Jardine 2015: 177).

By the time *Utopia* was printed in 1516, the educational reform pursued by the English *Graecistes* was by no means a *fait accompli*. Arthur Tilley energetically describes the 'storm of opposition' roused by the introduction of Greek at Oxford in the early years of the sixteenth century: 'The younger partisans of the old learning banded themselves together under the name of Trojans and mobbed the Grecians in the streets. The seniors

---

[5] See More's 'Letter to Dorp' (*CWM* 15.96).
[6] For a general treatment of *Utopia* as an expression of the educational philosophy of Erasmian humanism, see Parrish 2010: 589–605.

preached against Greek from the pulpit. Indeed, one preacher went so far as to denounce not only Greek, but all liberal learning. Logic and scholastic theology were, he said, the only deserving studies' (Tilley 1938: 234).

At this point More, who was in Abingdon with Henry's court, entered the lists on the side of the Greeks, writing the letter addressed to the University of Oxford which has already been quoted. More stresses the utility of a humanist training in rhetoric for lawyers and preachers, and the necessity of Greek for the study of Scripture. He argues that 'the most original thinkers and the most diligent interpreters of their thoughts were Greek'; no translation, however good, can substitute for the original (*CWM* 15.143). More's intervention was not merely literary, for he brought the matter to Henry's attention, 'with the result that royal letters were addressed to the university forbidding under severe penalties the students of Greek to be molested' (Tilley 1938: 235).

In light of this, the facility and enthusiasm with which the Utopians take to Greek is clearly exemplary. Hythloday concludes: 'I have a feeling they picked up Greek more easily because it was somewhat related to their own tongue [...] I suspect their race descends from the Greeks because, in the names of the cities and in official titles, they retain some vestiges of the Greek tongue' (More 1995: 181). This is, of course, a tongue-in-cheek moment, an opportunity for More to nudge any readers who have not yet noticed the Greek puns embedded throughout *Utopia*. But still, as Jane Raisch puts it, to someone of More's inclinations, 'this depiction of Greek learning as unchallenged and seamlessly integrated into Utopian society must have also had a genuine appeal' (Raisch 2016: 943).

The Library Without Walls

Hythloday's books, however, represent more than a humanist reading list. He tells us that the Sophocles, at least, is 'in the small typeface of the Aldine edition' ('minisculis Aldi formulis'), and later talks about 'showing [the Utopians] the books printed on paper in Aldine letters' ('ostenderemus eis libris chartaceis impressas ab Aldo literas') (More 1995: 182–183). These descriptions draw attention to one of the most famous innovations of the Aldine Press, set up by Aldus Manutius in Venice: its Greek type. Printing in Greek, with its breathings, accents, and subscripts, presented considerable technical challenges to a printing process designed around the greater regularity of Latin. Early pioneers tried various experiments: most strikingly, Janus Lascaris printed a number of editions entirely in capitals, reviving Greek inscriptional letters for the purpose. Aldus himself said of his critics in the preface to his 1496 edition of Theocritus, Hesiod, and Theognis: 'I would not wish them anything worse than that they too should one day print Greek texts' (Manutius 2016: 24–25).

The 'small typeface' of the Sophocles is actually the fourth instantiation of the Aldine Greek typeface, premiered in his edition of Sophocles in 1502. This had been somewhat simplified in comparison to previous versions, and was attractive, clear, and easy to read. According to Nicholas Barker, it was based on Aldus' own handwriting, but he also detects the influence of the type-cutter, Francesco Griffo, on the design: 'Liberated at last from the drudgery of following the polymorphous and idiosyncratic forms of the Greek scribes, [Griffo] gave it a simplicity and uniformity revolutionary in his time' (N. Barker 1992: 62). The Sophocles, Euripides, and Homer also formed part of one of Aldus' most famous innovations: the classical library in the portable octavo format. The Aldine octavos were not necessarily cheaper than larger volumes, but the smaller format took books out of the library and into the world.[7] These texts, presented by themselves without learned commentaries, were aimed not at cloistered academics but at the educated gentleman, perhaps holding a political office, and the travelling scholar. In his 1503 catalogue Aldus himself called them *libelli portatiles*, or 'portable little books' (Manutius 1975: Tav. X–XIII). Erasmus saw Aldus as striving to create a library without walls; as he said in his *Adages*: 'Aldus is building a library which knows no walls save those of the world itself' (*CWE* 33.10).

Having Hythloday carry these Aldine texts to Utopia, then, is an imaginative fulfilment of this promise, sending them even beyond the boundaries of the known world. What has not always been recognized, however, is that not just some but all of Hythloday's books represent Aldine editions. J. B. Trapp has pointed out that by the putative date of Hythloday's final voyage to Utopia—7 May 1503—not all the books from his list had appeared in print. Specifically, the Aldine Plato, Herodian, Hesychius, and Plutarch had not yet seen the light of day. He concludes, whimsically, that Hythloday must have either 'supplied these works in 'manuscript, which the context seems to make unlikely, or they had been pre-ordered and were sent on, which seems still less likely, or, Utopia being Utopia, he had found a remarkable book-seller there' (Trapp 2002: 260). But each of these solutions, of course, quite misses the point. By the time More began to write *Utopia* in May 1515, they had all had time to issue from the Aldine Press.[8]

That same year saw the death of Aldus Manutius himself, on 6 February. His ambition had been nothing less than to print, often for the first time, 'all the best Greek books'.[9] Thus Hythloday's travelling library can be seen as a paean to his achievements.[10] In his letter to Martin Dorp, dated 21 October 1515, More wrote that 'Aldus Manutius the Roman was one of the greatest' of the humanist printers ('Aldus Manutius Rhomanus erat in primis') (*CWM* 15.94–95). The departure from the internal chronology of the narrative noticed by Trapp is in the service of doing justice to the true significance of Aldus' library without walls. More, perhaps, was particularly able to appreciate the

---

[7] M. Lowry (1979: 142–146) has a helpful discussion of the issue of cost.
[8] Lascaris (1495), Aristotle (1495–8), Theophrastus (1497), Aristophanes (1498), Dioscorides (1499), Thucydides (1502), Sophocles (1502), Herodotus (1502), Herodian (1503), Lucian (1503), Euripides (1503), Homer (1504), Plutarch (1509), Plato (1513), Hesychius (1514).
[9] *[O]ptimi quique Graecorum libri*, in his preface to Lascaris' Greek grammar (1495); πάσας τὰς τῶν Ἑλλήνων ἀρίστας βίβλους, in his preface to Musaeus' *Hero and Leander* (c.1495/7) (Manutius 2016: 4–5, 8–10).
[10] The circumstance of Aldus' recent death was pointed out by Lupton (More 1895a: 218 n.), but the connection has not so far been developed fully.

effects of the Aldine project: Erasmus laments, in a prefatory epistle to *Utopia*, that More had never been to Italy, renowned as a cradle of humanist learning (More 1995: 4–5). But, as the reference to the recent edition of Hesychius shows, the Aldine editions brought this cutting-edge scholarship swiftly even to a remote island like England—or Utopia.[11]

Utopia, England, and *ultima* Thule

In the prefatory epistle to his 1507 edition of Erasmus' Latin translations of Euripides' *Hecuba* and *Iphigenia in Aulis*, Aldus lifts a joke from Juvenal. In the Roman author, 'Thule now speaks of hiring a teacher of rhetoric' ('de conducendo loquitur iam rhetore Thule', Satire 15.112). 'Thule' in Latin thought represented the extreme north, located somewhere north of Britain, as in Strabo's *Geographica* 1.4; the implication is that even so backward a place as Thule is now *talking* about hiring someone to teach the sophisticated art of rhetoric. Aldus modifies the line, so that 'Thule is now dealing with hiring a teacher of rhetoric' ('ut de conducendo tractet iam rhetore Thule'): in these even more enlightened times, Thule has at last finished talking about it and is now in the process of actually hiring someone to teach a humanist programme of rhetoric. Erasmus' translations, partly undertaken during a stay at More's house in 1505–6, were also dedicated to William Warham, the Archbishop of Canterbury, and were thus closely linked to England; Aldus' joke plays into stereotypes of England as an intellectual backwater at the beginning of the sixteenth century. In fact, Erasmus himself had been offered a post teaching Greek at Cambridge, so that the joke comes to seem very specific.[12]

It is the peculiar geographical unfixity of Thule in the classical tradition that enables Aldus to perform this deft manoeuvre. Theodore Cachey draws attention to 'Thule's liminal status, located at the very ends of the earth and on the border between geographical truth and literary fiction', as acquiring particular resonance in the Renaissance, 'especially during the period of the discoveries and explorations' (Cachey 2003: 80). Virgil in the *Georgics* (1.30) referred to it as *ultima* ('furthest') *Thule*, and the epithet stuck, expressing 'the aura of uncertainty surrounding Thule, which led to its assuming symbolic rather than geographic resonance' (Cachey 2003: 80; see also Romm 1992: esp. 121 ff.). Utopia is imagined as occupying a similarly distant and liminal space, a Thule for the age of exploration. The text weaves together real and imaginary worlds, so that Hythloday travels to Utopia with Vespucci and argues with Cardinal Morton, and the real Peter Giles adopts the voice of the fictional Peter Giles in the prefatory material. In

---

[11] More's own library is now lost, but it seems likely that he owned or had access to the volumes mentioned by Hythloday through his humanist connections. It has been suggested that Hesychius lies behind some of the names in *Utopia* (W. Allen 1967).

[12] He had already been offered the position in 1506, the year the first edition of his Euripides translations was printed, and eventually took it up between 1511 and 1514.

a wonderful detail, Giles specifies in his epistle to Jerome Busleyden that he cannot confirm the precise location of Utopia, because due to 'an unlucky accident' he missed it: at the very moment that Hythloday mentioned it, 'one of the company, who I suppose had caught cold on shipboard, coughed so loudly that some of Raphael's words escaped me' (More 1995: 27).[13] The grossly physical bodily function interrupts the fantasy at the very moment that it threatens to spill over into reality.[14]

In spite of the Thule-like remoteness of their island home, the Utopians have access to the most up-to-date humanist scholarship, as represented by the Aldine Greeks. Jennifer Summit (2008: 73) points out that in its dependence on European imports of classical texts, Utopia reproduces the market condition of England in the early sixteenth century. The stereotype implied by Aldus' joke about Thule may partly explain why English printers initially declined to print Greek (and indeed Latin) classical texts. England was not rich in classical manuscript resources, and English scholars did not want 'homegrown' editions but prestigious Continental ones which would enable them to participate in Europe-wide conversations in a way that had only become possible since the advent of print. A strong industry therefore grew up around importing books to fill this gap in the market. Even a century later, the newly established Bodleian Library in Oxford was admired not for its manuscripts but for its printed collections (see Grafton 2009b: 3). Conversely, *Utopia* itself, aimed at an international humanist readership, was not printed in England but initially in Leuven by Thierry Martens (1516), then in Paris by Gilles de Gourmont (1517), and then in Basel by Johann Froben (1518). All three locations were hubs of humanist industry, and well suited to More's project.

As David Norbrook (2002: 26) has put it, 'in writing the *Utopia* More left the English monarchy and became a citizen in the republic of humanist letters'. The changes of location, from Louvain to Paris to Basel, all centres of printing and of humanist learning, reflect the unfixed location of the Republic of Letters, which exists through the exchanges of humanists with each other and with the medium of print. Grafton's (2009a: 6) description of the Republic of Letters as 'a palimpsest of people, books, and objects in motion' is captured in the paratextual material of the early editions of *Utopia*. The circulation of printed texts, whether new humanist works like More's, or the latest editions of classical texts being produced by the Aldine Press, was of vital importance to the Republic of Letters. It was especially key for widening access to areas that had previously been seen as benighted; the Aldine editions carried by Hythloday represent a passport for English scholars like More into the humanist Republic of Letters, conferring the ability to participate in the humanist dialogues taking place across Europe.

---

[13] 'comitam quispiam clarius ob frigus opinor naviagtione collectum tussiens, dicentis voces aliquot intercepit'. This translation uses a passive construction, but *intercepit* ('intercepted') is active, enacting a positive intervention.

[14] Halpern interprets this moment rather more violently as 'the body's revolt against Utopia' (1991: 149).

The Republic of Letters

The term *respublica litterarum* is first attested in 1417, but did not enter into wider usage until the turn of the century (see Burke 1999: 8). As Grafton observes, 'the Republic itself [...] really began to take shape in the consciousness of scholars around 1500, as Erasmus became the leader of a self-conscious avant-garde of scholars bent on reforming the Church and the universities' (Grafton 2009b: 16). Erasmus himself did much to popularize the concept. In *Antibarbari* (written in 1495 but not printed until 1520), an extended passage depicts the *literaria Res p[ublica]* as being under attack from various enemies (*CWE* 1/1.68 ff.). He evidently had this concept in mind in a passage in the *Adages* under the heading *Festina lente* ('Hurry slowly' or 'More haste less speed') in praise of humanist labours in general, and Aldus' labours in particular. He compares those 'who by their valour protect or even extend the boundaries of their country' ('qui respublicas sua virtute vel tuentur, vel etiam augent') to the one 'who restores a literature in ruins' ('qui literas collapsas vindicat') (*CWE* 33.10; 2/3.18); the words *respublicas* and *literas* occupy the same place grammatically in their respective clauses, once again invoking the idea of the 'Republic of Letters'. This man, Erasmus grandly declares, 'is engaged on a thing sacred and immortal, and works for the benefit not of one province only but of all nations everywhere and of all succeeding ages' (*CWE* 2/3.10). The Republic of Letters is presented as a collaborative, transnational, transhistorical humanist enterprise.

On this grandiose scale, the Republic of Letters existed primarily on a conceptual level: it was, as Peter Burke puts it, 'what we might call an invisible or "imagined community"' (Burke 1999: 8). In practical terms, the Republic of Letters was performed through interconnected scholarly networks. The most significant of these, when it comes to *Utopia* at least, are the English *Graecistes*, the Aldine 'academy' based in Venice, and the Northern circle of humanists centred around Erasmus. Between them, they form the major cultural and intellectual contexts which gave rise to *Utopia*. These were not, of course, separate, and there was considerable overlap and movement between them. The key figure linking these three networks and *Utopia* was Erasmus. As well as spending time in England, he also visited the Aldine Press in 1507 and stayed for nine months, working on a new and expanded edition of his collection of *Adages*. He vividly describes the atmosphere of international scholarly collaboration in a common cause characteristic of his idea of the Republic of Letters, describing how Aldus was sent manuscripts and money from all over Europe: 'What scholar does not support Aldus in his efforts toward noble ends? Who does not contribute something to make his work lighter?' (*CWE* 33.14). This generosity, he says, was extended to him too during his stay: 'how many learned men came to me to supply me with authors that had not yet been printed, and whom they thought I could use!' (14). Aldus himself 'had nothing in his treasure of books which he did not share', and Erasmus even 'felt the kind help of certain people who were unknown to me either by face or name' (14).

More sent his completed *Utopia* to Erasmus in late 1516; Erasmus mobilized his own extensive network of contacts to produce a series of laudatory epistles for the work, and saw the first few editions through the press.[15] Thus, in its early printed editions, *Utopia* is presented as being at the centre of a series of conversations and correspondence carried out among some of the leading luminaries of Northern European humanism. (This network was so strongly associated with Erasmus that it is often referred to as the Erasmian Republic of Letters.) The first edition, which was printed by Thierry Martens in Louvain in December 1516, begins with a prefatory epistle from Peter Giles to Busleyden, a wealthy Dutchman whom More had also met on his embassy to the Netherlands. Giles played an important role in the editing and publication of this first edition, and worked as a corrector for Martens's press. In turn, Jean Desmarez, a teacher at the University of Louvain, writes to Giles. Desmarez also contributed a poem, as did two more Dutch humanists, Gerard Geldenhouwer (who also supervised *Utopia* through the press) and Cornelius Graphey. Then there is a letter from Busleyden to More, and finally the letter from More to Giles which serves as a preface to the work. The 1517 edition (sent by Erasmus to be printed by de Gourmont in Paris) added an epistle from Guillaume Budé to Thomas Lupset, a young English humanist tasked with preparing the edition, and a second epistle from More to Giles. The 1518 Basel edition contributed further epistles from Erasmus to the printer, Johann Froben, and from Beatus Rhenanus to a fellow German humanist, Willibald Pirckheimer.

The text of *Utopia*, then, is preceded by an ostentatious display of its humanist connections. If epistolary exchanges between humanists 'constituted the fragile but vital canals that connected and animated intellectual commerce in the far-flung parts of the Republic [of Letters]' (Grafton 2009b: 22), then *Utopia* fashions itself as a significant confluence. The fluctuations in the prefatory material among the first three editions of *Utopia*—with items being added, dropped, and moved—maintain the impression of a text at the centre of an ongoing humanist conversation. Raisch observes that '*Utopia*'s paratexts clearly model the primacy of textual analysis and scholarly labor in the production of an ideal intellectual community', so that in fact it is often 'in the paratexts more than in the text itself that *Utopia* seems to be at its most utopian' (Raisch 2016: 938).

The authors of the paratextual materials are all collaborators in the Utopian illusion, and none more so than Peter Giles, whose contributions make the fictional Giles appear to step out of the pages of the main text and into the prefatory material. In his letter, Giles also says that he has added some marginal notes (More 1995: 27), so that his collaboration with More on the Utopian project continues into the text itself; visually, readers encountered a conversation between humanists taking place on the page. The earliest editions of *Utopia* contain around two hundred printed marginal notes, most of which draw explicit contrasts between the way Utopian society is arranged and the way 'we' do things 'today'. This in itself is at odds with More's treatment of Utopia as being geographically distant but temporally contemporary to his own society. The notes add another

---

[15] For the early Latin editions of *Utopia*, see Taylor in this volume and Roggen 2008: 14–31.

voice into the text, one which is not that of More the author, nor Morus the character, who expresses a much more sceptical view of Utopia at the end of Book Two. This effect is enhanced visually by the different typeface used for the notes: where the main text is printed in roman, the notes are in black letter. If the notes are by Giles, then the setting of the work as a dialogue between More, Giles, and Hythloday is actualized through these textual interventions.[16]

Within the main text itself, we are presented with a series of conversations between humanists. Book One opens with a brief description of the diplomatic negotiations which had taken More to the Netherlands in 1515. But the narrative quickly moves from Bruges to Antwerp, from diplomatic to humanist circles. In Antwerp, Morus meets Peter Giles, who introduces him to Hythloday, and the text unfolds as a dialogue between the three men in the idyllic setting of More's garden. In Book One, further dialogues proliferate: contained within More's narrative of the dialogue in the garden are Hythloday's narratives of the dialogues in Cardinal Morton's house, and in the French and Macarian councils, before the successive dialogues give way to the account of Utopia which takes up Book Two.[17] As the text comes back to the garden in Antwerp, the dialogue is brought to a rather unsatisfactory close: as Hythloday finishes talking, Morus is left with a number of objections. But he does not raise these with Hythloday, because he sees that Hythloday is tired, and foresees that he might not take contradiction well; instead, 'with praise for [the Utopians'] way of life and his account of it, I took him by the hand and led him in to supper' (More 1995: 249).

It is central to the meaning and purpose of *Utopia* that its dialogues remain unresolved; as Chloë Houston puts it, 'More's use of the dialogue form, with its multiple voices and shifting narration, exerts a rhetorical control over the reader which refuses to allow the identification of More himself with any one position' (C. Houston 2014: 15). The text simply ceases: an ending without resolution. But the way that More draws attention to the arbitrariness of the conclusion and the moral cowardice of Morus underlines the necessity for further discussion, here avoided. Morus' subsequent words open up the possibility, and indeed the strong desirability, of future dialogues on the subject: 'I said that we would find some other time for thinking of these matters more deeply, and for talking them over in more detail. Would that this would happen some day!' (More 1995: 249). Morus finishes by claiming that, while he does not agree with everything Hythloday has said, 'in the Utopian commonwealth there are very many features that in our own societies I would wish rather than expect to see' (249). As Cathy Shrank has argued, 'the questions left hanging as to which Utopian policies Morus

---

[16] The title page to the second edition in 1517 claims that they are by Erasmus, though this could be an error or a clever marketing move—having the intellectual giant of Northern humanism on the front page might not be a bad idea for book sales. For the authorship of the marginal notes, see also Taylor in this volume.

[17] Cathy Shrank observes that 'after an initial scene-setting, many dialogues abandon that conversational mode: turn-taking falls away and dominant characters hold sway, uninterrupted for pages on end' (2013: 28).

would wish implemented in England can be seen as a prompt to further discussion, beyond the confines of the text', so that 'the breakdown of dialogue within the text is necessary precisely to encourage conversation back in the "real" world' (Shrank 2013: 35). The reader is invited to join the humanist conversations of *Utopia*.

The Coming of the Book to Utopia

Raisch identifies '*Utopia*'s investment in constructing communities' as emerging not only 'in the friendly correspondence among fellow-intellectuals that constitute the paratexts', and 'in sixteenth-century Antwerp in book 1', but also in the way that 'Greek scholarship produces community on the island of Utopia in book 2' (Raisch 2016: 930). As we have seen, Hythloday brings the enthusiastic Utopians a capsule library of Aldine Greek texts which provides them with the essential humanist curriculum. But the coming of the book to Utopia is not quite as straightforward an affair as this implies. For a start, not all of Hythloday's books arrive unscathed. His copy of Theophrastus' treatise *On Plants* was unfortunately 'somewhat mutilated' (*in locis mutilum*) during the course of the voyage, since he 'carelessly left it lying around, a monkey got hold of it, and from sheer mischief ripped out a few pages here and there and tore them up' (More 1995: 180–181).

This monkey has been seen as a key focal point for the interpretation of the passage concerning the Utopians' achievements in Greek. On a narrative level, the reported incident 'provides', as Louis Marin puts it, 'a very powerful "effect of reality"', paradoxically through its very absurdity: 'It is as if the truth of the narrative, far from insisting on the likeness between the real and rational, demanded instead absurdity as the criterium of reality' (Marin 1984: 177). More may well have been writing from experience, since he himself 'kept at home a large monkey' (*CWE* 40.1043), immortalized in a portrait of the family by Holbein.[18] We might, then, interpret Hythloday's monkey as a charming dash of realism designed to add depth to More's description of Hythloday's voyages. But, as Marin (1984: 175) explains, in its very character as 'such a perfectly accidental and insignificant event', the incident with the monkey arouses the suspicions of the reader; and 'meanings abound once suspicion sets in'. Thus Marin interprets it as a symbol for the contingency of the Western cultural tradition: 'The humanist library (and along with it Western culture) is more perfectly *transmitted* to Utopia because a monkey mutilates Theophrastus' (177). Summit adds that Theophrastus is a particularly 'apt object of textual mutilation', since his work 'was known to the West only through fragments' until

---

[18] On the Holbein portrait, see D. R. Smith 2005: 484–506. Smith finds the monkey 'scampering up Dame Alice More's skirt' in Holbein's original sketch for the painting 'anarchic', producing a 'disruptive effect' (484, 489, 500). Observing that it is one of the later additions to the sketch, he argues that its inclusion was requested by More himself (489). An etching of the drawing (now in the Kunstmuseum Basel) can be found at https://www.rct.uk/collection/659104/the-family-of-thomas-more.

the fifteenth century; it 'became part of the humanist canon when Aldus published it in an edition of 1497, a copy of which was owned and annotated by Erasmus' (Summit 2008: 75, 74). The monkey effectively undoes the work of collecting, editing, and preserving the works of classical antiquity undertaken by the Aldine Press, returning Theophrastus to his medieval fragmented state. In this sense, the incident highlights the significance of the Aldine project: More's contemporaries can laugh, secure in the knowledge that damage to one copy of Theophrastus is now insignificant, while at the same time being reminded that they have only escaped being in the position of the Utopians through the efforts of Aldus and other proponents of humanism.

The monkey itself turns out to be a particularly fertile metaphor. As Marin puts it: 'The monkey also carries within him a long and rich tradition: *simia-similis*. He is the caricature of identity in representation. He is the figure of figure, the double of figure: he reflects himself in a ludicrous mirror image' (Marin 1984: 179). As a result, 'the monkey is a negative Utopian, and the Utopian who goes "back to the school of the West" of Greece and of modernity, is a positive monkey' (180). Anne Lake Prescott, similarly, suggests that monkeys are 'funny as failed—or, worse, satirical—imitators of ourselves' (Prescott 2003: 431 n.). Summit additionally draws attention to the classical resonances of the Latin word *cercopithecus*, usually translated as 'monkey', or 'ape': 'In classical literature, the Kerkopes were deceptive dwarves whom Jupiter transformed into monkeys' (Summit 2008: 76). Thus, 'as men turned into monkeys, the Kerkopes reverse the civilizing mission that Hythloday believes he is carrying out' (76). These associations of the monkey as imitator have lent support to the argument in Yoran (2010: 160) that 'while the explicit argumentation of *Utopia* provides a vision of the ideal Erasmian social order, there is also a hidden level of meaning, one which contradicts central notions of Erasmian humanism and subverts, moreover, the premises of humanist discourse'. Though Yoran does not mention the monkey, other critics have found it to be the vehicle for just such a subversion of humanist discourse. Summit (2008: 76), for instance, concludes that the monkey and the Kerkopes 'also critique [Hythloday's] mission, suggesting that reading natural philosophy does not elevate men's wisdom but reduces them to the level of animals'.[19] Similarly, Nicole Morgan (1994: 42) argues that the passage subversively suggests that the damage done by the monkey undermines the authority accorded to ancient texts by the humanist movement.

But rather than questioning the value of the contents of Hythloday's books, the monkey can more persuasively be seen to reflect upon the figure of the reader. The monkey is effectively an overly literal reader: he 'materializes the text', mistaking the leaves of a book *On Plants* for leaves which might make up his natural diet. In his prefatory letter to Giles, More relates that a certain professor of theology has arranged to be sent by the Pope to be bishop of the Utopians. The bishop, like the monkey, has read *Utopia* too literally. Many years later, in his *Confutacyon of Tyndales Answere* (1532),

---

[19] Summit (2008: 77) also observes that in 1556 Robinson translated the Latin *cercopithecus* as 'mormosett'—an anagram of 'T[h]omas More'—thus making the monkey 'a figure for More himself'.

More expressed considerable anxiety over the danger that bad readers can be harmed even by good books: 'all be yt there be none harme therin | folke yet beynge (as they be) geven to take harme of that that is good' (*CWM* 8.179). The monkey functions as another emblem of the incompetent reader, who, like the bishop, consumes a text without comprehending it, and if not receiving actual harm, certainly without benefiting from it.

This interpretation of the monkey receives further support from an important classical source. Among Hythloday's books is a copy of Lucian, which is highlighted as being of special interest to the Utopians: they were 'delighted with the witty persiflage of Lucian' ('Luciani quoque facetiis ac lepore capiuntur') (More 1995: 180–181). More and Erasmus had translated a number of Lucian's dialogues between them, which were first printed in 1506, and Lucian is recognized as a significant influence on *Utopia*. *Utopia* can helpfully be characterized as an exercise in the 'serious play' (*serio ludere*) practised by Lucian, and the monkey, which is described as *ludibundus* ('playful'), is emblematic of the Lucianic games that More's text plays with its readers. Raisch (2016: 945) has productively drawn attention to an episode in Lucian's *A True Story* in which the narrator loses a third epic poem by Homer, but there is another parallel which has not yet been suggested. Lucian's *The Ignorant Book-Collector* is an invective against a wealthy man who buys books and goes through the motions of reading them in the hope of gaining a reputation for learning, but is incapable of understanding or benefiting from them. Lucian complains: ' "A monkey is always a monkey," says the proverb, "even if he has birth-tokens of gold." Although you have a book in your hand and read all the time, you do not understand a single thing that you read' (Lucian 1921: 179).

Despite the best efforts of Hythloday's multivalent monkey, the Greek books reach Utopia mostly intact. Once they arrive, it is not simply their contents from which the Utopians benefit. Hythloday explains that 'while we were showing them the books printed on paper in Aldine letters, we talked about what paper is made of and how letters are printed, though without going into details, for none of us had had any practical experience of either skill'; the Utopians, however, 'with great sharpness of mind [...] immediately conceived how to do it' (More 1995: 183). Thus, they began 'to make paper and print with type' ('iam chartam ilico facere et literas imprimere tentarunt') (184–185). The books can be 'read' as material objects which contain the traces of their own production: the process is deciphered from the product. The Aldine texts serve as examples through which the best printing practices can be divined. When the Utopians master the art of printing and set up their own press, they are effectively recreating an idealized version of Aldus' press in Venice, immortalizing his life's work in the no-place of Utopia.

But, as with so much else in Utopia, this apparently idealized vision of scholarly industry has unsettling undertones. Hythloday reports that the Utopians soon 'became so proficient that, if they had the texts of the Greek authors, they would have no lack of volumes. But now they have no more than those I mentioned—which, however, they have reprinted in thousands of copies' (185). Restricted to the books that Hythloday had brought, the Utopians are unable to progress, but are limited to forever reprinting these Aldine editions. Even with regard to their exemplary enthusiasm for Greek, where More seems most unambiguously to hold the Utopians up as an example, a note of anxiety creeps in: Utopia is always in danger of falling into an unproductive, or endlessly but fruitlessly productive, stasis. The success of the Utopian system explicitly rests upon its isolationism, represented geographically by the digging of the channel to turn the peninsula into an island (see More 1995: 111). Although Hythloday asserts that 'any sightseer coming to their land who has some special intellectual gift, or who has travelled widely and knows about many countries, is sure of a warm welcome'—as his own experience corroborates (185)—the fact is that the tight control of their geographical borders restricts intellectual as well as economic exchange. Hythloday relates that 'as for the export trade, they prefer to do their own transportation, instead of letting strangers come there to fetch the goods', explaining that 'by carrying their own cargoes, they are able to learn more about foreign countries on all sides and keep their own navigational skills from getting rusty' (185). This also effectively prevents contamination of the Utopian system through tightly controlling contact with the outside world, restricting it to a limited number of people and largely keeping out 'strangers'. But the result of this is that the Republic of Utopia cannot become part of the Republic of Letters, since the latter relies on the free exchange of knowledge across international borders. The political conditions which produce such an ideal community of Greek scholars simultaneously prevent this community from realizing its true potential.

This close linking of processes of intellectual and economic exchange is not incidental. For all its idealism, the Republic of Letters was intimately bound up with systems of economic exchange. Grafton writes that 'the Republic of Letters stood, in the first instance, for a kind of intellectual market—one in which values depended, in theory at least, not on a writer's rank but on the quality of his or her work' (Grafton 2009b: 24). The figurative intellectual market existed alongside a more literal one: the humanist citizens of the Republic of Letters wrote to each other exchanging money, recommending each other for teaching positions, and seeking patronage. Meanwhile, Lucien Febvre and Henri-Jean Martin offer a pertinent reminder that 'from its earliest days printing existed as an industry, governed by the same rules as any other industry; the book was a piece of merchandise which men produced before anything else to earn a living, even when they were (as with Aldus and the Estiennes) scholars and humanists at the same time' (Febvre and Martin 1997: 109).

It is telling, then, that Hythloday's account of his introduction of Greek books to Utopia is coloured by the language of economic exchange. The passage is framed by references to trade: he begins by saying that he brought with him 'a good-sized packed of books instead of merchandise' ('librorum sarcinam mediocrem loco mercium') (More 1995: 180–181). The Utopians, of course, do not deal in 'merchandise' (*merx*) amongst themselves, since in their system of communal living everything is freely available and there is no need to exchange money or goods. Hythloday recognizes this, and so brings books instead. But his language here, as elsewhere, reveals that he himself is unable to free his mind from the economic systems of sixteenth-century Europe.[20] Books take the

---

[20] Compare, for example, the passage in which Hythloday compares the Utopian custom of prospective spouses viewing each other naked to the process of buying a colt (More 1995: 189).

place of merchandise, in such a way that it is not clear whether the substitution occurs because of their difference or because of their similarity. At the end of the passage, Hythloday observes that 'few merchants go there to trade', for, he asks, 'what could they import, except iron—or else gold and silver, which everyone would rather take home than send abroad?' (185). Hythloday and his companions, of course, introduce the inventions of printing and paper-making to the Utopians, which are presented as clear improvements over their previous system. In a manoeuvre characteristic of the colonizer, Hythloday frames this transference of knowledge in economic terms: the Utopians 'owe' (*debent*) these arts to his party (182).

The fact that Hythloday is unable to escape the language of trade and economic exchange signifies more than a failure of imagination on his part. It registers a distinct ambivalence about the entanglement of the Republic of Letters in economic systems of exchange—systems in which *Utopia* itself is equally implicated. The title page of the 1516 edition refers to the work as a 'golden little book' (*libellus aureus*), a conventional enough advertisement of the moral and intellectual worth of its contents. In light of Hythloday's equation of books with merchandise, however, the baser connotations of monetary value may be activated. And when we remember that the Utopians use gold to make chamber pots, the inherent value of a golden book is distinctly unsettled. A Renaissance trope with classical origins identifies waste paper (from worthless writings) as destined to be used as toilet paper, while the leaves of a book eaten by a monkey will presumably emerge as excrement eventually.[21] As a text, *Utopia* positions itself as a site of humanist production, a commodious forum in the Republic of Letters, and at the same time slyly suggests that it might, in the end, be a golden book read by a monkey.

Conclusion

An early sixteenth-century reader, taking up *Utopia*, held in their hands a microcosm of the Republic of Letters. In its pages, humanists from across Europe collaborated on a Utopian project. The illusion of the reality of Utopia is created by appealing to the reader's empirical experience of the reality of *Utopia*, with its map and linguistic sample. *Utopia*'s conceptual investment in its own physical qualities is mirrored in its insistence on the material properties of Hythloday's Greek books. On the one hand, the introduction of Greek books to Utopia allows the Utopians to demonstrate how a society which truly values the advancement of knowledge would respond to the advances in technology and spread of resources that had been taking place in Europe during the fifteenth

---

[21] On the waste-paper trope, see Reynolds 2017. Freud elaborated on the apparent psychological connections between gold and excrement in his 1908 essay entitled 'Character and Anal Erotism' (Freud 1959: 167–176). Freud mentions the proverbial *Dukantensheisser*, or 'shitter of gold ducats', who is found in visual culture from at least the fifteenth century: V. Allen (2007: 94) finds one depicted on a misericord from the late fifteenth century in a church in Amsterdam.

and early sixteenth centuries. The irony is that it is not quite clear what benefit, other than pleasure, the Utopians will gain from their new books: their posited descent from the Greeks effectively short-circuits the processes of constructive emulation espoused by European humanists. Even here, where we would most expect Utopian practices to be held up for unequivocal praise, there is an unsettling undercurrent. This does not, however, reflect scepticism about the value of the Greek books themselves, or the humanist project they represent. Rather, the fundamental tensions arise from the Utopians' intellectual commitment to humanist pursuits on the one hand, and political refusal to participate in relationships of exchange with other nations on the other. *Utopia*'s playful engagement with its own materiality and that of the Greek books it describes encourages the development of an active reader, one who is not a monkey, nor even a Utopian, but an engaged citizen of the Republic of Letters.

CHAPTER 3

NEC MINUS SALUTARIS QUAM FESTIVUS

Wit, Style, and the Body in More's Utopia

ANDREW ZURCHER

To the third Latin edition of Thomas More's *Utopia*, published by Johann Froben in Basel in 1518, the printer added a collection of epigrams; this body of short poems and translations was thereafter re-edited—some poems deleted, new supplied—and published as a separate volume in 1520, entitled *Epigrammata*. More is thought to have begun composing these Latin poems about twenty years before, and certainly by 1509, when he dedicated to Henry VIII at his accession a *carmen* and some verses on kingship, later combined in the 1518 collection. Other poems reflect the sorts of reading and writing, often political in tone and bent, that characterize his letters and other works from this period—particularly, of course, *Utopia* (1516). And there are among the epigrams many points of contact with the concerns of *Utopia*, not least in a subgroup of verses preoccupied with political insights, particularly the dangers of tyranny; these poems, with titles such as 'Sola Mors Tyrannicida Est' ('Death Alone Kills Tyrants'), 'Sollicitam Esse Tyranni Vitam' ('The Life of a Tyrant is Troubled'), 'Tyrannum in Somno Nihil Differre a Plebeio' ('The Sleeping Tyrant Does Not Differ from a Subject'), and 'Regem non Satellitium Sed Virtus Reddit Tutum' ('A King is Preserved Not by His Retainers, But by His Virtues'), speak directly to the sorts of claims Hythloday makes to Morus in Book One of Utopia.[1] But such conspicuous points of contact and overlap between the epigrams and More's dialogue tell only part of a more complex story about tensions in More's writing between private and public discourse, implicit and explicit

---

[1] See also 'De Rege et Rustico', an epigrammatic fable about a peasant who, attending the public procession of a king, and failing to discern the mere man from surrounding crowds and courtiers, exclaims, 'Ille mihi picta veste videtur homo' ('To me he seems just a man in ornate clothes'); the parallel with Utopian disdain for the opulent display of foreign ambassadors in Book Two is striking. For More's focus on kingship and tyranny in his literary works, including these epigrams, see Baumann 1985.

meaning. The pairing of the *Epigrammata* and *Utopia*—the 'Libellus vere aureus, nec minus salutaris quam festivus, de optimo rei publicae statu deque nova insula Utopia'—invites closer inspection not only of More's epigrams, but also of the stylistic and hermeneutic conventions of epigrammatic writing, and how they might condition or structure our understanding of More's *libellus*.

Studies of the epigram as a characteristic, even constitutive, mode of humanist discourse emphasize, along with its brevity, its ephemerality: its inscription in its contemporary historical, social, and political moment. Other studies—including the work of early modern literary critics and theorists—stress a more concrete kind of inscription: the origins of epigram (and epigrammatic style) in monumental epigraphy (Colie 1974: 80–96; Cummings 2017). Both these almost universal strands in the critical history of epigrammatic writing thus locate the beginning, and meaning, of the genre in the intimate encounter between *res* and *verba*, thing and word. In this light, epigrammatic writing might be thought particularly important to the development of humanist discourse because of its focus, in multiple senses, on style: not just the highly intellectual rhetorical brilliance that produces what sixteenth-century scholar Julius Caesar Scaliger called the *argutia* ('brilliance', 'point'; from the Latin *arguere*, 'to make clear') of the epigram,[2] but—going deeper—the origin of the Latin word *stylus* in the Indo-European root *stig-*, giving us Greek *stizein* ('to prick'); Latin *instigo* ('goad, spur'); and various English terms derived from these cognate terms ('instigate', 'stimulus', 'style'). Trenchant, mordant wits of the humanist tradition, famous across fifteenth- and sixteenth-century Europe for the brilliance and acuity of their writing, hold the epigram at their hearts; and, as many literary historians observe, the epigram was a favourite genre for humanist philosophers, poets, and dramatists throughout the period, and across many vernaculars.

Not all epigrammatists took their cue from the Roman master Martial, whose biting, satirical teeth made his poems the model of *argutia*. After publication of the Planudean anthology in 1494, European epigrammatists could set before their writing-desks a Greek tradition, one nothing so partial to morsure as Martial, but instead typified by brevity, elegance, neatness, brilliance, and—especially—wit: *ironia* and *aporia* (from the Greek for 'no passage', hence a rhetorical or conceptual perplexity). For Kathryn Gutzwiller (1998: 8), these epigrams are distinctively and acutely marked by 'indeterminacy of meaning' arising from tensions between their material and historical closure and their literary placement and reproduction. This heightened tension between historical application and literary or aesthetic detachment made the epigram a byword for cunning and brilliance, so that it was celebrated in Rome for the virtues Cicero ascribes to Philodemus' poetry in his attack on Piso: 'He goes on to write a poem so witty, so neat, so elegant, that nothing could be more brilliant' ('poema porro facit ita festivum, ita concinnum, ita elegans, ut nihil fieri possit argutius', Cicero 1909: 29). We find Beatus

---

[2] 'Epigrammatis duae virtutes peculiares: brevitas & argutia' ('The epigram has two distinctive virtues, brevity and wit') (Scaliger 1561: 170).

Rhenanus, More's admirer and author of the preface to More's *Epigrammata*, introducing his friend's poems in the same terms: 'But indeed, as has not escaped you, the epigram should have brilliance joined with brevity, should be witty, and thereupon should close up everything with little exclamations, which the Greeks call *epiphonemata*' ('Sed enim, id quod te non latet, argutiam habeat epigramma cum brevitate conjunctam, sit festivum, & acclamatiunculis, quae epiphonemata Graeci vocant, subinde claudatur').[3] Essential to the Greek epigram, along with *argutia*, were *brevitas* (brevity), *festivitas* (wittiness), *elegantia* (elegance), and *concinnitas* (neatness), where the chief place—both for Cicero and Rhenanus—goes to wittiness. It is unsurprising, then, to find More repeatedly titling many of his epigrams, in both the 1518 and 1520 versions, with the phrase 'e Graeco' ('from the Greek'); he is keen to advertise the Greek commitment of his poems not to a cutting critique of contemporary characters or customs, but to (even more demanding) simultaneous attack and retreat: the *equipollentia* (in logical and epistemic terms, 'equality of force or power') of a style so sharp that it razors an ultimately indiscernible line.[4]

The application of the *Epigrammata* to *Utopia* in 1518, then, emerges not as a casual textual pairing, but as a decisive framing of the text of More's dialogue with a kind of interpretative key. But with the medical connotations of the Latin *salutaris* ('healthful, salubrious') in mind, the allusion to Cicero's *Ad Pisonem*, above, sounds an important—and ultimately cautious—note. Cicero attacked Piso, viciously, for his Epicurean habits and filthy gaggle (*sordidissimi greges*) of hangers-on; as we have seen, Cicero connects his contempt for their pursuit of bodily pleasure with the stylistic brilliance of the neat Philodemus, capable of turning the perfect epigram. This coordination of Greek epigrammatic style with the shame (or shaming) of the material body is a pervasive feature of Roman anxiety about the inheritance of Greek culture; it is also a connection to which Quintilian turns at a peculiar moment in Book XII of the *Institutio Oratoria* that seemingly holds particular resonance for More. Acknowledging the *gratia sermonis* ('grace of style') of Attic Greek, Quintilian encourages Latin writers to make up with conceit that which they lack in language: 'Since we cannot be so delicate, let us be stronger. If they beat us for subtlety, let us prevail by weight' ('non possumus esse tam graciles: simus fortiores. Subtilitate vincimur; valeamus pondere', Quintilian 1922: 12.10.35–6). The naturalness of Greek simplicity Quintilian then connects with the artless speech of intimacy:

> There are still some critics who deny that any form of eloquence is purely natural, except that which closely resembles the ordinary speech of everyday life, which we use to our friends, our wives, our children and our slaves, a language, that is to say, which

---

[3] Rhenanus in More 1520: 3. Quintilian describes *epiphonema* as 'an exclamation attached to the close of a statement or a proof by way of climax' ('est enim epiphonema rei narratae vel probatae summa acclamatio', Quintilian 1922: 8.5.9).

[4] For More's probable ownership of a manuscript of the *Palatine Anthology* (a gift from Desiderius Erasmus in 1509), see Cameron 1993: 178–201; cf. G. McDonald 2013.

contents itself with expressing the purpose of the mind without seeking to discover anything in the way of elaborate and far-fetched phraseology. And they hold that whatever is added to this simplicity lays the speaker open to the charge of affectation and pretentious ostentation of speech, void of all sincerity and elaborated merely for the sake of the words, although the sole duty assigned to words by nature is to be the servants of thought. Such language may be compared to the bodies of athletes, which although they develop their strength by exercise and diet, are of unnatural growth and abnormal in appearance. (12.10.40–1)

The nexus of elements here—simplicity in style, common speech with one's intimates, and the artificiality of the conditioned human body—establishes a blueprint for More's thinking about meaning and style throughout *Utopia*. In repeatedly coordinating these elements in both books of *Utopia*, More draws readers back to epigram and its traditional tensions between *argutia*, *festivitas*, and the intractable infirmity of materiality.

***

A short way into the 1520 collection of More's epigrams, readers encounter verses titled 'In Efflatum Ventris e Graeco' (More 1520: 30). This epigram (number 21), 'On Wind of the Bowels, from the Greek', translates Nicarchus, a first-century poet known to modern readers through the *Greek Anthology*. More's version of the poem, like its original, takes a swipe at the pride of kings:

> A fart retained in the bowels too long will kill you; whereas a fart quickly expelled will save you. If a fart can save or destroy you, is a fart not equal to dreaded kings?

> (Te crepitus perdit, nimium se ventre retentes.
> Te propere emissus servat item crepitus.
> Si crepitus servare potest & perdere. nunquid.
> Terrificis crepitus regibus aequa potest?)

The power to save or spill, to condemn or pardon, is one of the defining marks of the sovereignty of rulers. Here, for both Nicarchus and More, this supreme power is imagined as no different from, and no better than, the flatulence of human bowels. In this sense, the poem is satirical, insisting with disparaging economy on the embodied frailty of even the most powerful men. The clarity of this message, a comparison structured by perpendicular syntax that even a child could parse easily, More adopts from his source:

> A fart stopped up too long can kill; but a fart that speaks its stuttering music saves. So, if a fart can save, and on the other hand, kill, does a fart not hold a power equal to kings?

> (pordē apoktennei pollous adiexodos ousa:
> pordē kai sōzei traulon hieisa melos.
> oukoun ei sōzei, kai apoktennei pali pordē,
> tois Basileusin isēn pordē echei dunamin.)

Nicarchus' childish repetition of *pordē* ('fart'), interrupting every line, functions stylistically like the giggle-inducing flatulence gag of Roman farce. The slapstick demands crude composition, achieved through the schematic repetition of *apokteinein* ('to kill') and *sōzein* ('to save'), and the metapoetic and oxymoronic construction of the poem as *traulon melos* ('stuttering music'). More creates the same effect with his repetition of *crepitus*, 'crack', even intensifying the humour in the final line by wedging the word between *terrificis* and *regibus*, recreating syntactically the awkward escape of air from a pompous body in the very performance of its dread spectacle.

Though in a tight space and context of a generally pedantic fidelity to his source, More also alters the terms of Nicarchus' presentation, destabilizing the application of the epigram. Nicarchus' epigram contrasts wind that is *adiexodos*—'without a through way'—and wind that 'speaks' (*hiēmi*). This contrast, sounding in the terminology of music and music-making, connects a fart erupting to producing melody on, say, a wind instrument. More's verse, instead, focuses much more schematically and without this witty, dense wordplay on an opposition between interior and exterior; either the farter retains (*retentes*) the wind, or expels (*emissus*) it. Here the unthroughfaresomeness of the *crepitus* is not at stake; rather our understanding is drawn to something that, if held *within*, kills, but if allowed to come *out*, saves. By this means More's epigram facilitates not only comparison between the *crepitus* and kingly power, but a counter-reading that implicates his own epigrammatic practice. The high-stakes tension between holding something in, and giving it passage, is, after all, a problem not for kings—who can say anything with impunity—but for courtiers, who must ever remain conscious of the actionability of their words. How to speak without danger is the courtier's whole craft. Moreover, the epigram in More's version combines this fundamental courtly problem with the dynamics of decorum, for learning how to negotiate the body's awkward transgressions within social and political space—indeed, the very tagging of the body's functions as indecorous, as a constitution of that public space—is the bedrock of propriety. It is unsurprising, then, that the word More uses to translate *pordē*—*crepitus*—derives from the verb *crepere*: 'to rattle, crack, creak', but also, figuratively, 'to fart', and 'to talk noisily and without meaning, to prate'.

More's epigram on the *crepitus* thus gains by its schematic reimagination of Nicarchus' original an allegorical potential ambiguating its *epiphōnēma*, or witty conclusion. The poem turns back on itself, at once making a commonplace sally against kings and staging a complex ironization of that attack that tags the poem as indecorous, the unwelcome intrusion of the private into public space, a shameful and prating thing to be politely disregarded. This is typical of many of the *Epigrammata*, and of More's collection as a whole. For example, a later poem in the collection, translating verses by (pseudo-)Lucian, illustrates the ignorance of the fool, the *fatuus* or *mōros*, who is suffering from an infestation of fleas:

> ON THE FOOL, FROM THE GREEK
> Morio, whom the fleas bite, extinguishes his lamp.
> Now, he says, those fleas can't see me anymore.

> (IN FATUUM E GRAECO
> Quem mordent pulices extinguit Morio lychnon.
> Non me, inquit, cernent amplius hi pulices.)
>
> (More 1520: 49)

Interpretations of More's translation tend to focus on the wordplay created by More's allusion to his own name, not only in *Morio*—the fool—but also in the first syllable of *mordent*, 'they bite' (McCutcheon 2015a: 227–228). The same onomastic wit appears elsewhere in the collection, in puns on *mors* (death) and *mora* (delay). At a literal level, the fool's foolishness is exposed in his belief that lack of (visible) exposure will protect him from the fleas. The associations with More's name, however, suggest that the poem also functions as a metaphor for the epigrams themselves, and that More—perhaps assailed by the dangerous bites of knowing readers—can defend himself by making his meaning less explicit. The fool, here, becomes a little wise, precisely by being too foolish to speak clearly. So much is evident in (pseudo-)Lucian's original: 'The fool, bitten by many fleas, extinguishes his lamp, and says, "You see me no more!" ' ('esbese ton luchnon mōros, psullōn hupo pollōn | daknomenos, lexas: ouketi me blepete') (*Greek Anthology* 1916–27: 11.432).

But this epigram, like 'In Efflatum Ventris', turns back on itself, ironizing its apparent meaning. The poem humbly offers More himself as its flea-bitten subject, but satirical conventions also suggest that the terms can be reversed, and that the king laughing at his jester may, in fact, wear the motley. More has added to his translation more than the play on his own name. The Latin verbs he chooses to translate Greek *daknein* ('bite') and *blepein* ('see')—*mordere* and *cernere*—are regularly used in Latin in figurative senses connected to literary interpretation. *Mordere* can signify gaining purchase, or traction, in a material ground or—more metaphorically—in understanding. So Seneca urges Lucilius in *Epistulae morales* 78, 'Interim hoc tene, hoc morde' ('Meanwhile, hold fast to this thought and grip it close') (Seneca 1989: 2.78.29). It can also be used figuratively to signify the 'bite' or 'sting' inflicted by an insult, jest, mock, or satire, and in this sense appears throughout the works of Terence, Juvenal, Horace, Ovid, and Cicero, as in Juvenal's Satire 9.10, where the poet recalls Naevolus at the dinner table enjoying himself with a 'ioco mordente' ('biting jest'). Thus in biting poor Morio, the fleas might gain a kind of purchase on him—grasping his meaning—while at the same time stinging and ridiculing him. *Cernere*, in turn, literally means 'to separate, sift', and like its Greek cognate *krinein* (which gives us 'critic' and 'criticism'), is used figuratively to mean 'to perceive, see' and—by extension—'to understand, comprehend, judge, decide' (Lewis and Short 1879). More's use of these two verbs not only emphasizes the allegorical extension of his epigram, which comes insistently into focus as a subtle, paradoxical musing on ambiguity and interpretation, but also reverses the direction of its application. Through a conventional fool-king figure such as Midas—the subject of Erasmus' presentation of the fool convention in *Praise of Folly* (1511), and a commonplace exemplum of the topos in this period—we may understand that the foolishness of More's Morio *really* describes the conventional satirical contract operative in the Tudor court: attacks on the royal person are permitted precisely because they are not acknowledged. Leave the lights off, and More is safe precisely because his king, too, is safe. His *pulices* can get no injurious purchase on him—fool that he is—because they cannot in the darkness of his folly be seen to bite their other victim.

More's epigrams 'In Fatuum' and 'In Efflatum Ventris', then, exploit their style, diction, sources, and generic conventions to reverse their apparent application in a witty meditation on the operation of the *Epigrammata* as a whole. They are similar in another way, too. Both poems deal with the embarrassing condition of the human body by negotiating its exposure. Turn off the light, jokes the fool, and I'm preserved from shame. And yet it's precisely because the fool's body is on the page, as it were, that the epigram has any force at all. To return to More's crepitous imagery, it's not clear whether the meaning has been retained privately, or expressed publicly; has More created a stink, or not? Not every one of the over two hundred poems in More's *Epigrammata* reflects on the conditions and perils of poetic utterance, on the propriety of exposure, but the overall collection participates in the tensions that I have been describing, and in a way that offers clear parallels for a reading of *Utopia*, the work with which More's epigrams were originally published. Any gathering of epigrams is, by nature, miscellaneous. Miscellaneity, like the fool's motley, covers the fool's body (or body of his discourse), both revealing him for a fool and concealing the body from exposure. Dispersal or cancellation of meaning is the meaning, and what is most evidently revealed about the fool's sense is his reluctance, or inability, to establish that it is, in fact, nonsense. More's *Epigrammata* has been repeatedly attacked by critics and historians for its instability of tone, subject, meaning, and form. Some readers seek to excuse More from these charges by supposing that a subgroup of poems—the explicitly political poems dealing with kings, royal power, and tyranny—constitute the writer's real focus, which he carefully packaged in a great deal of nonsense to soften and disarm its potential charge. What these readings, both hostile and sympathetic, fail to notice is that miscellaneity is not simply a packaging in the *Epigrammata*, but the matter itself. For More, instability is a mode in terms at once generic (eclecticism, miscellaneity), political (tyrannical caprice), epistemic (scepticism), and hermeneutic (irony). And at the centre of this instability, at least in the epigrams discussed here, is the inconvenient intrusion of the embarrassing—because material—human body.

***

In a sense, the *Epigrammata* provide for the 1518 edition of More's *Utopia* another paratext (like the letters, alphabet, woodcuts, and other ancillary documents framing the text), structuring our interpretation of the dialogue. The conversation between Hythloday and Morus reveals the same preoccupations as the epigrams, with unrelenting consistency. Just before Book One begins, readers are presented with a short prefatory letter from More to his friend Peter Giles, who he claims first introduced him to Hythloday. This letter begins by establishing the text of *Utopia* as constrained by the same human limitations that produced the eclecticism of the *Epigrammata*. Bodies, More points out, exist in time, if only just:

> Howe beit to the dyspatchynge of thys so lytell busynes my other cares and troubles did leave almooste lesse, then no leasure. Whyles I doo daylie bestowe my tyme abowte lawe matters; some to pleade, some to heare, some as an arbytratour wyth myne awarde to determyne, some as an umpier or a judge with my sentence finallye to discusse. Whiles I go one way to see and visite my frend: an other way about mine owne privat affaires. Whiles I spend almost al the day abrode emonges other, and the residue at home among mine own: I leave to meselfe, I meane to my boke no time. For when I am come home, I muste commen with my wife, chatte with my chyldren, and talke wyth my servauntes. All the whyche thynges I reken and accompte emonge busynes, forasmuche as they muste of necessytye be done: and done muste they nedes be, oneles a man wyll be a straunger in hys owne house. (More 1551: †7v–8r)

The moment of literary composition is here nested within a delicate allusion to Quintilian's comments on natural or authentic speech in Book XII of the *Institutio Oratoria*. But this moment of literary composition is also one that More considers his most private, as evidenced by the homology created in a zeugma present in both the Latin and English texts: 'I leave to meselfe, I meane to my boke no time' ('relinquo mihi, hoc est, literis, nihil') (More 1551: †7v; 1516: a3r). *Outopos* is a product of *ouchronos*, a no-time hour, a private space of 'meselfe' defined precisely by the exclusion of all other activities and relations. This is a privacy even deeper than the conscience he must discharge in his equitable judgements, a privacy deeper than his friend, deeper than his 'privat affaires'. It is a privacy more private than his domestic life 'at home among mine own'—for even there, More says, he is at work, even while he 'commen[s] with [his] wife, chatte[s] with [his] chyldren, and talke[s] wyth [his] servauntes', all of which, as he says, 'I reken and accompte emonge busyness' ('inter negotia numero'). We are presumably called to question whether or not More achieves his duty to his wife and children and avoids being to them merely a 'straunger' (*peregrinus*), by massing his conversation with them among his public offices, manifold social duties, and ordering of his servants. To any humanistically trained reader—that is, readers that More must have imagined for his Latin dialogue in 1516—the stated anxiety about More's status in his house, that he might become *peregrinus*, that he had, in fact, become *peregrinus* even in seeking to avoid it, must have conjured the loss of another kind of relation, one summed in a word that lies at the centre of humanist writing, and especially that of More's intellectual circle: *familiaris*. In seeking to be *non peregrinus*, that is, more properly, *non alienus* or 'not a stranger' amongst his family, does More achieve *familiaritas*? If so, why count these relations *inter negotia*? Or is his most private hour, his most intimate moment, really that with his book? Can he only be himself when he is, at last, in moments stolen from sleep and meat, to-himself? Who is there, in *outopia*, to be familiar with?

The paradox More creates in his attempt to be *non peregrinus* amongst his *familiares* is one writ large across humanist intellectual culture. Kathy Eden's *Renaissance Rediscovery of Intimacy* (2012) charts the progress of the familiar or intimate style, almost as a badge of humanist self-identification and attainment, from the writings of Petrarch through those of Erasmus, to Michel de Montaigne's *Essais*. Eden sees the intimate letter, and familiar style in which it is written, as the mark of humanist writers: that which distinguishes humanist epistolarity from the *ars dictaminis* that preceded it. But the cultivation of an intimate style is not the same as intimacy itself; it is only the performance of intimacy, a stylistic representation of intimacy assumed in order to participate in certain coded exchanges, a rhetoric of privacy assumed to perfect very public business, that is, the constitution and ongoing renewal of elite social and intellectual cliques. For this reason, More's meditation on *familiaritas* in his letter to Giles—as the allusion to Quintilian should suggest—emerges as a carefully calibrated, and a consummate, performance: More and Giles were casual acquaintances who knew one another through intermediate contacts, who had been thrown temporarily together during More's participation in treaty negotiations in Bruges in 1515. To write to him promising a love greater than 'ever I dyd' rings for us with irony, in an age in which love has meaning only as a sincerely felt expression of an inward self, and not as a socially constructed and rhetorically performed relation between associates. More's blurring of the boundary between 'busynes' and *familiaritas*, then, is a version of the broader humanist tension between the rhetorical (and particularly epistolary) profession of intimacy, and the real intimacy that gave that profession, perhaps only for a season, its powerful social force.

More connects these commonplaces, in his letter to Giles, to the problem of style. The plainness and sincerity of his style, he claims, is a consequence of the simple operation he has been performing—that is, transcribing Hythloday's oral discourse, a methodical and almost mechanical process not permitting any exornation or laboured eloquence:

> For you knewe welenough, that I was already disbourdened of all the labour & study belonging to the invention in this work, and that I had no nede at all to trouble my braynes about the disposition, or conveyaunce of the matter: & therfore had herein nothing els to do, but only to rehearse those things, which you and I togethers hard maister Raphaell tel and declare. Wherefore there was no cause whie I shold study to set forth the matter with eloquence: for asmuch as his talke cold not be fine & eloquent, being firste not studied for, but sodein and unpremeditate, and then, as you know, of a man better sene in the greke language, then in the latine tong. And my writing, the nigher it shold approche to his homely playne, and simple speche, somuch the nigher shold it go to the truth: whiche is the only marke, wherunto I do and ought to direct all my travail and study herin. (More 1551: †6v–7r)

More's representation of the style appropriate to narrating Hythloday's speech—that is, the familiar style, the 'sodein and unpremeditate' style that Petrarch had developed in his *Epistolae familiares*—cultivates the paradox characteristic of Erasmian epistolary composition. All More's 'travail and study' must be to 'approche' a 'homely playne, and simple speche'; insofar as he labours, it will be to avoid the appearance of labour. The stylistic sleight-of-self distinctive to humanist epistolary practice articulated here, More frames in the same terms in an epigram, 'Ad Quendam Poetam Extemporalem' ('to a certain extemporal poet'): 'You warn us that you wrote these verses extemporally? | Your book tells us this, you being quiet' ('Hos te scripsisse mones ex tempore versus?

| Nam liber hoc loquitur, te reticente, tuus') (More 1520: 96). The best poetry seems extemporaneous, elegantly immediate; this poetry, quips More, instead sounds hurried, and the poet's protestation only highlights his incompetence. More's combination of casual, frank speech with the density and economy of composition required by the epigrammatic couplet indicates, meanwhile, his mastery in the very art in which his rival is said to be deficient. This paradoxical effect—the refined achievement of the natural, the studied production of the sudden, and the artificiality of the artless—appears in More's letter to Giles as an adaptation not merely of epistolary, but also of epigrammatic, convention.

It is no secret among critical readers of More's work that *Utopia*'s style is fundamentally litotic in nature. Litotes, the figure of diminution, often associated with the double negative, features in several landmark studies of the book, the most influential of which is certainly Stephen Greenblatt's *Renaissance Self-Fashioning* (1980). Building on the work of critics such as Elizabeth McCutcheon (1971, 1983), Greenblatt sees More's use of litotes exemplifying an anamorphic technique that both reveals and conceals the origins of *Utopia* in sociohistorical forces that the book 'is designed to render invisible'. Litotes, the figure of simplicity, is the animating spirit (in both ethical and poetic terms) of Greek epigram; from Callimachus onwards, humility and brevity structured the distinctive grace of epigrammatic style (Campbell 2019). My own understanding of the function of litotes in the stylistic fabric of *Utopia* is, therefore, that it illustrates and performs the commonplace humanist stylistic paradox I have been discussing. Litotes lies at the centre of More's first rhetorical posture to Giles; in seeking to be *non peregrinus*, More never says he wishes to achieve *familiaritas*, but implies it by double negation: to be a member of the family is not to be a stranger, isn't it not? From the start, litotes acts as a stylistic marker of the primacy of style in the matter of More's work, an insistence that the medium is also the message. Although its junior by some two generations, George Puttenham's *Arte of English Poesie* (1589)—the first substantive English treatment of the figure of litotes—offers a valuable gloss to More's practice in *Utopia*. Moving from emphasis to litotes, Puttenham writes:

> As by the former figure we use to enforce our sence, so by another we temper our sence with wordes of such moderation, as in appearaunce it abateth it but not in deede, and is by the figure *Liptote*, which therefore I call the *Moderator*, and becomes us many times better to speake in that sort quallified, than if we spake it by more forcible termes, and neverthelesse is equipolent in sence. (Puttenham 1589: 153)

For Puttenham, the essence of the figure is its moderation, its qualification of meaning, but this moderation or qualification only (of course) affects the 'appearaunce' of the thing being described, and not the thing 'in deede'. In other words (literally), the effect of the figure is to widen the gap between the actual value of a thing, and the abated appearance, imposing a burden of inference on auditors or readers, who must make up the abatement to realize the true 'equipollence' of the thing and its representation. The valuation of the litotic thing, then, is the work of auditors/readers, and not speakers/writers.

By contrast, Puttenham's description of emphasis—with which litotes is regularly paired by early modern rhetoricians, following Quintilian's *Institutio Oratoria* (9.2.3)—attempts to collapse the distance between word and thing, removing the burden of valuation from auditors or readers:

> And one notable meane to affect the minde, is to inforce the sence of any thing by a word of more than ordinary efficacie, and nevertheles is not apparent, but as it were, secretly implyed, as he that said thus of a faire Lady:
>
> *O rare beautie, ô grace, and curtesie.*
>
> And by a very evill man thus.
>
> *O sinne it selfe, not wretch, but wretchednes.*
>
> Whereas if he had said thus, *O gratious, courteous and beautifull woman*: and *O sinfull and wretched man*, it had bene all to one effect, yet not with such force and efficacie, to speake by the denominative, as by the thing it selfe. (Puttenham 1589: 153)

Puttenham relies on hyperbole as he concludes this description, but in one sense his assertion matches his examples: the *kind* of emphasis he practises here, in both illustrations, substitutes the thing he praises in a person (beauty, grace, courtesy, sin, wretchedness) for the person endowed with that thing. Emphasis in Puttenham's account thus gets close—as close as can be achieved in language—to speaking 'as by the thing itselfe'. If emphasis is to be coordinated with litotes as its opposite, then Puttenham's account of that figure is—fittingly, by contrast—to be understood as a mode of speaking a thing by negating the representation of the thing, that is, by negating its absence. If we stop thinking about litotes as understatement, or as the figure of asserting presence by denying the absence of thing; if we instead focus on the early modern account of the figure as a means of breaking the connection between things and words, it instantly comes into focus as a performance of the characteristic humanist epistolary and epigrammatic operation. I will use art to demonstrate that I use no art, as Polonius will later say; I will study not merely to seem, but to *be* 'unpremeditate', writes More. Both speakers insist that by having no meaning, they can be understood as meaningful; similarly, litotic speech disowns things so that auditors or readers may infer them, disowns their absence to imply their presence. It is not what is said, but the act of not saying it that creates the opportunity for inference.

The importance of observing this subtle shift in the operation of litotic style lies in the way More connects a style of speaking to a habit of thinking about the relation between people and things. Central to the philosophy of Hythloday's account of Utopia lies an economic and social vision of 'commoning' that makes what is said *familiariter*—that is, intimately, unpremeditatedly—seem *alienum*—that is, strange. As Morus and Hythloday reach the climax of their discussion of counsel towards the end of Book One, Hythloday explicitly links a 'strange' or 'foreign' way of speaking, the style of the *peregrinus*, to the social structure of private ownership in Henrician England. Morus advises Hythloday to offer counsel to the princes of Europe, telling him that his wide experience as a traveller will make him indispensable to courts such as Henry's. Hythloday protests:

> If so be that I shoulde speake those thynges that Plato fayneth in hys weale publique: or that the utopians do in theires, thies thinges thoughe they were (as they be in dede) better, yet they myghte seme spoken owt of place. Forasmuch as here amonges us, everye man hath hys possessyons severall to hymselfe, & there all thinges be common. (More 1551: F6v–7r)

In his choice of the adverbial phrase 'owt of place', Ralph Robinson's translation connects Hythloday's style to the *ou-topos* of his peregrine persona. For Robinson, these things that he might say would have 'no place'. The Latin original puts it differently; the difference is, I think, important:

> Quod si aut ea dicerem, quae fingit Plato in sua repu[blica] aut ea quae faciunt Utopienses in sua, haec quanq[uam] essent, u[t] certe sunt, meliora, tame[n] aliena videri possint, q[uod] hic singuloru[m] privatae sunt possessiones, illic omnia sunt communia. (More 1516: E1r)

These things that Hythloday might say, though they might be *meliora* ('better'), nevertheless 'may seem strange' or 'foreign', that is, *aliena*, the opposite of *familiares*. The supposed intimacy and frankness of Hythloday's style of speaking will be what makes the things he says *aliena*: the opposite of frank, the opposite of intimate. This transformation, moreover, is the *result* of contemporary European ideas about property: 'forasmuch' or 'because' (*quod*) 'everye man hath hys possessyons severall to hymselfe, & there'—that is, in Utopia—'all thinges be common'. The inferential cooperation of the litotic style, which brings speaker and auditor, writer and reader together in an intimate relation, seems to depend on the relation of persons to objects, the structures by which things are held to be associated (or not) with the people who have, handle, exchange, and lose them.

In Book Two of *Utopia*, Hythloday presents an account of Utopia distinctive for the total displacement of the private by the public. This feature of the Utopian 'commonwealth' is as well understood as it is, in Hythloday's account, explicit. Utopians do not own their houses, or the things that fill their houses. They 'common' together in public halls, instead of taking their meat, and enjoying the intimate conversation that might accompany that meat, in private. The conventional markers of individuality—dress, family relation, religious belief—are entirely displaced by constitutionally stipulated norms, which produce entirely social persons who can be said, truly and absolutely, to hold all things in common. More presents in *Utopia*, then, a kind of absolute caricature, writ large across the whole of the republic, of the society pictured in the first of Erasmus' adages, that friends hold all things in common: *amicorum communia omnia*. It is this difference in object relations which makes 'famylier communication' possible in Utopian civic spaces, whereas it is completely impossible—that is, without a place—in the councils of European princes.

More sets up a clear comparison, turning on the Latin word *familiaris*, between different conciliar styles in two famous passages from Books One and Two. In the first, at the climax of Book One, Morus responds to Hythloday's reticence to engage in public life by admonishing him about the difference between humanist *colloquia* and princely *consilia*:

> And to speake as I thynke, truly I can not alowe that such communicatyon shall be used, or suche cownsell geven, as you be suere shall never be regarded nor receaved. For how can so straunge informations be profitable, or how can they be beaten into their headdes, whose myndes be all reddye prevented with cleane contrarye persuasyons? Thys schole philosophie is not unpleasaunte emonge fryndes in famylier communication [*in familiari colloquio*], but in the counselles of kynges [*in consiliis principum*], where greate matters be debated and reasoned wyth great aucthorytye, thies thynges have no place. That is yt whyche I mente (quod he) when I said phylosophye hadde no place amonge kinges. (More 1551: F5r)

Morus' warning to Hythloday follows directly on a series of case studies that Hythloday presents to illustrate the benefits of reducing a king's personal property in order to encourage the commonweal. While he does not make the claim explicitly, Morus insists that Hythloday's counsel will fail because European princes labour under a *diversa persuasio*—Robinson's 'contrarye persuasyons'—that is, that kings should pursue their own wealth and grandeur, amassing as much money and power as possible. The identification of persona with property makes speech *in familiari colloquio* impossible.

By contrast, in another famous passage, in Book Two, Hythloday describes the arrival of foreign ambassadors to Utopia, and the hilarity that ensues as they process down the boulevards of Amaurot dressed in the splendour befitting their royal deputation:

> For to the iyes of all the utopians, excepte very fewe, whiche had bene in other contreys for some resonable cause, al that gorgeousnes of apparrel semed shamefull and reprochefull. In so much that they most reverently saluted the vylest, and most abject of them for lordes: passing over the Ambassadours themselfes without any honour: judging them be their wearing of golden cheynes to be bondemen. Yea you should have sene children also that had caste away their peerles and pretious stones, when they sawe the like sticking upon the Ambassadours cappes: digge and pushe their mothers under the sides sayinge thus to them. Loke mother how great a lubbor doth yet were peerles and pretious stoones, as though he were a litel child still. But the mother, yea and that also in good earnest: peace sone saith she: I thynk he be some of the Ambassadours fooles. Some fownde fawte at their golden cheynes as to no use nor purpose: beynge so small and weake, that a bondeman myghte easelye breake them, and agayne so wyde and large that when it pleased him he myght cast them of, and runne awaye at lybertye whether he wolde. But when the Ambassadoures hadde bene there a daye or .ij. and sawe so greate abundaunce of gold so lyghtelye estymed, yea in no lesse reproche then yt was wyth them in honour: and besydes that, more golde in the cheynes and gyves of one fugytyve bondeman, then all the costelye ornamentes of them .iij. was worth: they beganne to abate theyre currage, and for verye shame layde awaye all that gorgyouse arraye wherof theye were so prowde. And specyallye when they hadde talkede famylyerlye wyth the Utopyans, and hadde learnede all theyre fassyons and opynyons. (L1r–v)

In the delight we—in company with early Tudor readers—must take in the picture of this liberating world-turned-upside-down, it is easy to miss what I take to be one of the passage's crucial elements: the ambassadors' conversion from one perspective on person–thing relations, to its opposite. The 'famylier communication' that these three visitors have with the Utopians depends on, and is constructed by, the prevailing contempt for personal property. As often in More's work, the contrastive parallel between the two passages is exact, and artfully constructed.

This artful construction, illustrating More's consummate control of his dialogue, again turns our attention from the varied, even contrary, arguments presented over the course of Morus' and Hythloday's discussion to the style in which that discussion is framed. Artfulness bespeaks intention; evidence of the maker's hand implies some purpose behind the traces of the making made. We are, after all—especially after reading the chummy humanist epistles framing the text in its various early Latin editions—primed to consider ourselves as standing in relation to More's work in *Utopia* just as Morus himself stood in relation to Hythloday. Like More, we have come into a garden, a secluded and privileged space where we are permitted to raise arguments, try perspectives, and dare to perceive truths that in the normal course of civic and political life would be too dangerous, offensive, or, at least, *interested*, to articulate.[5] I think this prompts reflection on More's own relation to the material object in which his varied and even contrary arguments are inscribed: the book of *Utopia*. Is this a private object, one that tends to create value in a celebrated humanist writer to be renowned above others for his superlative learning and eloquence? Or is it a public document to be disowned and cast off as Utopian children do their pearls and precious stones? Has More made a stink? Has he extinguished the lamp? Entangled with these questions is some judgement—that is, our judgement—about the purpose of the work, on which any assessment of its value must depend. It was a commonplace of humanist epistolary practice, in a formula derived from the fourth-century Greek writer Libanius, that letters mediated between absent friends, making them present to one another: 'The letter is a conversation between absent persons' ('Epistola est absentis ad absentem colloquium', Erasmus 1521: A2r). In that sense, letters, and above all familiar letters, were said to contain and transmit some part of the writer's self. More's deconstruction of the pretensions of humanist epistolary familiarity takes on new urgency in a dialogue also preoccupied with the relation between public and private, self and thing, the possibility and value of real intimacy. The philosophical crisis at the centre of the reading of *Utopia*, then, might be said to be not the economic question of the distribution of wealth, nor the social question of the organization of the public weal, nor the political question of how to speak to princes, but the literary question of how to mean what you write. Or, to put it better, these may all be understood as versions, in More's *Utopia*, of the same question.

---

[5] For further consideration of the significance of the garden as a discursive space, see Morgan in this volume.

We have seen already how the litotic style of absence-negation allows More to become *familiaris* (*non peregrinus*) with his reader. More's dense use of litotes, so amply documented by McCutcheon, is only one of the rhetorical techniques on which he relies to structure his paradoxical negotiation of familiarity and alienation, privacy and publicity. The other—if anything, more emphatic and visible—resource is the commonplace. More's resort to adage, proverb, aphorism, and commonplace is so widespread in *Utopia*, and in so many cunning forms displayed, that (at least in my experience) readers tend not to notice it. I have already noted the organization of the whole dialogue on the plan of Erasmus' adage, *amicorum communia omnia* (or in More's phrase, *omnia sunt communia*). This is only one of many adages that More recruits in the course of the work. As Stephanie Elsky observes in her study of commonplaces and common law in *Utopia*, More begins Book One with a proverb.[6] Introducing his fellow ambassador to Flanders, Cuthbert Tunstall, More praises his virtue and learning by refusing to do so,

> not bycause I do feare that small credence shalbe geven to the testymony that commyth owt of a frindes mouthe: but bicause hys vertue and lernyng be greater and of more excellencye, than that I am able to prayse them: and also in all places so famous, and so perfectlye well knowne, that they nede not nor ought not of me to be praysed, onles I wolde seme to shew and set furth the brightenes of the sonne wyth a candell, as the Proverbe sayth. (More 1551: B1r–v)

More's combination of litotes and proverb dazzles: to praise Tunstall would be ineffective, therefore by omitting to praise him More will fail to be ineffective, and in so failing will prove effective—but effective in such a way, in fact, that the candle he has not held up, though weaker than the sun, by not being held up has nonetheless succeeded in outshining the sun. Commonplaces, as More points out, mean nothing precisely because everyone knows them already. You might as well not speak at all. The proverb, like the epigrams scrutinized earlier, sustains its force precisely by undoing itself. The tight synthesis of litotic paradox and proverbial illustration, in this opening passage, demonstrates how the two rhetorical strategies will function together throughout the work.

More's penchant for commonplaces in *Utopia* has, itself, become a commonplace of critical responses to his dialogue. What has not gone much remarked, by contrast, is the association between his use of commonplaces and the inconveniences of the body that characterize familiarity not only in the *Epigrammata*, but also in the corpulent rapacity of an unjust prince, or faecal opulence of a golden toilet. Two examples, plucked from

---

[6] Elsky (2013: 184) argues that because 'proverbs engender a discursive commons', they function as 'the discursive counterpart to More's effort to imagine a political commons rooted in custom'. Elsky does not profess to offer a full catalogue of More's proverbs or even his debts to Erasmus' *Adagia*; but her discussion fails to note some of the most conspicuous, and to her discussion relevant, examples, such as 'summum ius, summa iniuria' ('the most rigorous law is the greatest injury'), a common law maxim and important proverb in Erasmus' *Adagia* (1.10.25), which also features in *Utopia*, Book One at a crucial moment in Hythloday's narration of his argument with the lawyer in Morton's house.

many, demonstrate the habitual recurrence of More's dialogue to these associations. First, the conference at Cardinal Morton's house recounted by Hythloday in Book One, in which a fool merrily winds up a friar to the amusement of the Cardinal and his household, turns on two proverbs, one of which—like so many of Elsky's examples—is linked to Erasmus' *Adagia*. The conversation is occasioned by Hythloday's outrage that, in England at the time, a starving man could be sentenced to death for stealing a loaf of bread. Erasmus' *Adagia* sheds striking light on this conversation:

> Viro esurienti necesse furari [...] A starving man is forced to be a thief. Suidas classifies this as a proverb suited to those who are driven by extreme necessity to do something. For example, someone who confesses he has lied, may say, 'What was I to do? Either I had to lie or descend to the worst disgrace. A hungry man must steal.' Or someone greedy for fame may publish other people's work as his, because he can produce nothing outstanding of his own. (3.5.65; *CWE* 35.104–105)

The whole conversation, grounded in a proverb of Suidas, turns on the inconvenience of the material body, so insistent that it drives a man to theft and, thus, to his death. The thing he seeks to avoid his death, as Hythloday argues, causes it. But this proverb in Erasmus' hands also transpires, again, to implicate More himself, who—in the lengthy preamble to Giles where he insists that he has only recorded, verbatim, Hythloday's actual speech—perfectly illustrates the thieving author. Hythloday's outrage at the imposition of capital punishment on starving thieves thus works overtime, as it were, as a defence of the transcriber; 'don't hang the famished man' becomes 'don't shoot the messenger'. At the centre of this elaboration of a proverb—a conversation dominating Book One—stands the starving body. (Maybe More shouldn't steal so much time from his meat?)

This vignette ends in the well-known *contentio* between the scoffing fool and short-tempered friar, where another bout of commonplacing takes place before the fool is put in his place (by the Cardinal) by being displaced. The fool, daring to equate mendicant friars with lowly beggars, arouses the friar's vehement anger. Scorning Morton's entreaties and counsel, the friar works himself into an ever more salivary lather by citing scripture at his opponent, culminating in a quotation taken from Proverbs 26:5: 'answer a fool according to his folly'. This biblical proverb is delivered nested within two references to an Old Testament passage that itself centres, again, on the shame of the body:

> And it is song in the church. The skorners of Helizeus [Elisha], whiles he went up into the house of god felt the zeale of the bald, as peradventur this skorning villain ribauld shal feel. [...] For if many skorners of Helizeus, which was but one bald man, felt the zeal of the balde, howe much more shall one skorner of many frears feele, amonge whom be many bald men? (More 1551: F3v)

This allusion to 2 Kings 2:23 recalls the anecdote of Elisha who, when mocked by children on the road for his bald head, cursed them, with the result that bears issued from the woods and tore forty-two of the boys in pieces. Male fragility is rarely so violent on so trivial a cause as this, but that appears to be More's point: far from *salutaris* and *festivus*, Elisha's lack of mirth produces only death. It may at first seem odd that a healthy and merry dialogue should reach a rhetorical climax of this kind—that is to say, one that cheerlessly tears up bodies—in a tight coordination of proverb, commonplace, citation, and exposure. But these elements prepare us perfectly for the close of Book Two, where Hythloday describes the Utopians' religious beliefs and practices, noting in thinly veiled parody their capacious, dark churches; empty form of prayer; and farcically reduced doctrinal consensus. In insisting only on monotheism and the immortality of the soul, Utopians effectively reduce the Apostolic Creed to its first and last elements ('Credo in Deum Patrem omnipotentem [...] vitam aeternam'), disembowelling it precisely of those interior elements—the Incarnation, materiality of Christ's body, and its progress through suffering, death, and burial—that make it compelling to human affection and emulation.

Seen thus, More's investigation of the tensions between persons and things—focused as they are in *Utopia* around problems of style, familiarity and strangeness, public and private—seems to critique one of the fundamental tenets of the community of sixteenth-century men of letters we today know as humanists. Erasmus' familiar style and emphasis on intimacy, which as Eden (2012) shows is the foundational principle not only of his account of rhetoric but also of his theology, was predicated on an ideology of *communitas*. More's litotic style in *Utopia*, along with his quasi-satirical portrait of a republic that takes the concept of *res publica* (public things/affairs) to its extreme, seemingly insists instead on a residual, if incoherent, sentimentality for the flesh, property, and private selfhood. If we can take him to mean anything at all, he seems to suggest, this recoil into the private must be that meaning's consequence. In the concluding moments of *Utopia*, as Hythloday closes his discussion, Morus leaves his residual questions unspoken. More could be said. More will be left unsaid. But this inevitable inexhaustibility of the topic, and perforce of the persons discussing it, More pairs with a brief reflection on the relationship between money and the public good:

> thoughe manye thinges came to my mind which in the manners and lawes of that people semed to be instituted & founded of no good reason, not only in the fassion of their chevalry & in their sacrifices and religions, and in other of their lawes, but allso, yea & chieffely in that which is the principall fondacion of all their ordinaunces, that is to saye in the communitie of theire liffe and livinge, without anny occupieng of money, by the whyche thinge onely [*qua una re*] all nobilitie, magnificence wourship honour and majestie, the true ornamentes and honoures as the common opinion is of a common wealth utterly be overthrowen and destroyed. (More 1551: S3r–v)

A thing, money, lies in the *publica opinio* ('common opinion') at the very foundation of the *respublica*, such that the dispensing with this thing takes with it a great number of immaterial and incontrovertibly positive qualities. Making sense of this statement, as many critics have commented, is a difficult task. It is too simple to say that Morus retreats with a sigh into the world-as-it-is, because this world is characterized by precisely that *communitas*—the *publica opinio*—that Utopia in Hythloday's account privileges. As a worthless thing deriving all its value from attribution—that is, the hopes, purposes, and fears held by the people who desire and amass it—money is emblematic of the simple human weakness that More seemingly diagnoses, in a tone not devoid of compassion, in the weak *corpus* of humanist *communitas*. We have care for the body, even the flatulent and lousy body, and for the balding head. We have sentimental relations with things.

Perhaps the neatest illustration of the frail human sentiment about things—standing, for me, as *Utopia*'s greatest legacy—emerges as an irony arising from More's own biography. Hythloday's account of Utopia stresses categorically the Utopians' rationalist approach to the immortality of the soul and consequent worthlessness of the body. The immortality and primacy of the soul might be said, in fact, to be the only religious principle Utopus considered absolute when framing the Utopian constitution:

> Savinge that he earnestly and straytelye chardged them, that no man shoulde conceave so vile and base an opinion of the dignitie of mans nature as to thinke that the sowles do dye and perishe with the bodye: or that the worlde runneth at al aventures governed by no divine providence. And therfore thei beleve that after this lyfe vices be extreamelye punyshed & vertues bountyfully rewarded. Hym that is of a contrary opinion they counte not in the numbre of men, as one that hath avaled the hyghe nature of his sowle to the vielnes of brute beastes bodies: muche lesse in the numbre of their citiziens, whoes lawes & ordenaunces if it were not for feare he wold nothing at al esteme. For yow may be suer that he wil study other with crafte prevely to mock, or els violently to breake the commen lawes of his countrey, in whom remayneth no further feare then of the lawes, nor no further hope then of the bodye. (O4r–v)

In another neatly constructed, contrastive parallel, then, Morus pairs his own resignation to material sentiment, at the end of the work, with Utopus' commitment to the immaterial soul. The whole of Utopian common law, the whole of the *respublica*, with all its 'nobilitie, magnificence wourship honour and majestie', depends for Utopus, if not for More, on the contemptible body, to be cast away in an absolute commitment to the dignity of the immaterial. Ultimately, then, what is perhaps the greatest memento mori emerging from *Utopia*, in both senses of the phrase, comes in the fate of More's own body which, following his execution for refusing to swear the Oath of Allegiance, was returned, in pieces, to his devoted, and materially sentimental, daughter, Margaret Roper. 'As for [his] head', writes Anthony à Wood, drawing on the account in Thomas Stapleton's *Tre Thomae* (1588):

> it was set upon a pole on London-bridge, where abiding about 14 days, was then privily bought by the said Margaret, and by her for a time carefully preserv'd in a leaden box, but afterwards with great devotion 'twas put into a vault (the burying place of the Ropers) under a chapel joyning to St. Dunstan's church in Canterbury, where it doth yet remain, standing in the said box on the coffin of Margaret his daughter buried there. [...] One More of Hartfordshire (descended from him) had one of his chaps, and was by him among other rarities carefully preserv'd till the

'presbyterian' rebellion broke out in 1642. Jasper and Ellis Heywood, Jesuits, sons of Jo. Heywood the noted poet in the time of Hen. 8, had one of the teeth of the said sir Tho. More, but they being loth to part with their right to each other, the tooth fell asunder and divided of itself. (1813: 1.86)

Wood's account makes clear that More's family preserved every part of his body: the corpse, which was buried; the head, which Margaret kept, spicing it to keep it fresh until it was interred with her own corpse; the lower jaw, which found its way into the hands of Cressacre More; even the tooth he had lost during life, which the Heywood boys miraculously parted between them.

More's challenge to the humanist principle of *communitas*, then, was a simple human one. From its introductory paratexts to marginal annotations, *Utopia* playfully erases the individual self, and above all the human body, equating the self with the literary person, More with Morus: 'I leave to meselfe, I meane to my boke no time' ('Relinquo mihi, hoc est, literis, nihil') (More 1551: †7v; 1516: a3r). But among the proverbs and commonplaces, enigmatic ironies and ludic litotes, More repeatedly returns—as his daughter did, and as epigram does—to the vulnerable, often humiliating materiality of some one. By framing his dialogue on the best state of a commonweal with the *Epigrammata*, More invites readers to note the debt of both genres to litotes, to understand *festivitas* (wit) in connection with *argutia* (brilliance), and—perhaps above all—to recall the foundation of both dialogue and epigram in actual, embodied, material experience, without which (for all the promises of the *res publica*) there can be neither wit, nor health.

CHAPTER 4

THE RELIGIONS OF THE UTOPIANS

Sin and Salvation in Thomas More's Utopia

DAVID HARRIS SACKS

THE first readers of *Utopia*'s elegant Latin came from Europe's educated lay and clerical public, nearly all men, who possessed the command of classical language and literature needed to follow the carefully wrought dialogue in Book One and the brilliantly laid-out narrative in Book Two. It is a cunning work in which More set his readers puzzles, many posed, as we shall see, by his Latin word choices. The most important conundrum is raised by the work's Latin title—*De optimo reipublicae statu deque nova insula Utopia*—in early printed editions. Did More wish readers to side with Hythloday and take 'the new island of Utopia' to represent 'the best state of a commonwealth'? The conjunction *deque* ('and') left the answer ambiguous. Critical to this discussion has been how to judge the description of religion in Book Two. Based on the analysis of this subject offered in this chapter, my answer to More's implied question is that in his work he sided with his namesake Morus' doubts not just about the possibility of bringing a Utopian regime into being in the world, but also about the value of some of its central features.

PATTERNING A WHOLE COMMONWEALTH

Among *Utopia*'s most compelling qualities has been its capacity to convince readers not just that they are privy to an actual conversation between people they might meet, but also that Utopia is a place they might actually visit. Early in the book's history, around 1580, Philip Sidney singled out *Utopia* as a work of fiction for this last characteristic: its 'way of patterning a commonwealth', showing how its virtuous qualities functioned together, that he found 'most absolute', i.e. 'complete' or 'perfect' (Sidney 1973: 86–87). He indicated the same by spelling the title of More's book as *Eutopia* (86 n); Thomas

Wilson also used *Eutopia* in all editions of his *Arte of Rhetorique* 1553–85 (T. Wilson 1553: 100r; 1909: 199). Sidney, well educated in the Greek language, certainly knew that *eutopia* means 'good place' in contrast to *utopia* ('no-place'). The same pun appeared in the front matter of early Latin editions in the short poem provided by Anemolius, the fictive 'windy' Utopian poet (More 1995: 18–19).[1]

Utopia's narrator—'Morus'—acknowledges at the book's end that there are things described that he would want (*optarim*) to see in his own country. But as with much else, his statement is ambiguous, since he also acknowledges that he does not hope for (*sperarim*) or expect to see them (248–249). Ralph Robinson in the first translation into English (More 1551, 1556) renders the line as 'So must I needs confess and grant that many things be in the Utopian weal public, which in our cities I may rather wish for than hope after' (More 1999: 202). The gap between what one might desire and what one can actually look forward to demands interpretation. More himself called attention to this puzzle in the letter to Peter Giles that he provided for the second Latin edition, published in Paris (More 1517).[2] There More describes an unnamed, perhaps fictional, critic who singled out certain details of his work for censure, approving others, while raising doubts whether Utopia is real or fictitious. More's comment reinforces this critic's scepticism by playing a double game, simultaneously advancing Utopia as a real place while highlighting the account as a rhetorical performance. The passage stresses the fact that in *Utopia* we learn about the Utopian way of life at third-hand: in More-the-author's narrative of More-the-character's transcription of Hythloday's account (More 1995: 26–27).

Giles raised a similar puzzle in his prefatory letter to the humanist statesman Jerome Busleyden, one of the intellectual allies Desiderius Erasmus recruited to support More's book.[3] There Giles praises the picture 'sketched by More's pen' for making him as knowledgeable of Utopia and its customs as if he actually lived there. He could 'scarcely believe' that Hythloday 'saw as much in the five years he lived on the island as can be seen in More's description' (1517: 24–27). His remarks emphasize the supposed truthfulness of More's text, while simultaneously calling it into doubt. We are meant to ask how an author merely offering a written report of someone else's verbal account could describe it more effectively than the original narrator, thereby convincing readers that they might actually live there. The effect is enhanced by the fact that Utopia's actual geography is unspecified. More's epistle to Giles said he had forgotten to inquire about its location and Hythloday had neglected to say (34–35). However, Giles's letter to Busleyden explains that, when Hythloday mentioned it, he was prevented from hearing by someone coughing, while More was interrupted by a servant whispering in his ear (26–27). This verbal playfulness leaves open whether More-the-author shared Hythloday's favourable view of Utopia's communism or followed More-the-character's scepticism.

---

[1] For more on Anemolius' poem, see Hobbs and Taylor in this volume.
[2] This letter only appeared in this edition.
[3] See Taylor in this volume.

Nevertheless, a number of *Utopia*'s earliest readers believed More endorsed Utopian communism, or its underlying principles, as 'the best state of a commonwealth'. Busleyden, for example, took it that More praised Utopia as a 'perfect commonwealth', a 'model [...] of proper conduct' whose 'great strength [...] lies in the fact that [...] no one has anything of his own' (More 1995: 252–253). Among other early endorsements of More's Latin text, two further ones frame the text as favouring the Utopian constitution. Jean Desmarez, public orator and professor at the University of Louvain, singling out the fact, attested in the text, that 'Utopians have begun to accept our religion', express the 'wish that [...] we might adopt their system of ordering the commonwealth': this development 'might easily be made', he says, if 'a number of distinguished and persuasive theologians were sent to that island' to 'invigorate the faith of Christ, which is already springing up there [...] and then bring back to us their customs and institutions' (262–263). The second is the letter (written for publication in *Utopia*'s 1517 edition) to the English scholar Thomas Lupset, one of Erasmus' numerous literary allies, from Guillaume Budé, the French lawyer and humanist, who shared Busleyden's and Desmarez's belief that More favoured what Budé called the Utopians' 'Pythagorean rule of mutual charity and community'. Budé, like Desmarez, claims that the Utopian regime embodies 'truly Christian customs and authentic wisdom' which, if 'fixed [...] in the minds of all mortals' by 'the gods', would cause the 'withering away of pride, greed, idiot competition and almost all the other deadly weapons of our hellish adversary' (More 1995: 12–15). The reference to Pythagoreanism almost certainly derives from Erasmus' focus on the theme in the 1515 edition of his *Adagia* (*CWE* 31.29–50; Olin 1989; Wootton 1998; 1999: 6–13).

Forms of Worship

Despite their differences, then, all three early commentators regarded the Utopian community of property as embodying Christianity's central moral principle: Christ's admonition to 'love thy neighbour as thyself' (KJV: Mark 22:31; Matthew 22:39). Several jokingly called attention to the role of Hythloday to whom, as Budé says, More 'assigned the whole thing' (More 1995: 16–17), a point also made by Desmarez and Beatus Rhenanus, another humanist in Erasmus' circle, who supplied a further letter in 1518. None, however, emphasize the central fiction of *Utopia*, which frames Book Two as an eyewitness account of an actual place visited by Hythloday, 'a Portuguese' and Amerigo Vespucci's 'constant companion on the last three of his four voyages'. He is described as one of twenty-four men Vespucci left behind on the coast of what is now Brazil, 'the farthest point of the last voyage'; he then travelled 'through many countries' with five companions, by an unspecified route, possibly following Vasco da Gama or anticipating a circumnavigation, eventually returning home from the Indian Ocean via Taprobane (Sri Lanka) and Calicut on India's south-west coast (44–47, 47 n.; Parks 1938: 226). More was thus able to draw on the accounts of early voyages—of both Vespucci and

Columbus recounted in the parts of Peter Martyr d'Anghiera's *De Orbe Novo* already in print—to give Hythloday's narrative the character of a first-hand ethnographic report.[4] Verisimilitude was also advanced in the published text by the inclusion of a map of the island and by *Utopia*'s most imaginative feature: a quatrain in Utopian printed in the Utopian alphabet, invented for this purpose, and transliterated in roman type (More 1995: 20–21, 22–23, 23 n.). The resulting text thus looks back to ancient examples—fictive and non-fictive—and anticipates later developments in travel-writing (Das 2019: 19–92).

Another feature of the work, used from *Utopia*'s first edition onwards, are the subheadings employed in Book Two. The equivalent of chapter titles, they were frequently used by Thierry Martens, *Utopia*'s first printer, when publishing complicated texts. In 1516, Martens used them in not only in *Utopia* but also in Erasmus' *Institutio Principis Christiani*. But while the use of the subheadings derives from Martens's practice, their wording and placement almost certainly was supplied either by Erasmus, to whom More had transmitted his manuscript (their succinct style is similar to those in the *Institutio*), or by Giles, who earlier had worked with Martens and served on this occasion as *Utopia*'s corrector (Holtrop 1867: 44–45). However, since More resided with Giles in Antwerp while drafting Book Two, and Erasmus was visiting More in London a month or so before he completed the manuscript, it is probable that More was not only aware that subheadings would be used to shape the description of Utopia and its people, but also approved of their placement and wording. Certainly, the subheadings were unchanged in later editions, suggesting that More was content with them (More 1995: 30–31; 1965a: xv–xvi; Hexter 1952: 99–102).

There are no subheadings in Book One: they first appear in Book Two, after Hythloday's introductory descriptions—of Utopia's geography, farming practices, food and drink, and brief mention of Utopus as the founder of the island's constitution (More 1995: 108–114)—mimicking the style of Vespucci's published reports. Eight sections of varying lengths are then subtitled—the last entitled *De Religionibus Utopiensium* ('Of the Religions of the Utopians')—before the work concludes with Hythloday's encomium for the regime, and More's final ambiguous comments. The longest of these sections, filling nearly eighteen pages in 1516, is ostensibly about travel, but ranges widely over a host of issues including Utopian trading activities, attitudes about money, and ethical practices. We shall return to it, since its references to ancient philosophy—Epicureanism and Stoicism—bear directly on the religious themes addressed later. Several of the other sections are almost as miscellaneous. However, the section on Utopian religions, also very substantial—ten pages in 1516—focuses closely and coherently on its theme. It consummates Hythloday's description of the Utopian regime and passionate advocacy for its property-less way of life, where 'everything belongs to everybody' (240–241), serving as his answer to whether Utopia represents (for him) 'the best state of a commonwealth'.

---

[4] Vespucci 1907; 1916; d'Anghiera 1587: 1912. For more on *Utopia* and travel-writing, see Hadfield in this volume.

Concluding his discussion of Utopian religions, Hythloday described the islanders' practices of reverential worship in their churches and the prayer publicly performed in them, emphasizing the unity of Utopian society (238–239). Regardless of their different 'forms of religion', they all believe in one supreme god: although some are polytheistic, 'the vast majority believe in a single divinity, unknown, eternal, infinite, inexplicable, beyond the grasp of the human mind, and diffused throughout the universe, not physically, but in influence, origin, increase, progress, changes and ends of all things' (218–219). Hythloday reports that 'all alike call him Mythra', who, as St Jerome and Erasmus said, is the supreme being in ancient Persian religion and, associated with the spirit of light, the force for the highest good in the universe (218–219, 219 n. 115; More 1965a: 517–518). One of More's sources here is the First Decade of d'Anghiera *De Orbe Novo*, originally published in 1511, where it is reported that indigenous peoples, who 'adored visible stars and the heavens', also believed in a single God 'whom they represent as one, eternal, omnipotent, and invisible' (d'Anghiera 1912: 1.166–168; More 1965a: 516).

Discussing Utopian religions, More posed a number of conundrums and complications for his readers. The first relates to the use of 'religions' in the plural. Multiple cults exist among the Utopians, Hythloday states: some 'worship as a god the sun, others the moon, still others the planets'; others worship a human 'conspicuous for virtue or glory' as supreme among a pantheon of deities (More 1995: 218–219). While the Latin paraphrases wording used in d'Anghiera's First Decade, More was highly selective in drawing on this text, omitting, among other things, descriptions of the indigenous population's violent attacks on Europeans, the suspected presence of cannibals, idolatry, and what d'Anghiera called the inhabitants' myths and 'vain superstitions', including their supposed belief that the living dead walked among them in the dark (d'Anghiera 1587: 87–89; 1912: 1.166–168) . Describing the religious outlooks of the Utopians, then, More omitted evidence from his sources that would have called into doubt the degree to which the islanders, employing reason alone, had arrived at the truths of natural theology.

The plural 'religions' acknowledges that some Utopians arrived at their views from direct observation of physical bodies in the heavens, while the majority, through use of their reason, had reached a greater degree of philosophical or metaphysical abstraction. This treatment of the subject allows readers to imagine Utopia manifesting a spectrum of beliefs all pointing to the same fundamental conviction in the existence of a single supreme being (Baker-Smith 2000: 190, 191). This transforms diversity into unity, paving the way for the next move: the rapid conversion of many Utopians to Christianity. According to Hythloday, Utopians found Christianity to have deep affinity with 'the sect that most prevails among them' (More 1995: 220–221). 'After they heard […] the name of Christ,' Hythloday says, 'and learned of his teachings, his life, his miracles, and the no less marvellous constancy of the many martyrs whose blood, freely shed, had drawn so many nations into their religion, you would not believe how eagerly they assented to it' (218–219). He suggests that this may have resulted not just because they were 'influenced by the fact that Christ approved of his followers' communal way of life', but as the result of the 'secret inspiration of God' (220–221). Busleyden, Desmarez, and Budé all seem to have this passage in mind when suggesting that More himself endorsed the Utopian regime as the best form of commonwealth. Rhenanus, writing his letter of endorsement for the 1518 Basel editions, put this same point more succinctly: *Utopia*'s 'teachings', he said, 'are perhaps less philosophical than those of others, but [...] more Christian' (258–259).

Utopians who 'eagerly assented' to Christ's teachings understood that their full conversion to Christianity required the presence of an ordained priest to perform the sacraments, especially the Eucharist, confession, and penance. Hythloday reports that they 'disputed warmly whether a man chosen from among themselves' could attain the sacerdotal authority to give the sacraments their efficacy 'without the dispatch of a Christian bishop' and 'seemed about to elect one' when Hythloday departed (218–221). However, as More and his readers well knew, ordaining a priest in the Catholic Church requires consecration by the hands of a bishop, who in turn must be ordained by other bishops acting in continuous succession from Christ's Apostles (221 n.; More 1965a: 520). Utopians, using reason alone, thus appear confused about what was necessary for the next step towards salvation. More hints at this gap in Utopian religious understanding in his joking prefatory letter to Giles, where he reports that a devout professor of theology was seeking to be sent as bishop to Utopia by the Pope to 'further the growth of our religion there'. Further confusion is added by the fact that the Latin word Hythloday uses for 'bishop' is *pontifex*, high priest, not *episcopus*, the word More used in his prefatory letter (More 1995: 34–35). *Episcopus* unambiguously refers to a 'Christian bishop'. *Pontifex*, an office in ancient Roman religion, could refer to the Pope, but is used in *Utopia* three times to designate the office of the island's high priest (149, 194, 230). We are on notice, then, to be wary in interpreting Utopians' actions and what Hythloday says about them.

'Almost all the Utopians', Hythloday reports next, 'are absolutely convinced that human bliss after death will be enormous' and 'mourn over a death only if they see that the person was torn of life anxiously and unwillingly'. As he explains, they take such behaviour to indicate that the soul is without hope, conscious of wrongdoing, and dreading a painful end. They also believe God could not be 'pleased with the coming of one who, when he is summoned, does not come gladly, but is dragged off reluctantly and against his will. Such a death fills the onlookers with horror, and they carry the corpse out to burial in melancholy silence.' After asking God to show 'mercy on his spirit and pardon his infirmities, they cover the body with earth'. Their response is very different for 'someone who dies blithely and full of good hope': they 'carry his body cheerfully away, singing and commending the dead man's soul to God', before cremating him and placing at the site a column listing his achievements and honours. Returning home, they talk of the deceased's character and deeds; 'no part of his life is mentioned more frequently or more gladly than his joyful death' (224–227).

Although Utopians believed consciousness of wrongdoing could trouble some individuals, Hythloday's account leaves unanswered whether, like Christians, they possessed a sense of sin, i.e. of wrongdoing against God from which they could through faith be absolved and redeemed. Some translations treat their condition as manifestations of a 'guilty conscience' (More 1965a: 222–223). But this reading anticipates what might be said among Christians in More's own day. The Latin itself reads *male conscia*: 'conscious of guilt' (224–225). The passage, that is, depicts their troubled souls as suffering from hopeless despair, an error in itself since it implies the absence of faith in God's goodness. The same can be said about those going joyfully to their deaths, since for Christians life was a godly gift that should not be lightly abandoned. More, contemplating Jesus' Passion, would later say that when Christ commanded 'his disciples in no wise to be afrayd of death [...] he ment not that they should in no case once shrynk at death: but that should not so shrink & flee from temporal death: that by forsakynge the faith, they shuld fal in endless deth forever' (More 1557: 1354).[5]

Hythloday's account of Utopian attitudes to death is closely related to the treatment of Utopian philosophy and theology in the lengthy miscellaneous section ostensibly devoted to 'The Travels of the Utopians' (More 1995: 144–185). Early in that section, Hythloday states that Utopians came to their values 'partly from their upbringing', 'partly from instruction and good books' (154–155). Later in this section, we learn that,

> with the help of philosophy, they explore the secrets of nature [...] gratifying not only themselves but the author and maker of nature, who they suppose [...] like other artists [...] created this beautiful mechanism of the world to be admired—and by whom, if not by man, who is alone in being able to appreciate so great a thing? (182–183)

Here the text implicitly stresses that Utopians, lacking the revelations in the Book of Scripture, rely on the Book of Nature, accessible to observation and reason, to gain knowledge of God through his creation. Nevertheless, on such topics as the causes of weather, tides, and saltiness of the sea, as well as 'the origins and nature of the heavens and the earth, they have various opinions [...] as our ancient philosophers did'. Like them, they disagree with one another. They also disagree among themselves 'when they propose a new theory' (154–157). Studying the Book of Nature, then, does not always yield certainty, as suggested by the marginal note to this passage supplied by Erasmus or Giles, 'Physica omnia incertissma': 'Physics is the most uncertain study of all' (158–159).

Discussing Utopian views on moral philosophy, Hythloday notes that they 'carry on the same arguments as we do', asking questions concerning the nature of the 'good' and especially 'what to think of human happiness, and whether it consists of one thing or more' (158–159). Here More alludes to the comparison of Stoic and Epicurean philosophy on the subject of human ends in Cicero's *De finibus bonorum et malorem* ('On the Ends of Good and Evil'). Issues discussed there by Cicero also occupied the conversation in *Utopia*'s first book. Underpinning the debate there is a central question, indebted to Stoic thought as explored by Cicero, regarding the relationship between the ethical and the expedient: between *honestas* and *utilitas*, to use the Latin, a major issue for humanists in More's day. In Book One, Hythloday implicitly holds that the moral excellence of the

---

[5] This passage of the *Treatise* (omitted from *CWM* 13), written in Latin, was left in manuscript; William Rastell's edition of More's *Works* (1557) printed this translation by More's niece Mary Basset.

Utopian regime is the most useful means for attaining human happiness, which in effect treats the opposition between *honestas* and *utilitas* as a false dichotomy (100–105).[6] However, according to Hythloday, Utopians eschewed the restraint of the passions and quiet endurance of external contingencies commonly associated with Stoicism: rather, they 'seem too much inclined to the view which favours pleasure in which they conclude that all or the most important part of human happiness consists' (158–159). That is, in their moral philosophy, Utopians adopted an Epicurean position, which—long held to be self-indulgent and disgraceful—had come under favourable discussion among Italian and northern humanists in the fifteenth and early sixteenth century, including Erasmus (159 n.).[7] Here More again drew on Vespucci's ethnographical comments, who in his *Four Voyages* styled indigenous peoples as Epicureans, 'since their life is so entirely given over to pleasure' (Vespucci 1907: 97).

Vespucci wrote that the people he encountered were not idolaters (Vespucci 1916: 6). In Hythloday's report More followed this lead; in Utopian places of worship, he says, 'no images of the gods are seen' (More 1995: 234–235). More thus favours Vespucci's account over d'Anghiera's *De orbe novo*, which describes the use of idols on islands visited by Columbus (d'Anghiera 1587: 87–89; 1912: 1.166–168). Nevertheless, Utopian practices and outlook were markedly different from the peoples Vespucci described, not only in the diversity of their religions, but also in worshipping collectively in the equivalent of churches, where, Hythloday says, they burned incense, scattered perfumes, and displayed 'a great number of candles' in the belief that 'sweet smells, light and other such rituals somehow elevate the human mind and lift it with a livelier devotion towards the adoration of God' (More 1995: 236–239). Their worship, then, had much in common with ceremonial practices of the Catholic Church in More's time.

Utopians are also more focused on their philosophical goal of favouring pleasure than the peoples whom Vespucci described as 'liv[ing] according to nature', and who 'may be called Epicureans rather than Stoics' (1916: 6). This remark is puzzling, since living according to nature is a Stoic not Epicurean view.[8] Addressing this topic, More exploited ambiguities and possible contradictions in the Utopians' views. They take care, Hythloday says, to keep 'a lesser pleasure from standing in the way of a greater one' and avoid 'pleasures that are inevitably followed by pain'. Here they follow an Epicurean rule, especially in believing that 'happiness' is 'found [...] only in good and honest pleasure' and that 'virtue itself [...] draws our nature to pleasure of this sort, as to the supreme good'. They distinguish their view, we are told, from the 'school which declares that virtue is itself happiness', i.e. from Stoics. Hythloday then adds that 'when an individual obeys the dictates of reason in choosing one thing and avoiding another, he is following nature' (More 1995: 160–163). Accordingly, Utopians 'define virtue as living according to nature' and believe that 'God created us to that end'. Above all, they hold that reason incites us 'to love and venerate the Divine Majesty to whom we owe our existence and

---

[6] Logan 1983: 51–52, 108–109 n., 179–180; Ribeiro 2014: 66–67; Skinner 1978: 2.113–148, 192–195.
[7] Surtz 1957: 13–14; 1949a; 1949b; D. C. Allen 1944; Logan 1983: 144–147, 154–163; Kraye 1988: 374–386.
[8] Kraye 1988: 360; Sellars 2006: 27, 92–95, 99–104, 125–129; J. M. Cooper 2012: 150–158, 166–184, 186.

our capacity for happiness'. The accompanying marginal note—stating these views are 'like Stoic doctrine' (162–163)—highlights the issue. The comment represents a philosophical and theological warning since, as Erasmus later argued, the ancient Stoic view made humans rather than God logically responsible for their own happiness, whereas Christian doctrine held humans to be subject to the workings of Providence, receiving their greatest blessings as a divine gift (Kraye 1988: 369; Seneca 1529: a2r–6v). When Erasmus' colloquy 'Epicureus' (1533) defended Epicureanism, it stressed that 'true pleasure' comes only to those who live righteously, since 'only righteousness […] reconciles God, the source of the supreme good, to man' (*CWE* 40.1075–1076). Erasmus' reasoning combines the primacy Epicureans gave to pleasure with the primacy Stoics gave to virtue, which—as the colloquy argues—is possible only for believing Christians. 'There are no people more Epicurean than godly Christians', says Hedonius, Erasmus' spokesperson in the dialogue, because there is nothing more blessed than a good conscience in amity with God (*CWE* 40.1079).

Hythloday recounts that Utopians sought support for their philosophical opinions 'from their religion', which 'is serious and strict, indeed almost stern and forbidding'. In this they were not just like Stoics, noted for their asceticism, but also like ideal Epicureans who valued the pleasures of the mind over those of the body. Hythloday also says that Utopians never consider 'true happiness' without joining 'the rational arguments of philosophy' to their 'religious principles', without which 'they think […] reason […] is weak and defective' (More 1995: 158–161). Importantly, 'the principles they invoke' contrast with one of the central doctrines of ancient Epicureanism, which held that the soul dies with the body. As Hythloday notes, Utopians believe that the human soul is not just 'by God's beneficence born for happiness', but also 'is immortal', and that humans are posthumously rewarded for virtues and punished for shameful acts: 'Though these are indeed religious principles, they think reason leads us to believe and accept them'. Their reasoning, we are told, is instrumental, since they hold that 'if these beliefs were rejected, no one would be so stupid as not to feel that he could seek pleasure, regardless of right or wrong' (160–161).

However, in treating these issues, More's Latin word choices again posed interpretative puzzles. Here, the word used for acts receiving punishment is the plural of the noun *flagitium* (160), often translated into English as 'sins' (161) or 'crimes' (More 1965a: 163). Although *flagitium* could mean a shameful act, outrage, or offence against decency—and in this meaning could designate 'sin'—it originally referred to 'burning desire' or 'heat of passion' and had wide-ranging applications associating it with disgracing or dishonouring a person, including in a public demonstration of disapproval outside the door of a house. In most Christian texts written in Latin in More's day, *pecco, peccare* is most commonly used for 'sin'. Forms of this word appear three times in *Utopia*, Book Two. Twice, the word refers to an ignorant error or this-worldly crime (More 1995: 112–113, 192–193). Only in the third case—'*pecasse fatentur sese*'—is 'sin' an appropriate possible translation: the Latin can be rendered as 'confess their sins'. Nevertheless, read in context, its meaning is ambiguous, since it refers to the rituals followed in Utopian households on the day of 'The Last Feast' when, before going to church, wives prostrate themselves before their husbands, and children before their parents, to acknowledge offences of commission or negligence and beg forgiveness. Confession is not made to a divine being with sacred powers to absolve wrongs. Instead, it represents the acknowledgement of any errors made by subordinates in relations with their superiors: there is no equivalent ritual for male heads of households. The passage proceeds to say that this ritual removes 'any cloud of anger or resentment arisen in the family', enabling participation in the Last Feast service with a clear mind and untroubled conscience. However, nothing is said to clarify from whom, or what, might come the 'swift and terrible punishment' Utopians fear if they attend religious services while in 'hatred or anger toward anyone' (236–237). For learned Christians, steeped in Augustine's view of original sin, the language used here left open to doubt just how well Utopians' reason and grasp of natural theology informed their understanding of the human condition.

Toleration and Heresy

In Hythloday's account, the present history of peaceable religious diversity on Utopia began only after Utopus conquered the island, then called Abraxa, a name adapted from second-century Greek Gnosticism where it referred to the highest of 365 heavens (More 1995: 110–111, 111 n.; More 1965a: 386; Baker-Smith 2000: 55 n.). Previously, the inhabitants, not yet Utopians, 'were continually squabbling over religious matters' and 'easy to conquer [...] because the different sects were too busy fighting one another to oppose him'. Once Utopus gained victory, therefore, 'he prescribed by law that everyone may cultivate the religion of his choice'. They were permitted to seek converts, provided they did so 'quietly, modestly, and without insulting others'. Acts of persuasion could be vigorously pursued, but abuse or violence to advance one's cause was forbidden, and 'anyone who fights wantonly about religion' was to be 'punished by exile or slavery' (More 1995: 222–223).

This passage sometimes is taken to reflect More's own views on religious toleration in 1516—that 'wonderful year of Erasmian reform' (Chambers 1935: 121–125)—when, before Luther's attack on indulgences darkened the skies, there were high hopes that learning and peace would bring a better world into being. According to Hythloday, Utopus imposed a toleration in the belief it 'would benefit religion itself'. Because he was uncertain 'whether God likes diverse and manifold forms of worship and hence inspires different people with different ways', he held it 'arrogant folly to force conformity with his own beliefs on everyone else by threats of violence'. He was convinced that 'if one religion really is true and the rest false', the truth would 'prevail by its own natural strength' (More 1995: 222–225). This view closely parallels Aquinas' argument in *Summa Theologica* against compelling infidels to believe, since belief of necessity is voluntary (2.2 Q.10 A.8: Aquinas 1946: 2.1218–1219; Malcolm 2019: 48, 48 n.). In some critics' judgement, More, in keeping with this well-attested principle, remained intellectually committed throughout his life to toleration as the ideal to be followed, since it allowed for the Christian Church to be perfected (Fox 1993: 70–73; 1982: 65–66; Kessler 2002: 208). However, although Utopians are forbidden to use violence to advance religious views, their religious freedom is limited by 'a solemn and strict law against anyone who should sink so far below the dignity of human nature as to think that the soul perishes with the body, or that the universe is ruled by blind chance, not divine providence'. In keeping with this law, they also hold 'that after this life vices will be punished and virtue rewarded' (More 1995: 222–225). This reference to the Utopians' instrumentalist doctrine of the afterlife comes just before Hythloday's summative encomium for its regime, which presents a self-interested reason for upholding community of property, since, Hythoday implies, it reduced to a bare minimum the temptation to commit acts of vice against others and made performing acts of virtue necessary for material well-being.

Accordingly, Utopian laws made provisions against atheists: such an individual was not considered 'even one of the human race', not counted among Utopia's citizens, and barred from honours, offices, or any public responsibilities. It was believed that having 'degraded the sublimity of his own soul to the base level of a beast's wretched body', he would 'openly despise all the laws and customs of society, if not prevented by fear' of punishment in the afterlife. 'Who can doubt', Hythloday argues, 'that a man who has nothing to fear but the law, and no hope of life beyond the grave, will do anything he can to evade his country's laws by craft or to break them by violence, in order to gratify his own personal greed?' Such a person is 'regarded as low and torpid', but not physically punished or coerced into denouncing his view, since Utopians hold that 'no one can choose to believe by a mere act of the will' and 'it is one of their oldest rules that no one should suffer for his religion'. Utopians acknowledge the potential danger of atheism but do not seek to extirpate it. Instead, the atheist is encouraged 'to argue in favour of his opinion', but only in private 'in the presence of priests and other important persons, not the common people'. There is confidence, we read, that this practice will eventually allow reason to triumph over his madness (222–225).

However, as is well known, a decade later, once the Reformation was underway in England, More, while serving as a senior royal counsellor and then Lord Chancellor, was a major scourge of Protestants, savage in promoting their prosecution as heretics (Marius 1984: xxiv, 337, 347, 386–406).[9] Since 'Christ's Church hath the true doctrine already', More wrote in *A Dialogue Concerning Heresies* (1529), it was not necessary to 'give audience' to those who would 'dispute [...] for it or against it'. He added that 'outrages and mischiefs' resulting from heresies are 'the cause that princes and people' have justifiably punished them by burning. Where Christianity could 'be peaceably preached'—as permitted among the Turks—he argued that 'faith of Christ' would increase, but where a sect used violence to oppose truth, he advocated completely suppressing it as the 'plain enemy to Christ'. Because the peril from heretics would quickly grow very great, princes, he argued, were 'deeply bounden that they shall not suffer their people to be seduced and corrupted' by them (*CWM* 1.345–346, 405–406,

---

[9] For More's responses to heresy, see also Paul in this volume.

415–416; J. W. Allen 1971: 75–76; J. Marshall 2006: 234). More returned to this theme in his *Apologye* (1533), where he identified heresies committed by Christians with treason against God 'accounted as great a cryme as [...] treason [...] agaynst any worldly man' (*CWM* 9.136), and also in his *Debellacyon of Salem and Bizance* (*CWM* 10.1467; J. Marshall 2006: 234). No one, More implied, could rely on the testimony of a heretic in a temporal court, even in cases of murder. More's position on heresy, then, was consistent with Aquinas' view that while heresy is a sin from which repentance is possible, contumacious heretics are dangers to the health of church and state and should be delivered to secular authority for temporal punishments, including execution (*Summa Theologica* 2.2 Q.11. A.3; 2.2. Q.64. A.2; Aquinas 1946: 2.1226–1227; 1466–1467). Some commentators have consequently argued that More believed toleration was appropriate among pagans—such as Utopians—who lacked revelation, but that it should be forbidden among Christians, who already possessed the truth, since permitting diversity of religious views could only advance ignorance and error (More 1995: 223 n.). One version of this argumentative line holds that freedom to proselytize, practised among the Utopians, also provided the necessary opportunity for Christian missionaries to bring converts into church membership, but that once Christianity had prevailed, punishment for heresy would follow (Surtz 1957: 40–78). However, others suggest that More's sanguine hopes in 1516 were shattered by Reformation events and moved him decisively against toleration (Greenblatt 1980: 52–53; Baker-Smith 2000: 191; Fox 1993: 70–73; Wootton 1999: 31–33).

Undoubtedly, in the period after Luther first protested against indulgences in 1517, profound religious differences emerged in Europe and hardened under circumstances of deepening intellectual and religious conflict. More vigorously participated, starting with his *Responsio ad Lutherum*, written in 1523 as Henry VIII's servant and counsellor, in which he responded, under two separate pseudonyms, to Luther's insulting attack on the English king (Marius 1984: 276–291). After More became Lord Chancellor in 1529, he not only continued his vituperative verbal battles against the Protestants in works such as his *Apologye* and *Debellacyon* (both printed in 1533) but also violently attacked their persons (Marius 1984: 351–406). Arguably, his most important intervention in these publishing wars was his *Confutacyon of Tyndales Answere*, published in three parts in 1532 and 1532 (Marius 1984: 292–350). However, it is clear that even before he knew of Luther—indeed before writing *Utopia*—More was aware of the danger of heresy and heretics to both church and state from his experience as London's undersheriff (chief legal officer of the Sheriffs' Court) from 1510 to 1518 (Marius 1984: 53–54). In 1514, he became involved in the notorious case of Richard Hunne, a London merchant tailor found hanged while incarcerated in Lollard's Tower, the bishop of London's prison in St Paul's Cathedral (P. Marshall 2017: 88–92; Marius 1984: 123–133; *CWM* 9.215–246). Controversies surrounding the case, which continued into 1515, resulted in the king's personal intervention after two separate conferences involving representations from Parliament, royal judges, and the clergy failed to yield a conclusion. With Cardinal Wolsey's assistance, Henry ended the matter at a conference at Barnard's Castle in London (P. Marshall 2017: 93–95; Marius 1984: 133–135). At the time, More was just weeks away from the mission to the Low Countries on which he would begin writing *Utopia*: More's commission for that embassy is dated 7 May 1515.

Years later, in his *Dialogue concerning Heresies* (1529), More argued that Hunne had not been murdered as the London coroner's jury concluded, but had killed himself, and was, in fact, a heretic rightly charged and condemned by the ecclesiastical authorities. He knew the case 'from top to toe', as he put it, having talked on diverse occasions with many of the parties, and attending diverse examinations concerning it, including at St Paul's when the Mayor and Aldermen of London condemned the deceased Hunne as a heretic and ordered his body to be burned. More said he subsequently examined an Essex carpenter accused of robbery in London's Sheriffs' Court, who 'confessed that he hadde longe holden dyvers heresyes' which 'he herd rede' in a London conventicle attended by Hunne himself. More found 'not honest' Hunne's 'Faith toward Christ': fortunately, the 'goodness of god' had revealed his mischief. More's point was not just that Hunne had been guilty of heresy and the sin of self-murder but that he was a danger to religion (*CWM* 6.316–330; Marius 1984: 135–141). More returned to the case in 1533 in *The Supplicacyon of Soulys*, siding again with the clergy's judgement against Hunne (*CWM* 10.116–117, 132–136), and also more briefly in his *Apologye*. In the latter, he attributed a 'great vayngloryous lykynge of hym selfe' to Hunne, whose spirit of pride, played upon by the 'gostely enymye the devyl', led to his suicide (*CWM* 9.126). Although his comments on the case came fifteen years and more after the events, his detailed, circumstantial descriptions strongly suggest that he had considered Hunne a heretic at the time, regarded the Church's measures against him as justified. They provide evidence that More was as unprepared to tolerate heresy before 1516 as he was years later as Lord Chancellor.

The subject of toleration surfaces elsewhere in the description of the Utopians' religions. After many of them converted to Christianity, Hythloday reports, one of the newly baptized 'took upon himself to preach the Christian religion publicly, with more zeal than discretion'. Hythloday and his colleagues 'warned him not to do so', to no avail: he worked himself up into an impassioned fury, setting 'our religion above the rest', condemning 'all others as profane', and calling their followers 'impious and sacrilegious', deserving of consignment to eternal fires. Eventually he was tried 'on a charge, not of despising their religion, but of creating a public disorder' and sentenced to exile (More 1995: 220–223). That is, he was not treated according to the standards employed against criminals, for whom punishment was enslavement, but judged a danger to the good order of the Utopian community and removed from it, arguably to continue his proselytizing elsewhere. He was punished, then, albeit without being executed, for acting too aggressively in keeping with his religious conscience.

Did More have an example or analogy in mind? Since in 1510 he had published a life of Pico della Mirandola, who until his death in 1494 was one of Giralamo Savonarola's followers, More was undoubtedly aware of Savonarola, who was executed in Florence in 1498; a summary of Savonarola's funeral sermon for Mirandola is printed in the final chapter of the *Life* (*CWM* 1.73–75; Copenhaver 2019: 167, 183–185). Savonarola's story was widely known among humanists, church officials, and counsellors in European states.

Although excommunicated as a schismatic and heretic, he was not burned at the stake, but convicted as a criminal by government and ecclesiastical officials and hanged with two followers, whose bodies were then burned. His execution was as much for the zealotry of his disruptive actions in the city and his challenges to ecclesiastical authority as for heresy (Weinstein 2011: 226–317; 1970: 247–288). More may have had Savonarola in mind when he singled out the behaviour rather than ideas of the Utopian zealot for special attention.

Prayer, Suicide, and the Commonwealth

'The Religions of the Utopians' concludes with a description of services celebrated in Utopia's churches: the 'Last feast', at which the islanders give thanks for their prosperity in the previous month or year, and the 'First feast', at the beginning of the next month or year, at which they 'pray for prosperity and happiness in the month or year just beginning' (More 1995: 234–237). At these services they sing hymns accompanied by musical instruments; then 'the priest and the people together recite certain fixed forms of prayer, so composed that when they all repeat in unison each individual can apply to himself'. The Latin word for church used here—and in Hythloday's earlier account of Utopian sociability (142)—is *templum* (236), not *ecclesia*, the standard word for 'church' in More's day; the plural form is also used in the marginal note, *Templa cusismodo* (234). *Templum* refers to the shrine or location at which religious observance took place. Use of *ecclesia*, which means 'assembly', would have emphasized the community of believers gathered for prayer. On Utopia, with its fifty-four cities, there was no single church to which all believers belonged, even for those who shared the same theology.

Hythloday states that in their prayer each Utopian 'acknowledges God to be the creator and ruler of the universe and the author of all good things' (238–239). The Latin word used for this deity is a form of *Deus*, as in the Vulgate Genesis 1:1. The prayer must be offered in public worship by the monotheists among the Utopians, a majority among the islanders. By this stage in the discussion, therefore, attention has dropped away from the polytheistic sects accepting the existence of a chief deity who, like Zeus/Jupiter, is the highest but not the only divine being. Each person praying thanks God for placing 'him in the happiest of commonwealths', inspired by the truest religious ideas, and asks that if a society or religion 'more acceptable to God' exists, to be led to it. The link thus drawn between Utopia's religion and its constitution meant that resistance to its theology or regime would have dire consequences for its stability, even survival. The prayer asks that 'if their form of society is best and their religious the truest' then 'God will keep him steadfast, and bring other mortals to the same way of life and the same religious faith'. The prayer ends with worshippers wishing for 'an easy death', but asks that they 'be brought to him soon', if it please God, 'even by the hardest possible death, rather than be kept away from him longer, even by the most prosperous of earthly careers'. Those praying then 'prostrate themselves on the ground' and 'after a little while [...] rise and go to lunch', spending the rest of the day 'in games and military training' (240-241). Engaging in such practices of sociability after church services resembles activities traditionally practised in More's day on the Sabbath in English parishes, about which Puritan Sabbatarians would later complain (Homans 1942: 353-401; Underdown 1985: 45-72; C. Hill 1964: 141-211).

Hythloday's account of this prayer immediately precedes his encomium for Utopia's property-less economy which frees Utopians 'to live joyfully and peacefully, free from anxieties, and without worries about making a living' (More 1995: 242-243). Hythloday had 'no doubt', 'that every man's perception about where his true interest lies, along with the authority of Christ our Saviour [...] would long ago have brought the whole world to adopt the laws of this commonwealth, were it not for one single monster, the prime plague and begetter of all others—I mean Pride' (244-247). The hindrance, then, is sin. In Hythloday's description, the Utopian regime had reduced to the barest minimum incentives to commit sinful acts, but because it did so in the absence of knowledge of Christ, it achieved this without offering a means to eliminate sinfulness. More made this apparent by pointedly retaining sinning in Utopia, not just by giving it a criminal justice system (151-152, 184-185, 190-193), but by emphasizing suicide as a permitted practice (186-189).

Utopians believe, Hythloday says, that someone suffering incurably from 'excruciating and unremitting pain' has 'outlived his own death' and becomes 'unequal to any of life's duties, a burden to himself and others'. In this circumstance, they regard suicide 'a wise act, since for him death would put an end not to pleasure but to agony'. Also, because 'he would be obeying the counsel of the priests, who are the interpreters of God's will', it would be 'pious and holy' (86-87, 224-225). This passage, it has been suggested, relates to the Utopians' prayer for an early death (More 1965a: 558). However, as More knew, for Christians self-slaughter represented the gravest insult to God, the abandonment of hope in His mercy (Hexter 1952: 71-72; Skinner 1987: 150-151, 184-187, 190-193). Hythloday himself used this point in Book One, arguing against the death penalty: 'God', he says, 'has forbidden each of us not only to take the life of another but also to take his own life' (More 1995: 68-69, 187 n.). That Utopians accept suicide as an honourable way to avoid pain calls into question what exactly is meant by the claim that Utopian religious views have affinity with Christianity.

How readers should judge the Utopians' religious outlook is further complicated by Hythloday endorsing their way of life as desirable for Christians and expressing optimism for Christianity's continued survival on the island. Although he acknowledged that pride—which 'measures prosperity not by what she has but by what others lack'—'is too deeply fixed in human nature to be easily plucked out', he claims nevertheless that Utopians had somehow been 'lucky' enough to escape from it, maintaining a community of friends among whom all things are in common. Hythloday's language in this encomium sets several conceptual traps. One sentence suffices as illustration: 'Through the plan of living which they have adopted, they have laid the foundations of a commonwealth that not only is very happy, but also, so far as human prescience can tell, likely to last forever.' In Latin 'last forever' is *aeternum duratura*, i.e. will endure eternally (246–247). A literal translation emphasizes the 'eternal duration' of the regime, an oxymoron: if something is eternal, it has no beginning or end, and therefore no duration. Hythloday's claim also is inherently implausible. As Augustine implied in his distinction between the eternal and earthly city, no earthly regime, not even the visible Church, can be eternal, since all earthly institutions are composed of those who break and those who keep God's commandments. Moreover, all present-day communities will disappear with the end of time (Augustine 1960: 305–317; 1998: 987–991; cf. More 1965a: 565–566). *Aeternum duratura* suggests, therefore, that Utopia exists outside ordinary human time. The qualification that this outcome is 'likely', and therefore not certain, cannot save it from being logically impossible in the natural world. Only the 'Heavenly City'—Augustine's 'City of God'—can qualify as eternal.

Budé's letter highlighted this conceptual problem. He had heard, he says, that 'the island of Utopia […] is also called Udepotia', meaning 'Neverland' in Greek. He also called Utopia 'Hagnopolis', i.e. 'holy city' or 'city of saints', a name connecting it with the heavenly city in Augustine's *City of God*. 'Content with its own customs and possessions', Budé says, Utopia is 'blessedly innocent, leading a celestial life, as it were—lower than heaven, indeed, but far above the smoke and stir of this known world' (More 1995: 12–13; 13 n.) The implication is that Utopia ('no-place') is a Platonic Form or idea: not existent in a pure form anywhere in the world. As Aristotle emphasized in his *Physics*, 'Forms […] are nowhere' (3.4.203a7–9; Aristotle 1984: 1.346). Budé thus concluded that Utopia serves as 'a seed bed […] of elegant and useful concepts' for application in the present where possible, but incapable of full realization (More 1995: 18–19).

Hythloday's forecast of Utopia's eternal duration is designated as a presentment (*praesagium*), a term commonly employed for a divination or divinely inspired prophecy (246–247). However, his prediction is about worldly, inherently uncertain contingencies. At best, it is something to be wished for rather than expected, to paraphrase Morus' final observation (248–249, 249 n.). Here, then, More signals the impossibility of bringing a Heavenly City into being in this world in the absence of God's providential intervention. Without directly answering whether Utopia is also *eutopia*— a 'happy' or 'fortunate place': the 'best state of a commonwealth'—he asks his readers to decide if there might be a means of transforming society into a truly 'happy place' in the present world (Sacks 2017: 168–171).

As near as Utopian religion seems to Christianity, on close inspection its theology and moral prescriptions combine Epicurean and Stoic doctrines and beliefs, following Epicureans in letting pleasure be their guide, Stoics in living according to God's perfect rationality embodied in nature—a combination of competing opposites. However, both philosophical schools acknowledged suicide as an acceptable way to end life (Nussbaum 2009: 140–141, 197, 435–438; Rist 1969: 233–255). As Martha Nussbaum emphasizes, Epicureanism and Stoicism offer followers a cure for the sufferings of the soul resulting not just from false beliefs but the impossible, unachievable desires that hinder a human's flourishing life: they employ rational critique to free the soul to gain its natural ends

(Nussbaum 2009: 13–47). However, Christianity as understood by More is a theology of devotion and obedience. Whatever its therapeutic value, as a cure of souls, it looks to salvation achieved through Christ's suffering and purgation of sin as its goal, not to the practice of virtue or enjoyment of pleasure for their own sakes. Whatever benefits might come from adopting the Utopian regime—an issue about which Morus harboured serious doubts— More-the-author brought the work's larger meaning into perspective by prefacing Book Two with the debate in Book One about whether a virtuous scholar should become a statesman (Sacks 2017: 171). The resulting text thus explores the relationship of means to ends and practice to theory in ways that questioned at once the possibility of social reform solely through reasoned argument and persuasion and the belief in free will on which those methods depend. As intractable as these issues were in 1516, they only became more so in the aftermath of the publication of Luther's *Ninety-Five Theses* in 1517.

CHAPTER 5

'NOTHING IS PRIVATE ANYWHERE'

Utopia *in the Context of More's Thought*

JOANNE PAUL

THIS chapter seeks to elucidate the message of *Utopia* by reading the text in the context of the rest of More's work.[1] There are those, such as Wayne A. Rebhorn, who maintain that the dialogue form and names of his characters allowed More to place 'distance between himself and his ideas' (More 2005: xviii), or, as Han van Ruler and Giulia Sissa argue, that '*Utopia* offered a subject-matter in many ways unconventional, not to say wholly alien, to Thomas More himself' (van Ruler and Sissa 2017a: 7–22). This chapter will show that this distance was not as great as suggested.

Much has, of course, been written on various aspects of More's wider context in 1516, including humanism, rhetoric, travel writing, and politics.[2] However, little work, relatively speaking, has been done to place *Utopia* in the context of More's thought.[3] In doing so, I suggest that *Utopia*, though enigmatic, is not wholly anomalous. More uses the text as a way of advancing one of his central and recurring arguments: that there is a moral priority to what is held in common, over and above what is private to the individual. This argument has been recognized in *Utopia* (de Bom 2017; Baker-Smith 2000: 137–141, 203–204), but often without much emphasis, and not in the context of More's other works. For More, focusing on what is held in common reflects the true reality of

---

[1] Elements of what follow are developed from Paul 2016. My thanks to the organizers and participants of the events at which previous versions of this paper were presented, including 'Utopia: History, Theory, and Future' (Oxford), the Sixteenth Century Society Conference (Bruges), History of Political Ideas Seminar (IHR, London), and 'Authority Revisted' (Leuven).

[2] On humanism, see Kristeller 1980; Weil Baker 1999; Baker-Smith 2000; Skinner 2002b: 2.213–244; Parrish 2010. On rhetoric, see McCutcheon 1977; Kinney 1979; Wegemer 1990; Logan 1994. On travel writing, see Gradziel 2013; C. Houston 2014; and Hadfield in this volume. On politics, see Warner 1996; Gerard and Sterling 2005.

[3] Exceptions include Wegemer 1990: 288–306; Curtright 2013; Phélippeau 2016b; Sissa 2017: 25–70.

the world, not the fantasy of social convention that we have created for ourselves, which emphasizes what can be individually possessed. In *Utopia*, More creates a fantastic island that represents the eternal ideals that he sees in operation beneath the worldly 'stage play' of pride and inequality, not as a prescriptive programme, but as a reminder. *Utopia*, in short, operates like the *memento mori* of More's earlier works, and is broadly consistent with the message of his later religious polemics.

Multiple Mores?

Arguments about the interpretation of *Utopia* are too plentiful to name. A number place *Utopia* in its historic and intellectual context, noting More's debts to Plato, Cicero, Augustine, and others, and the ways in which these authors were taken up by More's humanist peers. Very few, however, have attempted to put *Utopia* in the context of More's thought as a whole. *Utopia* is often presented almost tragically as the last and the only of More's great humanist works, as More appears to transform into another author entirely in the 1520s. This 'multiple Mores' thesis has been roundly critiqued—for example by Travis Curtright (2013: 2–12)—and yet its legacy remains. The split between More's 'humanist phase', ending around 1520, and his 'polemical phase', lasting until his death in 1535, has meant that a sense of More's oeuvre has been obscured. The only way in which comparisons are typically made between these two 'phases' of work is in showing the depth of this transformation, and More's outright rejection of *Utopia* in particular. Much, for instance, has been made of the marginal gloss in the 1523 edition of the *Responsio ad Lutherum*, which suggests that Luther's invisible church must have been seen 'in Utopia' (*CWM* 5.118), and his comment in *The Confutacyon of Tyndales Answere* that 'I wolde not onely [burn] my derlynges [Erasmus'] bokes but myne owne also, helpe to burne them both wyth myne owne handes, rather then folke sholde (though thorow theyr own faute) take any harme of them, seying that I se them lykely in these dayes so to do' (*CWM* 8.179).

There are indeed reasons to be cautious in attempting to read *Utopia* in the context of More's works as a whole, or indeed reading any single work in the context of a thinker's oeuvre. We tread dangerously on the boundaries of Quentin Skinner's 'mythology of coherence' (2002b: 2.67–72) in attempting to do so, though the intention here is to note the historical evidence for some degree of consistency in basic principles, without insisting on a perfectly coherent or closed system. These problems are especially apparent when attempting to look at an earlier text in the context of later ones.[4] When it comes to More, we do have to address a significant change in context in the 1520s, namely the Reformation. More participated in the debate at Henry VIII's request, answering Luther's rejoinder to the king—*Contra Henricum Regum Anglie* (1522)—in

---

[4] My thanks to Richard Tuck for pointing this out.

the *Responsio ad Lutherum* (1523). After the *Responsio*, with the single exception of the *Letter to Bugenhagen* (an extensive text written in 1526 but printed posthumously), More did not make another volley into these debates for the following six years. When he did, it was, once again, by official request: his friend Cuthbert Tunstall, bishop of London, asked him to defend the Church against heretical books. This request launched More properly into the debate, and he penned millions of words on the topic in the period from 1529 to 1533. In addition, from the mid-1520s More's involvement in the fight against heresy was not restricted to the pen. In 1526 he led a raid in search of heretical books, and in 1528 he searched William Tyndale's former home. Under More's Chancellorship, six evangelicals were burned in England (three in London), and More endorsed such measures. There were also rumours that More took a direct hand in the torture of evangelical prisoners.[5] He denied this, though noted that he had certainly punished heretics, just as he would punish any criminal who would be likely to cause more pain if he were allowed to go free (*CWM* 9.117). This does at first seem a far cry from the More who created Utopia: an island in which religious toleration was limited only by the outlawing of atheism and zealotry.

There are powerful reasons, however, why we may not want to erect an impenetrable divide across the 1520s. First, this line is largely post hoc.[6] Contemporaries generally did not see Reformation debates as wholly distinct from the 'humanist-scholastic' debates which we now think of as preceding them (Rummel 1998: 9–10). There was no division between polemics on scholarship and those on religion: after all, both debates shared a focus on scriptural interpretation, among other things, and the similarities in vehement language between the two debates cannot be denied (Rummel 1998: 5). Too strong a delineation, then, between a 'humanist' and a 'polemic' phase in More's career, using the Reformation as the boundary, creates anachronistic and potentially obfuscating divisions. After all, the humanist debates were certainly 'polemical', and the Reformation disputes still strongly 'humanist', and the same can be said of More's work as well (Baumann 2015; Rummel 1998: 12).

The desire to overemphasize the change More underwent in the 1520s stems largely from an aversion to More's later activities as polemicist and heresy-hunter. More was a friend of Erasmus, to whom many evangelicals looked for theological guidance (even if Erasmus himself refused them explicit endorsement). The complaint that, as Matthew DeCoursey puts it, 'More abandoned his Erasmianism when he became a defender of the church' begins with Tyndale, whose disappointment in More is palpable (DeCoursey 2010: 18). Throughout the sixteenth and the seventeenth centuries, the humanists were associated with evangelicalism (and, it should be noted, republicanism), and it was the scholastics—More's opponents—who were associated with Catholicism(and with absolutism) (Rummel 1998: 9–10; Curtis 2006). More presented, and still presents, a problem for this narrative.

---

[5] For More's involvement in heresy-hunting, see Guy 2000: 118–122; Rex 2011: 105.
[6] With thanks to Greta Kroeker for her unpublished research on this topic.

It becomes easier to suggest that the reasonable humanist More gave way to a zealous Catholic More in the 1520s than to acknowledge that More saw a consistency between the two positions. The eighteenth-century philosopher David Hume, for instance, acknowledged a paradox in More; he 'is at once an object deserving our compassion, and an instance of the usual progress of men's sentiments during that age', for he possessed both an 'elegant genius and a familiar acquaintance with the noble spirit of antiquity' and had 'in the course of events, been so irritated by polemics' that he had 'thrown into such a superstitious attachment to the ancient faith, that few inquisitors have been guilty of greater violence in their persecution of heresy'(Hume 1983: 3.216).

Attempts to overcome the 'apparent tensions between the attitude [More] adopted in *Utopia* and his behaviour towards Tyndale and the rest', as G. R. Elton (2003: 177) put it, have often flirted with anachronism as various parties attempt to praise or condemn More by modern standards. Elton himself criticized R. W. Chambers's suggestion that 'it is precisely More's tolerance that makes him, on true Utopian principles, intolerant of the Reformation' (Chambers 1935: 252–253, quoted in Elton 1984: 177) and instead responded by asserting the contrary: *Utopia* was not tolerant and neither was More. Separating out the humanist More from the saint More helps to preserve *Utopia* from More's later unseemly religious zeal.

Contrastingly, this chapter maintains that the 1520s represented not so much a break between More's 'humanist' and 'polemical' phases as a shift in his approach. In More's writings before his involvement in the Reformation debates he critiques those who take hierarchy and political order too seriously; after that point, he is arguing against those who do not take them seriously enough. Throughout, however, More seeks to prioritize what is held in common over what is individual, the reversal of which he takes to be a sign of the most pernicious vice of all—pride—which has the potential to both tear apart commonwealths and damn Christian souls.

Before moving on to an analysis of More's works, it is worth thinking more deeply about what we mean by 'what is held in common'. There are at least three (overlapping) ways in which this idea appears in the texts which follow. First, there is humanity's common fate in death, which leads More to more general conclusions about mortals' common or equal standing outside worldly affairs. Those worldly affairs, and especially the inequalities established within them, are built largely upon public opinion, and here a second use of 'common' can be located. Public opinion can either be founded on prideful, individualistic motives, or on a more divinely inspired common sense, which takes seriously mortals' common fate and thus equality. Finally, if public opinion rests on eternal principles of equality and commonality, then—third—the common good will become the object of political and social structures (as well as guiding one's life choices) rather than individual good. That this is the central message of *Utopia* becomes clear only when it is read in the context of More's other works.

Memento Mori: Remembering the Commonality of Death in More's Early Works

In More's view, most people fundamentally confuse what they ought to take as 'real', resulting in the predominance of that mother of all sin: pride. By reorienting our perspective to what is eternal, and away from what is worldly, More maintains that we can see past the 'pageantry' or 'stage play' of this world to real and eternal principles, namely our equality and commonality. This was consistent with Northern humanist thought more widely, which took as its 'main targets' instances where 'a public sign becomes a totem or substitute for the real thing' (Baker-Smith 2000: 44), and we might think here of the extended sections in Erasmus' *Praise of Folly* (1511) and *Education of a Christian Prince* (1516), where he takes aim at kings who place more emphasis on the material expressions of kingship than what they are meant to represent. As he writes in *The Education of a Christian Prince*:

> If all that makes a king is a chain, a sceptre, robes of royal purple, and a train of attendants, what after all is to prevent the actors in a drama who come on the stage with all the pomp of state from being regarded as real kings?[...] It is the spirit that is right for a prince: being like a father to the state. (Erasmus 1997: 17.)

Like many of his contemporaries, More used memento mori as a way of recalling attention from the temporal to the eternal. This remembrance of death together with the pageant of life metaphors can be found in More's translations of Lucian, specifically his 1506 translation of *Necromantia*, or *Menippus*, a text which—like *Utopia*—plays with the line between reality and fiction. In a central passage of the piece, the main character travels to the Afterlife and is struck by what he sees. The bones of all who have lived are piled 'one on top of another, ill-defined, unidentified, retaining no longer any trace of earthy beauty' (*CWM* 3/1.176). It is impossible for him to identify who had been a king or a hero, and who had been a servant or a slave. He concludes that

> human life is like a long pageant, and that all its trappings are supplied and distributed by Fortune, who arrays the participants in various costumes of many colours. Taking one person, it may be, she attired him royally, placing a tiara upon his head, giving him body-guards, and encircling his brow with the diadem; but upon another she puts the costume of a slave [...]. And often, in the very middle of the pageant, she exchanges the costumes of several players; instead of allowing them to finish the pageant in the parts that had been assigned to them, she re-appareils them [...]. For a brief space she lets them use their costumes, but when the time of the pageant is over, each gives back the properties and lays off the costume along with his body, becoming what he was before his birth, no different from his neighbour. (176)

Lucian's metaphor of the pageant or stage play becomes one of More's most repeated images. He puts it to good use in his description of pride in the *Four Last Things*, written around 1522, but unfinished and published only after More's death. This text reflects on the importance of remembering the Christian four last things: death, judgement, heaven, and hell. More suggests that, in order to avoid sin, and especially pride, the 'root' of all sin, one should remember the nearness of death, which will take away all worldly trappings:

> If thou shouldst perceive that one were earnestly proud of the wearing of the gay golden gown, while the lorel playeth the lord in a stage play, wouldst thou not laugh at his folly, considering that thou art very sure that when the play is done he shall go walk a knave in his old coat? Now thou thinkest thyself wise enough while thou art proud in thy player's garment, and forgettest that when thy play is done, thou shalt go forth as poor as he. Nor thou remembrest not that thy pageant may happen to be done as soon as his. (*CWM* 1.156)

Finding this example 'too merry' for the subject, More employs a second, also oft-used metaphor, that of life as a prison, with the same message: 'for, young, old, poor and rich, merry and sad, prince, page, pope and poor soul priest, now one, now other, sometimes a great rabble at once, without order, without respect of age or of estate, all stripped stark naked and shifted out in a sheet, be put to death' (156). As the jailer says to the prisoners, 'all your pride is because you forget that it is a prison' (157).

In death, the great and the lowly become equals. This equality is the 'true figure', the 'very nature' of the world, which we take for 'fantasy' because of 'men's false opinion', but, if we took it for reality, people would 'bear themselves not much higher in their hearts for any rule or authority that they bear in this world' (158). More argues for a reversal of our understanding of what is reality and what is fantasy. The so-called real world is artificial, whereas the world we cannot see—the world beyond death—is the true reality.

The confusion between fantasy and reality has pernicious effects: primarily, it fosters pride. For More, drawing on Augustine, pride is the root of all sin. It is an essentially comparative and competitive vice: since pride is loving one's own superiority, it resents all others and is only satisfied when it the person possessed of it is superior to another (Lunn-Rockliffe 2013).[7] As he writes in *Utopia*: 'Pride [*superbia*] measures prosperity not by her own advantages but by others' disadvantages' (*CWM* 4.243).[8] 'Pride would not consent to be made even a goddess if no poor wretches were left for her to domineer over and scoff at' (243). Pride, in short, will always be at another's expense (T. I. White 1982: 346). For this reason, it is a vice that necessarily cuts across the bonds that unite people. Pride makes us interested solely in what is our own and asks us to focus on what separates us from other people. The inequality it draws on and fosters takes away from the common feeling that can be found in a recognition of essential equality. For More,

---

[7] Many thanks also to Gillian Clark for her explanation of Augustine's view of pride.
[8] Latin from facing pages of same edition.

it is the ultimate political, social, and religious problem. Pride inspires the scholastics, as More writes in his 'Letter to Dorp' in the same year as *Utopia*, to 'crown themselves victors just because we do not know in what sense, against all common sense, they have secretly agreed to construe our own words' (*CWM* 15.37). As Stephanie Elsky has pointed out, such scholastics commit the same misdemeanour as 'those noblemen, gentlemen, and abbots whom Hythloday refers to in *Utopia*', who close off common land 'and strip the English equivalent of the *vulgus* of what is rightfully theirs' (Elsky 2013: 195). Pride causes the wealthy and privileged to think themselves better than their neighbours simply because of the 'borrowed ware' that fortune has temporarily bestowed upon them, as he writes in his *Fortune Verses* of 1504 (*CWM* 1.40; cf. 13.9), and—from More's perspective—it motivates evangelicals to side with their own judgement, over the collective judgement of the entire Church. Like scholastics, he writes in the *Responsio*, the heretics demonstrate an 'arrogance before God' (*CWM* 5.205). As he writes in his *Confutacyon of Tyndales Answere*, Lutheranism tells 'every obstinate heretyke, every pratelynge fole, every smaterer in scrypture' that they 'understandeth the scripture better' than 'all the generall counsayles' and 'all the hole corps of crystendome' (*CWM* 8.343). Pride cuts across the bonds that ought to unite people, destroying commonwealth and Church in the process.

Central to these ideas of commonality is More's emphasis on a cluster of concepts including *publica opinio*, *sensus communis*, and *consensus*. In commenting on these themes, More draws on a rich classical tradition which links public opinion, consensus, and community, including in Cicero, Quintilian, and Seneca (Kempshall 1999: 286). The public opinion, common sense, and custom or consensus of a people has the power to hold a community together, and its fragmentation through the workings of pride is what shatters that community. For instance, it is custom that determines the meaning of language, the meaning that the scholastics reject (Remer 2009: 19; Kapust 2011: 97). God, too, speaks through the common custom of the Church, rejected by the evangelicals, and as More suggests—for instance in his *History of King Richard the Third*—the people's consent is essential to the unity of the commonwealth (More: *CWM* 2.79). Pride works against these concepts; those who espouse what is common knowledge will never find acclaim, so the prideful invent new interpretations in order to stand out from the crowd, so that they might, as More writes in his *Life of Pico* (1510) 'winne the favour of the commune peple & the commendations of folys' (*CWM* 1.61). Their pride destroys the unifying potential of consensus. For this reason More is in favour of censorship: the spread of ideas generated by pride can get in the way of the people's instinctive understanding of truth, because they are easily swayed by self-interest. In the *Confutacyon*, More goes as far as to suggest an innate ability within people to understand the truth of matters, a 'secrete inward instyncte of the spiryte of god' (*CWM* 8.381).

For More, European custom has become corrupted by prideful self-interest. Individual property ownership often becomes the focus for his critique and that of other humanists: it is an artificial custom that fosters pride and divides the community. As Baker-Smith has suggested, in Hythloday's critique in *Utopia*, money, 'by the means of its symbolic representation of value', serves to subvert 'the common interest' and allows the 'parasitical' to dominate the productive (Baker-Smith 2000: 204). This is especially evident in *Utopia* and More's later works, noted in the following sections, but it is equally clear in his early poems.[9] As he writes in the Latin verse, 'On Equality in Death': 'Though you conquer the world even to the pillars of Hercules, still the amount of earth which ultimately will be yours is the same as any man's. You will die as Irus's [the beggar's] equal, not a penny richer; and your land (yours no longer) will consume you' (*CWM* 3/2.125). All possessions and material possessions pass away in death: 'Just as surely as I came on earth naked, so surely naked shall I quit it. Why do I struggle in vain, knowing as I do that death is naked?', he writes in a response to William Lily's 'On Death' (85); and again, in his own 'On Death': 'He is dreaming who thinks that in this life he is rich; and when death wakes him up, he sees at once how poor he is' (145). The lessons of the epigrams are the same as in More's other early works: life is a pageant of artificiality, which masks our inherent equality.

COMMONALITY IN *UTOPIA*: PUBLIC VERSUS PRIVATE INTERESTS

Utopia, as a fantastic island, highlights the illusory nature of our so-called 'real world'. It is a society built on institutions which keep Utopians focused on what is held in common, over what is their own. It is this central theme which not only unites *Utopia* with More's other works, but also unifies the two books of *Utopia*.

In the first book, 'Morus'—the persona in the dialogue (as distinct from More-the-author)—and Hythloday debate whether or not it is Hythloday's duty to give his service to his commonwealth. Morus advances the view that even if it is to one's disadvantage to serve the commonwealth, it remains a duty to do so: 'it seems to me you will do what is worthy of you and this generous and truly philosophic spirit of yours if you so order your life as to apply your talent and industry to the public interest [*publicis rebus*], even if it involves some personal disadvantages to yourself' (*CWM* 4.57). Hythloday, however, does not wish to leave the peace and freedom he enjoys independently of the court; secondly, he does not think that he would do any good if he did: 'I have no such ability as you ascribe to me and, if I had ever so much, still, in disturbing my own peace and quiet, I should not promote the public interest [*publicam rem*]' (57). Monarchs are only concerned with war and acquisition, and courtiers with personal profit and flattery. He would end up either speaking counsel that was too far from the interests and intentions of monarchs or being forced to repeat the corrupt advice of sycophantic counsellors.

Morus is forced to agree: Hythloday would indeed fail to persuade them. The issue is with how he delivers his counsel, for 'such ideas should [not] be thrust on people,

---

[9] More's Latin epigrams were largely composed between 1500 and 1520 and published alongside *Utopia* in 1518 (*CWM* 3/2.10–12).

or such advice given, as you are positive will never be listened to' (99). Instead of 'this academic philosophy', which thinks that 'everything is suitable for every place', an adviser must adopt a 'more civil philosophy [*philosophia civilior*]', 'which knows its stage, adapts itself to the play in hand, and performs its role neatly and appropriately', or 'with decorum [*cum decorum*]'—an idea that runs closely alongside the humanist emphasis on common usage (99).[10] Whereas the scholastics were ignoring the dictates of *decorum* by refusing to adapt their language to a larger audience, the humanist speaker ought to adjust high-minded or universal principles to realities particular to the situation in hand. As Morus puts it: 'If you cannot pluck up wrongheaded opinion [*opinio*] by the root, if you cannot cure according to your heart's desire vices of long standing, yet you must not on that account desert the commonwealth' (99). Morus champions acting in the public interest, regardless of the self-interest of Hythloday or of those he would seek to influence.

Hythloday, however, persists, suggesting that to adopt this approach would be to become corrupt himself. In Hythloday's eyes, there cannot possibly be any room for an 'indirect approach' when people remain greedy and proud, and people will always be greedy and proud where there is private property. Only common property will solve the problem of corruption in the commonwealth: 'wherever you have private property and all men measure all things by cash values, there it is scarcely possible for a commonwealth to have justice or prosperity' (103). Hythloday therefore begins to 'ponder on the extremely wise and holy institutions of the Utopians', who hold all property in common (103). And so the debate over counsel turns into the discussion of the commonwealth of Utopia in Book Two.

In Utopia, unlike in Europe, all citizens are equal and all things are held in common. The paratextual letters also reinforce the idea that greed for personal gain separates one from his neighbour, 'with whom he is joined by rights of citizenship', as Guillaume Budé writes to Thomas Lupset (7). In Utopia, the 'common interest' is served because 'all men have all things in common', and thus 'every action, whether public or private, regards not the greed of the many or the caprice of the few' but 'is totally directed to the maintenance of one uniform justice, equality, and communion' (35). The Utopians have consequently been able to transform their land through shared work: as one marginal note—added by either Erasmus or Peter Giles (More 1989: 125 n.)—observes, 'What is Common to All is Born Lightly' (*More CWM* 4.113). Accordingly, the Utopians are not willing to cut up Utopia according to property lines. The doors to their homes are not locked and as a result 'nothing is private anywhere' (121).[11] This idea of public and private maps on to the distinction between what is held in common and what belongs to the individual.

Political power is also shared, mitigating the pernicious influence of personal interest. Political affairs cannot be discussed outside the public assemblies, in order to avoid tyranny, commonly defined by humanists as ruling according to one's own will and interest

---

[10] The translations of *philosophia civilior* and *cum decorum* are my own.
[11] This is my own translation of '*nihil est umquam privati*'.

rather than the good of all (Erasmus 1997: 25–28, 53; 1993: 104–105). Political decisions in Utopia are not made on the day when they are debated, so people will not vote obstinately and self-servingly, according to the opinion they voiced during the debate, but rather upon reflection on the good of the commonwealth as a whole; nor will a person 'give more thought to defending his opinion than to supporting what is for the good of the commonwealth' (*CWM* 4.125). Like much else in Utopia, the system is designed to place 'the public welfare' over individual interest. This includes warfare, in which the Utopian soldier's family accompanies him to war, breaking down the division between public service and private affairs. The custom of inspecting one's spouse naked before the wedding serves a similar purpose.[12]

Essential to achieving a system that prioritizes public welfare over private interest is the change in 'public opinion' between More's world and Utopia. As Morus states at the end of *Utopia*,

> many things came to my mind which seemed very absurdly established in the customs and laws of the people described [...] most of all in that feature which is the principle foundation of their whole structure. I mean their common life and subsistence—without any exchange of money. This latter alone utterly overthrows all the nobility, magnificence, splendor, and majesty which are, in the estimation of the common people [*ut publica est opinio*], the true glories and ornaments of the commonwealth. (274)

This passage has long been recognized as being central to understanding More's intentions in the text (Skinner 2002b: 2.213–244; Logan 2014: 242), though interpretation of its meaning varies widely. T. I. White is amongst those scholars who read this comment as an example of More's well-known irony, maintaining that More usually condemns public opinion. He cites More's comments elsewhere to support the idea that public opinion is 'an unreliable guide to morality' and that the 'virtuous man does not care about public opinion; indeed, his virtue usually flies in the face of public opinion' (T. I. White 1978: 141). White further adds that More's philosophical training would have also informed him that the 'argument from public opinion is one of the weakest that can be offered' (142). In contrast, when placed in the context of his other works, we see that public opinion is fundamental to the creation of the 'stage play' of worldly life, which we encountered in More's earlier works. Society's values, for More, are decided by the consensus of a people, rightly or wrongly. As Hythloday notes, in Europe it is 'futile consensus' that determines things 'to be sweet to them in spite of being against nature (as though they had the power to change the nature of things as they do their names)' (*CWM* 4.167). It is this 'consensus' or 'opinion' that is at the heart of such values. There is a 'false idea of pleasure [*falsa voluptatis opinio*]' and a 'meaningless nobility [*vana nobilitas*]', which is created by those who have a 'belief of nobility [*nobilitatis opinio*]' (169). Because Utopians are committed to 'natural' pleasures, they see through this façade of imagined

---

[12] Many thanks to Quentin Skinner for drawing my attention to these examples.

pleasure generated by 'perverse habit' (173). The way in which public opinion in Utopia is used to ensure authentic valuations is central to More's overall point. For More, public opinion can either reflect these fundamental truths, as in Utopia, or it can present a world of falsity and illusion, as in Europe.

Utopia is held together by justice, the 'strongest sinew of the commonwealth', which is defined by Utopians' acknowledgement of their fundamental equality. Injustice is defined as 'depriv[ing] others of their pleasure to secure your own' (197), and so justice comes from the desire to secure others' right to happiness, in line with or even before your own. In other words, as Hythloday puts it, 'nature surely bids you take constant care not to further your own advantages as to cause disadvantage to your fellows' (197). For this reason, Utopians do not see the need for treaties—this command of nature should be enough—and there is also little need for laws. In place of long and complex legal codes, in Utopia the citizens are 'trained': 'They have very few laws because very few are needed for persons so educated [*instituere*]' (195), an idea that goes far beyond 'schooling', and comes closer to what we might now think of as socialization. One of the most important agents of public opinion in Utopia is the priest. Priests are in charge of the 'influence of honor' and 'take the greatest pains from the very first to instil into children's minds, while still tender and pliable, good opinions [*opinio*] which are also useful for the preservation of the commonwealth' (229). These opinions, Hythloday reports, once 'firmly implanted in children [...] accompany them all through their adult lives and are of great help in watching over the condition of the commonwealth', which cannot decay, except 'from wrong attitudes' or 'perverse opinions' (229).[13]

The greatest and most lasting example of the significance of changing public opinion in is in the Utopians' treatment of precious metals and gems: as it is noted in the margin, 'Human Imagination [*Opinio*] Gives Value to Gems or Takes It Away' (169). Gems are given to children to play with, so that when they grow older, 'they lay them aside, not by any order of their parents, but through their own feeling of shame' (153); similarly, gold and silver are used for chamber pots and slaves' chains, and 'thus by every means in their power they make gold and silver a mark of ill fame' (153). When ambassadors come to visit Utopia in their gold chains and gem-studded jewellery, children giggle and adults thus mistake them for fools and slaves.

Unlike the cultural norms in *Utopia*, such as those surrounding gems and precious metals, those generated by European institutions encourage vices that eradicate the natural bonds that unite it, so that the commonwealth is torn apart, through enclosure or through expansionist policies. Whereas 'in Utopia, where nothing is private, they seriously concern themselves with public affairs [*negotium*]' and public opinion works towards the good of the commonwealth (239), outside Utopia, as Hythloday states, 'men talk freely of the public welfare—but look to their private interests only' (239). This is, as Richard McCabe puts it, the 'European paradox' that (in Europe) 'public opinion works against public interest' (McCabe 1988: 633–639). The most important of these vices,

---

[13] The translation of *ex perversis opinionibus* is my own.

as we might have expected, is pride. It is the 'one single monster, the chief progenitor of all plagues' that—in Hythloday's eyes—has prevented the adoption of the customs of the Utopians (*More 1965a:CWM* 4.245). The Utopians have eradicated pride, but in Europe, Hythloday concludes, 'Pride is too deeply fixed in men to be easily plucked out'. This is, however, precisely the language that Morus had used in response to Hythloday's objections in Book One: 'if you cannot pluck up wrongheaded opinion [*opinions pravae*] by the root […] yet you must not on that account desert the commonwealth' (99). This parallels Morus' closing observation that we cannot 'expect' to see Utopian reforms anytime soon (or at all). So what is to be done? More does not resolve the debate between Hythloday and Morus on this point, and all the reader is left with is the ambiguity of his final line: 'wishing' rather than 'expecting' to see Utopia appear in Europe.

Commonality in More's Later Works

Although consideration of More's early and contemporary works helps to solve the question of the central theme of *Utopia*—attention to what is held in common—it does not help us to understand More's own stance in regard to it. Although we have contested the validity of the 'multiple Mores' theory, in reading *Utopia*, we are confronted with two or perhaps even three more Mores within the text itself: the narrator, the author, and—arguably—Hythloday.[14] We can, however, use comments that More makes in less enigmatic texts as corroborative evidence to work out his meaning in *Utopia*.

More's puzzling ending to *Utopia* is echoed by a similar statement in his *Apologye* of 1533. There More tells his reader that it would be wonderful if the world were filled with people who were 'so good' that there were no faults and no heresy needing punishment. Unfortunately, 'thys is more easy to wish, than lykely to loke for' (*More CWM* 9.166). Unlike in *Utopia*, in the *Apologye* More goes on to explain what this means. He writes that, because of this reality, all one can do is 'labour to make hym self better, and charytably somewhat eyther part bear with other' (166). In some ways this suggestion is counter-intuitive, as it demands an attention on to one's own mindset that is seemingly at odds with More's focus on the common. However, the shift towards what is held in common has to begin with the individual (assuming that one does not live in Utopia). It is an internal reorganization of priorities, drawn in large part from More's reading of Augustine, as Kathy Eden (2001: 128–134) has shown: what is common and shared must be prioritized over that which is one's own. Eden points out that for Augustine the accumulation of goods, as well as attaining fame or favour and accruing political power, is not to be sought for its own sake, but is acceptable as means to attaining a higher end: 'Whereas those Christians who choose the monastic life choose the common ownership of material property, all those who live good Christian lives share whatever is true as

---

[14] In the Utopian language, 'he' means 'I'; see Hobbs in this volume.

their common intellectual property' (134). One does not have to live in a monastic community or Utopia to live the principles of equality and commonality.

More repeats this idea in his own works, often with reference to both property and the active life. In the *Letter to a Monk*, written three years after *Utopia*, More writes in reference to monastic living, as in Augustine, that 'God showed great foresight when he instituted all things in common' and 'Christ showed as much when he tried to recall mortals again to what is common from what is private' (*CWM* 15.279). This is because 'corrupt mortal nature cannot cherish what is private without detriment to what is common' (279). Once we 'call anything our own', our interests are diverted 'from the service of the common good [*communium cultu rerum*]' (279). More's point is not to suggest that property *should* be held in common, but that the lesson of a discussion of common property serves as a reminder to value common things (such as the common good) over individual ones, including the common good over our own. This lesson is reflected as well, he suggests, in the choice between active and contemplative lives. In choosing the contemplative life, 'God may find that what you have been doing is avoiding responsibility', by 'wrapping your talent up in a napkin, thus wasting it inside for fear of losing it out-of-doors' (303). Both these habits fuel 'personal pride, the most dangerous habit there is' and place faith in private interest over and above 'the Christian religion', which is shared by all (303). Whether in one considering the good of the commonwealth or the good life, the focus should be on the common.

These lessons are repeated, with some variations, in the *Dialoge of Comfort*, written during More's imprisonment in the Tower of London in 1534–5. Although here More adopts a more suspicious view of the active life, a wholly contemplative life is still condemned as self-serving. Through the character of Anthony, he disparages those who are not willing to trust in God enough to face a world of temptation, 'wherby for faynt hart they leve of good besynes, wherin they were well occupied | & under pretext (as it semeth to them self) of humble hart & mekenes, & servyng god in contemplacion & silence, they seke their own ease & erthly rest', an accusation that could be easily levelled at Hythloday (*CWM* 12.161). More adds that, if a man *truly* feels that he cannot do his duty publicly without falling into temptation, then he ought to retire from public life, but only after he has trusted in God enough to have made an attempt. One finds the same avoidance of extremes in the case of *negotium*, the opposite of contemplation, which Anthony says can be 'the name of a devill that is ever ful of besynes in temptyng folke to much evull besynes' (167). If both contemplation and action are temptations to pursue ungodly paths, then the surest method is to trust in God and attempt to navigate between them both: 'for those temptacions, while he that is temptid foloweth them not | the fight agaynst them serveth a man for mater of merite and reward in hevyn' (170). More's dialogue then turns immediately to the issue of ownership. Anthony suggests that economic inequality is in fact necessary to the commonwealth; there must be 'men of substaunce [...] for els mo beggers shall you have' (179). He gives an Aristotelian rejection of common property, arguing that it would lead to stagnation and indolence.

But it is the mindset that matters, not the economic reality. Anthony gives an example similar to the Lucianic illustrations from More's early work: if one of two beggars is given a home and fine clothes on a temporary loan, the two are still equal, as that property does not really belong to the fortunate beggar. So, too, all people are equal despite economic inequalities: 'in this world, betwene the rychest & the most pore, the difference is scant so much', because nothing truly belongs to us (163). What is important is how you view your place in the world, internalizing this fundamental Lucianic equality: 'yf a man kepe riches aboute hym for a glory & rialtie of the world [...] takyng the porer for the lack therof | as one farr worse than hym selfe: such a mynd is very vayne folysh pride' (184). However, if, on the other hand, he does not love his riches but uses them for the benefit of the commonwealth, then he has done as much as, or even more than, one who gives his riches away: 'yf there be a man [...] that hath unto riches no love | but havyng it fall habundantly unto hym, taketh to his own parte no greate pleasure therof', but bestows it liberally and keeps a hospitable house, 'this mans havyng of riches I might me thinketh in merite match in a maner, with an other mans forsakyng of all' (185). Like Augustine, More suggests that we ought not to consider the 'outward goods of fortune'—such as 'riches, good name, honest estimation, honourable fame & authority'—as important for our present life, but rather 'by the good use thereof, to make them matter of our merit with god's help in the life after to come' (209). It is about an orientation of the mind and soul away from what is private and towards what is common.

More also carries this lesson into another of his last works, *A Treatise upon the Passion*, likewise written in the Tower but left unfinished on More's death. There he condemns those who internalize the false and artificial inequalities of this world: 'howe much more foolish abusion is ther in that pryde, by which we worldlye folke looke vp on height, and solemnelye set by our selfe, with diepe disdayne of other farre better men, onely for very vayn worldly tryfles that properly be not our own?' (*CWM* 13.8). He lists those things from which people derive this sense of pride over one another—several of which had also appeared in *Utopia*—and demonstrates how foolish it is to measure one's worth over that of others, when we consider that it is not, in fact, even one's own property. Recalling the example of the pageant, or the beggar's borrowed estates, More writes that, 'as men maye call hym a foole that beareth hymselfe proude, because he jetteth about in a borowed gown, so may we be wel called very fooles all, if we beare us proude of any thing that we have here' (8–9). Nothing in this world actually belongs to us; it is all 'borowed ware' from God (9), the same phrase he had used in his 1504 verses about fortune (*CWM* 1.40; see above), and which must be returned at the end of our lives. Private ownership is a fiction. In this way Utopia is more 'real' than Europe.

And here we return to the idea of the stage play. More draws this metaphor not just from Lucian, but from Cicero, for whom it designates a way of negotiating between higher truths and the realities of one's situation; of particular importance is *decorum*, the idea that we already saw is deeply connected to public opinion (Cicero 1991: 37; see Skinner 2002b: vol. 2, ch. 8). For Cicero, *decorum* involves an acceptance of reality: including circumstance, audience, and one's own talents. In that way, acting with *decorum* is to take inspiration from actors, who 'do not choose the best plays, but those that are most suited' (Cicero 1991: 44–45). Essential to the performance of one's public duty is the analogy of the play-actor; one's actions and words must be mitigated by an

FIG. 5.1. Ambrosius Holbein, map of *Utopia*, in Thomas More, *De optimo reip. Statu, deque nova insula utopia* (Basel: Johann Froben, November-December 1518), The Bodleian Libraries, University of Oxford, Wood 639, p. 12.

awareness of role and audience. More takes this further and makes it the fundamental lesson of his works: to see and work within the falsity of the world around one, while recognizing it as such.

These lessons, in *Utopia* and in More's later works, are related, then, to those of his poetry and translations of Lucian. The short 'pageant' of life and the dangerous nature of pride are all foundational to More's comments, in *Utopia*, about a reorientation towards 'common things'. There is no clearer sign of this connection than in the map produced by Ambrosius Holbein and published with the 1518 edition of *Utopia* (see Fig. 5.1; contrast Fig. 9.1). The 1518 map of the island bears an uncanny resemblance to a skull, which is 'most apparent to the half-shut eye, and to the subliminal effect of a sidelong glance', as it is in Hans Holbein's *Ambassadors* (Bishop 2005: 109–110). The island itself is the main part of the skull, with the two cities and the labels pendant forming the dark sockets of the eyes. The ship in the foreground forms the toothy grin. It is a memento mori, designed to remind people of their impending deaths (Bishop 2005), a fear that—notably—the Utopians do not share. *Utopia*, like the skull, reminds us that nothing is truly our own, inviting us to lead lives dedicated to the commonwealth. Like More's other works, *Utopia* is designed to be a reminder of our 'real' priorities and our commonality.

CHAPTER 6

UTOPIA AND TRAVEL WRITING

ANDREW HADFIELD

TRAVELLERS' tales and travel accounts are embedded deep within the structure of *Utopia*. Reference to the explorations of the world which had taken place in the past few decades serves to situate Thomas More's work within a wider context of exploration and the expansion of knowledge as well as—paradoxically—to undercut the substance of Utopia and represent it as an imaginary island within an ironic context. Early readers who consumed travel narratives alongside *Utopia* would have been unsettled, not knowing whether they were encountering a real or fictional place. *Utopia* opens with the description of an encounter between 'Morus' (More's textual persona) and Peter Giles after mass at Notre-Dame Cathedral in Antwerp. Morus—as More indeed was—is in Flanders as spokesman for Henry VIII, accompanied by Cuthbert Tunstall, who has just been made Master of the Rolls. They meet a delegation sent by Charles, Prince of Castile (Charles I of Spain, later Holy Roman Emperor Charles V), in Bruges, to sort out a series of important trade disagreements and, during a hiatus in negotiations, Morus heads off on unspecified business to Antwerp where he meets his younger friend, Giles, who has been in conversation with a bearded and sun-tanned man. Giles is praised extravagantly as a man who is 'cultured, virtuous and courteous to all', 'open, trustworthy, loyal and affectionate' with 'his intimates' so that 'it would be hard to find another friend like him anywhere' (More 1989: 9). Giles explains that the bearded man is not a sea captain as Morus thinks but a great student of Greek, Raphael Hythloday, who is a traveller more like Plato than Palinurus, Aeneas' ill-fated pilot who fell overboard and drowned after dozing off at the helm, later meeting his master when he voyages to the underworld (Virgil, *Aeneid* 6.337–83).

Indeed, even before we learn about the Utopians, Hythloday speaks of the Polylerites—from *polus* (much) and *leros* (nonsense)—he encountered on his travels to Persia in a discussion with Cardinal John Morton about the nature of punishment. The Polyrites, according to Hythloday, do not punish criminals harshly but put them to work on beneficial public projects, in marked contrast to the ways in which criminals were treated in England (Briggs et al. 1996: pt 1). The policy, according to Hythloday, is 'mild and practical [...] for the aim of punishment is to destroy vices and save men' (More 1989: 24). The criminals accept their punishment and many are easily rehabilitated and return to society with no stigma attached to their earlier transgressions. Hythloday admits that not all of the assembled company were persuaded that this penal code could work, the unnamed lawyer arguing that 'such a system could never be practised in England without putting the commonwealth in serious peril' (25). Of course, we will never discover who was right. We have a fictional character reporting on a fictional voyage in a fictional conversation. As some elements are real (Persia, Cardinal Morton), the reader is unsettled and discombobulated even before we reach the main subject of the dialogue. How are we to understand the law enforcement policy of the Polyrites? Is More starting a debate about crime and punishment; indicating that the Polyrites' way *might* be a better way of treating criminals than current policies in England; or actually recommending what they do? The episode prepares the reader for the voyage to Utopia, warning them that they need to be receptive to new ideas, but also on their guard, as they will encounter many mysteries and wonders both real and imagined that they will need to decode and assess.

Hythloday has travelled to the Americas with Amerigo Vespucci on three of his four voyages, the genesis of the story of Utopia which follows:

> On the last voyage he did not return home with the commander. After much persuasion and expostulation he got Amerigo's permission to be one of the twenty-four men who were left in a garrison at the farthest point of the last voyage. Being marooned in this way was altogether agreeable to him, as he was more eager to pursue his travels than afraid of death. He would often say, 'The man who has no grave is covered by the sky', and 'The road to heaven is equally short from all places'. Yet this frame of mind would have cost him dear, if God had not been gracious to him. After Vespucci's departure he travelled through many countries with five companions from the garrison. At last, by strange good fortune, he got via Ceylon to Calicut, where by good luck he found some Portuguese ships; and so, beyond anyone's expectations, he returned to his own country. (10–11)

This opening sequence provides a series of details which set the scene for the representation of Utopia. More casts himself as a busy man of affairs, actively involved in the king's business and so a striking contrast to the solitary unencumbered life of Hythloday, a difference which paves the way for the debate between the value of the active and the contemplative life which concludes the first book of *Utopia*.[1] More is very careful to use a series of truthful/plausible details in his description of his experience: his service to the king, the negotiating teams from England and Flanders, the church of Notre-Dame, and the appearance of his friend, Giles. It is then left to the reader to determine at what point, if any, the description turns from truth to fiction. The depiction of Hythloday as

---

[1] For more on this debate, see Paul in this volume.

a weather-beaten explorer, the man who knows more about 'strange peoples and unexplored lands' (9) than anyone alive, might trigger our suspicions, or it might simply be a truthful representation of such a figure likely to be encountered in major ports such as Antwerp, one of the major new cities of Europe (Mols 1974: 16). Nonetheless, Hythloday's interest in philosophy, his belief in the superiority of Greek over Latin culture, and resemblance to Plato as a traveller that Giles notes, would surely alert more astute readers that all is no longer quite what it seems. Plato was indeed a traveller in the Mediterranean, spending twelve peripatetic years after Socrates' death, but he was better known for *The Republic*, an account of the imaginary ideal state (A. E. Taylor 1926/2013: 4).

Giles's account of Hythloday's travels already hints at an intriguing combination of the factual and the fictitious and philosophical. We learn of his contentment with his own company and his desire to reach the furthest point from the known world, where he is able to reproduce gnomic wisdom from the ancients in describing the world as a giant grave and heaven being equidistant from all places. We also learn that he is rescued after a long, complicated, and dangerous journey to Ceylon (modern-day Sri Lanka) via Calicut (or Kozhikode), the chief western seaport on the Indian coast. Calicut was best known as the port reached on 20 May 1498 by Vasco da Gama (c.1460s–1524), the Portuguese explorer and the first European to sail to India (da Gama 1947: 26). Ceylon had a rather different place in the European imagination of the period, as it featured prominently in Sir John Mandeville's account of his fantastic travels, a work More had read and which influenced *Utopia* (D. R. Howard 1971: 1).

In contrast to the factual, sober, and commercially inspired account of Marco Polo, the extraordinarily popular and influential *Mandeville's Travels* concentrated on the marvels of the East, the fantastic and scarcely credible places and creatures that the traveller who ventured beyond the world known to Europeans would encounter. Accordingly, its veracity was disputed even at this early stage in the history of travel writing.[2] Later, it was included in the first edition of Richard Hakluyt's *Principal Navigations* (1589), but was ejected from the second, revised edition (1598–1600). Mandeville alleged that he had travelled to Ceylon, which he describes as a large island, full of 'waste and wilderness' in which 'there are great numbers of dragons, crocodiles and other kinds of reptiles' (Mandeville 1983: 135). Most significantly the island contains a high mountain which has a large lake on its summit. The lake was created from the tears of Adam and Eve who wept for a hundred years after they were expelled from Paradise. There is an abundance of precious stones at the bottom of the lake, hard to reach because the lake is populated with crocodiles and snakes. However, every year the king gives the poor people of Ceylon permission to dive for jewels, which they do, having first anointed themselves with lemon juice which protects them from the hostile creatures in the lake. A river runs down the mountain bringing pearls and other precious stones. The sea surrounding

---

[2] On Mandeville in the context of late medieval travel writing, see Labarge 1982: 3–5.

Ceylon is so high that 'it looks to men who see it as if it hung in the air on the point of falling and covering the earth' (136).

Hythloday's voyages are therefore carefully situated between the wonders of the real and the mythical. Travellers and travel writers read travel writing so that encounters were anticipated and then recounted in terms of what had already been written (C. Houston 2009: 82–98). More's *Utopia* gives an indication of the impact which recent travel accounts were having on the European imagination and the understanding of the Continent's place in an expanding world, and the use of representations of far-flung inaccessible places to explore new, strange, and challenging ideas. While Plato's *Republic* stood at one extreme, a vision of a rational society demonstrating ideal philosophical principles in action, Mandeville's *Travels* stood at the other, revealing a world of miracles, monsters, and things beyond normal explanation, with, perhaps, Marco Polo's *Travels* somewhere in between, a mixture of 'travel guide, fact and fiction' (Ohler 1989: 209). Hythloday's description of Utopia—produced in response to Morus' and Giles's questions about his travels—form the substance of Book Two, after the debate about service and government in Book One, which was undoubtedly inserted to contextualize the account of Utopia (Hexter 1952: 18–21). The fictional Morus makes it clear what kind of information he has extracted from Hythloday and what sort of travel writing book we are about to read:

> We asked him many eager questions [...] and he answered us willingly enough. We made no enquiries, however, about monsters, which are the routine of travellers' tales, Scyllas, ravenous Celaenos, man-eating Lestrygonians and that sort of monstrosity you can hardly avoid, but to find governments wisely established and sensibly ruled is not so easy. While he told us of many ill-considered usages in these new-found nations, he also described quite a few other customs from which our own cities, nations, races and kingdoms might take lessons in order to correct their errors. (More 1989: 12)

Monsters were the subject of much medieval travel writing, strange creatures which seemed unnatural and so were either demonic or wonders which God had created to make people think about the nature of creation (Wittkower 1942). They were invariably represented in waste places far from human settlement such as deserts and the margins of maps, whether harmless and intriguing such as Sciapods (giants in Ethiopia and India who used their one colossal foot to shield themselves from the fierce sun), or aggressive and threatening, such as dragons or sea monsters which lured ships to their doom (see Brotton 2012: ch. 3). More's monsters—Scyllas, Celaenos, Lestrygonians—are all taken from the *Odyssey* and the *Aeneid*, to show that tales of such creatures belong to classical myth not modern-day reality.[3] As Hythloday asserts, the area from which he has returned is replete with monstrous creatures, especially early on in their epic voyage:

---

[3] Scylla was a six-headed sea monster which lived in the Straits of Messina (Homer, *Odyssey* 12.73–100, 234–59); Celano was a harpy, a monstrous bird with a woman's face (*Aeneid* 3.209–58); the Lestrygonians were giant cannibals (*Odyssey* 10.76–132).

Under the equator and as far on both sides of the line as the sun moves, there lie vast empty deserts, scorched with the perpetual heat. The whole region is desolate and squalid, grim and uncultivated, inhabited by wild beasts, serpents and men no less wild and dangerous than the beasts themselves. But as they went on, conditions grew milder. The heat grew less fierce, the earth greener, the creatures less savage. (More 1989: 11)

As Hythloday moves beyond the margins of the known, mapped world, he discovers hitherto hidden civilizations and the people become more like Europeans in nature and society, even though they have not had the benefit of Christian revelation. *Utopia* will show its readers a strange civilization, not a collection of marvels and mysteries, transporting them to a remote place which will remind them of a time before God intervened to transform the world. The book, as Hythloday makes clear, will reveal people who are almost like us but not quite, providing useful lessons to set against the sensational and—for both More and Morus—pointless nature of so much contemporary travel writing which is either false or misleading (probably both), and monstrous in its nature. Readers are warned that they, like Hythloday, should pay more attention to Plato than Mandeville.

The sustained references to Amerigo Vespucci (1454–1512) place the discovery of Utopia in terms of the modern discovery of the New World. Vespucci was an Italian explorer and cartographer who travelled on a number of voyages to South America (some of which may be fictional) in the service of the Spanish and Portuguese crowns around the year 1500. Letters detailing his exploits circulated throughout Europe in the decade before *Utopia* was published so More is situating his fictional work at the forefront of knowledge of the world. Vespucci—whose first name gave rise to the name 'America'—was seen by many as a figure whose significance rivalled that of Christopher Columbus as he, unlike Columbus, realized that the lands to which they both sailed were part of a new continent and not the far side of the lands of the emperor of the East, the Great Khan.[4] The writings associated with Vespucci and Columbus represent the indigenous Americans as either ignorant and docile, eager to cooperate with the Europeans or irredeemably savage, the cannibals of legend and ancient history (most significantly in Herodotus) who were now thought to have resurfaced in the New World (F. Barker et al. 1998; Herodotus 1972: 304–309). Columbus describes the people he encounters in Cuba on his first voyage as 'simple as animals':

They have no religion and are not idolaters; but all believe that power and goodness dwell in the sky and they are firmly convinced that I have come from the sky with these ships and people. In this belief they gave me a good reception everywhere, once they had overcome their fear; and this is not because they are stupid—far from it, they are men of great intelligence, for they navigate all those seas, and give a

---

[4] On Vespucci, see Dinneen 2003; Markham 1894. On Columbus, see Lemos 1998; Cohen 1988.

marvellously good account of everything—but because they have never before seen men clothed or ships like these. (Columbus 1988: 118)

These are the 'good' natives, ready to be converted and colonized, their religion close enough to Christianity to make it easy for them to be converted: or, rather, they are represented to the authorities in Portugal as people who can be converted and governed with little effort. In marked contrast are those represented in a letter to the city of Seville from Diego Alvarez Chanca (Columbus' physician on his second journey), which also describes them as animals, but of a more alien kind as they 'have not the intelligence to find a proper place to live'. They build houses on the seashore in a 'surprisingly primitive way' and it is a miracle that they survive (Chanca 1988: 147).[5] Chanca sees evidence of cannibalism everywhere in the West Indies, even though this belief often proves mistaken:

> One captain separated himself from the party with six men, not knowing that any information had been gained. He and his companions got lost and could not find their way back until, after four days, they struck the coast, which they followed until they rejoined the fleet. We thought that they were dead and eaten by Caribs, for there seemed no other explanation of their disappearance, since among them were pilots, sailors capable of making a voyage to and from Spain by the stars, and we didn't think they could get lost in so small a space. (134)

It soon becomes obvious that explorers' credulity regarding cannibals were exploited by the people they encountered, as can be seen in Chanca's account:

> We asked the women who were held prisoners on this island what kind of people these were [i.e., the inhabitants of the island they have just sailed to]; and they replied that they were Caribs. When they understood that we hated these people on account of their cannibalism, they were highly delighted; and after that, if any Carib man or woman was brought in, they quietly told us that they were Caribs. For even here, where all were in our power, they showed the fear of a conquered people, and thus we learnt from the women which were Caribs and which were not. (135)

The European world view thus made it easy for indigenous peoples to use them to fight their wars: Chanca does not state exactly what happened next but it is clear that the Europeans joined forces with the 'friendly' inhabitants against the 'hostile' Caribs (Hulme 1986: ch. 1).

More draws on such accounts in *Utopia* to create a work that is significantly different in substance but which always leads readers back to the questions that travel writing habitually raised. How and why did societies differ? Did other societies have better ideas about life and government than one's own? Was there a danger of finding the

---

[5] On Chanca (c.1463–c.1515), see Ruiz 1998.

exotic too attractive? Does travel really broaden the mind? Evidence of early editions indeed suggests that editors, translators, and readers all understood that *Utopia* served as a practical—albeit difficult and unusual—guide to politics and government, not an account of monsters, miracles, exotic people, or docile and hostile savages (T. Cave 2008d: 127, 141, and *passim*). Indeed, many of the details of Utopian society, and accounts of their behaviour, might have been consciously written in opposition to descriptions of the absence of work in many American societies, including those provided by Vespucci (Markham 1894: 9–10). Hythloday frequently represents the Utopians as a people who are so committed to work and self-improvement that they labour hard even—or, perhaps, especially—in their hours of leisure:

> The other hours of the day, when they are not working, eating, or sleeping, are left to each man's individual discretion, provided he does not waste his free time in roistering or sloth [*non quo per luxum, aut segnitiem abutatur*] but uses it properly in some occupation that pleases him. Generally these periods are devoted to intellectual activity. For they have an established custom of giving public lectures before daybreak; attendance at these lectures is required only of those who have been specially chosen to devote themselves to learning, but a great many other people of all kinds, both men and women, choose voluntarily to attend. Depending on their interests, some go to one lecture, some to another. But if anyone would rather devote his spare time to his trade, as many do, who don't care for the intellectual life, this is not discouraged; in fact, such persons are commended as specially useful to the commonwealth. (More 1989: 51)

The Utopians are ideal counterparts of Europeans, holding up a mirror which shames those living in the Old World. Like most English schoolboys and university students of the period they get up early to attend lectures (Vives 1970: 1–18); however, they do so voluntarily and with enthusiasm, making best use of the time they have. The emphasis is on the great value of education and lifelong learning which every Utopian desires, unless they are engaged in other fruitful activities which benefit the commonwealth. The pursuit of selfish, greedy individual pleasures, such as gambling, is unthinkable and so does not need to be forbidden—although the Utopians do play games which are like chess and one in which 'the vices fight a battle against the virtues' (More 1989: 52; Fitzmaurice 2003: 1). Hythloday reveals that he cannot abide the notion of 'waste', a concept which appears frequently in a colonial context. Here, Hythloday equates waste with idleness: the failure of the individual to better themselves and the society in which they live. The notion of 'waste' was also applied to land. Wasteland was not being put to work by its owners and so could be appropriated by those who would use it more productively. This principle underlay ideas about agriculture outlined in popular sixteenth-century manuals such as Thomas Tusser's *Five Hundred Good Points of Husbandry* (1557), published in the same decade as the first English translation of *Utopia* (1551) and which contrasted the productive use of the land as the basis for an ordered society with the anarchy, chaos, and disorder generated by idleness and waste (Tusser 1984: 11–12 and *passim*). As John Patrick Montaño points out in his study of English colonialism in Ireland (Montaño

2011: 55–56), the notion of waste was central to English justifications of their right to conquer and control their neighbours, which they derived from the *Laudabiliter*, the papal bull which granted English kings suzerainty over Ireland in 1155 in order to bring the Irish under the control of the papacy and stem their allegedly evil habits.[6] Societies in the Americas were often depicted as idle and unproductive, sometimes negatively in aggressively expansionist writing, sometimes more positively, as in Michel de Montaigne's famous description of the Brazilian cannibals (post-dating *Utopia*), reproduced later in Shakespeare's *The Tempest* (1611) when Gonzalo imagines that he might be a benign ruler of the island on which the Italian courtiers are shipwrecked (2.1.144–69). Montaigne, in his essay 'Of the Cannibals', contemplates the superiority of nature to culture, through a discussion of the practice of selective breeding. The 'cannibals'

> are even savage, as we call those fruits wild, which nature of herself and of her ordinary progress hath produced. Whereas indeed they are those which ourselves have altered by our artificial devices and diverted from their common order we should rather term savage. In those are the true and most profitable virtues and natural properties most lively and vigorous, which in these we have bastardized, applying them to the pleasure of our corrupted taste. And if notwithstanding, in diverse fruits of those countries that were never tilled, we shall find that in respect of ours they are most excellent and as delicate unto our taste, there is no reason art should gain the point of honour of our great and puissant mother Nature [...]. It is a nation, would I answer *Plato*, that hath no kind of traffic, no knowledge of letters, no intelligence of numbers, no name of magistrate, nor of tracts, no successions, no dividences, no occupation but idle; no respect of kindred, but common; no apparel, but natural; no manuring of lands, no use of wine, corn or metal. The very words that import lying, falsehood, treason, dissimulation, covetousness, envy, detraction, and pardon were never heard amongst them. (Montaigne 2014: 60–61)

In representing nature as benign and her fruits as wholesome and nourishing without human interference, Montaigne was consciously adopting a familiar and long-established European tradition which celebrated the natural world and lamented the rise of society and civilization. The myth was most famously and easily accessible in Ovid's description in the *Metamorphoses* of the Golden Age, a time before the dawn of history:

> In the beginning was the Golden Age, when men of their own accord, without threat of punishment, without laws, maintained good faith and did what was right. There were no penalties to be afraid of, no bronze tablets were erected, carrying threats of legal action, no crowd of wrong-doers, anxious for mercy, trembled before the face of their judge: indeed there were no judges, men lived securely without them. Never

---

[6] Gerald of Wales (Giraldus Cambrensis), the most influential supporter of Henry II's right to govern Ireland, reproduced the *Laudabiliter* in his *Expugnatio Hibernica*, and emphasized the colonial mission of the English to save the Irish from leaving their 'waste'.

yet had any pine tree, cut down from its home on the mountains, been launched on ocean's waves, to visit foreign lands: men knew only their own shore. Their cities were not yet surrounded by sheer moats, they had no straight brass trumpets, no coiling brass horns, no helmets and no swords [...]. The earth itself, without compulsion, untouched by the hoe, unfurrowed by any share, produced all things spontaneously, and men were content with foods that grew without cultivation. They gathered arbute berries and mountain strawberries, wild cherries and blackberries that cling to thorny bramble bushes: or acorns, fallen from Jupiter's spreading oak. (Ovid 1995: 31–32)

Ovid's description when translated to the New World, transforming a chronological narrative into a spatial one, had its own inbuilt paradox: in order to witness the new Golden Age the traveller was, of course, distinguished from those who could experience through the acquisition of the means of transport over the Atlantic. But everyone could understand the lure of this myth, the fantasy that unpleasant work was something that was unnatural and unnecessary, most powerfully represented in the popular story of the land of Cockaigne (accounts of which circulated from the thirteenth century onwards), an earthly paradise in which the rivers flowed wine, ripe fruit fell from trees into peoples' waiting hands, and roast pigs with carving knives in their sides ran around squealing 'Eat me! Eat me!' (Morton 1978: 1–45).

Montaigne's essay—published in 1580, a few decades after the first two French translations of *Utopia*, and a few years before its third—might even have been conceived in opposition to More's text, a work which validates the ideal republic of Plato over travellers' tales of the strange and unexpected, emphasizing the value of work, civilization, and productivity over the pleasures and delights of the Golden Age. Whether conscious or not, the relationship between the substance of the two works demonstrates the complicated interactions between different modes of travel writing, and shows that every representation is already mediated by conflicting traditions. The Utopians, far from being the innocent creatures of a Golden Age, are themselves eager to colonize their neighbours. In this way, the people Hythloday came face to face with, travelling beyond the lands encountered by Columbus and Vespucci, were much more like contemporary Europeans than those who dwelled in the Americas, not least in their use of 'waste' as a justification for colonization, one of the many jokes in More's fable (Fox 1982: 57).

The Utopians embark on colonial enterprises when they feel mounting population pressure, a motive which links them closely to their European counterparts as the need to find more living space for people was frequently cited as a reason for establishing settlements in other countries (K. R. Andrews 1984; Hadfield 1998: 10–12).[7] Conscious of the need to oversee and control the size of their population, Utopians decree that each metropolis should consist of 'six thousand households' with each household 'containing between ten and sixteen adults' (More 1989: 55). This means that each city has between

---

[7] The following three paragraphs are a revised version of material in Hadfield 1998.

60,000 and 96,000 people, making most Utopian cities larger than London, which had a population of *c.*50,000–60,000 people in Henry VIII's reign (Rappaport 1989: 61). The next largest cities, Norwich and Bristol, had populations in the region of 9,000–12,000 (Hadfield 2017a: 62). More would appear to be emphasizing the fictional nature of the Utopians' ability to regulate their society, especially as this is achieved 'by transferring individuals from a household with too many into a household with not enough' and urban dwellers to rural areas (More 1989: 55–56), a rational approach that clearly ignores normal affective relationships between people and imagines them as interchangeable numbers. More's close relationship with his own family and household was often noted by contemporaries (Chambers 1963: 167–181).

We should therefore be sceptical of taking the description of the Utopians' colonial policies at face value as if they were to be endorsed or adopted by European powers:

> And if the population throughout the entire island exceeds the quota, they enrol citizens out of every city and plant a colony under their own laws on the mainland near them, whenever the natives have plenty of unoccupied and uncultivated land. Those natives who want to live with the Utopians are taken in. When such a merger occurs the two peoples gradually and easily blend together, sharing the same way of life and customs, much to the advantage of both. For by their policies the Utopians make the land yield an abundance for all, though previously it had seemed too barren and paltry even to support the natives. But those who refuse to live under their laws the Utopians drive out of the land they claim for themselves; and on those who resist them, they declare war. The Utopians say it's perfectly justifiable to make war on people who leave their land idle and waste [*inane ac vacuum*] yet forbid the use and possession of it to others who, by the law of nature, ought to be supported from it. (More 1989: 56)

If More has any European country in mind here it can only be Ireland, especially given the geographical representation of Utopia as 'an island separated from the continent by a channel', making it rather like England (Fox 1982: 56; Montaño 2011: 70; Knapp 1992: 21). Ireland was the one significant overseas territory which England claimed and in which the English had established colonies, although they really only controlled the area around Dublin, the Pale. English monarchs had generally been reluctant to sponsor overseas voyages, regarding them as over-speculative, risky investments unlikely to provide a return on their investment, although 'in his own thrifty fashion' Henry VII did provide some support for John Cabot's voyages of discovery in the 1490s (Wernham 1966: 74; S. E. Morison 1971: 157–209; E. Jones 2010).[8] In effect there was no English tradition of transatlantic colonialism on which to draw when More was writing *Utopia*, as 'no serious attempt was made to settle in the Americas until Sir Humphrey Gilbert's expedition of 1583' (Pagden 1998: 34). Even the Spanish, who were the most advanced colonial power in Europe, had only just completed their conquest of Cuba in 1515 and

---

[8] For earlier English colonial/imperial exploits, see also Hower in this volume.

established an extensive network of colonies only after *Utopia* was published (Trevor Davies 1967: ch. 4).

For a long time Ireland had been regarded by the English as a country full of wasteland ready to be colonized, and there was a belief that if colonization was extensive enough then a fruitful collaboration between natives and newcomers would lead to the transformation of Irish society, making it a more stable, fruitful, and Anglicized country which would benefit all its inhabitants (Hadfield 1999). But even in Ireland there was little colonial activity of the sort More describes in *Utopia* taking place while he was writing it. More was writing during the period of Kildare Ascendancy. Ireland was governed from the Dublin Pale by the Anglo-Irish elite, the Lord Deputy almost invariably being the Fitzgerald earl of Kildare. Gerald, Earl of Kildare, was Lord Deputy almost continuously from 1496 until 1520, eclipsing the family's main rivals in Ireland, the Butlers of Ormond. English deputies were only occasionally appointed, with Thomas Howard, third Duke of Norfolk, undertaking the role from 1520 to 1522, until the Revolt of Silken Thomas in 1534 ended the power of the Kildares and saw the rise of a more aggressively interventionist English policy which involved more direct rule from London, the influx of 'New' English settlers, and periodic attempts to establish colonial settlements (Ellis 1985: 85–108; McCorristine 1987). The Lord Deputy did indeed pursue policies in line with the Utopians on his land, 'driving out Gaelic interlopers, constructing castles and other defences, and settling his own tenants on previously waste land' (Connolly 2007: 68). Kildare's actions are probably best read less as examples of colonial practice than as an indication of the close relationship between domestic and colonial policies in the early sixteenth century, a point also made in *Utopia*.

Given the context in which More was writing *Utopia* and, more significantly, the ironies which surround his representation of Utopian colonial practice, it is hard to read the Utopians' arguments as a serious recommendation for colonial expansion. Stephen Greenblatt's judgement that More's writings 'clearly represent a sustained and repeated impulse towards the unsettling of reality' (Greenblatt 1980: 26) describes the experience of reading *Utopia* with unerring accuracy. Rather, More is pointing out here a logical, possible solution to an economic problem which it is claimed is destroying the social and economic infrastructure of England. Hythloday reports a discussion which took place in Cardinal Morton's palace immediately after the suppression of the Cornish Revolt in 1497, a rebellion inspired by hostility to extremely high taxes which was 'put down with great slaughter of the poor folk involved' (More 1989: 15; see also A. Fletcher 1983: 10–12). Hythloday objects to the defence, given by a lawyer, of harshly punitive measures undertaken to control theft, claiming that the poor have no reasonable means of gainful employment. When his interlocutor objects that farming will provide people with an easily obtainable mode of employment, or—if not agriculture—the army, Hythloday counters that war is best avoided and having a standing army is pointless and ruinously expensive; nor, in any case, does this get to the root of the problem, which is sheep. When the Cardinal asks how Hythloday's thinking works, he explains:

> Your sheep [...] that commonly are so meek and eat so little; now, as I hear, they have become so greedy and fierce that they devour men themselves. They devastate and depopulate fields, houses and towns. For in whatever parts of the land sheep yield the finest and thus the most expensive wool, there the nobility and gentry, yes, and even some abbots though otherwise holy men, are not content with the old rents that the land yielded to their predecessors. Living in idleness and luxury without doing society any good no longer satisfies them; they have to do positive evil. For they leave no land free for the plough: they enclose every acre for pasture; they destroy houses and abolish towns, keeping only the churches—and those for sheep barns. And as if enough of your land were not already wasted on forests and game-preserves, these worthy men turn all human habitations and cultivated fields back to wilderness [*solitudinem*]. (More 1989: 18–19)

This is a complicated and subtle critical passage which assumes particular importance when read alongside the Utopians' belief in their right to establish colonies: in particular, the discussion of 'waste'. The Utopians argue that they need to colonize because of the pressure of population, meaning that they have the right to appropriate wasteland in other countries which could be reclaimed to support human life. In England, according to Hythloday, the upper classes are transforming good farming land into wasteland for their own pleasures, using the law to enforce the enclosure of vast spaces and evict tenants and small farmers, many of whom, according to Hythloday, become beggars and criminals. The Utopians justify their actions in terms of hard work and ability to use land properly. The English upper classes, in contrast, are idle parasites who have managed to accumulate far too many of the nation's resources for their own gain. What emerges, when we put the two sections of the text together, is that reasons for colonization may be more complicated than its proponents assume and that economic systems are more closely connected than a straightforward division between the domestic and the colonial.

Hythloday concludes his analysis of England's economic woes with a savage, albeit familiar, attack on the rich:

> To make this hideous poverty worse, it exists side by side with wanton luxury. The servants of noblemen, tradespeople, even some farmers—people of every social rank—are given to ostentatious dress and gluttonous eating. Look at the cook-shops, the bawdy houses and those other places just as bad, the wine-bars and beer-halls. Look at all the crooked games of chance like dice, cards, backgammon, tennis, bowling and quoits, in which money slips away so fast. Don't all these pastimes lead their addicts straight to robbery? Banish these blights, make those who have ruined farmhouses and villages restore them or rent them to someone who will rebuild. Restrict the right of the rich to buy up anything and everything, and then to exercise a kind of monopoly. Let fewer people be brought up in idleness. Let agriculture be restored, and the wool-manufacture revived, so there will be useful work for those now idle. (20–21)

For Hythloday, the solution is as simple as it is logical: idleness needs to be eliminated and the best way to achieve this is through the strict control of conspicuous consumption.

Economic ills are the mainsprings of crime and if such problems are rooted out then people will realize it is in their best interests to conform and act in the interests of society as a whole. The obverse of this selfish accumulation is the rational and sensible behaviour of the Utopians, who manage the population properly. While the English have let foolish games flourish, the Utopians all understand that they are as pernicious a blight on society as they are a waste of time. They even have solutions for depopulation, bringing people back from the colonies to restore numbers. This drastic solution has only been necessary twice in their history, 'both times in consequence of a frightful plague' (156).

Hythloday is not, of course, to be trusted entirely, which is why his belief in the value of colonization cannot be taken as that of More. Cardinal Morton, a man who—in real life—More liked and admired (Chambers 1963: 54–57), opposes Hythloday's ideas:

> 'My dear Raphael, I'd be glad to hear why you think theft should not be punished with death, or what other punishment you think would be more suitable. For I'm sure even you don't think it should go punished entirely. Even as it is, fear of death does not restrain malefactors; once they were sure of their lives, as you propose, what force or fear could withhold them? They would look on a lighter penalty as an invitation to commit more crimes, almost a reward.' (More 1989: 21–22)

Morton has identified what many would argue is the central flaw in Hythloday's argument: people have identities, feelings, ideas, prejudices, and souls. They are responsible for their actions and cannot be represented as if they have no control over their actions, are incapable of making choices, and have no sympathetic relationship to other people or their environment. Just as people will choose to behave well or not, to obey or break the law, to follow a moral code or ignore it, so will they be resistant to logical but insensitive plans such as the Utopians' plans to move people from one household to another, from one part of the country to another, from the country to the city or the city to the country, and from their nation to a colony. Hythloday's analysis of the economic problems which afflict English society in the early sixteenth century are surely accurate and acute; his solution is somewhat more problematic, as the Cardinal recognizes. The Utopians, in Hythloday's account, are eager to punish their own criminals more harshly than those of other people they govern because 'their crimes are worse and deserve stricter punishment because, as it is argued, they had an excellent education and the best of moral training, yet still couldn't be restrained from wrongdoing' (80). The Utopians do not quite conform to Hythloday's initially untarnished image.

The representation of colonial expansion in *Utopia* has to be seen in terms of wider debates about human nature, individual responsibility, and the soul in More's writing, not simply in terms of travel writing and representations of other cultures.[9] In some ways this is a trivial and obvious point because debates about other cultures, especially those discovered by Europeans in the Americas, invariably led to serious reflection on

---

[9] For the importance of the soul in More's writing and thinking, see Paul in this volume.

the nature of mankind, God's plans for the universe, and the nature of salvation. The Spanish colonization of South America, for example, led to vociferous and aggressive debates between diametrically opposed thinkers about the identity of the peoples found living on the continent. Were they natural men, innocent and pure, a reward from God to the truly faithful enabling the Church to intervene and secure their souls? Or were they natural slaves, somewhere between beasts and men in the great chain of being, capable of undertaking menial tasks but not of achieving parity with Europeans who had been given them by God to use as they saw fit (see Pagden 1986)?

More is exploring similar issues in *Utopia*. The Utopians have a variety of religious beliefs, some worship the sun, some the moon, and some the planets, others elevating historical figures to the status of deities.[10] Most, however, believe in 'a single power, unknown, eternal, infinite, inexplicable far beyond the grasp of the human mind', known as Mithra (More 1989: 96). In doing so More is representing the Utopians in terms of the docile and friendly indigenous peoples discovered in the New World, who were simple rational creatures ready to be converted to Christianity. Columbus refers to some friendly inhabitants encountered on his first voyage (1492–3) who he believes can 'easily be made Christians, for they appeared to me to have no religion', here their lack of belief being an advantage because there is no barrier to remove which obstructs the true faith (Columbus 1988: 56). Columbus' physician Chanca provides a longer description of peoples encountered on the second voyage (1493–6):

> These Indians seem so well disposed that they could be converted if we had an interpreter, for they imitate everything that we do. They bend their knees at the altars, and at the *Ave Maria* and other moments, and cross themselves. They say that they wish to be Christians, although actually they are idolaters. There are idols of all kinds in their houses. When I ask them what these are they answer that they belong to *Turey*, that is to say to the sky. I once made a show of wanting to throw these in the fire, which so upset them that they were on the point of tears. They also think that whatever we bring comes from the sky, for they call it all *Turey*, that is to say sky. (Chanca 1988: 154–155)

Here the indigenous people's adherence to their primitive/pagan beliefs is a sign of their imminent conversion.

More pushes such accounts to their logical conclusions in *Utopia*, forcing readers to imagine how those without Christian revelation would behave when confronted with the truth. Of course, most are ready to be converted and the Utopians are nothing if not tolerant of diverse religious beliefs and practices. However, there is a problem: that of the zealot. Hythloday describes one recent convert who, after his baptism, insists on preaching the Christian faith 'with more zeal than discretion', eventually deciding that he needs to condemn all other religions as profane and not just promote Christian belief. Despite the warnings from the Europeans, he continues promoting his convictions,

---

[10] For more on religion in Utopia, and More's attitude to religion, see Harris Sacks in this volume.

is arrested and tried on a charge 'not of despising their religion, but of creating a public disorder', and exiled, 'For it is one of their oldest rules that no one should suffer for his religion' (More 1989: 97).

What should we make of this incident? More was famously intolerant in his later debates with William Tyndale, and clearly had no intention of tolerating Protestantism (see Hadfield 2017b: 115–125). Is there an inconsistency? It is unlikely. More is following through the consequences of having to consider innocent and rational people who have not had the benefit of Christian revelation. For them toleration is logical but this is not a luxury in which the true Christian can indulge, as there is a truth which needs to be articulated. The question this incident raises is less one of absolute truth versus relativism and more an issue of what duties a Christian has to defend and promote their faith, one More was prepared to die for in 1535. More was surely more on the side of the banished Christian Utopian than Hythloday but he may not have felt that Christians—in 1516—needed to be quite so evangelical.

To reinforce this point it is also worth considering the Utopians' belief in the ethics of suicide. Marco Polo describes an encounter with the people of Manzi in South China who have such a pronounced sense of their honour that it is acceptable to kill oneself to avenge one's honour, a practice which can rebound to the suicide's advantage when a 'rich and powerful enemy may honour him in death and thus ensure him similar honours in another world' (Polo 1958: 225). In such a culture suicide is a logical choice, and the same is true in Utopia. When a Utopian has an incurable disease 'public officials come and urge the invalid not to endure further agony [...] This would be a wise act, they say, since for him death puts an end, not to pleasure, but to agony' (More 1989: 80–81). In doing so the suicide is 'obeying the advice of priests who are interpreters of God's will' (81). The last phrase provides readers of *Utopia* with a crucial clue: suicide makes sense for Utopians who are rational and base their understanding of morality on a Utilitarian conception of the balance of pleasure and pain, but is not appropriate for terminally ill Christians who would receive very different advice from their priests.

Utopia routinely refers to episodes in and issues raised in contemporary travel accounts, as might be expected. Travel writing—the accounts of Mandeville, Polo, Columbus, and Vespucci in particular—was a vital component of More's intellectual world when he created Utopian society, a statement which seems obvious enough. What is more important is that the questions raised by encounters with peoples from the Americas and elsewhere determine most of the crucial debates in the book: what is the nature of justice and how can it be achieved; is equality a desirable goal; what is the relationship between the individual and society; and, most significantly, what might a society without the advantage of Christian revelation look like, and what might Christians learn from it? *Utopia* is not a work that can be straightforwardly mapped onto modes of travel writing: it is far too sophisticated and subtle to be reduced to any such genre or type of writing. Nonetheless, neglecting to read More's work in terms of travel and colonial writing—in particular, representations of the Americas—leaves out a significant element of its story.

CHAPTER 7

UTOPIA'S EMPIRE

Thomas More's Text and the Early British Atlantic World, c.1510–1625

JESSICA S. HOWER

IN 1626, less than a year into the reign of Charles I, the Oxford-educated writer and colonial theorist William Vaughan dedicated a piece to his 'Great Monarch'. Published under the pseudonym 'Orpheus Junior', who describes himself as a countryman of Wales, *The Golden Fleece* opens with hyperbolic praise: Vaughan lauds his prince as 'the most Noble, | Mightie, and hopefull King | of Great Britaine', endows him 'with Apollo's lore', celebrates the 'Projectours rare' that Charles has at his disposal, and compares him to his namesake, the Holy Roman Emperor, Charles V (Vaughan 1626: A2r–v). With biblical references, classical allusions, and calls on more recent imperial history and literature, it was a telling and apt start to Vaughan's lengthy and often circuitous allegorical argument in favour of British colonization in the New World.[1]

Vaughan wrote at a crucial juncture in the history of British expansion across the Atlantic. Charles's father, James VI and I, had achieved a union of the English and Scottish crowns that fell short of what he and others had hoped, and numerous ventures, to the east and west, were fledging, with limited aid and oversight (Canny 1998; Croft 2003; Kupperman 2007). This was particularly true of Vaughan's concern: Newfoundland, specifically the Avalon Peninsula, where six years prior, in 1616, the author had purchased land from the London and Bristol Company of adventurers patented by James for settlement of the territory. In a nod to his Welsh roots, Vaughan dubbed his new colony 'Cambriol' (from 'Cambria') and endeavoured to promote, plant, and perfect its organization across 1617–18. By 1619, however, the enterprise was struggling, even collapsing, a reality that imbues the *Golden Fleece*, and its appeal to a royal and non-royal readership, with some urgency and desperation. In this climate,

---

[1] For more on *Utopia* and empire, see Hadfield, Lutz, and Weaver-Hightower and Bajaber in this volume.

Vaughan rested his appeal on history, and on one very particular history in particular. From his writing style, to his precedents, exempla, and textual allusions, Vaughan's book was steeped in the figures, events, language, and literature of the previous century. Across the three parts of his treatise, Vaughan cited the hopes and deeds of Henry VIII and Elizabeth I, their respective chief ministers Thomas Cromwell and William Cecil, mid- and late-sixteenth-century English statesmen like Thomas Smith and Francis Walsingham, the same era's maritime adventurers like Martin Frobisher, John Hawkins, and Francis Drake, as well as other 'brave' figures under whom 'our English found a Golden age' (Vaughan 1626: 77). In order to save his New Wales, Vaughan's text even resurrected several of these figures to appear before Apollo to testify to the ways in which colonization, especially in Newfoundland, would improve, enrich, and assist the domestic commonwealth.

Vaughan's literary career and colonial journey had begun around the turn of the century when, as a student at Oxford and in continental Europe, he began writing poetry and philosophy. His most famous composition, *The Golden-Grove* (1600), took the form of an Aristotelian commentary on the present condition of civil society, politics, and morality and, crucially, set the context and stage for the later *Golden Fleece*. Vaughan's outlook was gloomy, describing a nation imperilled by 'Heretiques and Schismatiques' (Vaughan 1600: F4r) with their 'Divelish device' and 'Romish Bishop' (F5r) and disloyal, uncivil subjects who 'doe by all shameful acts, and false counsels, suborne their countrymen to conspiracies against their Prince and Commonwealth' (Q6r), while those who till the land, in pursuit of the most pleasant and highly regarded lives, are oppressed by greedy landlords, such that 'yeomanrie is decayed, hospitalitie gone to wracke, and husbandrie almost quite fallen' (T4v). 'If the Common-wealth be destroyed,' he warned, 'both we and our families must likewise come to utter destruction. Let this serve for a watchword' (Q5v–6r).

A quarter-century later, Vaughan spied a remedy for precisely those ills. In order for the realm, which he explicitly construed as British in a reference to his own Welshness and to his monarch's claims, to survive and flourish, it needed convenient land for its godly inhabitants to live on, rich soil for them to till, agricultural plenty for them to reap, temperate air for them to breathe, expansive and bountiful seas for them to fish in, a vent for its idle and poor, profits for its coffers, an outlet for excess supply, a source for raw materials and tradeable goods like metals, animal skins, naval stores, and spices, and a haven secured from enemies: in short, an external realm to reinforce the internal. His Cambriol colony was presented as the overseas tonic to cure 'the Diseases of the Common-wealth' (Vaughan 1626: A4v) or, as the subtitle of *The Golden Fleece* puts it, a corrective for 'the Errours of Religion, and Vices and Decayes of the Kingdome, and lastly the wayes to get wealth, and to restore Trading so much complayned of [...] For the general and perpetuall Good of Great Britaine'. His mouthpiece, Orpheus Junior, explains,

> I saw that God had reservd the Newfoundland for us Britaines, as the next land beyond Ireland, and not above nine or tenne dayes saile from thence. I saw that he had

bestowed a large portion for this Countries mariage with our Kingdomes, even this great Fishing, that by this meanes it might be frequented and inhabited the sooner by us. And I verily thinke, that his Heavenly providence ordained this Iland not without a Mystery for us of Great Britaine, that Ilanders should dwel in Ilands. (pt 3, 5)

Fashioning a latter-day Jason's quest for 'our Colchos', Newfoundland, Vaughan described it as 'Great Britaines Indies, never to be exhausted dry' and capable, once planted, of ensuring 'that Great Britaines Monarchy might in a short time arrive to as great riches as the Spanish' (pt 3, 9–10). Where else, the author asked rhetorically, could settlements—where colonists can 'live to help themselves, and benefit their Country'— be more quickly erected and at lesser charge? (14). 'If with kind words your Majestie approve | This Golden Fleece sprung from a subjects love', then Cambriol would surely become the key to Britain's national and imperial greatness (95).

Although he wrote for a new audience in a new quarter-century, Vaughan's arguments and examples were firmly rooted in the colonial past, and not only of the most recent Jacobean or Elizabethan sort. He borrowed heavily from the projects and polemics of his immediate predecessors, especially Humphrey Gilbert and Walter Ralegh, but these mentions were buried deep within the work. Much more prominent were the precedents of early Tudor literature, in particular *Utopia* (even as Vaughan defines his project against More's book). His prefatory poem insists:

> This no Eutopia is
> [......]
> Wee bring Your Kingdomes
> By true Receits; which You will rellish well,
> If Humours ranke by Physicke You expell.
> In pithy fresh Conceits Your mind may joy,
> When sundry Troupes of weightie Cares annoy. (A2v)

Vaughan went on to cite Utopia the place and book no less than four more times: in a Latin version of his dedicatory verses to Charles, where he chose to write it as 'Eutopiam' (A4r); in an 'Epigram upon the Golden Fleece, moralized by the Authour for the good of Great Britaine', where he explains how the mythical hero Jason 'From Westerne Colchos brings the Golden Fleece; | Which no Eutopia is, nor Fairy-land' (B3r); in a chapter on 'the Impurity of the Church Militant', where it features for the staunchly anti-Catholic author as an example of a form of religious living, untenable since the death of St Paul, whereby 'you would have an equalitie, as in Sir Thomas Moore Eutopia of Degrees of Livings, under pretext of the Apostles paritie, that none of them should be greater then the other, every one would be a Pope in his Parish' (135); and in the conclusion to his First Part, where the author defended his choice to write 'of serious matters in an extraordinarie forme', adding 'If these reason cannot prevaile, but that still they will mutter, and seeke a hole where none is, I must referre them to the reading of Sir Thomas Moores Eutopia' (146, 148). At each turn, Vaughan's recourse to a book over one hundred years old was a significant decision, and it served to yoke a mid-1620s Stuart colonial discourse and venture to a Tudor text of the 1510s in a powerful, but not wholly original, way.

The Golden Fleece was not the first time that *Utopia* and a budding British imperialism were so intimately linked. Indeed, it was not even the first time that *Utopia* and Newfoundland were twinned. Yet though it ranks among the most enigmatic and contested works in Renaissance literature, More's text is still understudied among scholars of early British imperial expansion. Artificially separated from its full Atlantic-wide context and treated as the purview of literary critics, historians of domestic England, and students of political theory, the piece remains somewhat remote—a fiction. This chapter seeks to reposition the work within debates about imperialism. It examines the 1510s as a watershed of British imperial trial and error—to which More's text contributed—and *Utopia*'s continued relevance for theorists and adventurers across the Tudor and early Stuart period. Privileging a selection of critical moments and milieus in which the book was written, disseminated, consumed, and deployed, this chapter demonstrates how *Utopia* can shed new light on the origins of the British Empire in the sixteenth and early seventeenth centuries and vice versa.

***

Distilling the mass of opinions regarding More's text into a memorable list, Alistair Fox wrote that scholars have paradoxically found 'its function as a paradigm, its reformist practicality, its medievalism, its modernity, its desirability, its detestability, its seriousness, its frivolity as a *jeu d'espirt*, its modified Platonism, its Aristotelianism, and its Augustinianism' (Fox 1982: 50). Since then, the tendency for *Utopia* to function, in Robert Shephard's analogy, 'as a magic mirror in which readers have beheld what they desired most or sometimes what they feared most' (Shephard 1995: 843) has not abated, nor has its ability, in Terence Cave's rendering, to shapeshift and 'travel: it adapts itself to the interests and tastes of its new readers to an extent that very few other works of the period can rival' (T. Cave 2008a: 3). For all that, little attention has been paid to *Utopia* in an Atlantic-wide or British imperial framework, in the 1510s or beyond, or to appreciate its apparent popularity and usefulness in that sphere, whether as a means of inspiring colonial adventure, promoting colonial scheming, or delegitimizing colonial pursuits.[2]

Concurrently, scholars have dramatically upended traditional narratives of exploration, 'discovery', nation- and empire-building, early modern and modern. Those at work in British imperial history have challenged the once unambiguous distinction between centre and periphery, metropole and colony, effectively dismantling any view of the colonizer–colonized relationship as simple or linear from superior to inferior as well as the existence of unquestioned European hegemony. Yet their efforts privilege certain places and later periods (K. Wilson 2004; J. Thomson 2007; Howe 2009). At the same time, the rise of Atlantic History has reconceptualized the early modern

---

[2] Exceptions include Devereux 1976; Konecsni 1976; A. Cave 1991; Mayer 1991; Knapp 1992; Hadfield 1998; J. C. Davis 2000; with briefer analysis in Quinn 1966, 1976; M. C. Fuller 1995; Armitage 2000; Mitsi 2005.

experience, revealing patterns, processes, and peoples obscured by a nation-state-centric or regional-oriented methodology, uncovering the entangled paths of British, Spanish, Portuguese, French, and Dutch imperialism in competition and collaboration with one another, as well as a broader cosmopolitanism not bounded by national identity.[3] However, scholarship on the British Atlantic has most successfully probed the era after the establishment of a permanent, settlement-style colony in the territory that ultimately became the United States of America and westward enterprise from Ireland to Anglo-America, elevating those stories over earlier projects elsewhere and inaccurately positioning the British as frustrated latecomers in this Ocean basin—itself an immensely various, artificially invented, and potentially problematic unit of analysis (Games 2006a, 2006b; Greene and Morgan 2009). Finally, the 'New British History'—coined by J. G. A. Pocock (1975a) for the complex, plural history of the peoples, nations, and cultures situated along the Anglo-Celtic frontier and their global exchanges—has fixed on religious pluralism within the Atlantic Archipelago Britain and Ireland, state-building between 1603 and 1707 or 1801, and the emergence of a British identity.[4] At the same time, historiography on the sixteenth century still remains somewhat dominated, even dictated, by debates concerning the break with Rome and all that followed in Church, state, and society, an emphasis that leaves Tudor Studies and, more specifically, the study of principal characters like More, stubbornly insular, their overseas contexts understudied.

Here, at the intersection of these turns and limits, lies part of the trouble still haunting *Utopia*. By assuming that English/British imperial engagement with the wider Atlantic world only began in earnest after Jamestown in 1607, the Union of the Crowns in 1603, or Munster and Roanoke in the 1580s, that everything prior was purely theoretical or failed in practice, and therefore blunted in significance, or that early American or Irish activities were in any way divorced from domestic or continental European currents, we miss vital contexts, national and imperial, in which *Utopia* was forged, circulated, and called upon—contexts that can help us to better understand the text, its meanings and applications, and its legacies. Writing at a time of unquestioned ferment regarding 'Britain' and its empire that followed the accession of James I in 1603 and that of his son in 1625, Vaughan reminds us of *Utopia*'s relevance to New World colonial voyaging and highlights the way in which Stuart interactions abroad constituted a self-conscious evolution of ideas and trends already at work during the Tudor period, a process in which More's text played a vital role. I do not mean to suggest that empire or an Atlantic methodology are *Utopia*'s Rosetta Stone, the means by which we will finally unlock More's book, in all of its nuance and complexity. Nor am I suggesting that the examples offered below are exhaustive, the only points at which Tudor or Stuart authors and adventurers

---

[3] See Andrews et al. 1979; Canny 1988; Pietschmann 2002; Bailyn 2005; Mancke and Shammas 2005; Elliott 2006; Gould 2007; Armitage and Braddick 2009.

[4] Kearney 1995; Ellis and Barber 1995; Bradshaw and Morrill 1996; Bradshaw and Roberts 1998; Burgess 1999; Kidd 1999; Smyth 2001; Steffen 2001; Dawson 2002; Ohlmeyer and Macinnes 2002; Kumar 2003; Ellis with Maginn 2007.

invoked the book in an imperial context. Rather, I submit that by better understanding the fuller, early British Atlantic world in which it was written and read, we can come to a fuller understanding of the nature, significance, and utility of *Utopia* and of the empire created alongside it.

***

More thought, travelled, and wrote through a world much marked by the style of kingship that Henry VIII pursued in the early years of his reign and by the wider milieu that surrounded them both. Though it was the elder Henry Tudor who won his crown on the battlefield, war and martial display fuelled the younger, who was eager to prove himself on a grand stage and equipped with the requisite (relative) domestic stability, financial stores, foreign allies, and foreign adversaries to do so: on 26 April 1509, five days after the accession, the Venetian Ambassador Andrea Badoer characterized Henry VIII as 'magnificent, liberal and a great enemy of the French' (*LP* 1.5), glossing on 6 December that 'he is 18 years old, liberal, warlike and loved by his subjects, provided with money and eager for war with the King of France [...] the King wishes to attack' (*LP* 1.264); as Polydore Vergil put it in his *Anglica Historia* 'the king, in the flower of his youth and abounding in wealth and power, thought the war should be undertaken' and his councillors agreed, 'partly so that the king's keenness for warfare might not be destroyed, for at the time he placed more value on military science than on the other arts, and partly so England would not be stigmatized for ingratitude because she refused to give her protection to the common prelate of the Christian community' (Vergil 2010: 27.5).

A more secure dynastic footing, an impulse for exploration and annexation of 'new' as well as 'old' worlds and markets, military and missionary opportunism, chivalric airs, and humanist intellectual currents all served as motivators, ultimately bearing fruit across the Channel in Tournai, a city previously held by the Valois king, Louis XII. In late June 1513, Henry launched a successful invasion in concert with Holy Roman Emperor Maximilian I, moving south-east from Calais with great performance and spectacle, political and spiritual, intended to legitimize the cause as well as Henry's worthiness, even equal standing, alongside the Holy Roman Emperor (*LP* 1.2391: item 4284; *LP* 1, appendix, 25). After defeating the French at the Battle of the Spurs and taking Thérouanne, the army besieged Tournai, where, according to Edward Hall, 'the kyng of England and of Fraunce commaunded them to yelde to hym his citee & to receave him as there naturall lord, or he woulde put them and ther citee to swerde, fyer, and bloude' (E. Hall 1548: 36r). That September, Clerk of the Signet Brian Tuke recorded that 'this opulent, strong, fair and extensive city of Tournai surrendered' (Hinds 1912: no. 661) while contemporary John Taylor noted how Maximilian delayed his entry so 'that he might not detract from the King of England's glory' (*LP* 1.2391: item 4284). As Maximilian, Duke of Milan, surmised in a letter to Henry on 17 November 1513, the victory was all the more pleasant for a near-simultaneous victory against the Scots at Flodden (TNA SP 1/7, 41r; *LP* 1.2464: item 4579). Bernard André celebrated the two events in Latin, comparing Henry, 'victorious in France and Scotland', to Julius Caesar and Augustus, and adorned his title with royal arms supported by a red Cadwaladr dragon (for the family's Welsh origins) and white Richmond greyhound (for Henry VII's father, Edmund Tudor, Earl of Richmond) and topped with a closed imperial crown as well as red Lancaster roses, white York roses, and red-and-white Tudor roses, pressing the British and imperial significance of the event (CP 277/1).

A renowned commercial centre situated along the River Scheldt and the seat of a powerful bishopric, Tournai was targeted by Henry on the basis of England's historic claims to French territory, its economic and geostrategic advantage, and as a route to further expansion at the expense of a continental European rival (France) and a native population (the Tournaisiens) deemed inferior in politics, culture, and religion. There, the Henrician state undertook a roughly five-year-long experiment in overseas governance, accruing experience in the theory and practice of empire-building for participants and observers.[5] The Crown and its officials articulated and defended royal sovereignty over all matters and all personnel, temporal and spiritual, including the right to rule by governor; to make policy via Parliament at Westminster; and to appoint the city's bishop. Further to that, Henry and his deputies imported English-born subjects as soldiers, artisans, and administrators; attempted to overhaul the region's legal and judicial systems to adhere to domestic English standards; and pressed the pregnant imagery of the closed imperial crown.

The Treaty of Capitulation of 23 September 1513 set the stage for what was to follow, demanding all inhabitants, clergy and laity, renounce the so-called King of France, take 'Henry, together with his heirs, and successors for their real King natural and sovereign Lord [… with all] rights and sovereignties, dignities, prerogatives, royal preeminences and jurisdiction' and monies, and support a Tudor garrison of whatever size and duration Henry pleased, or depart within twenty days for 'countries not currently hostile' to the king or his kingdoms (Hocquet 1900: 397, 399, 400). Those who remained were compelled to swear an oath to Henry as *supremus rex* ('supreme king'), obeying his laws, defending his regime, and seeking absolution from him alone, under pain of excommunication (TNA SP 1/230, 65r–66v; *LP* 1.2319; Cruickshank 1971: 40; Mayer 1995: 14).[6] Such sweeping claims and elastic jurisdiction endowed the king with a supremacy that he lacked at home, where Parliament and Church (among others) circumscribed his power, and poised the city along with other Tudor territories against enemy 'Others'. Handpicked to preside over the city and its reform package as governor, lieutenant, or lord deputy was Edward Poynings (Hocquet 1900: 405–406; *LP* 1.2336). An experienced executor of Tudor rule abroad (in Calais and Ireland), Poynings was, like his title, an English import to Tournai. His reputation was built on his ostensible success in vanquishing sedition, organizing and controlling native inhabitants, and Anglicizing laws and norms, especially in Ireland. Endowed with and emboldened by new authority in a new territory, Poynings was to be the vehicle of Henrician empire in Tournai,

---

[5] For comparison to Calais, see Grummitt 2002; Rose 2008.
[6] A draft is cited here; the oath as administered does not survive.

against 'the comyn peopyll' there, whom English cleric and statesman Richard Sampson deemed 'soo wylde' (TNA SP 1/9, 70r; *LP* 1.3246: item 5386). Playing with two definitions of empire—both as a political theory of complete sovereignty and omnicompetent supremacy and as a marker of territorial expansion and rule over multiple areas—Henry used Tournai to assert his 'superiorite regale preeminence jurisdicion and autorite that we have in the region and domynion of Torney', where 'al causes be determynable within the same and no appeale or resorte [...] elsewhere can have plase' in an early 1517 letter to Silvestro de'Gigli, absentee bishop of Worcester, Henry's representative in Rome to Pope Leo X (TNA SP 1/14, 249r–v; *LP* 2.2871).

The Henrician governance of Tournai was seminal for its ambitious reckonings with the nature and extent of royal power, spiritual and temporal, sovereign and supreme, thus foreshadowing what was ultimately propounded during the English Reformation. It was equally significant for engaging with the broader theory and iconographical representation of empire and the practical realities of ruling a subject people in a foreign territory. Nonetheless, the episode has slipped through the cracks of multiple historiographies. It has been dismissed as immature, futile posturing, skimmed over as a sorry failure, lumped into the medieval period as a renewal of the Hundred Years War (Elton 1955, 1977; Scarisbrick 1968; Cruickshank 1971), fought over as either a teleological point of origin 'on the road to 1534', the year deemed by many to be the most critical in the break with Rome, creation of the Royal Supremacy, and foundation of the Church of England (Mayer 1991, 1995), or nothing novel at all (Davies 1998), and, most commonly, ignored entirely as a meaningless tangent. The effect is to miss the importance of the prolonged project, even in its own time, one that also gave rise to *Utopia* and Atlantic-wide scheming.

Back in England, in 1513, the very year he began his *History of King Richard the Third*, Thomas More was watching and responded to the government's first moves in Tournai with rather intrepid ambivalence. His epigram 'On the Surrender of Tournai to Henry VIII, King of England' declared, 'Warlike Caesar vanquished you, Tournai, till then unconquered, but not without disaster on both sides. Henry, a king both mightier and better than great Caesar, has taken you without bloodshed. The king felt that he had gained honor by taking you, and you yourself felt it no less advantageous to be taken' (cited in Wegemer 2011: 110). Superficially, More lauded Henry as Caesar's superior, but More's use of the verb 'felt'—*sensit* in the original Latin—rather than a stronger verb or sentence construction, mitigated the effect, indicating that the king might be deluding himself, feeling an honour that was not actually there. Further, by identifying his monarch as King of England alone, rather than 'King of France and England and Lord of Ireland', as Henry carefully styled himself in the Treaty of Capitulation, the author implicitly questioned the legitimacy of the effort and of any Tudor claim beyond England. More's disapproval grows palpable when the epigram is paired with another one also penned in 1513. 'On Lust for Power' impugned, 'Among many kings there will be scarcely one, if there is really one, who is satisfied to have one kingdom. And yet among many kings there will be scarcely one, if there is really one, who rules a single kingdom well' (cited in Wegemer 2011: 110). More was thus engaged with the Tournai project early on, both appreciating and questioning the significance of the venture.

It was less than two years later, while on a trade embassy to Flanders on behalf of the King's Council and Company of Merchant Adventurers, that More began *Utopia* (Hexter 1952: 15; Paul 2017: 30). The journey found him in the presence of Desiderius Erasmus, Cuthbert Tunstall, Peter Giles, and others (Baker-Smith 1991: 31–33, 120–121) and in cosmopolitan centres like Antwerp where knowledge spread about the New World (Quinn 1976: 75). On the very same trip, he also visited Tournai (Erasmus 1901–18: 2.256–262; *LP* 2.1552). The connection was neither coincidental nor fleeting. In 1515, Henry replaced Poynings with William Blount, fourth Baron Mountjoy, another royal favourite and Calais veteran but also a major literary patron (Carley 2008). The appointment helped usher northern humanism to Tournai, as Mountjoy used the city to entertain leading Renaissance scholars like Erasmus and More. The governor worked (in vain) to secure a prebend for the former, who was then preparing his *Novum Instrumentum* (1516), and eagerly welcomed the latter's 'book on the Island of Utopia' (Erasmus 1901–18: 2.231; *LP* 2.1331; TNA SP 1/13, 224r; *LP* 2.2066, Erasmus 1901–18: 3.347–348; *LP* 2.3981). 'I have not read it yet,' Mountjoy admitted, 'being overwhelmed with business, but shall do so soon, so that until I can enjoy his society, I may at any rate visit my More in Utopia' (Erasmus 1901–18: 2.452; *LP* 2.2748). As Dominic Baker-Smith (1991: 36) has noted, this letter, signed from 'Tournay, 4 January [1517]', is the 'first recorded allusion to the printed text,' which had appeared in December 1516. Further, on 2 March 1518, also from Tournai, Sampson wrote of 'More, whose wit and learning are so universally known', perhaps indicating *Utopia*'s wider readership there (Erasmus 1901–18: 3.276; *LP* 2.3982). It would have been fitting. More's book and the Henrician city were concurrent experiments in empire-building overseas. Yet less restrained by realities on the ground than his monarch, and beneath a narrative cloak of irony and abstraction, More both looked back to the ancients and across the Atlantic to confront the ills currently facing the sixteenth-century commonwealth. He blended fact and fiction to issue a stark critique of his king, kingdom, and their nascent empire, the text's ludic nature and imperial narrative emerging side by side and closely linked. By setting much of his story in a colony founded by a conquering King Utopus on an island 'in that newefonnde parte of the worlde whiche is scaselye so farre from us beyonde the lyne equinoctiall, as owre lyfe and manners be dissidente from theirs' (More 1551: O4r), relating it through an adventurous Raphael Hythloday, 'a Portugalle borne who 'for the desyre that he hadde to see and knowe the farre contreys of the worlde [...] joyned him selfe in companye wyth Amerike vespuce, and in the .iii. laste voyages of those iiii. that be nowe in prynte and abrode in everye mans handes' (B3v), and including various paratexts like a map, alphabet, and corroborating letters (Roggen 2008), More afforded his imagined state a manner of plausibility. At the same time, he played with invention and the Greek language to name the island a good or fortunate place that is also nowhere or no-place and its proponent an archangel who is also a destroyer or pedlar of nonsense (Baker-Smith 2011: 143–144; Paul 2017: 34–35).

Much in the vein of More's earlier epigrams, the book obliquely censured the Tournai venture. In Book One, Hythloday condemned 'the moste parte of all princes [who] have more delyte in warlike matters and feates of chevalrie [...] than in the good feates of peace, and employe muche more study howe by right or by wrong to enlarge their dominions, than howe well and peaceablie to rule and governe that they have all redie' (More 1551: B8v–C1r) and warned of bad, bellicose soldiers, as Roman and other histories showed, 'for not only the empire, but also the fieldys and cityes of all thies, by divers occasyons have bene ouerrunned and destroyed of their owne armies before hand had in a reddines' (C5v). Describing Utopian warfare in Book Two, he noted how easy it is to raise war against a near-neighbour, 'under the coloure of some olde tytle of ryghte, suche as kynges doo never lacke' (P1v). Yet there are shades to *Utopia* and to the behaviours of Hythloday's Utopians. While clearly indicting improper expansion and warning that the home nation must always take priority, the book also offered a potential justification of imperialism in the form pursued by the Utopians. This was not a world without empire. To the contrary, it began with conquest, founded by a 'kyng Utopus whose name as conquerour the Iland beereth […] which also brought the rude & wild people to that excellent perfection, in al good fassions, humanitie, & civile gentilnes, wherin they now go beyond al the people of the world' (G6r), and legitimized continued colonial growth in multiple circumstances. According to the Utopian rubric, imperial expansion was permissible, even necessary, as a means to ease overpopulation at home, spread superlative laws and ways of life, work 'waste & unoccupied grounde', drive out those who disagree (I5v), and to liberate a people from tyranny (O2v). Indeed, Hythloday clarifies, 'they counte this the moste just cause of warre, when any people holdeth a piece of grounde voyde and vacuant to no good nor profitable use, kepyng other from the use and possession of it, whiche nothwithstandyng by the lawe of nature ought thereof to be nowryshed & relieved' (I6r). As David Armitage argued, these passages made More 'the first author in Britain to recover the term *colonia* in its Roman sense of a scion transplanted from one community into an alien soil'; in doing so, he offered an '"agriculturalist" argument in favor of colonization and dispossession [that] was used well into the eighteenth century' (Armitage 1998: 108). At work in an Atlantic realm that bore some resemblance to England, with its island geography, waterways, and urban system, More (1551: H1v–4v) offered readers a powerful image of a legitimate empire in the New World.

***

More's musings on empire did not end in this text nor in France. Most immediately, they may have engendered a true 'Utopian Voyage': the first American project of Henry VIII's reign (Devereux 1976). As *Utopia* reached print in Louvain and circulated in Tournai, the author's brother-in-law, the lawyer and publisher John Rastell, organized an expedition to 'this newe landes founde lately' that 'Ben callyd America, bycause only | Americus dyd furst them fynde' (Rastell 1848: 31–32). In an idealistic amalgamation of John Cabot and Raphael Hythloday, he departed in mid-1517 for a planned three-year stint with royal support, at least two ships, victuals, soldiers, textiles, tools, and, most fascinatingly, a printer (Devereux 1976: 119–123; Williamson 1929: 85–88). Judging by his supplies and his account of his travels in the *Four Elements* (written c.1519), Rastell must have envisioned a combination of trade, occupation, colonization, and discovery: as a latter-day Utopus, he and his men would conquer, build English-style fortifications and homes, instruct via the written word, and find the north-west passage to Asia. But despite a letter of recommendation from the Crown and support from two London merchants, the crew forced anchor at Waterford and refused the crossing: a fitting, if ironic, use of another site of Tudor imperial ambition (Devereux 1976: 120–121; Clough 2004).

Rastell's play *The Four Elements*, written in Ireland and printed under his mermaid shop sign in 1520, memorialized his legitimacy and purpose. Ranking the benefits of his venture, Rastell began by wistfully reflecting upon the immortal fame that would have followed if 'Englyshemen | Myght have ben the furst of all' to 'take possessyon' and make 'furst buyldynge and habytacion' in the New World, befitting contemporary European thought in his erasure of any indigenous claims to the land upon which they lived (Rastell 1848: 29). He then pivoted quickly to the national glory and royal honour such an exploit would have brought, 'Bothe to the realme and to the kynge, | To have had his domynyon extendynge | There into so farre a grounde,' and imbued such a move with legal legitimacy, describing the territory as the precise place that 'The moste wyse prynce the vii. Herry | Causyd furst for to be founde' (29). From there, the author expanded his scope to envelop both the temporal and spiritual realms; now, the indigenous population inhabiting North America suddenly did emerge, for they served his purpose as a subject of reform and conversion from barbarity and immorality to civility and Christianity. Rastell charged,

> What a great meritoryouse dede
> It were to have the people instructed
> To lyve more vertuously,
> And to lerne to knowe of men the maner,
> And also to knowe God theyr Maker,
> Whiche as yet lyve all bestly. (29–30)

Here was a multipronged and multifaceted ideological argument in favour of English empire across the Atlantic Ocean.

Rastell never made it past Ireland nor did he use the words 'empire' or 'colony', but his ideas, imagery, and personal ties to More, a scholar who offered significant contemporary commentary on territorial expansion, all clarify his venture as among the earliest such schemes for the New World, launched at a particularly dynamic moment for imperial experimentation. For now, the very landscape that had engendered Rastell's attempt also assured its neglect, as an unsettled Tournai took priority. However, the collapse of its occupation and return of the city to France in 1519 injected new energy, ideas, and cash into fallow plots on both sides of the Atlantic.

***

Through the mid-sixteenth century, the vision worked out in print and in practice in the 1510s survived, reworked to fit the circumstances and exigencies of new but related contexts. In 1551, Ralph Robinson produced the first English edition of *Utopia* dedicated to William Cecil, then a principal secretary to Edward VI. As Terence Cave (2008b), Andrew Hadfield (1998: 84–85), and others (e.g. Guy 2000: 14, 92–94) have argued, the translation demonstrates Robinson's hope for patronage, a desire to see the book more widely disseminated as relevant to Tudor statecraft (in his words: 'frutefull & profitable' to the 'avauncement & commoditie of the publique wealth of my native countrey', More 1551: ✠3r), and its ongoing popularity in elite discourse, alongside and in dialogue with a growing body of non-fictional travel accounts in England.[7] Indeed, that corpus was soon to include Richard Eden's 1555 translation of Peter Martyr d'Anghiera's *Decades of the Newe Worlde or West India*, described by Gillian T. Cell as that 'which, more than any other single book, stimulated English curiosity about America' (1969: 35), and in which Richard Eden noted that he had 'not for every woorde asked counsel | Of eloquent Eliot or syr Thomas Moore' (R. Eden 1555: 374r).

Straddling the Edwardian and Elizabethan regimes, Cecil, Eden, and Robinson were part of a crucial circle of humanist scholars and statesmen who helped bring *Utopia* to bear on national and imperial projects in the second half of the 1550s. With Cecil, chief among them was Thomas Smith, who c.1549 and c.1562–5 wrote two treatises on the form, state, and improvement of English politics, governance, economy, and society: the *Discourse of the Commonwealth* and *De Republica Anglorum*. Both were informed by and explicitly reference *Utopia*; they also both presaged the author's shift, by the early 1570s, towards the colonization of Ireland's Ards Peninsula as the means to further the nation and commonwealth of England on a Utopian model. In the *Discourse of the Commonwealth*, Thomas Smith adopted the genre of dialogue to explore current socio-economic and political problems, his 'doctor' providing authoritative answers to the ills of England, which was a real place, unlike 'such a countrie as Eutopia was imagined to be' (T. Smith 1929: 107). With arguments that nevertheless echo More's view of colonisation, Smith's doctor contends that a strong, superior, and wiser people will 'have the soverayngtie over the rude and unlearned [...;] they that be pollitique and civill doe maister the rest': 'theire empires', like those of the Greeks and Romans, are those that 'spred abroade the widest, and longest did continewe' (23). He also stresses the importance of foreign goods and markets, balanced trade, and overseas travel for an island nation (24, 46–48, 61–65, 80). *De Republica Anglorum* (written in the 1560s and printed in 1583) in turn offers a close study of English law and its institutions, especially its uniquely mixed parliamentary–monarchical rule and superior emphasis on counsel and active subjecthood. Viewed in relation to Smith's other texts and broader colonial agenda, it might be seen to indicate (albeit implicitly) how such a commonwealth and civil society could justify expansion and settlement into less evolved areas (Quinn 1945: 545–546; 1976: 77–81; H. Morgan 1985: 261). As with the *Discourse*, Smith distinguishes his text from More's: the political system described in *De Republica Anglorum* is 'not in that sort as Plato [...] nor as Sir Thomas More his Utopia being feigned common wealths,

---

[7] For more on Robinson's translation, see Bishop and Cavanagh in this volume.

such as never was nor never shall be, vaine imaginations, phantasies of Philosophers to occupie the time and to exercise their wittes' (T. Smith 1906: 102).

In early November 1565, shortly after completing *De Republica Anglorum*, Smith revealed in a letter to Cecil that in his mind,

> [Ireland] will not be well governed, but with good force, prompte execucion Integrity and wisdom. And in my mynd needeth nothinge more then to have more colonies. To augment our tongue, our lawes, and our religion in that Isle, which thre be the true bandes of the commonwelth, whereby the Romaynes conquered and kept longe tyme a greate parte of the worlde. (TNA SP 70/81, 6v; *CSPF* 7.1654)

Not long after, Smith petitioned the Crown with a group of associates to 'obtaine Arde and other landes therto adjoyninge at their owne charges and perils, and to make the same civill and peopled with naturall Englishe men borne' (Kingsford 1912: 12). A grant in the Ulster territory followed in November 1571, as Smith rushed to promote his project in print, with *A Letter sent by I.B. gentleman*. Pulling together strands from his two domestic tracts and earlier theories for Irish reform (Armitage 2000: 50; H. Morgan 1985: 274), while again returning to dialogue form and invoking *Utopia*, Smith argued that God's providence, ancient conquest, law, the degeneration of Old English settlers, native barbarity and rebellion had prepared Ireland for new English rule, just as the home nation faced overpopulation. Though Smith had never before visited Ireland (H. Morgan 1985: 268), the text depicts 'a large Cuntrie, commended wonderfully for fertilenesse and commodious' (T. Smith 1571: A3r), with a pleasant climate, abundant waterways, fruitful soil, fish and fowl (B1v, D1r); timber, stone, plaster, and slate for building (D1r); and natural environmental defences much like the English coast (C1v), all apt for English-style garrisoning and occupation, permanent plantation, law, and governance (B1v, E3r–4r); 'it lacketh only inhabitants, manurance [landholding and cultivation], and pollicie,' observes I.B.'s interlocutor, 'Maister Smith' (a representation of the author's son) (B1v). Much as 'England was ones as uncivill as Ireland now is [... until] colonies of the Roymaynes brought [...] ther lawes & orderes'—as Smith wrote to William Fitzwillian in November 1572 (TNA SP 63/38, 70r), the *Letter* maintained that each of his colonists would plant, rule, and serve as 'a helper and mainteyner of Civilitie' in Ireland, thereby invoking the classical model and agriculturalist arguments employed by More (T. Smith 1571: D4r). He then made the comparison explicit: 'How say you now,' 'Smith' asks, 'have I not set forth to you another *Eutopia*?' (E1r). His spelling, as Cathy Shrank has shown, indicates that the author was playing with the Greek to turn More's 'No-Place' into a 'Good Place' (Shrank 2004: 176).

Although Smith's campaign rallied supporters and settlers, the project soon struggled: in late August 1572, Smith's son launched with just 100 men and, despite protestations—made in the letter to Fitzwilliam—that they 'neyther sought to expell nor to destroy the Yrish race but to kepe them in [quiet], in order, in virtuous labour, And in Justice, And to teach them our englishe lawes and civilitie', the settlement met quick resistance and the venture disintegrated (TNA SP 63/38, 69v). However, Smith's failure had imbued participants and observers with theory and practice in empire-building, explicitly bringing *Utopia* to bear on a new half-century of imperial expansion. Indeed, the Ireland–*Utopia* connection remained particularly strong. In late 1599, amid Tyrone's Rebellion, the statesman Robert Cecil—son of the counsellor to whom Robinson had dedicated his translation—labelled the earl of Tyrone's twenty-two-article scheme for a Roman Catholic kingdom of Ireland—principally run by Irishmen complete with the allowances of trade, travel, landholding, employment, and military service of Englishmen—as 'Ewtopia' (TNA SP 63/206, 153v; H. Morgan 1993, 2004). Whether Cecil did so to imply impossibility or colonization, ideal or idyll, cannot be said with certainty. Either way, the gloss powerfully recalls a lengthy history of Tudor imperial thought on both sides of the Atlantic.

Yet fittingly, the most poignant, dramatic, and ironic (if also apocryphal) turn comes to us from the New World. In June 1583, intent on enlarging Elizabeth's dominion, revenue, Protestant faith across the Atlantic, Humphrey Gilbert departed Plymouth with five ships, over 250 men (including craftsmen), various things 'to delight the Savage people' (Hakluyt 1598–1600: 3.145), and 'a token from her Majesty an ancor guyded by a Lady' (Quinn 1940: 2.348). The adventurer had first sketched and defended his plan some two decades before, in *A Discourse of a Discoverie for a new Passage to Cataia*, a learned exposition based on classical, medieval, and early modern sources that argued for the existence of a north-west passage to the East and for the legitimacy, suitability, and advantages of Elizabethan exploration and habitation there. When Gilbert's *Discourse* appeared in print in 1576, it was prefaced by a letter from Gilbert to his brother John, dated 30 June 1566 (H. Gilbert 1576: B4r), intended, as Mary C. Fuller (1995: 20–21) has argued, to underscore the credibility of the 'proofes' that followed, yet which also revealed the tract's historical and literary genealogy. 'Sir,' Gilbert began, 'you might justly have charged mee with an unsetled head if I had at any time taken in hand, to discover *Utopia*, or any countrey fained by imagination: But *Cataia* is none such, it is a country, well knowen to be described and set foorth by all modern *Geographers*' (H. Gilbert 1576: 3¶3r). Undertaking that project in 1583, Gilbert set course for 'those Northerly countreys of America', 'remote and heathen lands' found by Cabot in 1497 and according to the sailor Edward Hayes, who accompanied Gilbert, ostensibly reserved by God for the 'English nation' to plant and reduce to 'Christian civility' (Hakluyt 1598–1600: 3.145, 146, 144). Hayes described their good success: before a crowd of 'both English and strangers', Gilbert took possession of Newfoundland's 'harbour of *S. John*, and 200 leagues every way, invested the Queenes Majestie with the title and dignitie thereof', and declared the territory subject to the law, government, and Church of England (3.151). The promising start deteriorated, however, as Gilbert lost one of his vessels and his crew's support. They set sail for home, and into a storm. From a surviving ship, Hayes watched as his 'Generall sitting abafe with a booke in hand, cried out unto us in the *Hind* (so oft as we did approch within hearing) *We are as neere to heaven by sea as by land*', before— later that night—his 'Frigat was devoured and swallowed up of the Sea'. In the days prior, Gilbert had been 'very confident, and setled in the beliefe of inestimable good by this voyage' and those that were sure to follow (3.159). Though such assuredness was misplaced, the Newfoundland project did outlive Gilbert, much as it predated him. *Utopia* demonstrates both points. Gilbert's last words were Cicero's—and the very same offered by More in Book One, as he relates Hythloday's decision to stay behind in the New World: Hythloday was 'one that toke more thoughte and care for travaylyng, then dyinge: havyng customablye in hys mouthe theis sayinges. He that hathe no grave ys covered wyth the skie, and The way to heaven owte of all places is of like lenghth and distance' (More 1551: B4r). Armitage (1998: 107–108) has argued that the humanist Gilbert was studied enough to quote Cicero without mediation, but according to David Beers Quinn (1940: 1.89 n.) and others, it was More's text that Gilbert gripped as he drowned.

***

In the next century, Stuart subjects went on to establish the first lasting British colonies in North America, to expand and intensify the plantation of Ireland, and to further their projects in the East: all important developments for nation and empire, but ones very much built on past theory and example, positive and negative, factual and fictional, concrete and abstract, including More's *Utopia*. Uses of the book's title, form, and substance were vast and varied, yet the text remained yoked to overseas contexts, ideas, and themes. As the explorer and promoter of Guiana, Lawrence Keymis, averred in 1596, it was no longer the reign of Henry VII, when

> the strange report of a West *Indies* or new world abounding with great treasure should entice us to beleeve it: perhaps it might be imputed for some blame to the gravitie of wise men, lightly to be carried with the perswasion and hope of a new found *Utopia*, by such a one as *Columbus* was being an alien, and manie wayes subject to suspition. (Keymis 1596: A3r)

Rather, New World offerings were real, reported by 'our own Countriman'. Or maybe, as the poet and polemicist Thomas Scot suggested in 1616, 'the *Chameleon* [who] is in *England* a Familist, at *Amsterdam* a Brownist, further on an Anabaptist [...] must finde out *Sir Thomas Mores Utopia* [...] and be an *Elder* there' (Scot 1615: E5v): in such a scheme, exporting sectarians abroad to found dissident colonies was a way to protect the safety and security of the domestic realm and its Church. And yet, cautioned the Munster planter and soldier John Harrington in 1605, even with English law, civility, and rule in Ireland, 'Neyther will yowr Lordships thinke I dream an Eutopia heer, that neyther hath been nor ys lyke to bee' (John Harrington 1879: 6). The original text had been forged in a moment of (overlooked) empire-building and, as Vaughan's *Golden Fleece* reminds us, it remained pertinent for future imperial initiatives and dreams, as a powerful reference point, potential pathway, even disclaimer.

CHAPTER 8

THE URBAN CONTEXT FOR *UTOPIA*

The English Urban System, 1450–1516

ELIZA HARTRICH

UTOPIA is undeniably an 'urban' text.[1] At the most basic level, the fictional republic of Utopia described in Book Two consists of fifty-four cities, with the largest being the capital at Amaurot (More 1965a: 112–113, 116–117). As Sarah Rees Jones (2001: 118) has noted, More, through the voice of the character of Raphael Hythloday, fixates on conditions of urban life when describing Utopian society, with very little of the text devoted to the organization of rural society or agriculture. On a second level, *Utopia* stands in a long line of political treatises that use the city as a microcosm of the ideal commonwealth. Aristotle's *Politics* (especially Book VII), arising from the world of the ancient Greek city state, saw the interaction of people in a city as the fundamental expression of 'civil' or 'political' society. When identifying the characteristics of the ideal polity Aristotle found it important to discuss water supply, topography, fortifications, and other aspects of the urban physical environment alongside more abstract issues like civic virtue. This method of using the city to outline the features of the ideal commonwealth was also present in Plato's *Republic* and Cicero's *De Re Publica*, and was revived in medieval scholasticism, most famously in Marsilius of Padua's fourteenth-century *Defensor Pacis*. The humanist rage for classical scholarship brought new energy to the 'city as ideal commonwealth' trope, with Leonardo Bruni (1978: 135–175) famously grafting attributes of Aelius Aristides' ancient Athens and the city from Aristotle's *Politics* onto fifteenth-century Florence in his *Laudatio Florentinae Urbis*.[2] In *Utopia*, More's extensive description of

---

[1] Many thanks are due to Joel Halcomb, Stuart Palmer, and Phil Withington for their helpful comments on earlier drafts of this chapter. I am especially grateful to Dr Palmer for allowing me to consult his unpublished thesis.

[2] For explorations of this mode of civic humanism, see Baron 1966; Grafton 1991: 12–20; Skinner 1987: 123–157; 2002b: 2.10–38, 126–134, 214–244.

the republic's capital of Amaurot also drew heavily from Aristotle. *Utopia*, more broadly, is a text in dialogue with these classical and post-classical political treatises on the city as commonwealth; it is both an iteration of this venerable tradition and, at times, a satire of it (Logan 1983: 74–270).

Until the 1990s, scholars discussing 'urban' aspects to *Utopia* tended to focus on its debts to Aristotelian and Renaissance humanist discourses on the abstract 'city' (a snapshot of the pre-1995 landscape of *Utopia* studies can be found in More 1995: xlii–xlvi). Over the last three decades, however, there is increasing recognition that another, less abstract urban context may have influenced the content and ideas of *Utopia*: late medieval London. After all, More was undersheriff of London when he wrote *Utopia* in 1516, and at the beginning and end of the piece he proudly proclaims the narrator Morus to be 'citizen and sheriff of the famous city of Great Britain, London' (More 1965a: 46–47, 246–247). More's family had been established in London for more than four generations on both his maternal and paternal sides, making him more thoroughly a Londoner than virtually any other person residing in the city during the early sixteenth century (C. Barron 2011: 3–7; Ramsay 1982: 269, 272–276). Moreover, the description of Utopia's capital, Amaurot, resembles London quite closely: it is a city positioned on a gentle slope near a tidal river, and the governing structure of 200 syphogrants, twenty tranibors/protophylarchs, and one governor brings to mind London's common council of around 188 citizens, council of twenty-four aldermen, and one mayor (More 1965a: 116–123).[3] Lawrence Manley (1995: 23–62) has argued that *Utopia* represented the first example of a self-consciously London-centric cultural movement that emerged in the early sixteenth century. Rees Jones (2001: 117–135) goes further still, maintaining not only that More's description of the city of Amaurot in Book Two was a commentary on late medieval London, but also that the very philosophy of the text, in particular its condemnation of private property and advocacy of communalism, reflected the discourses employed by London's own civic government. In stressing the nature of More as a London writer and *Utopia* as a London text, Manley and Rees Jones form part of a broader scholarly movement of the 1990s–2010s that has reinterpreted canonical late medieval and early modern texts as 'London literature': a genre aimed at London merchants and members of the civic government and reflecting their ideals.[4]

Utopia, then, was far from unique either in its use of urban landscapes to map social relations or in its engagement with London civic culture. What does distinguish *Utopia*, however, is its focus not just on one individual city but on an urban system (Logan 1983: 245). Where classical and humanist treatises viewed the ideal commonwealth as something manifested in the city as a discrete and enclosed space, *Utopia* suggested that harmonious relationships *between* towns were as crucial to a fair society as harmonious relationships *within* them. One of the few scholars of More to recognize the critical

---

[3] The similarity of London and Amaurot is discussed in Manley 1995: 40–41; Rees Jones 2001: 121–122, 124; for the structure of London's civic government, see C. Barron 2004: 129–158.

[4] For examples of this approach, see Meale 1996: 181–227; Hanna 2005; Benson 2006: 147–168; Butterfield 2006; Mardock 2008; Crawforth et al. 2014; Salkeld 2018.

importance of interurban relationships to *Utopia* was Russell Ames in his 1949 book *Citizen Thomas More and His Utopia*. According to Ames (86–103), the land of Utopia should be viewed as 'a nation of cities or as a league of cities', and he looked to the Swiss Confederation, the Hanseatic League, the Swabian League, the Castilian Comuneros of the 1520–1 uprising, and other continental urban leagues as sources of inspiration for More. Ames saw medieval urban leagues through a Marxist lens as bulwarks against the dominance of aristocratic feudalism, and in arguing that More looked to these conglomerations for inspiration Ames advanced his broader point that More's *Utopia* embodied a primitive communist ethos. Regardless of whether *Utopia* constitutes one of the world's first communist texts, however, Ames did identify an important aspect of More's work that most subsequent critics have neglected: that a principal concern of *Utopia* is how towns interact with one another and the policies they put in place to ensure the collective welfare of an urban system.

This chapter follows Ames in viewing interurban relationships as key to the political philosophy expressed in *Utopia*. Where Ames looked to continental Europe for examples of interurban cooperation and competition that may have influenced More, this chapter takes a different tack, and instead explores how the experiences of English towns may have moulded More's vision for Utopia. Easily forgotten in the recent scholarly focus on London as a cradle for medieval and early modern literary production and as an influence on its content is the fact that London, although by far the largest of England's cities and the centre of its manuscript and printed book trade, was nevertheless enmeshed in a network of urban centres dotted throughout the country.[5] Other towns, such as Bristol, Coventry, Nottingham, or York, to name only a few, had bustling marketplaces, trade guilds, and civic governments—references to these spaces and institutions, or adoption of the discourses associated with them, in literary texts could stem as much from an author's engagement with this wider urban system as with circumstances specific to London. Moreover, authors whose writing was influenced by the milieu of the capital would have to address London's relationship with England's other cities and towns. London did not exist in a vacuum, and in the early sixteenth century—when More was writing *Utopia*—it was becoming more intertwined with provincial urban centres rather than less.

This chapter discusses the ways in which *Utopia* acts as a commentary not just on London, but also on the English urban network of which London was the central node. The first section of the chapter identifies the passages of *Utopia* that outline the relationships between towns in the fictional polity, and compares the political structures underlying Utopian interurban relationships to those present in More's England. The government and social practices in individual Utopian cities is not discussed at length, as these topics receive significant attention in Rees Jones's work (2001: 117–135). The second section places these passages within the more specific chronological context in which More was writing:

---

[5] Rare examples of scholarship that interpret literature in a non-London civic context include Withington 2009b, 2010a; Palmer 2016: 32–34.

namely, England in the years 1450 to 1516. It argues that *Utopia* bears witness to a period of heightened tension between English towns in the late fifteenth and early sixteenth centuries, when population growth and a shifting economy disrupted established trade routes and hierarchies. More uses the communitarian ethos of Utopia to satirize and criticize the self-interested and sectional impulses that created conflict between English towns in 1450–1516, but he also recognizes the inherent and unsolvable difficulties of maintaining a growing economy while keeping interurban rivalries at bay.

***

While Book One contains much material that would have resonated with English townspeople of the late fifteenth and early sixteenth centuries, it is Book Two of *Utopia* (that is, Hythloday's description of the land of Utopia, its laws, and the habits of its people) that delineates interactions between towns. Early on in Book Two, it is made clear that the island of Utopia comprises fifty-four cities (*civitates*). All of these cities are interdependent: economically, culturally, and politically. That these towns closely monitor each other's activities is apparent from the fact that not only do all fifty-four cities speak the same language and have the same laws, but they even follow the same street plans and look the same. Hythloday goes so far as to claim that anyone 'who knows one of the cities will know them all, since they are exactly alike insofar as the terrain permits'. Because of these commonalities among the towns of Utopia, Hythloday provides a description only of Amaurot, on the assumption that all the other Utopian towns share its basic features (More 1965a: 116–117).

In spite of this declared concentration on Amaurot, *Utopia* is remarkable for detailing the relationships *between* the fifty-four cities within the Utopian economy rather than focusing exclusively on the maintenance of prosperity and order *within* each city as an individual unit. The island features an urban system designed to ensure that the prosperity of any one town does not injure the prospects of another. The cities are spread out across the expanse of the island in such a way that there is at least 24 miles between each city, but with the caveat that no city should be more than a day's walk from one of the other cities. This spatial distribution is meant to produce stasis within the urban system, a stasis achieved by limiting competition. Each city is provided with hinterlands with which to feed itself that span over a 12-mile radius from the city, and Hythloday makes it clear that 'no city has any desire to extend its territory' (112–113). As such, the exponential growth of any one town to the detriment of another becomes impossible because no urban centre is capable of altering its supply chains in order to support a larger populace or expanding economy. The absence of expansionist ambitions for Utopian cities is also explained by the imposition of limits on the number of residents for each city, preventing a city from needing to acquire new hinterlands to feed a growing citizenry. Each city was to have 6,000 households, with each household containing between ten and sixteen adults.[6] When a city was

[6] A minor is defined as anyone below the age of marriage, which is set at 18 years of age for women and 22 for men. It may be implied that adults are defined as women over the age of 18 and men over the age of 22. See More 1965a: 143, 187.

deemed to have become overpopulated, individuals would be sent to live in cities that were underpopulated. Moreover, if too many people were living in Utopia, then some people from each city would found a colony on a site featuring sparsely populated or uncultivated land. Conversely, if cities in Utopia were unable to reach a certain level of population without reducing another city to a dangerously low population, then people would be moved from the colonies to make up for the shortage (134–137). The ideal size and population of a city state were themes that had appeared in Aristotle, but in the *Politics* (7.4–6) it is purely the welfare of that city state that dictates these numbers, with no consideration of ensuring prosperity for other urban centres. In this regard, *Utopia* is decidedly different from the classical, scholastic, and humanist texts it otherwise imitates. Where these texts (e.g. Plato, *Republic* 5.530–1; Marsilius, *Defensor Pacis* 1.5.8–9) focused on the individual city or city state as a discrete unit and discussed economic relationships or political relationships between cities predominantly in relation to war, *Utopia* places economic equality between towns at the heart of the 'ideal' polity.

As we shall see below, the symbiotic economic relationship between Utopia's cities may well have been intended as a pointed criticism of the cut-throat competition between towns that was endemic in the English economy of the late fifteenth and early sixteenth centuries. It need not follow, however, that More himself viewed the Utopian economy as a model to emulate. Utopia's urban system is, in practical terms, inherently unsustainable. The cities in Utopia are surprisingly large, ranging in population from 60,000 adults at minimum to 96,000 at maximum. Once children and slaves are included in these tallies, every one of Utopia's cities would have contained upwards of 100,000 people. Of English cities, only London approached anywhere near this high a population; England's second-most populous city, Norwich, had an estimated population of 8,540 in 1524–5 (Dyer 2000: 275), less than one-tenth of the typical Utopian city. In Utopia, each of these metropolises is given lands within a 12-mile radius to supply its needs; only if it is unusually distant from other cities is it provided with more acreage for this purpose, and, as discussed, Utopians are said to never seek to expand upon these allocations. According to Derek Keene (1989: 106–107), the narrowest possible definition of medieval London's hinterlands would encompass a 50-mile radius from the City, far greater than the 12-mile radius of territory that is judged to meet the needs of a Utopian city with a higher population! Even provincial towns like Canterbury, Colchester, and Northampton—with estimated populations of 4,700; 4,210; and 2,860 respectively in 1524–5 (Dyer 2000: 275)—seem to have drawn their supplies from a radius of 25 to 30 miles (Galloway 2001: 112). Considering that Utopia is roughly the same size, if not shape, of England (Goodey 1970: 15–30), it is difficult to imagine that all of Utopia's large towns would have found sufficient sustenance from their 12-mile radius of hinterlands to prevent them from seeking to acquire resources from agricultural areas belonging to other cities. The passages on Utopia's economy may thus constitute one of the famous ambiguities in More's text: while the urban system in Utopia is in many respects an ideal that highlights the injustices of early sixteenth-century England, More was also perhaps acknowledging the impossibility of enacting any functional alternative (Logan 1983: 245–246).[7]

To have any hope of operating an urban system predicated on the redistribution of population between cities, there needed to be a strict monitoring of in- and out-migration. In Utopia such regulatory power is vested in the urban government, but in a way much different from the mechanisms employed in early sixteenth-century England. Utopians who wished to travel from one city to another needed to receive a letter from the governor of their own city authorizing their period of leave and specifying a day of return. People who went outside the boundaries (*fines*) of their city without the governor's permission were to be brought back and punished. But, while migration is strictly controlled, the idea of an urban 'franchise'—that is, of rights to travel, trade, and political participation possessed exclusively by citizens of a given town—is not present. In Utopia, once someone has arrived in a new city, he or she has full rights there. Those who stay in a city for more than a day are welcome to set up shop there and are not resented by the tradespeople already established in the city (More 1965a: 144–147).

This lack of an urban franchise in Utopia represented a clear departure from contemporary practice in late medieval and early modern England. Individual towns in England received charters from the Crown which afforded exclusive political and economic rights to those who had taken oaths as freemen (also known as 'citizens' or 'burgesses') of the town. Only citizens of that town could vote in civic elections or hold office, and only citizens could run their own shops within the town or buy or sell goods by retail. Although citizenship could be purchased from the civic government, it was usually gained through long-standing association with the town concerned: by being the child of a citizen, marrying a citizen's widow, or serving an apprenticeship with a member of one of the town's craft guilds (Kowaleski 1990: 185–189; Barry 2000: 186–192; Liddy 2017: 44–50). Not all residents of a town were citizens: indeed, in Exeter only around 19 per cent of male heads of household held citizen status (Kowaleski 1990: 186). Citizenship thus restricted the exercise of the full range of economic activities in a town to a particular subset of residents, in addition to preventing outsiders from trading in the town. Being a citizen of *any* one town did, however, permit that citizen to exercise certain privileges in other towns under the rule of the English Crown, including the right to trade in other chartered towns without paying some of the tolls and duties typically extracted from non-citizens. To claim this privilege, merchants and artisans who arrived in a new town to sell their wares would sometimes be required to present to the civic government certificates confirming that they possessed the freedom of another town (Liddy 2017: 42–43). This process of checking certificates echoes the written permission that residents of Utopia's cities had to obtain and carry with them in order to travel to another city. The structures of urban citizenship present in late medieval

---

[7] For the debate surrounding whether More intended for Utopia to represent an ideal society, see Logan 1983 contra Skinner 2002b: 2.213–244.

and early modern England nevertheless precluded the type of economy envisioned for Utopia. It would have been virtually impossible for an Englishman or Englishwoman to travel to a new town and be able to set up shop or practise their craft there almost immediately without being subject to any restrictions, charges, or penalties, as the inhabitants of Utopia were able to do.

Indeed, *Utopia* is remarkable for its rather ambivalent attitude to urban citizenship (contra Rees Jones 2001: 117–135), given the institution's prominence in fifteenth- and sixteenth-century England. Citizenship was the cornerstone of urban culture in late medieval and early modern England. Christian Liddy (2017) has written that urban politics in late medieval England was dominated by disputes over the duties expected of and rights accorded to citizens, while Phil Withington (2005) and Jonathan Barry (2000: 181–196) have argued that standards of civil behaviour and ideas of good governance in early modern England were moulded by the associational culture of urban citizenship. Morus, of course, describes himself as a citizen of London in the opening and closing of Book Two, but otherwise the word *civis* ('citizen') and its derivatives appear only sixteen times in the length of the book (More 1965a: 112–113, 134–139, 184–185, 200–203, 206–209, 214–215, 220–221, 230–231). On these occasions, *civis* refers to any resident of the city (or even any non-enslaved resident of Utopia) rather than only to those who are sworn members of a small privileged group. In fact, Hythloday never attempts to define the term or the values associated with it. In never defining 'citizenship', *Utopia* presents a stark contrast not only to the obsession of English civic governments in policing access to citizenship, but also to thinkers such as Aristotle (in *Politics* 3.1, 3, 7) and Marsilius of Padua (in *Defensor Pacis* 1.4) who made a point of identifying which groups within a city would not be deemed part of civil society (Logan 1983: 176–177). Notable, as well, is the fact that the documents that accorded rights to citizens of an English town—urban charters—do not feature in the cities of Utopia, despite the fact that Amaurot is described as having kept detailed records for 1,760 years (More 1965a: 120–121). In taking away the trappings of urban citizenship and franchises from Utopia, More was also pursuing two aspects of his wider political vision: the removal of intermediate authorities between the family and the polity, and the creation of political order according to reason rather than inherited customs and privileges (Hexter 1973: 104; Manley 1995: 37–39; Bradshaw 1991: 123).

Without charters and citizenship, Utopia required a different mechanism to regulate its urban system. Interurban representative assemblies ensured that relations between Utopian cities were conducted in the interests of all, and not to the advantage of any one city. Each year every city in Utopia selected three 'old and experienced' residents to go to the capital of Amaurot for a meeting of the senate 'to discuss the affairs of common interest to the island' (*tractatum de rebus insulae communibus*) (More 1965a: 112–113). This senate is the body responsible for monitoring the economies and populations of the different cities to make sure that no individual city is suffering undue hardship: 'they first determine what commodity is in plenty in each particular place and again where on the island the crops have been meager. They at once fill up the scarcity of one place by the surplus of another' (146–147).

In fact, the maintenance of economic equality between Utopia's cities constitutes the only clearly elucidated function of the senate. The 'common interest' of the island is defined purely as the regulation of interurban relationships, and the assembly meant to determine matters of 'common interest to the island' consists solely of representatives from cities. In this formulation, the Utopian senate is very different from the English parliament (as described in Cavill 2009). Parliament consisted of two representatives from each borough (with a notable exception being the four from London), but also featured elected representatives from each county, in addition to the House of Lords. Representation in England, therefore, derived only in part from towns. The English parliament did discuss matters 'of common interest to the island', but the subjects that fell under this category were much more varied than those brought before Utopia's senate. Sometimes, issues of common interest that appeared before the English parliament did concern relationships between towns, and there was a tradition from the fourteenth and fifteenth centuries of parliamentary petitions equating the 'common good' or 'common weal' of the realm with the commercial interests of merchants and urban officials (C. Fletcher 2014: 102–103; Hartrich 2019: 97). But, just as often, parliament was granting taxation to the monarch or assessing the petitions of nobles and clergy: the 'common interest' mulled over by the English parliament was far greater than the sum of interurban connections.

The English parliament was, of course, not the only assembly with which More would have been familiar, and he may have drawn inspiration from the representative institutions of continental urban leagues. Associations such as the Four Members of Flanders and the Hanseatic League held assemblies in which representation was based primarily (but not exclusively) on towns and where the principal business discussed often concerned the resolution of disputes between member towns (Dollinger 1970; Dumolyn 2008: 5–23; Blockmans 1978: 189–215). England, too, had some tradition of urban leagues. From the mid-fourteenth century, the confederation of south-eastern coastal towns known as the Cinque Ports—consisting of the head ports of Hastings, Romney, Hythe, Dover, Sandwich, Winchelsea, and Rye, along with smaller 'member' towns linked to one of the head ports—held an assembly of town representatives known as a 'Brodull' or 'Brotherhood' at least twice a year to determine collective policy, apportion the financial contributions each town should make to the Cinque Ports' expenses, and arbitrate disputes between towns (K. M. E. Murray 1935: 139–89; Hull 1966: 31–32, 50, 71–73, 75, 81, 84, 97–98, 100, 111, 123, 136, 139, 152). In the very year *Utopia* was written—1516—More may well have had dealings with the Brodhull. The Merchant Adventurers, the London-dominated association of merchants of which More was a member and whose legal interests he often represented, came into conflict with the Cinque Ports when they seized the goods of John Pyham of Sandwich and Peter Maister of Winchelsea, and the Cinque Ports threatened to take goods from the Merchant Adventurers in retaliation (Hull 1966: 161). The Utopian senate may also have been a nostalgic nod to the fourteenth-century English 'estates of merchants': assemblies held intermittently until the early 1380s in which wool merchants from towns across England formulated common policies and gave their consent for the Crown to levy subsidies on commerce (Unwin 1918: 179–255; Liddy 2001: 331–345). Regardless of the source of More's inspiration, though, the prominence of an interurban assembly in Utopia represented a deviation both from the English parliament and from the bulk of classical and humanist political treatises. It was but one of many features of Utopia that highlighted the significance of balance within an urban system for any 'ideal' commonwealth.

***

In short, Utopia was a society that had little regard for urban franchises and instead took great pains to ensure equality between towns. More's inclusion of these features—unique to 'city as commonwealth' texts and at odds with contemporary practice—can be interpreted as a critical comment on the prevalence of interurban tensions in England in 1516. The English urban system was undergoing a period of recalibration in the late fifteenth and early sixteenth centuries, with shifting economic dynamics between towns making different franchised groups especially desperate to preserve their own privileges. The key change occurring at this time was the increased importance of London in the English economy (Manley 1995: 5, 23–25, 48). Between 1450 and 1516, London grew significantly in population and increased its share of England's export trade (summarized in Britnell 2004: 334, 518–519; Oldland 2014: 55–92). A little under 24 per cent of cloth exported by denizen merchants in 1449–50 shipped from London, but by 1515–16 this proportion had grown to an astonishing 70 per cent (Carus-Wilson and Coleman 1963: 97, 114). Demographic change is more difficult to trace, but it is estimated that 1 in every 66 residents of England lived in London in 1300, as compared to 1 in 40 by 1500 (Nightingale 1996: 105). The result of these trends was a concentration of capital in London. Estimates based on tax assessments have London holding 2 per cent of England's wealth in 1334 and 8.9 per cent in 1515, and these estimates are extremely conservative, as they do not include the expanding Middlesex suburbs as part of London's total (R. S. Schofield 1965: 508).

London's rise to prominence appeared to come at the expense of England's provincial towns, leading many historians to christen the fifteenth and early sixteenth centuries a period of 'urban decline' (e.g. Dobson 1977: 1–22; Phythian-Adams 1979: 16–30; Kermode 1987: 51–73; Goddard 2016). The loss of England's lands in France in the early 1450s disrupted the wine trade essential to ports like Bristol (Sacks 1991: 19–32). From 1450, therefore, the English economy became oriented around trade with Antwerp, a route controlled by London merchants to the virtual exclusion of their provincial counterparts (Goddard 2016: 197; Britnell 1998: 95–96). More broadly, the European-wide recession and bullion famine of the 1440s and 1450s reduced the amount of coin in circulation in England, and hence the availability of credit; loans became dominated by London merchants, since bullion existed in greater quantities in the capital.[8] In turn, with coin and credit less present outside London, provincial fairs lost much of their

---

[8] See Nightingale 1990: 560–575; 1996: 103–106; 1997: 634–642, 647, and Kermode 1991: 496–501; 1994: 72–88; Bolton 2011 presents an opposing view.: 144–164

appeal, and it became increasingly common for chapmen to bring goods from other parts of England to London for export and then purchase goods in London to distribute in the localities (Nightingale 1996: 103–104). As London came to monopolize credit provision and export trade, industrial production moved closer to the capital in order to reduce transport costs. Clothmaking that had once occurred in provincial urban centres like Coventry was now taking place in the Essex or Suffolk countryside, and often under the aegis of London merchants with newly purchased rural properties (Nightingale 1996: 103–106; Britnell 1998: 95–100, 110–111; Oldland 2018: 1–22). Small towns located near these hubs for rural clothmaking became the urban success stories of the 1460s to 1520s; Lavenham in Suffolk, heavily patronized by London merchants, grew in population and importance, while larger and more established regional capitals like York dwindled (Palliser 1979: 201–218; Phythian-Adams 1979: 16–19; Nightingale 2010: 4–6; Goddard 2016: 216–218). There were, of course, numerous exceptions to the general trend of provincial urban malaise (Goddard 2016: 202–203): Exeter famously maintained a healthy trade throughout the fifteenth century (Carus-Wilson 1963), and York's artisans experienced an economic boom at the same time as York's merchants and clothworkers faced hard times (Swanson 1989: 24–25, 45–52, 148–150, 173–175).

What seems to be the case, then, is that these economic conditions—and especially the concentration of trade in London—led not to a uniform 'urban decline', but rather a restructuring of relationships between English towns, from which some groups benefited and others suffered (Dyer 2000: 282–286). The ways in which residents from English towns did business with London, with local urban centres, and with their hinterlands were all shifting at the same time, producing friction at many different interfaces. As we shall see, residents of York, Hull, Bristol, Norwich, and other towns were convinced that their towns had been allowed to wither in order to feed a greedy and bloated metropolis. It was in precisely this context that More composed *Utopia*, and the rational and equitable redistribution of resources between towns in the fictional republic stood as a reflection on and rebuke to the disparities within the urban system of late medieval and early modern England. Indeed, Books One and Two of *Utopia* complement one another in that each contemplates the challenges faced by the changing English economy at the beginning of the sixteenth century: Book One from the perspective of the rural economy in its famous passages lamenting the enclosure of common lands for the purposes of large-scale sheep farming (More 1965a: 64–71), and Book Two from the perspective of the urban economy in its subtle criticism of interurban inequalities.

The most common response of English civic governments to these economic changes was to assert their own chartered privileges more aggressively and seek to challenge those possessed by others. In particular, the late fifteenth and early sixteenth centuries witnessed a spike in toll disputes between English towns, as civic governments questioned the rights of citizens of other towns to be exempt from paying additional tariffs. Coventry complained on numerous occasions in the 1490s that the civic governments of Bristol, Gloucester, and Worcester were charging illegal tolls on Coventry merchants trading in their towns, and these conflicts were severe enough to warrant appearances before Henry VII and Prince Arthur of Wales (M. D. Harris

1907–13: 549–552, 592, 594–595, 599–600). Although Nottingham resolved a disagreement with Coventry over whether their burgesses would be exempt from tolls in one another's towns in 1452, its civic government devoted much of its energies in 1480–1500 to similar disputes with the nearby towns of Lincoln and Retford (Stevenson et al. 1883–1956: 2.310–17, 348–353, 360–362, 396, 398, 420–421; 3.236–237, 266, 275–276, 279–280, 284, 304–308, 315, 450–452). York and Hull were engaged in a comparably long-lasting quarrel concerning the liability of the York Merchant Adventurers to pay additional customs when selling their goods in Hull, leading York to cite its own 'poverte' and 'decay' in attempts to get the Crown to rule in its favour (Sellers 1918: 109, 118–121). In some ways, these toll disputes were not entirely alien to the Utopian practices described by Hythloday. After all, the urban governments of Utopia monitored travel between towns through a rigorous licensing system. The frequent toll disputes in late medieval England nevertheless contravened one of the central tenets of the republic of Utopia: that no town should prize its individual interests over those of the urban system as a whole. It is understandable that, in an environment in which towns were bickering constantly over their respective privileges, More should envisage a commonwealth in which such privileges were entirely absent.

It is, of course, reasonable to doubt that More was following news of toll disputes in Coventry or Nottingham assiduously in the years before he wrote *Utopia*. Similar debates over interurban inequality, chartered privileges, and economic protectionism, however, were taking place in environments much more familiar to More: the London Mercers' Company and Merchant Adventurers. In 1509, seven years before the publication of *Utopia* and one year before the beginning of his tenure as London's under-sheriff, More was granted membership of the Mercers' Company of London (Lyell and Watney 1936: 320). The Mercers were a guild of London cloth merchants who had gained enormously in power and influence over the course of the fifteenth century due to the concentration of overseas trade in London and the eclipse of English wool exports by exports of finished cloth. On account of these economic trends, by the early sixteenth century the London Mercers had become the dominant voice in the English Merchant Adventurers, a loose organization of English merchants who engaged in overseas trade; this dominance angered both merchants from provincial towns and London merchants who specialized in goods other than cloth (A. F. Sutton 2002: 25–46). Between 1509 and 1517, More acted as legal counsel and negotiator for both the London Mercers and the Merchant Adventurers on a number of occasions (Lyell and Watney 1936: 329–335; cf. Ames 1949: 184–186; Ramsay 1982: 282–285; A. F. Sutton 2005: 333–334).

Most famously, More was part of the negotiating team sent to Bruges in 1515 by the English Crown and the Merchant Adventurers to reach a trade agreement with the representatives of Prince Charles of Castile (the future King Charles I of Spain and Holy Roman Emperor Charles V) (Surtz 1953: 272–297). It was during this mission that More wrote *Utopia*, and, indeed, the event serves as the premise for the text. During the 1515 mission there was a break in negotiations that allowed More to visit Peter Giles in Antwerp, and it is within the context of this visit that in *Utopia* Morus meets Hythloday and learns about the land of Utopia (More 1965a: 46–51). Trade tolls were one of the chief points of discussion during the 1515 negotiations. English merchants were charged tolls from multiple territories when trading in the Low Countries, but the 1515 embassy aimed to ensure that, when crossing the River Scheldt, English merchants paid only one toll (Surtz 1953: 275–277, 285, 287–288; *LP* 2: items 204, 723). Discussion of tolls during the embassy brought up the issue of interurban equality. In June 1515, the Provost of Cassel, one of Charles's negotiators, lamented that the proliferation of tolls was causing foreign merchants to desert Bruges, which contributed to the city's decay while Antwerp flourished (*LP* 2: item 581; discussed in Surtz 1953: 287–288). The Provost's conversation with the English commission in Bruges took place within a month of More's arrival in the city, and three months later, in September 1515, More left Bruges for Antwerp, where he wrote Book Two of *Utopia* (Surtz 1953: 279, 287–288, 290; Hexter 1952: 26–30). Considering that it is within Book Two that More outlines the relationships between towns in Utopia and the measures to be put in place to ensure equality between them, it is entirely feasible that the urban system outlined in *Utopia* was crafted as More reflected on the difficult toll disputes prominent in the 1515 negotiations. In the same way that the Utopian senate drew from both continental and English precedents, so, too, did More's meditations on interurban relationships act as a commentary on transitional periods in Habsburg as well as English urban systems.

While the Mercers and Merchant Adventurers were negotiating tolls with foreign powers, they were also involved in a number of bitter disputes concerning the relationship between London merchants and their counterparts from provincial English towns. There was a long history of protests by merchants from provincial capitals against the power of Londoners within the Merchant Adventurers' Company, but such complaints became more frequent and more vociferous in the late fifteenth and early sixteenth centuries. Merchant Adventurers from towns in northern England submitted a petition to parliament in 1478 against London's alleged control of the organization. Traditionally, they maintained, the Merchant Adventurers of England elected two governors, one representing London and the other representing merchants north of the Trent (especially those from York, Hull, Beverley, and Scarborough). In 1478, though, there was only one governor: John Pickering, a London mercer. Furthermore, the merchants from northern towns lamented that Pickering operated the English Merchant Adventurers in the interests of London alone, and to the detriment of merchants from other English towns (Sellers 1918: 75–80; discussed in A. F. Sutton 2009: 220–223, 227–228; Kermode 1998: 252–253).

Further tensions emerged in 1486, when Bristol traders complained to the royal council that the London Merchant Adventurers were unreliable trading partners who paid 'in Cardes, tenys balles, fysshehokes, bristilles, tasells and suche other simple wares' rather than cash, which they claimed resulted in 'grete hurte & losse' to Bristol (Lyell and Watney 1936: 294–295; A. F. Sutton 2005: 284). At the 1497 Parliament, merchants from English provincial towns banded together to submit a petition claiming that the London Merchant Adventurers prevented non-London merchants from attending foreign fairs unless they first paid the exorbitant fee of £20 to the London branch of the Merchant Adventurers' Company. The petition maintained that the citizens of London acted 'by confederacie made amonge theym self of their uncharitable and inordinate covetise for their singuler profite and lucre, contrarie to every Englisshemanes libertie', and that their actions shut out provincial merchants from the cloth trade 'by reason wherof all the cities, townes and burghs of this realme in effecte be falle into great povertie, ruyne and decaye' (Given-Wilson 2005: 1497 Parliament, item 10; A. F. Sutton 2005: 341). Conflict within the Merchant Adventurers' Company between merchants of different towns came to a head in 1509–10, the very year that More became a London mercer. At that time, the Merchant Adventurers of Norwich complained that at meetings of the Company abroad, the London merchants deliberately ignored the opinions voiced by provincial merchants. The Norwich Merchant Adventurers feared that 'the marchants of the cytte of London wyll bynde alle marchants of Englend att there wylle and pleasure […] to the intent to wery us'. The complaint was made at the 1510 Parliament, where More sat as an MP for London, and the Norwich merchants were soon joined in their animosity by the merchants of York, Hull, Beverley, and Newcastle (Sellers 1918: 121–126; cf. Cavill 2009: 165).

In addition to these disputes within the Merchant Adventurers' Company, London Mercers also were party to a series of conflicts in the 1470s to 1490s over whether London citizens should be allowed to go to provincial towns and fairs to trade their goods. Wealthier merchants in London tended to favour such a prohibition, believing that it would improve London's economy by forcing provincial merchants to travel to the City (A. F. Sutton 2005: 215–216). In 1487, the London Common Council forbade any London citizen from selling goods at markets or fairs outside the capital for a period of seven years, on pain of a £100 fine (Sharpe 1899–1912: vol. L, 240). The commons of England successfully petitioned parliament in 1487 to render London's ordinance null and void. They claimed that the London Common Council had acted for 'their syngler lucre and avayle', and that the ordinance would bring 'utter destruccion' to the economies of Salisbury, Bristol, Oxford, Cambridge, Nottingham, Ely, Coventry, and other towns that hosted popular fairs and markets (Given-Wilson 2005: 1487 Parliament, item 25; cf Cavill 2009: 165).

In the years immediately before the composition of *Utopia*, therefore, More was part of an organization beset with conflicts over economic equality between towns. Moreover, the interurban squabbling in the Merchant Adventurers' Company was only one manifestation of a wider tendency for increased competition among English towns in the period 1450–1516, apparent in the frequency of toll disputes and in the 1487 contention over Londoners' travel to provincial fairs. That such tensions prompted disillusionment with traditional forms of urban citizenship (and the trading rights associated with it) becomes more than understandable, and also helps to explain the importance of equality between urban centres to the 'ideal' commonwealth described in *Utopia*. The central premise of Utopia—both as fictional realm and as text—is that no entity should take more than it needs; that this premise is explored very often through an investigation of interurban relationships suggests that More's intellectual experiments were a pointed response to the shifting and fractious English urban system of his day, and even to similar conflicts besetting continental towns.

In doing so, More and his *Utopia* stand at odds with the work of Aristotle and other political tracts that focus on the city or city state as a discrete community, and not as an entity whose own interests must coexist alongside those of other urban centres holding equal claim to represent the 'common good'. The innovation of *Utopia* as a work of political philosophy thus lies not so much in its advocacy of an extreme version of the rhetoric of citizenship and community that imbued the legislation passed by London's civic government, as Rees Jones (2001: 117–135) contends, but rather in its repudiation of the very idea that any one city could comprise an 'ideal' commonwealth in and of itself. In describing the 'ideal' political community not as a single city but as a system of cities, *Utopia* went against both mainstream political thought and the practices of the London civic government of which More was a part.

CHAPTER 9

UTOPIA UNBOUND

The Fabrication of the First Latin Editions, 1516–1519

ANDREW W. TAYLOR

In Thomas More's lifetime, five Latin editions of *Utopia* appeared in quick succession: (1) Louvain: Dirk (Thierry) Martens, December 1516; (2) Paris: Gilles de Gourmont, *c.* September 1517; (3–4) Basel: Johann Froben, March and November 1518;[1] (5) Florence: heirs of Filippo Giunta, July 1519.[2] This chapter examines these Latin editions (the only ones from More's lifetime), exploring the nexus of relationships which shaped the text: the product of a collective humanist endeavour, orchestrated—for the most part—by More's friend, the humanist Desiderius Erasmus.

BEFORE *UTOPIA*

The genesis of *Utopia* was as rooted in humanist circles as its early publication history. The work was famously begun during More's embassy to the Low Countries (12 May–24 October 1515) led by Cuthbert Tunstall; but it also evolved amidst a humanist literary spat. Around September 1514, Maarten van Dorp wrote to Erasmus (*CWE* 3: Ep. 304) criticizing his 1511 *Moriae Encomium* ('Praise of Folly'), the work—its Latin title punning on More's name—Erasmus dedicated to More; completed at his house in Bucklersbury; and which, he said, More urged him to publish.[3] The quarrel between Dorp and Erasmus may have been staged, especially as Dorp was 'still one of Erasmus' official *castigatores* [proof-correctors] at the height of his "dispute" with him' (Jardine 1993: 111–112). Indeed, Dorp's

---

[1] The colophon of the second Froben *Utopia* is dated November (More 1518b: U6v); the rest of that continuously paginated volume—the epigrams of More, then Erasmus—bears a separate colophon dated December (K6r): critics refer to the volume as the November or December edition.

[2] For indispensable accounts of these editions, see More 1965a: clxxxiii–cxc; 1995: xxxiii–xli, 270–276.

[3] Letters are cited by number and the volume of *CWE* in which they appear.

letter concludes by informing Erasmus that he has seen Erasmus' *Disticha Catonis*—the first work in *Opuscula aliquot* (September 1514)—through Martens's presses. In his dedicatory letter to the *Disticha*, to Jean de Nève, Erasmus refers to Dorp as *Dorpius noster*: 'my Dorp' (*CWE* 3: Ep. 298). However, a rift apparently developed. 'Dorp's nonsense you shall hear about shortly,' Erasmus wrote in October 1516 to Peter Giles (a figure destined to appear in *Utopia* and—like Dorp—an editor/proof-corrector at Martens's press): 'I never saw a man whose friendship was more unfriendly. Tunstall, having read the stuff he addressed to me and his answer to me, abominates the man so much that he can scarcely bear to hear him mentioned' (*CWE* 4: Ep. 477). Dorp's initial letter about the *Moria* and an amplified version of Erasmus' response—*Epistola ad Dorpium* (*CWE* 3: Ep. 337)—were included in Martens's reprinting in October 1515 of Erasmus' *Enarratio allegorica in primum psalmum* ('Allegorical Exposition on the First Psalm'), dedicated to Erasmus' friend Beatus Rhenanus (another figure destined to appear in *Utopia*); it then appeared in all early editions of the *Moria* from Froben's 1516 edition onwards.

Dorp's attack on the *Moria* also elicited More's lengthy, unprinted epistle defending his friend's work. The date and location of More's 'Letter to Dorp'—Bruges, 21 October—places this response to Dorp's second letter to Erasmus (*CWE* 3: Ep. 347, 27 August 1515) in the final weeks of More's embassy to the Low Countries when More also drafted his first version of *Utopia* (what became Book Two). More's 'Letter' bridges the *Moria* and growth of More's own paradoxical satire. Dorp objected to Erasmus' satire of ignorant scholastic theologians, insisting 'I can produce many men here who can leave their books behind and dispute with anyone on a text of Scripture simply on the strength of their memories' (*CWE* 3: Ep. 347). More's 'Letter' responds with a tableau akin to the fictionalized recollection of Morton's household later included in Book One of *Utopia*. An unnamed Italian merchant, 'as learned as he is rich (and he certainly is rich)'—perhaps based on More's friend Antonio Buonvisi—debates with a distinguished disputant from a religious order who, at the start of dinner, declares himself 'ready to dispute *pro* and *contra* upon any topic'.[4] More delightedly relates how the merchant, realizing the theologian's poor grasp of Scripture, 'started to play with the fellow', inventing brief supporting texts, which the theologian interpreted in earnest, failing to notice their spuriousness and positing that his interpretation agreed with the thirteenth-century biblical exegetist Nicolas de Lyra (*CWM* 15.51–55); the punning allusion—through de Lyra—to the image of a lyre-playing ass, signifying someone too stupid to understand what they hear, would have been unmistakable for humanist readers.

Louvain 1516: What Are Friends For?

How More and Buonvisi's table talk shaped *Utopia* must remain speculation; there were doubtless other conversations with sympathetic friends. More's surviving letters offer

---

[4] For more on Buonvisi/Bonvisi, see Shrank in this volume.

very little on *Utopia*'s genesis, composition, publication, or revision. Indeed, More's first extant letter to Erasmus dates from mid-February 1516 (*CWE* 3: Ep. 388), some months after writing Book Two and the opening of Book One, whilst 'at leisure [*per ocium*]'—as Erasmus put it in his 1519 pen portrait of More for Ulrich von Hutten (*CWE* 7: Ep. 999)—but possibly before he had gone very far in expanding Book One, once back in London. Nonetheless, Erasmus' correspondence provides rich evidence of the collaborative effort behind the publication of *Utopia*, and the intellectual milieu that shaped it, even down to its name.

The first edition (Louvain, December 1516) derived from the manuscript More sent Erasmus with a letter dated 3 September (*CWE* 4: Ep. 461), in which he called the work *Nusquama* ('Nowhere'). 'Do what you can for it', More urged Erasmus. More's subsequent letters solicit news of progress. In a letter written around 20 September (*CWE* 4: Ep. 467), More expressly requested 'glowing testimonials, [...] not only from several literary men but also from people well-known for the part they have taken in public affairs'. More's offshoring of *Utopia* contrasts with the *Moria*, which Erasmus repeatedly revised, enlarged, and republished: once the original manuscript left More's hands, his authorial control over the work's mutating form became increasingly tenuous, limited possibly to minor textual corrections, and a second letter to Giles for the Paris edition (then cut by Froben).

Erasmus informed More from Antwerp on 2 October (*CWE* 4: Ep. 474) that the 'Island' would be seen to, adding in postscript that Giles was 'delighted with your *Nusquama*'. By 17 October (*CWE* 4: Ep. 477), Erasmus could tell Giles, 'I am getting the *Nusquama* ready; mind you send me a preface, but addressed to someone other than me, Busleyden for choice'. Giles's resulting letter to Busleyden from Antwerp (1 Nov. 1516) called the work More's 'island of Utopia' (*Utopiam insulam*). More, meanwhile, was eager to learn how a right-minded coterie regarded his work: 'I am delighted to hear that Pieter [Giles] approves of my *Nusquama*; if men such as he like it, I shall begin to like it myself', he wrote to Erasmus on 31 October 1516 (*CWE* 4: Ep. 481). 'I should like to know whether Tunstall approves,' he continues (he had asked before), 'and Busleyden, and your chancellor [Jean Le Sauvage]':

> that it should win their approval is more than I dared hope, being men so gifted that they hold high office in their own countries, unless they were to favour it because in such a polity as I have invented men like themselves, so cultivated and so upright, would certainly be at the head, whereas in their own countries, however great they may be (and great men they surely are), they always have to suffer great good-for-nothings as their equals—not to say, superiors—in power and influence.

For More, appreciation of *Utopia* required the honourable desire to rule the free, rather than the subjected, but, alluding to Hythlodaean discourse, he also entertains the possibility that 'the opposite way of thinking' could be 'deeply implanted in them by their own success', in which case the approval of Erasmus—his second self—will be more than enough: 'I think I could live happily with you in any wilderness'.

Thankfully, Tunstall's approval—calling the work 'Utopia' (More et al. 1947: 85, Ep. 28)—soon reached More. Yet Tunstall did not enter *Utopia*'s paratextual world, unlike Busleyden, whose letter addressed More 'from my house in Mechelen, 1516'. His covering note to Erasmus (*CWE* 4: Ep. 484, 9 November) set its shortcomings—a risk to reputation and self-respect—against its 'more than obvious proof of my devotion to you', inviting Erasmus to polish it where required. Although the letter's praising of More as a counsellor—combining learning and experience—echoes Morus' commendation of Hythloday in Book One (More 1995: 52–53), Busleyden focuses on Book Two as an ideal (*idea*) or perfect (*absolutissima*) commonwealth. Unlike Giles's letter to him, the Platonic emphasis of Busleyden is uncomplicated by Lucianic irony, which only flickers towards the letter's close, where he considers the fall of commonwealths ('if we have any') avoidable only if they adopt the Utopian pattern provided by More.

On 12 November, Gerard Geldenhouwer—like Dorp and Giles, a proof-corrector for Martens—also called the work 'Utopia' when informing Erasmus (in Brussels) that printing was under way (*CWE* 4: Ep. 487), news Erasmus conveyed to Giles on 18 November (*CWE* 4: Ep. 491): '*Utopia* in manibus typographi' ('*Utopia* is in the hands of the printer'). Paludanus (Jean Desmarez) similarly opens his Utopian letter to Giles (1 December) 'I have read the *Utopia* of your friend More [*Utopiam Mori tui*]' (More 1965a: 26–27). *Utopia* became, then, the work's short title, but had 'Nusquama' already been revised by More to 'Utopia' in the manuscript he sent? What of other 'Greek nonsense' in the island's chorography, such as 'Amaurot' and 'Anyder' in More's letter to Giles? The possibility of widespread editorial intervention is suggested by the residue of the phrase 'In senatu Mentirano' in 1516 (G3r) changed thereafter to 'In senatu Amaurotico': etymologically, the Greek adjective suggests being unknown or shadowy; the Latin feigning or deceiving (Freeman 2007: 6–7).

The paratexts in this first edition certainly testify to collaboration. These 'additions' to More's work recruit reputable Northern humanists to suggest the seriousness of the work whilst displaying their playful participation in the fiction. However, whilst these contributions seem 'deliberately designed to control the reader's interpretation' (P. R. Allen 1963: 91, 100), their history over these first five editions is far from one of simple accretion, more of ongoing manipulation and shifting perspectives. They also seem to have been collated at the last moment, since—whilst Book One opens neatly at the start of quire 'b'—the amount of material requires an unsigned quire ahead of quire 'a'. This material comprises the 'UTOPIAE INSULAE FIGURA' (Fig. 9.1), by an anonymous artist probably associated with Martens; Utopian alphabet, tetrastichon (four-line poem) in the Utopian language, with Latin translation; hexastichon (six-line poem) by the Utopian poet laureate Anemolius (Hythloday's nephew by his sister); Giles's letter to Busleyden; Paludanus' [Desmarez's] letter to Giles; Noviomagus' [Geldenhouwer's] poem on *Utopia*; Cornelius Grapheus' [de Schrijver's] poem to the reader; Busleyden's letter to More; and finally, as 'PRAEFATIO', More's letter to Giles. More's letter, lacking place and date, and—like the two books of *Utopia*—bearing glosses that Giles's letter states he added, appears to drift away from the preceding prefatory material towards the 'fiction' on whose threshold it floats. Giles may also claim authorship of the Utopian alphabet and tetrastichon, if there is truth in Giles's claim (in the letter to Busleyden) that their generation followed More's departure.

FIG. 9.1. Map of *Utopia*, in Thomas More, *Libellus vere aureus nec minus salutaris quam festivus de optimo rei[publicae] statu deq[ue] nova insula Utopia* (Louvain: Thierry Martens, 1516), The Bodleian Libraries, University of Oxford, Arch. B.e.44, sig. A1v.

Erasmus absented himself from the volume, despite his exertions to get it published. *Utopia* was consequently presented as by an author detached from the Louvain circle, though well known as Erasmus' friend (Jardine 1993: 121). Nevertheless, some readers associated *Utopia* more closely with Erasmus than he designed. When Erasmus wrote to More from Antwerp on 1 March 1517 (*CWE* 4: Ep. 543) for revisions for a second edition of *Utopia*, he included a letter to Luigi Marliano, physician to Charles of Burgundy (Charles I of Spain from 1516; Holy Roman Emperor Charles V from 1519), who 'suspects the first book of the *Utopia* of coming from me'. Had Marliano's suspicions been raised by the opening of Book One, where Charles is praised as 'most serene', and Henry VIII as 'most invincible' and 'most adorned with all the accomplishments of an outstanding prince'? Around March 1516, Charles had received Erasmus' dedication of his *Institutio principis Christiani* ('Education of a Christian Prince'), printed by Froben in Basel. Erasmus had also, in his adage *Scarabeus* (3.7.1) added to the expanded *Adagia* of 1515, included among 'the string of magnificent lies' the additions *invictissimus* ('most invincible') and *serenissimus* ('most serene') to royal titles. Furthermore, the title page of the 1514 Strasbourg edition of Erasmus' *Moria* advertised it as 'A truly golden little book, no less learned and wholesome than merry' ('Libellus vere aureus, nec minus eruditus, et salutaris, quam festivus'), a formulation echoed on the first edition of *Utopia*: 'Libellus vere aureus nec minus salutaris quam festivus'. Such allusive potential could lead readers like Marliano to attribute *Utopia*—or parts of it, given the contrast between its two Books—to Erasmus, not least because Erasmus' *Moria*, now in its ninth edition, had placed centre stage his friendship with More. This association was then further orchestrated in print (see Erasmus 1979: 40–64), including printed editions of Erasmus' correspondence, the first of which—*Epistolae aliquot illustrium virorum ad Erasmum Roterodamum, et huius ad illos*—was compiled by Giles even as Erasmus was considering prefatory materials for *Utopia*.

Comprising twenty-one letters (seven by Erasmus), the *Epistolae* was printed by Martens in October 1516 and preserves the earliest surviving letter from More to Erasmus (*CWE* 3: Ep. 388, London, c.17 February 1516). More's letter was retained for the more substantial epistolary collection, *Aliquot epistolae* (= *Epistolae elegantes* (1517)). It replies efficiently to three of Erasmus' and drops names of the influential and/or learned, including 'our friend' Richard Pace (*Paceus noster*); Henry VIII; Cardinal Wolsey (Archbishop of York); Archbishop William Warham; Lord Mountjoy (William Blount); Giles; Thomas Linacre; Rhenanus; and Thomas Ruthall (Bishop of Durham). Mention of More's wife adds a familiar touch. More dwells on difficulties in securing Erasmus a benefice 'adequate either to your wants or to the high opinion held of you by our great men', and on his own 'mission' to Flanders, where *Utopia* was conceived and where the conversation with Hythloday is set. Despite this, no mention is made of literary business: only the frustrations of being away from home longer than expected and the unsuitability of married men like himself for such posts. Yet warmly recorded in relation to the mission are 'the prolonged association with Tunstall', the intimacy struck up with Busleyden (also memorialized in his epigrams) and with Giles, 'such a good scholar and so amusing and modest and such a good friend', who sent him, he states, Erasmus' *Epistola ad Dorpium*. More professes, rhetorically or otherwise, a wish to have met Dorp: 'a man whom I approve of to a surprising degree, not only for his exceptional learning but on many other grounds, not least because by criticizing your *Moria* he gave me the opportunity of writing something in your defence'. This same ironic performativity is found in More's own 'Letter to Dorp', which ends with apologies for having to interrupt its composition and a lack of polish befitting its learned recipient on account of More's summons home.

More's letter to Erasmus acquires a literary-political charge that conducts across not just Erasmus' works, but to More's *Utopia* itself, as—amongst other things—it extends greetings to Rhenanus and records the progress in Latin and Greek of his servant John Clement, allegedly present at the conversation with Hythloday. These resonances with *Utopia* may be sensed in More's opening apology for his unresponsiveness, which teases away at faithfulness, truth, and knowledge of others:

> Since you left us, dearest Erasmus, I have received three letters from you in all. If I were to say I had sent you three answers, you will perhaps not believe me, even if I lie in the most sanctimonious manner, especially as you know me so well for a very idle correspondent, and not so morbidly devoted to the truth that I would as soon commit parricide as utter a modest fib.

Precisely this kind of ironic self-deprecation and flirtation with truth resounds in More's prefatory letter to Giles in *Utopia*, which opens with the words 'Pudet me' ('I am ashamed') and includes Clement's querying of More's recollection of Hythloday's account of the span of the bridge over the River Anyder:

> If you [Giles] do not remember, I shall put down, as I have actually done, what I myself seem to remember. Just as I shall take great pains to have nothing incorrect [*falsi*] in the book, so, if there is doubt about anything, I shall rather tell an objective falsehood than an intentional lie [*potius mendacium dicam quam mentiar*]—for I would rather be honest than wise [*bonus esse quam prudens*]. (More 1965a: 40–41)

Here, More reverses Lucian's assertion in *A True History*—his parodying of travellers' tales that has been seen as marking 'the birth of Western utopian fiction' (Marsh 1998: 193)—that 'at least in one respect I shall be truthful, in admitting that I am lying. Thus I think that by freely admitting that nothing I say is true, I can avoid being accused of it by other people' (1.4, trans. Costa 2009: 204). So nice a point was this that Giles—did Erasmus have a hand?—supplied a marginal gloss: 'Note the Theological distinction between a deliberate lie and an untruth' ('Nota Theologicam differentiam inter mentiri & mendacium dicere'). Far from theological, except for those wishing to make any discussion of truth a theological rather than moral matter, this echoes Aulus Gellius' *Attic Nights* (11.11), one of More's favourite works.

Preparatory Letters: From Louvain 1516 to Paris 1517 and Guillaume Budé

By 15 December, More was daily expecting copies of *Utopia* (*CWE* 4: Ep. 502, to Erasmus,). By 4 January 1517, at least Mountjoy, Erasmus' great supporter and dedicatee of his prestigious Aldine *Adagia* (1508), had received one at Tournai from Erasmus, but had yet to read it (*CWE* 4: Ep. 508). Doubtless, More soon had occasion to acknowledge receipt of his copies, although no letter survives. His next to Erasmus (13 January) is brief, reporting thanks sent to Busleyden, and requesting that Erasmus do likewise to Desmarez and Giles, 'for they wished you to have the credit of what they wrote' (*CWE* 4: Ep. 513). Humanist rhetoric privileged knowledge of others through their familiar writing over actual face-to-face encounter: of Lyster and Rhenanus, Erasmus confessed, 'I feel I love them more and know them much better from what you have told me and from their writings than many people I meet every day' (*CWE* 3: Ep. 388). In Erasmian circles, epistolary discourse—never quite private—was part of self-presentation, whether through the circulation of original letters, manuscript copies, or their inclusion in printed collections. Epitext and peritext thus come into dialogue.[5]

Publication of Erasmus' third, more substantial collection of letters certainly sets the scene for the second, Paris edition of *Utopia* and the coup of eliciting a prefatory letter from the illustrious French humanist Budé. From Antwerp on 5 March, Giles dedicated *Aliquot epistolae sanequam elegantes* (= *Epistolae elegantes* (Louvain: Martens, April 1517)) to Antonius Clava, advertising the epistolary 'tournament of eloquence' within between the 'two paladins of learning', Budé and Erasmus (*CWE* 3.351). The volume included Clava's letter to Erasmus (6 Feb. 1517) in which he repined, 'I instructed a bookseller with whom I am very friendly to send [*Utopia*] to me as soon as ever he could' (*CWE* 4: Ep. 524), Erasmus responding 'you will feel you have been suddenly transported into another world; everything there is so different' (*CWE* 4: Ep. 530). Another letter by Erasmus (21 Feb. 1517) urges Budé to buy a copy: 'do not grudge the leisure to read it, for you will not regret the trouble taken' (*CWE* 4: Ep. 534). That letter also conveyed Giles's admiration for Budé and a roll call of Erasmus' English humanist supporters, including Linacre, and anticipates the Paris edition of Linacre's Latin translation of Galen's *De sanitate tuenda* ('On Hygiene'). Erasmus' and Budé's exchange from summer 1516 (*CWE* 4: Epp. 403, 421, 441), printed in Martens's *Epistolae ad Erasmum* (1516), was extended by four more letters (*CWE* 4: Epp. 435, 480, 493, 531), plus additional paired exchanges, further broadening the French milieu: between Francis Deloynes and Erasmus (*CWE* 4: Epp. 494, 535), instigated by Budé; Budé and Erasmus (*CWE* 4: Epp. 522, 534); Guillaume Cop, an early translator of Galen, and Erasmus (*CWE* 4: Epp. 523, 537), where Erasmus again recommends *Utopia* and flags Linacre's publication; and Erasmus' exchange with the new bishop of Bayeux, Luigi di Canossa (*CWE* 4: Epp. 489, 538), who was tempting Erasmus with a place in François I's household or his own. But despite the Gallic emphasis of *Epistolae elegantes* and the groundwork laid for approaching Budé, Erasmus' mind was then more on Basel than Paris.

On 1 March 1517, Erasmus demanded that More revise the copy of *Utopia* he had sent him, so a transcription could be forwarded 'either to Basel or, if you prefer, to Paris' (*CWE* 4: Ep. 543). Erasmus certainly preferred Froben for his own works, but may have

---

[5] 'Peritext' comprises paratextual elements within the bounds of a book; 'epitext' material (including letters or reviews) beyond those bounds (Génette 1997).

sensed that reprinting *Utopia* was tied to Linacre's Galen. More may well have discussed the matter during Erasmus' English visit to receive his papal dispensation on 9 April; Erasmus departed at the end of the month, possibly with More's revised copy. If both Paris and Basel editions were agreed, the outcomes proved very different. On 30 May, Erasmus wrote to More from Antwerp about having sent *Utopia* and their shared *Epigrammata* to Basel (*CWE* 4: Ep. 584). As the Yale editors noted, the Paris edition contains, 'with a few slight differences, all the readings which appear in the [Froben] editions of 1518', implying—if we assume that Froben's March edition was not set from the Paris one (but see below)—that another copy likewise annotated by More was with Lupset in Paris (More 1965a: clxxxv–clxxxvi). From Louvain during summer 1517, Erasmus maintained regular contact with Froben's press in Basel, updating More in early July (*CWE* 5: Ep. 597) about the printing of his *Lucubrationes* (*Utopia*, *Epigrammata*, and Lucian). That spring (*CWE* 4: Ep. 571), Erasmus had prepared the ground for Tunstall opening an exchange of lengthy, erudite epistles with Budé, elegantly mixing Latin and Greek. Although intimate with those involved, Tunstall remained aloof from *Utopia*, just as he was elsewhere when 'Morus' and 'Giles' met with Hythloday. Instead, it was another eminent English humanist, Linacre, and his therapeutic business that figured in Budé's prefatory letter for More's 'healthful' work in 1517, Galenic matters also preoccupying the exchange between Budé and Linacre later published in *Epistolae Budaei* (1520). Budé's printed letters extend the humanistic network of learned friendship in which *Utopia* was embedded; comparison of the two highlights the interplay of 'real' and 'fictive' self-presentation in More's serio-ludic work.

Linacre, Lupset, and Lucubrations, Paris 1517: The Second Edition

Budé knew Linacre personally, but the way Budé refers mid-1516 to 'your friend Linacre' (not 'our') when relating to Erasmus his conversations with the Englishman and his gift to Linacre of his own *De asse*—the first thoroughgoing account of the values of ancient Greek and Roman coinage, published on 15 March 1515 (*CWE* 4: Ep. 435)—suggests that their relationship was then dormant. Linacre's service as physician to Henry VIII's sister, Mary, had taken him to Paris almost two years earlier, probably crossing from Dover to Boulogne on 2 October 1514 en route to Mary's marriage to the elderly Louis XII (who promptly died on 1 January), and returning with her at the start of May. Linacre's familiar letters are barely extant. *Epistolae Budaei* preserves an exchange of three (Budé 1520: B6v–C3v): Budé to Linacre (Paris, 10 July), Linacre to Budé (London, 8 June), Budé to Linacre (Paris, 9 September). The last must be from 1518, since it echoes remarks about Nicolas Bérault's imminent arrival in London on diplomatic business found in a letter from Budé dated 9 September 1518 (More et al. 1947: 131, Ep. 66), thanking More for two hounds he had sent and punning on More's name in the affectionate soubriquet *mi Oxymore* ('my oxymoron'). Linacre's letter of 8 June, meanwhile, belongs to 1517: it recalls Budé's gift of *De asse*, expresses gratitude for Budé correcting Lincacre's *De sanitate tuenda*, and includes an elegant Greek passage mentioning his gift of cramp rings, which he understands have been delivered. Budé's letter of 10 July arguably looks back to Linacre's June epistle; Budé apologizes that he had only received Linacre's letter on 6 July; he mentions working on *De sanitate tuenda*, and—matching Linacre—turns to Greek to acknowledge receipt of the rings. The bearer, presumably Lupset, is called 'the youth, whether your attendant, your scholar, or both' (Budé 1520: B8v); three weeks later this youth would be addressed as 'Lupset, most learned of young men' at the opening of Budé's Utopian letter, a rhetorical growth in familiarity plausibly licensed by encounters over Galen and Lupset's delivery of a gift-copy of *Utopia*, which Budé in the Utopian letter termed 'an appendix' to the 'former gift' of Linacre's work.

Budé's answering of Linacre's Greek with Greek was an exclusive epistolary embrace seen repeatedly in Budé's *Epistolae*. A heightened literary instance is found at the close of Budé's Utopian letter's exuberant dilation of More's (or rather Morus') ironic self-presentation as the amanuensis of the 'nonsense speaker' Hythloday:

> He feared that Hythloday himself, now fond of dwelling on the island of Udepotia, might some day suddenly appear, and be displeased and annoyed at More's unfairness in leaving him only the deflowered glory [*proapēnthismenon to kleos*] of this discovery. Such a persuasion is characteristic of men both good and wise [*agathōnte kai sophōn*]. (More 1965a: 12–13; translation adapted)

Whilst *Utopia* offers transliterated, self-cancelling Greek puns—the 'no-place' Utopia; 'waterless river' Anyder; 'spectral' city Amaurot; 'peopleless' governor Ademus; 'countryless' Achorians—Budé's letter demands full facility in Greek. Moreover, the issue of literary property is elevated from Hythloday's viewpoint in the preceding Latin: Hythloday could rightly complain that, if he decided to commit his own experiences to paper, More had 'left him a prematurely plucked and deflowered glory' ('gloriam sibi [...] praecerptam, praefloratamque relinqui'). The Latin gives the local clue to the Greek, particularly the recondite adjective *proapēnthismenon* ('deflowered'), but Budé's Latin also evokes More's like concern in his letter to Giles: 'I should certainly dislike to snatch away from him the flower and appeal of the novelty of his account' ('neque ego certe velim [...] florem illi gratiamque novitatis historiae suae praeripere'). But there's a twist. More alludes—the context is loquacity—to one of Pliny's letters: 'providendum est mihi ne gratiam novitatis et florem [...] praecerpam' ('I must make sure that I do not pluck ahead of time the appeal and flower of novelty', 5.20.8; emphasis added).

No mean scholar of Pliny, Budé registers More's Plinian allusion and, picking up *praecerpam*, repays it from Pliny's *Panegyricus* 58: *decus praecerptum praefloratumque* ('a prematurely plucked and deflowered glory'). Furthermore, Pliny's own borrowing of the following distinctive phrase from Quintilian's *Institutio Oratoria* (4.5.4), criticizing orators for telegraphing arguments, is also discernible in More's sentence: 'omnis in relicum gratia novitatis praecerpitur' ('all the appeal of novelty for the rest is reaped ahead of time'; emphasis added).[6] The sharpness and sophistication of Budé's response to More's work is evident not only in his reflections on the Utopian polity, but, as this example shows, also in appreciating 'the grace of his style, the polish of his diction'. It is not just Budé's turn to Greek that defines the exclusive literary domain, but also an acute sensitivity to the resources of literary expression: both propose a marriage of minds in keeping with the obligations of friendship Budé had recently explored in thanking Linacre for the gift of rings.

Budé's participation in *Utopia* may have been fostered by Linacre's recognition of the especially valued encouragement of Erasmus and Budé—the two lights of the age—in his dedication of *De sanitate tuenda* to Henry VIII (Galen 1517: A2v), which Lupset may have shown Budé. In the Utopian letter, Budé thanked Lupset for lending him Linacre's manuscripts for 'so long a time', although their reading had been hurried ('tumultuaria lectione ita percurri'). He wrote to Linacre on 10 July similarly lamenting the want of time (Budé 1520: B7v), confessing that only hours—not days—had been spent happily with Linacre's Galen. Reading Budé's letters against one another illuminates his careful, rhetorical reshaping of familiar discourse for the literary domain of *Utopia*, whether concerning cares impinging on his scholarly activities, or the relationship between ownership, labour, and profit. Thus, in the Utopian letter, Budé turns from the richer rewards (*maiorem [...] profectum*) of reviewing *De sanitate tuenda* to the profitable reading (*usui lectionis*) of More's work, which he took to his country estate. The demands of estate business—which had occupied him for more than a year (*alterum annum*)—are countered by his fascination in 'learning about and weighing the customs of the Utopians', so that he 'almost forgot and even dismissed entirely the management of household affairs [*paene rei familiaris procurationem intermiserim atque etiam abiecerim*]', realizing that 'all theory and practice of domestic economy, and all care whatever for the accumulation of possessions were nonsense [*cum nugas esse viderem artem omnem industriamque oeconomicam, omnemque omnino curam census ampliatricem*]'. Budé's Utopian letter here transposes matter from his 10 July letter to Linacre: 'Iam nunc <u>alterum annum</u> multa mihi negocia domesticae curae facessunt [...] nihil <u>paene rei familiaris</u> <u>procurationi</u> dederim' (Budé 1520: C1r; emphasis added). Both letters press at the limit—*paene* (almost)—of disengagement: the Utopian letter nudges this further, viewing Budé's duties and enrichment as *nugas* (nonsense, folly), the playfully emphatic repetition of *omnem* ('all', 'every') tilting at an absolute position ironicized in *Utopia* itself.

Budé's letter exemplifies receptivity to a vigorous critique of private ownership and corrupt laws defending the wealthy and licensing exploitation of the poor. At the close of Book Two, Hythloday attacks the begetter of all other sins: pride, a hellish serpent, a suckfish (*remora*), preventing conversion to a better way of life. Budé converts this to the simile of 'some inner and innate horsefly' (*oestro quodam intestino et congenito*) which has stung the human race, 'always grabbing something, taking it away, extorting

---

[6] For further resonances, see Whitton 2019: 92–94.

it, suing for it, squeezing it out, breaking it loose, gouging it away, twisting it off, snatching it, snitching it, filching it, pinching it, pilfering it, pouncing on it' ('quippiam semper abducat, abstrahat, abradat, abiuret, exprimat, extundat, exculpat, extorqueat, excutiat, excudat, subducat, suffuretur, suppilet, involet'; More 1965a: 6–7). Only the manic stotting of alliterative prefixes, rhyming verbal endings, and modulating vowels of Budé's Latin fully conveys the maddening distraction of this parasitical attack on citizenship and kinship.

Alert to *Utopia*'s Lucianic qualities, Budé also develops his own critical space. His remoter 'Udepotia' (Neverland) supplants 'Utopia', while his addition of Hagnapolis ('pure' or 'holy city') sounds millenarian—alluding to the 'new Jerusalem' of Revelation 21:2 ('kai tēn polin tēn hagian Ierousalēm kainēn')—so that the 'indirect' approach to reform Budé approves seems located primarily in stimulating readers' moral imagination, as he discovered on his estate (Baker-Smith 1991: 228–230). Budé's embracing More's work thus substitutes for their never having met, his faith in and affection for him depending on Giles's testimony and on More's sworn friendship with Erasmus ('amicus est iuratissimus'). As Budé tells Linacre, 'with Erasmus himself I have long ago formed an association of friendship [*societatem amicorum contraxi*] sealed by an exchange of letters' (More 1965a: 14–15). Through this epistolary rhetoric of intimacy these figures represent themselves to one another and to the world, a rhetoric exploiting the promise of authenticity to promote the power of fiction in pursuit of truth. Budé's letter not only approved of *Utopia*, but within these circles also artfully modulated and extended its 'very amusing and profitable' nature.

In a letter dated 15 September, Erasmus learned from Lupset that he had finished Galen and was now seeing that More's *Utopia* was republished (*CWE* 5: Ep. 664). The title page of Gourmont's edition advertises the virtues of this new edition: its handy format for men of affairs (*Enchiridii forma*: the form of a manual); its purging of textual errors; and addition of letters by Budé and More, as well as (apocryphally) annotations attributed to Erasmus, marginalia already present in the first edition. Due to its smaller octavo format, this edition lacked the *figura* of the island, Utopian alphabet, and accompanying poem, transcription, and translation. The paratexts therefore start with the *Hexastichon Anemolii*, followed by Budé's letter to Lupset; Noviomagus' and Grapheus' poems appear after Book Two, following a second, undated letter from More to Giles, and one from Busleyden to More. This arrangement gives prominence to Budé's letter. However, although Gourmont had pioneered printing in Greek in Paris over the previous decade, the font and setting were both crude, as the printing of Budé's Greek passage shows (Constantinidou 2015: 284–286; Botley 2010), and—despite claims that the edition was 'much more correct than before' (*multo correctius quam prius*)—it was riddled with typographical errors, resulting from hasty typesetting and inadequate proofing. Even the woefully incomplete errata are misfoliated. When Gourmont printed the first edition of Erasmus' *Moria* (1511), Erasmus blamed his English protégé Richard Croke for the shabby result: Lupset, tasked likewise with proofing both Galen (at Guillaume Le Rouge's press) and *Utopia* (*CWE* 4: Ep. 502), fared little better, as Erasmus would carp to More on finally inspecting the Paris edition in early 1518 (*CWE* 5: Ep. 785).

Yet for all the inadequacies of the Paris edition, publication elsewhere could have cost *Utopia* Budé's letter.

Between Paris and Basel

In 1517, Froben and the bookseller Wolfgang Lachner were eager for high-quality copy: Rhenanus sued Erasmus for 'new compositions, revisions, translations, your own and other people's', adding, 'If you wish anything of yours or your Lucian translations to be published here, write to the firm and say you would like it' (*CWE* 4: Ep. 575). Late that May, Erasmus' letter announcing his gift to More of Quentin Massys's diptych of Erasmus and Giles also conveyed that his servant Jacobus Nepos had taken More's works to Basel with his own (*CWE* 4: Ep. 584). Rhenanus wrote again from Basel on 8 July 1517, offering assistance despite strained relations with the press (*CWE* 5: Ep. 594). Erasmus kept More abreast of developments, reassuring him that Froben had been warned to give the works the sharpest oversight (*CWE* 5: Ep. 597). Growing increasingly impatient in Louvain that summer, Erasmus urged Rhenanus to 'see that they get on with the printing of what I sent, and especially that they make a good job of More's pieces' (*CWE* 5: Ep. 628, 23 Aug. 1517). The next day he composed a letter to Froben's corrector Wolfgang Angst (*CWE* 5: Ep. 634), requesting that Rhenanus compose a letter of commendation to serve as a preface to More's *Utopia* and *Epigrammata*, then dating 25 August his own short preface to the *Epigrammata*: a brief epistle addressed to Froben (*CWE* 5: Ep. 635), also sent to Angst.

Over the autumn, during which Erasmus seemed more concerned about securing a copy of Linacre's *De sanitate tuenda* than a Paris *Utopia* (*CWE* 5: Ep. 687), Froben certainly applied himself to Erasmus' *opuscula*, despite Erasmus' complaints that Froben was hoarding his manuscripts (*CWE* 5: Ep. 704A). Froben's plump quarto appeared in December 1517 (Sebastiani 2018: no. 68), comprising Erasmus' *Querela pacis* and *Declamatio de morte*, Erasmus' and More's Lucian translations (the bulk of the volume), and closing with More's response to Lucian's *Tyrannicida*. The *catalogus* on the verso of the title page advertises further works not in the volume: *Utopia*, More's *Epigrammatum liber* (the full title of which advertised William Lily's co-authorship of some parts), and Erasmus' *Epigrammata*: works which Rhenanus reported as being in press in a letter of 18 November to the learned Nuremburg patrician Willibald Pirckheimer (Rhenanus 1886: 98, Ep. 69). In place of these, an address from Froben, dated 6 December 1517, confesses that the volume would have grown too unwieldy and marred their presentation, and promises to publish them as soon as possible (Erasmus 1517b: 2L4v).

Froben's first edition of *Utopia* (Sebastiani 2018: no. 83) slipped to March 1518, after fourteen other volumes had been printed, including three by Erasmus (*In epistolam Pauli*; *Aliquot epistolae sanequam elegantes*; *Parabolae*). Erasmus' burst of letter writing to English patrons and friends on 5 March included sending More deep apologies from those at Basel over his *Utopia*, now underway, 'delayed', he claimed, 'for the elegant preface provided by Budé' (*CWE* 5: Ep. 785). Erasmus' mention of the Paris edition—finally seen, full of mistakes ('Vidi tandem Utopiam Parisiis excusam, sed mendose')—seems dismissively terse alongside his exhortation to read his latest exchange with Budé (enclosed), and reassurance over Froben's treatment of *Utopia*. Budé's preface was set from the Paris edition rather than manuscript (More 1965a: clxxxvi), so waiting for a copy may have compounded the initial delay in printing *Utopia*. The Paris *Utopia* arrived in Basel by mid-February, as Rhenanus refers to Budé's letter in his epistle, dated 23 February 1518, dedicating More's epigrams to Pirckheimer. If Angst had elicited a letter from Rhenanus the previous autumn for More's *Utopia* and *Epigrams* (as Erasmus requested), sight of Budé's no doubt prompted its rewriting, given its late date and emphasis on the work it now headed: More's *Epigrammata*. Although Budé's splendid preface had, as Rhenanus acknowledged, left little for him to add, he arguably takes over from More's second letter to Giles (omitted by Froben) the satirizing of readers of *Utopia* who question whether it is fact or fiction. The barbed quip with which Rhenanus caps his Utopian passage is reserved for those, like Pirckheimer, who know Greek: 'Do you not, then, welcome this wittiness of More, who can lead astray such men as these, not the ordinary run of men, but those esteemed by the multitude, especially theologians?' (*CWM* 3/2.76–77; translation adapted).

Froben's first edition of *Utopia* appeared as the first item in a continuously paginated volume, barring a minor hiccup following Book Two. More's epigrams, including More's and Lily's *Progymnasmata*, then Erasmus' follow. Both More's and Erasmus' *Epigrammata* have their own title pages, and the colophons of all three works give 'March' as the date of completion. To match Rhenanus' dedicatory epistle for More's epigrams, Froben supplied one 'to the reader' for Erasmus', dated 1 March. Although Budé's Utopian letter was prized, another new letter, Erasmus to Froben dated 25 August 1517 (*CWE* 5: Ep. 635), was placed ahead of it. It represents Erasmus' explicit, though modest, entry into the liminal space of *Utopia*, although the Paris title page claimed that edition had been thoroughly corrected through Erasmus' notes ('purgatio propter Erasmi annotationes'), possibly a reference to revisions entered into the Louvain copy Lupset took to Paris, rather than the printed marginalia claimed by Giles. Erasmus' Utopian letter to Froben projects the themes of friendship (*amicitia*)—a possible, but here ill-founded, anxiety over the clouding of critical judgment—and the business (*negotium*) of royal and domestic duties that blight the harvest of natural literary talent. In the subtle irony of wondering 'how he [More] found the time even to think of books', Erasmus thus anticipates More's letter to Giles later in the volume, but also looks ahead to his famous pen-portrait of More for Hutten (*CWE* 7: Ep. 999). The themes of Erasmus' letter and focus on the epigrams in Rhenanus' probably rendered Paludanus' rather derivative letter to Giles redundant. Its planned omission is evident from Erasmus' letter to Rhenanus from Louvain of 6 December 1517, addressing queries over the Utopian paratexts: 'Desmarez's [Paludanus'] things can be left out' (*CWE* 5: Ep. 732).

Such was the authority and diffusion of Froben's quarto editions of March and November 1518 that the ancillary pieces they omitted were doomed never to reappear in sixteenth-century print. But Froben's March edition also restored paratexts omitted from the Paris edition, where the smaller format precluded reuse of the Louvain woodcuts, and economy or expediency inhibited commissioning bespoke replacements. Froben's March edition, set it seems from an annotated Louvain copy, made three independent corrections not found in Paris. Evidence for a second copy being annotated by More comes from Pace's *De fructu*, printed by Froben in October 1517 (G3r). There, the interlocutor Paolo Bombasio says that he has seen a copy of *Utopia* with correction of *i* to *y* in *consydero* in More's own hand, as found in Froben's editions but not Paris (More 1995: xxxix, 273; 1965a: clxxxvii). As Bombasio was in Switzerland and thus near Pace in Constance in August 1517, just as Erasmus was writing to both Angst and Froben about printing More's works, including the revised *Utopia* he had sent, Bombasio could have seen the corrections and mentioned them to Pace then.

Basel: In the Frame

Dedicating his *De copia* to Froben's corrector Wilhelm Nesen (*CWE* 4: Ep. 462; Antwerp, 5 Sept. 1516), Erasmus stressed how his works should 'come before the public once again clothed in Froben's larger type and as accurate and elegant as may be. Let them at least give pleasure by their appearance'. Likewise, Erasmus' letter to Froben for *Utopia* expressed hope that More's works would be 'launched upon the world and upon future ages with the benefit of your typography' (*CWE* 5: Ep. 635). Froben's *Utopias* boasted typographical qualities rivalling those of Aldus Manutius in Venice (celebrated by More in the account of Greek works Hythloday took to Utopia, and by Erasmus in his adage *Festina lente*).[7] The aesthetic quality of Froben's publications was enhanced by the figurative borders used for title pages and decorative initials Froben had recently been commissioning from the most accomplished artists available. These, combined with assiduous mise-en-page and high standards of proofreading, became the hallmark of his firm.

The Froben volume is dominated by More. Its title page (Fig. 9.2) proclaims More's *Utopia*, followed by the *Epigrammata* of the 'most famous and most skilful man [*clarissimi dissertissimique viri*] Thomas More', only then and, sparingly, the *Epigrammata Des. Erasmi Roterodami* (Sebastiani 2018: no. 83). Indeed, Erasmus' name appears partly in lower case, whereas More's is fully capitalized for both his works. Yet the sumptuous framing woodcut of the title page promotes deeper Erasmian associations. Ambrosius Holbein's 'Lucretia et Tarquinius' was first seen in April 1517 fronting Erasmus' revised *De copia*, which Froben combined with *De ratione studii* (Hollstein 1954); it was reused for the internal title page of Erasmus' *De morte declamatio* in the *Querela pacis* volume (Erasmus 1517b: H1r) from which *Utopia* was bumped in December 1517. Internally, each prefatory paratextual element of *Utopia* is carefully set to

---

[7] For *Utopia* and the Aldine Press, see Suthren in this volume.

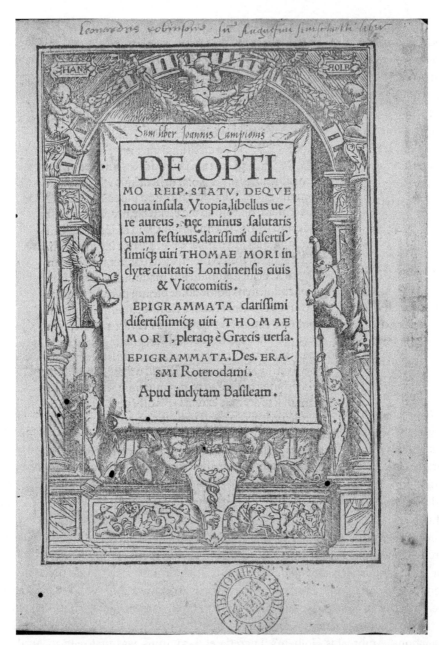

FIG. 9.2. Title page, Thomas More, *De optimo reip. Statu, deque nova insula utopia* (Basel: Johann Froben, November-December 1518), The Bodleian Libraries, University of Oxford, Wood 639.

commence on a fresh page, as in the Paris edition, but more elegantly here in the larger quarto format, with More's letter to Giles again the final piece.[8] In the Louvain edition, that letter's introduction stands curiously adrift at the bottom of a page, while the Paris edition drops the identification of More's letter as the preface, so that it appears as merely the final prefatory letter. Froben did not reinstate the 'PRAEFATIO' statement found in the Louvain edition, but instead demarked More's letter with a full-scale title page using the 'Triton Struggle' border (Fig. 9.3), probably Hans Holbein the Younger's first commission for Froben in 1516, used most recently for the title page of the November 1517 edition of Erasmus' *Moria* (Sebastiani 2018: no. 67). That volume included Gerard Listrius' (partly Erasmus') deflecting commentary on the *Moria*; Erasmus' *Epistola apologetica ad Martinum Dorpium*; and opened with two of those ancient precedents for Erasmus' satire mentioned in his expanded dedicatory letter to More: Seneca's *De morte Claudii Caesaris* and Synesius' *De laudibus calvitii*, translated by John Free (Phrea) (Erasmus 1979: 46–7, no. 11). The trompe l'œil of the 'Triton Struggle' border delightfully compounds the irony of More's epistolary fiction by presenting its opening as a sheet of paper or canvas held up by putti, while its recalling of the *Moria* volume evokes kinship with paradoxical encomium and Menippean satire.

Although the relationship between a work and its title-page border was far from fixed, the visual linking of *Moria* with *Utopia* seems specific: Erasmus' *Moria* and More's *Utopia* placed within the same frame, with Erasmus' involvement with Froben's edition of *Utopia* blazoned in his letter to Froben printed on the verso of the title page. When demand prompted Froben's reprinting of the *Utopia* volume that autumn, the 'complete and close resetting of the March edition' (More 1965a: cxc) included switching the works' title-page borders, further linking More and Erasmus: 'Triton Struggle' was used for the volume's title page as well as for More's letter to Giles; in place of 'Mutius & Porsenna', More's epigrams are fronted by Graf's 'Fool and Satyr', as in *Moria* 1515 and 1519 (Sebastiani 2018: no. 106).

In addition to the 'Lucretius et Tarquinus' frame, Ambrosius Holbein's work is also seen in the striking woodcut—new to the Froben editions—of the conversational scene at the opening of Book One of *Utopia* (Fig. 37.1). The labelling of the seated Giles, Hythloday, and More, attended by Clement, contributes further to the substantiation of the fiction and is informed by More's prefatory letter, nudging Giles—and arguably teasing us—about the presence of Clement, a member of More's household since 1514, 'who, as you know, was there with us, for I forbid him to be absent from any conversation in which there is some profit'. In More's letter, Clement is also reported attempting to correct More's misremembering of the width of the (waterless) river Anyder.

---

[8] Order of 1518 paratexts: Erasmus' letter to Froben; Bude's to Lupset; Anemolius' hexastichon; *Utopiae insulae tabula* (Fig. 5.1); Utopian alphabet, tetrastichon, translation; Busleyden's letter to Giles; More's to Giles.

FIG. 9.3. Opening page of More's letter to Giles, including the 'Triton Struggle' border by Hans Holbein the Younger, in Thomas More, *De optimo reip. Statu, deque nova insula utopia* (Basel: Johann Froben, November-December 1518), 17. The Bodleian Libraries, University of Oxford.

Basel, Winter 1518: More, Hutten, and Lucian

Froben's *Utopia* of winter 1518 tends to be the last early edition considered by modern editors. However, only André Prévost (More 1978a), seeing further authorial influence, based his edition on it (see More 1995: 98, 273–274). In addition to changing title-page borders, the winter edition followed and tidied up the March one: some pages have fresh catchwords betraying very minor changes in typesetting; careless page numbering was remedied; and further corrections outweighed the few fresh errors introduced (More 1965a: cxc). More's public profile received a further 'Utopian' fillip from Froben's press when it published Ulrich von Hutten's satirical works. In the coda of a dedicatory epistle to Erasmus (*CWE* 6: Ep. 863, 31 August 1518), the imperial secretary Jakob Spiegel greeted his friend and fellow Selestatian Rhenanus, and offered Hutten's ΟΥΤΙΣ, *Nemo* for Erasmus' recommendation to Froben; Hutten's *Aula* was to follow once printed. This ΟΥΤΙΣ, *Nemo*, a 'nobody' recalling More's 'no-place', was Hutten's rewriting, under the influence of Erasmus' *Moria*, of his earlier version, first published in 1510 in Erfurt (Jillings 1993). Although mentioned to Erasmus in 1515 (*CWE* 3: Ep. 365), composition was probably later, and it made its first appearance, with a handsome full-page Odyssean woodcut by Hans Weiditz, in imperial Augsburg in August 1518, printed by Johann Miller (Calmann 1960: 77–84). Froben printed it in quarto in September 1518 and January 1519 (Sebastiani 2018: nos. 97, 114) using Graf's 'Fool and Satyr' border for the title page, thus recalling Erasmus' *Moria*. Indeed, just as some had alleged Erasmian authorship of *Utopia*—'There were even men ready to give me More's *Utopia*, so universal is the rule that any new publication, willy nilly, must be mine' (*CWE* 6: Ep. 967, to Wolsey)—so Erasmus complained to Lorenzo Campeggi that *Nemo* was being attributed to him, despite Hutten's name on the title page (*CWE* 6: Ep. 961).

As Spiegel had intimated, Hutten's *Aula* followed, printed in Augsburg in mid-September 1518 by Grimm and Wirsung. Froben issued it in November (Sebastiani 2018: no. 101), just as he was handling *Utopia* again. Hutten's dialogue between the scholarly Castus ('Virtuous') and court-weary Misaulus ('Disliker of Palaces') resonates with More's 'dialogue of counsel' in Book One. Froben strengthened this association by capping Hutten's original dedicatory epistle to Heinrich Stromer with his own to More, dated 13 November 1518 (More et al. 1947: 132–133, Ep. 67). There Froben invokes Lucian's essay on dependent scholars, *De mercede conductis potentium familiaribus* ('On Salaried Posts in Great Houses'), pointing towards the elegant Latin version Erasmus had dedicated to Desmarez in 1506 (*CWE* 2: Ep. 197), before praising Hutten as Lucian reborn. A fitting recipient of Hutten's work, More is again portrayed as having been dragged from the Muses into Henry VIII's service, but also as the author of the work Froben is keen to advertise, *Utopia*: More's genius will be approved not just by Britons—the leading lights are then listed—but by the whole world (Hutten 1518b: A1v).

After Lucian: The Florentine *Utopia* 1519

Froben's letter thickens the humanistic texture around More's work; its dress south of the Alps was lighter. More's *Utopia* stands in uneasy relation to the ideals of Italian civic humanism (see E. Nelson 2006 for its emphatic rejection of them). The manifestation in Italy of the fifth and last lifetime Latin edition was influenced by factors other than those textual and personal relations shaping the work's migration from Louvain to Paris to Basel. In *Utopia* itself, cisalpine humanism—if we take the Roman view—is glimpsed in the recognition of Aldus Manutius' achievements in printing the literary monuments of Greek antiquity. Manutius is the numen pervading Hythloday's account of the Greek books he took in place of goods (*mercium*) on his fourth voyage: the Utopians prove particularly fond of Plutarch and Lucian's wit, and the model for printing is Aldine (More 1965a: 180–185). The Aldine Press issued Erasmus' *Moria* in August 1515 and the Lucian translations of Erasmus and More the following year, so an Aldine *Utopia* would have been fitting. But it was the heirs of Bernardo Giunta who published *Utopia* in Florence in July 1519 in an octavo edition which also included the Lucian translations. Giunta's learned editor Antonio Francini of Montevarchi (Varchiensis) probably provided scholarly oversight.

The Florentine *Utopia* is the third of five Erasmian volumes, secular and political, printed by the Giuntine Press between late 1518 and early 1520 (Connell 2020: 153): Euripides (December 1518, based on Aldine 1507); *Moria* (early 1519, based on Aldine 1515); Lucian-*Utopia* (July 1519; Lucian based on Aldine 1516); a humanist grammar (January 1520); a gathering of political works, including some Plutarchan essays (February 1520, based on Aldine 1518, adding *Sileni Alcibiadis* and *Oratio de virtute*). Although the complex relationship between Venetian and Florentine reception of Erasmian works cannot be pursued here, it is noteworthy that from around 1515 the Venetian patriciate saw publishing scholarly works as a way to cultivate the myth of Venice as a model republic and restore prestige lost following defeat at Agnadello in 1509 (Libby 1973: 7–8; see M. Lowry 1976: 414–416 for the impact of the defeat on Manutius). Manutius' ten-year privilege effectively passed with him in 1515, so, when Filippo Giunta died in 1517, his eldest son, the erudite Bernardo, appropriated swathes of Aldine territory. Thus, the Giuntine Press contributed similarly to Florentine prestige at a time when the younger Florentine generation reflected on Venice's mixed government in considering reform of its own (F. Gilbert 1968).

Textually, the Florentine *Utopia* follows Froben's March edition, but undoes the priority given there to the work. Its plain title page is headlined 'LUCIANI OPUSCULA ERASMO ROTERODAMO INTERPRETE', like the 1516 Aldine volume of the Lucian translations it follows (the 1506 Badius edition might also have been consulted, but Froben's recent *Querela pacis* volume was not). As in the Aldine, More seems the minor contributor, listed modestly after Erasmus' versions. The Giuntine also follows Aldine's signature mark of 'Erasmus' at the start of each quire, here extended to *Utopia* too, so that Erasmus haunts the whole volume. *Utopia*, a supplement to the Lucian and the final quarter of the volume, is even more modestly introduced than on the title page: directly after the 'FINIS' of More's *Declamatio* responding to Lucian's *Tyrannicida* appears the legend 'THOMAE MORI UTOPIA SEQUITUR' (More 1519: A8r); the verso is blank. Giles's letter to Busleyden appears next, followed by More's to Giles. All other prefatory matter found in Froben is missing, sweeping away its first thirteen pages, although what follows Book Two tracks Froben: Busleyden's letter to More, then Noviomagus' and Grapheus' epigrams. The compressed octavo format of the *libelli portatiles* (portable little books) pioneered by Manutius and emulated here in Florence accounts for the loss of the visual material, as with the Paris octavo, but perhaps not of the marginalia, as the Giuntine *Moria* copied the annotations squeezed into the Erasmian Aldine edition.

What kind of local repurposing does this pared-down paratext suggest? If the previous overloading of the *libellus aureus* with ancillary materials was itself ironic, that was perhaps a game less appreciated in Florence. Excising Erasmus' rather utilitarian letter to Froben is perhaps understandable, but cutting Budé's to Lupset—prized so much in the north—is less readily explained, especially as Linacre was to receive Francini's dedication of his Latin translation of Pollux's ten-book Greek lexicon, *Onomasticon*, in 1520. Its dedication to Linacre was prompted, Francini records, by Giampiero Machiavelli, who knew Linacre from his Italian days (1487–99), was still in contact in 1513, as a letter from Linacre testifies, and frequented Budé's *sodalité* in Paris 1514–15, when Linacre was there. Francini's dedicatory epistle also commended *Utopia* and More's versions of Lucian (the Giuntine package he probably edited), which only makes the loss of Budé's letter, in which Linacre figures, the more curious. Equally, the attentive reader of Giles's letter to Busleyden would be left wondering about the Utopian alphabet, Utopian quatrain, and annotations all mentioned there (but omitted from this edition).

Although *Utopia* keeps company with Lucian, serio-ludic continuities seem less important than the republican concern with tyranny that arches from Erasmus' and More's rivalrous responses to Lucian's *Tyrannicida* to *Utopia*'s anatomizing of monarchical government and its tendency to propagate and institutionalize corruption—although More addressed tyranny more trenchantly in his epigrams (available in the Froben volume employed for *Utopia*) than Lucian does in his declamation and More's response, where there is little on the justice or otherwise of overthrowing tyrants. Around the time the Giuntine *Utopia* appeared, power had shifted to Rome with the Medici papacy of Leo X (Giovanni di Lorenzo de' Medici, 1513–21), rendering Florence a disempowered satellite of papal policy (Scott Baker 2013: 72–81). The divisions between the Medici and Florentine office-holding class were only deepened by the military adventurism of the War of Urbino (1516–17). Medici policy also sought to place Lorenzo II de' Medici among international royalty; he was duke of Urbino while it remained a Medici possession, and his daughter Catherine (b. 1519) would become queen of France. Moreover, his appointment as Florentine captain general crossed a Rubicon, as citizens customarily did not assume military power. Ongoing unrest in Florence, pitted against its traditional ally (Urbino), with Lorenzo a potential dictator, reinvigorated debate on a more civic style of government. Appearing shortly after Lorenzo's unexpected death on 4 May, the Florentine *Utopia* of July would thus have fed the imaginations of an administrative class still considering itself a community of mature citizens serving the Florentine republic.

In this setting, both Carlo Dionisotti (1980) and Silvana Seidel Menchi (1987) regard the Giuntine *Utopia* and Erasmian works as political interventions sufficiently subversive to prompt the omission of prefatory sponsorship. Furthermore, Dionisotti (1980: 210–213) considered the unsold copies of the Florentine *Utopia* in the 1604 inventory evidence of suppression. Yet if such works were thought subversive, the Guintine imprint was far from disguised, and Francini mentions some of these volumes in the prefaces to others. Moreover, the lack of a preface to the Giuntine *Moria* (1518) arguably indicates little more than its closeness to the Aldine edition of 1515, from which it took its title and text, and which itself lacked a preface. The Aldine editors were responsible for other similar excisions, and where Manutius addressed readers in fresh preliminary materials, these were understandably shorn from the Florentine reprintings. Nonetheless, the want of fresh dedications perhaps suggests some kind of attenuation, as other contemporary works were addressed to Florentine political figures like Lorenzo Bartolini, Bartolomeo Cavalcanti, and Pierfrancesco Portinari, so the question of political charge remains open.

Although the Florentine *Utopia* appeared among Erasmian works and shares many concerns with Erasmus' *Institutio principis Christiani* (1516), its foundation in a 'moneyless economy' sets it radically apart from treatises on educating princes how to exercise power wisely and virtuously. Moreover, in the *Institutio*, Erasmus asserts that to avoid tyranny and promote subjects' interests, monarchy should be mixed with aristocracy and democracy, accepting the terms of the classical debate of the rule of the one, few, and many. Where Erasmus advocates restraining monarchical tendencies towards the pursuit of glory and wealth, *Utopia* utterly subverts the neo-Roman republican tradition by abolishing private property and the forms of justice that protect it. Like Plato's *Republic*, however, it is unclear how politically dangerous its radically different view was seen to be. Francesco Guicciardini's *Dialogo del reggimento di Firenze* ('Dialogue on the Government of Florence'), composed 1521–4 (Guicciardini 1994: x), debates the merits of rule by the one, few, or many. It falls short of explicit engagement with *Utopia*, but offers a teasing echo of Morus' closing words in *Utopia* when Barnardo del Nero reflects on rule by 'the one': 'They call it good when the person most capable of governing is preferred to all others—something that in our times one can desire more easily than one can hope to happen' (1994: 94; 'cosa che a' tempi nostri si può più facilmente desiderare che sperare', Guicciardini 1932: 97). Morus finishes with 'quae [...] optarim verius, quam sperarim': 'which I might more truly wish for than expect to see' (More 1965a: 246–247).

After five editions of *Utopia* in little more than thirty months, the gap of almost thirty years before the next (Louvain, 1548) is striking. In Florence, *Utopia* drifted out of More's and Erasmus' ken, deprived of much of its paratextual display of the *familia* of knowing participants. Elsewhere that summer Luther's theological challenge to papal authority and established doctrine became startlingly clear during the Leipzig Disputation (June–July 1519) debating Luther's Ninety-Five Theses. Both More and Erasmus would be drawn into these sharpening religious controversies; More also immediately suffered the literary attacks of Germain de Brie (Brixius), whose *Antimoros* (1519) included a page-by-page, mocking critique of apparent solecisms in the *Epigrammata* of 'Moros' (the fool), which accompanied *Utopia* and which itself suffered a few swipes. Meanwhile, Erasmus' hopes for the progress of 'good letters' had to contend with attacks on his *Annotationes in Novum Testamentum* by the conservative English theologian Edward Lee, as well as attempts to conflate humanist reform with Luther's challenge to the Church. More would soon be engaged in defending Catholicism, notably in Latin in the scurrilous *Responsio ad Lutherum* (1523), and later, against Tyndale, in increasingly voluminous vernacular works.

The contesting of truth and the push for certainty rendered the adversarial climate of the 1520s uncongenial to the play of paradox and irony in purposefully unresolved dialogues like *Utopia*. For those combating heresy, making matters 'as little bad as possible' (to cite Morus) was hardly sufficient. Yet even that deliberate understatement (litotes) belies a deeper pessimism in *Utopia*: that hopes for reform were ever to be frustrated by vested interests; that without abolishing private property, the *philosophia Christi* was bound to falter. Budé perhaps recognized this when renaming the island as 'Udepotia' (Neverland) and Amaurot 'Hagnapolis', foregrounding the work's meditative stimulation of the cloistered imagination rather than encouraging direct (or indirect) political engagement. A deep vein of satire in *Utopia* contrasts heathen achievement (through reason) with the failings of a European society that considered itself Christian. For the clarity and unaccommodating single-mindedness of his understanding of Christian revelation, More would go to the scaffold in 1535, so that when that octavo Latin *Utopia* appeared in Louvain in 1548, it was as the work of a martyr willing 'to lese good, lande and lyfe too, rather than to swere against my conscience' (More et al. 1947: 530, Ep. 206).

PART TWO

TRANSLATIONS AND EDITIONS, 1524–1799

CHAPTER 10

AD FONTES ET AD FUTURUM

A Survey of Latin Utopias

LUCY NICHOLAS

At the end of Book One of *Utopia*, almost certainly punning on More's name, Hythloday declares, 'If you had been with me in Utopia and had seen with your own eyes their customs [*mores*] and practices as I did'. It is arguable that to be truly in Utopia and see it through the eyes of the work's main narrator, Latin must be the entry point: this is the language in which the work was initially conceived, received, and assimilated. Although the Latin constitutes the main source for many of the translations into the vernaculars reviewed in this volume (at least until the eighteenth century), it is now often forgotten that *Utopia* was originally written in Latin, and indeed enjoyed a long afterlife in that language until well into the twentieth century. By returning to the Latin we are not only better placed to appreciate the original spirit of the work, its wordplay, and symbolic currency, but also to understand the men and women who continued to publish and read *Utopia* in Latin.[1]

This chapter examines *Utopia*'s Latin journey. It starts with Thomas More's conscious choice to write in Latin, suggesting that the Latin medium not only constituted the packaging but also encapsulated the very marrow, the message of the book. In contrast to many studies which focus only on the earliest Latin texts, it surveys Latin editions post-1518, well after More ceased to have any involvement in them.[2] The relative stability of the Latin text is noteworthy, and I argue that the Latin language is vital because it could retain the essential lineaments of the earliest incarnations of the work in a way that vernacular translations could not. At the same time, the particular motivations and contexts that impelled the production of new Latin editions stand in relation to and capture something of the concerns of their own time and place.

---

[1] For the symbolic quality of Latin see Waquet 2001; Burke 1991.
[2] One exception is Roggen 2008. However, this concentrates primarily on the paratexts and the survey extends only to 1631.

The Latin of *Utopia* and Later *Utopias*

Latin usage in the early modern period is a composite phenomenon worthy of some preliminary consideration. As Marie Delcourt insists in her Latin edition, 'More's Latin is a living language that must be studied as such' ('Le Latin de More est une langue vivante qu'il faut étudier comme telle', More 1936: 29). When More first penned *Utopia*, Latin was the lingua franca of early modern Europe: the primary mode of communication for the Church, law, science, international diplomacy, and the universal language of scholarship. Scholars often refer to the phenomena of 'diglossia', bilingualism in a native language and Latin; and also a yet broader multilingualism where Latin was used alongside a range of other tongues. Latin could be an instinctive mode both in which to write and—as with More, who used Latin at home—to speak. It coexisted with the array of European tongues, being both model and competitor for these vernaculars. At the same time, it could convey certain patterns of thought, connotations, and assumptions that are relevant for any evaluation of *Utopia* in Latin.

An important facet of Latin was the scholarly internationalism it could stimulate. Knowledge of Latin facilitated membership of a learned community—the *respublica litterarum*—and potentially enabled an international readership and reputation. The only truly 'European' language of the time, Latin crossed borders in ways no vernacular could. The *Utopia* project brought together a group of European humanists, all of whom shared the common bond of Latin: the Englishmen More and Thomas Lupset; the Dutch Desiderius Erasmus, Jerome (or Hieronymus) Busleyden, and Peter Giles; the French Guillaume Budé; the Swiss Johann Froben; the Germans Beatus Rhenanus and Willibald Pirckheimer.[3] The international compass of More's Latin is exemplified by the fact that *Utopia* was published during his lifetime in Louvain, Paris, Basel, and Florence, but not in England (then, relatively speaking, a cultural parvenu on the international stage).

The use of Latin also carried subtler connotations: through Latin a closer bond with classical learning could be forged, not least through a proximity to the language worlds of ancient texts (Waquet 2001: 178–179). It was through Latin that humanists could enter into a deeper dialogue with the classical world (Miller and Harp 2011: 13). By casting his work in elaborate and demanding Latin based upon an overwhelmingly classical vocabulary, syntax, and rhetoric, More could effectively harness classical literary topoi and genres.[4] Cramming the work with learned allusions to a variety of ancient authors including Plato, Aristotle, Lucian, Plutarch, Herodotus, Tacitus, Cicero, Seneca, and Pliny, he gave their words and thoughts an immediacy and revitalized instantiation

---

[3] Paul White (2014: 174) is less confident about Froben's grasp of Latin, but Froben clearly supported the language, publishing many works in Latin.

[4] For an assessment of *Utopia*'s Latin against standards of classical diction and syntax, see Monsuez 1966: 35–78.

more difficult to convey in a non-classical language. Perhaps more crucially as regards *Utopia*, Latin functioned as a conduit for specifically Greek ideas. A major activity of the Renaissance was Latinizing Greek texts, as seen in Budé's paratextual letter to Lupset, commenting on Thomas Linacre's achievement in rendering Galen's Greek into 'elegant Latin' (More 1965a: 5). More's *Utopia* embodied a commitment to the study of Greek literature (Andrew Taylor 2014: 1047), and ideas of Greek political philosophy and Lucianic approaches were potently refracted through the Latin.

Erasmus' deep involvement with *Utopia* has long been recognized.[5] Yet in many ways it is the Latin of *Utopia* that truly connects it with Erasmus' programme: for example, More's close adherence to the linguistic recommendations set out in Erasmus' *Copia* (Surtz 1967: 96–97). More's narrative also complied with Erasmus' recommendations about synonymy and enallage, figures of rhetoric, and metaphor, and More used imagery from, for example, medicine, agriculture, the animal kingdom, and navigation in a way that accorded with Erasmus' instructions about the suitability and range of metaphors in the first book of his *Copia* (Surtz 1967: 99–101). *Utopia* fell square with the prescriptions of the second book of Erasmus' *Copia*, which recommended, inter alia, vivid descriptions of persons and places (105–106). Erasmus approved of the use of sententiae (107), aphoristic phrases of the kind that were abundant in his own *Adagia* and *Moriae Encomium* ('Praise of Folly'; henceforth *Moria*); indeed, many striking phrases in More's *Utopia* have a proverbial ring.[6] *Utopia* also cleaved to the eclecticism of style that Erasmus advocated. Following strictures set out in Lorenzo Valla's 1471 *Elegantiarum Linguae Latinae* ('Elegancies of the Latin Language'), Erasmus advocated combining diction derived from a range of writers to create a compound texture (Tunberg 2017: 238). In *Utopia* the lexicon, though highly classical, is varied, drawing on an array of authors. There is also a close linguistic and generic nexus between *Utopia* and Erasmus' *Moria* (1511). Both works are replete with puns, their very titles signposting as much (Erasmus' playing on More's surname); and—as Eric Nelson argues—the Greek puns in *Utopia* do not just entertain: they organize (E. Nelson 2004: 20). The two works belong to an ancient genre of paradoxical humour inspired by Horace, who promoted the combination of pleasure and profit, and by Lucian, who advanced the notion of 'jesting out the truth' (McCutcheon 1983: 21; Goldhill 2002: 48, 60–107). Elizabeth McCutcheon has done more than many to alert readers to the fine texture of *Utopia*'s Latin, and the degree to which it embodies the serio-ludic (playfully serious) mode so prominent in Erasmus' *Moria*. She demonstrates how the prolific use of litotes—affirmation created by the negation of its opposite—helped to form a complex mindset that could more readily perceive ambiguities and paradox (McCutcheon 1977). Clarence Miller also illustrates how a tension of opposites (capturing an opposition of real and fantastical) is present in the composition of More's Latin sentences which range from the simple and brief to the labyrinthine, regularly going beyond what ordinary syntax can bear (Miller and Harp

---

[5] For Erasmus' involvement in the genesis and early printings of *Utopia*, see Taylor in this volume.
[6] See Zurcher in this volume.

2011: 11, 16). The very style of the Latin reveals close affinity with Erasmus and a hermeneutic which raised rather than answered questions (Skinner 1987).

A further dimension of Latin is the issue of insiders and outsiders. Scholars observe that, despite considerable interaction between Latin and vernacularity, Latin carried a different set of cultural signifiers to the vernacular (Burke 2004: 43–60). Many early modern texts written in Latin evince acute awareness of being composed in a tongue which could only be read by someone with Latin. Often such texts overtly included sections of Greek at points of greater sensitivity. The question of who did or did not understand the ancient languages was a live one in the sixteenth century, but *Utopia* foregrounded it in a noticeably explicit way. Hythloday, the fictional protagonist, portentously stressed that he 'was not untutored [*non indoctus*] in the Latin tongue but very well versed [*doctissimus*] in Greek' (More 1965a: 48–49). Many of the puns and place names could only be fully appreciated by those with Latin and Greek. In the text itself there is a joke about a friar's poor grasp of Latin (further highlighted in a marginal note), as he is depicted in Book One as misusing *zelus* (zeal) as if it were a neuter noun like *scelus* (crime), instead of using *zelum* (84–85). The Greek sentence at the end of Rhenanus' letter (where the witty fabrication of More's *Utopia* is openly acknowledged) encapsulates what is implicit in the whole *Utopia* project: namely that to read *Utopia* 'properly', Latin and Greek are required (12–13). Indeed, More later seems to have opposed *Utopia* being translated into English, which would have made it accessible to a wider, less learned readership (Logan 2011: 51).

Another fundamental aspect of *Utopia* is the ebullient display of Latinity. The presence of so many paratextual letters is a good index of this since, as scholars persuasively argue, epistles were often where oratory was most utilized (Knight and Tilg 2015: 128; Glomski 2017). Indeed, these very paratexts draw express attention to the quality of More's Latin. Gerard Geldenhouwer's poem refers to More as *disertus* ('eloquent') (More 1965a: 30); Giles's letter to Busleyden refers to More as a *homine facundissimo* ('man of great eloquence') (20–21); Budé's letter asserts that if Hythloday was the 'discoverer' of the island, More was the adorner, bestowing his style and polish of diction (*stilo orationeque*) (12–13). One possible reason why *Utopia* went through four editions within two years is because linguistic precision was deemed of such consequence: in each publication, minor corrections were made and forms were finessed (More 1965a: clxxxv–ix). Yet, as natural a language as Latin was for More and as exemplary as many adjudged his Latin (More 1978a: 248; 1965a: 579), the notion of good Latin style remained contested. Renaissance Latin continued to define itself throughout the sixteenth century, not least through a concerted repudiation of medieval practices and continual negotiation with the Latin of Christianity. The Latinity of *Utopia* had detractors, and a French humanist, Germaine de Brie (Brixius), in a long poem, *Antimorus*, questioned aspects of More's use of Latin, the deliberate use of the omega ω in the title—which looks like a backside—adding further insult (Marius 1984: 245–246). Brixius reproached More for a range of solecisms and barbarisms, including, for example, his use of the reflexive rather than a personal pronoun, a common feature of medieval Latin (More 1965a: 346, 416, 418). This was a high-level assault launched by one proficient Latinist against another, serving to highlight not just the contemporary importance of the use of Latin, but also how it was used in actual practice.

Latin was a language which the most powerful institutions across Europe—Church or State—employed to mediate their affairs.[7] As such, the language had strong associations with authority, and was imbued with considerable prestige. It followed that for individuals versed in the tongue, distinction in Latin might guarantee reputation and even status: a practised Latin style won credit not just for the author but for his/her place of origin too (Shrank 2004: 77). Latin was integral to self-fashioning and could be the way to secure advancement, as More had done in 1509, presenting a version of his Latin epigrams to the newly installed Henry VIII (E. Nelson 2004: 156). Authors seeking opportunities on the international stage also naturally used Latin. As the *Utopia* project would also eloquently demonstrate—a theme developed in the rest of this chapter—this applied equally to printers of works in Latin. The development of printing and humanism mutually influenced one another. The very idea of print played a powerful role in shaping rhetorical expressions of the humanist project which in turn could advertise the printing house's own refined partiality for classical learning. As successive regimes placed the comprehensive restoration of the ancient tongues at the centre of their programmes of education and cultural renewal, they also created new opportunities for those competent in them. With that development, however, and something More could not have predicted, Greek and Latin became increasingly bound up with certain political and religious ideologies, and their use became considerably more controversial as the Reformation progressed.

All the factors outlined here must be taken into account if the contexts for and impulses of later Latin editions of the *Utopia* are to be fully comprehended. Each of the areas discussed above can be related to any number of later Latin editions which this chapter now considers.

Latin in Subsequent Editions

Latin was an important mode of exchange and communication up until the eighteenth century. It should perhaps come as no surprise that More's *Utopia* continued to be published in Latin centuries after its original composition. Although neither More nor the coterie of friends involved in the first four editions participated in publications of *Utopia* after November 1518, a steady stream of Latin editions (often in clusters) went through the printing presses from 1519 to 1936: thirty-one in total, produced across Europe, from the Low Countries to Germany, Oxford to Paris.[8] There were many translations of *Utopia* into a multiplicity of languages (as this volume testifies),

---

[7] For some insights into this phenomenon in England, see McDiarmid 2007.
[8] See Berschin 2005: 377–387 and the International Thomas More Bibliography for *Utopia*: https://essentialmore.org/bibliographies last accessed Apr. 2018.

but certain places and people opted to retain the Latin, sometimes in parallel with vernacular editions.

Often the only information we have about these later Latin editions is the place of publication and identity of the printer, publisher, or bookseller. Sometimes the person financing the enterprise is named, occasionally the dedicatee or, thanks to an inscription, the owner of an individual copy. Although much can be inferred from the choice of title and paratexts selected, we can also glean insights from the arrangement of the Latin text itself, the aesthetics of form, choice of original Latin version or versions on which a particular edition relies, and inclusion of other texts besides *Utopia*. Accordingly, some of the analysis of these editions belongs to a broader history of the book.

In the vast majority of cases, the Latin text of *Utopia* deviates in no way from the earliest editions. Unlike translations into other languages, what requires explanation in the evolution of the Latin *Utopia* is not so much permutation as a pattern of stability, ironically often at key moments of historical flux. In the few instances where the Latin text of *Utopia* did undergo change, for example when sections of text were omitted, certain developments such as the Reformation must be confronted. In such cases, the Latin of *Utopia* could take on new nuances.

The next section reviews Latin editions adhering closely to the original *Utopia*. They are not discussed in chronological order but in ways that best illustrate the reasons for, and significance of, preserving the Latin. As I demonstrate, there was enormous variety in the times and places where subsequent Latin editions were published, but preserving the Latin appreciably reduced the cultural distance from the original author's milieu. Many of these Latin editions retained the conception and ideology of the original work more effectively than did vernacular translations. Indeed, sometimes the connotations of Latin underpinning the earliest editions were augmented and extended in later Latin editions.

Latin Communities and Internationalism

The original *Utopia* venture transcended national borders. Likewise, the essence of *Utopia*'s subsequent Latin dissemination could be said to be a European one. The international reach of the later Latin editions was extensive, around which those educated in Latin could coalesce. This section outlines some trends of this internationalism, not just identifying key locations of publication but also examining the cast of its Latin readership.

Some of the main hotbeds for publishing Latin *Utopias* were those where humanism had a pre-existing ascendancy. It is surely no coincidence that, of the eight sixteenth-century Latin editions published after More's death in 1535, six emerged from centres that had printed *Utopia* in his lifetime. Latin *Utopias* were published in Louvain in 1548 and

1565–6 (when a clutch of four appeared) and an edition was printed in Basel in 1563.[9] It is true that family ties connected these later editions with earlier ones: Louvain 1548 was financed by Arnold Birckmann's widow and the brother-in-law of Arnold's own brother, Franz, was Johannes Grapheus (de Schrijver), whose brother Cornelius authored a paratextual poem; Basel 1563 was printed by Froben's grandson, Nicolaus Episcopius (Roggen 2008: 16–17). However, Louvain and Basel were also locations pivotal in the promotion of Latin more generally. In Louvain, the Collegium Trium Linguarum ('College of the Three Languages'), founded in 1517 under Busleyden's patronage, helped foster the revival of the Literae Humaniores, particularly Latin, Greek, and Hebrew. Basel was another important humanist centre, not least because of its printing trade: Basel's printers boasted a large share of the European Latin book market (Weil Baker 1999: 302–303). Latin editions were repeatedly published in areas with colleges or universities whose primary business was promulgating Latin and Greek. A 1555 edition appeared in Cologne, a city where another college with a humanist focus, the Tricoronatum, had recently been established (1551); here again, as Vibeke Roggen (2008: 16) points out, its publication by the 'heirs of Birckmann' connects this edition with earlier *Utopias*. The 1663 Oxford edition published by William Hall had clear connections to that university: although Hall was not formally appointed by Oxford University Press, John Fell, one of the press's most famous executives, oversaw the edition (Gadd et al. 2013: 1.394), and two copies of this edition contain autographs of student owners—Will Vesey, undergraduate of Merton College, and Nathaniel Bridges, demy scholar at Magdalen—indicating the likely consumers of this print run.[10] The Foulis brothers who were responsible for printing the 1750 Glasgow edition were formally appointed as printers of Glasgow University (D. Murray 1913: 22). One brother, Andrew, studied classical languages at Glasgow, and many of the Foulis press's books were produced for scholars. As with Thierry Martens, *Utopia*'s first printer who provided many of the teaching manuals for the Collegium Trium Linguarum (Kirwan and Mullins 2015: 278), a good number of the later Latin *Utopias* were intended for a university market where Latin was in common currency.

While the Latin fraternities of higher education may have been a natural forum for Latin *Utopias*, some were destined for the nobility. This is evident not just from dedications (discussed later) but also owners' signatures. The manuscript signature of John Lumley (1534–1609), the Earl of Arundel's son-in-law, appears on the front page of a 1563 Latin edition from Basel, for example.[11] Consumers of *Utopia* were not, of course, always its readers: some were simply collectors. However, as the catalogue for Lumley's library observes, the linguistic range of his collection was narrow, suggesting that this aristocrat knew and read Latin. His collection reflects a more general attitude of the

---

[9] More 1548b, 1565a–b and 1566b–c, and 1563 respectively.
[10] These copies are held at Lincoln College (shelf mark o.9.33) and Balliol College (shelf mark 30.a.118) respectively.
[11] This copy is held by the British Library.

nobility who still regarded Latin as the language of culture and looked on its own vernacular as unworthy of the greatest minds (Jayne and Johnson 1956: 12).

University hubs and socially elite circles in Europe were not the only spheres where Latin thrived. Many Latin editions of *Utopia* emanated from cosmopolitan regions where Latin was dominant because of international connections. Frankfurt am Main was one, a vital outpost of the European book trade. Although there would be no university there until 1914, the city was fast becoming a crucial intellectual centre and wielded formidable international pull (Weidhass 2007: 43–44). It was not simply a key publishing city: many, including professors from a vast range of universities, came on buying trips to the twice-yearly book fair, a literary mecca not only within Germany but also for the intelligentsia of Europe (Weidhass 2007: 13). A Latin ode composed in 1574 by the Parisian humanist and printer Estienne (Henricus Stephanus) drew an explicit analogy between the book fair and classical Athens, describing the Muses summoning people to the books there (Weidhass 2007: 47–48). Three Latin editions of *Utopia* were published in Frankfurt (1601, 1670, and 1689), the latter two coinciding with an explosion in publishing in Frankfurt following the Thirty Years War (Weidhass 2007: 66). The Frankfurt Book Fair was also significant for a good number of other Latin *Utopias*. Franz, one of the Birckmanns (the family overseeing the publication of the 1548 Louvain and 1555 Cologne editions), was active in the great Frankfurt Book Fair and, as Roggen (2008: 16) suggests, may well have sold *Utopia* there for Froben. Johann Krafft the Elder of the Wittenberg Press—which produced a 1591 Latin *Utopia*—regularly attended the fair. The prominent Frankfurt bookseller Peter Kopff, who was commissioned by the Frankfurt Council to compile catalogue lists for the fair, financed three Latin editions of *Utopia*, printed in Frankfurt (1601), Hanover (1613), and Milan (1620).

The physical production of various Latin *Utopias* points to a relatively specific market of Latin readers. The original *Utopia* was never a very 'grand' book and even in its first incarnation it took a relatively modest form in terms of size, presentation, and binding. This was also true of later Latin *Utopias*. It was evidently not a luxury item intended for decorative purposes, to enhance the look of some opulent library. Copies of Latin *Utopias* tended to be workmanlike productions of a practical size (Roggen 2008: 19), bespeaking consumers who purchased copies with the express purpose of reading them, perhaps while on the go. At the same time, the commercial profile of the book is telling. To take the 1750 Glasgow *Utopia* as an example about which we have some concrete information: this was printed on paper of medium to good quality; wholesale it cost 1s. 6d.—slightly more than renting an unfurnished room in London for a week or buying a periwig—and retail 2s. 6d. (Gaskell 1986: 149).[12] This was no mean sum: only individuals of a certain level of financial security could justify its purchase, and there would certainly be little sense in someone without Latin investing in a copy.

---

[12] For the price comparison, see https://www.oldbaileyonline.org/static/Coinage.jsp#costofliving and www.oldbaileyonline.org, OA17501003, accessed 21 Aug. 2018.

Ludic Dimensions and Erasmus

One of the striking qualities of the original *Utopia* and its paratexts was the paradoxical humour underlying the narrative. However, over time, many versions of More's *Utopia* lost that ludic spirit so prominent in Erasmus and the classical literary tradition which he drew on; instead, *Utopia* became associated purely with an unproblematized ideal (Logan 2011: 162). In recent times, the work tends to be talked about in terms of the 'utopian' genre of speculative fiction that it spawned, as opposed to its relationship with Erasmian burlesque and classical paradigms of serio-satire and laughing gnomology. However, regarding the later Latin editions, such considerations may not be ignored, for many of them explicitly focus on the jocose-serious aspect of the original *Utopia* and even amplify it.

The most important example of the continuation of this tradition is the Hanover edition of 1619 (reprinted in Frankfurt in 1670). This edition incorporated *Utopia*, with many of the original paratexts, into a much larger body of works: a fantastically eccentric cornucopia of almost 700 tracts in two tomes. The editor of this compendium was Caspar Dornau, a Silesian orator and scholar of antiquity, philosophy, and medicine (Seidel 1994). The short title of the volume was *Amphitheatrum Sapientiae Socraticae Joco-seriae* ('The Amphitheatre of Joco-Serious Socratic Wisdom') but the longer title noted that, within the work, 'matters considered by people as either vile or vulgar are vindicated and decorated through the pleading of the pen' ('res, aut pro vilibus vulgo aut damnosis habitae, styli patrocinio vindicantur, exornantur'). This paradoxical theme runs through the collection, which includes (in verse and prose) many comical and satirical pieces that praise the unpraiseworthy, eulogizing animals such as the louse, body parts like the feet, painful physical conditions such as gout, and vices. In addition to these pseudo-encomia, Dornau juxtaposed excerpts of texts that were more serious in their purport—texts on, for example, Christian symbols such as the dove, palm leaf, rose, pearl, and oyster. Section headings under which Dornau arranged his texts effectively constitute a series of condensed paradoxes, with titles including *Nox et Somnus* ('Night and Sleep'), *Omnia* followed by *Aliquid*, then *Nihil* and *Nemo* ('All', 'Something', 'Nothing', 'No one'). Dornau explained that he had employed Socrates' name in his title to refer to the playful philosophical questioning of false opinions (Kivistö 2009: 29). Lucian is well represented in the collection. A quote from Horace's *Satires* on its title page—'ridentem dicere verum, quid vetat?' ('What is to prevent one from telling the truth as he laughs?', 1.1.24)—similarly captures the paradoxographical tradition of which Erasmus' *Moria* and More's *Utopia* were chief exponents. Indeed, in part two of the volume, Dornau included Erasmus' *Moria* in Latin under the heading *Stultitia* ('Stupidity').

Latin editions of *Utopia*, from the earliest to some of the latest, preserved a close affiliation with the tradition of playful profundity. The final Latin *Utopia* in More's lifetime, the 1519 Florence edition, published the work alongside More and Erasmus' translations of Lucian, although—as Roggen notes—this edition also had a distinctly political focus (Roggen 2008: 24; cf. Taylor in this volume). An edition printed in Paris and London in 1777 advertised on its title page the literary species it considered *Utopia* belonged to: *Desiderii & Thomae Mori Joco-Seria* ('the Serious Joking of Desiderius [Erasmus] and Thomas More'). Arguably too, the physical dimensions of many Latin *Utopias* epitomized the levity of More's work. A high proportion are very small. Some— and these include the editions of 1629, 1631, and 1663 from Cologne, Amsterdam, and Oxford respectively—are so minuscule—24mo, the size of an average playing card—that they immediately elicit a smile. They also marry jollity and gravity beautifully: a jeu d'esprit on the outside and deadly serious social satire on the inside. As Peter McCullough observed about the 1663 edition (a copy of which was owned by the Oxford student Vesey), a 'mind-boggling' skill was involved in typesetting this tiny book about 'nowhere', in which every single letter and punctuation mark represented a single piece of cast-metal delicately chosen from a type-case.[13] This was yet another way of magnifying the ludic timbre of the earliest editions. *Utopia* in Latin was, it seems, a much more faithful upholder of the witty paradoxicality of the work—as baffling as it was instructive—than many translations could ever be.

In many ways reintegrating More's *Utopia* back into the serio-ludic genre was part of a broader effort of the Latin editions to reassert the nexus between More's *Utopia* and Erasmus, especially the latter's *Moria*. In its original incarnation, *Utopia* was, as scholars have often noted, inextricably bound up with the broader Erasmian initiative. The year 1516 marked a point of maximum convergence of the trajectories of More and Erasmus, the time when their opinions and sentiments were most in harmony (More 1965a: xxvi). It is difficult to understand *Utopia* as anything other than a literary complement of Erasmus' *Moria*. However, as a direct consequence of the Reformation, as early as the mid-sixteenth century, many commentators began to minimize the relationship between the two men. Erasmus became associated with the reform movement; for those keen to present More as a Catholic martyr, a disassociation from Erasmus, whose orthodoxy was so suspect that all his writings were placed on the *Index of Prohibited Books*, was imperative. Despite this, many Latin editions maintained the connection. This was perhaps partly because More's Latin, with all its puns and aphorisms, was too self-evidently implicated in the Erasmian approach. Perhaps it was also bound up with a struggle by More's heirs over his posthumous reputation, with some wanting to present him simply as a humanist (as well as a reformer) in reaction to a recusant tradition which repudiated More's connection with Erasmus (McConica 1964).

The Oxford press which produced the 1663 Latin edition certainly viewed the work as the literary sibling of Erasmus' *Moria*: they reprinted the *Moria* in Latin the same year (Gadd et al. 2013: 1.394). It was, however, in the 1777 Paris–London edition (the *Joco-Seria* collection discussed above) that the sense of this pairing was most forcefully

---

[13] This was a bibliographic piece written for the webpages of Lincoln College, Oxford, and was only temporarily available.

conveyed. The publisher, Anne-Gabriel Meusnier de Querlon, whose initials appear on the first page, decided to combine in one volume Erasmus' *Moria* and (following that) *Utopia*. This alliance was explicitly discussed in the preface. De Querlon explained (in Latin): 'As soon as we had taken in hand that playful piece, *Praise of Folly*, written by Erasmus to be committed to the most elegant typeface, it was our intention to add the related narrative about Utopia by Thomas More' (More 1777: A1r). He described their writings as *perquam affinia* ('exceedingly allied') and *ut aiunt homogeneia* ('of the same species, as they say', A1v).[14] The volume also included a letter from Erasmus to More and many of the paratexts of the original *Utopia*, which de Querlon thought were composed almost entirely for humorous effect ('omnia fere composita ad iocum', A1v). There were other interesting dimensions of the Erasmus–More coupling that this Latin edition accentuated (discussed below), but the oxymoronic quality of the pieces was a vital one: at the end of de Querlon's *monitum editoris* ('admonition of the editor') was a Latin epigram by the Welsh epigrammatist John Owen (c.1564–c.1622/8) which juxtaposed notions of wisdom and stupidity: 'You first, Erasmus, wrote a Praise of Folly. That folly shows your intelligence' ('Stultitiae laudem scripsisti primus, Erasme: | Indicat ingenium Stultitia ipsa tuum').[15]

CLASSICAL HUMANISM, LATINITY: RENEWAL AND PRESTIGE

The original *Utopia* was in many ways an expression of classical humanism, conveyed in no small part by the Latin (and Greek) medium. The use of these languages in subsequent print runs of the *Utopia* was not just charmingly archaizing; it also constituted an attempt to reconnect with More's text. It also evoked a Renaissance enthusiasm for the culture and language of antiquity, and all its potential for regeneration.

It was often printers and editors who promoted this return to the ancients. All subsequent Latin editions continued to use the Greek font in those places where they reproduced materials from the original version that used Greek. The vast majority retained the paratextual letters and poems, literary forms redolent of the ancient world. Erasmus' praise of the Aldine Press and subsequent depiction of Froben's Basel Press as a crucible of humanist values and Renaissance scholarship established the ideal of the humanist printer (P. White 2014: 173, 180). Several printing enterprises which later published Latin *Utopias* followed suit. The printer of the 1563 Basel edition, Nicholas Bischoff, publishing under the name of Episcopius (meaning something like 'overseer' in Greek), specialized in humanist authors, like Poliziano (1454–94), whom he felt had

---

[14] *homogeneia* is technically a Greek term.
[15] The oxymoronic effect is possibly further heightened through the displacement of *-mus* ('mouse' in Latin) from Erasmus' name (now in the vocative) to the end of *primus* ('first').

helped restore the literature of ancient Greece and Rome (Coroleu 2014: 1). His edition of *Utopia* constitutes a veritable showcase of classicism. It was one of the first editions to integrate *Utopia* into a larger collection of More's works, in this case under the title *Lucubrationes*, a term meaning 'work undertaken at night by lamp-light', utilized initially by Cicero, but later made intellectually fashionable by Erasmus. *Utopia* appeared at the head of the volume, followed by More's *Progymnasmata* (Greek epigrams with translations into Latin by More and William Lily); the *Epigrammata*; translations from Lucian; More's *Declamatio Lucianicae respondens*; and certain *Epistulae* (starting with More's letter to Martin Dorp which defended Erasmus' use of Greek and was, in effect, an apology for humanism).

Nineteenth- and twentieth-century Latin editions were also attentive to the classical grain of the original *Utopia*, not least as a means to validate the very discipline of Classics. This was particularly true of English reprints. The 1895 Oxford *Utopia* was edited by J. H. Lupton, schoolmaster at St Paul's School (the first school in sixteenth-century England to teach Greek), and dedicated to Frederick Walker, the school's High Master, and Frederick Seebohm, author of the *Oxford Reformers* (1867), a celebrated disquisition on the lives of John Colet, Erasmus, and More. In the preface, Lupton commented that, in assembling this edition, the same care had been taken as he would have applied to a classical author, and he lauded *Utopia* as a 'true child of the Renaissance' (More 1895a: vii). *Utopia* was here central to an attempt to assert a close relationship between a public school and Oxford University based on a mutual commitment to classical learning. The 1910 London edition similarly celebrated the classical thrust of *Utopia*. A. C. Guthkelch, who wrote the introduction, clearly understood *Utopia* as the perfect expression of a Renaissance recovery of the Classics: 'During More's lifetime the world seemed to turn over in its sleep and open its eyes for a moment: it saw in antiquity a forgotten literature full of beauty and intelligence [...] then it went to sleep again' (More 1910a: xxi). He also highlighted More's love of Greek and stated that the most interesting part of *Utopia* was Book One where Platonic dialogues were imitated, 'set before us with some of the skill of Plato' (xxi, xxiv).

An important aspect of this nurturing of classical humanism was attention to the Latinity of the text, its accuracy, and even authenticity. The issue of accuracy is often reflected in statements on the front cover to the effect that the Latin text has been improved and corrected. The 1563 edition claimed it was *ab innumeris mendis repurgatae* ('purged of numerous errors'). The two Amsterdam editions of 1629 and 1631, Cologne edition of 1629, and Hamburg edition of 1752 all declared their texts *a mendis vindicata* ('set free from errors'). Of course, this goal of producing the most accurate form of Latin was important to the initial *Utopia* project, which in part went through so many editions because of Erasmus' desire to eliminate errors and perfect the Latin form.

The authenticity of Latin was another crucial consideration in many later Latin editions. One way to achieve this was through the choice of text: while many Latin editions broadly followed the November 1518 edition,[16] some expressly pledged

---

[16] More 1965a: cxc–cxci; however, I have noticed a number follow the post-1629 habit of using the superlative *iucundissime* rather than *dulcissime* (referring to Giles) at the end of More's letter.

allegiance to the first edition of 1516. These are the editions from Wittenberg 1591, Berlin 1895, and London 1910. Each uses the same title as 1516: *Libellus vere aureus nec minus salutaris quam festivus de optimo reip. Statu*, even reproducing the same layout, along with explicit references to 'Peter Aegidius' and 'Thedoricus Martinus', as on the 1516 title page.[17] Roggen (2008: 17) surmises that the Wittenberg printer or bookseller had obtained the 1516 edition. She says no more, but further explanation is surely necessary, since it is clear that the workshop also had another edition to hand, as the resultant edition included Budé's letter (not in the 1516 parerga). It is more probable that in all these cases editorial decisions were taken to pursue an *ad fontes* return to the initial source of the Latin. The Berlin edition certainly placed considerable emphasis on its dissemination of the first edition, the editio princeps.

For some later Latin editions, the best way to retrieve the most pristine form of Latin involved a more methodical approach of comparison and collation. The Paris–London 1777 version boasted on its title page that it was a 'work authentically printed using older editions of better note that have been collated' ('opus sincere expressum ex antiquioribus & melioris notae Editionibus collatis'), adding this had been undertaken 'with care and exertion' (*cura et studio*). The Berlin 1895 reprint was the first Latin edition to include a formal commentary about different versions. However, the edition where philological focus is most apparent was assembled by Delcourt in Paris, 1936. Delcourt was a classicist, interested primarily in philology; this training is very evident in her edition which places great emphasis on the Latin style and diction. As stated in the preface, she treated the earliest versions effectively as manuscripts, her choice of text wholly determined by *règles classiques* (classical rules). Her agenda is nicely summarized in her prefatory comment that 'grammatical notes are indispensable if one wants to grasp the movement of this language that is still alive, but on the verge of ossification' ('De notes grammaticales sont indispensables si l'on veut saisir le movement de cette langue encore vivante, mais a la veille de se scléroser'). She also devoted an appendix entirely to reviewing More's Latin vocabulary.

In other editions, attention to the Latin was implicated in much broader programmes of cultural renewal. One interesting example is the 1750 Glasgow edition, published by Robert and Andrew Foulis: a clear manifestation of the Scottish Enlightenment, and more particularly the Glasgow Enlightenment, animated in the main by the university there (Hook and Sher 1995: 11).[18] The Foulis university press—established by Robert in 1741—was reputed to be one of the finest printing houses in Europe. The brothers were deeply influenced by Frances Hutcheson (1694–1746), a brilliant Latinist, moralist, and leading figure in the Glasgow Enlightenment, who believed that 'the culture of the heart was the main end of all moral instruction' (Hook and Sher 1995: 45). The Foulis brothers shared this vision, and their great achievement was translating into print the values of the Hutchesonian Enlightenment (Hook and Sher 1995: 13). They published

---

[17] Berlin 1895 and London 1910 editions also reproduce the alphabet of *Utopia* (Fig. 1.1) and the 1910 edition the 1518 map of *Utopia* (Fig. 5.1).

[18] Compare Pin y Soler's Catalan project, discussed by Johnson in this volume.

a preponderance of Latin and Greek classics, many of which are listed at the back of their *Utopia* (Fairfull-Smith 2001: 41; D. Murray 1913: 9–10). They were the first to publish Greek in Glasgow (the 1743 edition of Demetrius' *De Elocutione*) and prided themselves on their scholarly approach, travelling to continental Europe to procure classical manuscripts. The list of Greek publications at the end of their *Utopia* emphasizes the 'pure Greek' they have used. The brothers' immersion in this world surely influenced their change of name from Faulls (or perhaps Faulds) to the more classically formulated 'Foulis', derived from the Greek term *phullon* or Latin *folium*, meaning 'leaf' but also (befitting two printers) the 'leaf of a page'.

The Foulis brothers' fastidiousness with proofreading and production won many plaudits; attention to detail was certainly on show in their *Utopia*. The use of the 'Scotch Roman' typeface was unique and sophisticated. They were also meticulous about formatting. Close comparison of this edition with others points to some very attentive reading of the Latin. Any medieval-sounding spellings, for example *negocia* and *precio*, are amended to fit more classical orthography (*negotia*; *pretio*).[19] Punctuation is amended, and certain phrases revisited: for example in Book Two, '[volumina] non infinita sufficiunt' ('their infinite volumes are not sufficient') has been changed to 'tantum non infinita non sufficiunt' ('practically infinite, but not sufficient'), which makes the sense clearer and more compelling on the ear. The Foulis' reputation for editing can be gleaned from the fact that the 1777 Paris–London edition explicitly cited theirs (A1v) and follows its lead in certain places (for example, in omitting Giles's letter to Busleyden).[20]

The Foulis' preoccupation with moral regeneration through linguistic purity was further evident in an English translation of *Utopia* published by Robert Foulis in 1743, seven years before the 1750 Latin version. This was a reprint of Gilbert Burnet's 1684 translation.[21] Burnet was a Scot and, as the volume proudly declared, 'Sometime Professor of Divinity at the University of Glasgow', two factors which surely attracted Robert to this text. But Burnet was also a distinguished linguist, fluent in Latin, Greek, and Hebrew, as well as Dutch and French. One wonders whether the new title given to *Utopia* in this edition—'A Philosophical Romance'—alludes in part to the Roman tongue, Latin: the root of the word 'romance' is *Romanicus*, meaning 'of Roman style'. A good portion of Robert's preface focuses on language, the theme with which it begins: 'There is no way of writing', he stated, 'so proper for the refining and polishing a Language as the translating of books into it, if he that undertakes it has a competent skill of the one Tongue and is a master of the other' (More 1743: 3). He then proceeded to celebrate the purification of

---

[19] More 1750: 1, 42. Some of these more classical adaptations first appear in Louvain 1548 but not all (for example, Louvain 1548 retains *syncerus* over the classical *sincerus*).

[20] It is unclear why this would have been omitted given the letter's clear humanist orientation; one possibility is the fact that in this epistle Giles claimed a significant role in the work's creation, and it may be that its eighteenth-century editors deemed this too confusing.

[21] For more on Burnet's translation, see Withington in this volume.

English that had occurred in recent years, noting, 'our language has fewer faults, and is more natural and proper than it was ever any time before' (5).

The Foulis publication of Burnet's translation is interesting for another reason: Burnet's preface—reproduced in the Foulis edition—raises important questions about the relationship between Latin and the vernacular. Robert made an explicit connection between classical languages and improving the vernacular, declaring that 'the French took no ill method when they intended to reform and beautify their language in setting their best writers on work to translate the Greek and Latin authors into it' (More 1743: 3–4). Tom Deneire has done much to draw attention to the complex interplay between Latin and the vernacular. He astutely highlights the paradox that the very rediscovery of Rome's linguistic refinement served to boost the development of the mother tongue (Deneire 2014: 1; cf. Castor and Cave 1984). The Foulis editions of the English and Latin *Utopia* might then be understood as allies in a common cause rather than competing discourses: both belonged to an overarching mission of cultivation; each worked to enhance linguistic and intellectual development in Scotland.

The reformative potential of More's *Utopia* was also relevant in a period of heightened national consciousness in the Netherlands: the Dutch Revolt from Habsburg domination. In the final stages of this great struggle for regional independence, two Latin editions (1629 and 1631) were published in Amsterdam, the most dynamic urban centre in the Netherlands and probably in Western Europe at the time.[22] It is very probable that these more recent *Utopias*—and the spate of vernacular editions printed there 1629–34—were expressions of a new national confidence. As Ronny Spaans and Terence Cave (2008a: 108) suggest, the republic depicted in *Utopia* became newly relevant for an emerging Dutch state. It may be possible to flesh this point out further, however. The act of reproducing the Latin *Utopia* might be a way to affirm local standing by staking the Low Countries' claim to the intellect, humanism, and fame of More and Erasmus, but Latin also offered an opportunity to assert international worth. Latin was useful for a small nation because it enabled that state to compete on the same footing as much larger nations with their emerging vernaculars (IJsewijn 2017: 4). Many scholars attest to the flowering of Latin and Greek that coincided with the Dutch Golden Age, which was itself a classical construct. As had been the case in the earliest phase of *Utopia* a century before, the Dutch emphasis on Latin in the early seventeenth century was bound up with both an investment in the idea of Europe and a deep sense of national pride (Deneire 2014: 275).

Individuals as well as regions could benefit from an association with the prestige and rhetorical flair of Latin. It was the Latin language of the original *Utopia* that initially signalled its importance to statesmen and governors, and Latin was a language via which patronage from such figures could be secured (McCutcheon 1983: 10). The negotiation of power and status in early modern Europe is an obvious dimension of some later Latin *Utopias*. The 1620 Milan edition is an obvious candidate. The dedicatory epistle from

---

[22] The 1631 edition was an exact copy of the 1629, and almost certainly pirated.

the printer and editor of the volume, Giovan Battista Bidelli, to Giulio Arese, president of the Milan Estate, makes a clear bid for beneficence (T. Cave 2008c: 274–275; Roggen 2008: 28–30). The letter is highly rhetorical in style, but it also makes explicit the relationship between the elegant Latinity, morality, and administration of the state that *Utopia* represented. Another example is the dedication of the 1777 Paris–London Latin edition to Jean-Frédéric Phélypeaux, first Count Maurepas, an important minister in the French court, by then chief adviser to Louis XVI. The editor De Querlon similarly asserted that humanist notion of the strong and necessary bond between classical learning and politics, writing that he bestows this 'political fable' to a 'man most well informed by nature, fortune and, through experience, political knowledge [...] a most sage judge, and similarly most assiduous in good arts' ('Fabulam politicam, Viro scilicet a natura, fortuna, usu politica scientia instructissimo [...] sagacissimo aestimatori, bonarum itidem artium studiosissimo', More 1777: title page 4). Drawing on a paragon of ancient patronage, he also likened Phélypeaux to Maecenas 'of that golden age of literature [*aureae literarum aetatis*]' and 'a most zealous protector and patron of learned men [*acerrimo literatorum praesidio fautore*]'. In both these cases, Latin's capacity to win kudos, political recognition, and support was articulated and reinforced through republishing *Utopia*.

Latin *Utopias* and the Reformation

So far in this chapter, the broad argument has been that the later Latin editions tended to cleave to or build on the character of the original Latin versions and what that connoted. Some Latin editions, however, became embroiled not just in the subsequent 'mythologizing' of More but also in the turbulent religious conflicts of the Reformation. These were of course tensions that the original collaborators in *Utopia* could not have envisaged.

Utopia was from the very beginning a text that experienced constant revision through translation and the reinterpretation that new renderings necessarily entailed. The substance of the subsequent Latin versions, by contrast, hardly altered at all. The 1563 Basel edition took some liberties with the marginalia, but did not tamper with the main text. It was, however, during the Counter-Reformation that some Latin editions underwent more significant modification. Although the post-Tridentine Church admired More for his heroic defence of the faith and ultimately canonized him, he was not an unproblematic figure. Certainly, when it came to *Utopia*, specific proposals had to be either explained away or overlooked if his golden *libellus* was to be unequivocally approved (Manuel and Manuel 1979: 151). Much of Book Two concerns religion. The 1565–6 Louvain editions (which were included at the very start of More's *Opera* published in those years) bear the marks of active censorship. Judicious redactions were made not just to marginalia and paratexts—for example, Erasmus' letter to Froben was omitted (possibly because of Erasmus' dubious standing for Catholics)—but also to the main text. The editions state as much before Book One, to the effect that these works by More, at least when corrected (*ita correcta*), could be presented to the reading public since they could now bring 'piety and a not profane pleasure' (*pietatem et delectationem non irreligiosam*). Excised from Book One is the section where the dialogue arguably becomes most ribald, as a theologian friar ridicules priests and, mocked in turn, irascibly draws on Scripture but exposes his own ignorance by using the wrong form of the Latin word *zelus*.[23] Roggen (2008: 26) also notes the insertion of *nonnulli* ('some') to qualify Hythloday's claim that preachers are clever men who adjust Christ's doctrines to people's morals. These passages were clearly offensive to the man responsible for censoring this work, Johannes Hentenius, a Dominican friar and professor of theology at Louvain. Catholic orthodoxy mattered to Hentenius. He had produced a Latin Vulgate Bible for official use and would in 1556 be appointed a leading member of the Inquisition. Another interesting facet of the Louvain editions was the packaging of More's *Utopia* into an ostensibly Catholic volume. As Roggen notes, an important objective of the Louvain *Opera* was to present More as a martyr, an objective 'underlined through the decision to locate his epitaph as the first among his works' (Roggen 2008: 25). The complete works also, naturally, included More's *Expositio Passionis Domini* ('Treatise upon the Passion'), a work closely associated with More's imprisonment in 1535 and an affirmation of the *catholica fides* (Santinello 1977) and his responses to Luther: the page heading 'IN LUTHERUM' consequently appears across a good third of the volume.

Other Latin editions must also be considered through the prism of Reformation politics. The passage excised from the 1565–6 Louvain editions was also omitted from the 1629 edition (apparently) published in Cologne by a printer going by the name of 'Cornelius Egmond', the title page of which indicated that it had been *expurgata* ('cleansed') in accordance with the Index of Prohibited Books and the corrections suggested by the cardinal archbishop of Toledo (Roggen 2008: 26–27). The printer's almost certainly fictitious name has been connected to the well-known Amsterdam printer Willem Blaeu. Indeed, this book shared the same form as the Amsterdam Latin edition of the same year that was definitely printed by Blaeu, with the exception of the omitted section. The sort of books Blaeu specialized in reveals a deep sympathy for the Jesuit cause. Forty-five of the fifty-six books (over 80 per cent) published by Blaeu were by Jesuits: thirty-four by the German Jesuit Jeremias Drexel; eleven by Robert Bellarmine, Italian Jesuit and cardinal of the Catholic Church (Begheyn 2014: 44). Jesuits, in particular, saw a spiritual bond between the brilliance of Latin in its purest form and its singular role as the language of the Church. In Reformed Amsterdam complaints were lodged to the city council in 1626–7 about the printing of such books (Begheyn 2014: 9). It was perhaps not then by chance that the 1629 edition of *Utopia* as amended along distinctly Catholic lines was given a fraudulent Cologne imprint by Blaeu. It seems likely that this 1629 'Cologne' edition was meant as a back-up measure to

---

[23] The omitted passage runs from *caeterum Theologus* to *nosque dimisit* (More 1965a: 82–84).

elude the Amsterdam authorities in the event that the Amsterdam edition did not make it past the censors.

In contrast to the Dutch printers of Catholic orientation who brought the Latin *Utopias* to press, the vernacular editions of *Utopia* published in the Netherlands at the same time as these Latin ones were much more 'Calvinist in tenor' (Spaans and Cave 2008a: 107). An association of the vernacular with Reformed circles and Latin with Catholics might be a natural conclusion here; Latin did, after all, become the language of the universal Roman Catholic Church in the Counter-Reformation, and the Jesuit movement became one of the most conspicuous guardians of Latin. However, as neo-Latin scholarship is now increasingly contending, such an oversimplification needs qualification (Waquet 2001: 78; Burke 1991: 27 ff.). Reformed religion was not a world without Latin, and many Protestants, committed as they were to rejecting Latin in the Church, were often better Latinists than the Catholics who were committed to maintaining it (Burke 1991: 24). In the case of *Utopia*, moreover, several Latin editions were produced by Protestants for Protestants. This includes the 1591 Wittenberg edition, from the printing house of Johann Krafft and his younger brother, who became the most important Reformation printers of the sixteenth century, Philip Melanchthon's writings comprising the bulk of their output.[24]

As Hugh Trevor-Roper reminds us, More's image was firmly divided by the politics of the Reformation, More being adopted by both Catholics and Protestants (1996: 17–18, and passim). Yet it is also possible to detect in the Latin *Utopias* traces of intra-confessional rivalry within Protestantism itself. The editor of the 1601 Frankfurt edition, Eberhard von Weyhe, had been expelled from Lutheran Wittenberg in 1591—the very year a Latin *Utopia* was published there—on account of his Calvinist leanings (Roggen 2008: 28). Ten years later, installed in Frankfurt, von Weyhe was instrumental in a republication. On the front of this edition was written the Latin 'nunc tandem bibliotaphis subreptum' ('now at last snatched from the graves of books'), possibly an assertion that this work was now being reappropriated for the Calvinist cause. Von Weyhe's name also appeared on the title page next to that of Maurice, Landgrave of Hesse, the ruler to whom it was dedicated. By 1605 Maurice had shifted allegiance from Lutheranism to Calvinism, and it is just possible that *Utopia* in Latin constituted a stepping stone in that journey of conversion: after all, many of the Utopians' religious practices accorded with Calvinism, including the abolition of aural confession, priestly celibacy, and worshipping images, as well as its promotion of electing priests. *Utopia* would again move through Calvinist channels in 1619 via the Wechel Press in Frankfurt: a Huguenot exile printing house which developed into one of the most important interfaces within the communication network of international Calvinism (Evans 1975).

It is perhaps unsurprising that the Latin text of *Utopia* should be co-opted by different religious confessions. Latin as a language retained deep links with religion throughout the early modern period and retained a sacrosanctity less available to the vernacular. Be

---

[24] The younger brother took charge in 1590.

that as it may, a final consideration must be that Latin was a useful tool for re-establishing a sense of unity in a religiously fragmented Europe. Dornau, editor of the Wechel press's Latin *Utopia* (1619), had Calvinist sympathies but also staunchly defended religious freedom, launching appeals during the first two decades of the seventeenth century not just for Protestant solidarity but also for Christian unity (Bahlcke 2016: 72–73). His inclusion of *Utopia* in a volume which, alongside the ancients, included writers of all Protestant colours—from Erasmus (viewed with suspicion by Catholics although he had never formally broken with that church), to Melanchthon (Luther's right-hand man in Wittenberg), Joachim Camerarius (intimate of Melanchthon), and Theodore Beza (Calvin's successor in Geneva)—certainly points to a unifying agenda. Such an approach was evidently not out of kilter with official support, for the work was published *cum privilegio* (with the permission of the Holy Roman Emperor). The capacity of Latin to transcend borders applied to religious as well as geographical boundaries. It is also worth remembering that many Latin editions emerged in the most religiously diverse and tolerant areas of Europe, including Amsterdam and Frankfurt.

Conclusion

This account of the Latin editions of *Utopia* is one of both continuity and transformation. In text and character, many Latin editions exhibit a constancy with the original: Latin *Utopias* were products of multilingual Europe and all the cross-cultural dynamics that multilingualism entailed, and were often the locus of Erasmian humanism and a high-spirited love of nonsense. They embodied a desire to connect with classical learning and languages, including Greek. Sometimes, publication of *Utopia* in Latin coincided with key historical phases, such as the Dutch Golden Age and Scottish Enlightenment, when the importance of Latinity was magnified and implicated in displays of national self-confidence and improvement. Occasionally, the Latin of later editions was altered and endowed with new, often religion-related, meanings and agendas. The journey of the Latin *Utopias* is a useful reminder of the fact that it is not the text itself that produces literary meaning but functional relations between the text and its author, readership, consumers, printers, editors, and its style (Deneire 2017: 38). A survey of the Latin *Utopias* in many ways mirrors the story of neo-Latin in the early modern period and all its attendant contradictions. Latin had international force but could also affirm national achievement. It was a language which could divide the educated from the uneducated and bestow prestige; but it could also work in parallel with the vernacular and consequently unite them. Latin was caught up in the conflicts of the Reformation and became a contested medium, yet it continued to be a language used by confessions of all shades.

Latin was commonly used until well into the eighteenth century. Its demise is a phenomenon only of recent times. This shift is reflected in two of the later Latin editions: Oxford 1895 included an English translation adjacent to the Latin text; London 1910 focused on the English and relegated the Latin to an appendix. Delcourt in the preface to her 1936 Latin edition openly declared her contempt for this subordination of Latin: 'For the English publishers, it is as if the Latin *Utopia* were an appendix to the old translation of Robynson, who is a little Amyot. But Amyot did not forget about Plutarch' ('Pour les éditeurs anglais tout se passe comme si L'Utopia latine était une annexe de la vieille traduction de Robynson, lequel est un peu leur Amyot'). It is considerably more challenging for those who inhabit a world now largely devoid of Latin study to appreciate that language's contours and dynamics. My hope is that this chapter has brought some of those to the fore again, but perhaps it is safer to conclude as More did: 'quandoquidem scribendi labore defunctus, nunc sero sapio' ('Since I have gone through the labour of writing, it is too late for me to be wise now') (More 1965a: 44–45).

CHAPTER 11

....

FROM PROTOTYPE TO GENRE

Translations and Imitations of Utopia *in Early Modern Germany (1524–1753)*

....

GABRIELA SCHMIDT

THOMAS More's *Utopia* was from the very outset an international enterprise. Written partly in Flanders, partly in England, published successively in Louvain (1516), Paris (1517), Basel (1518), and Florence (1519) with contributions by humanist scholars from four different countries, it has justly been called a 'European work', addressing concerns that could be taken up in various national, social and cultural contexts (Heyer 2009: 187; cf. T. Cave 2008a).[1] What has drawn much less attention is the crucial role played by early modern German-speaking areas, particularly the regions on the Upper Rhine, in the distribution and reception of More's work during the first century after its appearance. In fact, up to 1631, eight out of fifteen Latin single editions were issued by German presses, and it was in Upper Rhinish cities that the first vernacular translation was produced and that the earliest political pamphlets and literary works inspired by More's precedent began to appear. As Jörg Jochen Berns has pointed out (1995: 156), the early and strikingly diverse response to *Utopia* in this particular geographical area can be explained to a certain extent by its special cultural, political, and religious milieu. Marked by the close coexistence of various languages, creeds, and administrative systems, with a sophisticated agricultural production, as well as the influence of powerful mercantile and academic urban elites, the region naturally fostered discussions of social, legal, and religious reform and provided the ideal conditions for their articulation and distribution in print. At a later point, it was the influence of the Frankfurt and Leipzig book fairs as important international trading hubs and key sites for intellectual and cultural exchange (Terrahe 2010; Laeven 1992: 185–195) that proved decisive for the further popularization and adaptation of More's text and its gradual transformation into a literary genre of its own. In this chapter, I would thus like to foreground the early

---

[1] Unless otherwise specified, all translations from German and Latin sources are my own.

modern German reception of *Utopia* as an important showcase for the emergence of utopian fiction in its two contrasting manifestations which Andreas Heyer describes in a neologistic binary as 'archic' versus 'anarchic': the tradition of fictionalizing a serious, hierarchically ordered political ideal, and its satirical subversion, the creation of grotesque, levelling counter-worlds (cf. Heyer 2009: 186).

Erasmian Humanism in Local Colour: The First Vernacular Translation

Only eight years after its publication, in 1524, More's 'truly golden handbook' made its first appearance in the vernacular when the Basel humanist Claudius Cantiuncula, professor of civil law at the university, published his German translation under the title *Von der wunderbarlichen Innsel Utopia genant das ander Buch* ('About the Wonderful Island Called Utopia, the Second Book'). Cantiuncula's decision to translate only Book Two and leave out most of the accompanying letters and marginalia, thus reducing the narrative situation to an expository monologue, has been read as a fateful 'misunderstanding' or even wilful distortion of More's original design (Berns 1982: 106; Greschonig 2006: 123). As I will argue, however, this position needs some serious reconsideration. Not only is Cantiuncula's the only translation produced during More's lifetime, it would also be impossible not to notice how close the translator still was, both personally and geographically, to the intellectual milieu in which the book originated. If Cantiuncula's omissions and paratextual additions do effect a decisive shift in voice and theme, he nevertheless shares many of the central concerns that occupied the circle of humanists that produced *Utopia*, and some of their more subtle fiction markers are indeed still traceable between the lines. At the same time, Cantiuncula's version also successfully adapts the work to the local political concerns of his domain and appeals to the political hopes and apprehensions of his new citizen readership.

Born in the Lorraine city of Metz, Claudius Cantiuncula (or Claude Chansonnette) completed the first part of his legal studies at Louvain between 1512 and 1517, where he was elected dean of the College of Bachelors of Both Laws.[2] He was thus resident in the city and actively involved in university affairs when *Utopia* was first printed there by Thierry Martens in 1516. When moving to Basel the following year, he was personally recommended to Desiderius Erasmus in a letter dated 14 July 1518 (*CWE* 6: Ep. 852) by no less a figure than Maarten van Dorp, the Louvain humanist and theologian whose academic quarrel with Erasmus and More three years earlier had played a significant role in the genesis of *Utopia*.[3] Basel proved astonishingly fertile for Cantiuncula's legal

---

[2] On Cantiuncula's biography, see Thieme and Rowan 1985, as well as Kisch 1970: 23–97 (on whose account I mainly draw in the following sections). The most recent biographical sketch is Burmeister 2011.

[3] This quarrel is discussed further below; cf. Taylor in this volume.

career. He was offered the chair in Civil Law in October 1518, five months before he formally acquired his doctorate, and only one year later was elected rector of the university. Apart from being an influential member of the law faculty, Cantiuncula, like most Basel humanists, also worked as a corrector for the Basel presses. If not personally involved, he would certainly have followed the production and appearance of the two 1518 editions of More's *Utopia* and *Epigrams* with considerable interest. Among his close friends was Beatus Rhenanus, who contributed the prefatory letter to the *Epigrams* and had strong connections with the Lorraine school of humanist geographers; in the very same year that Cantiuncula's *Utopia* was written, Rhenanus encouraged Sebastian Münster to embark on his monumental *Cosmography* (Burmeister 2011: 461–462).

That Cantiuncula's friendship and intellectual affinity with Erasmus was more than a convenient career boost for the young lawyer is evident in his later habit of carrying a copy of Erasmus' New Testament with him on all his diplomatic journeys, which he annotated in the margins and liked to cite in his legal references (Kisch 1970: 114). It was in fact one of the distinctive and most original traits of Cantiuncula's legal thinking that he strove to reconcile law with philosophy (Kisch 1970: 17), basing his methodological reflections and legal practice on a firm ethical and biblical grounding. At the university, although he sought to avoid undue polemic, he was one of the chief proponents of the humanist *mos gallicus*, which advocated the historically informed and philologically competent study of the original sources of Roman law, judging and reflecting independently, instead of resorting to the extensive standard commentaries of late medieval Italian jurists (*mos italicus*). In his efforts to promote institutional reform, Cantiuncula strove to strengthen the position of civil law vis-à-vis canonistic studies, arguing for a deep synthesis rather than an innate opposition between theology and jurisprudence.

The clearest profile of his methodological views emerges from two short programmatic works he published in 1522: *Oratio Apologetica in patrocinium Juris Civilis*—a defence of civil law against attacks by theologians—and *De ratione studii legalis Paraenesis* ('An Exhortation on the Manner of Studying the Law')—a study guide for beginners, in which Cantiuncula portrays the ideal lawyer as a man with a sound humanist education and encyclopedic knowledge as well as a firm moral standing and practical experience (Cantiuncula 1522: D3r–E3v). The beginner should rely above all on authentic source texts (*ubique fontes petat*, F2r) rather than voluminous commentaries which Cantiuncula sharply criticizes (*tantum inutilium glossarum*, G3v). The chief objectives of legal practice and discourse must be clarity (G4v) and appropriateness (G2r), and to this end, linguistic competence (*cura verborum*) is just as important as legal expertise (*rerum sollicitudo*, G2v). The frequent references to Erasmus' theological writings interspersed in these reflections draw attention to the striking affinity between Cantiuncula's effort to redefine the relationship between theology, philology, and jurisprudence and Erasmus' own defence of his philological method against criticism from neo-scholastic theologians.

As Lisa Jardine (2015: 118–121) suggests, the publication of *Utopia* in Louvain has to be seen in immediate connection with precisely this defence, in particular the public polemic—whether real or staged—that developed in 1514–15 between Erasmus and the young theologian Dorp. As is well known, More contributed a decisive letter to this argument exactly during his 1515 Flemish embassy—the same event that also inspired *Utopia*.[4] We do not know whether Cantiuncula, who was at that time residing in Louvain and acquainted with Dorp, was informed about the contents of the letters that passed between the three scholars or whether he drew solely on Erasmus' later writings. In any case, a comparative reading of Cantiuncula's 1522 *Paraenesis* and More's 'Letter to Dorp', with its insistence on the complementarity of philology and theology, its critique of neo-scholastic glossaries, and its promotion of a source-based and communicable theology, demonstrates beyond any doubt that the translator was steeped in the very same intellectual climate as his author. A passage in *Utopia* that Cantiuncula seems to have found especially congenial is Hythloday's argument on the transparency of Utopian laws, which resonates particularly strongly with the 'Letter to Dorp'. Cantiuncula gives this passage, which is somewhat hidden in the 'De servis' ('On Slaves') section of the Latin *Utopia*, special prominence by furnishing it with a subtitle of its own, 'Von ihren gesatzen' ('Of Their Laws') (More 1524: K2r): this is the only one of Cantiuncula's section headings for which there is no equivalent either in the original text or in the Latin marginalia.

Another theme in which the intellectual proximity between author and translator becomes especially evident is Cantiuncula's insistence on the classical concept of equity. As the legal equivalent of the rhetorical norms of common usage (*sensus communis*) and propriety (*decorum*), which More puts centre stage in the 'Letter to Dorp', equity ensures that the application of legal norms is both fair, in the sense of equally just for all, and appropriate to the particular circumstances of each individual case. As has been pointed out, there is a certain tension inherent in these two differing uses of the term: while the case-oriented Aristotelian concept of *epikeia* ('reasonableness') stresses the principle of individuality, the more theoretical Ciceronian *aequitas* ('fairness') places the focus on the notion of equality (Majeske 2006: 2–3). The same tension can also be seen to permeate More's *Utopia* on all its textual levels, and the way Cantiuncula registers this tension in his translation of Book Two helps us understand something of his nuanced approach to More's work.

The problem of equity is discussed at three crucial points in the *Utopia* (Majeske 2006: 63–91). The most pertinent passage is the extensive debate on the appropriateness of capital punishment for theft in Book One, set at the dinner table of the English Lord Chancellor Cardinal Morton. In his plea for a mitigated law, the narrator Hythloday refers to the famous Ciceronian dictum *summum ius, summa iniuria* (which also features in Erasmus' *Adagia*), implying that the strictest justice, when not adapted to the circumstances, may in fact be the highest form of injustice (More 1965a: 72). The arguments Hythloday adduces to support his thesis (60–70) establish a strong connection between the lack of equity and the lack of social equality, to the extent that Hythloday, when he comes back to the concept in his peroration at the end of Book Two,

---

[4] For a concise summary of the polemic, its context and connection with *Utopia*, see Jardine 2015: 111–122 and Daniel Kinney's introduction in *CWM* 15.xix–xxviii.

equates ideal *aequitas* with absolute communism (238). The critique of this position as unrealistic by the persona 'Morus', who advocates a more case-oriented approach that 'adapts itself to the play at hand', is dismissed by Hythloday by means of another catchword from the classical *aequitas* debate: the 'leaden rule' of the builders of Lesbos, which they could bend at will (99). What Aristotle introduced as a positive example to praise legal flexibility is reversed by Hythloday to signify immoral arbitrariness. The tension between these two positions, for which there is no positive solution in the text of *Utopia*, finds an echo in the accompanying paratexts. In his 1517 prefatory letter to Thomas Lupset, the prominent French jurist Guillaume Budé seems to agree with Hythloday in singling out avarice as the key obstacle to true equity and proposing the communism of the early Christian community as the only possible solution (6–10). On the other hand, Budé also references Morus' opposite view when he ironically refers to Utopia as 'Udepotia' ('never-never land'), placing it 'outside the limits of the known world' (10–12).

Given that equity occupied such a central place in Cantiuncula's legal philosophy, it may therefore at first look like a surprising oversight that he chose to translate neither the paratext by his prominent Paris colleague Budé nor the legal discussion in Book One, which he dismisses as concerning matters specifically English and hence 'of no use for the understanding of the conditions of Utopia' (More 1524: A5v; trans. T. Cave 2008c: 159). However, if we examine the text more closely, the German translator turns out to be in fact much more aware of More's conceptual nuances than at first appears. The word he most often prefers for the Latin *aequitas* is 'billichkeit', which is the usual technical term, meaning as much as 'equitableness' (Grimm and Grimm, *s.v.*). A significant exception is, however, Hythloday's peroration in defence of communism, where Cantiuncula departs from his usual strategy and renders *hac aequitate* (More 1965a: 238) as 'diser glychheit' ('this equality') (More 1524: P2r), thus pinpointing Hythloday's egalitarian interpretation of the term.[5] Even more interesting is the way Cantiuncula references the classical equity debate in his own dedicatory letter to the Basel city council. The three virtues he singles out as key to the Utopians' happy commonwealth—common ownership, equal distribution of goods, and peaceful unity—and the three vices he urges his readers to avoid—strife, greed, and ambition (More 1524: A4v–5r; T. Cave 2008c: 157–159)—are in fact indirect quotations from Budé's 1517 Latin paratext, which contains two very similar triads. However, where Budé speaks of 'the equality of all things [...] among fellow citizens [...] absolute on all counts' (More 1965a: 11), Cantiuncula makes it very clear 'that the simple undifferentiated common ownership of all things, with no exceptions, [...] would be totally contrary to the humane living together of the citizens' (More 1524: A4v; trans. T. Cave 2008c: 157). To give this political point more weight, the translator resorts precisely to the classical Ciceronian argument about equity:

---

[5] Gregor Wintermonat, who, in his 1612 version, usually follows Cantiuncula's wording very closely, seems to have noted the inconsistency and silently corrected it to 'billigkeit' (More 1612: 200), without noticing the terminological nuance.

For when equality is not regulated, when the good and the bad, the well-born and the base, the wise and the foolish are received in the same way, then such an equality of the unequal is transformed into the highest form of inequality—much as, if one rigorously follows the letter of secular written law [...] (so that, for example, the mitigating circumstances of a fight are not taken into consideration), then in that case the highest form of justice is called the highest form of injustice and infamy. (More 1524: A4v; trans. T. Cave 2008c: 157)

What Cantiuncula appears to be doing here, then, is much more than conventional moralizing, as has usually been assumed; in fact, he turns both Budé's paratext and Hythloday's argument in Book One upside down, converting it into an argument for the impossibility—even injustice—of absolute communism. In doing so, Cantiuncula not only implicitly associates himself and More's text with one of the leading proponents of the humanist *mos gallicus*, but also continues the debate precisely where Budé left it in 1517, siding with More's persona Morus and proposing a reading that adapts Hythloday's political ideal to the actual conditions of an early modern European city-state. Despite its deliberate omission of Book One and the parerga, his translation thus clearly interacts with the whole of More's text, even though only readers closely familiar with the Latin original would have been able to appreciate the complexity of that response.

Less indirectly, the strong emphasis Cantiuncula lays on the third of his virtues in the prefatory letter, 'peaceful unity among the citizens living together' (More 1524: A4v; trans. T. Cave 2008c: 157), also directs his early readership of city officials to much more urgent political concerns. As a matter of fact, the translator presents his book to the city council as a farewell gift. Although the alleged reason for his decision to leave Basel is his obligation to care for his ailing father (More 1524: A3r; trans. T. Cave 2008c: 153), there are hints in his later correspondence (Thieme and Rowan 1985: 260) that the true reason for his departure may have been the rapid progress of the Reformation and the increasing religious tensions in the city.[6] The main inroad for reformed ideas in Basel had been its importance as a centre of print; Basel presses had started to distribute Lutheran writings from 1518 onwards. Another factor was the exceptionally strong influence of the merchant guilds in the city government, which had forced political independence from the city's bishop in 1521. From 1522 onwards, reformist preaching started to surge in some of the parishes, particularly those under the influence of the Franciscans, and more and more public breaches of church discipline occurred. When the Franciscan Provincial tried to intervene in 1523 by removing the local Guardian Konrad Pellikan from the city, the council resisted his attempt and reacted by appointing Pellikan, together with the openly Lutheran Johannes Oecolampadius, as theology professors, against the resistance of the university. When opposition between the religious parties became entrenched, the city council intended to mediate—with very

---

[6] *Pace* Burmeister (2011: 458–459), who affirms that there is no clear evidence for the existence of any other reason behind Cantiuncula's sudden departure than the one he cites in his preface. In the following historical summary I rely on accounts by Guggisberg (1982: 3–35) and Burnett (2016: 170–193).

limited success—by passing the so-called 'preaching ordinance', which Cantiuncula implicitly refers to in his preface (Salberg 2008: 37), obliging preachers to rely exclusively on Scripture and banishing all doctrinal polemics from the pulpit. Religious disturbances went along with growing social unrest in the countryside and among artisans in the city, where the weavers' guild started to agitate against the council's authority in the suburbs. This was the situation towards the end of 1523 when Cantiuncula turned his back on the city whose religious and social climate was probably becoming increasingly averse to his staunchly Catholic and conservative tastes.

Read against this background, the 1524 *Utopia*, which Cantiuncula offers to the council in lieu of a city encomium, becomes an urgent appeal for civic unity and religious moderation, in an attempt to summon all the authority of the former Erasmian humanist circle (now also split along confessional lines). It may seem significant that, in the same year, Cantiuncula also translated into French the *Exomologesis sive modus confitendi*, an expressly Catholic work by Erasmus about 'the manner of confession' (Erasmus 1524; Kisch 1970: 150). As has been pointed out, the addressee singled out in the dedication of his *Utopia*, Adelberg Meyer zum Pfeil (the first mayor of Basel elected without episcopal consent in 1521), was the most powerful representative of the moderately reformist faction of the 'gentlemen's guilds' within the council, trying to mediate between the conservative patricians and the more radical artisan guilds. His efforts were somewhat successful: the 1524/5 peasant's uprising was indeed muted relatively quickly and a degree of religious tolerance would prevail until the *Bildersturm*—an outbreak of iconoclasm—in 1529 (Salberg 2008: 36; Schüpbach-Guggenbühl 2010; Guggisberg 1982: 6).

The political context also provides us with another reason why Cantiuncula would have wanted to distance himself firmly in the dedication from Hythloday's plea for absolute communism. As Jörg Jochen Berns has shown, not only did More's *Utopia* strongly resonate with the discourse around the emergence of the first imperial civil law codex, the *Reichspolizeiordnung* of 1530, its more radical passages at the end of Book Two also bore some dangerously close similarities to the incendiary rhetoric of the pamphlets by Thomas Müntzer and others that were circulating on the eve of the Peasants' War (Berns 1982: 102–103, 107–109). Two of these pamphlets, the tenth and eleventh instalments of Johann Eberlin of Günzburg's *Fifteen Confederates*, printed at Basel in 1521, even had a fictional narrator called Psitacus ('Parrot') present a utopian fictional state called Wolfaria ('Welfare Land') with a radically levelling Lutheran regime existing 'somewhere within the Empire' (Berns 1995: 153; cf. Bell 1969; Saage 2001: 186–189). It seems logical, then, that the only dialogic element Cantiuncula introduces in his translation is the sceptical afterthought of the frame narrator 'Morus' at the very end, which marks the political enthusiasm of Hythloday's peroration with a strong caveat. The two speaker headings introduced before each concluding statement (More 1524: P1v, P4v) highlight the sharp contrast between the two positions and give further 'authorial' weight to the moderate view offered by Morus. In its endeavour to promote civic unity in the face of increasing social unrest and incendiary polemic, Cantiuncula's political approach arguably anticipates in many ways that of the first English translator, Ralph Robinson, nearly thirty years later (Schmidt 2018: 184–191).

This brings us back to the fraught question of Cantiuncula's generic misappropriation of More's text. It is certainly possible to read the 1524 *Utopia* as a political tract, another contribution to its period's lively discourse on imperial reform which, moreover, had the advantage of enriching the vernacular's rather limited vocabulary for expressing political realities (Goerlitz 2002: 408–413). This shift, or perhaps rather disambiguation, of genre is especially evident from one of the few original paratexts the translator chooses to include: Peter Giles's Utopian alphabet, presented under the German heading 'Der Utopianer Alphabet' (More 1524: A2r; see Fig. 11.1). While the woodcut letters and 'Quatrain in the Utopian Vernacular' from Froben's 1518 editions are faithfully reproduced, the Latin translation of Giles's Utopian poem is replaced by eight (metrically somewhat irregular) rhyming couplets in German. Lines 2–3, which in Latin signify as much as 'I alone of all countries have, without philosophy, | represented the city of philosophers for all mortals to see' (More 1965a: 18; my translation), are rendered by Cantiuncula as follows: 'Und ich eyntzig uff erden fry | Hab on die kunst Philosophy | Alln tötlichen menschen zkennen geben | Zů füren ein burgerlich leben' ('I, the only free city on earth | have, without philosophy, | revealed to all mortals | what it means to lead a civic life'). Rather than landing in Giles's playfully paradoxical philosophy-free city of philosophers, we have landed in a German free imperial city-state teaching us a well-ordered and respectable middle-class lifestyle (Grimm and Grimm, *s.v.* 'bürgerlich').

As unimaginative as this sounds, it nevertheless happens precisely in the middle of a paratext that is perhaps the boldest example of the ironic hide-and-seek game concerning the fictionality of More's island polity that the book's early contributors to the parerga indulged in. If we examine Cantiuncula's text closely and dispassionately enough, we can see him joining in this game. This begins with the very title. Not only does he (surprisingly) omit the political first part of the 1518 title *De optimo reipublicae statu* ('Of the Best State of a Commonweal'), he also replaces the neutral adjective 'new' (*nova*) that qualifies the island of Utopia in the second part of the Latin title with the word *wunderbarlich* (meaning as much as 'miraculous', 'extraordinary', but also 'strange' or 'inconceivable'; Grimm and Grimm, *s.v.*). In doing so, he literally takes up the metafictional jeu d'esprit of the original paratexts, since Budé's letter to Lupset had also referred to the creation of Utopia as *mirifica sors*—'a miraculous stroke of fortune' (More 1965a: 10). Similarly tongue-in-cheek, Cantiuncula describes his model state in the dedicatory epistle as that which 'was and *allegedly still is* the best organized' (More 1524: A5r; my italics). The preceding comparison with the ancient commonwealths of Sparta, Athens, and Rome, which would still exist had they followed the Utopian example (A4r; T. Cave 2008c: 155–157), is an indirect quotation from Busleyden's Latin letter to More (More 1965a: 34), but the hotchpotch of real and fictional references Cantiuncula adds to this suggests that he is deliberately continuing the joke (Salberg 2008: 38). Likewise, the conclusion of the dedicatory epistle, in adducing possible explanations for why the famous island of Utopia was never mentioned by classical geographers, takes up a point from Giles's letter to Busleyden (More 1965a: 24). At the same time, the translator considerably elaborates and expands Giles's point by introducing a whole range of modern European islands that have since changed their names (More 1524: A5v–6r; T. Cave 2008c: 161). It is

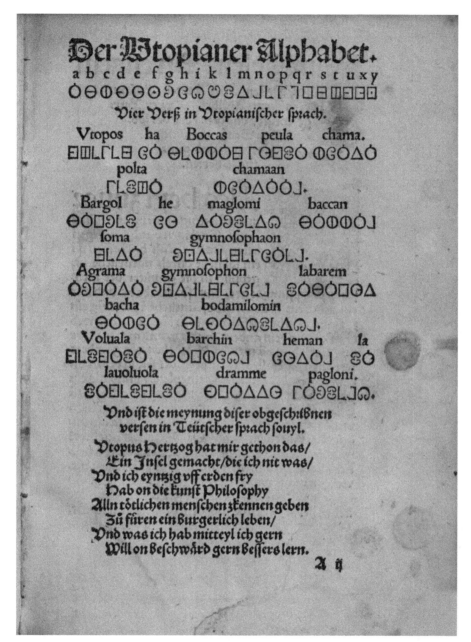

FIG. 11.1. Utopian alphabet and poem, in Thomas More, *Von der wunderbarlichen Innsel Utopia genant das ander Buch*, trans. Claudius Cantiuncula [Claude Chansonette] (Basel: Johann Bebel, 1524), sig. A2r. Bayerische Staatsbibliothek München, 4 Pol.g. 162 d, urn:nbn:de:bvb:12-bsb10166830-0.

thus quite evident that the first vernacular translator, rather than reducing More's multi-layered original to a mere 'historical document' (Berns 1982: 106), was in fact highly sensitive to the subtleties of *Utopia*'s generic play, and brought traces of them into his own version for his more sophisticated readers to notice and appreciate.

FROM POLITICS TO SATIRE: THE SECOND PHASE OF UTOPIAN RECEPTION IN GERMANY

We do not know how much Cantiuncula's translation, which never went through a second edition, resonated among its early readers.[7] Nevertheless, the Basel connection—alongside the growing influence of the Frankfurt Book Fair as one of the biggest hubs for the international Latin book trade—was to remain crucial both for the trajectory of the Latin *Utopia* and for its literary reception on German–Swiss soil.[8] In 1548, thirty years after the appearance of the first two Froben editions, a reissue was prepared in Louvain, including all the 1518 paratexts except the Utopian map and alphabet; this was closely followed, in 1555, by another very similar edition in Cologne. As Vibeke Roggen (2008: 16) has suggested, the decisive link between the first editions of *Utopia* and this second cluster was the Birckmann family of printers in Cologne, who had functioned as disseminators of Froben's books at the Frankfurt fair. Frankfurt and Hanau would produce another pair of single issues in 1601 and 1613, while a Basel printer closely associated with Froben, Nicolaus Episcopius, published the first collective edition of More's Latin writings in 1563, which would function as the decisive stimulant for the influential Louvain Latin *Opera* ('Works') of 1565.

It was also at Basel that the first full-blown literary utopia by a German author appeared in 1555. Caspar Stiblin's *Commentariolus de Eudaemonensium Republica* ('A Little Commentary on the Commonwealth of the Eudaimonians') takes its readers on a journey through the fictional countries of Aristotle, Plato, and Xenophon, before landing him in a storm on the island of Macaria with its capital Eudaimon (both meaning more or less 'blissful' or 'blessed place'). The place name is taken from a cursory reference of More's narrator Raphael Hythloday to a people called the Macarians living 'not far from Utopia' (More 1965a: 96). Although Stiblin's ideal state, through its emphasis on education and its unequivocal fictionality, is much closer to classical examples than to More's, certain aspects—especially the strong reliance on visual devices (including a woodcut illustration of Eudaimon's circular and symmetrical urban layout)—would prove

---

[7] Heiner Höfener is the only critic to assume that the Cantiuncula version had 'a broad readership', although he does not offer any evidence for this claim (Höfener 1980: iv). He is also the only one to notice that there is a direct link between Cantiuncula's and Wintermonat's later translation (see below).

[8] For the importance of the Frankfurt Book Fair to the dissemination of Latin *Utopias*, see Nicholas in this volume.

decisive for the later development of utopian fiction (Berns 1982: 111–113; Stiblin 1994: xlix–li). The most prominent of all German neo-Latin utopias, *Christianopolis*, by the Tübingen pastor Johann Valentin Andreae (1619), shares in fact many of the elements of Stiblin's little volume. Although it was published to the north of Basel, in Strasbourg, its emergence from the same geographical region suggests the existence of an intense intellectual exchange of utopian ideas in the neighbouring university towns of Strasbourg, Basel, Freiburg, and Tübingen. The even more famous Italian predecessor of Andreae's work, Tommaso Campanella's *Civitas Solis* ('City of the Sun'), a prison work composed in Italian in 1602 and subsequently turned into Latin, also owes its survival to the same south-western German intellectual culture. Its Latin manuscript version was smuggled into Germany by two Tübingen students and subsequently published at Frankfurt in 1623 (Berns 1982: 113–114).

What all these successive responses to More's prototype have in common is their unambiguously optimistic approach, including an idealized system of education, model urban planning, and an undisputed hierarchical social system. Although all of them provide their utopian accounts with a rudimentary fictional frame, their narrative structure—like that of Cantiuncula's translation—remains firmly monological; none attempts in any way to reproduce the polyphony and underlying ironies of More's original. However, in the meantime, there had also been a number of very different fictional responses in neighbouring European countries. In Italy, it was probably the publication of the 1519 Florence edition of *Utopia*, together with More's and Erasmus' translations from Lucian, that led to the foregrounding of *Utopia*'s satirical dimension in works such as Francesco Doni's *I Mondi* ('The Worlds') of 1552 (Gjerpe 2008: 51). French vernacular culture, too, had, from a very early stage, shown significant interest in the fictional and grotesque details of More's text, such as the Utopian language, alphabet, mock geography, and some of the more absurd social customs. These came to figure in such works as Geoffroy Tory's treatise on print design *Champfleury* (1529) and, most prominently, the first three instalments of Rabelais's *Gargantua and Pantagruel* series (1532–46) (Sellevold 2008a: 67).

It is via Rabelais that this second, satirical tradition of responses to *Utopia* first took root in German literary culture. The first translation, or rather free adaptation, of Rabelais in German was the *Affenteurliche und Ungeheurliche Geschichtschrift* (1575), a title which puns on 'ape' and 'adventurous' (*affenteurlich*) and evokes a narrative which is both 'monstrous' and/or 'unbelievable' (*ungeheurlich*). Written by the Strasbourg satirist Johann Fischart, this work is an extraordinary linguistic experiment, full of puns and paradoxes, which on its title page introduces the two mock heroes as *Königen inn Utopien und Ninenreich* ('Kings in Utopia and Nowhereland'). It also contains a fictional account of Rabelais's satirical, mock utopian Abbey of Thélème. The blending of elements from More's *Utopia* with vernacular satirical traditions was further perfected in the anonymous *Lalebuch* of 1597 (also sometimes ascribed to Fischart), a collection of carnivalesque merry tales set in a fictional town called Laleburg in a remote valley within the empire of Utopia, whose landscape is nevertheless unmistakably German. The citizens are said to descend from the Greeks, while their name contains a multilingual pun on Greek *lálein* ('to babble'), the German word *lallen* ('to slur', 'to babble'), and the dialect meaning of *Lale*, 'gaping fool' (Grimm and Grimm, *s.v.* 'lallen'; Berns 1995: 162–163). The *Lalebuch*'s community of fools is a veritable parody of the Utopians' celebration of humanist education, science, and social order—or at least of those readers who take More's ideal entirely at face value. It subverts Utopian society 'from within' (Berns 1995: 168) by throwing the satirical and grotesquely paradoxical elements of More's text into high relief (Dicke 2011) and thus creates a radical alternative to the dominant model of utopian discourse. The *Lalebuch*'s immediate successor, *Die Schiltbürger* ('The Citizens of Schilda') (1598), even announces its Morean credentials prominently on the title page by introducing its setting as 'Misnopotamia [Misrulepotomia] situated behind Utopia' and pretending to have been translated from 'Utopian or Rothwelsh [i.e. thieves' cant] into German'.

Both strands of utopian reception would meet during the first decades of the seventeenth century at the sites of the great book fairs at Frankfurt and Leipzig. As we have seen, it was at Frankfurt that the first Latin seventeenth-century edition of More's text appeared, emphatically advertised by the editor Eberhard von Weyhe as the long overdue reissue of an important classic, 'now at last snatched away from the grave of books' (see Roggen 2008: 28 on the possible private implications of this phrase; cf. Nicholas in this volume). Five years later, an anonymous work by one 'Mercurius Britannicus' appeared in the catalogue for the Frankfurt spring fair, allegedly printed in the city during the previous year by the heirs of Ascanius de Renialme. As we now know, this imprint was actually a fake, and the book—Joseph Hall's Menippean satire *Mundus Alter et Idem* ('Another World and Yet the Same')—was instead printed by Henry Lownes in London, where the publication of 'Satyres or Epigramms' happened to be illegal due to the so-called 'Bishops' Ban' of 1599 (McCabe 1980: 188).[9] Nevertheless, Hall's *Mundus* seemed to have been in such high demand at Frankfurt that a second edition was already prepared the following year by Wilhelm Antonius in the neighbouring town of Hanau (Wands 1980: 3–12).

Probably written in the last decade of the sixteenth century during Hall's Cambridge years (J. Hall 1981: xxi), the *Mundus*, like the *Lalebuch*, both imitates More's prototype and parodically inverts it. Like More's text, it allegedly reports the discovery of an unknown region, the fabled continent of Antarctica. Like the original *Utopia*, it contains a fictional frame narration, telling names, and an impressively sophisticated array of paratexts including five maps by the renowned engraver William Kip, nearly two hundred explanatory notes in the margin, an index of names, and several engravings of coins and inscriptions.[10] Hall's pseudoscientific paratextual apparatus seems to carry More's metafictional hide-and-seek game to extremes. As John Millar Wands observes, 'no other utopia [...] up to *Gulliver's Travels* tries so hard to make a fiction plausibly nonfictional' (Wands 1981: 89). On the other hand, however, what Hall offers his readers is

---

[9] On Renialme's importance as an importer of foreign books in London, see Roberts 2004.
[10] On Kip's life and work, see Worms 2004.

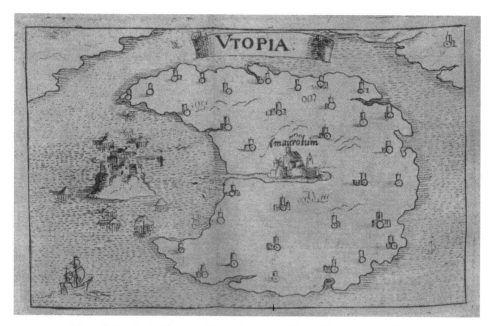

FIG. 11.2. Map of Utopia, in Thomas More, *De optimo Reipublicae Statu, Libellus vere aureus: Ordentliche vnd Außführliche Beschreibung Der vberaus herrlichen und gantz wunderbarlichen / doch wenigen bißhero bekandten Insul Utopia*, trans. Gregor Wintermonat (Leipzig: Henning Grosse, 1612), Bayerische Staatsbibliothek München, Pol.g. 670 f.

by no means a New World paradise, but a nightmarish and grotesque counter-world, embodying all the notorious vices of the old: 'another world and yet the same'.

The joint commercial success and mutual complementarity of the *Mundus* and *Utopia* seem to have been conspicuous enough for a prominent Leipzig publisher, Henning Grosse the Younger, to bring out both German translations in close succession in 1612 and 1613, advertising Hall's text as *Utopiae Pars II* (though erroneously ascribed to Alberico Gentili; see J. Hall 1981: xiii–xviii on this error). The translator of both works, Gregor Wintermonat, was a rather obscure figure, chiefly known for the publication of news, and local and church history (Salberg 2008: 43). Yet the two volumes have advertising appeal enough even without another prominent name on the title page. Both contain maps and engravings: the 1613 Hall reproduces all the illustrations and fold-out maps from the Latin editions; the 1612 More contains a new Utopian map by an unknown engraver (Fig. 11.2), a Utopian alphabet, and an engraving of More based on the Holbein portrait.[11] Both Wintermonat's title page (Fig. 11.3), with More's name and learned credentials printed in red, and the translator's preface with its list of famous admirers of More's work including Erasmus, Budé, and Jean Bodin, emphasize the book's status as an authoritative classic. On each title page

---

[11] On the maps, see Hiatt in this volume.

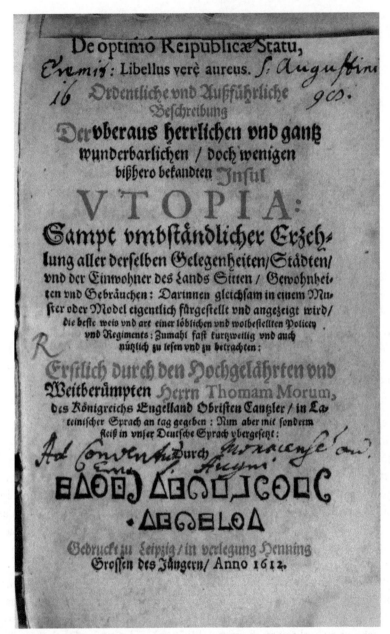

FIG. 11.3. Title page, Thomas More, *De optimo Reipublicae Statu, Libellus vere aureus. Ordentliche vnd Außführliche Beschreibung Der vberaus herrlichen und gantz wunderbarlichen / doch wenigen bißhero bekandten Insul UTOPIA*, trans. Gregor Wintermonat (Leipzig: Henning Grosse, 1612), Bayerische Staatsbibliothek München, Pol.g. 670 f, urn:nbn:de:bvb:12-bsb10770043-4.

the translator's name appears in Utopian characters: in the More volume hidden behind the nonsensical pseudonym of SMDYGMXIRNHDRH MXISOFM, in the Hall volume clearly identifiable (though with one slightly misprinted letter) as the clumsily Latinized GREGORIUM HUEMUMENSIUM (Fig. 11.4). Although this may be some kind of private joke, I would see in the 'emphatic anonymity' (Salberg 2008: 41) of the *Utopia* translation a deliberate generic hint associating the volume with similar literary devices familiar from popular satires such as the 1597 *Lalebuch*, whose alleged translator figures on the title page as 'Aabcdefghiklmnopqrstuwxyz'. That the island described in

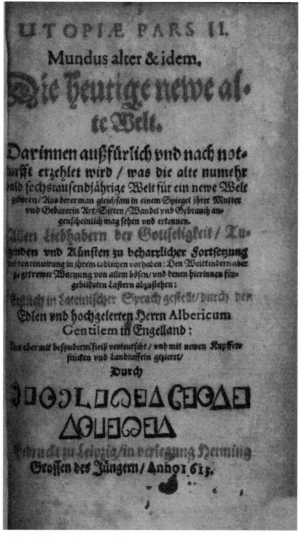

FIG. 11.4. Title page, Joseph Hall (attrib. Alberico Gentili), *Utopiae Pars II: Mundus alter & idem*, trans. Gregor Wintermonat (Leipzig: Henning Grosse, 1613), Staatliche Bibliothek Regensburg; 999/Philos.1049, urn:nbn:de:bvb:12-bsb11109903-0.

the book is meant to be read as real is made clear through its introduction as 'wonderful and most marvellous [*herrlichen und gantz wunderbarlichen*], but hitherto little known [*wenigen bißhero bekandten*]' (More 1612 π1r; trans. T. Cave 2008c: 163). This and the promise to provide 'a thorough presentation of the conditions [...], of its towns, and of the traditions, habits and customs of the inhabitants' activates a completely different set of stops in Wintermonat's readers than in Cantiuncula's: they would access the text as a contemporary travellers' account. All this makes the book highly marketable and points to the fact that Wintermonat's and Grosse's interest in publishing it seems to have been uncoupled from specific political or religious concerns and directed towards a national, rather than local, readership. After all, the book fairs were important commercial trendsetters. The Leipzig fair was around this time already well on course to outstrip its Frankfurt rival, and Grosse, as the official publisher of the fair catalogue, would have been perfectly aware of all the important sales trends (Salberg 2008: 41–42; Terrahe 2010: 193–194).

As far removed as all this seems to be from the context and concerns of Wintermonat's Basel predecessor, a close examination of the two German versions nevertheless reveals an astonishing degree of overlap. In fact, we get the impression that Wintermonat, rather than producing a version of his own, was carefully reworking the one by Cantiuncula—whom he also lists among his learned authorities in the preface (π2r)—and adapting it to the tastes and background of his new, broadened readership. Wintermonat's subdivision into sections follows exactly that of the 1524 Basel edition, often even literally, though he rephrases some of Cantiuncula's more obscure formulations, turning, for example, 'Von der Utopianer färt und wandlung' ('Of the Utopians' Wayfaring and Wandering') (More 1524: E2v) into 'Von der Utopianer Reisen' ('Of the Utopians' Travel') (More 1612: 61). He closely adheres to Cantiuncula's choice of words, even some of his characteristic doubles. Where Cantiuncula had expanded More's expression *aedificia neutiquam sordida* ('the buildings, far from mean') (More 1965a: 120) for Utopian houses into 'Die heüser vnnd gebeüw sind nitt schlecht oder nachgiltig' ('the houses and buildings are not bad or of poor quality') (More 1524: B4v), Wintermonat has exactly the same wording, only modernizing the spelling: 'Die Heuser und Gebeude seind nicht schlecht oder nachgültig' (More 1612: 25). On the other hand, he sometimes consciously smooths his predecessor's syntax and replaces some of his more cryptic localisms. Where More's Hythloday, to explain why a six-hour working day suffices in the Utopian economy, had referred, among other things, to the idle retainers of European noblemen using the term *caetrati* (More 1965a: 130), Cantiuncula renders this as 'Stradiotischen bůben' (More 1524: C4v), replacing a specific type of light-armed Roman soldier (bearing a particular shield, a *caetra*) by a specific type of early modern mercenary. Although Wintermonat follows Cantiuncula's next sentence very closely, he omits this particular reference, which he probably found too technical for his popular readership to understand (More 1612: 40). The close dependence of the two versions is perhaps most salient in the initial Utopian quatrain, whose iambic measure Wintermonat regularizes, while still attempting to follow Cantiuncula's wording wherever metrically possible. The verses on Plato's philosophical city already quoted above, 'Und ich eyntzig vff erden fry | Hab on die kunst Philosophy | Alln tötlichen menschen zkennen geben | Zů füren ein burgerlich leben' (More 1524: A2r), read in Wintermonat's German: 'Ich bin allein auff Erden frey | So ohn die Kunst Philosophey | Den Menschen hab zu erkennen gebn | Zu führen ein Politisch lebn' (More 1612: π4v).

Despite the striking resemblance between the two translations, Wintermonat is by no means a mere epigone; we clearly see him setting his own priorities. Although he takes over the suggestive word *wunderbarlich* from Cantiuncula's title, he enhances it with a whole series of further qualities to move his own 'Insul Utopia' into the direction of a travellers' account. Although he reinstates the first part of the 1518 title in Latin as a kind of homage to More's original, his own German title puts the word *UTOPIA* at the centre in red capitals, thus equating the book with the fictional place—as most modern but very few early modern editions do: previously, only the 1553 Antwerp translation and Barthélemy Aneaus's reissue of Jean Le Blond's French version (Lyons 1559) had titles thus clearly focused on More's neologism. Although he continues Cantiuncula's speculation about Utopia's geographical location in the preface, he spices it up with a topical piece of 'news from England', the recent discovery of a north-east passage to China (More 1612: ¶2v). The travel-book association is further strengthened through the reintroduction of the first part of Book One containing More's frame narrative and Hythloday's account of his previous travels with Amerigo Vespucci, whereas the ensuing political discussion between Hythloday, Morus, and Giles's textual persona is glossed over in only one sentence (9–10). To better guide his readers, Wintermonat adds a table of contents, running titles, and marginalia. While the latter usually function as a mere thematic reading aid, some are clearly meant to excite curiosity and display the translator's world knowledge, such as his annotation on the Utopians' artificial method of egg hatching: 'Similarly, it is still custom today in Cairo to hatch young chickens in the oven' (19). The 'learned' point is confirmed by a popular guide to the Holy Land, the *Reyßbuch deß heyligen Lands*, where indeed we find a marginal note 'young chickens hatched in ovens' on the page referenced by Wintermonat (Feyerabend 1584: 392r). Occasionally, though very rarely, Wintermonat's religious sympathies shine through. Where the Catholic Cantiuncula uses the words 'Bischof' ('Bishop') (More 1524: D4v) for More's 'high priest' (More 1965a: 140) and 'Bäpste' ('Popes') (More 1524: K3v) in a seemingly positive—though actually ironic—reference to popes' faithful adherence to treatises (More 1965a: 196), Wintermonat replaces these terms by the more neutral 'oberster Priester' ('high priest') (More 1612: 55) and 'Geistliche' ('clergy') (134). And where Cantiuncula's version renders Hythloday's criticism of the idleness of European priests and religious rather tamely as 'priester | und deren so man Religiosen nennet' ('priests and those that are called religious') (More 1524: C4v), Wintermonat uses the much more derogatory terms 'Ordensleut | Pfaffen und Münche' ('religious, shavelings, and monks') (More 1612: 39–40).

Overall, however, Wintermonat's reworking of his predecessor's translation is generic rather than religious or political. From a philosophical treatise on early modern statecraft, the German *Utopia* is evidently converted into a work of early modern fiction. More than anything, it is the close coupling of More's text with Hall's anti-utopian

Mundus that would be decisive in this respect. The relatedness between the two volumes is obvious not only from the title *Utopiae Pars II* in Wintermonat's Hall and the appearance of Utopian characters on both title pages, but also in the running titles of the 1613 volume, which read throughout: 'Von der Insel Utopia'. It is thus no surprise that the Frankfurt reissue of 1704 (and another, similar one of 1730) assembles both texts in one single volume (Pohl 2016: 501n.). Andreas Heyer has called Wintermonat's 'the first attempt at reconstructing the genre in itself by assembling several works under the umbrella term utopia' (Heyer 2009: 188). Others would follow suit: in 1619, Caspar Dornau decided to include More's work in a collection of mock-serious texts of all ages entitled *Amphitheatrum Sapientiae Socraticae Joco-Seriae* ('The Amphitheatre of Joco-Serious Socratic Wisdom') (Roggen 2008: 18).[12] And in 1643 the Utrecht publisher Johannes van Waesberg brought out a new edition of Hall's *Mundus*, appending to it, 'because of their similar subject matter' (J. Hall 1643: title page), Campanella's *Civitas Solis* and Francis Bacon's *Nova Atlantis*. It is interesting that, in what we might call the first anthology of early modern utopias, More's prototype seems to have fallen by the wayside.

OUTSTRIPPING *UTOPIA*: TRENDS IN SEVENTEENTH- AND EIGHTEENTH-CENTURY GERMAN 'UTOPIAN' FICTION

From the early seventeenth century on, the market for 'utopian' literature in early modern Germany would indeed be dominated by Hall's openly fictional and satirical approach. Apart from a series of new editions of the popular *Lalebuch* and *Schiltbürger* stories, an especially notable specimen of this discourse is the immensely popular *Utopia* by the Jesuit poet and dramatist Jakob Bidermann, first published in 1640.[13] Composed as a series of moralizing merry tales for schoolroom practice in the early 1600s, Bidermann's work is a succession of exuberant narrative episodes, loosely connected through a narrative frame, which in their entirety almost amount to a picaresque novel in the style of Petronius' *Satyricon* or Rabelais's *Gargantua and Pantagruel*. The *Utopia Didaci Bemardini, Seu Iacobi Bidermani* would nearly equal the publicity of More's, making it to eight editions before 1800, six printed in Germany, two in Italy, as well as a Polish (see Bidermann 1984: 3) and a plagiarized German version under the title *Bacchusia Oder Faßnacht-Land* ('Bacchusia or Carnival-Country') (1677). It would in its turn initiate a whole series of 'Jesuit counterutopias' (Reitinger 2007: 448). Around 1650, Johann Andreas Schnebelin, an officer in the Imperial Army, produced a loose adaptation of Hall's *Mundus* (drawing on both Hall and Bidermann) under the title *Erklärung*

---

[12] See Nicholas in this volume.
[13] On Bidermann's life and work, see Sieveke 2011.

der wunder-seltzamen Land-Charten Utopiae, so da ist das neu-entdeckte Schlarraffen-Land ('Explanation of the Strange and Wonderful Map of Utopia, which is the New-Found Land of Cockaigne'). This made complete the fusion of Hall's text with German popular satirical traditions already begun in Wintermonat's version of 1613 (Reitinger 2007: 441). What would create an even deeper impression than Schnebelin's book was the meticulously detailed fictional map in the shape of a fool's cap entitled 'Accurata Utopiae Tabula' that the cartographer Johann Baptist Homann produced to illustrate it in 1694.[14] Bound with Homann's *Atlas Novus* from 1716 onwards, it would remain popular for decades and continues to be reprinted to this day.

Schnebelin's and Bidermann's works are both illustrative of the overall developments in German utopian fiction after 1600. There seems to have been, perhaps already starting with Abraham Ortelius' 'Utopiae Typus' of 1595, an increasing interest in the visual elements of *Utopia*, especially the Utopian map. According to Franz Reitinger (2007: 441–449), this reflects a wider trend in seventeenth- and eighteenth-century German literary culture, where a combination of innovative map-making techniques and a certain predilection for allegorical mapping in Protestant devotional literature eventually made fictional maps a familiar feature. Utopian texts in this regard functioned as important catalysers, situated as they were at the interface between satire, narrative fiction, and religio-philosophical discourse. A second characteristic that we can make out in post-1600 utopias (both within Germany and elsewhere) is their increasing delight in narrative detail, mere storytelling for its own sake, leading to a gradual merging of the utopian tradition with novelistic genres.

As these seventeenth-century responses show, by 1650 we have come a long way from More's prototype, with the word 'Utopia' so far detached from its literary origins that it could function as a mere catchword in titles or imprints of philosophical treatises, polemical pamphlets, or satirical diatribes. A curious publication around 1700, *Utopia, Oder Entwurff Einer Paradigmatischen Policy* ('Utopia, or a Blueprint of Paradigmatic Policy'), posing like a Morean translation, could restrict itself to a pamphlet-like series of political theses (Morus 1700?; Pohl 2016: 495–496). And although a 'new and free translation' from 1753 by an unidentified author introducing themselves as 'J.B.K.' (*Des [...] Thomas Morus Utopien: in einer neuen und freyen Uebersetzung*) finally restores More's text in its original two-book and dialogic form, it essentially treats its model like a curiosity from the past. As the translator (who cites Henry Fielding's 1749 picaresque novel *Tom Jones* on the title page) observes in the preface, More's timeless political wisdom is certainly unquestionable. However, they cannot fail to remark that the storytelling skills of the author leave much to be desired in comparison with those of his more recent imitator Jonathan Swift:

---

[14] The map is best seen in colour; for an online copy see https://digital.library.cornell.edu/catalog/ss:3293788.

> If More all too often falls into the dry style of a philosopher and depicts the Utopians' way of life much to generally and without colour, Swift represents everything in the most pleasant episodes and lively accounts. His are the most exquisite narrative descriptions throughout, such as one will vainly look for in *Utopia*. (More 1753: 14)

Even though here still treated as a literary classic, More's prototype has at this point clearly been outstripped by its own literary progeny.

CHAPTER 12

RECEIVING MORE

Utopia *in Spain and New Spain*

DARCY KERN

IN 1515, while on embassy to Flanders, Thomas More began writing *Libellus vere aureus nec minus salutaris quam festivus de optimo statu reipublicae deque nova insula Utopia* (in English: 'A Truly Golden Account, as profitable as it is diverting, of the Best State of a Commonwealth and of the New Island of Utopia').[1] The embassy was to settle 'some differences of no slight import' between Henry VIII of England and Charles, 'the most serene prince [i.e. king] of Castile' (Charles I of Spain from 1516; Holy Roman Emperor Charles V from 1519), whose counsellor, Jerome Busleyden, appears as one of More's correspondents in the paratextual letters at the beginning of the book (More 2016b: 8). *Utopia* traced its intellectual descent from classical sources such as Plato's *Republic*, Cicero's *De officiis*, and Augustine's *City of God,* but it was also influenced by recent events, especially the Iberian exploration and colonization of the Americas.[2] Raphael Hythloday, the main (fictional) character of *Utopia*, from whom Morus the character learns 'so much about unknown peoples and lands', is a native of Portugal and alleges to have learned to sail while in the service of the explorer Amerigo Vespucci (originally a Florentine, but from 1505, a citizen of Castile). On his last voyage with Vespucci, Hythloday explains that he decided to remain 'at the farthest point' of the trip, that is, somewhere near modern-day Rio de Janeiro (10).

Given the contemporary context of Iberian exploration and More's diplomatic manoeuvres with the king of Castile, it is rather surprising that modern scholarship on the reception of *Utopia* in the Spanish kingdoms, especially Castile, the largest and the one colonizing the Americas, is limited. Very little work has been done since the great exertions of Marcel Bataillon on Spanish Erasmianism in the 1930s and Francisco López Estrada on More in the 1980s and early 1990s, though Randi Lise Davenport and Carlos

---

[1] All translations are mine unless otherwise noted.
[2] See chapters by Hobbs and Hadfield in this volume.

Cabanillas Cárdenas have looked briefly at the text's intersection with seventeenth-century Spanish Tacitism.[3] Guided by Charles I's motto, *Plus Ultra* (further beyond), this chapter traces *Utopia*'s appearance and reception in Spain and its American territories in the sixteenth and seventeenth centuries.

SIXTEENTH-CENTURY SPANISH TRANSLATIONS AND THE ABSENCE OF PRINT

Charles I became king of Spain in March 1516 and moved his Flemish court south of the Pyrenees the following year.[4] Humanists dominated both the royal court and the new Complutense University, founded in 1499 by Cardinal Francisco Jiménez de Cisneros (d. 1517), who was sometime regent for the king, head of the Order of Friars Minor (Franciscans)—whom he sought to reform morally and discipline in Castile—and sponsor of the Complutense Polyglot Bible, the first multilingual Bible in print (Ingram 2009: 6).[5] Cisneros repeatedly asked Erasmus to come to Spain, but though the great humanist considered the request, he never went (Bataillon 1950: 1.90, 95). Many Spanish clergy, scholars, bureaucrats, and courtiers nevertheless became Erasmian in their outlook on politics, reform, and good society. Arguably the most prominent Erasmians at court were Alfonso de Valdés and Alonso Manrique de Lara. Valdés was secretary to Charles I. Erasmus' work stimulated his desire for religious reform, especially of what he regarded as an unspiritual and dissolute papacy; he was also influenced by Erasmus' ideas on politics and war (Bataillon 1950: 1.427–472). Manrique was bishop of Córdoba from 1516 to 1523, at which point he became archbishop of Seville and Inquisitor General. While holding the latter positions, he became the dedicatory addressee of Juan Luis Vives's *De pacificatione* (Bruges, 1529). Vives, from a Spanish Jewish family that had converted to Catholicism (*conversos*), had long since left his homeland for England and the Low Countries, where he joined Erasmus' and More's humanist circle. Vives praised Manrique for his dignity, learning, nobility, and guardianship of the commonweal (Curtis 2008: 163–164). With wise, judicious oversight, he wrote, Manrique converted Seville into 'the centre of the world' and brought men and ideas from all over Europe to Spain (Sánchez Herrero 1992: 352; Guillén 2006: 88). The first three decades of the sixteenth century thus saw in Spain a flourishing, productive exchange of texts and ideas oriented towards educational, linguistic, political, and religious reform. Erasmus'

---

[3] Bataillon 1937 (trans. 1950); López Estrada 1980, 1992, 1996; Davenport and Cabanillas Cárdenas (2008: 114–117) argue that the Spanish perceived Tacitus to be dangerous because his works offered 'a covert way of passing on the Machiavellian message'. Nevertheless, he was translated and read often at the beginning of the seventeenth century.–

[4] The royal court was itinerant. It moved between cities such as Valladolid, Toledo, Burgos, Medina del Campo, and Seville.

[5] On Cisneros's reforms, particularly under Isabella and Ferdinand, see Turley 2014: 18–20.

networks and influence, combined with the desire of many elite Spaniards for widespread reform, laid the foundation for the reception of More's work.

Utopia first appeared in print at the end of 1516, when Thierry Martens, a printer in Louvain, published it at Erasmus' request.[6] A year later Gilles de Gourmont printed the text in Paris. Gourmont's edition was edited by Thomas Lupset, More's friend and fellow humanist, and had marginal notes written by Erasmus, but Erasmus later wrote that this version was 'full of inaccuracies' (Erasmus 1915: 240). In 1518 Johann Froben published two better versions in Basel. These editions contained both More's and Erasmus' *Epigrammata* and were the last editions More himself corrected; a fifth edition followed in Florence in 1519. The geography of *Utopia*'s early print history (Louvain, Paris, Basel, Florence) indicates that the book spread quickly throughout Europe. Printed vernacular translations soon followed in German (Basel, 1524), Italian (Venice, 1548), French (Paris, 1550), English (London, 1551, 1556), and Dutch (Antwerp, 1553). However, More's Latin text was never printed in Spain, and a Spanish vernacular translation did not appear in print until 1637. Royston Jones found this absence of printing in Spain significant. Spaniards, according to Jones, lacked interest in More's work and the Church discouraged them from reading it (R. O. Jones 1950: 478).

Jones, however, seems to have been unaware of two early vernacular translations. One was made by Vasco de Quiroga, a judge in the Second Audiencia (High Court) of New Spain from 1530 to 1535.[7] Quiroga was an important figure in the literary, educational, and social history of New Spain. He helped New Spain become an intellectual hub for exporting ideas back to Old Spain by bringing the printing press to the Americas, founding the first university in the territory, and accumulating a large library, which, like a good humanist, he shared with his fellow colonists (Warren 1963: 25; Ríos Castaño 2012: 26; S. Zavala 1955: 10–11). Quiroga's translation of *Utopia* is now lost, but he wrote in *Información en derecho* (1535), his report to Charles I/V, that he had translated the book 'to the letter', intending to mimic More's 'elegant style' (Quiroga 1939: 397). He intended to send his translation with the *Información*, but whether he did is not known. It may have crossed the Atlantic and reached Spain; it may have stayed in New Spain. He clearly hoped for a large audience, suggesting that everyone who could read Castilian Spanish ought to read it, as it was a practical guide for the economic and religious reform and good government of indigenous American communities (386). He was not alone in desiring reform and good government based on More's work. In 1532 the members of the Audiencia collectively and individually sent Empress Isabella, wife of Charles I/V, a description of New Spain and suggested it be divided into four provinces, reflecting the Utopian scheme (S. Zavala 1955: 13).

The other sixteenth-century vernacular translation can be found in the Royal Palace Library in Madrid; now known as the 'Gondomar Manuscript', it came to the Palace

---

[6] For the Latin editions of *Utopia* printed in More's lifetime, see Taylor in this volume.

[7] For practical purposes, from Hernán Cortés's conquest of the Aztec Empire in 1521 to the establishment of the viceroyalty in 1535, New Spain consisted of central Mexico, though the borders of the viceroyalty would extend from the modern south-western United States to modern Panama.

Library in the collection of Diego Sarmiento de Acuña, Count of Gondomar (1567–1626) (Davenport and Cabanillos Cárdenas 2008: 110).[8] The unknown translator(s) made the translation sometime between 1519 and 1535, when the fortunes of Erasmian humanists in Spain precipitously declined as the king struggled to deal with religious reform movements and their political fallout; the Inquisition increased its activities against Erasmians and alleged Lutherans in the late 1520s and early 1530s, though Manrique, as Inquisitor General, tried to temper the punishments against them until his death in 1538 (Bataillon 1950: 2.7–67). López Estrada (1992: 43–45) believed that the presence of this manuscript in the Royal Palace collection meant that it circulated among the elite at Charles I/V's court, while Davenport and Cabanillos Cárdenas (2008: 110) argue that the manuscript may have been 'the clean copy made for printing', since it contains two different hands with the second hand scrupulously correcting the first.

Whether the translator(s) of the Gondomar Manuscript intended it for print or manuscript circulation or both, it and Quiroga's translation probably were not printed for several reasons. First, market demand may have been low or uncertain. The Latin editions from Louvain and Basel both found their way to Iberia and likely proved sufficient to meet the needs of the educated elite or those with an interest in books and exploration, such as Hernando Colón, son of the explorer Cristóbal (aka Christopher Columbus), who founded the Columbian Library in Seville and purchased a copy of *Utopia* (1518b Basel edition) in Brussels (López Estrada 2001: 164). Colón travelled with the court of Charles I/V around Europe between 1520 and 1522. He was in the Low Countries several times and visited England once (Guillén 2006: 119–122). While in the Low Countries he purchased numerous Erasmian books, buying as many as nine in a single day (Bataillon 1950: 1.116 n.). The Columbian Library contains at least one other book from Froben's, Gourmont's and Martens's presses.[9] Colón corresponded with the Franciscan friar Juan de Zumárraga, who also owned a copy of the second Basel edition of *Utopia* (More 1518b) and who, in the late 1520s, became the first bishop, then archbishop, of New Spain. One of the last gifts Colón received before he died was a book from Zumárraga (Guillén 2006: 129). Zumárraga was also a close associate of Quiroga; both men had been at the royal court in the late 1520s and served together in New Spain in the 1530s. Like Manrique, both facilitated the circulation of literature from all over Europe among the Spanish. Thus, there were multiple Latin copies of *Utopia* circulating in Spain and New Spain and at least one, possibly two, manuscript translations circulating in Spain (if Quiroga's arrived with his *Información*).

The second reason that there was no sixteenth-century Spanish translation of *Utopia* in print may be due to the fact that its appearance in vernacular manuscripts coincided with a shift in the Spanish print industry. The printing press had arrived fairly quickly in Spain—Segovia had one by 1472—but Spain never became a leader in the print trade

---

[8] Real Biblioteca, Fondo Gondomar, RB II/1087.

[9] Conradus de Halberstadt's *Concordantiae Bibliorum* (Frobens, 1496), the *Constitutiones synodales Atrebatenses* (Martens, c.1500), and Maurus Honoratus Servius' *Index eorum que in hoc volumine continentur vocabula in Vergilium annotata* (Gourmont, c.1512) (Morera et al. 1999: 101, 199, 904).

(Wilkinson 2012: 78, 85–86). In the 1530s the centre of Spanish print shifted to Antwerp, specifically to the dominant Plantin Press. Christophe Plantin became the Royal Typographer for Charles I/V and 'chief censor of all his competitors' output' (Eisenstein 1979: 1.408). Meanwhile, Spanish printers suffered economically and often closed their operations. This was particularly true of the presses in Seville, even though all voyages to and from the Americas had to start and end in that city from 1503 on (Maillard Álvarez and Pérez García 2013: 273).

A third reason may be the worsening relations between Spain and England, as the marriage between Henry VIII and Catherine of Aragon, Charles I/V's aunt, broke down. Throughout the 1520s More took on greater political responsibilities and, at the time, it was unclear what role he might play in the king's manoeuvring. He was not yet the great Catholic hero and martyr he would become after his execution in 1535 (García Hernán 2016: 301), so reverence for his work and an urgency to print it were unlikely at the time that the first Spanish translations appeared in manuscript.

SIXTEENTH-CENTURY SPANISH HUMANISM, COLONIZATION, AND *UTOPIA*

The arrival of the Spanish in the Americas in 1492 initiated a complex, long-running debate about the land and the people who lived there. Europeans questioned who the indigenous Americans were, what rights they possessed, and how they should be treated legally, economically, and religiously. The theoretical debates on these issues were important and influential, but so too was the reality of Spanish practices in the Americas. Soon after Cristóbal Colón arrived, Spanish colonists established an economic system, known as the *encomienda*, that coerced indigenous labour.[10] This system engendered great exploitation. When Domingo Hurtado de Mendoza, the cardinal archbishop of Seville (1485–1502), heard reports that Spanish colonists were abusing the people of Hispaniola, he sent a group of Dominicans to stop the abuse. Legally, the friars had no authority to end the harsh labour regime on the island, but they strenuously preached against it. In response to the Dominicans' exertions, Spanish colonists chose a Franciscan, Alonso de Espinal, to represent them to Ferdinand II and refute the Dominicans, but the king was outraged by what he heard (Fernández Rodríguez 1994: 49). Under pressure from the Dominicans, the Castilian government enacted the

---

[10] The *encomienda* was a grant of labour rather than lands to Spanish colonizers and settlers. The grant gave a specific number of indigenous people to an *encomendero* (the Spaniard holding the grant) but did not identify the individuals within the community who had to fulfil the labour requirements. Indigenous leaders chose who worked and paid tribute. In return, the *encomenderos* were to help protect the community and to teach Castilian Spanish and Christianity to those who worked for them. Indigenous labourers retained legal rights under Spanish law and were not enslaved, though many were treated as poorly as slaves.

Leyes de Burgos in 1512. These laws forbade Spaniards from mistreating Amerindians under the *encomienda* and encouraged their conversion to Catholicism. A year later the Crown enacted the *Leyes Complementarios de Valladolid* to further protect the indigenous peoples (Fernández Rodríguez 1994: 61). In spite of these laws, the debate among Spaniards and Europeans about the status of Amerindians and how the Spanish should treat them persisted for the rest of the century. It also influenced the reception of *Utopia* in Spain.

Zumárraga and Martín de Valencia were Franciscans who read *Utopia*, likely the 1518 Basel edition which Zumárraga owned, and who were involved in Spain's colonization of the Americas, the latter as spiritual leader of 'the Twelve' Franciscans who arrived in 1524 and an inquisitorial commissioner from 1524 to 1526 (Tavárez 2011: 30; Morales 2001: 333–344; de Benavente Motolinia 2014). Zumárraga was 'an unusually well-educated member of his province' and a teacher in the Franciscan *studia generalia*, a sort of precursor to the modern university (V. Zavala 1985: 1.43; cf. Senocak 2012). Like Erasmus, he embraced humanist ideals, including the belief that the Bible should be read widely and in the vernacular. His publications from New Spain, the *Doctrina Breve* (1544) and the *Doctrina Cristiana* (1546), criticized the immoral behaviour of the Catholic hierarchy, a theme found in both Erasmus' works and More's early works. For example, in Book One of *Utopia*, Hythloday relates how the friars in England 'are the greatest vagabonds of all' and are overly sensitive to criticism, often resorting to threats or punishments against those who mock them, up to and including securing papal bulls to excommunicate their critics (More 2016b: 27). By contrast, the Utopians have few priests because 'their priests are of extraordinary holiness', and their religious celibates work constantly in the service of others (103). *Utopia*'s explicit, sweeping criticism of the mendicants did not deter Zumárraga—himself from a mendicant order—from securing a copy of the text, but it did lead one of the readers (possibly Zumárraga himself) to edit and annotate his copy.[11]

The annotations in Zumárraga's copy, like Quiroga's *Información*, show that the reader clearly understood the *salutaris* (helpful, wholesome) nature of More's work but missed its *festivus* (humorous) character. He underlined passages emphasizing *Utopia*'s seriousness while scoring out those that undermined the religious order of the Catholic Church. For example, in Guillaume Budé's letter to Lupset at the beginning of the book, where Budé thanks Lupset for sending him More's work and so drawing his attention to what will be diverting and profitable for future readers, Zumárraga's reader simply underlined 'and likely to be useful [or profitable] to future readers' (More 1518b/Z: 3). Quiroga offered a similar understanding in his *Información*, quoting the end of Budé's letter: 'In his [More's] history [...] we have a nursery of polite and useful institutions from which men may borrow customs and introduce and adapt them each to his own state' (Quiroga 1939: 397). Budé, of course, was playing on More's name in the Latin—*mores* (customs)—but Quiroga, like Zumárraga's annotator, missed Budé's playfulness

---

[11] Zumárraga's copy is now in the Benson Collection, University of Texas, Austin (shelf mark GZZ 321.07 M813D 1518): cited hereafter as More 1518b/Z. Warren (1963: 30) concluded that the handwriting is not Vasco de Quiroga's. I agree.

entirely. Fintan Warren (1963: 24–25) has argued that Quiroga was a man of great seriousness. Certainly, his treatment of Lucian in the *Información* reinforces this point. More 'was probably more widely read in his lifetime as the translator of Lucian than the author of *Utopia*' (Branham 1985: 23–24). Lucian, a professional sophist, practised oratory as entertainment, often with a heavy dose of satire. Quiroga references Lucian's *Saturnalia* frequently, but—unlike More—without the humour. This seriousness carried over to his reading of *Utopia*. For Zumárraga, Quiroga, and their circle of clerical and bureaucratic humanists, *Utopia* the book and Utopia the island offered readers a practical guide for social mores, culture, and political behaviour rather than a linguistic or philosophical diversion.

Zumárraga's reader found that *Utopia* offered guidance on three particular contemporary concerns. The first was gold and silver. More writes of the Macarian laws on gold and silver in Book One: 'On the day that their king first assumes office, he must take an oath confirmed by solemn ceremonies that he will never have in his treasury at any one time more than a thousand pounds in gold, or its equivalent in silver' (More 2016b: 35). Beside this passage Zumárraga's reader noted that this was 'the best instruction' (More 1518b/Z: 60). In Book Two, where More describes the Utopians' ambivalence to gold and silver (2016b: 62–63), Zumárraga's reader wrote, 'They have no use for money' (1518b/Z: 96). It is not hard to see why a reforming Franciscan would have found this passage important. It harks back to St Francis of Assisi's thirteenth-century Rule, which prohibited his followers from owning or even touching coin so as not to allow worldly goods to corrupt them, but extends a less restrictive limitation, in that it does not completely prohibit possession into the temporal sphere at a time when ever more quantities of gold and silver were beginning to trickle into the royal coffers from New Spain. Quiroga's *Información*, echoing *Utopia* and the notes made by Zumárraga's reader, commended indigenous Americans because 'they had no coins among them and disparaged gold and silver', using it only for social exchanges at parties (Quiroga 1939: 385). In this respect, then, the people of New Spain were closer to the Utopian ideal and easier to reform than contemporary Spaniards, who highly valued gold and silver.

The second concern was counsel. In Book One Zumárraga's reader marked a passage that depicted Morus chastising Hythloday for saying that there is no place for philosophy in royal councils. He underlined, blocked in the margin, and added the words *nota diligenter* ('note carefully') to Morus' argument that 'if you cannot pluck up bad ideas by the root, if you cannot cure long-standing evils as completely as you would like, you must not therefore abandon the commonwealth'. He likewise emphasized Morus' observation that 'it is impossible to make everything good unless all men are good, and that I don't expect to see for quite a few years yet' (More 1518b/Z: 62; 2016b: 36–37). Where Hythloday responds to Morus that Plato had warned wise men to avoid public business, as it corrupts and compromises men of goodwill and integrity, Zumárraga's reader highlighted the sentence, writing in the margin *notada doctrina Platonis* ('noted doctrine of Plato') (1518b/Z: 64; 2016b: 39).

The tension between good and evil, between being in the world but not of it, between the necessity to act on good ideas and the expectation of resistance to one's actions and ideas clearly emerges from this section and again reflects the struggle for the mendicant ideal, particularly in Spain. In the fifteenth century Spanish Franciscans had split between Observant friars and Conventual reformers (the former itinerant, the latter based in convents). The conflict became particularly pronounced in newly conquered Granada. Pope Leo X's bull *Ite vos in vineam meam* (1517) reunited the disparate factions under the control of the Observants but allowed the Conventuals space to practise their distinct Franciscan spirituality. Martín de Valencia, leader of 'the Twelve' in New Spain, was a Conventual Franciscan (Turley 2014: 30). For him and for a reformer like Zumárraga, More's text offered a clear enunciation of an enduring dilemma they faced. Once in New Spain Zumárraga set about evangelizing Amerindians with great energy, but this often required him to mediate between Spanish colonists who saw indigenous Americans as a necessary part of the economic system and labour regime and reforming clerics like Bartolomé de las Casas who argued vigorously for their natural rights (MacLachlan 1988: 55–59). Zumárraga himself believed the *encomienda* system needed significant reform, but he never sought to abolish it entirely, as Las Casas did, because Zumárraga was an *encomendero*, a colonist who formally held a right to indigenous labour and therefore profited from the system (Liss 1975: 79).[12] Towards the end of his life Zumárraga complained about being sent to the colonies and longed for the happiness of his convent in El Abrojo (Zumárraga 1951: 368; Turley 2014: 2). Steven Turley has observed that many of the Franciscans who migrated to the Americas ultimately found their mission work incompatible with their Order's eremitic spirituality not only because of the rigours of establishing a completely new church in a totally unfamiliar area but also because they had to mediate between Spaniards and indigenous Americans and between the various factions of Spanish colonists, particularly between Hernán Cortés and his opponents. This tension led to 'suffering and erratic behavior' as they tried to adapt to a new world that made little sense and saw less success converting indigenous peoples than they had hoped (Turley 2014: 3, 72–73). Judging from the notes in Zumárraga's copy of *Utopia*, he or another reader adhered to the Morean rhetorician's advocacy of good counsel and active engagement with the world while recognizing (and perhaps longing for) Plato's idealistic advice that good men withdraw from it.

What Zumárraga or his reader did not support was More's condemnation of mendicant corruption and canon law. As noted above, Hythloday denounced friars as the greatest vagabonds in all of England who should be arrested for their vagabondage and put to work. This was a bridge too far for Zumárraga's reader, who thoroughly scored it out. He did the same for an earlier line where a fool reports that the poor, the sick, and the elderly no longer ask him for money but let him pass 'without a word or hope', as if he were a priest, because they know he will not help them (More 1518b/Z: 51; 2016b: 27). Equating the fool's lack of charity with a priest's was obviously unacceptable to this reader. The reader also crossed out Budé's statement to Lupset that Christ's law of

---

[12] Las Casas initially held an *encomienda*, too, but he gave it up in 1515 after several interactions with the reforming Dominicans mentioned above.

communion among his followers 'undermined [...] all that body of civil and the more recent canon law worked out in so many vast volumes. Yet this is the law which we see now holding the fort of wisdom and ruling over our destinies' (More 1518b/Z: 7; 2016b: 120). To Budé, canon law was based not on Christian truth or the Catholic Church's maintenance of the apostolic tradition but on human artifice and novelty and was in direct opposition to Christ and his law. It is not hard to see why such a statement would be unpalatable for a clerical reader dedicated to the Church's claims about its authority.

Zumárraga's annotated *Utopia* and Quiroga's *Información* lead one to conclude that some sixteenth-century Spanish humanists read More's work with a seriousness that entirely ignored its playfulness and intellectually stimulating diversions. To them, *Utopia* served as a practical guide for engaging the world and improving society, though they individually and unofficially expurgated its criticisms of mendicants and canon law. That both Spanish and American society needed improving was beyond question, but there seems to have been greater hope of success with the peoples of the New World than with those of the Old. Influenced in part by reforms at the end of the fifteenth century as well as by Erasmian humanism and More's *Utopia*, Quiroga, the Audiencia, and the Franciscans sought to impose a regime on indigenous Americans that was not out of place with the Utopians' own experience of conquering and colonizing other communities.

More's Martyrdom and a New Translation

More's works continued to enter Spain throughout the sixteenth century. The library at the University of Seville (also known as the Universidad Hispalense) acquired at least two copies of More's *Omnia latina opera* printed at Louvain in 1566 (López Estrada 2001: 164). Meanwhile, *Utopia* was put to novel use. The Basque jurist Andrés de Poza (d. 1595) wrote a treatise in 1587 in which he described the clothing of young Basque women who walked around with short, uncovered hair, short shirts and skirts, and without a cloak. Normally such dress would be considered indecent, but, Poza writes, More gave a justification for it in *Utopia* when he described how potential marriage partners presented themselves naked to each other (one at a time, and always accompanied by an older man or woman of integrity) so that no hidden deformity would subsequently mar the marriage (Poza 1587: 37v–38r). Bataillon marvelled at Poza's audacity in comparing Basque popular dress to Utopian nudity, but the comparison allowed Poza to present regional attire as superior to that of the royal court because it was more natural, native, and practical, the single most consistent lesson in Spanish treatments of *Utopia* (Bataillon 1972: 57–58; López Estrada 1980: 47).

Meanwhile, More's status as a martyr for the faith, persecuted by a vicious English tyrant, grew. Several late sixteenth- and early seventeenth-century publications helped cement his reputation in Spain. Nicholas Sander, an English Catholic priest who left England in 1559 after the accession of Elizabeth I, wrote a tract, *De origine ac progressu Schismatis Anglicani* ('On the Origin and Progress of the English Schism'), detailing Henry VIII's divorce from Catherine of Aragon. Sander spent part of his exile in Spain at the court of Philip II (r. 1556–98), and his unfinished text, published multiple times in the 1580s and again in the early seventeenth century, became popular in the country. The Spanish Jesuit Pedro de Ribadeneira used Sander's work as a source for his own *Historia Ecclesiastica del scisma del Reyno de Inglaterra* ('Ecclesiastical History of the Schism of the Kingdom of England') (Madrid 1588) and added to the 1610 and 1628 editions of *De origine* (López Estrada 1996: 79–80). Ribadeneira's history is full of praise for More as a counsellor, a servant of the king, and a servant of God, but it never mentions *Utopia*. Likewise, the Sevillan poet Fernando de Herrera mentioned More's epigrams and Greek-to-Latin translations of Lucian but not *Utopia* in his biography *Vida y Muerte de Tomás Moro* (Seville, 1592; republished as *Vida de Thomas Moro* in Madrid, 1617). Despite the title, 'The Life and Death of Thomas More', Herrera (1617: 16) notes that he did not intend 'to write all of More's life' ('no es mi intento escrivar toto su vida'). The Spanish thus gradually adopted More as 'our invincible Martyr rebuk[ing] the stubborn waywardness of the British regions', as Cypriano Gutiérrez, a Jesuit who taught Scripture at the College of Santa Catalina in Córdoba, wrote (More 1637: 13v). Though the British had left him lying in red embers, More, like a phoenix, was reborn in Spain, according to Francisco Roco Campofrío y Córdoba, an alderman of Córdoba (16v). However, *Utopia* was not part of the martyr's repertoire, outside the Basque areas, at the end of the sixteenth century.

Neither Ribadeneira nor Herrera mentioned *Utopia* because Gaspar de Quiroga, the Inquisitor General, cardinal archbishop of Toledo, and nephew of Vasco de Quiroga, had placed the book on the *Index of Prohibited Books* in 1583 and included it in the *Index of Expurgated Books* in 1584.[13] The full entry for the 1583 prohibition reads: 'Thomas More, otherwise a pious and Catholic man, Utopia: unless expurgated' ('Thomae Mori [viri alias pii et catholici] Utopia: nisi repurgetur', G. Quiroga 1583: 60r). The beginning of the much longer entry in 1584 states that the book 'was written by Thomas More, a renowned man, and printed at Basel in 1563' ('Ex Thomae Mori, viri clarissimi, scriptis, in impres. Basileae apud Episcopium, anno. 1563'). It then lists the specifically expurgated lines, including the marginal note in Book Two that reads 'O priests far holier than our own' (*O sacerdotes nostris longè sanctiores*, G. Quiroga 1584: 193r).

Utopia disappeared from the *Index* in 1620 and did not reappear in the 1632 version (Sandoval y Rojas 1620; Zapata 1632). Its removal allowed the first Spanish translation to appear in print at Córdoba in 1637. Francisco de Quevedo, the prominent poet of the Spanish Baroque (1580–1660), owned a copy of *Utopia* (Louvain 1548), which he signed

---

[13] The Catholic Church began issuing lists banning specific books and/or authors in the 1550s as a means of standardizing the faith and asserting control over various factions that wanted reform and freedom in translation and authorship. Individual nations issued their own *Index of Prohibited Books* to supplement the Roman one. All were constantly revised and updated.

and annotated heavily. Like Quiroga and Zumárraga a century before him, Quevedo read *Utopia* as a serious treatise that could and should foster peace and good government in Spain if read and applied to political realities. Quevedo convinced Jerónimo Antonio de Medinilla i Porres, a bureaucrat in Córdoba and a knight of the Order of Santiago, to translate *Utopia* into Castilian Spanish, though Medinilla only translated the second book, either because Book One was too specific to England to translate for a Spanish audience or its style too playfully humanistic to serve the purpose of a practical political guide (López Estrada 1996: 85–86).[14] Quevedo also supplied prefatory material (More 1637: 1v, 10v–11v), as did many others, including Medinilla. The sheer amount of prefatory material in Medinilla's translation suggests that he circulated the manuscript widely among his friends and acquaintances as well as the proper religious and civil authorities. Medinilla informed his readers that in translating he had given more emphasis to 'the spirit of the author [More] than to his words' (4v–5r). He reaffirmed More's status as a 'holy martyr' but also included a 'note on chapter nine', declaring that 'some clauses' needed to be expurgated from the work because More portrayed the Utopians as 'permitting a variety of religions in their Republic'. His censored version attempted to maintain the 'Catholic sense of the Martyr [More]' by suggesting that More's diversity of religions actually meant the various groups and orders and local practices within the Roman Catholic Church (6v–7v). The official censor, Bartolomé Ximénez Patón, wrote that Medinilla had achieved the fidelity and elegance of style that Quiroga had earlier aspired to (and perhaps achieved) (21v–22r), but it is clear that the context of *Utopia* had shifted since the 1520s and 1530s. Where Quiroga and Zumárraga recognized the pagan religious diversity of the indigenous peoples of New Spain and sought to use *Utopia* to reorder their communities along Christian lines because it seemed to speak to the real situation in the Americas, Medinilla dropped the American context and reoriented the book to Europe and to a Spanish Catholic society that aggressively censored people and books while valorizing those who shared its faith.

Like Quiroga and Zúmarraga, Medinilla and those who wrote introductions to his translation saw the text as a practical guide for society, one that contained the 'precepts of governing', as Agustin de Galarça, a royal bureaucrat, wrote (More 1637: 17v–18r). Its relevance was more straightforward for readers of Medinilla's seventeenth-century translation than for readers of sixteenth-century versions (in Spanish and Latin). Since Book One, in which the character of Cardinal John Morton remarks on the entertaining linguistic diversions of his guests and offers ripostes to a lawyer and a friar at his table, no longer exists in the 1637 printing, the Spanish reader would have been at a loss to see the text as anything other than a treatise on government and communal organization. The loss of Book One also meant the loss of tension between worldly engagement and Platonic withdrawal and a change in Hythloday's nationality from Portuguese to Spanish. The former likely explains Jesuit enthusiasm for Medinilla's translation. Their

---

[14] For the practice of translating Book Two only, see also chapters by Schmidt and Shrank in this volume.

mission was worldly engagement; they did not face the same dilemma over engagement or withdrawal that had plagued the Conventual Franciscans in the previous century. Regarding the latter, the censor Patón's preface claimed Hythloday as a Spanish explorer, just as Gutiérrez claimed More had become a Spanish hero and martyr (More 1637: 9v). From 1580 to 1640 Portugal did belong to the Spanish Crown, but because Medinilla dropped the first book from the text, it was easy to claim Hythloday was Spanish without having to alter More's description of him as a sailor on Vespucci's voyages.

Comparing Sixteenth- and Seventeenth-Century Spanish Translations of *Utopia*

In addition to the loss of Book One, the 1637 Spanish translation is different in organization and language from the extant sixteenth-century one. The Gondomar Manuscript follows the order of the 1518 Basel edition. At the beginning of the translation are Peter Giles's letter to Jerome Busleyden and More's letter to Giles (the preface to the book), followed by the first book of *Utopia*. Missing are Erasmus' letter to Froben, Budé's letter to Lupset, the hexastichon (a six-line poem), the woodcut map of the island of Utopia, and the Utopian alphabet, all of which precede Giles's letters in the printed version. At the end of the second book is a translation of Busleyden's letter to More. The 1637 printing has none of these materials. In their place are many recommendations and laudatory poems about Medinilla and his work.

In Book Two, the only section the vernaculars have in common, the words and phrases used differ from each other, which in turn affects interpretation of the text. Near the beginning of the second book More writes that Utopus, the founder of Utopia, gave the island his name after conquering it and bringing its inhabitants to such a high level of humanity and culture that they soon surpassed all others (More 1518b: 71; 2016b: 44). The people that Utopus conquered were, according to the Gondomar translation, 'simple and wild' (*ruda y agreste*), but he 'taught' (*enseñó*) them such 'humanity' (*humanidad*) that they eventually 'exceeded all other mortals' (*exceder a todos los mortales*) (RB II/1087: C2r). In the 1637 version, Utopus no longer teaches the people but 'reduces the rustic and uncouth crowd to a human, civil manner of living' ('reduxo muchedumbre rustica y grossera a este manera de vivir humana, y civil', More 1637: 2r). The distinction here is important. In the sixteenth-century translation, Utopus teaches people who, though primitive, are nonetheless receptive to his civilizing instruction. It is a relationship that benefits both through a humanistic medium (teaching) and the emphasis is on growth (they 'exceeded'). In Medinilla's translation, the relationship has changed to one of power politics, where Utopus 'reduces' a non-individualized crowd to a (supposedly) human manner of living. There is nothing inspiring in Medinilla's exchange and really nothing out of line with contemporary Tacitism—the idea that the national interest is closely aligned with the power of the monarch—since Utopus is forcing the Abraxan crowd to live like all other men have lived.

Differences in phrasing in Book Two, chapter four ('Their Occupations') again emphasize the contrast between the Gondomar's focus on the individual citizen's development and Medinilla's prioritization of the ruler or state. More writes that Utopian magistrates shorten the workday (from six hours) if there is no need for the citizens of Utopia to make repairs to public infrastructure, since they cannot force citizens to perform useless labour. The goal of the republic is for all citizens to devote themselves as much as possible to the freedom and culture of the mind/spirit (More uses the word *anima*, which can mean either), not the labour of the body, for in the former lies the happiness of life (More 1518b: 85–86; 2016b: 56). In the Gondomar translation the goal of the republic is 'to relieve citizens of physical/bodily labour for which there is no necessity and to give them liberty of spirit' ('por que la orden de aquella republica tiene respecto a este fin principalmente de relebar alos ciudadanos del trabajo desu cuerpo no aviendo necessidad del y darles libertad de espiritu', RB II/1087: C6r). This purpose, for citizens to rise above the physicality of the body to the greater sphere of the *anima*, bears traces of fifteenth-century Florentine Neoplatonism, but how is one to reach such heights? Here the Gondomar translation makes explicit what More only implies. The translation states, 'Because such civil authorities do not exercise citizens against their will in superfluous labour' ('porque los tales Regidores no exercitan alos ciudadanos contra su voluntad en superfluo trabajo', RB II/1087: C6r). Utopian citizens have wills of their own, echoing Giovanni Pico della Mirandola's declaration in the 'Oration on the Dignity of Man' (1496) that human dignity lies in the will to choose what we become, ideally becoming like God. Thus, the Gondomar translation again expresses humanist conceits that mitigate the power of civil authorities. In the 1637 edition Medinilla dropped the will (*voluntad*), writing that 'magistrates do not bother citizens with useless work [...] because the aim of the republic is to satisfy public needs [...] and whatever time is left over from servile jobs is given to citizens to enjoy liberty and contemplation of the *anima*' ('Porque los Magistrados no ocupan a los Ciudadanos en travajos enutiles [...] pues que la institucion [...] desta Republica principalmente atiende solo a este fin, a que satisfechas las necessidades publicas [...] lo mas del tiempo que sobra de los empleos serviles, se reduzga a que los Ciudadanos gozen dela libertad, i contemplacion del anima', More 1637: 10r). The 1637 translation thus prioritizes public need over individual personal growth. Instead of the liberty of spirit so prominent in the Gondomar translation, Medinilla's work stresses the centrality and servile nature of public jobs.

The will (*voluntad*) appears again in the Gondomar translation in the very next chapter ('Social Relations'). More writes that if the population of Utopian cities exceeds the quota of 6,000 households, they enlist citizens from each city to plant colonies under Utopian law on the mainland, where natives have left land unoccupied and uncultivated. If the natives want to live with the Utopian settlers, they are accepted into the community. If they do not, the Utopians drive them out and, if necessary, make war on them (More 1518b: 87; 2016b: 57). The Gondomar translation states that the Utopian colonists ask their 'neighbours' if they would like to live with them; if so, the colonists are 'joined with those who come, of their will,' to the Utopian way of life and customs, and who 'easily develop' ('llamaron alos vezinos comarcanos quieren vivir conellos y juntados conlos que de su voluntad vienen con aquella orden de vida y con aquellas costumbres facilmente crescen', RB II/1087: C7v). Again the will (and the neighbourliness) drops from the 1637 translation. In this version the Utopian colonists invite the 'natives' (*los naturales de la tierra*) to live in their company if they would like ('si les agrada vivir en su compañia'). Those who accept the invitation and easily conform to the customs and laws are joined to them ('Aviendose juntado con los que acetan facilmente conforman en las costumbres, i leyes', 1637: 10v). The linguistic change is subtle but again emphasizes a legalistic power relationship between unequals. In the Gondomar translation the neighbours come of their own will and grow as they adopt the Utopian lifestyle and customs, whereas in Medinilla's translation the indigenous peoples accept and conform to Utopian customs and laws.

The translations of More's famous seventh chapter on Utopian slavery likewise distinguish the humanistic sixteenth-century version from its seventeenth-century counterpart.[15] Though both chapters are entitled *De los esclavos* ('On Slaves'), the vocabulary shows a marked difference. The Gondomar uses the word *siervos* four times, *esclavos* twice, the verb *servir* twice, and the noun *servidumbre* once in the section on slavery (RB II/1087: D8v). The Medinilla edition, by contrast, drops *siervos* entirely and uses *esclavos* three times, *esclavitud* once, *servir* once, and *servidumbre* twice (More 1637: 29r). The word *siervos* and its cognates had multiple meanings in the early sixteenth century, including 'servants', 'slaves', or 'serfs', the latter tied to the economic structure and land tenure of the Middle Ages. It could also refer to a person who belonged to a religious order or community in the Catholic Church. Pope Gregory I (r. 590–604) had even introduced the term to the papal title in the phrase 'servus servorum Dei' ('servant of the servants of God'). While *siervos* tied the text to medieval precedents, it also closely mirrored More's humanistic Latin. More entitled chapter seven *De Servis* (1518b: 119) and used the terms *servis*, *servorum*, and *servientem* throughout. Ambrogio Calepino's Latin dictionary, amended in the 1565 edition to include Italian, French, and Spanish words, supports the *servus/siervo* connection. For the entries on *servus* (noun and adjective), the Spanish is given as *siervo* and the definition as 'to whom freedom [*liber*] is opposed.' Only the exclusively feminine entry on *serva* gives the translation as *sierva* or *esclava* and states 'this is a slave-girl; all that serve are in bondage' (1565: 1000). Calepino's dictionary has no entry for *sclavus*, the Latin rendering of *esclavo* (981). Neither, it should be noted, does Alfonso de Palencia's 1490 *Universal vocabulario en latin y en romance*. Palencia only mentions the term *esclava* in the entry for a slave girl, just as Calepino's version does (449). Even Alonso Sánchez de la Ballesta's 1587 *Dictionario de vocablos castellanos, aplicados a la propiedad latina* has no entry for *esclavo*, but translates *siervo* as *servus* and gives several Spanish phrases (derived from Latin) that use the term (614). The Gondomar's use of *siervos* renders the text linguistically more flexible in interpretation,

---

[15] For the English translations of slavery, see Withington in this volume.

in that the status of the person so described could be legally and socially ambiguous, while also connecting it linguistically to Roman and medieval precedents.

Medinilla's use of *esclavos*, by contrast, refers exclusively to people who are entirely unfree and under the dominion of another. It reflects concurrent changes in Spanish dictionaries. Sebastián de Covarrubias Orozco published *Tesoro de la lengua castellana, o Española* in 1611. In it he included a long entry for *esclavo*, which he defined as 'el siervo, el cautivo' (captive). Covarrubias wrote that he understood *Sine Iure* to be the key phrase that defines a slave: a person without rights, because 'the slave is not his own, but [belongs to] his master, and to him [the slave] is prohibited any free act' (1611: 1.364r). More interesting is Covarrubias's definition of *siervo*: 'strictly, a slave' ('en rigor vale el esclavo') (2.28v). He has inverted the pre-eminence of the terms from what they had been in the previous century and now defines *siervo* exclusively in terms of slavery without any rights. Medinilla's reliance on *esclavo* renders his translation less historically grounded in the economic and social systems of the past, and more rigid with regard to the legal, social, political, and economic status of the person so described. It reflects a new type of slavery.

As a final example, the difference between the translations is immediately noticeable in the aforementioned ninth chapter on Utopian religion. Translated in the context of the recent and ongoing exploration and conquest of the Americas, the Gondomar version begins, 'The religions are not only varied and diverse throughout the whole island but in each city, where some worship the sun, others the moon, and others moving stars in place of God' ('Las religiones no solamente son varias y diversas en toda la ysla pero aun tambien en cada ciudad, por que unos adoran al sol y otros ala luna y otros a alguna delas estrellas erraticas en lugar de dios', RB II/1087: E7v). Medinilla simplified this by writing, 'There are various religions throughout the island and the cities, some worship the sun, others the moon, and others moving stars' ('Ay varias religiones no solo por la Isla, mas tambien en las Ciudades, unos adoran al Sol, otros la Luna, otros a alguna de las estrellas errantes', More 1637: 41r). He removed the final phrase 'in place of God', which is in More's original Latin (*dei vice*) (1518b: 140). For Medinilla, religious diversity existed only in the context of Catholicism and worship of the Christian God. One could not read of people who worshipped a natural body in place of God; such an idea might defeat the purpose of those who sought to reform Spanish society while under the watchful eye of the Inquisition.

Conclusion

In *Utopia*'s first 150 years Spanish bureaucrats, clerics, scholars, and courtiers on both sides of the Atlantic read it in Latin. Though its circulation may not have been as robust in Spain as it was in England, France, or the Low Countries, it nonetheless found a receptive audience. Some in this audience thought it worthwhile to translate *Utopia*, either to circulate in these same circles for non-Latin readers or for print publication for a more general audience. The Inquisition's interference in 1583 discouraged but did not eliminate interest in More's work and hindered publication of a vernacular translation, since one would need permission from the proper civil and religious authorities to go forward with such a text. It took the efforts of a famous patron, Quevedo, to see a translation through to print, but by the seventeenth century, general interest in *Utopia* seems to have declined, perhaps in part because of the perception that it was a practical guide for communal reform that would be difficult to effect in Spain. As Davenport and Cabanillas Cárdenas (2008: 113) have observed, the 1637 edition was not reprinted in Medinilla's lifetime, and there are few references to it in the seventeenth century. Another edition was not published until 1790. The extant translations themselves, along with Zumárraga's copy, suggest that people interpreted *Utopia* differently in the sixteenth and seventeenth centuries, though both used it as a practical guide for reform. For sixteenth-century Spanish readers it served as a real guide to a new world, one with all the possibilities for reform that More laid out. Though they read it with great seriousness, they also read it humanely and as applicable to individual human beings with souls and wills of their own. In the seventeenth century *Utopia* continued to serve as a basis for reform but without the Neoplatonic optimism and immediate application that American exploration had provided a century earlier. It now belonged to a society in which institutional power and reason of state governed human relations and limited human knowledge. Ultimately, Utopia, that elusive no-place, proved a chimera in Spain.

CHAPTER 13

UTOPIA IN SIXTEENTH-CENTURY ITALY

CATHY SHRANK

NORTHERN Italy was fertile ground for the transmission of Thomas More's *Utopia* in the sixteenth century.[1] The location for the last Latin edition published in More's lifetime (by the Giuntine Press in Florence in 1519), it was also the site for the printing of the first posthumous vernacular translation, by Ortensio Lando (Venice, 1548). This was only the second translation to be printed (after Claudius Cantiuncula's 1524 German translation) and the first to include both Books One and Two.[2] The Venetian presses would go on to see no less than six further editions before 1610, thanks to the inclusion of Lando's translation of Book Two as the final part of Francesco Sansovino's *Del governo*, first printed in 1561, with subsequent editions in 1566, 1567, 1578, 1583, and 1607, putting Venice at the top of the chart for early modern editions of *Utopia*, above London and Basel (both with three before 1600), a pre-eminence that reflects the dominance of the Venetian printing industry in sixteenth-century Europe as well as the market appeal of Sansovino's volume.

Whilst the popularity of Sansovino's version must owe at least something to the overall appeal of a work that he presented as a 'nuova Politica'—a sixteenth-century answer to Aristotle's *Politics* (Sansovino 1561: *3r)—the fact that Sansovino chose to include More's 'completely fiction[al]' (*tutta finta*) state at all, alongside actual polities from the early modern and ancient worlds, is testimony of its resonance for Italian readers. Scholars from Paul F. Grendler (1965) to Fabrizio Nevola (2019) have traced a long-standing Italian interest in devising ideal cities, found in works predating *Utopia*, such as Leon Battista Alberti's *De re aedificatoria* (printed in Latin in 1485), or Filarete's vision in the 1460s for a city, 'Sforzinda', which included social regulations alongside spatial planning. In addition, the intensely urban conception of Utopian governance (based as it is on the

---

[1] Unless otherwise stated, translations are my own. I am indebted to Alex Bamji and Ed Muir for their insights on a draft of this chapter.
[2] For the Florence edition, see Taylor in this volume; for Cantiuncula, see Schmidt in this volume.

island's fifty-four cities) presumably spoke to a culture where, in Paola Spinozzi's words, 'the only plausible identity in political and social terms was thriving on ideals of the city accomplished through the government of city-states such as Venice, Florence, and Rome' (Spinozzi 2016: 508). Further to that, there must have been particularly strong appeal for Lando's and Sansovino's most immediate readers: the Venetians. The Utopian political system, with a senate and a single elected ruler holding 'office for life', strongly resembled the Venetian constitution, whilst the vision of an island nation, enjoying a sustained civil peace and so renowned for its justice that its citizens are sought as magistrates by other countries (More 2016b: 50, 87), accords strongly with the 'myth of Venice': *la Serenissima*, the ideal, 'most serene' republic (Martin and Romano 2000: 2). Focusing on the 1548 and 1561 Italian editions, this chapter consequently explores the ways in which the sixteenth-century Italian *Utopias* were shaped by the cultural, intellectual, political, and religious contexts for which, and by which, they were produced.

1548: Eutopia *Ritrovata*

The 1548 translation strips away almost all the Latin paratexts, retaining only More's prefatory letter to Peter Giles. In the process, it effaces the pan-European humanist network that had collaborated in the production of the Latin *Utopias*. Printed anonymously, acknowledging neither its translator nor printer, the volume records a more scaled-down friendship than those celebrated in the Latin editions: namely, the relationship between Anton Francesco Doni (1513–74)—the man responsible for seeing this translation into print—and the dedicatee, the Ferrarese nobleman Geronimo Fava, in whose house the itinerant Doni 'had probably been a guest on one or more occasions' (Gjerpe 2008: 51 n.).[3] The discourse of friendship—so crucial to the self-presentation of More's humanist circle—is thus remodelled by Doni, who, from 1540—having abandoned a life as a monk and priest in Florence—pursued a 'wandering career, living by his pen and wits in northern Italy' (Grendler 1965: 483). Whilst he signs himself 'Your most affectionate Doni' (*vostro affettionatissimo Doni*), this is not a friendship of equals, but of patron and client: the pronouns used (*vostro, voi*) are respectful rather than intimate, and the gift of the book is 'not so much to preserve our friendship as in part to thank you for the favours I have received' ('non tanto da conserver l'amicitia, quanto a ringratiar vi in parte de beneficia ricevuti') (trans. Gjerpe and Klem, in Cave 2008c: 174–175). This dedication also downplays the political urgency of More's work: governing is placed on a purely domestic scale, as Doni remembers Fava's father 'governing [...] his family' (*ne governi della famiglia*) so effectively that his home is judged 'an excellent republic' (*un' ottima republica*). Fava himself, meanwhile, is invited to compare Utopia 'with the

---

[3] Kristin Gjerpe (2008: 48) surmises that the translation is printed by Aurelio Pincio, 'where Doni [...] had several books printed in the course of the following year'.

Republic of your home' ('facesse paragone con la Republica della casa vostra'). The selection of Fava as dedicatee is more than mere flattery of an obliging patron and his family, however. Fava's appearance in Doni's perplexing, teasing *Seconda Libraria*, printed seven years later in 1555, suggests a shared pleasure in the absurd. Fava features in an anecdote, comprising the entirety of Doni's entry on 'Fileremo' (aka Antonio Fregoso), which seems to point up the value of experience over book-learning (my use of 'seems' is advised: as Jonathan Bradbury observes, the tone and trustworthiness of information in the *Seconda Libraria*—much of which is 'fictional [or] fictitious' (Bradbury 2009: 94)— is hard to pin down). This anecdote relates how, travelling from Florence to Bologna on horseback, Doni and Fava fall into company with a man who will not shut up and who presses Fava to discover how he keeps his horse in such fine condition (Doni 1555: 34). When—after 'six or seven hours'—Fava is finally able to respond, his laconic and straightforward response ('hay and barley') causes Fava and Doni to 'cry with laughter', providing an epiphany about the deaths of Democritus (the laughing philosopher) and Heraclitus (the weeping philosopher) which reading a 'long discourse' on the matter— Fileremo's *Il riso di Democrito et pianto di Heraclito* (1513)—had failed to provide.

The low-key nature of Doni's Utopian paratext, muting the work's political valency and restricting the people connected to the edition to a cast of two (himself and Fava), nonetheless belies a much more extensive network, stretching from Venice to London, via Florence, Lucca, and Lyons: a network which, moreover, embodies the religious (and therefore political) fault lines of the early Reformation. Like Doni, the translator, Ortensio Lando (d. 1556–9), had abandoned religious orders (he had been an Augustinian monk and priest), turning—as did Doni—to 'earning his living from a sharp pen' (Gjerpe 2008: 56; cf Menchi 1994). Preserving the anonymity of the translator was not only wise, but necessary: Lando's heterodox views—evident from his claim in 1529 that he had 'translated "many writings" of Luther into Italian' and from his pseudonymous *Paradossi* (1543), in which he 'mocked the Venetian censors for forbidding the sermons of Ochino and the books of Luther and the anabaptists, while permitting the lascivious, immoral *Decameron*' (Grendler 1977: 72, 81)—had led to all his works being placed on the 1544 *Index of Forbidden Books* issued by the University of Paris (Ray 2009: 695), and it is telling that Lando is only publicly named as the actual translator of *Utopia* once, in the 1561 edition, a detail omitted from all subsequent editions. Sansovino, the editor of the 1561 volume, knew Lando (Grendler 1969: 142), so there is no reason to doubt the attribution (particularly in light of circumstantial evidence discussed below), but, as Kristin Gjerpe suggests, in subsequent editions 'the increasingly sharp confessional divide' probably 'made it unsuitable to name an author of heterodox beliefs', like Lando (Gjerpe 2008: 59).

Lando almost certainly encountered *Utopia*—if not the first time, then certainly memorably—whilst staying with Vincenzo Bonvisi/Buonvisi (1500–c.1573/6), the younger brother of More's bosom friend, the London-based Antonio Bonvisi (1487–1558), and part of a family of merchant bankers with headquarters in cities across Europe, including Rome, Lyons, Louvain, and London. Lando met Vincenzo in Lyons in 1534, where Gjerpe conjectures that Lando 'made the decision both to write in the vernacular and to become a translator', 'inspired perhaps' by his friend, the French scholar Étienne Dolet (Gjerpe 2008: 57), a man who similarly ran foul of the Inquisition, albeit fatally in Dolet's case: Dolet was executed for heresy in Paris in 1546. Lando returned with Vincenzo to the Bonvisis' home city, Lucca, where they were both resident in 1535, when news of More's death would have reached them (Luzzati 1972). They possibly even heard a first-hand account later that year, since Antonio also visited Lucca during his trip to northern Italy in autumn 1535–6 (C. T. Martin, rev. Morgan 2019). Certainly, it is after the mid-1530s that Lando started adopting Utopian-style pseudonyms, a device first used on the *Forcianae quaestiones* (1535), a dialogue—published under the name of 'Philalethes Polytopiensis' ('Lover of Truth, Citizen of Polytopia')—the title of which plays on Cicero's *Tusculanae Quaestiones*, and which alludes to the Bonvisis' estate, Villa Forci, in the hills to the north-west of Lucca where the conversations recorded allegedly took place.[4]

Mid-sixteenth-century Lucca was regarded by religious traditionalists as a city 'infected' with heresy, religious dissent that was fostered by mercantile families such as the Bonvisi (Adorni-Braccessi 1997: 339, 342). Vincenzo certainly seems to have harboured sympathies for reformist ideas (*le simpatie [...] per le idee della Riforma*, Luzzati 1972): in 1551 he was denounced for practices 'against the good customs and praiseworthy traditions of the blessed church of Rome' (*contra bonos mores et laudibilis consuetudines san[c]te romane ecclesie*) (cited in Baker-Smith 2006b: 235). Although 'the charges were dismissed', as Dominic Baker-Smith observes, 'there was no smoke without fire' (235). There is consequently a certain irony that *Utopia*, written by a man who would be martyred for his adherence to the 'old' faith, should be transmitted into Italian via cities like Lyons and Lucca, and networks of men, which were sympathetic to reform. Nonetheless, this conjunction of vernacularization and heterodoxy also underpins More's suspicion of translation, and his consequent desire, expressed in his *Confutacyon to Tyndales Answere* (1532), to withhold his works (and those of his friend Erasmus) from those who—being unable to understand them properly, as More would have it—might come to harm (*CWM* 8.179). But further to that, the religious affiliations of the Bonvisi brothers reflect the schism in the Church which (as we will see) would shape More's subsequent reception in early modern Italy. Whilst Vincenzo was allied with reform, his brother Antonio became strongly associated with opposition to it.

Antonio was a long-standing and intimate friend of More. More's final letter to him, written from the Tower, calls Antonio the 'apple of [his] eye' (*oculi mei pupilla*) and remembers how he has been 'not a geaste [guest] but a continuall nurslynge' in the Bonvisi house ('perpetuum Bonvisae domus non hospitem, sed alumnum'), although the length of time More gives—'almost this forty years' (*prope quadraginta*)—must refer to his acquaintance with the wider Bonvisi family (Antonio's cousins Lorenzo and Niccolò, and uncle Ludovico) since Antonio was only posted to London after 1505, when he would have been in his late teens (More 1565c: A6v, A6r; trans. More 1557: Z4v;

---

[4] For a list of texts published under Lando's Utopian pseudonyms, see Menchi 1996: 98–99.

cf. McCutcheon 1981: 39–40). Antonio was almost certainly the 'Italian merchant' (*Italum [...] mercatorem*), 'no less learned than he is rich (but he was very rich)' ('non minus doctum quam divitem; (erat autem ditissimus)'), celebrated in More's 1515 'Letter to Dorp', a defence of Erasmus' *Praise of Folly* (More 1625: 50). And Antonio is also probably the early reader of *Utopia* referred to in a lost letter, recorded only via Thomas Stapleton's late sixteenth-century biography, in a section on More's 'literary modesty', where More insists, with faux humility, that the 'great pleasure' that 'Anthony' has taken in *Utopia* 'arises from [...] affection rather than [...] judgement' (Stapleton 2020: 46). Antonio's life was thus intertwined with More's in various ways: philosophically, affectively, and materially. Their shared intellectual interests are evidenced by Antonio's probable reading of *Utopia* and appearance in the 'Letter to Dorp'. More certainly, Antonio stood godfather to More's grandson, Augustine, in 1533; and he bought a house, Crosby Place, from More in 1524, only to lease it back to members of the More circle—William Roper (More's son-in-law) and William Rastell (More's nephew and the editor of More's 1557 English *Workes*)—in 1547, as he prepared to leave England (Norman and Caroe 1908: n.p.). And, whilst he was permitted to do so, he supplied More and Archbishop John Fisher with food and wine whilst they were imprisoned in the Tower in 1534–5 for refusing to swear the Oath of Supremacy (*LP* 8.856), and sent More an expensive 'silke Chamlett gowne', which, according to More's ancestor Cresacre More, More initially put on for his execution, before being persuaded by the Lieutenant of the Tower to wear something less obviously lavish (C. More 1631?: 2X4r–v).

Antonio had been friendly with men on the other side of the confessional divide, including Thomas Cromwell, as well as supporters of a *via media*, such as the humanist Thomas Starkey (Mayer 2004); even after More's execution, Antonio would continue to send Cromwell information about political affairs in continental Europe.[5] However, in Susan Brigden's words, under the pressure of the Henrician Reformation 'he had to choose' a side, and—in doing so—'he became the "patron and second father" to London's ultra-Catholics' (Brigden 1989: 421). Certainly, after 1535, there are no records in the State Papers of gifts of gamebirds, such as partridges and pheasants, from Antonio to Cromwell.[6] The chronicler Charles Wriothesley (1508?–62) grouped Antonio amongst 'rank papists' (Wriothesley 1877: 34), and—in a speech after the reconciliation with the Church of Rome under Mary I in November 1554—Cardinal Pole lauded him as 'a special benefactor to all Catholic and good persons' (cited in Ford 1947: 235). Symptomatic of the services praised by Pole was the refuge offered by Antonio to members of the More circle in exile. During the Protestant regime of Edward VI, the Bonvisi household in Louvain was home to at least seven of that close-knit group: William Roper and his wife Margaret (More's eldest and favourite daughter); John Clement (More's one-time servant, allegedly present at the conversation with Hythloday recorded in *Utopia*), his wife Margaret née Giggs (More's adopted daughter), their daughter Winifred and her

---

[5] For examples of information supplied to Cromwell after 1535, see BL MS Cotton Vitellius B.XIV, 26r (7 Feb. 1536); TNA SP 1/102, 106r (28 Feb. 1536); SP 1/103, 156r (22 Apr. 1536) and 220r (3 May 1536).

[6] See e.g. TNA SP 1/80, 90r (8 Nov. 1533); SP 1/82, 143r (8 Feb. 1534).

husband William Rastell (More's nephew); and More's biographer Nicholas Harpsfield. As Katherine Forsyth surmises, Louvain was probably where 'Harpsfield began work on his biography' and 'the location for much of the planning and work towards the compilation of [More's 1557 English *Workes*]', and whilst Antonio 'was not directly involved in the production of More's *Workes*', he nonetheless contributed through the preservation of 'the More papers and manuscripts during the reign of Edward VI' (Forsyth 2018: 250, 249). These papers presumably included that final letter, written from the Tower. Emotively described in its heading as being written 'with a cole' (*carbona*), because More had been deprived of suitable writing equipment (More 1557: Z3v; 1566c: A6r), this letter is given a prominent—and dramatic—place as the very last text in the selection of More's correspondence in the 1566 Latin *Works*. This no doubt contributed to the significance given to Antonio in the subsequent Italian hagiographic treatment of More, including Giacomo Rossi's play about the life of More (*Tomaso Moro*), performed in the seminary at Lucca in 1692, which includes a scene in which Antonio receives and reads aloud More's final letter, and which culminates in a scene where 'More appears to Antonio in a vision and together they affirm the message of the play: that only the Eternal Good can satisfy the human heart' (Wheeler 1970: 21–22). Whilst the central role here accorded Antonio must have conveniently flattered its dedicatee, Cardinal Francesco Bonvisi, bishop of Lucca (Wheeler 1970: 23 n.), it nonetheless also speaks to the persistence of Antonio's association with More-the-martyr.

The 1548 translation is thus indebted to a mercantile network 'based in Lucca but with branches in Naples, Rome, Venice, Genoa, Lyons, Paris, Antwerp, and Nuremberg, as well as London' (Baker-Smith 2006a: 84). A work famously featuring a character who denounces the growth of sheep-farming and who applauds the Utopians for their indifference—even antipathy—towards money and material riches consequently owes its transmission into Italian to the connections of a family whose immense wealth was based on moneylending and trading in jewellery and high-quality woollen cloth (C. T. Martin, rev. Morgan 2019), and at least one of whom—Antonio, passing information to Henry VIII's government—was implicated in the very type of foreign policy derided by Hythloday in Book One. Patrons such as the Bonvisi brothers, like the Utopians, have the leisure to devote to intellectual pursuits and stimulating dinner-time conversations, but they have the means to do so precisely because they are able to exploit the kind of economic system that the Utopians reject.

Doni does not say exactly how the manuscript of the translation came into his hands, but Doni and Lando had become friendly after Doni read Lando's 1543 *Paradossi*, meeting in person shortly afterwards in Venice or Piacenza, and 'in 1544, Doni reports that he is preparing for the press an unnamed dialogue of a "M. Hortensio", who could be Ortensio Lando' (Gjerpe 2008: 57 and n.). The two writers had much in common. Both abandoned the cloistered life and became *poligrafi*, that is 'professional writers [...] who experimented with different genres and strived to produce texts that would appeal to a growing commercial market for vernacular works' (Ray 2009: 1695). Writers of this type 'did not enjoy court patronage', but 'tended to be lowborn men whose lives were characterised by uncertain finances, frequent travel, and a pervasive sense of being on the outside of mainstream culture' (E. Nelson 2006: 1042), a description with uncanny echoes of aspects of Hythloday's persona. Eric Nelson has also argued that Lando and Doni are part of a group of 'strident anti-Ciceronians', who—taking their cue from Erasmus' 1528 dialogue, *Ciceronianus*—were pitched against 'a large subset of Italian humanists—including eminences such as Pietro Bembo and Jacopo Sadoleto— whose enthusiasm for Cicero had reached such hyperbolic dimensions that they now insisted that all Latin writing should be based on Ciceronian models, and even that no word could properly be used in Latin prose if Cicero had not used it in his writings' (1042). This group included Lando's French friend Dolet, whose *Dialogus de imitatio Ciceroniana*, published in Lyons by Sébastien Gryphe in 1535 (shortly after Lando and Dolet had met each other in that city), features More as Erasmus' anti-Ciceronian mouthpiece. Two of Lando's own publications explicitly evoke Erasmus: the dialogue *Ciceronianus relegatus et revocatus* ('Cicero Banished and Recalled'), printed in 1534, also by Gryphe, and a dialogue on Erasmus' death, *In Desiderii Erasmi Roterodami funus* (1540), which satirically replays the Ciceronian/anti-Ciceronian debate by staging 'an imaginary conversation between two Italians, one a blind admirer of Erasmus, the other representing the prevailing Italian tendency to find fault with Erasmus on almost every ground' (Bietenholz 1971: 101). The *in utramque partem* style of *Funus* and its 'ambiguous and slippery language' (*un linguaggio così ambiguo e sfuggente*, Menchi 1974: 539) leave Lando's position on Erasmus less clear-cut than Nelson suggests (as does *Ciceronianus relegatus et revocatus*).[7] Nonetheless, the dialogue highlights the bad odour into which Erasmus was already slipping amongst orthodox adherents to the 'old' faith by the mid-sixteenth century, thanks to an association between Erasmianism and heterodoxy (Marsh 2008: 267; Bevan Zlatar 2012: 22–23). It also provides evidence of a further Bonvisi connection and of that family's sustained interest in Northern humanism, as the preface praises Antonio's and Vincenzo's brother, Ludovico, for 'his intimate knowledge of Erasmus' writings and his generous sponsorship of vernacular translations' (Baker-Smith 2006b: 254).[8]

Lando's characteristic mode is ambivalence: the 'apparent tendency to support both sides of the question' which, according to Conor Fahy 'achieves its most satisfactory literary expression in his *Paradossi*' (Fahy 1975: 30). However, despite Lando's penchant for the ludic and equivocal, the presentation of the 1548 translation flattens the ambiguity of More's *Utopia*. The elaborate epistolary paratext, in which More's humanist associates extend and elaborate on the game he has started, is removed, along with the frequently sardonic marginalia, and pseudo-documentary elements, such as the map, Utopian alphabet, and Utopian poetry. Lando's text also omits the final sentence, in which Morus vacillates over the Utopian project, articulating a mixed response to both the virtues of Utopia, and the feasibility of emulating its positive aspects:

---

[7] For the ambiguity of Lando's *Funus*, see Menchi 1974; Gilmont 2013: 389; for the ambiguity of Lando's *Ciceronianus relegatus et revocatus*, see Adorni-Braccesi and Ragagli 2004.

[8] Lando's description of Ludovico as 'compater meus' in *Miscellanae Questiones* (1550) points to a particularly intimate connection (*compater* = 'fellow godparent', *Medieval Latin Dictionary*).

> Meanwhile, while I can hardly agree with everything he said (though he is a man of unquestionable learning and enormous experience of human affairs), yet I freely confess that in the Utopian commonwealth there are very many features that in our own societies I would wish rather than expect to see. (More 2016b: 113)

In addition, Lando reduces the ironizing of Morus in the build-up to More's enigmatic ending by skipping over the lines in which (in the original) Morus confesses that he refrains from challenging Hythloday because he does not want his guest to think that he is intellectually insecure, 'recall[ing] that he had reproached certain people who were afraid they might not appear knowing enough unless they found something to criticise in the ideas of others'.

The way in which the Italian translation downplays the studied ambiguity of the Latin original is there from the outset. The Latin title announces that the work is 'On the Best State of a Republic and on the New Island of Utopia' (*de optimo reipublicae statu deque nova Insula Utopia*). The presence of the conjunction 'and' (*-que*) in the Latin title unsettles the connection between 'the best state of a republic' that the book discusses and 'the new island of Utopia' it describes: in the Latin the two things are not necessarily synonymous. In contrast, the 1548 title page announces 'The republic, recently "ritrovata" [I will return to that word], of the government of the island Eutopia, in which you can see new ways of governing states, ruling people, giving laws for senators, with great depth of wisdom' (*La republica nuovamente ritrovata, del governo dell'isola Eutopia, nella qual si vede nuovi modi di governare Stati, reggier Popoli, dar Leggi à i senatori, con molta profondità di Sapienza*) (trans. Gjerpe & Klem in Cave 2008c: 172–173). More's island is thus confidently dubbed 'Eutopia': good place, rather than no-place. This endorsement of the Utopian system is carried into Doni's dedicatory epistle, which commends the 'excellent Republic' (*ottima Republica*) of Utopia and the 'excellent manners, good laws, wise regulations, holy education, sincere government and men of noble spirit' which Fava will find within the book ('ottimi costumi, ordini buoni, reggimenti savi, amaestramenti santi, governo sincere, e huomini reali', More 1548a: 172–175). The playfulness of the Latin title page is further diminished by the description of its subject matter, in the Italian version, as 'no less useful than necessary' (*non meno utile che necessaria*), rather than 'no less beneficial than entertaining' (*nec minus salutaris quam festivus*) as in the Latin original.

Promoting the utility of the book extends into the table of contents 'of some of the principal things [*cose principali*] that the work contains' (A4r). This table picks out aspects presumably designed to appeal to its most immediate target market. Although the Venetian press was aimed at making money from a wider Italian readership and a growing demand for vernacular books, the Venetian readership on its doorstep was, as Simone Testa observes, particularly interested in 'geography and politics' (Testa 2015: 83). So, in Book One, attention is drawn to 'new types of sails' (*nuove vele di Navi*), referencing a fleeting mention of various kinds of vessel encountered on Hythloday's journey (More 2016b: 12); or we have the numerous entries on law and punishment in different places (six out of fourteen entries for Book One). The anatomization of the description of Utopia in Book Two begins enthusiastically: the opening description of the island (*c.*780 words of Latin) is broken into no less than five separate headings; the chapter on the cities of Utopia (*c.*640 words of Latin) into three; the brief chapter on Utopian officials (*c.*280 words of Latin) into two, and so on. This level of detail—extremely useful for guiding readers in the absence of the Latin marginalia—decreases dramatically about a third of the way through Book Two: from the item for the 'travels' (*pellegrinaggi*) of the Utopians onwards, the list follows the chapter headings of the Latin, rather than expanding on them.[9] Nevertheless, despite presenting the book as a blueprint for good government, the paratextual material contains some teasing hints of the work's elusiveness, besides the woodcut of the masked woman, a device associated with Doni, discussed in detail by Gjerpe (2008: 47, 52–53). The title page depicts its contents as a *storia*, a word which could indicate both 'a historie'—'a declaration of true things'—or 'a discourse, a tale' (Florio 1598: 92, 398). Similarly, the island Hythloday describes is *ritrovata*, that is either something real 'f[ou]nde out againe' or something 'invent[ed …,] devise[d]' (Florio 1598: 331).[10]

Although it consistently reduces the ludic ambiguity of More's work, Lando's translation is, as Thomas Wheeler (1970: 19) observes, 'generally accurate'. There are occasions when—presumably working at speed—Lando is tripped up by the familiar unfamiliarity of More's imagined land. For example, Lando fails to grasp More's use of the noun *conventus* to indicate, not (as is more usual) 'assembly', but the district surrounding each Utopian city. He consequently makes a nonsense of the explanation of how the Utopians maintain a steady population. Lando's Italian declares that 'there are six thousand [households] in each city, except the Senate' ('in ogni città ne sono seimillia [famiglie], eccetto il Senato', More 1548a: 31v); 'eccetto il Senato' is altered in the 1561 translation to 'nella città et nel contado' (More 1561: 185r), which—whilst still not capturing the precise sense of the Latin *excepto conventu* ('exclusive of the surrounding countryside') (More 2016b: 56)—at least restores the distinction between the urban and rural. However, Lando's translation is far from slapdash. It retains, for instance, at least some of the litotic habits that characterize More's original, as seen in constructions such as 'ne lo mandano via senza doni' ('they don't send him away without gifts', 1548a: 44v), translating 'neque inanem dimmitunt', More 1895a: 222), although the famous litotes in the opening sentence—referring to the 'differences of no slight import' (2016b: 8; *non exigui momenti*, 1895a: 19) between Henry VIII and Charles I of Spain (the catalyst for the encounter with Hythloday)—is flattened to 'certain disagreements' (*certa controversia*, 1548a: 8r).[11] This blunting of nuance is found elsewhere, as in the section on euthanasia, where the Latin—'sopiti sine mortis sensu solvuntur' (1895a: 224; 'having

---

[9] *Pellegrinaggi* (translating the Latin *peregrinatione*) denotes purposeful travels, in contrast to *viaggi*, journeys without a clear end. I am grateful to Ed Muir for pointing this out.

[10] For the tension between invention and discovery—and the ambiguity of the Latin verb *invenire* (to find, to contrive) on which this term/concept depends—see Scholar in this volume.

[11] For more on the rhetorical figure of litotes—affirming something by denying its negative—see Zurcher, Nicholas, and Morgan in this volume.

been put to sleep, [they] are freed from life without any sensation of dying', 2016b: 83)—is rendered as 'dormendo sono uccisi': 'sleeping they are killed' (1548a: 45r). Linguistic differences between Italian and Latin, compounded by semantic decisions, can also alter the tenor of the text, as in the passage on punishing adultery:

> id facinus ideo tam severe vindicant, quod futurum prospiciunt, ut rari in conjugalem amorem coalescerent amorem coalescerent, in quo aetatem omnem cum uno videant exigendam, et perferendas insuper qua sea res affert molestias, nisi a vago concubitu diligenter arceantur. (45r)
>
> (The reason they punish this offence so severely is that they suppose few people would join in married love—with confinement to a single partner and all the petty annoyances that married life involves—unless they were strictly restrained from promiscuous intercourse.) (2016b: 83)

The Italian translates 'cum uno' (1895a: 225; 'with one') as the feminine 'con una sola'. Whilst this could refer to 'one person' since the noun for person, *gente*, is feminine, the overriding impression is that it is the man who has agency, particularly when the noun phrase 'vago concubitu' ('promiscuous intercourse') is transformed into a verbal phrase 'giacersi hora con questa, hora con quella' ('to lie now with this one, now with that') (where *questa* and *quella* are again feminine).

There are moments when Lando expands on the original. There are three main types of embellishments. First, we have examples seemingly made for clarity, as when the compact Latin clause 'nisi si quis usus impediat' (1895a: 60; 'unless there is some need for them at home', 2016b: 61) becomes 'purche non sia qualche bisogna de l'opera sua' ('provided that there is no need for their labour', 1548a: 34r). Secondly, we have examples providing additional details that may reflect particular interests (be it of Lando's circle, or his target audience), as in the account of paper-making, which specifies the exact type of paper—*la carta bambacina* (43r), indicating the rags from which paper was made—where the Latin simply has *charta* or paper in general (1895a: 57). Thirdly, we have moments of colloquial expression, as in the Utopian indifference to wealth having been 'drunk in with milk in infancy' ('bevuto [...] co'late ne la fanciulezza', 1548a: 37r–v), where the Latin has the much less striking 'ex educatione conceperunt' (1895a: 183; 'picked up [...] from their upbringing', 2016b: 66).

More usually, however, Lando strives for concision, although Frank and Fritzie Manuel go too far when they suggest that his version is a 'bowdlerized paraphrase' (Manuel and Manuel 1979: 150). The impetus towards brevity may stem from a desire to produce a short, affordable work: printed in 'space-saving italics' (Gjerpe 2008: 47) and stripped of its marginalia and much of the paratext, including the bespoke woodcuts (the map, the Utopian alphabet), the volume comprises sixty leaves in octavo (7.5 sheets of paper), in contrast to fifty-four leaves in quarto for the 1516 Latin edition (13.5 sheets of paper). Lando trims back details that might be seen as redundant, for example omitting the information that Hythloday 'spent several months' in England ('aliquot menses ibi sum versatus', 1895a: 40), instead going directly to explaining when this was: namely, not long after the Cornish Rebellion (2016b: 15; 1548a: 12v). The sardonic observation that Hythloday is ridiculed 'even' (*quoque*) in England is similarly cut (1895a: 40), presumably as being irrelevant to an Italian readership, and descriptive passages frequently end up pruned, as in the account of 'idle retainers' (2016b: 18). Lando here omits the reference to the minority of labourers who are afraid of such men—namely, 'those whose physique isn't suited for strength and boldness, or whose spirit has been broken by the lack of means to support their families'—an aside which allows Hythloday to critique further the socio-economic set-up of sixteenth-century Europe. The famous tirade against enclosures is likewise reined in. More's Hythloday denounces those landowners who 'leave no land free from the plough' and who instead 'enclose every acre for pasture [...] destroy houses and abolish towns, keeping the churches—but only for sheep-barns' (19). Lando's Hythloday restricts this litany of crimes to 'destroy[ing] houses and cast[ing] down towns, in order to grant larger pastures to the sheep' ('rovinano le case, abbatteno le terre per lasciare à le pecore piu larghi paschi', 1548a: 14v).

Nonetheless, Lando's excisions and paraphrases may be about more than reducing word-count and streamlining the text. Enclosure is of less relevance to an Italian audience, where husbandry was a minor practice, farming was mixed cultivation, and most peasants lived in villages or towns, not on estates (Balestracci 1999). However, the wool trade it underpinned was one of the means by which Lando's patrons, the Bonvisis, had grown rich. Also telling is the way in which Lando substantially tones down Hythloday's attack on standing armies. Those who believe that it is a good idea to have men ready-trained for war are not—as in the Latin—derided as *morosophi* (1895a: 48; 'wise fools', 2016b: 18). The emotive description of 'men's throats [being] cut for no reason' is also omitted (*homines jugulandi gratis*, 1895a: 49); and an explicit reference to 'standing armies' (*exercitus*) is recast as *tali huomini* ('such men', 1548a: 14r). By the early sixteenth century, Italy was much more militarized than elsewhere in Europe, with the maintenance of standing armies crucial for city states such as Milan (Lando's birthplace) and Venice (where Lando's translation was printed). Indeed, the policy operated by both states 'of offering estates to their military captains to provide them with rural power bases and with quarters for their companies' (Mallett 2003: 73) sounds remarkably like the custom of keeping retainers so vilified by Hythloday.

That Lando's alterations might evidence an ideological position is further suggested by some rephrasing early in the text, in More's letter to Giles, which refers to 'our religion, which has made such a happy start there [in Utopia]' (2016b: 5; 'religionem nostram, feliciter ibi coeptam', 1895a: 7). Lando's translation distances itself from this confessional position. 'Our religion' becomes, more objectively, *la christiana religione* (1548a: 7r), and its establishment in Utopia is no longer treated as a 'happy' event: it is merely something that has 'begun there' (*ivi cominciata*). As Baker-Smith (2006a: 493) observes, Lando 'may well have been attracted by [*Utopia*'s] implicit criticism of the established order'. Certainly, that sense of critique is strongly present in Lando's own original contribution to Utopian fiction, his *Commentario delle piu notabili et mostruose cose d'Italia e altri luoghi* ('An Account of the Most Notable and Strange Things in Italy and Other Places'), published in 1548, the same year as his translation of *Utopia*. In this work, the narrator (a citizen of 'The Kingdom of the Lost') meets a Florentine who has been blown off course on a ship from Utopia. When this Florentine brings the narrator back to Italy, 'the travelogue becomes a catalogue of vices', as 'Lando shows himself to be [...] a critic of contemporary Italian society, the hypocrisy of the rich, the lifelessness of erudition and the absurdity of theological disputes' (Gjerpe 2008: 58). For Grendler, writers like Doni and Lando were 'writing at the depth of Italian discouragement from the sack of Rome in 1527 until peace in 1559', when the Treaty of Cateau-Cambrésis brought to an end the struggle between France and Spain for control of Italy (Grendler 1969: 177). He defines the intervening years as 'a period of pessimism and withdrawal' where 'critics of society' like Doni and Lando 'bitterly criticized Italian political leaders and argued that men should withdraw from the *vita civile* [civic life]' (178). Despite presenting *Utopia* as a 'useful' and 'necessary' text, the dedicatory epistle to the 1548 translation explicitly sets the lessons offered within a purely domestic context: Fava is not expected, or invited, to look beyond the government of his household to a wider, civic context. The circle around Lando to which the work is connected also has distinctly heterodox affiliations. There is, in other words, an oppositional, countercultural vein running through the 1548 Italian *Utopia*. In contrast, as the following section explores, when *Utopia* next appeared in Italian, in 1561, it was within a volume designed to equip and inform the would-be politician for the *vita activa* and *vita civile*, and which also aligns itself with religious orthodoxy.

1561: Histories 'useful and necessary to civil life'

In 1561, the Venetian-based writer and translator Francesco Sansovino included Book Two of Lando's translation in *Del governo de i regni e delle republiche cosi antiche come moderne* ('Of the Government of Kingdoms and Republics, Both Ancient and Modern'), the title page of which promises that—from its contents—readers could 'acquire knowledge of many individual histories which are useful and necessary to civil life' ('si ha cognitione di molte historie particolari, utili e necessarie al viver civile'). The description of Utopia appears as the final book, after descriptions of Rome (contemporary), France, Germany, England, Spain, Turkey, Persia, Tunisia, Venice, Rome (ancient), Switzerland, Ragusa, ancient Sparta, Genoa, ancient Athens, Fez, and Lucca. Sansovino (1561: *3r) presents this compilation to his readers as a 'nuova *Politica*': Aristotle's *Politics* updated for the cinquecento. As such, it was part of 'an efflorescence of popular history [that] occurred in the second half of sixteenth-century Italy', fuelled by 'the growth of the Venetian vernacular press' (Grendler 1969: 140).

Sansovino was a professional writer, 'work[ing] on his own initiative and liv[ing] on the income of his books', and who for two stretches of time—1560–70 (when *Del governo* as published) and 1578–81—operated his own printing press (Grendler 1969: 142). His

Governo is grounded in the culture of the Academia Veneziana, which 'was intended to play a substantial role in the education of young patricians and would-be politicians, attempting to create a centre for higher education and, more generally, an elite cultural institution in the heart of Venice' (Graheli 2013: 283). The Academia Veneziana was 'primarily a publishing venture' (284), and Sansovino's volume was entirely in tune with the 'pragmatic education that was to become a defining characteristic of the Venetian ruling class' (Testa 2015: 84). In the words of Grendler (1969: 162), 'sixteenth-century Italians were engrossed in the search for the perfect form of government'; *Del governo* 'provided in convenient format some raw materials' for such readers: 'with examples of many governments before him, the reader could discern for himself what was a good and bad' (161).

The volume is dedicated to Pier Francesco Ferrero (1513–66), from a noble Piedmontese family who were highly successful in exploiting the offices of the Church, for the advantage of both their immediate family and the duchy of Savoy (the Ferreros' use of church positions to promote their family interests is evident from the way in which they frequently transferred benefices from one family member to another).[12] Pier Francesco and his brother, Filiberto, both prospered in their ecclesiastical careers under the patronage of their uncle, Cardinal Bonificio Ferrero, one of three brothers in the Church. Pier Francesco's rise was further enabled by another relative, Cardinal Borromeo, who in 1560 obtained for him the position of papal legate to Venice, where he remained until March 1561, amongst other things intervening on behalf of Andrea Provana di Leynì, the military commander of Savoy, after he had ransacked two Venetian merchant ships in October 1560. Sansovino thus dedicated his volume—a work made for governors 'dealing with important affairs of state' (*maneggi delle cose importante dello stato*)—to a man of the cloth who was very much involved in state and church politics, and whose career was on the up: Sansovino's dedicatory epistle notes that the completion of his work coincided with news of Pier Francesco's exultation to cardinal (1561: *2r).

Book Eighteen of *Del governo* (the description of Utopia) is the only book to carry its own preface. Where the 1548 paratext had remembered More as a citizen of London (*Cittadino di Londra*) on the title page, and again in the title to Book One, Sansovino's preamble focuses on More, not only as citizen, but also—more prominently—as a martyr: at least half the short introduction is dedicated to celebrating More as 'a man of most saintly life, full of true justice and divine religion' ('huomo santissimo di vita, & pieno di vera giustitia, e di divina religione'), who died for his faith (trans. Gjerpe and Klem in Cave 2008c: 176–177). As with the 1548 translation, Sansovino's treatment of *Utopia* diminishes its ludic ambiguity, although not—as the earlier translation did— by earnestly presenting it as a 'useful' blueprint of an 'excellent republic', but by stating outright that it is a 'most pleasing fiction' (*piacevolissima fittione*), echoing the earlier address to the reader, where More's work was described, in even more absolute terms, as

---

[12] The biographical details in this paragraph are from Gnavi 1997.

'completely fictional' (*tutta finta*, More 1561: *3v). It is also in that prefatory address (but only in 1561) that Sansovino acknowledges Lando as the original translator. Sansovino explains to his readers that *Utopia* 'came into [his] hands already translated by someone else'—namely Lando, 'truly, a very learned man' (*huomo nel vero di molte lettere*)—and that he has 'only amended it a little' (*solamente [...] le ho racconciate alquanto*), because of the 'dialect' (*la sua lingua*) in which Lando was writing.

The Italian *Utopia* thus becomes caught up in the *questione della lingua*: the ongoing debate about what form the vernacular should take, a debate all the more pressing because of the 'process of standardisation of the literary language during the first half of the [sixteenth century]' (B. Richardson 1997: 181) and the accelerating pressures placed upon this by the growth of the print trade and the expanding market for vernacular texts. Printers more than anyone had a commercial stake in the outcome, and Sansovino pinned his own colours to the mast when he printed in 1562 (the year after the first edition of *Del governo*) *Le osservationi della lingua volgare di diversi huomini illustre* ('Observations about the Vernacular, by Various Famous Men'). These men comprised—in order—Pietro Bembo (1470–1547), Giovan Francesco Fortunio (c.1470–1517), Jacopo (aka Giacomo) Gabriele (1510–50), Rinaldo Corso (1525–82), and Alberto Accarisio (1497–1544).[13] All—regardless of their own regional origins—were proponents of the school of thought which held that written Italian should follow the model provided by trecento Tuscan and its three leading writers: Dante, Petrarch, and Boccaccio (the 'Tre corone', three crowns). Lando was Milanese, and his translation retains 'a Lombardy vocabulary and accent' (*di favella e accento Lombardo*, Scrivano 1980: 141). Sansovino consequently works to 'Tuscanize' Lando's prose, altering spelling and linguistic forms so that they align with those used by Bembo in his influential *Prose della volgar lingua* (1525), reprinted in Sansovino's *Osservationi*, where it is given pride of place as the very first text. In his version of *Utopia*, Sansovino consequently removes the more Latinate spellings that Lando favours, for example replacing *t* with *d*, so that *patroni* (from the Latin *patronus*, patron) becomes *padroni*; *c* with *g*, so that *luochi* (places, from the Latin *locus*) becomes *luoghi*; and substituting more Tuscan endings, so that Lando's *diligentia* (industry, from the Latin) becomes *diligenza*.[14] The orthographic alterations that Sansovino makes recurrently favour the forms found in Bembo's *Prose*: for example, the choice of *i quali* over *i quai* ('the which'); the spelling *lontana* (far) over *luntana*; or the tendency to elide prepositions with definite articles, so a phrase like *da l'altro* ('from the other') becomes *dall'altro*. Sansovino further tweaks Lando's semantic choices, substituting vocabulary authorized by texts such as Accarisio's *Vocabolario, grammatica et orthographie volgare* (1543) or Francesco Alunno's *Ricchezze della lingua volgare* (1543) on the grounds that they are words used in the works of one of the 'Tre corone'. Lando's *esterno* (foreigner) thus becomes *forestiero*, for instance; *turgurii* (huts),

---

[13] Sansovino's 1562 title page reverses the order in which Fortunio and Gabriele appear, and omits mention of Corso. Bembo and Gabriele were born in Venice; Fortunio, Pordenone (near Venice); Corso, Verona; Accarisio, Cento (in Emilia-Romagna); Sansovino, Rome (moving to Venice as a child).

[14] For the classicizing of spelling in Latin editions of *Utopia*, see Nicholas in this volume.

capanne; *epistola* (letter), *lettera*; *cerco* (around), *intorno*; *vilipeso* (vilified), *dispregiato* (1548a: 25v, 28r, 28v, 34r, 36r; 1561: 184v, 185v, 186r, 188v, 189v).[15]

Sansovino's adaptations extend beyond tinkering with Lando's vocabulary and spelling. His decision to reproduce only Book Two extracts the description of Utopia from its dialogic frame. The first-person voice remains, although some (but not all) of the snippets of pseudo-autobiography are cut, as when the narrator (unnamed in Sansovino's version) informs the reader that he spent five years resident in the Utopian capital of Amaurot (More 1548a: 27r; 2016b: 47). In contrast, the narrator's reminiscences about bringing Greek books, and printing, to Utopia remain (More 1561: 193r-v; 2016b: 79–81). Sansovino more systematically removes the second-person addresses, which help sustain the sense of conversation in the original (and in Lando's translation), even as Hythloday's voice dominates Book Two, transforming dialogue to monologue. For example, in Lando's version, in the account of the Utopians' work hours, Hythloday commands his audience that 'if you're not to make a mistake, you need to consider carefully', otherwise 'you could think that, with them working for only six hours, they're at a disadvantage when it comes to the essentials' ('non piglia te quivi errore, bisogno considerarvi attentamente. Potresti pensare che elli lavorando sei hore, patisseno disagio le cose necessarie', 1548a: 30r). Sansovino removes the second-person verb forms, rendering this (and other such passages) as a more generalized address, which is necessarily also more concise: 'if one's not to make an error, it's necessary to consider that although they only work six hours, they're not at a disadvantage when it comes to the essentials' ('non si pigli qui errore, bisogna considerar che quantunque lavorano solamente sei hore, non pasticano disagio delle cose necessarie', 1561: 186v). Lando's Italian here uses you-singular forms (*non piglia te*; *potresti*) alongside you-plural forms (*considerarvi*), which seemingly runs counter to the narrative frame (where Hythloday converses with plural interlocutors), information which is highlighted in Lando's version by the list of auditors supplied at the start of Book One, which tells us that the auditors of the conversation that follows comprise 'Giovanni Clementi. Hythloder. Tomaso Moro. Pietro Egidio' (1548a: 9r). (This paratextual element does not appear in the Latin.) The picture these pronouns depict is further complicated by the fact that, in Italian, you-plural forms (as with the French *vous* and early modern English *you*) could be used as a formal way of addressing an individual (in contrast to the informal *tu/thou*). However, the shift between singular and plural addressees is also present in the original Latin, which moves between the plural *erretis* ('you may make a mistake') and the singular *putes* ('you think') (1895a: 145). These changes in addressee might be a hangover resulting from the widely accepted scenario that More composed the bulk of Book Two before Book One (Hexter 1952). Alternatively, they could be seen to point up the difference between collective and individual thinking, and the need for the latter both to avoid error and to take personal responsibility for correcting it.

---

[15] None of Lando's choices here appear in W. Thomas 1550, a wordlist based on Accarisio and Alunno; all of Sansovino's alternatives do.

Manuel and Manuel have observed how Sansovino's substitution of *volontà* (will) for Lando's *voluttà* ('voluptuousness, sensuality, delight or worldly pleasure', Florio 1598: 456), 'a proper translation of the original [*voluptas*]', 'made utter nonsense of many of the sentences in More's discussion of *voluptas* in Utopia' (Manuel and Manuel 1979: 151). They suggest that this might have been a 'judicious' response in the light of the Council of Trent, which ('embod[ying] the ideals of the Counter-Reformation') would resume its third and final sitting in 1562 (Livingstone 2013). Proponents of the Counter-Reformation viewed the 'humanistic centers of Italy as locations "infected" with paganism, and sought to cleanse them' (de Armas 2002: 32). The Epicureanism underpinning the Utopians' attitude to pleasure would have sat awkwardly in this atmosphere, particularly in a work addressed to the newly appointed Cardinal Ferrero, a traditionalist in doctrinal matters, who in 1556 had served on the committee for reforming the papal court (the Curia), convened by Pope Paul IV (Gnavi 1997). The Counter-Reformation tenor of Sansovino's edition is also epitomized by the place at which he cuts off the work, at the end of the section on religion: 'When this prayer has been said, they prostrate themselves on the ground again; then after a little while they rise and go to lunch. The rest of the day they pass in games and military training' (2016b: 109; 'Fatta questa oratione, di nuovo si piegano in terra, & poco appresso levati, vanno a mangiare, il rimanente del giorno consumano in giuochi, & in essercitii militari', 1561: 201r). Sansovino's *Utopia* thus concludes on a militaristic note, as religion and military training go hand in hand.

Conclusion

Sansovino's version of *Utopia*, with its hagiographic treatment of More and alignment with religious orthodoxy, went on to have much greater reach than Lando's. *Del governo* was republished, in expanding editions, five more times before 1610, with *Utopia* always included as the final book, and the whole volume was translated into French in 1585, and again in 1611.[16] In contrast, Lando's two-book translation did not appear again in the early modern period. Nonetheless, the countercultural, heterodox strand found in Lando's translation, and the intellectual circle from which it arose, can be seen to survive in creative responses to *Utopia*, which built on an already well-established Italian genre of texts that 'theorized ideal cities and societies throughout the fifteenth century' (Spinozzi 2016: 505). Lando's own contribution, the *Commmentario* (1548), has been mentioned above. Doni would go on to write *I Mondi* (1552–3), a dialogue featuring seven different worlds, one of which is a 'wise-mad', or 'mad-wise' (*savio e pazzo*), world described in a dream.[17] Part I of Doni's *I Marmi* (1552), meanwhile, includes a dialogue

---

[16] For the influence of Sansovino's volume in early modern France, see Scholar in this volume.

[17] For the relationship between reason and folly, *Utopia* and Desiderius Erasmus' *Moriae Encomium* ('Praise of Folly'), see Taylor and Nicholas in this volume.

in which the interlocutors read from a book containing 'healthy laws' (*legge sante*), and which includes a character with Hythloday-ish tendencies called *Inquieto*, 'the restless one' (Grendler 1965: 481, 484). Nelson (2006: 1052) draws a convincing connection between Doni and Tommaso Campanella (1568–1639): 'one of the few authors of Utopias who acted on his ideas' (Gjerpe 2008: 64). Campanella's *Città del Sole* (written 1602, printed 1623) contains 'radically proto-communist' ideas, which he had previously attempted to put into practice in 1597, as the leader of a Calabrian rebellion against Spanish rule, which—in the process—also endeavoured to 'establish a society based on the community of goods (and wives), clearly inspired by More's Utopia'.[18] The ideological fissures, between orthodoxy and heterodoxy, glimpsed in the lives of the Bonvisi brothers—*Utopia*'s Italian patrons—are thus perpetuated in the varied Italian afterlives of More's text.

---

[18] For other examples of mid- to late-sixteenth-century Italian utopian fiction, including Francesco Patrizi's *La città felice* (1554) and Ludovico Agostino's *Dialoghi dell'Infinito* (written 1583–90), see B. Richardson 1997: 202–203.

CHAPTER 14

INVENTING *UTOPIA*
The Case of Early Modern France

RICHARD SCHOLAR

INVENTING *Utopia* in early modern France often meant translating the text.[1] This was a complex process activating the full range of meanings that French in the period lent to the verb *traduire*: it involved transportation, appropriation, and transformation. French translators, starting with Jean Le Blond in 1550, made Thomas More's Latin text available to readers of their native language and thus imported intellectual goods from the dominant international language of learning to the fledgling vernacular of an emerging European nation state. They viewed this work of importation not only as a contribution to the linguistic enrichment of French, but also as part of a broader cultural transfer of learning and other forms of 'soft power' (*translatio studii*) to accompany the movement of imperial power (*translatio imperii*) westwards, to Paris. Their work invariably brought the text across marked boundaries—of political geography, confessional allegiance, and genre—and relocated it in new settings. At times, as we shall see, it invented *Utopia* anew.

THE FIRST FRENCH TRANSLATIONS: AN OVERVIEW

Much of what has been just said of early modern France could be applied, *mutatis mutandis*, to France's neighbours in the same period. Le Blond was just one of numerous translators across western Europe who started, from the mid-sixteenth century onwards, to move *Utopia* out of the cosmopolitan, humanist, neo-Latin circumstances of

---

[1] The most important studies of this topic include Saulnier 1963; Hosington 1984; Céard 1996: 43–74; Sellevold 2008a.

its making and to bring the text closer to their local culture. Yet the intensity with which *Utopia* was translated in early modern France is unprecedented elsewhere. Three French versions appear in the second half of the sixteenth century alone: after its first printing in Paris in 1550, the translation of Le Blond (1502–53) underwent adaptation of its own when Barthélémy Aneau (1505?–61) published it in a revised edition of 1559 in his home town of Lyons; and Gabriel Chappuys (c.1546–1611) supplied the third version of *Utopia* by including a partial translation of Book Two as the final chapter in a comparative history of government first published in Paris in 1585, itself translated from Francesco Sansovino's widely read treatise on government, *Del governo*, first published in Venice in 1561 (reissued 1566, 1567, 1578, 1583, and 1607).[2] This unusually intense initial cluster of French translations yields a rich body of evidence that is of particular interest to reception history, as a critical method which traditionally accords greater hermeneutic importance to the first reception of a work (see Jauss 1982: 20). To the three sixteenth-century French versions just mentioned should be added two versions that appeared in the first half of the seventeenth century: the first is a 1611 French translation, printed in Paris, again translated from Sansovino's *Del governo*. Entitled *Du Gouvernement et Administration de divers estats, Royaumes et Republiques, tant anciennes que modernes* ('Of the Government and Administration of Various States, Kingdoms and Republics, both Ancient and Modern') translated by a certain—and otherwise unidentified—F.N.D., this work contains (as Sansovino's does) a rendering of the discourse by Raphael Hythloday in *Utopia*, Book Two. The second is a 1643 translation by Samuel Sorbière (1615–70), published in Amsterdam, of *Utopia* in its entirety.

What, then, might these first French translations of *Utopia*—when viewed as a cluster—be said to reveal of the text's broader reception history? They confirm that *Utopia* has been resilient enough to afford the wide variety of uses made of it, and that as it has done so, it has reflected the interests of its different users. They thus bear out the findings of a major collaborative study of the early modern German, Italian, French, English, Dutch, and Spanish versions of *Utopia*, introduced by Terence Cave, who recalls the etymological sense of the word 'resilience' when he says that *Utopia* is a text 'constantly rewinding its spring, renewing its forces', as it passes from one cultural moment to the next (T. Cave 2008a: 13). Cave initially sketches a distinction between two separate interpretative uses for the work, one tending to align it with the tradition of the ideal commonwealth in political philosophy—the so-called 'best state' exercise—associated with Plato, and the other to place it in the literary tradition of fictitious travel going back to Lucian (9–10).[3] The French cluster appears to support this distinction: Chappuys's version of *Utopia*, in presenting Hythloday's discourse on Utopia in Book Two as part of a comparative survey of government, points the work in the direction of political philosophy; Le Blond, by contrast, appeals immediately to the work's literary horizon of reception by, for example, adding a prefatory ten-line (*dixain*) verse in serio-comic praise

---

[2] For Sansovino's *Governo*, see Shrank in this volume.
[3] For the two approaches, see also Hadfield and Hobbs in this volume.

of the Utopians' saintly way of life. The two seventeenth-century French versions divide along the same lines: F.N.D. (in 1611) echoes Chappuys (and Sansovino) in aligning *Utopia* with political philosophy; Sorbière (in 1643) follows Aneau in reading *Utopia* as a literary fable; and we shall see that, in further ways, the 1611 and 1643 editions (printed in Paris and Amsterdam respectively) entrench various features of the sixteenth-century French cluster. Cave is quick to stress, however, that the distinction between these two interpretative uses does not hold in most early modern versions, which mix them, and he offers the early French paratexts as instructive here: all of them, he says with specific reference to Aneau's introductory note, 'revert insistently to the conception of *Utopia* as a heuristic text' and display to their readers the skills required to read the text in this way (T. Cave 2008a: 11). Herein, for Cave, lies the resilience of *Utopia*.

It is a particular achievement of Cave and his fellow contributors to have demonstrated how consistently instructive of wider context the paratexts of *Utopia* are. Their study shows how a complex set of materials, including the title page and illustrations, letters and poems of dedication and congratulation, maps of Utopia and scraps of Utopian writing, book and chapter headings, and marginal glosses, evolved in the very first Latin editions of the work and continued to do so in the subsequent vernacular versions across early modern Europe.[4] The author of the French chapter in that study, Kirsti Sellevold, concludes that the French translators 'provide us with an indispensable barometer for measuring the way in which More's work is successively reinserted into different cultural contexts' (Sellevold 2008a: 68). What remains to be fully explored, perhaps, is what the most appropriate conceptual model might be for understanding that process of successive cultural reinsertion in tracing a reception history that is concerned with text, and in particular *translated* text, as much as it is with paratext and context. What follows turns, for just such a conceptual model, to the notion of 'invention' as understood by the literary culture of early modern France.

INVENTION: A CONCEPTUAL CONJECTURE

From the vantage point offered by the first French translations, this chapter suggests that the early modern period witnesses the 'invention' of *Utopia*, in the complex sense that the period lends to that very term by holding in tension two apparently opposing processes: discovery and creation. One might view, as emblematic, the lexical invention of *utopia*—combining two Greek words, *ou* (not) and *topos* (place)—with the classical Latin suffix *-ia*. This invention was at once part discovery (the selection of the classical root words) and part creation (the play on those root words to make a fictitious place name). That the invention of *utopia* as a word combines discovery and creation is, I suggest, emblematic of a wider truth. It helps to account for the invention of *Utopia*, not

---

[4] For the early Latin editions, see Taylor in this volume.

only as a word, but as a text: one that discovers the old Greek thinking about the best form of the state even as it conceives of a New World that surpasses the Old in its forms of political life, and uncovers the serious problems of the present age even as it conceives of those problems as too serious always to be taken seriously. It helps, equally, to understand the travelling and shape-changing course of *Utopia* through history, for this is a travelling history of continuing invention, an invention that looks back to More's *Utopia* in the act of writing over it.

I readily concede that you might wish to look elsewhere for your conceptual model: to speech act theory, perhaps, as made famous by J. L. Austin and applied by Quentin Skinner (2002b: vol. 1) to the history of ideas; or (to cite just one further example) to the critical method of afterlives, developed by Cave and others in the wake of reception history (Holland and Scholar 2009). Whichever conceptual model you choose to adopt, however, you would be bound to want to explore—in a historically inflected study of reception—how the literary culture surrounding the objects of your study itself conceptualized the process of their composition and translation. Such an exploration leads to invention.

Invention has been extensively studied across a range of early modern disciplines and contexts.[5] Word historians such as Roland Greene and Grahame Castor agree that the term, by the sixteenth century, is caught up in a long and uneven process of change as it moves from its rhetorically-informed classical sense (the discovery of source material) to its modern sense (the creation or conception of something new).[6] For Greene, the process of semantic change was under way yet far from complete, so that 'the term contains the uncertainties of a period suspended between complementary but distinct notions of what it means to make customs, objects, or works of art' (Greene 2013: 22). Castor argues that sixteenth-century 'invention was still quite definitely a finding, a discovery, or a finding out, rather than a creating' (Castor 1964: 126). Yet his many examples of particular usage tend, in fact, to confirm Greene's view of sixteenth-century *invention*, which is that 'the tension built into the word does not compromise its meaning', but 'is that meaning' (Greene 2013: 19).

The literary culture of sixteenth-century France places discovery and creation in tension when it conceptualizes the composition and translation of literary texts. French writers of the period vigorously pursued theoretical questions about translation prompted by Italian humanists of the preceding century in the wake of Leonardo Bruni's *De interpretatione recta* ('Of the Correct Way to Translate'), c.1426 (Worth-Stylianou 1999: 128). The debate in France took on a national dimension as French writers sought to make their language and culture worthy of a European superpower and identified the imitation of prestigious models (principally, but not exclusively, classical ones) as the best means to achieve the betterment of French. How, though, was such *imitatio* best practised? And what role (if any) might translation play in the process? Etienne Dolet's

---

[5] Recommended studies are Castor 1964; Atkinson 2007; Greene 2013; Marr and Keller 2014.
[6] On rhetorical *inventio*, see Langer 1999: 136–144.

very short 1540 treatise on the subject views translation, within the broader framework of rhetoric and poetics, as 'a work of crafted imitation' if freed from the constraints of a literalist approach (Worth-Stylianou 1999: 129–130). Thomas Sebillet, in 1548, agreed. His rival Joachim Du Bellay, by contrast, argues in his *Deffence et illustration de la langue françoyse* (1549) that, while translations have usefully discovered the treasures of classical learning and made the revelations of Holy Scripture available for French readers (1.4), they are incapable of the higher task of bringing French to a state of literary perfection, for particular to each language is a certain *je-ne-sais-quoi* of eloquent style, which no translation can convey (1.5). Du Bellay recycles here the distinction traditional in rhetoric, between *inventio* (as discovery of source material) and *elocutio* (as the cultivation of eloquent style), and thus restricts translation to the lesser task of 'inventing' nonliterary foreign source materials in literal renderings for French readers. In the process, he also reasserts the literalist approach to translation, from which Dolet had freed it. All of this enables Du Bellay to exclude translation from the sphere of imitative writing and, ultimately, to present poetry as alone possessed of the energy necessary to cultivate French eloquence by imitating creatively prestigious foreign models.

Du Bellay's arguments set the agenda for later sixteenth-century debates in France. These debates frame the first French translations of *Utopia*, and each of the writers involved in the translations finds a way to counter the arguments of the *Deffence*, whether by setting out a direct response to (as is the case of Aneau in his *Quintil horatian* of 1551)[7] or by including (as Le Blond and Chappuys both do) refutations of Du Bellay in prefaces promoting the value of their work as translators. At various points, all of them call upon the language of invention, and—unlike the rhetorically minded Du Bellay—they do so, between them, in ways that indicate the full range of invention's meanings and its constitutive semantic tension. One might go further, indeed, and suggest that at times they actually foreground this tension in the word's meaning and exploit its possibilities—thereby actively intervening in the wider history of invention—by communicating to readers their sense of *Utopia* as a heuristic text that marries discovery and creation in a complex whole. All of them, for example, reveal sources of material for *Utopia* (such as Plato and Cicero) while declaring—as do the Latin paratexts (such as Anemolius' hexastichon)—that More's creation surpasses the achievements of its precursors; and all of them recognize that the heuristic nature of *Utopia* makes them inventors, too, who need in turn to situate their invention in relation to its antecedents.

In so doing, these translators may be said to institute a long French tradition of inventing *Utopia* anew, which includes but also exceeds their translations. That tradition looks outwards, in generic terms, to the independent and larger-scale French appropriations of More's work that appear in the century following the first publication of *Utopia*. These start in the first books—*Pantagruel* (1532) and *Gargantua* (1534)—of François Rabelais who, in a direct allusion to More's fiction, makes his giant hero Pantagruel the prince of Utopia. That allusion reveals the first of many telling differences

---

[7] The sections of the *Quintil horatian* relating to the *Deffence* are given in Du Bellay 2001: 304–361.

between More's text and Rabelais's appropriation, however, for, where More's Utopian commonwealth is a Venetian-style republic, Rabelais's is a monarchy.[8] The second such appropriation—to which we shall return—is the work of one of our early translators, Aneau, in his chivalric romance *Alector* (1560). Rabelais and Aneau relocate their borrowings from *Utopia* in generic settings (chronicle and chivalric romance) that are foreign to More's text. The *Histoire du Grand et Admirable Royaume d'Antangil* (1616), by the otherwise unidentified I.D.M.G.T., reads, by contrast, like a wholesale imitation of the form that Hythloday's discourse takes in *Utopia*, Book Two: namely, an account of a fictional land and its governance that is presented on its title page as a newly discovered country (*incogneu jusques a present*) and exemplary (*nompareille*). It is perhaps for this reason that *Antangil*, the third early large-scale appropriation of More's work in France, is generally identified as the country's first contribution to the new genre of the literary utopia (Saulnier 1963: 152–153; Jeanneret 1970: xiii).

Antangil shows how the French invention of *Utopia* can adumbrate its modern fortunes while also looking backwards, in time, to its own beginnings. Sorbière's 1643 translation of *Utopia* is similarly Janus-faced. As Sellevold observes, its publication in Amsterdam 'marks a shift into an alternative, cosmopolitan Francophone world that will reach its peak in the eighteenth century' (Sellevold 2008a: 86).[9] Sorbière recalls earlier interpretations of *Utopia* as a text that, in combining philosophical import and literary fiction, mixes—as the Horatian topos goes—profit and pleasure (T. Cave 2008c: 201).[10] Emphasizing for his part the pleasure of the text, he calls *Utopia* 'a fable as ingenuously invented [*ingenieusement inventée*] as one can find in books written solely to entertain', thus enshrining invention as a presiding term in the early modern French reception of the text. Sorbière presents these remarks about *Utopia* as indebted to the very first readings of the text 'by [Desiderius] Erasmus, [Guillaume] Budé, and all men of learning' (T. Cave 2008c: 198–199). Arguably, Sorbière's overt act of retrospection to the homages of More's humanist contemporaries is mediated here by a covert one to the cluster of early French versions of *Utopia*, for Le Blond in 1550 and Aneau in 1559 also associate Budé with the first reception of *Utopia* in France. They have the historical evidence on their side. The second edition of More's text was published in 1517 in Paris: France's capital was thus the setting for a major episode in the work's initial Latin diffusion throughout Europe. Thomas Lupset, who saw the Paris edition through the press of Gilles de Gourmont on Erasmus' behalf, elicited a long letter from Budé and added it prominently to the preliminaries of his edition, alongside other encomiastic letters by contemporary intellectual luminaries (More 1995: 271–272; T. Cave 2008c: 278). Sorbière's naming of Budé in 1643 thus continues a French tradition, by then well

---

[8] 'The particular republic that the Utopian arrangements would be most likely to call to mind was Venice, whose "mixed" constitution combined the institutions of Doge (the elected head of government), Senate, and Grand Council' (More 1995: 121 n.).

[9] For more on French literary culture in the Netherlands, see Verhaart in this volume.

[10] The source for this topos is Horace, *Ars poetica*, 343.

over a century old, of commending More's invention to French readers by looking back to its enthusiastic first reception by one of the country's most distinguished humanists.

LE BLOND'S MODEL OF THE HAPPY LIFE: PARIS 1550

Le Blond singles out Budé's letter by removing the other endorsements of humanist luminaries that surround it in the other early editions and by advertising it on the title page of his translation.[11] The translator chooses in that advertisement to draw attention to Budé's role in government, as if to put him on a par with More, who is described on the same title page as having been Chancellor of England as well as a distinguished humanist. Le Blond thus lends Budé's letter the character of a single authoritative interpretation of More's work. The paratexts of Paris 1550 run as follows: the title page; the privilege (granting the printer, Charles l'Angelier, the right to publish it); a prefatory note entitled 'To the Reader'; a summary of chapters; Budé's letter to Lupset; the translator's ten-line stanza (*dixain*); two long subheadings, one at the outset of the work proper and the other at its conclusion, each summarizing the work's contents and naming its translator; a second long subheading and Le Blond's motto, 'Hope for better things' (*Espoir en mieulx*), at the conclusion of the work proper; a second note, this one entitled 'From the Author [of the Translation] to the Reader'; and a detailed table of contents. There are two further paratexts scattered across the work as a whole: twelve elegant woodcuts, nine of which head the chapters of Book Two and illustrate scenes of life on Utopia; and the marginalia.[12]

Le Blond's translation of Budé's letter foregrounds an endorsement of More's work that is rich in invention. It recounts the discoveries that reading *Utopia* afforded Budé while he was having work done to his country house and which caused him almost to abandon in disgust the domestic chores of a landowner. It taught him (the famous legal commentator) to see that the law, as practised in Christian countries, only supports

---

[11] *La description de l'isle d'Utopie ou est comprins le miroer des republiques du monde, et l'exemplaire de vie heureuse: redigé par escript en stille Treselegant de grand' haultesse et majesté par illustre bon et sçavant personnage Thomas Morus citoyen de Londre et chancelier d'Angleterre Avec l'Espitre liminaire composée par Monsieur Budé maistre des requestes du feu Roy Francoys premier de ce nom* ('The description of the isle of Utopia, comprising the mirror for republics of the world and the model of a happy life set down in writing in a most elegant and elevated styles of great majesty by the illustrious, good, and learned Thomas Morus citizen of London and Chancellor of England, with the preliminary epistle composed by Monsieur Budé, Master of Requests of the late King Francis, the first of that name') (T. Cave 2008c: 182–183).

[12] The ordering of the paratexts in the BnF copy I have consulted of Paris 1550 (http://catalogue.bnf.fr/ark:/12148/cb309761123, last accessed on 28 Jun. 2023) differs from that given in T. Cave 2008c: 181–187. In particular, the note 'To the Reader' *precedes* Budé's letter in the BnF copy, thus resolving the anomaly Sellevold (2008a: 71 n.) observes in the wording of that note.

the material greed endemic in humans and therefore constitutes an affront to the 'rule of mutual charity and community property' that Christ passed down to his disciples. It revealed to him that the Christian alternative is to be found in a surprising place—the far-flung island of Utopia—which has organized itself according to the three 'divine institutions' of equality, dedication to peace, and contempt for money (More 1550: *2v-*8r; 1995: 6-19). This reading of More's work fundamentally aligns Utopian life with Christian revelation and vice versa (Garanderie 1989: 330). While developing in this way the moral import of More's text, Budé never loses sight of the literary playfulness with which it is dexterously intermingled to heuristic effect, and he reveals this intermingling not by commenting on it but by re-enacting it. He participates fully, for example, in the fiction—established in Book One of *Utopia*—that this is a true story of New World travel. It is in so doing that Budé uses the language of invention, describing Hythloday as having 'invented'—*inventé* (More 1550: *7r), *inventum* (More 1995: 16)—a model of the happy life by means of his foreign travel, and More as having adorned the model thanks to his eloquent style. Budé is here applying the distinction in rhetoric between *inventio* and *elocutio*—so by invention he means discovery—but he is clearly using the word in this sense with his tongue in cheek, since he knows full well that behind the travel narrative, featuring Hythloday the explorer in conversation with More the reporter, stands More the creator of the entire fictional world. Budé, we might say, here plays on the two senses of invention by presenting a creation as a discovery. He follows suit elsewhere in his letter: he claims to have heard that Utopia is also called Udepotia, thus adding Neverland to the risible names of Greek derivation that More invents for his Nowhere Island, and—in a characteristic intermingling of Christian moral import with creative literary play—he subsumes Amaurot and the other fifty-three identical cities of More's island under a new name of Greek derivation, Hagnopolis, thus rechristening Neverland as a City of Saints and adding a turn of his own inventive wit in emulation of More's.

Taken as a whole, Le Blond's paratexts carry powerful echoes of Budé's letter, not least its spirit of invention. Le Blond discovers important things in Budé's letter: the phrasing 'model of the happy life', for his translation of More's title, a description possibly inspired by Jean Desmarez's (aka Paludanus') letter to Peter Giles, printed in the first two Latin editions (Céard 1996: 47-48); reasons for considering 'this little book to be worth reading' (and therefore translating); and praise for the 'saintly life of the Utopians', which he versifies in his *dixain*. Sellevold suggests that, by thus appropriating Budé's letter, 'Le Blond may have wanted, among other things, to promote its evangelical message at the very moment when the non-schismatic French pre-reformers known as "evangelicals" were on the point of extinction' (Sellevold 2008a: 73). This may well be so, though Le Blond chose to dilute the message as he promoted it, toning down—particularly in the marginalia—some more of the overtly anticlerical statements in *Utopia* with which the evangelical message might well have been associated (Hosington 1984: 122, 131). This choice was surely prudent for a Catholic translator to make when, with Catholic France on the verge of schism, such criticisms might be attributed to sympathy for the cause of Luther, Calvin, and company.

That Le Blond chooses to put Budé's evangelical celebration of Utopian saintliness into verse, meanwhile, reflects the literary creativity with which Le Blond makes his discoveries, in Budé and elsewhere, and communicates these to his readers. Le Blond's version of *Utopia* makes two remarkable contributions. The first is its reversal of the order whereby the early Latin titles promise a discourse 'on the best state of a commonwealth' (*de optimo reipublicae statu*) before naming the 'new island' visited by Hythloday. By advertising the text's description of that island first, the Le Blond edition 'contributes to the progressive shift towards the emergence of "Utopia" as the distinctive name of the work' (Sellevold 2008a: 70). The second of his edition's contributions lies in its deployment of translation in the service of enriching French eloquence. Brenda Hosington, who has produced the most sustained textual study to date of the early French translations, declares Le Blond's translation 'both elegant and learned' (Hosington 1984: 122). In his note 'From the Author to the Reader', Le Blond comments on his practice as a translator, defending his use of paraphrase to clarify the meaning of the source text and his recourse to rare terms and neologisms, observing that 'if we only used standard terms common to everybody, our language would not be enriched by one jot' (More 1550: 187). In promoting neologism as enriching French eloquence, Le Blond takes the same line as Du Bellay's *Deffence*, which appeared the previous year (Sellevold 2008a: 70). That similarity masks a crucial difference, however, for Du Bellay in that text excluded translation from the literary task of bringing French to a state of eloquence, as we have seen, whereas Le Blond pointedly assumes that translation has a legitimate role to play among the literary arts.

Le Blond had already defended the legitimacy of translation on this score, in the exuberant defence of French mounted in his 'preamble' to the 1549 edition of the *Livre de police humaine* ('The Book of Civil Government'), his translation (first published in 1544) of a fifteenth-century Italian treatise by Franciscus Patricius on the ideal commonwealth (Hallowell 1960: 90). A minor nobleman from Normandy living in Paris, Le Blond had published poetry in the 1530s without securing a literary reputation, and he proceeded to translate Valerius Maximus and a third neo-Latin work in addition to the *Livre de police humaine* and *Utopia*: Johann Caron's chronicle of the reign of François I (1553; Sellevold 2008a: 68). Le Blond's version of *Utopia*, when seen from the perspective of his publishing career, appears central to his self-fashioning as a vernacular writer. We might say, echoing his motto, that it enabled him to hope for better things. Making available to French readers an important Latin work—following the success of the *Livre*—which promised to be 'useful and profitable to the republic', thanks not only to its political and religious import but also to its elegance of style, whose presence in the source text Le Blond emphasizes in the title of his work and the French rendering of which would enable him to demonstrate the value to the kingdom of the translator's art: Le Blond's *Utopia* made all of that possible.

ANEAU'S REVISION OF FORMS: LYONS 1559

Le Blond's edition also gave Aneau the opportunity to fashion his version of *Utopia*. Among the changes he made to Paris 1550 in the revised 1559 edition, published by the

Protestant printer Jean Saugrain in Lyons, were the removal throughout of Le Blond's name and the substitution of Aneau's initials, 'M.B.A.', by which Aneau usually signed his works. This may suggest that he was trying to pass Le Blond's work off as his own; if this was the case, the tactic long proved successful (Hosington 1984: 119). Since, however, Aneau retains both Le Blond's motto and his *dixain*, the latter a prominent paratextual feature of Paris 1550, it seems inappropriate to talk of intellectual theft in this case. Perhaps we would do better to think of a 'translation' from one of sixteenth-century France's humanist centres (Paris) to the other (Lyons). Rector of the Collège de la Trinité, Aneau was a leading figure in Lyonnais humanist circles, an author in his own right, the translator of classical and neo-Latin authors (including Ovid and Erasmus), and an authority that printers across the city invited to revise translations and write prefaces (Biot 1995a: 12 n., 16 n.; 1995b). Perhaps, as Sellevold speculates, Saugrain 'saw the potential for market success in publishing another French version of *Utopia*' and built on his existing relationship with Aneau (Sellevold 2008a: 73). Or perhaps Aneau took the lead on this occasion. He was certainly already interested in More: his long encomium of Justice in Greek and Latin verse, *Juris Prudentia* (1554), features the Englishman as the modern inheritor of the tradition, started by Plato and continued by Cicero, of imagining a republic (*Respublica ficta*) 'not as ever was, but as should be' ('Non ea quae usquam sed qualis debeat esse') (cited in Biot 1995a: 14).

Aneau makes changes to the text and paratexts of Le Blond's *Utopia* that are, at times, extensive. Hosington points to Aneau's amplifications of Le Blond's already paraphrastic version. In general, she considers the two translations to be broadly similar, not only in their abundant style but also in their surprisingly high level of accuracy and their elevation of More's Latin to a more elegant register in French (Hosington 1984: 128, 133–134). Like Le Blond before him, it seems, Aneau viewed his *Utopia* as a chance to contribute to the invention of French eloquence.

The most visible of Aneau's changes to the paratexts concerns the title of the work: *La Republique d'Utopie, par Thomas Maure, chancelier d'Angleterre, Œuvre grandement utile et profitable, demonstrait le parfait estat d'une bien ordonnée politique: Traduite nouvellement de Latin en Françoys*. The 'isle' of Utopia, in Le Blond's rendering, has its political status as a 'republic' foregrounded in Aneau's title, and the phrase *de optimo reipublicae statu* in the Latin title is hyperbolically rendered as 'the perfect state of a well-ordered commonwealth', whilst a doublet emphasizes the utility and profit to be derived from the work. However striking these changes may seem, they should not be allowed to mask continuities; nor should their significance be exaggerated. Le Blond's inversion of the Latin title, which puts Utopia first, is preserved. Meanwhile, Aneau's revised title can hardly be said to signal a shift in his version of Utopia from pleasure to profit, since—as we will see—he has much to say in other paratexts about the pleasure of the text. The shift is, at most, one of distribution across the paratexts as a whole. These run as follows: the title page; Le Blond's *dixain* (now unattributed); an introductory 'Note explaining the Work, by M.B.A'; a subheading at the outset of the work proper; the work proper, followed by a long subheading and Le Blond's motto (now unattributed); a glossary of Utopian names; a summary of chapters; a detailed table of contents; and a list of errata. These paratexts carry both substitutions and omissions in relation to Paris

1550. The most important substitutions are of Aneau's introductory note and glossary for Le Blond's two prefatory notes. The most important omissions are the woodcuts—to which Saugrain presumably had no access—and Budé's letter to Lupset. As was the case of changes made to the title, here again we should not exaggerate the significance of the letter's omission, since Aneau draws upon the letter in his introductory note.

In both that note and the glossary, Aneau focuses on More's invention, which he examines more explicitly than his predecessors from a formal point of view. More, Aneau says, was 'a most cunning craftsman of ingenious invention and eloquence [*tressubtil ouvrier de ingenieusement inventer, et de bien dire*]' in his choice of 'the form of a chorographical fiction [*fiction chorographique*] of an island recently discovered and ruled in a very orderly fashion' to depict 'a most excellent form of government for a republic'.[13] Aneau is quick to assert that More did not intend the depiction of a replicable model—a blueprint—for government in the real world. To support this assertion, Aneau offers More's naming of his island Utopia ('which means of no place'), before turning, for confirmation, to Budé's letter: 'and Master Budé in his magnificent prefatory epistle to the work named it "Udepotia", that is, something that never existed'. Both men, he concludes, meant to say that 'there is not and never will be so well-formed a Republic' (T. Cave 2008c: 190–191).

Utopian naming is a feature of More's invention that Aneau makes the subject of the other important paratext that he writes for Lyons 1559: a 'Glossary [*Interpretation*] of Utopian names, explaining the proper names of people, things, and places invented [*inventez*] and made for pleasure [*formez à plaisir*] by the author with reference to the story of Utopia'.[14] Aneau transmits to his vernacular readers the learned pleasure of these names in gloss after gloss: *Amaurot*, which means 'obscure and unknown', is 'the name of a town unknown to all geography'; *Anydre* is 'a waterless river, a thing nobody has ever seen'; the *Macarians* are 'blessed in all their happiness, without owning anything; but where are they?', and so on (More 1559: Z1v). He ends his glossary with an interpretative overview:

> All of these names meaning non-existent or empty things, [...] which are forged and invented [*inventez*] rather than true, give us to understand that this Utopia is an invented republic [*invention de Republique*]—not such as is, ever was, or will be—skilfully disguised in the form of a historical narrative [...] so as to give an example of reform to present-day governments and other principal and public institutions. (Z2r)

---

[13] By *chorographique* Aneau means the precise topographical description of a place.

[14] This glossary, which was absent in the copies that Sellevold and Gro Bjørnerud Mo consulted, does not figure in their bilingual edition of the Lyons 1559 paratexts (T. Cave 2008c: 188–193). I refer to a Bibliothèque municipale de Lyon copy (http://numelyo.bm-lyon.fr/BML:BML_00GOO010013700110 0743553, last accessed on 9 Mar. 2018), which contains the glossary (More 1559: Z1r–2r). All translations of the glossary are mine.

This overview repeats, from the perspective of the names of *Utopia*, the conclusion of Aneau's introductory note: that More's invention has 'the delightful and useful aim of reprehending [...] the defects of present-day republics and of representing the archetype of a true form of government, which all others ought to conform themselves to, or at least approach as closely as possible' (T. Cave 2008c: 192–193). The final qualification of that sentence reaffirms Aneau's view that More intends by his 'archetype' no blueprint for government.

More's archetype instead works heuristically, as Aneau explained earlier in his note, in the same way as the conceptual figures of Stoic sage and Ciceronian orator: both of these, he says, 'are depicted in the form that would be appropriate to them in their absolute perfection, if human weakness could attain it; and those who come closest to it will be judged to be the most excellent in wisdom and the art of oratory'. The most excellent government in the real world, then, will be the one that strives most closely—and fails least—to represent the Utopian archetype. Each and every government will fail, however, human weakness being what it is. For this reason, Aneau now declares, More's portrayal is of a form of government 'not such as anything of the kind ever existed or is actually to be found in some place, but such as it ought to be everywhere', a point we have just seen him also making in the glossary (T. Cave 2008c: 190–191). Aneau's phrasing brings to mind his description in *Juris Prudentia*, quoted earlier, of Plato as imagining a republic 'not as ever was, but as should be', and thus founding a tradition of political philosopy continued by Cicero and, in modern times, More (Biot 1995a: 15). Cicero's reappearance in Aneau's introductory note, albeit as a writer on oratory rather than political philosophy, suggests a further connection between that text and the passage in *Juris Prudentia*. What seems to underlie that connection, meanwhile, is an awareness of the Platonist theory of Forms as it relates to political philosophy (see M. Schofield 2006). Aneau sees More as having portrayed, after Plato, a 'perfect archetype' in that sense: it is a Form, the like of which particular governments strive to be, but in respect of which they are always an imperfect representation.

While Aneau and Budé both read *Utopia* as a heuristic text, then, the difference between their treatments is striking. Budé's seems implicitly Aristotelian, by contrast with Aneau's, as well as explicitly Christian. Budé ends his letter likening More's work to a 'seedbed [...] of elegant and useful concepts' from which present and future ages 'will be able to borrow practices to be introduced into their own several nations and adapted for use there' (More 1995: 18–19; 1550: *7v). Budé here reveals a practical conception of politics akin to that of Aristotle in the *Politics*, where Aristotle argues—against idealistic predecessors—that it is just as important to reform existing constitutions as it is to form new ones, and that constitutional reform is the practical task of politicians (6.1.1289a1–7).

Aneau, who had discovered in Plato the philosopher grounds for seeing More's idea of Utopia as an archetypal Form, finds in Plato the poet the key to understanding More's invention in *Utopia* of a literary form. Aneau opens his introductory note by claiming that More designed his New World fiction to convey an image of political perfection in the same way as 'ancients poets, under the veil of mythological fable, concealed true philosophy' (T. Cave 2008c: 190–191). Humanists like Aneau identified Plato as a poet of precisely this kind (see Pantin 2010: 19). Aneau first places the author of *Utopia* in the same august tradition of philosophical poetry and then highlights a formal innovation he says More has introduced—the 'colour of historical probability'—which, Aneau argues, causes us to view as a 'true story' what is, in fact, an 'imaginary account' invented (*inventé*) by its author. He returns to this innovative aspect of More's fiction towards the end of his note, when he identifies the historical figures present in Book One of *Utopia* as further devices of verisimilitude, used by the author 'in order better to disguise and to make more plausible the excellently forged invention [*la controuvée bonne invention*] in the form of a historical narration' (T. Cave 2008c: 190–191, 192–193). Aneau repeatedly uses the language of invention in his note to distinguish More's fictional creation from the factual narration it purports to be. It might seem tempting to conclude from these uses that Aneau, in his attention to More's experiment with literary form, makes a decisive intervention in the wider history of invention by moving the word towards its modern sense. To succumb to that temptation, however, would mean overlooking the importance to Aneau's reading of his initial observation that More discovers the materials for his experiment in the ancient tradition of the philosophical fable. More, then, is 'a most cunning craftsman of ingenious invention' for Aneau, because he mixes invention's discoveries and creative possibilities together in the experiment with form that is *Utopia*.[15]

As has already been mentioned, Aneau comments on *Utopia* in ways that indicate the formal orientation of his independent works, including his chivalric romance *Alector* (1560). This is a thoroughly entertaining piece of French vernacular humanist prose fiction in which the author uses elements from *Utopia* as well as from previous examples of the 'best state' exercise (Fontaine in Aneau 1996: 2.760–7272). Of particular interest here is the experimentation with form that connects *Alector* to *Utopia* via Aneau's 1559 version. *Alector* takes as its main setting a circular city—Orbe—that Aneau subjects to an extensive description whose form he connects to that of *Utopia*. The term 'chorographical' coined in 1559 for More's fiction of place reappears in the title of chapter 24 in *Alector*: 'Chorographie de la ville d'Orbe' (More 1559: 124r–136v; see Biot 1995a: 23–27). What surrounds this chorographical description is a romance narrative which starts when our twice-born outsider hero, Alector, is surprised in his beloved's bedroom and fights off his assailants. He is brought to trial (chapters 2–4): the High Priest of Orbe, Croniel, sentences Alector to trial by fight with the enormous serpent that has long terrorized the city. Alector's triumphant slaying of the serpent follows the chorographical interlude of chapter 24. Sellevold is right to observe that Aneau's mixing of romance narrative with utopian chorography enables him to produce 'his own highly independent imitation' of *Utopia* (Sellevold 2008a: 78). This has implications both for Aneau's utopian chorography—into which the romance narrative introduces

---

[15] I can only half agree, therefore, with the gloss on *inventer*—as 'discovery'—given in T. Cave 2008c: 191 n.

a markedly dystopian element in the shape of the serpent—and for that narrative, which is shaped by utopian chorography in respect not only of its main setting, but also some of its central episodes. The trial, for example, produces—thanks to Orbe's High Priest—an outcome that satisfies both Alector and his accusers. Likewise, in More's fiction, the community leaders swiftly 'settle disputes between private parties', a feature of arrangements in Utopia that—as the marginalia in Aneau's version observe at this point—stands in marked contrast to legal wranglings in 'other countries' (More 1995: 122–123; 1559: 137). *Alector* is, in its formal creativity, an invention of a piece with *Utopia*.

CHAPPUYS'S RHAPSODY OF INVENTIONS: PARIS 1585

Chappuys includes his partial translation of *Utopia*, Book Two in a comparative survey of government entitled *L'Estat, description et gouvernement des royaumes et republiques du monde* ('The State, Description, and Government of the World's Kingdoms and Republics'), which he published in 1585 in Paris, dedicating the work to Henri III of France, the reigning monarch.[16] The first twenty-three chapters examine factual examples of government—kingdoms and republics—all over the world. *Utopia*, the subject of the twenty-fourth and final chapter, constitutes the sole fictional example. Chappuys speaks of *L'Estat* as an original work and claims to have translated More's writing from the Latin. These claims were taken at face value for centuries until Nathalie Hester (1996, 1998) showed that Chappuys's entire volume is in large part a disguised French translation of Sansovino's *Del governo* (in its 1583 edition) and that Chappuys took as his sole source for *Utopia* Sansovino's version of Ortensio Lando's 1548 Italian translation. In the foreword to his work, Chappuys acknowledges that 'in the composition of this book' he has incurred intellectual debts to certain French, Latin, and Italian sources (More 1598: A3v). That he frequently names more minor such sources in the main text, while only mentioning Sansovino glancingly on three occasions, confirms that he deliberately concealed his borrowing of the Venetian's feathers (Hester 1996: 659; Sellevold 2008b). Yet Chappuys asserts, in the foreword, that he has paid his intellectual debts in full and that this should silence the carping of his critics, 'who will call this a translation [*traduction*], ragbag, or rhapsody, rather than an invention [*invention*] or some such' (More 1598: A3r). Opposing translation and invention, as Chappuys does here, suggests that he takes the former to mean the linguistic transfer of an existing text and the latter to mean the creation of an original work (albeit one that draws on previous sources). It is at this moment in our sequence of texts, by a small irony of history, that an occurrence of the term *invention* has never in fact more clearly referred to a discovery.

---

[16] The work was reprinted in 1598, by Regnault Chaudiere in Paris. I refer to that edition in what follows. All translations are my own.

Many features of Chappuys's translation of *Utopia* are found in his Italian source (Hester 1996: 663–664). The most important of these is the removal of all of Book One and the finale of Book Two, extracting Hythloday's discourse on Utopia from the surrounding dialogue. This intervention changes, of course, the shape of the work. It also profoundly alters the Latin text's distribution of voice and persona in that it leaves Hythloday unspecified as the narrator of the discourse and tends, in his absence, to imply that the narrator is none other than More himself. Other features inherited from Sansovino include a cut to the text in two places, amounting to some eight lines, where the narrator—with implicit reference to Europe—criticizes lawyers (for being manipulative) and laws (for being subject to the manipulation of lawyers);[17] the reduction of the 'Religions of the Utopians' in More's chapter heading to just one religion;[18] and a cut of some twenty lines where the narrator recounts the spread of Christianity in the tolerant multifaith setting of Utopian society.[19]

There are respects, however, in which Chappuys modifies or even adds creatively to his Italian source. He does this most prominently in the paratexts. The main paratexts in *L'Estat* relevant to Chappuys's version of *Utopia* include the title page, a dedicatory epistle 'To the King', and a foreword to the whole work. The paratexts of the Utopian chapter run as follows: the title ('De la republique d'Utopie, estat et gouvernment d'icelle'); an introductory paragraph, unsignalled as such, at the beginning of the translated text of 'On the Republic of Utopia'; a sentence that signals the end of the chapter in the style of a conventional finis; a final index that operates as a retrospective table of contents for the chapter; and—accompanying the text—chapter heads and marginalia. The title of the Utopian chapter translates Sansovino's, while modifying it in a manner consistent with the title that Chappuys chose for the work as whole, thereby emphasizing that the work's central task—of describing the 'state and government' of the world's 'kingdoms and republics'—now takes as its object 'the Republic of Utopia'. The introductory paragraph translates Sansovino's presentation of More, which starts with the author's life and martyrdom before introducing his *Utopia*, although Chappuys reverses the running order of the two parts of Sansovino's presentation as if to foreground More's work (Hester 1996: 663). The marginalia, meanwhile, are—as far as I have been able to determine—Chappuys's creation: there are none in Sansovino's *Del governo*, whereas marginalia figure in all twenty-four chapters of Chappuys's work, and those that accompany his partial version of *Utopia* do not correspond to the glosses found in the margins of the early Latin editions and subsequently put into French by Le Blond in Paris 1550. I would add that it seems consistent with Hester's account to think that Chappuys decided marginalia should accompany the entire text of *L'Estat* and that, in their absence from the sole source used for his 'Utopia', he created them.

Chappuys's modifications and additions amount to an inventive reinsertion of *Utopia* into a new context: one that connects the Frenchman's self-fashioning to the

---

[17] Compare More 1995: 194 (ll. 26–7) and 196 (ll. 8–14) with More 1598: 310r.
[18] Compare More 1995: 218 (l. 1) with More 1598: 313v.
[19] Compare More 1995: 218 (l. 28) to 222 (l. 5) with More 1598: 314r.

wider political situation of France in the 1580s. Chappuys had secured royal patronage as historiographer to Henri III in 1583 (Sellevold 2008a: 68 n.). Meanwhile, in 1584, the contemporary bibliographer La Croix du Maine celebrated the contribution to French culture Chappuys was making 'through books of his own invention [*les Livres de son invention*] as much as his translations [*ses Traductions*]'.[20] He had some success, then, in fashioning himself as an author in service of the kingdom. Chappuys uses the mixed materials he draws on for the text and paratexts of *L'Estat* to display the range of expertise and counsel he offers as historiographer to the royal dedicatee of his work and those serving in the government of France at a time of exacerbated conflict between the country's Catholic majority and Protestant minority. The years 1583 to 1585 saw Henri III developing an agenda of moral and political reform and cultivating his reputation as a pious Catholic monarch in his struggle to assert his authority in the face of hard-line Catholics who were forming, in opposition, an extremist party called the Ligue (Greengrass 2007: 312–364). Chappuys's dedicatory epistle and foreword to *L'Estat* portray Henri III as a modern Augustus, devoted to learning even in the midst of war, and as a true defender of the Catholic faith from 'heretical innovations' (More 1598: A2r–v, A4v, A6r–v). While it is possible to see in this latter portrayal Chappuys's adoption of a pro-Ligue 'position of no compromise', as Sellevold (2008a: 80) does, it more plausibly reflects, perhaps, the image of Henri III that the king and his advisers wished to project in an attempt to placate Ligueur opposition. Chappuys, in this perspective, is showing that he can offer the reigning monarch an indirect source of comfort and wise counsel.

This certainly seems to be the posture Chappuys adopts in the marginal gloss he adds to the passage in *Utopia* that explains how, when war is declared upon the peace-loving Utopians, they have placards posted in enemy territory that 'promise immense rewards to anyone who will do away with the enemy prince' (More 1995: 204–205). Chappuys's gloss reads 'I do not consider such advice—to employ deceit and spread treachery—plausible [*probable*]' (More 1598: 311v). The sole occurrence in the marginalia of *L'Estat* of a first-person-singular judgement, this gloss makes an exceptionally personal authorial statement, but one nevertheless consistent with Chappuys's persona: it displays an unwillingness to condone regicide, even in an extreme situation, that Henri III would have surely welcomed.

In other respects, too, Chappuys's version of *Utopia* is crucial to his performance of political expertise. He describes More's work, in his foreword to *L'Estat*, as a pleasurable exercise undertaken by England's Lord Chancellor, in imitation of Plato, offering 'a true model and form, as it were, of a perfect Republic' (More 1598: A3r). While this cursory description appears to share Aneau's heuristic conception of More's work as a Platonic archetype, the overall effect of Chappuys's work is more akin to a much enlarged version of Budé's Aristotelian seedbed, offering concepts and examples for piecemeal application by political leaders: Chappuys hopes that his book will teach his readers, in their

---

[20] De Juvigny et al. 1772: 1.249; translation mine. La Croix du Maine is here repeating the opposition between translation and invention (quoted above) by Chappuys in the foreword to *L'Estat*.

exercise of power, 'where they might be inferior to others, and where they might surpass them, in order that they might take the opportunity to reform themselves [...] or to improve still further in what they do' (A3r). The further claim made is that these practical possibilities are significantly enhanced for readers of *L'Estat* by the book's introduction of a fictional case. The paragraph introducing 'On the Republic of Utopia' states that More viewed his fiction as a pleasing way of teaching people how to live better (311v). Chappuys aligns himself with this view. Assuming the role of the author here, he translates and recycles Sansovino's words to new effect. As Sellevold (2008a: 81) points out, Chappuys was by 1585 known for his 1578 French translation of Francesco Doni's imaginative prose work *I mondi* ('Worlds'), which contains its own Utopian fiction, 'Il mondo savio e pazzo' ('The Wise and Mad World'). Chappuys praised Doni's 'miraculous and all but divine invention', and highlighted—implicitly refuting Du Bellay in the process—his free adoption of a paraphrastic style to convey in French the subtleties of Doni's invention (Chappuys 1583: 2r, 4v–5v; translation mine). In 1585, resolved no longer to appear in print as a 'mere' translator, he is prepared to assert that *L'Estat* is his invention.

Chappuys's specific aim, in his version of *Utopia*, seems to have been to fashion himself as an author building on his previous experience as a translator of imaginative fiction so as to enhance the heuristic political value of his work. Chappuys's case thus serves—in all its specificity—to illustrate, once again, two characteristics that define the early modern French reception history of *Utopia*. This is a reception history that highlights changing attitudes towards, and practices of, translation. It reveals, in the process, how entangled the translation of *Utopia* was in the early modern French rhapsody of inventions.

CHAPTER 15

UTOPIA IN TUDOR LONDON

Ralph Robinson's Translations and Their Civic, Personal, and Political Contexts

JENNIFER BISHOP

THE first English translation of *Utopia* was published in London in 1551, with a revised edition in 1556. The text was translated from Latin by Ralph Robinson, a member of the London Goldsmiths' Company, and was published in collaboration with a group of his fellow citizens from across the City's livery companies. Although the two editions of Robinson's translation were published only five years apart, they appeared in very different political and religious contexts. The first edition was published during the Protestant reforming years of Edward VI, and the second edition appeared during the strongly Catholic reign of Mary I. Despite these changing circumstances, however, Robinson's *Utopia* remained enduringly popular, weathering the upheavals of national politics and religious change and appealing directly to a vernacular readership of citizens, freemen, and the urban 'middling sort' (Barry and Brooks 1994). This chapter shows that the English translation was both a product of, and a contribution to, a growing enthusiasm for civic humanism and practical reform centred in sixteenth-century London, and that as such it formed part of a wider discourse about 'good governance' and the best state of the commonwealth that characterized the political thought of the mid-Tudor period (Sacks 1999: 68).

Whereas Thomas More's original text of *Utopia* had been intended for an elite readership of Latinate humanists and scholars, Robinson's translation made the text accessible to a vernacular English readership for the first time. The two editions of 1551 and 1556 presented a newly imagined version of *Utopia*, removed from the intellectual milieu of the European Republic of Letters, and made available to an emerging 'middling sort' of reader—literate citizens, merchants, and artisans—many of whom lived and worked in the expanding metropolis of early modern London. Through an examination of the circumstances, people, and places connected with Robinson's *Utopia*, this chapter tracks the first two English editions as they moved through, and adapted to, the changing political, religious, and literary worlds of Edwardian and Marian England. The focus throughout is primarily on Robinson and his network, with a concluding section that considers some broader themes that are crucial for understanding both the 1551 and 1556 editions.

THE 1551 EDITION

This section explores the context of Robinson's 1551 translation, discussing the significance of the publication's timing, and the political and religious circumstances in which it appeared, but also emphasizing the importance of place: specifically, the English *Utopia*'s roots in the civic and corporate culture of mid-sixteenth-century London. As Terence Cave has noted, 'what is critical is that *Utopia* surfaces here at a particular site: not in a university, or in a great house [...] but at the point of intersection between an everyday world of literate but not Latinate culture and the very centre of government. Such an event is unlikely to occur accidentally' (T. Cave 2008b: 94).

The urban context of the English *Utopia*'s appearance echoes the urban character of much of the text, especially the civic hierarchies and systems of government described in Book Two. Sarah Rees Jones has compellingly argued that More based Utopia's capital city, Amaurot, on London, with a set of recognizable parallels running through from topography to social structures. Amaurot's hierarchical government, which is reproduced in every other Utopian city, closely echoes that of London. For instance, the system of syphogrants and tranibors—Amaurot's magistrates—parallels the governmental hierarchy of early modern London. The Utopian officers are elected from among the householders of their communities, just as parish officers and constables were elected by householders in London. Rees Jones has shown that the electoral council of 200 syphogrants mirrored London's Common Council, which consisted of over a hundred councillors chosen from each ward; and the tranibors are in turn the counterpart of London's aldermen (Rees Jones 2001: 122). Like London's mayor, sheriffs, and aldermen, the Utopian magistrates are elected and serve for a period of a year or two on rotation; although, More notes, 'lightlye they chaunge them not' (More 1551: H5r). The Utopian government is thus the equivalent of London's Court of Aldermen and Mayor's Court, supported by the Common Council, the livery companies, and the parishes.

The hierarchies described in *Utopia* closely echoed those with which More, as a lawyer and undersheriff of London, was familiar. He could see the potential benefits of such a system, but he was also fully aware of the problems posed by urban expansion, and the apparent disconnect between the aspirations of civic institutions and the reality of everyday governance. The obvious parallels between Amaurot and the contemporary reality of sixteenth-century London that More exposed in *Utopia* may therefore have served, as Rees Jones suggests, to 'remind Londoners of the higher purpose of their own civic institutions', especially in a time of rapid change (Rees Jones 2001: 122; cf. Manley 1995: 40–41). Even if More had not intended his book to be widely read in London, civic politics clearly played a central part in his thinking: what occupies him most in *Utopia* is arguably not the best form of government for a kingdom, but rather that of a city, or set of city states (Rees Jones 2001: 117).

It is clear that Robinson and his circle of friends intended to make *Utopia*'s connections with London even more explicit when they made the text available to a vernacular readership in the 1550s (J. Bishop 2011). The first English edition of 1551 made its links with the metropolis clear from the title page. Here the translator, Robinson, is described as a 'Citizein and Goldsmythe of London', and the sponsor of the publication, George Tadlowe, is identified as a 'Citezein and Haberdassher of the same Citie'. The book itself is marked 'Imprinted at London', and the title page directs readers to the shop of its publisher, Abraham Veale (himself a member of the London Drapers' Company), 'dwelling in pauls churchyarde at the sygne of the lambe'. The identification of *Utopia*'s producers as members of high-ranking livery companies emphasizes the translation's roots in the corporate world of early modern London; likewise, the publication address in St Paul's Churchyard, the hub of the English book trade, locates the translation firmly at the heart of the City's growing literary culture. Taken together, this information points towards a specifically urban context for the 'beste state of a publyque weale' with which the book itself is concerned.

Robinson was not originally from London. Like many other young men in the City, he had migrated to the capital as an apprentice in his early twenties, hoping to build a career and use his skills to support his family. Robinson was born in 1520 in Lincolnshire, where he attended Stamford and Grantham grammar schools before entering Corpus Christi College, Oxford, as an exhibitioner in 1536. He graduated BA in 1540 and MA in 1544 (Cook 1935: 104–109). He then moved to London, where he joined the Goldsmiths' Company as an apprentice to Sir Martin Bowes, a prominent City alderman and one of the Goldsmiths' Company's most powerful and influential members. From 1548 to 1551 Robinson worked as a clerk at the Tower Mint, where Bowes was under-treasurer, and in October 1551 he finished his apprenticeship and officially became a freeman and citizen of London. Achieving this status was a significant marker in Robinson's career: he had successfully transformed himself from a 'foreigner' in the City to an enfranchised citizen, with all the rights and responsibilities that this entailed. When he published his translation of *Utopia* that same year, he could finally describe himself with some pride as a 'citizen and goldsmith of London'.

Although there may have been much to celebrate, the year 1551 also marked a moment of uncertainty for Robinson. With his apprenticeship completed and his employment at the Royal Mint at an end, he was in need of secure employment. He had a wife and a young family to support. He wrote several letters to his former schoolmate William Cecil, now a member of the Privy Council and secretary to Edward VI, asking for his support and patronage.[1] He dedicated his translation of *Utopia* to Cecil, perhaps with

---

[1] For Robinson's letters to Cecil, see BL MS Lansdowne 2 (the Burghley papers), 129r–134r (items 57–9).

similar hopes for preferment or financial assistance. At the same time, he put himself forward as a candidate for the Goldsmiths' Company clerkship, a position which had just become vacant. In the end he was taken on as an under-clerk at the Goldsmiths' Company, responsible for various administrative jobs such as drawing up yearly financial accounts (J. Bishop 2016).

There are many reasons why Robinson might have chosen to publish his *Utopia* in 1551, but it is vital to remember that he would not have been able to produce the text on his own. Like many early modern publications, the English *Utopia* was a collaborative enterprise, brought into being by a circle of friends and colleagues who pooled their resources, skills, and connections to produce the final book. The title page and preface to the 1551 edition name the most important of these collaborators: a translator, dedicatee, sponsor, publisher, and printer. Exploring the connections between these figures helps to elucidate some of the ideals that lay behind the publication of *Utopia*, locating the translation in the Protestant, humanist, reforming milieu of Edwardian London.

The choice of Cecil—then one of Edward VI's secretaries of state—as the book's dedicatee in 1551 was politically expedient, as Robinson and his friends had good reason to be cautious about the reception of *Utopia*. More's Catholicism and his disgrace under Henry VIII made *Utopia* a potentially controversial book to publish during the strongly Protestant regime of Edward VI. Robinson addresses this issue directly in his prefatory letter to Cecil, explaining that the 'fruteful and profitable' lessons to be learned from *Utopia* itself outweighed the unfortunate 'obstinacie' of its author 'in certein principal pointes of Christian religion' (More 1551: +4r). This effectively made a separation between *Utopia* the book and More the man, freeing the text from the associations of its author and repackaging it as something useful in its own right, to be discovered by a new generation of readers. But this disclaimer may not have been enough. Although censorship of the press had been lifted in the early years of Edward's reign, controls had been reintroduced in 1549, and in 1551 a royal proclamation had ordered that no books were to be published in English 'unless the same be first allowed by his majesty or his Privy Council in writing' (Hughes and Larkin 1964: item 371). Robinson would have known that Cecil had acted as a censor of the press in 1549, and that he continued to exert some influence over the book trade as a member of the Privy Council from 1550 (Phillips 2001: 129–130). This might explain why, in his preface, Robinson asked Cecil to defend *Utopia* with all 'the sauffe conducte of [his] protection' (More 1551: +5r).

Perhaps more significantly than issues of censorship, moreover, the dedication to Cecil linked the English *Utopia* directly to a circle of statesmen who began their political careers in the government of Edward VI and rose again to prominence in the reign of Elizabeth I. This group, often referred to as the 'Cambridge connection' in recognition of their shared educational background, applied the ideas of civic humanism that they had encountered in their university days to the practical requirements of governance (Hudson: 1980). Although Robinson was not part of this group himself, he would have received a similar education at Corpus Christi College, Oxford, which had been founded in 1516 by Richard Fox—a close friend of More and Desiderius Erasmus—in order to promote humanist education. Like Cecil, Robinson was part of the first generation to have received this English humanist education at university, and it is likely that he would have shared similar ideas about the application of learning to the affairs of state. His translation of *Utopia* may have been intended to appeal to this group of Cambridge graduates working in government, to whom he had a tenuous connection through Cecil. At the very least, he would have been aware of Cecil's interest in classical writings on citizenship and governance. And presumably he also thought that Cecil would be sympathetic to a translation project that aimed to make political texts such as *Utopia* more widely available, and therefore better known, among a more diverse group of citizens (Cave 2008b: 93–94).

In his prefatory letter to Cecil, Robinson alludes to some of the motivations that lay behind his decision to translate and publish *Utopia*. He relays a story from Lucian about the philosopher Diogenes. Seeing his fellow Corinthians busy preparing to defend themselves against the invading armies of Philip of Macedonia, Diogenes upends the barrel he lives in, and begins tumbling and rolling it around. When asked what he is doing, he explains that, seeing everyone else so occupied with important matters of state, he is—even if only by imitating their activity—contributing in his own way to the common cause. Robinson then compares his own project of translating *Utopia* to Diogenes rolling his barrel around:

> yet I seing every sort, and kynde of people in theire vocation, & degree busilie occupied about the common wealthes affaires: & especially learned men dayly putting forth in writing newe inventions, & devises to the furtheraunce of thesame: thought it my bo[un]den duetie to God, & to my countrey so to tumble my tubbe. (More 1551: +3r)

Robinson's story allows him to explore the significance of translation not only as a literary practice but also as a politically impactful activity. Translation, or literary 'barrel rolling', could appear to be an unimportant or at least marginal endeavour. By tumbling his tub up and down a hill, Diogenes does not effect real political change. But this analogy is not so simple. By adding his own gloss on this story, Robinson appears to be suggesting that philosophical 'barrel rolling' *was* just as important—if not more so— than more obvious, direct forms of political action. It is clear he believed that his translation of *Utopia* was in fact a useful, profitable, and important contribution to the commonwealth; and that the ideas in the book were worth sharing.

Although Robinson's *Utopia* was formally dedicated to Cecil, it does not seem that Cecil instigated or promoted the publication. Instead, the real sponsor of the translation was the London citizen and haberdasher Tadlowe. Robinson explains in his preface that it was Tadlowe who masterminded the project, requesting the translation in the first instance, as he could not read Latin, and then persuading Robinson to publish the result once he had read it. A member of the London Haberdashers' Company, Tadlowe was an active businessman with an interest in social reform and governance. Although he trained as a haberdasher and kept up a line in haberdashery goods, he also pursued several other occupations during his career, including running a tavern in London where he hosted plays and interludes. He imported wines from the Continent, leased rooms, and dealt in property throughout the City. The details of Tadlowe's early life and education are unknown: Robinson stated in his preface to *Utopia* that his friend did not have any Latin, so it must be assumed that he did not attend grammar school or university. His interest in *Utopia* coincided with his entry into the world of politics: he served as an MP in the House of Commons for the first time in 1547, and then again in 1554 and 1555. He was a member of London's Common Council, where he made a speech in 1549 (in response to the turmoil caused by the fall of Thomas Seymour, Protector Somerset), evoking an incident from *Fabyan's Chronicle* and recommending that the council 'thincke of things past to avoyde the daunger of thinges to come', an intervention—based on sound humanistic principles of using the lessons of history to shape current policy—which earns him the accolade of being 'a wise and good Citizen' (Foxe 1583: 1369).[2] He also acted as warden, surveyor, and governor of London's Royal Hospitals, playing an active role in their refoundation under Edward VI. Tadlowe's participation in local and national politics was concurrent with a wider trend that saw citizens taking an increasingly active role in legislation and reform and applying humanist ideas in a practical context (Loach 1991: 83).

It is highly likely that Tadlowe, rather than Cecil, is representative of both the intended and the actual readership of Robinson's *Utopia* in 1551. University-educated statesmen such as Cecil would have been able to read *Utopia* in its original Latin and would not have need of an English translation. Rather, it was men like Tadlowe—active and influential in their own spheres, with a practical interest in everyday civic governance and reform, but without the training in classical languages to access many important texts—who were the core readership of Robinson's work. In this sense, the English *Utopia* forms part of a wave of translations of classical and humanist works in the mid-sixteenth century—not least the edition of Thucydides translated by another 'citizen and goldsmith of London', Thomas Nicholls, in 1550.

It was Tadlowe who drove the production of Robinson's *Utopia* at every stage, and he appears to have been the point of mutual connection that held the group together. Veale, the first publisher and seller of Robinson's translation, was one of his close friends and bore witness to Tadlowe's will in 1557 (TNA PROB 11/39). Veale was a member of the London Drapers' Company, but he worked as a stationer, and set up as a publisher and bookseller in St Paul's Churchyard around 1550.[3] *Utopia* was one of his very first publications in a career lasting until the mid-1580s. His catalogue over these three decades contains a mixture of humanism, Protestantism, and practical, everyday texts, many translated into English from Latin or modern European languages. Much of Veale's output was religious, with a strong Protestant leaning: in 1551, the year of *Utopia*'s

---

[2] Cf. Hall and Grafton 1809: 2.523; Holinshed 1807–8: 3.1018. Foxe calls Tadlow 'George Stadlowe' (which is then followed by Holinshed; he is anonymous in Hall and Grafton).

[3] Veale remained a member of the Drapers' Company even after the incorporation of the Stationers' Company in 1557. Several of his apprentices in the Drapers' Company also went on to work in the book trade, but were forced to transfer to the Stationers' Company in the 1570s. See G. D. Johnson 1988: 2–17.

publication, Veale also published *Acts of the English Votaries*, by the hard-line reformer John Bale, and in the following year he published the Bible in English, and two works by Miles Coverdale. In addition to religious works, he also published various translations from classical authors and humanists including Juan Luis Vives and Erasmus. He had a steady line in books of cookery, herbals, and medicine, some of these also in translation, and he produced several cheap interludes and books of verse.

Like many publishers at the time Veale did not own a printing press himself, but had his books printed elsewhere before selling them at his shop in St Paul's. The printer of the 1551 edition of *Utopia* was Stephen Mierdman, a foreigner in London originally from Hooge Mierde in North Brabant (Hoppe 1948: 212–213). Mierdman had trained in Antwerp as an apprentice to his father-in-law Mattheus Crom, who specialized in printing Bibles and evangelical books. Mierdman and Crom had been active in the English Protestant book trade during Henry VIII's reign. Taking commissions from English Protestant authors abroad, they produced some thirty English-language religious texts between 1537 and 1546 and shipped them clandestinely to England (Pettegree 2002: 171). Charles V's clampdown on evangelical activity and English printing from 1546 forced Crom's business to close, and Mierdman migrated to London with his wife, Elizabeth. He obtained letters of denization in 1550, and was granted a five-year royal privilege to work as a printer in London (Page 1893: 177). This privilege allowed him to 'employ printers, English and foreign', a right usually denied to foreigners (*CPR, Edward* 3.314). Mierdman's output during his time in London was considerable, and he produced more than eighty works from his press between 1548 and 1553 (Kirk and Kirk 1900: 161; Pettegree 1992: 91 n.). He worked for and with a number of well-established printers and publishers in London including Edward Whitchurch, John Day, and Richard Grafton. Mierdman's involvement with the first edition of *Utopia* ties the translation closely in to the print culture of Edwardian London: Protestant, strongly driven by Continental migrant printers, with a flourishing of vernacular, affordable texts. Mierdman had a royal licence, as well as connections with prominent printers and stationers, attributes which helped to imbue the first edition of *Utopia* with legitimacy and status.

The final member of the English *Utopia*'s circle is Martin Bowes, Robinson's master and long-term patron and Tadlowe's business partner. Bowes is a key member of the group because he appears to have been the sole mutual acquaintance connecting Robinson and Tadlowe prior to *Utopia*'s publication in 1551. By the time of Robinson's apprenticeship with Bowes in 1544, Tadlowe was leasing several London properties from Bowes, including a tavern where he hosted interludes and plays (*LP* 14/1: g.1354(52)). It was likely to have been Bowes who introduced the two men, perhaps with a deliberate view to facilitating *Utopia*'s publication, or simply in the course of their business acquaintance. Second to Cecil, Bowes was certainly the most powerful and influential of Robinson's connections. He was one of the Goldsmiths' Company's most prominent members, and also held civic office, serving as an alderman for Langbourne ward from 1536, Sheriff of London in 1540, and Mayor in 1545–6. He was closely involved in social reform, and instigated several schemes for poor relief, devising a system of parochial collections for poor relief to be regulated by London's aldermen in 1547, and planning to create a 'brotherhood' for the poor along similar lines to European fraternities (Slack 1988: 120–121). Bowes was also one of the key movers behind the foundation of the Royal Hospitals in London, drawing up successive orders for their regulation and becoming comptroller-general when the hospitals reached completion in 1557 (Slack 1980: 110).

This connection with the Royal Hospitals provides a further point of interaction between Tadlowe and Bowes; they sat on several of the same committees and worked together closely during the early stages of the hospitals' refoundation. Under Bowes's authorization, Tadlowe was responsible for purchasing the royal letters patent for St Bartholomew's in 1547.[4] This close involvement in the implementation of practical schemes for social reform and poor relief links Tadlowe's and Bowes's interests directly with the need for commonwealth renewal raised in Book One of *Utopia*.

THE 1556 EDITION

The second edition of the English *Utopia* appeared in 1556, under the Catholic regime of Mary I. The text was revised and amended, with some additional material translated from the Latin version including four verses in 'the Utopian tongue' and three further poems translated into English. As well as these changes and additions to the text itself, it is clear that *Utopia*'s producers had repackaged the second edition to suit the new conditions under which it appeared, and to appeal to a new set of readers. The title page to the second edition signals some of these changes. Robinson is described as a former fellow of Oxford University, rather than as a goldsmith of London, and Cecil and Tadlowe are no longer named as sponsors of the text. The dedicatory letter to Cecil was removed and replaced with an address from Robinson to the 'gentle reader', in which he explains his reasons for publishing a revised edition. He apologizes for the 'rude' and 'base' translation of 1551, and places the blame for any mistakes on Tadlowe, claiming that he had produced that translation 'to please my sayde frendes judgemente, then myne owne. To the meanesse of whose leaninge I thoughte it my part to submit, and attemper my stile' (More 1556: A2r–v).[5]

The second edition was still published by Veale and sold from his shop at St Paul's, but in 1556 the printer had changed. The Protestant Dutchman Mierdman was no longer resident in London. After the accession of Mary I, and her drive to exile Protestant foreigners from the City, Mierdman moved back to the Continent to settle in Emden (E. G. Duff 1905: 105). His departure was part of a wider change in the City, as during Mary's reign the number of stationers in London was reduced by half (Loach 1986: 137). For those foreign printers who stayed in the City, many had their licences revoked as part of the effort by the Marian regime to stem the flow of Protestant printing and take control

---

[4] London, St Bartholomew's Hospital Archives, Treasurer's Accounts, 1547–61: 1r–4v.
[5] Although Tadlowe is not named, there is no evidence of his having fallen out with Robinson, and it is likely that he was still involved in the second edition.

of the book trade. By withdrawing the patents of 'undesirable printers' (both foreign and English) and granting them instead to stationers sympathetic to the new regime who would promote the reinstation of Catholicism, the direction of the book trade was changed very quickly (Took 1978: 224). This was the context in which the second edition of *Utopia* appeared, and it was printed by a beneficiary of these changes: the English stationer and specialist in books of common law, Richard Tottel.

Tottel was a member of the Stationers' Company and had served his apprenticeship as a stationer in London (Greening 2009). He set up his workshop in 1553 at the sign of the Hand and Star, located on the north side of Fleet Street within Temple Bar, close to the Inns of Court. In April 1553, a few months before Edward VI's death, Tottel was granted the exclusive right to print common law books in London, a privilege that was renewed by Mary in 1556 and again by Elizabeth in 1559.[6] Tottel was therefore a safe choice to print *Utopia*: he had royal protection, and was sanctioned by the new regime. It is also significant that Tottel was closely connected with a group of elite Catholic lawyers, many of whom had returned to England from exile on the Continent when Mary came to the throne. He was associated with a group at Lincoln's Inn that included William Rastell (More's nephew) and William Roper (More's son-in-law). Tottel's involvement with *Utopia* may therefore be explained through his connections with More's family and supporters and their—if not his own—Catholic sympathies.[7] Together with Rastell, Tottel published More's *A Dialogue of Comfort* in 1553, and a collected English *Works* in 1557. His involvement with *Utopia* therefore formed part of a larger project to make More's writings available to an English audience: in this case, a Catholic audience sympathetic to More's religious writings and beliefs.

Tottel's involvement with the second edition of *Utopia* significantly changes how we understand the timing and presentation of the text. He had useful connections with More's circle, and he had been granted a royal privilege for printing by Mary I, affording the publication no small measure of protection and legitimacy. Just as significant, however, is the possibility that Tottel could have introduced Robinson's translation to a new circle of readers: not only Catholic elites sympathetic to More and interested in his written work more generally, but also a wider network of humanist educated gentlemen, lawyers, and legal students based in and around the Inns of Court. Jessica Winston has shown that the Inns of Court were emerging during the mid-to-late sixteenth century as a hub of literary production, a flourishing particularly associated with a new generation of university-trained thinkers and writers keen to apply their humanist learning to practical social problems (Winston 2016: 7–8, 50–52; cf. Shannon 2009). Robinson and Veale were perhaps at the forefront of this trend, using Tottel's proximity to the Inns and his connections with lawyers and writers to find a new market for *Utopia*.

The prospect of this new readership for *Utopia* may have been the motivation for Robinson and Veale to produce a new edition of the translation in 1556. A connection

---

[6] *CPR, Philip and Mary* 3.18; *CPR, Elizabeth* 1.62–3.
[7] For an argument that Tottel was not Catholic himself, see Took 1978: 246.

with the Inns of Court men, a significant market for literary and humanist works, is certainly a more convincing explanation for the second edition of *Utopia* than any enthusiasm by Robinson and Veale for rehabilitating More's reputation under the Catholic Marian regime. Veale remained emphatically Protestant, and although his religious publications largely stopped under Mary—replaced with interludes and practical medical and cookery textbooks—his Protestant publications quickly picked up again once Elizabeth came to the throne.

Robinson's religious beliefs are slightly more opaque, but there is no evidence that he took advantage of the new religious climate to significantly alter his presentation of *Utopia*. Although his dedicatory letter to Cecil was removed, the book was not dedicated to anyone in Mary's government; and Robinson makes no mention of More or his religious views in his new preface. We can assume from this that Robinson was not seeking political preferment with this second edition, and neither was he attempting to reframe *Utopia* as the work of a Catholic writer.

Robinson's unwillingness to associate his translation with Mary's Catholic government is clear from some changes that he made to the text of the second edition. In his original 1551 letter to Cecil, Robinson had praised his former schoolmate's 'godlye dysposytyon, and vertuous qualytyes', before recommending *Utopia* itself as a 'frutefull and godly' book (More 1551: +5r–v). He concluded with the wish that Cecil and his heirs 'long and joyfully continue in all godliness and prosperity' (+6r). Robinson also included the words 'godly' and 'godlyness' throughout the text of *Utopia* and prominently inserted the phrase 'Godly governement' into the heading of Book Two, a phrase to which nothing in More's Latin corresponds (C5r; cf. Weil Baker 1999: 109). The language of 'godly' government was common throughout the Edwardian reformation, and has often been linked to a mix of religious and political reform espoused by a core group of Protestant preachers and writers associated with the regime. In the 1556 edition of *Utopia*, the phrase 'Godly governement' in Book Two was removed and replaced with 'politick government' (More 1556: G5v). As David Weil Baker has argued, this change of wording is indicative of Robinson's attempt to align *Utopia* with the classical, secular tradition of Aristotle and Plato, rather than with any explicitly Christian form of government (Weil Baker 1999: 110).

This change of wording serves to separate the ideas contained within *Utopia* from Mary I's Catholic government. Although the word 'godly' had carried explicitly Protestant connotations during the Edwardian reformation, it also had the potential to be used in a Catholic context. In William Rastell's preface to the *English Works* of More, published in 1557, for instance, he dedicates the book to Queen Mary and uses the word 'godly' five times in two pages. More is referred to as a 'wyse and godlie man', whose 'worthy workes and godly ende' are deserving of praise, and Rastell affirms his loyalty to 'your Maiesties most godly purpose': that is, the restoration of the Catholic faith (More 1557: C2r–v). Robinson's change from describing *Utopia* as a 'Godly' government in 1551 to a 'politick' one in 1556 could in this context have been a means by which to effectively distance *Utopia* from the Catholic revivals implemented by the Marian regime.

In place of the dedication to Cecil, the 1556 *Utopia* was dedicated to the 'gentle reader'. This change has been read by some scholars as an attempt by Robinson to enhance his social standing, and to distance himself from the unlearned circle of citizens who produced the 1551 edition. This interpretation has also been applied to Robinson's change of occupational descriptor on the title page of the 1556 edition, from 'goldsmith of London' to 'fellowe of Corpus Christi College in Oxford'. However, it is unlikely that these changes represented any significant shift in Robinson's aspirations or career. Rather, in 1556 Robinson was further strengthening his citizen ties, not cutting them: he was still closely involved with the Goldsmiths' Company and would soon receive a promotion to the office of company clerk—a position he had been petitioning for at least since his apprenticeship ended in 1551. It is more likely that the address to the gentle reader was a nod to the Inns of Court men and their circle—the new readers of Robinson's translation—than an attempt by Robinson to distance himself from his citizen status.

Finally, there were some entirely new additions to the second edition. These include marginal notes throughout the text, translated poems from the Latin edition, and, at the very end of the book, a new note from 'the Printer to the Reader'. This is a brief statement apologizing that the letters of the Utopian alphabet could not be included in the book, because 'their characters we have not' (More 1556: S8r). It is likely that this was Tottel's invention. Tottel had literary aspirations: he edited the songs and sonnets in his celebrated Miscellany of 1557, assigning titles and making other revisions and alterations to the texts (May 2009). His contribution to *Utopia*'s paratexts (including the addition of the epithet 'wittie' to the description of the work on the 1556 title page) suggests that he read More's book as humanist play and satire, rather than a handbook for governance, and that he was signalling his understanding of and participation in the literary game.

Conclusion

The two editions of the English *Utopia* were in some ways shaped by the sharply contrasting religious and political climates of the Edwardian and Marian regimes. These changes affected the way that the book was presented, modified some of the language that was used (or not used), and contributed to changes in the physical publication (most notably the change of printer). But despite these differences, Robinson's translation was published substantially unaltered and managed to remain relevant despite changing and volatile political circumstances. Part of the explanation for this, as David Harris Sacks has observed, is that on matters of high politics and religion, *Utopia* remained 'very much a book of the previous age' (Sacks 1999: 59): that is, concerned with issues that would have had immediate resonance in the early sixteenth century, but that were less relevant in a post-Reformation environment. The parts of *Utopia* that retained their impact, on the other hand, were the descriptions of civic life and governance, which were still directly relevant to the translation's mid-century readers; and, also, the social and economic issues—of poverty, crime, and property—that translated forcefully, and even radically, into the mid-sixteenth-century context.

The middle decades of the sixteenth century were defined by social unrest and economic distress, prompted in large part by enclosure, dearth, inflation, and debasement. In 1549, two years before Robinson's translation first appeared, there had been risings and rebellions that used the language of 'commonwealth' to agitate for widespread and radical change. Read in this context, the English *Utopia* has been placed as part of a wider body of complaint literature addressing topical social ills and suggesting controversial methods of reform. Weil Baker, for instance, has claimed that Robinson's translation is an example of a radical social critique, written in language that would have recalled to its sixteenth-century audience recent threats to the social order—albeit that these references were presented obliquely, 'under the guise of translation rather than originality' (Weil Baker 1999: 226). Other historians have taken a similar approach. Andy Wood has argued that the text appropriated and reflected the rhetoric associated with the 1549 rebellions and claims that Robinson's translation 'echoes popular political speech' (A. Wood 2007: 148); and Joshua Phillips has suggested that the English *Utopia* 'may have been dangerous because it sounded too much like the utterances of rebels and malcontents' (Phillips 2001: 131). These connotations are certainly present in the 1551 and 1556 editions of *Utopia*, and an awareness of the potentially radical meaning of 'commonwealth' would have been clear to Robinson and his circle, especially given that the book touched on politically sensitive themes such as enclosure. The proximity of the publication to the riots and unrest of 1549 may have contributed to Robinson's professed nervousness as he committed his translation to Cecil's 'safe conduct' and protection. But although the word commonwealth was in some ways evocative of rebellion and social disruption, it was at the same time a much broader, more inclusive concept, with a longer tradition of usage. It was not always controversial in its application. There is a strong tradition of civic humanism and reform that *Utopia* taps into that was equally important (Withington 2010b: ch. 5).

This chapter has reconstructed Robinson's position in a milieu of active civic humanists, with *Utopia* his own contribution to the reforming agenda being carried out by his friends in London. In his hands it was a practical text, designed to provide active citizens with inspiration and aspirations for social change. While he did not expect it to be read as a simple blueprint to be followed to the letter, he does seem to have identified it as a useful and profitable text on many levels. By translating *Utopia* into the vernacular and making it available to a broader readership, the project of reforming the commonwealth became a collective effort: something that could be implemented by a diverse body of citizens and the urban middling sort, acting within the law—rescuing the project of 'commonwealth' reform from the dichotomous rhetorical struggle between rebels and statesmen.

Robinson and his friends were certainly not the only ones to be caught up in an inclusive and wide-reaching enthusiasm for enacting models for social change. The mid-sixteenth century saw a proliferation of ideas and plans for commonwealth reform and restructuring across multiple spheres. This was noted by Thomas Smith, who complained to the Duchess of Somerset in 1550 about the great number of men who 'kneel upon your grace's carpets and devise commonwealths as they like, and are angry that other men be not so hasty to run straight as their brains crow' (cited in Brigden 2009: 458). This formulation anticipates Robinson's words to Cecil in his 1551 preface, that he had lately observed 'every sort and kynde of people in theire vocation and degree busilie occupied about the common wealthes affairs: and especially learned men dayly putting forth in writing newe inventions, and devices to the furtherance of the same' (More 1551: +3r). But the production of the first English translation of *Utopia* by these Londoners is significant all the same. As at once officeholders in their own spheres of civic governance, key players in the daily administration of institutions, and participants in national political institutions based in London, Robinson and his milieu operated in a 'little commonwealth' of their own—composed of even smaller commonwealths and corporate groups (the livery companies being a prime example)—that was also the hub of England's urban 'corporate system' (Withington 2005; cf. Hartrich in this volume).

Viewed in these terms, the first English editions of *Utopia* arguably did not speak primarily to national politics events—the struggle of rebels against the Crown in 1549, or the change of monarch and religion in 1553—but rather offered a point of reflection on the structures and role of civic politics: the place of London's citizens in what Patrick Collinson (1994) has labelled England's 'monarchical republic'. As Andrew Gordon has noted, if we look at Londoners writing about London, we can see 'how closely they identified with the city, bearing out the position that early modern citizenship was above all a citizenship of towns and cities, rather than nations' (Gordon and Stack 2007: 118). The first English *Utopias* were books about good government and the best state of a commonwealth, but understood primarily in relation to the structure of cities rather than the nation, and in the way that cities could bring good governance to the nation through parliament and law. The book made sense in 1551 *and* 1556 because the concerns of Londoners were broadly similar across this period: how to retain the independence and autonomy of the City in relation to the Crown; how best to self-govern; how to reform and structure key social and political institutions; and how to understand the importance of citizenship and the meaning of 'commonwealth' in a changing world.

CHAPTER 16

DIALOGUE, DEBATE, AND ORALITY IN RALPH ROBINSON'S *UTOPIAS*

DERMOT CAVANAGH

For more than a century, readers of English encountered More's *Utopia* in Ralph Robinson's translation first published in 1551 and revised and reissued in 1556. This chapter explores its style and mode. Firstly (building on Jennifer Bishop's chapter in this volume), it emphasizes that both author and translator were citizens of London and that Robinson's primary intention is to make *Utopia*'s civic concerns accessible. Second, it argues that the revised edition expands, rather than constrains, its promotion of dialogue and debate. Robinson's translation is both a major contribution to the dissemination of *Utopia* and a forceful articulation of its public concerns.

The title page of the 1551 edition of *Utopia* clearly signals its civic milieu. It declares that the original Latin text composed 'by Syr Thomas More knyght' has been Englished by Ralph Robinson, 'Citizein and Goldsmythe of London', at the request of his friend George Tadlowe, 'Citezein & haberdasshher of the same Citie'. This local act of fellowship will now diffuse its benefits more widely as vernacular readers gain access to *Utopia*'s account of 'the beste state of a publyque weale'. It is this aspect of More's writing that makes it most 'fruteful', the term cited first on the title page and used subsequently throughout the preface to denote the burgeoning, generative force of its ideas: those 'good, and holsome lessons, which be there in great plenty, and aboundaunce' (More 1551: +4r).

This presentation of the text seems fitting given that More was renowned as a citizen of London. He acted as one of the City's two undersheriffs, an office that was proclaimed in handsome capitals on the title page of the 1518 edition of *Utopia* and is emblazoned again at the conclusion of the work. Robinson's 1551 translation also affirms his more modest association with the Goldsmiths' Company, one of the 'Great Twelve' of the City's livery companies. In brief, after graduating from Corpus Christi College, Oxford in 1540, and being elected to a probationary fellowship two years later, Robinson left the university and was apprenticed to Sir Martin Bowes, the master and under-treasurer of the Tower mint in 1544, so beginning his lifelong involvement with the company. He was admitted into the livery in 1557, on being made under-clerk, and subsequently lived rent-free in the clerk's house attached to Goldsmiths' Hall from 1560 until his death in 1576 (Bennell 2004).[1] These were humble achievements in comparison to the author of *Utopia*, but London also provided the foundation for More's career (Ames 1949; C. Barron 2011). More too belonged to one of the 'Great Twelve', having been granted membership of the powerful Mercers' Company in 1509, a sign of his considerable standing within the City (Ramsay 1982). As many commentators recognize, however far More's imagination reaches in *Utopia*, it remains grounded in the corporate life of sixteenth-century London (Manley 1995; Rees Jones 2001).[2]

The traditions and practices associated with civic life, and especially with the livery companies, have been at the forefront of much recent social and cultural history (Withington 2005; T. Hill 2011). Jennifer Bishop has shown how important this context was for Robinson's translation, especially during the Edwardian period (1547–53) when the reform of local and national government was the subject of energetic discussion and action by citizens like George Tadlowe. Bishop demonstrates how *Utopia*'s concern with the 'publyque weale' spoke to Robinson's circle as they debated how 'humanist theory and political practice' might be best integrated (J. Bishop 2011: 938). In the 1551 edition, Robinson acknowledges the inspiration he derived from witnessing 'every sort, and kynde of people in theire vocation, and degree busilie occupied about the common wealthes affaires', including the endeavours of 'learned men dayly putting forth in writing newe inventions, and devises' (More 1551: +3r). The value of his translation too will be judged by the contribution it makes to 'the avauncement and commoditie of the publique wealth of my native countrey'.

A further dimension to these concerns emerges in its dedication to William Cecil, secretary to Edward VI and a member of the Privy Council, whose support is elicited to grant this provocative work 'sauffe conducte' (+5r). Robinson had a personal connection to Cecil deriving from the chantry schooling they shared in Grantham and Stamford—he had previously sought his assistance on at least two occasions—and he reminds his eminent contemporary of all 'that was betwene you and me in the time of our childhoode, being then scolefellowes togethers' (+5v; King 1982: 108–111). In this instance, however, his claim of past friendship involved more than the pursuit of favour. As Neil Rhodes has shown, the aspiration to expand 'the country's resources of knowledge' flourished in the mid-Tudor period and was expressed in a tradition of 'translating for the commonwealth' that was sponsored increasingly by Cecil (Rhodes 2018: 128). Erasmus' 1511 *Moriae Encomium* ('Praise of Folly'), a work closely affiliated to and influential upon *Utopia*, had been translated in 1549 by Sir Thomas Chaloner, an acquaintance of Cecil, who declared his intention to bestow an 'englisshe liverey upon this

---

[1] For further details of Robinson's biography, see Bishop in this volume.
[2] See also Hartrich and Bishop in this volume.

Latine boke' (Erasmus 1549: A2r).[3] Robinson's translation participates in this broader movement and, as we shall see, its vivid, popular style provides further compelling testimony to how deeply it was inspired by the social concerns that dominated Citizen More's great work of fiction.

However, Robinson's *Utopia* is not defined exclusively by a single moment: a substantially revised edition appeared five years later in the radically different context of Marian England (1553–8). During this period, the censorship of material considered to be heretical or seditious was expanding dramatically to include familiar landmarks such as the Edwardian Books of Common Prayer (1549, 1552) and Edward Hall's *Chronicle* (first published in 1542). Action was being taken against the printers of such works as well and Abraham Veale, who printed both editions of Robinson's *Utopia*, had swiftly terminated his production of Protestant moral tracts (Duffy 2009: 29–56; T. Cave 2008b: 94–95). At the same time, More's reputation was being energetically restored, a project that included the publication in 1557 of his *English Workes* in William Rastell's edition (A. Dillon 2002: 36–52).

The moment was timely, therefore, for Robinson to reissue his translation even if this required some effacement of its origins in an Edwardian civic moment. The 1556 text was shorn of its dedication to Cecil, who no longer held office, and the new preface revoked its earlier strictures on More's religious convictions. Admittedly, these had been expressed temperately. The author's ferocious polemical writing and his persecution of heresy had been overlooked, but Robinson noted that More 'could not or rather would not see the shining light' of Reformation and 'did rather cheuse to perseuer, and continue in his wilfull and stubbourne obstinacie even to the very death', even if this judgement was passed quickly and as 'a thing much to be lamented' (More 1551: +3v–4r). In the revised preface to the 1556 edition, such statements were withdrawn. In the most substantial discussion of this edition, Gabriela Schmidt (2018) has shown that it also softens the satirical account of established religion presented in the first version by making strategic amendments both to the translation and to its printed marginalia. On this view, the later version is a largely pragmatic attempt to broaden the work's topical appeal in transformed market conditions.

However, this interpretation misses other emphases of the 1556 *Utopia* and so constrains its larger significance. The second half of this chapter will demonstrate how Robinson not only preserved but also expanded the civic ethos of his work, notably its commitment to dialogue and debate. He achieves this by including more of the paratext that had accompanied More's original version of the work, most notably by freely translating, amending, and adding to *Utopia*'s copious marginal glosses (see Fig. 16.1). This material possesses multivalent implications that extend beyond its being read as an expression of largely pragmatic or acquiescent attitudes: I will return to this issue. However, I will begin by considering the broader rhetorical mode of his translation as it is presented in both versions. Robinson's *Utopia* is an undervalued work

---

[3] For the connections between *Praise of Folly* and *Utopia*, see Taylor in this volume.

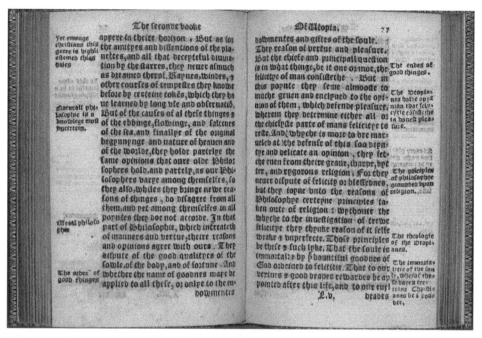

FIG. 16.1. Thomas More, *A frutefull pleasaunt, and wittie worke, of the beste state of a publique weale, and of the new yle, called Utopia*, trans. Ralph Robinson (London: [Richard Tottel] for Abraham Veale, 1556), The Huntington Library, San Marino, California, call number 12572, sigs L4v-L5r.

whose resourceful, creative dialogue with its precursor—More's *Utopia*—merits further investigation. It uses the vernacular to dramatize *Utopia*'s radical reappraisal of the world, and of our responsibilities towards it, but finds an equally eloquent voice with which to acknowledge the questions, predicaments, and challenges this produces. This commitment remains as forceful in the 1556 text as in its first iteration: Robinson's work continues to draw imaginatively on the rhetorical resources afforded by *Utopia* to express, as well as to explore, its urgent concern with the ills that afflict the commonwealth and the most effective means to remedy them.

English *Utopia*

In the letter to Peter Giles that prefaces *Utopia*, More apologizes for the delay in sending him the manuscript. After all, his task was simply to transcribe Raphael Hythloday's testimony, along with the discussion it provoked, without intervention because 'the nigher it shold approche to his [i.e. Hythloday's] homely playne, and simple speche, somuch the nigher shold it go to the trueth' (More 1551: +7r). This seemingly casual statement indicates that the reader should be wary. In such a subtly meditated composition as

Utopia, whose primary speaker is imaginary, the correspondence between plain truth and plain words is unlikely to be direct: so it proves. The speech and writing presented in this intricately designed and self-qualifying text require continuous evaluation and the author's discourse is no exception.

Robinson both admired and reflected on the 'eloquent latine stiele' of *Utopia* as much as its 'fruteful and profitable' content (+4r); or, rather, he understood that these were inseparable. In the 1551 preface, the translator doubts his ability to convey 'all the grace and pleasure of the eloquence, wherwith the matter in latine is finely set forth' and the result will be that 'the frutefulnes of the matter itselfe' will be much 'diminished, and appayred [impaired]'. It was equally important to preserve *Utopia*'s intriguing staging of the argument: 'the wittie invencion, and fine conveiaunce, or disposition of the matter'. Yet Robinson ensured his version of *Utopia* met these challenges by honouring More's commitment to the spoken word as the guiding principle of his style: his free translation draws energy throughout from a vigorous, colloquial use of the vernacular. This intention is signalled from the outset by adding the adjectives 'homely, playne, and simple' to More's terse observation of Hythloday's 'casual simplicity' of style (*neglectam simplicitatem*) and by the subsequent addition of a marginal gloss, in the 1556 text, to mark the significance of this passage 'Trueth loveth simplicitie and playnes' (More 1556: A4v; 1995: 31).[4] In this respect, Robinson releases More's text from the scholarly edifice of Latin to make it speak in a popular and contemporary voice.

To achieve this, the translator permeates the register of his *Utopia* with familiar usage. In Book One, for example, where there is more immediate dialogue and multivocality, there are continuous reminders of the work's orality, with frequent markers of on-going discussion. 'Naye god forbedde (quod peter) [...] Well I perceyve plainlye friend Raphaell (quod I)' are Robinson's renderings of 'Bona verba, inquit Petrus' (' "Well said", Peter replied'); 'Tum ego, Perspicuum est, inquam, [...] mi Raphael' ('Then I said, "It is clear, my dear Raphael" '), so adding idiomatic flexibility to the stiffer formality of More's Latin (More 1551: B7v–8r; 1995: 51, 53). Slang is used as well. For example, Hythloday mocks the practice of counsel at European courts because in such environments maintaining place matters more than practical wisdom and speakers fear 'that ever after they should be counted for very diserdes [dizzards/fools]' if some well-founded proposal is countenanced without or against their approval (More 1551: C1v).[5] In making such forceful statements Robinson creates a memorably irreverent voice for Hythloday. He imbricates his speech with a stinging use of insult, 'prowde lewde overthwarte and waywarde judgementes'; 'archedoltes'; 'nigeshe penny fethers' (C2r, C5v, L2v);[6] adjectival energy, 'chiding skolding, railing and reviling'; 'wrangling,

---

[4] All citations of More's Latin, along with its literal English translation by Robert Adams, are to More 1995.

[5] Robinson here translates 'post illa pro stultis plane sint habendi' ('henceforth they would look like simpletons') (More 1995: 53).

[6] Robinson's renderings of 'superba, absurda ac morosa' ('proud, obstinate, ridiculous'); 'sordidos atque avaros' ('mean and grasping') (More 1995: 55, 155). 'Archedoltes' is an addition to the Latin.

quarelling brawling and chiding' (E3r, F3r);[7] proverbial phrasing, 'by howke or crooke'; 'towchyd on the quicke, and hit on the gawl'; 'An other cummeth in wyth his v [five] egges'; 'For where money beareth all the swing' (C7v, E3r, E6r, I1v),[8] and a vibrant use of idioms, including additions such as 'pestiferous morreyn [murrain]'; 'dayly occupieng and chaffayre [trading]' (C8r, F4v).

This adoption of colloquial speech is not merely a local, demotic colouring applied to Hythloday's words. His language is also popular in a deeper sense because it is infused by his commitment to the 'weal public' or 'commonwealth', Robinson's renderings of More's 'republica'. Much of the translation's energy derives from Hythloday's levelling vivacity of tone: this expresses his stance towards the world as clearly as his observations. For example, Hythloday denounces how 'a great numbre of gentilmen, which can not be content to lyve ydle them selves like dorres [drones]' shamelessly exploit their tenants, 'whom they polle and shave to the quycke by reysyng their rentes', whilst these same 'gentilmen (I say) [...] only live in ydilnes'; as well as intensifying the orality of Hythloday's expression, the final clause is Robinson's scathing reiteration (C4r).[9] Hythloday excoriates the profligate employment of useless servants by the indolent rich purely to enhance their status: they 'carry about with them at their tayles a great flocke or trayne of ydell and loytrynge servynge men' (C4r).[10] The fate of these superfluous retinues is characterized vividly. Once they have lost favour, become ill, or their master has died, they 'starve for hunger, or manfully playe the theaves [...] untyll they have worne threde bare their apparell and also appayred their health', rendering them unsuitable for further service 'because of their pale and sicke faces and patched cotes' (C4v).[11] Robinson dramatizes the fate of these unfortunates with a characteristic use of doublets, the emphatic repetition of linked or related words, to add expressive force to More's Latin. In this passage, the lot of these superfluous men is captured vividly as a chain of doublets expands in a rhythmical indulgence of verbal ornament whose excesses are curtailed by the ominous concluding monosyllables:

---

[7] Robinson's expansions of 'conviciis' ('abusing'; literally 'loud noises') and 'rixarum' ('squabbling') (More 1995: 79, 93).

[8] 'by howke or crooke' and 'An [...] egges' are Robinson's additions; 'towchyd [...] gawl' is an expansion of 'perfusus aceto' ('stung by the vinegar') (More 1995: 79), an allusion to Horace, *Satire* 1.7.32; 'where [...] swing' is an idiomatic rendering of 'ubi omnia pecuniis metimur' ('where money is the measure of everything') (More 1995: 129).

[9] 'augendis reditibus ad vivum usque radunt' ('by increasing their rents they shave them to the quick'); Adams's translation adopts the less literal 'bleed white' (More 1995: 59).

[10] 'immensam quoque otiosorum stipatorum turbam circumferunt' (they 'drag around with them a great train of idle servants') (More 1995: 59).

[11] 'illi esuriunt strenue nisi strenue latrocinentur [...] Siquidem ubi errando paululum vestes ac valetudinem attrivere, morbo iam squalidos atque obsitos pannis, neque generosi dignantur accipere' (they 'set about starving, unless they set about stealing [...] Then when a wandering life has taken the edge off their health and the gloss off their clothes, when their faces look worn and their garments are tattered, men of rank will not care to engage them') (More 1995: 59).

And husbandmen dare not sett them a worke; knowyng well ynough that he is nothynge mete to doo trewe and faythfull service to a poore man wyth a spade and a mattocke for small wages and harde fare, whyche beynge deynteley and tenderly pampered up in ydilenes and pleasure, was wont with a sworde and a buckeler by hys syde to jette through the strete with a bragging loke and to thynke hym selfe to good to be any mans mate. (C4v–5r)[12]

Unlike More's text, the translation concludes with the emphasis firmly on the abject condition of the discarded retainer, rather than the man who will not hire him.

This instance exemplifies Robinson's ability to ensure that More's Latin retains immediacy and force in the vernacular and also how versatile he can be in adding implication. His version ensures that Hythloday's most acerbic insights into corruption, waste, and inequality are endowed with an uninhibitedly pugnacious tone that exposes the illusions that sustain privilege. In Book Two, Hythloday tells the famously droll story of the foreign ambassadors whose arrival in Utopia, swathed in gold and finery, creates a disconcerting impression when their hosts assume they are bondmen or fools whose servile station is signalled by their worthless insignia. '[H]ow great a lubber doth yet were peerles and pretious stoones,' a Utopian child exclaims on seeing these exalted emissaries, 'as though he were a litel child still' (L1r).[13] The conclusion that Hythloday draws about European values is expressed caustically and with added orality: 'In so muche that a lumpyshe blockeheded churle, and whyche hath no more wytte then an asse, yea, and as full of noughteynes and folyshenes, shall have nevertheles many wyse and good men in subjectyon, and bondage, onlye for thys, bycause he hathe a greate heape of golde' (L2r).[14] Even more absurd is the pride taken in nobility given that the status it bestows is acquired regardless of merit. Indeed, it may be devoid of any material basis, a point given far more graphic expression than in the original: 'And though their auncetours left them not one fote of lande, or els they themselves have pyssed it agaynste the walles, yet they thynke themselves not the lesse noble therefore of one heare [hair]'

---

[12] 'neque audent rustici: non ignari eum qui, molliter educates in otio ac deliciis, solitus sit accinctus acinace ac caetra totam viciniam vultu nebulonico despicere et contemnere omnes prae se, haudquaquam idoneum fore qui cum ligone ac marra maligna mercede ac victu parco, fideliter inserviat pauperi' ('country folk dare not [engage them] [...] for they don't have to be told that one who has been raised softly to idle pleasures, who has been used to swaggering about like a bully with sword and buckler, is likely to look down on the whole neighbourhood and despise everybody else as beneath him. Such a man can't be put to work with spade and mattock; he will not serve a poor man faithfully for scant wages and sparse diet') (More 1995: 59).

[13] 'quam magnus nebulo margaritis adhuc et gemmulis utitur, ac si esset puerulus' ('that big lout [...], who's still wearing pearls and jewels as if he were a little boy') (More 1995: 153).

[14] 'usqueadeo ut plumbeus quispiam et cui non plus ingenii sit quam stipiti nec minus etiam improbus quam stultus, multos tamen et sapientes et bonos viros in servitute habeat, ob id dumtaxat quod ei magnus contigit aureorum numismatum cumulus' (They are surprised 'that a dunderhead who has no more brains than a post, and who is as vicious as he is foolish, should command a great many wise and good men, simply because he happens to have a big pile of gold coins') (More 1995: 155).

(M1r).¹⁵ This indifference to rank and to the constraints imposed by artificial decorum, in language and in life, distinguishes Hythloday's discourse. Everyone he encounters or observes is addressed and appraised as a fellow citizen whose virtues or failings are assessed in terms of their contribution to the public welfare.

Much of the force and imagination of Robinson's translation derives, therefore, from Hythloday's portrayal as an impassioned English-speaking citizen who is unconstrained by deference. However, the translator also needs to show Hythloday's ability to command a variety of registers, including his ability to ventriloquize the verbal characteristics of other speakers, especially so in the dialogues that occur or that are recollected or imagined in Book One. Robinson meets this demand. For instance, Hythloday's outrage at an economy dedicated to private profit is expressed through a fervent use of *copia* to enumerate the degrading forms of consumption that exploit and debase popular appetites (cf. T. Cave 2008b: 102–103). This monstrous litany expands notably upon More's text and concludes with a prophetic outcry against injustice and an appeal for reform:

> almoste the ploughemen of the countrye, with all other sortes of people, use muche straunge and prowde newe fanglenes in their apparell, and to muche prodigal riotte and sumptuous fare at their table. Nowe bawdes, qweynes, hoores, harlottes, strumpettes, brothelhouses, stewes, and yet an other stewes, wine-tavernes, ale houses, and tipling houses, with so many noughty, lewde, and unlawfull games, as dice, cardes, tables, tennyes, bolles, coytes [quoits] [...] Caste out thies pernycious abomynacyons [...] Suffer not thies ryche men to bye up all, to ingrosse and forestalle, and with theyr monopolye to kepe the market alone as please them. (More 1551: D1r–v)¹⁶

The debate that Hythloday provokes offers Robinson further opportunities to dramatize conflicting viewpoints on the commonwealth through vernacular usage. Hythloday's open and familiar speech is juxtaposed with other modes of discourse that possess telling degrees of contrast or commonalty with it. In Book One, the lawyer in Cardinal Morton's household, who contests Hythloday's fervent denunciation of the social injustice he has observed during his sojourn in England, finds his usually

---

¹⁵ 'nec pilo quidem minus sibi nobiles videntur etiamsi maiores nihil inde reliquerint aut relictum ipsi obligurierint' ('Even if these ancestors have left them no estates to inherit, or if they've squandered all of their inheritance, they don't consider themselves a bit less noble'), (More 1995: 169).

¹⁶ 'et ipsis propemodum rusticis et omnibus denique ordinibus, multum est insolentis apparatus in vestibus, nimius in victu luxus. Iam ganea, lustra, lupanar et aliud lupanar tabernae vinariae, cervisiariae, postremo tot improbi ludi, alea, charta, fritillus, pila, sphaera, discus [...]. Has perniciosas pestes eicite [...] Refrenate coemptiones istas divitum ac velut monopolii exercendi licentiam' ('even some farmers—people of every social rank—are given to ostentatious dress and gourmandising. Look at the cook-shops, the brothels, the bawdy houses and those other places just as bad, the wine-bars and ale-houses. Look at all the crooked games of chance like dice, cards, backgammon, tennis, bowling and quoits. [...] Banish these blights. [...] Restrict the right of the rich to buy up anything and everything, and then to exercise a kind of monopoly') (More 1995: 65–67).

imposing discourse checked. This is a speaker who is 'more dylygent in rehersynge, then aunswerynge' and more intent on advancing his reputation than pursuing truth (D2r). Hythloday recollects being disparaged as a foreigner: 'In dede syr (quod he) yow have sayd well beinge but a straunger, and one that myght rather here somme thynge of thyes matters, then have anye exacte or perfecte knowledge of the same, as I will incontinent by open proffe make manifest and playn.' The pompous use of 'incontinent'—Robinson's substitution for 'paucis verbis' ('in a few words')—makes evident that the lawyer's discourse is signally devoid of plainness with its windy repetitions ('I wyll reherse', 'I wyll declare', 'I wyll aunswere', 'I wyll begynne'), ostentatious use of legalese, formal organization, and studied condescension: 'in what thynge yowe be deceaved, through lacke of knowledge, in all our fassions, maners and customes' (D2r–v).[17] The alarming long-windedness of his preamble is mercifully cut short by Cardinal Morton who speaks with admirable succinctness and candour whilst parodying the lawyer's vocabulary: 'hold your peace (quod the Cardynall) for by lyke *yowe wyll* make no shorte aunswere, whiche make such a begynnyng' (D2v; emphasis added). To witness this overbearing speaker being silenced is a comic pleasure, but if prolixity is a form of discourtesy, does this also sound a cautionary note for the loquacious Hythloday? If care for the listener is one way of expressing care for the common good, the Cardinal's intervention warns against indulging in unreciprocated monologue at the expense of dialogue.

This implication is drawn out more fully by the interlocutor Morus' speech in *Utopia* which is also compared subtly with Hythloday's. Robinson creates a dry and mordant register for the author's persona, as in his laconic concession of how Hythloday's painstaking and humane counsel would be received at court: 'So God helpe me not very thankefully (quod I)' (E8v), adding a more conversational pitch to More's Latin ('Profecto non valde pronis, inquam': ' "Not very enthusiastically, I'm sure," said I' (More 1995: 87). Morus confesses readily his admiration for Hythloday: 'I have in no lesse reverence and estimatyon a man that is of your mind, then anny of them al that be so high in power and aucthoritie' (More 1551: B8r). However, he opposes Hythloday, in a controversy with far-reaching repercussions, to uphold the view that 'good cownselles greatly healpe and further the common wealthe' with an impressive display of eloquence that is well served by Robinson (E4v). Hythloday's refusal to tailor his advice to the context in which it is delivered, or to accept compromise, means that it elicits the response it anticipates, producing only 'deaffe hearers' (F5r). This is to give up on both counsel and dialogue as lost causes. Morus' discourse is also given impressive colloquial force to question Hythloday's impatience that the frank communication between friends, that is being enjoyed in this exchange, should also hold within counsels of state. Equally, it is futile to advance challenging ideas or examples when the speaker is already assured that his effort will be wasted: 'nor yow muste not laboure to dryve into their heades newe and straunge informatyons, whyche yow knowe well shalbe nothynge regarded wyth them

---

[17] Robinson expands on More's Latin to draw out the lawyer's disdain; the Latin merely reads: 'in rebus imposuit tibi nostrarum rerum ignoratio' ('how you have been misled by ignorance of our ways') (More 1995: 67).

that be of cleane contrary mindes' (F6r).[18] For Morus, differences in rhetorical contexts need to be addressed if one wishes to advance the common benefit. Robinson adds an idiomatic touch to Morus' famous analogy between misguided counsel and an actor appearing in the wrong play. Surely such a maladroit speaker would do better to remain silent 'then by rehersynge that, which served nother for the tyme nor place to have made suche a tragycall comedye or gallymalfreye [hodgepodge]?' (F5v).[19] To encounter insincerity and the cynical pursuit of advantage is inevitable in public life, but this should not be used as an occasion for retreat and Morus' eloquence on this point is intensified by Robinson's familiar use of doublets:

> Yf evell opynyons and noughty persuasions can not be utterly and quyte pluckede owte of their hartes, if you can not [...] remedye vyces, whiche use and custome hath confirmed: yet for this cause yow must not leave and forsake the common wealth: yow must not forsake the shippe in a tempeste, bycause yowe can not rule and kepe downe the wyndes. (F6r)[20]

Plainness can be used well or badly along with other modes of speech. There are a range of rhetorical means that should be called upon to meet the world in its own terms and to negotiate flexibly with disagreement, indifference, and opposition. This requires the determination to seek as much commonalty of purpose as is possible in any given circumstance.

More's rehearsal of these arguments in *Utopia* was profoundly influential: it identified a tension that would endure between humanists who, on the one hand, envisaged counsel and dialogue as irreplaceable resources for advancing the common good and those, on the other, who saw them as either futile or useful only insofar as they equipped individuals with the skills to pursue advancement (Withington 2009a; Lupić 2019). In *Utopia*, Morus defends movingly the potential of humanist counsel and one wonders at the continuing, if changing, significance of this argument for Robinson, his circle, and his readers. The commendation of public obligations was doubtless of immediate and urgent interest to the translator and his associates in the highly charged Edwardian civic moment of 1551. To find the author's persona speaking equally forcefully that perseverance is needed in unpropitious times may have had a different, if equally compelling,

---

[18] 'Quid enim prodesse possit aut quomodo in illorum pectus influere sermo tam insolens, quorum praeoccupavit animos atque insedit penitus diversa persuasio?' ('What good can it do? When your listeners are already prepossessed against you and firmly convinced of opposite opinions, how can you win over their minds with such out-of-the-way speeches?'), (More 1995: 95).

[19] 'nonne praestiterit egisse mutam personam quam aliena recitando talem fecisse tragicomoediam?' ('Wouldn't it be better to take a silent role than to say something inappropriate and thus turn the play into a tragicomedy') (More 1995: 97).

[20] 'Si radicitus evelli non possint opiniones pravae nec receptis usu vitiis mederi queas ex animi tui sententia, non ideo tamen deserenda respubica est, et in tempestate navis destituenda est, quoniam ventos inhibere non possis' ('If you cannot pluck bad ideas up by the root, or cure long-standing evils to your heart's content, you must not therefore abandon the commonwealth. Don't give up the ship in a storm because you cannot hold back the winds') (More 1995: 97).

resonance in 1556. It is intriguing to find Morus insisting that even the most intransigent circumstances will pass and new occasions for intervention will arise. The citizen and counsellor should remain ready for service and, in the meantime, there remains the possibility for small gains, 'and that whyche yowe can not turne to good' may still be ameliorated, 'so to ordre it that it be not very badde. For it is not possible for all thynges to be well, onles all men were good. Which I thynke wil not be yet thys good many yeares' (More 1551: F6v).

Glossing Utopia

Morus' affirmation of resilience at the end of Book One may have held new implications for Robinson, therefore, as he revised his work on *Utopia* for publication in 1556. As was noted earlier, this edition modified his earlier text to help ensure a favourable reception in Marian England. The title page passes over Robinson's status as a citizen in favour of his good standing as a 'sometime fellowe of Corpus Christi College in Oxford'; More is also awarded more honorific tribute as a 'right worthie and famous' knight. *Utopia* is described as 'pleasaunt, and wittie' as well as 'frutefull'; the latter term no longer appears in the preface, and a more discerning 'gentle reader' is addressed in a worldly, knowing manner rather than as a fellow citizen (More 1556: A2r). The origins of the work are also described differently. The London citizen George Tadlowe is no longer mentioned; instead, an anonymous friend is recollected as requesting the translation strictly for 'his owne private use' (A2r). If the earlier version contained simplification and errors, these are attributed, rather condescendingly, to the translator's struggle to 'attemper [his] stile' to 'the meanesse' of his friend's learning. Robinson also disavows any ambition for the public circulation of his work. His hope was that his friend 'wolde have kepte it secrete to hym self alone'; how this 'rude and base' version ever appeared is explained awkwardly: 'yet fortune so ruled the matter that to Imprintinge it came, and that partly against my wyll' (A2r–v).

However, the signals contained in the new paratextual materials are not unmixed. If the revised preface dispenses with any criticism of More's religious beliefs (such as were contained in the 1551 edition), it has nothing to say in their favour or of his martyrdom. There are also additional reminders of the author's civic stature in the new materials added to the text. Versions of the poems by More's friends, Cornelius Grapheus and 'Noviomagus' (Gerhard Geldenhauer), are newly translated, with their fulsome tributes to 'the worthie clerke Sir Thomas More […] In whom London well glory maye' ('Morus, Londini gloria prima sui') and whose reputation ensures 'Londons immortal glorye,' a stronger version than the Latin ('Morus Londinae nobilitatis honos') (More 1556: S7r–v; 1995: 256). Giles's letter to Jerome Busleyden is also added with its affirmation of the work's 'singular prudence' in revealing 'all the originall causes and fountaynes […] whereof both issueth and springeth the mortall confusion and utter decaye of a common wealth', along with its equally insightful disclosure of how 'the avauncement and wealthy state of the same may rise and growe' (More 1556: S4v–5r). Terence Cave (2008b: 96) speculates that Robinson's translation of this spirited tribute may pay oblique homage to William Cecil (the dedicatee of the 1551 edition) who had also been, like the addressee Busleyden, a counsellor to a monarch during the brief reign of Edward VI. Giles's letter certainly appeals to all those who dedicate themselves to the common good: 'no man is more fitte and meete, then you with good counselles to further and avaunce the commen wealth' (More 1556: S6r).

The language of public benefit remains in the revised paratextual materials, therefore, and it continues to be expressed fulsomely in the translation. Indeed, the work's affirmation of dialogue is more expansive in one crucial respect. Robinson's most prominent addition to his revised version of *Utopia* was the inclusion of the extensive marginal commentary presented in More's text (McKinnon 1970; McCutcheon 2015b). These glosses were probably prepared by Erasmus and/or Giles and their effect is intriguing; they add a further, if less-noted, dimension to this already multilayered work.[21] By responding seriously, if often wittily, throughout, these comments add to the 'reality effect' created both by Hythloday's presence and by his detailed description of Utopia. Robinson demonstrates a striking degree of inventiveness in finding vernacular equivalents for the original marginalia. However, in exploring this new space for composition and commentary, the translator also embraces the opportunity it offers for broaching further independent dialogue and thought. This occurs to different degrees of intensity, sometimes by amending the original commentary to inflect its tone and perspective, but also by composing glosses of his own invention, an intention declared on the title page, 'divers notes in the margent augmented', showing that 'he must have reflected on the meaning and function of the glosses' (T. Cave 2008b: 96). This creative supplement to the text and paratext is especially substantial in Book One, where the text's emphasis on familiar discussion between new and old friends, along with the recollection (or postulation) of more combustible verbal exchanges, seem to have inspired the translator: the proliferation of marginalia in Robinson's Book One is particularly striking because marginalia is used more sparingly in the Latin text at that point. In short, in the 1556 version immediacy and orality returned as pervasive and continuous features of the entire work.

This potentiality is abundantly present in the original glosses. In these instances, the commentator who provides them is not responding to the text after the event, so to speak, but is present within it: speaking out to share companionably with the reader the immediacy of their reactions. Consequently, the voice in the margins is part of the circle of amity portrayed in the text, yet reaches beyond it, acting as a friend to the work by responding to it so receptively and also to the reader by sharing these perceptions and by acting as a guide. The glosses explain references, underline important points or turns in the argument ('Marke this well', More 1556: M7v), identify helpful parallels, and elucidate or distil key observations: 'This geere smelleth of Plato his communitie'; 'Shippes

---

[21] For further information on the authorship of the marginalia, see Suthren and Taylor in this volume.

of straunge fassions' (H4r, B6v). In so doing, these comments convey a quick and observant attention to the flow of argument. They model the active engagement needed to glean the most from the work and, crucially, encourage the reader to become a participant as well.

These aspects of the glosses provide the translator with a pattern to follow, of course, but also with a set of possibilities to be developed. When Hythloday comments disdainfully on European economies 'where money beareth all the swinge', Robinson responds forcefully to the energy of the original Latin—'Prudentissime dictum' ('A very shrewd observation') (More 1995: 129)—by adding that this is 'Wonderfull wittely spoken,' stressing the orality of Hythloday's words (More 1556: I2r). Similarly, the story of how the impressive effect sought by the foreign ambassadors to Utopia unravels is applauded: 'O wittie head' (L1v), although we can note a modulation of perspective in this comment which the original text provides in Greek ('O techniten' ('O what a craftsman!') (More 1995: 153)) in order to applaud the author's skill, but in Robinson's version might equally apply to the boy who makes the observation.[22] When Hythloday discusses the Utopians contempt for 'precious' stones, the marginal comment expresses the significance of this attitude by again using doublets to accentuate the implications of the Latin: 'The opinion and fansie of people doth augment and diminishe the price and estimacion of precious stones' (More 1556: M1v) ('Opinio hominum pretium addit aut adimit gemmis' ('Popular opinion gives gems their value or takes it away') (More 1995: 169)). 'The mutual recourse of kindness' is Robinson's comment on how the continual exchange of benefits underlies the cohesiveness and generosity of Utopian life (More 1556: L7v), making more explicit the affective element of the relationship.[23] The principle that underpins this mutuality is recognized boldly in the English as well as the Latin gloss: 'Equalitie is the cause that every man hath enoughe' (K4v).[24]

In expressing their moment-by-moment reactions, the glosses often convey the emotional force of the speech and dialogue that is being encountered in *Utopia*. As well as being explanatory, therefore, these comments express how the pleasures and challenges of the text are being experienced. Robinson augments or adds to these expressions of excitement at hearing the 'marvellous' (a much-repeated term) narrative being recounted by Hythloday in Book Two and of delight being taken in the startling insights that emerge. 'A marvelous straunge opinion touching the soules of brute beastes' is the reaction recorded to the Utopian belief that animals possess souls, even if of a lower kind (Q5r).[25] Similarly, the gloss notes animatedly, 'A marvelous straunge fashion in chusinge magistrates', amplifying the Latin, as Utopian constitutional arrangements are

---

[22] I owe this observation to Cathy Shrank.

[23] 'Officia vitae mutua' ('Mutual assistance') (More 1995: 165).

[24] 'Aequabilitas facit ut omnibus sufficiat' ('Equality for all results in enough for each') (More 1995: 145).

[25] Expanding on the Latin: 'Mira opinio de animabus brutorum' ('A strange opinion about the souls of animals') (More 1995: 225).

elucidated, before emphasizing further the conclusion that 'Tyranny in a well-ordered weale publique utterlie to be abhorred' (H5v).[26]

In Book One, especially, Robinson displays a marked degree of initiative and imagination in his response to the glosses. He expands, deletes, adapts, and revises the existing comments and adds significantly to them as well, more than doubling the amount (from twenty-seven to sixty-five). This transforms the role of the commentator in this phase of the work. In the original text, the annotations in Latin (and sometimes Greek) are economical: figures of speech are noted, some key points are underlined, proper names and places are added, allusions are glossed, and the irascible Friar's blundering misuse of Latin is mocked (More 1995: 79). In Robinson's version, this scholarly, if admiring, presence becomes a strident vernacular speaker who intervenes candidly throughout: observing and commenting freely on matters that concern the commonwealth. This confident tone is established at the outset when a set of additional comments are added to More's prefatory letter to Giles as if striking up a conversation. These include sympathetic recognition of 'The authours busines and lettes' and of inexorable temporal pressures: 'Meate and slepe: great wasters of time' (More 1556: A5r–v). When More's letter alludes to the ludicrous Rowland Phillips, the Latin marginal comment notes tersely, 'Sanctus ambitus' ('A holy suit') (More 1995: 35); Robinson chooses to expand on this in an informal tone: 'It is thoughte of some that here is unfainedly ment the late famous vicare of Croydon in Surrey' (More 1556: A7r). The fussy, and perhaps parodic, original gloss on the theological distinction More makes between inadvertent and deliberate lying becomes the blunt 'A diversitie betwene making a lye, and telling a lie' (A6v).[27]

Inaugurating his practice as a commentator in this way is a bold gesture on Robinson's part that changes the reading experience of Book One as a stream of comments imitate, modulate, and expand the tones and emphases found in the original glosses. Robinson also takes pains to make the marginalia more accessible. He dispenses with or amends the identification of classical allusions in the original text. For example, the reference to Horace is dropped (More 1995: 79) and the erudite identification of Livy as a source during the discussion of capital punishment (69) becomes simply 'Straite lawes not allowable' (More 1556: D4r). Hythloday's colloquial voice is much more readily reciprocated in the margins as well. His denunciation of how debased forms of popular consumption are promoted and indulged, noted earlier, is echoed in the gloss (for which there is no equivalent in the Latin): 'Baudes, whores, wine taverns, alehouses, and unlawful games be very mothers of theves' (D2r). Familiarity of tone is frequent too, such as 'A privie nippe for them that do otherwise' (D5v), for which there is no counterpart in the original, or the terse 'Triptakers' ('faultfinders') added to Hythloday's account of

---

[26] 'Mira ratio creandi magistratus' ('A notable way of electing officials'); 'Tyrannis invisa bene institutae reipublicae' ('Tyranny hateful to the well-ordered commonwealth') (More 1995: 123).

[27] 'Nota theologicam differentiam inter mentiri et mendacium dicere' ('Note the theological distinction between a deliberate lie and an untruth') (More 1995: 35).

how court counsellors routinely disdain advice proffered by rivals by appealing to tradition or custom (C2v).

The attention paid by the commentary also intensifies at significant junctures. For example, the glosses begin to multiply during Hythloday's denunciations of enclosure and 'dearth' in Book One as it becomes evident that laws are 'not made according to equitie' (C4r), and marginal notes are added for which there is no equivalent in the Latin (e.g. 'Idlenesse the mother of theves'; 'Landlordes by the way checked for Rent-raisyng'; 'Of Idle serving men come theves'; C5r). This enacts how thought is being stimulated by Hythloday's discourse on the injustices endured by the commonwealth and also being taken in radical directions; these are emphasized in the English version. Seemingly incurable social ills are gradually revealed to have causes and this process is tracked in Robinson's marginalia as Hythloday leads the auditor and reader back to the roots of the problem: 'The decaye of husbandry causeth beggery, which is the mother of vagaboundes and theves'; 'Rich men ingrossers and forestallers'; 'Povertye the mother of debate and decay of realmes' (C8v, D2v, F3v). This initiates the drawing of further parallels and the making of independent conclusions, connections, and associations— for instance 'That thefte ought not to be punished by death' (D4r)—and modulations of tone when, for example, the plainly descriptive 'Utopiensium instituta' (More 1995: 98) becomes the ringing 'The Utopian weal publique' (More 1556: F7r). These reactions often testify to the force of Hythloday's rhetoric and to fascination with the way his arguments develop and accumulate evidence. 'A worthy and commendable punishment of theves in the weale publique of Polylerites in Persia,' the gloss notes glowingly (D5r), expanding considerably on the neutrally informative Latin.[28] 'A notable example, and worthy to be folowed', advises another on the Achorians (E7v), accentuating the original.[29]

This process also illuminates another important quality of the original glosses throughout both books: if they convey how the work is being read in the moment, this also means that it is being interpreted as a contemporary text. The commentator makes frequent allusions and comparisons to present conditions and practices, especially so in Book Two, as if Hythloday's recollection of Utopia describes a civilization from the past, like classical antiquity (More 1995: 113 n.). Robinson follows this set of temporal implications carefully. 'But this nowadaies is the grounde of all mischiefe' (a fairly literal translation of 'At hinc hodie pestis rerumpbulicarum omnium') is the comment on how urban space is regulated in Utopia to ensure that cities are evenly spaced out and that the inhabitants see themselves as stewards ('good husbandes' ('agricolas')) rather than 'owners' ('dominos') of the land around them without any appetite for expansion (More 1556: G7v; 1995: 112). The satirical comment on astrology is made in a more intemperate tone than the Latin: 'Yet amonge Christians this geere [rubbish] is highly esteemed thies daies' (More 1556: L4v).[30] A more rueful comment is made on the Utopian contempt

---

[28] 'Respublica Polyleritarum apud Persas' ('The Polylerite society near the Persians') (More 1995: 71).
[29] 'Exemplum adnotandum' ('A notable example') (More 1995: 87).
[30] At hi regnant inter Christianos hodie' ('Yet these astrologers are revered by Christians to this day') (More 1995: 157).

for gambling, 'But nowadaies diceplay is the pastime of princes' (I1r), along with an equally sorrowful or perhaps exasperated reflection on their exemplary disdain for hunting as well in contrast to Robinson's contemporaries: 'Hunting the basest parte of boucheri among the Utopians, and yet this is nowe the exercise of most noble men' (M2v).[31] The Utopians' organization of the household is also preferred: 'So might we well be discharged and eased of the ydle company of servyngmen', the gloss notes (I6v), transforming into an aspiration what is a simple observation in the Latin ('Sic excludi potest otiosa turba ministrorum' ('Thus they eliminate crowds of idle servants') (More 1995: 137)).

Yet the glosses are not an echo chamber: they are also a space for independent reflection on the actions that will most benefit the commonwealth; persuasive argument is acknowledged wherever it may be found. The gloss affirms the objections made by Morus to Hythloday's approach to counsel by expanding the original reference to 'Philosophia scholastica' (More 1995: 94) into the declarative 'Schole philosophye in the consultations of princes hath no place' (More 1556: F5v). Similarly, unease is registered with the Utopian disavowal of private property which dispenses with any notion of personal ownership or private space.[32] Robinson adds a perhaps equivocal gloss when Hythloday is describing variants of Utopian religious sects who choose, on the one hand, a life of celibacy, work, vegetarianism, and contemplation and, on the other, a less strict, and more admired, order who tolerate marriage and worldly pleasures: 'It is not all one to be wise and good' (Q7v). When the Utopian toleration of atheism is described 'because they be persuaded, that it is in no mans power to beleve what he list', the commentator seems flummoxed and adds a further gloss to the Latin: 'A very strange sayinge' (Q4v).

Robinson's translation was born out of a moment of heightened civic awareness. It contributed to, and was inspired by, the argumentative resources that early modern citizens needed to guide their actions and attending to its expression brings us closer to their ideals and idioms. The continuities between the two versions, in this respect, are important to observe and the differences between them have been overstated (Weil Baker 1999). Robinson can be seen to share the spirit of other contemporary commonwealth-minded authors like William Baldwin and William Bullein (see Gresham 1986; Withington 2009a). Indeed, in his receptivity to the playful paratext of *Utopia*, Robinson is also in accord with these writers' explorations of different formal means to multiply responses and to facilitate debate, including glossing. In so doing, they espoused literature's role in 'shaping a commonwealth of active, morally engaged

---

[31] 'At nunc alea principum lusus est' ('But now dicing is the sport of princes') (More 1995: 129); and, expanding considerably on the Latin, 'At haec hodie ars est deorum aulicorum' ('Yet today this is the chosen art of our court-divinities') (171).

[32] Both the Latin and the English version share a disparaging tone on this point: 'This geere smelleth of Plato, his communitie' (More 1556: H4r); 'Haec sapiunt communitatem Platonis' ('This smacks of Plato's community') (More 1995: 119).

readers' who were enabled to deliberate and to draw their own conclusions (Griffiths 2014: 16).

If the effect of *Utopia*'s original glosses is to enlist the reader into a collaborative interchange, Robinson's ongoing dialogue with the work expands on this intention and defines it in his own terms. The experience of dialogue—how to listen, how to respond, how to adjudicate multiple points of view, and how to intervene constructively—takes on further significance and scope in the 1556 text. In the second version of the translation, Robinson was inspired by the orality of the glosses: their modelling of a civil speaking voice that is observant and frank without being disruptive, participatory and open-minded whilst remaining independent. In both versions of his translation, therefore, Robinson ensures that vernacular readers are included in the conversation portrayed and produced by *Utopia* and are able to discuss its observations, arguments, and proposals on equal terms with the text's interlocutors.

CHAPTER 17

'HET ONBEKENT EN WONDERLIJK EYLAND'

Frans van Hoogstraten's Translation of Utopia (1677)

WIEP VAN BUNGE

The first Dutch translation of Thomas More's *Utopia* appeared in Antwerp in 1553 with the publisher Hans de Laet, announced on the title page as *The Utopia of Thomas Morus, in his time Chancellor of England: a book most profitable and pleasing to read, especially for those who in the present day have to rule a town and district, a purpose which it is above all suited to serve. Now translated for the first time into Dutch.*[1] This translation—by an anonymous author—was reprinted by de Laet in 1562, after which the same text was published in Amsterdam in 1629, and in Hoorn in 1630 and 1634. After more than a century, the second Dutch translation was issued in Rotterdam in 1677 by Frans van Hoogstraten, entitled: *The unknown and marvellous Island of Utopia, discovered by Rafaël Hythlodeus and written as a dialogue by the learned Thomas More, Chancellor of England at the time of King Henry VIII. Translated into Dutch by F.v.H.*[2] Worldcat lists twenty-six extant copies of this edition in public libraries across the globe, and no doubt several dozens of copies have survived in private collections, as the title appears regularly in antiquarian booksellers' catalogues. In 1700 a second edition was produced in Amsterdam by Wilhelm Linning van Koppenol. This is a beautiful and fluent translation, preceded by two quotes singing the praises of More: one in Dutch by Gerardus Noviomagus or Geldenhauer (1482–1542), the Latin original of which had adorned the

---

[1] *De Utopie van Thomas Morus in zijnen tijden Cancellier van Enghelant: een boeck seer profijtelijck ende vermakelijck om lesen, bysondere den ghenen die heensdaechs een stadt ende ghemeynte hebben te regeren, daer hy meestendeel toe dienende is. Nu eerst ouerghesedt in neder Duytssche.* The translations is from Cave 2008c: 221; Spaans and Cave 2008a provides a full account of this translation and the various editions.

[2] *Het onbekent en wonderlijk Eyland Utopia, Ontdekt door Rafaël Hythlodeus, en by t'samenspraeke beschreven door den geleerden Tomas Morus, Kancelier van Engeland, ten tijde van Koning Hendrik den achtsten. In Nederduits vertaelt door F. v. H.* Unless otherwise stated, translations are my own.

first edition in 1516, and the other in Latin by the Portuguese bishop Jéronimo Osorio (1506–80), taken from Osorio's polemic with Walter Haddon (1515–72), which resulted from Osorio's appeal in 1562 to Queen Elizabeth to return to the Church of Rome (Osorio 1569).

It would seem that by the time the 1677 Rotterdam edition appeared, More's reputation among Dutch literati was well established. Leendert Strengholt has demonstrated that More's *Epigrams* were often referred to, and he has traced More's presence in such major Dutch authors as Roemer Visscher (1547–1620), Jacob Cats (1577–1660), Constantijn Huygens (1596–1687), Jacobus Revius (1586–1658), and Geerard Brandt (1626–85) (Strengholt 1989; cf. Visscher 2013: 82–84). In addition, Cats, by far the most popular poet of the seventeenth-century Dutch Republic, discussed the remarks made in *Utopia* on marriages (Cats 1637). In the middle of the century two plays in Dutch were published on the tragedy of More's death, focusing on the former Chancellor's 'steadfast' conscientiousness: in 1659 Jan Jacobsz. Schipper (1617–69) published his *Morus*, and in 1660 Hendrik Bruno (1620–64) produced his *Treur-spel Thomas Morus* ('The Tragedy of Thomas More'), based on the 1641 French play *Thomas Morus ou le Triomphe de la foi et de la constance* ('Thomas More or the Triumph of Faith and Constancy') by Jean Puget de la Serre (1594–1665). H. Glazemaker (1619–82), the translator of the philosophers René Descartes (1596–1650) and Baruch/Benedictus de Spinoza (1632–77), would later publish a translation of his own: *Thomas Morus of de Zegepraal des geloofs en stantvastigheit* (Amsterdam, 1668).

There is, however, little to suggest any substantial interest in *Utopia* among seventeenth-century Dutch political thinkers, who—being able to access the text in Latin—of course did not need a translation into Dutch. There are two potential reasons for the neglect of *Utopia* in the Netherlands prior to 1677, by which time Spinoza was dead (passing away in The Hague in February that year, whilst working on a *Tractatus politicus* of his own) and Pieter de La Court (1618–85) had already published his main work (Kossmann 1960/2000; cf. Mulier 1980; A. Weststeijn 2012; James 2012). Dutch republicans such as Spinoza, who did own a copy of *Utopia* (Vereeniging Het Spinozahuis 1914), and the de la Court brothers were fiercely realistic in their political outlook—perhaps Pieter Corneliszoon Plockhoy's (1625–?) and Franciscus van den Enden's (1602–74) 1662 proposals for a Dutch settlement in the New Netherlands in America being the exception, although neither of them refers explicitly to More (Séguy 1968; Mertens 2012; van Bunge 2012: ch. 4). In fact, de la Court repudiated More's *Utopia*, explicitly arguing that it was at best 'a republic in the air' and that its proposed collectivization of property was 'alien to human nature' (A. Weststeijn 2012: 63, 230). Their Orangist counterparts—supporters of the royal House of Orange—were, on the other hand, on the whole strict Calvinists, so there is every reason to assume they were loath to refer to any champion of 'Popery'.

More's imaginary travel tale only started to capture the Dutch imagination in the early eighteenth century. *Beschryvinge van het magtig Koninkryk Krinke Kesmes* ('Description of the Mighty Monarchy Krinke Kesmes') (1708), by Hendrik Smeeks (1645–1721), which incidentally smacked of 'Spinozism' on account of its mockery of theology, is generally assumed to have set the trend.[3] This is not to say that More was never quoted. Daniel Jonktys (1611–54), for instance, a Dordrecht and Rotterdam physician, in 1651 published a plea against the use of torture in criminal law, to which he added a piece on More's feelings about the cruelty of executing thieves (Jonktys 1651; Spierenburg 1978: 147–152). Another exception to the general lack of interest in More's *Utopia* during the Golden Age of the Dutch Republic was Johannes de Mey (1617–78), a highly original Calvinist minister and doctor of medicine from Zeeland with a deep interest in natural philosophy and Cartesianism in particular. De Mey was both a cousin and a pupil of Descartes's one-time friend and mentor Isaac Beeckman (1588–1637) (van Berkel 2013). After having served as minister he was appointed professor of philosophy at the Illustrious School of Middelburg in 1672. One of de Mey's many publications was entitled *Euzooia* ('Living Well') and contained a general theory on the well-being of individuals, communities, and commonwealths. It first appeared in 1674 and was obviously inspired by More. Although de Mey feared that More's proposal to end private property 'was more desirable than feasible', he explicitly supported the Englishman's ideas about the need in religious affairs to concentrate on the *essentialia*, and he borrowed from *Utopia* a number of practical measures as well (de Mey 1704; see Zuidervaart 2001). De Mey was well connected—a friend, for instance, of Pieter de la Court, accompanying him on his 1642 grand tour to France—and admired by many of his contemporaries, including the Rotterdam poet Joachim Oudaen (1628–92), who wrote a laudatory poem prefacing de Mey's collected works (1680–81) as well as a funerary poem after his friend's passing.

So why did F.v.H., that is Frans van Hoogstraten (1632–96), produce a new translation of *Utopia*? And why in 1677? He actually tells us why in a Dutch poem: 'Op het uitgeven der Nederduytsche vertaelinge van Morus Utopia' ('On Publishing the Dutch Translation of More's *Utopia*'). The poem is dedicated, not to More, but to his Dutch friend Desiderius Erasmus. 'How happy you would be,' van Hoogstraten avers, 'if you could visit Rotterdam today. For your native city has not just erected a famous statue in your honour, it now also celebrates the memory of your dear friend [More]', who, or so van Hoogstraten claims, had been falsely accused of betraying an ungrateful prince, whom he had always served loyally. So van Hoogstraten at least conveys the impression that the main purpose of issuing a new translation of *Utopia* was his desire to remind the Dutch reading audience of Erasmus, rather than More, and this impression is only further corroborated by the fact that in 1676 van Hoogstraten had actually embarked on the publication of a series of *Erasmiana*, including a Dutch translation of the *Moriae Encomium* ('Praise of Folly') (1676) and Daniel de Breen's (1594–1664) *Compendium theologiae Erasmicae* (1677; two separate Dutch translations were to follow in 1679; see Trapman 1993), as well as a Dutch translation of Erasmus' *Enchiridion militis Christiani* ('Handbook of a Christian Knight') (1677).

---

[3] See e.g. Buijnsters 1969; Barend-van Haeften 1990; Israel 2001: 320–322; van Eijnatten 2003: 240–245; Hanou 2002: 73–94.

The Rotterdam statue of Erasmus referred to in van Hoogstraten's poem dated from 1622, but in 1677 it had been re-erected, an occasion that sparked a true renaissance of Erasmianism in Rotterdam (van der Blom 1982). In order to gauge its significance, let us first take a closer look at van Hoogstraten, who was closely involved in the festivities surrounding the city's greatest son (Erasmus was born in Rotterdam, the illegitimate son of a priest), the circles in which van Hoogstraten moved, and the religious tensions of the 1650s–70s.[4] The van Hoogstratens originated from Antwerp in Flanders, where they were first recorded in 1534. In the winter of 1584–5, during the siege of Antwerp by the Spanish forces, they moved to Amsterdam, after at least one relative, Franchoys van Hoogstraten (1541–1632), had already settled in the Netherlands—in Dordrecht—as early as 1572. The van Hoogstratens were relatively well off: in particular, Franchoys's practice as a money changer appears to have left the family with a handsome fortune. Franchoys's great-grandson Frans or François was born in The Hague in 1632, the son of Dirk van Hoogstraten (1596–1640), a fairly successful Mennonite jeweller and painter.[5]

We know next to nothing about Frans's early life, part of which was spent in Dordrecht, after the untimely death of his father Dirk. Frans's brother Samuel (1627–78), with whom he would remain in contact throughout his life, would become an important painter, trained by Rembrandt (1606–69) and working in Germany, Vienna, and London. Samuel also composed a major book on the art of painting, *Inleyding to de Hooge Schoole der Schilderkonst* ('Introduction to the Academy of Painting'), published by his brother Frans in 1678 (T. Weststeijn 2008). It seems Frans became an apprentice with the Dordrecht book printer Abraham Andriesz (1614–62) (Thissen 1994: 67–68, 109–110). Dordrecht boasted a lively literary community in which Mennonites played an important part. In 1656 van Hoogstraten married and settled in Rotterdam, where in 1657 he opened a bookshop, and possibly a printing house (Thissen 1994: 68). Within a year he published his first book, *De schole der zedelycke deught* ('The School of Moral Virtue'), aimed at children in need of further instruction regarding 'the fear of the Lord', which would go into eighteen editions (Thissen 1994: 249). Its author was Tieleman van Bracht (1625–64), a Dordrecht cloth merchant and Mennonite preacher known for his piety. Van Hoogstraten's second publication was a Mennonite confession, but his third book, produced in 1659, hailed from an altogether different background: *Il Libro de la vanidad del mundo* ('The Book about the Vanity of the World') (1562) by Diego de Estella (1524–78), translated by van Hoogstraten himself, was a classic title by a noted Franciscan mystic. In the preface to the second edition of 1665 van Hoogstraten claimed to have translated and published this work because it seemed to him the best way to become intimately acquainted with its contents, which mattered greatly to him personally (see Thissen 1994: 85, 204–206). Van Hoogstraten's religious severity, including his

---

[4] This section draws on Thissen 1994—a splendid study of the seventeenth-century network of the van Hoogstraten family—and Zijlmans 1999, a fascinating analysis of Frans van Hoogstraten's Rotterdam circle of friends.

[5] Mennonites were a Protestant sect which emphasized adult baptism and rejected Church organization, military service, and public office.

rejection of worldly values, was no exception in the literary and religious circle of friends he joined upon arrival in Rotterdam, essentially made up of *chrétiens sans Église*: the Collegiant Johan Hartigveld (1618–78), the son of a rich mayor was to become famous for his personal frugality and for the generosity with which he parted with his fortune (van Bunge 1990b: reg. i.v).[6] It was very much in this vein that van Hoogstraten, in 1668, published *Voorhof der Ziele* ('Portal of the Soul'), an extremely pious emblem book, one of the first publications of the Haarlem engraver Romeyn de Hooghe (1645–1708; see van Nierop et al. 2008), and that in 1674 he produced a translation of Justus Lipsius' *De Constantia* (1583).

By this time, however, van Hoogstraten had converted to Roman Catholicism, and over the next three decades many *Catholica* were to be produced by his firm, including—in 1670 and 1675—translations of *Manuductio ad coelum* ('A Guide to Heaven') (1668) and *Principia et documenta vitae Christiani* ('The Principles of Christianity') (1673) by the Italian Cistercian cardinal Giovanni Bona (1604–79); Thomas à Kempis's *De imitatione Christi* (1674); and the Jesuit ascetic Achille Gagliari's *Breve Compendio* ('Brief Compendium') (1674). De Mey's friend, the poet Joachim Oudaen, a prominent member of van Hoogstraten's Rotterdam network known for his violently anti-Catholic sentiments, does not appear to have taken exception to this (Melles 1958). Van Hoogstraten remained a dear friend, a true 'Erasmian', devoted to the essence of the Christian faith and most of all concerned to practise its moral demands. During the late 1650s and 1660s, van Hoogstraten's bookshop served as the epicentre of a closely knit circle of friends. Besides Hartigveld and Oudaen, this group was made up of some twenty self-styled 'Erasmians', including the young Adriaan Paets (1631–86), Jacob Ostens (1630–78), and Johannes (1609–70) and Isaac Naeranus (dates unknown) (Roldanus 1935; van Bunge 1990a, 2004; Visser 2011: ch. 11). Paets, a Remonstrant, was to become mayor of Rotterdam, director of the Dutch East India Company, and ambassador of the States General in Madrid as well as the man who ensured that the Huguenot philosopher Pierre Bayle came to Rotterdam in 1681; Ostens was a surgeon, a future correspondent of Spinoza, and a Mennonite minister who was widely held to be a Socinian; the Naerani were booksellers and publishers, related to several prominent Remonstrant ministers.[7]

When van Hoogstraten set up shop in Rotterdam in the late 1650s, Hartigveld, Oudaen, Paets, Ostens, and Johannes Naeranus were all deeply implicated in a furious local dispute. Since it was largely fought by pamphlets, it turned into a very public feud whose origins lay in a *Placcaet* (decree), issued by the States of Holland in 1653,

---

[6] The Collegiants were an association mostly of Arminians and Anabaptists, founded in the village of Rijnsburg in 1619; they took their name from the meetings (colleges) at which everyone was free to speak on religious matters. Arminians followed the teachings of Jacobus Arminius (1560–1609), a Dutch Protestant theologian, who rejected Calvinist ideas of predestination. Anabaptists is a term for members of various Christian groups who rejected the validity of infant baptism, because the baptized person needed to able to understand the sacrament.

[7] Remonstrants were followers of the theologian Jacobus Arminius, who in 1610 formally proposed the Five Articles of Remonstrance against the teaching of Calvin; Socinians denied the divinity of Christ.

that made the proliferation of Socinianism a criminal offence (van Bunge 1990b: ch. 1; Visser 2011: ch. 11). As a consequence of this decree, the Remonstrant community of Rotterdam started reconsidering its so-called 'Friday college', an informal, weekly gathering where individual believers freely discussed their faith. This 'college' was inspired by the colleges first held by so-called *collegianten* in the village of Rijnsburg near Leiden. By the middle of the century their example has inspired Collegiants all over Holland and Utrecht, and it was common knowledge that their gatherings were frequented by men and women, of whom some held Socinian sympathies.[8] Some of the participants of the Friday colleges were no Remonstrants at all, but Mennonites, such as Ostens, who as early as 1651 had publicly advertised his sympathy for the 'Polish Brethren', members of the Minor Reformed Church of Poland (1565–1658), who—amongst other things—did not believe in the divine Trinity of Father, Son, and Holy Ghost. Samuel Lansbergen (1588–1669), the rather authoritarian minister of the Rotterdam Remonstrants, meanwhile, had come to feel that—now Socinianism had been officially outlawed—the Friday college put the entire community at risk. Following the Synod of Dordrecht (aka Dort) in 1618–19, Arminianism had effectively been banned, and the official establishment of a Remonstrant Fraternity in 1630 was still pretty recent.[9]

In 1654 the matter was discussed at the national assembly of the Remonstrants, which felt that its well-established tradition of toleration should not be put in jeopardy, but Lansbergen refused to take heed: the Friday college was closed down indefinitely. This caused considerable grief among the wider community especially since Lansbergen resorted to blackmail: if the Fraternity failed to listen to him, he would stop paying the annual contribution of the large Rotterdam community to the national Fraternity. Hartigveld, Johannes Naeranus, and several other prominent Erasmians parted with the Remonstrant community, feeling it had betrayed its heritage. They now established an independent, truly Rijnsburger college, while several Collegiants joined the Waterlander Mennonites, led by Ostens. In many ways Ostens was the crucial figure in the theological conflicts rocking Rotterdam during the 1650s and 1660s. Hated by the local Calvinist ministry, which held no doubts regarding his Socinian leanings, feared by the Remonstrants, anxious not to be associated with the Polish Brethren, he also met with growing resistance among his fellow Mennonites. He made a living as a surgeon—in 1661 his friend Johannes Naeranus published a translation Ostens had made of three medical handbooks—but he was mainly known for his attempts to establish a truly tolerant Church. As early as 1651 he had published a remarkable dialogue *Liefde-Son, Omstralende de Hoedanigheyt der tegenwoordige genaamde Christenheyt* ('Love-Sun Shining on the Condition of Today's Christianity'). This argued for the necessity of practising toleration since the Bible clearly indicates the difference between necessary

---

[8] See van Slee 1895/1980; Hylkema 1900-2/1978; Kühler 1912/1980; Kolakowski 1969; Fix 1991. For a more general account of the anti-Socinian campaign unleashed in 1653, Israel 1995: 909–916. We now know that the Rotterdam Collegiants were indeed in direct contact with several original Socinians, including, for instance, Stanislaus Lubieniecki (1623–75). See Jörgensen 1968; van Bunge 2020.

[9] For a definition of Arminianism, see n. 6.

and non-necessary articles of faith and leaves no doubt as to the Christian duty to exchange our amour propre for love of God.

Putting this irenic project into practice, however, turned out to be something of a challenge. Having arrived in Rotterdam in 1651 at the age of 21, Ostens was suspended as a *Vlaams* (Flemish) Mennonite minister as early as 1655, upon which he joined the more liberal Waterlanders, where he was instrumental in the continuation of the Collegiant meetings of his friends, many of whom were actually Remonstrants or former Remonstrants. In 1665 even the very liberal Waterlander Mennonites had had enough of Ostens's wayward behaviour. Ostens, for instance, baptized people in the Mennonite consistory who subsequently joined the Remonstrants. He repeatedly attempted to realize a merger with the local Remonstrants; he wrote several incendiary pamphlets in an Utrecht polemic concerning the Socinian tendencies among the local Mennonites (Ostens 1662, 1665); and in Rotterdam he ended up with a tiny community of his own, counting some twenty to thirty members. Once it turned out that he was a friend of Spinoza, who addressed his famous letter 43 to Ostens, his reputation was ruined, for Spinoza was widely held to have been an atheist. Until well into the eighteenth century, Ostens would be referred to as an 'Atheist' himself (Spinoza 1985–2016: 2.385–390; de Vet 1980: 176–180).

Ostens's career appears to illustrate the paradox of Protestant irenicism: more often than not, the desire to unite in the name of brotherly love and Christian toleration provoked violent quarrels and endless schisms. In particular during the 'Year of Disaster', 1672 (so-called because the Dutch Republic faced total defeat by the combined forces of the French and English), the religious tensions between the different Protestant sects took on a new dimension. Whilst Paets was fortunate to reside as an ambassador in faraway Madrid, once French troops had reached Utrecht and Orangist mobs took to the streets of the major cities of Holland, the other Remonstrant regents were attacked on the streets, their houses sacked, and several of them had to take refuge in Antwerp, in neighbouring Flanders (van Bunge 1990b: 67–71; Zijlmans 1999: 166–168). In dozens of pamphlets both Ostens and Oudaen were accused of plotting treacherous activities, undermining the very survival of the Dutch Republic. Isaac Naeranus actually spent three weeks in jail for having published one of Oudaen's more outspoken political pamphlets. Unsurprisingly, the Calvinist ministry of Rotterdam felt now the time had come to squash the Arminian, Socinian, and libertine supporters of the republican statesman Johan de Witt (1626–72), who was lynched and cannibalized by an Orangist mob in The Hague on 20 August (Prud'homme van Reine 2013).

Jori Zijlmans has demonstrated how close the links were among the Rotterdam 'Erasmians' who met at van Hoogstraten's bookshop. Oudaen, who owned a tile factory appears to have been the leading literary light of this coterie (Zijlmans 1999: 152–158). He was an erudite, eminently sociable poet with a passion for Roman history, who after having served in Haarlem as secretary to Petrus Scriverius (1576–1660), one of Erasmus' earliest biographers (Langereis 2001; Koning 2011), settled in Rotterdam in the mid-1650s. His cabinet of curiosities and coin collection were to draw a regular stream of visitors—he would publish a book, *Roomsche Mogentheid* ('Rome's Empire') in 1663, illustrated with many dozens of pictures of coins (Tadema 2004)—and his friends included the Dutch 'Prince of Poetry', Joost van den Vondel (1587–1679) from Amsterdam, as well as a host of other Dutch literati. What is more, Oudaen clearly served as a source of inspiration to a younger generation of Rotterdam authors such as Frans van Hoogstraten's sons David (1658–1724) and Jan (1662–1736), who would both turn into accomplished poets in their own right.

The social status of these Rotterdam Erasmians appears to have varied considerably, with rich and distinguished members of the regent aristocracy such as Paets and Hartigveld mingling amicably with the tile-maker Oudaen and a surgeon such as Ostens. They were held together by their joint dedication to a humanist, biblical Christianity, based on a minimal dogmatic foundation and allowing for a maximum of mutual toleration (Zijlmans 1999: 161–166). Cultivating individual piety and shunning any display of worldly fortune, they shared a great reverence for Erasmus. In doing so they continued a Rotterdam tradition which had started soon after Erasmus' death in Basel in 1536: the house at the Wijde Kerkstraat in which Erasmus was born was visited by countless admirers, including Philip of Habsburg (later Philip II of Spain) in 1549. Erasmus' portrait adorned Rotterdam city hall, and as early as 1557 a statue in stone was erected, replacing an earlier wooden statue of *Erasmus Roterodamus*—the first statue erected for a non-royal in the Netherlands. (It was hollow and when Philip came to admire it, a boy, hidden inside, recited a poem making it look as if Erasmus was addressing the prince.) When this second statue was destroyed by marauding Spanish troops in 1572, it was replaced by yet another wooden one which by the end of the sixteenth century was replaced once more by a statue in stone. In 1618 the city council ordered the production of what was to become the fifth and final statue, this time executed in bronze by the famous architect and sculptor from Amsterdam, Hendrick de Keyser (1565–1621).

It is this sculpture, completed in 1622, which to this day stands in front of the Lawrence church in Rotterdam (van der Blom 1982). When it was first installed, however, Calvinist theologians strongly protested as they regarded Erasmus as a progenitor of Arminianism, which had just been outlawed at the Synod of Dordrecht. Strict Protestants were simply unable to forgive Erasmus for not having joined the Reformation. Typically, however, the Rotterdam regents would not be instructed by clergymen on how to do their work, although in 1674, when Orangist mobs were still roaming the streets, they felt it safest to temporarily remove the statue, after which some minor damage was repaired. In 1677, the statue was re-erected. What is more, it was put on a new pedestal. The great scholar and poet Nicolaas Heinsius the Elder (1621–80) composed a poem which was carved into the pedestal, and Oudaen produced a Dutch translation as well as a separate booklet for the occasion, entitled *Den Grooten Rotterdammer In zyn Geboorte-stad herstelt* ('The Great Rotterdammer Restored in his Birthplace'), published by Isaac Naeranus. To all intents and purposes, Frans van Hoogstraten's publication of More's *Utopia* was part of the festivities: recall his reference to Erasmus' statue and his launching of a whole series of *Erasmiana* in 1676. Van Hoogstraten and his friends were only too relieved that the troubles of 1672 were over and done with, and they were eager to remind Rotterdam to take pride in its greatest son.

Over the centuries, few European cities have been as tenacious as Rotterdam has been since the sixteenth century to associate its *imago* with one of its sons or daughters—even though Erasmus left his native city at the tender age of 2, never to return. But once Erasmus started to style himself 'Roterodamus' (from 1510, but with growing insistence in the 1520s), and once he became famous, the local elites cultivated his memory (van Bunge 2013). In seventeenth-century Rotterdam Erasmus became a perfect source of civic pride since it was one of the Dutch cities in which orthodox Calvinists failed to seize power: Paets was only one of many local magistrates with Arminian leanings, and once the Dutch theologians Dirck Volckerstszoon Coornhert (1522–90) and Hugo Grotius (1583–1645) had appropriated Erasmus' heritage, he became very much part of the intellectual self-image of the liberal elites ruling Holland. When Grotius in October 1631 briefly returned from exile in France, the first city in the Dutch Republic he visited was Rotterdam, where from 1613 to 1616 he had served as pensionary (the equivalent of an English mayor). Upon arrival, he immediately set out for Erasmus' statue, which only fifteen years previously had been commissioned, largely thanks to him:

> My first visit to Rotterdam was to show my affection for the memory of Erasmus. I went to see the statue of the man who had so well shown us the way to a measured Reformation, never binding himself on disputable questions to one side or another. We Hollanders cannot thank this man enough, and I hold myself fortunate that I can from afar understand his virtue. (cited in Manfield 1979: 143; cf. Trapman 1999: ch. 4; Nellen 2007: 364–371)

When in 1692 Pierre Bayle—nicknamed *le philosophe de Rotterdam* and no Arminian at all—was facing dismissal from the Illustrious School of Rotterdam, he invoked Erasmus' memory in attempting to dissuade the local regents from firing him (Bayle 1996–2016: 8.676–678). At the time, Bayle was working day and night on the *Dictionnaire historique et critique*, which was to be published in 1697. Quite apart from the fact, or so Bayle argued, that it would simply be 'un-Erasmian' to fire the first professor of history and philosophy Rotterdam ever appointed—the Illustrious School had only been established in 1681—he pointed that he was working on a major dictionary, in which he would demonstrate how important Erasmus has always been to the city of Rotterdam. The letter Bayle sent to one of the local regents responsible for the school was indeed accompanied by a preprint version of some of the entries to be included in the *Dictionaire*, entitled *Projet et fragmens d'un Dictionaire critique*. For obvious reasons, the article on Erasmus took pride of place in this (Bayle 1692: 225–296).[10]

Unfortunately, Bayle's letter was addressed to the staunchly Orangist Jacob van Zuijlen van Nijevelt (1642–95), one of the most corrupt regents to rule the city, and Bayle was fired regardless. However, his appropriation of Erasmus once more demonstrated

---

[10] Bayle 1692: 225–296. Unfortunately, Bayle's letter was addressed to one of the most corrupt regents ever to rule the city, the staunchly Orangist Jacob van Zuijlen van Nijevelt (1642–95) (Bayle 1999–2016: 8.676–678). On Bayle's highly influential rendering of Erasmus' life and work, see Manfield 1979: 8.

the local topicality of invoking the memory of *Erasmus Roterodamus*. To Frans van Hoogstraten, however, the Erasmian renaissance of 1677 yielded the perfect occasion to remind the Dutch reading public of that other early sixteenth-century Catholic author, intimately connected to Erasmus and steadfast in his conscience. In particular the frank acknowledgement of religious plurality among the inhabitants of *Utopia* must have appealed to van Hoogstraten: as More wrote, 'There are several different religions on the island, and indeed, in each town' (More 1965b: 117). Once Christianity is introduced into Utopia, it meets with little opposition, until of course, one zealot starts calling for a prohibition of other religions. 'He was duly convicted and sentenced to exile—for one of the most ancient principles of their constitution is religious toleration', since one of the first things Utopia's founder Utopus did when he took control was to issue a law 'by which everyone was allowed to practice what religion he liked':

> He didn't presume to say which creed was right. Apparently he considered it possible that God made different people believe different things, because he wanted to be worshipped in many different ways. But he was evidently quite certain that it was stupid and arrogant to bully everyone else into adopting one's own particular creed. It seemed to him perfectly obvious that, even if there was only one true religion, and all the rest were nonsense, truth would eventually prevail of its own accord—as long as the matter was discussed calmly and reasonably. (More 1965b: 119)

Perhaps van Hoogstraten's translation even provides us with a clue as to why he converted to Roman Catholicism. Hazardous as it is to speculate about anyone's motives for religious conversion, especially during the early modern period when religious identity mattered politically in the way that it did, we can at least try to analyse the contexts in which they occurred. Becoming a Catholic in the Dutch Republic was tantamount to joining a religious denomination which was officially discriminated against: Catholics were ineligible for public office; their religious gatherings were at best 'tolerated'; they were not allowed to study at, let alone be employed by, any of the Dutch universities; and so on.[11] In 1592 the Jesuits had officially launched the *Missio Hollandica* ('Dutch mission'), which sought to win back Protestant coverts to the Church of Rome. On the other hand, the tolerant policies of the Dutch Republic, allowing a wide variety of Christian denominations to coexist, by its very nature included the danger of apostasy and as a consequence conversions were not uncommon (Kooi 2007; 2012: ch. 4). Protestant church councils were of course concerned about their members relapsing into Catholicism, but as they were only able to impose disciplinary measures affecting the confessional status of their flock, they were acutely aware of the risks involved in fraternizing with Catholics, who made up nearly half of the population of the Dutch Republic (Roodenburg 1990: 149–166).

Some twenty years prior to van Hoogstraten's conversion, the greatest poet of the Dutch Golden Age, Oudaen's Amsterdam friend Vondel, had done precisely the

---

[11] See e.g. Frijhoff & Spies 1999: 375–393; van Nierop 2002: 102–111; Parker 2008; van Gennip 2014.

same thing: born a Mennonite, living among Remonstrants, he had become a Roman Catholic, producing a massive body of scholarly literature as a result. In a recent analysis, Judith Pollmann weighs the various possibilities which might account for Vondel's conversion, and she points to a rather casual remark made by Vondel's biographer, the Remonstrant Geerard Brandt (1626–85), another friend of Oudaen's, according to whom Vondel had come to feel 'that there was no certainty to be had about religion, unless one were prepared to accept an infallible judge and explainer of all disputed points, and acknowledged on earth one Stadtholder of Christ, and that this led to the Pope' (Pollmann 2012: 98). Similar sentiments, Pollmann argues, appear to have inspired the female poet Maria Tesselschade Roemers Visscher (1594–1649) to join the Catholic Church almost simultaneously with Vondel:

> In Vondel and Tessel, then, we can detect the outline of one route by which moderate Protestants in a multiconfessional society might end up converting to Catholicism. Like many Protestants before them had done when confronted with the disagreements between the churches, they thought that one might reach consensus about a core of essential beliefs. However, whereas this moved some Christians to argue that no one could decide for another person what the truth in religion was, Vondel and Tessel were yearning for authority and unity, and were prepared to grant this to Rome. (99)[12]

Apparently, to some Protestants living in the Golden Age of the Dutch Republic, returning to Catholicism presented the most viable solution to the religious and political tensions resulting from the confessional strife, which in turn could only occur as a consequence of the intellectual freedom characteristic of that day and age. Thus, van Hoogstraten's decision to launch a literary offensive of *Erasmiana* fitted hand in glove with both his new-found Catholic identity and his dissident past. It even provided him with the opportunity to draw attention to Erasmus' English friend, whose *Utopia* conveyed the idea of a Catholic—i.e. universal—Christianity, able perhaps to put an end to the 'geschillen en twisten' ('disputes and arguments') among fellow Christians, which only lead to grief and bitterness, as he put it in the preface of his 1659 translation of De Estella's *De la vanidad* (Thissen 1994: 205).

More's scathing criticism of man's greed and lust for power no doubt also dovetailed nicely with van Hoogstraten's own leanings towards an ascetic, spiritual Christianity. But in view of the specific occasion at which *Utopia* was relaunched in Rotterdam, it would seem that van Hoogstraten was inspired most of all by the work's irenic vision of a Catholic Christianity. In a short poem on Adrian VI (1459–1523), the only Dutchman ever to have risen to the papacy, van Hoogstraten duly stressed the man's pacifism, calling him 'een vreebeminner en verfoeier van den twist' ('a lover of peace and an enemy of strife').[13] Erasmus, van Hoogstraten had argued in 1677, should be admired most of all

---

[12] For Tesselschade, see Smits-Veldt 1994.
[13] This poem appeared in van Hoogstraten's *Mengeldichten* ('Miscellany of Poems'), appended to his edition of Joseph Hall, *De Schoole der Wereld* (Dordrecht, 1682).

as he 'never established a church of his own' (van Hoogstraten 1682: 45; Thissen 1994: 206). This remark seems to have been prepared already in his book of emblems of 1668, arguably van Hoogstraten's most personal work. One of the emblems concerns Proverbs 1:7: 'The fear of the Lord is the beginning of knowledge.' In the poem accompanying the phrase, van Hoogstraten skilfully comments on the origins of the Reformation, arguing that 'Mother Church' has suffered more from its own believers than it has from 'Pagan, Turk or Jew':

> If you seek wisdom, give up the appearance
> Of knowledge: remember the dying scholar
> Who honoured Luther, spitting fire and flames,
> With this golden lesson, fitting the mouth
> Of a sage, ready
> To depart and to offer to the Keeper of all souls
> His soul: Dear Brother,
> Go into your cell and beg God
> Forgiveness: have mercy upon me!
>
> (van Hoogstraten 1668: 61)[14]

The 'dying scholar' van Hoogstraten cites here was the theologian Albert Krantz (c.1450–1517), whose deathbed advice to Luther is recorded in Willem Baudaurtius' *Apophtegmata Christiana* (1605), which enjoyed many reprints, but these were sentiments that clearly resonated with More's own suspicions of religious evangelism rooted, as he saw it, in man's terrible propensity for pride.[15]

---

[14] 'Indienge wijsheit zoekt, laat ingebeelden waen | Van kennis vaeren: denk aan zeecker krank'Geleerde, | Die Luther, daer hy vyer en vlammen spoog, vereerde | Met deze gulde les, wel voegende den mond | Van eenen Wijzen, die gereet en vaerdigh stont | Van hier te scheiden, en aen aller zielen Hoeder | Zijn ziel te offeren: Mijn welbeminde Broeder, | Gaet in uw Kloostercel: roept God aen, smeekt hem vry: | Weest my genadigh: Heere, ontferm u over my!'

[15] See Paul in this volume.

CHAPTER 18

UTOPIA AND GILBERT BURNET IN 1684

PHIL WITHINGTON

'I have now much leisure, and want diversion, so I have bestowed some of my hours upon Translations, in which I have proposed no ill Patterns to my self: but the Reader will be best able to judge whether I have copied skilfully after such Originals' (More 1684: A5v). So explained Gilbert Burnet in his preface to his translation of Thomas More's *Utopia*, published anonymously in 1684. It was a significant moment in the history of *Utopia*. The only previous English translations of More's Latin original had been by Ralph Robinson in 1551 and 1556.[1] Although these had been republished in 1596, 1624, and 1639, there had been no subsequent attempt to render *Utopia* into what Burnet called 'more Modern English' (A7v). Thereafter, Burnet's edition quickly became the definitive version of the text for readers not only in England, Scotland, and Ireland, but also in North America. Two versions were published in 1684, followed by a third in 1685; and after 1700 it became the base text for editions of *Utopia* published in Dublin (1737, 1747), Glasgow (1743, 1762), Edinburgh (1743), and Oxford (1751, 1753) as well as London (1795). Likewise, Thomas Jefferson, the primary author of *The Declaration of Independence,* owned not only a Latin edition of *Utopia* (Cologne, 1555) but also Robert Foulis's 1743 edition of Burnet's translation.[2] Put simply, Burnet translated *Utopia* for the North Atlantic Enlightenment.

Despite this not insignificant claim to fame, the 1684 translation has received little critical attention from either students of *Utopia* or historians of Restoration politics (though see Dodds 2017: 183–185). This neglect is surprising for a number of reasons. First, Burnet translated *Utopia* as a leading Protestant churchman, historian, and inveterate penman who was deeply embroiled in the great political dramas and intellectual

---

[1] See Bishop and Cavanagh in this volume.
[2] Library of Congress shelf marks: Jefferson collection HX811 1516 .A516 and HX811 1516 .E743. See also the chapter by Weaver-Hightower and Bajaber in this volume. For Foulis, see Nicholas in this volume.

developments of the day. Five years earlier, in 1679, he had published the first of his two-volume *History of the Reformation of the Church of England*: a publishing sensation that was dedicated to the king, received votes of thanks from both Houses of Parliament, and went into numerous new editions and 'abridged' versions (Greig 2004). *Reformation* added to Burnet's reputation as a powerful polemicist and popular metropolitan preacher. Burnet was also a canny networker who looked to maintain client and patronage networks across the political spectrum. All of which begs the question why a Protestant writer as eminent as Burnet suddenly had 'much leisure' in the first place and, more, why he chose to 'divert' himself by translating the 'little book' of a Catholic humanist who—as Burnet himself had shown in his *Reformation*—had steadfastly opposed the forces for reformation over 150 years earlier.

Second, as the politicized reception of his *Reformation* indicates, Burnet translated *Utopia* at an especially fractious moment in national public life—'at so hot a time', to use one of his favourite political adjectives (about more of which below) (Airy 1900: 288). Forty-two years since the outbreak of civil war, thirty-five years since Charles I was executed, and twenty-three years since the coronation of the restored Charles II, *Utopia* was published in a city once again experiencing extreme political tension and apparent constitutional crisis. It was only three years since parliament had looked to exclude Charles II's brother—James, Duke of York—from inheriting the crown on the grounds of his Catholicism; and we know (with the benefit of hindsight) that it was only four years until William of Orange used military force to initiate the 'Glorious Revolution' and make the same brother—now James II—abdicate the throne. Burnet was deeply implicated in the politics of both 'exclusion' and 'revolution': a man who began the 1680s a friend of the royal court; who became alienated from the Stuart brothers during the exclusion crisis, and was even suspected of colluding with plotters against the Crown in 1683; who embarked on a voluntary exile in 1684, only to return to England at the 'Glorious Revolution' as private chaplain to the triumphant William of Orange; and who is now recognized as one of the founding fathers of the 'Whig' version of British constitutional history. In circumstances such as these, it is certainly worth investigating why he translated a new *Utopia* for London's reading public in 1684.

Third, beyond the authorial and contextual questions raised by the translation, there is the issue of Burnet's linguistic and semantic impact on the text and what these, in turn, suggest about cultural developments since the 1550s and Robinson's editions. Because as well as developing a prominent public profile, Burnet was also very much a product of a certain strand of contemporary intellectual culture: as a high-achieving pupil of Scottish humanism; as a Fellow of the Royal Society in London; as a European man of letters; as a close friend and ally of a network of scholarly churchmen sometimes known as 'Latitudinarians' (who—whilst orthodox themselves—were indifferent to particular creeds and forms of church government or worship). When Burnet sat down to translate *Utopia*, that is, he did so with a set of scholarly skills and semantic assumptions that inevitably shaped the rendition of More's Latin in particular and historically specific ways (Withington 2017). Although they worked from a shared original text or texts, the contexts and semantics in which and by which Robinson and Burnet 'Englished' *Utopia* were demonstrably different. It follows that understanding the specifics of the text can in turn illuminate the political and intellectual cultures to which Burnet's translation contributed, as well as the powerful overlaps between political and intellectual life in the period.

This chapter addresses these issues in three stages. The first two sections place Burnet and his translation in political context. They are particularly concerned with identifying some of the reasons why such a savvy political operator and prolific writer should have regarded *Utopia* an appropriate and timely investment of his considerable energy and skills. The third section then moves beyond the immediate political circumstances of the translation to some of the broader changes in early modern culture and society that it reveals. It does so by comparing Burnet's 'modern' version to that by Robinson—a 'text' which Burnet was 'once apt to think' had 'been done by Sir *Thomas More* himself' given it was 'in the English of his Age, and not unlike his Stile' (More 1684: A6r).[3] To this end, the chapter focuses on one of Burnet's linguistic modernizations in particular: the introduction of 'slave' into *Utopia*'s English transcript. The chapter argues that Burnet's scholarly agenda to modernize *Utopia* was not in contradistinction to his political motivations. Rather, politics and scholarliness were intertwined. As such, his book provides valuable insight into how a 'Renaissance' text was rewritten to speak to an early 'Enlightenment' audience—but in ways that exemplified a profound appreciation of the ancients.

Burnet and *Utopia* in Context

Gilbert Burnet was born in 1643 in Edinburgh to an eminent judge and 'puritan' Episcopalian, Robert Burnet, and Rachel Johnston, sister of Lord Wariston.[4] He spent his formative years under the formidable tuition of his father and took his MA in Marischal College, Aberdeen, graduating in 1657. After his father's death in 1661, Burnet broadened his horizons, visiting London and the Low Countries and becoming acquainted with the intellectual ferment of the age. Returning to Scotland, he made his Scottish reputation as a minister and professor of divinity, as a protégé of John Maitland (second Earl of Lauderdale, Charles's secretary of state in Restoration Scotland), and as a religious writer and historian: his first major work is *The Memoirs of the Dukes of Hamilton*, printed in 1677. Through Lauderdale's influence Burnet was introduced to the royal court in London in 1673 and impressed the king and his brother enough to be made a royal chaplain. A year later, however, Burnet broke with Lauderdale and was accordingly removed from his chaplaincy. Instead, he was offered lectureships in the City of London (in the parish of St Clement Danes) and the Rolls Chapel, and it was on this

---

[3] It is not clear whether Burnet is referring to Robinson's 1551 or 1556 text.
[4] The best single account of Burnet's life is Greig 2004.

basis that he was able to continue his burgeoning career as a religious controversialist and historian. As is shown below, it was as a preacher and historian that he began his translation of *Utopia*, probably in the second half of 1683.

Before turning to the specific moment of translation, it is worth outlining the intellectual formation of the 40-year-old translator. Unsurprisingly for a highly educated seventeenth-century churchman, a key feature of Burnet's 'mental furniture' was his familiarity with 'ancient' learning and languages. In his unpublished 'Draught of my own life' Burnet recalled that his father, Robert, 'made the teaching me a great part of his care', with the result that 'before I was ten year old I was master of that tongue [Latin] and of the Classic Authors'. At 'the College of New Aberdeen' Burnet then 'went thro the common methods of the Aristotelian Philosophy with no small applause, and passed Master of Arts some months before I was fourteen' (Foxcroft 1902: 454). With his two brothers already a lawyer and a physician, Burnet's father 'wished we might be all of different professions'; although Burnet studied law for a year, he duly opted 'to apply [him]self to Divinity' with 'a hard course of study'. This involved reading the entire Bible 'with several Commentaries', studying controversies, going 'thro several bodies of School Divinity', and reading 'many volumes of History of all sorts'. Before he was 18 years old, Burnet was able to pass the 'course of trials' required of 'Expectant preachers' in Scotland. These included practical and critical preaching, disputing in Latin, 'Scripture History', a 'Hebrew Psalm […] to expound', and examination on 'the Greek Testament'. After the death of his father, Burnet was befriended by the moderate Presbyterian preacher James Nairn, who 'recommended also the reading of Plato and the Platonists' where Burnet 'found noble entertainment'. His knowledge was deepened further by another mentor, Bishop Robert Leighton, who 'advised [him] to read all the Apologies and the short Treatises of the Fathers of the first three centuries' (455–457, 461–462).

Burnet's ancient learning was a lifelong source of pride and distinction that he sought to impart to his own sons, who were fully versed in 'both Latin and Greek' before they each attended Cambridge or Oxford colleges (Foxcroft 1902: 511). But the same familiarity was also fundamental to his vision of the modern Church, which he believed should retain the values and structures of its 'primitive' origins, and to modern manners and discourse—including religious controversy—which should be characterized by the classical virtues of moderation and civility (471–472, 455). Such learning was not simply preferable, but necessary. In his *Reformation*, Burnet explained that Thomas More—as the man 'of rare vertues, and excellent parts' capable of writing *Utopia*—nevertheless 'became superstitiously devoted to the interests and passions of the Popish Clergy' because 'he was no Divine at all' and 'knew nothing of Antiquity' (Airy 1900: 355). Burnet likewise disparaged his Scottish Presbyterian contemporaries as 'generally a grave and sober sort of men; they had little learning among them, but that of systems, commentaries, and the Aristotelian philosophy; the reformers were the ancientist authors they read' (Foxcroft 1902: 31). But he was equally 'offended with the method the Bishops took' in Restoration Scotland: they 'observed none of the Primitive rules, while yet they fetched the chief arguments for their Order from those times' (472). Travelling to England in the early 1660s, Burnet instead found spiritual and intellectual succour amongst those he styled 'the most eminent of the young Clergy'. As he noted, 'I grew well acquainted with [John] Tillotson and [Edward] Stillingfleet [... Benjamin] Whichcote and [John] Wilkins were very free with me, and I easily went into the notions of the Latitudinarians' (463). Martin Griffin has shown that 'Latitude-men' was coined as an insult for a certain kind of mid-seventeenth-century Cambridge-trained clergyman or moralist. They were criticized for making religion too reasonable; for tending to a Pelagian view of human salvation (where humans had free will to effect their salvation); and for having a 'permissive and lax' attitude to church governance and liturgy (Griffin 1992: 8–9). These traits were not pejorative for Burnet, who was one of the first writers to take the label as normative. He particularly celebrated the imperative of moderation and comprehension when it came to the beliefs of others, but demonstrated, also, a queasiness about 'enthusiasm'—the faith in revelation over reason—as well as hostility to 'Popish' superstition and any kind of doctrinal bullying (Foxcroft 1902: 473, 93).

Burnet developed these principles within a wider intellectual milieu that included the diverse range of comparatively equable denominations in the Low Countries, which he encountered first-hand in 1664, and the Royal Society, of which he became a fellow the same year (Foxcroft 1902: 90–95). And just as his immersion in the ancients served as the basis for his modernity, so Burnet's religious ideas complemented his interest in philosophy and mathematics—which be began teaching himself in the early 1660s— and also 'the nature of language in general and of ours in particular' (461, 487). Burnet accredited his linguistic interests to another Latitudinarian friend, Dr William Lloyd, who in the later 1660s introduced him to '[John] Wilkins Philosophical language and Real Character and had the truest notions of a correct stile of any man I ever saw' (487).[5] According to Burnet, it was a pivotal moment in his development as a writer. Not only did he now keep 'close to his [Lloyd's] rules and so came to have the reputation of a correct writer as to stile', he also 'never published any book without shewing it to several persons before it went to the press', most usually Lloyd and Tillotson (487).

London in the 1670s was, in many respects, an ideal environment for an ambitious and articulate churchman to apply his broader learning and redoubtable stylistic 'rules'. The confessional distrust and divisions that characterized the 1640s and 1650s had resurfaced, generating intense public debate conducted in print. As Burnet recalled, 'I wrote many little books which were all so well received that they sold well and helped to support me, so that tho I had no great plenty about me yet I was in no want of anything': 'I got thro all these years in a very easy manner' (Foxcroft 1902: 487–488). But this writerly success was not without its ironies. Whereas Burnet's 'Latitudinarianism' pleaded 'mutual forbearance' between denominations and 'parties', the public appetite for 'little books' was based on an endemic and even ideological fear of an alternative version of Christianity—Catholicism—combined with an apparently ingrained incapacity of Protestant 'parties' to tolerate each other, be they Dissenters, Nonconformists,

---

[5] John Wilkins, *An Essay Towards a Real Character and a Philosophical Language* (1668).

Low Episcopalian, or High Anglicans (Greig 2013; Goldie 1991; Goldie et al. 1990). With his politicized histories and sermons, Burnet was hardly in the business of pouring oil on troubled waters. By the end of the decade, moreover, the kind of political and public fame increasingly enjoyed by Burnet was also dangerous, even fatal. On the one hand, from the 'Great Fire' (1666) to the 'cabal' at Whitehall in the 1670s to the 'Popish Plot' (1678–81), the public was gripped by fears of conspiracies apparently intending to introduce popery, slavery, and arbitrary government (Knights 1994). On the other hand, with the allegations of Titus Oates about the Popish Plot, a tactic of what might be called judicial murder was instigated by Anthony Ashley-Cooper, the first Earl of Shaftesbury, to try Catholic suspects for treason. The immediate result was at least twenty-two political executions—the last body of Catholic martyrs in English history—and a groundswell of opinion for excluding the Catholic James from the throne. By 1683, however, the focus of accusation had shifted, with the same persecutory tactics now deployed by Stuart loyalists and 'Tories' to attack those campaigning to exclude James and 'Whigs' (as the parties became known). In particular, allegations of a 'Rye House Plot' in the summer of 1683 eventually led to thirteen violent deaths by law and numerous incarcerations and exiles.

The Rye House Plot was an alleged plan to assassinate the Stuart brothers on their return to London from Newmarket races and to install the Duke of Monmouth, the king's illegitimate but Protestant son, on the throne. In the trials for treason that followed, Burnet lost 'the two best friends I had in the world'—William Lord Russell (executed) and Arthur Capel, Earl of Essex (suicide) (Airy 1900: 372, 288). Indeed, when news of 'that unhappy matter broke [...] those who knew in what friendship I had lived with them did all expect to see me clapped up' (Foxcroft 1902: 488). The involvement of Burnet and his friends in the bloody saga provided the immediate context for his translation of *Utopia*. This is true emotionally, in terms of how the fatal maltreatment of Capel and Russell (as Burnet and other Whigs viewed it) affected Burnet; practically, in terms of what Burnet felt safe to publish in the light of the executions; and politically, in terms of the ways in which More's text was a timely and resonant contribution to current political and confessional debates.

That Burnet was affected by the treatment of his 'two best friends' is apparent simply from the disproportionate amount of space he gives it in his memoirs of Restoration and post-Revolutionary politics. In what became a touchstone of Whig historiography, the Rye House Plot warranted as many as thirty-six pages (including editors' footnotes), with eighteen pages detailing the imprisonment, trial, and execution of Russell (Airy 1900: 349–386, 368–386). This compares, in contrast, to only nineteen pages devoted to the climactic illness, death, and assessment of Charles II (whom Burnet likened to the Roman tyrant Tiberius temperamentally, physically, and as a ruler who at 'the end of his life [...] became cruel') (470, 455–474). Burnet was aware of indulging his memory of Russell, 'that great and good man: on which I have perhaps enlarged too copiously: but the great esteem I had for him, and the share I had in this matter, will, I hope, excuse it' (384). Burnet's memoir accordingly contributed to the story of Russell's martyrdom. However, it also reflected the trauma of not simply losing a friend but also acting, along with Tillotson, as Russell's confidant and confessor in the days before his execution. In the published memoir, Russell's behaviour is as mannered and controlled as Burnet's studied 'stile' (382–383). But in the account Burnet kept for the 'private use' of Russell's wife, Lady Rachel Russell, there was, as Burnet put it, less 'choice of words or exactness of method' (Chatsworth R/1/5). Burnet instead described more intimate and affecting moments: how Russell 'entered upon the seriousest discourses I ever heard' about death and dying (1b); how Russell claimed to be glad not to have fled 'for he could not live from his wife and children and friends, that was all the happiness he saw in life' (2a); how talk of his wife 'saw his heart so near failing him' that 'sometimes I saw a tear in his eye and he would turn about and presently change the discourse'; how his final dinner was followed by 'long and pleasant discourse of his two daughters' (2b–c). The pathos is palpable. Burnet worried that 'when he saw us that were about him not able to contain our grief though we did what we could that he who was so tender himselfe was not by that more softened' (2c). He remembered Russell fumbling with his watch as he promised it to Burnet: 'the ring in which the ribbon goes broke in his hands which he thought a little strange' (3a).

Russell was executed at Lincoln's Inn Fields on 31 July 1683. Thereafter, Burnet's 'private' grief combined with anger at the political 'heat' that had led to Russell's death and the real fear that he would be next on the scaffold (Foxcroft 1902: 488). According to Burnet, he and Tillotson were interrogated by the Stuart brothers about their contribution to Russell's published speech, and Burnet was pilloried by loyalist pamphleteers in the press (Burnet 1683; Airy 1900: 384–386). So deep were the suspicions that Burnet was on the verge of publishing the private narrative written for Lady Russell in order to reveal the 'truth' of Russell's 'behaviour after his sentence and his execution'—written 'nakedly and without any Artifice'—when he was 'advised by all my friends to write no answer, but to bear the malice that was vented upon me with silence; which I resolved to do' (Chatsworth R/1/5; Airy 1900: 386). Instead, he 'built a Laboratory and for above a year I run thro some courses of Chemistry which helped me in my Philosophical notions, was a pleasant amusement to me and furnished me with a good excuse for staying much at home' (Foxcroft 1902: 489). And it was at this point that he translated and published *Utopia* (514).

The Problem of 'Heat'

Burnet's *Utopia* was first published in 1684 by Richard Chiswell and sold at the Rose and Crown in St Paul's Churchyard. Chiswell reissued the book twice in 1685, both times to be sold by George Powell 'over against Lincoln's Inn Gate in Chancery Lane'. Comparison of the three texts—copies of which are all held at the British Library—point to the publication of one edition, based on a single print-run, rather than three new editions of the book. Although each issue has a different title page, the typesetting and pagination are identical for each, although in RB.23.a.3170 the '1' on page 190 has slipped during printing.[6] Whereas previous editions of Robinson's English translation had embedded the name of the island in a longer clause, such as *A most pleasant, fruitful, and wittie worke, of the best state of a publique weale, and of the new yle called Utopia* (1556 and 1597) or *The common-wealth of Utopia* (1639), Chiswell now led with a bold and capitalized 'UTOPIA' followed by 'written in Latin by SIR THOMAS MORE, CHANCELLOR OF ENGLAND: Translated into English'. This focus on Utopia and More was accentuated by the fact that the translator of all three issues was anonymous. Indeed, it is unclear how well known Burnet's involvement with the translation would have been, though eighteenth-century editions that used the text attributed the translation to Burnet, and one subsequent owner of the 1684 book noted 'This book was translated by Dr Gilbert Burnet afterwards Bishop of Salisbury' (BL 1472.aa.46). Anonymity protected Burnet politically, but it also indicates that *Utopia* was a recognized 'brand' by the late seventeenth century. Chiswell was one of the most entrepreneurial and successful bookmen of the era, pioneering wholesale merchandising and developing transatlantic markets (Armory 2004). He had already helped turn Burnet's *Reformation* into a bestseller, commissioning new editions and more accessible 'abridged' versions after the first volume appeared in 1679, and clearly felt *Utopia* to be a viable commercial enterprise. He also retained a network of scholarly clerical authors in the Latitudinarian vein. Powell, the bookseller, is a more elusive, with the handful of titles associated with him limited to 1685 and 1686.[7]

Frustratingly, Burnet never explains which Latin edition he used as his source text.[8] He nevertheless made clear the practical reasons for turning to translation in his 'Preface'. On the one hand, the scholarship required was a form of self-censorship and authorial policing in a time of acute personal and public danger. As he put it:

> When a Man writes his own Thoughts, the heat of his Fancy, and the quickness of his Mind, carry him so much after the Notions themselves, that for the most part he is too warm to judg of the aptness of Words, and the justness of Figures; so that he either neglects these too much, or overdoes them: But when a Man translates, he has none of these Heats about him. (More 1684: A3r–v)

On the other hand, the content of the text could hardly be blamed on the translator:

> For as the Translators of *Plutarch's Hero's*, or of *Tullies Offices*, are not concerned, in either the Maxims, or in the Actions that they relate; so I, who only tell, in the best English I can, what *Sir Thomas More* writ in very Elegant Latin, must leave his Thoughts and Notions to the Reader's censure, and do think myself liable for nothing but the fidelity of the Translation. (A7v–8r)

---

[6] The BL copies are *Utopia* (1684), Wing M2691 (BL shelf mark 1476.b.34]; *Utopia* (1685), Wing M2692 (BL shelf mark RB.23.a.31730); *Utopia* (1685), not in Wing catalogue (BL shelf mark 1472.aa.46].

[7] It is intriguing that the last titles sold by George Powell the bookseller, in 1686, coincide with the start of the career of the celebrated Restoration actor George Powell (Backscheider 2004).

[8] The Latin text used in this chapter is More 1895a, based on the first and second Latin editions.

As importantly, Burnet held More in the same kind of esteem that he held Russell (and quite possibly himself): as 'one of the greatest Men that this Island has produced' (A5v). In *Reformation*, Burnet distinguished between the older More who opposed and persecuted English reformers and the 'youth' who 'had freer thoughts of things, as appears by his *Utopia*, and his Letters to *Erasmus*' (Burnet 1679: 2Y1r). The younger More should be respected for his 'probity and learning' as well as 'justice, contempt of money, humility, and a true generosity of mind' (2Y1v). Burnet also noted that, just as Russell was undone by a modern-day Tiberius, so More suffered 'cruel proceedings' at the whim of 'so ill a man, and so cruel a Prince' (C2r). In this rendering, More was not a Catholic martyr so much as the victim of tyranny. Russell likewise died for 'an opinion, that a Free nation, like this might Defend their Religion, & Liberties, when invaded & taken from them, tho under pretence & colour of Law'; More 'only for denying [Henry VIII's] Supremacy' (Chatsworth, R/1/3, 2; Burnet 1679: C2r). Who better, then, to unleash on the Restoration public than More, one of the 'Glories of his Nation' (C2v)?

The 'freer thoughts' of More meant nothing, of course, unless they spoke to the present. Burnet accordingly explained that *Utopia*

> seemed to me contain so many fine and well-digested Notions, that I thought it might be no unkind nor ill entertainment to the Nation, to put a Book in their Hands, to which they have so good a Title, and which has a very common fate upon it, to be more known and admired all the World over, than here at Home. (More 1684: A5v–A6r)

Burnet was explicit—perhaps dangerously so—about at least one lesson to be learned from the volume, advising that the 'tenderest part of the whole Work, was the representation he gives of *Henry* the Seventh's Court' as a place of wise counsel and good government (A7r). Referring to the dialogue of counsel in the first book of *Utopia*, Burnet thought it particularly telling that when More

> ventured to write so freely of the Father in the Son's reign, and to give such an *Idea* of Government under the haughtiest Prince [Henry VIII], and the most impatient of uneasy Restraints that ever reigned in *England*, who yet was so far from being displeased with him for it, that as he made him long his particular Friend, so he employed him in all his Affairs afterwards, and raised him to be L. Chancellor. (A7v)

Burnet even here glossed over Henry's subsequent tyranny to suggest his receptiveness to good counsel: a point clearly aimed at Charles II.

A second, more submerged resonance of *Utopia* was the capacity of its citizens to avoid 'heat' in their public and religious affairs. The concept of 'heat'—whereby human or social bodies acted on sensory and emotional impulses rather than reason—was an important political trope for Burnet and, indeed, his friends (Foxcroft 1902: 473). In his memoirs, for example, he typically noted that, just as the Popish Plot and 'exclusion crisis' made it clear 'how mad and fatal a thing it is to run violently into a torrent, and in a heat to do those things which may give a general disgust', so the loyalist reaction in support of James 'shewed how little men could build on popular heats, which have their ebbings and flowings, and their hot and cold fits, almost as constantly as seas or fevers have' (Airy 1900: 287). Likewise, in his dying speech Russell used 'heat' repeatedly: he implored all 'sincere Protestants' to 'lay aside their Heats, and agree against the Common Enemy' (Russell 1683: 2); he admitted that at the meeting for which he was to be executed, 'there were things said by some with much more Heat, than Judgement, which I did sufficiently disapprove' (3); he reassured the crowd that, since the very start of the legal process against him, he knew that 'the Heat in that Matter would produce something of this kind' (4); and so on.

In Burnet's translation of *Utopia*, the problem of heat was addressed directly: indeed, Burnet deliberately inserted the term in places that Robinson had not used it. The narrator Hythloday described, for example, how the Utopians were so judicious that neighbouring countries employed them as their magistrates 'for their own happiness and safety'. This was because Utopians 'being strangers among them, *are not engaged in any of their Heats or Animosities*: And it is certain, that when Public Judicatories are swayed, either by partial Affections, or by Avarice, there must follow upon it a dissolution of all Justice, which is the chief Sinew of Society' (More 1684: L8r; emphasis added). Robinson had used the construction 'nor yet be moved other with favour, or malyce towardes annye man' (More 1551: O3r). Likewise, Restoration readers would have learned that 'one of their [Utopian] ancientest Laws, [is] that no Man ought to be punished for his Religion (More 1684: N4v–5r). Rather 'every Man might be of what Religion he pleased, and might endeavour to draw others to it by the force of Argument, and by amicable and modest ways, but without bitterness against those of other Opinions' (N5r). It was explained that 'This Law was made by *Utopus*, not only for preserving the Publick Peace, which he saw suffered much by *daily Contentions and Irreconcilable Heats* in these Matters, but because he thought the Interest of Religion it self required it' (emphasis added). It transpired that while Hythloday was in Utopia, only one man was punished for breaking this 'ancientist' of laws. Perhaps unsurprisingly, it was a convert to Christianity: 'He being newly baptized, did [...] dispute publickly concerning the Christian Religion, with more zeal than discretion; *and with so much heat, that he not only preferred our Worship to theirs, but condemned all their Rites as profane*' (N4v; emphasis added). Punishment followed not because he 'disparaged their Religion, but for his inflaming the People to Sedition'. The irony would not have been lost on Burnet's readers, especially those of a Latitudinarian bent.

Burnet's other publications at this time also dealt with the problem of belligerent, uncivil, and potentially tyrannous Christians: Catholics in particular, but also Protestants. His biography of William Bedell, the scholarly and tolerant bishop of Kilmore who died during the Irish Rebellion of 1641, contributed to a lineage of compassionate and 'modest' Episcopalians with the right 'spirit and temper' to exert 'pastoral care', encourage the 'reformation of abuses', and 'discourse' with all denominations without raising 'Heats and Disputes' (Burnet 1685b: A6v–7r). Burnet's sermon for 5 November 1684 (the anniversary of the 1605 Gunpowder Plot) formulaically warned against the

'Church of *Rome* [...] as a Lion going about seeking how to devour all that differ from it' (Burnet 1684: B1r). But he also suggested 'that the late Rebellion [against Charles I] was managed with a Popish, that is Bloody Spirit', giving 'scope to Passion and Rage, to Jealousy and Mistrust' (D2r–v). Popery was 'a bloody Conspiracy against the Souls and Bodies of men'—'a Tyranny upon the tenderest Part of our Natures, our Reason'—but in opposing it, men should not fall into the trap of imitating its cruelties and 'Persecuting Spirit' (D3r, B1v, D1v). Viewed in these terms, the lessons of Utopian society, like the lessons of Henry VII's court, were salutary.

The Language of Slavery

Burnet translated *Utopia* because its exemplar of counsel and moderation was timely and because, at a moment of such public 'heat' and danger, it was safer and possibly more authoritative to use the voice of More than his own. Having outlined the context for translation, it is now time to consider the effect of Burnet's ventriloquism on the vernacular transcript of *Utopia*: how, in looking to convert More's 'Elegant' Latin with 'fidelity' into 'Modern' English, Burnet also produced a text that was significantly different from Robinson's translations of the 1550s (More 1685: A8r, A7v). Elsewhere I have shown that Burnet single-handedly turned More's text into a book about 'happiness', using the term nineteen times when Robinson never used it at all (Withington 2017: 23). Here we can focus on another important Utopian concept—'slavery'—and ask why the word 'slave' appears as many as twenty-six times in the 1684 edition of *Utopia* compared to only twice in the editions translated in 1551 and 1556.

The first point to note is that Burnet's linguistic choices were never accidental: he was a careful translator who was familiar with the contemporary scholarship on language and lexicology and self-conscious of his role in the modernization of English. In his 'Preface' to *Utopia*, for example, he compared the rigorous French 'Method' to 'reform and beautify their Language' with the more ramshackle and incidental development of English (More 1684: A3v). Whereas French regimes had long ago set 'their best Writers on Work to translate the Greek and Latin Authors into it', the English, according to Burnet, had lurched from one generation of flawed literature to another: from the 'fulsome Pedantry under which it laboured long ago' to the 'trifling way of dark and unintelligible Wit that came after that' to the 'extravagance of Canting that succeeded this' (A3v–4r). The possibility of 'a sublime pitch' (known today as the Elizabethan and Jacobean Renaissance) was diverted into a 'strong but false Rhetorick' by the twin 'places' of 'the Stage' and 'the Pulpit': two predominant genres from which 'the Rule and Measure of Speech is generally taken'. More recently, however, even 'that florid strain is almost worn out, and is become now as ridiculous as it was once admired' (A4r). Despite Burnet's political suspicions of Charles II (as published after Charles's death), in 1684 he nevertheless accorded his monarch significant and constructive cultural power: Charles II 'is so great a Judg, that his single approbation or dislike has almost as great an Authority over our Language, as his Prerogative gives him over the Coin' (A5r).[9] As a consequence, 'our Language has, like a rich Wine, wrought out its Tartar, and is insensibly brought to a Purity', but without 'the Expense and Labour that the French have undergone' (A4v-5r).

One example of this was that although 'the present Masters of the Stage [...] all acknowledge that they come far short of *B. Jonson, Fletcher and Beaumont* [...] Their Language is now certainly properer, and more natural than it was formerly' (A5r). Modernizing the English *Utopia* anew was another opportunity to demonstrate linguistic and literary progress. For help, Burnet could consult with writerly friends like Lloyd and Tillotson and also draw on the semantic and stylistic precepts outlined in Wilkins's *Essay Towards a Real Character and a Philosophical Language*, the methodology—as noted above—that Burnet attributed to his 'reputation' as a stylish writer. Published for the Royal Society in 1668, Wilkins's *Essay* had a threefold agenda: to provide tables of definitions of words and their synonyms that corresponded to the phenomena—conceptual or substantive—they described (Wilkins 1668: A2r, B2v); to establish a '*Natural Grammar*, as might be suited to the Philosophy of Speech, abstracting from those many unnecessary rules belonging to instituted Language' (B2v); and to encourage the development of a lingua franca that would enable transnational 'conversing' or '*Commerce*' (A2v-B1v). Wilkins positioned his approach in the tradition of Renaissance lexicology and linguistic reform, encouraging the Royal Society to compete with the 'Dictionary Making' of other 'famous Assemblies consisting of the great Wits of their *Age* and *Nations*'—in particular the 'Academies' in Italy and France (A2r). While particularly concerned with English semantics, Wilkins also strove to understand 'the *Universal Character*' of linguistic organization in at least three respects (B2r): that there was a single order of knowledge to be represented through recognized words and synonyms in any particular vernacular; that for any vernacular there were general rules of language to facilitate 'philosophical' communication in speech and writing; and that there might ultimately emerge a single transnational language that would enable different speakers properly to understand each other. In each instance, the 'reduction' of language to absolutes would rid the modern world of the conflicts, confusions, and obfuscations that stemmed either from the wilful manipulation and misuse of language or, in the long term, the problem of miscomprehension due to the 'vast multitude of Languages that are in the world' (B1r).

The result was a complicated book that was part historical linguistics, part grammar, part experiment, part encyclopedia, and part English dictionary and thesaurus. That Burnet was a devotee of the *Essay* helps explain with unusual certainty his preference for the language of 'slave'. In the lexicological tables designed by Wilkins, 'slave' appears as either the 'head term' or main antonym of a number of semantic clusters under the broad heading of 'Civil Relations': 'That Relation arising from the associating of Families under Government for mutual benefit and defence' (Wilkins 1668: 2L4r).

---

[9] Burnet refers to John Dryden, *Of Dramatic Poesie, an Essay* (1668).

Most importantly, 'slave' sat at the very bottom of the sociopolitical structure sketched by Wilkins, below the '*Lower* sort; considered *Aggregately*' (levels 7 and 8), as part of the '*Conditions of men; as having a right to dispose of themselves: or not*' (level 9). Here it headed a list of words that constituted the antithesis ('or *not*'): '*SLAVE, emancipate, manumit, servile, illiberal, Bondman, Bondage, Thraldom, enthrall, enslave, serve, Droyl, Drudge*' (2L4v). Thereafter 'Slave' and 'Enslave' were given as the antonyms of 'Free' and 'Enfranchize' (2V1r) and the terminology also featured in a set of vocabularies that included 'Remedying' ('Un-captivate, Un-slave, Un-imprison; [antonym] Parturition', 3E1r); 'Emancipate' ('Un-slave', 3F1r); 'Enthrall' and 'Inthrall' ('Slave (make)', 3F1v, 3I3v); 'Patron, of *Dependent*' ('*of Slave*, (Master)', 3L4v); 'Ransom' ('Price for un-slaving', 3N2r]; and 'Redeem' ('Buy liberty [...] Un-captivate [...] Un-slave', 3N3r). It also had a complicated position in vocabularies based around 'Serve'. It was distinct from 'Servant' and 'Souldier'; was the antonym of hired work; and was given as the exemplar of 'subjection' (3O4v). It also fitted into vocabularies of '*Servile*' ('Servant [...] Slave [...] Villain') and 'Servitude' ('Slave (thing)'). In contrast to the ubiquity of 'slave', medieval synonyms like 'Bondman' and 'Thrall' were listed only once, as freestanding words, and, even then, were defined for the reader as 'Slave' (3B3r, 3R2r).

With 'slave' such a dominant English term for types of unfreedom, it is hardly surprising that Burnet used it so extensively—and exclusively—in his translation. But as Table 18.1 shows, this was not the case for Robinson in the 1550s, who instead used 'serving man' where Burnet used 'slave' in Book One (in the historical discussions of government and society set in England) and 'bondman' instead of 'slave' in Book Two (in the descriptions of Utopian society). Robinson never stated his linguistic and literary influences explicitly, though Jennifer Bishop (2011) has recovered his close involvement with a network of reforming London citizens based around the Goldsmiths' Company (to which Robinson became clerk in 1556) at the time he wrote *Utopia*. Nor did he have the kind of linguistic and lexicological resource available to Burnet. But there is enough

Table 18.1 Comparative Uses of 'Slave' and Synonyms in Early English Translations of *Utopia*

Word	1551 edition	1639 edition	1684 edition
Slave	2	2	26
Slavery	1	1	10
Bondman	17	19	0
Bondage	14	14	0
Serving man	14	15	0
Varlet	0	0	1

Sources: More 1551, More 1639 (based on Robinson's 1556 translation, but the edition closest to Burnet's translation), and More 1684.

circumstantial evidence to show that while 'slave' was certainly available for Robinson to use, it had not yet achieved vernacular pre-eminence. In the nearest equivalent to Wilkins's *Essay*, Thomas Elyot's hugely influential Latin–English *Dictionary*, it was 'bondman' and 'bondage' (rather than slave and slavery) that translated *Servitia* and *Servitus*; and for other terms, such as *Serviliter* and *Dulia*, Elyot gave the words together (i.e. as 'bondman or slave') (Elyot 1538: Z4r, G1r). Likewise, Naomi Tadmor has shown that in William Tyndale's English translation of the Bible—published in 1540 and most likely known by Robinson's London milieu—it was languages of 'service' and 'bondage' rather than 'slavery' that were used to translate Hebraic concepts of unfreedom (Tadmor 2010: 101). The 1547 'Slavery Act'—which explicitly threatened to make 'slaves' of 'vagabonds' who either refused work or who ran away from work—had to be repealed in the subsequent parliament (1550), in part because the language of 'slave' was so incongruent (Davies 1966). During the uprisings and rebellion of 1549, rebels declared against the vestiges of feudal unfreedom through the language of 'bondmen' rather than slave (Whittle 2010: 24). And, perhaps most tellingly, when another member of the Goldsmiths' Company, Thomas Nicholls, undertook to translate Thucydides' *History* in 1550, like Robinson he preferred 'bondman' over 'slave'.

As Wilkins's comprehensive survey of English semantics suggests, between the 1550s and 1660s 'slave' eclipsed 'bondman' and 'serving man' as the English term for unfreedom. A preliminary survey of EEBO-TCP shows that as late as the 1530s 'bondman' appears more frequently in printed texts than 'slave', but by the 1550s 'slave' accounts for 70 per cent of descriptors of unfreedom, rising to 90 per cent by the 1620s.[10] When Thomas Hobbes looked to replace Nicholls's translation of Thucydides' *History* with his own—*Eight Books of the Peloponnesian War* (1629)—it is no coincidence that his term of choice was 'slave' rather than 'bondman'. Although there is no space here to explain this semantic transformation, what can be noted is its effect on More's Englished text. In Burnet's translation, 'slave' conflates a range of sociopolitical conditions as inherently and similarly unfree: convicted felons set to public and private labour; counsellors to princes who are servile rather than independent with their advice; and citizens of realms beyond Utopia who have either been captured in war or volunteered themselves into slavery and now serve in Utopian households.

In each instance, Burnet is consistent in following the original Latin of More. Robinson, in contrast, is much more creative in his translation: not only does he use 'serving man'—rather than slave—to describe enslaved felons (*servi*); controversially, 'serving man' also describes the idle retainers and dependents of lords who contribute nothing of value to the commonwealth (Burnet refers to them as 'idle Fellows' and 'idle Gentlemen') (More 1684: C5r, C6v). 'Bondman', in the meantime, defines the condition of servile counsellors and ordinary household slaves, but in using that term, Robinson omits one of More's best Latin puns. This is at the beginning of the 'tender'

---

[10] Figures based on a survey of EEBO-TCP in February 2019.

section on counsel to which Burnet directed readers in his Preface. As Burnet translates it, Hythloday asserts

> I think my Friends ought to rest contented with this, and not to expect that for their sakes I should enslave my self to any King whatsoever. Soft and fair, said *Peter*, I do not mean that you should be a Slave [*servio*] to any King, but only that you should assist them [*inservio*], and be useful to them [friends and kinfolk]. The change of the Word, said [Hythloday], does not alter the Matter. (More 1684: C2r)

Robinson had written:

> I think [my friends …] owghte to hold them contentyd and not to requyre nor to looke that […] I shoulde […] gyve my selfe in bondage to kynges. Naye god forbedde (quod peter) it is not my mynd you shoulde be in bondage to kynges, but as a retaynoure to them at youre pleasure whyche sewrelye I thynke is the nygheste waye that you can devyse howe to bestowe youre tyme fruitfully. (More 1551: B7v–8r)

As a result, Hythloday's pessimistic view that all political service involves slavery is elided by Robinson. Finally, when Robinson occasionally does use the term 'slave', it is to describe utter servility rather than a specific legal status, as in 'the most vile slave and abject drevell of all in [a master's] housholde' (translating More's *nebulonum*, 'idler') (L2v); which Burnet more accurately describes as the 'meanest Varlet' (More 1684: I3r).

These semantic decisions inevitably changed the place, tenor, and role of servility in *Utopia*. Robinson differentiated between two kinds of unfreedom—the service of idle gentlemen and convicted felons (serving men) and within royal courts and private households (bondmen)—and reserved 'slave' to describe the most extreme forms of abasement, whether experienced by a legally defined 'slave' or not. Burnet did not share these qualms about the word 'slave'; nor did he distinguish between different kinds of *servus* or conflate gentlemen retainers with convicted thieves. Instead, he adhered to the semantic precepts outlined by Wilkins and used the hegemonic term for unfreedom in order to follow the Latin.

The result was a more accurate reproduction of the topography of *servus* sketched by More. It also meant that whereas Robinson mostly delimited 'bondman' to the Utopian imaginary of Book Two, 'slave' in 1684 transected the two books, Burnet embedding it in 'the tenderest parts of the whole work': the discussions of 'an *Idea* of Government' in Tudor England. In so doing, he made 'slavery' a historical as well as a Utopian possibility and probably expressed his own view of the concept. In other of his works printed before *Utopia*, for example, he linked the term pejoratively to the tyranny of overbearing monarchs and, in particular, papal imperium and enthralment: the slavery that Russell and Capel died opposing and which Hythloday associated with servile counsel (Burnet 1682: 185; 1685a: 28). But he also recognized the utility of slavery as a tool of punishment and reform, noting that while some thought the 1547 'Slavery Act' 'against Vagabonds was too severe, and contrary to that common liberty, of which the *English* Nation has been always very sensible [...] it could not be denied but extrem Diseases required extream Remedies'; that, 'perhaps there is no punishment too severe for Persons that are in health, and yet prefer a loitering course of life to an honest employment' (Burnet 1681: G2r).

Conclusion: Happiness and Slavery

Burnet's insertion of 'slave' into the text of Utopia reflected a long-term linguistic shift that was particularly resonant at the moment of translation. Indeed, in using advanced humanistic skills to translate a quintessential Renaissance text, Burnet articulated a defining—perhaps the defining—paradox of early Enlightenment culture. For the monied, propertied, and independent classes the imperative of freedom—political, religious, intellectual—made slavery abhorrent. But for the very same people the requirements of labour made slavery, or versions of it, a social and economic necessity. If this was true of England in the 1550s then it was even more so for the English Atlantic by the 1680s.

In retrospect, indeed, the 1680s was an important decade for slavery in the English-speaking world. In the face of persistent resistance from slaves, and with profits of the plantation economy paramount, the governing assembly in Jamaica passed the Slave Act in 1684 (the same year as Burnet's translation first appeared in print). Described by Edward Rugemer as 'the missing link in the history of early English slave law', and building on prior acts in Barbados and the Jamaican Servant Act (1681), the legislation codified the fundamental differences between white indentured servants (contracted to work for colonial masters for a specified number of years) and black slaves; established elaborate and vicious mechanisms for capturing and punishing slave runaways; and confirmed slaves as chattels that could be hired, bought, and sold like any other property (Rugemer 2013: 430, 449–450).[11] Subsequently adopted by colonists in South Carolina, it was a crucial plank in the legal scaffolding of the transatlantic slave economy for the next two hundred or so years. In the meantime, Thomas Tryon published his *Friendly Advice to the Gentlemen Planters of the East and West Indies* in three parts, two of which consisted of excoriating denunciations of the brutality, inhumanity, and hypocrisy of the slave economy and the racism that justified it. Articulating 'the Complaints of the Negro-Slaves' now experiencing 'this Apostacy from the Dignity of the Humane Nature' (Tryon 1684: F8v), Tryon railed against the perversion of 'Labour' into a 'perpetual Plague to destroy Nature, and make Life a Torment, and Death a Courtesy' (G4v). He concluded that the only possible differences by which Christians could legitimate such oppressions were colour and learning: the one a product of 'climate', the other of 'custom and education' (I4v–I5r). That is, that they were no justification at all.

---

[11] Thanks to Rosie Knight for this reference and discussions about slavery in early America.

Racist, capitalist, and pragmatic, the burgeoning political economy of transatlantic slavery was very different to the punitive, reformatory, and rational institution envisaged by More and Englished, in different ways, by Robinson and Burnet. Burnet's text had contemporary resonance all the same. This was true personally, in that many of his patrons, friends, clients, and associates were invested in colonial initiatives. It was also true ideologically, in that at least two of them, Ashley-Cooper and John Locke, were involved in drafting *The Fundamental Constitutions of Carolina* in 1669: a document that envisaged 'an idea' of the colony in the same way that *Utopia* elaborated an 'idea of Government'. The similarities were not merely generic. As in *Utopia*, two of the key features of *Fundamental Constitutions* were the valorization of consultative and participatory citizenship and its commitment both to avoiding political heat and securing Christian liberty by enforcing religious toleration and interconfessional civility (items 95 to 109). A third was that slavery be recognized as the joists of this civil and spiritual freedom. While slaves could join churches 'as fully members as any freeman [... still ...] Every freeman of Carolina shall have absolute power and authority over his negro slaves, of what opinion or religion soever' (item 110) (J. Locke 1997: 177–180). That is, *Fundamental Constitutions*, like Burnet's *Utopia*, was a text about freedom and unfreedom for the English-speaking Enlightenment. The only difference between the two was that while 'slavery' in Utopia punished idleness and criminality, in Carolina, like the Caribbean, it subjugated and expropriated black labour. As Thomas Jefferson would have read on the title page of his own copy of Burnet's translation, Utopia was a place designed for the happiness of its citizens: it was 'THE HAPPY REPUBLIC', no less (More 1743). But it was a happiness dependent on the enslavement of others.

CHAPTER 19

FROM HUMANISM TO ENLIGHTENMENT

Nicolas Gueudeville and His Translation of Thomas More's Utopia

FLORIS VERHAART

THE relative obscurity of the translator and publicist Nicolas Gueudeville (1652–1721?) in modern-day scholarship is such that even the author of the only book-length study about him—Aubrey Rosenberg—believed his life and work had a representative rather than an independent value. For Rosenberg, Gueudeville might have enjoyed some literary renown in his own days, but he had no lasting impact on the development of European thought in the long run; on the contrary, by looking at Gueudeville we can learn more about those insignificant Huguenot intellectuals who tried to scrape together a living with their knowledge of French and Latin in the Dutch Republic at the turn of the eighteenth century (Rosenberg 1982: 1–2). In recent years, Gueudeville's name has gained slightly more notoriety among students of the eighteenth century since Jonathan Israel devoted a couple of pages to him (Israel 2001: 579–580), discussing him as part of the 'progress of the radical enlightenment' during the period 1680–1750. Gueudeville's 'radicalism' was characterized by 'a strongly anti-monarchical republican attitude combined with implacable hostility to ecclesiastical power and revealed religion'. Yet at the same time, his ideas were very often conveyed with reference to earlier humanist and classical writings or even through translations and adaptations of such works, including Plautus' plays, Desiderius Erasmus' *Colloquies* and *Praise of Folly*, and Thomas More's *Utopia*—activities referred to by Israel in a single line: 'In later years, he spent much time working on translations of Erasmus' (580). This chapter will be devoted to Gueudeville's translation of More's *Utopia*, which was first published in 1715 in Leiden by Pieter van der Aa. In what follows, it will be explained how this translation fits within its translator's life and interests, as well as within the interests of the publisher. Finally, an analysis will be offered of the key characteristics of the translation itself.[1]

LIFE

Nicolas Gueudeville was born to a Catholic family in Rouen in 1652.[2] He grew up in very modest circumstances and his decision to join a Benedictine monastery not far from Rouen at Jumièges therefore seems to have been inspired at least as much by a desire for a stable future as by religious zeal. Monastic life did not agree with Gueudeville and his exposure to Protestant writings—Aubrey Rosenberg mentions Pierre Jurieu (1637–1713) in particular—seem to have brought about a religious crisis that made him turn his back on Catholicism (Rosenberg 1982: 4). According to Gueudeville's *Motifs de la conversion* (1689), in which he later explained his personal development from Catholicism to Protestantism, divine providence allowed him to meet a Protestant who helped him to complete his spiritual journey. He escaped from the monastery of Saint-Martin-de-Sées, to which he apparently had moved from Jumièges, and eventually managed to travel to safety in the United Provinces (or Dutch Republic). It should be remembered that the *Motifs* was addressed to Gueudeville's Reformed co-religionists. The Catholic Nicolas Lenglet Du Fresnoy later claimed that Gueudeville had once confided to him that he would have never moved to the United Provinces if it was not to escape the consequences of some 'roguery' (*friponnerie*) he had committed in France (Lenglet Du Fresnoy 1734: 1.176).

Unfortunately, we do not know what this mischief might have been and, whatever the exact circumstances of Gueudeville's departure or flight from France were, he made his way to Rotterdam in 1689 and on 18 July of that year he addressed the local congregation of the Reformed Church, into which he had been accepted. The text of his address was published as *Les Motifs de la conversion*. At the time of Gueudeville's arrival, there were tensions within the Protestant Refuge between Pierre Jurieu and Pierre Bayle (1647–1706) about the relationship of refugees with France and about the nature of religious toleration.[3] Jurieu believed that the Reformed were entitled to being tolerated simply because they were right—at least in Jurieu's view. This was the right of the justified conscience, which stood in opposition to the right of the erring conscience, the idea that even someone whose religious views were wrong should be tolerated. That was the view taken by Bayle (van der Lugt 2016: 71). Gueudeville sided with Bayle, which foreshadows the inclusive conception of toleration that he would defend in his writings. In the years

---

[1] References to Gueudeville's translation are from the first edition (Leiden, 1715); translations from French are my own.
[2] A fuller account of Gueudeville's life can be found in Rosenberg 1982: 3–10.
[3] For more on Bayle, see van Bunge in this volume.

following his arrival in the United Provinces, he made a living by teaching Latin and keeping lodgers and got married in 1691.

From the late 1690s, Gueudeville also embarked on a writing career which covered a substantial range of genres and types of publications. The first of these are works of journalism, such as *L'Esprit des Cours de l'Europe*, a periodical which appeared from 1699 until 1710 and in which Gueudeville discussed the latest news—and gossip— from across Europe. It was so critical of Louis XIV's France that it became the object of a diplomatic row between the Dutch Republic and France (Rosenberg 1982: 7). The second category consists of works on geographical topics. Gueudeville was the editor of and contributor to the works of Louis-Armand de Lom d'Arce, baron de Lahontan (1666–before 1716), giving them a particular philosophical twist, as we will see below. He also supplied parts of the text of an *Atlas historique* (1705–20) and the *Nouveau Théâtre du monde* (1713). Next are works of literary criticism, the main example of which is Gueudeville's *Critique générale des Avantures de Télémaque* (1700), a discussion of François Fénelon's (1651–1715) novel of the same name.[4] Gueudeville criticized the literary aspects of the *Télémaque*, but agreed with much of its veiled criticism of Louis XIV's government. In fact, he used Fénelon's work as the starting point for a scathing attack on French absolutism. Fourth are works of a moral and satirical nature, including the anonymous *Dialogues des morts d'un tour nouveau* (1709), inspired by the *Dialogues of the Dead* written by the second-century sophist Lucian of Samosata. In the final category, we find translations of several works from the Renaissance and classical antiquity: Erasmus' *Praise of Folly* and *Colloquies* in 1713 and 1720 respectively, More's *Utopia* (1715), and plays by Plautus (1719). Although at first sight the sheer variety of different types of publications may stand out, all of these works share Gueudeville's characteristic style, interests, and points of view.

Throughout his life, Gueudeville struggled to make ends meet. In fact, some other members of the Protestant French community linked his financial difficulties with his allegedly immoral behaviour. After Gueudeville's death—allegedly from alcohol abuse—Jean Le Clerc, a professor at the Remonstrant Seminary in Amsterdam and the man behind several scholarly journals, believed people like Gueudeville gave Protestants a bad name:

> He died in the same way as he had lived, just like Gabillon, another former monk, who was no better than he was. I believed it was necessary to mention that on this occasion [...] to make sure that people do not think this kind of person is highly rated among Protestants.[5]

---

[4] For more on Fénelon's utopian novel, see Hill and Pohl in this volume.

[5] 'Il est mort à peu près, comme il avoit vêcu, aussi bien que Gabillon, autre Moine défroqué, qui ne valoit pas mieux que lui. J'ai crû devoir dire cela [...] afin qu'on ne crût pas que cette sorte de gens est fort approuvée, parmi les Protestans' (Le Clerc 1724: 222). Frédéric-Auguste Gabillon (*fl.* 1700) was a former monk who like Gueudeville had considerable financial difficulties. He became particularly notorious in Europe for travelling through England while pretending to be Le Clerc, so that he could benefit from the hospitality of people who thought they were hosting the famous scholar (Grafton 2001: 156–157).

It seems fair to say therefore that Gueudeville was a controversial figure. In the following sections it will become apparent why.

Works and Ideas

Gueudeville's ideas and interests relate to four fields: politics, religion, morality, and geography. Regarding politics and religion, it will not come as a surprise that he felt a strong dislike towards Louis XIV and his Catholic fervour which had led, in October 1685, to the Edict of Fontainebleau (also known as the Revocation of the Edict of Nantes, which in 1598 had granted French Protestants, Huguenots, the right to practise their religion in France without interference from the state). Gueudeville's aversion to the Sun King was mostly inspired by Louis's absolutism, in contrast to the English system in which the king's powers were subject to checks and balances, or the republican system of the United Provinces (Yardeni 1972: 603). The system created by Louis XIV was unprecedented (*trop nouvelle*) and with noticeable irony Gueudeville remarked that the way in which this monarch reigned was so 'extraordinary' (*extraordinaire*) that there was no need to 'fear that its memory might perish' ('avoir lieu de craindre que la mémoire en périsse jamais') (*L'Esprit des Cours de l'Europe* 1699–1710: 1.34 [June–Dec. 1699]). He used the well-known metaphor of the state as a body. In this case the body may look healthy on the outside, but is very weak on the inside, while the head (Louis XIV) can do as it wants (*L'Esprit* 1699–1710: 4.144 [Jan.–Apr. 1701]). The only way to change the situation was to live in accordance with reason (*raison*), for then the French would see that it was not in their interest to have the most splendid king in the world while the rest of the country was living in misery (*L'Esprit* 1699–1710: 12.405 [Jan.–June 1705]). The emphasis on reason and a focus on the common rather than the individual interest form a link across the works and thinking of Gueudeville.

Gueudeville believed that France's eagerly hoped-for defeat in the War of the Spanish Succession (1701–14) would trigger the insight among the French that they suffered merely for the illusions of one man (*L'Esprit* 1699–1710: 11.637–638 [July–Dec. 1704]). This brings us to another reason for the feelings of hostility towards the Sun King. Louis XIV was also the most daunting European enemy of Gueudeville's adopted home country. Although Gueudeville paid lip service to impartiality in his accounts of the political developments, he saw no problem in explicitly stating that all his sympathy lay with the Dutch (*L'Esprit* 1699–1710: 9.193 [July–Dec. 1703]). His periodical even created a diplomatic incident between the United Provinces and France. The cause was a deeply sarcastic passage in *L'Esprit des Cours* published in the April issue of 1701 on the capitation or 'head tax', which had been reintroduced by Louis XIV in order to finance the War of the Spanish Succession (see McCollim 2012: 37–44). Gueudeville printed the declaration that announced this measure (*L'Esprit* 1699–1710: 4.373–390) followed by his own commentary (4.390–412). With barely concealed irony he remarks how very kind the king has been to tell his subjects that he is in financial trouble and that they must show him that he has a place 'in their wallet as much as in their heart' (4.391–392). He makes a mock comparison between the French kings of the past and Louis XIV. Under Louis's predecessors, the people were richer, 'but how much does the fatness of the people matter compared to the glory of the king' ('qu'est ce que la graisse du peuple en comparaison de la gloire du Roi', 4.392). Not only is this ironic account of the capitation a fitting example of Gueudeville's obsession with Louis XIV and the need to prioritize the prosperity of the collective interest of the people of a country over its king; it is also typical of his approach of criticizing through parody.

Seeing such words as an affront to his country, the French ambassador, Jean-Antoine de Mesmes, comte d'Avaux, turned to the States General (the Dutch legislature) to ask for the suppression of the periodical, while trying to minimize publicity as this might harm French prestige (Rosenberg 1982: 18–19). In a letter from May 1701, d'Avaux claimed that Anthonie Heinsius, Grand Pensionary (the most important official in the United Provinces) had granted the request, but Gueudeville's periodical simply continued to be published under a different name: *Nouvelles des cours de l'Europe*.

Although the journalist Gueudeville also claimed to write about religion without bias, his anti-Catholicism is apparent in many of his works:

> The author will engage in religious matters least of all and is content to keep it a secret which one he thinks is the best and in which one he wants to live and die. He will not touch upon the religion of others and will do justice to all those who follow their conscience.[6]

Theological arguments for his Reformed beliefs are most easily found in the aforementioned *Motifs de la conversion* and include both an eager acceptance of *sola scriptura* (which held that Scripture was the only authority for Christian doctrine and practice) and a rejection of the idea that good deeds contribute to salvation (Rosenberg 1982: 12–13). The most notable aspect of Gueudeville's anti-Catholicism is his anticlericalism. An example is his account in his *Esprit des cours* for August 1705 of how the canons of the cathedral of Urbino were given a raise in income by Pope Clement XI. Gueudeville mocks the worldliness of these clergymen—'a good fat canon is a worthy object of generosity'—and quotes a passage from Juvenal's *Satire* 7.59–65 on poverty (*L'Esprit* 1699–1710: 13.139–142 [July–Dec. 1705]). Such a critique of the clergy is evident in More's *Utopia* in the original, but as will become apparent below, Gueudeville expanded it in his translation.

Gueudeville's citation of Juvenal is also an example of another important aspect of his works and way of thinking: he was steeped in classical and humanist culture and his writings are scattered with references to and quotations from Latin authors both from

---

[6] 'La Religion est la chose dont il se mêlera le moins, content de renfermer dans son Coeur celle qu'il croit la meilleure, & dans laquelle il veut vivre & mourir; il ne touchera point à celle des autres, & il rendra justice à tous ceux qui suivent les mouvemens de la conscience' (*L'Esprit des Cours* 1699–1710: 1.246).

antiquity and from the Renaissance. In *L'Esprit des Cours* for May 1700, Gueudeville quotes an epigram by the Florentine humanist Angelo Poliziano (1454–94): 'Marsilio hears the mass and you, Domizio, dismiss it. Who could doubt which of the two is more religious? You are so much more religious as it is less to hear good things than to do them.'[7] As Gueudeville explains, these lines are an epigram which Poliziano (aka Politien) wrote for his fellow humanist Domizio Calderini (1446–1478).[8] Calderini was a professor in Rome under popes Paul II and Sixtus IV and was notoriously indifferent to religion. Pressed by his friends, he went to mass, but said that he was going to see the 'common error' (see Vives 1543: 119).

Poliziano's epigram draws a contrast between those who hear the mass and those who only go half-heartedly, and hinges on the different meanings of *facere*, since *missam facere* does not mean 'to celebrate mass' (that would be *missam celebrare*) but 'to dismiss'. In the final line of the poem, *bona facere* simply means 'to do good deeds', which is, of course, better than merely hearing about good deeds. Gueudeville quotes this poem with an eye to an edict issued by Louis XIV in order to force his subjects to show more respect for sacred places and the celebration of mass. In a number of witty anecdotes, Gueudeville tells us that many in French churches do not seem to take religious celebration seriously and go to a mass as if it were the theatre, giving the vicar a round of applause when they liked his 'performance' and hissing at him when they did not (*L'Esprit* 1699–1710: 2.487–488 [Jan.–June 1700]). Before we become too enthusiastic about Gueudeville's skill as an interpreter of an obscure Renaissance poem, it should be pointed out that this poem and its proper interpretation had been discussed in the entry on Caldérinus (Remark B) in Bayle's *Dictionnaire historique et critique*, first published in 1697, which, as Rosenberg (1982: 252 n.) demonstrates, was Gueudeville's dependable treasure trove of historical and literary facts and anecdotes. This passage thus offers us a glimpse into Gueudeville's Latin learning, his sources, and his broader interest in the use of Renaissance literature to address contemporary issues, also apparent in his treatment of *Utopia*.

Next on our list of elements that help us understand Gueudeville's translation of More's work are his interest in geography and morality, which in his case are very closely connected, since his writings on geographic topics were strongly moral in character and largely inspired by a desire to hold up a mirror to his European contemporaries. His contributions to the *Atlas historique* often took the form of idealized descriptions of non-Western societies. A good example is his idyllic description of the inhabitants of Virginia who lived tranquil lives and were content with their available resources until English colonizers taught them greed and avarice:

> Content with little, this people was unfamiliar with the cares and concerns caused by the desire for luxury and ambition, and fulfilling their needs, which were restricted

---

[7] 'Audit Marsilius missam, missam facis illam | Tu, Domiti. Magis est religiosus uter, | Quis dubitet? Tanto es tu religiosior illo, | Quanto audire minus est bona quam facere' (Poliziano 1553: 592).

[8] Marsilio has not been identified.

to what was simple and necessary, required no effort or labour. However, this sweet tranquillity was soon disrupted by the arrival of the English, who had exposed themselves to the perils of a long journey out of a desire for gain and taught these peoples what avarice and greed can do to people.[9]

Apart from the blissful existence of the indigenous population of Virginia, Gueudeville also informs us in the same volume about the 'agreeable' religion of the Hottentots (6.74), the down-to-earth wedding customs in Madagascar (6.149), and the great fertility of the Abyssinians (6.2). Each of these examples is linked to a political or moral observation. In the case of the Hottentots, it is the joy they experience in practising their religion: worshipping one's god or gods should be a source of delight rather than fear. The example of Madagascan marriage customs demonstrates Christians should not be so obsessed with a woman's virginity when marrying and that it is fine for women to have control over their own bodies. Finally, the Abyssinians are discussed in connection with Gueudeville's theory that people who are not oppressed by their prince have both the energy and means available to have larger families.

Probably the best-known example of a thinly veiled attempt to teach Westerners a lesson about natural religion, morality, and the division of riches and possessions is Gueudeville's additions and revisions to the *Nouveaux voyages dans L'Amerique Septentrionale* by Louis Armand, baron de Lahontan (first edition 1703). Of particular interest is a dialogue between Lahontan and Adario, a 'distinguished savage' (*sauvage distingué*). Lahontan and Adario discuss a wide range of issues regarding society, such as religion and law. The conversation on religion is largely an attack on its organized form as spread by the Jesuits. Adario does not understand why Western religion and laws have become so heavily codified and complicated. Doing what is good is simple as long as you follow the 'natural impression engraved on our souls, which prescribes or forbids a thing according to whether it is in accordance with or opposed to justice and right reason'.[10]

We have already seen Gueudeville's concern with the opposition between common and individual interest as expressed in his criticisms of Louis XIV. Adario highlights this opposition to Lahontan as one of the central problems that is keeping the French from living together in harmony, namely the distinction between what is yours and what is mine (*le Tien et le Mien*). Instead Adario proposes a system in which each village has 'a collective storage of goods' for the community as a whole from which the head of every household will only pick as little or as much as he needs for his family (*L'Esprit* 1699–1710: 2.276). A similar communist system revolving round heads of a household

---

[9] 'Content de peu, il [i.e. ce people] ignoroit les soins & les inquiétudes que causent le luxe & l'ambition; & leurs besoins se bornant au simple nécessaire, ne leur donnoient ni peine ni travail pour y subvenir. Mais cette douce tranquillité a bien-tôt été troublée par l'arrivée des Anglois, qui s'exposant aux périls d'une longue Navigation par le desir du gain; ont apris à ces Peuples ce que peut l'avarice & la cupidité sur les hommes' (Châtelain 1719: 6.97).

[10] 'Quand tu cites les Loix n'entens-tu pas cette impression naturelle gravée dans nos Ames, qui nous prescrit ou qui nous défend une chose suivant que cette chose est conforme ou opposée à la justice & à la droite raison?' (Lahontan 1705: 2.241).

can also, of course, be found in More's *Utopia*. Although Gueudeville was the editor rather than the author of these dialogues, it is nevertheless apparent and in line with the scholarly consensus on Gueudeville that he strongly agreed with the views expressed by Adario. He also experimented with the dialogue form himself in his *Esprit des Cours*, where in February 1702 he introduced a 'sensible Indian' (*Indien sensé*) who criticized the Catholic preparations at Lent and forced his European interlocutor at least partly to agree with him (*L'Esprit* 1699–1710: 6.127–130 [Jan.–June 1702]; Rosenberg 1982: 126).

These elements combined explain why *Utopia* as a whole appealed to Gueudeville. Both as a work of Renaissance humanism and as a description of a (fictional) non-Western culture, this book allowed him to denounce the wrongs and injustices of his own age and culture in exactly the same ways as he had done throughout his career as a writer. Furthermore, anticlericalism, questions regarding the division of the earth's riches, and the fate of ordinary workers as well as religious toleration are all apparent in the way in which Gueudeville appropriated *Utopia* for his own agenda.

The final element that deserves to be mentioned in order to understand Gueudeville as a translator of More's work is his style. He had an insuperable tendency to digress, add burlesque and comical elements, and use neologisms, which some contemporaries appreciated, but most serious minds found very annoying, as exemplified by the reviews of the *Atlas historique* for which Gueudeville wrote many contributions. Henri Basnage de Beauval (1657–1710) wrote in his *Histoire des ouvrages des savants*: 'Mr Gueudeville writes with much fire. In everything he writes there is much brilliance and liveliness. One could even say there would be more sense [*esprit*] if there were a little less of it' (Basnage de Beauval 1704: 499). The reviewer for the *Journal des Savants* was even less understanding and believed Gueudeville's contributions should be separated from the rest of the work, as they were 'not very instructive' and full of 'jokes' and 'expressions that are supposed to be funny and only make those laugh who think like him and have the same prejudices' (*Journal des Savants* 1715: 106–113).

From *Utopia* to *Utopie*

With this background in mind, we can now turn to the translation of More's *Utopia*. It was printed and published by Pieter van der Aa (1659–1733), who was based in Leiden and had started his career with the publication of works on medicine, the natural sciences, and editions of classical Latin authors. Examples include the famous *Traité de la lumière* ('Treatise on Light') by Christiaan Huygens (1690), the *Pharmacia* and *Chymia medico-physica* (both in 1684; reprinted in 1688) by the Leiden chemist Jacobus le Mort, and an edition of the collected works of Cicero in 1692. Among students of book history, however, he has become most famous for a number of large, prestigious projects on which he embarked from the 1690s onwards. In 1692, he issued a new edition of Louis Moréri's *Grand dictionnaire historique*. This was followed by the *Thesaurus antiquitatum romanarum* in nine volumes, the first of which was published in 1694, and the *Thesaurus antiquitatum graecarum* in thirteen volumes (1697–1702). From 1703 to 1706, an edition came out of Erasmus' *Opera Omnia*. Another important focus for Van der Aa was the printing of works of a geographical nature, such as the *Délices de l'Espagne et du Portugal* (1707).

Van der Aa can thus be characterized as a printer who had the organizational talent and sense of entrepreneurship that allowed him to produce prestigious, large-scale publications, many of which were written in Latin. Among these large, expensive volumes, Gueudeville's translation of More's *Utopia* and its modest octavo format may seem a bit of an oddity. However, such a seemingly modest project nevertheless served a purpose for Van der Aa. His multi-volume projects were risky enterprises demanding considerable investment of money and time and interspersing such projects with smaller undertakings, such as the *Utopie*, created more financial stability for his firm. At the same time, they allowed this publisher to reach a far wider audience than his more learned and expensive publications and acted as a billboard that would hopefully induce readers to more expensive purchases. For this reason, the *Utopie* as well as the other translations which Gueudeville produced for Van der Aa contain extensive catalogues of the firm's other publications. The fact that the *Utopie* was a relatively modest and low-risk enterprise for Van der Aa is further confirmed by the engravings in this work. Although these have been identified as the work of the Leiden engraver Frans van Bleyswyck (1671–1746), one of the foremost engravers in the city, a comparison between the engravings in the *Utopie* and other more prestigious projects shows that the commissioner (Van der Aa) clearly asked for relatively simple representations and was more interested in quantity than in quality (Lewine 1898: 375; Streng 1990: 123).

Van der Aa and Gueudeville had already worked together before the *Utopie*. Van der Aa was responsible for the printing and publication of the *Nouveau Théâtre du monde* (1713), which has already been mentioned as one of the collaborative projects in which Gueudeville was involved. Gueudeville's other translation projects were also published by Van der Aa. Each of these served a commercial purpose similar to the *Utopie*, namely to provide a reliable source of income for the printing firm and to enlarge its target clientele. The *Utopie* was preceded in this sequence by Gueudeville's French translation of Erasmus' *Praise of Folly—Éloge de la folie—*in 1713. This publication must have been a commercial success, since it was reprinted twice within the next twenty years and was also pirated numerous times (Rosenberg 1982: 167–207; Hoftijzer 1999: 46). The popularity of the *Éloge de la folie* must have been an important financial stimulus for Van der Aa both to bring out a work of a character similar to Erasmus' masterpiece and to have it translated by Gueudeville. Further evidence of Van der Aa's hope of commercial success is the fact that he requested a privilege. In the Dutch Republic such privileges were not a requirement for publication—as was the case in France—but offered publishers protection against pirated editions. In practice, a privilege was only rarely requested, as it required a financial investment from the publisher and the copyright of publishers was generally properly observed. Publishers therefore only took the step of requesting a privilege for extra protection in the case of expensive and prestigious projects that had required a considerable investment and publications that may not have been expensive to produce but were expected to be particularly popular and profitable, as well as easy to reproduce by other parties (Lankhorst 1983: 66–68). The *Utopie* would have obviously belonged to the second category.

Paratexts in Gueudeville's *Utopie*

My discussion of the paratexts will focus on the prefatory material, which includes the title page, the publisher's dedicatory letter, the translator's introduction, and finally Gueudeville's life of More. Van der Aa's dedicatory letter is addressed to Jacques Emmeri, baron of Wassenaar. Van der Aa had good reasons to dedicate Gueudeville's translation to this Dutch nobleman. In 1712, Abraham Elzevier, the final descendant of the famous dynasty of Leiden printers, died and Van der Aa wanted to replace him as the official printer for the University of Leiden. As part of his efforts to reach this goal, he tried to obtain the support of the barons Van Wassenaar Obdam and Van Wassenaer, two branches of one of the most noble families of the Dutch Republic, with much influence on the administration of the University of Leiden (Hoftijzer 1999: 26–27). This dedicatory letter is therefore part of Van der Aa's strategy to fulfil this ambition and was not without success. On 8 May 1715, the year in which the *Utopie* came out in print, Van der Aa was appointed as the official printer of the university (Hoftijzer 1999: 28). In the dedication itself, Van der Aa falsely claims that Gueudeville's was the first French translation of *Utopia* to appear in print (More 1715: *8r).[11] It is possible he was unaware of earlier translations, in particular the one by Samuel Sorbière, published by Jan Blaeu in Amsterdam in 1643. It is equally possible that it was just a ploy to claim more originality for this translation. Finally, Van der Aa mentions that the idea of translating the *Utopia* was his own and that he approached Gueudeville to take up the project for him (*8v–*9r). This might be one of the explanations why Gueudeville's commissioned translation was so much longer than More's original, for if Van der Aa and Gueudeville had agreed that the latter would be paid per sheet, then he would actually have had a financial incentive to make his translation as long as possible.[12]

The paratexts written by Gueudeville are a clear reflection of the issues we have already seen. On the title page, More's work is presented as an

---

[11] For an overview of early modern French translations of *Utopia*, see Hosington 1984; Sellevold 2008a; Phélippeau 2016a; and Scholar in this volume.

[12] Although there is no remaining evidence that demonstrates such an arrangement was made in the specific case of Van der Aa and Gueudeville, it was very common among Dutch book producers to pay authors, translators, and correctors *par feuille*. Lankhorst (1983: 64) gives the examples of Richard Simon (1638–1712) who was paid in this manner for his work by the Rotterdam publisher Reinier Leers (1654–1714), and Michel Le Vassor (1648?–1718), who asked Pierre Bayle to inform the same publisher if he could be paid in this manner.

ingenious idea to remedy the misfortune of men and to give them complete happiness. This work contains the outline of a state, the laws, habits, and customs of which are entirely aimed at making life in human societies as pleasant as possible. [It is a] state that will definitely become reality, as soon as mortals will behave themselves according to reason.[13]

Gueudeville's introduction to the translation starts by arguing that Mother Nature has not been equally kind to all human beings: some of us are 'lame', 'blind', or generally 'infirm'. In addition, Gueudeville refers to ownership (*proprieté*), greed, and ambition as the three pests of civil society. The Utopians had found a way to overcome these problems by bringing the individual and common interest together.[14] Utopia does not have a prince who uses 'arbitrary power' (*le Pouvoir Arbitraire*) to squeeze so much money from his subjects 'to provide for his own luxury and pleasures' ('fournir à son luxe e à ses plaisirs', 2*2v). Instead, the Utopian prince acts as a primus inter pares who safeguards the careful balance reached on the island. In Utopia, there is not a small group of people amassing riches while others suffer in poverty, since all goods are public property (2*3r–2*4r). Gueudeville admits that the *Utopia* is a work of fiction, but stresses that its author More was a 'friend of man' (*ami de l'homme*). Of course, it is unlikely, perhaps impossible even, that a place like Utopia will ever exist, but it is a sketch of how, in theory at least, the ideal state could become reality (2*6v–2*7r).

The life of More is, of course, a very interesting piece, not least because it is the biography of a Catholic martyr written by a Protestant. Gueudeville sketches a contrast between More and two other major historical figures, Cardinal Wolsey and Henry VIII. The image that emerges of Wolsey is one of an overambitious clergyman who fell from grace and 'went off to bring to the dead his ambitious plan to become pope' ('Thomas Wolsey [...] s'en alla porter chez les Morts son dessein ambitieux de Papauté', 2*11r). More, by contrast, did not approve of the 'usurped power' (*la Puissance usurpée*) of the papacy, but wanted to avoid any further schisms within the Christian Church (3*2r–v). Henry VIII acts as a Louis XIV *avant la lettre*:

> This monarch, the most absolute perhaps to ever occupy the throne of England and who under the pretence and image of liberty reigned like a despot, this monarch

---

[13] 'L'Utopie de Thomas Morus, Chancelier d'Angleterre; Idée ingenieuse pour remedier au malheur des Hommes; & pour leur procurer une felicité complette. Cet Ouvrage contient le plan d'une république dont les Lois, les Usages, & les Coutumes tendent uniquement à faire faire aux Societez Humaines le passage de la Vie dans toute la douceur imaginable. Republique, qui deviendra infailliblement réelle des que les mortels se conduiront par la Raison.'

[14] 'Ses Loix, ses Coutumes, ses Usages ne tendent pas plus à la conservation, & à la sureté commune qu'à la sureté des Particuliers; & l'Ordre est si sagement etabli; les précautions & les mesures si bien prises, que chaque Citoïen trouve toûjours son *bien être* dans la Conduite Générale' (2*2v).

made the Representative Body confirm everything he had done and in addition Parliament declared him to be the Head of the Church.[15]

Seen from this perspective, More's tragedy was that he did not die primarily for his religious ideals and loyalty to Catholicism; he was simply the victim of the very kind of tyrant that in his *Utopia* he had tried to overcome: 'he was given an ignoble funeral, the victim in this respect of fate and the target of the king's wrath, even though, by the way, he deserved an end to his life as glorious as a tyrant made it humiliating'.[16] The presentation of both More and his *Utopia* thus fits in nicely with the framework of Gueudeville's thought: More is depicted as an independent-minded man who opposed not only the assertive mixture of politics and religion that Wolsey represented but also the absolutism of Henry VIII.

Gueudeville's Translation

In his preface, Gueudeville declared that his was no 'exact' (*exacte*) translation (2*8r). He stated that he has avoided any formulations that—in his view—would have gone against the author's intention, but his work should nevertheless be seen as 'a free translation' (*une Traduction libre*, 2*8r), although he rebukes any readers who might call it a 'paraphrase' (*parafrase*, 2*8r). He also admitted that occasionally he struggled with More's 'Ciceronian' Latin. He had always tried to capture the essence of what in his view More had intended, but was occasionally forced to 'guess' (*deviné*) what the Englishman might have meant (2*8r–v). Although the *Utopie* contains the occasional mistake in its translation, Gueudeville was a competent Latinist and many translations of key terms reveal a better and more accurate understanding of More's Latin than earlier translations by Jean Le Blond and Gabriel Chappuys, as Brenda Hosington (1984: 128) has demonstrated.[17] The reason Gueudeville's translation is nevertheless far removed from the Latin original is his typical digressive style full of absurd and satirical elements, which also characterized his rendering of More's work.

---

[15] 'Ce Monarque, le plus absolu, peut-être qui ait jamais occupé le Trône d'Angleterre; & qui sous l'ombre, sous l'image de la liberté, Gouvernoit despotiquement, ce Monarque fit confirmer par le Corps Representatif tout ce qu'il avoit fait; & de plus le Parlement le déclara Chef de l'Eglise' (3*12r–v).

[16] 'Il lui échut une Sépulture ignominieuse; en cela le jouët de la Fortune, la victime de la fureur du Roi; & d'ailleurs méritant, par son innocence, & par ses services, une fin aussi glorieuse, qu'un Tiran la rendit infame' (3*8r).

[17] An example of one of Gueudeville's misinterpretations can be found in More 1715: 80, where the non-existence of private property in Plato's state and Utopia is contrasted with the reality of contemporary Europe. Gueudeville misinterprets the Latin words *hic* and *illic* and thinks a comparison is being made between Utopia and Plato's ideas rather than between Utopia and Plato on the one hand and contemporary Europe on the other.

Hythloday's explanation of Utopian marriage customs, for example, turned out to be a great opportunity for Gueudeville to digress. When two Utopians want to marry, they are required to see each other naked beforehand:

> Whether she be widow or virgin, the woman is shown naked to the suitor by a responsible and respectable matron; and similarly some honourable man presents the suitor naked to the woman. We laughed at this custom and called it absurd.[18]

In Gueudeville's translation this becomes:

> A prudish and venerable matron shows the suitor his mistress *en pure nature*, that is entirely naked, and in turn a man of good habits, a man of good character, shows to the girl or widow his male display [*l'étalage viril*]. He takes off his shirt and presents himself to her to contemplate and examine from head to toe. We could not keep a straight face when we were told about this beautiful spectacle of the earthly paradise before the inconceivable fall of father Adam. We could not even refrain from telling them that that custom was silly and impertinent.[19]

This passage exemplifies Gueudeville's recurrent desire to enliven More's original and make it more direct, especially when sex and the human body are concerned. Many of Gueudeville's adaptations also serve a more practical purpose to make the *Utopia* more accessible, as they clarify transitions or remove references that may puzzle those who do not have a thorough training in classical culture.[20]

The most telling digressions, however, are those that reveal Gueudeville's concerns and interests with regard to his own age. These have already been discussed for his oeuvre as a whole and include anticlericalism, the religious policies of Louis XIV, and the economic position of workers. In Book Two of *Utopia*, Hythloday mentions several categories of idlers, among them clergymen: 'Then there is the lazy gang of priests and so-called religious.'[21] Gueudeville goes much further, however:

---

[18] 'Mulierem enim, seu virgo seu vidua sit, gravis et honesta matrona proco nudam exhibet, ac probus aliquis vir vicissim nudum puellae procum sistit. Hunc morem quum velut ineptum ridentes improbaremus' (More 1995: 188–189).

[19] 'Une prude & vénérable Matrone fait voir à l'amant sa Maitresse, en pure nature, c'est à dire toute nuë; & réciproquement, un homme de bonnes moeurs, un homme de probité, montre à la fille, où à la veuve l'étalage viril; il lui ôte la chemise, & le lui presente à contempler, à examiner depuis la tête jusqu'aux piés. Nous ne pouvions garder nôtre serieux en aprenant ce beau Spectacle du Paradis terrestre avant l'inconcevable chute du Pere Adam: nous ne pûmes, même, nous empêcher de leur dire que cet usage-là étoit sot & impertinent' (More 1715: 226).

[20] For examples of transitions that have been made explicit, see More 1715: 132, 222. An example of references omitted by Gueudeville can be found in More 1995: 41 (on the Roman general Manlius and the stoa) and 90 (on Crassus).

[21] 'Ad haec sacerdotum ac religiosorum, quos vocant, quanta quamque otiosa turba!' (More 1995: 128–129).

In addition, there are the ministers involved in worship, cardinals, archbishops, abbots, prelates, priests, monks, or the religious, as you like. Bring all these members confined and separated from society together in your mind and, good God, what an enormous quantity of idle mortals, the majority of whom only think about earthly delights and the pleasure of the five senses of Nature.[22]

The *Utopie* thus makes the anticlericalism that had already been present in the Latin original much more explicit and an important role for Gueudeville's digressions is thus to turn this work into a Protestant attack of Catholicism. The contrast between the working conditions of workmen in Utopia and elsewhere receives a similarly emphatic treatment. *Utopia* reads: 'No one has to be exhausted with endless toil from early morning to late at night like a beast of burden. Such wretchedness, really worse than slavery, is the common lot of workmen almost everywhere except in Utopia.'[23] This passage is turned into a veritable denunciation of working conditions for labourers:

They do not see themselves as beasts that are meant to toil and carry heavy loads under the threat of whiplashes. They do not tire themselves out as one does with horses. Actually, there is no unhappier, more woeful, more burdensome existence than being reduced to the fate of spending your days in ongoing labour. It is the existence of a slave who with his rest and liberty pays for the short pleasure of breathing in the knowledge that he is miserable. Let's say it with a sentiment of humanity: alas! Nevertheless, it is the fate of workers almost everywhere, but not of the Utopians.[24]

As a member of the Huguenot émigré community in the United Provinces, Gueudeville's biggest preoccupation was understandably with the religious policies of Louis XIV, especially the Revocation of the Edict of Nantes. In Book Two, we find a description of the founder of Utopia, Utopus, who established a tradition of religious tolerance among his people. Gueudeville bursts out in a long digression—not found in More's original—in which he condemns the use of force in religious matters:

Because you are convinced of the truth of an article in your catechism, you want the whole world to believe it too? To tell the truth, there is both extravagance and

---

[22] 'De plus: les Ministres du Culte, Cardinaux, Archevêques, Abbez, Prelats, Prêtres, Moines, ou Religieux, comme il vous plaira: rassemblez en idée tous ces Membres Séquestrés, & separez du Train Commun: Bon dieu, quelle prodigieuse quantité de Mortels oisifs, & dont le plus grand Nombre ne pense qu'aux Délices, & qu'au plaisir des cinq sens de Nature' (More 1715: 127).

[23] 'nec ab summo mane tamen ad multam usque noctem perpetuo labore velut iumenta fatigatus. Nam ea plus quam servilis aerumna est, quae tame ubique fere opificum vita est, exceptis Utopiensibus' (More 1995: 126–127).

[24] 'Ils ne se regardent pas comme des bêtes destinées à trainer, & à porter sous les coups; ils ne se fatiguent pas comme on lasse les chevaux. Effectivement, il n'est point de destinée plus malheureuse, plus affligeante, plus accablante, que d'être reduit par le sort à passer les jours dans un travail perpetuël; c'est vivre dans la condition d'un pauvre esclave qui païe de son repos & de sa liberté, le petit & court plaisir de respirer en se connoissant miserable. Disons le par un sentiment d'humanité: helas! c'est neanmoins preque par tout le destin des Ouvriers. Ce n'est pas celui des Utopiens' (More 1715: 121).

foolishness in that conviction. You might as well force a blind man, a one-eyed man, a cross-eyed man, a man, in short, who has no eyesight, a squint, or poor eyesight; force this man, I say, to have eyes as good, as healthy, as sharp, and of equal rightness as yours, according to your own presumption. Give him that eyesight or just leave him alone.[25]

It is not just the sheer length of the digression—it continues for several pages—but also the passionate tone, full of repetition, that shows this was an issue that was very close to his heart. In the first place, this passage is an expression of outrage about the treatment of the Huguenots by the French authorities in Gueudeville's age, but it also echoes a more specific context of a debate within the Huguenot community at the turn of the eighteenth century about the justification of religious toleration. The protagonists of this debate were Jurieu and Bayle, who—like Gueudeville—had been forced to flee from France for their Protestant beliefs. Gueudeville knew both men personally and was thoroughly familiar with their work. As mentioned above, Jurieu argued that the reason Protestants should be tolerated by countries with a Catholic majority was simply that the Protestants were right and the Catholics were wrong. Bayle, however, came up with a much more intricate and sweeping theory in defence of freedom of conscience, known as the doctrine or justification of the erring conscience: even when someone's convictions were demonstrably wrong, that person should not be forced to act against his or her conscience (van der Lugt 2016: 117–156). Gueudeville's use of a comparison between religious conscience and people whose eyesight has been seriously impaired is a reference to his preference for Bayle's ideas over Jurieu's and that even the apparently erroneous conscience should be respected. Digressions such as this one therefore both present a critique of Catholic intolerance and reflect tensions among Protestants.

Reception

Van der Aa's commercial instinct was right and *Utopie* was a commercial success. In 1716, Van der Aa sold his privilege for Gueudeville's translation to the Wetstein firm in Amsterdam, which reissued the work in 1717. Another Amsterdam printer and bookseller, François L'Honoré, subsequently acquired the privilege and brought out a revised edition in 1730 (Rosenberg 1982: 105, 208–122).

In the realm of reviews and journals, however, Gueudeville's burlesque approach and exuberant style made his oeuvre as a whole, and his translations in particular, highly

---

[25] 'A cause que vous êtes persuadés d'un Article de vôtre Catéchisme, vous voulez que tout le Monde le soit aussi? En verité, il y a la de l'extravagance & de la sotise: forcez, donc aussi un Aveugle, un Borgne, un Louche; enfin, un homme qui a la vuë éteinte, ou de travers, ou malade, forcez le, dis-je, d'avoir les yeux, aussi bons, aussi sains, aussi perçans, & d'une aussi grande justeste que les vôtres, à ce que vous prétendez; donnez lui cela, ou laissez le en repos' (More 1715: 292–293).

controversial among contemporary scholars and scholarly reviewers. Le Clerc, for example, could partly forgive Gueudeville for this style in his translation of Erasmus' *Praise of Folly*, because it is Folly herself who speaks here (Le Clerc 1717: 7.214–215). However, the same approach was much less appropriate in the case of More's *Utopia* and he therefore advised his readers to turn to Sorbière's older translation from 1643 (7.211).[26] That in the eighteenth century More's *Utopia* was seen as a serious political and moral critique of society, in which too ample a use of humour, neologisms, and digressions was therefore unacceptable, can also be concluded from other professional opinions. The French politician and publicist Jean-Nicolas Démeunier (1751–1814) believed that Gueudeville's 'pleasing tone' (*ton plaisant*) was 'ill-suited to a moral book' (*peu convenable à un livre moral*) (Démeunier 1788: 4.675). Perhaps unsurprisingly, the most negative judgement was expressed in the *Journal de Trévoux*, an academic journal largely written and edited by Jesuits. Here Gueudeville's work was dismissed as 'a mixture of trivial expressions and bad jokes' (*un mélange d'expressions triviales & de mauvaises plaisanteries*) (*Journal de Trévoux* 1718: 83).

These were the views of Gueudeville's readers who were part of Europe's scholarly elite in the eighteenth century. Those interested in popularizing the literature of Renaissance humanism, however, were more approving. An example is the *Bibliothèque universelle des romans*, an eighteenth-century take on *Reader's Digest*, which appeared between 1775 and 1789 and offered its readers extracts and summaries of novels and narrative fiction ranging from ancient to contemporary works of literature (see M. Hall 2002; A. Martin 1985). The issue for February 1776 contained an extract from More's *Utopia*. The translation that formed the basis of the extract was that of Gueudeville, since it was 'the best translation that we currently have' ('jusqu'à présent, la meilleure Traduction que nous ayons'), although the editors also claimed to have occasionally returned to the original Latin (*Bibliothèque universelle* 1776: 17.15). Earlier translations such as those of Sorbière and Le Blond—wrongly ascribed to Barthélémy Aneau—were dismissed as 'bad' (*mauvaise*) and 'inexact' (*pas exacte*) (17.14).

The next French translation to be produced was by Thomas Rousseau (*c*.1750–1800), first published in 1780.[27] The second edition (1789) contains a preface in which Rousseau refers to Gueudeville's translation as 'inaccurate'(*infidele*) (More 1789: xi), while he himself had translated More's work 'literally, including its beauties and shortcomings' (*littéralement [...] avec ses beautés, & ses défauts*, xii). However, Rousseau was not as scrupulous a translator as he would like us to believe. Like Gueudeville before him, he dramatized, digressed, and introduced vocabulary that would have been unfamiliar to More and in some cases even contrary to his convictions (see Gury 1976: 79–86, esp. 85 n.). He even inserted quotations from eighteenth-century authors into the main text of his *Utopie*.[28] The result was a translation that was geared to promoting the views of

---

[26] For more on Sorbière's translation, see Scholar in this volume.
[27] For more on Rousseau's translation, see Astbury in this volume.
[28] See e.g. More 1789: 86 for a quotation from *Le légataire universel* (1706) by Jean-François Regnard (1655–1709).

French Revolutionary thinkers. Although Rousseau was dismissive of Gueudeville's translation, he therefore worked in the same spirit as his predecessor: after Gueudeville had turned *Utopia* into the mouthpiece of the French émigré community in the Dutch Republic in the 1710s, Rousseau did the same for his intellectual and cultural allies in the late eighteenth century.

Conclusion

Gueudeville's translation did not constitute a radical change in how *Utopia* was read. The richness of More's masterpiece is such that the core of what was important to Gueudeville was already present in the Latin text. His changes therefore consist of digressions that expand on existing themes and arguments, while largely remaining within the spirit of the original. Rather, the translation's reception—popular among general readers and treated with disdain by scholars—demonstrates how in the eighteenth-century public sphere the *chefs d'œuvre* of learned Renaissance literature could be enjoyed regardless of the views of the intellectual elite. As described in this chapter, these additions reflect the translator's concerns and interests as well as those of the émigré community to which he belonged. Furthermore, the translation is important for the history of how the Latin original of *Utopia* was read. After all, Gueudeville's digressions serve as markers of those parts of More's work that apparently struck a chord with him and those in his environment. Ironically, therefore, the very digressions that made this translation so unbearable to Gueudeville's scholarly contemporaries make the *Utopie* a riveting document for present-day students of both eighteenth-century history and of *Utopia*. As such, it deserves its own chapter in the history of the reception of More's work.

CHAPTER 20

THOMAS ROUSSEAU, TRANSLATOR OF AN ENLIGHTENED *UTOPIA*

KATHERINE ASTBURY

SIXTEENTH- and seventeenth-century French translations of Thomas More's *Utopia* have received scholarly attention (e.g. Sellevold 2008a; Hosington 1984), as have the considerable number of imitations, borrowings, and utopian projects of the eighteenth century in France (e.g. Baczko et al. 2016), but until now very little attention has been paid to the work of Thomas Rousseau (1750–1800), who produced a translation of *Utopia* in 1780 and republished it with a new title and introduction in December 1789, just five months after the fall of the Bastille and the start of the French Revolution at a time when many felt that the regeneration of the nation was close to being complete.[1] The translation was his first foray into publishing and was intended to launch his career as a man of letters. This chapter will explore how Rousseau adapted More's text to suit better his intended readers in Enlightenment France and how it influenced his other literary and political activities in the years leading up to and during the French Revolution.

We have few biographical details about Rousseau. In 1787, in correspondence relating to his request for a pension, he describes himself as 'born without fortune, without support, without credit' ('né sans fortune, sans appui, sans credit').[2] In soliciting financial support as reward for his literary endeavours, he here wrote that he had spent twenty years devoting 'all my time, all the work of my feeble talents to the public good' ('tous mon tems, tous les travaux de mes faibles talens au bien public') and claimed that he had always preferred noble poverty to making money through the writing of immoral works. He explains that he made a promise 'to devote his time, his sleepless nights, his work to the search for truths useful to his fellow men, to defending taste, morals, and the

[1] The publication was listed in the *Mercure français*, 30 Jan. 1790.
[2] Archives nationales de France, F17/1212, dossier 10. See Chappey and Lilti 2010. All translations from French are my own.

religion of our fathers—this is how I began my careers in letters' ('de ne consacrer mon tems, mes veilles et mes travaux qu'à la recherche des vérités utiles à mes semblables, à la deffense du gout, des moeurs et du culte de nos peres—c'est ainsi que j'ai débutés dans la carriere des lettres'). This would suggest that Rousseau began his literary activity in the late 1760s. The catalogue of the Bibliothèque nationale de France suggests he began his literary career with anonymous play-writing, though nineteenth-century literary biographies do not include the plays attributed to him. The catalogue credits him with the one-act verse drama *Momus* (1765): if his birthdate of 1750 is correct, then he wrote and published this very young. Other potential plays include *Les Deux sœurs* (1774) and *L'Heureux Jour ou la fête des citoyens* (1774). However, the former is said to be by M. M*, not a pseudonym Rousseau ever uses later, and Antoine-Alexandre Barbier's *Dictionnaire des anonymes* suggests 'Marandon?' a more likely author (Barbier 1882: 1.930). The latter is, according to Martineau de Soleinne's *Bibliothèque dramatique*, 'printed for the author but not sold' ('imprimé pour l'auteur et non vendu', Soleinne 1844: 2.171) which does not tally with Rousseau being poor and without patronage. Furthermore, the tone of the plays does not sit with the statement quoted above from 1787 and there is no other evidence to suggest that Rousseau published anything before 1780. The *Journal encyclopédique* (1781 [15 June]: 536) calls him a new author when reviewing his *Lettre sur les spectacles*. All things considered, the information available to us suggests that his first publication is indeed the translation of *Utopia*.

Publication and Reception

It was not uncommon for aspiring men of letters in Enlightenment France to begin their careers with translations or adaptations of works they hoped would get them noticed. Rousseau was encouraged to provide a more accurate translation of *Utopia* than that produced by Nicolas Gueudeville by the writer and man of letters Meusnier de Querlon, himself an occasional translator of Latin texts (Guitton 1999), who died shortly before Rousseau's translation appeared in print.[3] In 1780, Rousseau published his translation, printed in Paris by Alexandre Jombert, entitled *Tableau du meilleur gouvernement possible, ou l'Utopie de Thomas Morus, Chancellier d'Angleterre*. Proclaiming its contents as depicting 'the best government possible', it was dedicated to Charles Gravier, comte de Vergennes, who at the time was busy overseeing French involvement in the American War of Independence (1775–83). Rousseau's strategy was in theory a good one: a new translation of a work that would be seen as useful to one of Louis XVI's most important ministers (Murphy 1982; Price 2009). In the dedication, Rousseau presents Vergennes as a good citizen (*bon citoyen*), good minister (*bon ministre*), and friend of humanity (*ami*

---

[3] See preface to the second edition of 1789 (More 1789a). For Gueudeville's translation, see Verhaart in this volume.

de l'humanité) who follows More's principles in his administration of the nation's foreign affairs. Although Vergennes is seen by Munro Price as conservative—a 'bitter foe of the Enlightenment' (Price 2009: 19), a defender of the monarchical tradition and royal authority (57), and thus a perhaps surprising choice for a work exploring alternative means of government—Rousseau dedicated the volume to Vergennes because of the minister's interest in developing trade and commerce, a theme that would run through Rousseau's later work.

Despite the dedication to the increasingly powerful Vergennes, the work did not make the impact Rousseau undoubtedly hoped it would. Although it is reviewed in the principal literary journal of the time, the *Mercure de France*, on 12 August 1780, the reviewer is not especially flattering. The review opens declaring that More's *Utopia* is 'nothing other than a plan for a Republic imitating that of Plato' ('n'est autre chose que le plan d'une République à l'imitation de celle de Platon', 74). This belittling of More's originality is not untypical of French responses to his text. The writers of the French Enlightenment expended considerable energy thinking about ways of governing better but often without referring directly to More's work (Hartig and Soboul 1976). Voltaire, for instance, admitted to Claude Adrien Hélvetius that he had not read *Utopia* (letter of 6 July 1739; Dainard et al. 2009) and accused More of being a superstitious persecutor in his *Essai sur les mœurs* ('Essay on Customs') (1756: 3, ch. 135). Voltaire's *Encyclopédie* (1774), the most important publishing venture of the century and arguably the most useful source of Enlightenment thought, only refers to *Utopia* twice, and one of those references is about a point of grammar rather than about the content of the work. For Antoine Hatzenberger, this is 'a deliberate exclusion due to a philosophic incompatibility' ('une exclusion délibérée due à une incompatibilité philosophique') as the Enlightenment *philosophes* wanted to focus on the real rather than the imaginary (Hatzenberger 2012: 101), though reference to More's text is made in the later *Encyclopédie méthodique*, where it is presented as a 'political novel' (*roman politique*) (Démeunier 1784: v).[4]

The *Mercure* reviewer of Rousseau's translation on 12 August 1780 claimed that *Utopia* 'can hardly interest today' ('ne peut guères intéresser aujourd'hui') because in their view the principles of morality and political economy it contained had already been demonstrated so many times in so many works that More's text had been superseded. Rousseau is criticized for having done nothing other than polish Gueudeville's 1715 translation when instead he should have been shortening it 'to make it easier to read and to make it clearer to see what useful content is within it' ('afin de le rendre plus aisé à lire, et de faire mieux connoître ce qu'il renferme d'utile, 75). Modern assessments of the translation have not been much kinder. Thierry Pacquot criticizes Rousseau, because he 'adapts *Utopia* more than he translates it and passes off his own ideas in the name of Thomas More' ('adapte *L'Utopie* plus qu'il ne la traduit et fait ainsi passer ses propres idées au nom de Thomas More'); this is all the more unfortunate for Pacquot because

---

[4] Cf. entry 'Economique', Baczko et al. 2016.

Rousseau's edition was to be the basis of the first Russian translation, produced in St Petersburg in 1789 (Pacquot 2007: 31). Baczko et al.'s 1,406-page *Dictionnaire critique de l'Utopie* (2016) does not include a single reference to Rousseau; and the only scholarly article to focus on him (Gury 1976) sees the 1780 edition in the light of the re-edition of 1789 and above all as a work of propaganda from a revolutionary, anachronistically casting propagandist aims back on to the 1780 text.[5] While some of Gury's assessments of Rousseau's translation are, nevertheless, valid, we need to untangle the two editions of the text in order to understand better the translation strategies undertaken by Rousseau without forcing him into a revolutionary paradigm.

The 1780 Edition

Unfortunately, we cannot know which edition of *Utopia* Rousseau was using as the basis for his translation but a comparison between Rousseau's translation and More's text reveals that Rousseau situated himself in a long line of eighteenth-century French translators who were more concerned with their target audience than the source text. To make his literary reputation, Rousseau needed to translate elegantly but also make the text relevant to 1780s France. As a result, 'More often disappears behind Rousseau' ('More disparaît souvent derrière Rousseau', Gury 1976: 80); but this should not be seen as something negative so much as an opportunity to understand how More's work resonated with Rousseau and how Rousseau, as an aspiring man of letters in eighteenth-century Paris, interpreted the text.

Although in the second edition of 1789, Rousseau claimed to have translated More literally, from the opening pages of Rousseau's 1780 text (which cuts out the prefatory material and begins directly with Book One) we can see that he has his eighteenth-century French audience in mind. The praise of Henry VIII is toned down—after all, he had been at war with France repeatedly during his reign. In Rousseau, he is simply someone whom England sees as one of its 'greatest' (*plus grands*) kings (More 1780: 1); the notion of invincibility is absent. On the other hand, the description of Georges de Themsecke is expanded: Rousseau adds that he had more knowledge 'of law of peoples and kings' ('du droit des gens et des souverains') than anyone and that 'he was, in a word, the cleverest and most skilful statesman of his century' ('c'était, en un mot, l'homme d'état le plus habile et le plus consommé de son siècle', 3). This addition to the description, coming just a few pages after the dedication to Vergennes, is clearly aiming to speak more of Louis XVI's minister than the early sixteenth-century Provost of Cassel.

Stylistically, Rousseau aims for immediacy by writing much more of Hythloday's account in the first person but he also regularly extends analogies. For example, in the

---

[5] Phélippeau 2016a: 304 also sees Rousseau's translation as 'expressing the ideas of the French Revolution'; cf. Minerva 1992 which sees 1789 Rousseau's translation as a *programme politique* but does not consider the text of the translation or the earlier edition.

discussion of why Hythloday does not enter the service of the king, the line 'the crow loves his fledgling and the ape his cub' (More 2016b: 14) becomes 'ainsi le corbeau caresse ses poussins, qu'il couvre affectueusement avec son aile; ainsi le sapajou s'admire, avec une sorte de complaisance, dans les petits monstres qui lui doivent le jour' (More 1780: 21): 'thus the crow caresses its fledglings which it covers affectionately with its wing; thus the capuchin admires itself with a sort of kind indulgence in the little monsters who owe it their lives'. We also see a tendency to increase the emotive effect. For instance, when discussing the nefarious effects of enclosure, More talks of villagers who have to 'leave the only homes familiar to them' (2016b: 19) but in Rousseau's version they leave 'those cottages which were for so long happy locations, where they have so often, under the auspices of work and simple nature, tasted the pleasures of innocence' ('ces cabanes si long-tems heureuses, où ils ont tant de fois, sous les auspices du travail & de la simple nature, goûté les plaisirs de l'innocence', 1780: 38). In the discussion on the death penalty, Hythloday interjects to make the arguments more personal. Thus 'If they say the thief suffers, not for the money, but for violation of justice and transgression of laws, then this extreme justice should properly be called extreme injury' (2016b: 22) becomes 'En vain m'alleguera-t-on qu'on punit dans celui qui dérobe, moins son vol, proprement dit, que l'infraction qu'il a faite aux loix: *je réponds* à cette objection, qu'une justice extrême est une extrême injustice' (1780: 49; emphasis added): 'in vain will they put forward to me that one punishes in he who steals less the theft proper than the infraction committed against the law: *I reply* to this objection that an extreme justice is an extreme injustice'. Similarly, the thief's reasoning for killing is given in the first person in the French (1780: 52) and whilst More's lawyer shakes his head and pulls a wry face (2016b: 26), Rousseau uses the verb *s'écrier* (to exclaim) and the lawyer speaks 'whilst wringing his hands and making I don't know what sort of grimace' ('en se tordant les poings et en faisant je ne sais quelle grimace', 1780: 63).

There are at times slight misreadings of the original. For instance, the explanation that Peter Giles's 'conversation is so pleasant, and so witty without malice, that the ardent desire I felt to see again my native country, my home, my wife and my children (from whom I had been separated for more than four months) was much eased by his most agreeable company and delightful talk' (2016b: 9) in French suggests he was enjoying Giles's company so much, he could not bring himself to go home ('je ne pouvois me résoudre encore à céder au besoin qui me pressait de retourner dans ma Patrie, pour y embrasser ma femme et mes enfans', 1780: 4). But the changes to the meaning of More's text seem to be entirely intentional rather than the result of poor translation. Book Two is, on the whole, more accurately translated with fewer additions from Rousseau. This is largely because Book Two presents Utopia whilst Book One's discussions are primarily about England. Rousseau sets out to make the social comment of Book One relevant to eighteenth-century France. His translation was published in the midst of the American Revolutionary War—America had declared independence and France was still fighting Britain—and this global political context gives an immediacy to the ideals of Enlightened social improvement which underpin many of Rousseau's additions. He asks, for instance, 'may not a man of our time have on certain objects, without imminent danger, views which are more judicious and more useful than those of our forebears?' ('l'homme de notre siècle ne peut-il, sans un danger imminent, avoir sur de certains objets des vues plus judicieuses & plus utiles que celles de nos pères?', 1780: 22). More's original paragraph mentioned simply the wisdom of our ancestors (2016b: 15), whereas Rousseau extends this to the concept of utility. Later in Book One, Rousseau reiterates the eighteenth-century French ideal of *philosophie*: philosophers should 'enlighten princes and help them with their advice' ('éclairer les princes de leurs lumières et les aider de leurs conseils', 1780: 74): the English simply says 'assist kings with their counsels' (2016b: 29). The verb *éclairer* has clear connotations within the French Enlightenment. In Denis Diderot and Jean le Rond D'Alembert's *Encyclopédie* (1751), the entry on the word *éclairé* makes clear that it is not education alone that makes an enlightened man but the ability to apply that knowledge usefully. Similarly, More's attempts to persuade Raphael that his advice would be 'of the greatest advantage to the public welfare' (2016b: 29) are extended by Rousseau to incorporate the notion of happiness, a key component of the American Declaration of Independence of 1776 (and subsequently the 1789 Declaration of the Rights of Man and the Citizen). If he were to advise the king, not only would Hythloday 'fulfil all the duties which honour and your position as citizen impose equally' ('remplir tous les devoirs que vous imposent également l'honneur et la qualité de citoyen'), but he would at the same time become 'the man most capable of being worthy of people and empires and of contributing to the happiness of humanity in general' ('l'homme du monde le plus capable de bien mériter des peuples et des empires, et de contribuer au bonheur de l'humanité en general', 1780: 73–74). Again, if we look to the *Encyclopédie* for clarification of what Rousseau might mean, we find that *bonheur* in a mid-eighteenth-century context 'is taken here to mean a state or situation which we would like to see continue forever unchanged' (Pestre 2003).

Eighteenth-century notions of freedom also find their place in the translation. For Rousseau, freedom is 'the most sacred possession of all reasonable creatures' ('le bien le plus sacré de tout être raisonnable', 1780: 91), his addition to the translation. Where More declares that 'riches and liberty make people less patient to endure harsh and unjust commands, whereas poverty and want blunt their spirits, make them docile, and grind out of the oppressed the lofty spirit of rebellion' (2016b: 34), Rousseau turns the sentence around to focus on the need for people to rebel, presaging the Revolution of just a few years later:

> It is the hard extremities of indigence, it is the cruel humiliations which man suffers, pressed by famine and need, which cause him to lose his spirit, which debase his soul, wear down his courage, remove from him, in a word, even the idea of those noble and generous sentiments which, making him see freedom as the most sacred possession of all reasonable creatures, lead him to break the chains being prepared for him and to flee far from the despot who intended them to be used on him.

> (Ce sont les dures extrémités de l'indigence, ce sont les humiliations cruelles qu'éprouve l'homme, pressé par la disette & par le besoin qui abâtardissent son esprit, avilissent son ame, énervent son courage, lui ôtent, en un mot, jusqu'à l'idée de

ces sentimens nobles et généreux qui, lui faisant envisager la liberté comme le bien le plus sacré de tout être raisonnable, le portent à briser les fers que l'on lui prépare, & à fuir loin du despote qui les lui destinait.) (1780: 91)

The translated text thus repeatedly bears witness to some of the key concepts of French eighteenth-century thought: happiness, freedom, and Enlightenment.[6] Furthermore, Rousseau's vocabulary on Utopian religion seems to come straight from Voltaire. Where More writes, 'those who have not accepted Christianity make no effort to restrain others from it, nor do they criticise new converts to it' (2016b: 99), Rousseau reformulates this: 'their first principle in religion is tolerance. […] They punish not only fanaticism but even indiscrete zeal' ('leur premier principe en fait de religion est la tolérance […] Ils punissent non seulement le fanatisme mais même le zele indiscret', 1780: 297). Early in the text he adds a footnote to the introductory material on Hythloday in which he attacks the Inquisition: in More, Hythloday finds himself at Calicut 'by strange good fortune' (2016b: 11) whilst Rousseau's explorer suffers 'much fatigue and many tribulations' (*bien des fatigues et des tribulations*) at the hands of the Inquisition (1780: 8) for believing in the Antipodes having actually been there. Rousseau also expands noticeably on the section on the Supreme Being. While More writes, 'Him they call their parent, and to him alone they attribute the origin, increase, progress, changes and ends of all things; they do not offer divine honours to any other' (2016b: 98), Rousseau, as Gury (1976: 81) has pointed out, echoes his namesake Jean-Jacques's (no relation) *Profession de foi d'un vicaire savoyard* published as part of *Émile* in 1762:

> it is he who created the world, who established this marvellous harmony which reigns in all its parts; it is he who regulates the path of the stars, who made the insurmountable barrier which separates the elements, who fixed the limits of the two oceans, it is he who prepares those unexpected events which cause us such surprise and which lead to those revolutions which all human prudence cannot foresee. Nature only offers us a circle of continuous vicissitudes, the centuries pass, the ages become compressed and merge into each other, death devours all beings; everything that breathes begins, grows, declines and ends: only God, always surrounded by his glory, is not subject to change.
>
> (C'est lui qui créa le monde, qui établit cette harmonie merveilleuse qui regne dans toutes ses parties; c'est lui qui règle le cours des astres, qui a posé la barriere insurmontable qui sépare les éléments, qui a fixé les bornes aux deux mers, c'est lui qui prépare ces événemens inattendus qui nous jettent dans la derniere surprise, et qui amene ces révolutions que toute la prudence humaine ne sauroit prévoir. La nature ne nous offre qu'un cercle de vicissitudes continuelles, les siecles s'écoulent, les âges se pressent et se confondent, la mort dévore tous les êtres; tout ce qui respire, commence, croît, décline et finit: Dieu seul, toujours environné de sa gloire, n'est sujet à aucun changement.) (J.-J. Rousseau 1762b: 293–294)

---

[6] For these themes, cf. Withington in this volume.

There are echoes of Jean-Jacques, too, in Thomas's reflections on property that are not to be found in the original, which is much more restrained. More, reflecting on Plato's belief that 'the one and only path to the public welfare lies through equal allocation of goods', has Hythloday express doubt whether it can be achieved: 'I doubt such equality can ever be achieved where property belongs to individuals' (More 2016b: 40). In contrast, Rousseau has Hythloday launch straight from Plato into a condemnation of the notion of property as the root of inequality: 'this unfortunate right of mine and yours is the fertile and eternal source of quarrels, fateful divisions, robbery, assassinations, wars, devastations, fires, massacres, in a word all the abominations that make our universe a true place of horror' ('ce malheureux droit du tien et du mien est la source féconde et éternelle des querelles, des divisions funestes, des brigandages, des assassinats, des guerres, des dévastations, des incendies, des massacres enfin, de toutes les abominations, qui font de notre univers un vrai séjour d'horreur', More 1780: 110–111).[7] More's text is thus infused with Enlightenment discourse on tolerance, religion, property, and becomes a resolutely eighteenth-century text in the process.

The French context of the 1780s is made clear repeatedly and, in so doing, Rousseau reveals his political standpoint. He is interested in the creation of 'wise institutions, useful establishments, and admirable regulation' ('des institutions sages, des établissemens utiles, de la police admirable', 1780: 13), ideas which represent an expansion of the original phrase: 'wise and prudent provisions that he observed among the civilised nations' (2016b: 12). More's 'well and wisely trained citizens' (12) become 'prudent, enlightened, hardworking nations whose government justly deserves praise' ('nations prudentes, éclairées, laborieuses, dont le gouvernement mérite à juste titre des éloges', 1780: 14). The notion of 'citizen' is almost always translated by 'nation', in line with Rousseau's strategic positioning as man of letters looking to improve the relationship between the monarch and his people, rather than as the republican he would become a decade later. While the labour of the poor benefits the 'public'—i.e. the wider community—in More (2016b: 40), it benefits *la patrie* in Rousseau (1780: 112). The translator implies that not just education but also hard work is the key to the nation's future, and peace alone is nothing without commerce and abundance, two concepts added to the translation at this point. When More writes about rents, Rousseau rewrites the section to present the nobility firmly as French eighteenth-century *seigneurs*: 'miserly when it is a question of their obligations and prodigious to the point of ruining themselves when it is a question of their own pleasures' ('avares lorsqu'il s'agit d'obliger, prodigues jusqu'à se ruiner lorsqu'il est question de leurs plaisirs', 1780: 28). In a pure addition to the translation, he talks of how they 'have no other talent than that of pressurizing their farmers, and reducing them to begging in order to triple their revenues and thereby sustain their ludicrous expenses' ('n'ont d'autre talent que celui de pressurer leurs malheureux fermiers, de les réduire à la mendicité, pour tripler leurs revenus, et pouvoir soutenir ainsi leurs folles

---

[7] There is also perhaps a nod towards Diderot's *Supplément au voyage de Bougainville* (written 1772). Clothing differs for the married, widowed, and the single for Rousseau (1780: 140–141), but only for married and single people in More (2016b: 51).

dépenses', 29). He writes of the dangers of ostentatious wealth which has made villagers ashamed of their mediocrity and destroyed the barriers between the orders that make up French society. He omits reference to the wool trade which was specific to Britain and instead talks of how 'the height of misfortune is to see unbridled luxury these days triumphing insolently amongst you' ('le comble du malheur est de voir le luxe effréné triompher insolemment aujhourd'hui parmi vous', 43), railing against the avidity of the indolent rich, 'whose insolent prosperity is an insult to public misfortune' ('dont l'insolente prospérité insulte au malheur public', 45).

In his attack on hunting, Rousseau is harsher on the nobility than More in his original, in part because of the context in France where such privileges were increasingly resented. While More describes taking pleasure from hunting as springing 'from a cruel disposition, or else finally produces cruelty' (2016b: 75), Rousseau says that having a taste for killing prey for pleasure is 'always proof of a hard soul and a ferocious character' ('toujours la preuve d'une ame dure et d'un caractère féroce') and even if a huntsman retains his sensibility, he will in time acquire 'cruel and barbaric feelings' ('sentiments cruels et barbares', 1780: 207). Rousseau is also harsher on lawyers than More, explicitly accusing them of using 'insidious comments to have the guilty exonerated and the innocent condemned' ('commentaires insidieux [...] à faire absoudre le coupable et à faire condamner l'innocent', 251). More simply calls lawyers 'a class of men whose trade it is to manipulate cases and multiply quibbles' (2016b: 86), but Rousseau ladens them with emotive adjectives such as 'avaricious' (*avares*), 'insatiable' (*insatiables*), 'dangerous' (*dangereux*), and calls them 'vermin' (*vermine*) (1780: 250).

The temporal gap between More's original text and the 1780 translation encourages Rousseau to update cultural references. He quotes the seventeenth-century playwright Jean-François Regnard when discussing how to get people to agree with your view (1780: 101) and, when discussing misers, expands on More to include explicit reference to Molière's Harpagon from the play *L'Avare* (1668). Rousseau extends the image of the miser looking at his hoard (202) and adds his own comment on 'harpagons' or misers: 'is it not clear that all misers are determined idiots and the most foolish of dupes?' ('n'est-il pas clair que tout avare est un imbécille décidé et la plus sotte des dupes?', 204). There is no analagous judgement in the original. Rousseau sometimes also adds elements to remind his audience of Paris. After Hythloday has presented the Polylerites' treatment of thieves, Cardinal Morton says the ideas are worth an experiment: 'I think it would not be a bad idea to treat vagabonds this way too, for though we have passed many laws against them, they have had no real effect as yet' (2016b: 26). In the French, the focus is more emotive and Rousseau clearly has Paris in mind as he adds in an explicit mention of the capital that is absent in the original:

> I even believe that these measures would give us the means to effect an advantageous change in that crowd of vagabonds, strays, and homeless who swarm around the *streets of the capital* and against whom we have pronounced so many *devastating judgements* without any effect up to now.

> (Je crois même que ces mesures nous fourniraient encore le moyen d'opérer un changement avantageux dans cette foule de vagabonds, d'errans et de gens sans aveu qui fourmillent sur *le pavé de la capitale*, et contre lesquels nous avons, sans aucun fruit jusqu'à ce jour, prononcé tant *d'arrêts foudroyants*.) (1780: 64; emphasis added)

These examples show how the translator's views on social injustice surface repeatedly. Rousseau's reflections on the monarchy also pepper the translation but, very much in the vein of mainstream French Enlightenment, look to reform from within. Although subsequently Rousseau espoused radical Jacobin views on the Republic, in 1780 he was happy to use Louis XVI as a way to literary success. The translation, therefore, tones down More's criticism of kings. More wrote that 'from boyhood' kings are 'infected with false values' and 'seeds of evil and corruption' (2016b: 29), whilst Rousseau talks of a 'tight circle of ideas and vulgar opinions which he had been given to suck on with his milk' ('cercle étroit des idées, des opinions vulgaires qu'on lui aura fait sucer avec le lait') and of the 'administration's vices' ('vices de l'administration', 1780: 75–76), placing the blame more firmly on advisers than the monarch himself. Whilst More writes that a king should 'improve [his kingdom] as much as possible, and make it as flourishing as it could conceivably be made' (2016b: 32), Rousseau expands on this idea and addresses Louis XVI directly:

> Maintain peace, grace your lands through the protection with which you honour sciences and the fine arts, enrich your subjects by applying yourself to making commerce flourish; lead France to the highest point possible of splendour and prosperity through a wise administration: love your people that they may love you, revere you, and thank you. Be accessible and generous always so that in the shadow of your august throne all your subjects form but a single family with you as the father.
>
> (maintenez la paix, ornez vos Etats par la protection particulière dont vous devez honorez les sciences et les beaux arts, enrichissez vos sujets, en vous appliquant à faire fleurir la commerce; portez enfin, par une sage administration, la France au plus haut point de splendeur et de prospérité où elle puisse atteindre: aimez vos peuples, qu'ils vous aiment, qu'ils vous révèrent et vous bénissent. Soyez toujours accessible et bienfaisant, qu'à l'ombre de votre trône auguste tous vos sujets ne forment qu'une même famille, dont vous serez le père.) (1780: 83–84)

Rousseau's references to the king make it clear that he sees Utopia as a model, and not as a 'flawed commonwealth' (More 2016b: xii). Throughout the translation, Rousseau lessens the divide between Hythloday's views and those of 'Morus' (More's in-text persona) so that there is very little of More's 'disassociat[ion of] himself from Utopia' (xii). Rousseau adapts More's text to suit his own philosophy and to advocate social reform and so smooths out some of the tensions in the original. For instance, when at the end of Book One More's Hythloday suggests that the Utopians' 'readiness to learn is, I think, the really important reason for their being better governed and living more happily than we do' (42), in the French translation there is no mention of 'readiness to learn', no qualifying 'I think'. We find instead a plea for reform: 'as long as our governments do not model themselves on theirs, we will never have the promise of enjoying the abundance and prosperity which [Utopia] always enjoys' ('tant que nos gouvernemens ne se modéleront pas sur le sien, nous ne devons jamais nous promettre de jouir de l'abondance et la prospérité qui sera toujours son partage', 1780: 118). Rousseau also incorporates his own ideas on political economy into the translation, stressing the importance of commerce, which 'alone makes the true wealth of a kingdom' ('seul fait la véritable richesse d'un royaume', 97), a theme he will pick up in subsequent writings.

BETWEEN ONE *UTOPIA* AND THE NEXT

Rousseau followed his publication of *Utopia* with a number of strategic publications aimed at cementing his literary career. For instance, the same year, he published a *Discours au roi* in which he attacked luxury and praised Louis XVI for standing up to the English and for making France flourish once more. In 1781 he played on his shared surname with Jean-Jacques Rousseau to publish a *Lettre à M* sur le spectacle des boulevards*, which serves as response to Jean-Jacques's *Lettre à M d'Alembert sur les spectacles* (1758). He once again presents Louis XVI's reign as promising to be one of 'charity' (*bienfaisance*) and 'justice' and quotes from *Utopia* when reflecting on the relationship between theatre and morality:

> In tracing the picture of the abuses and disorders caused by the lesser theatres, it seemed to me that I found myself in the time when the illustrious T. Morus, Chancellor of England declared 'the height of misery is to see unbridled luxury now triumph insolently amongst us'.
>
> (En traçant le tableau des abus et des désordres qu'engendrent les trétaux, il m'a semblé me trouver à l'époque où se trouvait l'illustre T. Morus, Chancelier d'Angleterre, lorsqu'il s'écriait « le comble du malheur est de voir le luxe effréné, triompher insolemment aujourd'hui parmi nous ») (1781: 63)

Rousseau declares the current century superior to More's not least because France has a virtuous king who both loves truth and is a 'good father' (*bon père*, 67). He concludes that if the country had a second national theatre to replace the boulevard stages it could reach great heights, stressing that this is not a 'beautiful dream' (*beau rêve*) like Utopia but a 'beneficial change' (*changement heureux*) that is actually achievable (81). These ideas are endorsed by Pierre Rousseau (no relation) in the *Journal encyclopédique* (1781 [15 June]: 536–537).

The references to *Utopia* are perhaps a marketing ploy to send readers back to his translation, and the morality and patriotism that Rousseau displays in the *Letter* are consistent with the additions he made to More's text. His interest in commerce as a way of ensuring the glory of the nation is also sustained, as are his beliefs in religious tolerance. In 1787, he published *Dissertation sur le commerce*, translating Girolamo

Belloni's *De commercatio dissertatio* (1750); the *Mercure de France* on 12 May 1787 declared, 'circumstances make the principles it contains more interesting than ever' ('les circonstances rendent plus intéressans que jamais les principes qu'elle renferme', 94). He also wrote a further essay to Louis XVI, the *Discours au Roi sur la protection qu'il accorde au commerce* (1787), which was quickly followed by a *Précis historique sur l'édit de Nantes* (1788), written 'to convince us of the advantages of tolerance' ('pour nous convaincre des avantages de la tolerance') and praising Louis XVI—'father of all his people' (*père de tous ses peuples*)—for revoking the Edict of Nantes and allowing freedom of religion. For Rousseau, freedom of religion will create prosperity:

> Foreigners will rush once more to place their gold and their money in our coffers, industry will be rewarded, merchants will get richer, the king's rights will increase day by day, commerce will take off brilliantly, the power and glory of the nation will grow, and the general happiness of the French, of this calm, sociable and sensitive people will rest on unshakeable foundations!
>
> (Les Etrangers accourront de nouveau déposer leur or et leur argent dans nos coffres, l'industrie sera récompensée, le négociant s'enrichira, les droits du roi augmenteront de jour en jour, le commerce prendra le plus brillant essor, la puissance et la gloire de la nation s'étendront, et le bonheur général des Français, de ce peuple doux, liant et sensible, posera enfin sur des fondemens inébranlables!) (1788: 41)

A poem on trade followed, *Les Fastes du commerce*, the result of years of work, according to Rousseau,[8] and the author was described positively by the *Journal encyclopédique* on 15 September 1788 as having 'talent, warmth and nobility in his sentiments' ('du talent, de la chaleur et de la noblesse dans les sentimens', 356).

Rousseau is typical of a number of men of letters in the 1780s who hoped to get themselves noticed by commenting on the political and economic situation in France whilst flattering the king in the hope of a pension for their usefulness. He remained in a difficult position financially, even if his work was noticed by the literary periodicals and other aspiring writers, most notably the 'would-be *philosophe*' Jacques-Pierre Brissot de Warville (Darnton 1991: 192). In 1782, Brissot included extracts from More, explicitly taken from Rousseau's translation in his collection of texts on criminal law, the *Bibliothèque philosophique, du législateur, du politique, du jurisconsulte* (9.4). The extracts taken from *Utopia* were then republished in an article in the *Journal encyclopédique* (15 November 1784). For Brissot, in *Utopia*, there was 'a host of good principles' (*une foule de bonnes principes*) that show More was a man ahead of his time (9.6). Brissot reflects on corruption at court and the impossibility of philosophers serving there, on shared property, tolerance, and education, and approves of More's stance on divorce. He includes seven lengthy extracts from Rousseau's translation: on theft, the origins and causes of crime, slaves, punishment for adultery, ways of rewarding virtue, laws, and religious tolerance. His engagement with More, through Rousseau, sets out ideas for legal, religious,

---

[8] AN, F17/1212, dossier 10, no. 10.

and social reform, and forms what Leonore Loft describes as Brissot's 'training as a polemicist' (Loft 2002: 198). Rousseau, in turn, would highlight precisely these sections as being the most just and the most to be admired by good politicians (*bons politiques*) in his preface to the second edition of his translation (More 1789a: xxi).

THE FRENCH REVOLUTION

Although Rousseau and Brissot would represent opposing views of the radical revolutionary phase of 1793, in 1789 the Revolution provided each of them with an opportunity to become the acclaimed man of letters they had aspired to. The Revolution led to a swift change of tone in Rousseau's writings. He launched an ode, *La Liberté française* (1789) with a disdainful 'cowardly and ferocious despotism | Cease to irritate my view' ('lache et féroce despotisme, | Cesse d'irriter mes regards'), which sits uneasily with his praise of Louis XVI just a couple of years earlier. At the end of 1789, a time when the regeneration of the nation was the focus of attention and there was a real sense that the Revolution was almost over, he reissued his translation of More, entitled this time *Du meilleur Gouvernement possible, ou la nouvelle isle d'Utopie, de Thomas Morus*. It was published by J. Blanchon, the publisher he had used for his ode to Liberty. The *Mercure français* of 30 January 1790 mentions the new publication in a more flattering light than the first edition, deeming the translation 'the closest which has appeared of a highly regarded work' ('la plus exacte qui ait paru d'un Ouvrage estimé', 219).

Questions of 'the best government possible' were most definitely in the air in late 1789. As Rousseau reflects, 'everyone wants to be politician, reformer, legislator' ('chacun veut être politique, réformateur, léglislateur', More 1789a: vii). The publication of a *Recueil de différens principes qui constituent un gouvernement libre, et régi par de bonnes loix* ('Collection of Different Principles Which Constitute a Free Government Ruled by Good Laws'), was announced in the *Mercure de France* on 14 November 1789, and on 1 December the *Journal encyclopédique* talked of 'le meilleur gouvernement possible' in a review of Bernardin de Saint-Pierre's *Vœux d'un solitaire*. Rousseau's new edition was intended to mine this revolutionary seam. The new edition opened with a translator's preface which begins: 'all men seem at this moment in time to want to take a few steps towards happiness' ('tous les hommes paraissent vouloir faire en ce moment quelques pas vers le bonheur', More 1789a: vii). He explains his rationale for re-editing the text:

> I do not advocate adopting all of the principles of the famous and unfortunate Chancellor of England but I remain convinced that most of the main ideas of his Utopia are marked by justice and reason. In this political novel we find profound views, wisely traced and solidly established plans regarding a number of important points concerning administration; we find truths that are timeless and valid for all peoples. It is because of this conviction that I determined to produce a second edition of the translation of this profound work that I undertook ten years ago.

(Je suis bien éloigné d'adopter tous les principes du célebre & infortuné Chancelier d'Angleterre; mais je n'en fuis pas moins persuadé que la plupart des grandes idées de son Utopie portent l'empreinte de la justice & de la raison. On trouve dans ce Roman politique, des vues profondes, des plans sagement tracés, solidement établis, sur plusieurs points importans de l'Administration; on y rencontre enfin des vérités qui sont de tous les tems, & qui sont bonnes pour tous les peuples. C'est d'après cette persuasion, que je me suis déterminé à faire faire une seconde édition de la traduction que j'ai entreprise, il y a dix ans, de ce profond ouvrage.)

The title removes the idea that the work presents a picture (*tableau*) of good government which was present in the title of the original translation. The new title is closer to the title of More's Latin original and appears to French readers as more definitive and the text more demonstrative 'du meilleur gouvernement possible'. The principal change to the edition, beyond the title, lies in the addition of a table of contents, making it easier to consult. This is all the more important because Rousseau presents the text as essential reading for those in the public domain:

> all ministers, magistrates, and others in public office should know it by heart; they will find sure rules for their conduct in all circumstances and will draw from it important maxims which contain, in a sense, the seeds of public happiness.
>
> (tous les Ministres, les Magistrats, & autres personnes en place devraient le posséder par cœur; ils y trouveraient des regles sûres pour leur conduite, dans toutes les circonstances, & y puiseraient ces grandes maximes, qui renferment, en quelque façon, les germes de la félicité publique.) (xxii)

The text thus becomes 'a perfect legislative code suited to remedying abuses' ('un code parfait de législation propre à remédier aux abus', 14). To this end Rousseau adds his own marginal section headings that provide guides to themes such as 'causes of revolutions' (*causes des révolutions*) and definitions of both despotism (*du despotisme*) and true philosophy (*de la vraie philosophie*). The translation itself is unchanged from the 1780 edition but the paratext in the margin draws attention in a new way to what he considers to be the key aspects. Even in the first edition, Rousseau, in the section on the wealth of kings (More 2016b: 34), had included the idea of despotism:

> An awful and barbaric despotism worthy of a Crassus is at the root of all the opinions offered in the council. What horrible maxims are not uttered? 'A king', one says, 'can never be rich enough because he is obliged, to maintain his crown and his dignity, to maintain at all times formidable armies which are ready to march at the first signal.
>
> (Le despotisme affreux & barbare, digne d'un Crassus est le fondement de tous les avis proposés dans ce Conseil. Quelles horribles maximes n'y débite-t-on pas? « Un Roi, dit-on, ne saurait jamais être assez riche, parce qu'il est obligé, pour le maintien & la dignité de sa Couronne, d'entretenir en tout tems des armées formidables, prêtes à marcher au premier signal. ») (More 1789a: 76)

The addition of the marginal heading, however, draws readers' attention more firmly to the notion of despotism which, in a revolutionary context, acquires connotations unintended in the 1780 translation. For example, the Affair of the Diamond Necklace (1785) and the virulent pamphleteering of the later 1780s criticizing the monarchy—and Marie Antoinette in particular—gives a whole new urgency to discussions of monarchical wealth.[9]

Similarly, the addition of the heading *causes des révolutions* in the context of 1789 brings home more starkly Rousseau's expansion of More's ideas on poverty. Hythloday's cynical suggestion that poverty is deliberately maintained to 'grind out of the oppressed the lofty spirit of rebellion' (More 2016b: 34) is extended in Rousseau and made more explicitly revolutionary. More had written:

> They are absolutely wrong in thinking that the people's poverty guarantees public peace: experience shows the contrary. Where will you find more squabbling than among beggars? Who is more eager to change things than the person who is most discontented with his present position? Who is more reckless about creating disorder than the man who knows he has nothing to lose and thinks he may have something to gain? (34–35)

Rousseau revises as follows:

> The misery of the people is, we are told, the safest way of ensuring royal authority. What nonsense, what horror! Have those miserly and fierce men who have the audacity to talk this way ever consulted experience? Without a doubt, no. It would have taught them that it is misery that creates both the hatred one feels for the sovereign and the seditions that tear apart the heart of the kingdom. Who would wish for, who would speed up with more enthusiasm those revolutions that change the face of empires than those who bear impatiently the heavy yoke under which they suffer? Encouraged by the hope of finding some occasion to improve their lot in the upheaval of things, who spreads the fire of rebellion with more audacity and rapidity in all the veins of the state than he who has nothing to lose?
>
> (La misere des Peuples, nous dit-on, est le plus sûr appui de l'autorité royale? Quelle absurdité, quelle horreur! Les hommes avares et farouches qui ont l'audace de nous parler ainsi, ont-ils jamais consulté l'expérience? Non, sans doute; elle leur aurait appris que c'est la misere elle-même qui enfante, & la haîne qu'on porte au Souverain, et les séditions qui déchirent le coeur de son Royaume. Qui doit souhaiter, qui doit accélérer avec plus d'ardeur ces révolutions qui changent la face des empires, que ceux qui supportent impatiemment le joug appésanti sous lequel ils gémissent? Encouragé par l'espoir de trouver quelqu'occasion d'améliorer son sort dans le bouleversement des affaires, qui porte avec plus d'audace et de rapidité dans tous les veines de l'Etat le feu de la rébellion, que celui qui n'a rien à perdre.) (More 1789a: 78)

---

[9] For more on how Marie Antoinette's reputation for frivolous expenditure was exacerbated by a plot by Jeanne de la Motte to acquire a diamond necklace through the Cardinal de Rohan, see Beckman 2014; on the virulent antimonarchy pamphlets, see C. Thomas 2001.

For Irmgard Hartig and Albert Soboul, in presenting *Utopia* as a handbook for the construction of a new society, Rousseau's text becomes the 'negation of utopia, in so far as it suppresses the contradiction between utopia and reality' ('négation de l'utopie, dans la mesure où elle supprime la contradiction entre utopie et réalité', Hartig and Soboul 1976: 179). It is certainly the case that the marginal headings encourage readers to see the text as advocating an egalitarian vision of society. Whilst the text itself is unchanged from the first edition (the only difference is that the incorrect typesetting of the first few lines is corrected), the context in which it is read has changed. Even the 'enlightened' first edition lessened the semi-comic intellectual exchange about the various possible ways of organizing society that are to be found in More, but the revised title and chapter headings in 1789 take this further and make the text a blueprint rather than a scholarly game.

Rousseau reissued his translation because he wanted to make a contribution to the regeneration of the nation that was taking place in 1789. He continued to publish during the Revolutionary decade with a desire to bring to fruition Enlightenment ideals of education with works he considered 'useful to the instruction of the people eager for enlightenment' ('utiles à l'instruction du peuple avide de lumières', Rousseau An. II). As so many men of letters did at the time, he turned his hand to journalism, responsible for, amongst others, the *Premier journal de la convention ou Le Point du jour* (1792) and *Le Mensonge et la vérité* and *Journal de la Montagne* (1794). The Société des Jacobins nominated Rousseau to work with the committee of public instruction which was created to organize a reform of the education system. He was presented to the National Convention as a man who 'combines revolutionary ardour, complete integrity, hard work, and the qualities of a man of letters' ('réunit l'ardeur révolutionnaire, la probité la plus intègre, l'activité du travail, et les qualités d'un homme de lettres') and who is 'known for his patriotic works even before the revolution' ('connu par des ouvrages patriotiques dès avant la revolution').[10] In addition to fulfilling public roles and acting as archivist to the Société des Jacobins, he wrote political plays such as *A bas la calotte ou les déprêtrisés*, performed at the Variétés amusantes in 1794, though he ensured that they avoided the pitfalls of immoral theatre he had condemned in his 1781 letter about the boulevard theatres. Above all, he made his reputation as a writer of patriotic songs, distributed via a dedicated journal, *Les Chants du patriotisme*, which Laura Mason (1996: 115) has declared 'a model of revolutionary pedagogy'. Strongly recommended by the *Annales patriotiques et littéraires de la France, et affaires politiques de l'Europe*, Rousseau's collection of songs was revered as an 'ingenious production which contains the whole history of the revolution' ('ingénieuse production, qui renfermera toute l'histoire de la révolution').[11]

---

[10] *Journal des débats et des décrets, ou Récrit de ce qui s'est passé aux séances de l'assemblée nationale depuis le 17 juin 1789, jusqu'au premier septembre de la même année*, vol. 54, Séance du Octidi 28 Prairial, An II, 427.

[11] *Annales patriotiques et littéraires de la France*, suppl. to vol. 104 (13 Apr. 1792: 465).

Despite the wide-scale distribution of his patriotic songs and his close involvement with the Société des Jacobins, Rousseau survived the radical phase of the Revolution. He continued to write and to advocate the neutrality of writers who publish 'in defence of principles, to support the government adopted by the people, to propagate those grand truths upon which rest both the prosperity of nations and the happiness of individuals' ('à la défense des principes, au soutien du gouvernement adopté par le peuple, à la propagation des grandes vérités sur lesquelles reposent également la prospérité des nations et le bonheur des êtres', 1796: 10–11). Like so many other minor writers of the period, Rousseau was, to use the phrase of Jean-Luc Chappey (2015: 13), a 'writer in revolution' (*écrivain en révolution*). He had found a purpose during the early years of the Revolution and continued to be convinced by the power of the written word in educating the nation. 'I wrote to instruct and not to be dragged off to be executed', he stated in An V in the *Censure de la Convention nationale* ('J'écrivais pour instruire et non pas pour me faire trainer au supplice'). He published the pedagogic *Le livre utile et agréable pour la jeunesse* (An VII) for 'a people whose political and moral existence it is proposed to renew' ('un peuple dont on se propose de renouveler l'existence politique et morale', (p.i), and he explained in 1792 that all he wanted to do was be 'useful to my fellow men and be worthy of my country' ('utile à mes semblables, de bien mériter de mon pays').

Although Rousseau had always had a focus on education—he expanded More's educational programme for the Utopians, for instance, giving full-time students a focus not just on liberal arts but also philosophy and metaphysics—by the moderate republican phase of the Revolution, known as the Directory (1795–9), he had, as many other minor writers like him, become a republican pedagogue who had moved away from seeing Utopia as achievable.[12] Nevertheless, he remained a writer who wanted to improve society, joining the Portique républicain in 1799, a literary society which aimed to mobilize neo-Jacobin writers to promote the importance of the arts in saving the Republic. Education was at the heart of the society's project (Chappey 2004), and in many ways, Rousseau's involvement with it represents the culmination of a coherent literary project. As an ardent believer in Enlightenment notions of progress, he had been profoundly marked by his translation of More's text in 1780 and this engagement with the concept of Utopia found its natural outlet in the revolutionary decade where he was able to channel ideas of social injustice and the importance of education into attempting to change the status quo.

---

[12] For more on *Utopia* and the Directory, see Chappey 2013.

PART THREE

TRANSLATIONS AND EDITIONS AFTER 1800

CHAPTER 21

FALSE FRIENDS (AND THEIR USES)

Thomas More's Utopia *Among the Victorians*

MARCUS WAITHE

SURPRISINGLY few English translations of Thomas More's *Utopia* (1516) were made in the nineteenth century. The British Library catalogue lists no new version between Arthur Cayley's (More 1808a) and Harold and Zoe Paget's (More 1909). Mid-nineteenth-century readers were largely content to take Gilbert Burnet's translation of 1684 as their standard, while, from the 1890s, Ralph Robinson's revised 1556 translation underwent a revival that lasted into the Edwardian period.[1] But what the nineteenth century lacked in fresh renderings, it made up for in what might broadly be termed 'cultural translation'. Coined originally by anthropologists to name the process of negotiation—of cultural meanings, equivalencies, differences—arising when social systems encounter one another, it has been applied more recently to evoke the extra-linguistic work of translation (Beidelman 1971; Burke 2009: 30). The effort is less to construe foreign terms than to make sense of, and to domesticate, an otherwise incommensurable cultural load. While translation of an ancient text precludes the answering analysis of an anthropological meeting, the late nineteenth century witnessed a period of intense engagement with More's *Utopia*, during which editors, readers, and public figures absorbed and realigned More's priorities through practices of popular allusion, critical commentary, and republication.

Writing on cultural translation, Peter Burke quotes a pertinent observation of the seventeenth-century translator Nicolas d'Ablancourt: 'Different times', he proposed, 'do not just require different words but also different thoughts, and ambassadors usually dress in the fashion of the country to which they are sent' (Burke 2009: 30). Victorian

---

[1] For Burnet's translation, see Withington in this volume; for Robinson's, see Bishop and Cavanagh in this volume.

editors and readers happily reclothed More's 'ambassadors', and on occasion sent them home without an audience. Their almost total neglect of Book One is illustrative, although there were precedents: Claude Chausonette's (aka Cantiuncula's) German translation, printed in Basel in 1524 (and the first vernacular translation—the only one to appear in More's lifetime), comprised only Book Two (Salberg 2008: 32), and early excerption practices presented Book Two as a stand-alone contribution to governmental theory, as seen in Francesco Sansovino's *Del Governo* (1561).[2] Nonetheless, the Victorians inherited, and developed to its fullest extent, a mythic conception of the work, one that prioritized utopian news over More's more inscrutable legacy. Broadly speaking, *Utopia* was conflated with 'utopia', here understood as a complete view of ideal social conditions.

If this was cultural translation, it was distinguished by a remarkable inattention to the fact of linguistic translation. Derived from a Latin text conceived in Antwerp, and published first in Louvain, many Victorian editions still presented *Utopia* as a classic of English letters. Despite the scholarly precedent of T. F. Dibdin's heavily annotated 1808 edition, few editors registered the implications of choosing one translation over another. Deeper concerns—such as the choice of Latin edition, the inclusion of early paratexts, or even the fact that *Utopia* was not the work's original title—were barely registered (T. Cave 2008c: xii).[3] Such niceties conflicted with the work's settled status, its ability to stand for an ideal or purist position unencumbered by worldly concerns. J. H. Lupton's English–Latin parallel text of 1895 seems an exception: as Lupton's preface noted, it exercised 'the same exact care that is looked for, as a matter of course, in editing a classical author' (More 1895a: vii). Instead of offering a new translation, however, Lupton applied a doubly antiquarian logic. He reprinted Robinson on the grounds 'of its representing an early period of English', but did so using the rarely seen first edition of 1551, for 'advantage of freshness' (ix).[4]

This chapter attends to the more revealing instances of selectivity and misinterpretation that flow from these conditions of republication. The aim is not to expose a faulty or partial translation in favour of one more compelling. Nor is it to propose a council of despair, along the lines of Wilhelm von Humboldt's remark in a letter to A. W. Schwegel (23 July 1796) that 'all translation seems to me simply an attempt to solve an impossible task' (cited in Wilss 1982: 35). Without diminishing the technical and ethical challenges involved in linguistic translation, the advantage of thinking more broadly about cultural encounter is that all versions of the text, however idiosyncratic, may be seen as generative, less corruptions of an original code than mutations productive of new life. The sheer instability of the text in question—considering its Latin variants, its changing title, its primary readership in translation—lends interest to its entire life, and afterlife. Misunderstandings become cultural opportunities, and blind spots yield new

---

[2] For Sansovino's version, see chapters by Scholar and Shrank in this volume.

[3] It was not until 1624 that an English edition appeared under the title of *Utopia* (T. Cave 2008b: 87).

[4] T. F. Dibdin's edition also used the 1551 edition of Robinson, albeit stressing its 'scarcity' (More 1808b: iv).

perspectives. This is apparent especially in the political sphere. The last decades of the nineteenth century witnessed an unusual convergence of Radical, conservative, and socialist readings: a wide spectrum of interest that puzzles, until understood as a function of matters not just lost, but also gained, in translation.

Layman's Terms

Writing in the *Faber Book of Utopias*, John Carey observes that 'Utopia means *nowhere* or no-place', but 'has often been taken to mean *good place*, through confusion of its first syllable with the Greek *eu* as in *euphemism* or *eulogy*' (1999: xvi). What Carey blithely dismisses as a misreading, most critics have taken for a deliberate pun (see Kumar 1991: 1). Still, it is worth querying the grounds for the assumption that utopia is a good place. To take at random one of many thousand press references, a piece in the weekly newspaper *The Era* on 'Competition and the Stage' from 9 July 1892 reports that 'we are as far as ever from Sir Thomas More's Utopia' (7). The author relies on a common understanding that reaching *Utopia* means reaching 'utopia'. The idea that More's vision signified a state of general happiness, formed at the outer reaches of idealism, even informed debating points in Parliament. Arguing for a defensive military capacity, and citing the Utopians' provisions for using force, the Liberal MP for Middlesex, Bernal Osborne, remarked in 1852 that he 'could not imagine that anybody, either in that House or out of it, would be more Utopian than the Utopians themselves'.[5] Here, as in so many other cases, the debater's conception of the 'utopian' relies on an allusion to More, but treats his work as if it were a manifesto. Acknowledging this quality in the layman's sense of utopia, J. S. Mill observed in Parliament that 'what is commonly called Utopian is something too good to be practicable' (Mill 1870: 109). The word 'commonly' registers the kind of 'mix-up' that Carey supposes, one that necessitates Mill's own coinage of 'dystopians', a term signifying those who favour what 'is too bad to be practicable' (109). 'Dystopia' has been recuperated or converted to mean something quite different today, in signifying a 'bad place' all too likely to arise if we make the wrong decisions.

This sense of a settled meaning at odds with the ambiguity of More's actual text interacts with a circular tendency that sees *Utopia* attributed to a genre defined exclusively by itself. On 7 April 1882, the *Daily News* observed of Anthony Trollope's *The Fixed Period* (1882) that 'the book belongs to the long line of fictions of the stamp of Sir Thomas More's "Utopia," describing, as it does, an imaginary country wherein society is organized upon fanciful conditions' (6). The untroubled linkage of More's book to an associated adjective and genre contributed to its fame. *Utopia* became an obvious inclusion among the many 'libraries' of literary classics compiled by publishers towards the

---

[5] Bernal Osborne, Militia Bill, House of Commons debate, 7 June 1852, *Hansard*, lines 173–4 <http://hansard.millbanksystems.com/commons/1852/jun/07/militia-bill>, accessed 21 Dec. 2017.

end of the century. As Lupton's glossary of Tudor English implies, the archaic mould of Robinson's translation allowed it to stand for the thing itself (More 1895a: 323–326). On 26 April 1890, *The Graphic* reported that 'Mr. Walter Scott has done well to include so celebrated a reconstruction of society as Sir Thomas More's "Utopia" [Robinson's 1556 translation] in his excellent series of Camelot classics' (480); on 13 April 1898, it reported the book's addition, again in Robinson's 1556 translation, to J. M. Dent's Temple Classics series (245). On 17 January 1891, the *Preston Guardian* noted the publication of *Utopia* in Cassell's National Library, an edition recommended for its 'particularly entertaining' biographical sketch of More. Edited in the late 1880s by Henry Morley—a professor of English at University College London—it used Burnet's translation on the grounds that it was 'translated with more literary skill' than Robinson had achieved (More 1889: 8). Though noting the Greek etymology of Hythloday's name (he renders it 'knowing in trifles'), Morley distinguished frivolities from political messages: 'under the veil of a playful fiction', he observed, 'the talk is intensely earnest, and abounds in practical suggestion' (9), while beneath the 'ideal communism', there 'lies a noble English argument' (10). Stressing the earlier composition of Book Two in 1515, he characterized Book One (1516) as 'introductory' (8), a kind of explanatory afterthought.

The appearance of *Utopia* in anthologies also signalled 'classic' status. These began with J. A. St John's 1838 and 1852 editions of Burnet's translation (printed under the title *Utopia: or the Happy Republic, a Philosophical Romance*), to which was 'added' Francis Bacon's *New Atlantis* (first published posthumously in 1627) and—in the second edition—also Plato's *Republic*. Predating Morley's 1889 edition of *Utopia* for Cassell's National Library was his earlier project—his influential and much reissued *Ideal Commonwealths*—which appeared in 1885, a volume that collected Burnet's *Utopia* alongside Plutarch's *Life of Lycurgus*, Bacon's *New Atlantis*, Tommaso Campanella's *City of the Sun* (1602), and Joseph Hall's *Mundus Alter et Idem* ('Another World and Yet the Same') (*c.*1605). If these versions appealed to a relatively safe understanding of the literary classic, their pricing and marketing targeted a lower middle-class and aspiring working-class audience. This reflected both a fashion for listing 'great books' useful for self-education, and a need to determine the scope of English studies, a new discipline understood initially as 'poor man's classics' (Waller 2006: 172–173).[6] Opposite the title page of Morley's edition were listed the other authors edited by him in Cassell's National Library, among them Xenophon, Plutarch, Edmund Spenser, William Shakespeare, Bacon, Voltaire, Daniel Defoe, Joseph Addison, Thomas Carlyle, and Charles Dickens, but also less familiar works such as William Petty's *Essays on Mankind* (1682) and *The Amber Witch*, and Lady Duff Gordon's translation of Wilhelm Meinhold's *Maria Schweidler* (1838). The Arnoldian internationalism of this selection sits curiously and suggestively beside inside-cover advertisements for *The Practical Rabbit Keeper* by 'Cuniculus' (the name

---

[6] The Regius chair of rhetoric and belles-lettres was established at the University of Edinburgh in 1762, and lectures in English literature were offered at mechanics' institutes in the early nineteenth century; but it was not until 1865, when a proper endowment marked Morley's succession to David Masson's chair at University College London, that the discipline of English began to assume its modern form.

meaning 'rabbit' in Latin), and L. Wright's *The Practical Poultry Keeper: A Complete and Standard Guide to the Management of Poultry, whether for Domestic Use, the Market, or Exhibition*. Given More's own interest in how matters should be managed, the focus on practical affairs and animal husbandry makes sense; but the conjunction of utopianism, self-education, and rabbit-keeping evidently positions this paperback at a location carefully poised between subjects more usually kept apart. A similar spirit pervades an article on 'A Working Man's Library', published in *Reynolds Newspaper* on 25 December 1898 (2): it included *Utopia* in a catalogue of books suitable for occupying the leisure time of working men. Eleven months after noticing Morley's edition, on 5 December 1891 the *Preston Guardian* reported a lecture, by Mr Phythian, that drew comparison between *Utopia* and the aims of the burgeoning Co-operative Movement. More's portrait of a moneyless and property-less economy naturally appealed to the kind of audience that could just about afford a paperback at 3*d*. Apart from the advertising possibilities, reliance on early translations of *Utopia* and other 'classics' out of copyright assisted the profitability—and affordability—of such ventures. In these circumstances, the culturally silent Englishing of a neo-Latin work acquired a complex significance, informed variously by factors commercial, antiquarian, canonical, and social.

Utopia on Handmade Paper

While *Utopia*'s appeal may easily be read along these politico-social lines (whether for 'ideal communism' or a 'noble English argument'), it was never confined to them. Several kinds of attraction were often felt by the same audience at the same time. Convergence between social radicalism and emerging cultures of the literary classic also played a part in more rarefied contexts: for instance, in the life and work of William Morris. In a list of 'The Best Hundred Books', published in the *Pall Mall Gazette* on 2 February 1886, Morris included *Utopia* at No. 51, categorizing it with works by Carlyle and John Ruskin as among those which 'I don't know how to class' (2). As a revolutionary socialist—and indeed one who would later publish *News from Nowhere; Or, An Epoch of Rest, Being Some Chapters from a Utopian Romance* (1890)—Morris was more than usually attuned to the radical import of More's *Utopia*.[7] But he was also interested in it as a work of literature. Its inclusion in his fine bookmaking venture, the Kelmscott Press, signalled an effort to combine literary with political canonization. Published in 1893, the Kelmscott edition used Robinson's 1556 version, an original copy of which Morris held in his personal library. This is not surprising in itself, since many Victorian editions employed Robinson's revised text; but Morris and the volume's editor, F. S. Ellis, took the less usual step of reproducing the marginal headings that Robinson added to that edition, perhaps influenced by Morris's intimate relationship with the layout of a book he kept at

---

[7] For more on Morris and utopianism, see Hanson in this volume.

home.[8] The same format inspired the marginal key added to *News from Nowhere* in its Kelmscott version (1892). Three hundred paper copies of the Kelmscott *Utopia* were printed, and eight in vellum; all were bound in limp vellum, with silk ties. This, clearly, is a world away from 3*d*. copies aimed at would-be rabbit-keepers. The popularity of More's book ensured that sales were buoyant, and that the edition required no subvention. William Peterson estimates that Morris made £45 on the whole print run of 300 copies: that is, around £6,000 in today's money.[9]

While Morris and Ellis scrupulously registered the source of their text, they engaged equally in practices of recreation and reimagination. Bare of ornament by comparison with the well-known Kelmscott *Chaucer* (1896), the Kelmscott *Utopia* was nevertheless unlike any other modern edition. Its typeface, 'Chaucer', introduces a stylistic countercurrent, the Gothic forms hinting at medieval manuscript culture rather than the Renaissance print culture conjured by Morris's 'Golden Type'. The woodcut designs of the ornamental capitals invoke a world of craft rather than mechanical reproduction (see Fig. 21.1). The marginal text and headings appear in a deep red highlight; and an alternating leaf motif marks the paragraph breaks. Robinson's 1556 edition used ornamental capitals and display type in headings, and its face is likewise Gothic (see Fig. 16.1); however, the flourishes are fewer, and the meaning of black letter's nod to handwritten precedent largely effaced by its status as the then ubiquitous English type.[10] Moreover, Morris and Ellis did not actually work from the original edition, but from a reset 1556 edition edited by Edward Arber in 1869. Arber restricted black-letter text to the page headers and his ornamental capitals are of Victorian design. He also included Robinson's marginal headings, which in itself supplies a more mundane basis for their appearance in the Kelmscott edition. Morris's copy of Arber survives, its text marked up to indicate the placing of leaf motifs, and additional ornamental capitals.[11] Textual changes are also evident, as where Morris overrides Arber and Robinson by decapitalizing the initial letter in 'Iron', and justifies the decoratively centred closing lines of each chapter; or where he reverts to older usage, as when returning Arber's 'th[e] entente' to Robinson's 'thentente' (More 1556: 91; 1869: 121; 1893: 189). On the previous page, he avoids a misplaced archaism by retaining the word 'wonders' (used in Arber and Robinson) in answer to Ellis's marked query, 'refer to Mr Morris if he would make this "wondrous" ' (More 1556: 91; 1869: 120; 1893: 189). And while Robinson's editions (and Arber's reprint)

---

[8] See Peterson and Peterson, 'The Library of William Morris: A Catalogue', <https://williammorrislibrary.wordpress.com/2014/03/21/¶-more-utopia-1556/>, accessed 21 Mar. 2018.

[9] Peterson notes that 'Morris's gross receipts from More's *Utopia*, an octavo published in an edition of 300 copies (thirty shillings) and eight vellum copies (ten guineas), could not have been less than £300, whereas it cost only about £255 to produce' (Peterson 1991: 201).

[10] For a discussion of black letter's later evolution as a 'nostalgic' face, see Lesser 2006: 99–126.

[11] The bookplate in Morris's copy reads 'The text from which the Kelmscott Press edition of "Utopia" was set up, with pencil directions as to initials etc in the autograph of William Morris'. The book is now in a private collection; page images of annotations are available at Peterson and Peterson, 'The Library of William Morris: A Catalogue', accessed 21 Mar. 2018. For an example of marking up, see the ornamental 'F' in 'For manye' (More 1556: 91; 1869: 121; 1893: 190).

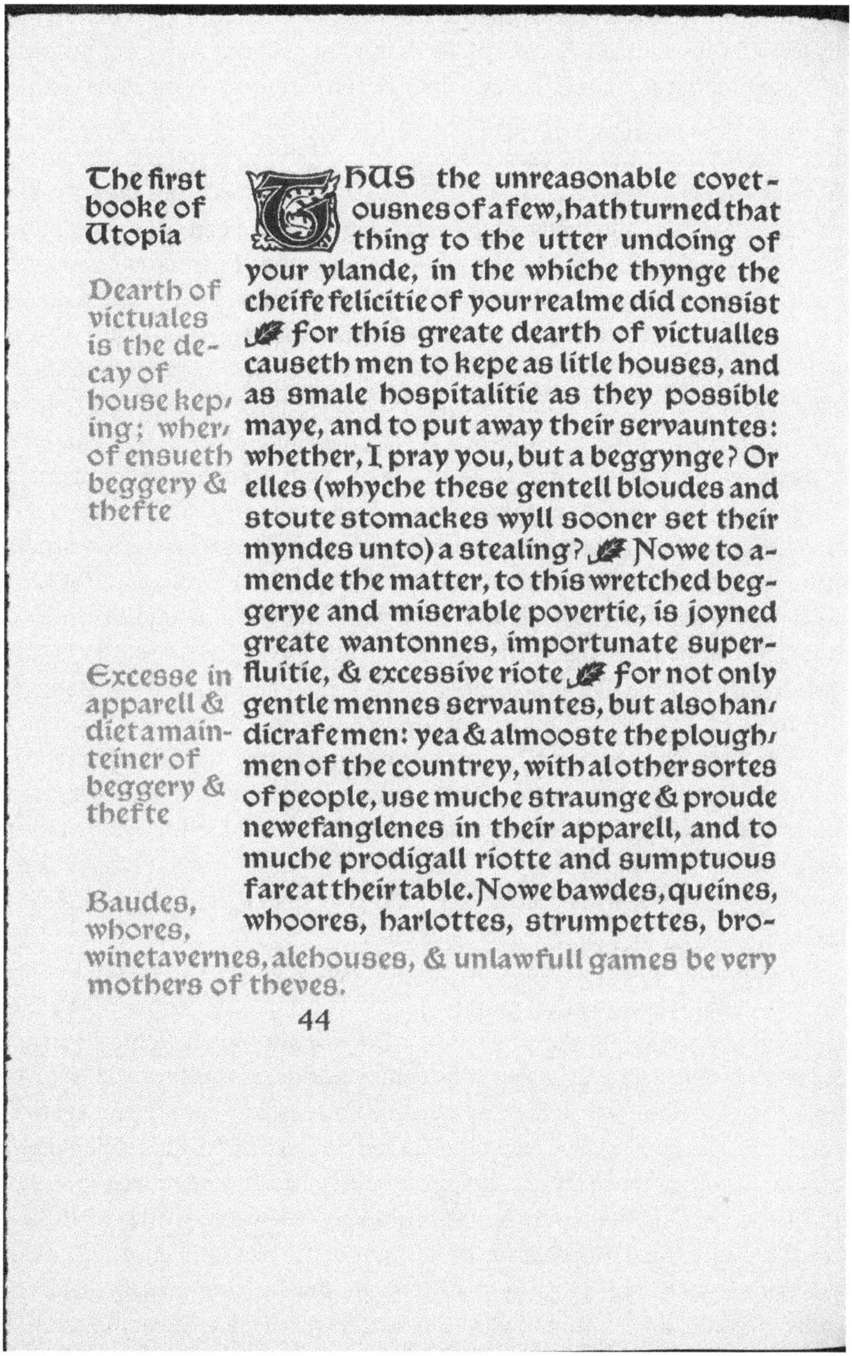

> The first booke of Utopia
>
> THUS the unreasonable covetousnes of a few, hath turned that thing to the utter undoing of your ylande, in the whiche thynge the cheife felicitie of your realme did consist
>
> *Dearth of victuales is the decay of house keping; wherof ensueth beggery & thefte*
>
> for this greate dearth of victualles causeth men to kepe as litle houses, and as smale hospitalitie as they possible maye, and to put away their servauntes: whether, I pray you, but a beggynge? Or elles (whyche these gentell bloudes and stoute stomackes wyll sooner set their myndes unto) a stealing? Nowe to amende the matter, to this wretched beggerye and miserable povertie, is joyned greate wantonnes, importunate superfluitie, & excessive riote
>
> *Excesse in apparell & diet a mainteiner of beggery & thefte*
>
> for not only gentle mennes servauntes, but also handicrafe men: yea & almooste the ploughmen of the countrey, with al other sortes of people, use muche straunge & proude newefanglenes in their apparell, and to muche prodigall riotte and sumptuous fare at their table. Nowe bawdes, queines,
>
> *Baudes, whores,*
>
> whoores, harlottes, strumpettes, browinetavernes, alehouses, & unlawfull games be very mothers of theves.
>
> 44

FIG. 21.1. Thomas More, *Utopia*, trans. Ralph Robinson, ed. F. S. Ellis (Hammersmith: Kelmscott Press, 1893), The Bodleian Libraries, University of Oxford, Kelmscott Press e.12, p. 44.

omitted the 'Utopia Insulae Figura' (map of Utopia) published with the 1516 text, Morris initially looked back to that principle of illustration in planning a chart of his own design (Peterson 1991: 154). Though subsequently dropped, the intention alone confirms a creative rather than reconstructive approach to the edition's format and apparatus.

Morris's departures from his textual source had a habit nevertheless of converging with Robinson's own forms of licence. As Elizabeth McCutcheon observes, 'Robinson himself comes very close to being a fellow participant of the text he is translating; he even enters into dialogue with it by way of his own marginalia', while at the same time 'making it more conservative and facilitating running comparisons that the marginal comments added in 1556 make even more explicit' (McCutcheon 1992: 106).[12] This sense of a participatory agenda entailed a great deal more than applying a fine binding to an existing text. Certainly, the new and luxuriant housing implied reverence for an increasingly popular literary classic, a quality that attracted the interest of an Eton master, who according to Aymer Vallance ordered forty copies, 'with the intention of distributing them as prizes among the boys of the college' (Vallance 1897: 149). And the aesthetic intrusion of medievalism was evidently uncontroversial, along with the technically inflammatory but historically remote 'communism' of Raphael Hythloday. But Morris's Foreword proved another matter. It addressed political questions, and to some extent took a socialist audience for granted: 'the Utopia', it suggests, 'is a necessary part of a Socialist's library'; indeed, it had become 'a Socialist tract familiar to […] meetings and debating rooms' (More 1893: iii–iv).[13] As Vallance explains, 'when the work appeared with a compromisingly Socialistic introduction by Morris, the [Eton] order, from motives of prudence, had to be cancelled' (Vallance 1897: 149). The incident starkly demonstrates the forms of cultural reconciliation at work in Morris's vision of the text. At least in his mind's eye, *Utopia* functioned simultaneously as a literary classic—and in that capacity a volume 'safe' for schoolboys—and as an early entry in an emerging (and, to some minds, dangerous) canon of socialist texts.

Morris's Foreword offers, all the same, an unusually sophisticated account of republication as a cultural and political gesture. Frankly acknowledging the work's filtered status, the first sentence invokes not 'More's *Utopia*', but 'Ralph Robinson's translation of More's *Utopia*' (1893: iii). Even as he commends its lessons for socialists, Morris recognizes that the book was written by a 'man who resisted what has seemed to most the progressive movement of his own time' (iii–iv). Indeed, he concludes that the value of *Utopia* as 'a book for the study of sociology is rather historic than prophetic' (iv). Such editorial self-consciousness has its limits: Hythloday's views are treated as if they are equivalent to More's, and Morris gives no account of the relation between Book One's dialogic method and Book Two's monologic form. But his commentary stands apart from other accounts in refusing to view the text as 'a charming literary exercise' (iii), whether hopelessly antiquarian or vaguely deracinated. Rather, it takes account of a

---

[12] For more on Robinson's dialogue with the text, see Cavanagh in this volume.
[13] For one such meeting, in nineteenth-century Japan, see Sako in this volume.

great 'change of ideas concerning "the best state of the publique weal"', and the ways in which this threw 'a fresh light upon the book' (iii). In this manner Morris acknowledges a recreative vision: the text is a message that changes over time, its meanings interacting with the present in new and unpredictable ways.

THOMAS MORE: CHARTIST, COMMUNIST, AND GENTLEMAN FARMER

By mediating the relation between his own present and More's past, Morris hoped to explain how a proto-communistic work came to be written by a man with 'a curiously blended savour of Cato the Censor and a mediaeval monk' (More 1893: vi). This ambition touches on the larger question of the work's political complexity and adaptability. What was it about More's vision that held the attention of so many different groups, ranging from working-class Radicals to middle-class socialists and Eton schoolmasters? One answer lies in the congruence between his moralized account of work in the new society and the Gospel of Labour: that multifaceted, but nevertheless quintessential, concern of Victorian bourgeoisie and Radical alike. A further possibility dwells in the broad social and political reach of Victorian medievalism, a topic discussed in what follows as it pertains to utopian experiments and land reform.[14]

Following in a long line of English Radicals who viewed participation in labour as a sovereign act, the Chartists happily embraced More's critique of aristocratic idleness. An edition of the *Chartist Circular* (Glasgow), published on 13 June 1840, reported that 'In Sir Thomas More's "Utopia", we find [...] that our titled Aristocrats are "the same yesterday, to-day, and for ever"' (156). The author then quotes Hythloday's observation that 'There are a great number of noblemen among you that are themselves as idle as drones—that subsist on other men's labour, on the labour of tenants, whom, to raise revenues, they pare to the quick'. In an address on 'Pauperism & its Proposed Remedies', given at the Bradford Mechanics' Institution, W. E. Forster argued similarly that the claims of labour were not just sacred, but deserving of proprietorial reward: 'When Englishmen are Thomas Mores,' he intoned, 'England will be a Utopia' (*Manchester Times*, 14 Oct. 1848: 3).

The Chartists recognized a grievance, and a claim to enfranchisement, in the spectacle of an idle aristocracy. By contrast, their sympathizers in the Establishment— Carlyle and Benjamin Disraeli among them—interpreted working-class discontent as a cause for the renewal of a feudal principle. Rather than conceding to social levelling, they urged landowners to renew the duties and responsibilities entailed by benevolent overlordship. These distinct traditions, of Radical and Tory Radical, combined curiously as new generations of writers were drawn into the late Victorian revival of agrarian

---

[14] For a broader discussion of medievalism in the period, see Waithe 2016: 21–37.

thinking. Morris, for one, recognized an affinity between Romantic complaints about enclosure and Hythloday's criticism of greedy landowners who depopulated field and farm in order to rear sheep (More 1893: v, 39–40). The labour and the land argument converged in Morris's analysis: by taking hands off the plough, More's contemporaries were turning England into a 'grazing farm for the moneyed gentry' (More 1893: v). Radicalism and Romanticism reconnected with monasticism on the common ground of opposition to free-market liberalism. This is not to suggest that all agrarianism was neo-feudal. Edward Carpenter resisted both the modern and the ancient system of land ownership by going 'back to the land' in the course of market gardening experiments at Millthorpe, south of Sheffield.[15] In *Progress and Poverty* (1879), Henry George argued that the 'economic rent', or unearned income, derived from land should be taxed and shared equally (George 1884: 319). This does not sound like a defence of the old order, but Carpenter was influenced by Ruskin and Morris, while George's emphasis on land as the key to social problems was congruent with Ruskin's thinking, as also with More's (see H. Rose 1891).

Recourse to medievalism upset the usual distinctions between modern political categories. Of all those who took an interest in More's *Utopia*, Ruskin epitomizes an unusual convergence of causes. Admitting himself 'a Communist of the old school—the reddest also of the red', he identified equally as a 'violent Tory of the old school', a believer in restored but responsible hierarchy (Ruskin 1903–12: 27.116; 35.13). In Letter 6 (June 1871) of *Fors Clavigera*—his sequence of letters to the workmen and labourers of Great Britain—Ruskin described More as 'a country gentleman, living on his farm, at Chelsea' ('somewhere near Cheyne Row'), and 'a stout Catholic; and, singularly enough, also a Communist' (27.113). The apparently innocuous mention of Cheyne Row was a mischievous nod to the well-known residential address and authoritarian politics of Thomas Carlyle. In the next letter (July 1871), Ruskin contrasted the ethos of the Paris Commune with the 'law of old Communism' propounded by this 'farmer', More (27.120).[16] And he offered his own translation from More's Latin, to the effect that 'The chief, and almost the only business of government, is to take care that no man may live idle' (27.118). In the process, Ruskin scotched the claims of an article in the *Liverpool Daily Post*, discussed in Letter 6 of *Fors Clavigera*, whose offence was to suggest that 'the only cure for Liberty is more liberty' (27.106 n.), itself a paraphrase of Thomas Babington Macaulay's remark that 'There is only one cure for the evils which newly acquired freedom produces; and that cure is freedom' (Macaulay 1932: 34). Steering this peculiar course between communism and reaction, Ruskin influenced many of the utopian landholding settlements of the late nineteenth and early twentieth centuries (D. Hardy 2000: 21, 111, 129). And he went on to found the Guild of St George, an organization whose very name evokes the 'mediaeval Communist tradition, the spirit of association' that his

---

[15] For a discussion of Carpenter's life and ideals, see Rowbotham 2008.
[16] The Paris Commune (est. 18 Mar. 1871) was based on principles of direct democracy and declared independence from the national government (Hawkins 2021). It ended in massacre in May 1871 (Kerr and Wright 2015: 'Paris Commune').

socialist discipline, Morris, recognized in *Utopia* (More 1893: iv). The guild sought to put unemployed labour back on the land, to make it fertile again; Ruskin announced that lands donated to the guild by his sympathizers would be 'cultivated by Englishmen, with their own hands' (Ruskin 1903–12: 27.95). Carlylean echoes of planting the wilderness chime here with the philanthropic movements of the day, and its New Imperialism. The guild's all-encompassing social vision—and Ruskin's associated experiments in land reclamation at Brantwood, Coniston Water—recalls the social and territorial engineering of More's Utopus. It stands as such in contrast to Hythoday's picture of an English landscape depopulated by stock grazing.

The Utopian prohibition on hunting for pleasure and the ban on animal sacrifices appealed to a related strand of late nineteenth-century radicalism. Amid a general turn towards dietary ethics, Ruskin campaigned against vivisection at the University of Oxford; Carpenter went further, in popularizing vegetarianism and Eastern philosophy (Rowbotham 2008: 310). The Utopian attention to pleasure in measuring happiness reveals a yet more surprising affinity. Whether More intended an 'Epicurean' allusion has been a matter of scholarly debate: Richard Marius observes that 'More did not mention Epicurus or Epicureanism in *Utopia*, and despite the resolute efforts of some recent writers to make More an Epicurean of the spirit, the idea that pleasure was the goal of human life was neither radical nor uncommon in the Middle Ages and the Renaissance' (Marius 1999: 174). But the notes to Dibdin's influential 1808 edition make a ready connection in stating that 'The author takes the side of EPICURVS' in an often misunderstood controversy (More 1808b: 235). It was a topic re-energized in the late eighteenth century, as Dibdin and his Victorian successors would have recognized, by Jeremy Bentham's 'felicific calculus' (Rosen 1996: lv): his assertion in the 1789 *Introduction to the Principles of Morals and Legislation* that 'Nature has placed mankind under the governance of two sovereign masters, *pain* and *pleasure*' (Bentham 1996: 11). This, in turn, was subject to unlikely revamping through the Morrisian reading of Ruskin's teaching, in his preface to Ruskin's *Nature of Gothic* (1892), that 'art is the expression of man's pleasure in labour' (Morris 1936: 292). From this quite contrary direction, More's emphasis on pleasure was received as a happy anticipation of a better life, as opposed to a grim prefiguring of utilitarianism and the dismal science. Once again, More's *Utopia* revealed an unusual strength of appeal across intellectual and political dividing lines.

The Utopian confidence in a benign authority—one that controls and orders society through household heads, and through regulation of the number of households—found its counterpart in the late Victorian and Edwardian turn towards centrally planned communities. More imagined Amaurot as a city of houses with large gardens behind them. Mediated through Owenite and Fourierist experiments, these ideas re-emerged in the Edwardian Garden City movement, whose combined medievalism and rationalism was realized at Letchworth in Hertfordshire.[17] The originator of the movement,

---

[17] For more on the political valence of Garden City architecture, see Waithe 2006: 181–193.

Ebenezer Howard, completed the circle in *Garden Cities of Tomorrow* (first printed in 1898 entitled *To-Morrow: A Peaceful Path to Real Reform*). This work invoked Ruskin's 1865 vision of 'sanitary and remedial action in the households that we have', and of a new city with 'a belt of beautiful garden and orchard round the walls' (E. Howard 1902: 20). Further topical connections concerned population planning. After-echoes of More's interest in this subject are apparent not just in Thomas Malthus' early nineteenth-century theories of scarcity and population growth, but also in Morris's contrasting idea of malleable potential, as expressed in his dream of a London regreened and de-intensified by slum clearance, and in Howard's vision of a new and independent city equipped with its own industries (E. Howard 1902: 12). The lingering influence of demography is likewise witnessed by Howard's allusion in *Garden Cities of Tomorrow* to the proceedings of the 'Demographic Congress' (12). H. G. Wells's *A Modern Utopia* (1905) expresses a similar outlook, with its quadrangular inns and 'common garden' system, all devised in the hope that rationalism might extend to the management of space, population, and community (Wells 2005: 148).

False Friends

Many popular movements of the mid- to late nineteenth century discovered a kind of archaic futurism in More's text, a sign of things to come. Among other causes, *Utopia* gave succour to suffrage campaigns, communistic thinking, demographic anxiety, ruralism, vegetarianism, and urban planning. So many apparent affinities could leave Victorian readers vulnerable to forms of misrecognition and misconstruction, a danger not lessened by an increasing dependence on Robinson's English editions and an associated tendency to take his early English prose as the word of More himself. Returning to the practice and the metaphor of translation, such hazards are comparable to the trap known in language learning as the *faux ami*, or 'false friend', a danger that arises when 'a word or expression in one language [...] has the same or similar form in another' (*OED*).

Attempts to understand the past are prone to similar issues. An impression of familiarity may encourage us to see only the things we expect to see. In the process, we miss or misconstrue sources of real difference. Of all those discussing More's *Utopia* in this period, Morris and Wells were the most attuned to the possibility that our embrace of perfection could mislead us. This more sceptical awareness reflected their appreciation of *Utopia*'s literariness. They recognized a narrative whose truth claims were hedged by a framing dialogue, itself gathered in another country by the character 'Morus'. Morris's *News from Nowhere* relies initially on the perspective of 'a friend', one William Guest, who bears a striking resemblance to Morris himself (Morris 1910–15: 16.3). Morris thus incorporates an unusually developed 'Lucianic temper', a mode glossed by Dominic Baker-Smith as an 'interpenetration between the actual world [...] and the imaginary world' and 'the introduction of fanciful names [...] which make their own oblique comment on the main theme' (Baker-Smith 2011: 143). In a further playful elision, Guest tells the tale in the first person, replicating the transition of *Utopia*, Book Two. Wells's *A Modern Utopia* likewise employs the device of a 'Voice', which is declaredly '*not to be taken as the Voice of the ostensible author*' (Wells 2005: 7). In these ways, Morris and Wells reveal *Utopia*'s intrinsic status as 'translation', understood here in the sense of a work already fundamentally and enigmatically committed to mediation.

For the most part, though, the tricksy or ludic elements that dwell in this literariness went unacknowledged by *Utopia*'s Victorian readers. And the more obviously perverse outcomes of cultural translation were not much appreciated. Despite being a master of provocation, Ruskin missed that same quality in Hythloday's diatribe against sheep-farming. Earlier in the century, Chartist readings fell prey to a different kind of wishful thinking, in confusing the Utopian insistence on labour-as-communal-imperative with labour in its post-Lockean construction as a process conferring property on the doer (see J. Locke 1988: 289–293). It was a small leap from there to the nineteenth-century connection between property ownership and voter enfranchisement, but not one More could have envisaged or sanctioned. In an 1885 lecture on 'Sir Thomas More & His Utopia', the clergyman and freethinker Arthur Wollaston Hutton treated 'the "New Learning" of the sixteenth century in relation to social reform' in his own day. Such comparisons, as we have seen, proved seductive for many; but it is not obvious why the Utopian model of society should align meaningfully with nineteenth-century conceptions of amelioration. Even setting aside the reservations of the character 'Morus', the society described by Hythloday was neither equalitarian nor aspiring to be so. Instead, it sustained a notionally just hierarchy in conditions of geographical isolation and social stasis.

Inconvenient aspects of More's vision went largely unremarked. The triumph, by the 1860s, of abolitionist and democratic principles meant that the basis of Utopian wealth in slave labour was at once beyond the pale and too close to home. It follows that the use of the death penalty and the whip to drive the slave population received little notice in accounts that stressed More's humanitarian credentials. Oscar Wilde's 'The Soul of Man Under Socialism' (1891) was a notable exception: it described the new machine age in approving terms as a slave economy without human slaves (O. Wilde 2003: 1183). A perfect society, Wilde implied, would always require the nasty work to be done by somebody, or something, else. But the human element runs unavoidably through *Utopia*'s history of translation: numerous instances of the word 'slave' in Burnet's translation contrast with the feudal terms favoured by Robinson, in 'bondsman' and 'servingman'.[18] More's Latin navigates these possibilities in a more balanced way. At points, the term *servus* (slave) is used, as in 'In hac aula ministeria omnia in quibus paulo plus sordis aut laboris est obeunt servi' ('In this hall, slaves do all the particularly dirty and heavy chores', More 1995: 140–141, 152). His terms vary, however, and contain discrepancies. Discussing a passage in Book Two that assigns the slaughtering of animals at market,

---

[18] For more on the vocabulary of slavery, see Kern and Withington in this volume.

the editors of the Cambridge Latin text note that 'The bondsmen (Latin *famuli*), who are mentioned only here, should possibly be distinguished from the slaves (Latin *servi*) who are referred to several times' (More 1995: 139, 140). But then they also note Hythloday's observation 'that the Utopians have assigned hunting "to their butchers, who, as I said before, are all slaves" (*servi*)'. Late Victorian use of Robinson's translation conveniently suppressed More's Latinate invocation of classical slavery—and Burnet's more lively awareness of a colonial growth area—in favour of a domestic or feudal service less likely to conjure the system of African slavery, itself abolished in the British Empire as recently as 1833.

William Gladstone, himself the son of a major slave owner, and an advocate for the West Indian interest at the beginning of his parliamentary career, remarked pertinently that

> We must beware of confounding those conceptions of a slavery maintained wholesale for the purposes of commerce, which our experience supplies, with its earliest form [among the Greeks], in which the number of slaves would seem to have been small, and their ranks to have been recruited principally by war, with slight and casual aid from kidnapping. (Gladstone 1858: 3.72–73)

In these ways, translations of More's *Utopia* were poised ambiguously and dangerously between three contexts for slavery and servitude, whose interrelation was not settled: the Roman system, the feudal system, and the recently abolished British system.

Utopia Repurposed

Both democratic and anti-democratic Victorians found things to like in More's *Utopia*: it delivered a vision of communism pleasing to conservatives as well as Radicals, to admirers of Sparta and lovers of Reform. This multivalent power reflected its radically translated condition. In several ways, Robinson himself symbolized this strange journey: a grammar-school boy and graduate of Corpus Christi College, Oxford, he became a member of the Goldsmiths' Company, and latterly a clerk working for the company. Hence his description as a 'citizein and goldsmyth of London' on the title page of the 1551 edition. This may have been 'an insecure and ill-remunerated job', as Terence Cave puts it (2008d: 89), but the misalignments are striking: while in the employ of the company, he translated a work in which iron is rated more highly than gold, and in which the goldsmith—whether as craftsman or financier—is said to make his living by doing nothing at all. With each subsequent engagement, or editorial participation, further ironies accumulate, so that the unorthodox uses of this text seem less like an abuse than a repurposing, the productive employment of a falsity already built into its structure. As Lawrence Venuti remarks, 'Translation [...] always involves a process of domestication, an exchange of source-language intelligibilities for target-language ones', such that 'domestication need not mean assimilation'. Rather, 'It can also mean resistance' (Venuti 2008: 177).

In Wells's case, the resistance was deliberate, indeed self-conscious. He borrowed the urban planning and gardens from More, but questioned 'the old fixity' (Wells 2005: 39). 'To Sir Thomas More,' the Voice observes, 'we should seem a breed of nomads.' The message of 'Those former Utopists', who 'were bitterly against gold', is rejected (54). In other cases, the resistance is less intentional than a product of unforeseen interactions between cultural contexts, reflecting partial assimilations of a past that dwells, like a foreign language, in another country. That the moral force of the Chartist and the late Victorian 'back to the lander' found ready affirmation in More's vision may suggest selective reading. It may even depend on blind or false readings. But these responses remain, in their own way, productive, the fruit of a generative capacity that exists in the text apart from its propositional content. Equally, the element of happenstance and dispersed authority resulting from the text's vernacularization meant that preconceptions apparently mistaken from the point of view of Robinson or Burnet could sometimes be justified against the Latin. Why, for instance, were nineteenth-century radicals so drawn to an imaginary society ruled by a 'prince', this being the term employed in the English versions consulted by these groups? McCutcheon (1992: 106) notes that the 'princeps' of More's Latin—meaning 'first official or governor'—does not necessarily imply monarchy. In Robinson's hands, it follows, Utopia's 'eponymous founder [...] becomes a king, rather than a law-giver—a change of real import for our understanding of the history of utopian thought and of More's ideas about government' (106). Cases of this kind reveal the peculiarly fugitive nature of a text whose terms of description and political notions are complicated by its source in a classical language. The usual precepts governing correctness of interpretation are destabilized almost limitlessly, so that a naïve reading can transform curiously into an original, or etymological, one.

More's canonization by publishers as an English literary worthy may seem to avoid *Utopia*'s socially and linguistically foreign aspect. But the associated sense of cultural sanction was precisely what made it so useful and appealing to Radical audiences. Turning the world upside down was less daunting when it observed time-honoured precedent. In making the case that More's book should appear in every socialist's library, Morris recognized this possibility. Though he insisted that More was a man belonging to a different age—indeed, a man of divided loyalties not easy to assimilate to present debates—he too sensed a political power in literary prestige. Morris's friend, Walter Crane, remarked in 1911 that 'Those who have been accustomed to regard [Morris] [...] as a dangerous revolutionary might be referred to the writings of John Ball, and Sir Thomas More, his predecessors in England's history, who upheld the claims of labour and simple life, against waste, want, and luxury' (Crane 1911: 41). This might seem a mobilization of the concept of 'the classic' to close down opinions that ruffle feathers. But Crane adds that 'it was a conservative clinging to the really solid foundations of a happy human life which made Morris a Socialist as much as artistic conviction and study of modern economics' (41). In this way, the projection of current political categories on to a remote past could generate truths by virtue of their imperfect fit. The imperfectness cut both ways, of course: Morris's socialism set its sights on a condition of happy stasis. He opposed the disruptive forces of economic liberalism. And, though he signed up to Marx's dialectical account of historical movement, his version of the post-revolutionary future was at least partly understood as 'an epoch of rest' (the subtitle of *News from Nowhere*). In this respect, he too was aligned imperfectly with the political categories of his time.

Conclusion

Most of the examples discussed in this chapter fall between two scholarly editions: Dibdin's edition of 1808 and Lupton's of 1895, both of which employed Robinson's 1551 translation. In the first half of the nineteenth century, Burnet's translation came back into favour—notably, for the comparative purpose of anthologization—while Robinson's 1556 edition acquired prominence towards the end of the century. Each translation possessed a different cultural and political valence, despite the fact that editors rarely spelt out the reasons for their choice of text. Robinson's 1551 edition possessed a rare or antiquarian interest; Burnet's translation encouraged comparative studies devoted to experiments in political philosophy and government; and Robinson's 1556 edition served the idea of *Utopia* as an early classic of English letters. But these are not absolute distinctions. The text's modern functions depended to a great extent on an avoidance of its radically translated condition, reflecting a shared, or inherited, understanding that More's *Utopia* was also 'utopia', and that 'utopia' was Book Two. Equally, the fact of translation was likely to be de-emphasized as More was recruited to a new pantheon of English letters.

Such emphases were on one level partial, or mistaken, in particular as they perpetuated the contingencies of one translation over another. But they also fostered a generative, participatory, even recreative, relationship with *Utopia*, one oddly in keeping with the freedoms Robinson allowed himself, and the transformations dramatized by the content and medium of the original Latin. Two principal sources of interest recur in the period: readings motivated by political hopes and readings that conferred canonical status. In many cases, these possibilities were mutually reinforcing. Chartists and late nineteenth-century Radicals were attracted by the authority it granted to communitarian positions, while publishers of 'classic' literature found a convenient audience among aspiring readers not previously admitted to educational opportunity. The encounter with *Utopia* as false friend thus takes on the appearance less of a fault than a heuristic process; it diagnoses the reforming priorities of the present, while mixing reverence with recreation, and distortion with accidental accuracy. These effects, as I have shown, centre on a link between labour and enfranchisement that is actually foreign to More's priorities. The Kelmscott *Utopia* hosts a convergence of these tendencies in their most developed form: an expensive, finely printed book whose Foreword is also a political pamphlet, albeit one self-conscious and qualified. Apart from illustrating a surprising link between literary prestige and revolutionary politics, the reception of More's *Utopia* provides an enabling context for this convergence through the political breadth of its appeal. It illuminates thereby the common ground that could be shared by a socialist, in Morris, and a 'Tory of the old school'. This, in itself, reflects a reading—no doubt a contentious reading—of More less as a new man than as one whose radicalism recurs to the soil like the 'root' of the word's etymology.

CHAPTER 22

THE CULTURAL POLITICS OF TRANSLATION

Translating Thomas More's Utopia *into German in the Late Nineteenth Century*

JANET STEWART

IN 1896 a new German translation of Thomas More's *Utopia* was published by Max Ernst in Munich under the imprint 'Verlag für Gesellschaftswissenschaft' (More 1896).[1] The translation was undertaken by Ignaz Wessely (1841–1900), a Viennese-born writer and professional translator, under the editorship of a young Eduard Fuchs (1870–1940), who was later to become a cultural historian and collector of caricatures and erotic art, recognized by Walter Benjamin in 1937 for his anticipation of an historical materialist approach to the study of art (see Benjamin 1975). The source text for the translation, heralded by Fuchs (1896: xvii–xix) as the first complete scholarly translation of More's *Utopia* into German, was the November 1518 edition of *Utopia*, published in Basel by Johann Froben. This chapter traces the genesis, production, and reception of this translation, showing how the text was conceived and received in line with a particular 'translation culture' (Prunč 1997, 2000) that governed the set norms, conventions, and values framing the interactions of those involved in its translation. The 'translation culture' within which the Fuchs–Wessely edition of More's *Utopia* was produced must itself be understood: first, against the backdrop of a nascent social democratic movement seeking to establish itself in the changing, and at times hostile, political environment of a recently united Germany; second, in the light of a particular view of adult education emerging from social democratic circles; and third, in the context of burgeoning interest in utopian thought in the German-speaking area that developed, in part at least, in response to the major sociocultural shifts that went hand in hand with the rapid

---

[1] This translation resurfaced in 1945 and is still being reprinted in Germany; recent editions were published by Nikol in 2011, the Europäischer Literaturverlag in 2015, and Dearbooks in 2016.

industrialization of this area in the late nineteenth century, the so-called *Gründerzeit* (Saage 2001–4; Leucht 2016).

Offering a critical appraisal of the prevalence of utopianism in late nineteenth-century Germany, Ernst Bloch characterizes the *Gründerzeit* and its aftermath as a time of 'partial' utopias, of utopias that posited societies without social, gender, or ethnic divisions, but that retained the liberal bourgeois world view and associated political forms: 'The partial utopias of today', claims Bloch (1995: 585), 'repeatedly exhibit dreams of emancipation.' The latter half of the nineteenth century in the German-speaking area certainly witnessed a flourishing of emancipatory future visions of different kinds, with a number of utopian works written in response to the central issues of the time, such as the effects of technology-led industrialization, colonial expansion, and the so-called 'Woman Question'. In this period, the rise of utopianism played itself out in three main directions: first, in the genre of literary utopias; second, in a series of practical experiments in utopian living; and third, in a set of discursive texts examining the concept of Utopia with a relatively high level of abstraction, from a range of disciplinary and political positions (Saage 2001: 4). These manifestations of utopianism in the German-speaking area formed an important intellectual context for the production of the Fuchs–Wessely translation of More's *Utopia*.

Before turning to a detailed engagement with the translation itself, it will be useful to note in greater detail the literary utopias, practical utopian projects, and discursive discussions of the concept of utopia that emerged in late nineteenth-century Germany, dwelling, in particular, on two key academic encounters with More's *Utopia* that influenced Fuchs's project to produce a new German translation of the work: a new Latin edition of *Utopia* edited by Victor Michels and Theobald Ziegler (1895) and, most importantly, *Thomas More und seine Utopie* ('Thomas More and His Utopia'), Karl Kautsky's critical Marxist analysis of More's *Utopia* (1888).

A number of prominent literary utopias were produced in Germany in the late nineteenth century. Drawing on the seminal future-oriented interventions of early nineteenth-century reformers such as Robert Owen, Jean-Baptiste Joseph Fourier, and Henri de Saint-Simon, literary works such as Ferdinand Amersin's 1874 *Das Land der Freiheit* ('The Land of Freedom'), Theodor Hertzka's 1889 *Freiland: ein sociales Zukunftsbild* ('Freeland: A Social Anticipation'), and Theodor Herzl's (1902) *Altneuland* ('The Old New Land') offered their German-speaking readership representations of utopia, using and developing established tropes of the genre. In *Das Land der Freiheit*, Amersin relates the tale of a young man who establishes a new society on an island, leaving behind the technical progress of the nineteenth century, while in *Freiland*, Hertzka, a leading liberal economist, provides a fictional account of a celebrated utopian European colony located in Kenya (Jackson 1980), and in *Altneuland*, Herzl tells the story of a Jewish intellectual who passes through Palestine on his outward and return voyages to a Pacific island on which he spends twenty years. These were popular works of fiction; *Freiland*, for example, went through ten German editions in seven years (Gabriel 2012: 9), enjoying similar success in Germany to Edward Bellamy's international bestseller, *Looking Backward* (1888), the most prominent example of a literary utopia produced in the late nineteenth century.

The popularity of utopian fiction in this period saw it also begin to exert a demonstrable *practical* influence in the German-speaking world as it was doing elsewhere (Wegner 2002). Hertzka, for example, was able to capitalize upon his publishing success with *Freiland* by founding a political movement to take forward the project imagined in the novel (Rosner 2006: 116). A number of affiliated groups swiftly established themselves across Europe, and subsequently an expedition to Africa was mounted with the aim of founding an experimental colony there (Rosner 2006: 116; Leucht 2016: 4–5). Although this experiment failed, the movement's central idea inspired the sociologist Franz Oppenheimer (1895) to propose that Hertzka's experiment could be realized in Germany through the nascent settlement movement (*Siedlungsbewegung*), which sought to reform capitalism from the inside through a return to working the land (Haselbach 1985). Meanwhile, the ideas laid out in Theodor Herzl's *Altneuland*, identified by Jeremy Stowlow as 'one of the earliest and most detailed representations of a possible Jewish society in a land belonging to the Jews' (Stowlow 1997: 56), formed part of a set of works that laid the basis for the realization of a separate Zionist state.

The literary utopias and practical experiments in utopian living that flourished in the last decade of the nineteenth century were accompanied by a renewed and vigorous discursive engagement with the concept of utopia. Newspapers and scholarly periodicals from across the political spectrum carried articles debating the merit of the concept itself, while academics such as the professor of law Friedrich Kleinwächter (1891), the jurist Arthur von Kirchenheim (1892), and the legal philosopher Rudolf Stammler (1892), produced monographs in which they offered sustained reflection on the genre of the literary utopia, tracing the tale of the evolution of literary utopias up to the present day. Survey works such as these were supplemented by studies focusing on individual literary utopias. The most influential of the latter was undoubtedly *Thomas More und seine Utopie*, in which Kautsky, the German Social Democratic Party's foremost Marxist theorist, set out to claim the value of More's sixteenth-century work for contemporary debates on the nature of modern socialism and its antecedents.

This undertaking was part of a larger ambivalence within Marxist thinking regarding the concept of utopia and its popular manifestations, which begins with Karl Marx's own writing. Even as he was sketching out his utopian vision in the *Communist Manifesto* in 1848, Marx and his co-author, Friedrich Engels, criticized the 'purely Utopian' thinking of the early French and British socialists, from whom they wished to distance themselves (Marx and Engels 1969). Drawing on the work of Luca Meldolesi (1982), Immanuel Wallerstein contends that, despite their critique of utopian thinking, 'Marx and [Friedrich] Engels were extraordinarily Saint-Simonian in their visions of a moral, productivist, intellectual utopia' and, moreover, that the antecedent for their visions was More's 'pioneer treatise' (Wallerstein 1986: 1302). Indeed, Wallerstein identifies More's text as the prevalent Marxist utopia in the time of Marx, which, he maintains, receded in importance only after Marx's death in 1883, when orthodox Marxism took up the language of Engels to denounce utopia as an 'ideological deception' (1303) or, at the very least, as in Kautsky's dismissal of utopian fiction, a 'harmless distraction' (Kautsky 1889: 268). This did not mean, however, that the concept of utopia was absent from Marxist thinking about 'scientific socialism'. On the contrary, August Bebel's 1892 *Die Frau und der Sozialismus* ('Women under Socialism') set out a blueprint for a socialist future, while, as Peter Schwartz maintains, the arguments Kautsky put forward in *Thomas More und seine Utopie* were of seminal importance for his project to establish a respectable intellectual basis for the development of modern socialism (Schwartz 1989: 45).

In *Thomas More und seine Utopie*, Kautsky offers an account of *Utopia* as a product of a particular historical moment, arguing that More's sensitivity towards the material and social conditions of his own age enabled him to anticipate modern socialism, and so counter those who would see in More's writing simply a reiteration of the socialist thought of antiquity. Kautsky's influential study received a mixed reception in the German-speaking countries at the time of its publication (Steenson 1978). On the one hand, his account of More's life and work was received favourably in social democratic and certain academic circles, confirming the importance of his approach to this canonical work. As one pertinent example, Victor Michels, professor of German at Jena, and Theobald Ziegler, professor of philosophy in Strasbourg, the editors of a new Latin edition of More's *Utopia* (1895), note the value of Kautsky's study and maintain in their introduction that he is 'correct to place in question the specifically platonic character of Utopia and to declare More's communism modern, rather than platonic' (More 1895: xxv).[2] On the other hand, however, Kautsky's study was received in more conservative circles with suspicion, at best, and downright hostility, at worst. In an era in which the socialist movement was engaged in a struggle to ensure its political legitimacy, Kautsky's proclamation of the modernity of More's text was regarded as unduly provocative in some parts of the German-speaking world, leading it to fall foul of the censor. As reported in the *Wiener Zeitung*'s official gazette of 16 April 1890, the District Court in Eger put in place an order to prevent the circulation of *Thomas More und seine Utopie*. Meanwhile, the Austrian social democratic newspaper, the *Arbeiterzeitung*, reported that when Kautsky gave a talk to the Association of Bookbinders in Vienna, 'the government's representative, Police Commissioner Feldmann, interrupted the speaker on numerous occasions' (N.N. 1889: 2). Such examples provide an indication of the sense of political threat to the establishment associated with Kautsky's interpretation of More's *Utopia* at this time.

In the German-speaking lands in the late nineteenth century, then, More's *Utopia* was regarded as both a celebrated literary monument and a potentially seditious text lending itself to radical interpretation. As such, it undoubtedly exerted a particular fascination upon Fuchs, who may have been only 25 years old when he took on the project of producing a new German translation of More's *Utopia*, but was already no stranger to the power of text and the attendant dangers of bringing material felt to be incendiary into the public sphere. By the time the Fuchs–Wessely translation appeared in 1896, Fuchs had already spent three terms in prison, on charges of treason brought initially under Germany's punitive Anti-Socialist Laws that were in place from 1878 to 1890. Born in

---

[2] All translations from German are my own, unless otherwise indicated.

modest circumstances in Göppingen in the south of Germany in 1870, Fuchs moved to nearby Stuttgart to take up work as an apprentice bookkeeper in a printing company at a young age. Here, as Thomas Huonker (1985: 9–12) details, he became involved in radical anarchist political circles, producing and distributing incendiary political pamphlets. He was caught and charged with lèse-majesté in 1888, serving a five-month prison sentence in Heilbronn (19). After that incident, his political allegiance shifted from anarchy to social democracy, but he continued to engage in political activities that saw him fall foul of the authorities and serve a second five-month prison sentence, this time in Rothenburg (24). Through his political contacts, he moved to Munich in 1890 to become a bookkeeper with the social democratic newspaper, the *Münchner Post*, where he moved in circles that included the leading Social Democrat MP Georg von Vollmar (34). In Munich, Fuchs found a place for himself in the burgeoning intellectual scene in Schwabing, where he rose quickly from bookkeeper to editor of the *Süddeutscher Postillon* (32), a popular biweekly satirical illustrated paper aimed at the working classes (Hake 2017: 104–105). During this period, he spent a third stretch in prison for treason, this time spending a full ten months behind bars in Nuremberg (Huonker 1985: 47–51).

On his release from prison, Fuchs began to develop further his writing and editorial activities in a number of directions. He sought to extend his interest in art history by placing longer articles in the *Süddeutscher Postillon*. At the same time, he continued to pursue his political interests, publishing political poetry in the *Süddeutscher Postillon*, and collaborating with Karl Kaiser and Ernst Klaar to produce an anthology of political poetry under the title *Aus dem Klassenkampf* ('From the Class Struggle') (Fuchs et al. 1894). Moving beyond the confines of the *Süddeutscher Postillon*, he conceived and edited a series of publications for Max Ernst's Munich-based publishing house, the Verlag für Gesellschaftswissenschaft, under the title *Sammlung gesellschaftwissenschaftlicher Aufsätze* ('Collected Sociological Essays'). This imprint was part of an ambitious plan to establish a press for social democratic literature in Munich to rival Dietz in Stuttgart and other similar enterprises elsewhere in Germany (Huonker 1985: 294–295). Leading Social Democrats including Vollmar gave their blessing to the series. Running to fifteen issues in total, the series made a significant contribution to the discussion and distribution of social democratic thought (295). In the eighth issue, Fuchs offered insight into his ambition for the series in the form of a programmatic editorial statement that laid out his purposely eclectic design: 'Whether idealist or materialist in orientation, whether Christian socialism or armchair socialism [*Kathedersozialismus*], whether utopian or modern rational socialists—all views will be given a platform' (Fuchs 1894: 5).

As Fuchs explains, the series was designed to include both new articles, on topics such as historical materialism and anti-Semitism, and reproductions of essays he judged to be of lasting sociological value (Fuchs 1894: 6), with a focus on texts that could be claimed as 'the utopian antecedents of modern socialism' (Huonker 1985: 298). Explaining his decision to reprint past works, Fuchs claimed, with a nod to Bebel, that in troubled times there is often a need to look back to the imagined world of the past to understand the present and find ways forward in the future (Fuchs 1894: 3). As well as reproducing key German-language works by authors such as Wilhelm

Weitling and Georg Büchner, Fuchs commissioned new translations of two classical works of utopian literature: Tommaso Campanella's *City of the Sun* (1900)—written in Italian in 1602 and first published in Latin translation in 1623—and Thomas More's *Utopia* (1896).

Fuchs's main inspiration in commissioning this translation was Kautsky's *Thomas More und seine Utopie*. The introduction to the translation opens with Fuchs proclaiming the seminal importance of Kautsky's work for Thomas More's reception in the German-speaking countries in the late nineteenth century and concludes by restating Kautsky's description of More as the antecedent of modern socialism: 'The greatest man of his time created the plan, the greatest movement in the history of the world. Modern socialism appropriated this and has taken as its basis More's central idea—common property' (Fuchs 1896: xxii). Elsewhere in the introduction, Fuchs offers details of More's life as further evidence of his commitment to examining the conditions of possibility for the development of modern socialism. Reflecting on More's execution, for example, Fuchs claims that he died neither as a Catholic martyr nor as the sworn enemy of the Reformation, but as 'a friend of the people [*Volksfreund*], as one for whom the well-being of the people was more important than the King's favour' (xi).

Fuchs's indebtedness to Kautsky extended beyond his knowledge of the views put forward in *Thomas More und seine Zeit*, however. As is revealed in a set of letters now lodged in the Karl Kautsky archive in Amsterdam (Kautsky 1894–1908), Fuchs was in direct correspondence with Kautsky as he prepared his introduction to the translation. In a letter dated 22 October 1895, Fuchs enquired whether Kautsky might be able to provide him with English-language literature on More's *Utopia* not readily available in Munich, while on 26 March 1896, he sought general advice on formulating his introduction. His letter reveals some doubt in his own ability to undertake this task; he asks Kautsky if there might be a safer—or more experienced—pair of hands to write the foreword and wonders whether Kautsky himself might be interested in taking this on. Kautsky, however, had already publicly indicated his confidence in Fuchs. In a review of the new Michels–Ziegler Latin edition of More's *Utopia* written for the *Neue Rundschau*, Kautsky (1895–6: 794) remarked: 'We have just received word that a publishing house aligned with us politically [*parteigenössischer Verlag*] is preparing a new translation [of More's *Utopia*] that is in good hands.'

Fuchs's editorial foreword, as he himself confesses, drew heavily on both the introduction to the Michels–Ziegler (1895b) Latin edition of More's *Utopia* and Kautsky's *Thomas More und seine Utopie* (Fuchs 1896: iv). The foreword runs to nineteen pages and is divided into four sections: a set of introductory remarks, including biographical details for More; an account of the genesis of *Utopia*; a brief publication history, including information on previous German translations; and a short set of reflections on the content of the text and the author's intentions. While offering a markedly less detailed introduction to More's *Utopia* than Michels and Ziegler, Fuchs was evidently keen to claim scholarly legitimation for his new German edition by demonstrating his editorial prowess—or at the very least, his talent as a collector—through offering a detailed account of the source text used for the translation.

The source text used by Fuchs and Wessely was the November 1518 edition of *Utopia*. While scholarship now usually regards the March 1518 edition, the last edition in which More had a hand, to be the most definitive version of the text (More 1965a: clxxxii–cxciv), Fuchs claims in his introduction that the November 1518 edition was the 'most carefully revised version of the text produced during More's lifetime' (Fuchs 1896: xix). Fuchs provides no detail as to how this version of the text came into his possession, but he notes that Michels and Ziegler did not have access to it when preparing their Latin edition, which was based on the 1516 edition of Utopia (More 1895: xlii). And indeed, in their introduction, Michels and Ziegler, citing the work of Lina Berger (1879b), remark that although contemporary scholarly literature on *Utopia* mentions a fourth edition published in November 1518, they had been unable to find a copy to verify its existence. Fuchs states that he sent his edition of *Utopia* to Michels, who authenticated it as an example of the November 1518 edition, enabling Fuchs, with some satisfaction, to supplement the scholarship of Michels and Ziegler by declaring definitively: 'Thus four separate Latin editions [of Utopia] appeared within two years' (1896: xix). Further stamping his authority on the question of *Utopia*'s genealogy, he proceeds to note that although meriting no mention in the Michels–Ziegler Latin edition, the 'Robynson' English translation references a fifth edition that was apparently published in Vienna in 1519 (xx).[3]

Fuchs prided himself on having produced the first complete scholarly translation of *Utopia* into German (1896: iii). The earliest German translations, he observed, had focused on Book Two only, while the most recent German translation, carried out by Hermann Kothe for Reclam in 1846, included both books, but not the paratexts. In contrast, the Fuchs–Wessely translation comprised not only Books One and Two, but also the ancillary material, marginal notes, and photographic reproductions of the illustrations that accompanied the 1518 edition of the text. In positioning these materials, Fuchs and Wessely reported that they had taken care to replicate the order in which they appeared in that edition after the title page and before the beginning of Book One: the letters from Desiderius Erasmus to Johann Froben and Guillame Budé to Thomas Lupset were followed by a translation of the hexistichon attributed to the poet laureate, Anemolius; photographic reproductions of Ambrosius Holbein's map of Utopia and of the Utopian alphabet; and finally, the letters from Jerome Busleyden to Peter Giles and from More to Giles. This accords with the account of the 1518 edition offered by Surtz (More 1965a: clxxxviii). Additionally, the text offers what Fuchs (1896: xiii) claims to be the first full German translation of the letter from More to Giles that was contained in the 1517 Paris edition of *Utopia*, where it appeared following the text of Book Two, as recorded by Surz (More 1965a: clxxxvi). In the Fuchs–Wessely translation, this letter appeared as a long footnote to Fuchs's (1896: xiii–xv) account of *Utopia*'s genesis.

---

[3] The only 1519 edition was printed in Florence; Surtz declares this edition 'of no independent value' (More 1965a: cxc).

The Fuchs–Wessely translation included six photographic reproductions in all, five of which appeared in the 1518 Froben edition of *Utopia*. In his introduction, Fuchs provided brief information on these images, noting correctly that the map of Utopia and the depiction of the Utopian alphabet are both 'probably' works by Ambrosius Holbein, as is the woodcut depicting Hythloday, Morus, and Giles in conversation in Antwerp that appears on the opening page of Book One (Fig. 37.1; Fuchs 1896: xx). The two woodcut borders that appear on pages 1 and 19 of the translation respectively, and the printer's mark that appears at the end of the volume, on the other hand, are attributed by Fuchs to Hans Holbein [the Younger]. While this is correct in the case of the two woodcuts, the printer's mark was designed for Froben not by Holbein, but by Urs Graf (see Hollstein 1977: 171). The final image that accompanied the Fuchs–Wessely translation, a photographic reproduction of a portrait of Thomas More, did not appear in the 1518 source text. Fuchs (1896: xx) claims this image, which he positioned as a frontispiece to the translation, was 'a reproduction of the famous portrait that Holbein completed while visiting Thomas More's residence (1525–8)'. This is, however, incorrect. The image is not a reproduction of this portrait; nor yet is it one of the many engravings based on the portrait, or other related works by Holbein, and produced 'after Holbein' (see Stanley Morison 1963). It is actually one of the most well known of the 'false engravings' of More in circulation, depicting a heavy-faced, thick-jowled figure, wearing a fur tippet and pointed cap. The clothing of this sixteenth-century figure may have borne some resemblance to that worn by More, but according to Stanley Morison (1963: 70), 'there the resemblance ceases'. A potential source for the frontispiece might be an engraving produced by Johann Heinrich Lips for Johann Casper Lavater from a work by Christian von Mechel (see Sandgathe 1992). Morison lists this as one of a number of prominent 'false engravings' of More, commenting that von Mechel 'should have known better' than to produce this work. The image, labelled as a portrait of Thomas More, was included in the French translation of Lavater's influential *Essays on Physiognomy* (1793: vol. 2, plate 53), with which Fuchs would have been acquainted through his interest in visual culture, in general, and caricature, in particular (see Fuchs 1902, 1903).

Fuchs's editorial decision to include images and extensive ancillary material in the 1896 translation was reflective of his own emergent practice as a collector and publisher of visual culture (see Benjamin 1975). His decision was praised by a number of reviewers, but also drew criticism from some quarters. An anonymous review that appeared in *Vorwärts*, the daily newspaper of the German Social Democratic Party, took issue with the translation on grounds of cost, suggesting that without the marginal notes, the letters from Erasmus and others, and the reproductions of images taken from older editions of the text—all of which was 'not by More and therefore had little to do with the actual description of Utopia'—the volume would have been more affordable and so more 'suitable for distribution to German workers'; at a cost of 2Mk, the reviewer feared that the Fuchs–Wessely translation would not enjoy 'the circulation that one would have wished for Thomas More's *Utopia*' (N.N. 1896: 3). It is telling that the reviewer did not level the same criticism at the Michels–Ziegler Latin edition of the text; at 3,60Mk, it was substantially more expensive than the German translation, but it was, of course, targeted at the academic market, rather than the workers' education sector.

The *Vorwaerts* review situates the production of the Fuchs–Wessely translation in the wider context of discussions and disagreements within the social democratic movement—and left-wing circles more generally—about the nature of education to be provided for the working classes. In particular, the question of the role of (bourgeois) culture in an emancipatory educational programme was the subject of intense debate, with important contributions from Wilhelm Liebknecht, Franz Mehring, and others (Emig 1980; Hake 2017: 155–173). This debate, in turn, was situated in wider deliberations taking place in Germany at the turn of the twentieth century on the nature of culture and, concomitantly, the definition and scope of cultural history (*Kulturgeschichte*) and its relationship to other disciplines, including sociology (see Bruch et al. 1989; Hake 2017). As he made the transition from journalism to academic writing, Fuchs self-identified as a cultural historian; his first full-length books were subtitled *eine Kulturgeschichte* ('a cultural history') (Fuchs 1902, 1903; see also Zingarelli 1976). His decision to publish new translations of More's and Campanella's canonical works must therefore be understood in the context of these debates and, given his own political leanings, of nineteenth-century socialism's infatuation with past culture, which included a fascination with classical antiquity mediated, as Sabine Hake (2017: 100) argues, through Weimar Classicism and romanticism.

Fuchs was enamoured of the possibility of a proletarian reinterpretation of bourgeois culture; this found expression not only in his translations of classical literature, but also in works such as his poem 'Der Prometheus unserer Zeit' ('The Prometheus of our Time'), first published in the *Süddeutscher Postillon* in 1892 (Hake 2017: 100–101). Focusing on a figure with a prominent place in the socialist imaginary, Fuchs's poem offers a vision in which violence is confronted by 'the sharp arrow of knowledge', to bring about the liberation of the proletariat (Fuchs 1892).[4] In other words, he offers a vision in which the acquisition of particular forms of bourgeois cultural knowledge by the working class is posited as a path towards emancipation. His later activities as a collector of caricatures and erotic art would see him undermine this view; as Benjamin would later recognize, he became a collector of works from 'border disciplines' that served to question the tenets of traditional art history (Benjamin 1975: 36–37). This, argues Benjamin, opened up the possibility of breaking the constraints on scholarship imposed by an emphasis on cultural history understood as 'cultural heritage', as it was in the debates prevalent in left-wing circles in the early twentieth century (see Schwartz 2006: 121–122):

> Cultural history, to be sure, enlarges the weight of the treasure which accumulates on the back of humanity. Yet cultural history does not provide the strength to shake off this burden in order to be able to take control of it. The same is true for the socialist

---

[4] An English translation of this poem is offered by Hake 2017: 100.

educational efforts at the turn of the century which were guided by the star of cultural history. (Benjamin 1975: 36)

While Fuchs's activities as publisher and collector placed him, in Benjamin's eyes, as a herald of an alternative historical materialist approach to art, he was also—and remained—convinced of the intellectual and political value of classicism and other key tenets of bourgeois cultural heritage, as indeed, was Benjamin himself (Schwartz 2006: 121). Fuchs's work in putting together a collection of sociological essays that included the translation of More's *Utopia*, and the care that he took to demonstrate a working philological knowledge of the source text, are evidence of his commitment to curating cultural heritage. In this, he was joined by Wessely, the professional translator and linguist commissioned to render More's Latin text into German.

Unlike Fuchs, whose work, thanks largely to Benjamin, has received some scholarly attention, Wessely is a somewhat elusive figure, who, in line with Lawrence Venuti's (1995) much-cited theory of the 'invisibility of the translator', does not merit a note in major German biographical dictionaries. A brief biographical sketch published in 1956 describes Wessely variously as a lexicographer, translator, philologist, publisher of foreign language dictionaries, and writer (Springer 1956: 1530). Born in Vienna in 1841, he studied law and philology in the city, before moving to Leipzig, Munich and, finally, Berlin, where he died in 1900. He was living in Munich when working on his translation of More's *Utopia*; the municipal Address Book for Munich (Königliche Polizei-Direktion 1890: 389) lists Wessely's address as Augustenstrasse 109, the same street in the bohemian quarter of the city that was home to Fuchs from 1890 to 1894 (Huonker 1985: 27). Prior to moving to Munich, Wessely learned his trade as a translator and lexicographer in Leipzig, where he lived from around 1866. In November of that year, he wrote to the major Leipzig-based publisher Brockhaus, seeking employment, mentioning his publishing experience in the fields of art and literature, and indicating that he was motivated to pursue the contact with Brockhaus through his long-standing acquaintance with Rudolf Weigel in Leipzig.[5]

During his time in Leipzig, Wessely produced a number of dictionaries, including English–German, English–Italian, English–French, English–Spanish, and English–Swedish pocket dictionaries and a major German reference work, the *Grammatisch-Stilistisches Wörterbuch der Deutschen Sprache* (Wessely 1883). Translations upon which he worked include Charles Dickens's *Christmas Carol* and *David Copperfield*, Walter Scott's *The Talisman*, James Fenimore Cooper's *The Prairie* and *The Pioneers*, and Louisa M. Alcott's popular children's books, *Little Women* and *Little Men*. In translating these works of popular fiction, Wessely was imbricated in the larger 'translation industry' that had sprung up in the first half of the nineteenth century in Germany, where the

---

[5] Letter from Ignaz Emanuel Wessely to Brockhaus, dated 6 Nov. 1866. The letter, which runs to two pages, was offered for sale on ZVAB by Eberhard Köstler Autographen & Bücher in 2018. It is likely that Wessely is here referring to Rudolf Weigel, the Leipzig-based print-dealer, publisher, and collector, descendant of the long-established Weigel dynasty, who died in 1867 (Tschackert 1896).

commercialization of literary life led to translations of works for popular consumption being churned out as efficiently and swiftly as possible (Bachleitner 1989: 6). On many of these works, Wessely is credited with 'overseeing' or 'revising' the translation, an activity that indicates a relatively high professional standing, albeit in a field that carried little prestige. Indeed, according to Bachleitner (11), literary translation was largely regarded as a task to be undertaken by failed writers, a profile that Wessely appears to fit, in part at least. It is clear that he tried his hand as a poet and playwright; several of his poems are to be found in the manuscript section of the Vienna City library, in the papers of the Jewish Bohemian writer (and translator from Serbian into German) Ludwig August Frankl von Hochwart, while a manuscript copy of a play that Wessely wrote while living in Munich is held in the Herzogin Anna Amalia Library of the Klassik Stiftung, Weimar. In the catalogues of various libraries worldwide, Wessely also appears as the author of a series of works on art history published in Leipzig in the late nineteenth century. This is, however, an understandable cataloguing error; these studies were actually the work of Joseph Eduard Wessely, but in the printing style of late nineteenth-century Germany it is difficult to distinguish between I. E. Wessely and J. E. Wessely.

Wessely may not have been the author of scholarly works on art history. He did, however, enjoy an academic career alongside his work as a translator of popular literature. There was another type of literary translator at work in the nineteenth century. Translating from canonical texts such as the classics or Shakespeare, these translators enjoyed greater prestige than their counterparts working with popular fiction (Bachleitner 1989: 6–7; see also Kitzbichler et al. 2009). Wessely was involved in work of this kind, collaborating on the translation into German of the works of Aristophanes with his teacher, the celebrated—if sometimes controversial—scholar, translator, and professor of German, Johannes Minckwitz (Minckwitz and Wessely 1885–c.1875),[6] as well as engaging in scholarly reflection on the art of translation. According to his entry in the *Allgemeine Deutsche Biographie*, Minckwitz was recognized by Alexander von Humboldt in 1857 as 'the foremost translator of the classics after J. H. Voß' (Fränkel 1906: 413). Like Minckwitz, Wessely was a key contributor to *Összehasonlitó Irodalomtörtenélmi Lapok* or *Acta comparationis litterarum universarum*, a new journal of comparative literature edited by Hugo Meltzl (who also studied with Minckwitz) and Samuel Brassai and published in Klausenberg in Siebenbürgen.[7] An important early work in the development of comparative literature as a discipline, the journal

---

[6] Wessely translated vols 6–10 of the works of Aristophanes. On the connection between Minckwitz and Wessely, see Fassel 2006: 446. See also 'Meltzl von Lomnitz, Hugo von', *Kulturportal Ost-West*, https://kulturportal-west-ost.eu/biographien/meltzl-von-lomnitz-hugo-von-2, accessed 17 Sept. 2018.

[7] Wessely was listed on the title page of the first issue (15 Jan. 1877) as one of a group of collaborators that also included Dr Wilhelm Schott (Berlin), Dr J. Minckwitz (Leipzig), Dr Giuseppe Cassone (Sicily), Dr O. Hóman (Klausenburg), Sándor Imre (Klausenburg), Dr P. Mayet (Tokyo), Dr E. Wessely (Leipzig), Dr Johannes Scherr (Zurich), Dr P. Avenarius (Leipzig), Dr Fraccaroli (Sicily), Dr V. Thomsen (Copenhagen). http://documente.bcucluj.ro/web/bibdigit/periodice/osszehasonlitoirodalomtortenelmi/, accessed 17 Sept. 2018.

was strongly committed to multilingualism and to translation, accepting articles and translated texts in a wide range of languages (Damrosch 2007; Fassel 2005; Lehnert 1982).

Wessely wrote a number of articles for the journal, including an extended meditation on the practice of translating classical Latin poetry that sheds some light on his approach to translating More's *Utopia* (Wessely 1878). Proceeding from his own translation of selected odes by Horatio, Wessely set out to present 'examples of a completely new, authentically German and truly poetic way of translating the work of this most classical of all Latin poets' (1878: 458). To describe his method, Wessely draws on the concept of *Nachdichtung*, or 'rewriting', to signify an approach designed to enable him to attend to the 'objective' or 'universal' element of the poetic (458), while simultaneously rendering this in a form 'palatable to modern tastes' (460). In invoking the concept of *Nachdichtung*, he is careful to differentiate his use of this term from the practice of 'rewriting' classical texts without reference to the source text, while simultaneously insisting upon the creative aspect of translation that, as Benjamin (1996) would later recognize, has the capacity to extend the target language.

When Wessely describes his translation method as 'authentically German', he is situating his remarks in the context of larger debates about the practice and status of translation. In the nineteenth century, a distinctively German understanding of translation developed, according to which the German language, precisely because of its flexibility, is uniquely well placed to show the semantic, metric, and grammatical structures of the source text in the translation (Kitzbichler et al. 2009: 6). In the work of prominent nineteenth-century theorists of translation and language such as Johann Heinrich Voß and Wilhelm Humboldt, a clear view emerged of translation's role in the building of a culture and of a language; deficits in the German language, it was argued, could be countered through reconstructing the metrics and the structures of classical source texts. This view had certainly shifted somewhat by the end of the nineteenth century, by which time the works of Johann Wolfgang von Goethe (1749–1832) and Friedrich Schiller (1759–1805) had been recognized as German classics. However, translation of classical literature into German was still thought to have an important cultural political role to play in establishing morals and cultural norms (Kitzbichler et al. 2009: 7).

By the end of the nineteenth century, as we have seen, More's neo-Latin text had attained the status of a classic work of literature. Wessely's commitment to producing a translation adequate to the status of the source text emerges clearly from his translator's notes, which formed an important part of the translation's paratextual apparatus. There was general consensus amongst reviewers of the work that Wessely was quite successful in realizing his ambition. Kautsky and others certainly judged Wessely's translation to be far superior to the 1846 Kothe translation, which, Kautsky noted dismissively, 'may have cost only 40 pfennig, but was not worth even tuppence' (Kautsky 1889: 257; see also N.N. 1896). Wessely contributed to the general sense of dissatisfaction with Kothe's translation in his translator's notes. In his explanation of More's reference to Galen's *Microtechne*, Wessely notes that this is erroneously—and amusingly—translated by Kothe as 'a male individual, "the Microtechne", while—*pour comble de Plaisir*—Galen becomes a "Gaul" ' (More 1896: 116). Wessely then comments: 'the producer of this "translation" reveals yet again that he has no idea about something that occurs in *Utopia*. But the reader really just has to accept this with this translator, who managed to produce his German version without reference to the original Latin text' (116).[8]

Wessely was clearly eager to ensure that his own scholarly qualification to undertake this translation task could not be questioned. He provides extensive explanations of the wordplay involved in More's choice of names for the characters and locations that appear in the text and offers detailed notes on references to classical literature as well as on historical figures mentioned in the text. At times, he also takes it upon himself to provide an interpretation of More's intentions, as in his contextualization of the *Parva Logicalia* mentioned in the text's description of the Utopians' education. With reference to the provenance of the work he translates as the 'Foundations of Logic' ('Anfangsgründen der Logik') and to a letter written in Latin by More, Wessely offers reflection on More's critique of the scholastic dialecticians (More 1896: 98).[9] In a second extended translator's note, he goes on to consider More's contribution to the long-running philosophical debate over universals that pitted 'realism', which holds that universals have a 'real substantial existence independently of being thought', against 'nominalism', which maintains that 'universals have no existence independently of being thought' (Flew et al. 1979, cited in Keiper 1994: 5). Wessely situates More's thought 'on the side of nominalism', the ascendancy of which, Wessely claims, changed the nature of the humanities in the fifteenth and sixteenth centuries, establishing the basis of the human sciences in their modern incarnation (More 1896: 98–99). At other points, Wessely's notes are designed to supplement existing knowledge, as in the case of his discussion of the identity of Gerardus Noviomagus, the author of one of the poems included in the ancillary materials. Wessely identifies Noviomagus as Gerhard Geldenhauer (1482–1517), drawing on Michels and Ziegler as his source, but then proceeds to note that there are two other possible identities for this figure; in some works, Wessely indicates, he is suggested to be Gerhard Bronchrost (1494–1570), professor of mathematics in Rostock, while in others, he has been identified as Listrius van Nimwegen, a friend of Erasmus (More 1896: 168).

In the translated text, Wessely retains the Latin name, Gerardus Noviomagus, for this figure, as he does consistently for all proper nouns. This decision may at first appear to contradict Wessely's reflections on the practice of translation offered in the *Acta comparationis litterarum universarum*, where he emphasized the importance of producing translated language that is 'authentically German'. It certainly did not find favour with contemporary reviewers: writing in the *Neue Zeit*, Kautsky criticized Wessely's decision to preserve the ancient Roman meaning of Latin terms rather than providing translations that would be better aligned with the sixteenth-century context in which More was writing: why, asks Kautsky, was Lusitanien not translated as Portugal, or Gallien as France (Kautsky 1896–7: 826)? This contributes to Kautsky's

---

[8] Kautsky (1889: 257) claims that Kothe translated from a French edition of *Utopia*. For more on Kothe's translation, see Nethercott in this volume.

[9] The letter referred to here by Wessely in general terms is likely to be More's open letter to Maarten van Dorp, composed in 1515. The letter is reproduced and translated in *CWM* 15.

overall impression of a translated text in which, at times, the language is disjointed to the point of compromising understanding. His criticism found an echo with the anonymous reviewer for *Vorwärts*, who noted that the language of the translated text had 'a musty whiff of the Middle Ages about it' (N.N. 1896: 3).

A more generous reading of Wessely's translation choices, however, might choose to focus on how the translated text sets out to draw attention to its status as a translation of a source text that is itself the product of multiple layers of translation. As Marina Leslie argues, More's *Utopia* is 'a place that can only be apprehended in translation or described or enacted through translation' (Leslie 1998: 58). The complex forms of translation at play in *Utopia*—from Utopian to Latin, from Greek to Latin, from the oral to the written form, from the Utopian to the European sociocultural context—situate the work in the context of the concerns of the sixteenth-century translator, for whom, Leslie argues, translation 'was—in all senses of the word—a radical act' (68). Through translation decisions such as his choice to retain the Latin names of the fictional characters and places that appear in the text, and to use footnotes to explain the puns upon which these names are based, Wessely draws attention to the poetics of translation at work in *Utopia* at the intersection of the translatable and the untranslatable. In his wider reflections on translation method, as we have seen, his main concern was how to integrate the 'truly poetic' with the 'authentically German' (Wessely 1878). In electing to translate a text in which the poetics and politics of translation are played out in terms of both form and content, Wessely was able to develop his method further, demonstrating his view of the cultural political importance of both the practice of translation and critical reflection upon translation, which, as Leslie argues, are crucial facets of More's *Utopia*, which 'obsessed as it is with its origins and with measuring the distance from the source, will offer both a narrative and a graphic commentary on the linguistic, literary and sociohistorical processes of translation as humanist method and subject' (Leslie 1998: 58).

In developing her argument about the importance of translation in More's *Utopia*, Leslie highlights the devices deployed in the text to foreground the question of distance from source. Amongst others, these include the decision to employ the fictional figure of 'Morus' as Hythloday's eager but sceptical interlocutor, whose role in the narrative structure is, in part, to provide a distancing gloss on the tale of the Utopians recounted to him. In a well-known passage at the end of Book Two, Morus provides a list of the things that he purports to have found absurd in the Utopians' system of social organization, although, he maintains, he did not find it appropriate to articulate any fundamental criticism of Hythloday's account. At this point in the narrative, More's *Utopia* walks a careful line between criticism and affirmation, distance and closeness, rejection and acceptance of difference. And at this point in the Fuchs–Wessely translation, an additional paratextual device is added that further underscores the way in which the source text mediates between distance and closeness. The main objection voiced by Morus to the Utopians' form of social organization was to 'ihre gemeinsame Lebensweise' (More 1896: 162). In Wessely's translation, the adjective *gemeinsam*('communal') is chosen to render the Latin *communi*. This lexical choice finds an echo in other translations, both into German and into English; Kothe, for example, translates the phrase, rather awkwardly, as 'die Gemeinschaft des Lebens' ('the community of life') (More 1846: 155), while Robert Adams (More 2016b: 113) offers 'the communal living'. Something rather curious, however, occurs in the Fuchs–Wessely translation, which appears to offer a clarification of the translation choice for the Latin *communi*: a footnote keyed to the adjective *gemeinsam* notes emphatically 'd[as] i[st] kommunistisch' ('i.e., communist'). No further commentary is provided.

This deceptively simple footnote, I argue, functions to perform an additional layer of the translated text's complex engagement with the question of translatability. At first glance, 'communist' may initially appear to be offered simply as a clarification of the translator's choice of vocabulary and the inclusion of this footnote may then appear to conflate the terms 'communal' and 'communist'. On closer consideration, however, it becomes clear that this single-word footnote also functions to highlight the gap between the two terms, adding to the cultural politics of translation played out in the text through the ongoing dialogue between editor and translator, translator and author, and translated text and 'original' that characterizes the work. The footnote obfuscates as much as it clarifies. When considering this footnote, there are two distinct but connected translation choices that merit attention: first, the use of the term *kommunistisch* and second, the decision to locate that term in a footnote rather than in the main text. Employing the adjective *kommunistisch* serves to situate the translated text in its contemporary political context, establishing a connection both with prominent left-wing thinkers (not least Marx and Engels, the authors of the *Communist Manifesto* published in the wake of revolutionary activity across Europe in the mid-nineteenth century) and with the wider field of nineteenth-century utopianism and its antecedents discussed at the outset of this chapter. The decision to locate the adjective *kommunistisch* in a footnote, meanwhile, is likely to be a consequence of the controversial nature of the term as it was used in the late nineteenth century. The entry on 'Kommunismus' contained in the 1895 edition of Meyer's *Conversationslexikon*—a useful barometer of the themes and topics under discussion in the German public sphere at the time of publication—first traces the origins of the term to Plato and then to More, before offering an overwhelmingly critical account of contemporary communism. Using the term *kommunistisch*, but placing it in a footnote, allows the translation to perform More's *Utopia* as a foundational tract of nineteenth-century socialist thought, while simultaneously distancing itself from that claim. Just as More employed a number of narrative devices to distance himself from the radical perspective put forward in *Utopia*, so the 1896 translation seeks to both perform the text's political import and distance itself from a bold interpretation of its politics.

The publication of their translation of *Utopia* gained Fuchs and Wessely recognition in left-wing circles. At a time in which the punitive Anti-Socialist Laws had only recently been lifted and there was clear evidence that the establishment was suspicious of Kautsky's interpretation of More's *Utopia*, there were, however, risks involved in producing a new German translation of the text. Perhaps for this reason, neither Fuchs nor Wessely offered in their paratextual materials any sustained engagement with the larger contemporary political questions raised by the text. They do not appear to address, for example, the pressing and problematic issues for a late nineteenth-century reading of More's *Utopia* identified by Michels and Ziegler in the introduction to their new Latin edition of the text, such as the 'Woman Question', the issue of slavery, and ideas about sustainability (More 1895b: xxx– xxxiii). Instead, Fuchs, in his introduction, and Wessely, in his translator's notes, appear to focus more on the philological angle, which could be interpreted as a retreat from the overtly political thrust of *Utopia*. And yet, the decision to undertake this translation was also clearly politically motivated. For them, the very act of translating the text and thereby inserting it into contemporary political discourse is a radical act. As we have seen, Fuchs and Wessely moved in political circles of different kinds; while Fuchs was actively involved in anarchist and, later, social democratic politics, Wessely was engaged theoretically and practically in the politics of world literature. Their different ways of being political came together in the 1890s in relation to the nascent social democratic workers' education movement and its desire to reclaim the cultural heritage proper to it. In this context, Fuch and Wessely were united in their belief in the political potential of translation. It is, then, little wonder that they were drawn to More's *Utopia*, a text that foregrounds the political power of translation. Their translation, the first complete translation of *Utopia* into German, aimed to make the text available to a new set of readers in order to foster the creation and emancipation of a politically engaged working class in late nineteenth-century Germany.

CHAPTER 23

NOT JUST A LIGHT-HEARTED JOKE

Russian Moreana from the Age of Karamzin to the Rise of Social Democracy and Lenin's 'Stele of Freedom'

FRANCES NETHERCOTT

In 1918, with Lenin's approval, the name of Thomas More was one of nineteen 'outstanding thinkers and personalities in the struggle for the liberation of workers' to be inscribed on an obelisk in the Alexander Gardens, just outside the Kremlin walls.[1] Officially unveiled to mark the first anniversary of the October Revolution, the memorial plaque effectively authorized a series of publications about *Utopia* as one of the key antecedents to Soviet Communism. Thereafter, a steady stream of interpretative studies and bibliographical surveys, as well as a number of didactically titled histories of socialism, such as 'From Thomas More to Lenin' (Gorev 1922) and 'Utopian and Scientific Communism' (Volgin 1928), appeared in large print runs.[2] All of them confirmed More's reputation as one of the chief precursors of Soviet socio-economic organization. Celebrated as 'the first to raise the banner of socialism in a modern bourgeois Europe' (Levitskii 1925: 108), for readers and interpreters, particularly during the first two decades of the new regime—a period often characterized as the most 'utopian' of the Soviet experiment—there was little doubt that the ideas about equality, happiness,

---

[1] The list was compiled by the prominent Bolshevik Vladimir Friche. Other names included Tommaso Campanella; Karl Marx; Friedrich Engels; Charles Fourier; Clause Henri de Rouvroy, comte de Saint-Simon; the Leveller Gerrard Winstanley; and various nineteenth-century Russian revolutionary thinkers-cum-activists. The obelisk was originally completed in 1914 to commemorate the three-hundredth anniversary of the Romanov dynasty. The rebranding by Lenin as a 'stele of freedom' was one of his early measures to eradicate any vestiges of the imperial past. However, mutatis mutandis, in 2013, the obelisk was dismantled on Putin's orders, and has since been replaced with a replica of the pre-revolutionary monument dedicated to the Russian tsars.

[2] Other examples include Svyatlovskii 1923; Levitskii 1925. Translations from the Russian throughout this chapter are my own.

property and labour that More set out in his famous work made him a powerful model to emulate.

If the fascination, post-October 1917, with More's tale of an egalitarian society may be described in terms of a perceived common cause, the origins of Russian Moreana in the late eighteenth century, and the subsequent ebb and flow of interest in *Utopia* during the course of the nineteenth and early twentieth centuries, are arguably more instructive of a domestic history marked by political conservatism and the unattended consequences on sociopolitical thought of a controlled, top-down policy of modernization. There are many factors to consider here, but among the most important to bear in mind insofar as they present a useful setting for analysing the sequence of Russian translations and interpretations of More's work are: (1) the impact on public discourse of official conservative reaction to the French Revolution of 1789; (2) the social and political repercussions of Alexander II's programme of reforms launched in the early 1860s, namely, the emancipation of the serfs and the question of the peasant commune (*obshchina*), the introduction of trial by jury, and the granting of greater university autonomy; (3) the consolidation of a network of institutions of higher learning facilitating the formation of a community of learning and intellectual debate with Western peers; and (4) the emergence of the revolutionary, radical intelligentsia as conduits for the introduction on to Russian soil of European political thought such as Utopian socialism, Marxism, and social democracy. (With reference to this last factor, it is worth noting that, in his account of the genesis of capitalism in the first volume of *Capital*, Karl Marx treated More's characterization of enclosure as a reliable source, a point which rarely passed unnoticed by Russian and Soviet commentators committed to foregrounding the contemporary relevance of More's ideas.) Two further considerations worth mentioning relative to the Russian reception of Thomas More concern the rise of public opinion or a public sphere (*obshchestvennost*) during the closing decades of the nineteenth century, and last but not least, the ethos of mass education after 1900. The phases, then, of Russian Moreana in the late imperial era as encapsulated in the production of translations suggest that Russian readers clearly recognized the importance (and/or potential danger) of his thought well before his inclusion in the pantheon of revolutionary thinkers by the Bolsheviks.

I begin with a brief overview of the first known Russian translation of *Utopia* (1789; repr. 1790): a bibliographical rarity about which we have little information aside from a fairly cryptic, yet revelatory, review by the late eighteenth- and early nineteenth-century novelist and official historiographer, Nikolai Karamzin. Indeed, later translators seemed to have been unaware of its existence, even though the main libraries in St Petersburg and Moscow possessed copies of it, and we do come across references to it in late nineteenth-century specialist literature. But these are few and far between. A major part of this chapter focuses on the interpretative 'scholarly' study and translation by the historian and left-wing thinker Evgenii Tarle (Tarle 1901; More 1901). Mistakenly touted by the author as the 'first' Russian translation and misleadingly presented as 'translated from the Latin', Tarle's thesis became embroiled in a scandal involving (university) politics and personal vendetta. The third translation, by Aleksandr G. Genkel' in collaboration with N. A. Maksheeva (1903, 1905, 1918, 1923), entered the canon as the 'Vulgate' version (Volgin, in More 1935b: 28). Intended for a wide readership, it was dismissed by peers as slipshod and flawed. Notwithstanding, its publication in four editions (at the height of revolution, the onset of the Red Terror, and as Bolshevik Russia embarked on its New Economic Policy) meant that it occupied a prominent position in the literature about *Utopia*. This was, in turn, superseded in 1935 by the publication of what must be considered the first rigorous and integral translation from the Latin into Russian by the classical philologist A. I. Malein. With an introduction by V. P. Volgin, it was published to mark the four hundredth anniversary of More's death. Based on the 1518 Basel edition, the translation was published by the Academy of Sciences in two subsequent editions (1947, 1953). Although faithful to the Latin, the translation was, at Malein's own admission, marred by cumbersome sounding loanwords (More 1935b: 30). It was finally superseded in 1978 by the translation of Judith Kagan, a highly respected classical philologist, but with an otherwise 'standard' commentary—namely, using the parameters of 'scientific communism' to assess the work—by I. N. Osinovskii, author of further books on More (Osinovskii 1985), and on More, utopian communism, humanism, and Reformation (Osinovskii 1978).

'I HAVE SEEN A LAND WHERE PEOPLE LIVE AS THEY SHOULD LIVE': KARAMZIN'S COMMENTARY ON *UTOPIA*

In 1791, Nikolai Karamzin (1766–1826), one of Russia's foremost public intellectuals during the reigns of Catherine the Great and Alexander I, published a review of an anonymous, abridged translation of More's tale in his *Moscow Journal*, an influential periodical which, by virtue of its numerous reviews of foreign (predominantly French) literature, played a major role in familiarizing Russian readers with European thought and culture (Vallich 1977; Karp 1987). Entitled *Portrait of the Best Possible Form of Governance or Utopia* (*Kartina vsevozmozhnogo luchshego pravleniya ili Utopii*) and published in 1789 by the well-known St Petersburg publisher Johan Karlovich Schnor (More 1789b), this translation was from Thomas Rousseau's French translation (1780, 1789), itself based on an English translation.[3] The book, it appears, was a commercial success, and to meet public demand it was reprinted the following year under the considerably longer title, *The Philosopher Raphael Hythloday's Travels in the New World, and a Description of Noteworthy Curiosities and of the Wise Governance of the Life of the Peace-Loving Inhabitants on the Isle of Utopia* (*Filosofa Rafaila Gitlode stranstvovanie v Novom Svete i opisanie luibopytstva dostoinykh primechanii i blagorazumnykh ustanovlenii zhizni miroliubivago naroda ostrova Utopii*) (More 1790a). Despite the change in title, the translation in the two editions—a largely faithful rendering of the French, albeit with a tendency to 'neutralize' some of the polemics in Book One—remained unchanged (Vallich 1977: 244).

It is important to note that if, after 1800, Karamzin used his position as Alexander I's official historiographer to uphold the principles of autocracy, in the 1780s and early

---

[3] For Rousseau's translation, see Astbury in this volume.

1790s he was regarded as an Enlightenment and 'liberal' oppositional figure. It was this political world view, which, according to the Soviet critic E. I. Vallich (1977), informed his commentary of *Utopia*, even though in his opening remarks he seemed to dismiss More's ideas as fanciful, contradictory, and a pale shadow of Plato's imagined ideal state (Karamzin 1791: 359). In Vallich's view, this was, in fact, a tactic to put to rest any suspicions the censor might have had. Indeed, in the course of his review, which comprised an informative summary—'to which, it is hoped, the reader will not object' (359)—and some biographical information about More not included in the translation, Karamzin offered virtually no commentary on some of the potentially tendentious themes pertaining to 'democratic rule', the problem of tyranny, obligatory labour, the principles of equitable distribution of goods, and the provision of welfare for all citizens: instead, he focused on less controversial issues such as marriage and war.

However, as Vallich suggests, Karamzin's seemingly anodyne reading of *Utopia* actually belied his deeper understanding of the work which was based on a familiarity with the original Latin: his excursus on marriage, for example, drew on passages that were missing from both Rousseau's and the Russian translation—which Karamzin (1791: 365) criticized for its Gallicisms and poor command of both the French and Russian languages —suggesting that he either had the Latin to hand or was summarizing from memory. Vallich also makes a compelling case to argue that the underlying purpose of Karamzin's review was to provide his readers with cryptic pointers as to the potentially subversive social and political significance of the tale for the present day. A case in point concerns his loose rendering of a passage towards the end of Book One. According to Vallich, the phrase 'I have seen a land where people live as they should live', which Karamzin included as a quotation from the translation, was, in fact, his own invention. As Vallich notes, the Russian translation read: 'were you to travel to Utopia you would not encounter a people with a more enlightened, or just society' (Vallich 1977: 253). Albeit a subtle alteration, the preceptive tone it acquired in Karamzin's rendering was enough for the discerning reader to appreciate from his follow-up remarks on law, customs, and the economic structures forming the scaffolding, so to speak, of communal ownership (a term he mentions just once), that the real value of More's tale was his vision of a society without private property. In view of the political situation at home and abroad, it is perhaps understandable that Karamzin's review relied rather more on oblique inference than any open suggestion of the lessons that More's imagined isle might have for the Russia of his day. Revolution was then unfolding in France, and memory of the Pugachev Rebellion (1773–5) was still recent. This had pitted serfs against landlords in part as a response to Catherine the Great's *Nakaz* (Instruction) of 1767 in which she famously established the inviolability of private property as the special monopoly and privilege of the nobility (Pipes 2000); in 1782 she had extended these rights even further to include not only to the surface of the lands and their products but also to anything lying beneath it such as minerals (Pravilova 2014: 24).

From Idealism and Utopian Socialism to Populism: Russian Commentaries (1830s–1860s)

Other than this brief 'Karamzin episode', information about this early period of Russian Moreana is patchy. Judging by accounts, the 1789 and 1790 editions disappeared from circulation (although, as I have mentioned, copies were held in the major libraries), and the few commentaries on *Utopia* dating from the 1830s seem to have been based on the Latin: these included 'Thomas More and His Utopia' ('Tomas Morus i ego Utopiya', 1837)—an anonymous fifty-page essay on More which included passing reference to Saint-Simonianism, and Fourierism—and K. A. Nevolin's short entry for the 1839 *Encyclopedia of Jurisprudence* in which he noted that More's model for the ideal state was Plato (Nevolin 1857: 232). In 1860, a long essay about More's life and work appeared in the weekly *Russian Word* (*Russkoe Slovo*) (1859–66), a magazine popular with a nascent populist intelligentsia committed to social revolution based on the peasant commune and the distinctively agrarian features of Russian social organization.[4] The explicit aim of the author, V. G. Avsenko, was to revive interest in a figure whose importance, he argued, had been overshadowed by other big names of the European Renaissance, such as Desiderius Erasmus, Niccolò Machiavelli, Francesco Petrarca, and Giovanni Boccaccio. In the spirit of 'life writes the book', Avsenko gave a detailed account—mostly reliant on Thomas Stapleton's *Vita et obitus Thomae Mori* (1588)—of More's upbringing and 'moral character' (his abhorrence for the dissolute lifestyle of his student peers at university; his personal asceticism) as the basis for elucidating some of the key themes in *Utopia*. For the reader, however, Avsenko's psychological, and mostly sympathetic, portrait of More as a man apart is strangely at odds with the judgemental tone running through his five-page summary of *Utopia* itself. If he acknowledged Book One as a masterful vindication of humane and noble ideas—especially on account of its arguments against harsh punishments for minor crimes—Book Two, in his view, was riddled with ridiculous fantasies, and exposed an author who was not always 'noble and humane' in his deliberations (Avsenko 1860: 41–42). For example, More's counsel to cut off the ear of a convict as a deterrent to escape (a practice, which, Avsenko noted, 'even in Turkey is a form of punishment, not a preventative measure'), significantly diminished More's stature as one of the finest philosophers of the ancient and modern eras (46).

Avsenko's presentation of the Utopian economy was possibly the most damning of all, and is worth quoting in full:

> In the economic sphere we see the most infantile, immature notions of national wealth placed under the sign of mercantilism. The absence of an agricultural class,

---

[4] The publication was shut down in 1866 following the first assassination attempt on Alexander II.

> any understanding of the true meaning of money, the unwieldy organization of state funds based on the export of grain products—none of this differs from the illusions of other mercantilists of his age. Given its lack of any meaningful philosophical analysis, More's *Utopia* could not have had an enduring moral influence on society. What might it give his contemporaries beyond passing amusement? The First Book went unnoticed, while the Second [...] had no social application whatsoever, least of all in England—famous for its circumspect political reforms and highly developed principle of individual freedom. (47)

In sum, for Avsenko, More's only originality was a view of society and human nature, which, however, was 'crudely corporeal' (*grubo-chuvstvennyi*) to the point of the most revolting cynicism:

> Thomas More looks at society rather like an amateur in horse rearing views his stables. In no way should the work be compared to the writings of Plato, Aristotle, Cicero, Rousseau, or Locke; rather it is a literary fantasy, which has passing similarities with a whole host of writers ranging from Plato to the *domostroi* of Archpriest Sylvester; if anything, it has more in common with Fénelon's *Aventures de Télémaque*. (46)[5]

Where, then, Avsenko had the greatest difficulty was in reconciling the 'soaring philosophical heights' of the first book of More's work with the 'contemptible' aspirations in the second: in his view, it was almost impossible to believe that they were written by one and the same person (41).

Historicizing More, Ideologizing More: Late Nineteenth- and Early Twentieth-Century Assessments

Two seemingly disparate factors—the consolidation of scholarship during the second half of the nineteenth century and the rise of social democracy—assured *Utopia*'s high standing in the Russian canon. Even the most cursory overview of university-related publications, from introductions and summaries in so-called thick journals (*publitsistika*) and 'encyclopedic dictionaries' to monographs and transcripts of lecture courses, suggests that the Russian scholarly community was fully up to date with recent Western literature about More and his legacy.[6] Beyond academia, the questions More

---

[5] Archpriest Sylvester was the author of a set of rules for Russian households during the reign of Ivan the Terrible. For more on the association between Fénelon's *Télémaque* and *Utopia*, see chapters by Hill, Pohl, and Verhaart in this volume.

[6] See e.g. Yanzhul 1890; Gogotskii 1857–73: 3.518–522; Chicherin 1890; Jakovenko 1891.

raised resonated with contemporary intelligentsia debates about the peasantry, the challenge to autocracy, and questions of social equality. Fuelled by the socio-economic consequences of Alexander II's Emancipation Act (1861)—namely, the worsening impoverishment of large parts of the rural community—and articulated in the categories of social democratic thought, these debates also generated works of utopian fiction, the most famous and most influential of which was undoubtedly Nikolai Chernyhevskii's celebrated novel, *What Is To Be Done?* (1863). Depicting a future society based on communal, egalitarian principles, it became a staple for Russian Marxists. As scholars have noted, if Lenin used Marx's *Das Kapital* (1867) as an intellectual template for the development of Bolshevism, it was in Chernyshevskii's novel that he discovered an emotional dynamic for the cause of revolution that was in many respects far more powerful (Frank 1990).

By the end of the nineteenth century, these parallel sites of reception for *Utopia* began to overlap. Among the reasons for this was the shift in historical study from political issues to questions relating to society and the economy—dominant figures in the field included P. G. Vinogradov (1854-1925), specializing in the history of medieval England; D. M. Petrushevskii (1863-1942); and A. N. Savin (1873-1923)—and the appointment to professorial chairs of scholars with broadly populist and democratic affiliations. Prominent amongst these appointments were the legal Marxist and economic historian Mikhail Tugan-Baranovskii (1865-1919), the historian and sociologist Nikolai Kareev (1850-1931), and the celebrated historian of Russia Vasilii Kliuchevskii (1841-1911), the latter two sharing broadly populist, democratic views. Arguably, a pivotal 'moment' in bridging university and sociopolitical discourses, and of immediate relevance to the question of More's Russian reception, was Karl Kautsky's study, *Thomas More und seine Utopie* (1888), in which he explicitly aligned the ideas of *Utopia* with the origins of social democracy.[7] Published in several editions, and quickly translated into Russian, alongside his 1895 co-authored multi-volume *Die Vorlaufer des neueren Sozialismus* ('The Forerunners of Modern Socialism'), it remained an authoritative statement on the history of socialism, and of More as one of its founding fathers, until the late 1920s when Kautsky was proclaimed persona non grata on account of his hostility to Soviet Bolshevism and the October Revolution. As I discuss below, Kautsky's study provided Tarle, author of the first twentieth-century translation, with a framework within which to develop his own interpretation of the significance of More's text for the socio-economic historian. However, if Tarle accepted the underlying premise of Kautsky's approach, as a practising historian he also challenged Kautsky's reading on the grounds that he ignored the actual experiences that shaped the world of men and women in sixteenth-century England for the sake of a priori categories pertaining to modes of production and class struggle.

---

[7] For more on Kautsky, see chapters by Stewart and Moir in this volume.

SCIENCE, UNIVERSITY POLITICS, AND PERSONAL VENDETTA: EVGENII TARLE

Evgenii Tarle (1874–1955) studied history at Kiev University, and it was under the supervision of the early modernist Ivan V. Luchitskii—a specialist in French agrarian history, Catholicism, and Calvinism—that he began work on his Masters dissertation on More in 1898. In the early stages of his work, Tarle benefited from research trips abroad, notably to the British Museum library, where he collated archival material, and familiarized himself with Western literature on the topic. He had completed the dissertation by the end of 1900. Entitled *The Social Views of Thomas More in Connection with the Economic Conditions of His Age*, it was published under the auspices of the left-wing (legal Marxist and social democratic) literary and popular science journal, *God's World* (*Mir bozhii*) in the spring of 1901 in readiness for his viva examination, which took place in the autumn of the same year.[8]

Tarle's aim was to explore the connections between 'real fact' and 'theory', namely, the ways in which the socio-economic and political reality of Tudor England gave rise to a theory premised on radically different principles of labour, welfare, justice, and rights. As he put it: 'by studying More's era and his career it may be possible for the historian to discern "methodological strands" as he engages in the difficult task of analysing the reasons for change in social theory, past and present' (Tarle 1957: 122–123).[9] It was Tarle's view that, with one exception—Kautsky—no one to date had taken this approach; that is, to use the work both as a valid historical source for understanding the Tudor world and as a resource for charting developments in social theory. The dominant trend in Western literature, he claimed, with reference to the French academician and literary critic Jean Marie Napoléon Désiré Nisard (1806–88), was to treat *Utopia* as the 'lighthearted pleasantry of a scholar' ('l'aimable jeu d'esprit d'un érudit', Tarle 1957: 220; Nisard 1855).[10] In its scope, then, Tarle's monograph was undeniably ambitious. An opening account of More's life prior to *Utopia*—together with an outline of the economy and society in early sixteenth-century England (namely, the agrarian crisis triggered by the rise of enclosures and the transfer of the centre of economic gravity from the countryside to towns)—provided two 'contextual frames' within which to analyse the work. The next three chapters—a summary of the book, a discussion of More's intellectual resources together with a bibliographical review of recent nineteenth-century literature about him, and a survey of the place of *Utopia* in the history of social theory (from

---

[8] *Obshchestvennie vozzreniya Tomasa Mora v svyazi s ekonomicheskom sostoyaniem ego vremeni. Prilozheniya. Perevod 'Utopii' s latinskogo, rukopis' sovremennika o Tomase More*. My quotations are taken from the edition included in Tarle 1957: 121–265, 717–729.

[9] See also the foreword to Tarle 1957 by A. S. Erusalimskii (xiv).

[10] Alekseev 1955 claims that, well before Tarle, Zhukovskii (1866: 73) had made a similar point on the underlying seriousness of the work.

Tommaso Campanella and Francis Bacon, in the sixteenth and seventeenth centuries, to Charles Fourier and Étienne Cabet, in the eighteenth and nineteenth)—formed the central plank of Tarle's thesis, while a concluding chapter charted the main events of More's life after *Utopia*, his trial and execution, against a backdrop of Church–state relations at the onset of the Reformation.

In the pivotal fourth chapter, 'The Literary Sources of the Utopian State', Tarle used what was ostensibly a discussion of the *status quaestionis* of research in Russia and Europe to foreground the groundbreaking nature of his thesis. Few scholars, he claimed, irrespective of whether their approach was informed by socialist thought or inspired by More's canonization in 1886, had assessed the importance of Plato's *Republic*, *Critias*, *Timaeus*, and *Laws* or of St Augustine's *De Civitate Dei* as models for *Utopia*.[11] A second line of enquiry concerned the viability of *Utopia* as a source for the socio-economic historian:

> We must prove this by real facts, and if we argue that in his positive ideals we see a reflection of More's contemporary social environment, then, likewise, we have to evidence this. For, informing the positive ideals of *Utopia* were multiple factors—emotive and intellectual responses, literary influences as well as More's own creativity itself. (Tarle 1957: 221)

However, judging by the critique of his peers, Tarle failed to meet expectations on either count. In support of his claims concerning influence, he relied exclusively on textual similarities and verbal coincidences. And if his insistence on a multi-pronged approach to bear out his thesis concerning the importance of More's intellectual biography as the basis for his critical observations in *Utopia* seemed more promising, what followed was a strikingly combative diatribe against Kautsky: the one author he had singled out for adopting a comparable understanding of the work. Conceding that Kautsky was the first to regard *Utopia* as a refractor of More's social and economic environment, and that, from a methodological point of view, his book stood on more solid scientific ground than any other study to date, Tarle was quick to point out that the absence of any reference to the literature on the economic history of England made it difficult for the reader to ascertain the rationale for his hypotheses and assertions. If what Kautsky wrote about merchant capital was largely correct, where did he get the idea that trade relations between nations 'constitute a national language'? And where did he get the idea that the sixteenth century was a 'fight to the death' (*Todeskampf*) between feudalism and capitalism? Or that the principles of European absolutism had close causal links with the principles of capitalist production (which, Tarle added, did not exist in the fourteenth

---

[11] Tarle's critique singled out von Rudhart 1852, Manning 1851, Seebohm 1869, Bridgett 1891, W. Hutton 1895—recent biographical accounts which he dismissed for failing to analyse More's models for *Utopia*—and the historians/social theorists Adler 1899, Shtein 1899, Mohl 1855–8, Taine 1864 (who made no mention of More at all), Brink 1877–93, as well as the work of two eminent Russian scholars: the historian of juridical thought Boris Chicherin (1828–1904), and the historian and social theorist Robert Vipper (1859–1954).

and fifteenth centuries): 'Here we encounter the hallmarks of Kautsky's prose. Knowing full well that there is no class struggle in *Utopia*, he sets out regardless, relying on a variety of verbal antics, to present this supposed battle of interests as the entirety of More's ideals' (221). For Tarle, such a caricature and ideologically driven reductionism betrayed low-level scholarship.[12]

Tarle conceived the inclusion of a translation of *Utopia* in the appendix to his dissertation as an opportunity to demonstrate his skillset as promising young scholar: 'So as not to fall back on a descriptive account of *Utopia* we have translated the treatise into Russian,' he declared (121). His translation, he claimed, was based on the Latin text—the first of its kind in Russian—which he had accessed via a reprint of the editio princeps published in Berlin in the *Lateinische Literaturdenkmaler des XV und XVI Jahrhunderts* (1895). Tarle was therefore keen to stress a major point of difference between his own rigorous translation and the 1790 version which, he added, could not be found in any of the major libraries. As we shall see, for his examiners—specialists in classical philology and early modern history—this was one of several claims which lacked foundation: given his scholarly pretensions Tarle should have known that both the Public Library in St Petersburg and Russian State Library in Moscow held copies. Initial reviews of the published dissertation and translation in the press, though, were favourable: bar a few minor errors, Tarle had produced a readable translation that was significant for making the subject matter of *Utopia* accessible to a wider reading public. The review by Vasily Solomin, a contributor to *National Economy* (*Narodnoe Khozyaistvo*), a moderately left-wing social science journal specializing in questions of political economy, was fairly typical in this regard. Solomin called it a capital piece of research, the best study on More to have appeared either in Russia or abroad in the last few years, and he singled out Tarle's historical-literary survey of More's place in the history of social thought as especially impressive. For Solomin, Tarle had convincingly demonstrated the importance of More for modern-day communism: 'At the heart of More's endeavour to balance the interests of the individual and the state was a communistic economy [*khozyaistvennyi stroi*], disdain for private property, communal labour, shared tools of production and acquired assets, the moral obligation of labour, and a system of "social utilitarianism" ' (Solomin 1901: 180).

Rather more surprising, perhaps, was that four months later in the October issue of the same journal, a second, extended review of the translation appeared which can only be described as excoriating (Vodovozov 1901). The author, Vasily Vodovozov (1864–1933), a well-known *publitsist* (essayist) and left-wing activist, had clearly gone through the translation with a fine-toothed comb in order to spotlight every single mistake. For example: *castellum* was translated as 'New Castile', which, Vodovozov pointed out, was a historic region in Spain, and later, in 1534, the original name for Peru; 'Calicut' (Caliquit/ Kozhikode) was transformed into 'Calcutta', which, Vodovozov noted, did not exist until the late seventeenth century. 'Secondary ideas' for *secundae intentiones* did not

---

[12] See also Alekseev 1955: 23.

make sense; referring to J. H. Lupton's authoritative 1895 English translation and commentary (a study which, as Vodovozov pointed out, Tarle had obviously not consulted), he suggested 'general ideas' or 'concepts' as a better alternative. Tarle had confused the length with the width of the river on the island. He translated both *civitas* and *urbs* as 'town' (*gorod*), meaning that he lost sight of the federal structure of utopia. Worse still were missing sections, notably the matter of physical health as a supreme good.

On the basis of these lapses, distortions, and misreadings, Vodovozov argued that Tarle had, in fact, based his translation on the rather poor German 1846 translation by Hermann Kothe.[13] The similarities between the two were uncanny. Moreover, as an interpreter of *Utopia*, Tarle's claims to originality either betrayed his ignorance of existing analyses (in addition to Lupton, Tarle was unaware of I. Wessely's 1896 German translation), or involved what amounted to breaches of scholarly practice. In Vodovozov's view, Tarle's contention that More was the first true opponent of the death penalty was simply wrong; the parallels he drew between More and St Augustine were completely without foundation, and exposed his unfamiliarity with the work of the latter; and he exaggerated the influence of Plato. Had he been more familiar with the literature—for example, Eduard Zeller (1875), who argued that More's ethical principle was Epicurean rather than Platonic, Lina Berger (1879a), or Lupton, not to mention the foreword to the *Lateinische Literaturdenkmaler* edition from which Tarle claimed to have worked—he would not have committed these errors. Worst of all, for Vodovozov, was Tarle's misrepresentation of Kautsky's arguments concerning the economic causes of the Reformation. Not only did Tarle distort Kautsky's views, making false claims that Kautsky was ignorant of the literature, he also misquoted him. Finally, if, by his inclusion of so many Latin, Greek, and German words and an impressive scientific apparatus, Tarle had hoped to dazzle the reader with his erudition, closer inspection revealed that the intellectual scaffolding of his study was actually incredibly flimsy, and could collapse at any moment.

Why did Vodovozov do this? In his review he referred to the viva examination, which he had attended alongside other members of the public and journalists (the practice in Russia). Aside from Tarle's supervisor, Luchitskii, and the official 'opponent', the professor of Western European literature N. P. Dashkevich, all the examiners found fault with the thesis. In his account, Vodovozov singled out the main objections raised by the panel of assessors: the textual analogies Tarle used in his discussion of More's intellectual resources, namely Plato and St Augustine, were of the most primitive kind, of as much value as a comparison between apples and oranges. But it was Tarle's seriously flawed translation that was subject to the most damning criticism. Georgii Chelpanov, professor of philosophy, and the Latinist Adol'f Sonni confirmed that Tarle had not translated from the Latin, but from a second-rate German translation, and that he had both reproduced and amplified the howlers. How, in the end, he obtained his Masters degree despite considerable opposition was, Vodovozov suggested, the work

---

[13] For Kothe's and Wessely's translations, see Stewart in this volume.

of backstage machinations by his supervisor, Luchitskii. Certainly, reports of the viva which appeared in the left-wing press expressed little doubt that the criticisms of Tarle were politically motivated: the young scholar was regarded by conservative-minded professors (and the police department which oversaw proceedings) as a subversive social democrat to whom teaching responsibilities should not be granted. The right-wing press, by contrast, as Vodovozov noted, ridiculed the affair.

Recent studies have demonstrated that Vodovozov's account of Tarle's disastrous performance at his viva was slightly disingenuous, and that the blistering force of his attack was, in fact, fuelled by personal vendetta (Kaganovich 2014: 28–38; see also Kucherenko 1977: 60–68; Tarle 1957: v–xxxv). Vodovozov and Tarle were erstwhile friends with a shared political and ideological affinity for social democracy. In April 1900, they were both arrested for their role as 'discussants' to a talk ('Ibsen as a moralist') to be delivered in Kiev by the revolutionary activist and thinker Anatolii Lunacharskii. Forewarned, the police stormed the venue and arrested those present. In his memoir account of the episode, Vodovozov, who shared a prison cell with Tarle, described his friend's state of fretful agitation and anxiety over the fact that he would not be able to take up his scholarship to travel abroad, and feared that his academic career was over. He even threatened suicide, and entreated Vodovozov to alert the prison authorities about this. Alarmed, the police speeded up the process of interrogation and released him within two days. The others remained in prison, and on their release were placed under police surveillance. The suggestion, then, is that Vodovozov was (falsely, it seems) led to believe rumours that during his interrogation Tarle had informed on the other political prisoners. Driven, then, by a sense of betrayal, he encouraged rumours that Tarle had not, in fact, done the translation of *Utopia* himself, but had handed over the task to his wife. This also explains why he was prepared to humiliate Tarle during the viva when he took the floor to challenge his erstwhile friend's integrity as a scholar and translator (Kaganovich 2014: 31–32).

Unlike Vodovozov and the viva examiners, most Soviet assessments of Tarle's translation accepted that he had worked from the Latin, only falling back on the Kothe translation when he got stuck. That said, the most commonly used epithets to describe the end result are 'hasty' (*naspekh*) and 'not very successful' (*malo udachnyi*).[14] Given the conditions in which he completed the dissertation and translation, this is perhaps not surprising. Tarle was given a suspended sentence, lost the right to teach, and in August 1900, following a period of house arrest on his father-in-law's estate in the region of Kherson, was exiled to Warsaw where he had limited access to materials.[15] As B. Kaganovich argues, it was also clear from Tarle's repeated requests to Luchitskii that he wanted to defend the thesis as soon as possible (that is, by May 1901), in the hope that this would lead to the lifting of the police injunction, and allow him to resume a university

---

[14] See Volgin in More 1935b: 27; Alekseev 1955; Osinovskii's introduction in More 1978b: 5–81.

[15] Tarle's letters to Luchitskii from this period (autumn 1900–spring 1901) mention that he had managed to obtain materials from the London Record Office, and that he had access to dictionaries of medieval Latin.

career. It remains, though, that this more reasoned explanation fails to account for one, quite pertinent, observation Vodovozov made in his review: had Tarle read Kautsky more attentively (whose monograph, incidentally, Vodovozov called the 'best study to date—albeit not without weaknesses') he would have been forewarned that Kothe's translation was three times removed from the original, and that he had compounded existing errors with distortions of his own (Vodovozov 1901: 6–7). As Vodovozov reminded his readers, Kothe, who was seemingly unaware that *Utopia* had been written in Latin, had produced his translation from a French translation, which itself was most likely a translation from Gilbert Burnet's 1684 English version.[16]

Tarle never returned to More or the sixteenth century. As a professor and researcher, he specialized in modern European and Russian military, diplomatic, and socio-economic history, and is perhaps best known for his studies of the Napoleonic Wars. His *Complete Works* published posthumously (a hefty twelve volumes, 1957–62) established him as one of the most prodigious, yet complex, historians of his age. Accused of placing historical knowledge in service to Stalinism in the 1930s (his 1936 biography of Napoleon was read as a paean of praise for the Red Tsar), he was also a victim of the regime, and was arrested and incarcerated along with many other falsely indicted historians for plotting against the regime in the so-called Academic Affair of 1929–31. If his ill-fated translation of *Utopia* was never re-edited during his lifetime (it was included in the *Complete Works*), its reputation as a slipshod piece of work was perpetuated owing to its inclusion in a succession of Soviet bibliographical studies, literary surveys, and interpretative studies in which the questionable hypotheses he had advanced were signalled as points of contention.[17] Ironically, in the end, what gave Tarle's study lasting relevance were the points he had in common with Kautsky: their shared underlying premise that More's work was a window on to (and critique of) the socio-economic reality of early sixteenth-century England, and not a light-hearted pleasantry, anticipated Soviet interpretations, all of which championed a view of More as a pioneering figure in the struggle for social justice.

MORE FOR THE MASSES: A. G. GENKEL''S 'VULGATE' TRANSLATION AND EARLY SOVIET INTERPRETATION

Almost contemporary with Tarle's thesis and translation was the 'Vulgate version' published by Aleksandr Germanovich Genkel' (1872–1927). A botanist by training, and during the Soviet era recognized as the founder of the faculty of agricultural science

---

[16] For Burnet's translation, see Withington in this volume.
[17] This accusation recurs in the commentaries by Levitskii (1925), Volgin (1928), Alekseev (1955), and Osinovskii (1978, 1985).

and botany at the University of Perm, Genkel' was deeply committed to the cause of public education, and dedicated most of his life to the topic. Alongside writings on plant morphology, he published over two hundred 'popular-scientific' essays on a whole range of subjects, from literature and poetry to politics and pedagogy (including, in 1906, *Narodnoe obrazovanie na zapade i u nas*, 'On the characteristics of public education in the West and in Russia'). His decision to offer a readable translation of *Utopia* for a wider, non-specialist readership may, then, be understood in terms of a conviction in its contemporary relevance to socialism, and thus its value as an instructional tool for a mass audience of workers.

Genkel' was fully aware of Tarle's study. In the preface to the first edition, he claimed that his own text was actually ready for publication in 1898, prior to Tarle's, but, as he put it, he wanted to 'cross-check' his translation with as many editions of the original as possible, and it was only in the summer of 1900 that he was able to travel abroad to compare his translation with various editions held in Western libraries (in his preface, he mentioned by name only the Royal Library of Sweden in Stockholm). At this point he required a further eighteen months to revise his translation, during which time Tarle's version appeared: 'However, we ascribe such importance to More's book that we decided to come out with our own translation; as the cornerstone of the modern world view, classical works require the utmost amount of exposure, and every new study can contribute to this' (More 1903: preface [n.p.]).

If the publication of a second edition of Genkel''s translation in 1905 suggests there was a demand for More's *Utopia* among a growing readership, its high profile also left it vulnerable to some acerbic criticism. A review by Professor Sonni (one of Tarle's examiners), once again demonstrated on the basis of textual evidence that the translation was modelled entirely on Kothe (Sonni 1905). To make this point, Sonni compared passages from the original (in the *Lateinische Literaturdenkmaler* edition) with, first, his own literal translation, then Kothe's translation, and finally Genkel''s. Not only did Genkel' reproduce some of the howlers present in Kothe's translation, but it was also clear that in places he did not even understand the German. Where he did consult the original his knowledge of Latin was not up to scratch.[18] The upshot was that More's irony was lost on him. Perhaps, though, it was the manner in which the publishers of Genkel''s translation had tinkered with Holbein's famous portrait of More included in the frontispiece that exasperated the scholar the most. As Sonni complained, 'the portrait [...] in the book frontispiece bears no resemblance to any of the images of the great humanist that have come down to us: the author of *Utopia* has been given a moustache!' (Sonni 1905: 393).[19]

---

[18] Criticism of a poor grasp of Latin was a recurring theme in the reviews, and may, in part, be explained by educational practices, which, since the second half of the 1870s, placed a major emphasis on the study of ancient Greek and Latin. Contemporaries, however, frequently complained that instruction consisted in rote learning of grammar, which killed rather than awakened interest in the subject.

[19] Despite Sonni's remonstrations, the moustache was still there in the final 1923 edition. See Fig. 0.1.

For Sonni and Soviet commentators, the most effective part of Genkel''s contribution to the literature on More was the informative and rather more accurate biographical sketch written by his collaborator, Maksheeva. As Volgin writes in his introduction to Malein's 1935 translation, 'the translation by A. G. Genkel'' wins you over by its style. Easy to read, it gives the impression of an original modern-day work. But that, unfortunately, is its only merit' (More 1935b: 28). Notwithstanding this harsh criticism, the accessible style and, more importantly, the underlying message of More's work—taken at face value—secured its popularity among a novice readership. This was no truer than in the immediate aftermath of Revolution: the re-edition, in 1918, of Genkel''s translation by the Petrograd Soviet of workers and Red Army deputies, and a further reprint by the Kharkov-based publishing house Proletariat in 1923, just as the new Soviet Russia was entering a period of recovery after the civil war and harsh economic measures of war communism, were both timely reminders of the goal of revolution and a vindication of the heady optimism accompanying the belief that a golden age of communism was, at last, well within reach. Surveys and interpretative literature dating from this period captured this mood. As V. Levitskii wrote:

> More was the first, some four hundred years ago, to formulate clearly and concisely the goal of socialism as the most equitable and rational form of social organization based on the transformation of the land, together with all the means and tools of production, into common ownership [*obshchaya obshchestvennaya sobstvennost*]. (Levitskii 1925: 5)

The titles and subject matter of works of fiction, for example, Yakov Okunev's *The World to Come* (1923), Innokentii Zhukov's *Voyage of the 'Red Star' Detachment to the Land of Marvels* (1924), or *In a Thousand Years* by Viktor Nikolskii (1925) also reflect the utopian spirit of the early 1920s: possibly the most famous novel from this period was *Journey of My Brother Alexis to the Land of a Peasant Utopia* by the economist Alexander Chayanov (1920). Importantly, unlike the ancients and certain utopian socialists, it was More's vision of socialism in terms of production (rather than distribution) and the economy on a national scale (*natsional'noe gosudarstvennoe khozyaistvo*) that made him the perfect interlocutor for modern-day scientific socialists. More's achievement was to formulate the goal of socialism as the return of the land, together with the means and tools of production, to common ownership (Levitskii 1925: 10, 5).

In one of the earliest works of synthesis on the history of socialism (1922), Boris Gorev drew clear parallels between More and Marx to the point where they are virtually indistinguishable. Both men, he wrote, were witness to radical shifts in European society and politics:

> In some instances, the religious wars and peasant uprisings in the age of Sir Thomas More carried the banner of universal equality and common ownership. In England, greedy landowners destroyed the peasantry by evicting them en masse from their land. As a result, large crowds of homeless vagrants began to wander the streets

begging for alms, sometimes even reduced to stealing. Their government was merciless towards them even though it was responsible for turning them into beggars. […] More was one of the first to grasp a point which Marx later developed in great detail, namely that every 'contemporary state is a conspiracy of the rich, who, on the pretext of the common good pursue their own advantage'. Where More (and the utopian socialists) failed, however, was in his inability to countenance the revolutionary potential of the people. Instead, he vested his hopes in the good offices of a benevolent ruler. We know that, to this day, such rulers from the governing classes have never been found. Even so, the working class completely assimilated the ideal of the great English communist in its new and perfected form of Marx and Engels's scientific socialism. These ideas will come to fruition in the worldwide proletarian revolution that is just beginning. (Gorev 1922: 5–6, 9–10)

If, for the modern-day reader, the terms of Gorev's remarks, cited here, barely stand up to scrutiny, it is easy to appreciate that for a novice readership in the early 1920s their underlying optimism and rallying spirit must have been irresistible. As I mentioned at the beginning of this chapter, thanks to Lenin, More had earned his place in the Soviet pantheon of revolutionary thinkers: it was, therefore, de rigueur in publications intended for a mass readership to include reminders of Lenin's wisdom in such matters, to insist on the historical precedents of modern-day socialism, and to offer assurances of a brighter future for the ordinary man.

Conclusion

'No one better than Kautsky in his *Forerunners of Modern Socialism*', Levitskii wrote, 'captured the significance of More's tale' (Levitskii 1925: 109). Written a few years prior to Kautsky's ousting from the Soviet hall of fame, Levitskii's remark serves as a reminder of possibly the most enduring feature of Russian and post-revolutionary appraisals of *Utopia*: it was not a joke. In Kautsky's words, as cited by Levitskii (1925: 109): 'Even though bourgeois historians treat it as a light-hearted joke, it became a major turning point in the history of human thought. In the history of socialism it announced a new era […] imparting to socialism a form that has since conquered the world.' Reading More through the lens of Soviet communism, then, required dismissing West European studies (which characteristically reduced his ideal state to a Christian ethic, or an intellectual game) and foregrounding More as a socio-economic thinker by transposing his story to the registers of class struggle, and, of course, by aligning his ideas (albeit with due deference) with those of Marx.[20] Any insurmountable incompatibilities between More and modern-day socialism (notably between More's religious convictions

---

[20] See Gorev 1922 (cited above); Osinovskii in More 1978b: 'More opposed the feudal-absolutist structure with the communist ideal of "Utopia". However, at that time, the bearer of these ideas, the proto-proletariat, was not capable of "independent political action"' (80).

and Soviet atheism) were negotiated simply by returning him to his historical context. Ultimately, what counted, and what became standard in the literature (and analysed with varying degrees of finesse), was More's critique of social inequality, his condemnation of the detrimental effects of large-scale expropriation by a social caste based on private property and exploitation (an allusion to the rise of enclosures), and the impoverishment of the peasantry. From there it required only the smallest leap of imagination to conclude that 'More's project expressed the antagonism between a "proto-proletariat" [*predproletariat*] and a growing bourgeoisie' (Osinovskii in More 1978b: 23).

CHAPTER 24

UTOPIA IN EAST CENTRAL EUROPE
The Hungarian Scene

ZSOLT CZIGÁNYIK

The present chapter discusses the influence of Thomas More's *Utopia* and utopian thought in Hungarian literature and culture with a special emphasis on the interaction of literature and political thought, especially concerning freedom of religion.[1] When we reflect on *Utopia*'s reception in Hungary in the past five hundred years, we naturally focus on the East Central European region more widely (that is, roughly speaking, the present-day Poland, Czech Republic, Slovakia, Hungary, the former Yugoslavian area, Romania, and the Ukraine, although the extent and borders of the region are subject to debate). This region is historically and culturally intertwined, the various nations living in this area having a strong mutual influence, despite differences between languages. The reception of *Utopia* reflects the cultural heritage of East Central Europe. As the examples below will show, the historically multicultural field of Hungary (as the historical region) extends to areas in present-day Slovakia and Romania (and five other countries), and the authors that contributed to the reception of *Utopia* in Hungarian literature and culture are not only Hungarians, but also of Greek, Czech, and Croatian origin, representing much of the variety of the region.

First of all, a detailed (though not definitive) overview is given of utopian works in Hungarian literature, including some foreign authors active in Hungary. Before the first Hungarian translation, the Latin text of *Utopia* played a role in Hungary (Latin had a significant function in Hungarian culture: until 1844 it was the official language of the country). As Csaba Maczelka (2017: 59–60) argues, *Utopia*'s influence can be observed as continuously present in Hungarian literature from the sixteenth century onwards

---

[1] The writing of this chapter was supported by the Humanities Initiative Fellowship of Central European University. The author wishes to express his gratitude to the university founded by George Soros. While completing the chapter, the author was supported by the Gerda Henkel Foundation. Some material appears in Cziganyik 2023, which contains a more detailed analysis of Hungarian utopian literature. Unless otherwise stated, English translations are the author's.

despite the fact that the first mention of the term *utopia* in a Hungarian text dates from 1791, almost three centuries after the publication of More's book (Maczelka 2019: 9). Utopian notions were particularly influential in Hungary in the nineteenth century and in the analysis emphasis is laid on the works of dramatist Imre Madách (1823–64) and the most popular novel writer of his time, Mór Jókai (1825–1904). The twentieth century saw the rise and domination of the dystopian genre: here the works of writers and poets Frigyes Karinthy (1887–1938), Mihály Babits (1883–1941) and writer and mechanical engineer Sándor Szathmári (1897–1974) will be discussed briefly. This is followed by an analysis of the Hungarian translations of *Utopia*, and particular emphasis will be laid on the role of religious denominations in its reception.[2] It will also be argued that utopia and dystopia appear as complementary, rather than opposing, concepts in Hungarian utopian works. Utopianism is not a mainstream element of Hungarian culture, yet its role is not marginal either. Within Hungarian literature utopian works often appear in the oeuvres of major writers, yet criticism tends to focus on other works and consider the utopian elements as secondary to a writer's work. This has resulted in a relative isolation of utopian impulses within Hungarian literature and the fact that so far no contiguous utopian and/or dystopian tradition has been established by literary scholarship.

This relative isolation of utopian elements within Hungarian culture becomes even more clear when we examine the international reception of Hungarian literature. Without going into details it may be established that whereas Hungarian composers such as Ferenc Liszt (1811–66) or Béla Bartók (1881–1945), scientists like Albert Szent-Györgyi (1893–1986) or Mihály Csíkszentmihályi (1934–2021), or even footballers as Ferenc Puskás (1927–2006) are well known outside the borders of Hungary and offer a significant contribution to universal or European culture, Hungarian writers, poets, or dramatists are fairly unknown beyond the language community. So, in an international context the Hungarian utopian tradition is doubly isolated and exerts only minor influence. The one important exception to this rule is Imre Madách's play *The Tragedy of Man* (1862), which has been translated into a number of languages and performed in many theatres around the world: partly for this reason the utopian elements of the play are emphasized here, whereas the rest of the chapter dealing with the utopian aspects of Hungarian literature serves as a reminder that valuable treasures lie outside the focus of interest of international scholars and the wider public alike.

The widespread cultural division of Europe into East and West stemming from the Enlightenment (see Wolff 1994) is a simplification, and we have a more accurate picture if we reflect on the existence of a separate Central European region that mediates between Western and Eastern power and cultural structures (Szűcs 1983). This liminal position of Central Europe is the background for a hybridity which can be traced in the reception of More's *Utopia*. In this chapter I use the term liminality as an expansion on Van Gennep's and Turner's concept, the way Árpád Szakolczai conceptualizes it as 'permanent liminality', arguing that the experience of in-betweenness may become permanent in certain large-scale societies (Szakolczai 2000: 220; 2009: 148). Permanent

---

[2] For the effect of confessional allegiances on the reception of *Utopia*, compare esp. chapters by Shrank, van Bunge, Verhaart, and Withington in this volume.

liminality characterizes Central Europe, a territory where societies are in the state of constant change from structures of totalitarian/controlled societies and democracy, between Eastern and Western patterns of building society, between the Occident and the Orient. Balázs Trencsényi highlights some typically Central European features such as the 'eternal debate' between local cultures and imported ideas, and modernity perceived as being 'related to the idea of a temporal and spatial lag and the imperative of following the already existing models of the "civilized West" ' (Trencsényi et al. 2016: 4). This results in the import of Western ideas, yet they have to be 'renegotiated'. This renegotiation process is present in the reception of the utopian ideals presented in More's work, particularly how the notions of religious freedom are treated in Central Europe.

THE SIXTEENTH-CENTURY RECEPTION OF *UTOPIA* IN THE FRAMEWORK OF RELIGIOUS DISPUTES

When the origins of Hungarian utopianism are to be mapped, some historical facts need to be clarified. The territory of Hungary before the First World War was almost three times as large as its present territory, and historically important cultural centres, such as Kolozsvár (Cluj) or Kassa (Kosice) now lie outside the current borders of the country. This explains why the first utopian elements of Hungarian literature were written in cities that are today part of Romania. To understand the historical context it must also be mentioned that the central part of the country was invaded by the Ottoman Empire following the disastrous Battle of Mohács in 1526. More was familiar with the situation in Central Europe, and particularly in Hungary. In 1527 Jerome Laski (also known as Hieronim Laszky), a diplomat of Polish origin in the service of King János Szapolyai of Hungary (1526–40), visited the court of Henry VIII (Szőcs 2004). Little is known about the details of this visit, except that Henry politely refused the appeal for help against the Turks. More was the Speaker of the House of Commons at this time and very active in diplomatic matters; it is more than likely that he conversed with the ambassador from Hungary and that his knowledge about this distant country originates with Laski. As Szőcs (2004: 431) argues, Hungary was too distant for Henry to be considered important, but close enough for More to become the venue of his last major work, *A Dialogue of Comfort against Tribulation*, written a few years later under very different circumstances. In this dialogue, two Hungarian noblemen prepare to die in battle against the Turks, offering a spiritual model to More, who was also ready to die for reasons of conscience—something he considered more valuable than his life. Yet More's knowledge of Hungary may have had even deeper roots as well, as John Morton, Archbishop of Canterbury, whom More served as a page in the 1490s—and whom Hythloday recalls visiting in Book One of *Utopia*—had been stationed as a diplomat in Hungary in 1474 at the court of King Matthias Corvinus (1458–90). As Attila Fáj argues, there is a tradition in Hungary that the model for Utopia (or at least, for the person of Utopus) is the rule of Matthias of Hungary (Fáj 2004: 12; cf. Balázs et al. 2016: 317). This legend is based on the account of the island of Utopia given by Hythloday 'that their land was not always surrounded by the sea. But Utopus, who conquered the country [...], also changed its geography' (More 2002: 42). Another argument is that the shape of the island of Utopia is described as resembling a crescent which is more or less also true of the historical territory of Hungary surrounded by the stretch of the Carpathian Mountains, which creates something of an island for non-Indo-European Hungarians in the sea of alien languages. Despite its references to Hungary, the full text of *A Dialogue of Comfort against Tribulation* only became available in Hungarian in 2004, and is not very well known outside scholarly circles (Tóta 2002).

The Ottoman rule of Hungary began in the sixteenth century: it lasted more than 150 years, during which time the cultural centres of Hungary shifted to the unoccupied territories in the north (much of which is present-day Slovakia) and to the semi-independent Principality of Transylvania, where the level of religious tolerance was exceptionally high in comparison to contemporary practice elsewhere in Europe. It was in 1568 at the assembly of Torda in Transylvania that for the first time in Europe freedom of religion was codified,[3] providing high levels of freedom to most Protestant denominations, including the antitrinitarians or Unitarians, who were mostly persecuted elsewhere in Europe for their rejection of the concept of the Holy Trinity. This religious tolerance in multicultural Transylvania, a semi-independent principality that had to balance itself between the Catholic Habsburg Empire and the Ottoman Empire, had a number of political and cultural causes, among which the role of More's *Utopia* is not insignificant. Such is the context of the first utopian writings in Hungarian literature: books that were written by foreign authors, primarily the antitrinitarian theologian Jacobus Paleologus (also known as Giacomo da Chio, 1520–85), who had been born in Greece, became a Dominican friar (but later he renounced his vows), and played an extremely active role in the religious debates in Europe in the late sixteenth century. He worked in Transylvania between 1573 and 1575, and wrote, amongst other works, a dialogue entitled *Catechesis Christianae dierum duodecim* ('Twelve Days of Christian Catechesis', 1574), which is one of the most extensive summaries of antitrinitarian theology.[4] The protagonist of one part of this highly satirical book, Telephus, a South American Indian (a representative of the classical 'noble savage'), describes the life of Indian communities before the Spanish conquest in utopian terms. In this description, the life of Indians was simple, but rational and moral, before the irrationalities of Catholicism and European civilization ruined their morally superior culture. The inhabitants of this utopian South American country did not know warfare, did not exercise international commerce, and did not use money. As a result, greed, and hunger for power were unknown amongst them. Their family lives were harmonious, primarily because the example of the

---

[3] Today Turda, Romania, but also known as Thorenburg.
[4] For more on Paleologus, see Balázs 2009 and Dostálová 1971.

unnatural celibacy of the clergy (the main target of Paleologus) did not poison their lives. Mihály Balázs considers both this utopian description of the pre-Columbian religious life of Mexicans and the wider requirement of religious tolerance to be influenced by More's *Utopia*; hence he claims that Paleologus is the first major figure in the reception of More in Hungarian culture (Balázs 2009: 118).[5] Iván Horváth argues that another major (yet unfinished) work of Paleologus, *Disputatio scholastica* ('Scholastic Dispute', 1575) was also inspired by More's *Utopia* (Horváth 2007: 178). The setting of this dispute is a fictional city built of gold and gems and the vivid images and exciting episodes exceed in imagination the requirements of theological disputes and fit into the tradition of utopian literature.

The story of the influence of *Utopia* in Hungarian culture is continued in Transylvania by another writer of foreign origin, Johannes Comenius (1592–1670, also known as Jan Kamensky), whom Dagmar Čapkova (1970: 33) claims as the first modern scholar of pedagogy. He is relevant in the reception of *Utopia* because of his (alleged) Hungarian ancestry and also his activities in Hungary in the 1650s, when he was the leading professor of the Protestant college of Sárospatak in the north of Hungary (although his major utopian work, *The Labyrinth of the World and the Paradise of the Heart* (1623), was not written in Hungary). More important for our purpose is his pamphlet dedicated to Prince György Rákóczi II (ruler of Transylvania 1648–60), *Gentis Felicitas* ('The Happiness of the Nation', 1659), that contrasts the miserable state of Transylvania with its possible happiness, a condition that is described in utopian terms: 'the nation realizing the magnificence of human nature [...] is] seeking to mount the highest level of blessed glory' (Balázs Trencsényi 2010: 256).[6] The treatise (written in the form of an admonition) is usually analysed as a discussion of the concept of the nation (Urbánek 2005), but it uses the two-part structure well known from More's *Utopia* where the problems facing contemporary England are contrasted with the happy state of Utopia. In Comenius' treatise the wretched state of current affairs in Hungary and Transylvania is also compared to a utopian ideal. As Balázs Trencsényi (2010: 526) reminds us, for Comenius blessedness is not merely a spiritual state, but also has concrete political-institutional features, and he lists eighteen markers of *felicitas*, such as the land being densely populated, the people having peaceful manners and being governed by good laws, and good magistrates not seeking to subjugate their own people. Economic prosperity and education also play a significant role in the life of a happy nation. Given that similar features characterize the inhabitants of Utopia, it is entirely possible that More's work served as a model for the pattern offered by Comenius.

The influence of *Utopia* can also be demonstrated in the works of Miklós Zrínyi (1620–64), the most significant epic poet in the seventeenth century and a descendant of an important Croatian-Hungarian family (Czigány 1984). Krisztina Kaposi (2012) convincingly argues that Zrínyi had read More's book and its influences can

---

[5] Balázs also proves that More's *Utopia* was available in libraries in sixteenth-century Kolozsvár.
[6] For a discussion of *Utopia* and happiness, see also Withington in this volume.

be found in some of his works. In her analysis of the paratexts in the works of Zrínyi she points out a number of important parallels. She argues that the prosaic introduction of Zrínyi's chief epic poem, *The Peril of Sziget* (*Szigeti veszedelem*, 1651) includes allusions to the paratexts of More's *Utopia*, for instance, when he compares his own feelings towards his work to the crow's and the monkey's love of their offspring (Kaposi 2012: 436).[7] Even if Zrínyi's library did not include *Utopia*, Kaposi reflects on one of Zrínyi's most popular epigrams ('Befed ez kék ég'—'The blue sky covers me'), which includes allusions to Cicero, but in a form that differs from the original in *Tusculan Disputations*. Rather, the quotation Zrínyi uses corresponds to a part of More's *Utopia*.[8] It is also an allusion to Cicero in a modified form, so Zrínyi quotes More and not Cicero.

If *Utopia*'s Latin text influenced major scholars and poets in Hungary in the seventeenth century, then More also features in a book published in 1790 in Kassa (present-day Kosice in Slovakia) entitled *Thomas Morus, olim Angliae cancellarius, juvenem principem docet, quid facto opus sit, ut sceptro admovendus, sibi gloriam, salutem regno, subditis felicitatem pariat* ('Thomas More, the former Lord Chancellor of England teaches the young prince what to do through the power of his dignity to gain glory for himself, prosperity for his kingdom and happiness for his subjects'). The author is Ferenc Szuhányi (1742–1824), teacher, theologian, and Jesuit until the dissolution of the order in 1773.[9] In this book of more than 300 octavo pages, More, former Lord Chancellor of England, teaches a prospective king of Hungary (in the historical context probably Leopold II, who ruled from 1790 to 1792). The introduction includes More's biography, based on accounts by Thomas Stapleton and Gilbert Burnet, and the rest of the book is a treatise in political philosophy in the form of advice to an enlightened ruler. Balázs (2016: 319) argues that Szuhányi follows the example of the German writer and historiographer David Fassmann (1685–1744), who also wrote a dialogue in 1724 in Leipzig in which More gives political advice (see also Havas 2011). Despite the quotations from More's *Utopia*, Szuhányi's text reflects the situation of eighteenth-century Hungary rather than sixteenth-century England. A central notion of Szuhányi is that the goal of government is the happiness of the nation which lies in the harmony between the ruler and the ruled (Comenius is not quoted, but very similar suggestions appear

---

[7] 'Et certe sic est a natura comparatum, ut sua cuique inventa blandiantur. Sic et corvo suus arridet pullus et suus simiae catulus placet' (More 2009a: 9); 'It is only natural, of course, that each man should think his own inventions best: the crow loves his fledgling and the ape his cub' (More 2002: 14).

[8] 'Itaque relictus est, uti obtemperaretur animo eius, peregrinationis magis quam sepulchri curioso. Quippe cui haec assidue sunt in ore, Caelo tegitur qui non habet urnam, et undique ad superos tantundem esse viae' (More 2009a: 6); 'Being left in this way was altogether agreeable to him, as he was more concerned about his travels than his tomb. He would often say, "The man who has no grave is covered by the sky", and "Wherever you start from, the road to heaven is the same length" ' (More 2002: 10).

[9] The Latin text available via the University of Debrecen Electronic Archive, https://dea.lib.unideb.hu/dea.

in his *Gentis Felicitas* discussed above, and the same idea of the enlightened ruler is present in György Bessenyei's *Tariménes*, discussed below). This harmony is achieved if the government is submitted to 'Divina Lex', the divine law that appears as a form of natural law in Szuhányi's argument. When the details of such a rule are discussed, the preference of peace above war is emphasized, along with the importance of the material wealth of the subjects and the necessity that the ruler be surrounded by loyal and trustworthy—rather than greedy and self-interested—persons. Szuhányi's argument centres around the good ruler as the cornerstone of good government; in contrast, in *Utopia*, the behaviour of the Utopians and the rules of society are more important. But when Szuhányi's 'Thomas More' argues that perfection cannot be achieved and that it is difficult to rule according to the norms of Plato, the allusions to *Utopia* are obvious (Balázs 2016: 321). Nonetheless, György Vajda (1916) argues that the influence of More's *Utopia* is rather indirect in Szuhányi's work, as the statements of his work that may be references to *Utopia* are very general and hence could be found almost anywhere; More's name only appears here for its authority. Certainly, as László Havas argues (2011: 340), Szuhányi's book is an important witness to the fact that More was highly honoured in Hungary well before his canonization: in Catholic circles (the majority religion in Hungary), primarily because of his perseverance in defending the Catholic faith, and in Protestant circles (a significant minority in Hungary), because of the idea of religious tolerance present in *Utopia*.

Utopia in Nineteenth- and Twentieth-Century Hungarian Literature

The first proper utopia written in Hungary in Hungarian is *Tariménes utazása* ('The Travels of Tariménes', 1804) by György Bessenyei (1747–1811), described by Lóránt Czigány (1984: 85) as a 'bitter satire', in which (being his last work) the ageing Bessenyei reflects on his own failures besides the contemporary social and political situation. But *Tariménes utazása* remained hidden for more than a century for a reason not uncommon in the history of Hungarian literature: censorship. It only appeared in 1930, when the Habsburg monarchy could no longer see a danger in the publication of this satirical piece of political fiction. As a result, what could have been an important writing in the history of nineteenth-century Hungarian utopianism, appeared as a freshly published text in the twentieth century, fuelling interest in utopian notions in the 1930s and 1940s. Bessenyei, a significant writer of the Hungarian Enlightenment (cf. Czigány 1984: 82), presents a rationally governed, enlightened state in the fictional country called Totoposz (where it is not difficult to recognize the name of Utopus). Bessenyei's work initiated a tradition of utopian voyages in Hungarian literature, a tradition that would later be marked by gulliveriads, narratives that pretend to be sequels of Jonathan Swift's work. Bessenyei drew inspiration from France (François Fénelon, Montesquieu, Jean-Jacques Rousseau) as well as from England (primarily More and Swift).[10]

The hero of Bessenyei's book, Tariménes, is a student and traveller who arrives in an ideal country where the goal of government is the common good of all: 'The only aim of secular law is to enable people to live together, and live based on their own income, without predation' (Bessenyei 1953: 373). In this pseudo-Hobbesian utopia, civilization is seen as a development on nature, serving the individual's happiness, while uncivilized people live a chaotic life. Bessenyei presents no Rousseauesque longing for a natural state of mankind: natural life is seen as abominable. The 'uncivilized' nations are described in similar terms to how Swift's Gulliver describes Yahoos: dirty, unintelligent, aggressive animals. Civilization is presented as a limitation on the freedom of the individual for the harmony of the community; manners are explained as a system to channel and limit the expression of negative feelings towards each other: without manners the cooperation of society towards the common good would be seriously hindered. The harmony of Totoposz is based on an understanding of the coherence of society which, even though hierarchical, is meant to serve the benefit of all. The king of the neighbouring country Jajgádia harshly criticizes the queen of Totoposz when he argues that 'she does not rule over her people, but she serves them' (422). The neighbouring Jajgádia (whose name wittily indicates 'the country of sorrows' in Hungarian) is the dystopian model within the fictional framework that corresponds to the everyday reality in early nineteenth-century Hungary, subjugated to Habsburg rule: power stems from the enslavement of people, and coercive force is naturally used by those in power. As the king of the land of sorrows puts it: 'my wealth stems from the poverty of my people' (422). This is not the case in the utopian Totoposz, where the goal of society is understood as the happiness of all in the pursuit of the common good, and where a harmonious and non-oppressive co-existence results. The central idea of Totoposz, that 'the fortune of one person does not serve the misfortune of other' (337), is both the opposite of what Bessenyei experienced in everyday life and a notion brought from the utopian perfection of More's people: the narrative structure is very similar to the sixteenth-century model in the sense that Bessenyei considers the situation of his country miserable and offers a better model. The disposition of the implied author of *Tariménes utazása* seems to differ from that of *Utopia* in that the preference for the rule of Queen Arténis is obvious, whereas there is quite some ambiguity in the case of More. Utopia is the ideal for Hythloday (whose name ironically means 'an expert in nonsense'), whereas the character 'Morus' is not always enthusiastic about it and it has never been clear how the author relates to the country depicted in his book. There is no character named Bessenyei in *Tariménes utazása*, and even though the protagonist's guide, Master Kukumedóniás, bears a lot of resemblance to the ageing author of the book, he does not explicitly express the author's views, even though the preference for the rule of the Enlightened queen is articulated.

---

[10] For more on Fénelon, see esp. Hill and Pohl in this volume; for Montesquieu, see Pohl in this volume; for J.-J. Rousseau, see Pohl and Ramiro Avilés in this volume.

The positive ideal that is so emphatically present in Bessenyei's book is less obvious in the most popular and internationally best-known piece of Hungarian utopian literature: a philosophical drama written in 1862 by Imre Madách (1823–64), entitled *Az ember tragédiája* ('The Tragedy of Man'). The play, which includes a number of utopian elements, is considered the most important Hungarian drama to this day, and it is known round the world as it has been translated into seventeen languages. (In England the 'Bloomsbury Group' showed an interest in Madách, with the play first published in English by Virginia and Leonard Woolf's Hogarth Press in 1933.[11]) The play spells out a complex allegory of mankind's history as Adam and Eve, the first human couple, travel through space and time visiting instances of human history. Their journey begins in the Garden of Eden, and after the original sin, which is presented as a conscious revolt, it includes, amongst other sites, the building of the pyramids in Egypt, the ancient societies of Athens and Rome, but also scenes of modern history such as the French Revolution. This journey in time and space also takes us to the Phalanstère, the utopian community envisioned by Charles Fourier (1772–1837), a French utopian socialist philosopher. Madách highlights the dystopian and oppressive aspects of this fictional ideal community: Madách's Phalanstère is a place where creativity is considered dangerous and the inhabitants are forced into conformity. The artist Michelangelo, for instance, is made to carve identical legs for chairs, and Plato has to tend the cattle. The utopian attempt of Phalanstère is presented by Madách as one of the many failed political aspirations that keep turning into an oppressive system in the history of mankind. As Erika Gottlieb argues, the play is 'a romantic precursor of the dystopian fiction of the twentieth century, as it demonstrates the continuous interaction between utopian and dystopian perspectives in the numerous political dreams of Messianism that inevitably turn into the nightmares of dictatorship' (Gottlieb 2001: 44). Gottlieb also highlights the play's 'consistent dialectic between aspirations and disillusionment', with the thinking of the masses continuously violating the development of the ideas of great minds (46). Utopia's oscillation between the positive and the negative, inherent in More's consciously ambivalent term (Abensour 2008), is naturally present in the play where political aspirations keep resulting in dystopian forms of oppression which prevail over utopia in all ages of mankind, including the future. Madách's play exemplifies Roland Schaer's definition of utopia, which states that utopian literature is a 'dialectic of dream and nightmare—best and worst of possible worlds' (Schaer 2001: 6). It is also a prime example of the Central European hybridity of utopian and dystopian structures. The dialectic of Madách's drama is present in the explicitly suggested hope that the occurrences implicitly do not support. But hopelessness does not prevail either, as humanity keeps surviving dictatorships and a will for new beginnings is always maintained.

The utopian impulse in late nineteenth-century Hungarian literature remained strong, especially through the work of the most prolific and most popular nineteenth-century

---

[11] For a more contemporary English translation by George Szirtes, see Madách 1998. The popularity of *The Tragedy of Man* was further enhanced by an animated movie directed by Marcell Jankovics and released in 2011 (under the same title).

writer in Hungary, Mór (Maurus) Jókai (1825–1904).[12] Even though his popularity has been fading since the second part of the twentieth century, and recently his critical acclaim has been questioned as well (cf. Zsuppán 2017: 111), he remains one of the cornerstones of Hungarian literature. His relationship to utopia is quite typical in modern Hungarian literature: like many other major writers, he tried his hand at writing utopian fiction, yet these attempts remain fairly marginal within his oeuvre. Despite this marginality, one of his major novels, *Aranyember* ('Timar's Two Worlds', 1872) includes a location named 'Senki Szigete' ('The Ownerless Island'). It is described as a small, hidden island on the River Danube, isolated from society: this is where the protagonist finds the happiness that he misses in the outside world despite his economic and social successes. The Ownerless Island is a utopian place, but more an escapist critique of capitalist society of the late nineteenth century than a well-defined model for an alternative society. Yet in Jókai's following work, *A jövő század regénye* ('The Novel of the Century to Come'), a monumental work of some eight hundred pages which began to be published in serialized form in 1872, a complex utopian model is described. The novel depicts the Austro-Hungarian Monarchy in an imagined future a hundred years after the book was written, yet most of the technical details are unchanged, with one major exception: the invention of the flying machine. This particular technical aspect thoroughly changes the life of mankind and leads to eternal peace on earth.

Jókai's optimistic belief is typical of the utopian literature of the nineteenth century (the more critical voices of Edward Bellamy or William Morris appearing only towards the end of that century), and the role of technology particularly links Jókai to contemporary French writer Jules Verne (1828–1905), who wrote of the electrical flying machine in *Robur the Conqueror* (1886) more than a decade after Jókai's book. For Jókai, however, the importance of technological progress lies in its social and political consequences: they are never praised for their own sake unlike in most of Verne's works. The social and political consequences of the invention of the flying machine are indeed utopian: with warfare made meaningless (as it is not possible to defend cities against the flying machines), a time of eternal peace ensues with prosperity, as the abolition of all borders and diminishing distances bring a limitless circulation of goods and information, which results in a state of universal happiness. Optimistic as he is, Jókai consciously links his work to the utopian tradition of More, Swift, and Tommaso Campanella in the preface to his book, which also serves a similar function to More's Book One of *Utopia* in listing contemporary problems, to which the solution comes in the form of the utopian construction. We may note that during the eighteenth and nineteenth centuries in Hungarian utopian literature the role of religion continuously diminishes. Whereas in the sixteenth and seventeenth centuries religion was of central importance in the reception of *Utopia*, it is less significant for Bessenyei and absolutely marginal in the case of Jókai.

---

[12] For more details on Jókai's utopian fiction, see Czigányik 2015.

In twentieth-century Hungarian literature, the utopian impulse mostly takes the shape of dystopian works.[13] Frigyes Karinthy (1887–1938), popular writer, poet, and humorist of the first half of the twentieth century, contributed two short yet significant works to Hungarian utopian literature. *Utazás Faremidoba* ('Voyage to Faremido', 1916) enriches the tradition of gulliveriads. But in Karinthy's work 'the delightful adventures of an optimistic Mr Gulliver turn into the bitter history of a self-destructive humankind' (Hartvig 2013: 33). Karinthy's Gulliver travels to a harmonious world inhabited by inorganic intellect, thus offering the first depiction of robots, before Karel Čapek invented the term in his *R.U.R.* in 1920. The perfect working of the intellect is the ultimate aim of the satirical world of Faremido, and organic life is seen as seriously threatening the perfection that only machines may achieve. In *Capillária* (1921), Karinthy satirizes the female–male relationship as a basic aspect of human life. The book includes a preface in the form of a letter written to H. G. Wells about the fractious relationship of the two sexes in European culture. Within the narrative, Gulliver discovers an alternative world in the form of an underwater queendom of women where men and women form two different species, women ruling and enjoying the comfort that is made possible by the services of their male counterpart. The dominant position of women, the satirical reversal of the contemporary political situation, however, does not lead to harmony, but emphasizes the miserable situation of humankind.

The tradition of the gulliveriads is continued by Sándor Szathmári (1897–1974), a mechanical engineer who wrote a number of significant utopian and science fiction works, the most important being *Kazohinia* ('Voyage to Kazohinia', 1941).[14] The book, following the tradition of island fiction present in More's *Utopia* as well, depicts a positivistic and extremely rational world that turns out to be a hell of boredom for the traveller. The inhabitants know nothing about emotions, symbols, or abstract notions such as the past. All their material needs (including sexual needs) are fulfilled, and the inhabitants cooperate to make the harmonious society run smoothly, yet they live in personal isolation. When the protagonist learns of the existence of another society that the majority treat as a lunatic asylum, he believes it would satisfy him, yet he only finds a dystopia of uninhibited frenzy. Szathmári, while offering a satire on his contemporary society, demonstrates the inhuman nature of both extremes: the exaggeration of the role of the rational intellect but also that of the lack of rational control in the life of society.

The presence of More's legacy in twentieth-century Hungarian literature is combined with reflections on the tragic historical experiences of the age, resulting in negative utopias. A significant dystopian novel was written by the leading poet Mihály Babits (1883–1941), entitled *Elza pilóta* ('Pilot Elza', 1933), which depicts a world of endless war resembling George Orwell's *Nineteen Eighty-Four* (yet written almost twenty years earlier). Warfare lasting for generations becomes the natural state of affairs all over the world, making the conditions of humanity unendurable. Tibor Déry (1894–1977)

---

[13] For a more detailed account, see Czigányik 2023 or Kosznai 1994.
[14] The book is available in English (e.g. Szathmári 2012). For a more detailed discussion, see Czigányik 2017.

wrote *G.A. úr X-ben* ('Mr. A.G. in X', 1964) while he was serving a prison sentence for his activities during the 1956 Revolution. The novel depicts a surrealistic world of anti-consumerism where the inhabitants, who embrace a strong death wish, look for discomfort in all aspects of their lives. The optimism that was strongly present in Jókai's work in the late nineteenth century becomes scarce in twentieth-century Hungarian literature, whereas images of absurdity are prevalent.

The Hungarian Translations of *Utopia*

As we have seen, *Utopia* had a considerable impact on Hungarian literature, even though the book was not available in Hungarian until the twentieth century and the Latin editions of it were all imported. The first translation (by Ferenc Kelen) was published in 1910, followed a generation later by two others, László Geréb in 1941 and Tibor Kardos in 1943 (Cziványik 2016). *Utopia* was always published in an annotated form, often with introductions and/or afterwords of high scholarly standard, and the basis of the translations was always the Latin text, usually the 1518 Froben edition or Victor Michels and Theobald Ziegler's 1895 critical edition printed in Berlin. The presence of the paratext varies according to translation: More's letter to Peter Giles is usually translated, yet most of the other parerga are ignored. Recent editions are often illustrated, with images usually based on the 1518 Froben edition. In the next section of the chapter I briefly compare the translations; I analyse how More and *Utopia* appear in them, and how this influences the general perception of More in Hungary, first locating him as a major figure in social philosophy, later (essentially from the 1960s on) focusing on the literary merits and ironical features of his book.

The first translator of *Utopia* was Ferenc Kelen (1873–1958), who translated literary works from German, French, and English into Hungarian, including the work of Oscar Wilde and Guy de Maupassant.[15] His translation is precise but cumbersome. It appeared in 1910 as a part of a series of philosophical writers by the prestigious Franklin Company in Budapest, in cooperation with the Hungarian Academy of Sciences. Both the quality and the style of the text, and the afterword along with the notes (also authored by Kelen), place More's *Utopia* in a serious philosophical tradition. The translation is accurate and scholarly, yet not very reader-friendly, with a large number of archaic expressions and cumbersome sentence structures. The sixty-page afterword is a scholarly study on the life of More and the importance of his *Utopia* in the European literary tradition. It includes a detailed biography of the author (based on accounts by William Roper, Thomas Stapleton, and Cresacre More), and locates *Utopia* as a work of social philosophy in the sixteenth-century humanistic tradition, emphasizing its relation to Plato's

---

[15] Compare the career of Wesseley, discussed by Stewart in this volume, and of Inoue, discussed by Sako in this volume.

Republic, but defines Utopia's ethics as Epicurean. It is also emphasized that Utopia is a communistic ideal and its ethos rationalistic, as exemplified by the treatment of religion as an essentially private matter.

Taking the stylistic features of Kelen's text into consideration, it is small surprise that a generation later, in 1941, a new translation by László Geréb (1905–62), writer, translator, and literary historian was published. This translation took the demands of the wider public into account, the foreword (written by the translator) locating the author in his historical context, praising the harmony of the literary imagination and the wisdom of statesmen. The text is fluent and accessible even today, yet a number of disturbing dashes appear in it—about two per page on average. Their presence is explained in an endnote: 'Our text gives the full Utopia, but not fully. We have left out nothing from Morus' train of thought, but have shortened the lengthier reasonings and meticulous details for our impatient age' (More 1941: 80). Indeed, most of the dashes mark the absence of short passages: one or two sentences that mostly do not violate the integrity of the text. Yet towards the end of Book One, one single dash marks a truncation of several pages: the discussion concerning the negative effects of private property. In the absence of this important discussion, the readers of Geréb's translation will not learn that the text supports communal ownership of property. This serious truncation may be due to either censorship or self-censorship, yet the strictly anti-communist political regime in 1940s Hungary may also account for it.

With a popular but abridged edition and a less accessible older text in the market, it is no wonder that after merely two years, in 1943, another translation was published, this time prepared by Tibor Kardos (1908–73), a renowned literary historian of the Renaissance. This text, which combines Kelen's professionalism with Geréb's modern fluency, became the standard Hungarian text for More's *Utopia* (published since 1943 in no less than seven editions, with a revised edition in 1963 with modifications in sentence structure and paragraphing that further enhanced the text's accessibility for the modern reader). As Ákos Farkas argues, 'Kardos's stylistically uncharged, and therefore timeless, version of Hungarian provides his translation with an aura of linguistic universality' (Farkas 1992: 170). The new translations (and revisions) move towards a more accessible text, not giving up the scholarly ideal (unless in the form of truncations in Geréb's case), but placing the emphasis on the literary qualities of the text, emphasizing the harmony between literary imagination and philosophical thought.

The duality of reception that wavers between the literary and the scholarly is well represented in the anthologies published in Hungary where excerpts of *Utopia* are included. Besides the first translation of 1910, published as a part of a series of philosophical writers, excerpts from More's text also appeared in collections of social philosophy, as in the collection of extracts by early modern British philosophers, translated by András Bodor (1915–99), professor of classical philology, and published in 1952, where approximately twenty pages of More's text appear alongside selections from the works of Francis Bacon, Thomas Hobbes, and John Locke. This philosophical tradition is further represented by Zoltán Bíró's *Fejezetek a társadalomfilozófiai gondolkodás történetéből* ('Chapters from the History of Social Philosophy', 1989), an anthology of social philosophers for university students of economics, where an excerpt of *Utopia* is placed in the company of extracts from Plato, Niccolò Machiavelli, and René Descartes.[16]

At other times, however, *Utopia* featured in literary anthologies. A good example of this is a 1960 anthology of English literature for students, where a short excerpt of More's text is shown as a piece of Renaissance English literature, with Edmund Spenser and Sir Philip Sidney as neighbours (Lutter 1960). This approach is also present in a collection that appeared in 1992 where More is presented in the company of Petrarch, Boccaccio, and Shakespeare as a major writer representing a significant literary tradition of the Renaissance (Borbála Trencsényi 1992). As we can see, *Utopia* in Hungary is equally important as a literary and as a scholarly-philosophical text, and no clear tendency can be observed in its treatment by editors and publishers. Rather, it is a versatile text, as can be seen by the appearance of a short section of *Utopia* in a collection concerning the history of education (Komlósi 1978), alongside texts by the neurologist and educator Edouard Claparéde (1873–1940), and Maria Montessori (1870–1952), founder of the 'Montessori' method of education.

THE CATHOLIC RECEPTION OF MORE IN THE NINETEENTH AND TWENTIETH CENTURIES

As we saw in the overview of early modern Hungarian literature, More was important both for Catholics and Protestants. More's work played a significant role in the religious debates in Hungarian Protestantism in the sixteenth century, where the focus was primarily on the policies of religious toleration outlined in Book Two, policies that were modelled in sixteenth-century Transylvania. The Catholic reception of More, especially after his canonization in 1935, is also significant. Although this focuses on More's character, *Utopia* is not ignored. The first Hungarian book on More was published by the official publisher of the Catholic Church in 1859: a translation (via French) of *Sir Thomas More: His Life and Times* (1839), by the Catholic man of letters William Joseph Walter (1789–1846). In the year of his canonization, a short *Life of Saint Thomas More* (*Morus Szent Tamás élete*) was published (P.K. 1935), followed three years later by his inclusion in a volume entitled *Korunk szentjei* ('Saints of Our Times', 1938, edited by the Piarist Antal Schütz, a leading theologian in Hungary in the first half of the twentieth century. Here, More—along with a handful of other saints from past centuries, such as Robert Bellarmin (1542–1621) and Albert the Great (1200–80)—appears in the company of modern saints of the nineteenth century, such as Thérèse of Lisieux (1873–97) and Bernadette Soubirous (1844–79). The volume, which

---

[16] See also Kovács 2005, where an extract from *Utopia* features in 'an overview of the history of philosophy for A Levels'.

merited republication in 1939 and 1940, emphasizes the need for real models in the context of modern celebrity culture, and More is presented as an example to follow. Schütz, referring to Norwegian writer and Nobel Laureate Sigrid Undset (1882–1942), argues that people always have a need for heroes, and instead of deifying movie stars and record-breakers, he recommends the reverence of saints (Schütz 1938: 1). The example of More is highlighted for combining humanism with Christian faith, truthfulness with serenity, and heroism with meekness. More recognizes the sufferings of common people (*Utopia* is presented as a satire on contemporary England) and silently revolts against the usurpation of power by the king.

The public influence of the Catholic Church radically diminished after the Communist takeover in 1948, yet More as an exemplary figure was meant to counterbalance the new hagiographies of Communist leaders. In 1950, two years after a strongly anticlerical Stalinist-type dictatorship was introduced in Hungary, painter Pál C. Molnár (1894–1981) was commissioned by the parish priest to produce a painting for a side-altar of the Jáki chapel, a chapel in a touristic area of Budapest. The painting, entitled *The Good Death*, features, amongst other figures, More and his daughter Margaret. The martyr of the Catholic Church, who died by the wish of Henry VIII who could be seen as a political tyrant, had a significant message in a similar political situation of dictatorship (Csillag 2008). Cinema also played a role in More's reception as an exemplary figure in Hungary. Fred Zinnemann's film *A Man for All Seasons* (1966), winner of six Academy Awards, premiered in Hungary in 1968, and it was broadcast several times on TV in the 1990s. The film is based on the biographical play of the same title by Robert Bolt (and adapted by Bolt himself).[17]

The end of the dictatorial regime in Hungary in 1990 brought a renewed interest within the Catholic Church in the person of More, who was often presented as an example of the Christian politician (in 2000, Pope John Paul II would declare More the patron saint of politicians). During the dictatorship, being a politician meant being a member of the atheistic party (named the Hungarian Socialist Workers' Party after 1956), and was hence unacceptable for a practising Catholic. Even though officially the government of Hungary accepted the right to freedom of religion, party members and anyone of significant standing or influence (especially teachers) were discouraged from practising religion, which was considered a strictly private affair. These two factors created a vacuum for politically active members of the Catholic Church in 1990, and More looked like an attractive (if distant) example for a Catholic public personality taking his faith seriously. In this context, the writing of *Utopia* did not play a central role, yet its existence was not marginalized either. In 1992, a translation of Mario V. Pucci's 1984 Italian biography of More was published in Hungarian (and republished in 1996). The book focuses on More's perseverance and martyrdom, but a short chapter also informs the reader of the island of Utopia. In 1993, a year after Pucci's book (and a year before the second free elections in Hungary), *Thomas*

---

[17] Published in Hungarian under the title *Kinek se nap, se szél* in the translation of István Vas in 1969.

More: Der Heilige des Gewissens (1979), by the Swiss Protestant theologian and writer Walter Nigg, was published in Hungarian, by the publisher of the Franciscan Order, entitled *A lelkiismeret szentje* ('The Saint of Conscience'). The book is based on the sixteenth-century biography by the theologian Thomas Stapleton (1535–98), and similarly to Pucci's book, focuses on the clash between More and Henry VIII, but also has a short treatment of *Utopia*. It is emphasized here (Nigg 1993: 26) that *Utopia* includes a number of humorous elements and not all its statements can be claimed to reflect More's opinion. Nigg particularly rejects the Communist interpretation of Karl Kautsky, claiming that an unbiased reading focuses on the critical aspect of the book that is based on More's Christian humanism.[18] In the same year, the Benedictine Dávid Söveges published a significant scholarly work on the history of spirituality. Just like Pucci and Nigg, he also emphasizes More's perseverance and humanism, and as usual in the religious reception, the role of *Utopia* is not central to the treatment. More (Söveges 1993: 187) is presented a prime example of sixteenth-century Christian humanism alongside Desiderius Erasmus and the Benedictine mystic and monastic reformer Ludovicus Blosius, or Lois de Bois (1506–66). Söveges emphasizes More's erudition, family life, humour, and perseverance. *Utopia* is only mentioned in passing (its religion is not Christian but universally human). More's prayers are noted for the influence of Carthusians, and mention is made of the *Dialogue of Comfort* as being of special importance for Hungarians.

Conclusion

Utopia has been present in Hungarian literature and culture since the sixteenth century. Its influence has been most significant in the debates of the Reformation, particularly those concerning freedom of religion, and the example of More was important both for Protestants and Catholics. Yet his influence is present beyond religious disputes in many areas of Hungarian literature and culture. The liminal position of Central Europe between East and West is manifest in the renegotiation of utopian ideals: the notion of religious freedom was particularly important in the sixteenth century, but More has a recurring importance for religious communities. There is, however, a duality observable in the reception of *Utopia*: it is presented either as a significant work of a social philosopher, or (almost opposing the previous approach) as a significant piece of Renaissance literature, as a piece of fantastical fiction. These approaches are present in the translations, but also in various anthologies where excerpts from *Utopia* are included. The duality is often resolved in the harmonious coexistence of the philosophical and imaginative element in utopian fiction. Another aspect of the cultural hybridity typical

---

[18] For a discussion of Kautsky's interpretation of *Utopia*, see chapters by Stewart, Nethercott, and Moir in this volume.

of Central European liminality is the duality of utopia and its opposite, dystopia, which may be manifestly present within the same work. This hybridity can be observed in the works of Madách and Szathmári. The influence of *Utopia* became particularly strong in the nineteenth century, yet its function never became dominant or mainstream. Utopian works still contribute to Hungarian and Central European culture in a significant manner, illuminating the relationship between the individual and the collective in suggestive and peculiarly pertinent ways.

CHAPTER 25

A CATALAN IN SEARCH OF HUMANISTS

Josep Pin i Soler's Translation of More's Utopia *(1912)*

P. LOUISE JOHNSON

JOSEP Pin i Soler's Catalan *Utopia* was the first new translation of Thomas More's text to appear on the Iberian peninsula since the Castilian version of Book Two by Jerónimo Antonio Medinilla y Porres (Córdoba 1637; reprinted in Madrid 1790 and 1805), and it was the first printed translation of Book One in Iberia. Pin (self-styled 'Josep') was born in Tarragona in 1842, and died in Barcelona in 1927. He studied at the Barcelona Conciliary Seminary, where he continued the Latin education begun as a young child at the house of a pharmacist neighbour, 'Dr Martí' (Cavallé 1994: 410). While a student in Madrid in 1865, he was involved in the so-called St Daniel's Night demonstrations (10 April) which were brutally put down by the military. Students, Krausists,[1] and democrats had protested against the removal of Emilio Castelar from his chair in history at the Complutense University of Madrid following his publication of an article critical of Queen Isabel II, and subsequently against the departure of the rector of the university, Juan Manuel Montalbán, and the government's imposition of the Marqués de Zafra in his place (Pérez Vidal 1951: 95; cf. 'Don Emilio Castelar' 1879). Pin went into exile, settling in Marseilles, where he obtained employment at the Spanish Consulate, and studied and practised architecture. According to Manuel de Montoliu (1947), Pin cultivated links with Occitan language and culture,[2] and while away from Spain his desire to participate in the movement for the normalization of Catalan as a language of cultural intercourse (Anguera 1994: 108) was already manifest in contributions to the

---

[1] The doctrine of Krausism, promoting an education free from dogma, was progressive, humanistic, and hugely influential to Spanish educational reform. It was introduced to the country by philosopher Julián Sanz del Río who had spent time with members of the Krausist circle at Heidelberg in 1843.
[2] The Biblioteca de Catalunya has evidence of limited correspondence between Pin and Frédéric Mistral dated 1888 and 1904. BC MS 4514/1.

Reus newspaper *La Prensa*.³ In 1875 he married Alice de Latour, a native of Brussels, and this connection with Belgium would lead him to make an impassioned defence of the country and a fierce denunciation of German aggression in his presidential address to the Barcelona Jocs Florals ('Floral Games') in 1915.

Pin returned to Barcelona around 1887, before settling there with his family in 1890, having published an important trilogy of novels in Catalan (*La família dels Garrigas*, 1887⁴ *Jaume: novela cathalana*, 1888; *Niobe: novela catalana*, 1889), as well as numerous plays which saw the influence of French naturalism and a shift from rural settings to a theatre of urban customs (Litvak 1968: 279, 283). Lily Litvak, however, considers Pin's naturalism to be 'spiritual' and far removed from that of Émile Zola, the leading proponent of French naturalism. Along similar lines, Manuel de Montoliu (1947: 8, 10) maintains that Pin resisted naturalism and was the first to treat rural themes from an urban perspective. —Montoliu was elected to the Academia de Buenas Letras in Barcelona following Pin's death in 1927, which explains his very accommodating tone. Jaume Vidal Alcover, more circumspect in his appreciation, refers to the novels as 'difficult to classify within the Catalan literary context of the time' ('difícilment classificables dins la literatura catalana de l'època', Vidal Alcover 1980 [27 Apr.]: 25), a context characterized by a movement from literary Romanticism to naturalism, realism, and Catalan *modernisme*. The challenge presented by Pin in terms of establishing both his literary contribution and politico-cultural affiliations is exacerbated, as Vidal Alcover suggests, by his manifest dislike of the linguistic authorities of his day:

> In literature, adhering rigorously to the norms that govern the good use of language is not necessarily the measure of writing well, especially when those norms are as questionable as any linguistic standard imposed from above. Pin i Soler was unlucky enough to think differently from the mandarins of his time.
>
> (Literàriament, adequar-se amb tot rigor a la normativa que regeix el bon ús del llenguatge no és, necessàriament, escriure bé; sobretot quan aquesta normativa és tan discutible com, d'altra banda, ho pugui ser i ho sigui qualsevol normativa lingüística imposada. Pin i Soler va ser un escriptor que no va tenir l'encert de pensar com pensaven els mandarins del seu temps.) (25)

---

[3] Pin is reported to have received an invitation from a friend to contribute to the Castilian-language *La Prensa* while in Geneva around 1866–7 (Cassany 1992: 310), before the Spanish 'Glorious Revolution' of 1868 in which Isabel II was deposed. His insistence on writing in Catalan displeased one editor, who had wanted an article 'in pure, authentic Castilian' ('algo en puro y castizo castellano') (Pin, cited in Cassany 1992: 310). Translations throughout this chapter are my own.

[4] Josephine de Boer comments of the Spanish translation by Carmen de Villalobos that 'the melodramatic story of the decline and fall of the family of rich cultivators, due to the stubborn despotism of the father, is so unrealistic [...] that one wonders why it was chosen out of the wealth of significant Catalan novels of the pre- and post-war eras for one of the rare Spanish versions of this genre' (Boer 1955: 458). *La família dels Garrigas* has been republished several times; the second and third volumes, while largely well received, are less known.

The desire to plough his own furrow undoubtedly extended to his literary production, and in some measure explains the ambivalence of responses to his work; as Enric Cassany (1992: 313) remarks, Pin did not adopt a positivistic theory of reality in his novels (that is, in spite of his association with naturalism), but rather upheld the Romantic principle of the absolute freedom of the creator. He concludes,

> the author behaves as the absolute ruler of the novelistic space, not just as a demiurge, but as a subject who can co-opt the novel without any kind of constraint, as a platform for direct expression. The freedom he is allowed by the genre is extreme, and he is prepared to use and abuse it.
>
> (l'autor actua com a senyor absolut de l'espai novel·lesc, no solament com a demiürg, sinó com a subjecte que pot disposar sense restriccions de la novel·la com a plataforma d'expressió directa. La llibertat que li concedeix el gènere és extrema, i està disposat a usar-ne i abusar-ne.) (313–314)

The Biblioteca d'Humanistes

Pin i Soler was 70 years of age in 1912 when his translation of *Utopia* was published by Llibreria L'Avenç as the fifth volume of the Biblioteca d'Humanistes, a series which seems to have been entirely Pin's initiative, and for which he was wholly responsible, translating all the works himself. The series made available, for the first time, Catalan translations of (mainly) sixteenth-century humanist works, and contained ten volumes in total. As Joaquim Mallafrè observes, Pin performed judiciously the roles of 'publisher, curator, translator, scholar and prologuist' for the works (Cavallé and Mallafrè 1994: 169), in other words applying the same absolute control to the process Cassany observes above in relation to his novels. The series was a hugely significant task. The decision to adopt the 'Biblioteca d'Humanistes' designation must have been Pin's, since no single publisher owned it, and it was at the time—and I would argue should still be seen as—'one of the most unified and original contributions to Catalan letters' ('una de les incorporacions més unitàries i originals a les lletres catalanes' (Cavallé and Mallafrè 1994: 169). The volumes published prior to *Utopia* were translations of Erasmus: *Elogi de la Follía* ('Praise of Folly', 1910); *Col·loquis familiars* 1ª série and *Col·loquis familiars* 2ª série ('Colloquies', 1911–12); and *Llibre de civilitat pueril* ('On Civility in Children', 1912).[5] All contain introductory material of varying length.

Volume 6 was a translation of the *Diàlechs* by the Valencian humanist Joan Lluís Vives[6] (1915) who was, like Erasmus, a friend of More. The introduction that precedes

---

[5] All titles are given as they appear on the title page or manuscript, that is, in pre-normative Catalan. For the ongoing, posthumous association of More and Erasmus, see esp. Shrank, van Bunge, and Verhaart in this volume.

[6] The Valencian form of the name is given here.

the translation seems to have formed the basis of a lecture read on Pin's admission to the Real Academia de Buenas Letras in Barcelona in February 1914. As Joaquim Mallafrè has noted, Pin then moved away from what would have been a more obvious order of humanist works after Vives, to publish two lesser-known works: *Lo Philobiblon* (1916) by Richard de Bury (aka Richard Aungerville, 1287–1345) and the *Diàlechs de les armes y llinatges de la noblesa d'Espanya* (1917) by the sixteenth-century humanist Antoni Agustí i Albanell, before the final two volumes, Niccolò Machiavelli's *Lo princep* (1920) and *Traduccions* (1921).[7] Pin left an introductory commentary on El Brocense (Francisco Sánchez de la Brozas, 1523–1600) in manuscript version which remains unpublished, and some preparatory notes for a proposed twelfth volume on the monks of the Montserrat monastery in the sixteenth and seventeenth centuries. It seems likely that Pin's interest in such a volume derived from his friendship and correspondence with the Benedictine Anselm Maria Albareda, later cardinal and prefect of the Vatican Library, from the time Albareda was at Montserrat. In the later letters, Albareda addresses Pin as 'my dear uncle', and Pin sends him drafts of his work for comment. The earliest letter consulted is dated 1915 and refers to Vives's *Diàlechs* (BC MS 4514/2).[8]

Many of the translations, although not *Utopia*, are parallel texts. Of the three different publishers involved—Henrich y Compania, Llibreria L'Avenç, and Llibreria antiga y moderna de S. Babra—L'Avenç, the publisher of *Utopia* (as well as of *Col·loquis* and the *Llibre de civilitat pueril*), is the most interesting in terms of its explicit contribution to the modernization of the Catalan language.[9] The publishing house grew out of the nineteenth-century initiative of *L'Avens* (later normativized to *L'Avenç*), an influential Catalan review which positioned itself as a gateway to the European avant-garde, adopting and promoting the linguistic reforms of Pompeu Fabra (1868–1948), which sought to unify the language around the Barcelona standard, narrowing the gap between written and spoken varieties through orthographical, lexical, and grammatical reform. I have found no evidence to explain the move from L'Avenç to S. Babra after 1912, although it seems reasonable to suppose that the publication of Fabra's influential norms in 1913 and the backing of L'Avenç for these, might have made any further business with the publisher extremely difficult, given Pin's trenchant opposition to this evolving institutionalization of Catalan language (of which more below), although Caballeria and Codina (1994: 89) note that L'Avenç was by now in decline before its demise in 1915.

---

[7] Cavallé and Mallafrè (1994: 170–173) give a detailed exploration of what Pin's plans may have been for the series.

[8] In Pin i Soler (1947: 25), Pin's son, Armand Pin de Latour, refers to Albareda in a note to the corresponding entry as 'Un dels "nebots literaris" del meu pare' ('one of my father's "literary nephews"'). Martí i Castell (2017: 34) considers Albareda to be literally Pin's uncle, which is highly unlikely given their respective dates (Albareda 1892–1966; Pin 1842–1927).

[9] Cavallé (1994: 409) asserts erroneously that all volumes in the series except *Utopia* were published by Henrich. According to Caballeria i Ferré and Codina i Cantijoch (1994: 85), the Henrich house emerged from the nineteenth-century Catalan 'Renaixença' and published most of its titles in Castilian. S[alvador] Babra (1874–1930) was an antiquarian bookseller and publisher with a shop on Canuda street, Barcelona.

The motivation behind the Biblioteca d'Humanistes can be traced to comments made by Pin in his introductions to Machiavelli's *Lo príncep* and to Erasmus' *Llibre de civilitat pueril*. In the first, Pin talks about 'the great good we could do for our country' ('lo gran bé que feríem a la nostra patria') by addressing the absence of such publications in Catalan. This concern in turn is related to remarks made by the Enlightenment pedagogue Baldiri Reixac in his 1749 *Instruccions per la ensenyansa dels minyons* ('Guidelines for Teaching Children'), and recalled by Pin in the *Llibre de civilitat pueril* (Erasmus 1912: x): Catalans had abdicated their responsibility by not translating works into their language (Reixac advocated the prioritization of Catalan over Latin and Castilian), and had also been remiss in composing worthwhile works in Castilian or Latin instead of Catalan, 'as if the Catalan Nation did not deserve or need to be as educated as any other' ('com si la Nació Cathalana no meresqués o no tingués la necessitat de ser tan instruhida com quiscuna de les demés').[10] Pere Anguera (1994: 135) suggests that there was almost certainly a financial motive at play as well in Pin's decision, and this would hardly be surprising given that Pin was a self-made man, and the Catalan literary market could sustain few professional writers at the time (see, for example, Domingo 1996: 20, 48; Martí i Castell 2017: 12–15).

Pin reaffirmed his loyalty to the Catalan language at intervals thereafter, both discursively and in his creative practice. It seems certain that many of the translations existed in draft or partial form some time before their eventual publication, and Joan Cavallé (1994: 410) suggests that stronger even than Pin's 'seduction' by the humanists, was his attraction to translation as an activity, to 'the pleasure of language'.

Pin and the Catalan Language

Pin's *Utopia* was published at a time when the Catalan language was undergoing significant reform, or 'normativization', as the process became known. Following the emergence of political nationalism in Catalonia in the late nineteenth century and related attempts to modernize the Catalan language, Fabra had published his *Gramática de la lengua catalana* (in Spanish) in 1912. The following year the Philological Section of the Institut d'Estudis Catalans (IEC), in which Fabra, along with the section's first president, Mallorcan Mossèn Antoni Maria Alcover, was the driving force, published its *Normes ortogràfiques*, rules for regularizing Catalan spelling, which were current until November 2016, when the IEC controversially released a set of revised norms, followed by a new grammar. Pin's *Utopia* is written, then, in pre-standardized Catalan which presents no great difficulty to the twenty-first-century reader but does exhibit some inconsistencies.[11] A contemporary reviewer of the Catalan *Utopia*, Alfred Opisso,

---

[10] Cited by Pin in Erasmus 1912: ix; cf. Cavallé and Mallafrè 1994: 170.
[11] For the analogous involvement of *Utopia* in sixteenth-century debates about language, see Shrank in this volume.

remarks that Pin i Soler 'writes admirably, in a prose which itself demonstrates the equality between Catalan and better cultivated languages' ('escribe de una manera admirable, en una prosa que bastaría por si sola á demostrar la igualdad entre la lengua catalana y los idiomas mejor cultivados', Opisso 1912 [9 Oct.]: 6); his translations of Erasmus and More are considered to be as elegant as the originals; and in what amounts to a panegyric, Opisso exalts Pin's erudition and good taste in creating a richness of expression that languages attain '[only] after long centuries of perfecting' ('después de largos siglos de perfeccionamiento'), without having to 'disinter words and phrases buried long ago or resort to terms used only in regional dialects' ('No es el escritor que desentierra frases o vocablos de luengos años sepultados, ó que va en busca de voces sólo usados en dialectos comarcales'). In short, 'Pin's love for the Catalan language has ensured that it lacks nothing that other languages possess' ('el amor de Pin y Soler al catalán le ha llevado á hacer que no carezca de lo que poseen las demás lenguas'). A primary subtext of Opisso's review is the status of the Catalan language as it emerged from the eighteenth and nineteenth centuries following absolutist repression, and the rather hit-and-miss attempts that had been made in the nineteenth century particularly to look to the past, to the Golden Age of Joan Martorell and Bernat Metge, in an attempt to inspire a renaissance of Catalan language and culture. In fact, Opisso makes this genealogy explicit, positioning Pin as a direct descendant of the most important figures in Catalan letters. A contemporaneous, unsigned review in *La Vanguardia* newspaper (7 Sept. 1912) underlines Pin's contribution in similar terms.

Mallorcan intellectual Gabriel Alomar, originator of the term 'futurism', dedicated a column in *El Poble Català* over consecutive days to *Utopia*, with Pin's translation as pretext. He considers it 'little-known' (Alomar 1912a [7 Oct.]), the 'puerile fantasy of a learned man', characterized by the same innocence as 'scientific fantasies about men from Mars' (Alomar 1912b [8 Oct.]), but is otherwise gracious towards Pin as translator. Pin retained a press cutting of the second column amongst his papers which he annotated, saying '[Alomar] hasn't understood *Utopia* and does not know Thomas More' (BC MS 4511/4).

It is Pin's attitude to the process of linguistic reform that sees him at his most animated. With justification critics have referred to his arrogant and disdainful bearing, and 'irascible' character, particularly in his later years (e.g. Domingo i Clua 1981: 113; Anguera 1994: 105). Some of this is to be expected given that to a large extent he frames his Biblioteca d'Humanistes as a service to Catalan bibliography, and of course to the Catalan language as he understands and writes it. His most virulent contributions on the subject post-date the publication of his translation of *Utopia*, which is free of such digressions, but an indicative comment can be found footnoted in the introductory essay to his translation of Erasmus' *Praise of Folly*, published in 1910 (as *Elogi de la Follíía*). Here he questions the tendency of certain 'modernists' to introduce foreign words into Catalan — for 'foreign' we read Gallicisms — to avoid using a perfectly good Catalan word which happens to be graphically similar to its Castilian equivalent. In (Pin's) established Catalan usage, for example, 'serious' was translated as *seriós* and *seriosa* (*serio* and *seria* in Castilian), whereas the modernizers favoured *greu* (by analogy with the French *grave*, according to Pin). The implication is that such changes responded to political imperative rather than linguistic logic, and sought to establish a distance and difference between modern Catalan and Castilian, following almost two centuries of Castilian dominance. This was an accusation levelled frequently at the orthographic reforms to come, not only by Pin i Soler. At the same time, Pin does not show the same degree of sensitivity to Castilian borrowings, which are numerous, as Anguera (1994: 110) observes.

The introduction to *Elogi de la Follíía* is notable for other reasons as, *pace* Opisso, Pin asks the reader to appreciate the work he has undertaken to bring back into the language idioms, maxims, and other turns of phrase long since forgotten, and to polish and shine certain linguistic 'gems' so that they are fit for purpose in the present day (Erasmus 1910: lii). Pin's response to reforms proposed by both the IEC and the more conservative Acadèmia de la Llengua Catalana was frequently marked by ingenious logic, one instance of which became memorialized in the way in which he represented his name (a practice insisted on by his surviving son, Armand Pin de Latour, in publishing his father's work posthumously): thus 'Pin y Soler' was preferred to 'Pin i Soler' because he saw the more modern Latin *i* as functioning as a *barra*, separating elements, and therefore in conflict with its copulative function (which the Greek *y* achieved).[12] In this same introduction to *Elogi de la Follíía*, and by way of justifying the translation, Pin had complained of Erasmus' lack of influence in Catalonia. He sent the draft to Eugeni d'Ors (writer, philosopher, and later Falange-affiliated intellectual), who reminded Pin that he had dedicated the first book of his *Glosari* (1907) to Erasmus.[13] Pin made good the omission, but stood by his comment about D'Ors's lack of explicit engagement with Erasmus' work (see Domingo 2005: 13; Erasmus 1910: xlvii).

Finally, the complex question of Pin's political allegiance helps us to begin to understand why he is a relatively forgotten figure in the present day. Anguera (1994) is helpful in this regard: in the nineteenth century and in exile, Pin was a fierce advocate of the Catalan language and of schooling in Catalan, as we have seen. On his return to Spain, his belief system can probably best be described as conservative Catalanist (unlike Alomar, for example), fiercely protective of literary regionalism but viscerally opposed to political nationalism (Anguera 1994: 112). The Biblioteca d'Humanistes was itself an initiative in service to 'la nostra pàtria' which would elevate its standing amongst other scholars publishing in Catalan, and of course strengthen Pin's profile too. Upon being admitted to the Acadèmia de Bones Lletres (or 'Buenas Letras') in Barcelona, he broke with traditional hegemonic use of Spanish to deliver his speech in Catalan, 'with valiant belligerence' (*amb ardida bel·ligerància*), according to Anguera (1994: 112). His campaign against Fabra's linguistic reforms led him to join

---

[12] See Pin's annotations to the Acadèmia de la Llengua Catalana's (undated) pamphlet, *Sobre normativa*, detailing proposed orthographic reforms (BC MS 4431/3).

[13] Falangism was 'a right-wing Spanish movement that developed in the early 1930s under the leadership of José Primo de Rivera, and sought to reproduce German and Italian fascism in Spain. Opposed to the Republican regime, it supported Franco's Nationalist coup of 1936' (John Scott 2015).

the revived Acadèmia de la Llengua Catalana (1915), and in 1916 he was a signatory to the organization's rival *Regles ortogràfiques*. In his annotations to early drafts of these rules, it is fair to say that Pin is no less forthright than he had been in his criticisms of Fabra (in, for example, the combative 1913 'Protesta contra les normes ortogràfiques' published in the *Diario de Reus*). Pin's militancy on behalf of Catalan is beyond doubt. What is more unusual—and, as Anguera suggests, has not been much studied—is his stance as both *catalanista* and *espanyolista*, which he adjudges to be compatible (if not unproblematically so):

> Pin is a precursor of a fairly widespread ideological typology which is nevertheless little studied, or rather, deliberately ignored, by scholars: those who feel Catalan, aggressively so, in linguistic, cultural, and emotional affairs, and at the same time Spanish, even Spanish nationalist, in politics. In his life this duality was shared by most people, except, fundamentally, that while the majority did so instinctively, some perhaps adopted the position consciously; Pin was completely aware of this dual militancy and vaunted it.
>
> (Pin és com un precursor d'una tipologia ideològica força extensa, però poc estudiada i sobretot voluntàriament deixada de banda pels analistes: la dels qui se senten catalans, fins i tot catalans bel·ligerants, en els aspectes lingüístic, cultural i sentimental, i alhora espanyols, també si cal espanyolistes, en el polític. En el seu temps aquesta dualitat era compartida per la pràctica totalitat de la ciutadania, però amb la diferència fonamental que metre la majoria ho eren d'esma, alguns fins it tot potser ho eren de manera assumida; Pin era del tot conscient de la militància dual i se'n vanava.) (Anguera 1994: 150)

Following the Francoist victory in the Spanish Civil War, this dual allegiance—or the Spanish dimension of it—allowed Pin to be lionized as a true patriot, as Manuel de Montoliu demonstrated in 1943, in a speech on the occasion of the hanging of Pin's portrait in the Municipal Corporation of Tarragona (see esp. Montoliu 1947: 19–20). The speech is powerfully propagandistic and exaggerates Pin's literary significance, but it also underlines a perception that Pin was always independent, his 'own man', and thus all the more valuable as a 'good' Catalan in Francoist terms, and an asset to Francoist letters. In the period immediately after the Second World War, Francoist censorship meant that few original works were published in Catalan, yet in 1946 Pin's 1913 speech 'Protesta contra les normes ortogràfiques' saw the light as a pamphlet, its scornful critique of the modernizers clearly finding favour with the authorities of the day. Pin's son Armand also arranged the edition and publication of *Comentaris sobre llibres y autors* in 1947. It was not until 2002 that Pin i Soler's most important works began to be republished by Arola, a Tarragona-based publishing house. Although the prefatory commentaries on Erasmus and More appear in *Articles, pròlegs i estudis* (2007), the translations themselves, arguably the most significant of Pin's achievements, are not included. Cassany, in his review of the publishing project, talks of 'a very complete collection of his *original* work in Catalan' (my emphasis; 'una col·lecció molt completa de l'obra original catalana', Cassany 2004: 250) which partly explains the omission. The cost of preparing and publishing the translations would also undoubtedly be an issue, but the general neglect of such an important body of translated work is nevertheless difficult to comprehend.

The Translation

Pin's version of *Utopia* appeared in 1912, and there was no new Spanish translation until 1937 (Davenport and Cabanillas Cárdenas 2008: 113). It is curious, as Cavallé and Mallafrè indicate, that often missing from the extensive introductions Pin appended to his translations of the humanists is an indication of the specific source text used, and details of other editions, translations, and auxiliary materials consulted (Cavallé and Mallafrè 1994: 173–174). This is particularly the case with *Utopia*, for which as noted, there is no parallel text. Cavallé and Mallafrè add that Pin knows the writers he translates very well, and his extensive library contained early, collectible editions of both originals and translations (174). Mallafrè himself translated and edited a trilingual edition of *Utopia*—Latin original, Robinson's English translation, and a new Spanish translation (More 1977a)—and is responsible for the only detailed, if tentative, study of Pin's Catalan translation to date, at slightly over five printed pages in length. The identity of the original edition consulted by Pin is particularly interesting. Mallafrè proposes, with some hesitation, that Pin translated directly from the Latin:

> [Pin] follows and sometimes compares his version with the Latin original (for example 'coses no gaire interessants' [things of scant interest] is contrasted in a note with ' … erant enim ridicula' […]). This doesn't mean to say that he didn't consult other translations. He knew Robinson's well, for example, and cites him occasionally […], and we might perhaps find traces of another.
>
> (El segueix i alguna vegada compara la seva solució amb l'original llatí (per exemple 'coses no gaire interessants' és contrastat en nota: '… erant enim ridicula' […]). Això no vol dir que no consultés alguna solució d'altres traduccions. Coneixia bé la de Robinson, per exemple, que cita alguna vegada […] i potser hi trobaríem ressons d'alguna altra.) (Cavallé and Mallafrè 1994: 176)

There are several points of note here. First, as detailed in the posthumously published, annotated personal library catalogue, *Comentaris sobre llibres y autors* (Pin i Soler 1947: 157–159), and as noted by Mallafrè, Pin possessed two Latin editions of *Utopia*. These were duplicate copies of Joseph Lupton's bilingual English and Latin edition published by the Clarendon Press in 1895, which reproduces Robinson's translation, with the March 1518 Latin version (printed at Basel) at the foot of the page, together with Lupton's notes. On this evidence, Pin does not seem to have possessed a 'bibliophile' or collectible edition of *Utopia* (whereas he did own, for example, a 1515 edition of Erasmus' *Moriae Encomium* ('Praise of Folly')). The Biblioteca de Catalunya holds an incomplete Basel December 1518 edition of *Utopia* which bears the seal of the Inquisition from 1613 and is marked with the stamp of the Episcopal Library of Barcelona, but there is no clear indication that Pin had access either to this or any other early edition. As we have seen, Mallafrè acknowledges Pin's familiarity with Robinson's translation, and this is borne out in Pin's introductory commentary to his Catalan translation, where we find an apparently amused reference to Robinson's spelling of 'Fyrste Boke' and 'Second Boke' (More 1912: xii).

Pin's volume brings together a 'Breu comentari sobre la vida y obres de Sir Thomas More' ('Brief Commentary on the Life and Works of Sir Thomas More') which runs from pp. vii to xlvi, the letter to Peter Giles ('Epístola liminar' ('Liminal Epistle')) as well as both Book One and Book Two, headed 'Lo primer llibre de la comunicació de Rafael Hitlodeu sobre la millor forma de la cosa pública' ('The First Book of Raphael Hythloday's Communication on the Best State of the Republic') and 'Llibre segon' ('Second Book') respectively. It also contains eight plates. Four are facsimiles of the illustrations from the 1518 editions (the title page; map of Utopia (see Fig. 5.1); garden scene (see Fig. 37.1); and Utopian alphabet and quatrain (see Fig. 1.1)). Three are from the 1715 French translation by Nicolas Gueudeville (depicting Amaurot, the golden chains worn by slaves, and a Utopian temple). One is a reproduction of Hans Holbein the Younger's sketch of More.[14] These may of course have been reproduced from Lupton. The end material includes a bibliography 'taken from the best English bibliographies' ('extreta de les millors bibliografíes angleses') of editions in Latin, German, Italian, French, Dutch, Castilian, Russian, and English (129–135), together with a note on the initial reception of *Utopia* and its rapid reprinting, and an appreciation of Pin's copy of the 1805 Repullés edition of Medinilla's translation, a gift from his friend Pau Font de Rubinat. Pin acknowledges 'distilling the essence of many works in the biographical section' ('concentrant en la part biogràfica lo essencial de moltíssims llibres'), and underlines his task in service to 'our versatile, beautiful and most noble Catalan language' ('la nostra dúctil, hermosa y nobilíssima Llengua Catalana'), trusting that his own rendering will not be the last (136).[15] Details of the illustrations are given following the table of contents, together with a list of volumes published and forthcoming in the Biblioteca d'Humanistes. The edition, in terms of its paratexts at least, has some scholarly intent.

According to *Comentaris sobre llibres i autors*, Pin's library contained a total of eighteen English editions (including the Lupton); three French editions (Samuel Sorbière's 1643 translation; Gueudeville's 1715; and the Paris 1888 edition which reproduces Thomas

---

[14] The original (c.1526–7) is in the Royal Collection, https://www.rct.uk/collection/912268/sir-thomas-more-1478-1535.

[15] Recent Catalan versions include those of Joan Valls i Royo, translated from the Castilian (More 1988); Joan Manuel del Pozo, translated from the Latin (More 2009b); Núria Gómez Llauger, also apparently translated from the Latin (More 2016a). Neither Gómez Llauger nor the author of her introduction, David Gálvez, make reference to previous Catalan versions. Del Pozo acknowledges having had sight of a photocopy of Pin's manuscript, and of the published version, but does not engage explicitly with any part of Pin's work.

Rousseau's 1789 translation); and two Castilian (Medinilla's 1637 translation of Book Two only, and two copies of Repullés's 1805 reproduction of this edition—'reproducció de l'anterior', More 1805: 154).[16] In addition, Pin owned Fernando de Herrera's *Vida*,[17] and three other biographical works. We know with certainty that, for his translation of Book Two, Pin consulted the Madrid 1805 Repullés edition of Medinilla's version, which closes in combative mode with an admonishment from Martial's Epigrams: 'carpere vel noli nostra, vel ede tua', the preceding line of which reads 'cum tua non edas, carpis mea carmina, Laeli'; 'although you do not publish your own, you criticize my poems, Laelius; either don't criticize mine or publish your own'.[18] Pin is clearly taken by this bullish posturing, and reproduces it at the end of his manuscript (BC MS 4480, fo. 90), but presumably reconsiders since the epigram is absent from the published book. At least one other issue suggests that there was cautious treatment of the Repullés edition: in Book Two, in the section on the religions of the Utopians, Pin follows Medinilla in adopting the singular 'De la religió', but when Medinilla attributes responsibility for decreeing freedom of religion to the Utopians themselves, rather than to Utopus, Pin avoids this error or interpretation in the Catalan. This reattribution of agency in the two key phrases—'The Utopians [...] made this edict' and 'The Utopians made such a statute'—seems to derive from the version of Book Two contained in Francesco Sansovino's *Del governo* (Venice 1561 and subsequent reissues), which has 'Gli Utopiensi [...] fecero un'editto' and 'Fecero gli Utopiensi tale statuto' (More 1561: 193v). Sansovino essentially reproduces Ortensio Lando's vernacular original published in collaboration with Francesco Doni in 1548, but introduces a number of linguistic 'improvements'.[19] However, the translations in respect of this peculiarity ('Utopiensi') are identical (see More 1548a: 54r), meaning that Sansovino either did not notice or did not object to the rendering.[20] The Louvain 1516 edition has 'Utopiensis' rather than 'Utopus' (Basel 1518) at both mentions (with the singular verbs 'instituit' and 'sanxit', More 1516: I4r). It seems possible that Lando consulted Louvain 1516 and derived an Italian plural from it; or less likely, and for some unknown reason, reinterpreted a later edition. The Gondomar Manuscript and published French translations consulted all have Utopus as agent.[21] It is surely too much of a coincidence that Medinilla might separately have consulted Louvain 1516 and introduced the same

---

[16] For Sorbière, see Scholar in this volume; for Gueudeville, Verhaart; for Rousseau, Astbury; for Medinilla, Kern.

[17] In the end material Pin notes that the *Vida* is the second edition (1617, the first having been published in Seville in 1592). The entry for More in *Comentaris sobre llibres i autors* clarifies that this was another gift from Font i Rubinat, in 1913 (Pin i Soler 1947: 27).

[18] Both the Castilian and Catalan acknowledge the quotation with the form 'Marcial. lib.I Epig. 93'. The Loeb Classics bilingual edition has it as Epigram 91. See also Davenport and Cabanillas Cardénas 2008: 112 n. 12.

[19] For more on Lando's and Sansovino's versions, see Shrank in this volume.

[20] Note that in the second mention of the Utopian statutes, Lupton's collation of the first edition (1516) erroneously reads 'Utopien*ses*', rather than 'Utopien*sis*' (More 1895a: 272 n.).

[21] The Gondomar MS (Real Biblioteca, Fondo Gondomar, RB II/1087) can be consulted in facsimile via the permanent link at https://realbiblioteca.patrimonionacional.es/cgi-bin/koha/opac-detail.pl?biblionumber=21760. The Gondomar Manuscript also has the unmediated title 'De las religiones de los de Utopía' for the section on religion, and accurately gives thirteen for the number of the priests (below).

translational change as Lando from whichever edition he used. It is much more credible, therefore, that Medinilla based at least some of his translation on the Italian. Medinilla also erroneously has 'thirty' priests, instead of thirteen, in what appears to be a clear misreading of the Italian *tredici* (or the Latin *tredecim*) later in the same section on religions (the early Latin editions have *tredecim*).[22] Lydia Hunt (1991: 27) observes that 'Medinilla was considered [...] very expert in Latin, poetry and astronomy', and therefore the 'mistranslations'—notably *sabios* (wise) for *sanctiores* (holy)—she identifies must, she supposes, be motivated: that is, ascribable to Medinilla's specific world view, even if this influence is unconscious. However, we cannot completely disregard issues of unmotivated inaccuracy, and these will be important to bear in mind for Pin too.

Translation Approach

Mallafrè summarizes Pin's translation 'methodology' under the headings 'Condensació' (Condensation), 'Lectures dubtoses' (Questionable Readings), and 'Flexibilitat i expressivitat' (Flexibility and Expressiveness) (Cavallé and Mallafrè 1994: 177–180). Thus, Pin respects the sense of the original, but is often more direct and abbreviates some sections (177–178), perhaps, comments Mallafrè, 'out of a certain prudishness' (178). However, since Pin quite faithfully translates the section describing the Utopians being inspected naked before marriage (More 2016b: 83), it is far from clear what other misgivings Mallafrè is referring to. He identifies relatively few errors of translation and minimizes their importance in the work as a whole (Cavallé and Mallafrè 1994: 179); and instead draws attention to the use of informative paraphrase, creative elaboration, and idiomatic or vulgar phrasing. Overall, he concludes that Pin 'is faithful, but not so that the original expression restricts his Catalan rendering' ('És fidel, sense deixar, però, que l'expressió original engavanyi la seva expressió catalana', 180). For his part, Pin finds that More's prose 'dawdles' in places. He adopts the device commonly seen in sixteenth-century prefaces of asking friends for their impressions of his manuscript, whereupon they urge him to publish, in order to 'increase the number of good books translated into our language', and to 'concentrate the translation, polish it until it is refined and flowing [*llisquenta*]' (More 1912: xi). He remarks on some 'tautologies' in the original which he will suppress in the interests of a more accessible read, but in *Utopia*, there is little

It does not contain Martial's epigram. French translations consulted—Jean Le Blond (1559), Sorbière (1643), Rousseau (1888 edn)—all have the conventional rendering of Utopus as agent.

[22] López Estrada (1965: 308) also makes this observation of Medinilla's *Utopia*, commenting that some other numerical measurements are changed. He puts forward the possibility that Medinilla was working from a different manuscript or different version from the one he himself is using (Basel 1518). Davenport and Cabanillas Cárdenas (2008: 112) maintain that the Gondomar Manuscript seems to be based on a 1518 edition because it replicates the error of 'twenty' for 'twelve' miles contained in these, and assert that Medinilla's base text could not have been earlier than 1518 for the same reason.

detailed comment on individual translation problems, certainly in comparison with his edition of Erasmus' *Praise of Folly*.

We can draw limited conclusions from short samples of text (here, More's letter to Giles and the section on religion) which may indicate Pin's method, in line with Mallafrè. At the beginning of the letter, as More apologizes to Giles for his tardiness, Pin writes 'six months' instead of 'six weeks'. At the end, his rendering of the feast metaphor—about ungrateful readers—is also confused. As Mallafrè suggests, there is a tendency towards abbreviation: in the first paragraph of the section on religion in his descriptions of the two religious sects (where circumspection may well motivate the omission of certain details); and in his account of priests in battle. On women priests, Pin's rendering suggests that both elderly widows and village maidens are eligible for the priesthood, rather than just the former; and there is licence in his expanded translation of the policy of maintaining twilight in churches: 'mentres que la llum esmortuhida eleva l'ànima a Déu, *qu'es origen de tota claror*' ('while the shrouded brightness lifts the soul to God, *who is the origin of all light*'; emphasis added to indicate the addition). Consistent with his tactic of making More a friend of Spain, Pin adds a note: 'Without doing so deliberately, he praises our churches' ('Alaba, sense ferho expressament, les nostres iglesies', More 1912: 117). The description of the Utopians' singing in church, and of the musical accompaniment, loses the balance ('some sweeter [...] some less sweet') in Pin's Catalan: the musical instruments, he says 'are much superior to ours' (120), and the text is otherwise condensed. The content of the closing prayer is vastly simplified: the section on dying is reduced to 'let their last moments not be cruel' (121), and the lengthy description of the distribution of wealth in the Republic of Utopia, compared with other so-called republics, is also considerably shortened with a loss of detail.

Pin and the 'English Character'

At the beginning of his prefatory commentary, Pin refers to More as 'Thomas More' or simply 'More', but once he has described the translation context, he switches consciously to 'Thomas Morus', explaining that this was the form More's friends used, and he thus aligns himself with them (More 1912: xii). 'Morus' is retained in the main text. Despite this declaration, however, and while 'Morus' dominates in the prefatory commentary, there remains some slippage to variations on 'More'. Thus, there is little sense that Pin respects the convention of distinguishing between the historical More and More the interlocutor, suggesting rather that he views his use of 'Morus' as an expression of something akin to loyalty. According to a note on the manuscript, the translation was sent for printing on 5 May 1912 (BC MS 4480: 1r). While many quotations are marked as such in the introductory essay, their source is often not given, but Pin's wider references indicate a significant breadth of reading across the Romance languages and English, and he seems sympathetic to the English in general, notwithstanding More's martyrdom, punctuating his essay with moments of irony and sarcasm. The by-now conventional reference to the commutation of More's sentence to a 'senzilla decapitació' (More 1912: xl) for example (which echoes the French 'simple décapitation' of Eugène Muller's introduction to the French edition of 1888, a copy of which Pin owned), is acknowledged as 'tant bell geste' ('such a beautiful gesture') (xl). As a general observation, Pin is more sympathetically inclined towards More on account of the Englishman's acquaintance with Vives, of whom More writes warmly in correspondence with Erasmus, and whom Pin would later translate (the introductory essay to the *Diàlechs* (1915) seeks to establish the moral superiority of Vives in comparison with Erasmus, of whom Pin is particularly critical). He clearly believed Erasmus to have been born in Gouda (as opposed merely to being conceived there), and saw his attachment to Rotterdam as a forgetting, or worse, betrayal of his origins. This seems quite gratuitous, but it allows Pin to speak in contrasting terms of Vives's rootedness, of his being a loyal son both of Spain and of his 'Region'—by which Pin means Valencia—and of its places, customs, and language. Vives claims never to have forgotten the language his mother taught him (Valencian), and Pin remarks that there is no better vehicle for learning than one's maternal tongue (Pin i Soler 1915: v–lxi). This is a clear reflection—or projection—of Pin's own dual affiliation, to both Catalonia and Spain.

Pin's introductory essay to *Utopia* begins in anecdotal mode, demonstrating implicitly an awareness of the framing devices employed by More: Pin recalls a trip by sea to Granada, via Seville, in which he visited the Cartuja and gazed on bloody pictures representing scenes from Pedro Calderón de la Barca's play *La Cisma de Inglaterra* ('The English Schism'), first performed in 1627. Pin explains that he took inspiration from the pictures and, returning to his lodgings, began to compose his introduction to the life and works of More, so that he could append it to the translation which he claims to have completed some considerable time before. He draws a connection between the grove of trees where he is sitting—planted, so he says, by Charles V, Catherine of Aragon's nephew—and the history of More, Henry VIII's faithful servant. The second section of the commentary discusses Pin's approach to the translation itself, to More's text as a work of fiction and as a work which exemplifies 'English' character. The third and most substantial section recounts More's life, and specifically his rise to a position of influence at Henry's court.

Pin says that it is obvious from the first lines that *Utopia* is a work of fiction, a *fábula* or fable—a term also used by Sorbière—given away by the fantastical names and toponyms (Pin explains Amaurot with the adjective *emboyrat* meaning 'foggy', interpreting the name as a direct allusion to London).[23] Further footnotes to the main body of the text also relate features of Utopian life and customs explicitly to England and the English (More 1912: 68 n., 87 n., 107 n.). Such explication aside, More's invented characters and places serve, Pin says, to 'rip veils asunder', to make way for eloquent protests against the 'tyranny, extorsion and egotism of those who at that time governed the Christian states' (xiv), ideas that were suggested to More by Seneca 'the Cordoban', according to Pin, who here again seeks a rapprochement between Spain and England as a way of ensuring a more favourable

---

[23] '[L]a Capital d'*Utopia*, lloch no existent, s'anomena *Amaurota*, obscur, sense visió, emboyrat, alusió a Londres' (Pin i Soler in More 1912: xiv).

reception for his translation.[24] Over and above any educational or literary importance we would wish to bestow on *Utopia*, the work has another significant function, he says: 'to bear complete witness to the English mentality', within which 'dissimulation' or an 'exaggerated correctness', an impassiveness and imperturbability, are key (xv). He underlines the quintessential Englishness of More, calling him 'a faithful mirror of that society' (xvi) in which Oliver Goldsmith's *The Vicar of Wakefield* (1766) would later pass as a model of charity (Pin appears to be referring to the book, rather than the character, although this may simply be imprecise expression), and where the adventures of Daniel Defoe's Robinson Crusoe are learned by heart, including his first words to Friday (summarized as 'call me Master') (xvii). Pin's intention, however, is apparently not to criticize Defoe, but to express gratitude for the narrator's kind words about the Spanish, which contrasted with prevailing accounts of Spanish cruelty in colonial Mexico and Peru (xvii).

Pin remarks that '[More] formulates in his book moral norms, religious principles which would be improper of a non-English Catholic contemporary of his; but which in his country were doubtless quite usual ways of thinking' ('formula en son llibre normes morals, principis religiosos, impropis d'un Católich no anglés contemporani seu; pero que a la seva terra eren sens dubte maneres usuals de pensar', xvii–xviii). He further comments that Utopian approaches to military conflict, to giving one's word, to international relations (including subsidizing one's allies at times of conflict),[25] and to trade—remembering that Catalan urban centres strove to compete with Manchester in the textile industry in the nineteenth century—'were by 1516 so completely English as to have been sucked with the mother's milk, learnt in school, studied in depth and later moulded in other maxims by the Florentine Machiavelli' ('eren ja en 1516 tant de mena angleses, que xuclades amb la llet materna, apreses a l'escola, estudiades a fons y enmotllades despres en altres máximes del Florentí Machiavelli', xviii).[26] Joan Manuel del Pozo, author of the second Latin-to-Catalan translation of *Utopia* (2009b), reads More quite differently, suggesting that his vision was diametrically opposed to that of his contemporary Machiavelli (in *The Prince*), insisting as he did on the separation of politics and ethics ('estava donant la resposta frontalment oposada al *Príncep* de Machiavel, contemporani seu, que pretén la total autonomia de la política en relació a l'ètica', More 2009b: 29). From our perspective, Pin's concern appears to be to unite More and Machiavelli in their contribution to 'Englishness'. Thus, he writes that just as the ideological 'yeast' of *Utopia* is English in its essence, so the ideological 'yeast' of the *Prince* is consonant with the English way of thinking (More 1912: xx). Both works, he says,

---

[24] Lucius Annaeus Seneca (aka Seneca the Younger), the Roman philosopher, statesman, and playwright, was born in the Andalusian city of Córdoba in 65 CE.

[25] Pin refers to the pound sterling as the 'Cavalry of St George', a reference to the 'Golden Cavalry of St George', used to describe the subsidies paid to other European states in the eighteenth and nineteenth centuries, particularly during the Napoleonic Wars (1803–15).

[26] For *Utopia* as an expression of 'British' attitudes to foreign policy and in relation to Machiavelli's *Prince*, see also Moir in this volume.

have contributed to forming successive generations of writers, philosophers, English men of government who, honest in their personal business, faithful in servicing their individual duties, sacrifice without scruple the most respectable collectivities to the greater good of the English.

(han contribuit a formar successives generacions d'escriptors, de filosofs, d'homens de Gubern anglesos, que personalment honests, fidels cumplidors de llurs deures individuals, sacrifican sense escrupol les més respectables collectivitats en benefici de la collectivitat anglesa.) (xx)

According to Pin, these behavioural characteristics culminated in the Victorian era and are beginning to wane at the start of the twentieth century, not because they are now without value, but because other nations are adopting the English example.

The hybrid nature of *Utopia*, as both 'a fiction and a collection of useful maxims', is indeed paradoxical, admits Pin, but also 'of huge transcendence' (xxviii). The decision to publish the work must have been made by More when 'suitably bound with English essence, it seemed to him time to present his fellow countrymen with that faithful echo of what many English at the time were thinking' ('ben amarrat d'essencia anglesa li semblá oportú donar als seus compatricis aquell eco fidel de lo que molts anglesos del seu temps pensavan', xxviii). Thus, once again Pin seems to suggest that More's work is in line with thinking within certain echelons of English society, regardless of its wider resonances and interlocutors.

Final Words

It could be argued that Pin's humanist reading of More illuminates his own position on language, through an appeal to a plurilingual pre-nation-state version of the state. But Pin's exile from Spain was also a major determining factor in this sense, together with his alienation from the literary and linguistic establishment which was never fully resolved when he returned to Catalonia. As part of the process of refamiliarization, for example, Pin frequented the Barcelona Athenaeum, and in 1905 affirmed the legitimacy of his own language, referring to 'that case of ethnic persistence manifest in my own speech, which is as though I had never moved from Catalonia' ('aquell cas de persistència ètnica que's demostrava en mon parlar, igual que si may m'hagués mogut de Catalunya', Pin i Soler 1905). The optimism underpinning such a performative declaration did not last, as we have seen. Thus, we might say that linguistic authenticity became bound up with a sense of identity and belonging, and any suggestion of rejection strengthened his identification with a larger entity (i.e. Spain). Ultimately, Pin's positioning between Catalonia and Spain, or within Catalonia and Spain, is itself an example of a utopian dream, in the context of a push towards the one-nation one-state model that was actually in the ascendant during the later decades of his life.

CHAPTER 26

THE HISTORICAL FALLACY

Utopia *and the Problem of Fiction in Weimar Germany*

CAT MOIR

THE publication in 1922 of Gerhard Ritter's new German translation of Thomas More's *Utopia* could not have been timelier. As the historian and political theorist Hermann Oncken acknowledged in his introduction to the volume, in the aftermath of the First World War, thinkers and politicians were preoccupied with the shape the new world order would take. In this context, the age-old question of the ideal state, and More's exemplary engagement with it, acquired new relevance. In his introduction, Oncken put forward a bold new argument. He claimed that More's *Utopia* should be read as a meditation on sixteenth-century British foreign policy. Although influential at the time, particularly in Germany, this view has since been widely discredited. Eric Voeglin claimed Oncken's 'gross mistake' was to misrecognize a fundamental difference in political mindset between the 'insular' British and the 'continental' Europeans (Voeglin 2002 10.197). Meanwhile Richard Saage (2006) has diagnosed the failure of Oncken's interpretation in its proximity to the ideological objectives of a nascent National Socialism.

This chapter challenges these views by reassessing the role of fiction in More's *Utopia*. The first section of the chapter examines the question of fiction in the utopian genre. The second section then sets the scene for the 1922 German edition, and discusses Ritter's translator's preface. The third section of the chapter examines Oncken's argument, while the fourth section deals with its reception and criticism, including in Ritter's later work. In contrast to Voeglin, Saage, and the later Ritter, this chapter argues that the failure of Oncken's interpretation lies not in its mistaken methods or ideology, but rather in its lack of regard for the literary character of the work. It concludes that the historical fallacy of the Oncken–Ritter reading demonstrates the limits to which *Utopia* as a work—indeed a genre—of fiction refuses to be subjected.

Fiction in the Utopian Genre

The radio adaptation of H. G. Wells's science fiction novel *The War of the Worlds* is famous for causing widespread alarm among American audiences when it was broadcast in October 1938. The opening section of the hour-long play, which retold Wells's story of a Martian invasion of the earth, was presented as a series of news bulletins interrupting another programme. A weather report and recording of a dance band are interspersed by news flashes about strange explosions on Mars. Fictional Princeton astronomy professor Richard Pierson dismisses speculation about life on Mars in an interview with reporter Carl Phillips, but news of strange activities grows more intense. The supposedly live broadcast covers the landing of a cylindrical meteorite in New Jersey. With crowds gathered at the site, a Martian is declared to be emerging from the extraterrestrial craft, as Phillips's shouts about incoming flames are cut off mid-sentence. By the time the show had finished, the station was receiving reports of mass panic in the streets: with global political tensions running high in the years prior to the Second World War, thanks to the clever framing of the story, some listeners had mistaken it for a genuine alien invasion.

As surprising as it may seem, the model for such framing techniques was first provided by More's fictional account of the 'new island of utopia', which appeared in Latin in 1516, then in vernacular translations from 1524. More's main narrative—an account of an island in the New World, where an ideal state was supposed to be established—is embellished with maps, poems in an invented utopian language, and actual correspondence in which More and his contemporaries indulge his premise. These parerga are the written blueprint of the devices later used in the radio adaptation of Wells's story: they lend a certain atmosphere of veracity to a work that deliberately plays with the boundary between imagination and reality.

In important respects, the works of More and Wells both belong to a genre of writing in which serious political considerations are tested out under the exotic conditions of fiction. That More's prank was met with less credulity than the *War of the Worlds* broadcast is largely a matter of the changing nature of mass media. The twentieth-century audience listening to Wells's tale was large, diverse, not personally known to the producers of the show, let alone to Wells himself, and radio was still a relatively new medium, particularly for drama: reactions to the piece could hardly have been predicted in advance. Meanwhile, the sixteenth-century audience reading More's original Latin work was small and, where not personally known to the author (and, as More's extensive correspondence demonstrates, many of his readers were), it was nevertheless culturally homogenous and uniformly erudite enough to know what the text was up to and be in on the joke. Still, even then the skill of More's portrayal may have had some almost fooled: when Paul Turner omitted Jerome Busleyden's letter to More—part of the early paratext—from the Penguin Classics edition (first printed in 1965), it was because Busleyden seemed 'to take Utopia literally, as a model of political organization, not symbolically, as a mere moral fable' (More 2003: xxvii). The trick to interpreting Utopia, of course, consists in recognizing that it is neither blueprint nor whimsy, and certainly neither apart from the other.

The literary form of *Utopia*—both the work and the genre—has always been crucial to its success, not least because literary utopias do what abstract theories of the good society usually refuse to: they portray it in detail, thus exposing the weaknesses and problems that underlie its perfect veneer. Unlike a work of theory, a work of fiction employs devices that are meant to remind us (even if they sometimes fail, as happened with the *War of the Worlds* broadcast), that utopia is not only, indeed sometimes not even, a *eu-topos* (good place): it is primarily an *ou-topos* (no-place).

Reinhart Koselleck (2002) pinpoints the onset of the decline of the literary utopia in the moment when, in the eighteenth century, speculative philosophies of history emerged, predicting that all that could be imagined in the good society would be achieved in a real, historical future. Krishan Kumar (2010) has argued in a similar vein that it is no coincidence if the literary utopia's twentieth-century demise followed the rise in the nineteenth of actual utopian movements that seemed to put dreams of the ideal state into practice. What good were storybooks when, in the French Revolution and its aftermath, it seemed that new worlds could be constructed not just in the pages of books but on the ground? This sentiment clearly motivated that anti-utopian utopian Karl Marx when, asked why he did not provide a more detailed outline of what a future communist society would look like, replied that he did not 'write recipes [*Rezepte*] for the cook-shops of the future' (Marx 1996: 35.17).[1]

More's *Utopia* is certainly no futuristic cookbook: in a time when Europeans did and could still imagine the existence of distant, undiscovered, exotic islands, there was no need for them yet to project fantasies about improved social organization into the future. More importantly, though, and unlike Marx later, More was convinced of the necessity of fiction to his enterprise: his ruses to make the narrative appear more realistic are—as is the paradox of realism generally—all the more indicative of its invented character. They signal to the reader that this is a serious but playful thought experiment: 'as entertaining [*festivus*] as it is instructive [*salutaris*]', as More put it in the work's original, full title.

But what instruction does More's entertainment offer? What would it be like to live in the republic of Utopia? There would certainly be undeniable material benefits of living in a welfare state in which food, clothing, housing, healthcare, and education are provided freely, and where the working day is just six hours long. Even these advantages have some downsides, though: restricted production and equitable distribution mean that everyone in Utopia wears the same colourless clothes. Meanwhile, although More, like Marx, gives us no cookbook, the food in Utopia, which Raphael Hythloday describes as 'quite reasonable', is 'provided at the public expense' only because 'convicts work

---

[1] The German word *Rezepte* can mean both 'receipts' and 'recipes'. The translation has been adapted here to the latter option, which was in more common use in the nineteenth century, and is more appropriate in the context of the sentence. Translations throughout are my own, unless otherwise stated.

as servants' of society (More 2003: 30).[2] Personal liberties are heavily restricted, and women and children are considered public property. Of course, the aspiration to realism of utopian works means that the visions they project are always closely correlated to the historical imagination of the age in which they are produced: in sixteenth-century England, women and children were indeed considered property, at least in theory, and one might argue that More's inability to see beyond this and other horizons of human freedom makes him merely unremarkably authoritarian for his own time.

That More's Utopia is ostensibly not a perfect society does not mean, however, that its author did not intend it as a vision of an ideal state, as some commentators have argued. In what was considered the authoritative English-language study on *Utopia* for much of the second half of the twentieth century, H. W. Donner (1945) argued in this vein that More's aim was not to praise Utopian institutions, but to demonstrate their absurdity in order that improved Christian ones might emerge to surpass them. Later, George M. Logan (1983) would claim that More's work was prescriptive neither with respect to utopian society nor to Christian humanism, but was simply concerned with the age-old political question of how best to counsel a king. Aspects of these arguments are certainly convincing. One of the main functions of utopian writing is undoubtedly that of critique, and dressing political criticism in artistic form has always been a favoured way to escape censorship. Indeed, it is precisely *Utopia*'s literary accoutrements that identify More's work as belonging to that oldest genre of political writing, the discourse on the ideal commonwealth dating back to Plato's dialogue on the *Republic*. Nevertheless, it seems an unnecessary stretch to deny More's wager any measure of earnestness. As Turner reminds us, in an age in which the nobility enjoyed vast hereditary wealth, while thousands of people starved, and social mobility was almost non-existent, a certain amount of austerity such as we find in Utopia might have been seen as a small price to pay in return for a measure of social justice (More 2003: xix–xx). More recently, Lawrence Wilde has built on this line of interpretation, arguing that the 'fictional form of *Utopia* may disguise its serious intent but it should not diminish it' (L. Wilde 2017: 2). For Wilde, More's work is an honest plea for social justice in a world driven by greed and the lust for power.

Yet even if we accept that *Utopia* presents *a* vision of an ideal state, it is clearly far from intended to be *the* vision. As More has the Utopians say in their communal prayer, 'If I am wrong, and if some other [...] social system would be better [...] I pray Thee in Thy goodness to let me know it', and indeed the polyvocal structure of the work enables multiple, complex perspectives to emerge (More 2003: 109). Thus although Hythloday presents communal ownership as one of the most attractive features of Utopian society, his conscientious counterpart 'Morus' (More's in-text persona) raises important objections to dispensing with private property: the prospects of shortages, of idleness, and of rioting in the absence of an adequate system of distribution. As a work of fiction,

---

[2] For the shifting terminology used to translate *servi* (here rendered 'convicts'), see also Kern, Withington, and Waithe in this volume.

More's *Utopia* can perform multiple tasks at once, extolling the virtues of communal ownership while simultaneously considering its potential problems. For all the inspirational rhetoric in the *Communist Manifesto*, its status as a piece of political propaganda prevented it from indulging in the same luxury.

Fiction, then, is inherent to what *Utopia* is and does, a fact that far from diminishes its critical or theoretical power. Interpretations of the text that neglect this dimension are bound to err in some respect, since they almost always seek to single out one voice at the expense of all others. Paradoxically, of course, there is also always an element of selective focus at play in the reception history of a work like More's, not least because each age sees most clearly in it those features that reflect its present concerns. Oncken's interpretation, which accompanied Ritter's 1922 translation of *Utopia*, is perhaps an exemplary case study of these issues.

Ritter's 1922 Translation

In 1922, the shadow of the First World War still hung heavily over the young Weimar Republic, the first democratic state in German history, which existed from 1919 until the Nazi *Machtergreifung* ('seizure of power') in 1933. At the forefront of public consciousness was the question of how Germany would meet its reparations obligations under the Treaty of Versailles, a source of shame and guilt for many German conservatives who believed the Social Democratic (SPD) government had betrayed national pride and victory on the battlefield by capitulating. The matter was made more difficult by the dire economic situation in which Germany found itself. Already in May 1922, Germany had to negotiate an international loan to pay its debts. In November, as inflation spiralled out of control, the loan had to be renegotiated. The wages of ordinary workers were almost worthless. In spring, strikes broke out in north Germany, Baden, and Berlin, but were quickly quashed by the authorities.

In this atmosphere of instability, confrontations between left and right were becoming more open and violent. In June, Minister for Foreign Affairs Walter Rathenau was murdered by members of the far-right Organization Consul, also responsible for the assassination of Finance Minister Matthias Erzberger a year earlier. Rathenau's was one in a series of political attacks in 1922 that helped to foment popular unrest, and although the Weimar Republic had what was in many respects the most liberal constitution in the world at that time, in moments of crisis like this, Article 48 allowed the president to mandate a state of emergency without consulting the Reichstag (the German parliament). Between 1919 and 1925, President Friedrich Ebert used Article 48 a total of 136 times. While the provision allowed order to be temporarily restored in moments of panic, this was often only achieved through the disproportionate use of force, which in the long run revealed the weakness of the system. What kind of a state can maintain order without sacrificing freedom? That age-old question of political theory was being lived out in visceral reality in the Weimar Republic. It was the perfect moment for a new translation of More's *Utopia*.

As Ritter notes in his translator's preface to the 1922 edition, *Utopia*—particularly the second book—had already been translated into German several times (More 1922: 46). In fact, German was the very first vernacular language into which More's work was translated from Latin, in 1524 by Claudius Cantiuncula (1496–1560), an ecclesiastical notary from Metz.[3] Cantiuncula was a renowned humanist scholar, acquainted with More's friend Erasmus, with whom he corresponded alongside other European intellectuals of his day, including More. A judicial and political reformer, Cantiuncula's apparent motives in translating *Utopia*, and in particular his omission of the first book, may nevertheless display a certain conservatism for its time. Helmuth Kiesel has suggested that many early German translations of *Utopia* omitted the first book because they were concerned to focus on the imaginative content, which was intended to play an instructive role for public figures in the genre of a mirror for princes, rather than on the potentially more incendiary content of Book One, with its sociopolitical critique of European courts and their politics (Kiesel 1979: 61–66).[4] Seen in this light, that Cantiuncula dedicated his translation of Book Two to the mayor of Basel, a town he believed was dangerously radicalized by its support for the Protestant Reformation, suggests he intended it as a cautionary gesture. Whatever Cantiuncula's true motives were, however, his edition indicates the extent to which, as Nicole Pohl has recognized, the translation history of *Utopia* into German 'reflects contemporaneous political debates and anxieties' (Pohl 2016: 493). Ritter's translation is no different.

A staunch German nationalist, Ritter completed his PhD in history at the University of Heidelberg under the supervision of Hermann Oncken in 1911. Published in 1913 as *Die preussischen Konservativen und Bismarcks deutsche Politik* ('The Prussian Conservatives and Bismarck's German Policy'), Ritter's study dealt with Otto von Bismarck's fraught relationship with the Prussian Junker class (the landed nobility) from which he came in the period 1858–76, during which Bismarck became Prussian minister-president then the first Chancellor of a united Germany. At the heart of the book is the question of allegiance to those who hold power: it was an issue that would occupy Ritter throughout his career and personal life.

A member of the national-liberal German People's Party in the Weimar Republic, today Ritter would be called a national conservative: he believed strongly in obedience to authority and the value of tradition, was a monarchist and critical of democracy, as well as being incidentally also deeply anti-Catholic. Like many Germans, Ritter found it difficult to come to terms with his country's defeat after serving as an infantryman in the First World War (Schwabe 1994: 84). He believed the Weimar Republic was doomed to fail because Germany lacked a republican tradition (Weeks 1999: 996). Although a

---

[3] For Cantiuncula's (aka Chansonette's) translation—the only translation printed in More's lifetime—see Schmidt in this volume.

[4] The other early German translation—also of Book Two only—is by Gregor Wintermonat (1612). See Schmidt in this volume.

nationalist himself, during the Weimar years Ritter opposed the radical ideology of the nationalist Pan-German League (Schwabe 1994: 84). He nevertheless initially supported Nazism as a bulwark against what he saw as the perils of socialism, breaking with the party only after it pursued his mentor Oncken and attacked the power of the Church (see Conrad 2005: 44; Weeks 1999: 997).

Ritter's ideological orientation is clear from his preface: one of the justifications he puts forward for offering a new translation is that what he claimed was the most recent complete German translation of More's *Utopia*, by Ignaz Emanuel Wessely in 1896, 'was probably supposed to serve the propagation of socialist ideas' (More 1922: 46).[5] To be sure, Wessely's translation was prefaced by the socialist cultural historian Eduard Fuchs, who, as editor of the satirical newspaper the *Süddeutscher Postillon* and the socialist weekly *Vorwärts*, was particularly interested in political satire. Fuchs was also inspired by communist theorist Karl Kautsky's work *Thomas More und seine Utopie* (1888), in which Kautsky strongly emphasized the significance of More's text for the socialist tradition. Despite Ritter's perception, however, the influence of Wessely's edition in propagating socialism seems to have been limited. Writing in *Vorwärts*, an anonymous critic attacked the translation, and claimed that Fuchs's introduction was little more than a rehash of Kautsky (Pohl 2016: 497). For his part, Ritter dismissed Wessely's translation as a 'not exactly unsolid, but rather rushed and quite clumsy piece of work' that did not do justice to the sophistication of More's Latin, and was occasionally inaccurate (More 1922: 46). A new translation, he argued, must 'try to be stylistically more readable and freer, while at the same time being far more precise grammatically and in terms of accuracy'. This is clearly the task Ritter set for himself in his new rendition, which drew extensively on the 1895 critical edition published by Victor Michels and Theobald Ziegler.

Ritter's decision to work with the Michels–Ziegler volume is significant because it is part of a translation strategy that already signals the thrust of the interpretation he shared with Oncken. Ritter notes that, whereas Wessely had translated the 1518 edition of *Utopia* commissioned by Erasmus, the Michels–Ziegler volume returned to the earlier, 1516 version (More 1922: 47). Although Ritter insists that his choice to use Michels–Ziegler over Wessely is motivated by linguistic rather than political factors, there is clearly more going on. For one thing, he claims that, having compared the two editions, the differences between them are 'negligible', an assertion that appears hardly credible from the perspective of contemporary More scholarship. As Elizabeth McCutcheon has shown in her detailed work on the topic, the 1516 and 1518 Latin editions are immediately strikingly different on account of the different arrangement of the parerga, the poems, letters, illustrations, and figures that surround the main text. 'Items that loom large in

---

[5] For Wessely's translation, Fuchs's introduction to it, and the influence of Kautsky, see Stewart in this volume. In fact, a more recent translation had appeared in 1920, by Tony Noah, the same woman who translated works from French (Montaigne, Rolland) and English (H. G. Scheffauer, Frank Harris's biography of Oscar Wilde) into German. Noah's translation of Utopia was praised by the socialist newspaper *Die Neue Zeit* (1921: 39.216), edited by Karl Kautsky; see Pohl 2016: 498.

the first edition disappear in the second', McCutcheon (2015b: 134) confirms, 'while new letters are added', and there is a 'new arrangement of the material'. It is unlikely that Ritter himself had access to the Latin works, but since the Michels–Ziegler and Wessely volumes reproduce these differences between the parerga, they would have been visible to him in translation. And while such amendments may appear trivial, as McCutcheon argues, the editorial decisions that frame the text tell us much about the context and possible intentions of its ever-evolving interpretation.

Ritter chooses to omit the parerga entirely. Only More's letter to Peter Giles (Aegidius in Ritter's version, retaining his Latinized name), which was included as the original preface, is retained here: Giles's letter to Busleyden, and Busleyden's to More, are both omitted, as is the utopian alphabet and the accompanying quatrain written in the invented utopian language. Ritter justifies his decision by claiming that it would be necessary to reproduce More's entire correspondence concerning *Utopia* in order to faithfully assess the significance of the work's paratextual material (More 1922: 48). Perhaps there is something in that assertion, though what it shows if anything is that Ritter was far from insensitive to the significance of the parerga: his decision to omit everything not verifiably of More's hand implies the recognition that any selection of additional material is necessarily partial. By the same token, so is his own selection, which as it turns out is explicitly linked to the rejection of the literary value of the text.

Ritter notes that older editions of *Utopia* were often illustrated and accompanied by 'sometimes more, sometimes fewer additions to the text and preface, befitting the taste of the age', and although he concedes that such features might be 'of literary-historical interest', he insists that 'they are entirely unproductive for the purpose of a politically oriented edition' (More 1922: 48). The reason for this, according to Ritter, is that these paratextual elements contribute unhelpfully to the 'fiction propagated by More himself that his report merely reproduces the story recounted by Hythloday'. Moreover, Ritter argues that the additional letters, which heap praise on More's talent as a writer, overemphasize his significance as an author, inviting the reader to simply identify the ideas put forward in the work as More's own. Even the snippet of utopian language, which Ritter believed stemmed from More, is rejected as a 'joke' and a 'mystification of the reader' without serious purpose. Yet if Ritter was concerned to avoid reading *Utopia* as the direct expression of More's personal vision, which his omission of the laudatory letters suggests, then surely it was counterproductive to excise the very code that undermines this danger? After all, in Utopian *he* means 'I'.[6] The inclusion of the language at the very beginning thus sets up the premise of polyvocality that makes the text resist reduction to a single viewpoint.

What Ritter clearly objects to here is any suggestion that the fictional aspects of *Utopia* might be relevant to a serious interpretation of the work. This is perhaps not incidental when we consider that it is the fiction that allows the text to consider the virtues

---

[6] See the Utopian quatrain in the parerga (Fig. 1.1), with its interlinear transliteration and Latin translation.

of communal ownership, at least notionally. Seen in the light of his earlier comments on Wessely, Ritter's decision to disavow the literary dimension of More's work in line with Oncken's reductively historicist reading appears ideologically motivated. In an age in which political extremes were vying openly for legitimacy, everything about Ritter's preface seems to insist that More's *Utopia* should not be read as a book about the merits of communism.

Oncken's Argument

In comparison to Ritter, whose objection to socialism comes through strongly in his translator's preface, his teacher Oncken was relatively well disposed to social democracy, even if his own political commitments were not social democratic per se. His first book, a biography of trade union leader Ferdinand Lassalle (1825–64), printed in 1904, tackled a risky subject at a time when social democracy was seen by many liberals and conservatives as a threat to the established order. Yet Oncken's scrupulous sources criticism, and his detailed analysis of Lassalle's complex personality, including the significance of his Jewish background and the problems associated with emancipation and assimilation in the *Kaiserreich* (Second Reich, 1871–1918), put his biography beyond reproach. Oncken was sympathetic to Lassalle's effort to bridge the gap between the state and the working class in the interest of national unity and cast him as a figure whose politics fell somewhere 'between Marx and Bismarck', as the subtitle of the 1966 edition put it.

Oncken was trained by the neo-Rankean Max Lenz (1850–1932), and—having succeeded to Lenz's newly vacated seat—in his first address to the Prussian Academy of Sciences, Oncken praised his teacher for having brought about a 'renaissance' of the historical scholarship of 'the master' Leopold von Ranke (1795–1886), a torch he declared himself proud to take up.[7] Ranke had sought to put history on a firm scholarly basis, emphasizing fidelity to the sources as the only way to guarantee objectivity. In the post-Rankean years when Heinrich von Treitschke (1834–96) had dominated history in Berlin, the discipline had largely been put in the service of German nationalist ideology. By advocating a return to Ranke in his academy speech, Oncken therefore subtly distanced himself from this perspective. Elsewhere, he was more explicit. In a programmatic 1904 essay entitled 'Politics, History, and Public Opinion', Oncken rejected the idea that history should serve a nationalist agenda, insisting that the historian should be objective in the treatment of the source material, allowing the national attitude to be visible only in the text's written style.

---

[7] Neo-Rankeans aimed 'to free history of its political aims and to base it on the foundations of objective, contemplative study' (Iggers 1988: 45).

Oncken's avowed suspicion of style and his fetishization of the source evidently fed into his interpretation of *Utopia*, which he articulated in two works both published in 1922: his introduction to Ritter's translation, and the text of a speech published as *Die Utopia des Thomas Morus und das Machtproblem in der Staatslehre*. The former was more general, comprehensive, and detailed, but it shared with the second, shorter work the same basic orientation: both read *Utopia* through an explicitly historical lens as a *staatsphilosophisches Werk*, that is, a work concerned to elaborate a theory of the state. The independent essay differed perhaps most significantly from the introduction to Ritter's translation in that it omitted any discussion of the source history, a point on which, as we will see, Oncken's argument hinged substantially, if problematically.

In his introduction to Ritter's translation, Oncken observes that More's *Utopia* had over time become synonymous with a particular kind of 'literary form' concerned with presenting the features of the ideal state (More 1922: 5). This, he argued, had led to the work being considered almost exclusively from this 'very narrow perspective', in which it was 'to a certain extent dissolved from its intellectual and temporal conditions' and read 'primarily in the context of the novels of state [*Staatsromane*] that reach from antiquity down into our own time'. Contrary to this approach, Oncken favoured a 'historical-political evaluation' of *Utopia*, that would examine it initially as an 'entirely individual case' and only then proceed to the general problems it raised.

Oncken's method was influenced by Wilhelm Windelband's conception of the logic of history as modelled on the humanities rather than the hard sciences. In a context in which the rise of the modern natural sciences was forcing older disciplines such as history and philosophy to question their institutional place and the specificity of their method, Windelband had distinguished between nomothetic disciplines, which aim to derive general laws according to which particular phenomena can be explained and understood, and idiographic ones, which seek to understand the meaning of contingent, unique, and often culturally or subjectively variable phenomena. Whereas the natural sciences were ranged among the nomothetic disciplines, Windelband put the humanities, including history, in the idiographic category. It was a contentious matter, and in the 1890s a dispute about methodology (*Methodenstreit*) broke out after Karl Lamprecht published the first volume of his *Deutsche Geschichte*. There, Lamprecht positioned the broad sweep of cultural and economic history as more important than personal and political history, rejecting Ranke's descriptive method in favour of a more genetic approach. In short, Lamprecht was less interested in reconstructing the details of a particular era or event, and more concerned with trying to uncover the underlying laws or tendencies according to which events took place. His approach to history was at least partly nomothetic, rather than purely idiographic, and it aroused vigorous opposition. Alongside Friedrich Meinecke (1862–1954), Lenz, and Max Weber (1864–1920), Oncken was one of Lamprecht's sharpest critics, and the same methodological predilection for the specific and contextual that galvanized him against Lamprecht motivated his approach to reading *Utopia* (Hirsch 1946; Studt 1999).

Oncken's treatment of *Utopia* as an individual case began with a reassessment of the circumstances under which the text was composed. Oncken claims that Book Two, the discourse on utopian society, was produced in the Netherlands before Book One, which was written later in London.[8] This he sees as significant because in the intervening period More was offered a post in the government of Henry VIII, a turn of events that, Oncken argued, caused More to revise Book Two's vision of a communistic welfare state existing in pure island isolation in light of his new priorities, and to draft a more realistic introduction that might make his ideas for reform appear more plausible.

Oncken claims that More was an advocate of a welfare state at home, a policy that might be achievable on an island like Britain, but only if the state had no wish to maximize its foreign influence. However, according to Oncken, More's ministerial ambitions forced him to accept that no state exists in isolation, and from a foreign-policy perspective war and trade, rather than welfare, were the order of the day. The revisions More made to his putative *Ur-Utopia* thus resulted, so Oncken argued, in a political philosophy whose positions on domestic versus foreign policy were highly inconsistent and potentially even incompatible. Oncken claims that More's communistic utopian state is ultimately revealed to be based on 'the most modern individualistic desire for acquisition' through its engagement in trade with outside states of the 'old order', and that thereby the 'thoughts of political engineering of the reformer More [...] emerge from their intellectual compromise' (More 1922: 31). Ultimately, he argues that the inconsistencies in the book must be understood through the lens of the personal tensions within More himself, between the idealist who imagined Utopia as a *Friedensstaat* (state of peace) and the pragmatist who, sensing an opportunity to play *Realpolitik*, reimagined it as a *Herrschaftsstaat* (state of domination), incorporating elements of a class society and a world-political frame into Book Two in his revisions.

Yet if Oncken's historicized reading of *Utopia* ostensibly stems from his conception of history as concerned with detail rather than form, it is striking that he has little evidence for his claims about More's revisions. Indeed, he freely admits that he 'assumes' More revised Book Two when writing Book One in the wake of his offer of a political office (More 1922: 31). That nowhere is source evidence for this assumption cited suggests a more than purely historical perspective was at work. A consideration of the book's publication context is significant here. Ritter's translation of *Utopia* was the first volume in the series Klassiker der Politik, whose purpose, according to the advertising brochure distributed by the publisher Reimar Hobbing, was to 'contribute to the task of politically educating the German nation and of teaching how to think politically', and 'above all to be an aid to political leaders who [...] wish to devote themselves to the resurgence of the fatherland' (Sawada 1967: 152, 160). As co-editor of the Klassiker series alongside Meinecke, Oncken would have been instrumental in shaping the focus of the series, and he further set the tone by contributing the introduction to its very first volume. By 1922, then, it would seem that Oncken's earlier reservations about putting history to

---

[8] More 1922: 11–15. This differs slightly from the account in *CWM* 4, which argues that the introduction to Book One (5 pages) and the discourse of Book Two (70 pages) were produced in the Netherlands in 1515, followed in 1516 by the Dialogue of Counsel in Book One (30 pages) and Book Two's Peroration and Conclusion, both written when More was back in England (xxvii–xli).

political uses had significantly relaxed. Why might this have happened, and what are its implications for understanding his reading of *Utopia*?

The short answer to the first question must surely be: the First World War. That the conflict brought about a fundamental shift in Oncken's perceptions and allegiances can be seen in the fact that, whereas prior to the war he had been something of an Anglophile, in favour of a rapprochement between Britain and Germany, after the Asquith Government entered the war on the side of Germany's enemies, he began to hold Britain equally responsible for the origins of the conflict. In a piece published in translation in the *New York Times* in 1916, Oncken argued that English, not German, militarism was the major threat to world peace. Whereas the German army, according to Oncken, was 'peaceful by nature', being based on the principle of military service—a 'leveler of inequalities', that made war appear particularly tragic because it 'affects all'—the English army was an 'army of conquest' that relied on mercenary labour drawn from all corners of empire by an aristocratic officer class. In his own day, Oncken argued,

> the Englishmen are using throughout the world the tried methods of their system. They drag tens of thousands of Hindu troops to France and Belgium to figure worthily on European soil at the side of the French Turcos and the Russian Tartar hordes. They ship as freight upon their ships Senegalese negroes to the German colony of Kamerun and seek to hold Egypt, which does not belong to them, by means of coupling together unwilling Hindu regiments and Australian volunteers; they turn the Japanese loose against Kiao-Chau and the South Sea Islands. Compare that with the manner in which, for the defense of our outpost which was lost to the overwhelming yellow odds, a few thousand men, true unto the death to the call of the Fatherland, hurried up from offices and factories throughout East Asia: then you will clearly realize the moral difference between the German and the English systems; or, to use the formula of *The Morning Post*, the difference between 'militarism and the abuse of militarism'. (Oncken 1916 [9 Apr.]: 1)

Here Oncken already invoked More, whom he pitted as the proponent of mercenary armies against Niccolò Machiavelli as the founder of the principle of military service. Whereas Machiavelli 'knew that the national deliverance of Italy could only be accomplished by national military service', his contemporary More 'explains how the island people of the Utopians, heartily detesting war, prefer the system of hired mercenary races'. According to Oncken (1916: 1), More's 'recipe [...] stands at the entrance gateway of the entire modern war history of Great Britain'. Hostility towards Britain, particularly in relation to its colonial and foreign policy during the First World War, thus appears to have motivated Oncken's reinterpretation of *Utopia* to a significant degree. In his introduction, Oncken presents More as the originator of a peculiarly British approach to foreign policy, apparently both realistic and moralizing at once.[9] In *Die Utopia des Thomas*

---

[9] For *Utopia* as an expression of the 'English character', and in relation to Machiavelli, see also Johnson in this volume.

Morus, he even suggested that More was able to envisage, four hundred years hence, Britain's position of global domination (Oncken 1922: 389).

Oncken's analysis of Morean duplicity reveals much about the peculiar ideological complexion of Weimar Germany. On the one hand, his critique of Britain's employment of mercenaries appears motivated by a sense of ressentiment vis-à-vis its imperial influence. Almost in the name of the colonized, Oncken seems to assert himself against British barbarism, lingering, nevertheless, on cases—Kiautschou (in China); the South Sea Islands—of German possessions lost in the war. On the other hand, however, Oncken's indignation against the 'aristocratic' British seems underpinned by a view of military service to the nation as a socially unifying, even 'democratic' force (Oncken 1916).

Admittedly, Oncken's concessions to socialism were heavily tinged with nationalism. When he argued in an address to Berlin students on the tenth anniversary of the republican Weimar constitution that the living standards of the underprivileged masses must be improved, he did so on decidedly integrational grounds: 'Whoever speaks of the nation must include the whole nation' (Oncken 1935: 113). Yet Oncken nevertheless saw the nation defined in civic rather than ethnic terms. 'We deem it our national duty', he continued there, 'to affirm unanimously our allegiance to the constitution as the only legitimate foundation of our national existence and particularly to the ideal of unity and liberty which forms its basis' (104). Thus although Oncken shared the bitterness concerning Germany's treatment after the war that motivated many, including Ritter, to embrace National Socialism, his allegiance to the constitution of Weimar strongly differentiates Oncken's politics from those of the nascent Nazi movement, for whom the democratic Weimar constitution was an affront against German nationhood. Indeed, despite his enthusiastic nationalism—which as we have seen increasingly influenced his view of history after the First World War, and also included an expansionist, 'greater German' (*großdeutsche*) agenda—Oncken rejected the Nazis' *völkisch*-racist conception of history, and felt deeply uncomfortable witnessing the party's rise in the years he spent in Munich between 1923 and 1928 (Hirsch 1946: 154–155). In 1935, Oncken criticized the Nazi state in a speech to the German Philosophical Society, saying that it sanctioned historical revisionism and encouraged biased scholarship. He was dismissed from his post as a result, dying in exile ten years later.

Reception of the 1922 Edition

The complexity of Oncken's position only made his political interpretation of *Utopia* a more appealing object of engagement for his contemporaries and successors. His line of argument was adopted by Meinecke in his 1925 *Die Idee der Staatsräson in der neueren Geschichte* ('The Concept of "the Reason of State" in Modern History'); by Ottmar Dietrich in his 1926 *Geschichte der Ethik* ('History of Ethics'); and by Friedrich Brie in his 1924 'Deismus und Atheismus in der englischen Renaissance' ('Deism and

Atheism and in the English Renaissance') and 1928 *Imperialistische Strömungen in der englischen Literatur* ('Imperialist Tendencies in English Literature'), although Brie later revised his view (Donner 1945: 100). In 1930, Oncken's former student, Michael Freund (1902–72), who like many of his generation switched his allegiance from social democracy to National Socialism during the course of his life, read *Utopia* as indicative of the fact that Britain's island position and its class society had prevented a theory of state power from emerging there in the 'unconcealed intensity and grandiose unilateralism' that it had assumed among Continental nations (Freund 1930: 254). Meanwhile, if Nazi jurist Ernst Rudolf Huber (1903–90) criticized Oncken's perspective, it was only because as Huber saw it Oncken had ignored that it was only the exploitation of other countries that enabled the Utopians to realize their social ideals (see Donner 1945: 98).

Perhaps the best-known reception of Oncken's theory was by Ritter himself, however, whose *Machtstaat und Utopie* ('Power State and Utopia', 1941) revised Oncken's view only mildly. Ritter differed from Oncken in that he did not regard *Utopia* as the political programme of More the ministerial candidate, and he broadly rejected Oncken's theory of a proto-*Utopia* in which More's revisions transformed a *Wohlfahrtsstaat* (welfare state) into a *Herrschaftsstaat* (state of domination). Nevertheless, Ritter broadly continued in Oncken's tradition of reading *Utopia* through an exclusively historical-political lens, and in fact he pushed the typology implicit in Oncken, and developed more systematically by Freund, much further than either. Ultimately, Ritter argues that Machiavelli and More were the prototypical representatives of peculiarly 'Continental' and 'insular' political philosophies which, although deeply interconnected, are nevertheless opposed according to an 'inner lawfulness' that was only revealed by the atrocities of the First World War (Ritter 1941: 141). For Ritter, a supporter of National Socialism at the time he wrote *Machtstaat und Utopie*, Germany's abandonment of moral veneer in matters of foreign policy represented a positive development in that it united the interests of nation and state in a single political philosophy.

Reading Oncken's introduction to *Utopia* almost exclusively through the lens of Ritter's development of it, Richard Saage (2006) has interpreted Oncken as himself much closer to a nascent Nazi ideology than is arguably the case. To be sure, Oncken was the source of the comparison between More and Machiavelli that Ritter took up. In his introduction to the 1922 edition of *Utopia*, Oncken argued that although More seeks to make himself appear anti-Machiavellian by advocating a communistic welfare state, in the final assessment he merely disguised his true ultra-Machiavellian intentions—British world domination—under a thin veneer of morality. As Oncken saw it, this exercise in so-called 'liberal imperialism' had been repeated in the context of the First World War and its build-up by Richard Haldane (British secretary of state for war, 1905–12), H. H. Asquith (prime minister, 1908–16), and Edward Grey (foreign secretary, 1905–16), who, as he argued already in his *New York Times* piece,

> emphatically took up the idea of the English responsibility to educate peoples to freedom. Yet another world mission, which combines the idea of the nation being a chosen people with idealistic humanitarian goals, letting power apparently disappear

behind some such ethos, but never fearing to take a new 'burden' of responsibility on its shoulders, in order ultimately to achieve the most violent world domination since the age of the Roman Empire. (Oncken 1916: 1)

According to Saage, Oncken read More's example as a demonstration of the fact that power cannot be outrun and is better embraced than dissimulated—in other words, as directly anticipating Ritter's argument (Saage 2006: 46). He claims that Oncken drew concrete lessons from More for Germany in 1922, namely that it should not be imagined that the establishment of a German republic or a League of Nations had banished power politics from the scene. 'What Oncken implied is clear,' Saage argues: 'after its military defeat of 1918, the German Empire must re-establish itself as a power state [*Machtstaat*]' (47). When he claims that this goal resulted only a few years later in the establishment of the Third Reich, Saage clearly aligns Oncken ideologically with Nazism.

Saage's direct references to Oncken are sparse, remaining limited to *Die Utopia des Thomas Morus*, and not including his fuller introduction to Ritter's translation of *Utopia*. As a result, Saage's critique rather misrepresents Oncken's position, failing to take into account either Oncken's hostile stance towards Britain in 1922 or his disdain for National Socialism.[10] The former surely suggests some genuine critique of British foreign policy, and not only oblique praise. By identifying More with his erstwhile friend Haldane, and the hated Grey and Asquith—figures associated with what he saw as Germany's unfair defeat and exclusive burden of guilt—Oncken could well be seen to be arguing that Germany should *not* pursue this path to power. Meanwhile, Saage's claim about Oncken's ideological proximity to Nazism seems overstretched given the latter's obvious mistrust of the regime and eventual persecution by it.

In an obituary published in 1946, Felix Hirsch claimed that Oncken's criticism of Nazism had begun much earlier than 1935, even if it became more direct with time. In December 1933, Oncken gave an address to the Prussian Academy of Sciences on Oliver Cromwell as statesman that Hirsch argued was intended to be read as a coded critique of Nazism. 'Oncken analysed the personality and policies of the Lord Protector with whom the Nazi "intelligentsia" liked to compare Adolf Hitler', Hirsch explains, and although the speaker 'never mentioned the name of the German tyrant nor his promise that the German *Reich* would last a thousand years', he nevertheless observed that after Cromwell died, his English revolution became merely an episode (Hirsch 1946: 157). According to Hirsch, 'Oncken's audience quickly grasped what the speaker was intending to convey' with this 'historical parallel', namely that Nazism would not deliver the mighty future it promised to the German people.

Perhaps Oncken's comments on *Utopia* can also be read in this vein: after all, by 1922 precisely the rhetoric of which Oncken claimed to be suspicious—a national 'chosenness' to carry out a 'world-historical mission' that would establish a new Roman

---

[10] This is also the position taken by Sawada 1967: 151–152.

Empire—was prominent not in Britain but in Germany, above all in the growing Nazi movement. From this perspective, Oncken's interpretation of *Utopia* can be seen to perform an even more complex critique of global politics post-First World War than has previously been acknowledged: perhaps fitting for an introduction that read *Utopia* primarily as a text about the 'eternal antithesis between political ideal and political reality', and emphatically not as the novel of state par excellence (More 1922: 45). If Ritter's rejection of the importance of literary form served to downplay the significance of *Utopia*'s exploration of the virtues of communal ownership, perhaps Oncken's interpretation disguised the ambiguity of his own ideological commitments? Certainly, Oncken was no satirist, a fact that doubtless contributed to his inability to adequately appreciate *Utopia*. Yet there is just as much 'cant' in Oncken's own writing as there was in More's, which only makes attempts to erase ambiguity from his position more challenging.

Nevertheless, Oncken's account of *Utopia* was clearly intended to be a discursive, rather than a creative, text, and by 1922 he was evidently committed to a vision of history as politically instructive, even if this was sometimes at odds with his insistence on the objectivity of source analysis. Given these insights, it is entirely legitimate to unpick his errors by analysing both the internal consistency of his argument and the framework of his own ideological commitments. However, Saage arguably shares a certain weakness with Oncken's other critics who have mostly sought to refute his interpretation based on the accuracy of his arguments rather than the logic of his premise. To be sure, Oswald Bendemann's 1929 refutation of Oncken's thesis of an *Ur-Utopia* is all the more compelling because it is based on detailed source evidence. Meanwhile, commentators such as Donner have raised important objections against the substance of Oncken's claims, both about various aspects of *Utopia* and about British history more broadly. So, for instance, Donner rebukes Oncken's argument that the Utopians wage war on foreign peoples under the dishonest auspices of freeing them from tyranny, insisting that it is 'in defence of law and order that the Utopians take up their arms, neither for intervention, nor expansion' (Donner 1945: 99). And again, when in his *Die Utopia des Thomas Morus* Oncken ostentatiously refuses to provide contextual evidence of the English brutality in warfare that would prove More's overtures to humanist idealism are misleading, Donner claims that such evidence is not necessary. The 'only historical argument', he claims, 'is the practice of Henry VIII and his contemporaries, and that is exactly what More is attacking with his biting satire' (101). It is a point made already in 1915 by Oncken's contemporary Werner Sombart, who observed that since the reader 'never knows with More where his seriousness ends and his mockery begins', the apparent ideal of warfare presented in Utopia could just as easily signal his 'derision of the warmongerers whom the great chancellor saw rising through the ranks and gaining influence among his countrymen' (Sombart 1915: 33).

Herein, it seems to me, is the real key to understanding why the Oncken–Ritter line of interpretation failed: because it did not recognize *Utopia* as a literary work in which More's own views, where indeed they can be said to be represented, are dispersed among multiple characters and subject positions.[11] Both Oncken and Ritter take *Utopia* as a whole to be indicative of More's personal convictions in a way that is borne out by neither the text nor the extensive scholarship on it. Oncken himself comes close to perceiving his own error when, in the *New York Times* article, he observes that the Utopians hire mercenaries 'at a price so high that nobody is able to pay it' (Oncken 1916: 1). Yet rather than considering whether this absurd conceit may in fact suggest that the text is using fiction to engage in a criticism of mercenary warfare, Oncken instead concludes that More disingenuously 'consoles himself with the thought that the use of this method has the edifying advantage that it will ultimately eliminate this pest from the world'. Of course, Oncken is referring here to the character Morus, More's avatar, whose views, however, are not to be simply conflated with the author's.

As Stephen Greenblatt has argued in his intricate examination of the literary construction of Renaissance selves, though Hythloday is carefully crafted as the 'fictional character' in opposition to Morus' supposedly authentic voice, in their discussion on the question of state service, it is nevertheless Hythloday who 'speaks for directness' in the matter of counselling a king, while the 'real' Morus advocates 'submission to fiction' and 'accommodation to the play at hand', confounding any easy association of one voice with More's own (Greenblatt 2005: 34–35). Interestingly, Greenblatt, too, accepts a version of Oncken's thesis according to which this dialogue stages More's internal deliberations about entering into government (36). Nevertheless, in his assertion that the realistic character Morus represents More's fictional public self, while the larger-than-life Hythloday gives voice to some of the real, though radical, designs of the historical More, Greenblatt captures the narratological complexity of a text whose meaning cannot be easily attributed to either authorial intention or the historical context of production. In doing just that, Oncken and Ritter succumbed to a historical fallacy in their interpretation of *Utopia*, and in the process they paradoxically overdetermined the work's significance for understanding the political context of their own time.

---

[11] Karl Vorländer's argument (1926)—that it is Oncken's implicit fusion of historical and philosophical perspectives that compromises his interpretation—also does not address the problem of fiction.

CHAPTER 27

JAPANESE TRANSLATIONS OF MORE'S *UTOPIA*

TERUHITO SAKO

IN the early 1990s, when I enrolled in a master's programme to start my academic career, my ambition was to be a theoretical sociologist: more particularly, to formulate a theory of social life in late capitalist settings. Acquainting myself with Talcott Parsons's influential *Structure of Social Action* (first published in 1937), however, I quickly ran into some conceptual and methodological problems centring on the relationship between social theory and social 'reality'. Parsons seemed to accuse—falsely—social theorists like Thomas Hobbes (1558–1679) and Herbert Spencer (1820–1903) of confusing the societies they prescribed or theorized with the societies they lived in or expected to develop in the near future (Parsons 1968: 4, 93–94; Spencer 1893: 563; Hobbes 1968: 228–229). Even more troubling, a fundamental assumption of Parsons's thought seemed to be that the models of society outlined by sociologists should somehow epitomize the laws and structures of the society inhabited by the sociologist: it was on this basis that he criticized the theories of Spencer and Hobbes as *unreal* and *fictional* (even though both writers were aware of the *unreality* and *fictionality* of their accounts).

This conceit, it transpired, was a feature of much contemporary theoretical sociology: just as Parsons's own social system theory was blamed as unreal and fictional in the 1960s, so more recent theories by Anthony Giddens (1938–) and Niklas Luhmann (1927–98) have been charged with excessive abstractness and being unfit to describe social reality. As such, it seemed to me that the priority for theoretical sociologists was not to formulate yet another model of society that would be condemned for failing to capture the nature of social reality, so much as to address the fundamental relationship between theories and practices and how that relationship is studied and understood.

In my own work I have done this in two ways. One method has been to use quantitative-statistical methods on the language of social thought over time, to clarify what thinkers meant when they used particular words. This has involved developing a computer-assisted statistical technique of processing natural language texts: what is popularly known as 'text-mining', 'text analytics', or 'data-mining' (see Sako 2018).

Secondly, I have built on the theoretical potential of Max Weber's 'ideal type' to clarify some of the positive implications contained in classical social theories by the likes of Hobbes and Spencer. An 'ideal type' describes the essence of a phenomenon rather than its every empirical detail, and a good example of the method is Karl Mannheim's *Ideology and Utopia* (1936). This separated utopian mentalities into four types: 'Chiliast'—*waiting* for God's decision; 'Liberal'—*aiming* for the realization of certain ideals; 'Conservative'—*ignoring* all the reflexive thoughts about contemporary society; and 'Socialist-Communist'—*waiting* for the predestined transformation of society (Mannheim 1997: 173–226).

Although Mannheim's typology is somewhat crude, it nevertheless made the key insight that readers' attitudes towards theoretical models of society are much more important than the models themselves or, indeed, the intentions of the theorist. Over the past century and a half, for example, Marxist interpretations of Karl Marx and Friedrich Engels's vision of communism have differed and conflicted wildly. For example, Position A (an academic Marxist attitude) posits that communism shall be realized as a necessary consequence of dialectical developments in the capitalist economic system. Position B (a militant Marxist attitude) argues that we should make it happen in reality through the revolutionary efforts of the proletariat. Position C (an anti-revolutionist attitude) rests on a belief that our present social world is good enough and there is no serious need to modify it. Position D (a dilettante attitude) holds that it is enough for us to know that we can live our social life in some ways differently from the present one. Position E (the twentieth-century theoretical sociologist attitude) asserts that Marx and Engel's vision does or does not epitomize our society enough.

By concentrating on the reader's attitude towards social models—in this case, that of Marx and Engels—we suspend judgement on the evaluation of the model itself. As importantly, we can trace the history of any given model of society across time and space. For instance, we can describe the Chinese medieval history of the imagery of *The Peach Blossom Spring*—Tao Yuanming's fifth-century fable depicting a 'utopian' land—as a sequence of changes in readers' attitudes to the book over time (Swartz 2008). When Tao Yuanming formulated his idea of the land of peach blossoms, he apparently borrowed the imagery of 'small country with a small population' from the philosopher Laozi (c.571–471 BCE). But Tao denied Laozi's insistence on the feasibility of it. Tao thought it would be sufficient for the land of peach blossoms to exist at the bottom of one's soul. During the Tang Dynasty (618–907), the idea of *The Peach Blossom Spring* came to be associated with the ascetic lives of Taoist monks who lived in seclusion. During the Northern Song Dynasty (960–1127), it was understood by Wang Anshi (1021–86) to be the ancient ideal state of human community that could no longer be rehabilitated. We are similarly able to clarify the synchronic distribution of types (or factions) of Christian radicals in medieval Western Europe, as did Norman Cohn (1970). And we can describe the modern Japanese history of Thomas More's *Utopia* (1516) in the same way.

That is what I do here. What follows recounts the succession of translations of *Utopia* into Japanese between 1882 and 1993, and the way the book was positioned—and repositioned—in relation to different ideological and intellectual movements and

Table 27.1. Books and translations printed in Meiji Japan

	Meiji 00s	Meiji 10s	Meiji 20s	Meiji 30s	Meiji 40s
Total number of book publications	10,153	41,940	45,045	40,981	41,669
Translations as a percentage of total number of book publications	20.7%	9.6%	8.2%	5.8%	5.2%

priorities.[1] I show that from the 1880s, *Utopia* became an extremely significant book for Japanese readers: one of the most visible and popular texts imported from the West and a coded means to critique contemporary Japanese society. In the second half of the twentieth century, this critical function became obsolete as freedom of thought and speech became permissible and material prosperity made social reform less urgent. In the meantime, translations became more scholarly and academic: even as translators strove to render *Utopia* in its own terms, the text became removed from wider society.

Utopia in the Meiji Period (1868–1912)

In the mid-nineteenth century the two Anglo-Chinese Wars (the 'Opium Wars', 1840–2 and 1856–60) made the Japanese aware that modernization and Westernization might be necessary to survive European expansion into East Asia. The Japanese leaders launched several projects to achieve this aim. One of them was the systematic translation of Western books. During the forty-five years of the Meiji period (1868–1912), over 4,500 titles—1,115 British; 859 French; 756 Russian; 536 German; 425 American (as far as can be confirmed)—were translated and published in Japanese.[2] As a result, a large proportion of the Japanese population—not only a handful of ultra high-grade intellectuals, but also urban middle-class and local elites—successfully learned about the ideas associated with Western modernization and industrialization (Kawato and Nakabayashi 2001).

During the earliest stage, Japanese leaders concentrated on acquiring Western practical knowledge that addressed immediate needs. And as time went on, their interest widened steadily. Table 27.1 shows the importance of translated books during the earliest stage of Japanese modernization. The right scale and the broken line show the total number of titles published in Meiji Japan. The left scale and the solid line show the proportion of translated books over that period. Table 27.2 shows the genres of the published translations.

---

[1] For *Utopia* in nineteenth-century Japan (in relation to China), see also Ma in this volume.
[2] See *NDL Online* (*Japanese National Diet Library Online Bibliographical Information Service*) <https://ndlonline.ndl.go.jp>

Table 27.2. Genres of translations printed in Meiji Japan

	Meiji 00s	Meiji 10s	Meiji 20s	Meiji 30s	Meiji 40s
Law	224	455	220	97	49
Medicine	306	403	345	289	103
English Literature	15	117	267	173	297
English Language	54	228	377	207	196
Moral Philosophy	101	53	68	98	148
Christianity	18	78	261	166	203

In the first decade of the Meiji period, we can see the large proportion of books about medicine (and pharmacy) and law (and jurisprudence). These subject areas were the highest priority for the Meiji regime because of their immediate usefulness. Medicine was essential both to military growth and vitality, and for coping with the health implications of urbanization, with Japanese cities growing rapidly at the time. Incorporating the Western legal system was indispensable to reforming and representing the regime as a modern sovereign state able to interact on a level playing field with Western imperial powers. As time went on, translations of medical and legal texts declined and the number of works that can be classified as English language and literature, Christianity, and moral philosophy grew significantly. This suggests that over the Meiji period, the pressures of 'top-down' practical modernization and Westernization were followed by 'bottom-up' cultural modernization and Westernization.

From the Meiji period up to the present day, More's *Utopia* has been translated and published in Japanese over ten times. This makes it one of the three most popular translations, with only two titles exceeding it: Adam Smith's 1776 *Wealth of Nations* (over fifteen publications) and William Shakespeare's late Elizabethan play *Hamlet* (thirteen publications). We do not have reliable data for the sales figures of those titles, but the numbers of released versions eloquently demonstrate the extent the influence of More's *Utopia* had upon modern Japanese culture.

The first Japanese translation of *Utopia* (More 1882; Meiji 15[3]) was entitled *A Tale of Good Government* (*Ryo Seifu Dan*).[4] The translator was Tsutomu Inoue (1850–1928). Inoue's translation was republished the following year (Meiji 16) under the new title of *A Tale of the Organization of New Government* (*Sin Seifu Soshiki Dan*) (More 1883). These two editions were abridged translations of Books One and Two using Ralph Robinson's English edition of *Utopia* (More 1551). Prior to 1882, other than practical books, we find

---

[3] The Gengo system of dating has two elements: the first identifies the era; the second identifies the year within that era. The Meiji period ran 1868-1912; Taisho, 1912-1926; Showa, 1926-1989; Heisei, 1989-2019.

[4] Unless otherwise stated, all translations from Japanese are my own.

only six or seven Japanese translations of books of English literature and philosophy, including works by David Hume (1711–76), John Stuart Mill (1806–73), Jeremy Bentham (1748–1832), and Herbert Spencer.[5] As such, Inoue's translations were one of the earliest sources for Japanese readers to learn about (early) modern Western sociopolitical thought.

Inoue was a shrewd translator who knew that the title of a translation was important to the commercial success of the book. In 1883 (Meiji 16), for example, when he published the translation of William Shakespeare's *The Merchant of Venice* (c.1596–9), he used the Japanese title *A Criminal Trial of the Case of Pawning of the Human Flesh: A Strange Western Story* (*Jin-Niku Shichi-Ire Saiban: Seiyo Chinsetsu*). According to hearsay, it sold over fifty thousand copies—a big hit—because of this outlandish Japanese title (Yokoyama 1961: 92). It is significant, then, that Inoue chose the titles *A Tale of Good Government* and *A Tale of the Organizing of New Government* for the 1882 and 1883 editions respectively. Why 'government'? And why did he change the qualifier from 'good' to 'new'? The use of the term 'government' would have resonated with the most likely readers of the book at the time. One of the Meiji regime's most significant reforms was the importation of meritocracy into central government. Almost all the other sectors—including local government and influential private business enterprises—kept discrimination by birth and rank. Of necessity, therefore, the most able young men—the core of the reading public—sought employment in the central government offices.

If the term 'government' was quite an effective draw to attract the attention of these readers, why did Inoue replace 'good government' with 'new government'? First, the phrase 'new government' invoked the current reforms of the Meiji Japanese central government, accentuating the contemporary relevance of the text. Secondly, 'good' (or 'bad') was, perhaps, too evaluative, and could be understood by the authorities as a criticism of the present regime, especially as the first translation was published just five years after the subjugation in 1877 of the regime's last and most serious rebellion: the Satsuma Rebellion or Seinan War, led by disaffected samurai who were concerned with the direction the Meiji regime was taking. 'New' was an altogether less provocative moniker. Whether it prepared readers for the content of the text is another question. But while it did not explain how to get a job in central government, some readers may have been excited by the unforeseen developments in Hythloday's storytelling. Indeed, Inoue may well have thought it apposite for those educated young men who devoted themselves to going up the bureaucratic career ladder to develop a critical perspective on the regime. This is because Inoue was not only commercially astute but also, it seems, a man on an ideological mission. He understood English, French, German, Russian, Chinese, and Esperanto and published no fewer than four hundred translations (an almost incredible number), including texts by Shakespeare, Daniel Defoe (1660–1731), Jules Verne

---

[5] These texts can be retrieved from the *NDL Digital Collection*. <http://dl.ndl.go.jp/search/>

(1828–1905), and J. W. Goethe (1749–1832).[6] Such an oeuvre suggests a man with liberal and progressive inclinations.

The third Japanese *Utopia* (More 1894) was translated in Meiji 27 by Tamikichi Ogiwara (dates of birth and death unknown) under the title *An Ideal State* (*Riso-Teki Kokka*). Like Inoue, Ogiwara chose the Robinson edition as his source text and summarized Books One and Two. In its opening page, Ogiwara drew the readers' attention to the different implications between the original title and the Japanese title:

> The original title of this book is *Utopia*. On the one hand, *Utopia* is referred to as a fantasy, a castle in the air. On the other hand, the author [More] wrote the story as if *Utopia* is the name of a country. So, I could name the Japanese title simply 'Yuutopia'. I did not do so, just because it sounds unfamiliar for the Japanese readers. (More 1894: 1)

Here, Ogiwara presented the selection of the term 'ideal state' as his third and reluctant choice. However, his real intention might have been the opposite: he was simply providing an excuse to the censors for using the term 'ideal state'. In addition, Ogiwara's explanation might have been an indirect criticism of Inoue's somewhat misleading title. By using the term 'ideal state', Ogiwara presented *Utopia* not as a book for jobseekers, but as a work of political philosophy.

The fears that Inoue and Ogiwara felt about censorship were far from groundless. In fact, Yushu Morita (1882–1954), a Christian socialist, journalist, and later translator of More (1929a), recalled an event involving Toshihiko Sakai (1871–1933), Hitoshi Yamakawa (1880–1958), and Kanson Arahata (1887–1981)—three major figures in the Japanese socialist movement—at the end of the Meiji period as follows:

> I remember one summer night of 1907. That night we held a lecture meeting concerning socialism, at some place very close to the main campus of the Imperial University of Tokyo. In the plan, Sakai, Yamakawa, and Arahata were expected to be the presenters. But as soon as the curtain-raiser [Morita himself] started to talk about Thomas More's *Utopia*, the police authority issued a winding-up order. (Morita, in More 1929a: 45)[7]

The young educated people who held this meeting placed More's *Utopia* in the (pre)history of modern socialism. It was what Inoue and Ogiwara may have intended for their translations all along. Certainly, translations of *Utopia* preceded Japanese translations of the works of Karl Marx (1818–83), Friedrich Engels (1820–95), and the Victorian socialist William Morris (1834–96). Morris's *News from Nowhere* (1890) was translated and

---

[6] Inoue translated most of the 400 books. However, it is known that one of Inoue's nephews, Roan Uchida (1868–1929)—later a famous novelist—translated several books for Inoue and allowed him to publish it under his own name. See Yokoyama 1961: 92.

[7] For *Utopia* as 'a Socialist tract familiar to [...] meetings and debating rooms' in nineteenth-century Britain, see William Morris in More 1893: iii–iv (cited by Waithe in this volume).

published by Sakai in 1904 under the title *The Ideal Country* (*Riso-Kyo*). Two years later, Sakai translated and published Engels's 1880 *Socialism: Utopian and Scientific* under the title *Scientific Socialism* (*Kagaku-Teki Shakai-Shugi*). The high officials of the police regarded More's *Utopia* as one of the foundational texts of this burgeoning canon of socialist texts translated into Japanese.

In 1910, several hundred socialists and anarchists were arrested on the suspicion of an assassination attempt on the Meiji emperor (the High Treason Incident). Of those arrested, twenty-six were prosecuted and twelve executed. The incident was an important moment in the modern history of civil protest in Japan, bringing to a halt a flourishing tradition of criticism and reform. Today we know that the police and prosecutors trumped up at least twenty-two charges out of twenty-six (Gavin and Middleton 2013: 1–7; Sumiya 1974: 251–284). Their intention was obvious: to suppress all kinds of nonconformist thought. At the time, however, the majority of people stood by the authorities, and treated the various kinds of reformers alike as in the same category as the Russian terrorist organization Narodnaya Volya (the People's Will) who killed Tsar Alexander II with a bomb in 1881.

Utopia in the Taisho Period (1912–1926) and Early Showa (1926–1945)

While the social reform movements suffered the dark years of suppression after the High Treason Incident (1910), the fourth Japanese translation of *Utopia* (More 1914) appeared in Taisho 3, also based on the Robinson edition. The translator was Masatake Mikami (1867–1946). Mikami entitled the book *Yuutopia*, the title Ogiwara had ostensibly rejected in 1894. At the start of the work we find five testimonial letters by influential figures of the time, including two members of the House of Representatives (the lower house in the Japanese parliament): Chifuyu Watanabe (1876–1940) of the Pro-government party (Rikken Seiyukai) and Minoru Yoneda (1863–1926) of the group affiliated with no party (Mumyo Kurabu). These letters emphasized the oldness and satirical quality of More's *Utopia* and the honesty of More's personality. They nicely reflect the social movement of the time: Taisho Comprehensivism (Taisho Kyoyo-Shugi).

Taisho Comprehensivism was a movement encouraging young elites to acquire wider knowledge and to avoid the evils of specialization and bureaucracy. For conservative elders who remembered the premodern elites—and who had been proud to recite the entire lines of the *Four Books* and *Five Classics* of Confucianism—modern university men appeared rigid and narrow. Therefore, the conservatives welcomed the rise of Taisho Comprehensivism. On the opposite side, younger nonconformists and their sympathizers found in the movement a loophole that made it possible to justify their readings of radical books. Using Taisho Comprehensivism prudently, Mikami reintroduced More's *Utopia* to Japanese readers. In the process, he helped to reconstruct modern reformist social thought after the 1910 High Treason Incident.

According to conservative logic, Japanese elites could expand their learning with foreign books written by men of wisdom: that is why the five testimonials of Mikami's More (1914) emphasized More's righteous personality. In his recommendation of the book, Chifuyu Watanabe wrote: 'More was [...] not only virtuous and devout, but also wise and practical. His true intention was not to criticize the rulers of his time, but to have hope to build a better society' (More 1914: 3). Another recommender, Minoru Yoneda, wrote: 'In the bloody age of Henry VIII's reign, More was one of the few who stood on his own two feet. Even after he resigned from the Chancellorship (1532), More persisted in his belief, manifested his disapproval against the Act of Supremacy (1534)' (More 1914: 22). These endorsements might have successfully eased the general reading public's tendency to mistakenly equate social reformers with extreme terrorists. The same logic revered antiquity: hence the testimonials underscored that More's *Utopia* was 400 years old. In addition, the testimonials highlighted More's loyal martyrdom and undeserved punishment by Henry VIII, and Mikami prudently bundled into the book More's biography written by Maurice Adams (More 1890a). In sum, it is no exaggeration to claim that the publication of Mikami's *Utopia* was a touchstone of Japanese freedom of thought and speech at the time.

The fifth and sixth Japanese translations of *Utopia* appeared simultaneously in 1929 (Showa 4) in two series of 'great works of all times and places', with a seventh appearing in 1934 (Showa 9). One, translated by Yuzo Murayama (1887–1958) (More 1929b) was volume 50 of the 124-volume *Selected Works of World Great Thinkers* (*Sekai Dai-Shiso Zenshu*), published by the Shunju-Sha publishing company between 1927 and 1937. Founded in 1918 with the surge of Taisho Comprehensivism, it established a hugely profitable business model, producing series of world's classics in Japanese translations. Murayama's *Utopia* was consequently bundled together in one volume with Tommaso Campanella, *The City of the Sun* (*La città del Sole*, 1602); Morris, *News from Nowhere*; and Francis Bacon, *New Atlantis* (1627). The other translation of 1929—Yushu Morita's *Utopia* (More 1929a), in which he recalls the 1907 censorship of a meeting that mentioned *Utopia*—was the first volume of the forty-volume *Selected Works of Great Social Thinkers* (*Shakai-Shiso Zenshu*), published by the Heibon-Sha publishing company between 1928 and 1933. Founded in 1914, the Heibon-Sha excelled in publications of practical pocket dictionaries and concise encyclopedias for the general public. In 1920s the company ventured into publishing Japanese contemporary popular literature, and used that as a base for emulating the Shunju-Sha business model of translations of world's classics. Like Murayama's *Utopia*, Morita's translation appeared in a compilation volume with Morris's *News from Nowhere*, Campanella's *City of the Sun*, and—instead of Bacon's *New Atlantis*—Edward Bellamy's utopian novel *Looking Backward* (1888). Murayama's and Morita's translations of *Utopia* can be seen as the greatest crystallizations of Taisho Comprehensivism. And the manner in which More's work was anthologized with other texts by both the Shunju-Sha and the Heibon-Sha clearly show the significant role that his *Utopia* played in Japanese social thought in early Showa (from the late 1920s to mid-1940s). At the time, More's *Utopia* was the second starting point of the modern Japanese history of progressivism and socialism.

Murayama's *Utopia* (More 1929b) contains rich commentaries on the biography of More, analysis and interpretations of *Utopia*, and evaluations of its influences. Among those commentaries included in the volume, the influential literary critic Asatori Kato (1886–1938) contributed an interesting analysis. We may summarize Kato's analysis in three points. First, Kato argued that the concept of Utopia was already well known among the Japanese reading public, so just copying the English pronunciation of utopia in Japanese as 'Yuutopia' was sufficient to explain and introduce the work—a statement which confirms the impact of Mikami's translation (More 1914), which went under that title, after the High Treason Incident (1910). Secondly, Kato distinguished the 'utopian type of novel (including More)' as a genre of literary art from the 'futurist type of novel (including Verne)'. In the 'futurist type of novel', the most important feature of the drawn fictional world is feasibility or realizability. In contrast, the 'utopian type of novel' emphasized not feasibility but the logical consistency and ideality of the drawn imaginary world. Thirdly, Kato perceived that 'utopian literature' flourishes in eras of 'anxiety', and he diagnosed his own time as exactly such an unsettled era. During this time a series of tragedies struck Japan, including the Great Kanto Earthquake of 1923 (over 100,000 people killed) and Showa Financial Crisis (1927–30); the Rice Price Crash (1930–1) was to follow shortly after. In the middle of these crises, a rich popular culture flourished among the affluent urban populace[8] and, at the same time, the influence of the military authority expanded in Japanese politics and diplomacy.

Related to all those points, it is noteworthy that in 1931 a Protestant cleric, Iwasaburo Okino (1876–1956) published a popular book entitled *A Fable of Utopias* (*Yuutopia Monogatan*). As the name of the publisher—the Housewife's Companion (Shufu-no-Tomo-Sha)—suggests, the company specialized in publishing books for women and for those unfamiliar with academic books and texts written in foreign languages. Okino's book provided synopses of the imagery of utopias of all ages and various countries, and argued that human history developed the ideas of utopia from mere fancy into realizable social aims. Okino's book and Kato's commentary in Murayama's edition (More 1929b) suggest that by the beginning of the Showa period the term 'utopia' had taken a firm hold not only on Japanese literates, but also on the wider population. Moreover, they understood *Utopia* in the way that the handful of urban highbrows in 1907 had grasped: all through human history there had been countless utopian visions and efforts to reform society, and the present day was no exception.

In the preface of his translation of *Utopia*, Morita openly declared the great leap of revolutionary socialism in contemporary Japan: 'Within two decades [from the High

---

[8] In early Showa, some people were disturbed by a contemporary culture they categorized as 'Erotic, Grotesque, and Nonsense'. They disapproved of young women dressing in what they saw as a revealing way and striding out in the city streets; of popular novels openly describing sexual activities; and the sensationalist treatment of bizarre murder cases in newspapers and magazines. Alternatively, these phenomena could be read as signs of emancipation from traditional oppression.

Treason Incident until the early Showa], our socialist comrades increased several hundred times in number. A thousand emotions are crowding into my mind' (More 1929a: 4). This statement reveals why, in his contribution to Murayama's *Utopia* (More 1929b), Kato introduced a new distinction between the 'utopian type of novel' and the 'futurist type of novel', instead of the dichotomy of 'utopia' and 'socialism'. Kato found that Japanese ordinary people understood More's *Utopia* as having a close affinity to modern revolutionary socialism. He and other reformers must have felt ambivalent about it: the equation of 'utopia' and 'socialism' was, in a sense, favourable; but it increased the risk of censorship. Kato therefore felt it was necessary to switch the cognitive framing to protect More's *Utopia* from governmental prohibition.

Kensho Honda (1897–1978), a professor of modern English literature at Hosei University, published in Showa 9 the seventh translation of *Utopia* (More 1934) with the Iwanami-Shoten publishing company. Based once again on the Robinson edition, the key aspect of Honda's *Utopia* was the publisher. The Iwanami was, and remains, the most prestigious academic publishing company in Japan: its publication of Honda's translation was an act of academic legitimation that indicated More's *Utopia* to be one of the prominent literary works of world history.

Utopia from Post-War Showa (1945–1989) to Heisei (1989–2018)

In the middle of the Great Depression (1929–33), the Japanese utopians—as revolutionary socialists—merged with radical traditionalists, creating the Japanese national socialist military regime, which would lead them into the catastrophe of the Second World War.[9] After a long and bitter war, in 1947 Japan amended their constitution. The new constitution guaranteed to the people of Japan freedom of speech, of religion, of thought, and of association, as well as respect for fundamental human rights. As noted above, More's *Utopia* held a special position in pre-war Japanese social thought, functioning as a touchstone of freedom of thought and speech from government censorship. Necessarily, after 1947, the Japanese attitude towards *Utopia* changed.

The eighth version of Japanese *Utopia* appeared in 1948 (Showa 23), reissued in 1957 (Showa 32), when Masao Hirai (1911–2005), a professor of modern English literature at the University of Tokyo, published his translation.[10] Hirai's translation was significant in two respects. First, he drew on John Churton Collins's 1904 English translation and Joseph H. Lupton's 1895 Latin–English edition as well as Robinson's sixteenth-century translation. Consulting multiple versions suggests the deepening of the post-war

---

[9] For detailed discussion, see G. A. Houston 1986; Tankha 2006.

[10] There seems no substantial difference in the main text of More 1948 and More 1957b, but More 1957b includes a new introduction by the translator Hirai.

Japanese academic treatment of *Utopia*. Prior to Hirai, all the translators relied on Robinson's edition only. Secondly, Hirai raised a question: 'Is More's *Utopia* really utopian?', by which Hirai means 'ideal' (More 1957b: 203). In fact, as Hirai pointed out, the Utopian system that More's Hythloday describes strictly prohibits the open discussion of political issues (Book Two, chapter three, 'Their Officials'), where we are told that 'it is a capital offence to make plans about public business outside the senate or the popular assembly' (More 2016b: 50). Secondly, there are limits on religious tolerance, there being no room for atheists—a lack of belief manifested by a denial of posthumous reward or punishment—who are excluded from public office, as being 'not even [...] of the human race' (Book Two, chapter nine, 'The Religions of the Utopians', 100). Thirdly, slavery exists unquestioningly (Book Two, chapter seven, 'Slaves'; cf. chapter five, 'Social Relations', where we are told that slaves undertake all the onerous and dirty domestic duties). Hirai concluded that all these were remnants of a medieval value system, and the true significance of More's *Utopia* was in the ambivalent coexistence of the medieval and the modern. The Japanese post-war dissipation of ideological tensions made it possible to read *Utopia* open-mindedly.

In Showa 44, a ninth version (More 1969) was translated by Akio Sawada (1928–2015), a professor of history at the University of Tsukuba, again showing the academic bent that translations of *Utopia* had taken from Honda's 1934 translation onwards. Based on Edward Surtz and J. H. Hexter's Latin–English edition for Yale University Press's *Complete Works of St Thomas More* (1965), Sawada's version was the first Japanese translation of *Utopia* to pay great attention to More's Latin. This is not an exceptional case. Generally speaking, before 1960s, Japanese importation of premodern Western culture had been from modern vernacular translations. Of course, there had been a small number of classical Greek and Latin scholars in Japanese universities. But all they could do was to share knowledge of Greek and Latin within their small academic circle. The situation changed in 1960s when the popularization of higher education began. A massive number of college students suddenly needed to learn about ancient Graeco-Roman thought and medieval European thought. To do so, they required Japanese books translated directly from Greek and Latin.

In addition, Sawada's *Utopia* was published by the Chuo-Koron publishing company (established in 1886) as the seventeenth volume of the eighty-one-volume series *The World's Great Books* (*Sekai No Meicho*), published between 1966 and 1976. Here—in response to the expansion of higher education in the late 1960s—we see the Chuo-Koron publishing company adopting the pre-war business model of the translation series of 'great works of all times and places' previously pursued by the Shunju-Sha and Heibon-Sha. In *The World's Great Books* series, *Utopia* appeared alongside *Praise of Folly* (1511), by More's friend and fellow scholar Desiderius Erasmus.[11] Thus, while Morita's and Murayama's translations (1929a, 1929b) combined More's *Utopia* with works of 'utopian'

---

[11] For the importance of this friendship to the production and reception of *Utopia*, see—amongst others—Taylor and van Bunge in this volume.

fiction from the seventeenth century onwards, Sawada's placed satirical works by More and Erasmus side by side. Probably Sawada and Chuo-Koron took Hirai's academic view on More's historical significance (putting his work alongside that of one of his contemporaries), rather than reverting to the pre-war social reformist interpretations of *Utopia*.

The last version that this chapter deals with is the tenth *Utopia* published in 1993 (Heisei 5): this is an extended and corrected version of Sawada's 1969 translation, which includes a Japanese translation of the paratextual poem 'Four Lines in the Utopian Tongue' and eight paratextual letters.[12] The transformation of *Utopia* from a popular cipher for socialism to the focus of scholarly expertise was complete.

Conclusion: A Miscellany of Japanese *Utopias*

As we have seen, the Japanese reading public crystallized their attitude towards More's *Utopia* in the early Showa period. Ironically, because the post-war constitution (1947) declared freedom of thought would be guaranteed, *Utopia* lost its practical function of disguised social critique. Under the post-war constitution, revolutionary political parties were decriminalized and people criticized government openly. However, even today, we find several remnants of the pre-war Japanese collective memory of the popular Utopia as sole guard wall for the idealistic social reformers, in some unexpected places. By way of conclusion, I give two examples: one comical, the other tragic.

Today, most Japanese people have a bath in their houses. Nevertheless, they still love to go to the public baths: it is one of the most familiar ways to take a pause of relaxation, just as much as having some glasses of beer and watching a football game. In 2016, the five hundredth anniversary of *Utopia*, there were over 25,000 public baths in the country. We find 'Utopias' here.

Table 27.3 shows the most frequent names of Japanese public baths (from a sample of 1,894): 'Utopia' won twelfth place, with at least ten of these public baths including 'Utopia' in their name (0.5 per cent).[13] This is especially significant given that the names

---

[12] These eight letters are: Erasmus to Johann Froben (25 Aug. 1517); Guillaume Budé to Thomas Lupset (31 July 1517); Peter Giles to Jerome Busleyden (1 Nov. 1516); Jean Desmarez (aka Paludanus) to Giles (1 Dec. 1516); Busleyden to More (1516); More's prefatory letter to Giles; a second letter from More to Giles, beginning 'Greetings' (1517); and Beatus Rhenanus to Willibald Pirckheimer (Feb. 1518). No lifetime edition of More's *Utopia* includes all these letters. See T. Cave 2008c: 278.

[13] There is no official complete list of Japanese public bathing facilities. I searched the internet and identified 1,894 facilities' names. What follows is the list of the public baths named *Utopia*, for the convenience of the readers who want to visit: *Yuutopia*, Hon-dori, Kure-shi, Hirosima-ken; *Yuutopia Niju-ichi*, Kameari, Adachi-ku, Tokyo-to; *Yuutopia Inariyu*, Hachiken-cho, Takayama-shi, Gifu-ken; *Yuutopia Uwa*, Akema, Uwa-shi, Ehime-ken; *Yuutopia Koto-Ura*, Kotouracho, Amagasaki-shi, Hyogo-ken; *Yuutopia Shiratama Onsen*, Gamo, Joto-ku, Osaka-shi; *Yuutopia Konakano*, Konakano, Hachinohe-shi, Aomori-ken; *Yuutopia Kirishima*, Chuo, Ohtsu-shi, Shiga-ken; *Yuutopia Nishifuna*, Nishifuna, Funabashi-shi, Chiba-ken; *Yuutopia Daigo*, Ishida-ouke-cho, Fushimi-ku, Kyoto-shi.

Table 27.3. Names of Public Bathhouses in Japan (2016) by Popularity

Rank	Name	Number
33	Waterfall	3
33	White Mountain	3
33	Broad-Minded God	3
33	King	3
33	Capital	3
30	Pure Water	4
30	God of Fortune	4
30	Beauty	4
26	Showa	5
26	Taisho	5
26	Shinto and Buddhism	5
26	Joy and Pleasure	5
21	Treasure	6
21	Great Peace	6
21	Fishery God	6
21	Conjugal Harmony	6
21	Fountain	6
17	Willow	7
17	Good Fortune	7
17	Paradise	7
17	Agricultural God	7
15	Jewel	8
15	Peace	8
14	Mt Fuji	9
12	Happiness	10
12	East	10
12	**UTOPIA**	10
10	Prosperity	11
10	Turtle	11
8	Green	12
8	Felicity	12
6	Crane	13
6	God of Wealth	13
5	Bamboo	14
4	Comfort	15
3	Rising Sun	32
2	Pine Tree	39
1	Flower	42

of facilities are supposed to be unique, to distinguish one from another (unlike Utopians' houses). Looking at the rankings, most of the frequently used names have associations with worldly benefits that can be classified in six types:

1. worldly benefits in general, such as felicity, happiness, joy, and pleasure;
2. benefits of nature, including the rising sun, agricultural god, fishery god, fountain, pure water, or waterfall;
3. perennial youth and long life, symbolized by pine, bamboo, crane, turtle, green, and Mount Fuji;[14]
4. prosperity, as found in gods of wealth, jewels, and treasure;
5. peaceful social relations: as in peace, great peace, conjugal harmony, broad mind;
6. beauty, as seen in flower, willow, or the physical, outer beauty of a human (especially female beauty).

It is not difficult to imagine the reasons why these names were chosen, given that bathing is regarded as a modest worldly benefit. The other set of names groups together Utopia, Buddhist paradise, Showa, Taisho, and the syncretic god of Shinto with Buddhism. This suggests that *Utopia* has been a proxy for the traditional Buddhist paradise since the Taisho period (1912–26) and through the Showa period (1926–89). For premodern Japanese people, the most widespread spiritual (as opposed to worldly) value system was Buddhism, and in the twentieth century, revolutionary socialism became an alternative value system. It was not difficult for the Japanese to convert one system of thought into another, because they have a rich history of syncretic systems of thought: for example, the syncretism of Shinto and Buddhism; the fusion of the Chinese writing system and indigenous notation system; the combination of Confucianism and Western sciences; and Utopianism and revolutionary socialism.

The second remnant of *Utopia* is more bitter, and that is the use of the idea of 'utopia' in newspaper advertisements selling real estate in the early 1970s. There are over twenty such advertisements in newspapers from 1971 to 1974. Just two, both from morning issues of the Tokyo edition of *Yomiuri Shimbun* (one of Japan's national newspapers), serve to illustrate the phenomenon. The first, from 15 April 1972, advertises a resort cottage in northern Japan: a typhoon-free and summer heat-free area. The accompanying image shows an open, unpopulated landscape (very different from crowded, urban Tokyo), with a substantial place name planted on it, reading 'Utopia'. The second, from 29 March 1973, uses the same term to advertise plots in a suburban residential area near Tokyo.

The Economic Miracle (1954–72) made Japan one of the most prosperous nations in the world. In the meantime, movements for radical social reform gradually ceased. The last was the student movement in the late 1960s which, as in other prosperous nations, was conducted by the post-war 'baby boomers' (in the Japanese case, born c.1947–9).

---

[14] In Japanese traditional folklore, pine and bamboo symbolize perennial youth, on the grounds that they are evergreen. Crane and turtle symbolize longevity, because they have long lives. The Japanese pronunciation of 'Fuji' refers to both 'Mount Fuji' and 'immortality'.

By the early 1970s, however, these Japanese baby boomers had found jobs in the giant Japanese corporations and were now encouraged to cast off their radical utopianism and—with tragic irony—purchase a new kind of utopia with money. These material utopias are segregated from political-economic-social tensions and the owners can enjoy worldly benefits as much as they like: to consume, to sleep, to procreate, to rear children, to enjoy vacations. It is noteworthy that today they are around 70 years of age, enjoying a stable living with pension; some may own a cottage. Their children, however, are now around 40 years of age and severely scarred by the economic downturn of the early 2000s, with many still economically dependent on their parents. Given that Japan is likely to be facing significant problems of impoverishment and inequality by 2030, a new page in the Japanese history of reading More's *Utopia* might well be about to be turned.

CHAPTER 28

THE MULTIPLE LIVES OF *UTOPIA* IN MODERN CHINA

TEHYUN MA

Since 2003, China's politically engaged citizens have been discussing Marx, Mao, and global politics on the popular message board *Wu You Zhi Xiang*: a website name that is generally translated into English as utopia. The concept of utopia has often been seen as central to Maoist thought. The Great Leap Forward, which took place between 1958 and 1961, sought to build a new socialist society in the countryside that would allow China to leapfrog the British economy in fifteen years and share the bounty of collective labour. Later, in 1968, Mao inaugurated the Cultural Revolution by calling on youths to smash old hierarchies and open up possibilities for a new egalitarian future. Both projects had catastrophic consequences. Tens of millions died from starvation during the Great Leap, while current estimates indicate that a million more perished in the violence of Cultural Revolution. Whatever the dystopian denouement, though, the utopian designs underpinning each project are not hard to discern.

Despite the utopian streak in Maoist policies, utopia as a concept in Chinese thought has a relatively short history. Difficult to translate into a Confucian vocabulary, the term only became common in East Asia in the late nineteenth century, and the work that gave it its name—Thomas More's 1516 text—would not be translated into Chinese until 1935, about half a century after it first appeared in Japanese.[1] While there is a growing body of work on the concept of utopia in China, More's place within that tradition has been less explored. Two brief notices in *Moreana* (Sawada 1974; Hsia 1981) pointed to the existence of a pair of Chinese translations: one, from 1935, in China, and the other, in 1965, a UNESCO-sponsored edition undertaken in Taiwan. However, due to their brevity neither of the *Moreana* pieces has room to offer either a close reading of the translation or a careful reconstruction of the context in which they appeared. Chinese scholars did not take up the baton themselves. Though R. Pho-chia Hsia acknowledged that More

---

[1] For Japanese translations of *Utopia*, see Sako in this volume.

was a significant figure 'in Chinese Marxist historical pedagogy', East Asian scholarship on him, he argued, remained scarce because of the 'general neglect of Renaissance and Reformation history' in both China and Taiwan (Hsia 1981: 108).

A flurry of recent studies have begun to fill in the gaps. Yi-Chun Liu (2016, 2017) has offered a forensic analysis of the process of translation, not only bringing to light previously unexplored editions, but also reading the subtle differences between them. To reveal how each translator aimed to shape readings, she picks up on distinctions in language, paratexts, and supplementary images between editions. Her work has provided us with a much fuller picture of the various translations of *Utopia* that circulated in China and indicates that while More's ideal society may have had less influence there than it did in Japan, it was nevertheless a well-known text. But like Hsia and Sawada, Liu's work thus far has had less to say on the historical context in which each translation appeared. Meanwhile, a speculative online piece by Eisel Mazard (2015) has pointed to the possible influence of More's *Utopia* on Mao, which he suggests the Great Helmsman may have encountered via Japanese anarchists. We now know a great deal more about how More's little book made its way into China. But the question of why each edition appeared is less clear. Given just how highly politicized the field of literary production was in both Republican and Maoist eras, this is a question worth asking.

This chapter builds on existing work by seeing utopian thought as a product of a new temporal relationship in China between past, present, and future. But in contrast to Liu, I focus less on the mechanics of translation, and more on showing how *Utopia*'s Chinese career might be mapped on to the transformation of the Qing domain first into a republic, then into a socialist state, and latterly into a post-Maoist mixed economy. I argue that *Utopia*, in the hands of Chinese interlocutors, has proven to be a malleable text. Whether through deliberate ambiguity or careful design it has been used as a way to critique or uphold China's rulers. Emphasizing especially the 1935 and the much less-explored 1956 translations, I make the case for reading *Utopia* as a product of particular moments in Chinese history. The 1935 edition, published in cosmopolitan Shanghai at the height of the Republic of China's Nationalist state-building, provided both a coded critique of authoritarianism and hints of admiration for a highly regulated and militarized society. The 1956 edition, meanwhile, can be seen as part of a propagandistic push to back collectivization in the countryside. Unlike in Japan, the text never served as a programmatic design for a new society, but its contemporary resonances would have been hard to miss for readers of each edition.

Utopia as a Concept

Westerners in China, who had reduced the empire to a semi-colony over the middle of the nineteenth century, were aware of More's work, and related it to their surroundings. In 1895 the Nanking Missionary Association heard the Revd J. C. Ferguson compare the Confucian classic *The Great Learning*, the 'Ideal Commonwealth' in Plato's *Republic*, and More's *Utopia*. Ferguson saw similarities between the three. In *The Great Learning*, which was written after Confucius' death by his students, Ferguson found much to praise, including its 'attention to the welfare of the people' and (in contrast to Plato's *Republic*) its exaltation of the family ahead of the state. But Ferguson saw More as 'more practical' than either of the two ancient texts, and while China was moving away from its Confucian past, England was moving towards eradicating the evils More documented. Ferguson, however, did not think More provided a guide to future action in either country, for 'the coming commonwealth would provide for the welfare of all by education [...] and by compulsory co-operation of capital and labor' (*North China Herald* 1895 [19 Apr.]: 58). More's work reappeared as Westerners tried to make sense of the anti-imperialist Boxer revolt in 1900. Noting that much in *Utopia* had since become true, the Revd F. L. Hawks Pott wondered whether utopian dreams in China too 'would in time, by the power of the new ideas and the new principles, be realised' (*North China Herald* 1900 [12 Dec.]: 1246–1247). Pott's utopia, though, was a China Christianized by missionary effort. Unlike Ferguson, he left little room for a utopia inspired by Chinese cosmology or political thought. By 1919, the *North China Herald*—China's main English-language newspaper—was calling More's *Utopia* 'that much talked-of, little read book' (1919 [27 Dec.]: 816).

Over the preceding decades, though, utopia as a concept had made its way into East Asian thought via a different route. It reached Japan first where More's work was embraced by social reformers as a blueprint for government-sponsored social engineering. Both China and Japan had been compelled to enter into commercial relations with Western powers in the middle of the nineteenth century. But whereas in China this process had been accelerated by a series of military defeats, which forced the Qing to surrender aspects of its territorial and economic sovereignty, Japan had embarked in 1868 on a rapid and highly successful programme of state-led modernization: the Meiji Restoration. Meiji reformers encouraged engagement with Western learning, and as Japan began to change, writers began to imagine a multitude of possible futures: Alfred Aldridge (1985) has counted twenty translations of utopian novels into Japanese in the 1890s.

In part, the vogue for utopian fiction probably came directly out of the popularity of More's work. *Utopia* itself was published in Japanese in the early 1880s and became one of the most influential texts of the period. Discussion of the book in Japan, though, can be traced back to 1874, and continued for the best part of fifty years (Ho 1991: 202). Over that half-century, *Utopia* tended to be used as a political manifesto in a manner that stripped it of its humanist context (Moichi 1999: 91). The prescriptive aims are evident in the work of translator Inoue Tsutomu (1850–1928), who published the earliest version under the title *A Tale of Good Government* (More 1882) and saw More's ideas as a way to push for social reforms. His second edition was retitled with the even more programmatic *On How to Organize a Good Government*. Later translations (by Tamikichi Ogiwara, 1894, and Masatake Mikami, 1914)—the former of which was named *The Ideal State*—were closer to the original (even if they omitted some sections and changed others), but they still lauded More's island 'as a paradigm for emulation'. The 1914 edition popularized the term utopia in Japanese and ensured More's tome was familiar to 'to nearly all the Japanese readers of Western literature' (Ho 1991: 213–214). Though More's *Utopia*, unlike many foreign works, did not enter China via a Japanese translation, the concept of utopia—and awareness of the text—may have come from Chinese interaction with their East Asian neighbour in the late nineteenth century. Chinese intellectuals often spent time in Japan as students or exiles—sometimes with sponsorship from Chinese authorities—and Inoue, who was also an avid translator of science fiction writers such as Jules Verne, was well known among the Chinese literati (Yan 2014: 142–143).

But the concept of utopia did not translate easily into Chinese. One of the first definitions of the term appeared in an English–Chinese dictionary by the German linguist and missionary Wilhelm Lobscheid in the late 1860s. In his multi-volume work, Lobscheid endeavoured to 'introduce a great number of words' that were 'previously unknown' to China as part of his design for the 'diffusion of general knowledge and the promotion of civilisation' (Tsz 2017). Lobscheid's work was unparalleled at the time: the dictionary encompassed 50,000 English terms, including keywords of the Western political lexicon like 'democracy', 'liberty', and 'Parliament', concepts that were unknown to China at the time. Utopia was among these Chinese neologisms, but was defined entirely in the idiom of traditional Chinese thought as a 'fabled island of immortals [*penglai*]', and 'a place of blissful happiness [*anleguo*]' (Lobscheid 1869: 1903). The pattern of mapping utopia onto existing Chinese concepts would recur over the following years among native writers too.

This particular definition of utopia owed something to Confucian and Buddhist understandings of temporality. Time in Chinese culture was perceived as cyclical rather than progressive: the passage of the years was more likely to lead to decay than development. Therefore, the ideal society in Confucian tradition lay in the past; the duty of those in the present lay in emulating precedent rather than working towards an unrealized future (Fokkema 2011: 24). Emperors who failed to live up to age-old prescriptions would lose the mandate of heaven and see their dynasties collapse. To break with the past was to invite disaster. Utopian Chinese fiction, if it could be styled as such, thus celebrated paradises that might be regained. Scholars have tended to single out *The Peach Blossom Spring* (421 BCE) as the best example: a classic of Chinese literature written during the political tumult of the Six Dynasties period that 'describes a simple, idyllic, and rustic way of life' (Fokkema 2011: 24; Ho 1983–6: 29). Nostalgia for a lost past, rather than a yearning for something new, marked the genre. The idea of the future 'as an open horizon'—a future that could escape the prison of the past—was therefore hard to imagine for those raised as good Confucians (Hammer 2011: 54). Buddhism, with its emphasis on rebirth and the next life, offered another way to think about an ideal society that was yet to be, so it is no surprise that early translators ransacked that faith's vocabulary to imbue utopia with Chinese meaning (Yan 2014: 143). Indeed, in 1903, the late imperial reformer Liang Qichao mentioned More's work in a letter to his counterpart Kang Youwei, but continued to use the Buddhist term *huayanjie* as an approximation of the concept (143). And even as late as 1913 the Buddhist connotation of utopia remained, according to a prominent dictionary, a 'place of blissful happiness' (143). The other place lay in cosmology rather than state and society.

Yet the imperial crisis of the late nineteenth century led to the emergence of a new temporality that made secular utopian thought possible. From the 1880s, the Qing suffered a series of military defeats: first to the French in 1885 and then to the Japanese in 1895. These reversals not only led to the loss of the tribute nations of Vietnam and Korea, but also opened China to further imperial encroachment. China's vulnerability triggered a territorial scramble among Western powers who carved out spheres of influence. The looming prospect of partition and dynastic demise led China's intellectual elite to challenge Confucian tradition (Rankin 2008). For them, humiliating defeats suggested that the likes of 'self-strengthening' reforms, which from 1860 had borrowed Western technology without threatening China's traditional culture, were no longer adequate. Many radical reformers began to question existing orthodoxies, first and foremost among those being reverence for the past. Such desire to save the empire inspired creative interpretations of Confucianism from figures like the late imperial reformer Kang: a man who, as we have seen, was well aware of More's work. In the 1890s Kang argued that Confucius had been misread, and insisted the ancient sage was really a progressive thinker (Zarrow 2012: 48–53). Kang's ambition, as Douwe Fokkema points out, was to 'break with the fatalism that resulted from the concept of history as a more or less cyclical movement of growth and decline' (Fokkema 2011: 276). For Kang, a new orthodoxy could underpin a Confucian modernism, which would legitimate change while still paying homage to the old authorities.

The new critical relationship with the past helps to explain the popularity of science fiction and other future-oriented genres in China around the turn of the century. Edward Bellamy's *Looking Backwards*, an 1888 bestseller in the United States, was also a huge hit in East Asia. In China, Bellamy's story was translated and serialized over the course of 1891–2 (Geng 2010: 406; Jiang 2013: 116). Its popularity led to its republication only two years later, and it remained influential into the 1930s, when it was mentioned in the preface to the first Chinese edition of More's *Utopia*. *Looking Backwards* is a quintessential work of modern utopian fiction. It follows a man who wakes up after a hundred years and finds himself in a highly industrialized socialist society in which the corruption and excesses of capitalism in Gilded Age America have been eradicated. The significance of the likes of Bellamy's work, David D. W. Wang has argued, lay in the way they introduced the 'future perfect mode of narrative' to China: a mode that allows authors to imagine 'not what *may* happen in the years to come but with what *will have* happened' (Wang 1998: 310). In doing so, *Looking Backwards* and other science fiction works opened up a 'new horizon for thinking out time and its possibilities' (312). Novels by Chinese authors at the turn of the century, such as Liang Qichao's *The Future of New China* (*Xin Zhongguo weilai ji*) (1902), have a similar temporal outlook (Wang 1998: 309). Some of these utopian works bear resemblance to More. Chen Tianhua's 1905 novel *Roar of the Lion*, for instance, is set on an island in which disciplined residents are trained in martial arts and adopt Western practices (Q. Wu 1995: 11). And though Kang's political treatise *The Book of Great Unity* or *The Book of the Commonweal* (*Datong*

Shu), which was written in the early 1900s, continued to use Buddhist terms to describe his ideal society, the author had come to conceive of time, Wang suggests, in decidedly modern terms 'as a unilinear process of development towards the future' (Wang 1998: 319; cf. Zarrow 2012: 47).

Hints of this new temporal mode are in the works of the eminent translator Yan Fu who gave utopia a lasting Chinese name. Yan was a prolific translator of Western political theory: he rendered John Stuart Mill's 1859 *On Liberty*, Montesquieu's 1750 *Spirit of the Laws*, and Adam Smith's 1776 *Wealth of Nations* into Chinese. As an intellectual familiar with Inoue in Japan, he was the first to introduce More's *Utopia* to the Chinese reading public in his translation of Thomas Huxley's 1893 *Evolution and Ethics*, which Yan published over the course of 1896–8. Scholars who have studied Yan's translation style have pointed out that his work often strayed from the spirit of the original text due to his preference for a classical Chinese writing style, his tendency to paraphrase, and his desire to influence how new ideas were received. He, like others at the time, did not shy away from borrowing from Chinese cosmology and classical literature to render concepts intelligible for a native audience (Huang 2003: 28, 31–33). Yet in introducing *Utopia* to China, Yan did not fall back on the classical imagery found in Lobscheid's dictionary. Instead, he chose to transliterate the word 'Utopia' into the Chinese: *wutuobang*. As Yi-Chun Liu has pointed out, this transliteration was far from haphazard. Yan sought to embody the concept of utopia in the word itself. The first character, *wu*, denotes 'darkness', but also evokes a sense of the 'unreal and nonexistence'. *Tuo*, meanwhile, means 'to entrust something [...] to another'. The third character, *bang*, 'designates a country or a place' (Liu 2016: 335). To elucidate the meaning, Yan wrote that 'utopia' means 'no such country, only exists in the mind'. The idealistic and illusory quality of utopia is evident (Yan 2014: 143; Liu 2016: 336). In short Yan's neologism, or this act of transliteration, was revolutionary in its attempt at indigenizing a future-oriented concept without reference to either a Confucian past or Buddhist paradise. It would be used in all the subsequent Chinese translations of More's book.

1935 Version

Although the first translation of *Utopia* itself did not take place until 1935, More's work had been discussed in some depth in Chinese sources before then. The fall of the Qing dynasty in 1911 led to the establishment of the Republic of China. Instability plagued the new state, and despite nationalist demands for a strong central authority, China divided into the rival fiefdoms of colonial powers and military strongmen. Recent interpretations of the 'warlord era' (*c*.1911–27), however, have emphasized the cultural and political innovations of the period. In 1919, anger at the failure of the victorious powers in the First World War to reward China for its contribution to the war effort sparked a wave of student protests, which became known as the May Fourth Movement. May Fourth intellectuals intensified the attacks on Confucianism and other manifestations of feudal culture that had begun to appear in the late Qing. Unlike Kang, who had tried to advocate reform within the confines of Chinese tradition, they rejected it entirely. While anti-colonial in their aspirations, the new generation of iconoclastic and politically active Chinese embraced ideas that had entered China from the West. Liberalism, democracy, and nationalism flourished alongside Bolshevik-inspired socialism and anarchism.

In this radical milieu More's *Utopia* began to attract attention. One 1928 work on the history of socialism by the leftist author and translator of Marx and Engels Wu Luping began its study of the early modern world with the text, and read Henry VIII's Chancellor in a tradition that extended forward to Gracchus Babeuf (1760–97), Henri de Saint-Simon (1760–1825), and Charles Fourier (1772–1837). Much in the manner of Marx and Engels, Wu read the Utopians as precursors to the scientific socialism of the modern world, and situated *Utopia* itself in struggles over the transition from feudalism to capitalism in England: a line that the later Maoist translation would echo. Wu's study provided a lengthy synopsis of More's work, which included translated excerpts from the book. Here he cast *Utopia* as a manifesto for a 'communistic society', and lauded the author as a genius (Wu L. 1930: 69, 59).

Wu published with a minor press, and his socialist sympathies would later see him arrested by the authorities, but such works on Western political theory intrigued a growing reading public. Shanghai, where *Utopia* was first translated into Chinese just five years after Wu's study, stood at the centre of republican intellectual culture; in the 1920s eclectic ideas circulated freely in its streets and cafés. Shanghai's cultural centrality is not surprising: it had grown rapidly after the Opium Wars of the mid-nineteenth century had seen large parts of the city ceded to foreign powers. The 'Paris of the East', as it became known, was a site of both colonial domination and resistance, characterized by hybridity and exchange. In 1921, for instance, the Chinese Communist Party held its first meeting in the heart of the French-ruled quarter. Unlike old imperial capitals like Beijing or Nanjing, Shanghai was first and foremost a place of capitalism and commerce, with its space organized according to the needs of trade. The city became a major publishing hub.

Publishing, however, was not purely a route to make money in Shanghai. Intellectuals in the trade from the late nineteenth century onwards saw themselves as circulators of ideas that would enlighten their readers and aid in the work of national construction (J. Li 2007: 143; Reed 2004: 205). Inspired by May Fourth protests, proponents of the New Library Movement set out to raise literacy levels by setting up public reading rooms. Knowledge, they believed, should no longer be monopolized by the Confucian-scholar gentry, but opened up to the masses (Liao 2009). From 1925 to the outbreak of the Sino-Japanese War in 1937 there was an increasing emphasis on access to education, which members of the ascendant Nationalist Party saw as a precondition for raising the political (and with it the patriotic) awareness of the people.

The combination of politics and print capitalism is evident in the work of the publishing house that produced the translation of More's text: Shanghai's powerful Commercial Press. Founded in 1897, the press published thousands of titles, many of which were translations of foreign works. Given the competitive nature of the industry, the press's leadership had to be business-savvy, and from the late 1920s onwards they produced cheap and accessible editions for mass readership (Reed 2004: 203). Their various series—Encyclopedic Books, World Literary Classics, and Chinese Translations of World Classics—included works by Homer, Jean-Jacques Rousseau, Carl von Clausewitz, Charles Darwin, Immanuel Kant, and Bertrand Russell. The output was eclectic, ranging from histories of Frederick the Great to work on child psychology, and included around 3,800 translated books—about a quarter of their total list (J. Li 2007: 42, 148). The press worked with well-known translators. Yan Fu, who transliterated 'utopia' into Chinese, was among the authors to publish with them in the early twentieth century. There was no doubt money to be made here, but the publisher embraced the ethos that public enlightenment offered a higher purpose than the mere pursuit of profit (J. Li 2007: 146–148). One influential figure at the press, Hu Shi—a prominent May Fourth intellectual, and a student of the American pragmatist John Dewey—helped to establish a compilation and translation office for the publishing house in 1920. Hu, like other revolutionaries and reformers at the time, wanted to vernacularize Chinese literature, an aim the Commercial Press's chair Wang Yunwu pursued with vigour (J. Li 2007: 41–42).

More's *Utopia* appeared in 1935 as part of the press's Chinese Translations of World Classics Series. The translator was Liu Lingsheng. Born in 1894, Liu studied at St John's University in Shanghai. Despite his time at an Anglican College, he may well have been familiar with Jesuit missionaries who played an active role in Chinese education in the period, and by 1927 he had acquired a position as a professor of literature at Jinlin Women's College in Nanjing, while also working with the Commercial Press. Eisel Mazard indicates that Liu worked from Japanese translations—a common way for Western texts to enter China—but Liu himself lists a series of English editions, including a 1910 edition from Everyman's Library (a popular series in China that the Commercial Press had in its library), as his sources (Mazard 2015; Gamsa 2011: 568). It is likely, though, that Liu would have at least been aware of Japanese versions too. In keeping with the practice of the Commercial Press, Liu's *Utopia* was pitched to a mass market. It is written in an accessible vernacular Chinese, cuts out entire sections such as More's opening greeting to Peter Giles, and focuses heavily on Books One and Two (rather than the paratext). Classical and Latin references are often omitted, and annotations guide the unfamiliar reader through the historical context, including the unsavoury habits of Henry VIII. The work would have been readable for a growing literate public.

Liu appears to have been in good standing with China's ruling authorities, though like any author at the time, he had to take care when venturing into political commentary. In 1927, Chiang Kai-shek's Northern Expedition had brought most of China under the control of the Chinese Nationalist Party (Guomindang or the GMD). Liu would remain loyal to the party, moving with the government to Sichuan when war with Japan broke out in 1937, and then joining it in exile on Taiwan when Mao's Communists triumphed in 1949. But the Nationalists were a fragmented organization and satisfying the various factions could prove tricky. The party's founder, Sun Yat-Sen, had envisaged a united, democratic, and socialist China, but he had rejected class struggle as a means to move towards that utopian future. Both Nationalists and Communists claimed to be the true heirs of Sun's vision, but Chiang, fresh from his military success, had turned on Mao's party in the late 1920s, murdered thousands of leftists, and chased the remnants into remote corners of the republic. Despite the socialist purge, leftists who clung to Sun's egalitarianism remained in the increasingly authoritarian GMD, though they vied for influence with factions that sought to emulate aspects of European fascism. Those rightist elements hoped to build a tightly regulated society bound together by the ethnic affinity of Han identity and a centralized party state, and were willing to rejuvenate Confucianism to instil respect for the nation. Yet almost all Chinese Nationalists saw their party as a vanguard leading China from its peasant past to a powerful future, even if the precise form modernization would take remained up for debate. And any intellectual who veered too close to a Bolshevik line risked being censored or worse.

Liu's preface, though hinting more than once at his own leftist sympathies, is marked by what was probably carefully calibrated ambiguity. More's wit is acknowledged, but Liu does not imply that *Utopia* is a satire, even as he argues it was a 'forerunner' to Jonathan Swift's *Gulliver's Travels* (More 1935a: 12). 'The sense of irony and humor', Mazard argues, 'disappeared entirely in the Chinese translations' (Mazard 2015; Hsia 1981: 107). The preface begins with a brief biography of More, before Liu moves to situate *Utopia* in a longer history that stretches back to Plato's *Republic*, moves forward through Augustine's *City of God*, and progresses through James Harrington's mid-seventeenth-century *Oceania* and early modern political theory to the utopian socialism of Babeuf and post-French Revolutionary thinkers. More is historically contextualized in Renaissance humanism but his ideas are also treated as transcendent. He is a man for all epochs (More 1935a: 7).

Perhaps aware of the risks involved of venturing too close to domestic politics, Liu does not attempt to locate More's ideas in Chinese tradition. Occasionally, he uses terms borrowed from Chinese philosophy, as when he critiques Utopians' belief that humanity is 'naturally born good' (More 1935a: 9). But More is situated instead entirely within the development of Western political theory and no direct attempt is made to compare or contrast him to East Asian figures. More could have easily been fitted into two recurring tropes of Chinese Confucian tradition: the sage adviser to the emperor (of whom the negative counterpart was the bad eunuch) and the prescriptive planner who set down rules for how to organize a harmonious society. The best known of the latter was, of course, Confucius himself, but others had established prescriptions for planning capital cities, for instance, that were largely followed into the Qing dynasty. While the republic abandoned the reverence for Confucian precedent, the GMD embraced modernist state planning, especially in the 1930s. Thus, while Liu did not relate More to any Chinese figures, he probably did not need to. The parallels would have been clear.

But Liu does not see More simply as a figure from the past to revere. He does say that much can be learned from *Utopia*. But his emphasis is on 'progress', a word that recurs in the preface, and indicates once more the temporal framing of utopian thought in China. Like earlier Chinese thinkers who had grappled with Bellamy (whom Liu mentions in his preface) the commentary is future-orientated. Liu is interested in More's vision of the society to come rather than seeking to emulate what once was. The translator, indeed, divides society up into three kinds of people. The first (and he surely has Confucians in mind here) revere the past. The second kind are content with the present. And the third kind are the utopian thinkers who imagine new futures. Liu clearly respected the last. Those that 'ridiculed' them, he argues, 'are spineless people'. The utopians may be small in number, 'but they all possess the determination to reform, the ardent ambition, the knowledge to innovate'. Above all they 'have the understanding of foresight', and 'society's progress is largely reliant' on their 'imaginaries' (More 1935a: 8–9). Liu was more critical of their method, which emphasized ethical reflection rather than a belief in a need to 'compete and fight': mobilization after all was central to both Nationalist and Communist projects (9). Yet Liu argued that utopian thinking, when allied to science and struggle, could help society to move towards a better future state, and augment 'the possibility of progress in political and social enterprises' (6). Utopianism 'is worthy of esteem and admiration' for practical reasons, he argues (7). Thus, we should learn from a centuries-old text not to replicate the past, but move to a new future.

With that vision of the future, Liu carefully navigated between different wings of the party while emphasizing the progressive possibilities of utopianism. The socialist elements to utopian thought are freely acknowledged, but unlike the later Chinese Communist translation, Liu distinguishes that brand of utopian thought from More's. He notes sympathetically liberal tendencies in More's society: the election of the Utopians' governor and the freedom of religion on the island (More 1935a: 11). And he sees these as prescient given the course European society would take over the following centuries: More for him is a precursor to Enlightenment thought as well as a prophet of scientific socialism (9). At points, though, he implicitly criticizes the lack of respect for individualism in More's ideal state (9, 10). Here, Liu may have been encoding critiques of the increasingly authoritarian and inegalitarian Nationalist regime in China. Nicola Spakowski has perceptively argued of the 1930s that discussion of utopias and utopian socialism was a way of 'criticising the regime without putting oneself at risk' (Spakowski 2019: 96). As an imaginary place, a utopia could be discussed critically in a way that the writer's own place could not be. More's elision of class conflict—which Marxist writers saw as a blind spot in his work—almost certainly made his *Utopia* more palatable to Chinese Nationalists and liberal intellectuals alike.

Furthermore, More's vision of a tightly disciplined society, which is less prominent in Liu's preface, echoes a more conservative strand of Guomindang thought. As war with Japan approached, Nationalist leaders sought to place society on a militarized footing. They aimed to 'spiritually mobilize' citizens, transforming the Chinese into a highly disciplined people who would rally to rescue the nation they loved while remaining immune from the corrupting allure of the Chinese Communists. For some, this led to an embrace of neo-Confucianism, which emphasized respect for authority. In 1934, the GMD had launched the New Life Movement, a mass campaign which, Arlif Dirlik and Brian Tsui have shown, tried to reform everyday behaviours like spitting, queue-jumping, and frivolous expenditure (Dirlik 1975; Tsui 2018: chs 1, 3). Internal self-discipline would manifest itself in service to the state, while the external imposition of rules would remake the individual. Some scholars have seen New Life as a manifestation of a Confucian fascism (Wakeman 1997).

Elements of New Life thought do creep into Liu's preface and the translation. Henry VIII is portrayed (perhaps not unfairly) as a lavish and wasteful king (More 1935a: 15). The highly regimented society of the Utopians, with its puritanical discipline, bore more than a passing resemblance to the Guomindang ideal in which individual cultivation and communal strength went hand in hand. Liu picks up on the way the Utopians subordinate the 'clan' to the higher interests of the 'nation' (11). Nationalists would surely have seen parallels here in their own project to transform into national citizens the 'unawakened' Chinese masses mired in the localism of kin and village.

Liu's *Utopia* could therefore be read as an endorsement of New Life-era civic discipline or as a thinly coded critique of a GMD that had strayed from the path of Sun's own utopian design. One suspects, if only from the emphasis given to the socialist and liberal elements of More's work, that Liu was more sympathetic to the latter, but the way the book was received by his contemporaries is unfortunately hard to trace. War with Japan two years after *Utopia*'s Chinese publication disrupted the Nationalists' state-building project and interrupted Shanghai's growth as a cosmopolitan intellectual centre. Yet the book was evidently popular enough to warrant a reprint in 1944, along with the wider series in which it had been published, despite the conflict in China still raging. By then, Japan was on the retreat across Asia and the Pacific, and within Nationalist and intellectual circles attention turned once more to future planning: How would Chinese society be reconstructed? What place would democracy and a written Constitution have in a new order? What role should the state play in economic life? Coupled with renewed interest in Western politics—alliance with the USA and Britain had seen Chinese planners discuss the relevance to their nation of the Beveridge Plan and New Deal—it is possible that republication reflected a wider interest in imagining a post-war future (Ma 2014). That post-war future, however, would not belong to Chinese Nationalists like Liu. Instead, the heirs would be Mao's Communists.

1956 Version

Although Mao's brand of Communism would come to embrace utopian themes, the early days of the People's Republic of China (PRC) were not noted for their utopian fiction. The Communist Party from 1949 onwards, Quingyun Wu notes, emphasized scientific socialism rather than 'bourgeois fantasies' (Q. Wu 1995: 11). Yet *Utopia* itself reappeared in a new translation in 1956 that blurred the boundaries between More's vision and Mao's. Much like the 1935 edition, some conjecture and context are required to make sense of the 1956 translation, but it seems highly likely that *Utopia* was enlisted as an ideological prop in the work of socialist transformation.

Utopia's Maoist translation was a product of the Sino-Soviet alliance that flourished in the early to mid-1950s before collapsing spectacularly towards the end of the decade. Friendship with the Soviet Union not only brought economic aid and technical advice, but also drew China into a series of cultural and intellectual exchanges with its socialist elder sibling. In the early years of the alliance students, artists, and writers moved across the borders of the Communist bloc, carrying with them new ideas and practices. Ideologically correct Soviet literature began to displace the decadent bourgeois romances of Republican-era China (He 2011: 397–398). Socialist realism now mingled with a brand of science fiction designed to stimulate youthful enthusiasm for industrial development (Jiang 2013: 120). In part, here publishers met the demand to learn from the USSR, but these translated works also provided a reliable source of income and helped booksellers to steer clear of troubles with the censors (Volland 2008: 62).

The process of translation, meanwhile, was centralized under the PRC. Translators, who in the early twentieth century had been amateurs who saw their work as one aspect of a wider intellectual calling, had professionalized in the 1930s, and after 1949 were organized—like many professions—into a single association for easier control and mobilization (Volland 2014: 141). From 1952 onwards, the National Compilation and Translation Bureau of the General Publication Administration became much more active in coordinating and standardizing work across the country, setting out titles to be published by various publishing houses (Volland 2014: 144–145). This coincided with the move to centralize the publishing industry by 1956, which was designed to whittle down the market and 'strategically direct' the reading public to select officially endorsed titles (He 2011: 400). As a result, translators were reduced to the role of 'translation workers' with very little autonomy (Volland 2014: 144–145).

Sanlian Shudian, the publisher of the 1956 edition, was a major producer of translated works in the early days of the PRC. The press typically listed over a hundred new books a year and was closely tied to Renmin Shuju (the People's Press), the 'publishing arm of the Party-state' (Volland 2014: 143). Sanlian Shudian produced a varied output, with essays on planning by the Commission on the Compilation of Chinese Economic Writing (1951) sitting alongside a *New Songbook* (1951) by the Music Office of the Central Theatre Research Department. Alongside such state-sanctioned work, the press published literary and theoretical works by Russian authors. Although the majority of its translated work came from the Soviet world, a handful of books were taken from English or German sources. These too were diverse to say the least, though generally reflected the author's affinity for—or significance to—Marxist analysis. Titles here included the victim of McCarthyism Philip Foner's *History of the American Labor Movement* (1947), Rodney Hilton's study of the Peasants' Revolt (*Bond Men Made Free*, 1973), and G. W. F. Hegel's theory of history. Only the occasional outlier like a biography of Benjamin Franklin stood clearly outside the socialist camp, although the bureau's interest here may have sprung from the attention Marx paid to the American printer in *A Contribution to a Critique of Political Economy*. More's *Utopia* was therefore not chosen accidentally: it was selected for its capacity to shed light on socialism. Moreover, though the 1956 edition used Ralph Robinson's English translation, the translator used the 1953 Russian edition published by the Soviet Academy of Sciences (USSR Akademii Nauk) for reference, and appears to have lifted the preface entirely from that Soviet-era text.[2]

The second translation into Chinese took place against the backdrop of momentous changes on the land. In the summer of 1955, Mao told the party conference of his plans for the 'Cooperative Transformation of Agriculture'. His speech inaugurated what became known as the 'socialist high tide', which led to the collectivization of most farms within a year. Gradual collectivization had been underway since 1953, but with the Great Helmsman frustrated at the modest pace of growth, and fearful that his plans for the rapid modernization of China were under threat, he pushed for an acceleration of the programme. Peasant farmers, who just years before had become small proprietors thanks to the Communists' early land reform, were encouraged to form mutual aid societies and pool their labour and resources (Selden 1993: 82–84, 91–94). Initially, the process moved slowly, and in the summer of 1955 only 14 per cent of Chinese households lived in small-scale cooperatives. By the end of 1956, however, 88 per cent of farming households had been reorganized into large-scale Soviet style collective farms that encompassed multiple villages (Selden 1993: 98; Yang 1996: 31). The collective farms differed in scale and type from the large-scale communes of the Great Leap Forward (1958–61). The former comprised on average 270 households, compared to over 7,000 for the latter (Yang 1996: 361). They lacked, too, the communal mess halls and crèches of their larger successors. Yet the collectivization campaign transformed the political economy of the countryside and set the path that the party would later follow with such catastrophic consequences. Already in 1955, indeed, Mao had projected the 'complete transformation' of Chinese farming from 'semi-socialist to fully socialist cooperatives' by the end of the decade (Zhongguo zhongyang bangongting 1957). While before, farmers had retained a modicum of economic independence in cooperative arrangements, now all property was to be held in common, and remuneration allocated on the basis of labour contributed. Labour itself was organized along militarized lines of brigades overseen by party cadre. Mao believed he had found a way to eliminate residual inequality: the bane of private property would finally disappear from rural society (Selden 1993: 84–85; Liu and Wang 2006: 729).

Utopia in its 1956 incarnation should be considered against the backdrop of this rural upheaval. Given the tight control over translation it seems highly likely that the release was deliberately designed to coincide with the 'socialist high tide'. In January, the People's Press—the parent publishing house to Sanlian Shudian—brought out *Socialist Upsurge in the China's Countryside*, a collection of essays with a preface by Mao, which were distributed to cadre in rural areas with a view to bringing an end to 'right conservatism' against the program (Zhongguo zhongyang bangongting 1956). Both translators and publishers understood the imperative for message discipline. Since mid-1954, the intellectual climate had encouraged conformity to the party line, and people were alert to the direction the political wind was blowing. Intellectual autonomy had been

---

[2] For the 1953 Russian edition, see Nethercott in this volume.

stymied by rectification campaigns and Mao's long-standing line that there was no such thing as art for art's sake made the propagandistic role of the writer explicit. Thought reform in the universities sought to strip foreign-trained academics of their bourgeois outlook and admiration for the West and remake deviant scholars into loyal followers of Marxist-Leninism (Walder 2015: 71–72). The attempt to bring intellectuals to heel climaxed in 1955 with a public and intense attack on the eminent writer Hu Feng, who had called for greater independence. Hu was a party member, an influential figure in the Chinese Writers' Union, and on the executive board of *People's Literature*, but found himself prosecuted and incarcerated for twenty years. The timing of the attack on Hu coincided with the socialist upsurge and sent a clear message to anyone who wished to spread a subversive message: 'He was used as a tool', Merle Goldman argues, 'in the campaign to bring the Party's collectivization of agriculture and nationalization of industry to fruition' (Goldman 1987: 241).

Utopia's translator, Dai Liuling, therefore had to tread carefully, especially as he carried the stigma of a Western education himself. Dai had taken an MA in English literature from Edinburgh in 1939 and specialized in the work of early modern authors. He translated Christopher Marlowe's Elizabethan drama *Dr Faustus*, for instance, in the same year as his *Utopia* (Zhang 2013: 44–45). Dai, however, showed his full commitment to the Communist cause. Like other writers at the time, he bowed to party pressure and in January 1955 penned an article in his university newspaper attacking a school of literary reform associated with one of the prominent targets of thought reform. And in the wake of the Anti-Rightist Movement of 1957, he joined nine other prominent literary professors in declaring their allegiance to Mao. Their article, 'We must plant the red flag of socialism on the teaching and research of Western languages', leaves little to the imagination. Dai and his peers accused some Chinese of still falling for the allure of the West and called for struggle within higher education to eradicate such sympathies (Feng et al. 1958: 253).

Dai's 1956 translation of *Utopia* was longer than Liu's 1935 edition, weighing in at 127 pages rather than 59. As a result, more of the original appears, with More's letter to Peter Giles now included, along with an appendix showing the author's correspondence with Erasmus. In part, this may be down to the publisher worrying more about politics than profits. Dai's rendering of the text is less accessible than its predecessor's but was never likely to reach a mass market. But the differences too may be down to the practices encouraged in the early Communist period. 'Direct translation'—as literal an adaptation of the text as possible—was seen as a way to overcome the supposed imprecision of Chinese itself (Volland 2009: 471). It seems probable too that a professional translator like Dai would have thought it safest to stick closely to the text, especially given that he had the ideologically sound Soviet version for reference. Footnotes generally provide historical context, though occasionally reflect on matters germane to the Marxist canon (More 1956: 160, 166–168). At points, the meaning of the English is subtly misrepresented in a manner that suits Maoist preoccupations. When it came to discussing how the islanders spent their free time, for instance, Utopians do not engage in 'some good science as shall please them', which was Robinson's wording (More 1895a:

143), but rather 'scientific research [*kexue yanjiu*]': a more fitting use of leisure during the first Five-Year Plan (More 1956: 67).

Indeed, though Dai translated the preface from the 1953 Soviet edition, the message the opening pages conveyed would have chimed with Mao's moves towards collectivization. *Reading Books Monthly*—a review magazine that ran from 1955 to 1960—certainly interpreted the work as ideologically attuned to the times. In 1956, it praised More's text as 'the earliest and one of the most important pieces of work on the development of socialism', and otherwise largely followed the preface (Song 1956: 17). That preface, much in the manner of Karl Kautsky, cast More as a communist visionary who had witnessed the dawn of capitalism in early modern England and apprehended its contradictions.[3] More's work is read as a critique of a process of primitive accumulation that displaced both the peasant and the handicraft worker (More 1956: 2, 6). On Utopia those contradictions are resolved and More is lauded as the representative of the oppressed masses. Both the preface and the reviewer express reservations: More is no scientific socialist, and fails to grasp the historical role of the proletariat and peasantry in bringing about socialism. For all his prescience, moreover, he cannot grasp the significance of productive forces in making a communist society possible (More 1956: 3, 9; Song 1956: 17). But on the whole he is welcomed into the socialist pantheon.

Readers would surely have had little difficulty in seeing More's *Utopia* in a Maoist vein. The language used in the preface to describe the aristocracy ('bloodsucking exploiters') echoed the class labelling of landlords in the Chinese countryside (More 1956: 4). When More is discussed in the preface as a perceptive and empathetic reader of rural social relations the parallels to Mao, whose 1926 *Report on the Peasant Movement in Hunan* similarly distilled the tendencies of village life, are implicit (More 1956: 14; Song 1956: 16). Both became visionaries whose manifestos for a future society are shaped by their acute understanding of the wrongs of the present one. Parallels abound too on the island of Utopia itself. Like collective farms, the Utopians have abolished private property, engage in voluntary but highly productive labour, and allocate resources from ability according to need (More 1956: 8). The combination of individual frugality and central command—which had appealed to the Nationalists a generation earlier—also made the work palatable to Chinese Communists (7). And the Utopians' monogamy would have been easy to read in light of the recent Marriage Law, which barred polygamy and gave women a right to divorce (Song 1956: 17).

Yet ultimately the ideal society did not lie in reorganizing kinship. 'It is not blood relations', the preface noted of Utopia, 'but economic unity that is the mark of a family' (More 1956: 8). Moreover, production is organized through individual towns rather than through the country as a whole, with the governing authorities then distributing the fruits of collective labour: a template that could easily be applied to the communes (7). Ma Lieying, in an appendix to the 1956 edition that largely recounted the history of translating *Utopia*, drew out the comparison more explicitly when he noted the

---

[3] For Kautsky, see Stewart and Moir in this volume.

'communal messes' on More's island (152). In such light, More could be seen as a prophet of the vast communes Mao was striving to establish. Mazard (2015) suggests that Mao may have drawn from More (perhaps via the interlocutors of Japanese anarchism) a desire to abolish money. But in 1956, at least, *Utopia* provided a prophecy of a society that in terms of its productive relations bore more than a passing resemblance to Mao's design for the land. The themes in More's work would later be echoed (without acknowledgement) in the Great Leap Forward. There, too, abundance, voluntarism, collective production and consumption would appear as Maoism embarked on its own utopian phase.

Utopia's Afterlives

Utopia's Chinese lives did not end in 1956. Dai's work was republished in 1982 in the PRC, and in 1997 in Taiwan, where it was denuded of its Marxist theorizing (Liu 2016: 334). A Taiwanese edition of 1966, sponsored by UNESCO and fronted by a preface translated from an earlier Japanese text, has also appeared (Hsia 1981: 107). More recent editions, according to Yi-Chun Liu, have also been published that are more faithful to the historical context. More's *Utopia*, meanwhile, continues to be reinterpreted to meet the needs of changing times. Scholarship in recent years has sometimes used a comparative lens viewing More in relation to works in the Chinese canon like *Peach Blossom Spring* (Liu 2016: 334). More continues to be read in a materialist vein—he was one of the 'petty bourgeoisie' who 'speaks for the toiling masses', scholars at Zhejiang University argued in 2016—but now he can be read as a visionary of socialism with Chinese characteristics. His Utopia is a 'wealthy public ownership society' which 'takes the road of common prosperity': it is a take on More that marries his apparent sympathies for communism with growth in the Reform Era (Fan and Qian 2016). In China, at least, More remains a man for all seasons. From anti-Confucian visionaries around the turn of the twentieth century through Republican era Nationalism and on to Maoist and post-Mao socialism, *Utopia* has provided a way to think about possible Chinese futures, though always in the context of the nation's present.

CHAPTER 29

UTOPIA AND UTOPIAN WRITING IN ARABIC

PETER HILL

This chapter will discuss the reception of Thomas More's *Utopia* in Arabic, and its interaction with other forms of writing we might describe as 'utopian'. The Arabic language of course possesses an old, rich literary culture, which contains many works predating More's *Utopia* which have since been compared to it, or described as 'utopian'. In particular, the tenth-century philosopher al-Farabi (d. 950/1) offered in his *al-Madina al-Fadila* ('The Virtuous City') a typology of ideal and non-ideal government strongly influenced, like More, by Plato.[1] *Hayy ibn Yaqzan* ('Alive, Son of Awake') by the twelfth-century writer Ibn Tufayl (d. 1185) is a philosophical tale of a man who grows up isolated from other humans on an island and teaches himself to reason. More generally, a vast and diverse body of 'mirrors for princes' literature, with antecedents in Sassanid and Indian traditions, offered precepts and models for good government.

More as Catholic Martyr

We will return later to these works and their interactions with More and other European utopian writers. But at the time of the original publication of, and European vogue for, More's *Utopia* in the sixteenth century and for three centuries thereafter, the links between Arabic literary culture and the European cultural ecumene—Renaissance Christendom and the world of the Enlightenment—were tenuous. In the year of *Utopia*'s first Latin publication, 1516, the Ottoman Empire conquered Syria; over the next two decades, it also came to control Egypt and the North African coast as far as Algiers. The Arabic-speaking lands of the Mediterranean were now under a Turkish-speaking

---

[1] Translations from Arabic are my own unless otherwise stated.

government: political contacts with Europe tended to pass through these channels. European merchants still flocked to cities like Aleppo and Cairo, and Christian pilgrims to the Holy Land, but they remained a relatively marginal element in a powerful and self-sufficient Ottoman Empire. Until the early nineteenth century, the major literary and translational links between Western European and Arabic culture were through the Catholic Church, which after the Council of Trent (1545–63) forged strong ties with Arabic-speaking Christians—not least as compensation for the lands lost to Protestantism (Heyberger 1994).

Accordingly, the first Arabic account of More passed through these channels, part of a wave of translations of classic works of Baroque Catholicism (Heyberger 1999). In the seventeenth century one of the Church's emissaries to Eastern Christians, Brice de Rennes, a French Capuchin missionary in Damascus, produced an abridged Arabic version of the classic Catholic Church history by Cardinal Cesare Baronio and others: the *Annales Ecclesiastici* (1588–1607). Brice's Arabic version of Bishop Henri de Sponde's continuation of this chronicle was printed by the Catholic missionary organization, the Congregation of Propaganda Fide in Rome, in 1671. Under the year 1535 it chronicles More's execution among the other iniquities committed by the heretic king of England, Henry VIII. More is described as 'master of the entire law [*shari'a*]', 'the second in the kingdom after the king, his name famous among all kings for his virtues and courage in affirming the truth and the righteous Christian law [*al-namus al-mustaqim al-masihi*]' (Sponde 1671: 3.830). But there is no mention of More's *Utopia*: there are a few references in the Latin *Annales*, but these do not make it into the Arabic abridgement.

Other Church historical works which mention More in a similar light were translated into Arabic, in manuscript at least, later: Cardinal Orsi's *Istoria ecclesiastica* in 1792, and Alfonso de Liguori's *Storia delle eresie* in 1852 (see Graf 1944: 3.235, 247, 491). The More encountered by Arabic-speaking clergy and educated laymen, from the seventeenth century into the nineteenth, was thus a man of distinction and learning and a Catholic martyr, but not the author of *Utopia*. This seems to have been the main image of More available in Arabic until very late in the nineteenth century.

Utopian Writing in the Arab Nahda

Before considering the very different version of More that was presented at that time, we should look at some important related developments that took place over the course of the nineteenth century. This was a period in which the Ottoman Empire, including its Arabic-speaking provinces, came increasingly under the influence of a rapidly changing Europe. This entailed both extension and centralization of the Ottoman state, increasing dominance by European commercial and financial interests, and European military expeditions, leading in some cases to imperial annexation (as with the French occupation of Algiers in 1830, and the British of Egypt in 1882). One aspect of this process was the emergence of an Arabic literary and cultural 'revival' (the Nahda), with multiplying intellectual contacts with both Europe and other lands, and the spread of printing and cultural societies. I will focus here on three related trends: the translation into Arabic of European works of 'utopian' literature and science fiction; the rediscovery of older Arabic 'utopian' writings; and the emergence of a new Arabic tradition of utopian and science fiction writing.

Many of the first and most enduringly popular works of European literature translated into Arabic in the nineteenth century were French and English didactic novels of the seventeenth and eighteenth centuries. These often had a strong utopian component: they had been written in an Enlightenment Europe which was familiar with both More's *Utopia* and at least one of the older Arabic works, *Hayy ibn Yaqzan*, translated into Latin by Edward Pococke as *Philosophus Autodidactus* in 1671 and into English, by George Keith, three years later. Proto-novels like François Fénelon's *Les Aventures de Télémaque* (1699), Daniel Defoe's *Robinson Crusoe* (1719), and Bernardin de Saint-Pierre's *Paul et Virginie* (1788), were popular on a European and often a global scale, and had a number of different incarnations in Arabic (P. Hill 2019). These began in the 1810s, when a small circle of Greek Orthodox Christian translators in the Egyptian port of Damietta began to chip away at the monopoly then held by the Catholic Church on translational traffic from Western European languages into Arabic. Along with other Enlightenment works, they translated *Télémaque*, François Fénelon's narrative of the education of Ulysses' son Telemachus, who under the guidance of his tutor Mentor encounters a number of societies around the Mediterranean which express different social and political principles. The Damietta circle also translated Jean-François Marmontel's deistical didactic novel *Bélisaire* (1767), based on the life of a Byzantine general (P. Hill 2015b).

The trend continued as new Arabic printing presses emerged outside the Lebanese monasteries and the Propaganda Fide of Rome, which had largely confined their output to devotional works. *Robinson Crusoe* was printed in Arabic by Protestant missionaries in 1835 and again in 1861, and *Télémaque* in a rhyming translation by the Egyptian educator al-Tahtawi, in a privately run Arabic newspaper (P. Hill 2015a). Successive versions of both *Télémaque* and *Paul et Virginie*, Bernardin de Saint-Pierre's romantic idyll of a virtuous natural life set on the island of Mauritius, followed in a rapidly expanding Arabic press and also in the theatre, over the later decades of the century (P. Hill 2018). They were also joined by Arabic translations of more recent European literature, including Jules Verne's science fiction, starting with his 1863 novel *Cinq semaines en ballon* in 1875 (Holt 2009); and an account of a decadent age coming to a violent end in Bulwer Lytton's 1834 *The Last Days of Pompeii*, on the eve of the twentieth century, in 1899.

Many of the same literati who were translating European texts were also rediscovering and publishing older Arabic ones. These included some from the 'mirrors for princes' tradition, like the fourteenth-century North African king Abu Hammu's *Wasitat al-suluk* ('Mediation of Conduct') published in 1862; Ibn Khaldun's famous *Muqaddima* (1867); *Hayy ibn Yaqzan* (1882); al-Ma'arri's *Risalat al-ghufran* ('Epistle of Forgiveness', 1903), in which the eleventh-century poet conducts dialogues with dead figures from Islamic history; and al-Farabi's *Virtuous City* (1906). Some tales, especially the more vernacular ones, had never lost their popularity in a manuscript and oral tradition but were now printed, like the eighth-century Ibn al-Muqaffa''s version of the animal fables of *Kalila and Dimna* (printed in 1834). Arab writers noted the similarities between these and the European translated works: *Télémaque* was compared by its translator al-Tahtawi and others to *Kalila and Dimna* and other mirrors for princes (P. Hill 2018). This notion of comparability or even equivalence between Arabic and European utopian works would be important later for the reception of More.

The third trend consisted of a modern tradition of Arabic utopian writing, drawing on both European and older Arabic sources. One early example was *Kitab Ghabat al-Haqq* ('Forest of Justice', 1865), written by the Aleppine Christian author Fransis Marrash, a few years after an outbreak of sectarian violence in Mount Lebanon and Damascus had been quelled with great violence by the modernizing Ottoman state. Marrash imagines an allegorized State of Civilization, which has just defeated its rival, the barbarous State of Slavery, in war. The state is ruled over by King Freedom and advised by a Philosopher from the City of Light, who outlines his vision for a civilized order in harmony with the laws of nature: this encompasses reforms in town planning, public health and education, the end of slavery, and the separation of religion and politics. The action centres around the trial of the defeated leaders of the Army of Slavery, who are allegorized vices, like Pride and Greed, condemned to be subdued to their opposite virtues, like Humility and Generosity. This appeared not long after the actual—and rather harsher—trials of the Druze and Muslim rebels of 1860 had been covered in detail in Syrian newspapers. It is evidently an allegory for what Arab intellectuals hoped the reforms then being enacted by the Ottoman Empire might become—with the aid of enlightened 'philosophers' such as themselves (P. Hill 2020: ch. 4).

Marrash was a pioneer, but by the early twentieth century there was a growing tradition of quasi-utopian writing in Arabic, in an intellectual atmosphere marked by the mushrooming of new periodicals and publishing ventures, and vigorous debates. These disputed the merits of Arab-Islamic versus Western civilization; European empires versus Ottomanism or nascent Arab nationalism; feminist versus patriarchal views of women's role in society; Darwin's evolutionism and Ludwig Büchner's materialism versus religious and spiritualist accounts of nature; and possessive individualism and capitalism versus both Islam and socialism or anarchism.[2] Writers were not always neatly divided into modernizers and traditionalists over these questions, though, and the literary scene gave rise to many interesting hybrids. Muhammad al-Muwaylihi's *'Isa ibn Hisham's Tale* (1898–1902) resurrects an Ottoman Pasha from early nineteenth-century Egypt to critique turn-of-the-century Cairo (R. Allen 1992). The Christian writer Mikha'il al-Saqqal and the Islamic modernist and spiritualist Shaykh Tantawi Jawhari wrote science fiction works imagining races of virtuous beings inhabiting Venus or Halley's comet (al-Saqqal 1907; Tantawi Jawhari 1912); a European orientalist would compare another of Tantawi Jawhari's works to al-Farabi and More (Tantawi Jawhari

---

[2] See Watenpaugh 2006; Booth 2001; Elshakry 2013; Khuri-Makdisi 2010.

1935). Others, like Muhammad al-Manfaluti in his story 'The City of Happiness', made references to older Arabic works like al-Farabi's (see Deheuvels 2007: 1.220–230).

The radical journalist Farah Antun (1874–1922) wrote two historical novels with utopian aspects. *The New World, or Mary Before the Annunciation* and *The New Jerusalem* were set in early Christian times and at the time of the Muslim conquest of Jerusalem and the Holy Land respectively, but also had contemporary overtones: the early twentieth century too, Antun implies, is the end of an era, and a new dispensation is at hand (Ballas 1985: 1). In another work, *Religion, Science, and Property: The Three Cities* (1903), Antun dramatizes this new dispensation in a vision of the cataclysm and rebirth of modern society. Religion and Science are portrayed as cities in conflict with one another; the third city, Property, is in the grips of the struggle between workers and capitalists. After an exploration of the rights and wrongs of these conflicts—including an exposition of Karl Marx's views on capital and labour—Antun imagines an apocalyptic war between the rival forces which destroys all three cities, followed by the ultimate rebuilding of a single, ideal city (see Deheuvels 1999). The terms had shifted since Marrash's utopia of 1865: for Marrash, civilization was a unitary force, faced with the task of subduing an external enemy, slavery, or barbarism. For Antun, the seeds of barbaric destruction lie in the tensions within modern capitalist civilization itself, in its 'three cities'. It is also largely in the men of science, rather than religious clerics, capitalists, or militant workers, that Antun sees hope for the future—a tendency we will find repeated in Arab radical thinking over the following decades.

More in the Arabic Encyclopedia

It was in this atmosphere of fin-de-siècle expectation and foreboding that More reappeared in Arabic, in a very different guise to that of de Rennes's Catholic martyr. In 1898 the Arabic encyclopedia *Da'irat al-Ma'arif* ('Circle of Sciences'), edited by the famous Beiruti Protestant man of letters Butrus al-Bustani and his son Salim, dedicated an entry to 'socialism' (S. al-Bustani 1898: 227–232). Its author, probably Salim al-Bustani, is clearly antipathetic to socialism, though cooperativism (*al-mu'ahada*) is perhaps less threatening than 'communism or pure socialism' (*al-kumunism aw al-ishtirakiyya al-mahda*) (227). Most of the article is dedicated to modern socialism: the doctrines of French Revolutionary communist Gracchus Babeuf (1760–97), the French social thinkers Henri de Saint-Simon (1760–1825) and Charles Fourier (1772–1837), the Scottish factory owner and social reformer Robert Owen (1771–1858), and the pioneering consumer cooperative of Rochdale in Lancashire (founded in 1844) are described in some detail. This is largely what Marx and Friedrich Engels had dubbed the 'utopian socialist' tradition, and was not itself new to Arabic readers. The Arabic press had long since offered discussions of socialism, anarchism, and events like the 1871 Paris Commune (Ayalon 1987). Back in the 1850s, the editor of the Beirut newspaper which had printed Fénelon's Enlightenment utopia had rejected the more radical visions proposed by Owen and Saint-Simon, describing the 'school of sharing' (*madhhab al-musharaka*: socialism or communism), along with the principles of the French Revolution, as a 'wilderness of impossible hopes' (P. Hill 2020: 195–197).

But al-Bustani also seems fascinated, perhaps despite himself, by socialism's fire-like ability to burst out unexpectedly 'and consume all that stands in its path', after having lain dormant for centuries (S. al-Bustani 1898: 231). In this vein he describes many historical examples of socialist upheavals from ancient and biblical times onwards, and here he mentions More's *Utopia*. He describes it as one of the writings which emerged around the time of the Peasants' War in Germany (1524–5)—an uprising inspired by radical Protestant ideas—and which formed a 'prelude' to the doctrines of modern socialism. It proposed 'the distribution of property [*tawzi' al-amwal*] and the purification of the order of human societies [*tanqih nizamat al-ijtima' al-insani*]'. It was based on 'the principle of equality [*musawat*] and kindliness to the subjects [*ra'iyya*]', and the notion of a Cockaigne-like paradise of abundance: 'all would be happy, revelling in the ease of security and luxury [*rati'in fi bahbuhat al-amn wa-l-rafahiyya*]' (227). With this alluring vision, More's *Utopia* thus offered one more example of socialism's worrying ability to break out unforeseen at any point in history.

DREAMS OF THE PHILOSOPHERS (1926)

This association of More's *Utopia* with socialism would persist through most of the twentieth century, as socialism came to loom larger in the Arab world. The cataclysm foreshadowed in works of the fin de siècle had come to pass in the shape of the First World War. The eastern Arabic provinces of the Ottoman Empire emerged as a new set of national states, but under the tutelage of European imperial powers: Syria and Lebanon as French League of Nations Mandates, Iraq and Palestine as British ones; and Egypt as formally independent but under close British control. The succeeding decades would be dominated by nationalist agitation against imperial rule, but other ideologies also appealed to the growing middle classes: socialism, inspired by both European and American reformist traditions, and the Communism of the Russian Revolution; and an Islamic reformism and revival movement which gave birth, in 1928, to the Muslim Brotherhood. The next two writers to offer summaries and partial translations of More's work in Arabic would place it within a tradition of utopian writing seen largely through a socialist lens, and particularly through the work of H. G. Wells, whose *A Modern Utopia* was published in 1905. At the same time, comparisons also began to be made between More and the tenth-century philosopher al-Farabi.

The first substantial account of the Western utopian tradition in Arabic came in 1926, with *Ahlam al-Falasifa* ('Dreams of the Philosophers') by the Egyptian journalist Salama Musa. Musa came from a wealthy Coptic Christian family in Zagazig in the Nile Delta. He was attracted to modern and scientific ideas from an early age, and in 1909 went to study in London, where he came under the influence, in particular, of three progressive tendencies in English intellectual life. These were the anti-religious Rationalist Press Association of John Robertson; the Fabian Society, whose biggest names at the time included Bernard Shaw and Wells; and the eugenics movement around the scientist Francis Galton (Egger 1986: 20–27). On his return to Egypt he became active in journalism, writing on a range of modern and controversial themes including socialism, evolution, and eugenics. Shortly after the First World War he became an editor of the long-established literary magazine *al-Hilal* ('The Crescent'). He entered briefly into organizational politics, taking a hand in founding the Egyptian Socialist Party in 1921, but as a Fabian gradualist he soon disagreed with communists who wanted the party to join the Bolshevik Third International, and was expelled (Egger 1986: 69–86; Elshakry 2013: 242–252). Stepping back again from active political commitment, he founded in 1929 his own magazine, *al-Majalla al-Jadida* ('The New Magazine'), which, as Israel Gershoni and James Jankowski write, came to occupy 'a unique niche in Egyptian intellectual discourse during the 1930s' (Gershoni and Jankowski 2009: 114). 'Relentlessly antitraditionalist and radically modernist', the journal appealed to both a 'select cohort of older Egyptian liberals' favourable to Westernization, and members of 'the growing educated and professional class of younger Egyptians', who preferred Musa's 'secular reformism' to either the established, tired-looking parliamentary parties or the more nativist radicalism of the Muslim Brothers or Young Egypt (a nationalist party founded in 1933).

Musa was also, in these years, especially attracted to the style and concerns of H. G. Wells, as well as being influenced by Shaw (Musa 1961: 76–77). As early as 1910 he had summarized a set of Wells's works in the Arabic press. But in the 1920s, in particular, as Vernon Egger writes, 'Musa seems to have discovered that Wells's concerns and proposals were distinctly relevant to his own career, and the influence of Wells on Musa's own social and political thought became increasingly pronounced' (Egger 1986: 88). He began deliberately modelling his editorials for *Kull Shay'* after Wells's 'futurist orientation'. Much of Musa's writing through the 1920s and 1930s may be seen less as belonging to a particular political position than as attempting to discern 'the shape of things to come', in Wells's phrase: the increase in centralized state control visible in Roosevelt's USA, Stalin's Russia, and Mussolini's Italy alike; or the growing importance of evolution in human history, expressed in biological discoveries and also Nazi eugenics programmes (see Musa 1936).

Musa's *Dreams of the Philosophers* (1926) summarizes a number of utopian works, from Plato and More to Wells and Shaw, by way of Johannes Andreae (1586–1654), Francis Bacon (1561–1626), Tommaso Campanella (1568–1639), and various nineteenth-century writers: Edward Bellamy (1850–98), William Morris (1834–96), and W. H. Hudson (1841–1922). Musa then offers his own historical and critical remarks on the utopian tradition, and finishes with a utopia of his own. His summary of More does not include Book One, but otherwise is accurate and detailed, covering all parts of Hythloday's description of Utopia (Musa 1926: 30–40). It is interspersed with Musa's own comments and evaluations. He criticizes freely those elements he sees as outdated or mistaken in More's vision—as he does with the other writers he describes in *Dreams of the Philosophers*—although perhaps seeing many as inevitable given the age in which More lived. More is unaware of the Malthusian law that means that natural population increase combined with unlimited food will soon lead to the poverty of the Utopians; his provisions for the enslavement of those who roam without permission is not well thought through: slavery has its uses in freeing the citizens from dirty tasks, but the despotism of masters over slaves will lead to the despotism of a prince over the masters (37–38). More's account of war is similarly marked by an age of discovery, colonization, and piracy; and he perhaps failed to appreciate the eugenic benefits of the military in his time: it sent the worst elements of society off to die in war (38–39). What Musa mainly admires in More's vision is his suppression of private property and its replacement by 'communism [*shuyuʿiyya*] of goods': it is the part where Hythloday speaks of this regime that he quotes directly, translating rather literally from Gilbert Burnet's late seventeenth-century English translation (34–35). He also seems to approve the fact that all Utopians must engage in agriculture, and that they spend their plentiful free time in 'the pursuit of the sciences and arts' (40).

Some of these more positive aspects of Musa's appreciation of More may have influenced his own utopian vision of Egypt, which concludes *Dreams of the Philosophers* (Musa 1926: 114–133). In his imagined Egypt, over 1,000 years in the future, most of the population lives in large agricultural communes: these are run on a socialist basis, and most people work very few hours (although individuals are allowed to work extra hours to gain extra pay); they spend most of their free time in study. Yet here the similarities with More's Utopia end. Musa's future Egypt is extremely technologically advanced: almost everyone possesses their own car or aeroplane; they live off specially bred fruits, irrigated by an aerial technology which causes clouds to rain on demand; the universal use of rubber has freed the streets and houses from dust. The government is composed of representatives of the different professional unions, apparently representing the equivalents of the technically skilled middle classes of Musa's day: doctors, biologists, agronomists, and merchants. These technicist and futuristic elements reflect Musa's Wellsian inspiration and what Vernon Egger calls his Fabian-influenced 'socialism for the middle classes' (Egger 1986: 47). Yet the most striking element of Musa's vision is that his new society is built around the principle of eugenics. This has caused its people to evolve into what Musa sees as a higher form of life: they have enormous heads, slender limbs, and only vestigial teeth. People may only have offspring on receipt of a government licence; when a child is born, it is examined by a medical committee, which rules it fit or unfit for life. The unfit—generally those whose heads are too small—are painlessly killed. Even their religion now consists of worshipping the principles of evolution.

Musa does show some uneasiness with this future order: he imagines waking up himself after a thousand-year sleep in the new society, and has difficulty reconciling himself to the absence of romantic love and family life, and the coldness with which unfit children are killed off. He is also painfully embarrassed by the fact that he himself, with his small head, large teeth, and beard, belongs to a lower stage of evolution than the people around him. But he expresses little doubt that what he is describing is a superior society, indeed a superior breed of beings. In these eugenicist aspects, we can discern the influence on Musa of Shaw and the Galtonians, as well as the pressure of the Darwinian tradition in modern Arab thinking since the 1880s (see Elshraky 2013).

The place of More's *Utopia* within Musa's vision is ambiguous: it is part of the utopian heritage, to be taken seriously and perhaps to be imitated in some aspects. But it is also clearly for Musa—as for Wells—severely dated, and superseded by more futuristic, technologically advanced, and for Musa biological-evolutionary visions of the future. More, he implies, is one of those utopian writers who were 'literati' (*udaba*'): the ideal is to combine this humanistic vision with 'science' (*'ilm*), as Plato, Wells, and Hudson did in their utopian visions (Musa 1926: 107). For Salim al-Bustani in his encyclopedia, More had been seen as one among many examples of socialism: as a timeless phenomenon, ready to blaze out at any period of human history. Radical writers in the early twentieth century were coming to see socialism as a future stage of human history, superior to the present, but one which, whether in the technicist, eugenicist, or Marxist versions, would decisively supersede old-fashioned visions like that of More.

More and al-Farabi (1928)

Musa was a confirmed 'Westernist': he mentions al-Farabi only in passing, to say that his *Virtuous City* derived from Plato but was modified by 'the dominant trend in his time', his somewhat dismissive phrase for Islam. In describing the utopian visions in *Dreams of the Philosophers*, he makes frequent use of the terms *hulm* ('dream') and *khayal* ('imagination'), but he also uses *tuba*. This word, often found in religious contexts, previously meant blessedness, good fortune, eternal life, or a pleasant life; its similarity in sound as well as meaning to 'utopia' led to its adoption as a translation of the term: its influence is particularly visible in the now accepted translation for the adjective 'utopian', *tubawi*. The other term with Arabic roots which came gradually to be associated with the idea of utopia was *al-Madina al-Fadila*—'the Virtuous City'—also used a few times by Musa in his preface (Musa 1926: 13). This was originally the title of al-Farabi's work, which was being rediscovered in the Arab world, as we have seen, from around the turn of the twentieth century. By the 1920s writers were beginning to compare it with More's *Utopia*: one author in an Egyptian newspaper apparently claimed that al-Farabi had in fact inspired More. This prompted a rebuttal and a careful scholarly comparison of al-Farabi's 'Virtuous City' and More's 'Island of Blessedness' (*jazirat al-tuba*) by the Lebanese Catholic scholar Fu'ad Ifram al-Bustani (1928).

Fu'ad al-Bustani was writing in the scholarly journal *al-Mashriq* ('The East'), under the editorship of the very learned and very reactionary Jesuit Louis Cheikho: a wholly different atmosphere to that of Musa's aggressively modernist publications. His article starts with an ironic reference to the habit of Arabs and other 'Easterners' of claiming that all the great civilizational achievements were theirs first, as in this case with the concept of utopia. He then sets out to show that the two works in question are in fact very different. He gives brief biographies of the authors and summaries of their works, including tables of contents: that of *Utopia* is a close translation of the contents of Burnet's English translation. He concludes that More certainly did not borrow from al-Farabi, although both men were inspired by Plato. Al-Farabi's vision was that of a pure philosopher, while More's was that of a social thinker, who looked at things 'from the point of view of administration, government and legislation', with a view to reforming the government of England in his time (F. al-Bustani 1928: 34). Unlike Musa, it seems that Fu'ad al-Bustani did not regard More as a 'utopian' in the pejorative sense: rather he was, unlike al-Farabi, a practical thinker and reformer. This positive assessment of More may have been influenced by his own aspirations to a moderate and pragmatic politics, as well as the Catholic ambience in which he was writing: certainly, he pays respectful homage to More's Catholic martyrdom (28).

This view was at odds with those who laid claim to a more modern and scientific vision than More's of how to design a better society: not just Musa, with his eugenicist fantasies, but also the proponents of a Marxist scientific socialism. The standard Marxist assessment of the 'utopian socialism' of Saint-Simon and Owen, as bold and radical but insufficiently materialist, was put forward in the short-lived Communist periodical *Ruh al-'Asr* ('Spirit of the Age') in 1930 (see Sa'id 1974: 47–48). In Naguib Mahfouz's classic novel set in 1940s Cairo, *Sugar Street*, an Egyptian Communist character accuses the Muslim Brothers of being 'utopian', like More, Louis Blanc, and Saint-Simon (Mahfouz 1994: 241).

THE LAND OF DREAMS (1939)

After Musa's summary, the next major version of More's *Utopia* presented to an Arabic reading public was an abridged translation in a 1939 work by Zaki Najib Mahmud. Mahmud's book, *Ard al-ahlam* ('The Land of Dreams'), dealt, like Musa's, with a broader tradition of utopianism, and read it to a great extent through the lens of H. G. Wells. Mahmud would later become known as the main Arab advocate of logical positivism and translator of the philosophical works of John Dewey (1859–1952) and Bertrand Russell (1872–1970). In the 1930s he had co-authored popularizing compilations on Greek and modern philosophy (Amin and Mahmud 1935, 1936), and translated Plato's *Dialogues* (Plato 1934–5). In 1938, the year before the publication of *The Land of Dreams*, Mahmud also published a translation of H. G. Wells's *The Work, Wealth and Happiness of Mankind*, as *al-Aghniya' wa-l-fuqara'* ('The Rich and the Poor').

The Land of Dreams, completed in 1939, consisted of abridged translations of seven classic utopian works: Plato's *Republic*, al-Farabi's *Virtuous City*, More's *Utopia*, Bacon's *New Atlantis* (printed 1626), Samuel Butler's *Erewhon* (1872), William Morris's *News from Nowhere* (1890), and finally Wells's *Modern Utopia*. This is clearly the English utopian tradition, with the addition of the Greek Plato and the Arab Farabi. And Mahmud, despite his later reputation for 'austere rationalism', clearly brought some political commitments to his treatment of it (Abdel-Malek and Kahla 2016: 67). His introduction to *The Land of Dreams* concludes:

If the reader should feel, after finishing reading this book, any dissatisfaction with the meagre, miserable, wretched existence [*'ish saqim shaqi ba'is*] that is our present situation, and should then feel the desire for change [*taghyir*] and reform [*islah*] in a socialist [*ishtiraki*] manner which recognizes the worth of individuals, leaves them their right to freedoms, and destroys hateful divisions amongst people [...] if the reader should feel anything of this after finishing reading the book, then I will have achieved my goal. (Mahmud 1977: 12)

This gives a clear sense of Mahmud's dissatisfaction with contemporary reality, which was shared by many in Egypt in the 1930s, a time in which the old elite parliamentary politics seemed incapable of overcoming the country's problems: poverty, a corrupt political system dominated by the Palace and the aristocratic landed families, and the continued British military occupation of the Suez Canal Zone. It also offers a thumbnail sketch of Mahmud's own views of a happier state of mankind, similar to Wells's in *A Modern Utopia*. The notion of balance between the rights of the collectivity and those of the individual which Mahmud refers to here is a major preoccupation of Wells's utopia. In his introduction to More's *Utopia* Mahmud, like Musa, repeats Wells's stricture (found in his 1908 introduction to Ralph Robinson's sixteenth-century translation) that More lacked imagination, as well as the claim that More aimed primarily to criticize sixteenth-century England and only secondarily to picture an 'ideal state' (*dawla muthla*) like Plato's (Mahmud 1977: 17–18).

Mahmud perhaps values More and this pre-Wellsian utopian tradition—including the Arabic al-Farabi—more highly than Musa. In his introduction to the abridged translation of *Utopia*, Mahmud writes, 'the book [...] contains solutions to important questions which occupy minds in this age'. These include the problem of leisure time and the limitation of the working day, the abolition of gold and silver (similar to those contemporaries who propose the abandonment of the gold standard); and More's urging that both domestic and foreign policies should be ruled by reason, not passion: 'this alone would be sufficient for humanity not to be exposed to the catastrophes and sufferings [*al-kawarith wa-l-alam*] which it is undergoing today' (Mahmud 1977: 18–19).

All the same, Mahmud's rather free translation shows clearly enough that it was the socialistic and other usable elements in More which he chiefly valued. He often translates More's language—from Robinson's English translation—into the terms of modern Arabic political terminology: 'The people of Utopia adopt the principle of socialism [*mabda' al-ishtirakiyya*], and thus you see that every person there has his needs fulfilled, or rather overwhelmed by the abundance of production [...] I agree with Plato insofar as he adopted socialism [*fima dhahaba ilayhi min ishtirakiyya*]' (More 1977b: 35).[3] Later, Christianity is said to preach 'the doctrine of communism [*madhhab*

---

[3] Cf. Robinson's English, on which Mahmud's translation is based: 'all thynges beyng ther common' (More 1895a: 105).

al-shuyu'iyya] which abolishes differences in property between men [*fawariq al-mal bayn al-rijal*]' (61).⁴

Wells's *Modern Utopia* contains several passages of reflection on and criticism of the earlier utopian tradition (largely Plato, More, and Morris): in translating these, it is notable that Mahmud translates Wells's 'old utopias' as 'the old Virtuous Cities [*al-mada'in al-fadila al-qadima*]', whereas Wells's own 'modern utopia' is invariably *al-yutubiya al-haditha*. Al-Farabi's title is here used, it seems, to stand in for the premodern, static, and limited utopias which Wells criticizes when he says that a modern utopia (*al-yutubiya al-haditha*) must necessarily allow for further development, and must necessarily be on the level of the planet rather than of an island (or city, as with al-Farabi). As with Musa, then, More's *Utopia* is ultimately consigned to a past phase of human civilization.

1952 AND AFTER

The Land of Dreams was originally published on the brink of war, in 1939, but would have far greater popularity later, in the wake of the seizure of power by a group of young Egyptian revolutionary army officers in 1952, a pattern soon to be repeated across the Arab world (see Batatu 1984). It was in the atmosphere of jubilation that followed the deposition of King Fu'ad—and before the new military regime's authoritarian characteristics had become fully apparent—that *The Land of Dreams* was reissued in the popular series 'Books for All' (*Kutub li-l-jami'*) in a run of 'several thousand copies' which—according to the author, at least—sold out quickly (Mahmud 1977: 7). For the sake of cheapness and portability the volume was cut down from the 1939 edition, losing the sections on Plato, al-Farabi, and Bacon: More's is thus the first and earliest 'utopia' to appear in the book.

As new nationalist governments came to power across the Arab lands and became more radical, especially from around 1958, they increasingly laid claim to one variety or another of 'socialism': from the 'Arab socialism' of Gamal Abdel Nasser in Egypt, the National Liberation Front in Algeria, or the Ba'th Party in Syria, to the brief ascendancy of the Communist Party in Iraq and the longer-lived Marxist-Leninist regime in South Yemen. As political projects which might well be described as 'utopian' multiplied, debates raged as to the nature of socialism and its relationship with nationalism, Marxism, and Islam, and in this context there was increasing interest in the nineteenth-century 'utopian socialists' and the broader Western utopian tradition. This can be seen in works such as leftist writer Luwis 'Awad's *Studies on Systems of Rule and Schools of Thought* (*Dirasat fi al-nuzum wa-l-madhahib*, 1962), which includes accounts of Saint-Simon, Fourier, Owen, and Étienne Cabet (1788–1856); or an early 1960s translation of

---

⁴ Robinson: 'all thynges commen [...] communitie' (More 1895a: 269).

Élie Halévy's 1948 classic *Histoire du socialisme européen* by the left Nasserist politician Jamal al-Atasi (Halévy 1962?). In the Egyptian press in the 1960s there appeared both Mahmud's abridgement of More (More 1963b), accounts of al-Farabi (Wafi 1963), and studies of more recent Western utopian literature by Angèle Butrus Sam'an, who would later make the first complete Arabic translation of More's *Utopia* (Sam'an 1965a, 1965b, 1966; More 1974).

Interesting for its positioning between three competing tendencies of Arab thought of the time—Marxism, liberalism, and Islam—is a study of utopian thinking by Fu'ad Muhammad Shibl, published at some point in the 1960s: *The Virtuous City: A Study of the Economic and Social System of the Utopian Writers*. This is based on standard English-language sources, such as American sociologist and urbanist Lewis Mumford (1895–1990), literary scholar Henry Morley (1822–94), and anarchist writer Marie Louise Berneri (1918–49), and follows the Western tradition from Plato to—once again—H. G. Wells. The influence of some Marxist ideas is plain: Shibl tries to show how utopias were products of their historical circumstances, rather than simply critiquing them for being outdated, as Musa tended to. He also cites and endorses Engels's critique of utopian socialists, however, for believing that their revelation of truth alone could effect reform, and ignoring social forces and the 'historical mission of capitalism to develop the productive forces' (Shibl [n.d.]: 141).

At the same time, Shibl's concern for the rights of the individual as against the state shows his consciousness of the defects of Stalinism, as well as of authoritarian Arab governments—perhaps influenced by anarchists like Berneri. His remark that More 'criticizes the government for keeping an army which tempts it to go to war to justify maintaining and spending [money] on it', might well have been seen as applicable to military-authoritarian Arab states (49). The utopian writers were ignorant, he concludes, of 'two great truths' which are especially apparent in the present age: the fact that technological progress does not bring about happiness, and the conflict between the individual and the state (142–143); William Morris, he notes, was one of the few utopian writers to critique state power (113). There is also a more subdued attempt to see how Western utopianism might relate to Islam: Shibl sees the Utopians' emphasis on a return to living in harmony with nature as divinely inspired; he wishes he had had space to include Islamic economic thought in the book, and for his title adopts the term *al-Madina al-Fadila* 'in emulation of the Islamic philosopher' al-Farabi (138, 143, 5).

Dystopia and the Utopian Horizon

In June 1967 the combined military forces of Egypt, Jordan, and Syria were crushingly and rapidly defeated by Israel. For many this meant disillusionment with utopian dreams of national liberation and socialism, and a return to retrenchment and pragmatism; for others, an intensified radicalism, visible especially in new revolutionary Palestinian movements. And for others—and indeed some of the same people—it meant a return to the older Arab and Islamic heritage, whether in a revaluation of literary and intellectual culture, the renewed spirituality of the Islamic revival (the Sahwa), or the political resurgence of different forms of Islamism. Shortly after the 1967 defeat, Ahmad Ra'if, a member of the Muslim Brotherhood imprisoned by the Nasserist state, wrote a work of Islamist science fiction which was performed by fellow members of the Brotherhood in their prison. Like Tantawi Jawhari's fictions several decades earlier, *The Fifth Dimension* (*al-Buʻd al-khamis*, published 1987) presented the life of inhabitants of another heavenly body—in this case Mars—as more moral and Islamic than that of earthlings (see Szyska 1995). This joined an Arabic tradition of science fiction which had continued to grow, especially from the 1940s, H. G. Wells's works again being one major influence (Barbaro 2013: 159). In later years, this literature has taken on a more dystopian tone, as it reflected on deepening social crisis and authoritarianism in Arab countries, down to Ahmad Khalid Tawfiq's famous 2008 novel *Utopia*, which portrays a dystopian Cairo divided into the gated community of the hedonistic, drug-fuelled rich—the 'utopia' of the ironic title—and 'the sea of poverty outside'. Since the genuinely utopian moment of the Arab uprisings of 2011 has given way to renewed autocracy and violence, this dystopian trend has only deepened (Alter 2016).

The questioning of modernist norms has also led to a sensitive revaluation of older Arabic traditions, including utopian ones. The Lebanese literary critic Faruq Saʻd wrote a study of al-Farabi and of the Western utopian tradition—perhaps the first major account to place the two alongside each other and give them equal weight. *With al-Farabi and the Virtuous Cities* was written during the Lebanese Civil War in 1975–6, partly in Lebanon and partly in exile, and published in 1982. The book is dedicated 'To wounded Lebanon [...] my dear homeland [...] | they thought they would succeed in making it into an "altered city" [*madina mubaddala*]. | But in vain! [...] | It will be forever a "virtuous city" ' (Saʻd 1982: 5). It concludes by asking: 'Finally [...] has the striving towards the virtuous city stopped?' And answers: 'In reality, and inevitably, the virtuous city has been and will remain always and forever the horizon of existential hope [*al-murtaja al-wujudi*] of humanity, the destination of the essential tendencies [*al-tawajjuhat al-kiyaniyya*] of humanity to attain happiness, love, health, sufficiency [*kifaya*], and peace' (122). The utopias of More and al-Farabi, for Saʻd, are no longer historically limited visions to be superseded by more modern ones—Marxist, Wellsian, or eugenicist—as they had been for most Arab writers through the twentieth century. His view of utopia resembles Salim al-Bustani's of socialism nearly eighty years previously, though with a more positive valuation: it is a continuous presence in human history, from the ancient world to the Islamic civilization of al-Farabi to the present day: a horizon always visible and never attained.

This may, indeed, be an apt image for the different versions of More and his *Utopia* which Arabic speakers had made and remade at different times, and in response to varying challenges. More can be taken as a kind of prism through which to observe different phases of development of Arabic culture and its interaction with the world beyond it. More, the Catholic martyr of the seventeenth century, belonged to a bid to bring Christian communities of the Ottoman Empire firmly into the embrace of the Church of Rome, at a time when relations with Western Europe were a relatively minor part of Ottoman life. More, the harbinger of unsettling socialist movements of the end of the nineteenth century, reflected the attempt of nineteenth-century Arab intellectuals to make themselves part of an orderly, prosperous, Western-dominated bourgeois civilization—to which socialism could only be a threat. More, the forerunner of Wellsian visions of technical progress of the 1920s and 1930s, then belonged to a new middle-class generation, exemplified by Salama Musa, which sought to appropriate more sweeping and radical solutions which went beyond the bounds both of capitalism and of existing human biology. The vogue of 'utopian' discussions from the 1950s to the 1970s responded to the partial achievement of a progressive and socialist vision of national liberation. The anxieties that emerged in some works of that period, and the placing of More alongside the Islamic philosopher Farabi, suggested the limits of that nationalist achievement, and a turn to cultural introspection with a renewed emphasis on the religious and the locally specific. Meanwhile, the surge of revolt that swept the Arab world in 2011—to the astonishment of practically all observers—reminds us that the utopian impulse, not unlike Salim al-Bustani's 'fire' of socialism, is apt to break out unpredictably, unannounced; it also tends to be followed, as in the present phase of authoritarian reaction, by the disenchantment of a dystopian mood.

PART FOUR
BEYOND *UTOPIA*

CHAPTER 30

EARLY MODERN UTOPIAN FICTION

Utopia *and* The Isle of Pines

CHLOË HOUSTON

INTRODUCTION

WHAT did 'utopia' mean in the early modern period? When the word was used in the decades following the 1516 publication of Thomas More's *De optimo rei publicae statu deque nova insula*, it sometimes referred directly to the imaginary island described in that text. Discussing purgatory in his *Actes and Monuments* (first published in 1570), for example, John Foxe writes: 'I do not [...] thinke, that [...] there is any such fourth place of Purgatory at all (unles it be in M. Mores Utopia)' (Foxe 1583: 1017). Here, More's fictional island is taken to mean a place that has no existence in reality, and this seems to have been the word's chief meaning during the early modern period, even when not directly associated with More by name or by reference to *Utopia* itself. Utopia's association with unreality was at least as present in early modern usage of the word as its association with an ideal or idealized society. Thomas Browne, in *Pseudodoxia Epidemica* (1646), states of the mythical phoenix that 'Some say it liveth in Aethiopia, others in Arabia, some [...] in Utopia' (Browne 1646: 132). Utopia, first and foremost, was no-place. In fact, texts that actively sought to portray either ideal, real, or conceptual locations or communities frequently distanced themselves from the concept of utopia. William Barlow, bishop of Lincoln, writing in 1601, sought to defend his fellow Protestants' belief in a Catholic church of Christ, for example, in these terms: 'I am assured that we all professe there is a Catholike church of Christ, not a *Platonicall utopia*, no where extant, but a company of Gods chosen every where scattered' (Barlow 1601: 108).

The writers and editors of travel literature knew all too well that to call a place utopian was to call its credibility into doubt. For Lawrence Keymis, in his *Relation of the second Voyage to Guiana*, the prospect of finding utopia in the New World was a seductive idea, but one that carried connotations of naïvety: 'it might be imputed for some blame to the gravity of wise men, lightly to bee carried with the perswasion and hope of a new found *Utopia*' (Keymis 1596, sig. A4). Samuel Purchas's *Purchas His Pilgrimage* (1613) uses 'utopia' to distinguish between 'true history' and fanciful imaginings, for example, in recounting the travels of Iambulus to the 'Islands of the Sun': 'The reports of this his voyage savour more of an *Utopia*, and *Plato's* common-wealth, then of true Historie' (Purchas 1613: 708). Travellers might long have hinted at the possibility of finding utopia abroad, but by the later 1500s, this dream was primarily associated with a naïve lack of judgement (C. Houston 2010).

In the seventeenth century, then, Utopia was not only emphatically not a real place, but often carried comic associations. In the literature of the period, 'utopia' is shorthand for a place that is ridiculous or fanciful, and is regularly employed for the purpose of satire, as is manifested by some examples from the 1630s. John Taylor, the Water Poet, uses 'Utopia' or 'Utopian' in a number of his poems; the following example describes 'A Figure-flinger, Cunning-man':

> He'le tell you wonders when you are alone,
> Of the Philosophers admired stone:
> And that it from Utopia did come,
> Brought to him by a Spirit, he sent to Rome.
>
> (J. Taylor 1630: 13)

Taylor refers to utopia in a similar manner in his poems 'A Bawd', 'A Whore', and 'In Praise of Hemp-seed', printed in the same collection. Richard Brathwait also uses 'Utopia' to mean an unreal or fanciful place, for satirical effect, in his poem 'To the Pious Memory of Sir Richard Hutton Knight'. The poem mocks a captain who claims to have travelled to 'Zealand' and 'Brabant' with the marginal note, 'These Countreys might have been in *Utopia* for ought he knew' (Brathwait 1641: B4r).

Robert Burton's exploration of the idea of utopia in *The Anatomy of Melancholy*, first published in 1621, also recognizes the comic and unrealistic aspects of utopia, even while Burton engages in constructing 'one of mine owne'.[1] Burton begins from the premise that there is a need for social reformation, 'some generall visiter in our age, that should reforme what is amis' (1989: 1.84). He enumerates the many changes to be desired, which touch on all aspects of life, including religion, arts, sciences, education, and morals, and plans 'a new *Atlantis*, a poeticall commonwealth of mine owne, in which I will freely domineere, build Citties, make Lawes, Statutes, as I list my selfe' (1.85). But this utopia is a private space, inaccessible to anyone else: in a mockery of the traditional ambiguity as to the utopian place's precise location, Burton jokes that he will choose a site: 'whose latitude shall be 45 degrees (I respect not minutes) in the midst of the temperate Zone, or perhaps under the *Aequator*, that Paradise of the world [...] the longitude for

---

[1] For more on Burton's use of utopia, see Patrick 1948; J. C. Davis 1981.

some reasons I will conceale' (1.86). While Burton constructs a utopia in order to criticize aspects of the status quo, he does not conceive it as a serious response to social ills. Burton identifies human beings as the primary block to creating an ideal society. Real people are 'partiall and passionate, mercilesse, covetous, corrupt, subject to love, hate, feare, favor, &c' (1.92). The creation of a utopia is an explicitly fictional and individual process, not one that is socially useful (C. Houston 2014). A little over a century after the term was first coined by More, 'utopia' had fully absorbed the meaning of something unrealistic or unfeasible.

Just as Burton saw the need for social reform, but did not perceive that utopia had a role in achieving it, so those engaged in actual social reform in the seventeenth century rejected the utopian form and the very word 'utopia' in projecting their images of better societies. Samuel Hartlib and his associates, including reformers such as John Dury and William Petty, evidently had More's *Utopia*, and other utopian literature, in mind when they spoke of the need for social reformation and outlined their plans for how it should be achieved. Writing in the 1640s, Hartlib maintained that More's *Utopia*, 'a most excellent Booke', could offer 'a true patterne of a rightly constituted Commonwealth and which might easily bee put in practice' (HP 28/1/19B, 28/1/20A). In specific terms, when thinking about the creation of ideal scientific institutions, Hartlib turned naturally to the utopian projections of Francis Bacon in his *New Atlantis* (1627). Indeed, he specifically refers to Bacon's Salomon's House in his planning for such institutions. In undated notes contained within the Hartlib Papers, Hartlib comments under the title 'Londons University': 'Arca Noa and House of Salomon or a Library of Representations' (HP 47/9/38A). However, he noted in his *Ephemerides* (1640) that utopian texts such as More's, or Tommaso Campanella's *The City of the Sun* (1623), needed to be improved or 'remedied' if they were to be of use to real people; they tended too much to ignore human defects, and focused on theory rather than practice (HP 30/4/57A, 57B). Despite these drawbacks, Hartlib viewed utopian texts as potentially useful 'counsels', advice to help society improve itself. Nonetheless, he was careful not to use the word 'utopia' to describe his own projected ideal societies or institutions, such as his 'Office of Address' (Hartlib 1647, 1648). Even the utopian text which was produced by the Hartlib circle via his associate Gabriel Plattes, *A Description of the Famous Kingdome of Macaria. Shewing its Excellent Government* (1641), largely ignores the conventions of the utopian form in favour of a direct portrayal of how England could—and, by implication, should—be run (Webster 1979; Boesky 1996). Utopian writings such as *Macaria*, and later James Harrington's *Oceana* (1656), steered as clear as they could of the word 'utopia' in an attempt to avoid its connotations of unreality, comedy, and blind optimism (C. Houston 2014).

The fact that the word 'utopia' became associated with fanciful imaginings rather than serious political thought did not mean that the early modern period did not produce a significant number of utopian texts, and a number of these were directly concerned with social reformation. The utopian writings of the early modern period take a wide range of forms. There are mock travel narratives, early forms of science fiction which project fantastic societies in other worlds, like Joseph Hall's *Mundus Alter Et Idem* ('Another world and yet the same') (1605) and Francis Godwin's *The Man in the Moone* (1638). There are works of political philosophy which present idealized societies as direct models for emulation, like *Macaria* and *Oceana*, and utopian dialogues of the later sixteenth century, which, like *Utopia*, highlighted problems with contemporary society and modelled solutions through imaginary foreign communities (Nicholls 1579; Lupton 1580). There are early utopian novels, like Samuel Gott's *Nova Solyma* (1648), which portrays an idealized society in Nova Solyma, or New Jerusalem; the experience of living in Nova Solyma is an education for its English visitors on the question of how to live a good life as individuals, as well as how to build an ideal community. The practice of imagining idealized societies in print proliferated in the seventeenth century, as the questions of the ideal society and the good life were explored in many forms of writing beyond the conventional utopia (C. Houston 2014).

It is tempting to see these various forms of utopian literature in the decades that followed 1516 as constituting a neat division of elements that were united in More's work: *Utopia*'s playfulness going into satirical travel narratives, and its political philosophy into works dedicated to social reform, for example. In fact, both overtly political and overtly fictional utopian writing of the early modern period continue to share interests, and, in particular, fictional or literary utopias often remain concerned with political questions, even when they seem to obscure such concerns. All utopian writing from this period took from *Utopia* a focus on the question of what it means to live a good life and a profound questioning of the status quo; and fictional utopias, forerunners of the utopian novel, remained close to *Utopia* in a number of ways.

While each utopian text needs to be understood within its own context, rather than treated solely as an example of utopian fiction, early modern utopian texts are often profitably discussed in comparison with one another, and a number of shared concerns can be identified even in utopian texts dating from the furthest limits of the early modern period. For the rest of this chapter, we will consider some similarities between More's *Utopia* and one of its strangest literary descendants: *The Isle of Pines* (1668), by the Civil War republican Henry Neville. There are manifest differences between the two texts including, for example, *Utopia*'s sustained and explicit interest in the immediate social context of the time of its production, compared to *Isle*'s comparative silence on this subject;[2] *Utopia*'s more sophisticated engagement with political and moral philosophy; *Isle*'s centring of the travel narrative format in place of the dialogue. Nonetheless, or perhaps in light of these differences, a number of similarities between the texts demonstrate the productivity of their comparison. An examination of both texts' earliest publication histories, their use of paratexts, their playing with generic boundaries, and their critique of representation shows that these two utopian texts share a number of qualities and interests, even if these are not immediately apparent.

---

[2] But for a reading of *Isle of Pines* which recognizes its political contexts and interests, see Mahlberg 2006b.

Utopia

The publishing history of the earliest editions of *Utopia* is complex.[3] J. H. Hexter's hypothesis that Book Two was written first, when More had leisure during his visit to the Low Countries in 1515, and that Book One followed later when time allowed on his return to England, has been widely accepted (Hexter 1952). It seems likely that More completed both parts of the manuscript by the late summer of 1516, with additions and amendments being made under pressure of time (Baker-Smith 2000). In September of that year, he sent the completed book, together with a preface addressed to Peter Giles, to his friend Erasmus in the Netherlands. Erasmus edited the text, adding marginal notes and requesting prefatory letters, including those from Giles and Jerome Busleyden. Gerard Geldenhauer (aka 'Noviomagus'), who also provided some verses, informed Erasmus that the book would be published by Thierry Martens in Louvain, and would include a map by 'an illustrious artist', Ambrosius Holbein (Baker-Smith 2000: 35). The first (Latin) edition appeared at Louvain at the end of 1516, and seems to have been immediately successful, with Erasmus planning a new edition straight away. There followed a Paris edition in 1517, two in Basel in 1518, and one in Florence the following year. The first editions of *Utopia* were thus the product of numerous hands, with a wealth of paratextual material (at least sixteen paratextual elements in the March 1518 edition printed at Basel, for example). The presence of paratextual material, and especially the use of prefaces, was something that later utopian fiction would frequently replicate. The preface was 'conventionally the place where such works reflect upon their own fictitious nature, which was probably necessitated by the ancient suspicion against travellers' tales', and 'a rumination on the truthfulness of the traveller's story in the prefatorial position is almost always found in utopias', probably dating back to Lucian's *True History* (Csaba 2013: 18). Given that it constitutes an effort on behalf of author, editor, and other contributors to shape the reader's response to the text, paratextual material forms an important layer of meaning in More's multifaceted utopia.

In particular, there are a number of ways in which the paratexts of *Utopia* destabilize the notion that Utopia itself represents an ideal society. The French humanist Guillaume Budé's letter to Thomas Lupset was first published in the second edition, printed at Paris in 1517, and was reproduced in subsequent versions, including the 1518 edition upon which the standard Yale text is based (C. Houston 2014). Budé introduces Utopia as follows: 'The island of Utopia, however, which I hear is also called Udepotia, is said (if the story is to be believed) still to preserve, by marvellous good fortune, access both in its public and its private life to the truly Christian customs and the authentic wisdom' (More 1989: 118–119). Budé presents an image of Utopia based on Christian ideals, and goes on to say that this has been achieved through community of property, love of peace, and contempt for gold and silver. He asserts, therefore, as Raphael Hythloday will later

---

[3] For a detailed account, see Taylor in this volume.

maintain, that the 'true wisdom' of Christianity amounts to little more than communality of possessions, a seeming simplicity which sounds a note of caution. In the same breath as commending the Utopians' Christianity, Budé puns on Utopia as 'Udepotia' or 'Neverland', and adds the cautionary aside 'if we are to believe' (*si credimus*) Hythloday's story (More 1895a: lxxxvii). Here Budé touches on one of the central problems of *Utopia*. The text pretends to represent a society structured in an ideal manner and open to Christianity, but in doing so it demands that we question the true purpose and wisdom of that religion. Budé goes on to wish that all societies could follow the basic principles of Utopian legislation and asks what sort of holiness the Utopians had to possess not to fall victim to avarice and cupidity. But rather than address this wish to God, he calls instead upon 'the powers above' (*superi*) and 'the immortal gods' (*divi immortales*), referring to people as 'mortals' and to the devil as 'the Stygian adversary'.[4] Budé's terms of reference are pagan and classical rather than Christian. He suggests that divine powers have behaved in a less kindly manner to the states of Christendom: 'Would that God, in his infinite goodness, had dealt as kindly with those regions which still keep and proudly proclaim their allegiance to the faith called by his holy name!' (More 1989: 119). If Christian societies could live like the Utopians, Budé suggests that 'the golden age of Saturn would return', continuing to offer a confused frame of reference for Utopia which is at once Christian and classical. How can Utopia be, as Budé claims, simultaneously 'one of the Fortunate Isles, near neighbour to the Elysian Fields' of classical culture and 'Hagnopolis', the holy city, 'blessedly innocent, leading its own exalted life' (119–120)? By collapsing the difference between Christian and classical frames of reference Budé questions how compatible the two really are, and undermines his own presentation of Utopia as a purely Christian example of good living.

Following this prefatory letter, there are several episodes in Book One that destabilize the presentation of Utopia as an ideal state. The text rarely makes the chronology of its publication explicit, but at times we are reminded that More knew already how Utopia would later appear when he was writing Book One. One such occasion happens early in Morus' account of Hythloday's narrative of his journeys. Morus says that while travelling, Hythloday introduced the magnetic compass to a people who had not previously known of its existence (More 1989: 12). It seemed at first a useful innovation, but the mariners, unused to their new tool, soon became incautious and ventured out in dangerous weather, so that 'this discovery, which they thought would be so advantageous to them, may become the cause of much mischief'. Read before Utopia has been encountered, this odd little anecdote may seem insignificant, but it serves as a momentary reminder that not all innovations are advantageous, and that what works well in one place does not always have the same positive function when transferred to another. The inclusion of the story about the compass and the reference to the dangers to be encountered on sea-journeys can be read as a criticism of the notion that travel is purely a beneficial experience. Morus reminds his audience that travelling can be

---

[4] For Latin, see More 1895a: lxxxviii.

dangerous; the cultural exchange represented by the use of the compass is potentially a difficult and hazardous process. This episode serves to counter the idea that one culture can only benefit from adopting the practices of another, a warning against taking the seemingly advanced habits of Utopia as recommendations for contemporary England.

More's drawing on the conventions of travel literature through his inclusion of the anecdote about the compass is just one example of the way in which his text plays with generic boundaries. The question of how to categorize *Utopia* generically and how to describe the genre of the literary utopia has occupied scholars for generations (Vieira 2010; Chordas 2010). More's borrowings from the conventions of travel writing—like the paratextual materials—frequently serve to threaten the notion that *Utopia* is a representation of an ideal society and enhance the instability of the text.[5] In his letter to Giles, for example, More employs the well-worn convention of travel literature that the author should emphasize the first-hand nature of his experience and thus the authenticity of his narrative, claiming that he is only repeating 'what you and I together heard Raphael describe' (More 1989: 3). More then makes a show of insisting that he has in spite of this been as truthful as possible in relating Hythloday's tale: 'For, as I've taken particular pains to avoid untruths in the book, so, if anything is in doubt, I'd rather make an honest mistake than say what I don't believe. In short, I'd rather be truthful than correct' (5).

This play at verisimilitude reminds the reader of the falsity associated with the genre of travel writing from classical times onwards: More's account of Utopia is based entirely on the experiences of another, and so his claim to be telling the truth at the expense of all other considerations is self-consciously false. Later, in conversation with Morus and Giles, Hythloday makes his own claim for truthfulness, asserting the authority of the eyewitness: 'you should have been with me in Utopia and seen with your own eyes their manners and customs, as I did—for I lived there more than five years' (40). In doing so he calls to mind the similar declaration of Lucian in the *True History*, where he claims the traveller's privilege of superior knowledge: 'Well, that is what it was like on the Moon. If you do not believe me, go and see for yourself' (Lucian 1990: 262). The similarity of these two claims reminds us that neither Lucian nor Hythloday has been to the society he imagines, and that neither society really exists. Like Lucian, who describes the 'Saladfowls' and the 'Garlic-gassers' he encounters (254–255), More uses comic names for the people and landmarks of Utopia, such as the River Anydrus ('waterless') and Utopia itself ('no-place'). In doing so, and in his ostentatious claims for truthfulness, More allies his text with Lucian's travel satires in which descriptions of the ideal society are so hyperbolic as to be ridiculous. Reminding us of the tradition of satirizing travel literature, More establishes the ironic and playful context in which his text must be read.

This context affects the degree to which Book Two of *Utopia* can be taken to provide solutions for the English social ills and problems that are debated in the dialogue of Book One. For example, through its use of irony, *Utopia* points to ways in which seemingly ideal Utopian customs are ill-fitted for its European readership. The playing

---

[5] For more on the relationship of *Utopia* to travel writing, see Hadfield in this volume.

of religious music is one such example. In Utopia, Hythloday states, the production of music in religious ceremonies involves an exact match between the method of expression and its subject:

> all their music, both vocal and instrumental, renders and expresses natural feelings and perfectly matches the sound to the subject. Whether the words of the psalm are cheerful, supplicatory, serene, troubled, mournful, or angry, the music represents the meaning through the melody so admirably that it penetrates and inspires the minds of the ardent hearers. (More 1989: 106)

Utopian religious music precisely 'matches the sound to the subject', or in the Latin, 'ita sonus accommodatur ad rem [...] ita rei sensum quendam melodiae forma repraesentat, ut animos auditorum mirum in modum afficiat, penetret, incendat' (More 1895a: 296). The music has an effect on the spirits of the listeners because it represents meaning with total accuracy. But the instruments that produce such music are entirely different to those known by Hythloday's own audience, being 'quite different in shape from those in our part of the world' and in many cases 'not even comparable' (More 1989: 106). The perfect capacity of Utopian music to replicate exactly its subject is thus unattainable for the European audience, and Utopian music itself cannot be replicated elsewhere. Their musical arts are, like the Utopians, separated from the known world (Jameson 1977).

Utopia also critiques its own facility to represent accurately by questioning the notion that the text itself can provide an exact or truthful representation of its subject. The paratextual materials frequently cast doubt on the text's capacity to represent Utopia correctly, and it seems appropriate that the text should place the question of its own veracity at its very beginning. The 'preface' of the 1516 and 1518 editions of *Utopia* was More's own letter to Giles, and the question of the text's truthfulness is raised immediately, in More's apology for not having managed to transcribe Hythloday's relation of Utopia as quickly as he would have liked. The credulous reader may believe More's claim in his opening paragraph that 'All I had to do was repeat what you and I together heard Raphael describe' (More 1989: 3), but by the time any reader has encountered the description of Utopia itself, it will be obvious that More's role in the creation of *Utopia* goes beyond that of scribe. When More states at the end of this opening paragraph that 'Truth in fact is the only quality at which I should have aimed, or did aim, in writing this book', it is impossible to miss the significance of that '*should* have aimed' (Latin: *debeo*, More 1895a: 2). The question of the text's truthfulness is foregrounded elsewhere in the paratextual materials: Giles's letter to Busleyden, for example, jokes that both he and More missed hearing Hythloday explain where the island was actually located when one of their company coughed at the wrong moment (More 1989: 25). More's letter also bemoans the fact that he does not know in which sea Utopia is situated: 'I am quite ashamed not to know even the name of the ocean where this island lies about which I've written so much' (5). *Utopia*'s paratext repeatedly questions the text's capacity for truthful representation. In this respect, *Utopia* itself exemplifies Kate Lilley's description of later early-modern utopian writing, that it 'offers a critique of the world as it is, and also of representation as it is' (Lilley 1992: 109).

The Isle of Pines

Neville's *Isle of Pines* appears to be a very different sort of text, describing a very different sort of place, from More's *Utopia* (Ladani 2014: 38). Recent scholarship on the text has often sought to emphasize its distinctiveness from what might be called 'the conventional literary utopia' or the 'static ideal societies familiar to European readers' (Scheckter 2011: 8). John Scheckter, in his recent critical edition of the text, suggests that it depicts a society balanced between order and chaos, which looks back on the past 'with both relief and further fear of disorder' (11). Susan Bruce, in her introduction to *Utopia, New Atlantis*, and *Isle of Pines* in *Three Early Modern Utopias* (1999), reads all three texts as engaged with a discourse of origins, interested in the genesis of the societies which they depict and in the roots of the utopian genre. Neville's utopian text frequently looks backwards to its forebears, despite the obvious care taken by Neville to distinguish the Isle of Pines from Utopia itself.

Though both texts depict a fictional encounter with a fictional island, located at some distance from the narrator's and reader's own society, Neville's Isle of Pines bears little relation to Utopia in terms of its physical environment, its inhabitants, and its social organization. Rather than being (like Utopia) an island deliberately cultivated and with a long history of human civilization, the Isle of Pines is a desert island, apparently discovered in 1589 by five survivors of a shipwreck and subsequently populated by them. The text begins with a letter purporting to be from Henry Cornelius Van Sloetten, a Dutch sailor whose ship was blown off course en route to the East Indies, 'and wracked near to the Coast of *Terra Australis, Incognita*' (Neville 1668: A2r). Finding themselves on the unknown island, Van Sloetten and his companions encounter a community of English-speaking people, numbering around 2,000 in total. Their leader, William Pine, explains that the island was originally discovered and populated by his grandfather, George Pine, and his four companions following their own shipwreck a century before. Pine and his fellow survivors, who are the daughter of his master, two maidservants, and an enslaved black woman, find life on the island to be remarkably comfortable, with abundant food and clement weather. George Pine's narration of this stage of the Isle's history has been read as an arcadia, with human inhabitants living at one with the natural world (Mahlberg 2012b: 61). Although Pine does eventually impose some rules on his many offspring, decreeing after a period of forty years, when the population has reached 560, that all members of the community must read the Bible once a month and refrain from marrying their siblings, he is a remarkably passive ruler, and the society demands little intervention from its patriarch. Following his death, however, the Isle of Pines encounters conflict, as Pine's descendants break the two rules that have been given to them and decline into social disorder; 'the idyll degenerates into a dystopian nightmare' (Denbo 2007: 158).

Despite the obvious differences between these two utopian locations, however, there are a number of resonances between the texts themselves which point to the ways in which More's presentation of his fictional island influenced subsequent utopian writing. The earliest version of Neville's *Isle of Pines* was first published in June 1668, 150 years after the expanded edition of More's *Utopia* was printed at Basel. This first publication consisted solely of the fictional narrative of George Pine, whose ship, like Van Sloetten's, is wrecked on its journey to the East Indies. In this narration, Pine describes how he and four fellow travellers set up a community on the deserted island. Eventually beginning sexual relations with each of the women, Pine becomes the patriarch of this society, which finally includes 1,789 of his descendants. By the end of the history, he has witnessed the deaths of all four of his consorts, and passed his narrative, along with his rulership of the island, to his eldest son.

Although this version (hereafter Part I) was presented on its own both in this original printing and in some later editions, it was quickly followed, in July 1668, by *A New and Further Discovery of The Isle of Pines*, which, as Scheckter has written, 'changes and complicates every angle of the original' (2011: xii). *A New and Further Discovery* (henceforth Part II) has for its narrator Cornelius Van Sloetten, the Dutch captain who reaches the island in 1667 and makes his own observations about the place and its inhabitants. Pine's original narrative is passed to the Dutch sailors by William Pine; this narrative is copied, but then apparently stolen, a gap in the pagination testifying to where it would have been included in Part II. Were this not complicated enough, there then appeared, just weeks later, a third publication, or Combined Version, in which Part I is inserted back into Part II, where, according to Van Sloetten, it should have been all along, and the entire text is again titled *The Isle of Pines*. In the Combined Version, the Dutch narrator is now called Henry Cornelius Van Sloetten, and, in addition to his narration and that of George Pine, the text includes some supplementary paratextual material in the form of two prefatory letters, an engraved frontispiece, a four-panel illustration of the plot of the entire work, and a coda. Like *Utopia*, the title page of the Combined Version continues to present it as a genuine travel narrative: 'The ISLE of PINES, OR, A late Discovery of a fourth ISLAND near *Terra Australis, Incognita* BY Henry Cornelius Van Sloetten'.

Like *Utopia*, *The Isle of Pines* was quickly translated out of its original language, with a number of editions appearing in Europe soon after its first publication (Mahlberg 2012a: 1–2). If the early publication history of the Latin *Utopia* is complex, with numerous editions following one another, and the second edition expanding on the first in terms of its paratext, then the early publication history of *The Isle of Pines* is convoluted in the extreme, as though Neville had taken the idea of a multilayered, multiple-edition fictional travel narrative and pushed it to the point of absurdity.

As with *Utopia*, the paratext of *The Isle of Pines* destabilizes the direct communication of information by the main narratives: in Scheckter's words, the 'transmission of information' is 'unsettled' (2011: 54). The two fictitious letters added to the Combined Version purport to be from a Dutch merchant, Abraham Keek, the '*Friend and Brother*' of their unnamed recipient (Neville 1668: A2v). Far from testifying to the authenticity of Van Sloetten or the veracity of his narrative, however, Keek's letters 'offer only a tentative, unsubstantiated version of events', naming neither Van Sloetten nor George Pine, nor the island in question (Scheckter 2011: 55). Keek apparently writes his first letter when Van Sloetten's ship has landed in at La Rochelle on its way to Amsterdam, having received an early report of Van Sloetten's narrative from '*a Merchant in this City*'; the second letter is written after the ship has sailed onwards for Amsterdam. Both letters, brief and apparently written in haste, undermine the veracity of the narrative which is to follow. For one thing, Keek misrepresents the position of the island, placing it in the north Atlantic, '*about 2 or 300 Leagues Northwest from* Cape Finis Terre', and the population, which he estimates at '*about* 2000 English *people*', rather than the figure of 'ten or twelve thousand persons' which is offered on the title page (Neville 1668: A2r–v). Keek recognizes that errors may have been made in the geographical calculations, which he will seek to correct: '*it may be that there may be some mistake in the number of the Leagues, as also of the exact point of the Compass, from* Cape Finis Terre; *I shall enquire more particularly about it*' (A2v). This calls to mind More's letter to Giles in *Utopia*, in which he regrets the fact that he may have made errors in the exact calculation of distances and measurements, and requests that Giles should verify these calculations via Hythloday. Keek's gross error in placing the Isle of Pines in the north Atlantic rather than the south-east Indian Ocean—in not only the wrong sea but the wrong hemisphere—is so inaccurate as to be entirely unbelievable, and strongly reminiscent of More's particular mention of the difficulty of fixing Utopia in an ocean. Like More's letter to Giles, which is apparently written before he has made the decision to put *Utopia* into print, Keek's letters exist in a fictional time located historically in between the completion of the narrative and before its actual publication. As Scheckter points out, by the time the reader encounters Keek's letters, they are 'factually irrelevant, useful only for their sense of pressure', much as More's letter is no longer factually accurate by the time it is encountered by the reader, serving to call attention to errors and inconsistencies rather than to lend veracity to the main narrative or clarify 'unfamiliar presumptions in [the] source text' (Scheckter 2011: 55).

The veracity of the text seems to have been the focus of its initial reception. On his copy of the Combined Version of *The Isle of Pines*, Anthony à Wood wrote: 'W[he]n this was first published 'twas look'd upon as a sham' (Neville 1668/W: A2r). Wood, like Pepys, may have had the text bound with other, genuine, travel narratives, but he clearly perceived it as a work of fiction (Mahlberg 2006a); shams were a popular form of writing in the Restoration, permitting as they did the expression of unorthodox or scandalous ideas and opinions (Loveman 2008). However, outside Neville's own circles, it seems that a number of readers were taken in by the text's pretence and 'believed that Utopia was a real place' (Chordas 2010: 66). Such readings would have been encouraged by the fact that, although Wood identified Neville as the author of the text, Neville himself never admitted to his authorship (D. Carey 2010: 203, 204; Mahlberg 2006a: 133–134). The earliest responses to *The Isle of Pines* constituted a discourse on its truthfulness, with at least one reader, Henri Justel, making a 'hopeful enquiry' about the island's existence and being disappointed eventually to learn of its falsity (D. Carey 2010: 204). Like *Utopia*, *The Isle of Pines* is a text which plays with generic boundaries; modern scholarship has considered it as a travel narrative, arcadia, utopia, Robinsonade (i.e. narrative about being marooned on a desert island), erotic fantasy, and political satire amongst other things (Fausett 1993; Mahlberg 2012b: 4). In considering the question of genre, Daniel Carey draws attention to Wood's classification of *The Isle of Pines* as a sham, noting 'the capacity of forged documents to move in an unsettling way between the generic boundaries that separate fiction and history, or fantasy and truth' (D. Carey 1993: 23). Like *Utopia*, *The Isle of Pines* is a text which disturbs the clear demarcation of genre and raises questions about the possibility of categorizing and indeed reliably making sense of written texts.

Lennard Davis argued in *Factual Fictions: The Origins of the English Novel* that the roots of the novel can be separated altogether from the category of fiction, with early novelists tending to claim that their works were true. In order to avoid the censure accorded to fictional literature, the novel instead affiliates itself with 'news', thus committing itself, in Davis's words, to the 'inherent doubleness and reflexivity' of 'an ambiguous form—a factual fiction which denied its fictionality and produced in its readers a characteristic uncertainty or ambivalence as to whether they were reading something true or false' (L. J. Davis 1983: 36). The utopian novel, which has its roots in the seventeenth-century utopian fictions that continued to be strongly influenced by *Utopia* itself, affiliates, like *Utopia*, with travel writing, also a genre which lies on the borders between fact and fiction. This affiliation with travel writing, the consequent 'inherent doubleness' of early modern utopian texts, and the uncertainty or ambivalence produced in their readership, are important ways in which these utopian novels, *The Isle of Pines* amongst them, had their origins in *Utopia*, a text which has an 'inherent doubleness' at its core. Like other utopian novels, *The Isle of Pines* is a fundamentally unstable text, having in common with *Utopia* its multiple layers of narration and narrative voices, complex paratexts, and generic unfixedness, which combine to destabilize a straightforward reading of the text.

The Isle of Pines also shares *Utopia*'s interest in the fallibility of representation and the text's capacity to denote anything with accuracy. This implicit critique of representation is present in the description of the island and in the main body of Van Sloetten's narrative, but it comes to the fore in the paratextual material, and especially the text's coda or Post-Script. In this Post-Script, we are told about a mistake made by the Isle of Pines' seventeenth-century inhabitants, who, on hearing the music of bagpipes, are convinced that the musical instrument is a living entity: 'to see the admiration of those naked people concerning them, would have striken you into admiration; long time it was before we could perswade them that it was not a living creature, although they were permitted to touch and feel it' (Neville 1668: 31). The inhabitants cannot understand that the music could be a representation, mimesis, rather than an actual being. Further blurring the boundaries between fact and fiction, Neville seems to have taken this anecdote from a contemporary travel narrative, *The Golden Coast*, which had been published three years previously, in which native people also confuse bagpipes with a living being

(Anon. 1665: 89; Mahlberg 2008: 136). Their belief that the music emanates from a creature is in both anecdotes a comment on the naïvety of the audience. The response of the inhabitants of the Isle of Pines is born of lack of experience, though not, we are told, of stupidity: 'and yet are the people very intelligible, retaining a great part of the Ingenuity and Gallantry of the English Nation, though they have not that happy means to express themselves' (Neville 1668: 31). In Neville's version of this story, the bagpipe-player is an Irishman who is 'un-English'd' by his time abroad and can no longer remember the English language, but has learned the bagpipes in England, remembered the technique, and taken the instrument to sea with him. The man himself possesses multiple identities, constituting a mixture of cultural, national, and linguistic characteristics. In retaining part of their English identity, the islanders apparently retain what the text perceives to be their native English intelligence, but they are unable to distinguish between reality and its simulacrum in listening to the bagpipes' music. The naked natives in the Post-Script stand in for the reader of the text, who may, like Henri Justel, naïvely believe that *The Isle of Pines* is a genuine travel narrative.

Conclusion

Like many other early modern utopias, including the island of Bensalem in Bacon's *New Atlantis*, Utopia and the Isle of Pines are societies that stand on the brink of being known. Each text revels in this position as both known and not-known, lying on the borders between the factual and the fictional, and resists simple categorization. These are undeniably very different utopias, written for different audiences, but they share an interest not only in the nature of the good life but also in more serious political and literary questions: to return to Lilley's formulation, they critique the world as it is, and they also critique representation as it is. Following *Utopia*, political and fictional utopias are distinct in some ways, but continue to be related by this shared interest in critiquing the world within a mode of writing that questions its own capacity for accurate representation. Fictional utopias are still political, in registering to a greater or lesser extent a dissatisfaction with the status quo, even when, like Morus, they are sceptical about plans for improvement.

CHAPTER 31

OF SURVIVAL AND LIVING TOGETHER
The Eighteenth-Century Utopian Novel

NICOLE POHL

IN 1516, Thomas More published his controversial book, *De optimo reipublicae statu deque nova insula Libellus vere aureus, nec minus salutaris quam festivus* ('Of the best state of a commonwealth and of the new island Utopia, truly a golden booklet, as beneficial as it is cheerful'). This small book gave a political/philosophical school of thought its name but also coined a literary genre which since its inception has been debated in form and function.[1] The schism between the form and function of the literary utopia, between its literariness and utopian speculation, which divides scholarly work on utopias but also utopian writers themselves, can be bridged by an understanding of utopia as literature of knowledge for living (*Lebenswissenschaft*). In this framework, literature presents and mediates collective human experiences and knowledge in aesthetic forms of expression as an extension of life sciences. Hans Ulrich Seeber (2017: 1–2) reminds us that literary utopias, particularly utopian fiction, carry, convey, and assemble the knowledge of experience, of survival (*Überlebenswissen*), and of living together (*Zusammenlebenswissen*) as society and a species. This knowledge is not expressed naïvely and untheorized but as Christoph Menke (2010) has argued, through a critical lens, underpinned and made possible, as I would argue, by specific aesthetic features. This aesthetic-critical stance emerges as the core of the literary utopia which, since More, had to negotiate the tension between sociopolitical theory and aesthetic expression.

The early novel of the eighteenth century developed from and reframed the fictional satire, romance, and prose fiction of the sixteenth and seventeenth centuries. It thus

---

[1] Scholars have debated if More himself named the book *Utopia* or if it was the editors or printers; for the naming of the work, see Taylor in this volume; for a summary of this debate, see Schölderle 2017. For an overview of utopia as a literary genre, see esp. Fortunati 2000.

started off as a complex hybrid, experimenting in the eighteenth century with satire, romance, the supernatural, travel writing (including the imaginary voyage), sentimentalism, and 'formal realism' to capture human experiences with verisimilitude and historical relevance. In the following, I will show that the utopian novel of the period taps into these concerns and integrates the 'literary' and 'political' into a polygeneric and polymodal literary genre that, as a literature of knowledge for living and surviving, not only reflects the issues of the day but is guided by a discourse on change. These concerns, as my case studies indicate, were debated across Europe in the period, in dialogue with each other.

The Beginnings: More's *Utopia*

Utopia was conceived during More's appointment in 1515 as a delegate to a conference on Anglo-Flemish commerce.[2] More famously composed Book Two, 'The Discourse on Utopia', first and concluded it in 1516 with Book One, which includes the 'Dialogue of Counsel' (Hexter 1952: 18–21). The book's unusual structure and composition, the title's pun on 'no-place' (*ou-topia*) and 'good place' (*eu-topia*), the use of ambivalent rhetorical strategies (such as litotes, a figure of speech which expresses a thought by denying its opposite), and double-coding of the place and character names—that is, their satirical meanings—create a truly open text that reflects critically on the possibility of a 'best state of a commonwealth'.[3]

Book One records the political and social ailments of early modern Europe through the eyes of the fictitious sailor Raphael Hythloday in debate with 'Morus' (More's textual persona) and Peter Giles. It echoes principal humanist debates on the best state government, civic self-government, social equality, and political wisdom in the light of the development of absolutism and early capitalism. Whereas in Book One, England is seen as held in the clutches of agrarian capitalism where sheep 'eat up and swallow down the very men themselves' (More 1992a: 26), the Utopians in Book Two recognize the true value of material goods and class distinction: 'for the smaller or finer thread of wool, which self-same wool (be it now in never so fine a spun thread) did once a sheep wear, and yet was she all that time no other thing than a sheep' (82). Some of these issues were also discussed by More's friends and contemporaries such as Desiderius Erasmus in *Adages* (*Chiliades Adagiorum*, 1502–32) or his *Praise of Folly* (1511). The paradigm governing the *Adages* was the principle of *amicorum communia omnia* ('Friends hold all things in common'), the spirit of true community that we also find in Utopia.

Since its conception, the multifaceted ambiguity of *Utopia* has puzzled philosophers and literary scholars alike. Satire and rhetorical ambivalence undercut the idea that

---

[2] For more on the embassy to Flanders, see Hower in this volume.
[3] For the rhetorical strategies used in *Utopia* (including litotes), see Zurcher in this volume.

Utopia is a simplistic 'Golden Handbook' for change. The dialogue between Books One and Two, the multiple perspectives in Book Two, and, finally, the unreliability of Hythloday as the 'nonsense pedlar' turn the text into a satirical musing on Utopian possibilities. As Morus states, closing his account:

> In the mean time, as I cannot agree and consent to all things that he [Hythloday] said, being else without doubt a man singularly well learned and also in all worldly matters exactly and profoundly experienced, so must I needs confess and grant that many things be in the Utopian weal-public which in our cities I may rather wish for than hope for. (More 1992a: 136–137)

But it is not only the utopian message which is multilayered and ambivalent (and thus in many ways pre-empts the critical utopia of the eighteenth century) but the dialogic form too.

Utopia is a dialogue, determined by literary forms and aesthetic and rhetorical strategies. Thus, in the case of More's *Utopia*, it is the dialogue as a literary and philosophical form which provides one obvious formal model for the text. Originating in Plato's dialogues, the medieval and Renaissance incarnations of dialogues are diverse and were clearly popular. As a well-versed vehicle for polemic, philosophical debates, poetic eloquence, and political persuasion, it lent itself ideally to the literary utopia of the Renaissance period, but with the development of the early novel, is pushed to the background by formal realism (see Watt 1957). Chlöe Houston argues that during the early modern period, utopia develops from '[philosophical] satire to utopia as an imaginative means to achieve social reform' by developing the dialogue into a narrative (C. Houston 2014: 10). Part of this transition from dialogue form to narrative is the assimilation of the already established travel narrative into utopian literature.

Early travel narrative, or more precisely imaginary voyages, by Homer, Herodotus, and Thucydides were parodied by Lucian in his second-century Menippean satire, *A True Story* (*Alethon diegematon*) which used the imaginary voyage (and indeed the lunar voyage) to reflect critically on his contemporary society (Marsh 1998: 181–210). Thus, as Northrop Frye (1957: 310) has proposed, the Menippean satire provided a useful literary form for More and later utopian writers such as Jonathan Swift. However, Vita Fortunati has made the case that whilst the satire (and the dialogue) is didactic and philosophical, as a literary form utopia 'unlike satire, [...] always aims, implicitly or explicitly, at a systematic description of society as it should be' (Fortunati 2000: 6). Therefore, if utopia has merely adopted elements of satire and the early modern dialogue, the question is now to define the utopian genre. Fortunati therefore asks:

> What are then the characteristics of the utopian genre? To propose a rough definition of utopian narrative, then, one might say that it is the detailed and systematic description—achieved either in a positive sense or in an ironic-negative (or

dystopian, anti-utopian) sense—of an alternative society, one which emerges in opposition to that within which the writer operates. (4)[4]

The key word here is 'description', a literary activity designed, as Louis Marin puts it, 'to project, into the language, a total and perfect presence to the spirit' (Marin 1973; cited in Fortunati 2000: 4). Discursive openness accompanied by mimesis allows for the formation of a narrative literary genre that juxtaposes the author's society with an alternative and, certainly in the case of More, better society. Given that the alternative society is either geographically remote (*eu/utopia*) or placed in the past/future (*eu/uchronia*), 'cognitive estrangement' in form and attitude contests the narrative verisimilitude and indicates utopia's relationship with romance, science fiction, and fantasy (Suvin 1979, 2014). As I will show, the eighteenth-century utopian novel seeks to bridge this gulf in different formal ways, including the embedding of micro-utopias within early novel forms, or imbuing the imaginary voyage and satire with formal realist features.

Thus, from the moment of its inception, utopia has been a hybrid literary genre evolving from and creating new generic features and formal structures whilst absorbing relevant historical and political debates and issues. Therefore, it lent itself particularly well to the emerging novel of the eighteenth century by experimenting with formal realism and introducing the idea of history and perfectibility to the utopian discourse *(eu/uchronia)*. Primitivist and nostalgic utopias, sentimental individualist utopias, voyage utopias, satires, anti-utopias, pornographic utopias (somatopias), feminist utopias, micro-utopias, and philosophical tales populate the fictional landscape of the eighteenth century.[5] In the following I will particularly look at the incarnations and reincarnations of the voyage utopia in the eighteenth-century novel of sensibility, imaginary voyage, satire, and critical utopia.[6]

Geographical Utopias

In the eighteenth century, the geographical utopia evolved into different models. Ethnological utopias speculated on diverse models of progressive socialization from a 'state of nature' culminating in what Adam Smith called the 'Age of Commerce', or simply, modern civil society. Natural histories of civil society developed an idea of a gradual progression of humanity through comparisons between European and non-Western societies.[7] Such narratives served to demarcate Western achievements in science and technology, the arts and culture: in short, what they perceived as civilization.

---

[4] Whilst formally, dystopia did not exist in eighteenth-century utopian literatures, we can identify the utopian satire in Daniel Defoe and the critical utopia in Robert Paltock and Voltaire. On the critical utopia in the eighteenth century, see Pohl 2007.
[5] On some of these subgenres, see Pohl 2010. On micro-utopias, see Racault 1991; Lewes 2000.
[6] I follow Fausett 1993 in using the term 'voyage utopia'.
[7] See e.g. Adam Smith, *On the Wealth of Nations* (1776); John Locke, *Of Civil Government* (1690); Montesquieu, *Réflexions sur la Monarchie universelle en Europe* (1724) and *De l'ésprit des lois* (1748);

This conjectural historiography justified and naturalized colonization of the 'New World', as we can see in More's *Utopia* (Seeber 2017). A more relativist representation of human nature and human values drew attention to fundamental geographical, climatic, and historical differences between peoples and cultures.[8] Within this framework, progress and the concept of civilization were redefined as relative, not absolute. Historical pessimism created utopias that idealized the 'state of nature' and defined society and civilization as progressive alienation from an original good: they thus opposed Thomas Hobbes's antisocial notion in *Leviathan* of the 'natural' man in that this version of utopia promised the regeneration to man's *status naturalis*. This primitivist dream of the ideal society was perhaps first expressed in Montaigne's essay 'Des Cannibales' (c.1580), and in the eighteenth century, in Jean-Jacques Rousseau's reconstruction of the *homme naturel*. Utopian novels such as Denis Vairasse's *History of the Sevarites* (1675, written in English) or Gabriel de Foigny's 1676 *La Terre austral connue* (translated by David Fausset in 1993 as *The Southern Land, Known*) document simple, virtuous, and self-sufficient communities, anticipating Rousseau's 'noble savage', as does Aphra Behn's essentialist description of the Indians in Surinam in her short prose fiction *Oroonoko* (1688), which portrays them in their innocency, simplicity, and non-aggression.

The eighteenth-century novel marries these primitivist discourses with the novel of sensibility such as Henry Mackenzie's *The Man of the World* (1773) and Sophie von La Roche's *Erscheinungen am See Oneida* (1798), the title of which would translate as 'Apparitions or Events at Lake Oneida'. For such writers, the idea of 'sympathy' binds intuitive human beings into a community of affectionate responsiveness to one another's joy and sorrow; the identification of the beholder with the pain of the sufferer extended and consolidated the human community of which both are a part by directing the immediate feelings of the responsive witness into sympathetic action, the requirements of moral duty. Anthony Ashley-Cooper, third Earl of Shaftesbury (1671–1713), and Rousseau posited the idea of sympathy and compassion (*pitié*) as the basis of a good human society that holds selfish individualism, or in Rousseau's words, *amour propre*, in check. As John Mullan explains, the novel of sensibility speaks to 'the need to imagine how private individuals might understand each other and learn to share each other's interests. If the novel developed as a genre that made significant the distinctive fate of a particular individual, then sentimentalism was the attempt to rescue that individual from isolation and selfishness' (Mullan 1996: 248). The complexity of this is particularly explored in Rousseau's *Les Rêveries du promeneur solitaire* ('The Reveries of a Solitary Walker', 1776–8). Here, Rousseau suggests that through solitary contemplation, civilized man regains his primitive sympathy and emphatic sociability. In Walk Six, however, he experiences the corruption of this sympathy, tracing in some ways the civilizing process of mankind. He starts off by experiencing 'his natural goodness combined with his

---

Jean-Jacques Rousseau, *Sur l'origine et les fondements de l'inégalité* (1755) and *Du Contrat Social* (1762); Adam Ferguson, *An Essay on the History of Civil Society* (1767); Thomas Hobbes, *Leviathan* (1651).

[8] See particularly Montesquieu.

excessive pity' in the face of human poverty and fragility (Butterworth 1992: 203). He then increasingly feels the pressing burden of obligation and duty:

> The conclusion I can draw from all these reflections is that I have never been truly fitted for social life, where there is nothing but irksome duty and obligation [...]. As long as I act freely I am good and do nothing but good, but as soon as I feel the yoke of necessity or human society I become rebellious, or rather recalcitrant, and then I am of no account. (Rousseau 1979: 103)

Thus, the literature of sensibility as a form of *Lebenswissenschaften* explores human society and human relations in action. However, despite the emphasis on empathy, sympathy, polite sensibility, and virtue, it also explored the dangerous excesses and corruption of these human emotions which result either in the private return to nature ('individualist utopias'), as Rousseau's solitary walker puts into effect, or the retreat of a like-minded few into micro-societies, as we have in the community at Clarens in Rousseau's *Julie ou La Nouvelle Héloïse* (1761).

Prefiguring the individualist utopias are the Robinsonades (named after Daniel Defoe's 1719 travel narrative *Robinson Crusoe*), with the German *Der abenteuerliche Simplicissimus Teutsch* (1668) by Hans Jakob Christoffel von Grimmelshausen as an early example.[9] The novel depicts the picaresque life journey of the protagonist Melchior Sternfels von Fuchshaim during the period of the Thirty Years War (1618–48). After a life of misery, warfare, and deceit in Germany, Japan, Macau, Egypt, Rome, Constantinople, and Moscow, Melchior reflects on his life, European society, faith, and the Church and decides to do a pilgrimage to Santiago de Compostela in Spain. On the way, he is shipwrecked, spends fifteen years, first with a companion, then alone on a remote island very much like the later Robinson Crusoe, and in the end, favours his solitary life to being rescued by a Dutch ship that happens upon him. Robinsonades—such as *Simplicissimus* and Defoe's *Robinson Crusoe*, but also Henry Neville's *The Isle of Pines* (1668), *Les Aventures de Télémaque* (1699) by François Fénelon, and Hendrik Smeeks's *Beschryvinge van het magtig Koningryk Krinke Kesmes* ('Description of the Mighty Kingdom of Krinke Kesme', 1708)—are formally indebted to the utopian satire and the imaginary voyage, but as individualist utopias they are fundamentally pessimistic about the perfectibility of human society (Blaim 2013; 2016: 6).[10]

The eighteenth-century answer to the individualist Robinsonade is the retirement from society explored by Rousseau's *Reveries* and *Julie*, and Voltaire's *Candide, ou l'Optimisme* (1759). Unlike the Robinsonade, the sentimental novel is invested in the innate sociability of man and projects its utopian hope onto the new worlds, shared by a small group of affectionate companions or exemplary indigenous peoples. The retreat is the refuge to the pastoral and the nostalgic. Henry Mackenzie's first novel, *The Man*

---

[9] The book is known in English as *Simplicius Simplicissimus*.
[10] For more on Fénelon, see Verhaart and Hill in this volume; for more on *The Isle of Pines*, see Houston in this volume.

of Feeling (1771), considers the 'man of feeling' as a virtuous opposite of the 'commercial' man, though at the same time, he emasculated his protagonist Harley through his self-absorbed and raw emotionality (Maurer 1998: 29). In his second novel, *The Man of the World* (1773), Mackenzie juxtaposes, rather schematically, the stoic and virtuous Cherokee Indians with the Europeans' self-indulgence in sentimentality to warn against the excesses of emotionality. After years of capture, Mackenzie's protagonist, William Annesly comes to idealize the Cherokee nation as a perfect society, 'where greatness cannot use oppression, nor wealth excite envy; where the desires are native to the heart, and the languor of satiety is unknown; where, if there is no refined sensation of delight, there is also no ideal source of calamity' (Mackenzie 1976: 2.183). Whilst the juxtaposition between the Cherokee and eighteenth-century Europeans functions as a critique of civilization and progress, it also embodies a nostalgia for lost innocence (G. A. Barker 1975: 67). This nostalgia is not anticipatory in the sense of Ernst Bloch (*Vorschein*) but harks back to an idealized state of nature. If Paradise or the Golden Age has been lost, then surely it could be found and thus it becomes a utopian paradigm. This quest for Paradise, embodied in the iconographic tropes of the Golden Age, was projected onto new worlds, be it the Americas or the Antipodes, with a wish to revert or at least halt the progress of civilization.[11]

One way of halting and reverting this debatable progress was education, as outlined in Rousseau's *Émile, ou De l'éducation* (1762). Jacques-Henri Bernardin de Saint-Pierre's novel *Paul et Virginie* (1788) is an explicitly pastoral novel (read as domestic fiction by Berman 2006: 57–87), which outlines the upbringing of two children—a new utopian generation—following Rousseau's principles. It responds to the exoticization of the South Seas, particularly after Louis-Antoine, Comte de Bougainville's popular, real-life travel account of his circumnavigation of the globe, *Le Voyage autour du monde, par la frégate La Boudeuse, et la flûte L'Étoile* (1771), and Denis Diderot's fictitious *Supplément au voyage de Bougainville* (written 1772, published 1796), subtitled 'a dialogue between A and B on the drawback of binding moral ideas to certain physical actions which bear none' (*dialogue entre A et B sur l'inconvénient d'attacher des idées morales à certaines actions physiques qui n'en comportent pas*). Vladimir Kapor suggests that Bougainville 'viewed Tahiti with a heavy philosophical investment, through an array of pre-existing concepts such as the "Noble Savage" or "state of nature", and reconstructed it accordingly, thus in turn shaping the abstract Tahitian mirage' (Kapor 2008: 227). Diderot fed into this construction of the Tahitian by using the utopian form of the dialogue to contrast the idealized society and harmony of Tahiti with the flawed and degenerate Europe. Both Bougainville and Diderot trade in the exotic to make a philosophical point. Bernardin de Saint-Pierre's *Paul et Virginie* infuses this exotic discourse with issues of education, sexuality, colonialism, and class whilst at the same time being much more accurate in the description of nature and the environment beyond the idealizing eighteenth-century iconography:

---

[11] For the utopia of sensibility more generally, see Bartolomeo 2007.

At twelve years of age Paul was more robust and intelligent than Europeans at fifteen, and where the Negro Domingue had merely cultivated, he had beautified. He went with him to the neighbouring woods to uproot young lemon- and orange-trees, tamarinds whose round tops are of such a lovely green, and custard-apple trees whose fruit contains a sweet cream with the fragrance of orange-blossoms. He set these trees, which had already grown quite tall, around the perimeter of their enclosure, where he had already planted the seeds of those trees that flower or fruit in their second year: agathis whose long bunches of white flowers hang down in a circle like the crystals of a chandelier; the Persian lilac whose clusters of blossoms, the colour of unbleached linen, rise straight into the air; and the papaw whose trunk bristles with green melons instead of branches and rises to a capital of broad leaves like those of the fig-tree. (Bernardin de Saint-Pierre 2005: 59)

Paul and Virginie represent the Rousseauesque children of nature who live in an Edenic harmonious society in Mauritius: a utopian, *petite societé* ('micro-society') amongst European settlers and slavery (Howells 2007: ch. 3). Despite the integration of simple human society into nature—seen in the quotation above—there are hierarchies. The Rousseauesque Paul is superior to the indigenous Domingue through an education that nurtured his innate quality of taste, natural virtue, and sympathy.[12] Another juxtaposition, the one between Europe and Eden, is set up through the narrative voice of a settler, and is further underscored by Virginie's sojourn in Europe and her epistolary exchanges with Paul during that time. These letters are reminiscent of Françoise de Graffigny's epistolary *Lettres d'une Péruvienne* (1747) that also contrast an Edenic Inca society with the 'barbaric' high society of eighteenth-century France in the letters of the captured Inca princess Zilia. Whilst *Lettres d'une Péruvienne* is Swiftian in essence, *Paul et Virginie* is sentimental. Paul and Virginie's correspondence documents that they have grown into sentimental and naïve adults who are but fragile utopians.[13]

Von La Roche was inspired by, and reworked, both Rousseau's *Julie* and Bernardin de Saint-Pierre's *Paul and Virginie*. Her novel *Erscheinungen am See Oneida* outlines a conjectural history of society from the Edenic union of the Wattines, who fled France during the French Revolution to the American wilderness, to the creation of a democratic community with other European immigrants. Von La Roche's story was loosely based on the real-life French émigrés, a husband and wife called Wattine, who fled to Lake Oneida, lived there in isolation for some years, and then founded a settlement. The story was most probably related to La Roche by her son Fritz who visited the Lake in 1794 and met the couple (Lange 1948). La Roche's novel so impressed Alexis de Tocqueville that he visited the site on his American travels with Gustave de Beaumont in the 1830s and composed the brief 'Journey to Lake Oneida', published posthumously in 1835.[14]

---

[12] On the issue of slavery and race in the novel, see Prasad 2009: 21–44.
[13] See also Sarah Fielding's *The Adventures of David Simple, Volume the Last* (1753), which like the novels of Mackenzie and Bernardin de Saint-Pierre, struggles with the concept of the utopia of sensibility. See Woodward 1992.
[14] For an English translation, see Tocqueville 1960.

La Roche's depiction of the indigenous people—the Oneida nation—serves as a complex contrast to the horrors of the Terror in France.[15] Whilst they are romanticized, idealized, and stereotyped, life at Oneida creates the possibility, as Alessa Johns has argued, of a feminocentric space founded on community, support, and nourishment (Johns 2003: 141–155). The cultural barriers between the Oneida nation and the European settlers become meaningless in the shared humanity of giving birth and nurturing life. Thus, as Linda Dietrick concludes, 'here among the indigenous inhabitants of America it seems possible to bring about what the French Revolution could not: the dream of returning to a natural state of equality and harmony' (Dietrick 2014: 26).

Mackenzie's, La Roche's, and Bernadin de Saint-Pierre's utopias are geographical micro-utopias. The schism between the new novelistic forms and utopian content/function is bridged by the insertion of micro-utopias. Indeed, as the micro-utopias draw on the nostalgic idea of Eden underpinned by a negative conjectural history of civilization, they complement and underscore the pastoral and sentimental elements of the novels.

Lunar and Subterranean Voyages

More fantastic projections of different and better worlds can be found in the lunar and subterranean voyages which emerged in the seventeenth century with Francis Godwin's *The Man in the Moone; or, A Discourse of a Voyage Thither by Domingo Gonsales the Speedy Messenger* (1638), John Wilkins's *The Discovery of a World in the Moone* (1638), and Cyranno de Bergerac's *L'autre monde ou L'Histoire comique des États et Empires de la Lune* ('The Other World, or; The Comic History of the States and Empires of the Moon', 1657). The lunar voyage continued in the eighteenth century with David Russen's *Iter lunare* ('Lunar Journey', 1703), Diego de Torres Villarroel's *Viaje fantástico del Gran Piscátor de Salamanca* ('The Fantastical Voyage of the Great Almanac-Writer of Salamanca', 1723), Robert Paltock's *The Life and Adventures of Peter Wilkins* (1751), and Voltaire's *Micromegas* (1752), the title of which would translate as the oxmoronic 'small-large'. These utopian speculations marry the imaginary voyage, the picaresque, astronomy, and astrology with satire and the early novel to reflect critically on their own worlds and societies.

Eberhard Kindermann adds an eschatological element to the lunar voyage in his 1744 *Die Geschwinde Reise auf dem Lufft-Schiff* ('The Swift Voyage on an Airship').[16]

---

[15] On the stereotyping of Native Americans in German literature, see esp. Zantop 1997.

[16] The full title is *Geschwinde Reise auf dem Lufft-Schiff nach der obern Welt, welche jüngsthin fünff Personen angestellet, um zu erfahren, ob es eine Wahrheit sey, daß der Planet Mars den 10. Jul. dieses Jahrs das erste mahl, so lange die Welt stehet, mit einem Trabanten oder Mond erschienen. Der untern Welt zu curieuser Gemüths-Ergötzung und Versicherung dieser Begebenheit mitgetheilet durch die allgemeine Fama* ('The Swift Voyage on an Airship to the Upper World, which five people recently undertook to learn if it is true that Planet Mars will appear for the first time on 10 July in this year with a Trabant [satellite]

Five allegorical travellers, Auditus, Visus, Odor, Gustus, and Tactus (the five senses), are encouraged by the Angel Fama (Reputation or Rumour) to build a spaceship based on six vacuum-filled spheres, not too dissimilar to Otto von Guericke's 'Magdeburg hemispheres', which he used to demonstrate atmospheric pressure in 1654. The travellers encounter different extraterrestrials, but the Martians epitomize the possible future of humankind, perfected through reason and Enlightenment. Mars is described as Paradise, not a nostalgic return to lost innocence but an eschatological future. Hania Siebenpfeiffer suggests that the 'first evidence of the human potential to learn is the fact of space travel itself, as it proves that mankind has begun to understand the true order of the universe' (Siebenpfeiffer 2013: 150; cf. 2008). Kindermann's science fiction novel—possibly the first one in German—offers the prospect of a rationalistic *civitas dei* on Mars, underpinned by the possibilities of modern technologies, Enlightenment, and natural theology.

If the lunar voyage went up, subterranean voyages extended the boundaries of the imaginary geography of utopia in the eighteenth century by going underground, as in the anonymous *Relation D'Un Voyage Du Pole Arctique Au Pole Antarctique Par Le Centre Du Monde* (1723); Charles De Fieux Mouhy's fantastical *Lamekis, ou Les voyages extraordinaires d'un égyptien dans la terre intérieure avec la découverte de l'isle des Sylphides* (1735–8), which details 'the extraordinary voyages of an Egyptian in the interior of the world with the discovery of the island of Sylphs'; and Giacomo Casanova's *L'Icosaméron* (1788). Whilst the planetary voyages were based, to a certain extent, on contemporary astrological and astronomical knowledge and technologies, the subterranean voyages were underpinned by classical and folkloric myths and, in the seventeenth century, by Hollow Earth theories proposed by Edmond Halley (1656–1742) and William Derham (1658–1735) (Standish 2006).[17] Thus, when Ludvig Holberg's protagonist Niels Klim falls into the underground world, he quickly concedes 'those men are right who hold the Earth to be hollow, and that within the shell or outward crust there is another lesser globe, and another firmament adorned with lesser sun, stars and planets' (Holberg 1960: 10).

Holberg's *Niels Klim's journey under the ground; being a narrative of his wonderful descent to the subterranean lands; together with an account of the sensible animals and trees inhabiting the planet Nazar and the firmament* was originally published in Latin as *Nicolai Klimii Iter Subterraneum* (1741) in Leipzig and Copenhagen anonymously, in fear of royal censorship. The book instantly became a success: it was translated into German in 1741, into Holberg's native Danish in 1742, went through many Latin reprints, and provided the inspiration for Jules Verne's 1864 *Voyage au centre de la Terre* (Jørgensen 1983). Holberg knew More's *Utopia* but *Niels Klim* is purely Swiftian; indeed Holberg himself compared *Niels Klim* to *Gulliver's Travels* in the Introduction to his

---

or moon. Told to the lower world as curious entertainment and assurance of this occurrence by the universal Fama').

[17] See Fitting 2010, 1996. Underground worlds are not alien to Nordic mythology; the Edda, for instance, features an underground world, Svartálfaheimr ('home of the dark elves').

1744 *Moralische Abhandlungen* ('Moral Reflections').[18] The tale of *Niels Klim* employs strategies of formal realism not too dissimilar from Defoe, comprising a narrative related by a first-person narrator and underpinned by letters, journals, and a manuscript. Other formal elements borrow from Lucian's *True History,* Cyrano de Bergerac, and, of course, Swift, with the hyperbolic description of different and curious civilizations which offer a multitude of utopian possibilities. James McNelis (1960: xlv) has suggested that 'Swift concentrates on man, Holberg on society'. The device of cognitive estrangement underscores the comprehensive critique of Denmark: as Holberg writes, 'In Germany, in France, and especially in England, [...] it is far easier to display the strength of the judgment and imagination than in our northern Kingdoms, where the force and spirit of a writer are checked and blunted by a most rigid censorship' (Holberg 1960: 15). When *Niels Klim* was slated as a mere fantastic tale, Holberg defended himself and wrote,

> If a man were to be moved to Saturn, Jupiter, or to the Moon and were to describe our Earth from his vantage point, would critics who were reviewing books in those planetary worlds, not also point out that the author was ignoring principles of verisimilitude and dreaming up completely nonsensical things which contradict nature and experience? At the sight of a human figure would they not be astounded and exclaim, 'Well, what a sight and fit for painting!' (Holberg 1926: 239; my translation)

As a critical utopia, a subgenre which we will explore later in more detail, Holberg does not offer simply one utopia but a range of different societies: Pyglossia, Martinia, Cocklecu, and Potu (Potu = Utop). These are subterranean worlds that explore the possibilities of enlightened absolutist rule, religious tolerance, and freedom of speech. The truly rational beings are the mobile trees, evoking the Treants in Norse mythology.[19] Only one nation of humans exists underground, and these, the Quamites, are debased creatures like Swift's Yahoos. The protagonist Niels Klim clothes the Quamites and teaches them useful arts—they learn to ride horses and make firearms—and they end up conquering the neighbouring nations, which are made up of cats, tigers, bears, roosters, and the like. But he is unable to lead them effectively and like Gulliver, returns to his own world, miserable and misanthropic.

Iceland had its own weird and wonderful subterranean voyages with Eiríkur Laxdal's Icelandic *Ólandssaga*, written after 1775, and the *Saga Ólafs Þórhallasonar* ('The Saga of Ölafur Þórhallason'), *c.*1788. The latter continues the fantastical utopian projection of the former 'Saga of No such Land' in a narrative that mixes the saga, romance, the picaresque, and the *Bildungsroman* with formal realist features. The *Saga Ólafs Þórhallasonar* embeds the underground world of an enlightened Elfin people, their laws, agriculture, customs, and science contrasted with the human world above, in a complex narrative

---

[18] Jacob Bidermann, whose work Holberg was also familiar with, published his comic rebuttal to More's *Utopia* as *Utopia Didaci Bemardini* in 1621.

[19] Holberg also wrote a poem entitled 'Metamorphosis', an imitation of Ovid, in which brutes and trees are transformed into humans.

structure reminiscent of Giovanni Boccaccio's *Decameron* (Eggertsdóttir 2006). Laxdal pays attention to gender—gender equality amongst the elfins is an accentuated feature—and natural sciences. Laxdal is known to have been familiar with Holberg's *Niels Klim* and to have had a translation of a manuscript of William Derham's *Physico-Theology* (1713), an extended argument for natural theology. Laxdal possibly knew Derham's *Astro-theology: or, A demonstration of the being and attributes of God, from a survey of the heavens* (1714) which suggested the possibility of the hollowness of Venus and thus infers the possibility of subterranean planetary life.[20] Laxdal thus married elements of the Icelandic sagas with the prophecies of astrotheology and natural theology, allowing for perfectibility and progress in a mythical past. The experimental mix of the Icelandic sagas, the tales of mythical folk above and underground, and the idealized depiction of simple and rustic communitarianism also became the food for later writers such as William Morris, who travelled to Iceland in 1870s and was fascinated by its culture and landscape.[21]

CRITICAL UTOPIAS AND *EU/UCHRONIAS*

Out of the anti-utopianism of the Robinsonades and the sceptical relativism of ethnographic utopias developed a critical utopianism. 'A central concern in the critical utopia', writes Tom Moylan, 'is the awareness of the limitations of the utopian tradition, so that these texts reject utopia as a blueprint while preserving it as a dream' (Moylan 2000: 83). Eighteenth-century critical utopianism was based on melioristic doctrines of perfectibility. Already in the seventeenth century, a historicist anthropology emerged that opposed the classical anthropology of a static human nature, specifically the Christian conception of a fallen humanity which in theory made any utopia impossible.[22] The idea of perfectibility was interpreted in the eighteenth century as both an innate characteristic and a moral duty, as both a passive, mechanistic faculty (David Hartley and Étienne Bonnot de Condillac) and an active, creative principle that drove the individual as well as society beyond mental and political slavery (Baruch Spinoza; John Locke; Adam Ferguson; Marie Jean Antoine Nicolas de Caritat, marquis de Condorcet; Immanuel Kant). Whether optimistic or pessimistic about human nature, eighteenth-century utopian writers grasped the idea of historical relativism and, more importantly, the changeableness of human nature—hence the importance of educating the utopian subject.

Philosophers such as Hobbes, Voltaire, and Ferguson highlighted, if in different ways, the human restlessness that rendered the classical idea of human nature, and thus the ideal of static utopianism in the shape of More's Utopia (with its inflexible systems),

---

[20] On the hollow Venus theory, see Fara 2007. On astrotheology and utopia, see Harrison 2014.
[21] For more on Morris, see Hanson and Waithe in this volume.
[22] See e.g. the work of Blaise Pascal whose political theology is essentially anti-utopian. See W. D. Wood 2013: 51–91.

futile. 'While he [man] appears equally fitted to every condition,' writes Adam Ferguson (1767: 1.1.10), 'he is upon his account unable to settle in any.' 'The activity and eagerness with which we press from one stage of life to another, and unwillingness to return on the paths we have trod' is, for Ferguson, an indicator that the lack of physical and intellectual stimulation is a grave obstacle to progress and perfectibility (1.1.61). And Voltaire vehemently argued in his *Lettres Philosophiques* (1734), especially in his piece on Pascal, for the need to revise the doctrine of original sin and the idea of human greatness that is only possible in man's original condition in the Garden of Eden or some remnant of that blissful state in fallen humanity. Paradise, the static utopia, a state of constant and unchangeable happiness and tranquillity, is, according to Voltaire, mere *ennui*, and counteracts the principle of perfectibility. 'Once again, 'tis impossible for mankind to continue in that suppos'd lethargy,' he wrote in 1733: ''tis upsurd to imagine it, and foolish to pretend to it. Man is born for action, as the fire tends upwards, and a stone downwards' (Voltaire 1994: 137). The concept of degeneration that is posited here is not Rousseau's negative anthropology, or the historical degeneration that the 'Querelle des Anciens et des Modernes' engaged with, but the idea of perfection as stasis. The restlessness that Hobbes, Ferguson, and Voltaire identify is not an aimless search for happiness but comes out of a modern desire for transgression and historical transformation. Kindermann's protagonists in *Die Geschwinde Reise* prove the point where vitality and inventiveness aid the realization of utopia. Indeed, the eighteenth-century critical utopia illustrates Ernst Bloch's anticipatory dialectic of the future.

This dialectic is exemplified in the episodic nature of eighteenth-century critical utopias where the protagonists travel through a range of utopias—these works consequently often take the shape of 'voyage utopias'—only to leave them at the end finding their utopia within themselves. Thus, whereas Gulliver and Niels Klim return to their worlds unenlightened and misanthropic, Voltaire's own sceptical *Candide* take us from the 'earthly paradise' (*paradis terrestre*) Thunder-Ten-Tronckh to El Dorado, 'a country better than Westphalia' ('un pays qui vaut mieux que la Vestphalie', my translation) to end in Candide's garden where utopia is cultivated, 'because, when man was put in the Garden of Eden, he was put there *ut operatur eum*, that is, so that he might work; this proves that man is not made for rest' ('car, quand l'homme fut mis dans le jardin d'Éden, il y fut mis *ut operaretur eum*, que pour qu'il travaillât; ce qui prouve que l'homme n'est pas né pour le repos' (Voltaire 2003: 83–84). In Samuel Johnson's oriental tale *The History of Rasselas, Prince of Abissinia* (1759), Rasselas and his companions reflect on their sojourn in the Happy Valley only to confirm that 'such [...] is the state of life, that none are happy but by the anticipation of change: the change itself is nothing; when we have made it, the next wish is to change again' (S. Johnson 2009: 102). Abbé Prévost's *Monsieur Cleveland* (1731–9) also explores a range of utopian loci and societies on his journeys to the paradisiacal Caribbean island of Sainte-Hélène, the island of Madeira, the native society of the Abaquis and the Nopandes in North America, and the commune of Fanny in Cuba. All utopian models, even the one created by Cleveland himself as the legislator of the Abaquis, are flawed and are based on an artificial and thus fragile model of harmony and order. These texts do not reject utopia per se but reflect the necessity of continual transformation, the necessity of what Johann Wolfgang von Goethe came to call *Bildung*. It is therefore no coincidence that these critical utopias borrow from the picaresque and the *Bildungsroman*—novels tracing the protagonist's development from childhood to adulthood—where individual evolution and growth is intertwined with social perfectibility (Temmer 1982).

This new emphasis on history-as-progress had a profound impact on the genre. The utopian novel of the eighteenth century witnesses a shift from *eu/utopia* to *eu/uchronia* that committed to the Kantian idea of 'man's emergence from his self-incurred immaturity' as a process and progress. Louis-Sébastien Mercier's 1770 *L'An 2440, rêve s'il en fut jamais* ('The Year 2440, A dream such as there never was') transformed Anne Robert Jacques Turgot's theory of progress into a specific utopian formula by projecting the image of a better society on to the year 2440 and, at the same time, providing a detailed and harsh critique of the Ancien Régime, the sociopolitical system of pre-Revolutionary France (Forsström 2002; Alkon 2010).

However, not all future projections were driven by this optimistic investment in the future. *Memoirs of the Twentieth Century* (1733) by the Irish writer Samuel Madden is possibly one of the earliest examples of time travel.[23] The frame narrative documents how a collection of letters written in the twentieth century were made accessible to the narrator, and how these 'authentic' documents are prophetic warnings to eighteenth-century monarchs and governments.[24] Prefaces are interspersed further during the five volumes, commenting and reflecting on the content of the 'future' letters and events. In his dedication, Madden selects the Prince of Wales as 'the Defender of our Faith' and of enlightened, rational civilization and prophesizes the totalitarian takeover of Europe by the Jesuits in the early nineteenth century, the collapse and conquest of the Ottoman Empire by the Tartars, and the decline of empires such as France and Poland in the time of a future George VI.[25] Madden's *Memoirs* is a curious mix of apocalyptic writing, satire, and advice to princes, using cognitive estrangement but undermining the claim of verisimilitude at the same time. Answering to the charge that 'these vast discoveries and improvements, these changes and revolutions of things below, which are mention'd in the subsequent letters, cannot possibly happen, nor consequently be true, many of them are so improbably', the narrator claims that therefore they must be true (Madden 1733: 550–551). Improbability becomes a measure for verisimilitude and realism (see Alkon 2010: 104).

---

[23] The full title is [Samuel Madden], *Memoirs of the Twentieth Century. Being Original Letters of State, under George the Sixth: Relating to the most Important Events in Great Britain and Europe, as to Church and State, Arts and Sciences, Trade, Taxes, and Treaties, Peace, and War: And Characters of the Greatest Persons of those Times; From the Middle of the Eighteenth, to the End of the Twentieth Century, and the World. Received and Revealed in the Year 1728; And now Published, for the Instruction of all Eminent Statesmen, Churchmen, Patriots, Politicians, Projectors, Papists, and Protestants* (London: Osborn and Longman, 1733).

[24] On the narrator in Madden and Mercier, see Kukkonen 2017: ch. 7.

[25] For a detailed study on Madden, see Ní Chuanacháin 2016: ch. 6.

With the development of the early novel and the raising of the stakes in terms of narrative complexity and generic diversity, Raymond Trousson has argued that 'utopia' 'only becomes a novel when it stops being a utopia' (cited in Racault 1991: 768; cf. Trousson 1993). We have seen that in fact the utopian novel of the eighteenth century tried to mediate its literariness with utopian forms and functions. This literary mediation is determined by the literary and historical, thus intertextual, contexts and, as Fortunati has stressed, is '*in fieri,* always evolving [...] into a more and more complex structure' (Fortunati 2000: 1; cf. Kuon 1986). These structures are polygeneric and polymodal, experimental and self-reflexive on form and function. The aim of both the early novel and the utopian novel is to collect the knowledge of human experience, of human survival (*Überlebenswissen*), and of living together (*Zusammenlebenswissen*) as society and a species.

CHAPTER 32

CONVERSATION, FORMATION, AND FORMS OF UTOPIA IN FIN-DE-SIÈCLE SOCIALIST JOURNALS

INGRID HANSON

On 12 February 1887, the Socialist League journal *Commonweal* included in its regular column of propaganda reports the following account from 'J.G.' (John Glasse) of a lecture that took place in Edinburgh on 31 January that year:

> James Campbell lectured on 'Social Utopias'. In a lecture instinct with the finest feeling and the richest imagination, he passed in review various ideals cherished in the past. Though the lecture was one which it might have been thought tended more to give enjoyment than to provoke discussion, there was nevertheless an animated discussion at its close. (Glasse 1887: 56)

In a journal that records, in that same year, the forced closure of socialist newspapers in Italy, the arrest of scores of socialists in Germany, the imprisonment of socialists in Holland, and the arrest, trial, and imprisonment of members of the Socialist League in Norwich for stirring up a crowd through political agitation, it is significant that 'animated discussion' is used as a marker of success.[1] Indeed the presence of post-talk discussion or opposition appears again and again in *The Commonweal*'s reports of local and regional meetings as a sign of health in the movement. Utopias, imagined or practised, are not remote, ideal spaces in this context, but permeable, interactive,

---

[1] See e.g. the following articles in *The Commonweal*: 'Socialist Condemnation', 14 May 1887 (155); 'The Labour Struggle: Germany', 2 July 1887 (215); 'Continental Notes: Germany', 13 Aug. 1887 (263); 'Continental Notes: Holland', 24 Sept. 1887 (311); 'Continental Notes: Italy', 3 Dec. 1887 (390); 'The Disturbances at Norwich', 22 Jan. 1887 (31); 'The Norwich Socialists', 29 Jan. 1887 (37).

amenable to criticism, and useful for the 'propagation of socialism', the central aim of *The Commonweal*, set out in its opening issue in February 1885 (1). William Morris's *News from Nowhere*, published serially in the newspaper, of which he was founder and editor, between 11 January and 4 October 1890, is itself set in the context of a 'brisk conversational discussion' between socialists 'up at the League' about 'the future of the fully-developed new society'—a deliberate echo, of course, of Thomas More's 'best state of a publique weale' (Morris 1910–15: 16.3).[2]

Six years later, a Manchester-based socialist newspaper, *The Clarion*, established in 1891, announced its intention of generating a new discussion about the ills and possibilities of society in its own Morris-inspired utopian series of columns entitled 'Merrie England'. *The Clarion*'s editor, Robert Blatchford, writing under the pseudonym 'Nunquam' ('Never')—a nicely playful use of Latin disavowal which resembles More's prepublication use of the title *Nusquama* ('Nowhere') instead of the Greek *Utopia*, but shifts the emphasis from place to time—set the columns in the context of a relationship between discussion and action.[3] In his headnote to a later edited collection of the articles, Blatchford argues that 'the great impediment to action is not discussion, but the want of that knowledge that is gained by discussion preparatory to action' (R. Blatchford 1908: 9). To generate that discussion, he addresses the 'Merrie England' series not to his socialist comrades but to the generic 'hard headed workman' John Smith, anticipating, in his opening column on 4 March 1893, the opposition he would encounter: 'Dear Mr Smith,—I am sorry to hear that you [...] call Socialism "Tommy-rot" [...]. Nevertheless, as you have good metal in you, and are very numerous, I mean to argue the point with you' (8). It is not only in the twenty-three columns of 'Merrie England' that Blatchford does this, however; rather, like *The Commonweal*, *The Clarion* engages its readers in numerous strands of conversation and argument about the present, the future, and the space between the two. In the act of generating this discussion, variously inviting and imagining reader responses, these two newspapers engage with their own political moment and the realities of its socialist and working-class readers as well as with utopias, both literary and actual, of the past and present, demonstrating a faith in the power of conversation central to More's own project in 1516.

As Chloë Houston (2014: 4) notes, More's *Utopia* 'was written as a dialogue in the open mode: questioning, discursive and self-critical'. While these characteristics of the sixteenth-century dialogue are not carried over precisely or wholesale into the nineteenth-century print spaces I discuss in this chapter—indeed Houston charts their gradual disappearance across the seventeenth century—they are present to varying degrees in their dialogic imaginings of the future not-quite-perfected state of society

---

[2] On Morris's use of this phrase of More's, see his Foreword to the Kelmscott edition (More 1893: iv). For more on nineteenth-century editions of *Utopia*, and Morris's in particular, see Waithe in this volume.

[3] Blatchford's nom de plume is shortened from 'Nunquam Dormio' (I never sleep), which he carried over from his job on *Bell's Life in London* (see L. Thompson 1951: 33); as Morrish (2001: 119) notes, More is still referring to *Nusquama* up to a few months before publication; see also Taylor in this volume. For the shift from geographic utopias to temporal utopias (*euchronias*), see Pohl in this volume.

as well as in their interactions with the present as a means of bringing about that future, post-political state. Hannah Arendt (1998: 26) notes that for the ancient Greeks, 'to be political, to live in a polis, meant that everything was decided through words and persuasion and not through force and violence'. Because argument signifies equality rather than coercion and the possibility for distinct views rather than a single, homogeneous one, it is central to the project of 'mak[ing] Socialists', described by Robert Blatchford (1908: 243) as 'the best way to realise Socialism'. This project is central to both journals, though generated by different means. *The Commonweal* conducts its conversation with readers in a tone of indignation, passionate seriousness, and intense social criticism, while *The Clarion* generates an alternative to mainstream social life and modes of action through a wide-ranging engagement with the cultural life and language of working people. I am not going to argue, as Elizabeth Carolyn Miller has done in relation to *The Commonweal*, that the newspapers under discussion here 'construct themselves as utopian spaces outside the "march of progress" narrative that had accrued to print and to capitalism' (Miller 2013: 40), but rather that they generate, through conversation, interaction, and discussion, what Fredric Jameson describes as a 'utopian wish' for a just and economically equal community characterized by a multiplicity of views and actions (Jameson 2005: 72). In the decade following the 1888 publication of the American socialist Edward Bellamy's influential utopia, *Looking Backward*, and Morris's answering 1890 text, *News from Nowhere*—a decade that saw a sudden proliferation of utopian texts and ideas—*The Clarion* and *The Commonweal* (the first making its triumphant entry into the increasingly crowded field of socialist print, the second heading towards decline) drew their readers into conversation with More's text, Morris's text, Bellamy's text, and the idea of Utopia. Differences in style, form, and content notwithstanding, both papers modelled and explored a 'plural' view of human and social relations characterized by the 'equality' and 'distinctness' Arendt (1998: 175–176) associates with plurality.[4]

In constructing their propaganda as discussion, *The Clarion* and *The Commonweal* resist the reification of relationships between writers and readers, initiators of action and doers of it: they insist on the humanness of their politics. Yet, while speech is, as Arendt (1998: 176) points out, an interaction unmediated by things, in which people reveal themselves '*qua* [as] men', it is nonetheless conducted here through the physical page, with its particular choice of layout, juxtapositions of articles, and inevitable capacity to have the last word. The very act of turning conversation into writing renders a newspaper more like an annotated map than a post-lecture discussion; nonetheless the emphasis of both papers on a dialectic of exposition and opposition leading to change allows them some of the fluid qualities of what Henri Lefebvre (1991: 73) describes as 'social space', produced by human interactions and, crucially, productive of new actions. While More's text, as Greg Walker shows, engages with a Menippean tradition of ambivalence and uncertainty 'to tease, surprise, and delight his intended scholarly

---

[4] For an account of the effects of Bellamy's book, see Beaumont 2012: 28–32, 121–150.

readership' (Walker 2010: 334), it also negotiates the space between what Dominic Baker-Smith describes as 'the problematic relationship between imagined worlds and mundane reality' (More 2012: xx). The insistent dialogism, internally and externally, of these nineteenth-century newspapers constructs that space as both unsettling play and teleological practice, relational but not aimless.

The conservative philosopher Michael Oakeshott describes human relationships as conversation, arguing that

> voices which speak in conversation do not compose a hierarchy. Conversation is not an enterprise designed to yield an extrinsic profit, a contest where a winner gets a prize, nor is it an activity of exegesis; it is an unrehearsed intellectual adventure. […] As with gambling, its significance lies neither in winning nor in losing, but in wagering. (Oakeshott 1991: 489–490)

Oakeshott's idealist conception, for all its appealing qualities, is problematic in its dissociation of speech from ends and in its failure to recognize the inevitability of hierarchies, open or hidden. While the conversation represented in and generated by these newspapers does partake of intellectual adventure, variously constructed, it also arises from a clearly expressed desire to win, in the form of converting its readers to socialism. Yet the power of socialist newspaper editors, like that of socialist lecturers, lies only in its capacity to move readers or listeners to action; the power to bring about change lies with readers. Owen Holland, discussing the utopian and politically purposeful context of *News from Nowhere*, quotes Angelika Bammer noting the need to 'reconceptualize the utopian in […] *this-worldly* terms, as a process that involves human agency' (Holland 2017: 14). For Morris and Blatchford as editors as well as writers, no such reconceptualizing was needed. Their utopian impulse to dialogue was rooted in a practice of human plurality and a commitment to 'agency as a collective process', as Holland notes.

MERRIE ENGLAND: *THE CLARION*'S CONVERSATION WITH MORRIS AND MORE

Although Blatchford's writings on socialism are clearly influenced by Morris, and as Noel Thompson (2006: 19) notes, his *Merrie England* 'had a decidedly Morrisian complexion' in its analysis of the problems of capitalism and its emphasis on the imbrication of work, pleasure, and beauty, *The Clarion*'s interaction with *News from Nowhere* in particular, and the idea of Utopia more broadly, is not merely one of imitation or agreement but of argument and evaluation. *The Clarion* illustration that accompanied Blatchford's 10 October 1896 obituary for Morris shows a female figure wearing loose Pre-Raphaelite-style dress, a sash reading 'socialism', and a Phrygian cap (symbolizing liberty) decked with a garland of laurel, leaning on a tombstone adorned with wreaths, topped with a paint palette and inscribed with Morris's name and dates. At the foot of the tombstone are a number of Morris's books, three of which have legible titles: *A Dream of John Ball*, *Signs of Change*, and *The Earthly Paradise*. While *News from Nowhere* might seem an obvious choice for inclusion in this memorial, it is characteristic of *The Clarion* that it is not among the visibly titled books (R. Blatchford 1896: 321). Blatchford, who describes Morris, seventeen years his senior, as 'my one hero' (325), repeated over and over in this obituary, 'he was our best man' (324–325). He clearly admired Morris and references to the older man run through his work; nonetheless, he makes no secret of the fact that *News from Nowhere*, though important, is far from his favourite of Morris's books.

It is not the content of *News from Nowhere* nor the idea of Utopia that left Blatchford less than convinced; indeed, not only did he draw on Morris's economic analysis for his 'Merrie England' series in 1893, he also wrote and published his own utopian novel, *The Sorcery Shop*, in 1907, demonstrating faith in the form. It is the style and tone of Morris's work that Blatchford critiques in his own conversations about the transformation of society through socialism. Devoting two of the eleven chapters of his collection of reviews, *My Favourite Books*, to Morris, Blatchford dwells at length on his favourite book, *A Dream of John Ball* (1888), and his favourite collection of poetry, *The Defence of Guenevere* (1858), but dismisses *News from Nowhere* with a brief sentence noting that 'in its own way, as a picture of an ideal commonwealth, "News from Nowhere" is a very beautiful and convincing piece of work' (R. Blatchford 1900: 93). Even Morris's widely admired tale of the Peasants' Revolt, *John Ball*, draws censure amidst the praise: 'Morris's limitations are, chiefly, a weakness of characterisation and an almost painful absence of humour […]. Never, so far as I am aware, in this book or in any other, has Morris woke us into laughter.' He insists on this as a failing: 'some readers may think that in such a dreamy, poetical, and elevated work, laughter would be as incongruous as in a church. For my part, I like an occasional smile' (108–110). The lightness of Blatchford's comment, like the throwaway 'in its own way' about *News from Nowhere*, belies a significant criticism, while at the same time inviting the reader to agree: who does not like 'the occasional smile'? While *John Ball* might certainly be read as a book devoid of comedy, a careful reading of *News from Nowhere* reveals a seam of self-deprecating humour, particularly in the treatment of dissenters from the utopian social project and the presentation of the narrator William Guest as an obvious stand-in for Morris, the latter a technique Blatchford picks up in *The Sorcery Shop*, as Chris Waters (1982: 28) has noted. What Morris does not do, as Blatchford and his fellow journalists on *The Clarion* do routinely, is banter.

Jonathan Rose records that Harry McShane, the Scottish trade unionist and Labour activist, started out as a socialist reading Henry Hyndman's *Justice* and another London-based newspaper, *The Socialist*, but 'like most working-class readers, he much preferred Blatchford's *Clarion*, where an unideological socialism was leavened with breezy articles on literature, freethought and science' (J. Rose 2010: 305). Although 'unideological' is a rather freighted term—and we might certainly see ideology at work in the paper's refusal to oppose warmongering jingoism during the Boer War of 1899–1902, and again in

1914—it is true that it set itself up as a paper of common sense and common language. It offers, Blatchford claims, 'a new journalism'. The New Journalism identified by Matthew Arnold in 1887 was characterized by 'ability, novelty, variety, sensation, sympathy, generous instincts', but marred, in his view, by one great fault: 'it is *feather-brained*' (Arnold 1887: 638–639). While Arnold's New Journalism is often associated with mainstream papers such as the *Pall Mall Gazette* under the editorship of W. T. Stead, Blatchford claims a new journalism for himself, and associates it with action: 'it is a new journalism […] created by the men risking this venture' he writes on 12 December 1891 (R. Blatchford 1891: 4). Its essence, as in Arnold's version, is 'variety', and it includes, crucially for Blatchford, a comic representation of current events: 'We would, therefore, beg our serious friends to remember that truth may lie under a smile as well as a frown, and to our merry friends would say that a jest is none the less hilarious when it comes from the heart' (4). The success, at least in terms of readership, of *The Clarion*'s approach is evident in its sales figures: it was one of the longest-running of the socialist newspapers, with a regular circulation of 34,000, rising to some 80,000 at its height, compared with 2,000–3,000 for *The Commonweal* (Reitz and Mutch 2009: 122–123; Mutch and Kelvin 2009: 136). Just at the moment when *The Commonweal* was struggling to maintain circulation and when variety was increasingly replaced by narrowness, *The Clarion* entered the conversation about 'the fully-developed new society', in a style other socialist newspapers, particularly those based in the north or written by northerners, would adopt or adapt over the following decades. It was a style that included not only humour but also in-jokes and banter between its writers, who took comic pseudonyms in the style of earlier radical writers but also of the mainstream press from which they came.[5]

Elizabeth Carolyn Miller, discussing the socialist print culture of the 1890s, asks 'can a print counterculture be autonomous without being irrelevant? In its oppositionality, does it risk marginality?' (Miller 2013: 168). The answer, for *The Clarion*, is an intense and comically inflected engagement with the everyday worlds of its readers as well as the past and the present. In an article of 16 March 1895 on the transformative and interactive power of laughter, the *Labour Leader*'s 'Merlin' argues that 'laughter cures the diseases of the mind as fresh air heals those of the body'. He argues that what is needed for a better society is 'a real meeting […] of sympathy and mutual understanding' between rich and poor in a spirit of comic self-criticism, and as an example of the effects of this kind of meeting, he argues that 'stout Robert Blatchford meets the rich and cultured Ruskin through his books and becomes cultured, and in his own very real way rich himself' (1895: 3). It is a richness Blatchford shares with his readers through his familiar and irreverent treatment of the greats of the socialist movement and other sages such as John Ruskin (1819–1900), Thomas Carlyle (1795–1881), and More. Like *The Commonweal*, *The Clarion* makes frequent reference to these heroic writers of the near and distant past,

---

[5] e.g. 'Dangle' (A. M. Thompson), 'Mont Blong' (Montagu Blatchford), 'The Bounder' and 'Quinbus Flestrin' ('Great Man-Mountain'), borrowed from *Gulliver's Travels* (Swift 2008: 29); the last two are noms de plume for E. F. Fay, as L. Thompson (1951: 118) notes in a throwaway comment. On comic conversational style in socialist journals, see K. Harris 2016: 119–120.

but in a tone very different from the reverent seriousness with which the London paper treats them.[6] A characteristic mingling of sympathy and comedy is evident in 'Tailoring Up to Date', a *Clarion* article of 28 May 1892 on sweatshops in which 'Quinbus Flestrin' suggests that 'Thomas Carlyle is not suitable reading for hot weather. No. The unsweetened Thomas should be taken during the winter months in small doses' (Fay 1892: 8). Having identified with its readers' imagined response to Carlyle's style, the article goes on to endorse his point of view as powerful and effective: 'he is too rich and nourishing for the hot weather—apt to induce a rush of blood to the head, to engender in all honest and fair-minded men a flux of anger against the things which be and the things which order them'. Readers are invited, by a kind of reverse psychology, to see themselves as partners in Carlyle's critique of society, applied in the rest of the article to work practices in the tailoring trade.[7]

In an unusually pessimistic column of 15 January 1898 archaically entitled, 'As I Lay A Thynkynge', Blatchford pursues a similar approach, but leaves the conversation unfinished. The article begins with an invocation of the idea of Utopia: 'It is pleasant picturing new Utopias with Imagination's paint-box, or taking goose-quill in hand and squaring the world's circle by the rules of logic' (R. Blatchford 1898: 21). This pleasant activity, however, is rather undermined by the hard realities of the world, shaped as it is by a history of oppression, as the article goes on to suggest: 'it is ill work suiting young dreams to old records, matching green justice against grey crime, or building up fair towers of intellectual pride on the quicksands of modern folly, or the rubbish heaps of ancient shame'. It concludes:

> In the reign of Henry VIII, Sir Thomas More wrote 'Utopia', and more than four centuries later William Morris wrote 'News from Nowhere'. Are we any nearer to the realisation of Utopia now than we were under the reign of Bluff King Hal? Human nature does not and will not alter, charm we never so wisely. (21)

Present action, Blatchford suggests here, is not compatible with airy visions of alternative worlds. Charming, in this column, is a deceptive and ineffective activity and readers are left to question quite what it is that might change human nature. In earlier articles, by contrast, Blatchford had urged on his readers the socially transformative potential of both Morris and More and outlined the malleability of human nature and the inevitability of socialism. In a collection of essays published in 1895, indeed, he argues that 'a good deal of the time spent over the daily paper and the sensational novel might bring a richer harvest if devoted to the writers of the old lost years. We often talk of [Edmund] Spenser and [...] of Sir Thomas More; but how many of us ever read the Faery Queen or Utopia?' (R. Blatchford 1895a: 120). In the hugely popular and widely read collected

---

[6] See K. Harris 2016 on a similar lightness of tone about the greatly admired Walt Whitman (122-4).
[7] The article quotes the secretary of the Amalgamated Society of Tailors, Mr Flynn, 'a Man with a capital M' (Fay 1892: 8), lamenting the actions of the 'Jew Sweater' in undercutting union prices with cheap labour. On the strain of anti-semitism in 'Quinbus Flestrin' 's writing, see Holmes 2016: 23.

essays of *Merrie England*, first published in book form in November 1893, Blatchford included an appendix of books he considered would enable readers to 'more fully enter into the spirit of "Merrie England" '. *News from Nowhere* is one of the eighteen listed books in early editions and Bellamy's *Looking Backward* is added to a whittled-down list of twelve by the 1908 edition.[8] Blatchford's questioning of utopian possibilities in 1898, then, is surely more than an expression of the disillusionment Laurence Thompson (1951: 146–149) suggests began to set in towards the end of the century. Rather, it is another use of utopian ideas in the 'education of desire' through the stimulation of discussion about alternative worlds and their capacity to raise questions that might lead to action.[9]

The newspaper's uses of the concept of Utopia across the 1890s are as plural as its editor's own. In his 'Answers to Correspondents' column of 13 February 1892, Blatchford replies to an unknown reader: ' "Glass-paper" asks Nunquam to write an ideal Socialistic romance. "Glass-paper" will find all he wants in William Morris's "News from Nowhere" ' (Blatchford 1892: 4). In April and May 1895, however, *The Clarion* serializes a rather different response to Morris's text. The columnist 'Mont Blong' (Montagu Blatchford, Robert's brother) puts his name to a dystopian tale, in which a traveller from the past arrives in the present and is able to compare it unfavourably to his own time. 'A Free Country: The return of a medieval serf to the modern day' begins with a self-conscious reference to Morris, both name-checking his utopian texts and distancing itself from them: 'In William Morris's "Dream of John Ball", a modern Englishman is carried back to the fourteenth century of our glorious country. In 'News from Nowhere' by the same author, a modern Englishman is lifted forward into the twenty-somethingth century of our still *more* glorious country' (M. Blatchford 1895 [27 Apr.]: 136). 'Mont Blong' continues: 'If you haven't read those stories be advised by one whose advice is not generally worth following and read them; they are both charming.' Like Blatchford's praise of Morris, this recommendation carries with it a subtle hint of depreciation in that use of 'charming': Morris's stories may please but they might also beguile. Once again the solution is to set them in conversation with the present concerns of readers through a direct address: 'I daresay you have often wondered—as I have—what an English serf of the Middle Ages would think of that freedom which we are supposed to enjoy in this nineteenth century, that freedom for which they longed and struggled, and often died in the fourteenth century'. 'Mont Blong' goes on to note that in telling the story, 'as I have not the literary art of William Morris, my rude clumsy attempt may be far from answering'. He makes use of the idea of Morris the expert to align himself more closely with his readers and invite their identification with his tale. At the same time, 'Mont Blong' borrows Morris's medievalism and offers an argument that reverses, in analysis though not in conclusion, Karl Marx and Friedrich Engels', suggesting that the apparent

---

[8] On *News from Nowhere*, see also 'Nunquam', 'An Unpractical Paper', *The Clarion*, 20 July 1895 (R. Blatchford 1895b: 232).

[9] On 'the education of desire', see Miguel Abensour's argument, outlined in E. P. Thompson 1977: 791.

gains of capitalism merely cloak the relations of slavery that were more apparent in the feudal era (see Marx and Engels 2012: 35–38).

'Mont Blong' 's story tells of a fourteenth-century swineherd, Wat Warton, whose name bears echoes of Wat Tyler, a key figure in the 1381 Peasants' Revolt described in Morris's *A Dream of John Ball*, with its riddling social critique and utopian imagination of a more just and equal world. Warton wakes up, like *News from Nowhere*'s Guest and Bellamy's Julian West, in the future, and is delighted to find that in the nineteenth century he is no longer a serf but a free man. Like Guest, Warton finds his understanding of language and concepts challenged: instead of the community of shared possessions he expects to find in a country described as 'free', he encounters the injustices of capitalism. Turned away from a tavern for attempting to help himself to a jug of beer, 'poor Wat was at a loss to perceive why in a free country some of the people should monopolise all the breakfast' (M. Blatchford 1895 [4 May]: 141). The comic tone and comical figure serve to highlight the injustices the time traveller encounters. He comes under suspicion for loitering in a village with no visible means of support and is thrown into prison where 'for some hours he sat confusedly striving to understand why in a free country a man should be locked up for being poor' (M. Blatchford 1895 [11 May]: 149). On his eventual escape, 'he discovered that freedom, the Englishman's birthright, is little more than a mockery to the majority of the English people; and that a *poor* free man of the nineteenth century has actually less liberty than a serf or bondman of the fourteenth' (149). Wat eventually dies, alone and in penury; passers-by come upon 'the poor battered unhandsome corpse, which was all that British freedom and commercial enterprise had left of Wat Warton' (M. Blatchford 1895 [25 May]: 165). 'Mont Blong' 's defamiliarization of the world does not imagine a future hope, but rather demonstrates the injustice of the present through a satirical, absurdist critique. Nonetheless it is a narrative of temporal displacement, rather than the spatial displacement central to More's work, that is put to use in this dystopian tale, in which the past bears the seeds of a more hopeful future. If, as Matthew Beaumont argues, utopian writing at the fin de siècle 'insinuates a troubling sense of absence into the present', this story evokes that absence not through 'the intrusion into the present of a future whose historical possibility has been suppressed by [...] ideological limits' (Beaumont 2012: 4) but through the intrusion of a past that demonstrates by contrast the social and structural failures of the present.

The commercialism of Victorian capitalism and the individualism that poses as freedom are repeated targets for attack, discussion, exposure, and opposition in the conversational spaces of *The Clarion* and its associated publications. Blatchford, discussing the errors of 'cheapness' in *Merrie England*, offers an ideal utopian vision that works in tandem with 'Mont Blong' 's satire, drawing on Marx's theory of labour and More's account of wealth in Utopia, as well as invoking familiar biblical narratives: 'in my Utopia, when Cain asked "Am I my brother's keeper", he would be answered with a stern affirmative. In my Utopia a thing would be considered cheap or dear according to the price it *cost*; and not according to the price that was paid for it' (R. Blatchford 1908: 117). The project of *The Clarion* (the subtitle of which is *A Weekly Illustrated Journal of Social Reform*), then, might be seen as the embodiment of this 'stern affirmative', a conversation with readers and between columnists designed to encourage working-class people to take responsibility for each other and for the state of society: not to bring about revolution, but to introduce 'reform', as the journal's subtitle suggests, and to 'make socialists' (R. Blatchford 1908: 243) who might in turn remake society.

The Commonweal, Conversation, and the Idea of the Strike

In the 1890s, while *The Clarion* and *Merrie England* together were reaching close to a million readers and drawing them into a demotic utopian conversation with writers of the past and present, *The Commonweal* was part of a differently evolving discussion, reflected in its changing subtitles, from 'the official journal of the Socialist League' in its first issue of February 1885 (1), through 'A Journal of Revolutionary Socialism' from December 1890 (385), and finally, in 1892, 'A Revolutionary Journal of Anarchist Communism' (37).[10] At the end of April 1892 the journal dropped its subtitle altogether, replacing it with an unattributed quotation from Morris: 'Have you not heard how it has gone with many a Cause before now: First, few men heed it; Next, most men contemn it; Lastly, all men ACCEPT IT—and the Cause is won' (Morris 1910–15: 22.118). The journal closed for lack of funds between September 1892 and May 1893, then limped on until 1894 with the restored subtitle 'A Revolutionary Journal of Anarchist-Communism', this time as a hyphenated compound noun. Revolution rather than social reform was always the programme of *The Commonweal*, and under the anarchist editorship of D. J. Nicoll after 1890, the image of the general strike became the central emblem of social transformation: references in *The Commonweal* to a general strike had risen year on year from just 1 in 1885 to 38 in 1889; in 1890 this leapt to 107. As H. H. Duncan wrote in *The Commonweal* on 4 June 1892:

> taking as our definition of a strike, simply a revolt against tyranny and injustice, and, in some cases, a desire to improve the condition of life, we find that the strike instead of being a feature of the present age, or as some people say, 'the work of the desperate anarchist', is of early origin, presumably dating from the very moment that man first conceived the idea of 'fettering a friend for a slave'. (Duncan 1892: 4)

It is an image that brings past and future together in the present; it becomes both critique and dream, the centre of a utopian conversation that focuses on the moment and means of social change, rather than the reasons for it or the possibilities after it.

---

[10] L. Thompson (1951: 99) notes that within a year of its publication as a book, 750,000 copies of *Merrie England* had been sold.

This emphasis did not represent in itself a break from the years of Morris's editorship but rather a development of the newspaper's support for strikes as a means to bring about more just working conditions. What is new is an intense and increasingly single focus on the general strike. On 12 March 1892, the front cover of the journal carries an article entitled 'The Great Strike: Anarchist Manifesto', which notes: 'to strike is good, to refuse to work for slave-drivers and robbers is a noble act of revolt'. It goes on to explain that the wealth the workers have made is theirs and urges them to 'take all land and capital; all is yours'. The manifesto makes a connection between the strike from labour and the necessity to resist violence, including if necessary by violent means: '*take the wealth* you have made and if the tyrants resist, if they shoot you down like dogs, the last weapons of the wretched, the torch and bomb will rid you of them forever' (*The Commonweal* 1892: 41). The paper's last substantial fictional offering, a play by the Paris Communard Louise Michel, entitled *The Strike* and published serially between 19 September 1891 and 20 February 1892, dramatizes just such a confrontation between rich and poor. Set 'outside a villa near Warsaw', the play's Prologue shows a young woman, Gertrude, shockingly betraying a revolution organized by her husband Vladimir and his friends (Michel 1891–2 [19 Sept. 1891]: 113). Just before his death, unaware of her betrayal, Vladimir challenges Gertrude's belief in the power of individualism. She insists on it, however: 'You, for example, follow your own bent,—towards Utopia,' she says. 'Is not the Utopia of one age ever the reality of the next?' cries Vladimir (113), a question to which the rest of the play is an affirmative answer.

The following scenes show Gertrude's marriage to a rich businessman, Eleazar, whom she helps to become yet more prosperous while working tirelessly to silence his revolutionary children. The play ends with her suicide by drowning in the Danube amid visions of Lady Macbeth, after the success of the people's revolution. It is a play that draws, like H. H. Duncan's article, on the identification of the strike, so familiar to readers, with revolution. A similar effect is achieved in Michel's poem 'To Battle' published in *The Commonweal* on 15 June 1889, which begins:

> Sound the alarum-bell, sound,
> Dash all your tools to the ground,
> And strike,
> strike!
>
> (Michel 1889: 189)

The strike, then, is an act of refusal in the laying down of tools and arms, and at the same time a metaphorical act of battle, as suggested by the title and poem's rhythm.[11]

By the time of the play's publication two years later, *The Commonweal* was carrying repeated injunctions to its readers to become more active in bringing about a general strike. On 14 June 1891 a 'mass meeting' on 'Strikes: Their Cause and Cure' was held

---

[11] See my discussion of this poem in Hanson 2013: 245.

at the Reformer's Tree in Hyde Park; Michel was one of the speakers. The contents of her talk, translated by Auguste Coulon,[12] are summarized in a short article by 'CWM' (Charles Mowbray) in *The Commonweal* on 20 June 1891, noting that she talked in detail about 'the new idea, "The General Strike". Our Comrade explained that in all past revolutions, people flew to arms and the barricades, but ignorance of economics and the true solution of the labour problem caused the failure of their efforts' (Mowbray 1891: 63). The dual meaning of the strike is made evident in Scene 4 of Michel's play, when the first revolution has been foiled and another is in preparation. Eleazar's adult son and daughter, urging their father to leave Gertrude, 'be brave', and join the revolution, hear 'Songs Outside' that echo the words and rhythm of 'To Battle':

> Ring! Ring! In the air! Ring!
> Tocsin of the iron age! Ring!
> Long live the strike!
> Long live the strike!
>
> (Michel 1891–2 [5 Dec. 1891]: 157)

The inclusion of the 'iron age' suggests here that the strike is not only the contemporary analogue of past revolutions, but also, like the blow of a hammer on metal, is creative and constructive. The song's second stanza in the play is a reworking of the final stanza of Michel's earlier poem, which begins, 'Nay, comrades, never give in' and goes on 'To battle! until we win | the world, | the world!' (Michel 1889: 189). The main action of the play shows the personal cost of freedom, while the words of its song emphasize the utopian, world-making power of the revolution:

> Men and women! Comrades, come!
> All of you in thousands come!
> The world is ours!
> The world is ours!
>
> (Michel 1891–2 [5 Dec. 1891]: 157)

'The world', here signifying the future that is to be won, is hardly imagined at all; instead, Michel concentrates on the moment of revolutionary triumph. As Jameson argues about contemporary utopias, 'the formal flaw—how to articulate the Utopian break in such a way that it is transformed into a practical-political transition—now becomes a rhetorical and political strength—in that it forces us precisely to concentrate on the break itself' (Jameson 2005: 232). The fragmentary form of the play, intensified by its uneven serialization among articles on the suffering of the workers and the power of a general strike, invites readers to bridge the gap between what John P. Clarke describes as 'the movement of ideas' and 'the movement of reality' in a sustained focus on the moment

---

[12] On Coulon's role as anarchist provocateur in the pay of the British Special Branch, see Bantman 2013: 104–106, 124.

of disruption through a withdrawal of labour (Clarke 2009: 15). For Michel, a utopian dream becomes a utopian reality in this one idea, 'concentrating the whole of socialism', as Georges Sorel would later advocate, 'in the drama of the general strike' (Sorel 1999: 113). The play, like the newspaper more broadly, conjures 'collections of images, which taken together and through intuition alone, [...] are capable of evoking the mass of sentiments which correspond to the different manifestations of the war undertaken by socialism against modern society' (113). Sorel justifies his insistence on the efficacy of the 'myth' of the general strike by comparing its effect with what he describes as 'the senseless hopes which the utopians have always held up before the dazzled eyes of the people' (118). For Sorel, 'utopias have no place in economic conflicts': detailed plans about the future, he argues, will not help the revolution; images and emotion, rather than conversation and discussion, are the motivating forces for change (129). If, however, the moment of disruption can be seen as utopian, conversations about the means of that break work alongside images of it to engage readers in the imagination of change.

On 20 February 1892, alongside the final instalment of *The Strike*, is an article by the German political exile Johann Most, entitled, 'Why I Am a Communist', one of a series of such articles written by anarchists and Communists across the 1890s and representative of their ongoing political wrangling over ideas.[13] Most argues that 'there are some misconceptions attached to the real meaning of Communism. There are some who, more or less, believe it to be some kind of Utopia, while others see in it [...] an all-fixing machinery of State'. Neither view, Most suggests, is accurate: 'modern Communists do not think of such Utopias as imagined by all those idealists from Thomas More down to Edward Bellamy; and they do not to propose to shape, in advance, the mode of action by the people of future ages' (Most 1892: 32). Among 'all those idealists', no doubt, would be some of the utopians lectured on by James Campbell in Edinburgh just a few years earlier. Most goes on to say that 'modern Communism is satisfied with proclaiming its principle of common possession of all wealth'—precisely the ground of More's society, where 'there is abundance for all since everything is divided equally' (More 2012: 52). It is not the social policy of More's Utopia or Bellamy's to which Most is responding in this article, however, but a common perception of Utopia as an unrealizable ideal, in order to dispel similarly inaccurate perceptions about anarchism, decried by some contemporary Communists as a political dream that failed to grasp the economic realities of a materialist conception of history. Most challenges this view by urging on readers the sound economic basis of his own ideals, noting that he is anti-statist, but that his anarchism arises necessarily out of Communism.[14] His defence of his position sounds like nothing more than Raphael Hythloday's defence to More of the Utopians' social organization and commonality of possession, which concludes: 'you have no conception of such a polity, or at least a distorted one' (More 2012: 53). Set alongside Michel's work, and in the wider context of the newspaper, Most's article works to suggest that it is not a

---

[13] See e.g. *The Why I Ams*: Morris, 'Why I am a Socialist' and Louisa Sarah Bevington, 'Why I Am an Expropriationist' (Morris 1894; Bevington 1894).

[14] On anarchist economics and anti-statism, see Kinna 1999.

comprehensive understanding of a future world that matters, but an unwavering vision of the object and end of desire, the details of which might nonetheless be under continuous and minute discussion.

Generating Utopian Conversation

As Jameson notes of utopian writings, 'the most reliable political test lies not in any judgement on the individual work in question so much as its capacity to generate new ones, Utopian visions that include those of the past, and modify or correct them' (Jameson 2005: xv). While *The Clarion* and *The Commonweal* create very different utopian discussions, both continue the conversation about utopia and social change, and both generate new utopian thinking, utopian tales, and utopian conversations, blurring the boundaries between the printed page and each newspaper's readers, inviting them to shape its contents and in turn a new social order. At the same time, the papers set themselves in dialogue with alternative ideas of Utopia through their advertisements.[15] In 1890 *The Commonweal* is particularly active in promoting utopian texts, as though in publishing *News from Nowhere*, it set in motion a conversation that can only be continued by reading it alongside not only *Looking Backward*, in the dialectical relationship that Jameson (2005: 143) describes as 'the eternal pair of Bellamy and Morris', but also other contemporary utopias.

On 15 November 1890, *The Commonweal* carries a large advertisement for John Petzler's *Life in Utopia*, described as a '1s[hilling] paper', but available on 'special terms to branches' (368). By December 1891, Petzler's book, first published in May 1890, is part of a mass Christmas Eve giveaway of 'books and pamphlets the price of which keep many of them out of [readers of *The Commonweal*'s] hands', at a special event in Hoxton. While twelve loose paper copies, unbound, and twelve bound copies of *News from Nowhere* are included, 100 copies of Petzler's book are available, suggesting that despite the special offers to branches, it has not sold well (*The Commonweal* 1891 [5 Dec.]: 160). The book's programmatic certainty and heavy-handed approach may have contributed to its unpopularity, although little evidence remains of readerly responses. In his introduction Petzler (1890: iii) notes that the book 'is to some extent based on Plato's Republic and Sir Thomas More's Utopia', and in the town square of this country there is a 'great colossal bronze statue of Sir Thomas More, the celebrated discoverer of Utopia and the wise reformer of her social institutions' (75); yet there is no trace here of More's intellectual critique or playfulness. While Petzler does introduce 'a novel and highly romantic mode of marriage, a subject which Bellamy did not touch in Looking Backward', his reworking of the marriage market, like the whole of his text, is rooted in an idea of authoritarian order, regulation, and completion: it takes the form of a mass ceremony of rational selection

---

[15] For more on *Utopia* and advertising, see Sako in this volume.

of mates, based on lists of accomplishments, traits, and interests, overseen by 'Utopia, your kind, generous, and solicitous mother' (iii, 109). There is no recognition here of the vagaries of sexual desire suggested by More's insistence on premarital viewing of the naked potential mate (More 2012: 92). In contrast to More's, Michel's, and Morris's various formal and stylistic gestures towards imperfection and incompletion, Petzler's tightly organized script works to shut down conversation rather than open it up.

While *The Commonweal* pressed copies of *Life in Utopia* on its readers, *The Clarion*, always more closely and specifically engaged with questions of gender, repeatedly advertised Jane Hulme Clapperton's *Margaret Dunmore: Or, a Socialist Home*, noting as it did so that this was a text widely and favourably reviewed in the mainstream press (*The Clarion* 1895 [16 Mar.]: 84). Published in 1888, the novel itself predates both Bellamy's and Morris's tales, but its repeated advertisement in socialist journals over the following years sets it in ongoing conversation with those texts and with the broader utopian conversation of fin-de-siècle socialism.[16] The socialist home of the title is a commune established in 1890, funded by the wealthy Margaret Dunmore and drawing in a range of young English men and women and older French revolutionaries, who begin the novel discussing the means and meaning of social change. Thérèse José writes to her friend Henri Martin, inviting him to join the proposed communal household: 'you are well acquainted with the various experiments already made by mankind in this direction, and their all but invariable failure'. She goes on to urge that 'the march of events [...] may make possible to-day, and easy to-morrow, what was impossible ten, five, or even one year ago' (Clapperton 1888: 23). Unlike Petzler's, Clapperton's is a world with permeable boundaries and a close connection to contemporary life; it offers no account of revolution, but suggests, as does *The Clarion*, that gradual change is possible through small-scale choices and communal conversation.

As Ruth Kinna notes, a common critique by writers on the utopian state is that it 'requires an unreasonable degree of consensus of its citizens, that it ignores trade-offs between competing moral values and leaves no room for genuine pluralism' (Kinna 2009: 226). Although this is true in individual texts, such as Petzler's, published or advertised in fin-de-siècle socialist journals, the very fact of their participation in the pluralistic world of newspaper publishing, lecture tours, and open-air propaganda of various kinds draws them into a participatory conversation that traverses different parts of contemporary culture. In January 1891, D. J. Nicoll, discussing the demise of feudalism in an article in *The Commonweal* entitled 'The Glorious Reformation', argues that 'the Utopia of More, in its wide range of speculation on every subject of human thought and action, tells us how thoroughly the narrowness and limitation of human life had broken down' (Nicoll 1891: 2). Utopia, in this conception, involves the capacity for imagination that goes beyond conventional norms, that engages with all aspects of life, and that takes risks. Ernst Bloch famously suggested that 'thinking means venturing

---

[16] However, *The Commonweal* does not advertise Clapperton's *Margaret Dunmore* at all, and Ernest Belfort Bax's journal *To-Day* cautions its readers to 'fight very shy' of this 'perfectly preposterous' book (*To-Day* 1888 [Mar.]: 92).

beyond. But in such a way that what already exists is not kept under or skated over. Not in its deprivation, let alone in moving out of it. Not in the causes of deprivation, let alone in the first signs of the change which is ripening within it' (Bloch 1986: 1.4). By the time *The Commonweal* closed for lack of funds in 1894, its emphasis on venturing beyond, on multiplicity and imperfection, which reached its apogee with the publication of *News from Nowhere* in 1890 and lingered on in Michel's invitational play, had been replaced by a narrowing viewpoint. Meanwhile *The Clarion* was so successful that it moved its publishing office to Fleet Street in 1895, before its own uneven decline set in following the journal's turn to pro-war jingoism in 1899 and again in 1914, with its concomitant closing down of plurality. Despite their 'all but invariable failure', what both achieved in the utopian moment of the 1890s was a lively and polyvocal discussion that continued and continues to resonate, generating new discussion about deprivation, future transformation, and the means of venturing beyond the safety of the known in pursuit of a better and more just world.

CHAPTER 33

UTOPIA, THE IMPERIAL SETTLER UTOPIA, AND IMPERIAL SETTLER SCIENCE FICTION

REBECCA WEAVER-HIGHTOWER AND MUSAB BAJABER

Utopus, who conquered the country and gave it his name (for it had been previously called Abraxa), and who brought its rude uncouth inhabitants to such a high level of culture and humanity that they now surpass almost any other people, also changed its geography. After winning the victory of his first assault, he had a channel cut fifteen miles wide where the land joined the continent, and thus caused the sea to flow around the country. He put not only the natives to work at this task but all his own soldiers too, so that the vanquished would not think the labor a disgrace. With the work divided among so many hands, the project was finished quickly, and the neighboring peoples, who at first had laughed at the folly of the undertaking, were struck with wonder and terror at its success. (More 2003: 42)

THE details presented in the above excerpt from Thomas More's 1516 proto-novel *Utopia* describe a colonized space similar to those established by real-life settler colonies in America, Australia, and parts of Africa. In the second book of *Utopia*, from which this passage is taken, through the words of traveller and former visitor to Utopia, Raphael Hythloday, More describes in detail the space's history and culture. Specifically, Hythloday tells how its leader and conqueror Utopus, in settler colonial fashion, invaded a peninsula and eradicated the culture of its 'rude and uncouth inhabitants', forcefully establishing his ideals to create Utopia (42). Readers are told that Utopus not only conquered and cultivated the peninsula; he also cut it off from the mainland: 'He had a channel cut fifteen miles wide [....] And thus caused the sea to flow around the country' (42), turning the peninsula into an island, easily fortified, separated, and contained to become the perfect space to establish a new and ideal settler society. Also in the logic of the settler colony, the now conquered people were incorporated into the settler culture, their former culture replaced with 'such a high level of culture and humanity' that they 'would surpass almost any other people', causing 'wonder and terror' in neighbouring countries (42). This superiority, so the Utopians tell Hythloday, leads the colonized to voluntarily embrace Utopian ideals so as to enjoy a quality of life found in no other culture.

More's work coined the term 'utopia', but it was not the first to depict the societal ideal the word has come to signify. Religious texts, myths, and philosophical treatises since antiquity have described isolated paradises.[1] What distinguishes More's work, however, is that it added an imperial dimension to this depiction.[2] Like other imperial powers, Utopia largely excludes itself from outside influence, with its inhabitants encountering travellers like Hythloday but able to reject elements of outside culture that contradict their ideology.[3] Nonetheless, despite this preferred isolationism, again like other imperial powers, Utopia forcefully projects itself onto peoples it presumes inferior for what it sees as natural and legitimate reasons, including overcrowding, defending allies, subduing enemies, and civilizing barbarians. In other words, through its policy of exclusion and expansion, Utopia establishes control over the direction of cultural and political influence. Utopians take their 'superior' culture to 'inferior' and weaker nations, but these nations cannot return the influence. This fantasy of the unidirectional influence of a 'superior' culture on an 'inferior' one is reflected in other colonial texts, including—two hundred years later—in Daniel Defoe's *Robinson Crusoe* (1719), in which Crusoe recreates his island as a little England, teaching everything about his language and culture to Friday, his indigenous and willing servant, instead of learning from Friday, the indigenous person with the knowledge of how to survive in that environment (Weaver-Hightower 2007).

But this unidirectional model also captured the imagination of real-world settler colonies who strove to halt the two-way cultural influence (and racial mixing) that inevitably results from colonization and cultural encounter. Considering the founding of the North American settler colonies, Annette Magid asserts in 'Thomas More in America' (2016), that More's work—which was published around the same time that Europeans set foot on the North American continent—was in line with the imperial aspirations and ambitions of many early American colonial settlers, who were seeking to establish new societies free of the problems that plagued Europe.[4] This chronological coincidence, however, does not mean that these settlers took what More wrote as blueprint for ideal colonization. As Bill Ashcroft (2017) indicates, early settlers did not deliberately cut themselves off from the mother country by altering the landscape as did More's early Utopians, nor did they lay out their cities in the manner More proposed. Yet, as Ashcroft

---

[1] See also Hadfield and Hobbes in this volume.
[2] See also Hower, Hadfield, and Lutz in this volume.
[3] In reality, imperial powers, like Britain, absorbed cultural elements from elsewhere, such as the use of tea and china, both imports but now considered essential parts of British culture. Yet for much of Britain's imperial history the notion of colonial influence was that it was unidirectional, with Britain spreading its culture across its empire in a 'civilizing mission'.
[4] For more on *Utopia* in sixteenth-century South America ('New Spain'), see Kern in this volume.

explains, the distance between early settlers and their mother country did allow them to entertain Moreish utopian ideals and concepts (180). And despite the fantasy of an empty and available space, a terra nullius, these settler colonies were created, as Ashcroft reminds us, 'at the expense of the indigenous people and flora and fauna' who were very much already in existence, just like the pre-inhabitants of *Utopia* (181). Even five hundred years after its publication, More's brand of utopianism continues to seep into the American cultural presumption that some societies have the right and mandate to influence or demolish inferior ones. As this chapter will show, this presumption has governed the development of the United States of America as a settler colony, and this presumption also continues to influence fantasies of the United States' future, as evident in its science fiction.

Though other critics have noted the influence of utopianism on early settler colonialists who attempted to establish utopias in the 'New World', little has been mentioned about *Utopia*'s influence on the variation of settler colony that this chapter identifies as 'the imperial settler utopia'.[5] As we will argue, unlike settler utopias like the Owenites, the Quakers, and others that were isolated and focused on inward development, imperial settler utopias are settler colonies that are so entranced by their own ideals that they envision their colonies as predestined to expand and dominate others on the merit of superiority. Hence, imperial utopian colonies tend to move beyond their original borders to colonize other spaces and clash with other colonies with different visions of idealism. These imperial settler utopias, this chapter argues, are found in both the real and fictional worlds of settler colonial cultures.

This chapter aims to establish that *Utopia*, as the original imperial settler utopia, influenced the development of real-world imperial settler utopias in the nineteenth and twentieth centuries and that, in return, these real-world settler colonies combined with the legacy of *Utopia* to contribute to the rise of a literary genre that often builds upon imperial settler colonial fantasies: namely, science fiction (Rider 2008). In particular, this chapter will look at how utopian ideology plays out in different contexts over time and will examine the real-world development of the imperial settler utopia through the example of the settler colonies that would eventually make up the United States. Throughout the chapter, we will consider the two primary and coexisting qualities of the imperial settler utopia: first, expansion, justified by a logic related to the utopian ideology of the colony and civilizing mission; and second, insularity, justified by the need to keep influence unidirectional. This chapter will culminate with examination of how the United States' imperial settler aspirations led to efforts to continue the nation's expansion into space, a fantasy best exemplified in the science fiction franchise *Star Trek*. As illustrations, we will examine in more detail two episodes of *Star Trek*, arguing that they show the fictional and real-world utopian attempts as dialectical and mutually reinforcing. The utopian fantasy first perpetuated through More's utopian fictional text soon played out through real-world actions. And these actions led to the continuation

---

[5] On settler utopianism, see Tower Sargent 2010a, 2010b; K. Hardy 2012; J. C. Davis 2000.

of the fantasy in imaginations of the future, which in turn continue to affect real-world actions. Ultimately, we hope to further the understanding of this cycle of influence begun by *Utopia* and showcase how More's work continues to guide the direction of history and literature five hundred years later.

The United States of America: An Imperial Settler Utopia in Action

This imperial settler utopia as it functioned in the real world can be best seen in the settler colonies that came to be known as the United States of America.[6] Throughout its more than four-hundred-year history, from the first colony established at Jamestown in 1607, what was called 'the New World' was settled by communities of immigrants in search of a better life, often with utopian dreams. The Massachusetts Bay Colony and communities of New Haven and Pennsylvania in the seventeenth century, for instance, were all established to be utopian, with the dream of greater religious freedom (W. E. Nelson 2005; R. Sutton 2004; Sreenivasan 2008). The Massachusetts Bay Colony was established first in 1628, and then New Haven in 1638 by a group of settlers who wanted a government more integrally connected to the Church. Pennsylvania was founded forty-three years later by William Penn in 1681, similarly with the utopian fantasy of religious tolerance for its Quaker majority. Of course, for the indigenous inhabitants of the settled space, the world was not 'new', the land not empty, and the settlements of European migrants not utopian. And for the slaves upon whose backs the nation was built, 'the New World' brought no better life. But both oppressed indigenes and exploited and enslaved people were crucial to More's Utopia, as well.[7]

Once the nation became established, other utopian communities were formed primarily by 'white' settlers as internal enclaves. The New Harmony colony of Owenists in Indiana (est. 1852), the Amana Colonies of Pietists in Iowa (est. 1850s), and others were settled but did not expand their reach into other territories.[8] Neither did the many Shaker communities in the nineteenth and twentieth centuries, nor the twentieth-century utopian communities of Twin Oaks in Virginia (from the 1960s to the present) and the Family of Mystic Arts in Oregon (1960s and 1970s). Each of these communities was established in its own time to create a space inside the United States that could be governed by 'utopian' principles of harmony and peace (R. Sutton 2004; Sreenivasan 2008). These spaces were not created in the vein of More's *Utopia* as imperial settler utopias in that they did not express or act on expansionist ideals but instead acted in the spirit of cooperation that the word 'utopia' has come to mistakenly carry. Thus, rather

---

[6] On the USA as a settler colony, see Hixson 2013; Rifkin 2014.
[7] For more on slavery and *Utopia*, see Kern, Withington, Waithe, and Lutz in this volume.
[8] See also Lutz in this volume on the Hutterite community.

than examining these isolated, ideal communities within the United States as 'utopian'—as they clearly fashioned themselves—we instead examine the larger nation itself as utopian in the vein of More's proto-novel, because the United States provides a particularly strong example of the imperial settler utopia that is at the same time insular and expansive.

This dialectical ideology reminds us that it is important to consider the spatiality of the utopian fantasy and how the United States as a nation has conceived of itself as an island, in its demands to expand westward throughout its continent; in its efforts to culturally, economically, and politically dominate its continental neighbours (Canada and Mexico); and through its increasingly impermeable borders that resist the encroachment of 'undesirable' immigrants. As Bill Ashcroft explains in 'Critical Utopias', the insularity of the original Utopia, represented by its island setting, reminds that 'although imagined, [Utopia] is a place, and spatial perfection requires boundaries, control, limits and direction' (Ashcroft 2007: 413). And so we turn to examining the United States, as an example of imperial utopian ideology.

The United States was imagined, so say its founding documents, on utopian ideals of democracy and freedom. The Declaration of Independence, written in 1776, was primarily penned by Thomas Jefferson, who, according to the Library of Congress list of his library contents, owned not one but two copies of More's *Utopia*—a Latin edition printed by the heirs of Arnold Birckmann (Cologne, 1555) and Robert Foulis's 1743 edition of Gilbert Burnet's 1684 English translation—leading one to assume that Jefferson read the book.[9] The second sentence of the Declaration clearly lays out the utopian ideals of the white men who dared to rebel against the great imperial power of Britain: 'We hold these truths to be self-evident, that all men are created equal, that they are endowed by their Creator with certain unalienable Rights, that among these are Life, Liberty and the pursuit of Happiness.' This famous sentence is followed by a long list of offences of the imperial power (Britain) against the 'upstart' colony, most of them overt but not unexpected acts of imperialism that England performed against all of its settler colonies, including exacting taxes from the colony and governing the colonized space from afar and without colonial input.

The preamble to the US Constitution, another of its founding documents created fifteen years later, also presents the nation to be founded on principles that can be traced back to More's *Utopia*. 'In Order to form a more perfect Union', the document begins, defending its own existence, the nation will 'establish Justice, ensure domestic Tranquility, provide for the common defense, promote the general Welfare, and secure the Blessings of Liberty to ourselves and our Posterity'. As has widely been recognized by historians and critics since then, these principles of freedom and equality were not extended to all inhabitants of the colonies, but excluded women, many people of colour, non-landowners, and especially the indigenous inhabitants of the land who preceded the settlers.

Though unrecognized by most historians, the United States' founding as an imperial settler utopia includes the dual insularity and expansiveness that can be traced back to More's

---

[9] Library of Congress shelf marks: Jefferson collection HX811 1516.A516 and HX811 1516.E743.

Utopia. From its beginning, the utopian ideals stated in its founding documents led to a fantasy of 'American exceptionalism', that is, the notion that the United States is different from the rest of the world, including other anglophone settler colonies. This difference creates an insular perception, since the country is isolated in its exceptionality. As Michael Adas explains, 'American exceptionalists tend to see the rise of the United States to global power as part of a larger teleological progression toward—depending on the observer and time frame in question—human virtue, utopian sublimity, civilization, development, or modernity' (Adas 2001: 1702). At the same time, this fantasy of exceptionalism is also expansive, in that it positions the United States as a model for the rest of the world. From the beginning of the nation's colonial settlement, one of its first colonial governors, John Winthrop, in the eighteenth century, well described this insular expansiveness of the imperial settler utopia in his edict for the Massachusetts Bay Colony: 'We shall', he proscribes, 'be as a city upon a hill, the eyes of all people are upon us' (W. E. Nelson 2005). The 'city on a hill' is, of course, a metaphor of a place insular, fortified, and contained, as was More's island, since the hill is separate and not part of a continuous landscape. But this metaphor is also expansive, since the city's model way of life would in this fantasy inevitably spread across the landscape. As Adas explains (quoting from one of Winthrop's sermons), Winthrop's description of Puritan exceptionalism at the same time 'stressed its lessons for the rest of humanity, lessons that he believed would be regarded as "a story and by-word through the world". The city, after all, was on high ground with the "eyes of all people" upon it' (Adas 2001: 1692). In this way, the city-on-a-hill metaphor exemplifies the simultaneous insularity and expansiveness of the imperial settler utopia that began with More's *Utopia*.

These coexistent desires for insularity and expansiveness have led to debates about the United States' place in the world since at least the mid-nineteenth century. As the nation grew over the eighteenth and nineteenth centuries, debates raged between those who wanted to respect the intentions of the 'Founding Fathers' for the United States not to get involved in world conflicts, especially those of Europe, and those who felt that the democratic ideals of the Founding Fathers were meant to be promoted throughout the world, at gunpoint, if necessary. As so well explained by Gary Nash et al. (2000: 519): 'Americans have rarely just focused on perfecting the good example at home, waiting for others to copy it. This requires patience and passivity, two traits not characteristic of Americans. Rather, throughout history, the American people have actively and sometimes forcefully imposed their ideas and institutions on others.' The nineteenth-century United States struggled with its identity as an imperial settler utopia. The expansive ideology and belief in the mission to spread utopian ideals, captured in the phrase 'Manifest Destiny', led to the spread of settler culture westward across the North American continent.[10] Acts like the Louisiana Purchase (1803) and the wars with Mexico

---

[10] Pratt (1927: 798) explained the origins of the phrase as follows: 'The author of the phrase "manifest destiny" was John L. O'Sullivan, editor in 1845–6 of the monthly *Democratic Review* and of the *New York Morning News*. The phrase first appeared in an editorial article in the *Democratic Review* for July–August, 1845. It was repeated in an editorial in the *Morning News* of December 27, 1845, in reference to the Oregon question.'

over Texas (1846) and California (1846-8); the belief that the indigenous people who already lived in those spaces were only an obstacle to be absorbed, surmounted, or moved as with the Trail of Tears (the forced displacements of indigenous peoples in 1831-50); and the establishment of the reservation system show the expansionist belief of US forces in the nineteenth century.

The United States' struggle with its imperial settler utopian tendencies—its isolationism and desire to spread the American way of life (especially its brand of representative capitalist democracy) around the world—have been threaded through its history. One of the more notable events in the nineteenth century exemplifying this struggle is the nation's dealings with the Philippines after the Spanish-American War (1898), specifically the national debate over whether or not to take the Philippines as a US territory or to grant them independence as promised when the indigenous Filipino people supported the United States against Spain. This internal debate led Rudyard Kipling to pen his paradigmatic imperialist text, 'The White Man's Burden', urging the United States to take the Philippines as a territory or colony, under the logic of duty as a 'white' nation, a logic that won out (Kipling 1899).

This practice of American expansion escalated after the US Civil War (1861-5), when Secretary of State William Seward argued for the United States to hold a 'commanding sway in the world' (Nash et al. 2000: 520). Seward put his ideals into practice with the purchase of Alaska from Russia in 1867. He also made inroads on Hawaii that would result in its annexation in 1898, and he had sights on Cuba and a future Panama Canal (520). Debates over the imperial aspirations of Seward and later Teddy Roosevelt (1858-1919) occurred in newspapers and other venues, led by anti-imperial ex-presidents such as Grover Cleveland (1837-1908); public intellectuals like William James (1842-1910), Samuel Gompers (1850-1924), Andrew Carnegie (1835-1919), and Jane Addams (1860-1935); and writers like Mark Twain (1835-1910) (Nashe et al. 2000: 527). So the United States continued to act on imperial fantasies, yet these ambitions were not uncontested.

Fantasies of expansion of American influence persisted in the twentieth century with the spread of American politics and culture across the globe, including the absorption of Hawaii and Alaska as states in 1959 and Puerto Rico, the Northern Mariana Islands, the US Virgin Islands, American Samoa, and Guam as territories. In the mid-late twentieth century, the areas of expansion reached into space.[11] As Alexander McDonald illustrates, these fantasies of conquering space did not begin with the Cold War in the 1950s and 1960s and the perceived competition between capitalism and communism, but have existed in American fantasies of expansion, pioneering, and colonization since the nation's founding (A. McDonald 2013: 20-22). Indeed, they can be traced at least as far back as Edward Everett Hale's 1869 novel *The Brick Moon*, published serially in

---

[11] Our purpose here is to examine direct political imperialism, but critics like Said (1993) and Hardt and Negri (2000) have persuasively argued for the existence of alternative forms of colonization that do not involve the spread of national governments into another space. Said discusses imperialism that is spread through culture. Hardt and Negri discuss economic imperialism, which they argue is superseding political imperialism in the twentieth century.

the *Atlantic Monthly*. Yet the push into space was certainly accelerated by the Cold War Space Race, as evidenced by John F. Kennedy's famous proclamation at Rice University on 12 September 1962 about going to the moon, where he characterized space and the moon in particular as frontiers to be 'explored and mastered'.[12]

It was this environment and this fantasy of the United States as an imperial settler utopia that spawned the series that will be the focus of the rest of this chapter: the cult classic *Star Trek*. At the series' beginning in the 1960s, the belief was that the next inevitable area for expansion for the United States was into outer space which is, not surprisingly, expressed in the opening credit voice-over of each episode of *The Original Series* with its famous call for exploration of 'the final frontier'[13].

STAR TREK, THE FEDERATION, AND IMPERIAL SETTLER COLONIALISM

We will now examine the cinematic analogue of the United States as an imperial settler utopia: the United Federation of Planets that is threaded through the *Star Trek* corpus. The creation of Gene Roddenberry in 1966 and spanning to date seven television series, thirteen films, and many novels, games, comics, and toys, *Star Trek* is one of the most successful science fiction franchises in existence, rivalled only by George Lucas's *Star Wars* franchise (1977–). Although Roddenberry's creation eventually grew out of his control and authorship and developed into a franchise influenced by many writers, contributors, and producers, his vision of the utopian future of Earth remains the heart of the *Star Trek* franchise. While he does not explicitly allude to More's *Utopia* or any utopian work in *Star Trek*, Roddenberry's idea of a future imperial, yet isolated, humanist utopia on Earth is an extension of More's idea of an imperial and isolated humanist utopia in the sixteenth century. Throughout his colourful life and his various interviews, Roddenberry proclaimed himself a humanist and an adamant defender of humanism; he was described by *The Humanist* as 'one of the most influential yet unheralded humanists of the twentieth century' whose creation is 'solidly based upon humanistic principles and ideas' (David 1991). We contend that Roddenberry's connection to humanism and his promotion of the basic principle that human beings are capable of solving their problems and progressing their society through rational thinking echoes More's *Utopia* and the subsequent utopian tradition.

---

[12] The speech can be viewed and a transcript found at the JFK Library website at https://www.jfklibrary.org/learn/about-jfk/historic-speeches/address-at-rice-university-on-the-nations-space-effort.

[13] For more on the influence of imperial narrative in science fiction, particularly *Star Trek*, see Byers 1987; Fulton 1994; Geraghty 2004.

The *Star Trek* universe begins in the twenty-third century in a world where technologically advanced humans founded a political United Federation of Planets ('The Federation') which Roddenberry envisions as an idealized futuristic version of the United Nations. This Federation involves more than 150 species of sentient creatures from a range of planets, most of which are humanoid.[14] Furthermore, many of the episodes and major events rotate around events in colonies or conflicts around colonies similar to contemporary and historical conflicts.[15] The Federation is the one constant across the many series, films, and other *Star Trek* products, with progressive ideals of racial inclusivity and harmony that would, Roddenberry speculates, dominate the future multicultural earth (David 1991). The Federation is a force for democratic values and a peaceful coexistence across the universe, as its far-flung member planets work to trade, travel, and talk across the species barrier. 'The Prime Directive', which mandates the non-interference or colonization of less technologically developed species, governs all exploration across the series so that members of the Federation are only allowed to colonize non-inhabited planets and explore space for peaceful purposes.

Yet, despite the constant presence and frequent invocation of the Prime Directive, its rules are nearly always broken. In episode after episode, viewers see how humans—often with the best of intentions, unlike other 'villainous' space empires such as the Borg or Romulans—interfere, disrupt, and destroy other cultures perceived as inferior, as did the Utopians. The Prime Directive is breached so often in the show that one might conclude that its presence is only meant to keep the influence in the direction opposite to Earth's utopia, which—in turn—isolates and protects Earth from incoming influence. Terrans (i.e. Americans), like Utopians, have achieved their utopia. They do not want others, even more advanced civilizations, to interfere with or disrupt it, any more than they might interfere with the development of others. Yet they see themselves as being responsible for spreading their imperial settler utopian ideals into space, thus bringing together the opposites of insularity and expansiveness characteristic of the imperial settler utopia.

A typical plot point of episodes across the *Star Trek* franchise involves using counter-utopias to highlight the superiority of the Federation's imperial settler utopia. In *Archaeologies of the Future* (2005), Fredrik Jameson argues that in order to understand utopias, one must have dystopias as contrast. Similarly, we argue here that the *Star Trek* shows need counter-utopias in order to fully illustrate and argue for the Federation as a successful utopia. Two episodes more than twenty years apart nicely illustrate this plot tendency: 'The Apple' (1967) from *Star Trek: The Original Series* and 'The Masterpiece Society' (1992) from *Star Trek: The Next Generation*. 'The Apple' (written by Max Erlich)

---

[14] One of the plot lines of *The Next Generation* explains this phenomenon by tracing the origins of much of the universe's life back to a proto-bipedal species that seeded hundreds of planets with life. So, under this logic, the bipedal species the humans encounter on other planets share a common ancestor.

[15] According to the official *Star Trek* website, the Federation of Planets has 700 colonies. Furthermore, many of the episodes and major events rotate around events in colonies or conflicts around colonies similar to real conflicts on Earth.

centres on a utopia of people indigenous to a planet, a utopia upset by contact with the Federation. Likewise, the 'Masterpiece Society' (written by James Kahn, Adam Belanoff, and Michael Piller) centres around the failure of a planetary utopia, but in this case a rogue utopian Federation settlement, also destroyed by contact with the larger imperial utopia of the Federation. These two episodes reaffirm what More has established in *Utopia*: that a successful utopia, whether indigenous or settler, cannot be sustained without being insular and expansive at the same time. Furthermore, analysing these two episodes from different series demonstrates that the integration of utopian ideals and settler imperial policies that More's *Utopia* intimated five centuries earlier is still held dear.

An episode from the second season of *The Original Series*, 'The Apple' centres on an encounter between the *Enterprise* crew and the inhabitants of a Garden of Eden-like utopia on Gamma Trianuli VI. This colony is indigenous in that it is not identified as a Federation settlement, but the inhabitants are phenotypically 'white', as were most actors and characters on American television of the 1960s. In this utopia, the inhabitants have lived for a thousand years under the protection and oppression of a god-machine, Vaal. They have provided the machine with fruits and vegetation; and Vaal in return has provided them with social stability, abundance, and happiness. Despite the stability and happiness present in this utopia, many members of the *Enterprise* think that the conditions on Gamma Trianuli VI are inhumane because, in the words of *Enterprise* doctor Leonard McCoy, this utopia is one of 'stagnation' that has left its population undeveloped for thousands of years. That is, in the utopian vision of the *Enterprise* team, without Darwinian struggle, the inhabitants of Gamma Trianuli VI have not progressed or evolved. James Kirk (the *Enterprise* captain) agrees and eventually destroys Vaal, leaving the newly independent inhabitants in disarray. As the starship team prepares to leave the planet, Kirk assures the inhabitants that all will be well and that with the help of the Federation, they will evolve and will be happy in a 'real' utopia under the Federation's hegemony and not the false god Vaal.

'The Masterpiece Society', an episode from season 5 of the 1990s spin-off, *The Next Generation*, shows a similar situation. In this episode, the *Enterprise* attempts to save a Federation human settler colony on Moab, a planet threatened by a stray fragment of a dead star. When the dispatch team of officers beams down to the colony, they find a genetically engineered utopia where every person is constructed to fulfil a specific duty, thus ensuring harmony and progress in the colony. This utopian settler colony has maintained a strict isolationist policy and has been successful for 200 years. Despite its success, however, and upon seeing the Enterprise, many of its residents request to leave Moab. The Federation, they think, is superior because of its expansive and adventurous spirit. But the sudden desertion of key members of Moab's population destroys the utopian society, and the story ends with a final note on the dangers and fallibility of isolationism and genetic manipulation and on the merits of the Federation's American-styled ideals of self-determination and exploration.

Both 'The Apple' and 'The Masterpiece Society' use counter-utopias to show the Federation as the ideal utopia: insular but also expansive and therefore successful.

In 'The Apple', the static culture on Gamma Trianuli VI did not progress for thousands of years because it was not expansive. Like More's Utopia, the planet is isolated and well protected, with a dangerous landscape planted with mines and poisonous roses to fend off intruders, and, as in *Utopia*, only the inhabitants of this planet know how to navigate its landscape. But unlike More's Utopia, Gamma Trianuli VI did not expand beyond its borders, protecting its isolation and leading to its downfall. These opposite utopias eventually collide, and the Federation comes out victorious because of its imperial 'civilizing' mission. In the end, when Kirk and his team bid farewell to the inhabitants who are left in chaos, he (in the vein of Utopus) assures them that they have achieved the 'correct' utopia, which is the one that he and McCoy see fit for them:

> You'll learn to care for yourselves, with our help. And there's no trick to putting fruit on trees. You might enjoy it. You'll learn to build for yourselves, think for yourselves, work for yourselves, and what you create is yours. That's what we call freedom. You'll like it, a lot. And you'll learn something about men and women, the way they're supposed to be. Caring for each other, being happy with each other, being good to each other. That's what we call love. You'll like that, too, a lot. You and your children. ('The Apple')

Here we see the civilizing mission at work in direct counter to the Prime Directive. The inhabitants of Gamma Trianuli VI, even though peaceful, are savages in the eyes of the *Enterprise* crew; and it is the duty of the imperialists (the Federation) to civilize them. The inhabitants of the new utopia will 'learn' how to care for themselves, with the 'help' of the Federation. They will learn to 'build' and 'think', and they will earn their 'freedom' and live 'the way they're supposed to be' (i.e. like the Federation). In other words, eventually the static, isolated, and passive utopian settler colony loses to the aggressive, dynamic, and expanding imperial utopian settler colony, showing that utopias cannot exist in isolation. Utopian settler colonies can only survive through imperial means: through aggression, through pushing boundaries and ideals on others, and through evolving to become stronger and more efficient by the day.

'The Masterpiece Society' further illustrates the legacy of More's utopian imperialism and how the *Star Trek* series used counter-utopias to demonstrate the superiority of the Federation. Here, however, the encroached upon utopia is not an indigenous one as in 'The Apple'. Moab is, rather, a Federation settlement that sought to establish itself on a strict isolation policy different from the Federation. The human settlers of Moab form an isolated utopia based on the best genetic and technological practices. However, the strict isolationist policy that rejects expansion and exploration brings its own demise. As a result of its isolation, the ideals of this utopia collapse in the face of the Federation's competition, even though Moab's inhabitants and environment are perfect and better structured than the Federation. Again, the endurance of the Federation's utopia results from its expansive aggressive policies that allow it to progress and upgrade, unlike Moab, which lost its edge because of its self-focus. Importantly, the citizens of Moab themselves affirm the superiority of the Federation imperial settler utopia, since they choose to leave Moab and join the Federation.

Despite the connection between utopian success and settler imperialism, it is important to mention that the producers of *Star Trek* were aware of the problematic dichotomy of insularity and expansiveness of utopian rhetoric and practice. Their ambivalence can be seen in the final dialogues in each episode where the captain of each ship reflects on the destruction caused to the utopias they encountered. For instance, in 'The Apple', the ship's first officer Spock and Doctor McCoy discuss the justification of destroying the native utopia:

> SPOCK: Doctor, you insist on applying human standards to non-human cultures. I remind you that humans are only a tiny minority in this galaxy.
> MCCOY: There are certain absolutes, Mister Spock, and one of them is the right of humanoids to a free and unchained environment, the right to have conditions which permit growth.
> SPOCK: Another is their right to choose a system which seems to work for them.
> MCCOY: [*addressing Capt. Kirk*] Jim, you're not just going to stand by and be blinded to what's going on here. These are humanoids, intelligent. They need to advance and grow. Don't you understand what my readings indicate? There's been no progress here in at least ten thousand years. This isn't life. It's stagnation.
> SPOCK: Doctor, these people are healthy and they are happy. Whatever you choose to call it, this system works, despite your emotional reaction to it.
> MCCOY: It might work for you, Mister Spock, but it doesn't work for me. Humanoids living so they can service a hunk of tin.

What we see in this discussion is that, as Spock continues to point out the utopian aspects of the planet and the logical right of its citizens to uphold their beliefs, McCoy emotionally argues that the utopia simply does not 'work' for him. Thus, he and Kirk decide to fix Gamma Trianuli VI and bring it in line with the imperial settler utopia of the Federation. Of course, the show was created within the context of the Vietnam War, when the American (utopian) state was waging war against another state that presented itself as utopian: the Communist confederation of the Soviet Union. *Star Trek: The Old Series* captures a different historical situation from that of More's *Utopia* but with a similar ideology at work.

In 'The Masterpiece Society' we see a homologous scenario, when Captain Jean-Luc Picard and Commander William T. Riker (the starship's first officer) reflect on the destruction they caused to the settler utopia of Moab:

> PICARD: If we ever needed reminding of the importance of the Prime Directive, it is now.
> RIKER: The Prime Directive doesn't apply. They're human.
> PICARD: Doesn't it? Our very presence may have damaged, even destroyed, their way of life. Whether or not we agree with that way of life or whether they're human or not is irrelevant, Number One. We are responsible.
> RIKER: We had to respond to the threat from the core fragment, didn't we?

PICARD: Of course we did. But in the end, we may have proved just as dangerous to that colony as any core fragment could ever have been.

Significantly, as with 'The Apple', this end provides a moment of ambivalence that reveals the awareness of the shows' writers and audience of the delicacy of their proposal. The United States in the 1990s was celebrating the fall of the Berlin Wall in 1989, its 'victory' in the first Gulf War in 1991, and was transitioning from the late stage capitalism of President Ronald Reagan, who, we should also remember, repeated the city-on-a-hill metaphor in both his election-eve speech in 1980 and his farewell address in 1989. The notion that the United States in spreading its ideology might be committing cultural imperialism was a question in the air during several of these events.

As well as the 'inferior' counter-utopias examined in 'The Apple' and 'The Masterpiece Society', however, we should mention that the *Star Trek* franchises also rely upon counter-utopias that are over-expansionist to again demonstrate that the Federation represents the best embodiment of expansionism and isolationism. The Borg, for instance, feature as villains in several *Star Trek* series. They are cyborgs that, like the Federation, consider themselves the embodiment of what they call 'perfection' and work to colonize other species by 'assimilating' them, with the same level of aggression as More's Utopus so that, as they intone, 'resistance is futile'. The Borg, we argue, indicate an act of disavowal on the part of the show's writers, who show that imperial settler behaviour taken to its extreme becomes villainous. Perhaps the new post-Communist overarching fear that the Borg represent is of losing individuality in the face of fanaticism or terrorism, reflecting newly emerging US fears during the making and screening of *The Next Generation* (1987–94). While the Federation is shown as an imperial settler utopia with good intentions, the Borg are shown to be imperial settler colonialists without good intentions.

Both 'The Apple' and 'The Masterpiece Society' stress that insular utopias are not sustainable. In many ways, the representation of the failure of these two utopias reflects the way American settlers sought to protect their utopian colonies. Early settlers saw that their utopias could not be sustained without being both insular and expansive. Hence, they declared independence from the British Empire and then began encroaching upon indigenous lands towards the west and then overseas and finally into space. We argue here that this insular and expansive utopian dichotomy that was articulated by More's *Utopia* seeped into settler colonial practices and the formation of the US imperial policy, and that it continues to haunt US fantasies of ideal situations up to this day.

Looking at how the fictional and real world are mutually constituted, *Star Trek*'s vision of the imperial settler utopia continues to reflect and inspire US foreign policy. In a piece on former US President Barack Obama, Charley Locke reminds us that in an interview in 2016 with *Wired*'s editor-in-chief Scott Dadich, Obama reveals his deep admiration of the *Star Trek* series and gives reasons about why the show has shaped his life and policies. According to Obama, it was 'hope', and the fantasy of 'commonality of humans' and 'the confidence and ability to solve problems', that makes the show great and which, he says, is what makes America great, too. 'That is what I love most about

America,' Obama explains, 'that spirit of "oh, we can figure this out." [...] If we ever lose that spirit, then we're gonna lose what is essential about America and what I think is essential about being human' (C. Locke 2016). To Obama, these American ideals are universal in that they represent humanity, thus implying that Americans do have the moral obligation to maintain and spread them (which Obama frequently did throughout his years of presidency).

What is relevant to our argument here, however, is that Obama's reference to *Star Trek* yet again illustrates that the dichotomy More's *Utopia* has created over the past 500 years, in suturing utopianism and imperial fantasies. In the twentieth and twenty-first centuries, the United States, as an imperial settler utopia, continues its struggle between the two poles of insularity and expansiveness as it considers both the role of immigration and its role as a leader in globalization.

CHAPTER 34

AWAY FROM THE ANCESTRAL HOME

Utopia and Philosophy in Bloch and Beyond

JOHAN SIEBERS

THE USES OF UTOPIA

IF Thomas More was the first to give a name to a tendency that runs through philosophical thinking since its beginnings, it is surely Ernst Bloch (1885–1977) who most comprehensively made it the basis of his thought, from his first book publication, *Spirit of Utopia* (1918), via his magnum opus *The Principle of Hope* (1959), to his last book, *Experimentum Mundi* (1975).[1] A contemporary understanding of what utopian thinking is about must take Bloch as the central meeting point. Both retrospectively and prospectively, all lines of utopian thinking come together in his unique oeuvre. This chapter will explore the nature of the utopian as it appears in Bloch's philosophy. We will see how his thinking, through a reflection on the utopian, enacts a decisive turnout of some of the long-standing dimensions of what is called 'philosophy' and into a future-oriented thinking for which, as yet, a clear name is lacking.

Philosophy has always stumbled and faltered at the threshold of the new; in the idea of utopia a radical thinking of the new has slowly been prepared until it found expression in Bloch's writings. Today, Bloch's writings continue to inspire a range of scholarly engagements and utilizations of utopia, from social theory to feminism and ecological and radical environmental thought. However, the main purpose of this chapter is to show how in Bloch's philosophy the core idea of More's *Utopia* is brought to explicit awareness and placed in a deeper and broader understanding of the nature of utopian thinking. Bloch brings *Utopia* back to itself and moves decisively beyond it. As More's

---

[1] All translations of Bloch are my own.

most explicit heir, he revolutionizes philosophical thinking by formulating in a general way the truth of no-place that is a good place by conceptualizing it in terms of not-yet being and not-yet conscious. In utopian thinking we connect to a world that is in process and to the dimensions of our consciousness and subconscious that have to do with longings, desires, anticipations, hunches, and intimations.

For Bloch, the world is radically unfinished in all its dimensions; being itself carries the feature of the 'not-yet'. At the heart of all existence and given with the meaning of being as such, lies an openness, a lack, a darkness, a drive to create, a question longing for an answer.

Bloch sometimes speaks of 'the darkness of the lived moment' to indicate the heart of existence (Siebers 2021). Precise and unambiguous words fail because of the nature of what we are talking about here. Think of the moment at the threshold of what comes next. You can't grasp it by the scruff of the neck. 'At the start, we can only whisper, otherwise we can't speak at all' (Bloch 1975: 11). The term *utopia* arose first in the realm of social and political thought, but it is important to see that the reason for this lies predominantly in the fact that, for us, the practical question of how to live together provides simply the most obvious encounter with the nature of not-yet being. More's *Utopia*, or more generally the social utopias, form the ancestral home, the *Stammhaus*, of all our utopias but they do not exhaust the utopian or make up the essence or principle of them (Bloch 1959: 375). All movement towards the new, all attempts to live a human life, involve the creation of relations: with others and with the world around us. As Bloch says, we move from 'I' to 'we' as the universe, in enacting the not-yet, brings about its own solidarity (Bloch 1975: 375). Togetherness resides in becoming and becoming is always a becoming of togetherness. It is quite easy to see that it should be so: try to imagine connectedness, whichever shape it may take, without some form of movement or becoming, and vice versa. There is, for Bloch, therefore an implicit directionality in all becoming, but not one towards a goal that is given in advance. The process of the world is teleological without a telos, and therefore open to the creative and free formation of goals, values, and aims as the expression of togetherness—goals that enhance or diminish the fullness of actualization. Bloch uses the word 'hope' to indicate this directedness in being. Not-yet being, the ontological rootedness of the utopian moment in reality and in our consciousness, thus becomes 'the principle of hope' (Bloch 1959).

Insofar as philosophical thinking has sought to fixate this processual openness in terms of familiar oppositions, such as actuality and possibility, is and ought, body and mind, passion and reason, self and other, matter and form, being and becoming or being and nothingness, reality and appearance, truth and persuasion, time and eternity, speech and writing, identity and difference—in other words, insofar as thinking has been 'philosophy'—it has reified and split off not-yet being into a transcendent realm and, with that, mythologized, idealized, and alienated it. Traditional philosophy breathes the spirit of authoritarianism; the spirit of utopia counteracts it. In the idea of the utopian, we find the kernel of a fundamental critique of the authoritarian abstractions bequeathed to contemporary culture by the institution of philosophy. No utopia without revolution. Bloch's commitment to the term 'materialism' for utopian thinking (in which he hears the 'mater' and matrix, the creative womb, of new being) and his rejection of philosophical idealism must be seen predominantly against this background. While he continues to speak of philosophy, his version of it has in many ways unrecognizably shifted from what used to be understood by that term. Philosophy becomes experimental: a compass in the creative advance of the world (Bloch 1975). Utopian consciousness, precisely because of its roots in the openness of not-yet being, lies at the basis of all liberation from enslavement and all ideology critique, even if in More's case, the moment of ideology critique has not yet been fully reflected. It exists in the text despite himself, we might say, in the carnivalesque, subversive unconscious of the text. No ideology can fully annihilate the utopian so it always remains available as the starting point of critique and at the same time all ideologies—from Hollywood to institutionalized religion—emerge as static, isolated fantasies of the hopeful longing that animates the not-yet.

Utopian moments, in the sense in which I have indicated them here, can be found everywhere in nature and in culture. Indeed, the fact of the existence of meaning or symbolization, and of human culture itself, reflects a utopian moment within the natural world (even though its hope is more often than not disappointed). In a brief text, no more than one page, 'Der scheidende Odysseus' ('Parting Odysseus'), Bloch gives us a utopian reading of the *Odyssey* 1.5 by way of example (Bloch 1968: 72–73): the Greek is usually translated in terms of Odysseus 'fighting for his life and the return of his comrades', but Bloch's recasting this as 'searching for his soul and the return of his companions' puts marked emphasis on Odysseus' *psyche*. In an 'un-Greek' way, or so Bloch reads this line, Odysseus is in search of himself and his home: he does not live in the presence of where he belongs, but in its absence, and this in a double way. Bloch points out that Homer distinguishes between Odysseus' search for his soul and for his way home. Ithaca is only the proximate, concrete goal that makes for a journey along which Odysseus encounters the hidden love for Nausicaa, which remains outspoken and 'entirely unbecome', as the utopian dimension of his existence. The not-yet, we might say, is in sense itself also clouded in not-yet being. In all process there is the goal that has not yet been reached and there is something that remains itself as-yet unbecome. Both moments together make up the utopian. We find such an explicit statement of the dual structure of the utopian for the first time in Bloch's work. More does not show an explicit awareness of it. However, in hindsight, we might say that the complex and satirical mirroring of England and Utopia in the text only works because of it. Perhaps the structure of the utopian in Bloch shows some parallels with the Lacanian object of desire that is constituted by its absence or loss. However, for Jacques Lacan (1901–81) the *objet petit a* remains forever out of reach while this type of finality would, for Bloch, precisely destroy the openness of the utopian. Hope is essential and hope makes life both possible and impossibly hard to bear, a duality that merely reflects the dual structure of the utopian itself (Lacan 2007). Thus, a utopian ethics would urge us to look for those moments in the process of our life and of the world where genuine hope exists, i.e. where something is at stake, might succeed, or fail. Bloch uses the terms *front*, *novum*, and *ultimum* to characterize these moments. At the front of realization, the new may come into existence, and the as-yet-unbecome ultimate may be intimated (Siebers 2012).

Both Lacan and Bloch were influenced in their youth by Hegel (1770–1831) and both departed from Hegel's claims of absolute knowledge. Lacan retains the dialectical triad in the relation between the real, the imaginary, and the symbolic and he also retains the conservative orientation on the constitutive role of remembrance, while evacuating all final content from the activity of remembrance. Bloch departs from Hegel more radically. While retaining the intimation of the ultimate, he does away with a logical, idealist notion of the dialectic and most emphatically with remembrance as the movement of the spirit. 'Hegel denied the future' (Bloch 1962: 7). *Front, novum,* and *ultimum* form the interdependent coordinates and beating heart of the creative, utopian process and might be said to be dialectically related (i.e. at once presupposing and contradicting each other) but because of their fully material, concrete existence they cannot be conceived of as concrete universals, as part of a logic of being as in Hegel. Their interrelation is dialectical only in a minimally committed sense, almost as an obligatory compliment or salute and even more to Karl Marx (1818–83) than to Hegel. We have to hear the oxymoronic irony in 'dialectical materialism' and hear it as laughter coming from the belly of the darkness of the lived moment.

'The swear word has to go,' Bloch declared in a television interview in 1967 with political scientist Iring Fetscher. 'Utopia' and 'utopian' as terms of abuse, relegating the recipient of it to the realm of unrealistic fantasy, impotent daydreaming, or misguided idealism—that had to go and the word restored, for the first time, to its true nobility as referring to something hardly ever explicitly stated, but always felt, throughout human history and across cultures, something without which we can't make sense of existence (Bloch 1978). That pejorative strain in the meaning of the term 'utopian' was of course also present in More. We might say that only the form of the story, which situated this no-place firmly if not locatable within England's emerging colonial realm, allowed the other strain—the strain of not-yet being, which gave the text its classic status—to shine through, despite the satire, the contemporary prejudices which are never critiqued by More, and the relentlessly unceasing display of wit. Utopia might be real, the form of the text says, and that was enough to ensure the word would never leave the earth. Bloch's thought surveyed the inner and outer workings of utopia, made its structure visible, and sensitized us to the ubiquitous presence of it in all spheres of action, meaning, and reality, in a vast, baroque, and infinitely meandering and coiling oeuvre that leaves no stone unturned to follow the trail of hope. Bloch liberated utopia from its ancestral home and all vestiges of *restitutio ad integrum*.

Today scholars in a wide range of disciplines find Bloch's generalized notion of utopia as not-yet being a useful instrument for their aims. In queer studies, José Muñoz's *Cruising Utopia: The Then and There of Queer Futurity*, first published in 2009, interpreted queering as a utopian figure of thought and practice, aimed at breaking open the present and its pragmatisms, often apparently beyond the need to justify themselves, in the name of a desired and loved future that can be better than the present. The queer emerges in this study as a temporal magnitude, always infused with promise and hope. Cat Moir, in *Ernst Bloch's Speculative Materialism: Ontology, Epistemology, Politics* (2019), made the ontology of not-yet being a contemporary voice in the debates in philosophy and political ontology that aim to restore a place for more open, creative, and imaginative forms of speculative thinking—and in politics— pointing out that Bloch used the phrase 'speculative materialism' long before contemporary authors started using it to describe their philosophical positions. In gender studies, Caitríona Ní Dhúill's *Sex in Imagined Spaces: Gender and Utopia from More to Bloch* (2010) examines the contrast between More's rational utopia—in which sexual desire is highly regulated, if not suppressed, as part of a more general mentality that seeks order as a counterweight to impending chaos—and Bloch's striving, loving, desirous, hopeful, and erotic transgression into the new. Her work mobilizes this contrast to point to the as-yet hardly explored utopian dimension of gender and sexuality, a sexual imaginary that has a vital role to play in liberating people to autonomous embodied existence and to an interpersonal sexual relationality without coercion, oppression, and damage.

Foucault pointed out that the body is the real subject of all utopias and he has also shown how the sexual body has, throughout history, been the subject of quite dystopian institutions (Foucault 1978, 2006). At the crossroads of utopia and dystopia we encounter human sexuality. Although Bloch himself did not write much about sex, and what he wrote bears the mark of his time and sociocultural station, contemporary scholarship is beginning to investigate gendered utopias of sex. It is becoming clear how much work still needs to be done for our sexual cultures and encounters to become positive, non-exploitative, and inclusive. Giving an explicit voice to sexuality's not-yet may help with this task. As another example in this short list of ways Bloch's generalized utopian philosophy is put to use in contemporary scholarship, Nicola Sayers's *The Promise of Nostalgia: Reminiscence, Longing and Hope in Contemporary American Culture* (2020), takes up the task of what Bloch called the 'rescue' of the past. Reading nostalgia against the grain as testimony to a kernel of hope that is forward-looking through the veil of an idealization of a past that never was, Sayers illustrates the relation between utopia and ideology as a productive one, which can be drawn upon to interpret contemporary popular culture as affirmative, without relapsing into the fatalism that has accrued to so much critical theory.

The most sustained elaboration of utopia into a method of analysis, however, has been carried out by Ruth Levitas in sociology. Levitas's classic study *The Concept of Utopia* (1990) played a formative role in establishing the now burgeoning field of utopian studies. It traces the historical development of the concept from its beginning before More, ultimately going back to Plato's theories of the ideal polis, via Francis Bacon (1561–1626), Immanuel Kant (1724–1804), Marx, and others to Bloch and other defenders, and detractors, in the twentieth century. Levitas analyses the totalitarian connotations of much twentieth-century utopian thinking and shows how the antidote to totalitarianism is not less utopias but better, more inclusive, and more holistic utopias. Since the publication of this study, Levitas has developed this view into a comprehensive sociological method which seeks to revitalize the early inspiration of sociology: 'the imaginary reconstitution of society', as practised for example in the work of William Morris and H. G. Wells, which Levitas places in radical contrast to the epistemic goals of most other approaches in sociology and social theory. For Levitas's utopian method, sociology is a creative and imaginative discipline.[2]

Levitas's 'The Imaginary Reconstitution of Society' (2005) and the later *Utopia as Method* (2013) identify three stages to the process. After a topic of inquiry has been identified (for example, health care), first an *archaeological* investigation takes place. How has health care been organized until now? Which historical developments can we ascertain? How do the existing health-care structure and its associated practices relate to other structural features of society and to the lived reality of people? The findings of this phase feed into the second, ontological phase, where the existing structures and practices are further interpreted in order to make explicit which conceptions of human flourishing and the good life they embody. The results then feed into the formulation of a new vision for the place of health care in human flourishing and the good life. This is the beginning of the imaginative work. What would 'health' and 'health care' mean if we think of them as part of the good life? Can we formulate a vision, however tentative, and can we think about how that vision could be rendered concrete? Social thought exercises here both a critical and a constitutive, or speculative, function and the critical and the speculative rely on each other. In the third, architectural phase, the imaginative vision is linked to concrete actions, policies, and institutions in order to explore what a reconstitution of society in the light of this imaginative vision would look like and would involve. More traditional empirical data and analyses can be utilized by the utopia-as-method approach at every step along the way, but the essential ingredient of imaginative, transformative thinking is added as a natural element of social thought. All sociology is sociology, also, of the future. It makes sense that it is so. Society consists of the social relations and activities of people. These always take place against a horizon of anticipation. If we understand by sociology the reflective elaboration of the members of a society of their social world, the anticipatory horizon needs to be constitutive of sociology itself, just as it is constitutive of the social world. Reading back into history and accounting adequately for the rhetorical aims More had in writing his book—aims which dictated his use of narrative and tropes—with Levitas we can see *Utopia* as an early experiment in the imaginative reconstitution of society, displaying all three elements of archaeology, ontology, and architecture.

A comprehensive overview of contemporary utopian literature cannot be attempted here. The American and European Utopian Studies societies, active since the 1970s and 1980s respectively, bear witness to the wealth of research and scholarship, which cannot all be brought under a single heading. These developments do illustrate that, with its starting point in More's polemical-political pastiche and the subsequent maturation of the concept by Bloch as a foundational philosophical one that is able to co-ordinate and reinterpret core aims and orientations in ontology, epistemology, ethics, and anthropology, the concept of utopia has become an indispensable critical and

---

[2] Cf. Unger's idea of 'social reconstruction', which is also an approach to social theory/sociology that emphasizes plasticity, creativity, and anti-naturalism, but not in terms of a notion of the utopian. Levitas 2005 discusses Unger.

speculative resource across the humanities and social sciences. Not all contemporary uses of utopia agree with the way Bloch interpreted the concept. There is, for example, a strong current within the critical theory of the Frankfurt School—going back to Theodor Adorno's reflections in *Minima Moralia* (first published in 1951) and other works—which emphasizes the necessity, but also unavailability, of utopian images and which seeks to hold on to the moment of truth of the utopian precisely in faithfulness to this unavailability. Currents in social philosophy and social thought that are congenial to this approach include Jean-Luc Nancy's (1986) notion of the inoperative community, Giorgio Agamben's (1998) reflections on the coming community, and Gillian Rose's (1981) thinking of the broken middle.[3] In all of these, the continued remembrance of the absence of a positive image of wholeness, freedom, or integral fulfilment is the only available access to utopia in the modern world. The link between the 'non-place' (*ou-topia*) and the good place (*eu-topia*) has been severed in the eyes of many of these theorists due to the atrocities and alienations of the modern age, and nothing has taken its place. For Bloch, as we have seen, this view must end in new totalitarianisms and a new authoritarianism, this time of the oracles of absence (cf. Jameson 1991). There is no pitting Hegel contra sociology, only a further development, along the lines set out by Levitas, for example, of the sociological imagination. However, the vitality of utopian thinking is underscored by the debates between these different views on our orientation to what is not yet but might be.

We started this chapter at the abstract end, tracing, still in a rather sketchy way, how the reflective recuperation of the idea of utopia has opened up a way of thinking about the new and the future that has few, if any, explicit precursors in the history of philosophy but that allows us to understand the history of philosophy in a particular way, as the distortion or encapsulation and rigor mortis of that drive for the new. I have argued elsewhere that the separation of philosophy and rhetoric, lamented by Cicero in the first century CE, which runs through the entirety of European intellectual and sociocultural history—the one concerned with truth, the other with persuasion—reflects this distortion (Siebers 2019b).[4] It is one consequence of an abstract, static, ideological way of thinking that, early on, nestled itself in European thought (and perhaps elsewhere as well), primarily motivated by the all-too-human desire for control and power as alleviation of fear and insecurity and, according to some, secondarily enabled by the emergence of script culture (Harris 1981). If we split up truth and persuasion we close off to ourselves the future as an open space of the new and of the creation of goals. Knowledge becomes—as it did in the history of philosophy—remembrance, and persuasion becomes a neutral tool to wield power and further interests, good or bad, egotistical or communal. Conversely, we might then argue, with the establishment of the utopian as a fundamental concept in philosophy, we should be able to overcome the abstract opposition between philosophy and rhetoric, truth and persuasion, and rethink the field

---

[3] For a comprehensive discussion, see Truskolaski 2021.
[4] Cf. Cicero's *De Oratore* for his early recognition of this point.

of human deliberation, conversation, and expression in terms of the interdependency of anticipation and communication: in the living, free interaction between persons the new can be encountered and inhabited. The resulting communicative action resolves the abstract separation of philosophy and rhetoric into a concrete praxis; in More's *Utopia* we see a glimpse of such a praxis in the framing of the discourse as a conversation between (more or less) equal participants, unlike a Socratic dialogue (Siebers 2013).

Communication gives us access to the utopian, and vice versa, in a privileged way. A reflection on spoken communication can make this especially clear. Walter Ong writes:

> The spoken word is somehow always radically inaccessible: if flees us, eludes our grasp, escapes when we try to immobilize it. [...] Besides interiority and mystery and holiness, the spoken word also signals hope. Knowledge grows by hope. For all knowledge is only arrested dialogue, framed ultimately in speech, in communication. I speak because I have hope in others. [...] Hope is the difference between information encoded in machines and real knowledge in the consciousness of man.
>
> Because it is framed in dialogue, knowledge even when most carefully formulated, or especially when most carefully formulated, promises more than it explicitly states. Seen as part of dialogue, as communication, as caught in the word, each statement of a truth looks forward to the next stage. [...] Because it is always an invitation as well as a vehicle of information, the word can never be concluded or put aside: it looks always into the future, ahead, anticipating further growth. At the level of sound, this state of affairs registers in the fact [...] that the word as sound is never present all at once. Sound exists only when it is going out of existence. This means of course that it exists also only when it is coming into existence. If we stop bringing sound into existence, actively producing it, it is no longer there. Sound is future-oriented, and thus hopeful. And, in accord with its natural habitat in the world of sound, so is the word. (Ong 1967: 314–316)

As we speak, we move at the front of the process of the world, bringing the new into being. Even in our most deliberate speech activity we cannot grasp the emergence of a word; somehow it is *there*. But in our speaking and listening we mould and shape our awareness, our lives, and our relationships with those around us. As inaccessible as the spoken word is, so, unavoidably, it is the gateway to shape the good life. Is the moment of speech, which is also always the moment of listening, not the most near and familiar instance of utopia, of the no-place that is a good place? Ludwig Wittgenstein (1889–1951) seems to have recognized this point to some extent: 'Can only those hope who can talk? Only those who have mastered the use of a language. That is to say, the phenomena of hope are modes of this complicated form of life' (Wittgenstein 1953: 224). I speak because I have hope in others; I can have hope in others, because we can speak and listen.

The activities of speaking and listening lie at the basis of a moral attitude towards others and ourselves, as Lisbeth Lipari (2014) has shown. When we speak and listen, we are together with others without merging with them, or having to share an identity. The communicative relation of speaking and listening is not dialectical, in the sense that a higher synthesis would be achieved on the basis of a prior contradiction. Even when we agree, and that is not always the case and not always the point when we talk with each other, we still remain each who we are. The communicative relation is paradoxical because it is at once a free giving and a withholding. In communication, distance and relation, independence and interdependence, rise and fall in tandem (Buber 1965). As we have seen, communication is a perpetual perishing and coming-to-be, oriented in anticipation towards the future. Insofar as speaking and listening provide the bedrock for the moral attitude, they do so partly because of their utopian, anticipatory character, opening up 'futures in the gaps of the present', by which we allow each other to be (N. Barron 2021).

To all these contemporary uses of utopia, More's text is the ancestral home, from which Bloch set free the spirit of utopia and provided the bearings for at least one particular form of creative, if not revolutionary, theory-praxis, aimed at, in Bloch's own often-used and remarkable phrase, which More would have loved for its irony as well as its promise and as an expression of true human freedom, 'changing the world into all recognition'.

Experimentum Mundi: Utopian Ethnographies

When philosophy turns into a creative practice of the new and when we understand such a practice as communicative—which means as an expressive practice of relationality and relating by which we can live our lives and live into an open future—philosophy becomes experimental. It is no coincidence that Bloch's last work bears the title 'the experiment of the world', *Experimentum Mundi*. Bloch will not have had a scientific experiment in mind, the testing of a hypothesis by factual confirmation, but rather the root meaning of the word: the action of trying something out (from the Latin *experior*: I try, I put to the test). Philosophy as experimental means philosophy as *suchend und versucherisch*, as we have seen above: as 'searching and trying'. In German both words share the verb *suchen*, literally to seek. As a practice, the utopian philosophy teaches us how to seek, how to hope (*docta spes*). It teaches us that utopia exists, as we have seen in our analysis of the moment of speaking, in the concrete here-and-now, and as the opening towards the future within that here-and-now. Our thinking, then, has to become as concrete as the present moment; it has to make its home there in order to give voice to utopian moment, allow it to contribute what it can and must to our perception of truth, and to infuse our actions with meaning and purpose. Bloch himself was keenly aware of the need for philosophy not only to make use of abstract or reflective reasoning and conceptual analysis—not only to seek to articulate what lies beyond immediately lived experience—but also to make room for stories that express precisely that lived experience. He used the term *fabelnd Denken* ('storytelling thought') to refer to it and claimed that certain things can only be talked about in stories. In order to emphasize the importance of the tale as well as of the abstract system, he placed his book *Traces* (2006), a collection of short stories about the not-yet as lived experience, at the beginning of the Collected Edition of this oeuvre, and *Experimentum Mundi*, his most abstract statement of the categories and principles of the utopian philosophy, at the end. In between these two pillars the entire arc of his thought is suspended.

Traces, I claim, is a work of philosophy as (auto)ethnography. It is a natural voice in the contemporary development of philosophy as ethnography, which Walter Feinberg defines as follows:

> Philosophical ethnography is a philosophy of the everyday and ethnography in the context of [...] discourse about coordinating meaning, evaluation, norms and action. Its basic assumption is that in the affairs of human beings truth, justice and beauty are not ultimate and fixed ends but [...] guideposts hopefully to more refined considerations and more adequate appreciation and decisions. (Feinberg 2006: 5)

In order to understand and work with these essentially shifting guideposts and to not lose ourselves in abstractions, ethnography has to be, or become, part of the modes of thought available to the utopian thinker. The very medium within which we may encounter the advance into the new is that of our daily, lived experience, and perhaps mostly those aspects of it where we relate to others. Philosophical ethnography is descriptive, not explanatory. In this aspect it links well to thinkers like Wittgenstein and Alfred North Whitehead (1861–1947), who have pointed out that philosophy is a descriptive activity: 'philosophy just puts everything before us' (Wittgenstein 1953: 126); 'philosophy is the elucidation of immediacy, the eliciting of self-evidence' (Whitehead 1938: 146). With other ethnographic work, it shares the characteristics of having an aesthetic component that is part of its expressive power, of being reflective and capturing a reality (L. Richardson 2016). Ethnographic practice as a way of thinking by giving thick descriptions also effectively resists premature attempts at systematization or conceptualization, while allowing for the slow work of allowing meaning to emerge through iterations of reading and writing, in some ways analogous to speaking and listening and equally capable of grounding a moral attitude towards the topic and the people at hand. Since the ethnographic thinker is herself involved, as a person, in the ethnographic work, this type of philosophy cannot be conducted in abstraction from the personal existence of the thinker and her willingness to know herself, including the willingness to acknowledge an irreducible element of not-knowing in this self-knowledge. Philosophical, or rather utopian, ethnography implies the willingness to work on oneself, on one's feelings, emotions, and unconscious dynamics, as a condition of the criteria of aesthetic, reflective, and real relevance and as a condition of being able to take up one's own voice in free, communicative interaction with others. Not that we first work on ourselves and only then start doing philosophical ethnography; rather the one is implied in the other.

As an example, let us look at a brief aphorism from Bloch's *Traces*:

Drawn out. Waiting likewise makes one desolate. But it can also make one drunk. Someone who stares too long at the door where he expects another to enter can become intoxicated. As by tuneless singing that draws and draws. Dark, where it draws us to; probably into nothing good. If the man, the woman, whom one awaits doesn't arrive, the clear disappointment doesn't really undo the intoxication. It only combines with its result, a particular kind of hangover that occurs here too. Against waiting, only hoping helps, which one must not only drink, but cook somewhat too. (Bloch 2006: 1–2)

Hope is a good breakfast but a bad dinner, the proverb has it. Cooking for someone keeps our hoping that they will come from turning into the inebriating chant of waiting. We move out of the darkness of the lived moment into a concrete future. We hope. We hope by doing something, something that is immediately linked to our physical well-being and our desire to share our life with others, with another. We cook. I cook, therefore I hope. When cooking, as here in this text, is a metaphor or metonymy, it works just the same. My love, whom I cooked dinner for, will soon arrive. My hope is an active hope; what does it matter if I fail, as long as I have worked and tried? But the chant of waiting draws us back into the dark. It is no good place and the wait is all too present, no no-place either. Too much fatal finality, too little agency, too little hope. Is philosophical idealism, like all ideologies, not the reaction to the disappointment of waiting for someone, something, that never comes, an anti-utopia, the dystopia of contemplation? We become desolate, drunk with homesickness; we project the object of our desire into another realm, to have commerce with beyond experience. The person who is waiting can expend their energy frantically doing nothing this way, like Miguel de Cervantes's Quixote chasing shadows on a never-ending journey to his love. Yet true love waits.

According to Lacan (2007), courtly love is the most elegant way of coming to terms with the fact that there is no sexual relation. The possibility of disappointment has been foreclosed by the assurance of the reality of love to such a degree that it can no longer bear fulfilment. Its fulfilment has, in this way and paradoxically, been fast-forwarded to circumvent the need for consummation, which, of course, could only be disappointed. The courtly lover has taken up refuge in the wait that now takes on the character of patience and that gives all the satisfaction the consummation promised. He or she *is no longer waiting, no longer hoping* and therefore 'in a good place'. But in our aphorism, there is no courtly love and the wait is not motivated by patience. Patience requires cooking, patience requires hope. It transforms waiting into watching over what is of value and loved, in the faith that, in time, it will come to fruition. 'Faith is the substance of things hoped for, the evidence of things not seen' (Hebrews 11:1). A wait that does not find its way to patience is frustrated and hung over from the start, at risk of desolation and paranoia. We need to cook, to orientate ourselves practically, actively to that which, or whom, we are hoping for. When we cook, we go out of ourselves and change the world. The aphorism's title, 'drawn out', plays with the *Langeweile*, the long while and bore of the wait as a drawn-out endurance and, by contrast, with being drawn out of oneself and into the world by active hoping, which may bring the arrival of the other person about. The aphorism shows us something about communication. I have to give freely of myself in order to have a chance at receiving freely from another. There are no guarantees. If I insist on having those, I won't encounter the other person: communication, togetherness, has to be a free gift between independent people, or it is no communication but at best the coordination of behaviour. As far as the encounter goes, there is only hope, but hope is active. Waiting inebriates; hope nourishes.

I know the moment Bloch describes here. I read the few lines he writes about it and start to see connections between their respective meanings as I, also actively, cook up my reading of them, in the hope of encountering a thought, if not the person who had it. The text reflects back on itself and grants me as reader a peek in the mirror. I have to do something if I am to learn something from it. The text has become, not a secondary reflection on daily life that takes place regardless of it, but a factor within daily life that allows me, via its careful description of a fleeting moment, to experience my life more fully and to find the right attitude that makes it possible for the new to come into my life. This vignette is through-and-through utopian. It even shows us that the passive wait is the dystopian attitude that intoxicates with false promises and isolation and leads only to a hangover when what was longed for does not arrive. The land of Cockaigne, where no one has to cook because the chicken fly fried through the air, is a case in point.[5]

The aphorism, however brief, is an example of thick description. Layers of meaning reinforce and counteract each other; we feel concretely that there is never an end to interpretation, and we even hesitate to use that word for what we do when we engage actively with what the text has to say to us. Only a patient and creative, personal engagement with this level of description can communicate the ideas and insights to us that illuminate a familiar moment like the one we are talking about here and materially change us, change our lives, as readers who arrive for dinner. We work on ourselves when we write, and read, a text such as this; we inhabit the utopian moment when we practise ethnography in this way. *Traces* is a work of literary communication but, like the calendar tales by which it was inspired, it is directed at its readers not only in a literary manner but also morally. Other modes of utopian ethnography must be imagined as well. Auto-ethnography, life writing, ethnographies of ecology, heritage, animals, love, and friendship: all of these and more can be, and are, conducted to give voice to the ubiquity of the not-yet, the heart of the utopian.

As the twenty-first century unfolds, cultural dynamics and global challenges force and enable us like never before to imagine different, new, better, more equal, respectful, and joyful ways to constitute how we live together as real, embodied, feeling, thinking, hoping, and acting persons, with each other, with the world around us, with what we know and don't know, with our past, present, and future and indeed, internally, with ourselves. The depth of articulation of the utopian that has been achieved since More, in what is itself a beautiful case of not-yet consciousness, gave a name to this elusive, creative moment of realization, and can give us hope that this work of the imagination will not come to a halt.

---

[5] For Cockaigne, see Hadfield and Hiatt in this volume.

CHAPTER 35

HUMAN RIGHTS AND/IN UTOPIA?

MIGUEL ANGEL RAMIRO AVILÉS

RAPHAEL Hythloday ends his description of the institutions, manners, and customs of the Utopians by saying: 'Now I have described to you, as exactly as I could, the structure of that commonwealth which I judge not merely the best but the only one which can rightly claim the name of a commonwealth' (More 1964: 146). What did Hythloday see in the island of Utopia to judge it not merely the best (*optimam*) but the only (*solam*) commonwealth entitled to call itself such? Did he envisage a society in which people enjoyed rights and freedoms as one of the benefits to be derived from living in a well-ordered society under the rule of law?

The question I would like to consider in this chapter is how Thomas More has contributed to *inventing* what we know today as human rights (Lynn Hunt 2007), which are our *ultimate* utopia, because

> when people hear the phrase 'human rights', they think of the highest moral precept and political ideas [...] a set of indispensable liberal freedoms, and sometimes more expansive principles of social protection [...] an agenda for improving the world, and bringing about a new one in which the dignity of each individual will enjoy secure international protection. It is a recognizably utopian program [...] this program draws on the image of a place that has not yet been called into being. (Moyn 2010: 1)

Our vision of utopias is therefore one of a place where inhabitants enjoy better living conditions, perhaps because they have rights and freedoms that are denied to them in real society, or perhaps because their basic needs (and also their desires in some cases) are satisfied, or perhaps because they have received a better education or public instruction. Despite the opinion expressed by Voltaire's Pangloss towards the end of chapter 5 of his *Candide* (1759)—that 'it's impossible that things would not be as they in fact are. Because everything is for the best'—reality is not the best of all possible worlds.[1] Accordingly, More's *Utopia* (1516) can be considered a speculative exercise on how to improve the form of government and people's lives. For this reason, in the sestet that Anemolius, poet laureate and nephew to Hythloday by his sister, writes on the island of Utopia, he says that the island surpasses the city imagined by Plato because it has better people, resources, and laws, and that it should be called Eutopia (i.e. 'good place').

Ascertaining the historical point at which rights became one of the standard topics in descriptions of ideal societies is linked to this question. The European Enlightenment (conventionally seen as beginning in the early eighteenth century) was the turning point in that respect, but given the originality of More's work, which was the first description of an imagined society in which the state and the law are the cornerstones of its construction (J. C. Davis 1981; Ramiro Avilés 2002), *Utopia* contains the prerequisites that J. C. Davis (2010: 42) mentions as being necessary for a rights-based society: the existence of laws, judgement based on authority, and some sort of coercive sanction. *Utopia* does not describe a Garden of Eden, but rather a political society: a place where, between its founding by King Utopos and the arrival of Hythloday, the life of the Utopians is governed by a range of laws and institutions imposed by a centralized authority (Tower Sargent 1982). These laws and institutions control many aspects of people's lives (how they can dress, the work they can do, whether they can travel, the length of their working day) and are able to prescribe and inflict punishments for breaches of these codes, including the death penalty.

As a result, a contemporary reader may conclude that rather than being a (e)utopia, this is instead a dystopia, considered in political terms as a form of government in which rights and freedoms are completely absent, in which the state has become an all-powerful and omnipresent Leviathan. As Gregory Claeys says,

> modern readers who peer closely into More's paradigmatic text discover much about which to be alarmed. Like the snake in the Garden of Eden, dystopian elements seem to lurk within Utopia [...] The country, we are informed, was founded by civilizing its barbarians and artificially isolating a peninsula, transforming it into a fortified island. Utopia remains an imperial power. When overpopulated it sends out colonies, seizing the uncultivated land of indigenous peoples, and driving out any who resist them. Well-paid mercenaries keep enemies at bay [...] Utopia's peace and plenitude now seem to rest upon war, empire, and the ruthless suppression of others. (Claeys 2017: 6)[2]

This interpretation—connecting utopian thought to tyranny, violence, and totalitarianism— is of growing influence in some circles which adhere to a certain way of understanding political liberalism and the relationship between the power of the state and the liberty of

---

[1] 'Car il est impossible que les choses ne soient pas où elles sont. Car tout est bien', Voltaire 2005: 17.
[2] For Utopia and colonization, see also Hadfield, Hower, and Weaver-Hightower and Bajaber in this volume.

its subjects, considering that where laws ends, liberty begins (Avineri 1962; Popper 1947; Berlin 1996).

The reading of More's *Utopia* which I am suggesting attempts to refute this idea. As Barbara Goodwin (1980) explains, there is not an inevitable connection between utopian thought and tyranny, violence, and totalitarianism. In my opinion, the status of rights and freedoms, and also of duties, is a recurrent theme through the history of utopian thought, because in their literary utopias, a number of utopian authors, beginning with More, discussed the limits of the action of the state or the freedom from arbitrary dominance: what we today call human rights.

Human Rights and Utopia

The Universal Declaration of Human Rights (1948) was not only an ethical and legal reaction to the Second World War, a conflict in which *c.*70–85 million people perished, making it the most destructive war to date, but also the culmination of a cumulative historical process which, according to Micheline Ishay, draws on very diverse philosophical, ethical, and religious contributions. One of the most important of these is the contribution made by the European Enlightenment (Ishay 2008: 7).

The Enlightenment was a turning point in the history of rights because, between 1689 and 1776, 'rights that had been viewed most often as the rights of a particular people—freeborn English men, for example—were transformed into human rights, universal natural rights, what the French called *les droits de l'homme* or the "rights of man" ' (Lynn Hunt 2007: 21–22). It was therefore in France that the use of the term *droits de l'homme* became widespread, especially after Jean Jacques Rousseau included it in his *Social Contract*, published in 1762 (Lynn Hunt 2007: 23–25). Although it is impossible to find in More's *Utopia* a theory of natural rights, because he had no real interest in elaborating philosophy of law like the sixteenth- and seventeenth-century legal theorists Francisco Suárez and Hugo Grotius (Eliav-Feldon 1982: 113), he nonetheless constructed a civic remedy for institutional flaws: Utopians need one ruler because there is evil, but the Ademus' power should be exercised in accordance with a humanely constructed legal system which has as its end the good of the Utopians.[3] In this sense, Hythloday says 'As a result, when in my heart I ponder on the extremely wise and holy institutions of the Utopians, among whom, with very few laws, affairs are ordered so aptly that virtue has its reward, and yet, with equality of distribution, all men have abundance of all things' (More 1964: 53).

---

[3] The term 'Ademus' is used to describe the chief magistrate of Utopia in More's letter to Peter Giles, which was only included in the 1517 edition; it means 'the prince without a people'.

The claims of natural rights would come later with the utopias written during the Enlightenment by James Burgh (1714–75), Thomas Northmore (1766–1851), and William Hodgson (1745–1851). However, we must remember that

> eighteenth-century people did not often use the expression 'human rights', and when they did, they usually meant something different by it than what we mean [...] During the eighteenth century, in English and in French 'human rights', 'rights of mankind', and 'rights of humanity' all proved to be too general to be of direct political use. They referred to what distinguished humans from the divine on one end of the scale and from animals on the other, rather than to politically relevant rights such as freedom of speech or the right to participate in politics. (Lynn Hunt 2007: 22–23)

Likewise, a number of issues that still concern us today and which began to be discussed during the Enlightenment can be glimpsed in More's *Utopia*. As Ishay (2008: 8) points out, 'now as then, we find ourselves pondering the roles of the state as both the guardian of basic rights and as the behemoth against which one's rights need to be defended'. This concern led to debates about issues such as religious freedom, the limits of private property, what kind of punishments could be imposed, and what level of social welfare must be provided.

Similarly, it was during the Enlightenment that the feeling that Lynn Hunt has considered as the basis for the birth of the philosophy of human rights began to emerge: the empathy towards other people that enables us to recognize them as equals. This empathy was also fostered in the literary sphere, as novels such as *Pamela, or Virtue Rewarded* (1740) and *Clarissa, or the History of a Young Lady* (1747–8) by Samuel Richardson, and *Julie, ou La Nouvelle Héloïse* (1761) by Jean Jacques Rousseau, made readers empathize with the characters because their most intimate feelings, and especially their desire for autonomy, were similar.[4] The foundations of a new social and political order were concealed in this process involving empathy and the conquest of new spaces of autonomy (Lynn Hunt 2007: 39).

The literary form that most utopians use as a distinctive feature allows them to empathize with the readers. As William Godwin in his account of the composition of *Caleb Williams* (1794) explains, after writing *Enquiry Concerning Political Justice* (1793) he conceived the idea of writing a book in which he would break down the ideas expressed there to transform people's minds about society: 'I will write a tale, that shall constitute an epoch in the mind of the reader, that no one, after he has read it, shall ever be exactly the same man that he was before' (W. Godwin 1998: 338).

More and the other authors who followed the institutional solution are interested in both the literary form and the subject of the role that the state should play. As Lyman Tower Sargent (1994) argues, the literary form is one of the recognizable 'faces' of utopianism, thereby embodying 'the artistic pretensions of the utopist' (Trousson 1995: 43). The use of the literary form in utopian thinking potentially enables readers to feel

---

[4] For a discussion of Rousseau's *Julie*, see Pohl in this volume.

empathy towards characters such as Hythloday, George Pine (in Henry Neville's *Isle of Pines*, 1668), Captain Longares (in the anonymous, undated *La Isla de Jauja*), and William Guest (in William Morris's *News from Nowhere*, 1890), as well as the people who live in each of the imaginary lands and whose lives are fabulous accounts presented as histories.

As for the role of the state and of the law, both More and other later authors who consciously or unconsciously followed his model made sure that there was no room for the idea of tyranny in their descriptions of imagined societies (J. C. Davis 1981). The state might be potentially limitless but in societies like those visualized by More, James Harrington (1611–77), Gerrard Winstanley (1609–76), and Henry Neville (1620–94), the power of the ruler had limits and tyranny was outlawed. According to Harrington's *Oceana* (1656), 'if the liberty of a man consists in the empire of his reason, the absence whereof would betray him unto bondage of his passions; then the liberty of a commonwealth consisteth in the empire of her laws, the absence whereof would betray her unto the lusts of tyrants' (James Harrington 1977: 170). In *The Law of Freedom in a Platform* (1652), Winstanley appealed to the magistrates to fight against tyranny using these words: 'Therefore, the work of all true Magistrates is to maintain the common Law, which is the root of right Government, and preservation and peace to everyone; and to cast out all self-ended principles and interests, which is Tyranny and Oppression, and which breaks common peace' (Winstanley 1965: 538). And lastly, in *The Isle of Pines* (1668), Neville found the islander John Phill guilty of 'divers ravishing and tyrannies', for which he was sentenced to death (Neville 1999: 202).

It is not until the Enlightenment that we can find descriptions of imagined societies in which the language of rights is explicitly included. English utopias of the Enlightenment, such as those attributed to Burgh, Northmore, and Hodgson contain the first descriptions of imagined societies, following the model begun by More, in which law and the state remain key elements in attaining the best form of government, but which include Enlightenment philosophy about the 'rights of man'. And the rights are part of the pursuit of happiness, as stated by Thomas Jefferson in *The unanimous Declaration of the thirteen united States of American* proclaimed in 1776, since happiness, according to John Locke's *Essay on the Human Understanding* (1689), could be understood as the foundation of all liberty (Book II, chapter 21: 'Of Power').

Burgh, who was connected to the 'Founding Fathers' of the United States of America Benjamin Franklin (1706–90) and John Adams (1735–1826), wrote *An Account of the First Settlement, Laws, Form of Government, and Police, of the Cessares, A People of South America* (1764). Burgh's utopia contains the language of rights and includes the most common political issues of the time regarding the best form of government, including the fight for the rule of law, the rejection of tyranny, the need to protect religious freedom, and the prohibition on torture. The imagined society is presented in a series of nine letters, dated between 28 September 1618 and 19 June 1620, allegedly from Vander Neck, one of the senators of the imagined republic. As told in the prefatory material of the tract, the story of the Cessares can be compared to More's *Utopia*, which affects its credibility: 'Some of my readers may perhaps view the following account of the CESSARES in much the same light with Sir T. MORE'S UTOPIA, rather as what a good man would wish a nation to be, than the true account of the state of one really existing' (Burgh 1994: 73). The author obliquely critics the English political system by extolling the virtues of a mythical South American republic (C. J. Hay 1979: 102), which is unknown because isolation is guaranteed by law: 'having made a law, that whoever discovers the passes which lead into their country, shall be put to death as a traitor, even though he were at the head of their republic' (Burgh 1994: 73). This republic would promote 'the happiness of a state' regulated according to the 'scheme of government, laws and establishment' which can serve as an example for the colonies added to the British Empire (74).

In his *Account*, Burgh tells how the Dutch explorer Vander Neck left his homeland hoping to be able to found a society with

> a form of Government, as would be productive of the most beneficial and salutary consequences to every individual. Such a design, every person who is not insensible of the feelings of humanity and benevolence, and lost to every worthy and generous sentiment, must highly applaud [...] by securing to them the delightful enjoyment of their civil and religious liberties, under the government of laws founded upon justice, goodness, wisdom, and equity; and by transmitting all these invaluable blessings to their posterity. (77)

Following the most classic patterns of contractualism, Burgh describes how legitimate political authority is based on voluntary agreement. This free, deliberative, and personal agreement can be seen twice in the Cessares' imagined society. First, inhabitants must consent before embarking on their voyage: 'Having thus engaged a sufficient number of persons to embark with us in our undertaking, we laid before them all [...] the difficulties which they must expect to encounter with [...] We therefore desired them to take some time, to weigh all these difficulties deliberately in their own minds' (82). And they also must consent when those who were chosen to found that new society met a second time as an assembly to approve the form of government and the laws of the new commonwealth before embarking on their voyage:

> We held a general assembly, in which the form of government and all the laws of our state, (drawn up some time before by Mr Alphen and myself) were read and carefully considered: and having made such alterations as were judged proper, the whole assembly expressed their approbation of them and all who were above 21 years of age sign'd them; expressing thereby their submission to them, and by that means became entitled to all the privileges of citizenship. Then to prevent any disputes on our arrival at the desired country, all the citizens proceeded to the election of the magistrates. (82–83)

The republic was a mixed or balanced government in order to get an equilibrium among the oppositional pure forms of government: monarchy (*the one*), aristocracy (*the few*), and democracy (*the many*). Like Polybus, Aristotle, and Cicero, and echoing

Harrington's *Oceana*, it is insisted that the surest way to prevent tyranny is through a proportionate mixture of these forms (Pocock 1975b). The pure forms are prone to degenerate, but a government that disperses power among the one, the few, and the many could prevent it. As explained in Burgh's *Account*, this particular form of government consists of a governor, who is hereditary, and senators, who are chosen by the citizens (Burgh 1994: 87). Burgh believed that a mixed constitution could yield liberty and happiness for all (C. J. Hay 1979: 102):

> Civil dissensions, turbulent factions, and precipitate determinations, are found by experience to be the constant effects of a popular government, we agreed that the citizens should chuse, out of their own body, a certain number of persons, called senators, who, in conjunction with the governor, should be invested with the supreme and legislative power. But as many inconveniences are also found to arise from the execution of the laws by a number of persons, in whose hands the supreme power is lodged; it was agreed to commit the executive power to one man only, whom we call the governor. But as the governor may not always be possessed of proper abilities to conduct the reins of government, or may be disposed to execute such schemes, as may be destructive to the public good: his power is limited, and his authority carefully restrained by our laws. (Burgh 1994: 88)

According to Vander Neck, it is the best form of government 'to secure our rights and liberties, to preserve a due balance, and keep a happy medium between the tyranny of arbitrary monarchy, the factions of aristocracy, and the anarchy, licentiousness, and wild tumults of a democracy' (88). This leads the author, who had allegedly obtained Vander Neck's letters, to conclude that it would be difficult to

> find a better form of government, where the liberty and happiness of every individual is more carefully consulted; where every tendency to vice and licentiousness is more effectually discouraged; and where more care is taken of the right education of the children, upon which the welfare of posterity greatly depends. What alterations may hereafter be introduced among us, when the present generation is dead [...] I cannot say. But happy will it be for our children, if they steadily pursue the same plan, adhere to the same laws, and suffer nothing to destroy that right disposition of the heart and mind, and that amiable simplicity of life and manners, which at present flourish among us. (136)

Northmore's *Memoirs of Planetes, Or a Sketch of the Laws and Manners of Makar* (1795) talks the language of rights still more explicitly. It narrates the expedition by Phileleutherus Devoniensis,[5] a fictional English ship's captain who is abandoned by his

---

[5] Northmore follows the word games found More's *Utopía*: the translation into English of the name of the ship's captain is 'Lover of liberty, from Dover'. I would like to thank Cathy Shrank for observing this point.

crew on an island south-east of the Cape of Good Hope. He makes his position clear on the very first page:

> With whatever degree of partiality I may view the form of government here presented to you, and how fondly soever I may imagine it, in the abstract, to be calculated to ensure the happiness of mankind, I am ready to allow that in the present institutions of society, philosophy has yet much to do to prepare the minds of men to receive it. (Northmore 1994: 139)

On his voyage he meets the inhabitants of Makar, a society that was founded after a revolution in which the people 'demanded a restitution of their rights, and that a new constitution should be founded upon those rights [...] and that a new code of laws should immediately be framed upon the rights of man' (172). Makar used the liberal thesis of limited government because it was considered a necessary evil: 'all governments were more or less usurpations upon the rights and liberties of mankind [and] Government therefore was manifestly an evil [but] this evil is become absolutely necessary' (177). Makar adopted a constitution according to which the rights and freedoms recognized for the people who live there limited the state in matters of religion ('the government has no right to interfere in matters of religion'; 'every religion be admitted'); in its legislative activity ('all laws were more or less infringements upon the rights of man, they recommended a reduction of the existing code to such a number of laws only as may be deemed after a strict investigation absolutely necessary to the well-being of the country in its present circumstances'); in the types of punishment that can be imposed ('the greatest punishment [...] be imprisonment'); in the procedure for imposing them ('every accused person be supposed innocent until he be convicted of guilt'; 'the accused be brought to trial as soon after the supposed commission of a crime as possible'); in the freedom of printing and the freedom of the press ('every valuable foreign work be translated into the Makar tongue'; 'the liberty of the press be unbounded') (177–182).

Finally, Hodgson's *The Commonwealth of Reason*, also printed in 1795, is likewise committed to the discourse of human rights. He wrote his tract while he was confined in the prison of Newgate, London, for sedition. In this case, the author echoes the language of the French Revolution, as it sets out a plan to implement a system of government

> set out with a declaration of rights, founded on the broad and permanent basis of LIBERTY, FRATERNITY and EQUALITY, as I conceive it is on the imperishable foundation of these rights alone, that those laws and regulations can be built, which shall truly and faithfully have for object, what ought to be considered the most important of all human pursuits—THE HAPPINESS OF THE HUMAN RACE LIVING TOGETHER IN SOCIETY. (W. Hodgson 1994: 215)

Unlike *Utopia* or Burgh's and Northmore's works, Hodgson's *Commonwealth* is not fictional in form. It is a manifesto containing a declaration like the American Declaration of Independence (1776) and the French Declaration of the Rights of Man and of the Citizen (1789), in a constitution that is considered the highest law in the legal system:

'The first business of the legislative body should be to frame a CONSTITUTION upon the sacred RIGHT OF MAN, and all LAWS and DECREES should be considered as null and of no effect that deviated from the principles of this constitution' (W. Hodgson 1994: 245). When he attributes supremacy to the constitution of the imagined society, Hodgson is taking up the content of article 6 of the Constitution of the United States (1787) to prevent Parliament, as it did the English one before the American Revolution, from passing laws and decrees that limit inherent rights.

Article 1 of the Constitution of Makar states that 'all men, when they come out of the hands of nature, are equal and free' and article 2 declares that 'the legitimate end of all association whatever, is the conservation of society, and the preservation of the natural and imprescriptible rights of each of its members: these rights are Liberty, Security and Resistance against oppression of every kind, and are founded on the nature of man' (W. Hodgson 1994: 215). The aim of this declaration of rights was not only to make a formal and public statement confirming the changes but also to bring about a transfer of sovereignty. As Lynn Hunt (2007: 116) affirms, 'the declarers claimed to be confirming rights that already existed and were unquestionable. But in so doing they effected a revolution in sovereignty and created an entirely new basis for government'. Article 3 therefore proclaims that 'The SOVEREIGNTY ought to reside in the majority of the citizens who compose a nation' (W. Hodgson 1994: 216).

Liberty is defined by Hodgson as 'the power of doing everything for the advantage of the individual which does not trench upon the rights of another', and the constitution says that the limits to the exercise thereof must be imposed by the law: 'the law, which, to be just, must be the expression of the will of the absolute majority of the citizens, fixes the boundaries to the actions of men' (W. Hodgson 1994: 216, article 4). The type of legal system proposed by Hodgson would be the exception to the general rule that Tower Sargent (1975: 91) attributes to most utopias, namely that 'if the law did not say expressly that you could do something, you could not do it'. In this sense, article 5 states that 'The law can acquire no right to forbid those actions which are not injurious to society. Everything that is not forbidden by the law, each citizen ought to be allowed to do with safety, and ought to be by the law guaranteed in doing; but no citizen ought to be obliged to do that which is not prescribed by the law made antecedent to the compulsion' (W. Hodgson 1994: 216). Article 6 proclaims equality before the law ('it ought to be the same for every citizen') followed by equal rights for all citizens ('every citizen being equal in rights') (216). Religious freedom is declared in article 8: 'Religion being a matter of opinion, ought to be free as the circumambient air. No citizen ought to be compelled to adopt any particular religious tenets, or be excluded from his rights as a citizen on account of his faith, while the manifestations of it does nor tend to injure the society of which he forms a part' (217). The principle of criminal legality is set out in article 9 ('no citizen ought to be accused, arrested, or detained, except in cases determined by the law, and according to the forms which shall be prescribed by the law'), and the humanization of criminal and procedural law is set out in articles 10 and 11 ('the law ought not to establish any punishment that is disproportioned to the crime committed', 'every citizen being presumed innocent until such time as a jury of his fellow-citizens shall have declared him guilty') (217). This entails the prohibition of the death penalty: 'As nothing can be more unnatural than that man should destroy his fellow man, so society, in my opinion, can never acquire the right of inflicting the punishment of death on any of its citizens [...] I should therefore propose the abolition of all capital punishment' (238). Article 12 also recognizes the right to free communication of thought and opinion, with the only restriction being that it is 'not injurious to the interest of individuals' (218). Another two aspects that were very important in the liberal thought of the time were the imposition of taxes for the maintenance of society ('society has a right to reimburse those expences which it incurs, by a levy on each of its citizens; this impost ought to be equally sustained by all the citizens, according to the abilities of each') and the protection of property ('every citizen has a right to the protection of society in the enjoyment of his property honestly acquired; no power can deprive him of any part of it, except when a majority of his fellow-citizens shall have declared it necessary to the safety of the state, and in that case, society is bound to make him an indemnity') (218–219).

In summary, Burgh, Northmore, and Hodgson show how constitutionalism meets utopianism (J. C. Davis 1991: 332). A constitution is the highest legal declaration formulated by the sovereign power and is the foundational moment of any political society. King Utopus and many others are Founding Fathers, like Franklin, Adams, and Thomas Jefferson (1743–1826). Once the constitution is in force, political power should be exercised in accordance with the rule of law, preventing corruption and enabling happiness, with the language of rights, freedoms, and liberties an inherent part of this common purpose.

Human Rights in Utopia

It is possible to argue, albeit cautiously and with caveats, that utopian thought has contributed to inventing what we now call human rights, and that the model of an imagined society begun by More in his work was possibly the first time that the conditions arose for a rights-based society (J. C. Davis 2010: 40). Like Burgh, Northmore, and Hodgson, in his text *Concerning the Best State of a Commonwealth and the New Island of Utopia*, More does not describe a fantastic world inhabited by extraordinary beings but one populated by human beings subject to political conditions. The purpose of his 'Truly Golden Handbook, No Less Beneficial than Entertaining' was to describe the institutional arrangement of a commonwealth. Accordingly,

> what [Hythloday] said he saw in each place would be a long tale to unfold and is not the purpose of this work. Perhaps on another occasion we shall tell his story, particularly whatever facts would be useful to readers, above all, those wise and prudent provisions which he noticed anywhere among nations living together in a civilized way. For on these subjects we eagerly inquired of him, and he no less readily discoursed; but about stale travellers' wonders we were nor curious. Scyllas and

greedy Celaenos and folk-devouring Laestrygones and similar frightful monsters are common enough, but well and wisely trained citizens are not everywhere to be found. (More 1964: 15)

And these institutional arrangements could be useful to reform England because 'there are many features that in our own societies I would like rather than expect to see' (152).

The reading I am suggesting attempts to show how the status of rights and freedoms, and also of duties, is a recurrent theme in More's *Utopia*. It is true that there is not a theory in the book about universal natural rights or a solemn declaration of the rights, liberties, and duties of the citizens who inhabit the imaginary island, but legal rules, like those enacted by King Utopus for the island of Utopia, can be seen as part of the process of awakening to a new world, as the germ of a *eunomic* (law-abiding) model of society: 'They have adopted such institutions of life as have laid the foundations of the commonwealth not only most happily, but also to last forever, as far as human prescience can forecast' (More 1964: 151). Is this why the Utopians are so happy?[6] One objection to this reading might be that in *Utopia*, More attempted to control all behaviour, and this control is achieved through the strict and inflexible enforcement of rules: 'Being under the eyes of all, people are bound either to be performing the usual labour or to be enjoying their leisure in a fashion not without decency' (83). *Utopia* envisages a system of legal rules controlling public and private behaviours (Ramiro Avilés 2001: 242). In More's *Utopia*, the state rules everything, even the most personal sphere (Tasso 1999: 310).

The question of whether human beings are really free on the island of Utopia, where every action may be controlled, must be seen from a historical perspective, because in contrast with twentieth-century attitudes, early modern European political thought did not assume that authority and liberty were antithetical (J. C. Davis 1992: 513). During the sixteenth and seventeenth centuries, 'in terms of civil liberty a congruence between liberty and law was sought in order to defend the subject from will and power [...] That the essence of freedom was to live under known rules and not to be subject to the arbitrary wills of other men was a commonplace formulation of the seventeenth century well before John Locke gave his own utterance to it' (J. C. Davis 1993: 28). It is the republican reading of the idea of liberty—of liberty before liberalism—in which law ensures freedom (Skinner 1998).

If we accept that freedom and authority are not antithetical, and that freedom is achieved not only by living with no interference but also by living under known rules in a society enabling people to enjoy their rights and freedoms and protecting them from tyranny, the laws in Utopia become tools of liberation rather than of oppression. Seen from this viewpoint, the legal system in Utopia guarantees and extends the liberty of utopian citizens (J. C Davis 1993: 29).

Utopia is a description of an imagined society that is much more complex than those that dispense with the law and the state (Ramiro Avilés 2002), precisely because

---

[6] For *Utopia* and the language of 'happiness', see Withington, Sacks, and Czigányik in this volume.

maintaining them gives it a marked political content. Hythloday's description of the Utopians' customs, manners, laws, and institutions enables a discussion of whether these people enjoyed any type of rights or freedoms, or whether the Ademus had unlimited power. The presence of a centralized authority and a legal system means that a discussion of rights is meaningful, since rights were considered as limits on the action of the state during the Enlightenment. This would explain why More's *Utopia* addresses issues such as the struggle for the rule of law, liberty of conscience, the humanization of criminal law, property rights, and resistance to oppression: these issues are discussed in the sections that follow.

THE STRUGGLE FOR THE RULE OF LAW

The struggle for the rule of law is the starting point since, in the real world, the maxim *princeps legibus solutus est* ('the ruler is unfettered by laws') set out by Jean Bodin (1530–96) was a prevalent political idea. In imaginary societies like the one visualized by More, the power of the ruler had limits. Utopia is an example of a well-ordered government because it is governed by laws and not by arms. Government is not a personal matter, but instead an institutional one, and the rulers are not above the law (A. B. Ferguson 1965: 16). Tyranny is outlawed, and More equates it with government by the force of arms: 'To take counsel on matters of common interest outside the senate or the popular assembly is considered a capital offense. The object of these measures, they say, is to prevent it from being easy, by a conspiracy between the governor and the tranibors [government officials] and by tyrannous oppression of the people, to change the order of the commonwealth' (More 1964: 67–68). The morality and personality of the ruler is therefore not the most important factor in attaining the best form for the commonwealth; the effectiveness of the institutional framework is vital. This is the point at which George Logan sees More diverging from Northern humanists because, '[they] were strongly committed to a personal rather than an institutional view of politics [...] More is going to stress instead the importance of non-personal factors—mores [customs] and institutions—in securing good government' (Logan 1983: 38–39). In this respect, the inhabitants of the island of Utopia 'are infinitely better than any other people at the time, but they are not significantly better by nature; they are better because their social institutions are better' (Tower Sargent 1975: 89).

The struggle for the rule of law entailed the reform of the entire legal system (Eliav-Feldon 1982: 109–111). A radical reform of society would be attained by the abolition of unfair and imperfect rules, and the adoption of new ones. The imperfections of the legal system thus condemned are both formal and material (Ramiro Avilés 2001: 239). Formal imperfections derive from problems connected with the complexities of law enforcement and the generation of elaborate codes; the law is imperfect because it is made up of rules which are hard to understand, lengthy texts, unfamiliar or unknown laws. The solution was to enact a code of a few comprehensible laws, which would be inexorably put in execution. Consequently:

> They have very few laws because very few are needed for persons so educated. The chief fault they find with other peoples is that almost innumerable books of laws and commentaries are not sufficient. They themselves think it most unfair that any group of men should be bound by laws which are either too numerous to be read through or too obscure to be understood by anyone. (More 1964: 114)

On the other hand, the main material problem of the legal system historically was the separation of law and justice. According to Giampaolo Zucchini, the crisis of early sixteenth-century legal systems was explicitly underlined by dramatizing this separation: a separation that the Utopians wished to abolish by creating social justice founded on citizens' virtue and the virtue of the new social and institutional systems (Zucchini 1986: 423). As More says through Hythloday, 'But if this agreement among men is to have such force as to exempt their henchmen from the obligation of the commandment, although without any precedent set by God they take the life of those who have been ordered by human enactment to be put to death, will not the law of God then be valid only so far as the law of man permits?' (More 1964: 30).

Freedom of Conscience

As regards liberty of conscience, Raymond Trousson points out that deism, the rejection of the Church, and pluralism of conscience are not exclusive features of Enlightenment utopias, because from More in the early sixteenth century to Robert Burton in the seventeenth, we find the same religious tolerance and plurality, and the same suspicions towards the Church (Trousson 1995: 20).[7] In *Utopia*, Hythloday tells us that freedom of conscience was one of the first enactments of King Utopus: 'From the very beginning, therefore, after he had gained the victory, he especially ordained that it should be lawful for every man to follow the religion of his choice [...]. They count this principle among their most ancient institutions, that no one should suffer for his religion' (More 1964: 133). Accordingly, on the island of Utopia, 'there are different kinds of religion not only on the island as a whole but also in each city. Some worship as god the sun, others the moon, others one of the planets', and they do not try to deter others from their religion (130, 132).[8] However, this liberty is not limitless since Utopus also enacted 'that no one should fall so far below the dignity of human nature as to believe that souls perish with the body or that the world is the mere sport of chance and not governed by any divine

---

[7] Burton's Utopian excursion is in his *Anatomy of Melancholy* (1621), D8v–E3r (in the section 'Democritus to the Reader').

[8] For a further discussion of religion in Utopia/*Utopia*, see Sacks in this volume.

providence' (134). The final reason that led Utopus to establish this freedom was to achieve social peace: 'Utopus had heard that before his arrival the inhabitants had been continually quarrelling among themselves about religion. He had observed that the universal dissensions between the individual sects who were fighting for their country had given him the opportunity of overcoming them all' (133). Hence a famous passage from *Utopia* describes how the island punishes those whose proselytizing is harmful to social peace, in the cautionary tale of one over-enthusiastic convert to Christianity:

> As soon as he was baptized, in spite of our advice to the contrary, he spoke publicly of Christ's religion with more zeal than discretion. He began to grow so warm in his preaching that not only did he prefer our worship to any other but he condemned all the rest outright. He proclaimed them to be profane in themselves and their followers to be impious and sacrilegious and worthy of everlasting fire. When he had long been preaching in this style, they arrested him, tried him, and convicted him not for despising their religion but for stirring up a riot among the people. His sentence after the verdict of guilty was exile. (132–133)

THE HUMANIZATION OF CRIMINAL LAW

Although the process of humanization is primarily associated with the eighteenth century (Tarello 1976: 383), some of the preconditions for a transformation of the criminal law are apparent in the sixteenth and seventeenth centuries. The humanization of the criminal law means a rationalization process of the enforcement of the laws in which penalties are severely and fairly kept. In this sense, the death penalty is enacted only for the severest crimes. More's *Utopia* expresses 'an aversion to the common European practice of hanging thieves and other offenders against property' (Eliav-Feldon 1982: 123). Renaissance humanism is full of criticism of a criminal law that is characterized by unequal application, ambiguity, torture, ineffectiveness, and disproportionality (125–126). In *Utopia*, we see a future Lord Chancellor rigorously attacking existing judicial practice, and by implication anticipating its humanization, when More says—again through Hythloday—that if equity has any meaning, not all offences are equal, and there is no similarity or connection between killing a man and robbing him of a coin. As he remarks,

> Surely everyone knows how absurd and even dangerous to the commonwealth it is that a thief and a murderer should receive the same punishment. Since the robber sees that he is in as great danger if merely condemned for theft as if he were convicted of murder as well, this single consideration impels him to murder the man whom otherwise he would only have robbed. Because he is in no more danger if caught, there is greater safety in putting the man out of the way and greater hope of covering up the crime if he leaves no one left to tell the tale. Thus while we endeavor to terrify thieves with excessive cruelty, we urge them on the destruction of honest citizens. (More 1964: 29–30)

Here, in 1516, we see the forerunners of the theses of Cesare Beccaria (1738–94) and Voltaire (1698–1778).

Property

The question of property is also a disputed issue in *Utopia*, because natural shortage is a hallmark of this model of imagined society. More did not trust nature to resolve political problems: it was necessary to find a new institutional system to create artificial abundance, meaning equality of distribution, or control of the appetite for ownership. To do so, he designed a new model of property. The new system would be fairer than the existing one, and through it More sought social justice and the common good with property as a cornerstone of his model of the ideal society (Eliav-Feldon 1982: 79). More's *Utopia* depicts private property as an endemic illness and therefore something to be abolished and replaced by a system of communal property. In this sense, More creates one of the most powerful images against private property: sheep devouring human beings. In the dialogue with Cardinal Morton in Book One, Hythloday says that sheep 'which are usually so tame and so cheaply fed, begin now, according to report, to be so greedy and wild that they devour human beings themselves and devastate and depopulate fields, houses, and towns' (More 1964: 24). For this reason Hythloday states:

> it appears to me that wherever you have private property and all men measure all things by cash values, there it is scarcely possible for a commonwealth to have justice or prosperity [...]. I am fully persuaded that no just and even distribution of goods can be made and that no happiness can be found in human affairs unless private property is utterly abolished. (52–53)

Resistance to Tyranny

Resistance to tyranny is also an important subject in *Utopia*, reflecting More's concerns with the perpetual maintenance of the best form of the commonwealth and freedom from arbitrary dominance. On the island of Utopia, new rules have been enacted in order to prevent the corruption of the *princeps* (Fenlon 1981: 453). For instance, the Ademus is elected to a post which is held for life but subject to legal oversight, because the Utopians know the prince is a fallible human: 'The governor holds office for life, unless ousted on suspicion of aiming at a tyranny' (More 1964: 67). On the island of Utopia, the law prohibits political debate outside the senate (67–68). People cannot be deprived of their liberty by having their actions determined by the arbitrary will of anyone other than the representatives of the body politic. As Quentin Skinner states, if you wish to maintain your liberty, you must ensure that you live under a political system in which there is no element of discretionary power, and hence no possibility that your civil rights will be dependent on the goodwill of a ruler, a ruling group, or any other agent of the state. You must live, in other words, under a system in which the sole power of making laws remains with the people or their accredited representatives, and in which all individual members of the body politic—rulers and citizens alike—remain equally subject to whatever laws they choose to impose upon themselves. If and only if you live under such a self-governing system will your rulers be deprived of any discretionary powers of coercion, and in consequence deprived of any tyrannical capacity to reduce you and your fellow-citizens to a condition of dependence on their goodwill, and hence to the status of slaves. (Skinner 1998: 74–75)

More thought that where the rule of law was observed, there would be political stability; tyranny, rule without the limits of the law, would be politically unstable. According to Tower Sargent (1984: 207), the fight against tyranny reflects the tension between what the prince ought to do and what he ought to refrain from doing. In *Utopia*, More used the dialogue between 'Morus' (More's dramatis persona) and Hythloday to discuss the limits of power; if the state is unavoidable, then it must be limited. *Utopia* is a book about autocratic power and how it might be possible to control it. In defence of the commonwealth and the struggle against tyranny, *Utopia* advocates the primacy of the public interest:

For this very reason, it belongs to the king to take more care for the welfare of his people than for his own [...] It is not consistent with the dignity of a king to exercise authority over beggars but over prosperous and happy subjects [...] to have a single person enjoy a life of pleasure and self-indulgence amid the groans and laments of all around him is to be the keeper, not of a kingdom, but of a jail. (More 1964: 46–47)

This critique avoided the use of the terms dictator or *tyrannus*—an exceptional and appreciated ruler—since the dictator's objective is to safeguard the commonwealth in times of extreme danger. The utopist confronts the τυραννος, i.e. the tyrant who is a usurper because he rebels against a lawful sovereign and rules only in his own interest (Baumann 1985: 111–112). According to Hythloday, this kind of tyrant is like a bad doctor because he does not know how to treat an illness without causing another one: 'In fine, as he is an incompetent physician who cannot cure one disease except by creating another, so he who cannot reform the lives of citizens in any other way than by depriving them of the good things of life must admit that he does not know how to rule free men' (More 1964: 47).

Conclusion

In this brief review, I have attempted to show that, while exercising due caution because of the risk of treating and discussing human rights anachronistically and because utopian thought has an ambivalent relationship with democracy and politics, it is nevertheless possible to establish a link between Thomas More, his *Utopia*, utopian thought, and the vindication of rights and liberties. This link became stronger and more apparent from the Enlightenment onwards, when it established an architectural way of understanding the construction of the imaginary society which leads to a dystopia when the rule of law, rights, and liberties are not respected. More's *Utopia* and the law-based utopias are not the secular hell created by twentieth-century totalitarian regimes because Utopian freedom from arbitrary dominance may be seen as a political ideal that embraces a new view of society with relevance even today.

CHAPTER 36

UTOPIA AND MORAL ECONOMY

MARTIN LUTZ

THE eminent British historian R. H. Tawney (1880–1962), one of the founding fathers of Economic History as an academic discipline, found much at fault with modern capitalism.[1] He lamented a loss of moral values in the economy since the Middle Ages, and the subordinance of the common good under individual self-interest. In *Religion and the Rise of Capitalism* (1926), Tawney used the example of the enclosure in English landownership—when formerly common land that was jointly used by villagers was converted into private property—to show how the emerging new economic order wreaked havoc on the rural population. It is in this context that Tawney related his historiographic analysis to Thomas More, who in Utopia's first book prominently addressed land enclosures in the dialogue with Raphael Hythloday, starkly criticizing their detrimental effect on the rural population of his time. As More had done four hundred years earlier, Tawney bitterly wrote about the social distress caused by the land enclosures, where the 'worst side of all such sudden and sweeping redistributions is that the individual is more or less at the mercy of the market, and can hardly help taking his pound of flesh' (Tawney 1926/1936: 139).

Tawney went on to become a prominent figure in the ongoing debate on 'moral economy'.[2] He stands in line with two other scholars, the Hungarian-born economist Karl Polanyi (1886–1964) and British social historian E. P. Thompson (1924–93), who

---

[1] I would like to thank Sünne Juterczenka, who first introduced me to More's *Utopia*. Phil Withington, Rüdiger Bergien, Johanna Biedermann, Paul Franke, Eva-Maria Kaiser, Moritz Hinsch, Tanja Skambraks, and Jasper Stange provided valuable input into this chapter. I would also like to thank the students in my class 'The Moral Economy of Utopian Communities in Modern America' at Humboldt University (summer 2021) for their inspiration. Finally, I am grateful for the productive work environment at Henning Petersen's *Remise*.

[2] In this chapter, 'moral economy' in quotation marks refers to the respective academic discourse. In other instances, the term is used more broadly, for example, in addressing historical cases of a specific moral economy.

were crucial in formulating an alternative interpretation of modern capitalism's emergence. Their accounts focused not on the positive impact of growth, technological progress, and efficiency gains, but rather on deprivation, inequality, unemployment, starvation, and social unrest. Many of these themes would be familiar to More, as well as to readers in the twenty-first century.

The moral economists' target was an economic system conventionally called 'modern capitalism' that gradually evolved in Europe over the course of centuries, with an accelerated dynamic from the late eighteenth century onwards. The German historian Reinhart Koselleck (1923–2006) called this transformative period between 1750 and 1850 *Sattelzeit* (literally, 'saddle time'). This period also brought on a new way of thinking about the economy. Moral philosophers, political theorists, and economists such as Adam Smith (1723–90), David Ricardo (1772–1823), and John Stuart Mill (1806–73) in the eighteenth and nineteenth centuries established a new liberal framework of classic economic liberalism. In this framework, the *Homo economicus* and private property play a crucial role. In classic and later neoclassic (also labelled neo-liberal) economics, the collective endeavour of self-interested, utility-maximizing individuals brings benefits to the economy and society as a whole (Moscati 2019; McCarraher 2019).

The moral economists begged to differ. Tawney wrote extensively about the plight of English peasants in the late Middle Ages who were driven from their customary use of common land. Polanyi took an interest in the Speenhamland laws from around 1800 as a rural response to widespread pauperism caused by high grain prices. Thompson in turn was interested in the formation of the English working class, and the oppression they suffered under terrible working conditions. As with More's *Utopia*, the moral economists' work combined the analytical aspect of observing the world and their interest in changing it for the better. Tawney, for example, engaged in workers' education and political activism from a Christian background. After the Second World War, Thompson was a prominent figure in the British Communist Party and the New Left movement.

By the end of the twentieth century, the moral economists' works were receiving renewed scholarly attention in the debate on 'moral economy'. It its broadest sense, scholars in this debate are interested in the impact of moral values on the economy. As a conceptual framework it relates to the way moral values shape economic choices, institutions, and practice. The social scientist Andrew Sayer (2010) argues that economic action is always influenced by moral dispositions and norms. From this perspective, every human is a *Homo moralis* when engaging in economic activity, guided by moral principles of what is right or wrong.

More had a strong influence on social and communist thinkers in the nineteenth and twentieth centuries, such as William Morris (1834–69) and Karl Kautsky (1854–1938). Yet, despite Tawney's reference to More in his critique of the enclosure movement, *Utopia* has been remarkably absent in twentieth-century debates in the more specific discourse on 'moral economy' (Rogan 2018: 3). Likewise, academic treatments of More's work often neglect the book's economic implications. The intellectual historian Quentin Skinner, for example, influentially interprets *Utopia* primarily as a contribution to political theory of the Renaissance age, not as a piece of political economy (Skinner 2002a: 123). The themes established by More, however, prominently address structural changes in an age of accelerating modernization, a process that Polanyi labelled 'the great transformation'. Moreover, More's dark depiction of the economic system in the early sixteenth century resonates with later critiques of modern capitalism up to the current debates on inequality in the twenty-first century. For this reason alone, anyone who is interested in moral critiques of the present economic system might well benefit from a close reading of Hythloday's account as a description of an alternative way of how to structure an economy.

This chapter connects More's economic themes in Utopia to the debate on 'moral economy' as it evolved from the early twentieth century to the present. It first outlines the main characteristics of Utopia's economy as imagined by More. It then provides an overview of the intellectual history of 'moral economy' from the original moral economists to the current debate. With the Hutterite case, an Anabaptist Christian group in North America, I will introduce one specific example of how a moral economy based on collective ownership of property continues to exist up to the present day. The final section assesses the potential for further research offered by 'moral economy'.

Utopia's Economy

Work is a grave responsibility in Utopia. With very few exceptions, everyone is expected to engage in productive activity, and idleness is highly disregarded (More 2014: 63–64). At the same time, citizens' workload is rather light. They spend three hours at work before lunch, and three more in the afternoon. As Hythloday emphasizes, 'everyone practices his [or her] trade diligently, but not working from early morning till late at night, exhausted by constant labor like a beast of burden' (61).[3] Instead, Utopia's citizens enjoy a long afternoon rest and recreational activities as well as eight hours of sleep at night. Yet, Utopians miraculously manage to produce an abundance of goods, keep their buildings and roads in meticulous order, and have eliminated poverty in their commonwealth.

The economy and its underlying moral conditions play a crucial role for More in framing his narrative. Book One immediately engages the reader in a fundamental critique of the prevalent economic conditions in the early sixteenth century. As Hythloday explains to the somewhat puzzled character 'Morus' and Peter Giles, the immense greed of the ruling class, and the deliberate marginalization of peasants through enclosures, leaves stealing as the only way for the impoverished to fulfil their material needs. Hythloday's initial reflections on inequality, starvation, and widespread pauperism provide an opener in how to imagine a perfect economy. This

---

[3] The insertion of the female pronoun is my own.

opener then serves as a backdrop for More to imagine a just economy in Book Two. Utopia's economy features prominently in Hythloday's account, particularly in the chapter on 'Occupations'. More placed this chapter relatively early on, reflecting the paramount importance of a functioning economy for Utopia's overall well-being. In addition, shorter passages relating to economic organization are scattered through Book Two, most prominently those dealing with Utopia's community of goods and the island's overall commonwealth.

From Hythloday's account, we gather substantial information about the structural foundations of Utopia's economy. The most fundamental feature, and the one that is perhaps most frequently related to in scholarship, is the absence of private property. Hythloday briefly refers to this striking characteristic on two occasions in Book One. There, we are also immediately confronted with scepticism when Morus points out that 'it seems to me that no one can live comfortably where everything is held in common. For how can there be any abundance of goods when everyone stops working because he is no longer motivated by making a profit' (More 2014: 48), echoing later conceptions of the utility-maximizing *Homo economicus*. More's own role in the dialogue represents his contemporaries' scepticism against abolishing private property.

Based on the fundamental principle of communal property, Utopia's internal economy is then portrayed as a frictionless process, where the production, distribution, and consumption of goods and services is coordinated by an invisible hand. The core unit in this process is the household. All adults are expected to be skilled in farming. In addition, every citizen—including women—follows a trade. In a rotation system, Utopians typically farm for two years and then return to the city (54). Gender seemingly played a subordinate role in assigning work tasks, although we learn a few details about the specific roles of women, who, 'as the weaker sex, engage in lighter crafts, mostly working with wool or linen. The other trades, which require more strength, are relegated to the men' (60). It is thus likely that women are primarily responsible for making clothing and preparing meals. There are also hints that children were assigned duties. For example, minors from the age of 5 on are responsible for serving meals. Older children usually take up their fathers' trade.

While the rural population produces its own food, city dwellers rely on marketplaces to obtain foodstuffs. In addition to food markets, each city district also houses a marketplace and warehouses for other commodities where each household takes the products it has produced (67). All transactions are non-monetary, as money is entirely absent. As Hythloday explains, everyone can obtain 'whatever he and his household need, and he takes away whatever he wants, paying no money and giving absolutely nothing in exchange for it' (68). In addition to providing an abundance of food, clothing, housing, and other necessities, public welfare plays a crucial role, prominently in public education and in health care. As Hythloday tells us, Utopians' 'first priority is the sick, who are cared for in public hospitals' (68). Given the surplus produced on the island, Utopians also engage in international trade, exporting 'vast quantities of grain, honey, wool, linen, timber, red and purple dye, fleece, wax, tallow, leather, and also livestock. They give one-seventh of all this to the poor in that country and sell the rest at a moderate price'

(73–74). Iron is the only major commodity that Utopians have to import, so in exchange for selling goods abroad they accumulate large amounts of silver and gold.

How can Utopians achieve such a phenomenal economic performance leading to seemingly universal welfare? Or, as Hythloday addresses his listeners, given the short six-hour workday in Utopia, 'you might think that there would necessarily be some shortage of supplies' (62–63). Hythloday then explains that the fact that this is far from the case is in part due to the much larger size of Utopia's workforce compared to other countries, where 'a large part of the population [...] live their lives in idleness' (63). Here he mentions women (a literary slap in the face for all the hard-working women back in the 'real world' engaged in household work, fieldwork, care work, and much else), noblemen, their retainers, priests, and feigning beggars. Hythloday states that 'if they all were put to work—and useful work at that—you can easily see how little time would be enough and more than enough time to produce all the goods required for human needs and conveniences' (63).

'Useful' (*utilis*) plays another crucial role in explaining Utopia's economic miracle.[4] Hythloday employs this term several times, as in the context of useful employment, useful inventions, useful trade, and useful branches of science. Utopians have seemingly eliminated everything that is inefficient and not useful to the common good. Here, Hythloday again provides a brief comparison with the real world of the early sixteenth century: just a minority of workers 'are occupied in necessary trades' and much productive work is directed towards 'over-indulgence and wanton luxury' (63). In contrast, Utopians are able to produce an abundance of goods and keep their buildings and roads in shape 'since the structure of the commonwealth is primarily designed to relieve all the citizens from as much bodily labor as possible, so that they can devote their time to the freedom and cultivation of the mind. For that, they think, constitutes a happy life' (66).

Given such a highly motivated, efficient, and disciplined population, few laws are necessary to administer the economy. Indeed, Hythloday only mentions one occasion when public authorities directly intervene. Every year, the senate in Amaurot decides on the distribution of surplus goods among the cities, and it ensures that surpluses and scarcity are addressed, essentially so that the whole island functions like a single household (73). In the final assessment, this system ensures that 'no one is a pauper or a beggar there, and though no one has anything, all are rich' (129–130).

The shining paradise that Hythloday unfolds is not without its dark spots. Most notoriously, slavery is crucial in the production process.[5] It becomes clear from Hythloday's account that enslaved people are responsible for all the 'grievous labor' (61), such as slaughtering and 'all the chores which are somewhat heavy or dirty' (69–70). Moreover, Utopians engaged in economic imperialism, deliberately waging war against their neighbours for territorial expansion.[6] Whenever the island's population increases too

---

[4] Ralph Robinson tellingly tends to translate this word as 'profitable', or with the doublet 'good and profitable' (More 1551, 1556).

[5] For more on *Utopia* and the vocabulary of slavery, see Kern, Withington, and Waithe in this volume.

[6] See also Hower, Hadfield, and Weaver Hightower and Bajaber in this volume.

much, new colonies are established on the continent on land acquired from the native population, if necessary by use of military force (67). Hence Gregory Claeys (2016: 405) appropriately considers Utopia an 'imperial power'.

Contemporaries of More recognized war and slavery—or at least serfdom—as ways to achieve economic goals. And yet in many ways Utopia provided a stark contrast to the economic realities of early sixteenth-century Europe. Frequent uprisings like the German Peasants' War (1524–5) were a clear indicator of social unrest stemming from economic conditions. At the end of Book Two of *Utopia*, Hythloday once more reminds his listeners of the bad conditions in Europe at the time (More 2014: 131). Against this backdrop, More painted a truly utopian picture of a society that seemingly had resolved its political, social, and economic turmoil and—as the book's title indicates—has achieved the 'best state' of a commonwealth. This remarkable efficiency is based on a set of underlying values that form the fundamental fabric of Utopia's economic ethos:

> to look out for your own good is prudent; to promote the public good is pious. But to deprive someone else of pleasure to promote your own is wrong; […] Finally, as religion makes clear to true believers, God will repay the loss of brief and paltry pleasures with enormous and never-ending joy. Following this line of reasoning and having considered the matter long and hard, they think that all our actions, including also our virtuous deeds, are directed toward pleasure as our happiness and final end. (83–84)

Hythloday's account of the Utopian economy leaves much to be desired. We only learn about the overall structures, not about the details of day-to-day work routines, as Clarence Miller critically comments in the introduction to the Yale edition (More 2014: xiv). We do not learn about the environmental impact or the depletion of natural resources. There is also only a brief indication that contraction and expansion of Utopia's population might be a sign of a Malthusian economy, where population growth leads to scarcity, starvation, and eventually a rebalancing of the population to match the available economic resources.

Nonetheless, *Utopia* opens up a vast array of fundamental economic issues and questions, ranging from private property versus common property and self-interest versus the common good to gender relations in the workplace and non-monetary transactions. As Tawney's brief reference to More's treatment of the English enclosures indicates, all these themes were central to the emerging field of 'moral economy' in the twentieth century.

Moralizing the Economy

Conceptualizations of 'the moral', 'the economy', and a benevolent commonwealth were not entirely new to the twentieth century. Recent conceptual history has unearthed a long-standing intellectual tradition going back to ancient Greece (Götz 2015: 148–151). Plato's *Republic* served as important reference point not only for Hythloday but also for countless philosophers, political theorists, and political economists. Aristotle prominently employed the idea of a common interest (*to koinê sympheron*) as opposed to individual utility maximization (Meikle 1995; S. T. Lowry 1987). Medieval Europe witnessed vivid reinterpretations of ancient thought and theological exegeses of what the Bible had to say about the economy, as Jerry Harp points out in his afterword to the Yale edition of *Utopia* (More 2014: 155–157). Referring to the Bible, Thomas Aquinas and other scholastics tirelessly spoke out against usury, for example. The debate on the *bonum commune* (common good) addressed the fundamental issues of how to constrain people's self-interest and a government's responsibility to pursue the common good for society at large. These debates were not merely confined to an abstract scholarly exchange. A prominent example of concrete economic practice is the Franciscan order that was founded in the early thirteenth century on the basis of moral notions of poverty and equality. It was also the Franciscans that from the mid-fifteenth century established a system of pawnshops to facilitate access to affordable credit in the Monti di Pietà (Skambraks 2023).

More and his Renaissance contemporaries thus drew on a long-standing European tradition of discerning the relationship between moral values and economic practice. The idea of a commons, for example, was not as utopian as one might think from a modern capitalist perspective. It was rather a prominent feature in Christian thought and part of the day-to-day rural real-life experience in the agricultural commons, where villages jointly administered land. Other moral perceptions, for example, of interest, usury, and equity also had a strong impact on economic practice. In his conceptual history of 'moral economy', Norbert Götz points out that from ancient Greece to early modern Europe

> The notion of economy was embedded in a pre-determined framework of social norms and not understood as an autonomous sphere of human agency. In ancient thought the term moral economy would, therefore, have been redundant. The middle ages did not advance beyond such a restricted view of economy, and in the early modern period a further emphasis of its agrarian connotations was common. (Götz 2015: 148)

According to Götz and Ute Frevert (2019a, 2019b), however, a distinctly new component had entered the discourse on the moral and the economy by the end of the early modern period. Cameralists, physiocrats, and eventually modern economics in the line of Adam Smith developed a new way of thinking about the economy. They conceptualized the economy based on a human 'propensity to barter and trade' (Smith), exposed to the 'Malthusian trap' of demographic expansion and contraction (Thomas Malthus, 1766–1834), the efficiency gains resulting from specialization and trade (Ricardo), and utilitarianism (Jeremy Bentham, 1748–1832, and Mill). As a result, the rational, utility-maximizing, and egotistical *Homo economicus* became an abstract model for human agency widely employed in academic economics, a model that continues to be used today.

It is important to note here that these thinkers did not conceive of the abstract model as representing actual human beings. Adam Smith still considered the relationship between moral values and human agency. He is most famous for his book *Inquiry in the Wealth of Nations* (1776), widely considered the foundation of modern economics. Seventeen years earlier, however, he published his first major work *The Theory of Moral Sentiments* (1759) where he claimed that even the most selfish person is guided by emotions and passions. Almost a century after Smith, Mill acknowledged that no political economist 'was ever so absurd as to suppose that mankind are really thus constituted' (Frevert 2019b: 23). A century later, John Maynard Keynes (1883–1946)—himself one of the most important economists of the twentieth century, famously wrote of the 'defunct economist' influencing 'practical men' in his *General Theory of Employment, Interest and Money* (1936: 383–384). Economics as an academic discipline, though, had to rely on stylized models based on abstraction, to further its scientific agenda. As Frevert pointedly states,

> To define the economic field as special, unique, independent, and separate from others served different ends. As much as it expressed the desire of academics to prove, establish, and monopolize their professional expertise, it accompanied and enhanced the process of functional differentiation that characterized the advent of modernity. Moreover, it co-produced the illusion that human activity could be neatly divided into different segments, with each segment obeying different 'laws' and criteria. What Mill had called '*conscience*, or feeling of duty' was thus, in theory, excluded from the economic sphere and might instead find its place in religious charity or welfare work. (Frevert 2019b: 23)

The Enlightenment thus constituted a crucial transitional period in economic thinking, separating premodern and early modern conceptualizations of a moral economy from a distinctly modern outlook on differentiated social spheres, each governed by its own premises, principles and 'laws'. Crucially, these developments made it possible to think of the moral and the economic as detached spheres of social life. Frevert and Götz accordingly argue that 'moral economy' as a concept 'was created when morality was detached from the notion of economy in the middle of the eighteenth century, since its signification was no longer self-evident' (Götz 2015: 149).

Unsurprisingly, then, the very term 'moral economy' itself first appeared in the writings of political philosopher Jean-Jacques Rousseau (1755), the philosopher and scientist Fortunato Bartolomeo de Félice (1769), and in the *Encyclopædia Britannica*'s third edition from 1797 (Götz 2015: 149–151; Frevert 2019b: 16–18). In the German original version of his important work *Religion within the Boundary of Pure Reason* (*Die Religion innerhalb der Grenzen der bloßen Vernunft*, 1793), Immanuel Kant (1724–1804) used the phrase *Angemessenheit des Lebenswandels* (literally, 'the appropriateness in conduct of life'), a term that was later translated as 'moral economy' in the English edition. While the meanings of 'moral economy' differed between the Enlightenment philosophers, Frevert (2019b: 18) contends that the overall motivation was that the 'modern concept of the economy [...] invited philosophers, economists, and others to think about its moral dimension'.

Beginning in the 1830s, the 'moral economy' gradually entered the sphere of economic thinking (Frevert 2019b: 17). Driving forces were the British social reformers Robert Owen (1771–1858) and James Bronterre O'Brien (1805–64), and the scientist Andrew Ure (1778–1857) through his book on *The Philosophy of Manufactures: Or, An Exposition of the Scientific, Moral, and Commercial Economy of the Factory System of Great Britain* (1835). In the following decades, Friedrich Engels (1820–95) and Karl Marx (1818–83) contributed their own moral critique of the modern capitalist system, as did Christian social reformers. Pope Leo XIII, for example, issued the encyclical *Rerum Novarum* in 1891, where he staunchly criticized the social and moral upheaval brought upon by industrialization. Regardless of their own Christian, socialist, or communist viewpoints, these critics wrestled with the overall process of liberal modernization that had led Europe into a seemingly unrestrained capitalist order.

From here, it was only a small conceptual step to 'moral economic' analyses of Tawney, Polanyi, and Thompson. All three focused on the fundamental changes brought about by the 'great transformation' in British society with the advancement individualization, commercialization, marketization, and industrialization. Their work combined the historiographic analysis of how the modern economy evolved in Britain and a distinct normative 'antipathy toward utilitarianism [...] understood as the tendency of Victorian political economy to privilege the pursuit of pecuniary gain over all other human motivations in envisaging social order, reducing society to a matrix of economic transactions' (Rogan 2018: 3). In other words, all three formulated an ardent moral critique of both modern scientific economics and the modern economic order.

As the first of these moral economists, Tawney set the stage in his work as an economic historian. Educated at prestigious English institutions (Rugby; Balliol College, Oxford), Tawney was a firm Anglican and strong adherent of Christian socialism. In addition to his academic position, he engaged in workers' education, influenced the public through popular books, and had a strong impact on policymaking. His work dealt with Protestantism's impact on economic development in the early modern period (Rogan 2018: 43–48). Like Max Weber (1864–1920), Tawney interpreted the Reformation and subsequent rise of Protestantism as a crucial period in the formation of modern capitalism. Contrary to Weber, who hailed the efficiency gains in the modernizing economy, Tawney greatly lamented the subsequent loss of moral values and adherence to the commonwealth. It is in this context that he formulated a strong critique of the enclosure movement that caused social distress, noting that the 'worst side of all such sudden and sweeping redistributions is that the individual is more or less at the mercy of the market, and can hardly help taking his pound of flesh' (Tawney 1926/1936: 139).

This critique of property privatization and the expansion of the market economy also plays an important role in Polanyi's thinking two decades later. Polanyi was born in Vienna (Rogan 2018: 57). Educated in law and economics, he sympathized with socialism and became an ardent critic of the Austrian School of economics. With the advancement of Austrian fascism, Polanyi emigrated to London in 1933. Like Tawney, he engaged in workers' education and after moving to the United States in 1940 he began work on *The Great Transformation* (1944), delineating the privatization of property, the encroaching market economy, and the disjunction of economic activity from its social context (Polanyi 1944/2001). For Polanyi, this 'disembedding' of the economic sphere from social relationships brought upon a countermovement of workers, artisans, and peasants that resulted in the great social uprisings of the nineteenth century and the gradual emergence of the modern welfare state (Sayer 2010: 81–82). Polanyi thus spoke of a 'double-movement', a dialectic process of marketization promoted by modern economics, and responsive attempts for social protection against the detrimental effects brought upon by the market.

Like Polanyi, E. P. Thompson hailed from a socialist background. He was a member of the Communist Party of Great Britain, breaking with the party only after the Soviet invasion of Hungary in 1956 (Rogan 2018: 148). In later decades, he became a prominent peace and nuclear disarmament activist. Thompson's *The Making of the English Working Class* (1963) was a landmark publication in the field of social history, making Thompson 'a giant of the English profession' (Rogan 2018: 57) and ensuring an international scholarly reputation. It was followed by 'The Moral Economy of the English Crowd in the Eighteenth Century' (1971), the single most important reference point in the debate on 'moral economy'. The article's empirical focus dealt with moral legitimizations of food riots. More fundamentally, it attacked the dominant viewpoints in economic history and economics at the time. In stark words, Thompson accused these disciplines of 'crass economic reductionism, obliterating the complexities of motive, behaviour, and function' in a 'schizoid intellectual climate'. The basic flaw of these econometric approaches, Thompson (1971: 78) contended, was 'an abbreviated view of economic man'. The solution to the problem was to reintegrate economic action's moral dimension into the analytical framework.

Tawney, Polanyi, and Thompson firmly stood in the tradition of social criticism going back to the nineteenth century (Rogan 2018: 3). Despite their difference (for example, Tawney's Christian socialism and Thompson's Marxism), all three combined the analytical aspect of unearthing moral economies in historiographic work with the normative agenda of shaping contemporary society. This tension between analysis and activism, while anything but 'value-free' in Weber's interpretation, greatly contributed to the three moral economists' fame in the academic world and beyond.

VALUES MATTER: THE CURRENT DEBATE

While E. P. Thompson was a historian of the 'long' eighteenth century, scholars quickly began applying 'moral economy' to different settings such as the analysis of retirement in the welfare state (Kohli 1987) or the labour movement (Swenson 1989). As Thompson reflected in *Customs in Common*, 'if I did father the term "moral economy" upon current academic discourse, the term has long forgotten its paternity. I will not disown it, but it has come of age and I am no longer answerable for its actions' (Thompson 1994: 351; cf. Frevert 2019a: 8; Götz 2015: 155–158). Recent conceptualizations draw 'moral economy's boundaries even wider. Sayer, for example, considers 'moral economy' to be 'the study of how economic activities of all kinds are influenced and structured by moral dispositions and norms, and how in turn those norms may be compromised, overridden or reinforced by economic pressures. On this definition, *all* economies—not merely pre- or non-capitalist ones—are moral economies' (Sayer 2010: 78). Frevert agrees that in this sense no economic system is value-free, and that 'moral propositions and value judgments are firmly entrenched in economic theory and practice. They structure, give meaning and approval to or criticize economic behavior, and they can encourage collective action' (Frevert 2019a: 9).

'Moral economy' in this wider understanding is not precisely a social scientific theory with a set of clearly defined hypotheses and methodologies, let alone universal 'laws'. I would rather consider it a conceptual lens that allows us to take a specific analytical look at one certain aspect of the economy: at the way moral values shape human agency. It is thus not surprising that morality plays an important role in recent approaches that stress the role of institutions for economic development. For example, in a volume *On Capitalism* commemorating the hundredth anniversary of Weber's *The Protestant Ethic and the Spirit of Capitalism*, the economic sociologists Victor Nee and Richard Swedberg stress the importance of moral values in upholding social institutions. They claim that 'if institutions are not properly anchored in the mores of society, they are without much force and power' (Nee and Swedberg 2007: 9).

Economic sociologists and anthropologists in particular were at the forefront of analysing the moral dimension of the economy in different settings. Jens Beckert, for example, speaks of a moral embeddedness of markets and argues that 'economies operate within the context of a moral universe that resists the logic of economic efficiency' (Beckert 2006: 13) In a similar way, Mark Granovetter—who popularized the concept of embeddedness in *Economic Sociology*—refers to Thompson's moral economy as challenging the rigid assumptions behind *Homo economicus*' seemingly 'rational' propensity to make choices. Mental constructs such as norms, values, and trust form the basis of social relationships, and Granovetter (2017: 26) contends that 'any understanding of the economy must come to grips with these important social forces'.

In anthropology, scholars draw on a long-standing tradition of addressing the moral dimension of exchange. Bronislaw Malinowski's seminal study on the *Argonauts of the Western Pacific* from 1922 remains a standard reference book that shows the reciprocal nature of transactions in the islanders' society. More recent works in anthropology look at the moral economy of immigration (Fassin 2005) and—more generally—stress the inherently embedded character of the economy in Polanyi's tradition (Carrier 2012: 362–364). Moreover, since the 1970s James Scott has helped to popularize the concept in political science (J. C. Scott 1976).

There is also a growing literature that addresses the moral dimension from the viewpoint of economic ethics and philosophy. The philosopher Michael Sandel, for example, paints a dark picture in 'The Moral Limits of Markets', criticizing 'the most powerful social and political tendencies of our time, namely the extension of markets and of market-oriented thinking to spheres of life once thought to lie beyond their reach' (Sandel 1998). Debra Satz (2010) and the economist Paul Zak (2008) have made similar interventions.

Frevert critically remarks, however, that these recent empirical applications and further conceptual developments in the relationship between moral values and economy have been largely confined to the social sciences. This holds true for both the purely academic discourse and scholars' public interventions. In both academic teaching and in research, 'moral economy' continues to play a subordinate role in the fields of economic and social history. Polanyi's concept of embeddedness, for example, is widely employed in the economic sociology but rarely discussed in historiography. The recent crises of modern capitalism—such as the 2008 financial crisis, the 2010 Euro crisis, and the ongoing climate crisis—have provoked broad debates on issues ranging from income equality to taxation, ethical consumption, and fair wages. Historians for the most part have been absent in these debates, despite the long-standing tradition of the relationship between moral values and the economy. It is thus to the point when Frevert asks, 'why then should historians remain aloof when the rest of society, as well as their colleagues in the social sciences and political philosophy, have embarked on a lively discussion of how markets and morals go together or not? What can they contribute to the discussion?' (Frevert 2019b: 15-16).

Still, there are several historiographic attempts to utilize the conceptual tradition of 'moral economy'. The moral foundations and implications of a household economy, for example, are an important focus in the historiography of antiquity, without explicitly applying 'moral economy' as a conceptual framework (Hinsch 2021; Von Reden 1995; Millett 1991). The topics of credit and usury feature prominently in this regard also in medieval and early modern history (Skambraks, forthcoming; Knäble 2019; Fontaine 2014). The 'new social history' of early modern Britain has examined how the moral basis of economic activity in the late medieval era came under increasing pressure from the sixteenth century onwards (Muldrew 1998; Wrightson 2000; Withington 2005). In modern and contemporary history scholars take the concept to address a wide range of themes. Frank Trentmann, for example, addresses the moral dimension in fair trade and modern consumption practices (Trentmann 2007, 2016, 2012). Other scholars look at the moral economy of gambling (Franke 2022), bankruptcy (Finger 2019), or the cultural history of tax morale (Schönhärl 2019).

Utopian Studies is another field of interdisciplinary research that directly connects to moral economy in modern societies. As defined by the Society for Utopian Studies, it is 'devoted to the study of utopianism in all its forms'.[7] This includes imagined utopias

---

[7] https://utopian-studies.org, last accessed 23 Aug. 2021. The society's journal *Utopian Studies* also regularly features economic themes.

in literary fiction and economics in real-life communities. Historical analyses tend to focus on small-scale intentional communities, such as the kibbutzim in Israel, European socialist communes, and American hippie or ethnic communities (Schwenkbeck 2021; Harison 2015; Pitzer 1997; Warhurst 1994). Religious groups and their moral vision of economy also feature prominently in Utopian Studies. The North American Hutterites likewise serve to exemplify a communal way of living based on collective ownership and strong moral values.

A Communal Utopia in Modern Practice: The Hutterite Moral Economy

More painted a picture of a society without individual profit-maximization, competitive markets, self-interest, and greed, at least if we only look at the island's internal economy. How utopian is such an ideal in the context of modern capitalism, an economic system that the moral economists so starkly criticized? In other words, is it possible for the infamous *Homo economicus* to break out from the current world to create something even vaguely like Hythloday's depiction of *Utopia*?

A glimpse into the diary of a German traveller to the American and Canadian West in the years 1930–1 offers one perspective. Eberhard Arnold (1883–1935), who sympathized with Christian socialism and was a staunch pacifist, had much to ponder on his journey. Indeed, with his home country descending into an abyss that would lead to the rise of the Nazi Party and the impact of the Great Depression all around him, his destination must have appeared to him like a true utopia. Nestled in the Great Plains of the USA and Canada, the visitor experienced the vision of a small-scale society based on communal property. There, all able-bodied members worked, including women and older children, contributing to the community's overall welfare.[8] They produced sufficiently to sustain their community and their commonwealth seemed to be in excellent shape. Arnold's diary does not report a single issue that blighted Depression-era America: no starvation, no homelessness, no unemployment, no social deprivation.

The communities in question were the Hutterite *Bruderhöfe* (literally, brethren farms): communal settlements based on Anabaptist Christianity (Janzen and Stanton 2010; Peter 1987; Bennett 1967; Peters 1965).[9] Arnold had experimented with communal living in the 1920s and founded the Rhön Bruderhof near Fulda, about 602 miles north-east of Frankfurt. His trip to America served the purpose of connecting the newly founded community in Germany to the historical Hutterite Church. Well versed in

---

[8] Arnold, 'Diary, Summer 1930', Mennonite Church USA Archives, Hist MSS I-447, Box 20: 6.
[9] Anabaptists were Christians who rejected the validity of infant baptism, because the baptized person needed to able to understand the sacrament. See also van Bunge in this volume.

Anabaptist history and belief, Arnold enthusiastically wrote that 'up till today the complete communism in production and consumption of every single Bruderhof [...] and also the absolute unity of faith of all 35 Bruderhöfe is as good as completely unshaken; one can almost say is preserved absolutely pure' (Arnold 'Diary Summer 1930': 170). This 'purity' of the Bruderhof community was firmly based on Anabaptist–Hutterite religious principles, in particular the central tenant to forgo individual property as outlined in Acts 4:32–5:

> And the multitude of them that believed were of one heart and of one soul: neither said any of them that ought of the things which he possessed was his own; but they had all things common. [...] Neither was there any among them that lacked: for as many as were possessors of lands or houses sold them, and brought the prices of the things that were sold, And laid them down at the apostles' feet: and distribution was made unto every man according as he had need. (KJV)

Not only did the Hutterites provide Arnold with a stark contrast to a capitalist world in turmoil, but Bruderhof communal economics more generally exemplified how moral values shape economic thinking, institutions, and practices.

The Hutterites' origin dates to the Reformation era in the 1520s in Central Europe, when a small group of radical Anabaptists founded the first commune in Moravia. There is no indication that the early Hutterites knew about More's *Utopia*, let alone were directly influenced by it (Von Schlachta 2003; Klassen 1964; Bender 1957; Friedmann 1956). Yet the publication of the text in 1516 and founding of the community about fifteen years later seem more than coincidental. This was a moment of reform and revolution, after all, and although they articulated it differently, both the early Anabaptists and More drew on shared heritage of a *bonum commune*. In thus fitting that Claeys (2016: 409) briefly refers to the Hutterites in his reflections on *Utopia*'s five hundredth anniversary.

After centuries of persecution and ensuing migration, the tiny Hutterite population ended up in the Dakota Territory in the 1870s. The three original Bruderhöfe, each consisting of between 100 and 150 people including children, then rapidly expanded across the northern plains and beyond. By the early twenty-first century, Hutterites numbered about 50,000 people in over 400 communal settlements. The *Gütergemeinschaft* (community of goods) is what sets the Hutterites apart from other Christian churches. In other ways, however, their moral grounding resembles the doctrines of Anabaptist and general Christian conservativism. It includes a patriarchical power hierarchy, clear gender roles, and a socially conservative stance on a wide range of issues (for example, their staunch rejection of homosexuality). Bruderhof governance evolved over centuries with a strong early modern tradition concerning offices and regulations. Contrary to More's Utopians 'who have very few laws' (More 2014: 46) a Hutterite Bruderhof is tightly governed by countless rules that are specified in the communal *Ordnung* (literally, order). Instructions range from attire and haircuts to constraints on using certain technologies. Deviation from the rules can result in severe punishment and even expulsion from the community.

In the introduction of the Yale edition of *Utopia*, Miller pointedly asks whether 'even if we thought it might work in Western nations, would we want to live in such a faceless and regimented society?' (More 2014: viii). Claeys likewise comments that Utopia 'is not really a *fun* place. It is a *safe* place. It offers repose. But the price is restraint' (Claeys 2016: 405). This assessment would most certainly hold true for an ordinary visitor who, unlike Arnold in 1930, had no personal investment in following the moral guidelines prescribed by Hutterite Christianity. Yet, the example of the Bruderhof community of goods has a certain appeal also to a wider public, as countless popular books, journalistic reports, and documentaries show.[10]

Tawney, Polanyi, and Thompson never wrote about the Hutterites (at least I could not find any references in their work), though Tawney in particular may well have been interested in this form of Christian communism. Other academics, however, took note of the Hutterite communal economy. One of them was historian Victor Peters, who in *All Things Common* (1965) provided one of the first systematic analyses of the Hutterite economic way of life in the context of modern American capitalism. It is no coincidence that the book's opener refers to More's *Utopia*, for Peters considered the Hutterite Bruderhof as

> Literally utopian, for it was Thomas More who wrote: 'For what can be more rich than to live joyfully and tranquilly without any worry, not fearful for his own livelihood, nor vexed and troubled with his wife's importunate complaints, not dreading poverty to his sons, nor anxious about his daughter's dowry? But instead to be secure about the livelihood and happiness of their wives, children, grandchildren, and their posterity which they handsomely assume will be a long time.' (Peters 1965: 102–103)

And yet, not all seems to have been as ideal in practice. Twenty-five years before Peters's scholarly account, Eberhard Arnold admiringly wrote about the impressive agricultural operations he observed, including a 'very large mill', a 'gigantic thresher', and 'the most modern motors' (Arnold 'Diary Summer 1930': 63–7). While this sophisticated (and likely quite expensive) modern equipment at first glance appeared to be highly beneficial for improving efficiency in production, a somewhat puzzled Arnold also noted a counter-perspective. It was voiced by an elder at Rockport Bruderhof who did not praise progress, but rather worried about decay, lamenting 'the no longer [*sic*] Hutterian school, the economic rationalization of the *Bruderhöfe*, the influence of the world and diminishing unity in the style of life and the waning influence of elders' (Arnold, 'Diary Summer 1930': 170).

From Arnold's perspective, trying to find an escape from the troubled circumstances in Germany, his puzzlement seems understandable. At the same time, the Rockport elder's concern was perfectly substantiated. By 1930, American Hutterites were far from isolated, even if their remote settlement location would appear to be. The Bruderhöfe

---

[10] See e.g. the BBC production *How to Get to Heaven with the Hutterites* (2013). A 1991 German documentary on the Hutterites is appropriately entitled *Kinder der Utopie* ('Children of Utopia').

were instead tightly connected with their environment, especially in economic terms. Hutterites produced for the market, and were in turn susceptible to volatile prices and competition. They took out loans, bought machinery, and in many other ways relied on exchange with the outside world. Hutterites thus were connected, much in the same way as Utopians, to a larger system beyond their community's boundaries. Seen in this picture of a wider world, both More's fictitious island economy and the real-life Bruderhof lose at least certain aspects of their 'utopian' character. It thus should not surprise us that Hutterites were confronted with beliefs, ideologies, and rationales that competed with or were in direct opposition to their own Anabaptist beliefs. How should a Hutterite discern the logic of economic growth, profit-maximization, expansion, and efficiency gains in a competitive environment? How could Hutterite moral values be compatible with the requirements of modern capitalism? And how would this eventually shape the 'purity' of the Bruderhof community that Arnold so greatly admired?

Contrary to More's static Utopia, where the values and institutions once established seemingly never changed, the Hutterite moral economy is in flux and contingent (Longhofer 1993). It is connected to the dynamic environment brought upon by market forces, government regulations, and technological innovations. The Hutterite elder's critical comment on the state of the Bruderhof in 1930 and the many regulations governing the communities serves as a reminder that maintaining a communal commonwealth in the real world requires constant attention, authority, and strong institutions. And yet, the underlying moral values that govern a Bruderhof economy have been remarkable persistent. The communal embeddedness of the Hutterite economy continued to hold despite modernization's impact on the most remote corners of Montana or Manitoba. In this sense, the Hutterites present a perfect example for students and scholars to assess the long-term capacity for 'embeddedness' between the sixteenth and twenty-first centuries.

IMPLICATIONS FOR FUTURE RESEARCH AND DEBATE

Twenty years after Thompson coined 'moral economy' as a term of modern academic analysis, the concept was considered to have 'come of age' (Gailus and Lindenberger 1994). Does that mean that thirty years later 'moral economy' is getting close to retirement? A look at the current debate reveals that, on the contrary, the concept continues to be shaped, applied, and reconfigured across disciplines. Perhaps more than ever, the end of capitalism's Golden Age, the crisis of the welfare state, the collapse of state socialism, rampant global inequality, and pending environmental doom require new reflections on the relationship between morality and economy.

At the same time, it is no longer appropriate, if it ever was, to consider academic economics as the primary scapegoat for capitalism's detrimental impact. Rapid advancements in the fields of behavioural economics, cognitive science, and psychology have greatly changed the way *Homo economicus* is modelled. The psychologist Daniel Kahneman is but one example of a researcher who has bridged the disciplines of human economic action, critically engaging with concepts of human selfishness, rationality, and utility. With Amon Twersky he developed prospect theory as an alternative approach that directly tackles the shortcomings of Rational Choice Theory. Prospect theory stresses people's loss-aversion in decision-making. It stands in contrast to the utility maximization hypothesis in Rational Choice Theory (Kahneman 2011, 2003). Newer conceptualizations of economic behaviour also consider the impact of emotions and not the least the underlying moral values that shape a person's economic preferences. In this sense, *Homo economicus* is always also *Homo moralis*.

This widened conceptualization of economic action coincided with new and critical assessments of modern economies. Ever since the Club of Rome published its groundbreaking report on the 'Limits to Growth' (Meadows et al. 1972), the environmental dangers of a depletion of natural resources have remained a prominent topic in scholarly and popular debate (Schmelzer 2016: 266). Countless research centres and think tanks are searching for economic alternatives.[11] In a sharp response against philosopher Francis Fukuyama's contention that after the downfall of the Soviet bloc the world had reached 'the end of history' (and entered a glorious age of enduring liberal capitalism) the economist Geoffrey Hodgson called for ongoing relevance of 'Utopian discourse' (G. Hodgson 1995: 197). In *Utopia for Realists* (2016), the bestselling author Rutger Bregman popularized utopian ideas such as a universal basic income to a wider audience. The economists Esa Mangeloja and Tomi Ovaska (2019) even consider More's *Utopia* to be a new classic in economic thinking.

While it might be a bit far-fetched to consider More a classic in economic thinking, the issue of collective ownership came back on the agenda of economic analysis with Elinor Ostrom's 1995 groundbreaking book *Governing the Commons*. Contrary to most modern economists and economic historians, Ostrom did not consider the collective sharing of resources in production as a problem per se. With the right institutions and careful governance, societies could successfully manage resources without overextending, polluting, or depleting them. Ostrom did not refer to *Utopia* in her analysis, instead focusing on real-life examples such as irrigation systems, fisheries, and communal pastures. Yet, her work has greatly influenced further research and applications on collective ownership. As the Hutterite example also shows, certain moral values and effective institutions can indeed stabilize communalism and collective management of property.

In the current debate on the sharing economy, joint ownership of property plays a major role. Other important themes in the critique of the current state of the economy

---

[11] These include the British Schumacher Center for a New Economics (https://centerforneweconomics.org), the German Laboratory for New Economic Ideas (https://konzeptwerk-neue-oekonomie.org/english), and the Institute for New Economic Thinking (https://www.ineteconomics.org) in the United States, all last accessed on 20 Aug. 2021.

and the quest for alternative solutions abound. These range from the Occupy Wallstreet movement's impetus to address the stark income inequality in Western societies (the '1 per cent') to the fair-trade movement and animal rights organizations that criticize the industrialized production of meat. Referring again to Frevert's critical assessment that these debates so far have been largely contained within the social sciences, it can be asked what role historians can play in this regard. The answer here is that only historical analysis can contribute long-term assessments of the relationship between the moral and the economic. For example, as Jo Guldi and David Armitage claim in their *History Manifesto*, the 'spectre of the short term' that is 'haunting our time' needs historical recalibration (Guldi and Armitage 2017: 1). History can provide people with 'coordinates by which they [can] understand the present and direct their actions towards the future', as 'a guide to life' (10). Only analysis over the *longue durée* can tell how utopian ideas such as communal property were implemented in the past, how they were governed, why they sometimes succeeded and more often failed. Thus, historiography can provide an important input in assessing the feasibility of seemingly pre- or early modern alternative approaches to the economy in a modern capitalist world.

More's *Utopia* does not offer a blueprint for a just economic system, if only because its slavery and violent imperialism are morally problematic. Yet, it deserves attention as it raises important questions regarding the rights and wrongs of how people sustain their livelihood through the production, distribution, and consumption of goods and services. Most important of all, it addresses timeless questions about what constitutes a just commonwealth and how a political economy should be governed. In this sense, *Utopia* offers more than just an old and fictitious account of a commonwealth based on collective ownership of property. Rather, it is a crucial intervention to contemporary debates about moral economy.

CHAPTER 37

UTOPIA AND ARCHITECTURE

DIANE MORGAN

For over five hundred years Utopia (the text and idea) has provoked discussions about where we are heading to (if anywhere at all). As we now know, Utopia might not be a destination we can or even want to reach.[1] To make the situation even more disorienting, yet also tantalizing and provocative, Immanuel Kant tells us that ideas per se are 'concept[s] of reason whose object can be met with nowhere in experience' (Kant 1977a: §3; cf. Caygill 1995: 236). Yet we still have to begin somewhere, 'from some point or another' (Mendelsohn 2017: 42). Often standard accounts of *Utopia* and architecture begin and end with a minimal, and therefore ultimately meaningless, account of Book Two. For example, Dominique Rouillard writes:

> In the classical utopias architecture serves an essentially narrative purpose. As such what is required of it is an efficient functionality as far as the distribution of space, hygiene, solidity comfort, etc. are concerned. [...] *The architectonic or decorative dimension has no importance in More's narrative*. It would even have damaged the equality of the treatment of individuals: the fifty-four cities which cover the island are 'built according to same plan and have the same aspect where the site permits'. (Rouillard 2006: 10; my translation, emphasis added)

Despite citing Hythloday's highly significant afterword ('where the site permits'), which drastically qualifies any idea of an imposed and fixed uniformity, Rouillard seems all too confident about knowing the layout of Utopia.[2] This is also the case of Ruth Eaton's *Cités idéales* ('Ideal Cities') which locks More's description of architecture to a

---

[1] See the famous statement by Oscar Wilde (1986: 34) about the importance of utopia as an endless and restless journeying in search of what we could call, following the film-maker Luis Buñuel, 'an obscure object of desire'.

[2] Marin's attentive reading of the description of Amaurot reveals the non-congruence of its blocks (*quartier*), streets, and districts, the conspicuous absence of its central markets and of the Prince's palace (Marin 1973: 27, 163–184). Marin thereby destabilizes the stereotypical view, held by Rouillard (and Eaton), of Utopian cities' predetermined layout.

transhistorical search for an ideal urban 'model' to then raise the dangers of standardization, suppression of individualism, and dominance of surveillance society, all deemed 'characteristics of utopian worlds' (Eaton 2001: 16–17). In *Architecture and Utopia*, it only takes Franco Borsi a few lines before he is evoking 'concentration-camp repression' and a few pages for King Utopus, 'the ideal leader', to 'prefigur[e] Hitler's *Mein Kampf* [*sic*]' (Borsi 1997: 7, 25).

Both Eaton's and Borsi's books are crammed full of fascinating images of a wide range of architectural forms from various periods, all more or less related to a largely misguided search for 'perfection' that is characterized as often 'arrogant' and 'megalomaniac' (Eaton 2001: 239, 241; cf. Coleman 2011: 8). Both end reflecting on the need to scale down ambition, engage with 'the human dimension', and protect the environment, at both local and global levels. These conclusions might be fair enough, but we have to ask ourselves whether, despite themselves, they are not in effect presenting an argument for the necessity of 'utopianism', rather than 'proving' why we should stay clear of it. Mind you, the nature of the 'it', of 'utopia', is far from clear in More's inaugural text. He certainly does not provide a simple definition of the term. We are instead provoked to debate what it might be and do. What is clear is that, due to their sweeping surveys, neither Eaton nor Borsi can adequately address the complexities and playfulness of More's text despite at times, and almost symptomatically in the case of Eaton, registering that Utopia's cities were only 'quasi-identical' and that More's text had a historical context (Eaton 2001: 14, 240). Both texts confirm Louis Marin's claim, in his indispensable *Utopiques: Jeux d'espaces*, that such readings reduce what are non-conceptual 'utopic figures' to static, 'complete' images of a supposed 'model' of 'social ideality, imaginary reverie, or political project' to then judge the ideas according to their 'possibility or impossibility of realization' (Marin 1973: 251–252). They fix the elaborate play of spaces, effacing any playfulness (21; cf. Marin 1984: xvi).

For Robert Hughes, the natural 'home' for the 'utopian impulse' was in architecture (Hughes 1980: 164). 'Painting can make us happy,' he continues, 'but building is the art we live in; it is the social art par excellence, the carapace of political fantasy, the exoskeleton of one's economic dreams. It is also the one art nobody can escape.' Yet, for Hughes (as for many others concerned with architecture) the 'utopian impulse' is situated in the past. For these writers and thinkers, something went seriously wrong: 'The culture of the twentieth century is littered with utopian schemes' (164). Hughes highlights what he sees as the failure of modernist architecture by using the word 'building', signalling that not much of what we live in, and with, actually qualifies as 'architecture' (the art form). For modernist thinkers such as Ernst Bloch, architecture as a 'social creation' stands out from other art forms (Bloch 1995: 2.737). Architecture is largely concerned with realizing actual buildings, but lamentably many buildings do not qualify to be considered architectural works of art. They lack the requisite aesthetic qualities; they fail to please, charm, stimulate, enhance our daily lives, let alone inspire us to search for something better.

Compared to other art forms, architecture has especially onerous responsibilities as it is so omnipresent, impinging on all aspects of our public and private lives. We could even say that the built environment gives society its various forms. We construct structures and systems, in our heads and in the physical world, to spatialize and conceptualize (conferring meaning on the world around us) by organizing and arranging it according to our needs and desires. We naturally invest in the spaces around us, wishing them to provide us with the best possible places for feeling good, at ease, safe, and comfortable in. It can easily be argued that architecture is the art form most vitally entwined with what it is for us humans to be alive on this planet. Yet, in Hughes's eyes, under dogmatic modernism, architecture, far from being life-enhancing and dream-fulfilling, became a living nightmare that one desperately wanted to escape from.[3] 'The utopian buck stops here,' he says, describing the planned city of Brasilia (Hughes 1980: 211). Brasilia stands as the 'emblematic' indictment of those 'who design for an imagined Future'. For Hughes, back in 1980, what seemed 'obvious' was that 'it is better to recycle what exists, to avoid mortgaging a workable past to a nonexistent Future, and to think small. In the life of cities, only conservatism is sanity'.

It is interesting to consider Hughes's words forty years on. He is not entirely wrong. Recycling what exists does not necessarily mean making do with the world as it is. Recycling can be creative, restorative, and to an extent transformative. In this context we could consider Patrick Geddes's remarks on the re-erection of Crosby Hall, Chelsea as a university hall of residence (interestingly on the site of More's own garden). Geddes considers this project to be 'no mere act of archaeological piety, still less of mere "restoration", but one of renewal; it is a purposeful symbol, a renewed initiative, Utopian and local, civic and academic in one' (Geddes 1915/2012: 374; cf. 369–373 for other references to More's influence). This type of architectural praxis is certainly one feasible and positive way of intervening in this world and helping to build a better 'civic spirit'. But is it 'utopian'? Does it really change the world? Is it not tinkering on the surface? Are not such initiatives easily recuperated within our ideologically enclosed system, when something more radical is needed?

Marin also raised doubts about whether social institutions are ultimately impervious to fundamental change. He begins *Utopiques* with an inspiring account of his experiences of 1968 at Nanterre University: 'a liberating explosion and an extra-temporal moment of overthrow [*renversement*]; it was also the seizure of every opportunity to speak [... T]hose who spoke [...] found themselves beyond themselves, beyond what they thought or believed' (Marin 1973: 15). However, soon after, he bluntly states that this 'revolutionary festival' was ultimately a failure, that the institutionalized university cannot be a catalyst for change (17). Whilst recognizing Marin's political engagement at that time and respecting the fact that his disillusionment arose from lived experience, we might nevertheless want to protest by retorting that, even if the ultimate outcome

---

[3] Abensour 2013: 24 writes that dogma is 'what seems good and appropriate and, it therefore goes without saying, what escapes all interrogation, all questioning, all examination, a fortiori all critique, because the order such as it is, as it presents itself, as it situates itself, as it produces and reproduces itself falls far short of all problematicity'. Utopia is an escape from this 'order': 'it ignores time and space' (25–26).

of such 'utopian' commitment is failure, such bids for change are still worthwhile, even most necessary, as pure expressions of the refusal of what is presented as the status quo: things as they supposedly are (and have to be). We might want to go yet further and bring in Fredric Jameson's provocative remark that failure is in itself crucially important as 'a way to encourage the analysis of our own situation and in particular its crippling effects on our sense of history and of the future' (cited in Moylan 1998: 74–77).

To return to recycling. Despite any discussion as to its ultimate impact—does refusing that plastic bag help offset the ecological crisis?—Hughes is surely right to suggest that wasting resources is a sign of insanity. Here he could have found support in key nineteenth-century utopian texts—Edward Bellamy's *Looking Backward* (1888); William Morris's *News from Nowhere* (1890)—which loudly protest against the tragic stupidity and injustice of waste, wasted resources, wasted opportunities, wasted energy, wasted lives, sheer wastefulness (Bellamy 1986: 166–178; 226–229; Morris 2004: 285–306; cf. Geddes 1995/2012: 72). Interestingly for us as readers of More, David Harvey also notes: 'I always thought that the purpose of More's *Utopia* was not to provide a blueprint for some future but to hold up for inspection the ridiculous waste and foolishness of his times, to insist that things could and must be better' (Harvey 2000: 281).

Hughes is similarly far from being content with the world as it presented itself to him back in the late 1970s. He characterizes his age as one of 'ideological cramp and historicist narrowness', 'constriction' (Hughes 1980: 406). He laments the 'appalling commercialism of the art world, its flight into corporate ethics and strategies' (409). We could readily agree with him now and relate these concerns to architecture, whose relation to economics is most ambivalent and often highly compromising. Bloch, writing twenty years earlier, during the aftermath of the Second World War and Nazi reign of terror, would not have been able to console Hughes. Bloch had grave doubts whether architecture could ever flourish in the 'hollow space of late capitalism': 'Only the beginnings of another society will make genuine architecture possible again,' he stated (Bloch 1995: 737; cf. Coleman 2013: 135–166). Nevertheless, a glimmer of hope can be detected in Hughes's text: he concludes regretting how dogmatic modernism rejects 'the benefits of the modernist spirit', its 'anxious and open discourse', its search for 'more ways' to 'act as a transformer between the self and nonself'. Something positive was happening during the 'utopian' period of early modernism after all: more reason to return to More's book and to hold on to the idea.

We began this chapter by alerting ourselves to the dangers of fixing More's *Utopia* in an image of a topos: that of the 'ideal city' which unsurprisingly turns out to be far from perfect. Like Rouillard et al., I too will venture into the text, but not to Book Two. Instead, I will head to what looks like another identifiable place, a garden, nominally situated in Antwerp. Far from being non-essential places of pleasure, gardens can be sites for addressing many urgent and conflictual global issues facing us today including, to cite T. D. Demos (2012),

> the corporate financialization of nature, realized by the patenting of genetically modified seeds by agriculture and pharmaceutical corporations; the production of

greenhouse gas emissions, via a monoculture- and export-based agribusiness reliant on the fossil-fuelled transportation industry and chemical fertilizers; and the destruction of unions and small-scale farmers, displaced by the mechanization and monopoly ownership of the means of production.

This garden can function as an 'imaginary focus' to kickstart our analysis of Utopia and Architecture, but we will have to guard ourselves against deluding ourselves that this 'place' does or could exist. As defined by Kant (1998: B672), a *focus imaginarius* lies outside the bounds of experience. It is a heuristic device for generating interest in 'maintaining the whole', that is, some sort of commonality which does not yet exist as such (Kant 1994: 51).[4] Although in this sense illusory, it could nonetheless be necessary as a means of extending our vision beyond experience, to then return us differently to this world, tracing 'new lines of flight' towards 'an other non-place [*vers un non-lieu autre*]' (Abensour 2000: 26). Such a garden might also permit us to discuss the implications of what Marin (1973: 23) calls 'utopian practice' defined as: this play in space, 'as an *a priori* form of external sensibility'. When Marin states that 'utopian practice is an architectonic, an art of systems' (25), he draws on Kant's *Critique of Pure Reason* where we are told that 'This schematism of our understanding with regard to appearances and their mere form is a hidden art in the depths of the human souls, whose true operations we can divine from nature and lay unveiled before our eyes *only with difficulty*' (Kant 1998: B181).

How can we understand this passage in relation to architecture and utopia? In this world we orientate ourselves at the level of images; these are produced 'through' and 'in accordance with' schemas which are 'as it were a monogram of pure *a priori* imagination' (B181). Images have to be connected with concepts 'to which they are in themselves never fully congruent' (B181). Schemas can never by captured by images. Images re-present. Marin envisages Utopia as a 'performative force', akin to a 'schema of transcendental imagination' freeing us from the clutches of ideological reproduction: 'in utopia we read the unfigurable figure of Infinite Liberty' (Marin 1993: 16). As he says: '*Utopia is not a topography but a topic*; not an imaginary place, as one often says, but an indeterminate place, or more precisely, the indetermination itself of place' (Marin 1973: 152). As such, utopia presents a crucial problem for figuration. We want our ideas to take on an evident shape and be clearly representable in this world so that they mean something tangible. However, this dogged search for meaning might be misplaced. George Bataille, for one, warns us that we are wrong to take even a dictionary as an authoritative source of meanings. He suggests that, despite our assumptions, a dictionary's function is far from giving clear precise, well-formed, and handy definitions of what things are. Instead, he writes: 'a dictionary begins when it no longer gives the meaning of words, but their tasks' (Bataille 1994: 31). By implication he seems to suggest that, as thinkers and would-be practitioners of utopia, we need to accept a degree of 'formlessness'. Maybe

---

[4] For a discussion of this Kantian transcendental utopia as a 'frame for thought' versus a more Deleuzian immanent model, see Buchanan's analysis of Jameson (1998: 21).

we should indeed follow his lead and see More's 'Utopia', not so much as a meaningful 'thing', but rather as being what 'serves to bring things down in the world, requiring that each thing have it form' (31).

We do so much want 'Utopia' to 'take shape' and we resist attempts such as More's and Bataille's to declassify the categories and terms with which we build and rebuild our customary world. Yet Marin insists that such displacements are the conditions of possibility for clearing a space for playful (more creative and freer) thought. This chapter therefore responds to the challenge of figuring Utopia by resisting form. Like Hythloday, it wanders; like *Utopia*, it is conversational in tone. Within it I interject jarring comments drawing attention to the unavoidable, but possibly productive, stressing and straining involved in holding together in a relation something usually categorized as a literary text—though More's work is also sometimes shelved under Philosophy or Political-utopian theory—and considerations about architectural theory and practice. Thinking about 'stress and strain' in relation to architecture can even lead us directly to 'utopian' approaches to the world such as those of the visionary engineer Buckminster Fuller. His writings on tensegrity (defined as continuous tension and discontinuous compression) destabilize conventional ideas about how our world is constructed (R. B. Fuller 1972: 133–152; 1999: 103, 394, 510–512).[5] Whereas we tend to think of tension as something to be reduced or even eliminated, especially when building structures (but also in human relations), and to favour what is more compact, solid, and apparently stronger, therefore more dependable, Fuller positivizes the former. He consequently defies centuries of building tradition which is primarily based on compression, the gradual amassing of blocks of material, regarding this cumbersome, ecologically unfriendly building method as indicative of antiquated 'solid thinking'.

Architecture is indeed conventionally tied to solid, grounded concerns in ways that other arts are not. It is far easier for literature to be distanced from ideological constraints and to engage more freely in intellectual speculation than it is for architecture, which tends to be pushed towards a different and more compromising form of speculation: that of property. However, even in the 'literary' world there are constraints. An instance presents itself here, in this very volume. In an ideal—a eutopic—world I would have had numerous lengthy footnotes in homage to the extensive paratexts that supplement, complement, compliment, add to and fill in, imitate, and further ironize More's urtext. These paratexts signal that *Utopia* is a collective endeavour to create a space whose form is sufficiently accommodating to air 'no less instructive than delightful' ideas that are still in the process of being shaped (More 2020: 3).[6] Such discursive notes would have signalled the collaborative nature of this chapter, the way that it is in dialogue with other writers. They would have captured a sense of More's short, but complex, multilayered, proliferating, and accumulative text. They would have required

---

[5] R. B. Fuller (1972: 133–152; 1999: 103, 394, 510–512) also challenges the isolationism associated with islands (like Utopia) and individualism.

[6] Similarly architecture is a collective venture; it should also make a contribution to improving society by opening up life-enhancing spaces (Piano 1985).

readers to flit between two places on the same page, just as More's *Utopia* demands that we move between spaces (here, there; now, then). Nevertheless, given Marin's powerful analysis of the political potential of utopian playfulness and how it can be easily be closed down by institutionalized formalization which tends to definitively place things, people, ideas (Marin 1973: 16–17), maybe the restrictive formatting—imposed by the form of the published volume, which eschews numerous long footnotes—is highly apposite, nay symbolic. After all, Morus advises Hythloday in Book One that an 'indirect' approach, that we could understand as a form of pragmatic compromise, is necessary in the world-as-it-is (More 2020: 66). But we might yet still balk at such restriction, as does Hythloday.

Let us resume tracing the 'figure' of the garden. It is hard to address—conceptualize? visualize?—this non-place behind every place, especially in 'architectural' form. Another risk with my 'garden' is that it that might not amount to anything different from all other gardens one can imagine, and/or that it is just my own personal foible.[7] The best I can do is to propose not entering the garden as part of the narrative flow in Book One, but to start by relocating it: placing it between the two books. After all, it is in the middle where connections are made (Deleuze with Parnet 1991: 106; Buchanan 1998: 20–21). Resituated in the middle, it would not be completely conflatable with the garden evoked in Book One. It would need to be radically transformed, although the demands placed on it might reveal it to be inadequately adaptable. It can longer be the garden of a king's emissary, or a walled-in enclosure with only one way out or in. Despite being distinct and secluded, both necessary characteristics for conferring on it a certain exceptionality, we could say that it has swinging doors, reminiscent of the Utopians' houses (More 2020: 81), inviting easy comings and goings across the two books. By so doing I am attempting to acknowledge the extensive scholarly debates about how to read, how to enter into, More's densely complex text.

It is difficult, if not impossible, to conceive of, and even more visualize, the already transformed garden in this new location (between the two books). How can one insert such a site there where one has only the end of Book One on one page and the opening sentences of Book Two on the next? Will it magically emerge from the folds that lead to the spine of the volume? What if in our particular edition we only have one side of a page which marks the end of Book One and straightaway, on turning overleaf, we find ourselves at the beginning of Book Two? Does this not further reduce our chances of constructing this place? If this is our case, there does not seem to be room for manoeuvre at all. This is a dilemma that has already confronted us: that of the relation between ideas in a text (here literary) and their 'figurative representations [*bildliche Vorstellungen*]'. For Aristotle in *De Anima* 'the soul never thinks without an image' (3.7, 431a, 14–17). According to Kant (1987: §77, 293), this 'image-neediness' underpins our (human) discursive understanding ('unser [...]

---

[7] For how fear of the simulacra and of projection ('social determination') haunt utopian thinking and how 'failure' is therefore necessary for marking the necessity of a space beyond the limits of what seems imaginatively possible from the standpoint of our now, see Jameson 2005: 289, 293; Buchanan 1998: 22.

diskursiver der Bilder bedürftiger Verstand (intellectus ectypus)'). In 'What is Orientation in Thinking?', a text that is not just about getting by in this world but also about getting to another world, one that promotes 'freedom of thought' in a 'community of others', Kant writes: 'However exalted we may wish our concepts to be, and however abstract we may make them in realm of the senses, they will continue to be associated with figurative representations [*Vorstellungen*]' (Kant 1994: 247, 237). We are evidently faced with a problem: we rely on forms, we are form-making, but how can we shape what does not yet exist, whose form is hopefully radically different from anything that we have hitherto experienced?

Buckminster Fuller, for whom utopianism was fundamental, said 'Form is a verb', i.e. form does things; it has an immediate impact on this world (R. B. Fuller 1999: 162–163);[8] for Nathaniel Coleman, utopia gives to architecture and the city 'a sense of purpose in improving the lot of individuals and groups' (Coleman 2011: 21). But how can our customary forms of orientation suffice for finding our way to and thereby building a radically transformed and improved world? There is no pathway to utopia. As Jameson (2004) says, the function of utopian thought is the revelation of 'the utopian leap, the gap between our empirical present and the utopian arrangements of this imaginary future'. It is difficult to apply these ideas to real-world architectural praxis. Architectural projects are determined by so many imperatives, a major one being that time is money (architecture requires plenty of both). An architectural project is such a complex combination, series, coordination of so many operations involving various teams of workers that finding time for what Aby Warburg calls *Denkraum* ('thinking space') is difficult. As Roland Recht explains, *Denkraum* is a distancing between oneself and one's world that enables one to orientate oneself in relation to it (Recht, in Warburg 2012: 11, 19). Recht draws attention to Warburg's maybe voluntary lapsus on the eve of his death. Warburg wrote (2012: 19): 'Kant: what is orientation in space (incorrect title)?' The space we are offered by More's text and paratexts, and as encountered after 500 years of historical reflection, we see 'through a glass, darkly'. We are obliged to consider future conditions of possibility for orientation both in thinking and in space: 'for we know in part' but cannot 'prophesy in part' (1 Corinthians 13).

To hold back the crushing weight of real-life imperatives bearing down on our topic 'Utopia and Architecture', to clear a space for reflection (*Denkraum*), I return to my more speculative mode to conjure the phantasmatic presence of the garden between the two books. Were we to visualize it, but somehow without latching on to images, it would emit special effects both backwards into Book One where they can rebound to traverse the whole text as an ostensible linear narrative, as well as in the other direction, into Book Two, where they can remain captured at the end if readers prefer. Some do. Equally possible is that, once they arrive at the end of Book Two, they make the long journey backwards, maybe bouncing off various points on the way, even remaining permanently

---

[8] For Fuller as 'anticipatory' in Bloch's sense, see R. B. Fuller 1999: 15.

at sea, as it were, free to circulate, never entirely settling down. To my mind, in More's short *Utopia* there is something akin to the epic 'ring composition' described by Daniel Mendelsohn (2017: 31–33) in relation to Homer's *Odyssey*. Of course, Hythloday—like Odysseus—is 'polytropos': a man 'of many turns'. All the elements are there in this most labile of texts to facilitate these various ways of reading and hence spatializing the text, to create variable relations with its ideas: here August Blanqui's intriguing proposition that 'only the chapter of bifurcations remains open to hope' springs to mind (Blanqui 2013: 147; cf. Abensour 2000: 437). The structure of More's text is fluid or floating, not grounded: 'Sometimes it's as if you're on familiar territory; sometimes you feel at sea, adrift in a featureless liquid void with no landmarks in sight' (Mendelsohn 2017: 41). All the more reason for locating the starting point for my analysis in the *phantasmatic* presence of the Antwerp garden: a temporary or atemporal interstitial space (that does not exclude others). It might be a good idea.

Not just a good idea. If it were to exist, it might be a potentially 'good place' (*eu-topos*) where people could come together to express themselves peacefully, despite their differences, with a view to improving society. Here Kant would surely correct our hesitant prevarication: 'if it were to exist'. For Kant, such a garden is a 'necessary idea' indicating 'what ought to be done' (Kant 1998: B373–375). Discussing Plato's *Republic*, he disputes the unfeasibility of the figure of the philosopher-king. For Kant utopian 'dreams', like More's, should not be dismissed out of hand for the very reason that they have not actually been properly tried in practice; they are therefore conceivable; moreover, it is 'the duty of the head of state (not of the citizens)' to 'continually approach such a state' (Kant 1994: 188).

Eutopia was a central concern for the town planner Geddes. He thought that the 'good place' was not only not nowhere (*ou-topos*) but also latently already there, all around us: 'Eutopia lies in the city around us; and it must be planned and realized, here or nowhere, by us as its citizens—each citizen of both the actual and the ideal city seen increasingly as one' (Geddes 1995/2012: vii; cf. Sullivan 2011: 167). Maybe Geddes was right: we do not need to look much further. Maybe it is indeed a question of cultivating the 'upgrowth' already in our world, so that it brings forth 'varied flower and fruit' in garden cities (Geddes 1995/2012: vi). Geddes was writing amidst the destruction of the First World War, which compounded the desolation of the 'paleotechnic age' with its 'predatory finance', mere 'money-wealth', and 'wasteful industry'. By contrast, garden cities represented an alternative, more peaceful, more cooperative way of life, a way of ending slum dwellings, creating real 'wealth and leisure', 'the bettering of man and his environment together' (73). Gardens were seen by Geddes as providing a 'wholesome and delightful contribution to the sustenance of their inhabitants'.[9] The realization of such good places relied on a thorough exploration and keen sense of the site's geographical and historical situation, acquired by surveying.[10] Geddes elaborated a

---

[9] More's Utopians are similarly devoted to their gardens (More 2020: 81).
[10] Cf. how Utopian city-planning responds to what 'the site permits', discussed at the start of this chapter.

rich definition of surveying. The process was concerned with 'the whole situation and life and community in past and present'; its function was to 'prepar[e] for the planning scheme which is to forecast, indeed largely decide its material future'. The survey was to resonate with 'civic feeling' (346), starkly contrasting with other all-too-heavy-handed impositions of town planning that give utopianism such a bad reputation. Geddes's sectional representations, rather than bird's-eye views, of 'utopian' cities (including More's) can change our perspective and thereby our assumptions about what architectural forms might be imaginable. Sectional representation reveals 'civic potential as "a drama in time" ' (Sullivan 2011: 173, citing Geddes).[11] Capturing such dramas permits a synoptic 'visualis[sation] and depict[ion of] the city from its smallest beginnings, in its immediate and wider setting'. The 'minuteness' of such details was important for Geddes (1995/2012: 360–361). Let us, however, bear in mind Jameson's point throughout—and that is the juggling act of this chapter—about how the function of utopian texts is

> to bring home, in local and determinate way, and with a fullness of concrete detail, our constitutional inability to imagine utopia itself, and this, not owing to any individual failure of imagination but as the result of the systemic, cultural and ideological closure of which we are all in one way or another prisoners. (Jameson 2005: 289; emphasis added)

Within utopian thinking, including Geddes's, the garden is a powerful symbol, so it feels right to focus on this figure in More's text, but we have also to try to hold on to Jameson's point about the unimaginability of utopia.

In the narrative itself the garden, a form of heterotopia (a world within a world, refracting that outside world), provides the occasion for an encounter which could in time possibly produce radical social and political transformation, for who is to know yet what the future has in store hopefully for us (along with others)? Such an unexpected, yet for many long-awaited, rupture with an apparent status quo—an extraction from an all-too-overbearing here-and-now—would defy the reservations of Morus and Peter Giles, who were at the scene. Indeed, the promising, yet fragile, vision of the archetypal garden risks dissolving before our eyes when we read the closing lines of the book. Behind Hythloday's back, as it were, Morus betrays his function as the objective describer of a historical event, or, more accurately as Book Two is concerned, as the self-effacing transcriber of Hythloday's words and—jettisoning any pretence at neutrality—passes judgement on what he has heard: in his view, 'not a few of the practices which arose from Utopian laws and customs and laws were patently absurd' (More 2020: 169). The central issue of 'their life in common without money' is deemed to 'utterly subvert

---

[11] In *Utopia* there are many detectable traces of 'dramas in time'; see Marin 1973: 213–245 on the Utopians' rich cultural history which problematizes greatly the myth of their insularity. They are also still living in the aftermath of two devastating epidemics that so traumatized the Utopians that they have been anxious about population levels ever since (More 2020: 92).

[...] the proper ornaments of any commonwealth', namely 'nobility, magnificence, splendour and majesty' (170). Bewilderingly, we discover that we have not been in safe hands after all: it would seem that Morus is a committed defender of the establishment, and therefore out of sympathy with Hythloday's radical stance on wealth, property, and social injustice. Yet apparently, according to Jameson (and Abensour) such 'bewilderment' is 'fruitful', integral to the utopian function, namely: 'to jar the mind into some heightened but unconceptualizable consciousness of its own powers, functions, aims, and structural limits' (Jameson 1977: 11).

These destabilizing revelations about Morus confound our impressions gathered from Book One where he explicitly solicited Hythloday to enter political life to advise those in power how to improve society. Nevertheless, despite his solid social standing as ambassador—a representative of the state—and as host of the interlude in the garden, Morus' personal insecurities are also revealed. He is not that sure of himself. Once Hythloday finishes speaking towards the end of Book Two, Morus refrains from comment: not just because Hythloday is tired and prickly (Morus states that it 'wasn't clear [...] whether he would tolerate a contrary view'), but also because he fears being associated with those individuals Hythloday has 'rebuked' who, not having any ideas of their own, resort to criticizing those of others, for the sake of having something to say (More 2020: 170). It could be that he senses his own vacuity. He therefore takes Hythloday by the hand to lead him into the house where supper has been prepared behind the scenes (by servants). This gesture is friendly enough: fitting testimony to the interesting and pleasant time—despite evident differences of opinion—spent in one another's company. Nevertheless, the vision of the garden at the end of a long afternoon appears dimmer, less vibrant.

Yet there were so many further issues that needed raising! When it comes to it, nothing has been properly discussed. Definitely no decisions were made; rather, many unresolved contradictions came to light. Marin is helpful here. For him the text sets up differences which it then holds apart in the form of a 'neutralization', thereby maintaining what he calls the 'distance of contradictions [*l'écart des contradictoires*]' (Marin 1973: 20–21, 34). Here Marin draws on Kant's 'Attempt to introduce the concept of negative magnitudes into philosophy' (Kant 1977b: 779–819; 2002: 203–241). In this essay Kant suggests that the form of 'negativity' arising from the non-resolution of issues is not to be seen as a lack, defect, or omission, but a powerfully suggestive 'robbing' or 'privation' of reconciliatory closure: an intense holding-open of a 'real opposition' which flags up the issues and stakes of a particular situation (Kant 1977b: 792–793; 2002: 220–221). Hence the non-resolution of, for example, the important question raised in More's text about whether those in power can be positively influenced by experienced, socially engaged 'utopian' thinkers should not be regarded as a failure. Better still, we should reassess our assumptions about what we take 'failure' to mean. Jameson for one encourages us to regard failure as productive, even necessary. Discussing the utopian dimension of Science Fiction, he proposes that 'by force of its failure we are returned all the more intensely to the real' (cited in Buchanan 1998: 21). But maybe we overstate the sense of 'failure' at the end of More's text? Maybe the vision of the garden scene is fading fast only because here, located at the end of the book, night is already closing in and it is a good time to head indoors?[12]

After all, not all is lost. Before they left the garden, Morus suggested postponing the discussion for another day, hopefully sooner rather than later. He has also muttered to us that, whilst not agreeing with everything that Hythloday said, he wishes that 'many features' could be adopted in 'our own cities', namely in England, but he doubts that they will be (More 2020: 170). We might therefore have the lingering feeling that at least nothing has been written off quite yet, that there seems to be agreement that the issues merit further deliberation. The garden might still be a befittingly promising place to return to and as such fulfil Ian Buchanan's definition of utopia's form: 'by virtue of being not yet', Utopia 'takes the form of a promise, or better a promising-machine' (Buchanan 1998: 22–23).

Of course, the story does not begin in the garden. It began in Bruges: there is a diplomatic and trading crisis, 'over matters that were far from trifling', between Spain and England (More 2020: 27). As ever when it is a question of alliances and power politics, this situation needs resolving as it could escalate into armed conflict. If one wants a topos, one can imagine the impressive building and attendant ceremonial trappings that shaped and coloured their meeting; doubtless, they had sumptuous meals in a banqueting hall to facilitate the digestion of the difficult issues that had to be worked through. These negotiations have been suspended, hopefully momentarily, so that representatives of the Spanish prince can go to Brussels to consult with him. There seems no particular reason for concern. Talks have not exactly broken down. One assumes that there is mutual respect. At least as far as Morus is concerned, they are all 'men of high standing' (27). He praises in particular the head of the Spanish delegation, Georges de Themsecke, for his eloquence, skill, talent, and long experience. So, although agreement has not as yet been successfully reached, overall it seems to have gone well enough, so far. Apparently not feeling especially anxious, Morus consequently takes time away from business, evading or interrupting the established order: the exiting from being which is the precondition for the utopian conversion (Abensour 2013: 27, 275).[13] For the time being, then, Morus is at leisure. He heads to Antwerp where his friend Giles resides. The friends happen to meet when Morus leaves the Gothic cathedral Notre-Dame. Here, in front of Notre-Dame, we will have to pause.

The figure of the Gothic cathedral resonates too loudly within utopian thought not to be remarked upon. My convoluted sentence with its 'not to be remarked upon' attempts

---

[12] The fading light at the end of More's text compares weakly with more spectacular, energetic moments of utopian eruption evoked elsewhere, e.g. Marin's 'flash of lightning' (1973: 21), Jameson's 'fireworks dissolving back into the night sky' (1977: 21; 2005: 94, referring to Adorno). 'Fading light' also fails to capture the 'overshooting' qualities of fireworks and lightning. Marcuse (1964: xi) defines 'transcend' and 'transcendence' as 'tendencies in theory and practice which in a given society "overshoot" the established universe of discourse and action towards its historical alternatives (real possibilities)'. To tap into such 'overshooting' aspects of More's text, due attention must be paid to its convoluted complexities which extend into the labyrinthine paratexts and commentaries it has propagated.

[13] For the idea of conversion in Utopia, see Zurcher in this volume.

to recognize the importance of litotes (affirmative statements using ostensibly negative constructions) in More's text. Dominic Baker-Smith (following Elizabeth McCutcheon) notes that there are 140 of them in the Latin text (including the opening statement of Book One that Henry VIII's differences with Charles V were of 'no slight importance' (*non exigui momenti*)).[14] Litotes are a means of 'pointing up tensions and contrasts which makes us pause, and equally to avoid blunt assertions' (Baker-Smith 2014a: 499). Pausing, interrupting a narrative, is politically important as it gives us critical distance, time to reflect and reorientate ourselves: another interstice, like the gap between Books One and Two, making space for *Denkraum*.

The cathedral is identified by Bloch as a residual 'guiding space' for architecture (Bloch 1995: 733). To take a few examples from utopian texts: for William Morris, it is 'a harmonious co-operative work of art', 'organic', built by the 'gildsmen of the Free Cities' (Morris 2004: 331, 337, 339); for Bloch, it symbolizes 'buoyancy and jubilation', the 'attempted construction of the depictiveness of a perfect space [...] of the organic excelsior with tree of life and community' (Bloch 1995: 724, 726). The Gothic cathedral was similarly important for German Expressionist architects in the early twentieth century. The architect Bruno Taut (1880–1938) proclaimed that 'The Gothic cathedral encompassed all artists, who, suffused with wonderful unity, found in the architectural structure of the cathedral a resounding collective rhythm' (cited in Washton Long 2013: 123).

More's lively and appealing sixteenth-century cathedral scene—the congregation dispersed into little groups across the square, conversing, occasional passers-by joining in—exemplifies what Geddes calls 'the city's pageant' (an integral aspect of its 'drama in time' mentioned above), something he deemed very important to reconstruct as part of the 'synoptic' vision needed to build eutopian garden cities: 'to assure such utopias we have to know our ground' (Geddes 1995/2012: 282, 320, 362). It is here, in front of the cathedral, where Morus is almost fortuitously introduced to Hythloday, who had already struck his eye and whom he rightly surmises is a well-travelled sailor. We can imagine the encounter in its shaped context. The fictional text stages many such architectural scenes (often unacknowledged by commentators, as is evident in the epigraph taken from Rouillard and the critical neglect of architectural spaces outside Book Two). In fact, we almost run the risk of being overwhelmed by images, our 'neediness' for images producing a situation where we are crowded out by them and totally absorbed by the details they represent.

This 'risk of being caught up in the given content' is especially prevalent when teaching utopian studies, as it is details which often intrigue and engage us (Moylan 1998: 2). Take the distracting detail found in Giles's paratextual letter to Jerome Busleyden which both corroborates Morus' retelling of Hythloday's tale and undermines it: according to Giles, the discussion about Utopia carried on over dinner and others were present. We know that servants were there as one whispered in Morus' ear at the crucial moment when the location of Utopia was named. But servants would not be seated, and there was at

---

[14] Cf. Zurcher in this volume.

least one other person at the table, party to the conversation: 'one of the company' with a bad cold, maybe caught on shipboard, so perhaps an acquaintance of Hythloday (More 2020: 20). There is overt, even excessive, textual playfulness, raising the annoying suspicion that we are being distracted by details—details that elude us to boot—from the major issues that came to light back in that garden.[15] This tactic might just mean that we become all the more determined to return to them as we maybe do not like being fobbed off in this way, but we also hopefully begin to see the political stakes at play in this text (albeit 'through a glass darkly').

But let us step back. We are not yet at the dinner table. Let us consequently proceed from the cathedral to the garden of Morus' temporary lodgings. It would be easy to visualize the type of house in Antwerp at that time: it is surely quite grand and comfortable as befits his status, but he is not entirely at home there; he has temporarily set up shop, as it were. It is here that he gets to know Hythloday first-hand, once they are all seated on a bench that is strangely covered by a layer of turf. This landscaping detail is also conspicuous: a bit like 'the most handsome and frequented church in Antwerp', but more disconcerting. It pokes through the modest description from outside, as if the author cannot resist registering his own predilection for a particular form of garden furniture. It complements what Baker-Smith aptly describes as a 'leaking' effect of the paratexts, whereby the fiction leaves its own world and 'appears to engage the real one, rather like those pictures in which a limb or a garment protrudes over the frame' (Baker-Smith 2014a: 492). It necessitates another break.

I find not only the turf strange: I am also unsettled by the seating of three people on one bench. Is Hythloday in the middle? In which case, Morus and Giles are obliged to position themselves obliquely, twisting their bodies to see and converse with him. It is certainly an informal, even intimate, arrangement as they might have to squeeze themselves to all fit (and Morus and Hythloday have only just met), but it hardly suggests a comfortable arrangement, although the woodcut from Johann Froben's 1518 Latin editions (Fig. 37.1) allays some of my worries as it depicts an L-shaped or curved bench. Despite my apparent frivolity, this scene raises an important issue. The organization of space is crucial when it comes to political debate, making or breaking chances for a positive outcome. Peace workers know the importance of creating safe but 'open', comfortable, and warm spaces for giving the time needed to discuss difficult and sometimes traumatic issues (Lederach 2005). War, conflict, suffering is the background to More's text: the *why* which necessitates what could be considered the central concern of the text, namely *how* to construct a different (better) society. What sort of space needs to be created for people to feel safe and/or at home? More's Utopians are apparently 'everywhere at home'; wherever they go they are 'warmly received' (More 2020: 98). By contrast Hythloday, who is more in our world, wanders restlessly. He cannot find peace. It is surmised by some that he did return home at one point but 'found the habits of his countrymen intolerable' (20). The text can be understood at this level of 'architectural'

---

[15] For potential distracting details, cf. Zurcher in this volume on 'miscellaneity'.

FIG. 37.1. Ambrosius Holbein, woodcut of the garden scene, in Thomas More, *De optimo reip. Statu, deque nova insula utopia* (Basel: Johann Froben, November-December 1518), The Bodleian Libraries, University of Oxford, Wood 639, p. 25.

intervention: as a debate about what spatial arrangements would need to be in place, given a space, so that that better world, hopefully radically different from this one, where people can feel at home and live peacefully together, becomes possible.

We resume the narrative. All three are seated, one hopes more or less comfortably. Hythloday, the restless traveller, who could be a kinsman of Ulysses, having accepted Morus' offer of hospitality, has also (like Morus and Giles) taken time out of his activities to recount his experiences.[16] We have already noted the importance of 'taking time' ('evading') as well as 'making space' (Dikeç et al. 2009). The garden is the space which offers this *epoché*, or produces a suspension of judgement. The adjacent house permitted easy serving of the welcoming lunch, which must have greatly contributed to a shared sense of well-being before the narration began and, as we know already, the supper served later helps round off the storytelling in a non-conflictual way by diverting attention away from the possibly contentious discussion. It is the garden that makes such discussion possible by giving it a place, but we would in turn have to stay there for longer, or return on another occasion, for any resolutions to be reached.

The garden thus gives a place for initial discussion, a place that is denied in the court, the real locus of political power and where a form of violence dominates and distorts relations. This important point requires further consolidation. I suggest turning to Abensour's writing on 'compacity' in totalitarian architecture that creates a 'mass society' and thereby suppresses politics (Abensour 1997: 50–53, drawing on Arendt). Compact buildings are to be contrasted with more 'porous' architectural forms, such as those Benjamin celebrates in Naples. He writes: 'buildings and actions interpenetrate in the courtyards, arcades and stairways. In everything, they preserve the scope [*Spielraum*, playspace] to become the theatre of new, unforeseen constellations' (Benjamin 2004: 416). We will remember that the houses of More's Utopians have swinging doors ('that yield to a touch of the hand'), opening 'both onto the street and into the garden', thereby permitting 'anyone to enter' (More 2020: 81). The architecture lends itself propitiously to agreeable sociable encounters. By contrast, the exchanges possible at court are far from fluid. Morus duly states: 'In a discussion among friends this sort of academic philosophy isn't without its appeal, but in the councils of princes where major issues are debated with great authority, it's quite out of place' (65). Hythloday's response is unreservedly corroborative: 'Exactly my point [...] philosophy has no place among princes'.

The problem is that the debate 'among friends' has no political force in the real world as it is constructed, and the more pragmatic 'indirect' or 'oblique' approach (*ductus obliquus*) advocated by Morus is unacceptable to Hythloday as we have already noted (More 2020: 66; cf. Abensour 2000: 47–48, 69–71). Morus' advised diplomacy is for Hythloday a compromising form of dissimulation, bordering on lying, reneging on the responsibility to express clearly what one thinks is right and wrong. Commenting on Hythloday's bleak description of political discussions in the institutions of power, Baker-Smith writes:

> How can idealism intrude on scenes like these? The effect is to give a wholly new turn to the old debate about action and retirement, *negotium* and *otium*: given the power of custom to construct the moral imagination (a point More returns to several times) and given that society is founded on custom, how can you introduce alternative values into such a closed system? (Baker-Smith 2014a: 499)

---

[16] For analyses of hospitality see Schérer 1993, 2004; Derrida 1997, 2001.

Again, this is, or rather should be, a central debate in architectural theory and praxis: 'how to introduce alternative values into a closed system?' Coleman convincingly suggests that even 'great architects'—such as Santiago Calatrava and Daniel Libeskind—can be 'fully ensnared within the logic of late capitalism' and consequentially be branded, meaning that their architectural oeuvres are turned into prized commodities, akin to the Louis Vuitton bag, recognizable by its signatured design (Coleman 2013: 149; 153). Be that as it may, rather than seeing the 'oblique approach' as unavoidable compromise with a given system that ultimately recuperates and defuses the force of alternatives, is it at all possible to radically reformulate our understanding of its potentiality so that it can destabilize conventional forms of thinking and doing? Such attempts were made by Claude Parent and Paul Virilio. In their collaborative projects in the 1960s—for example their church, Sainte-Bernadette du Banlay, Nevers (1963–6)—they highlighted the critical function of the oblique in architecture, often employing 'utopian' vocabulary. Parent intriguingly and inspiringly proclaimed that 'the oblique function has a past [...] imagine in the past this archaeology of the future [...] ONE MUST READ THE PAST AS A FUTURE TO DISCOVER' (Parent 2004: 5). In Parent's (and Virilio's) radically oblique analysis of temporality, the past—often taken to be a firm ground under our feet on which we are to continue to build more or less traditionally, i.e. according to what Baker-Smith calls 'custom'—erupts into as yet-to-be-explored potentiality. We are shaken in our assumptions and obliged not to conform as we no longer quite know where we stand. As Parent (2004: 47) says: 'The oblique function is the ARCHITECTURE OF EFFORT that wakes up and catalyses the human. It is the opposite of the enervating comfort that puts him to sleep and leads his mind to its death.'[17]

Parent and Virilio were surely right to insist that we need to wake up from such lethargy, otherwise we remain trapped, imprisoned, enclosed in an ideological system (Jameson 2004; Abensour 2000: 113–114, discussing Benjamin). Certainly, lethargy seems alien to More's Utopians, who are always on the move, busy learning, keenly alert to the pleasures of sound, sight, and smell, and the shape and loveliness of the universe. No wonder they sleep a sound eight hours (More 2020: 85, 110, 119). The significance of the sleeping–waking balance to Utopian thought—from More through Bellamy and Morris to contemporary thinkers such as Abensour and Harvey—gives us a lively sense of the cultural resonance of More's text through time. Given our 24/7 'culture', that keeps us on an often unproductive standby, the vision of a Golden Age arriving when we may finally hope 'to say good-bye to fear, tension, anxiety, overwork and sleepless nights' seems particularly appealing (Harvey 2000: 281; cf. Crary 2014).

Hence a good night's sleep followed by vigorous waking-up is needed for 'custom', or what we could also call 'ideological closure', to be disrupted so that the lively forms of utopian practice can take place. Utopianism is about creating such a 'space', but how? What sort of 'space' can and should be built and how would it engage in

---

[17] For a discussion of various 'architectural' attempts (including Parent's and Virilio's) to convert a closed-down, defensive 'bunker mentality', see D. Morgan 2015.

'praxis', that is, actually engage with this world? Again, what could be a more fundamental, 'grounded' question and, we might think, *grounding* question, in the sense of generating an impotent sense of not knowing 'how'? These are impossible questions to answer. When asked to comment on possible critique of the architectural system, Abensour point-blank responded: 'I will not be engaged in answering the difficult and real question about the relations between utopia and architecture' (Abensour 2013: 266). Such questions should nevertheless be asked. Having now done so, we will hastily retreat to the garden!

The garden scene is divided up into several episodes. I suggest the following breakdown: (1) the arrival in the garden (from the cathedral); (2) the sitting-down and initial discussion which reveals fundamental differences of opinion (including the so-called 'Debate of Counsel'); (3) the exiting of the garden and entry into the house (the break for lunch); (4) the return from lunch and, not the resumption of the previous discussion, but Hythloday's account of Utopia; (5) finally, the exiting of the garden for supper. It is almost not the same garden before and after lunch. It no longer hosts discussion. We have Hythloday's monologue; the others just listen. When Hythloday has finished, Giles says nothing and Morus does not care, or dare, to express his reservations. Instead, he hospitably, as well as diplomatically, escorts his guest into the house 'having praised [the Utopians'] way of life and [Hythloday's] exposition' (More 2020: 170). Morus also suggests they organize another occasion for proper discussion, intimating that Morus intended finding other conversational topics for the evening meal, although this transpires not to be the case, as revealed by Giles's letter to Busleyden (20), discussed above.

So what did the garden become in episode 4? This episode in fact comprises four parts, stretched out over both books: (4a) the return from lunch and getting settled (on that turf-covered bench); (4b) the putting into place of a state of attentive anticipation, what we can identify as a 'moment'; (4c) Hythloday's monologue; (4d) the polite after-remarks and Morus' private mutterings (addressed to us). What is happening in and to time and space in the isolated 'moment' (4b)—when, at the end of Book One, Hythloday 'sat silent and thoughtful a moment' (More 1992b: 30)[18]—before starting his monologue (Book Two)? For Marin this precise 'moment', just before Hythloday begins to speak, is 'an intensity-sign', an 'exiting out of the series'; we have duly located in the narrative the sequence of micro-details leading up to this extraordinary 'event' that 'presents' itself as a rupture from what has gone before (Marin 1984: xxiv). Suspended in time and space, this 'moment' cannot be entirely catered for and predicted: it is an 'instance of pure difference', creating a 'scene' (xxiv). It is a strange sort of 'scene' as we have left 'actors' behind and, even if we are still supposed to be in the garden, it has become irrelevant, a 'place outside place [*un lieu hors lieu*]' (Marin 1973: 20). This 'scene' is the wherein and whereby the very 'instant of pure difference' emerges which marks and registers

---

[18] Here I follow Adams's translation as he explicitly uses the word 'moment'; it features in Baker-Smith's translation, but implicitly: 'he sat briefly in silent thought and then began as follows'.

(here Marin refers to Bloch): 'the signal of the imminence of a fracture, an imminence which is immanence. It is present, but of an already arrived future' (Marin 1984: xxiv). It is a 'moment' seemingly promising potentially momentous effects. But Marin suggests that its significance comes before what is said. It does not even rely on the substance of Hythloday's ensuing account of the Utopians in (4c), or on the personality and credentials of the speaker. Marin writes, regarding this moment, that it is 'no matter what he says or how surprising is More's description of him' (xxiv). This 'moment' is an 'unsettling wound' in the text, that the text subsequently must do its best to account for, by 'covering' it, maybe so that we as readers do not lose our sense of bearings altogether. Following on from this moment, possibly anything could happen, or not. Our grounded sense of 'permanence', of being situated in a here-and-now that can be represented, has fallen away.

Of course, we should, in a chapter on 'Utopia and Architecture', leave the phantasmatic, 'schematic' garden and head into Book Two to track Hythloday's 'architectural' description of Utopia and the active life of its happy citizens. Once that was fully accounted for, we then should go back to Book One to compare what we have seen in Utopia with the desolate landscape of Tudor England, with its monstrous sheep who devour humans, pillage and destroy houses, cities, fields, and occupy churches, and the equally insatiable gluttonous rich in their luxurious palaces isolated in an apocalyptic wasteland across which we can detect roaming figures in desperate search for shelter, and perceive others raucously inebriating and obscenely gorging themselves in taverns, frenetically fornicating in brothels (More 2020: 42–44). Nevertheless, it seems to me more important to hold on to this empty, yet pregnant, 'moment'. We should not forget this hiatus that presents itself as a straining of our imagination and is so full of promise. It is the 'promise' behind the promise mentioned at the end of Book One (74). It is the precondition for change; it cannot be completely catered for, though some architectural arrangements can be put in place so that it is not pre-empted from the start. Twenty years ago, Jameson described the utopian moment as follows:

> We need, then, to posit a peculiar suspension of the political [...] it is this suspension, this separation of the political—in all its unchangeable immobility—from daily life and even from the lived and the existential, this externality that serves as the calm before the storm, the stillness the centre of the hurricane; and that allows us to take hitherto unimaginable mental liberties with structures whose actual modification or abolition scarcely seem on the cards. (Jameson 2004)

These COVID-induced times hardly feel 'calm' or 'still', despite the weight of immobility, and we would certainly be hard-pressed to compare them to the extra-temporal 'revolutionary festival' of 1968 as described by Marin (1973: 15). Yet is there maybe nevertheless something akin to the 'utopian political process' described by Jameson that we could identify: 'The reduction of all of us to that psychic gap or lack in which we all as subjects consist, but that we all expend a good deal of energy on trying to conceal from ourselves' (Jameson 2004). Whilst I am ill at ease with Jameson's universalizing 'we' here[19]—especially as I am about to latch on to it opportunistically for my final sentence (I imagine that many people live 'reduction' every day and feel 'ideological closure' most acutely)—is there any way that our current situation might be turned into a moment 'portentous of great changes' (Bellamy, cited in Harvey 2000: 281)? The 'moment' for radically rethinking and restructuring the world we have built for ourselves?

---

[19] Utopians, though they might be deemed a statistical, anonymous population, have no word for the supposedly universalizing 'man in general' (More 2020: 107).

CHAPTER 38

MAPPING UTOPIA

ALFRED HIATT

To map Utopia is arguably to fall into the same trap as the zealous theologian who, according to Thomas More's prefatory letter to Peter Giles, was so taken with news of the island that he wished to become its bishop (More 1995: 34). To give visual form to a 'no-place' (*ou-topos*) is to reduce it to the plane of realism, thereby distorting its joke, and traducing its purpose. In spatial and temporal terms, Utopia is on the threshold of Old and New Worlds, ancient, modern, and future all at once. In this state of optimal non-existence, it both invites and repels maps.

Maps, in truth, do not abound in the many editions of *Utopia*, and their relative paucity may well indicate a reluctance on the part of editors, map-makers, and other savants to over-literalize More's island.[1] There is, nevertheless, a long tradition of utopic mapping, of which the map of (More's) Utopia is only one, admittedly rather particular, example. While this contribution will primarily consider cartographic responses to More's text, the broader context should not be forgotten. For while More's *Utopia* is a remarkable product of early sixteenth-century humanism, it did not arise ex nihilo, and it bears notable affinities with earlier forms of utopic thought, as well as marked differences from them.

Two staples of medieval spatial representation, both undoubtedly known by More, are particularly important to consider in relation to Utopia. The earthly paradise was a consistent presence on medieval world maps from as early as the eighth century, generally appearing at the easternmost end of Asia, usually with some indication that it was no longer accessible to mortals (Scafi 2006). Like the location of Utopia, then, the Garden of Eden was a place that could be conjectured but never conclusively known. Much the same can be said of the *terra incognita* represented by the classical and medieval idea of the antipodes. The world map in Macrobius' fifth-century commentary on Cicero's *Dream of Scipio*, an image widely copied throughout the Middle Ages, shows not only the world of Europe, Africa, and Asia known to classical antiquity, but also

---

[1] But see Schmidt in this volume for maps in German translations and spin-offs.

unknown land in the southern hemisphere, part of which was thought to be inhabited by unknown (and unknowable) antipodal peoples (Macrobius 2001–3: 2.5–9; Hiatt 2008: 213–215). The clues given by Raphael Hythloday indicate that it is precisely in such a part of the world that Utopia is to be found (though, as More notes in his prefatory letter to Giles, Hythloday did not reveal its precise location there): the island is beneath the equator, in a temperate region conducive to cultural and technological attainment (More 1995: 34, 46–48). In addition to the earthly paradise and the temperate zone of the antipodeans, a further medieval model for Utopia was that of the monastery. The structure of Utopian society is, as has often been noted, deeply indebted to monastic practices, and the Utopians themselves are said to be impressed by monasticism (More 1995: 220). Only rare examples survive of medieval plans of monastic buildings, and for the most part these are utilitarian in nature (Skelton and Harvey 1986: 43–58, 141–146, 221–228; Fermon 2013: 582–584). However, an exception would appear to be the remarkable cloister plan of St Gall (Switzerland). Dated to 816–37, this image shows the abbey church and its precincts, including dormitories, scriptorium, refectory, infirmary, cemetery, gardens, and lodging for visiting monks. It seems not to have been a drawing of the actual buildings of the monastery, but something closer to a plan of an ideal monastic institution: self-contained, self-sustaining and, in its way, insular (Horn and Born 1979).

More, then, was not the first to conceive of a non-place in relation to real and known places (Lochrie 2016). But his distinctive combination of classical and medieval utopianism—crowned by his coinage of a term to describe the discourse, and framed by the context of early sixteenth-century New World exploration—marked a decisive departure from earlier traditions. Characteristically, More was both precise and vague in his description of the island's location and its topography. According to the account delivered by Hythloday in Book Two, Utopia has a central span of 200 miles across, tapering towards ends just 11 miles apart, with the result that the island has the form of a crescent, 'like a new moon'. The 'horns' (*cornua*) of the crescent form a bay, protected from the elements, making the inner coast 'one great harbour' (More 1995: 108–109). In the middle of the bay a large rock, surmounted by a garrisoned tower, rises above the water. One model for Utopia's harbour is likely to be the description of Brundisium (Brindisi) in the Roman poet Lucan's first-century *Civil War*. In this well-known and frequently illustrated passage of Lucan's poem (Gautier Dalché 2003), the land is said to form two 'horns', with which it encloses the waters of the Adriatic, and here too an island at the entrance to the harbour resists wind and waves, ensuring calm waters within (Lucan 1997: 2.610–627). In the *Civil War*, Brundisium serves as a synechdoche for Italy, and briefly as a refuge for Pompey the Great, who only narrowly escapes the clutches of the pursuing Julius Caesar by means of pre-dawn flight. None of these associations seems directly relevant to More's island, except that the figure of Caesar, a relentless breaker of natural order who attempts to block his enemy's escape by a massive landfill operation outside the harbour (Lucan 1997: 2.650–679), offers a parallel to Utopus, the founding father of Utopia.

For we learn that the island was not always an island. It was once the land of Abraxa, until the conqueror Utopus not only renamed the region after himself but also sundered it from the mainland by constructing a channel 15 miles wide (More 1995: 110). Having established the origin of its insularity, as well as its basic outline, Hythloday gives some details of Utopia's cities. There are fifty-four *civitates*, each 'identical in language, customs, institutions and laws' (*lingua, moribus, institutis, legibus prorsus eisdem*) and each built on the same plan, at a minimum of 24 miles apart (112–113). The only city to be named is the capital, Amaurot (variously translated as 'Ghost City', 'Shadow City', or even 'Mirage'), which lies 'in the middle of the island' (*in umbilico terrae*), and is the site of the island's annual assembly (*senatus*) (112–113). Almost square in shape, it sits on the river Anydros ('waterless'); a stone bridge across the river is placed at the most inland side, making the city accessible to ships. The city is walled, and internally divided into wards (*vici*). Its streets are 20 feet wide, and its houses three storeys high and flat-roofed, in rows with gardens behind (114–120). The Anydros—the only river to be given a name—rises from a spring a distance of 80 miles above Amaurot and, after absorbing tributaries, extends to a width of half a mile at the capital, before travelling a further 60 miles until it reaches the sea (116). Further information about the layout of cities emerges in the course of Hythloday's commentary. Each city is divided into four equal districts, in the middle of which is a market; each ward contains a hall, to which thirty families are assigned; there are four hospitals in each city, outside the walls; each city has a perimeter of at least 12 miles of farmland, extending in every direction (12, 136–138). Hythloday also mentions Utopian colonies on the mainland, set up to receive surplus population from the island, as well as neighbouring peoples with whom the Utopians interact: the Achorians ('No-Placers') to the south-east of Utopia; the more distant Anemolians ('Windy People'); the Macarenses ('Happy Ones') who live 'not far' from Utopia; the Zapoletes ('Busy Sellers'), a rough people living 500 miles east of Utopia who are useful as mercenaries; the Alaopolitans ('People of No Country'), and the Nephelogetes ('Cloud People') (84, 150–152, 94, 208–210, 202). Anyone interested in giving visual form to More's Utopia would find, in short, a clear sense of the island's shape and its distance from the mainland, as well as significant detail regarding its capital and a major river. Conversely, the potential map-maker would have to operate with a dearth of toponyms, and with no clarity regarding the distribution of the island's other cities, other than that there are fifty-three of them, no less than 24 miles apart, only occasionally appearing on the outer coast.

The earliest cartographic representations of Utopia are accordingly rather basic affairs, their authors apparently reluctant to supplement Hythloday's description with much further detail. Among the paratextual material that appeared in the first edition of 1516 was a woodcut map (Fig. 9.1). This image attempts to represent the 'crescent' of the island, separated from a seemingly populous continent by a brief channel. The most prominent feature of the interior is the Anydros river, whose course—from source (*fons Anydri*) to river mouth (*Ostium anydri*)—spans nearly the entire island. It encloses Amaurot (*civitas Amaurotum*), which dominates the centre of the island. Eight architectural vignettes represent other, unnamed cities on the island, while a rock with a tower protects the entrance to the bay formed by Utopia's 'horns', which is being rounded by two ships. Two years later, a revised version of the image appeared in the third edition of

Utopia (Fig. 5.1). On the 1518 map, which is attributed to Ambrosius Holbein, Anydros and Amaurot—the latter now an *urbs* (walled town or city) rather than a *civitas* (community of citizens)—retain their dominant position, with no further toponyms added. However, the position of the ships has been reversed, and crucially three figures now appear in the foreground of the image. One of these, who gestures towards the island, is labelled 'Hythlodaeus'. His companion is, presumably, Morus; the third figure, standing at some distance, may represent Giles, or perhaps More's servant, John Clement (who is recorded as being present at the conversation with Hythloday). This image has been interpreted as a 'memento mori', given the island's resemblance to a skull, with the ships now acting as a rictus (M. Bishop 2005). Emblematic rather than illustrative, like the 1516 map it explicates little of the text, instead acting as a point of entry and visual prompt to the account that follows it (McClung 1994; Gury 1974; Goodey 1970; Bony 1977; Padrón 2007). The figures in the foreground of the 1518 map serve the additional function of forming a bridge between the two books of *Utopia*, between the garden bench in Antwerp and the southern-hemisphere island described by Hythloday.

Subsequent editions of *Utopia* made little attempt to elaborate the cartographic response to the text any further. While the Leiden edition of 1715 eventually supplied aspects of Hythloday's description with a series of illustrations, including an engraving showing the bay of Utopia, only one later edition, Gregor Wintermonat's German translation of 1612, supplied a new map (Fig. 11.2; McClung 1994: 14–17).[2] This too was a relatively basic response to the text. Headed 'Utopia', it contains the single toponym 'Amaurotum' above a large, central city on a prominent but unmarked river. Thirty-four cities are marked at fairly regular intervals but, consistent with More's text, they remain unnamed. As in the 1516 and 1518 maps, a large rock with a tower protects the harbour, and the coastline of a nearby continent is visible. The map appears in preliminary matter after an engraving of More and immediately prior to the start of Book One, once again offering itself as a visual preface to the text, rather than a point of reference or commentary. The outstanding cartographic responses to Utopia were not, it transpires, destined to appear in editions of the text, but in independent productions roughly 400 years apart: at the end of the sixteenth century, and at the beginning of the twenty-first.

The 'Utopiae typus' of Abraham Ortelius

At the beginning of August 1595, the imperial counsellor and recently ennobled humanist Johannes Matthäus Wacker à Wackenfels wrote to his friend Jacob Monau to outline the contents of a map of Utopia forthcoming from the hands of the master cartographer Abraham Ortelius (Hessels 1887: 657–659 (no. 274)). In the letter, Wacker

---

[2] For Wintermonat's translation, see Schmidt in this volume.

claims to be the author (*auctor*) of the map, and he takes the opportunity to baptize it by supplying a list of toponyms. These place names, Wacker explained, followed a clear scheme, and were designed to serve a particular purpose:

> So I am sending you a list of the names of fifty-four of their towns, which it pleased me to establish in the following way: five are towns of Utopian lineage or conception [*oppida Utopianae originis sive notionis*]; five of ancient Greek; five each of Latin, German, Italian, French, Spanish, Belgic, Sarmatian, and Saracenic. By this means any nation [*gens*] may recognize something of itself in this Utopia. Because these towns [must] exceed the number 50 by four, I distributed the remaining names among friends: one town I named after you, one after Ortelius, one after my own name. The fourth I suppose will be taken up by the metropolis of Amaurotus. (Hessels 1887: 658 (no. 274); my translation)[3]

Wacker goes on to state that he has followed the same principle in devising names of rivers 'if our maker [Ortelius] perhaps wants to use them for irrigating the cities' ('si ijs uti forsan ad urbes irrigandas, Plastes noster vellet'). The list of Wacker's cities and rivers, contained in a *tabella* (a separate list, or perhaps a diagram) that originally accompanied the letter, no longer survives, but it is evident that it was used faithfully by Ortelius in the map he produced the following year (Fig. 38.1). By 23 March 1596, when Ortelius wrote from Antwerp to his nephew Jacob Cool in London, the map was nearly finished. Ortelius took the opportunity of his letter to Cool to confirm the opinion of William Camden (apparently conveyed to him by Cool) that he had made the map for friends including Monau and that he had done so unwillingly, adding that a further complication had been caused by the demand of the humanist Johannes Baptista Favolía to have his name added to those already on the island: 'I see he has not yet had enough of this kind of joke' ('Video eum nondum satiatum solitis nugis') (Hessels 1887: 680 (no. 286); my translation). The map had certainly been completed by October 1596, when Cool reported receipt of twelve copies of it, along with the same number of copies of Ortelius' map of ancient Germany (Hessels 1887: 696 (no. 294)). Thereafter the map of Utopia made by Ortelius seems for the most part to have disappeared from view, until a single copy resurfaced in 1981, when it was bought in London by a private collector (Kruyfhooft 1981; van den Broecke 2004). This map conforms to the scheme announced by Wacker, and shows that Ortelius did indeed add the name of 'Favolia' to the image, bringing the number of cities on the island up to fifty-five.

The apparently disparaging references to the map made by Ortelius have encouraged scholars to see the map of Utopia as a misstep almost instantly regretted, and perhaps even suppressed, by its creator (Kruyfhooft 1981; Karrow 1993: 25; Meurer 1998: 151; van den Broecke 2011: 684–687 (no. 234); Kruyfhooft 2016). Closer inspection of the surviving correspondence surrounding the map, as well as the artefact itself, suggests

---

[3] The complete text of the letter, both in the original Latin and in translation, appears in Appendix 38.2.

FIG. 38.1. Abraham Ortelius, 'Utopiae typus' (Antwerp, 1596), Coll. Charles Vreeken Fund, King Baudouin Foundation, entrusted to the Plantin-Moretus Museum, Antwerp, © Michel Wuyts & Bart Huysmans.

a more complex situation (Depuydt 2019). In the first place, there is every reason to see Wacker and Monau—and perhaps the former particularly—as the driving forces behind the map. Both the idea for the map and its content seem to have been almost entirely theirs. Secondly, it is now clear that, as well as the consignment sent to Cool in London, Ortelius sent copies of the map to his friends, including the Leiden humanist Bonaventura Vulcanius (Depuydt 2019: 244–245). The map apparently circulated independently of Ortelius' monumental *Theatrum Orbis Terrarum*, and its appendix of historical maps, the *Parergon*. Most intriguingly, one nineteenth-century witness, the Leipzig scholar Johannes Poeschel, states that he had found Ortelius' map enclosed within the 1518 Basel edition of More's *Utopia* that he was using, though it is unclear when this insertion had taken place (Poeschel 1878: 425; Depuydt 2019: 245). All in all, then, even if Ortelius' distancing remarks are taken seriously (the possibility of a kind of modesty topos cannot be ruled out), for its early modern and later readers the map clearly constituted a significant, if appropriately ludic, response to More's text.

The title of this 'Utopiae typus' explicitly acknowledges its debt to More, as well as the layers of narrative involved in its construction: it is produced 'from the narration of Raphael Hythloday, from the description of Thomas More, from the delineation of Abraham Ortelius' ('Utopiae typus, ex Narratione Raphaelis Hythlodaei, Descriptione D. Thomae Mori, Delineatione Abrahami Ortelij'). A cartouche in the lower left of the image records Ortelius' dedication of the map to Wacker, and the latter's presence is further reinforced by the appearance of a poem written by him, and offered 'to the viewer':

> Behold before you the delights of the earth: behold blessed realms!
> The world has nothing better or more beautiful.
> This is Utopia: citadel of peace; nest of Love,
> Justice, and harbour and shore of the supreme good.
> Praise other lands; revere this one, you who know it.
> The blessed life is secured in this place, or nowhere.
> I[oannes] M[attheus] [Wacker] à W[acken].f[els].[4]

The shape of the island, which is oriented to the south, remains faithful to More's description. On its southern coast, the land tapers into 'horns', thereby forming a bay, with the rock and tower at its centre not forgotten. More than previous cartographers, Ortelius has observed the narrowness of the channel cut by Utopus, with four ethnonyms—Zapoleti, Achorii, Anemolii, and Macarenses—deployed to mark an otherwise empty continent to the island's south. On the interior, however, significant supplementation of the text has taken place as a result of Wacker's toponyms. 'Amaurotus metropolis' occupies a central position, its stone bridge over the 'Anydrus fluvius' clearly marked. But on to the central stem of capital city and river a fully developed topography has been grafted. Wacker's place names not only fill the island, they have the effect of subdividing it into regions. For—whether following instruction by Wacker, or according to his own judgement—Ortelius grouped the names of cities and rivers by language. Thus, moving clockwise from the island's north-western segment, it is possible to discern the following sequence of regions: Utopian; Italian; German; Latin; Greek; Spanish; 'Belgic' (i.e. Flemish); 'Sarmatian' (i.e. Polish); and 'Saracenic' (Ottoman Turkish). Each region boasts the names of five cities in its language, along with a similar number of rivers. How serious a point was Wacker, Monau, and/or Ortelius, trying to make with this arrangement, and what is the effect on the viewer?

One might begin by looking again at Wacker's statement in his letter to Monau that the linguistic diversity on the map was intended to allow each *gens* to see something of itself 'in this Utopia'. While perhaps faithful to More's intention, then, the introduction of languages, especially when grouped in segments, operates by very different means, since it reinforces ethnic and linguistic identity. On the other hand, the consistent repetition, in multiple languages, of the negation of place ('Kein stadt', 'nulleville', 'Nusquamia', 'Nonnata', 'Udepolis'; 'sinaqua', 'Senzzaqua', 'Wasserlos', 'Onwaeter', 'Bezwoda', 'Sanseau'

---

[4] 'En tibi delicias mundi: regna ecce beata! | Queis melius, queis nil pulchrius orbis habet. | Haec illa Utopia est; arx pacis; nidus Amoris, | Justitiae, ac summi portus et ora boni. | Lauda alias terras; istanc cole qui sapis. Isto | Vel nulla fixa est Vita beata loco. | I.M.W. à W.f.'

etc.) drives home the central pun of 'utopia', and implies deliberate irony on the part of the map's creators, rather than pious hope. Wacker's choice of languages offers a snapshot of the preoccupations of a late sixteenth-century diplomat (and presumably some fellow feeling with More, by then a venerated martyr in both religious and intellectual terms, lies behind his commission of the map). He presents a mixture of classical and modern European languages, with Greek and Latin present but not accorded priority over vernacular tongues (English, tellingly, is excluded). The three obvious outliers—because either non-European or less widely spoken—are all identified in classicizing terms: 'Belgic', 'Sarmatian', and 'Saracenic'. The presence of Flemish is not surprising, given Ortelius' involvement and the map's publication in Antwerp, while Wacker's embassies to the Polish court (Lindner 1868; Evans 1973: 155; Trunz 1992: 24), and his proximity to Polish speakers in Breslau (at the time linguistically German), makes the choice of 'Sarmatian' readily explicable. The inclusion of 'Saracenic' may be the map's boldest gesture, particularly given the threat of the Ottoman Empire to Christian Europe at the time of the image's composition. Indeed, Wacker concludes his letter to Monau by recording his alarm at news of a Turkish ('Scythian') attack on the region of Podolia in eastern Europe (Hessels 1887: 658–659 (no. 274)). The nature of the 'Saracenic' toponyms included by Wacker has puzzled previous scholars (van den Broecke 2004; Depuydt 2019). Although 'lingua Sarazenica' would normally imply Arabic, the names are in fact Turkish. Their source has recently been identified by Nil Palabiyik as Johannes Leunclavius' *Annales Sultanorum Othmanidarum* ('Annals of the Ottoman Sultans'), published in Frankfurt in 1588, and well known to historians and orientalists, including Joseph Scaliger (Palabiyik 2021). Wacker appears to have used the list of place names that appears at the conclusion of Leunclavius' work to select the toponyms he deemed suitable for the map. Unlike the place names in the other languages, however, the 'Saracenic' toponyms on Ortelius' Utopia are not neologisms steeped in serio-ludic irony, but real places, albeit sometimes open to metaphoric reading ('sublime city', 'twisted castle', 'mirror lake').[5] The presence of these names on the map testifies to the level of interest in Ottoman language and culture felt by humanists such as Wacker, and his willingness to include Turkish words within a utopic scheme is certainly suggestive of an ecumenical impulse at odds with contemporary expressions of hostility towards the Ottoman empire. At the same time, the Turkish names on the map remain a foreign element, emanating not from erudite wordplay but from a recently published historical narrative, and comprising actual toponyms rather than no-places.

Finally, and crucially, the map of languages offered in Ortelius' Utopia crosses the confessional divides that marked late sixteenth-century Europe, in much the same way as the correspondence and maps of erudites such as Ortelius, Wacker, Monau, Camden, and many others (Shalev 2012). Wacker himself spanned the divide: born in Constance, raised in the reformed Lutheran church, he converted to Catholicism in 1592 for reasons that remain obscure, but which may be connected with increased levels

---

[5] See Appendix 38.1 for a full list.

of anti-intellectualism within Protestant circles (Trunz 1992: 24; cf. Lindner 1868: 330–332). By that time in his life, Wacker had moved from one humanist centre to another, starting in Vienna, before finding a flourishing scene, headed by Monau, in Breslau. Shortly after the publication of the map of Utopia, Wacker moved permanently to the court of Rudolf II in Prague, where he became one of the leading intellectuals at court, and where he consolidated his friendship with the astronomer Johannes Kepler (Evans 1973: 156; Trunz 1992: 24–25). The *typus Utopiae* produced by Ortelius may well, then, be seen as a jeu d'esprit on the part of Wacker, and one that—to follow Ortelius—was essentially nugatory. But, if so, it was a trifle emerging from the heart of humanist Europe, and in its multilingual, cross- or non-denominational way, it may have been an attempt to envisage, however briefly, another world and yet the same (to cite the title of Joseph Hall's satirical utopia *Mundus Alter et Idem*, c.1605). A world in which 'each may recognize something of himself', though whether that something amounted to a vision of improvement, or of laughing nihilism, remains open to question.

NOVA UTOPIA: SATIRE AND SPATIAL PLAY AFTER THE AGE OF MORE

The centuries following the publication of More's *Utopia* saw numerous imitations, adaptations, and reworkings of the central idea of an island community living according to norms markedly different to those of western Europe. Two kinds of mapping can be identified within this sprawling literature, increasingly dominated by the strain of Lucianic satire already evident in muted form in *Utopia*. The first type of map, well exemplified by the Protestant bishop Hall's *Mundus Alter et Idem*, was allegorical (J. Hall 1605, 1981). Hall used the sixteenth century's construction of a 'Terra Australis incognita' as the site for an exploration of the conspectus of sins prevalent in Catholic Europe. The maps that accompany *Mundus Alter et Idem* depict the landscape encountered by Hall's narrator, 'Mercurius Britannicus', with its regions of gluttonous Crapulia, female-governed Viraginia (in a play on New Guinea, also known as 'Aphrodysia Nova Gynia'), overpopulated Moronia, and thief-infested Lavernia. Undoubtedly indebted to *Utopia* (*Mundus Alter* begins with a three-way dialogue on the utility of travel), the 'other world' encountered by Mercurius is different in almost every respect to that of its model. The same can be said of the convergence of the notion of utopia with the 'Land of Cockaigne', a mythical land of plenty with strong medieval roots.[6] This connection appears to have been made at some point during the sixteenth century. Certainly, traces of Cockaigne can already be found on the map of Utopia published by Ortelius, in the shape of the towns of 'Cuccagnola' and 'Goliensdorp'. Seventeenth-century maps of Cockaigne—or its German variant 'Schlaraffenland'—such as Johann Baptist Homann's 'Accurata

---

[6] For more on Utopia and Cockaigne, see Hadfield in this volume.

Utopiae Tabula' of 1694, feature regions such as 'Magni Stomachi Imperium' (Empire of the Great Stomach), 'Stultorum Regnum' (Kingdom of Fools), and, as with Hall, 'Terra Sancta Incognita' (Holy Land, Unknown).

The alternative strategy to mapping no-places post-More was realist, depicting the imagined land alongside the emergent spaces of the New World. Thus the early editions of *Gulliver's Travels* included maps showing the positions of Liliput and Blefuscu, Brobdingnag, Laputa, Balnibarbi, Luggnagg and Glubbdubdribb, and finally Houyhnhnms Land, with their dates of discovery ranging from 1699 to 1711, in relation to actual geographical locations, such as the coasts of 'Di[e]mens Land' (the future Tasmania), New Holland (later Australia), North America, and Japan (Swift 1726: vol. 1, plates I, II; vol. 2, plates III, IV). Like More's Utopia, such maps invite the reader into a knowing game, in which the verisimilitude of the no-place is at once admired and rejected. But whereas More wrote at a moment in which the southern hemisphere abounded in conjecture, some new and much old, many reports, and little certainty, by the time of Swift its contours were known in broad detail, even if mega-fictions such as the Great Southern Land lingered in the cartographic imagination (Hiatt 2011).

It remains surprising that More's Utopia only became a site for rejuvenated cartographic invention in the first two decades of the twenty-first century. Had Ortelius' map attained a wider distribution, it may have inspired a more vigorous tradition of maps specifically dedicated to More's description of the island, rather than other versions and interpretations of Utopia. Conceivably, too, the early canonization of the paratext to More's work hindered imaginative responses (T. Cave 2008a). Whatever the reasons, it is revealing that the production of maps of Utopia over the past twenty years has for the most part been the work of professional artists; an exception is Johannes Stoffers's 'Nusquamia', where a Utopia-inspired map serves as a source of academic-philosophical meditation (Stoffers 2001). The idea of mapping, in the sense of a subjective response to the body's interaction with space, has become central to artistic production. A very large number of twentieth- and twenty-first-century artists have used maps of one kind or another in their works, frequently adapting existing images, but on occasion creating their own (Cosgrove 2005; Harmon 2009). This trend makes it entirely understandable that artists should turn to Utopia as the site for renewed examination. Three 'maps of Utopia' produced between 1998 and 2013 serve to show some of the different possibilities available at the meeting point between art, geography, and sometimes mordantly political satire.

The foundation of Satomi Matoba's 'Topographical Map of Utopia' (1998) is a map of the island of Oahu (Hawaii), with the crucial addition of a city map of Hiroshima, grafted on to the northern part of the island. The base map of Oahu, produced by the US Geological Survey in the 1950s, emphasizes the topography of the island, but also its heavy militarization, with military reservations, naval bases, and naval air stations. The map of Hiroshima has been conjoined to the map of Oahu with enough smoothness that it does not at first glance appear to be an intrusion; the road network on both maps appears to connect, and the division between the maps is blurred. However, Hiroshima's 'foreignness' has not been disguised: its colour scheme is different to the rest of the map, and it retains Japanese characters, rather than the English of the Oahu map. As a result of the translation of the Japanese city, Hiroshima and Pearl Harbor appear at opposite ends of the island. The map is clearly a commentary on the intertwined history of the two places, the bombing of one leading ultimately to the bombing, and subsequent American occupation, of the other, a history experienced personally by the artist, who was born in Hiroshima in 1960. Satomi's 'Utopia' is a companion piece to her 'Pearl Harbor/Hiroshima' (1998), in which, using the same maps deployed in the 'Topographical Map of Utopia', the two places are conjoined, with Hiroshima imposed over Waipahu on the north side of Pearl Harbor. Utopia in this representation is a bitterly ironic title, but it also signals the artist's act of creating a no-place, in order to meditate on the twentieth century's legacy of violence and mass destruction. The bright blue of the Pacific reminds that both places are found in the same ocean.

A more direct engagement with More's Utopia can be found in two artworks produced within a year of each other, Qiu Zhijie's 'Map of Utopia' (2012), and Stephen Walter's 'Nova Utopia' (2013). Visually similar and determinedly playful, the two works in fact take significantly different approaches to their subject. Zhijie's map anatomizes More's *Utopia*, identifying its sources and influences, while at the same time pluralizing the concept of utopia by moving across times and cultures (Fig. 38.2). The form of the island in many ways remains faithful to its base description in More's work, but the 'horns' of the island's bay have been wittily rendered as feet, from which a stubby pair of legs leads to a torso, beneath a smaller island which resembles a disembodied head. Zhijie's Utopia is divided into various utopian movements before, during, and after More (Hopfener 2018). At the centre of the torso is Plato's Republic, from which

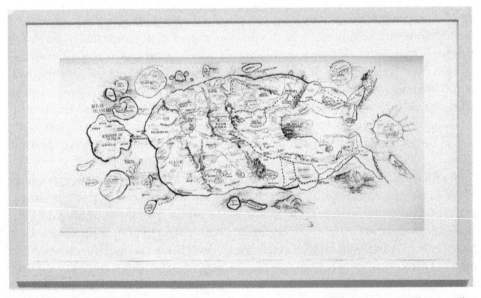

FIG. 38.2. Qiu Zhijie, 'Map of Utopia' (2012). Collection Van Abbemuseum, Findhoven, The Netherlands. Photo: Peter Cox.

a railway line leads to 'Cicero's Respublica' and 'Hegel's State of Nature', and then in two directions: one (left leg) to Marxism, Mao, and World Revolution, the other (right leg) to 'Market', 'Globalization', and 'The End of History'. Across a mountain range from Plato appears 'Guild Socialism' and acknowledgment of eighteenth- and nineteenth-century French socialistic utopias in the form of 'Saint Simon' (Henri de Saint-Simon, 1760–1825) and 'La Phalange', the latter a reference to the ideal society of Charles Fourier (1772–1837). On the other side of the mountain range, Zhijie introduces 'The Confucionist Harmonious World', 'Taiping Heaven Kingdom (1851–1864)', and 'Zaroaster', part of a region comprising the Golden Ages and pre-historical paradisical forms of various cultures, including the Garden of Eden and Shangri La. No longer a fundamentally European tradition, utopianism emerges as a phenomenon with many manifestations, and numerous prophets, some of which can be cast in provocative alignments, such as the 'Jungle of Hobbes' and 'The Gulf of Anarchist', situated a little beneath the body/island's anus. Utopia's disembodied head consists of the 'Christian's Kingdom of Heaven', accompanied by a run of islands representing equivalents in other religions (Islam, Buddhism, Hinduism, Taoism). At the other end of the 'body', the islands at the 'feet' of the main island derive from the utopian tradition: 'Utopia of Thomas More' itself ('Anonymous Election', 'Common Ownership', 'Meditation in Free Time', 'Free Education', 'Golden Toilet'); 'New Atlantis of Francis Bacon'; and 'The New Utopia of Technological Revolution'. It is not, ultimately, entirely clear with what degree of irony the artist views the figure he presents. At once a learned commentary and networking of interconnected and aligned movements spanning much of human history, Zhijie's 'Map of Utopia' seems to reserve judgement on the hopes, aspirations, failings, and underlying violence it arranges. The overriding impression is of a corpse floating in the water.

The energy of Walter's 'Nova Utopia' (Fig. 38.3) derives not so much from the history of utopian thought as from a profound engagement with Ortelius' 'Utopiae typus' of 1596 (Fig. 38.1). Walter has taken the shape and much of the interior configuration of Ortelius' map, shorn of the nearby mainland, as the basis for his image. However, he has made numerous modifications, transforming the interior into a richly textured and immensely detailed dystopia. The governing narrative of 'Nova Utopia' is that More's island underwent a capitalist revolution between 1890 and 1900.[7] The results are all too painfully evident. The island's ten regions—an echo, conscious or not, of the linguistic division of Ortelius' image—have become a site for rampant touristification, with everything, including history and art, now a commodity. At one end of the island, the coastlines of Prora and Activa offer a kind of Ibiza on steroids, with booze, music, dance, sex, and drugs the main attractions. At the other end, the region of 'Sacrum' is devoted to New Age spiritualist pursuits, including a 'Oneness Centre', 'Hippy Circle', 'Dignia

---

[7] Relevant inscriptions on the map include: 'Region of the Old Civil War', 'Memorial Cemetery', '1900 Final Battle', and 'Battlefield Tours'; near the city of Mellis is the 'Historical House of Savo the Priest—Father of the Capitalist Revolution (1890–1900), and Museum of Entrepreneurism. No trespassing'. Nearby hills are marked 'Once the hideout of the capitalist rebels'.

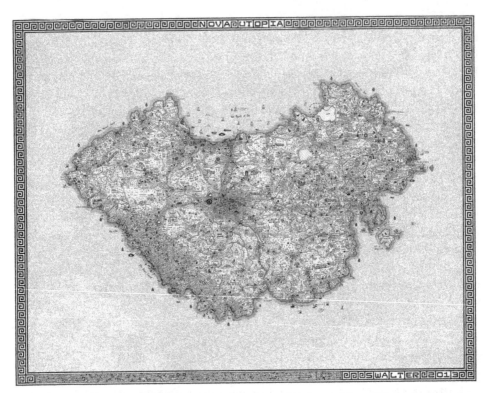

FIG. 38.3. Stephen Walter, 'Nova Utopia' (2013), British Library, Maps CC 6.a.91, © Stephen Walter, published by TAG Fine Arts.

'Euthanasia Tourism', 'Slow Food', and a 'Centre for the Ecology of Feelings'. The nearby region of 'Cosmo' appears to represent Sacrum's neo-liberal underbelly. Featuring the cities of Rosot ('Antiques', 'Literary Hotspot', 'Culture Vultures', 'Opera'), and of 'Venalia', it encompasses a 'Palace of Neo Liberalism' and 'Institute of Entrepreneurialism'. 'Cosmo' abuts the region of 'Temor' ('fear' in Spanish, a language used frequently on the map), whose upmarket attractions include mountaineering, hiking, and skiing. Temor's coastal region boasts a luxury tourist zone around the city of Orondo, with a country club, resort, 'chic villas', 'yacht haven', and an entirely privatized peninsula. The other side of the Bay of Orondo offers a more frankly depraved tourist landscape, with a 'Race Track rich men and their toys' next to 'real life sex slave hunts', alarmingly close to a 'Council for the Preservation of Romanticism', whose label appears beneath a Gothic steeple.

The theme of environmental degradation goes hand in hand with that of capitalistic excess. Near the teeming capital of 'Castillo Aire' (occupying the central position of Amaurot) is a contaminated lake, marked 'Disease' and 'Resort Closed', alongside a 'New Centre for Conservation and Research'. The region of 'Feo' (i.e. 'Ugly') bears the marks of heavy industrialization, and of increasing Chinese influence (Fig. 38.4). On the coast it is notable for the cities of Sforzinda ('Old Grandeur in Decline', 'Sewage Filtration',

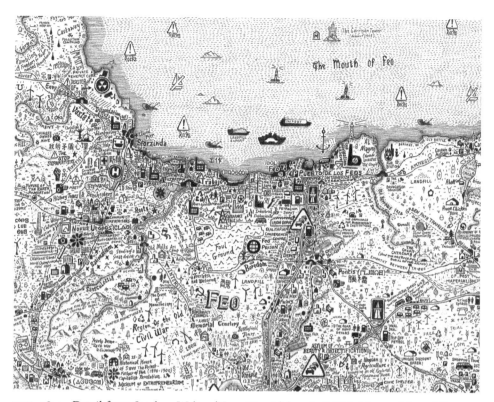

FIG. 38.4. Detail from Stephen Walter, 'Nova Utopia' (2013), British Library, Maps CC 6.a.91, © Stephen Walter, published by TAG Fine Arts.

'Internment Camp');[8] Trabajo ('Drink Problems'; 'Anti-Government Demos'), Feo ('They dress the same here'; 'Labour Stronghold'), and Al Magro ('Meagre'), a survival from Wacker's nomenclature, 'known locally as "Old Utopia" '. Inland can be found a Chinese-owned mine and a 'New Chinese development'. Like other parts of the island, Feo contains remnants of the island described by Hythloday, as well as more recent utopian manifestations. 'Communist Sympathizers' can be found south of the city of 'Novus Utopus', along with a 'permanent anti-capitalist demo'. The region of 'Sapientia', for the most part filled with tourist attractions for the aged such as ballroom dancing, cake shops, and 'Gilbert and Sullivan Vacationers', also contains 'The unpopulated City of Pruitt-Igoe', a reference to the iconic high-rise public housing complex built in St Louis, Missouri, in 1956, and demolished in the 1970s, poignantly located in the place of Ortelius/Wacker's 'Nondumia' ('Not-Yet City').

Outstandingly bleak, 'Nova Utopia' tends towards the allegory of Hall's *Mundus Alter*, with no escape from venality—certainly not through art, which along with the

---

[8] Sforzinda was an ideal city designed—but not built—for Francesco Sforza, Duke of Milan, by Antonio di Pietro Averlino, aka Filarete (c.1400–c.1469). For more on *Utopia* in Italy, see Shrank in this volume.

museum sector, is thoroughly implicated in capitalist expropriation of resources. The island contains two private art museums, one belonging to a 'Russian Oligarch' and the other to a 'Chinese Tycoon'. Walter's Utopia seems to share some of the anger of Satomi's 'Topographical map' and some of the necrology evident in Zhijie's map of Utopia. All three artists appear to view Utopia as a fundamentally flawed, indeed failed, concept, not only a no-place, but a no-longer place. There is considerable wit in their dissection of those flaws, and rather than a straightforward assault on the viability of More's text, it might be more accurate to see the New Utopia of the early twenty-first century as an incorporation of the social and political critique of Book One of *Utopia* into the depiction of the island in Book Two. That is, the disgust in Raphael's rejection of counsel in the Old World has an echo in the protest embodied in Satomi's gesture, as well as in the unrelenting scorn directed at touristic commodification in Walter's image. If this critique is less gentle than More's closing remark that there were Utopian practices that he 'would wish rather than expect' (More 1995: 249) to see in his own society, it is just as sharply pointed.

APPENDIX 38.1[9]

NAMES ON ORTELIUS' 'UTOPIAE TYPUS' (1596)

Cities

Utopian: Anemolia; Barzaneia (Barzanes City); Sysograntia (Syphogrant [i.e. Wise Elder or Dotard] City); Trapemeria (Turn to Foolishness?); Traniboria (Tranibor [i.e. Bencheater] City);

Italian: Ariavento (Airy); Belsogno (Dreamy); Castelvoto (Empty Castle); Cuccagnola (Little Cockaigne?); Nonnata (Unborn)

German: Keinstadt (No City); Larburg (Empty Town); Niemanzingen (Nobody's Place); Nindertheim (No One's Home); Onhausen (Without Houses)

Latin: Nondumia (Not-Yet City); Nullibia (Not-Here City); Nusquamia (Nowhere City); Quippeia (Anything City); Scilicetia (Doubtless City)

Greek: Madiapolis (Is Not a City); Midepopolis (Not Yet City); Midepolis (Not Even City); Udepolis (No City); Udepopolis (No Kind of City)

Spanish: Al magro (Meagre; also a place name in Andalusia); Aunno (Not Yet); Sombriosa (Shady); Ventadinada (Wind of Nothing); Villavazia (Empty Town)

'Belgic': Idelbeck (Empty Town); Ghendermonde (Not of the World); Goliensdorp (Glutton YTown?); Laerdael (Open Valley); Sottenbroeck (Fools' Swamp)

---

[9] I am very grateful to the following scholars for their advice on the translations of the names on Ortelius' map: Charles Burnett; J. Richard Green; Ladan Niayesh; Zur Shalev; Sebastian Sobecki. In particular, I must thank Nil Palabiyik, who identified the 'Saracenic' names, and whose translations of them are reproduced below, alongside the Latin of Wacker's source, Johanes Leunclavius' *Annales Sultanorum Othmanidarum*.

'Sarmatian': Iustrosczinia (*sic* for Lustrosczinia?: Mirror Land); Malagoscz (Inhospitable; also a place name in southern Poland); Niebylowna (Never Town); Nigdziemista (Nowhere Town); Utopowa (Utopian/Drowning City)

'Saracenic': Alaschezer (High City or Sublime City; Leunclavius, *Annales*, col. 316, line 12, 'urbs alta vel sublimis'); Caraoiluc (Black Noon; Leunclavius, *Annales*, col. 535, line 9, 'a nigra meridie', in fact Black/Strong Thigh); Gugertzinluc (Dove-Cote, Pigeon House; Leunclavius, *Annales*, col. 507, line 30, 'Columbarium'); Teggiurzair (Governor's Meadow; Leunclavius, *Annales*, col. 593, line 3, 'pratum'); Tzorlichisar (Twisted Castle; so Leunclavius, *Annales*, col. 220, lines 6–9, 'castellum distortum', in fact Mighty/Intractable Fortress)

French: Horsdumonde (Out of the World); Jamais (Never); Nulleville (No Town); Sansterre (Earthless); Pointhuys (No House)

Additional: Amaurotus metropolis (Dark/More); Favolia (Favolia); Manobia (Monau); Rotiliana (Ortelius); Saxirupia sive Tisvilaget ((Wacken)fels: Stony or Stone Province; Leunclavius, *Annales*, col. 318, line 34, 'regio saxosa')

Rivers

Utopian: Boriotranus flu. (Devouring Bench, cf Traniboria); Grantiophysus flu. (?Old Body, cf Sysograntia); Mapetrerius flu. (cf. Trapemeria); Moleanius flu. (cf. Artemolia); Zarbaneius flu. (cf. Barzaneia)

Italian: Senzzabarca flu. (Without Boat); Senzzagambaro flu. (Without (Cray)fish); Senzzaletto flu. (Without Bed); Senzzaqua flu. (Without Water); Senzzariva flu. (Without Bank)

German: Bettlos flu. (Bed-less); Fischlos flu. (Fish-less); Schiflos flu. (Ship-less); Uferlos flu. (Bank-less); Waßerlos flu. (Water-less)

Latin: Nullalueius flu. (*sic* for Nullalevius flu.) (No Bed); Nulliguttius flu. (No Drop); Nullipiscius flu. (No Fish); Nullirippius flu. (No Bank); Nulliscaphius flu. (No Boat)

Greek: Acheilus flu. (Bankless); Acytus flu. (Bedless); Amyndus flu.; Anaus flu. (Shipless); Astrangius flu. (Dropless)

Spanish: Simpescado flu. (Without Fish); Sinagua flu. (Without Water); Sinmadre flu. (Without Source); Sinnaos flu. (Without Ships); Sinrebera flu. (Without Bank)

'Belgic': Onloop flu. (Streamless); Onscheepken flu. (Shipless); Onvischken flu. (Fishless); Onwaeter flu. (Waterless)

'Sarmatian': Bezbrzega flu. (Shoreless); Bezlodz flu. (Shipless); Bezprizikoprow flu. (Ditchless); Bezriba flu. (Fishless); Bezwoda flu. (Waterless)

'Saracenic': Bogasu flu. (Bull water river; Leunclavius, *Annales*, col. 496, lines 50-51, 'tauri aqua'); Carasu flu. (Black water river; Leunclavius, *Annales*, col. 458, line 15, 'aqua nigra'); Einegioli flu. (Mirror lake; Leunclavius, *Annales*, col. 122, lines 21–23 and 31–34, 'instar speculi clara limpidaque ... aqua'); Saslidere flu. (River with reeds/rushes; Leunclavius, *Annales*, col. 892, lines 14–15, 'flumen aut aqua iuncosa'); Vlbad flu. (Great wind river; Leunclavius, *Annales*, col. 896, lines 57–58, 'magnus ventus')

French: Sansbatteau flu. (Without boat); Sanseau flu. (Without Water); Sanspoißon flu. (Without Fish); Sansrivage flu. (Without Bank)

Additional: Anydrus flu. (Waterless); Felsius flu. ((Wacken)fels); Mavonius flu. (Monau); Ortileus flu. (Ortelius)

APPENDIX 38.2

Johannes Wacker to Jacob Monau, 1 August 1595

The Latin text reproduced here is from Hessels 1887: 657–659. The English translation which follows is my own.

Nobilissimo atque ornatissimo uiro: Domino Jacobo Monau, patricio Vratislauiensj Domino affini et amico obseruandissimo et carissimo Breslam.

Cum uideam planè hoc uelle praestantissimum Dominum Ortelium nostrum, ut ego, qui auctor ipsi fui edendae in publicum σκϊαγραφίας uerè σκϊαγραφίας Vtopianae, ab obstetricio munere, quo primum functus sum; ad sacerdotalem quasi dignitatem accedam: et, quod in idiotismo nostro dicitur, partum etiam illum baptizem, urbesque Vtopianas proprijs suis nominibus insigniam: obtemperandum censui optimo atque ornatissimo uiro: et de re Geographica si umquam quisquam alius, praeclarissime merito.

[658] Itaque nomenclaturam ad te mitto quinquaginta quatuor illorum opidorum: quam ita instituere libuit, ut quinque sint opida Vtopianae originis siue notionis, quinque Graecae ueteris: totidem Latinae: totidem Germanicae: totidem Italicae: Gallicae: Hispanicae: Belgicae: Sarmaticae, Sarazenicae: ut hoc pacto quaeuis Gens, de suo aliquid in Vtopia ista agnosceret. Quia uerò quinquagenarium numerum quatuor ipsa opida excurrunt: illorum nomenclaturam inter amicos distribui: et unum quidem opidum, de tuo, unum de Ortelij, unum de meo nomine indigetauj. Quartum, Amaurotus metropolis, ut existimo occupabit.

Jam, ne simplicem insaniam insaniremus: fluuiorum quoque nomina fingere placuit: si ijs uti forsan ad urbes irrigandas, Plastes noster uellet. Qua de caussa ad notiones priorum Gentium et linguarum, fluminum quoque indigetationem accommodauimus: sicut ex infrascripta tabella prolixius apparebit. Tibi mi nobilissime Domine affinis, liberum facio: An haec ad Ortelium an ad Vtopum Gentis conditorem mittere uelis.

Non possum autem facere, quin te historiae mirificae simul et ridiculae admoneam. In Italia: nobis adolescentibus, duo fuere, spectatae nobilitatis iuuenes (quorum patriae parcimus) qui seriò, et extra omnem iocum affirmarent, se in Vtopia, et quidem Amaurothi per integrum annum et quod excurrit, fuisse. Quibus nos tum temporis fidem habere maluimus: quam ut uanitatem hominum pugnis ac ferro dilaceremus. Vtinam uero boni illj Vlysses nunc Antuerpiae essent: et cum Ortelio uiuerent. Longe enim certiora et luculentiora, de urbibus et fluminibus illis, et de tota insulae facie, quam nos, et quam ipse Hythlodeus alter αὐτόπτης, in medium afferre possent. Nunc cum intelligam illos in Vtopiam unde uenerant, redijsse: his nostris interea fruendum.

Te cum tuis rectè ualere opto; et me amare. Domino Ortelio plurimam ex me, et obseruantiae atque amoris plenissimam salutem. Theatrum unà cum hoc ἐπιμέτρῳ auidissime exspecto. Verberauit, hoc ipso momento, quo haec scribebam nos grauissimus nuncius; Schytas in Podoliae finibus maximo numero consedisse: et de perruptione cogitare: qui rumor utinam [659] falsus sit. Haec festinantissime scripsi. Vale. Nyssa. Calend. Sextilibus 1595.

(Since I saw clearly that our most outstanding Master Ortelius wished that I, who was the author of the soon to be published *skiagraphias* [sketch]—truly a Utopian *skiagraphias*— should leave my first post of midwife to enter the priestly role, and as it is put in our common speech, baptize that new birth, and identify the Utopian cities with their own names, I decided it was necessary to obey that excellent and most distinguished man, more deservedly famous in the field of Geography than anyone else.

So I am sending you a list of the names of fifty-four of their towns, which it pleased me to establish in the following way: five are towns of Utopian lineage or conception; five of ancient Greek; five each of Latin, German, Italian, French, Spanish, Belgic, Sarmatian, and Saracenic. By this means any nation may recognize something of itself in this Utopia. Because these towns [must] exceed the number 50 by four, I distributed the remaining names among friends: one town I named after you, one after Ortelius, one after my own name. The fourth I suppose will be taken up by the metropolis of Amaurotus.

Now, in order to complicate simple insanity, it pleased me to invent the names of rivers too, in case our Maker perhaps wants to use them for the purpose of irrigating the cities. For which reason, in addition to the conception of peoples and languages, we undertook the proclamation of rivers also, as will appear in more detail from the table written within. I give you, my most noble Lord and ally, the freedom to choose whether you want to send this to Ortelius, or rather to Utopus, the founder of the nation.

I am unable to do other than to remind you of a story at once remarkable and laughable. In Italy, when we were boys: there were two young men of genuine nobility (I forbear to mention their country) who used to affirm seriously, beyond any joke, that they had been in Utopia, and indeed in Amaurotus for an entire year and more. We chose at that time to have faith in the two, rather than lacerating the vanity of men with blows and iron. I wish that those two good Ulysses were now at Antwerp, and living with Ortelius. For they could bring foward far more certain and richer [information] about cities and those rivers, and about the entire surface of the island, than we [could], and than Hythloday himself, another eyewitness, [could]. Now since I understand they have returned to Utopia whence they came, enjoy these things of ours in the meantime.

I hope that you and yours rightly prosper and esteem me. To Master Ortelius from me many greetings, full of regard and of love. I await most eagerly a *Theatrum* [*Orbis Terrarum*] along with this addition. A most venerable messenger harassed me at this very moment when I was writing these lines. [He reports that] the Scythians have camped on the borders of Podolia in very great number, and that they are contemplating invasion; I hope to heaven this rumour is false. I wrote these lines very quickly. Farewell. Nysa. 1 August 1595.)

CHAPTER 39

CONTEMPORARY UTOPIANISM

An Island Renaissance

RHYS WILLIAMS

THERE is no site more typical of utopian thought than the island. The imaginary society requires a conceptual space both isolated and bounded, within which the imagination can do its work. So, King Utopus made the conditions of possibility for his utopia by cleaving an island from the mainland: 'Utopus [...] designed to separate them from the continent, and to bring the sea quite round them' (More 1890b: 90). This foundational act of separation is also the foundational act of utopian thought, creating the formal ground for difference to exist, pulling away, and beginning afresh. Following Gilles Deleuze (2004: 9), we can say that as islands are separated from continents, so islands provide a conceptual ground to separate ourselves from what exists; islands are deployed as sites of potential novelty.

From polis to island to nation to globe, the size and constitution of the bounded space in which utopia is thought has shifted with the conditions of the age. Along with this spatial transformation came a temporal one: the nineteenth century, with its political, industrial, and Darwinian revolutions, shunted utopian thought into the future, no longer an alternative but a horizon for transformative action in the here-and-now (Williams 2019b). As Franco Berardi argues, the prevailing understanding of the 'future' in the twentieth century was

> A psychological perception, which emerged in the cultural situation of progressive modernity, the cultural expectations [...] shaped in the conceptual frameworks of an ever progressing development [...]: the Hegelo-Marxist mythology of Aufhebung and instauration of the new totality of Communism; the bourgeois mythology of a linear development of welfare and democracy; the technocratic mythology of the all encompassing power of scientific knowledge. (Berardi 2011: 13)

No matter the ideological colouring, it seemed the present was putty in our collective hands, the future waiting to be moulded to our collective desires. This is no longer the case. The twentieth and twenty-first centuries have seen the collapse of communism, the dramatic failure of the free markets and the financial sector, austerity policies in the richest countries, the new rise of the far right across Europe and beyond, the collapse of belief in mainstream political establishments and in scientific expertise, the growing awareness of the structural inequalities of gender and race, and—perhaps the most severe curtailing of any fantasies of endless progress and omnipotence—the environmental and climate crisis. The utopian dreams of the recent past lie scattered like the grand works of Ozymandias. Apart from a pie-in-the-sky techno-utopianism that looks a great deal like toys for very rich boys, apocalypse reigns; the future flattens into a chronic present whose only linear resolution is ecological collapse, itself now invested with a perverse utopian desire: 'apocatopia, utopalypse', the world slate wipes itself clean (Miéville 2018).

The present certainly feels like an interregnum—though perhaps it always does, or always is—a period of flux in which certainties break down and new possibilities and forms emerge. We are today surrounded by ruins. Or at least—to be more cautious with the slippage between ontology and epistemology—we are surrounded by political and aesthetic strategies that position us in relation to a present-as-ruin, placing the Now in a post-apocalyptic frame, living in the aftermath, arguing through formal and aesthetic gestures that the status quo is already dead, and amongst this sea of rubbish we must find our island futures, and nurture them. Because contemporary utopianism, in a surprising turn of events, has returned to the island.

This chapter concerns itself with the contemporary return to islands in utopian thought, but with the twist that the islands are not empty containers any more, but busy sites of transformation; no longer peripheral, but central as an origin for a developing future. Further, they are legion. No single island provides the blueprint for a better future. Each 'better' is situational, deeply entangled in the place and the people that comprise it. Going beyond real islands, the chapter explores how the form and concept of the archipelago manifests itself in the act of curating as a key symptomatic logic of our time, extending far beyond the practices of the art world, drawing together elements to form a dialogue that opens up alternative futures.

Islands, Then and Now

For Eduard Glissant, ' "Archipelic thought" [...] endeavors to do justice to the world's diversity' and 'forms an antithesis to continental thought, which makes a claim to absoluteness and tries to force its worldview onto other countries' (Obrist 2012: 4). As a conceptual model, a key tenet of the emerging field of island studies, the archipelago pushes against the thought of empire that is a 'synthesis, serving to standardize', instead figuring 'a network of interrelationships between various traditions and perspectives' (5). And in true utopian style, it breaks with the repetition of the same, and is open to the future, open to the new and the unknowable other: 'It is not a recapitulation of something which existed in an obvious way. It is the quest for something we don't know yet' (5).

Islands have long been understood as peripheral, as 'remote and dependent on oft-distant mainlands' (Stratford 2013: 3). Hand in hand with this spatial grammar is a temporal one: the peripheral is also the past, while the centre, the mainland, the capital city, marks the civilized location of future production. Islands in this light are 'quaint bastions of conformity and antique tradition, savage gardens of sexual delight, [...] social backwaters, impoverished stepchildren of colonial empires' (P. Hay 2006: 27). From More's Utopia on, the colonial tradition heavily informs the shape of the utopian impulse.[1] Distant lands 'need to be occupied, conquered, and colonized', these 'isolated and backward' people and places need to be brought into the fold of civilization (Stratford 2013: 3–4). More's island is split from the mainland, so that the colonial project can gain its purchase: 'Utopus, that conquered it [...] brought the rude and uncivilised inhabitants into such a good government, and to that measure of politeness, that they now far excel all the rest of mankind' (More 1890b: 89). Islandness is thus typically understood as 'a dysfunctional state. [...] The island itself is seen to be a postcolonial trope, one traceable to Eurocentric assumptions of dominance' and marked by an assumption of 'obsolescence, hideboundedness or structures of chronic injustice' (P. Hay 2006: 28). If, in the past, islands were utopian spaces, it was not, in the last analysis, because of what we might find there, but because of what might be created there.

In the contemporary period, the role of islands in utopian thought has shifted. In an interregnum, in a time of uncertainty and epistemic shift, in a time of apocalypse, where the old world collapses and a new one is made, centres reverse polarity, to stand as the last bastions of a dying status quo. The barbarians are at the gate, the zombies are scaling the walls, and the stockpiles are running low. The old dream of a frictionless, smooth, and universally globalized world is giving way to one in which futures are differentiated from place to place, where resilience lies not in large-scale unification but in smaller-scale attention to place and community. Just as knowledge is situated, so are futures, as futures are a form of knowledge (Haraway 1988). In this new dispensation, islands are not to be colonized, but learnt from. They are 'advance indicators or extreme reproductions of what is future elsewhere', 'the first, the harbingers, the pioneers, the miner's canary' (Baldacchino 2007a and 2007b, cited in Watts 2014: 30). And no longer should we understand them as isolated, that hangover of the empire mentality, but rather as archipelagos, relational sites of 'connection, assemblage, mobility, and multiplicity' (Stratford 2013: 3) in which the flows of culture and creation are subject to constant innovation in each new situated island context. Islands do not stand alone: they are nodes in a transformational matrix, each different, yet each a part of something larger,

---

[1] For more on colonialism/imperialism and Utopia, see Hower, Hadfield, Lutz, and Weaver-Hightower and Bajaber in this volume.

and all, in their relative fragility, 'acutely aware of their own potential transience in time, whose finely tuned ecosystems are hypersensitive to change' (Watts 2014: 30).

The contrast between these two models of islands is a contrast between two politics, two modes of thought, and two ways of being in the world. Turning to the manifestation of archipelagic thought in culture, we find it articulated most clearly in the logic and practice of curating.

Curating Utopias

In the *New Left Review* in 2015, Fredric Jameson called curating the new dominant logic of the time, one thoroughly entangled with global finance capital. Whether this makes curational forms incapable of genuine utopian critique or perfectly positioned for it, is a difficult question, but it's what you do with it that probably counts. So, what is being done with it?

The year 2003 saw the appearance of *Utopia Station* curated by Molly Nesbit, Hans Ulrich Obrist, and Rirkrit Tiravanija at the Venice Biennale. The latest in a series of gatherings designed to create connections, tensions, and discussions around the idea of utopia, it was the most concrete—the most exhibition-like, the most constructed—to date. It was large, containing works by more than sixty individual artists, architects, and artists' groups, along with posters by another hundred, but was nonetheless conceptualized as unfinished: a way station rather than a destination; utopia as a process, catalyst, or fuel rather than a plan. The trace of the archipelago is clear; for the show, the curators were in conversation with Glissant, and together 'designed a new, alternative form of utopia consisting of a continuous dialogue' (Obrist 2012: 5). Curating is the art of suspending a series of diverse elements together so that they sit in tension, in complex relation, all speaking to each other—a dialogue, in which new thoughts and pathways emerge from the interrelationship, from the emergent network of meanings. Such is the archipelagic thrust of curating. Along with the artworks there were events, performances, talks, all geared to facilitate and inspire discussion and creation around the idea and the direction of utopianism in the present moment.

Enter 2015, and curating is an established big business—superstar curators like Obrist (see Obrist 2015) are seemingly everywhere, and academic work on curating has spawned entire courses dedicated to understanding and practising the craft. While utopianism has seen little overt traction in literature or film since the counterculture years in the 1960s and early 1970s (with some honourable exceptions, particularly for readers of the science fiction novels of Kim Stanley Robinson), it is a popular organizing topic for curated exhibitions. The curatorial impulse is one of the contemporary homes of the utopian. While *Utopia Station* continues to tour and manifest in various locations, exhibitions like Penny Woolcock's *Utopia* and Banksy's *Dismaland* appeared in 2015 in the United Kingdom, and across the Atlantic the *Museum of Capitalism* opened in Oakland in 2017 before touring. Just like *Utopia Station* before them, *Dismaland* and

Utopia were more than exhibitions. They incorporated into themselves spaces for radical political groups, evening events, and politically charged performances. In Banksy's case, the back-right quarter of the main arena was given over to a few spaces that contained posters, texts, and videos damning of the police state, an exhibition of 'radical banners', and a space to pick up leaflets and information, or radical magazines.[2] These were not out of place among the art, and there is no doubt that these tents provided exposure to these ideas—and crucially acted to normalize them, even glamorize them—for a number of people who would not otherwise encounter them. In Woolcock's case, local activist groups such as Sisters Uncut (a feminist group campaigning against domestic violence) were given evening platforms to speak, mingled with politicized celebrities like the comedian Russell Brand, musician Charlotte Church, and political journalist Owen Jones, lots of slam poetry, and live music. The curatorial here extends beyond the artworks themselves. Additive in nature, these exhibitions reach beyond themselves and into the world of politics and activism, drawing elements of the outside world into themselves, placing them in dialogue, and creating networks whose influence extends beyond the exhibitions in space and time.

The year 2016 marked the 500th anniversary of More's *Utopia*. There was a series of celebrations, including *UTOPIA 2016: A Year of Imagination and Possibility* at Somerset House in London, comprising a whole year of events, with a number of curated exhibitions responding to the theme. Some of these were more radically utopian than others (Williams 2016), pointing up the tension inherent in curation as a utopian mode: it is all too easy for productive tension to become flaccid constellation, a flat representational game that says nothing of the profound structural problems that lie underneath. With nothing of the subversive edge of their namesake, these exhibitions are always in danger of ending up as merely glorified design shows, their utopianism limited to a more comfortable desk or better working space, or diluted into purely aesthetic abstraction.

One of the more interesting versions of what we might call curatorial utopianism emerges from Afrofuturism. Starting with the music of Sun Ra and the collective P-Funk in the mid-twentieth century, Afrofuturism is now a prevalent aesthetic strategy shot through with political intent, spanning music, art, literature, film, and more. In tune with our eco-apocalyptic age, though with its origins firmly in the Middle Passage and slavery, a key strategy of Afrofuturism is temporal disruption and timeline remixing: to cast the present as post-apocalyptic; to shift into futures based on pasts lost or imaginary, (re)constructed from glimpses of alternative historical narratives in scattered cultural products, positing both a stolen heritage and reclaimed possibilities of the future. As Mark Dery states:

> For [Americans of African descent], the apocalypse happened a long, long time ago, when across the Atlantic's gulf alien intellects, 'cool and unsympathetic', regarded them with 'envious eyes' (as the Martians regard the Earth in War of the Worlds),

---

[2] See the archive website 'Dismaland' for further links, http://dismaland.co.uk/, last accessed 21 Oct. 2021.

prelude to beaming them aboard slave ships and transporting them across the wounded galaxies to a prison planet, a nightmare that in some respects has never ended. As Sun Ra said, 'It's after the end of the world; don't you know that yet?' (Dery 2016)

The absolute rupture that sits at the origin of Afrofuturism allows the artists freedom to create new archives, a new past, with new meanings: a crafted and selected resource, pertinent, and urgent for the needs of the present. This is done through a collecting and placing in tension—*curating*—fragments of the present, collectively opening a door to the potential for radical difference. Afrofuturism is in this sense both a radical future vision produced by a selective curatorial process, and a process of selection in the present guided by a radical future vision. An excellent recent example is Kapwani Kiwanga's art film series *Afrogalactica* (begun in 2011), narrated from the future by an anthropologist. Reimagining the history of Africa as one of technological modernity, the film narrates the fate of a lost space mission, which must reconstruct the culture of its past from the fragments remaining to it on board the ship. These fragments are precisely real-world examples of Afrofuturism from the real-world present and recent past. Thus, the act of curation here draws together these real elements in order to extrapolate a past that was not allowed to be, and a future that might still be hoped for. Note that here again, it is the gesture of apocalypse that frees up these fragments to be salvaged and reinterpreted, and a new narrative for a world renewed to be written.[3]

Perhaps the apotheosis of this new nexus of utopian curation, however, is Ben Rivers's *Slow Action* (2011). Beginning with the premise of catastrophically risen sea-levels, the art film aims to present a series of potential island utopias that arise in the aftermath. The most contemporary temporality of ecological collapse and rising sea levels here provides the opportunity to return to the origins of utopian thinking: bounded and isolated islands. Far from blank, however, these islands are inhabited by the ruins of our age and are less a series of blueprints than potentialities within utopian thought.

The four sections of the film mark out a range of potential utopian figures. The first island, 'Eleven', is founded on the valorization of pure rational, mathematical thought. But unlike a dystopian Fordist nightmare, here such valorization has led to a bare simplicity of life, the inhabitants devoting their time to stargazing at night, when the universe is revealed in all its truth. The second utopia, 'Society Islands', is a string of islands, each with a different social structure. The inhabitants are always aware of other possible utopias and are free to explore them at will. The uniqueness of these islands lies in the dominance of narrative as a social principle—to the extent that suicide is the normal mode of death, as the choice of how to seal your own narrative is considered a crucial one, with ramifications on how your life as a whole is understood. The third island, 'Kanzennashima', holds only one inhabitant, a self-professed madman, whose utopia manifests a complex temporality. For him, utopia can only be approached, never

---

[3] See e.g. 'The Institute of Things to Come', http://theinstituteofthingstocome.com/oldsite, last accessed 21 Oct. 2021.

reached, and it lies in the past: not as a golden age, but as the ruins of its own ruins whose restoration can only come about through constant efforts of rearticulation. These efforts themselves are the utopia, we understand. This baffling and beautiful idea—the doubling of a ruin—suggests a mode of agency able to engage with the remnants of the past and to expose within their ruins another: the ruins of imagined but unlived pasts, much like Kiwanga's artwork. To then live as an articulation of these alternatives is the utopian gesture, a redemption of the past in the present. Finally, the fourth island, 'Somerset', is in permanent, semi-ritualized revolution: utopia through a refusal to entrench. The old people fight and die in battle, while the young, unjaded by experience, govern. The principle here is the constant effort to reproduce and maintain that moment of perfect accord that marks the founding of a utopia: that moment of coming together of more than one individual and their desires, founded in a rejection of the present, symbiotic with the destruction of the old, and the maintaining of an open future not yet corrupted by its realization.

To create its utopias, the film uses footage of real places presented as future ruins. But they are present realities, which makes a ruin of the present and catapults us into a position of seeing the present as past, as ruins of a now-past age. The temporality is further complicated by the narrative present of the film being set even further into the future, looking back at these island utopias as curios, entries in a Great Encyclopedia of Utopias, diligently collected by a lineage of Curators. These future islands are thus present perfect: they will have been. The ecological catastrophe, and the socio-diversity that arises in aftermath, are thus certainties. But they are comprised of a collage of the present, with images of real ruined or other-worldly locations (the ecological wastelands, the plastic islands are already here) estranged through the camera's lingering eye, through clever juxtaposition and framing, through splicing with an alienating soundtrack salvaged from 1970s science fiction films (past representations of the future). All of this is presented under a guiding narrative written by Mark von Schlegell with no knowledge of the kind of footage Rivers was going to take, and which often opens up a rift between narrative and visual content that the viewer cannot reconcile, in the tension of which possible meanings proliferate. One can only guess what the narrative present of the film is like, but I would suggest that it be inferred as the organizing principle of the conflicting elements of the film: a post-utopian, curatorial perspective that manages to suspend within itself the formal and temporal tensions of ruin and futurity, apocalypse and utopia, submission and agency. It is a moment of enlightened balance, of perfect stillness amidst the storm.

The presence of so many competing and contradictory temporalities in the film, from past futures to present pasts, points to a dominant temporality that is comprised precisely of the variegated ruination of temporalities in the present. In turn, the organizing principle of the film as a series of future-perfect encyclopedia entries points to curatorial practice again, here as a potential ground for reasserting agency in the present. Jameson (2015: 120) has asserted that our era suffers from a 'collective loss of historicity' and pinpoints the rise of curatorial practice and form from art to financial derivatives as the definitive symptom. Such practice produces for Jameson a series of singularity events, objects that cannot be universalized, generalized, or totalized, and which speak of the effort and failure to map the postmodern experience of individuals and of communities, and of the relation between the two. The perfection of such an effort has surely long been the paradox at the heart of utopias. If Jameson is correct, and present conditions make this impossible effort the key political dilemma of our age's ruined temporality, then perhaps *Slow Action*, with its conscious effort to curate a series of resonant, yet pointedly singular (non-total, non-universal), utopian figures, is the appropriate mode in which to orient ourselves in the wasteland, with a view to future praxis.

Past Future-Bearing Islands

In the ecologically insecure present, the question of energy has come to the fore in any serious discussion of a better future. If we are to ameliorate, lessen, or just survive our negative impact upon the planet's ecology, the transition to sustainable modes of life, and in particular to sustainable energy systems, is paramount, and requiring of wholesale social changes far beyond the merely technical. Further, utopian imaginings now cannot be a matter only of human social organization, but also concern humanity's relationship to the non-human, and a just transition for one relates to a just transition for the other. The necessity of energy transition provides us with a historical moment of crisis in which opposing ideologies are wrestling over the future of society *via* the future of energy. The point is less whether renewable energy automatically equals a more just society, whatever that looks like, and more that the massive infrastructural changes ahead provide leverage to institute something different.

Our dependence upon fossil fuels has never been the only possible option. Alternatives have always presented themselves, only to become a forgotten railway siding as the train of progress sweeps along another track. Here we come back to islands, specifically the Isle of Bute. In 1813 the engineer Robert Thom bought the Rothesay Mills for a small sum, the industrial site bought cheap because water was unreliable according to the strict capitalist timetable, and coal was prohibitively expensive to ferry to the island. Thom endeavoured to 'turn the whole Isle of Bute into a testing ground for avant-garde water management schemes' (Malm 2015: 97). Thom constructed long and winding watercourses over the landscape. Rather than impinge too strongly upon the land, Thom preferred to 'simply follow the lines which nature points out' (Thom, cited in Malm 2015: 97). As Malm puts it: 'For Thom, dancing with the water as it flowed through the landscape appeared a form of art' (96). Here is the very definition of a situational future technology: it appears much simpler than the impressive engineering of a steam engine, but its complexity lies in its negotiation with place and people. Thom's most famous creation was the self-acting sluice, a float and sluice mechanism which constrained water when there was too much and released more when the levels dipped. In conjunction with the system of canals and ducts that traced the land, these self-acting sluices mark an early version of a kind of smart technology that integrates with the systems of the land rather than attempting to change them. It was a stunning success: the mills became very profitable, and Thom's system of water-management caught the eye of others (Malm 2015: 98–100).

In the 1820s, Thom was commissioned to carry out an ambitious project in Greenock, providing water for a series of empty sites, hoping to attract mill owners to set up shop there. While the mechanics of the project were yet again a success, and the cost of running a water mill clocked in at some one-eighth that of steam, the lots remained mostly empty. History's face turned from the alternative. There was a financial crisis (the Panic of 1825) that hit just at the moment of the site's completion, slowing the expansion of the trades and the building of new mills. But the most significant element was simply this: waterpower required cooperation among mill owners; it required an awareness of the needs of others, and a willingness to negotiate one's own individual desires with theirs. Of water and steam, the latter might have appeared the more advanced technology, but in terms of social relations, in terms of emotional and cognitive demand, it was by far the more brute, simple, and individualistic of the two. Steam won not because it was more advanced, but because it resonated with the desires of capitalists to have their sense of individual agency unencumbered by the needs of others: 'In short, a motive power that in many respects was indeed a welcome gift of nature [water] was often attended by a lack of independence in use and management, [with the attendant cost of] *emotional energy* from which steam-power users were entirely free' (L. Hunter, cited in Malm 2015: 119). In this way, the islands of renewable energy demand as well as figure a utopian element: they necessitate a care for the structures of social relations, a maintenance of interpersonal relations, of the technologies of human interactions that are the most complex. And this is the key utopian demand upon energy production: that it requires cooperation, and community, and an attention to place. Under the cosh of the contemporary ecological crisis, we finally see a return to the kind of futures that Thom's work seemed to promise; some of the most impressive are once again off the Scottish coast.

Future Islands in the Now

Following McKensie Wark's rather idiosyncratic definition, we might understand utopia 'to be a diagram, in pictorial or textual form, of a way of life that has actually been experienced, and which may be a fragment out of which to extrapolate a social form on a larger or deeper scale' (Wark 2014). In 2008, the Isle of Eigg, off the west coast of Scotland, became the world's first community to launch a renewable, off-grid electric system. On average, it runs on 90–5 per cent energy from solar, wind, and water. It is community-owned and community-run. When the system generates a surplus of power—a particularly windy day, a very wet week—heaters in the two churches, the community hall, and the pier lobby switch on automatically, keeping the shared spaces warm throughout the winter. The utopian and communal thrust of Eigg is clear, prompting the activist group Platform to ask 'could Eigg [...] be the Tredegar Medical Aid Society of energy?', referring to the future-bearing scheme that provided the model for the National Health Service in the United Kingdom (Platform 2015: 1).

In the case of Eigg, the community is so embedded in the energy production it has led to a decentring and sharing of expertise. The maintenance team is made up of non-experts who do other things day to day, have learnt on the job, and are not 'engineers' in any professional sense. While life is far from 'utopian' on Eigg, with the difficult climate, low income, and a heavy dependence on tourism, it has also become a symbol of hope and change for its landownership revolution, and its independent, renewable energy system. I visited the island for a couple of weeks on a field trip in 2019, and while I was there the leading members of the island's organizing council were busy dealing with not one but four separate visits from international documentary crews and reporters. The danger here is that the symbology of the island obscures its more difficult, more banal reality. But while life is not always easy on Eigg, and while running an island on consensus is a tough ask, nonetheless one of the original members of the island trust called it her 'utopia', and the others at the table agreed (Williams 2019a). As with any utopian transformation, the proof is the changes in people's actions, people's habits, and the way that the system 'provides for people's needs and does not entrench exploitation or rely on constant expansion' (Platform 2015: 5). Eigg did not have a huge amount but it certainly strove for this kind of systemic and individual transformation.

Skirt around the Scottish coast to the north-east and we arrive at Orkney, an archipelago whose island communities have 'positioned themselves [...] as an exemplar' of utopian energy futures (Watts 2018a: 8). For some twenty years now, Orkney islanders have lived in something like a science fictional future, with giant machines making renewable energy in their seas, coupled with experiments on land with wind generation and hydrogen cell production. No backwards periphery here! As an archipelago, Orkney breaks the model of isolated island utopias by understanding itself as a 'port of call for a planetary-wide archipelago of test-sites—thinking and working together [...] each with unique expertise and learning to be shared between them' (Watts 2018a: 10). Like Thom's Isle of Bute and the Isle of Eigg, the mode and means of energy production is tied to place and time and community: one that has sensibly turned profits from the oil industry into a staging post for surpassing it. This electricity can only be generated here, where the seas are rough and fast. As well as everyone being unusually well versed in energy generation and storage—'including the seven children of the local primary school who spoke knowledgeably about electrolysers and curtailment' (Auger and Hanna 2017)—Laura Watts points out that 'goodwill was also an infrastructure that kept the place going' (Watts 2018b). As ever this is the core of any utopian infrastructure—and one often overlooked in all the detail of systems and organizations. That Orkney is a piece of the future in the present can perhaps best be intuited from the attitudes of the people towards the present: as Watts (2018b) states, 'there is no talk about the end of the world, here. Instead, they jokingly comment that, in an apocalypse [the Orkney island of] Eday, with all its energy, would be a great place to be'.

CURATING A FUTURE IN THE PRESENT

To close, I look briefly at two acts of curating that are deeply utopian, isolating and identifying future-bearing 'islands' in the mess of the present, and bringing them together under the banner of utopian praxis. Firstly, Solarpunk. A tiny subgenre of science fiction, it exists almost wholly online, produced by amateur authors. Its ethos is one of a positive vision of the future, in which we have managed to solve our ecological problems and made the shift to a sustainable mode of life (for key examples, see Ulibarri 2018; Wagner and Wieland 2017). The texts produced by Solarpunk are not the main interest, however. That lies in the communities that have sprung up around the idea, and the way in which 'Solarpunk' has become a way of identifying a particular set of aesthetics, living practices, and innovations. It has become, in short, a lens that can be turned upon the world, isolating future-bearing elements of the present—a DIY solar boat, an opensource social media platform, a smart-tech approach to permaculture—and gathering them together into a curated presentation of a possible and desirable future.[4]

Secondly, we have the project 'Seeds of Good Anthropocenes'. As the website describes,

> Seeds [...] can be social initiatives, new technologies, economic tools, or socialecological projects, or organisations, movements or new ways of acting that appear to be making a substantial contribution towards creating a future that is just, prosperous, and sustainable.[5]

The seeds themselves are anything from permaculture in Cameroon to Melbourne's green city transition. The similarity in approach between Solarpunk and 'Seeds of Good Anthropocenes' is clear. The focus in both is on identifying utopian elements in the hereand-now, which can be encouraged and brought together to make a better future more plausible in the long run. In this way they are heirs to More's Utopia. In them all we recognize a global utopian imagination, networked and communal. Utopianism as a shared project: a constellation of fragments, a mood board, a dialogue between practices, and a vision that is inspired by and selective of those practices. In the contemporary period, utopia can only be global, but it still needs to be bounded and situated. One solution proposed by contemporary utopianism is a global archipelago of places, people, and practices, curated and in communication.

---

[4] See *Solarpunks*, https://solarpunks.net/, last accessed 21 Oct. 2021.
[5] https://goodanthropocenes.net/what-are-seeds/, last accessed 21 Oct. 2021.

APPENDIX

OUTLINE OF MORE'S *UTOPIA*

Preliminary Materials

In the early Latin edition More's text[1] is preceded by a shifting set of preliminary materials, variously including a map of Utopia; a Utopian alphabet; a poem in Utopian, with an interlinear transliteration and Latin translation; a poem by the Utopian poet laureate Anemolius; and letters and poems written by humanist contemporaries of More. Some editions after 1517 add paratextual material at the end of the work.[2]

The Prefatory Letter

More's first contribution to *Utopia* is a letter to his friend and fellow humanist in Antwerp, Peter Giles, apologizing for the delay in sending him the text of the book. Serving as the book's preface, the letter is important in setting up *Utopia*'s overarching joke: that it is a fictional account of conversations between the 'real-life' Giles and More with the imagined explorer-cum-philosopher Raphael Hythloday, that is nevertheless presented as if true. The letter then describes the busy public and domestic life of More (the reason why he has taken so long to finalize the manuscript); acknowledges difficulties remembering everything Hythloday had said (raising the fundamental tensions between truth, untruth, lying, and honesty); hints at the importance of Latin and especially Greek philosophy in shaping the text; and rehearses conventional worries about committing the manuscript to publication and having it misconstrued by hostile or unlearned readers. In so doing, the letter establishes the collaborative and allusive nature of the text and its dialogic and representational qualities: how More as author is trying to recollect and convey on the page a previous and fleeting (pretended) conversation.

Book One

The beginning of Book One finds the narrator More (an in-text persona hereafter known as Morus) as a London citizen who has been co-opted into negotiating the settlement of important trade disputes between Henry VIII of England and his Habsburg nephew-in-law Charles, then Duke of Burgundy (by the time *Utopia* was printed, he was nominally—if not formally—Charles I of Spain; in 1519 he became Charles V, Holy Roman Emperor). These negotiations take place in the city of Bruges. During a lull in negotiations, Morus visits Antwerp and—one day after Mass—encounters his friend, the humanist Giles, who introduces him to the enigmatic Portuguese 'Ulysses' or 'Plato', Raphael Hythloday: one-time companion of the Florentine explorer Amerigo Vespucci on his transatlantic travels, who had been left as

---

[1] This outline is based on More 2016b; quotations and page references in the Appendix relate to that edition.
[2] For an overview of the shifting Latin paratexts, see T. Cave 2008c.

one of twenty-four men in the garrison at the 'farthest point of [Vespucci's] last voyage' (10); he and five companions then travel through 'many countries', before making it back to Europe via Ceylon and Calicut. To continue their conversation, they return to Morus' lodgings and sit in the garden, on 'a bench covered in grassy turf', to talk (11).

Morus abbreviates his account of Hythloday's travels to focus on 'the customs and institutions of the Utopians' (13); but before he begins on those, he feels obliged to recount the exchange that leads up to that discussion. This part of the conversation begins when Giles diverts the talk towards the issue of government in Europe by observing that Hythloday's experiences and wisdom would make him an excellent royal counsellor. Hythloday forcefully demurs, equating 'service' (*servias*) to a monarch with 'servitude' (*inservias*) and observing that whereas kings value the 'arts of war' he could only counsel 'the arts of peace' (13–14).

This precipitates a discussion about the problems of giving and receiving counsel (frequently called 'The Debate of Counsel'), which Hythloday unexpectedly situates in England by beginning his explanation of his reluctance to enter royal service with an anecdote set during his alleged sojourn in the household of Cardinal John Morton, Archbishop of Canterbury (1486–1500) and, from 1487, Henry VII's Lord Chancellor, who mentored More and whom More greatly admired. Hythloday recounts a discussion he had with Morton and his advisers about punishing thieves in which he—famously—demonstrates the complicated set of socioeconomic forces (including enclosure) encouraging crime in contemporary England and so causing unprecedented numbers of executions. Hythloday draws on the example of the Persian 'Polylerites' ('People of Much Nonsense' in Greek), who condemn criminals to redemptive slavery and hard labour (25), as an alternative system of punishment to the death penalty. The idea is mocked until Morton shows interest in it; Hythloday's point is that whatever the merits of an argument, courtiers will always agree with the position taken by the man in charge (28).

Hythloday then elaborates on his unsuitability for political counsel—and the broader tension between political practice and philosophy—by contrasting the likely policies of a typical monarch (the king of France) against what should be the true priorities of a prince. Whereas in practice kings require advice about how to extend territory, wage wars, maintain armies, tax and dominate their people, Hythloday claims he could only counsel a monarch how to achieve peace, equity, and 'his people's welfare' (*popolo bene [. . .] suo*) (34). Morus counters that a counsellor is obliged not only to give good counsel but also to be realistic about what he can achieve in any given situation, to recognize and negotiate the circumstances in which he operates, and to present advice effectively, persuasively, and 'tactfully'. That way, 'what you cannot turn to good, you may at least make as little bad as possible' (37). Hythloday is scathing in return before making the surprising (and infamous) observation that 'wherever you have private property, and money is the measure of all things, it is hardly ever possible for a commonwealth to be just or prosperous' (39). More is sceptical—'It seems to me that people cannot possibly live well where all things are in common' (41)—and Hythloday promises that the example of the Utopians will prove his case. Giles and More are intrigued. They 'go to luncheon' and then return to the bench to hear Hythloday's description of Utopia, which he presents as 'the best state of a commonwealth' (42).

Book Two

Book Two consists of Hythloday's monologic description of Utopia, with a brief but important set of interjections by Morus at the very end. It has already been mentioned at the end of Book One that, twelve hundred years ago, some Romans and Egyptians were shipwrecked on the island, allowing the Utopians to learn 'every single art of the Roman empire' (42). Hythloday now outlines the geography and early history of Utopia: how—then called Abraxa—it was conquered and civilized by Utopus, who turned the peninsula into an island, named it after himself, and established a network of fifty-four cities, with the city of Amaurot as the capital hub (44–45). He describes how households rotate between town and country on a regular basis—with food production carefully controlled to meet demand—and the architectural structure and civic governance of the cities.

This is followed by a longer section discussing the 'occupations' of the Utopians: how everyone (men and women) is trained in farming, plus at least one additional urban trade; how only six hours a day are devoted to work, with the remainder (discounting eating, sleeping, and an hour's recreation) given to 'intellectual activity' such as public lectures; how all work is necessary, rather than superfluous; and how this balanced, with equitable distribution of labour producing everything Utopians need while providing adequate time for them to 'devote themselves to the freedom and culture of the mind' (56).

Having explained how the Utopians work, Hythloday turns to their 'social relations and their system of distributing goods' (56). As in late medieval England, the foundational institution of Utopian society is the patriarchal household. Less familiar to More's contemporaries is that households donate everything they produce to common markets (from which heads of household can take everything their household requires 'without any sort of compensation') and live in 'spacious halls' where they 'take their meals in common' (58). But if this section begins to unpack the nature of Utopian communalism, it also establishes the importance of Utopia's imperial power to its domestic arrangements. On the one hand, when the size and number of households becomes too large, the Utopians 'plant a colony under their own laws on the mainland near them'; and if the population should dramatically shrink—for example, because of plague (as has happened twice in their history)—they can bring 'people back from the colonies' (57). On the other hand, Hythloday almost inadvertently reveals that Utopia is a slave society: it is because enslaved people do dirty and menial work (like butchering animals, cleaning, and heavy chores) that Utopian citizens can learn trades, improve their minds, and participate fully 'in communal life' (57–59).

There then follows the longest section of Book Two. Ostensibly detailing 'the travels of the Utopians', Hythloday begins by explaining how individual mobility between the urban provinces is strictly regulated and how the island's economy is micromanaged centrally by the representative senate in Amaurot, which ensures the appropriate supply of goods domestically and controls foreign trade to the extent that 'the whole island is like a single family' (61–62). The section then becomes a complicated discussion about Utopian ideas of value, pleasure, and the nature of true happiness that is precipitated by a discussion of economic surplus. Hythloday explains that Utopians export surplus goods and receive not only products but also 'immense quantities of silver and gold', as well as 'cash', 'credit', and 'promissory notes', from other countries in return. However, the 'vast reserve of treasure' created by this balance of trade is used primarily to pay mercenary soldiers in times of war. Within Utopia itself, gold and silver carry no value beyond their intrinsic worth as metals (which is limited) and are used to make the basest artefacts: chamber pots, slaves' shackles, jewellery for criminals (63–64). This section includes the much-cited anecdote of the Anemolian ambassadors who initially think that their splendour will impress the Utopians, before realizing that—in Utopian eyes—it merely makes them look foolish (65). Rather, we are told, Utopians value learning over riches, and conceive of happiness in terms of 'good and honest pleasure' that corresponds to 'religious principles' (broadly defined) and 'living according to nature' (with virtue and reason) (69, 71,

70). Such pleasures are to be found in 'every state or movement of body and mind'. They include the capacity for contented reflection, intellectual curiosity, the pursuit of knowledge (both ancient and experiential), sensory exultation (especially music), as well as health, beauty, strength, and agility. But the Utopian list of 'false pleasure' is equally memorable. It includes devotion to finery and fashions, the pursuit of 'ceremonial honours', hoarding of artefacts and riches, gambling, and hunting (66, 73–74). Nor are there taverns or alehouses in Utopia (62).

If these values and sense of the good life underpin Utopian communism, then so, too, do the enslaved peoples discussed in the next section. These include prisoners of war captured by Utopians; Utopian citizens guilty of heinous crimes; criminals purchased from other countries; and 'drudges' from outside Utopia who choose to become enslaved there because living conditions are better. The section also includes some of the more extraordinary Utopian customs, at least when viewed from a late medieval Christian perspective: Utopians kill themselves if illness has made their life a continual 'torture' rather than a source of pleasure (82); prospective marriage partners inspect each other naked so they are 'protected from deception'; divorce is permissible (albeit unusual) if spouses have 'incompatible characters' (84), but adultery is punished with slavery and, if recurring, by death (85).

The section then turns to issues of punishment and law, Hythloday making the important observation that Utopians 'have few laws, for their training is such that very few suffice' (86). This reflects how the good behaviour and attitudes of the Utopians are habituated and naturalized through the formal education of children provided by priests and, as importantly, through their social 'institutions', 'customs', and 'manners' (104, 64). It also indicates the equitable nature of Utopian law, by which 'the most obvious interpretation of any law' is always 'the fairest'. As a result, 'in Utopia everyone is a legal expert' (87).

One corollary of this is that Utopians are in demand as magistrates in other countries. Another is that they never make treaties with other nations—believing 'men are united more firmly by good will than by pacts'—with More taking the opportunity to satirize European powers for their endless diplomatic shenanigans and 'for keeping treaties badly' (89). This leads smoothly into the penultimate section of Book Two, which deals with the reasons why Utopians go to war, and their methods of warfare. Hythloday explains that Utopians are much more likely to fight for the interests of their friends and allies than themselves (90–92). He also notes that, although both men and women undergo intensive military training in Utopia, the citizenry 'despise war as an activity fit only for beasts' (89). This means that when they do become embroiled in wars, Utopians employ fierce and ruthless mercenaries to supplement their own voluntary civic militias and use 'intelligence and rationality' rather than 'strength and ferocity' to undermine enemies. Stratagems include rewarding the assassination of prominent opposition leaders and statesmen, inciting domestic and dynastic dissension among their enemies, targeting the opposing general to end battles as quickly as possible, perfecting the tactic of setting (and avoiding) 'crafty ambushes', and always ensuring that battles are fought 'outside their own borders' (95–97).

This discussion of military practices viewed by Europeans as dishonourable but which, according to Utopian reasoning, are 'wise' and 'humane' leads inexorably to the concluding section, 'The religions of the Utopians' (92). This contains a description of the Utopians' religious beliefs, rituals, and offices followed by a few concluding pages in which Hythloday explains why Utopia is not simply the 'best' of commonwealths 'but indeed the only one that can rightfully claim that name' (109).

In terms of religious belief, Hythloday explains how Utopians generally share in the belief of 'a single divinity [...] beyond the grasp of the human mind' (98) which they nevertheless worship through different gods. This diversity is protected by law; reasonable and moderate debate is also encouraged and is expected to enable Utopians to find spiritual truth. What Utopians may not do is force their god or gods on others, either 'by threats or violence' (100). Hythloday notes how Utopians are nevertheless drawn to Christianity (it is like a sect that 'most prevails among them' and they are attracted to its approval of a 'communal way of life'); but he also describes how the one Utopian he saw arrested and exiled for violent religious zeal was a Christian convert (99)—a prescient intimation of things to come in contemporary Europe. Among Utopians there is widespread belief in 'bliss after death', that 'vices will be punished and virtues rewarded', that the dead move among the living, and that holiness is articulated through public service ('the active life') and hard labour (100–103). Like other public office holders, Utopian priests are elected by secret ballot: they form a select cadre of 'extraordinary holiness' (103) responsible for public worship, morality, and education. They also accompany Utopian armies to war—where they act to limit bloodshed, defend the defeated, and encourage peace—and preside over reverent and musical worship in huge and monumental cathedrals that serve as 'a single destination' for Utopians and their gods (104–108). Hythloday finishes his description of Utopia with an account of Utopian prayers, in which the happiness of the commonwealth and bliss after death take precedence over personal and 'earthly careers' (109).

This leads directly into perhaps the most controversial part of Book Two, in which Hythloday becomes increasingly impassioned about the qualities of Utopia as a commonwealth and the narrator responds, finally, with sceptical irony. According to Hythloday, Utopia's success stems from the absence of 'private business' ('everything belongs to everybody'): Utopians accordingly live without inequities or inequalities (for example, between the idle rich and labouring poor) or the psychological damage that relentless material competitiveness ('greed') and anxiety ('poverty') cause (109–110). But as importantly, Hythloday notes that through their education, institutions, and customs Utopians have managed to efface 'the one single monster' that 'is too deeply fixed in human nature to be easily plucked out' and which prevents Europeans from developing true commonwealths of their own: 'I mean Pride', whereby 'good fortune is dazzling only by contrast with the miseries of others' (112).

The narrator's concluding response to this eulogy cleverly confirms Hythloday's conjunction of social inequity and human pride by rejecting Utopia as a template for European commonwealths. The fundamental flaw of 'their whole system', the narrator opines, is that 'their communal living and their moneyless economy […] utterly subverts all the nobility, magnificence, splendour and majesty which (in the popular view) are the true ornaments and glory of any commonwealth' (113). Or to put that another way: to emulate Utopia would require not simply social and cultural revolution, but also the transformation of human nature.

Bibliography

Archival Sources

Archives nationales de France, F17/1212, dossier 10 (Thomas Rousseau, correspondence about a pension, 1787).
Biblioteca de Catalunya [BC] MS 4431/3 (copy of Acadèmia de la Llengua Catalana's pamphlet, *Sobre normative*, annotated by Josep Pin i Soler).
Biblioteca de Catalunya MS 4480 (Thomas More, *Utopia traducció catalana ara per primera volta estampada, precedida per un Comentari sobre l'autor y'l llibre*, trans. J. Pin i Soler).
Biblioteca de Catalunya MS 4511/4 ('Ressenyes periodístiques sobre les traduccions d'humanistes').
Biblioteca de Catalunya MS 4514/1 ('Esborranys cartes de Josep Pin i Soler').
Biblioteca de Catalunya MS 4514/2 ('Cartes adreçades a Josep Pin i Soler').
British Library MS Lansdowne 2 (the Burghley papers), 129r–134r (items 57–9: Ralph Robinson's letters to William Cecil).
Cecil Papers 277/1 (Bernard André, 'Invocatio de inclita invictissimi regis nostri Henrici octavi in Gallos et Scotos victoria', 1513).
Chatsworth R/1/3; R/1/5 (Papers of Gilbert Burnet and Lady Russell).
Hartlib Papers 28/1, https://www.dhi.ac.uk/hartlib (Samuel Hartlib, *Considerations Tending to the Happy Accomplishment of Englands Reformation in Church and State*, 1647)
Hartlib Papers 30/4, https://www.dhi.ac.uk/hartlib (Samuel Hartlib, *Ephemerides*, 1640)
Hartlib Papers 47/9/38A, https://www.dhi.ac.uk/hartlib (Samuel Hartlib, undated note on London University)
International Institute of Social History in Amsterdam, Karl Kautsky Papers, Arch00712, Inv. Nr. Dx 502–512 (Eduard Fuchs's correspondence with Karl Kautsky).
London, St Bartholomew's Hospital Archives, Treasurer's Accounts, 1547–61.
Mennonite Church USA Archives, Hist MSS I-447, Box 20, 6 (Eberhard Arnold, 'Diary, Summer 1930', English translation by Plough Publishing House, 1973).
Real Biblioteca, Fondo Gondomar, RB II/1087 ('Gondomar Manuscript': Anonymous Spanish translation of *Utopia*, c.1519–35).

Works by Thomas More

Printed Editions and Translations of Thomas More's *Utopia*

Cave, Terence (ed.) (2008c), *Thomas More's* Utopia *in Early Modern Europe: Paratext and Contexts*, Part II, 'The Paratexts' (Manchester: Manchester University Press), 145–280 [includes parallel translations of German, Italian, French, Dutch, and Spanish paratexts, and an account of the Latin paratexts].

International Thomas More Bibliography for *Utopia* at http://www3.telus.net/lakowski/Utopbib1.html

More, Thomas (1516), *Libellus vere aureus nec minus salutaris quam festivus de optimo reip[ublicae] statu, deq[ue] nova Insula Utopia* (Louvain: Thierry Martens) [Latin].

More, Thomas (1517), *De optimo reipublicae statu, deque nova insula utopia* (Paris: Gilles de Gourmont) [Latin].

More, Thomas (1518a), *De optimo reip. Statu deque nova insula utopia libellus vere aureus* (Basel: apud Johann Froben [Mar. edn]) [Latin].

More, Thomas (1518b), *De optimo reip. Statu, deque nova insula utopia, libellus vere aureus* (Basel: apud Johann Froben [Nov./Dec. edn]) [Latin].

More, Thomas (1518b/Z), Annotated copy of More 1518b, owned by Juan de Zumárraga. Benson Collection, University of Texas, Austin (shelf mark GZZ 321.07 M813D 1518) [Latin].

More, Thomas (1519), *De optimo Reipublicae statu deque nova insula Utopia libellus vere aureus*, in *Luciani opuscula Erasmo Roterodamo interprete* (Florence: Heirs of Filippo Giunta) [Latin].

More, Thomas (1524), *Von der wunderbarlichen Innsel Utopia genant das ander Buch*, trans. Claudius Cantiuncula (Basel: Johann Bebel) [German].

More, Thomas (1548a), *La republica nouvamente ritrovata, del governo dell'isola Eutopia*, trans. Ortensio Lando (Venice: [Aurelio Pincio?]) [Italian].

More, Thomas (1548b), *De optimo Reipublicae statu deque nova insula Utopia libellus vere aureus* (Louvain: Servatius Sassenus for Arnold Birckmann) [Latin].

More, Thomas (1550), *La description de l'isle d'Utopie ou est comprins le miroer des republiques du monde, et l'exemplaire de vie heureuse*, trans. Jean Le Blond (Paris: Charles l'Angelier) [French].

More, Thomas (1551), *A fruteful, and pleasaunt worke of the beste state of a publyque weale, and of the newe yle called Utopia*, trans. Ralph Robinson (London: [Sebastian Mierdman for] Abraham Veale) [English].

More, Thomas (1553), *De Utopie van Thomas Morus in zijnen tijden Cancellier van Enghelant: een boeck seer profijtelijck ende vermakelijck om lesen, bysondere den ghenen die heensdaechs een stadt ende ghemeynte hebben te regeren, daer hy meestendeel toe dienende is* (Antwerp: Hans de Laet) [Dutch].

More, Thomas (1555), *De optimo reipub. statu deque nova insula Utopia, libellus vere aureus, nec minus salutaris quam festivus* (Cologne: heirs of Arnold Birckmann) [Latin].

More, Thomas (1556), *A frutefull, pleasaunt, and witte worke, of the beste state of a publique weale, and of the new yle, called Utopia*, trans. Ralph Robinson (London: [Richard Tottel for] Abraham Veale) [English].

More, Thomas (1559), *La Republique d'Utopie, par Thomas Maure, chancelier d'Angleterre, Œuvre grandement utile et profitable, demonstrait le parfait estat d'une bien ordonnée politique*, [trans. Jean Le Blond], ed. Barthélemy Aneau (Lyons: Jean Saugrain) [French].

More, Thomas (1561), 'Del governo della Rep. d'Utopia', trans. Ortensio Lando, rev. Francesco Sansovino, in Francesco Sansovino, *Del governo de regni et delle republiche cosi antiche come moderne libri XVIII* (Venice: Francesco Sansovino) [Italian].

More, Thomas (1563), 'Utopiae libri II', in *Thomae Mori, Angliae ornamenti eximii, Lucubrationes ab innumeris mendis repurgatae. Vtopiae libri II. Progymnasmata. Epigrammata. Ex Luciano conuersas quaedam. Declamatio Lucianicae respondens. Epistolae. Quibus additae sunt duae aliorum epistolae, de uita, moribus & morte Mori, adiuncto rerum notabilium Indice* (Basel: Nicolaus Episcopius) [Latin].

More, Thomas (1565a), 'Utopia', in *Thomae Mori Angli, viri eruditionis pariter ac virtutis nominee clarissimi, Angliaeque olim cancellarii, Omnia, quae hucusque ad manus nostras pervenerunt, Latina Opera* (Louvain: Jean Bogard) [Latin].

More, Thomas (1565b), 'Utopia', in *Thomae Mori Angli, viri eruditionis pariter ac virtutis nominee clarissimi, Angliaeque olim cancellarii, Omnia, quae hucusque ad manus nostras pervenerunt, Latina Opera* (Louvain: Pierre Zangre) [Latin].

More, Thomas (1566a), 'Del governo della Rep. d'Utopia', [trans. Ortensio Lando,] rev. Francesco Sansovino, in Francesco Sansovino, *Del governo de regni et delle repubbliche antiche et moderne [...] libri XXI* (Venice: Giovan Battista and Marchiò Sessa and brothers) [Italian].

More, Thomas (1566b), 'Utopia', in *Thomae Mori Angli, viri eruditionis pariter ac virtutis nominee clarissimi, Angliaeque olim cancellarii, Omnia, quae hucusque ad manus nostras pervenerunt, Latina Opera* (Louvain: Jean Bogard) [Latin].

More, Thomas (1566c), 'Utopia', in *Thomae Mori Angli, viri eruditionis pariter ac virtutis nominee clarissimi, Angliaeque olim cancellarii, Omnia, quae hucusque ad manus nostras pervenerunt, Latina Opera* (Louvain: Pierre Zangre) [Latin].

More, Thomas (1567), 'Del governo della Rep. d'Utopia', [trans. Ortensio Lando], rev. Francesco Sansovino, in Francesco Sansovino, *Del governo de regni et delle repubbliche antiche et moderne [...] libri XXI* (Venice: Giovan Battista and Marchiò Sessa and brothers) [Italian].

More, Thomas (1578), 'Del governo della Rep. d'Utopia', [trans. Ortensio Lando], rev. Francesco Sansovino, in Francesco Sansovino, *Del governo et amministratione di diversi regni et republiche, cosi antiche come moderne [...] libri XXI* (Venice: Giovanni Antonio Bertano) [Italian].

More, Thomas (1583), 'Del governo della Rep. d'Utopia', [trans. Ortensio Lando], rev. Francesco Sansovino, in Francesco Sansovino, *Del governo et amministratione di diversi regni, et republiche, cosi antiche come moderne [...] libri XXII* (Venice: Altobello Salicato) [Italian].

More, Thomas (1585), 'De La Republique D'Utopie', trans. Gabriel Chappuys, in Gabriel Chappuys, *L'Estat, description et gouvernement des royaumes et republiques du monde, tant anciennes que modernes* (Paris: Pierre Cavellat) [French].

More, Thomas (1591), *Libellus vere aureus nec minus salutaris quam festiuus de optimo reip. statu, deque nova insula utopia* (Wittenberg: Johann Krafft).

More, Thomas (1597), *A most pleasant, fruitful, and wittie worke, of the best state of a publique weale, and of the new Yle called Utopia*, trans. Ralph Robinson (London: Thomas Creede) [English].

More, Thomas (1598), 'De La Republique d'Utopie', trans. Gabriel Chappuys, in Gabriel Chappuys (trans.), *L'Estat, description et gouvernement des royaumes et republiques du monde, tant anciennes que modernes* (Paris: Regnault Chaudière) [French].

More, Thomas (1601), *Illustris Viri Thomae Mori Regni Britanniarum Cancellarii, De Optimo Reipublicae Statu, Deque Nova Insula Utopia, Libri Duo*, ed. Eberhard von Weyhe (Frankfurt: Peter Kopf) [Latin].

More, Thomas (1607), 'Del governo della Rep. d'Utopia', [trans. Ortensio Lando], rev. Francesco Sansovino, in Francesco Sansovino, *Del governo et amministratione di diversi regni, et repubbliche, cosi antiche come moderne [...] libri XXII* (Venice: Altobello Salicato) [Italian].

More, Thomas (1611), 'Du gouvernment et administration de la Republique d'Ytopie', trans. F.N.D., in F.N.D (trans.), *Du Gouvernement et Administration de divers estats, Royaumes et Republiques, tant anciennes que modernes* (Paris: François Huby) [French].

More, Thomas (1612), *De optimo Reipublicae Statu, Libellus vere aureus: Ordentliche und Außführliche Beschreibung Der uberaus herrlichen und gantz wunderbarlichen, doch wenigen bißhero bekandten Insul Utopia*, trans. [Eszetts and Gregor Wintermonat] (Leipzig: Henning Grosse) [German].

More, Thomas (1613), *Libellus vere aureus nec minus salutaris quam festivus de optimo reip. statu, deque nova Insula Utopia* (Hanau: Jan de Haan for Peter Kopf) [Latin].

More, Thomas (1619), *De optimo reipublicae statu, deque nova insula Utopia, libri duo in*, Caspar Dornau *Amphitheatrum sapientiae socraticae joco-seriae*, vol. 1 (Hanau: David und Daniel Aubry/Clemens Schleich), 822–854.

More, Thomas (1620), *De optimo reipublicae statu, de que noua insula Vtopia, libri duo* (Milan: J. B. Bidellium).

More, Thomas (1620). *Illustris viri Thomae Mori Regni Britaniarum Cancellarii, De optimo reipublicae statu, de que noua insula Vtopia, libri duo: hac postremo editione Superiorum iussu emendati. Ad illustrissimum Senatus Mediolanensis Praesidem D.D. Iulium Aresium.* (Mediolani: Apud Ioannem Baptistam Bidellium). Available online at http://luna.folger.edu/luna/servlet/detail/FOLGERCM1~6~6~89278~106466:-Utopia-- Illustris-viri-Thomae-Mori. and https://play.google.com/store/books/details/Thomas_More_Illustris_viri_Thomae_Mori_De_ optimo_r?id=yNVnuWbCKrgC.

More, Thomas (1624), *Sir Thomas Moore's Utopia*, trans. Ralph Robinson (London: Bernard Alsop) [English].

More, Thomas (1629a), *Thomae Mori Utopia, a mendis vindicata* (Amsterdam: Willem Blaeuw) [Latin].

More, Thomas (1629b), *Thomae Mori Utopia, a mendis vindicate* (Cologne: 'Cornelius Egmond') [Latin].

More, Thomas (1631), *Thomae Mori Utopia, a mendis vindicata* (Amsterdam: Jan Jansson) [Latin].

More, Thomas (1637), *Utopia*, trans. Don Jerónimo Antonio Medinilla i Porres (Córdoba: Salvador de Cea) [Spanish].

More, Thomas (1639), *The Commonwealth of Utopia*, trans. Ralph Robinson (London: Bernard Alsop and T. Fawcet, to be sold by Wil. Sheares) [English].

More, Thomas (1663), *Thomae Morie Utopia, a mendis vindicata* (Oxford: William Hall for Francis Oxlad) [Latin].

More, Thomas (1643), *L'Utopie de Thomas Morus*, trans. Samuel Sorbière (Amsterdam: Jean Blaeu) [French].

More, Thomas (1677), *Het onbekent en wonderlijk Eyland Utopia, Ontdekt door Rafaël Hythlodeus, en by t'samenspraeke beschreven door den geleerden Tomas Morus, Kancelier van Engeland, ten tijde van Koning Hendrik den achtsten*, trans. Frans van Hoogstraten (Rotterdam: Frans van Hoogstraten) [Dutch].

More, Thomas (1684), *Utopia*, trans. Gilbert Burnet (London: for Richard Chiswell).

More, Thomas (1685), *Utopia*, trans. Gilbert Burnet (London: for Richard Chiswell, to be sold by George Powell).

More, Thomas (1704), *Ordentliche und Außführliche Beschreibung Der überaus herrlichen, und gantz wunderbahrlichen, doch wenigen Bißhero bekandten Insul Utopia* (Frankfurt: Henning Grosse) [German].

More, Thomas (1715), *L'Utopie de Thomas Morus, Chancelier d'Angleterre; Idée ingenieuse pour remedier au malheur des Hommes; et pour leur procurer une felicité complette. Cet Ouvrage contient Le Plan d'une République dont les Lois, lest Usages, et les Coutumes tendent uniquement à faire aux Societez Humaines le passage de la Vie dans toute la douceur imaginable. Republique, qui deviendra infalliblement réelle, des que les Mortels se conduiront par la Raison*, trans. Nicolas Gueudeville (Leiden: Pieter van der Aa) [French].

More, Thomas (1743), *Utopia: or the Happy Republic; a Philosophical Romance, in Two Books*, trans. Gilbert Burnet (Glasgow: Robert Foulis) [English].

More, Thomas (1750), *De Optimo reipublicae statu, deque nova insula Utopia* (Glasgow: Robert and Andrew Foulis) [Latin].

More, Thomas (1753), *Des Englischen Canzlers Thomas Morus Utopien: in einer neuen und freyen Uebersetzun*, trans. J.B.K. (Frankfurt: Heinrich Ludwig Brönner) [German].

More, Thomas (1777), *De optimo reipublicae statu, deque nova insula Utopia, libri duo* (Paris and London: Barbou) [Latin].

More, Thomas (1780), *Tableau du meilleur gouvernement possible, ou l'Utopie de Thomas Morus, Chancellier d'Angleterre*, trans. Thomas Rousseau (Paris: Alexandre Jombert) [French].

More, Thomas (1789a), *Du meilleur Gouvernement possible, ou la nouvelle isle d'Utopie, de Thomas Morus*, trans. Thomas Rousseau (Paris: J. Blanchon) [French].

More, Thomas (1789b), *Kartina vsevozmozhnogo luchshego pravleniya ili Utopii*, trans. Anon. (St Petersburg: Johan Karlovich Shnor) [Russian].

More, Thomas (1790a), *Filosofa Rafaila Gitlode stranstvovanie v Novom Svete i opisanie luibopytstva dostoinykh primechanii i blagorazumnykh ustanovlenii zhizni mirolyubivago naroda ostrova Utopii. Perevod s Anglinskogo yazyika. Sochinenie Toma Morisa*, trans. Anon. (St Petersburg: Johan Karlovich Shnor) [Russian].

More, Thomas (1790b), *La Utopia de Tomás Moro*, trans. Jéronimo Antonio Medinilla y Porres (Madrid: Pantaleon Aznar) [Spanish].

More, Thomas (1805), *La Utopia de Tomás Moro*, trans. Jéronimo Antonio Medinilla y Porres (Madrid: M. Repullés) [Spanish].

More, Thomas (1808a), *Memoirs of Sir Thomas More: with a New Translation of his Utopia, his History of King Richard III, and his Latin Poems*, trans. Arthur Cayley, 2 vols (London: Cadell and Davis) [English].

More, Thomas (1808b), *A most pleasant, fruitful, and witty work, of the best state of a public weal, and of the new isle called Utopia; written in Latin by the Right Worthy and Famous Sir Thomas More, Knight, [...]; with copious notes, and a biographical and literary introduction*, trans. Ralph Robinson, ed. T. F. Dibdin (London: William Bulmer for William Miller) [English].

More, Thomas (1838), *Utopia: or the Happy Republic, a Philosophical Romance* [trans. Gilbert Burnet], *To Which Is Added The New Atlantis, By Lord Bacon*, ed. J. A. St John (London: Joseph Rickerby) [English].

More, Thomas (1846), *Thomas Morus und sein berühmtes Werk Utopia. Aus dem Englischen übersetzt*, trans. Hermann Kothe, ed. Eduard Maria Oettinger (Leipzig: Universal Bibliothek) [German].

More, Thomas (1852), *Utopia: Or, The Happy Republic; A Philosophical Romance* [trans. Gilbert Burnet], *To Which Is Added, The New Atlantis by Lord Bacon. With an Analysis of Plato's Republic, and Copious Notes*, ed. J. A. St John (London: M. S. Rickerby) [English].

More, Thomas (1869), *Utopia. Translated into English by Ralph Robinson. His Second and Revised Edition, 1556: Preceded by the Title and Epistle of his First Edition, 1551*, ed. Edward Arber (London: A. Murray & Son) [English].

More, Thomas (1882), *Ryo Seifu Dan*, trans. Tsutomu Inoue (Nagoya: Shisei-Do) [Japanese].

More, Thomas (1883), *Shin Seifu Soshiki Dan*, trans. Tsutomu Inoue (Nagoya: Shisei-Do) [Japanese].

More, Thomas (1885), *Sir Thomas More's Utopia*, in Henry Morley (ed.), *Ideal Commonwealths: Plutarch's Lycurgus, More's Utopia, Bacon's New Atlantis, Campanella's City of the Sun, and a Fragment of Hall's Mundus Alter et Idem* (London: George Routledge and Sons) [English].

More, Thomas (1888), *Voyage a L'Ile D'Utopie*, [trans. Thomas Rousseau], introd. Eugène Muller (Paris: Delagrave) [printed with Bernadin de Saint-Pierre, *L'Arcadie*, 1781] [French].

More, Thomas (1889), *Sir Thomas More's Utopia*, trans. Gilbert Burnet, ed. Henry Morley (London: Cassell & Co.) [English].

More, Thomas (1890a), *The 'Utopia'* [trans. Ralph Robinson]; *and 'The History of Edward V*, ed. Maurice Adams (London: Walter Scott Publishing) [English].

More, Thomas (1890b), *More's Utopia*, in Henry Morley (ed.), *Ideal Commonwealths: Plutarch's Lycurgus, More's Utopia, Bacon's New Atlantis, Campanella's City of the Sun, and a Fragment of Hall's Mundus Alter et Idem* (London: George Routledge and Sons) [English].

More, Thomas (1893), *Utopia Written by Sir Thomas More*, trans. Ralph Robinson, ed. F. S. Ellis (Hammersmith: Kelmscott Press) [English].

More, Thomas (1894), *Riso-teki Kokka*, trans. Tamikichi Ogiwara (Tokyo: Hakubun-Kan) [Japanese].

More, Thomas (1895a), *The Utopia of Thomas More in Latin from the Edition of March 1518, and in English from the First Edition of Ralph Robynson's Translation of 1551 with Additional Translations, Introduction, and Notes*, ed. J. H. Lupton (Oxford: Clarendon Press) [Latin/English].

More, Thomas (1895b), *Utopia*, ed. Victor Michels and Theobald Ziegler (Berlin: Weidmann) [Latin].

More, Thomas (1896), *Utopia*, trans. Ignaz Emanuel Wessely, ed. Eduard Fuchs (Munich: Verlag der Gesellschaftswissenschaft) [German].

More, Thomas (1901), 'Utopii', trans. Evgenii Tarle, in Evgenii Tarle, *Obshchestvennie vozzreniya Tomasa Mora v svyazi s ekonomicheskom sostoyaniem ego vremeni. Prilozheniya. Perevod 'Utopii' s latinskogo, rukopis' sovremennika o Tomase More* (St Petersburg: Mir bozhii) [Russian].

More, Thomas (1903), *Utopiia*, trans. Aleksandr G. Genkel' (St Petersburg: Busellia) [Russian].

More, Thomas (1904), *Sir Thomas More's Utopia*, trans. Ralph Robinson, ed. John Churton Collins (Oxford: Clarendon Press) [English].

More, Thomas (1905), *Tomas Mor i ego utopiia*, trans. Aleksandr G. Genkel' (St Petersburg: Knigoizdatel'stvo M. V. Pirozkova) [Russian].

More, Thomas (1908), *Sir Thomas More's Utopia*, trans. Ralph Robinson, ed. John Churton Collins; introd. H. G. Wells (London: Blackie & Sons) [English].

More, Thomas (1909), *More's Millennium: Being the Utopia of Sir Thomas More Rendered into Modern English*, trans. Valerian Paget [pseud. of Harold and Zoe Paget] (London: Alston Rivers) [English].

More, Thomas (1910a), *The Utopia of Thomas More, Ralph Robinson's translation, with Roper's Life of More and some of his letters [...] To which is added the Latin text of the Utopia*, ed. George Sampson; introd. A. Guthkelch (London: G. Bell & Sons) [English/Latin].

More, Thomas (1910b), *Utopia*, trans. Ferenc Kelen (Budapest: Franklin) [Hungarian].

More, Thomas (1910c), *Utopia* [trans. Ralph Robinson], *with the 'Dialogue of Comfort'*, introd. John O'Hagan, Everyman's Library (London: J. M. Dent & Sons) [English].

More, Thomas (1912), *Utopia: Traducció catalana ara per primera volta estampada, precedida d'un comentari sobre l'autor y'l llibre*, trans. J. Pin i Soler (Barcelona: Tip. L'Avenç: Massó, Casas & Ca.) [Catalan].

More, Thomas (1914), *Yuutopia*, trans. Masatake Mikami (Tokyo: Rigyu-Shoin) [Japanese].
More, Thomas (1918), *Utopiia*, trans. Aleksandr G. Genkel' (Petrograd: Sovet rabochikh i krasnoarmeiskikh deputatov) [Russian].
More, Thomas (1920), *Utopia*, trans. Tony Noah (Zurich: Rascher) [German].
More, Thomas (1922), *Utopia*, trans. Gerhard Ritter, introd. Hermann Oncken (Berlin: R. Hobbing) [German].
More, Thomas (1923), *Tomas Mor i ego Utopiia*, trans. Aleksandr G. Genkel' (Kharkov: Proletariat) [Russian].
More, Thomas (1929a), *Yuutopia*, trans. Yushu Morita (Tokyo: Heibon-Sha) [Japanese].
More, Thomas (1929b), *Yuutopia*, trans. Yuzo Murayama (Tokyo: Shunju-Sha) [Japanese].
More, Thomas (1934), *Yuutopia*, trans. Kensho Honda (Tokyo: Iwanami-Shoten) [Japanese].
More, Thomas (1935a), *Wutuobang* [Utopia], trans. Liu Lingsheng (Shanghai: Shangwu yinshuguan) [Chinese].
More, Thomas (1935b), *Zolataia kniga stol'zhe poleznaia, kak zabavnaia, o nailuschshem ustroistve gosudrarstva i o novom ostrove Utopii*, trans. A. I. Malein, introd. V. P. Volgin (Moscow and Leningrad: Academia Moskva) [Russian].
More, Thomas (1936), *L'Utopie ou le traité de la meilleure forme de government*, ed. and trans. Marie Delcourt (Paris: E. Droz) [French/Latin].
More, Thomas (1939), 'Yutubiya', trans. and abridged Zaki Najib Mahmud, in *Ard al-ahlam* (Cairo: Dar al-Hilal) [Arabic].More, Thomas (1941), *Utopia*, trans. László Geréb (Budapest: Officina) [Hungarian].
More, Thomas (1943), *Utopia*, trans. Tibor Kardos (Budapest: Franklin) [Hungarian].
More, Thomas (1947), *Utopija*, ed. A. I. Malein, introd. V. P. Volgin (Moscow: Academy of Sciences) [Russian].
More, Thomas (1948), *Yuutopia*, trans. Masao Hirai (Tokyo: Iwanami-Shoten) (reissued as More 1957b) [Japanese].
More, Thomas (1953), *Utopija*, ed. A. I. Malein, introd. V. P. Volgin (Moscow: Academy of Sciences) [Russian].
More, Thomas (1956), *Wutuobang*, trans. Dai Liuling (Beijing: Sanlian Shudian) [Chinese].
More, Thomas (1957a), 'Utopii', trans. Evgenii Tarle, in Evgenii Tarle, *Akademik Evgenii Viktorovich Tarle, Sochineniya v dvenadtsati tomakh*, vol. 1 (Moscow: Academy of Sciences), 121–265, 717–729. [Russian].
More, Thomas (1957b), *Yuutopia*, trans. Masao Hirai (Tokyo: Iwanami-Shoten) (reissue of More 1948) [Japanese].
More, Thomas (1963a), *Utópia*, trans. Tibor Kardos (rev. edn, Budapest: Európa Könyvkiadó) [Hungarian].
More, Thomas (1963b), 'Yutubiya', trans. and abridged Zaki Najib Mahmud, *Turath al-insaniyya*, 5: 368–385. [Arabic].
More, Thomas (1964), *Utopia*, trans. Edward Surtz (New Haven: Yale University Press) [English].
More, Thomas (1965a), *Utopia*, ed. Edward Surtz and J. H. Hexter, in *The Yale Edition of the Complete Works of St Thomas More*, vol. 4 (New Haven: Yale University Press) [English/Latin].
More, Thomas (1965b), *Utopia*, trans. Paul Turner (Harmondsworth: Penguin) [English].
More, Thomas (1966), *Wutuobang*, trans. Xiangzhang Guo (Taipei: Tai Wan Zhonghua) [Chinese].
More, Thomas (1969), *Yuutopia*, trans. Akio Sawada (Tokyo: Chuo-Koron) [Japanese].

More, Thomas (1970), *La Description de l'isle d'Utopie*, trans. Jean Le Blond, ed. Michel Jeanneret (The Hague: S. R. Publishers) [French].
More, Thomas (1974), *Yutubiya*, trans. Angèle Butrus Sam'an (Cairo: Dar al-Ma'arif) [Arabic].
More, Thomas (1977a), *Utopia/Utopía*, ed. and trans. Joaquim Mallafrè Gavaldà (Barcelona: Bosch) [Latin/English [Robinson's trans.]/Spanish].
More, Thomas (1977b), 'Yutubiya', trans. and abridged Zaki Najib Mahmud, in *Ard al-ahlam* (Cairo: Dar al-Hilal) (first published 1939) [Arabic].
More, Thomas (1978a), *L'Utopie de Thomas More*, ed. and trans. André Prévost (Paris: Mame) [French].
More, Thomas (1978b), *Utopiya*, trans. Judith Kagan, commentary by I. N. Osinovskii (Moscow: Nauka) [Russian].
More, Thomas (1988), *Utopia*, trans. Joan Valls i Royo (Barcelona: La llar del llibre) [Catalan].
More, Thomas (1989), *Utopia*, trans. Robert M. Adams, ed. George M. Logan (Cambridge: Cambridge University Press) [English].
More, Thomas (1992a), *Utopia*, trans. Ralph Robinson (London: Everyman) [English].
More, Thomas (1992b), *Utopia*, trans. Robert M. Adams (New York: W. W. Norton & Co.) [English].
More, Thomas (1993), *Yuutopia*, trans. Akio Sawada (Tokyo: Chuo-Koron) [Japanese].
More, Thomas (1995), *Utopia: Latin Text and English Translation*, ed. George M. Logan, Robert M. Adams, and C. H. Millar, trans. Robert M. Adams (Cambridge: Cambridge University Press) [English/Latin].
More, Thomas (1999), *Utopia*, trans. Ralph Robinson, ed. David Harris Sacks (Bedford: St Martin's Press) [English].
More, Thomas (2002), trans. Robert M. Adams, ed. George M. Logan (2nd edn, Cambridge: Cambridge University Press) [English].
More, Thomas (2003), *Utopia*, trans. Paul Turner (London: Penguin) [English].
More, Thomas (2005), *Utopia*, ed. Wayne A. Rebhorn (New York: Barnes & Noble Classics) [English].
More, Thomas (2009a), *Utopia*, ed. Emilio Piccolo (Naples: Senecio) [Latin].
More, Thomas (2009b), *Utopia*, ed. and trans. Joan Manuel del Pozo (Barcelona: Accent) [Catalan].
More, Thomas (2011), *Utopia*, trans. Robert M. Adams, ed. George M. Logan (3rd edn, New York: W. W. Norton & Company) [English].
More, Thomas (2012), *Utopia*, trans. Dominic Baker-Smith (London: Penguin) [English].
More, Thomas (2014), *Utopia*, ed. and trans. Clarence H. Miller; afterword by Jerry Harp (2nd edn, New Haven: Yale University Press) [English].
More, Thomas (2016a), *Utopia*, trans. Núria Gómez Llauger, introd. David Gálvez (Barcelona: Angle Editions) [Catalan].
More, Thomas (2016b), *Utopia*, trans. Robert M. Adams, ed. George M. Logan (3rd edn, Cambridge: Cambridge University Press) [English].
More, Thomas (2020), *Utopia*, trans. D. Baker-Smith (London: Penguin) [English].

The Complete Works of St Thomas More (CWM)

CWM 1: Thomas More, *English Poems, Life of Pico, the Last Things*, ed. Anthony G. Edwards, Katherine Gardiner Rogers, and Clarence H. Miller (New Haven: Yale University Press, 1997).

CWM 3/1: Thomas More, *Translations of Lucian*, ed. Craig R. Thompson (New Haven: Yale University Press, 1974).
CWM 3/2: Thomas More, *Latin Poems*, ed. Clarence H. Miller et al. (New Haven: Yale University Press, 1984).
CWM 4: Thomas More, *Utopia*, ed. Edward Surtz and J. H. Hexter (New Haven: Yale University Press, 1977).
CWM 5: Thomas More, *Responsio ad Lutherum*, trans. Sister Scholastica Mandeville, ed. John Headley (New Haven: Yale University Press, 1969).
CWM 6/1-2: Thomas More, *A Dialogue Concerning Heresies*, ed. Thomas M. C. Lawler, Germain Marc'hadour, and Richard C. Marius (New Haven: Yale University Press, 1981).
CWM 7: Thomas More, *Letter to Bugenhagen, Supplication of Souls, Letter Against Frith*, ed. Frank Manley, Geramin Marc'hadour, Richard Marius, and Clarence H. Miller (New Haven: Yale University Press, 1990).
CWM 8: Thomas More, *The Confutation of Tyndale's Answer*, ed. Louis A. Schuster, Richard C. Marius, James Lusardi, and Richard J. Schoeck (New Haven: Yale University Press, 1973).
CWM 9: Thomas More, *The Apology*, ed. J. B. Trapp (New Haven: Yale University Press, 1979).
CWM 10: Thomas More, *The Debellation of Salem and Bizance*, ed. John Guy, Ralph Keen, Clarence H. Miller, and Ruth McGugan (New Haven: Yale University Press, 1987).
CWM 12: Thomas More, *Dialogue of Comfort Against Tribulation*, ed. Louis L. Martz and Frank Manley (New Haven: Yale University Press, 1977).
CWM 13: Thomas More, *Treatise on the Passion; Treatise on the Blessed Body; Instructions and Prayers*, ed. Garry E. Haupt (New Haven: Yale University Press, 1976).
CWM 15: Thomas More, *In Defense of Humanism: Letter to Martin Dorp, Letter to the University of Oxford, Letter to Edward Lee, Letter to a Monk: With a New Text and Translation of Historia Richardi Tertii*, ed. Daniel Kinney (New Haven: Yale University Press, 1986).

Other Works

More, Thomas (1520), *Epigrammata* (Basel: Johann Froben).
More, Thomas (1557), *The workes of Sir Thomas More Knyght, sometime Lorde Chauncellour of England, wrytten by him in the Englysh tonge*, ed. William Rastell (London: John Cawood, John Waly, and Richard Tottell).
More, Thomas (1563b), *Thomae Mori, Angliae ornamenti eximii, Lucubrationes ab innumeris mendis repurgatae . Vtopiae libri II. Progymnasmata. Epigrammata. Ex Luciano conuersas quaedam. Declamatio Lucianicae respondens. Epistolae. Quibus additae sunt duae aliorum epistolae, de uita, moribus & morte Mori, adiuncto rerum notabilium Indice* (Basel: Nicolaus Episcopius).
More, Thomas (1565c), *Thomae Mori Angli, viri eruditionis pariter ac virtutis nominee clarissimi, Angliaeque olim cancellarii, Omnia, quae hucusque ad manus nostras pervenerunt, Latina Opera* (Louvain: Jean Bogard).
More, Thomas (1566c), *Thomae Mori Angli, viri eruditionis pariter ac virtutis nominee clarissimi, Angliaeque olim cancellarii, Omnia, quae hucusque ad manus nostras pervenerunt, Latina Opera* (Louvain: Jean Bogard) [copyright shared with Pierre Zanngre].
More, Thomas (1625), *Dissertatio epistolica, de aliquot sui temporis theologastrorum ineptiis; deque correctione translationis Vulgatae N. Testamentis: ad Martinum Dorpium* (Leiden: Lugduni Batavorum).

More, Thomas (1961), *Selected Letters*, ed. Elizabeth Frances Rogers (New Haven: Yale University Press).
More, Thomas (2004), *Erősítő párbeszéd balsors idején*, trans. Zsuzsa Gergely (Budapest: Szent István Társulat; Kolozsvár: A Dunánál).
More, Thomas, et al. (1947), *The Correspondence of Sir Thomas More*, ed. Elizabeth Rogers (Princeton: Princeton University Press, 1947).

Works by Desiderius Erasmus

Collected Works (CWE)

CWE 1: The *Correspondence of Erasmus, Letters 1-141*, trans. R. A. B. Mynors and D. F. S. Thomson, annotated by W. K. Ferguson (Toronto: University of Toronto Press, 1974).
CWE 2: The *Correspondence of Erasmus, Letters 142-297*, trans. R. A. B. Mynors and D. F. S. Thomson, annotated by W. K. Ferguson (Toronto: University of Toronto Press, 1975).
CWE 3: The *Correspondence of Erasmus, Letters 298 to 445*, trans. R. A. B. Mynors and D. F. S. Thomson, annotated by James K. McConica (Toronto: University of Toronto Press, 1976).
CWE 4: The *Correspondence of Erasmus, Letters 446 to 593*, trans. R. A. B. Mynors and D. F. S. Thomson, annotated James K. McConica (Toronto: University of Toronto Press, 1977).
CWE 5: The *Correspondence of Erasmus, Letters 594 to 841*, trans. R. A. B. Mynors and D. F. S. Thomson, annotated Peter G. Bietenholz (Toronto: University of Toronto Press, 1979).
CWE 6: The *Correspondence of Erasmus, Letters 842-992*, trans. R. A. B. Mynors and D. F. S. Thomson, annotated Peter G. Bietenholz (Toronto: University of Toronto Press, 1982).
CWE 7: The *Correspondence of Erasmus, Letters 993-1121*, trans. R. A. B. Mynors, annotated Peter G. Bietenholz (Toronto: University of Toronto Press, 1987).
CWE 24: *Literary and Educational Writings, 2: Copia*, trans. and annotated Craig R. Thompson (Toronto: University of Toronto Press, 1978).
CWE 27: *Literary and Educational Writings, 5: Panegyricus, Moria, Julius exclusus, Institutio principis christiani, Querela pacis*, trans. and annotated A. H. T. Levi (Toronto: University of Toronto Press, 1986).
CWE 31: *Adages Ii1 to Iv100*, trans. Margaret Mann Phillips, ed. R. A. B. Mynors (Toronto: University of Toronto Press, 1982).
CWE 33: *Adages II.i.1 to 22.vi.100*, trans. and annotated R. A. B. Mynors (Toronto: University of Toronto Press, 1991).
CWE 39-40: *Colloquies*, ed. and trans. Craig R. Thompson, 2 vols (Toronto: University of Toronto Press, 1997).

Other Works

Erasmus, Desiderius (1511), *Moriae Encomium: Erasmi Roterodami declamatio* (Paris: Gilles de Gourmont).
Erasmus, Desiderius (1514), *Erasmi Roterodami mōrias enkōmion, id est Stultitae laus, Libellus vere aureus, nec minus eruditus, & salutaris, quam festivus, nuper ex ipsius autoris archetypis diligentissime restitutus* (Strasbourg: Matthias Schürer).

Erasmus, Desiderius (1516a), *Epistolae aliquot illustrium virorum ad Erasmum Roterodamum, & huius ad illos* (Basel: Johann Froben).

Erasmus, Desiderius (1516b), *Institutio principis Christiani saluberrimis referta praeceptis, per Erasmum Roterodamum, cum aliis nonnullis eodem pertinentibus, quorum catalogum in proxima reperies pagella* (Louvain: Thierry Martens) (Aug. edn).

Erasmus, Desiderius (1517a), *Aliquot epistolae sanequam elegantes Erasmi Roterodami & ad hunc aliorum eruditissimorum hominum antehac nunquam excusae praeter unam & alteram* (Louvain: Dirk (Thierry) Martens).

Erasmus, Desiderius (1517b), *Querela pacis undique gentium eiectae profligataeque: autore Erasmo Roterodamo. Cum quibusdam aliis, quorum catalogum proxima reperies pagella* (Basel: Froben).

Erasmus, Desiderius (1518), *Aliquot epistolae sanequam elegantes Erasmi Roterodami, & ad hunc aliorum eruditissimorum hominum* (Basel: Johann Froben).

Erasmus, Desiderius (1521), *Brevissima maximaque compendiaria conficiendarum epistolarum formula* (Landshut: Johann Weissenburger).

Erasmus, Desiderius (1524), *Maniere de se confesser par Monsieur Erasme roterodame premierement descripte en latin puis apres translatee en francois*, trans. Claude Chansonnette (Basel: Johannes Froben).

Erasmus, Desiderius (1549), *The praise of folie: Moriae Encomium a booke made in latine by that great clerke Erasmus Roterodame*, trans. Thomas Chaloner (London: Thomas Berthelet).

Erasmus, Desiderius (1676), *Moriae Encomium of de Lof der Zotheid* (Rotterdam: Frans van Hoogstraten).

Erasmus, Desiderius (1677), *Handboexhen van den Christelijke Ridder* (Rotterdam: Frans van Hoogstraten).

Erasmus, Desiderius (1713), *L'Éloge de la folie*, trans. Nicolas Gueudeville (Leiden: Pierre van der Aa).

Erasmus, Desiderius (1720), *Les Colloques*, trans. Nicolas Gueudeville (Leiden: Pierre van der Aa).

Erasmus, Desiderius (1901–18), *The Epistles of Erasmus*, ed. Francis Morgan Nichols, 3 vols (London: Longmans, Green & Co.).

Erasmus, Desiderius (1906–58), *Opus epistolarum Des. Erasmi Roterodami*, ed. P. S. Allen, H. M. Allen, and H. W. Garrod, 11 vols (Oxford: Oxford University Press).

Erasmus, Desiderius (1910), *Elogi de la Follía*, trans. J. Pin i Soler (Barcelona: Heinrich y Ca).

Erasmus, Desiderius (1912), *Llibre de civilitat pueril*, trans. J. Pin i Soler (Barcelona: L'Avenç).

Erasmus, Desiderius (1915), *Opus Epistolarum Des. Erasmi Roterodami*, vol. 3, ed. P. S. Allen (Oxford: Oxford University Press).

Erasmus, Desiderius (1969), *Chigu Raisan*, trans. Kazuo Watanabe and Kei Ninomiya (Tokyo: Heibon-Sha).

Erasmus, Desiderius (1979), *Encomium Moriae id est Stultitiae Laus*, ed. Clarence H. Miller, in *Opera Omnia Desiderii Erasmi Roterodami, Ordinis Quarti, Tomus Tertius* (Amsterdam: North-Holland).

Erasmus, Desiderius (1993), *Praise of Folly*, ed. A. H. T. Levi, trans. Betty Radice (London: Penguin).

Erasmus, Desiderius (1997), *The Education of a Christian Prince*, trans. Lisa Jardine (Cambridge: Cambridge University Press).

OTHER SOURCES

Abdel-Malek, Kamal, and Kahla, Mouna El (2016) (eds), *America in An Arab Mirror: Images of America in Arabic Travel Literature: An Anthology* (New York: Springer).
Abensour, Miguel (1997), *De la compacité: Architectures et régimes totalitaires* (Paris: Sens & Tonka).
Abensour, Miguel (2000), *L'Utopie de Thomas More à Walter Benjamin* (Paris: Sens & Tonka).
Abensour, Miguel (2008), 'Persistent Utopia', *Constellations*, 15: 406-421.
Abensour, Miguel (2013), *Utopiques II: L'Homme est un animal utopique* (Paris: Sens & Tonka).
Academy of American Franciscan History (1949), *The Americas*, 5/3, special issue dedicated to the memory of Don Fray Juan de Zumárraga, First Bishop and Archbishop of Mexico.
Accarisio, Alberto (1543), *Vocabolario, grammatica et orthographia de la lingua volgare* (Cento: Alberto Accarisio).
Adas, Michael (2001), 'From Settler Colony to Global Hegemon: Integrating the Exceptionalist Narrative of the American Experience into World History', *American Historical Review*, 106: 1692-1720.
Adler, G. (1899), *Geschichte des Sozializmus und Kommunismus, von Plato bis zur Gegenwart* (Leipzig: C. L. Hirschfeld).
Adorni-Braccesi, Simonetta (1997), 'Religious Refugees from Lucca in the Sixteenth Century: Political Strategies and Religious Proselytism', *Archive for Reformation History*, 88: 338-379.
Adorni-Braccesi, Simonetta, and Ragagli, Simone (2004), 'Lando, Ortensio', *Dizionario biografica degli Italiani* 63, https://www.treccani.it/biografico/.
Adorno, Theodor W. (2005), *Minima Moralia*, trans. E. F. N. Jephcott (London: Verso).
Affeld-Schmidt, Birgit (1991), *Fortschrittsutopien: Vom Wandel der utopischen Literatur im 19. Jahrhundert* (Stuttgart: Metzler).
Agamben, Giorgio (1998), *Homo Sacer: Sovereign Power and the Bare Life*, trans. Daniel Heller-Roazen (Stanford, CA: Stanford University Press).
Agustí i Albanell, Antoni (1917), *Diàlechs de les armes y llinatges de la noblesa d'Espanya*, trans. Josep Pin i Soler (Barcelona: Llibreria Antiga i Moderna de S. Babra).
Airy, Osmund (1900) (ed.), *Burnet's History of My Own Time: A New Edition Based on that of M. J. Routh*, vol. 2 (Oxford: Clarendon Press).
Aldridge, Alfred O. (1985), 'Utopianism in World Literature', in Masayuki Akiyama (ed.), *The Reemergence of World Literature: A Study of Asia and the West* (Tokyo: Nanundo), 161-205.
Alekseev, M. P. (1955), *Slavyanskie istochniki* Utopii *Tomasa Mora* (Moscow: Academy of Sciences).
Alexander, David (1991), 'Gene Roddenberry: Writer, Producer, Philosopher, Humanist', *The Humanist*, 51 (Mar.-Apr.): 5-30, https://web.archive.org/web/20060702000506/http://www.philosophysphere.com/humanist.html.
Alkon, Paul K. (2010), *Origins of Futuristic Fiction* (Athens, GA: University of Georgia Press).
Allen, Don Cameron (1944), 'The Rehabilitation of Epicurus and His Theory of Pleasures in the Early Renaissance', *Studies in Philology*, 41: 1-15.
Allen, J. W. (1971), *A History of Political Thought in the 16th Century* (Lanham, MD: sRowman and Littlefield).
Allen, Peter R. (1963), 'Utopia and European Humanism: The Function of the Prefatory Letters and Verses', *Studies in the Renaissance*, 10: 91-107.
Allen, Roger (1992), *A Period of Time* (Reading: Ithaca Press).
Allen, Valerie (2007), *On Farting: Language and Laughter in the Middle Ages* (Basingstoke: Palgrave Macmillan).

Allen, Ward (1967), 'Speculations on St. Thomas More's Use of Hesychius', *Philological Quarterly*, 46: 156–166.
Alomar, Gabriel (1912a), 'Utopia, la dècima musa (Notes al marge de *l'Utopia* de Thomás Morus, traduida per Pin y Soler)', *El Poble Català* (7 Oct.).
Alomar, Gabriel (1912b), 'Utopia, la dècima musa (Notes al marge de *l'Utopia* de Thomás Morus, traduida per Pin y Soler) [II]', *El Poble Català* (8 Oct.).
Alter, Alexandra (2016), 'Middle Eastern Writers Find Refuge in the Dystopian Novel', *New York Times* (29 May), https://www.nytimes.com/2016/05/30/books/middle-eastern-writers-find-refuge-in-the-dystopian-novel.html.
Alunno, Francesco (1543), *Richezze della lingua volgare* (Venice: Aldo).
Amersin, Ferdinand (1874), *Das Land der Freiheit* (Graz: Leykam-Josefsthal).
Ames, Russell (1949), *Citizen Thomas More and His Utopia* (Princeton: Princeton University Press).
Amin, Ahmad, and Mahmud, Zaki Najib (1935), *Qissat al-falsafa al-yunaniyya* (Cairo: Dar al-Kutub al-Misriiyya).
Amin, Ahmad, and Mahmud, Zaki Najib (1936), *Qissat al-falsafa al-haditha* (Cairo: Lajnat al-Ta'lif wa-l-Tarjama wa-l-Nashr).
Andreae, Johann Valentin (1619), *Reipublicae Christianopolitanae Descriptio* (Strasbourg: Lazarus Zetzner).
Andrews, K. R. (1984), *Trade, Plunder and Settlement: Maritime Enterprise and the Genesis of the British Empire, 1480–1630* (Cambridge: Cambridge University Press).
Andrews, K. R., Canny, Nicholas, and Hair, P. E. H. (1979) (eds), *The Westward Enterprise: English Activities in Ireland, the Atlantic, and America 1480–1650* (Detroit: Wayne State University Press).
Aneau, Barthélémy (1996), *Alector ou le Coq: Histoire fabuleuse*, 2 vols, ed. Marie Madeleine Fontaine (Geneva: Droz).
Anguera, Pere (1994), 'El pensament polític i social del novel·lista Josep Pin i Soler', in Francesc Roig i Queralt and Josep M. Domingo (eds), *Actes del Simposi Pin i Soler* (Tarragona: Institut d'Estudis Tarraconenses), 104–165.
Anon. (1597), *Das Lalebuch: Wunderseltzame, Abentheurliche, vnerhörte, vnd bißher vnbeschriebene Geschichten vnd Thaten der Lalen zu Laleburg [...] zusammen getragen, vnd auß Rohtwelscher in Deutsche Sprach gesetzt* (Frankfurt: Paul Brachfeld).
Anon. (1598), *Die Schiltbürger: Wunderselzame Abendtheurliche, vnerhörte, vnd bißher vnbeschriebene Geschichten vnd Thaten der obgemelten Schiltbürger; in Misnopotamia hinder Vtopia gelegen [...] zusammen getragen vnnd auß Vtopischer auch Rothwelscher in Deutsche Sprach gesetz* (Frankfurt am Main: Paul Brachfeld).
Anon. (1665), *The Golden Coast, or, A description of Guinney* (London: for S. Speed).
Anon. (1709), *Dialogues des morts d'un tour nouveau* (The Hague: Johnson).
Anon. (1765), *Momus* (Bordeaux: Labottiere).
Anon. (1774), *L'Heureux Jour ou la fête des citoyens* (Paris? [n.pub.]).
Anon. (1858?), *La Isla de Jauja* (Madrid: [n.pub.]).
Antun, Farah (1903), *Al-din wa-l-'ilm wa-l-mal: al-mudun al-thalath: Dhikr madinat al-din wa-madinat al-'ilm wa-madinat al-mal wa-ma jara bayna sukkaniha min al-niza'* (Alexandria: [n.pub.]).
Antun, Farah (1904), *Urushalim al-jadida, aw, fath al-'Arab Bayt al-Maqdis wa-l-rajul al-marid wa-l-Isra'iliyya al-jamila fiha* (Alexandria: [n.pub.]).
Antun, Farah (1906–8), 'Al-'Alam al-jadid aw Mariyam qabl al-tawba', *al-Jami'a*, 5–6.

Aquinas, Thomas (1946), *Summa Theologica*, trans. Fathers of the English Dominican Province, 3 vols (New York: Benzinger Brothers).
Arendt, Hannah (1998), *The Human Condition* (2nd edn, Chicago: Chicago University Press).
Aristophanes (1498), *Aristophanous Komodiai ennea* (Venice: Aldus Manutius).
Aristophanes (1998), *Clouds; Wasps; Peace*, ed. and trans. Jefferey Henderson (Cambridge MA: Harvard University Press).
Aristophanes (2002), *Frogs; Assemblywomen; Wealth*, ed. and trans. Jefferey Henderson (Cambridge MA: Harvard University Press).
Aristotle (1495–8), *Opera* (Venice: Aldus Manutius).
Aristotle (1932), *Politics*, trans. H. Rackham (Cambridge, MA: Harvard University Press).
Aristotle (1935), *Athenian Constitution; Eudemian Ethics; Virtues and Vices*, trans. H. Rackham (Cambridge MA: Harvard University Press).
Aristotle (1984), *Physics*, trans. R. P. Hardie and R. K. Gaye, in *The Complete Works of Aristotle: The Revised Oxford Translation*, ed. Jonathan Barnes, 2 vols, 1.315–446 (Princeton: Princeton University Press).
Armitage, David (1998), 'Literature and Empire', in Nicholas Canny (ed.), *The Origins of Empire: British Overseas Enterprise to the Close of the Seventeenth Century* (Oxford: Oxford University Press), 99–123.
Armitage, David (2000), *The Ideological Origins of the British Empire* (Cambridge: Cambridge University Press).
Armitage, David, and Braddick, Michael J. (2009) (eds), *The British Atlantic World, 1500–1800* (2nd edn, Basingstoke: Palgrave).
Armory, Hugh (2004), 'Richard Chiswell, the Elder (1640–1711)', in Oxford Dictionary of National Biography, www.oxforddnb.com.
Arnold, Matthew (1887), 'Up to Easter', *Nineteenth Century*, 21 (May): 629–643.
Ashcroft, Bill (2007), 'Critical Utopias', *Textual Studies*, 21: 411–431.
Ashcroft, Bill (2017), *Utopianism and Postcolonial Literature* (New York: Routledge).
Athenaeus (1989), *Deipnosophists*, trans. C. B. Gulick (Cambridge MA: Harvard University Press).
Atkinson, Catherine (2007), *Inventing Inventors in Renaissance Europe: Polydore Vergil's De inventoribus rerum* (Tübingen: Siebeck).
Auger, James, and Hanna, Julian (2017), 'Et in Orcadia Ego', *Crap Futures*. http://crapfutures.tumblr.com/post/167486881219/et-in-orcadia-ego, last accessed 31 July 2018.
Augustine (1960), *The City of God against the Pagans [. . .] with an English Translation*, vol. 6, trans. William Chase Green (Cambridge, MA: Harvard University Press).
Augustine (1998), *The City of God against the Pagans*, trans. and ed. R. W. Dyson (Cambridge: Cambridge University Press).
Avineri, S. (1962), 'War and Slavery in More's Utopia', *International Review of Social History*, 7: 260–290.
Avs'enko, V. G. (1860), 'Thomas Mor', *Russkoe slovo*, 11: 30–65.
Ayalon, A. (1987), 'From Fitna to Thawra', *Studia Islamica*, 66: 145–174.
Bachleitner, Norbert (1989), ' "Übersetzungsfabriken". Das deutsche Übersetzungswesen in der ersten Hälfte des 19. Jahrhunderts', *Internationales Archiv für Sozialgeschichte der deutschen Literatur*, 14: 1–49.
Backscheider, Paula R. (2004), 'George Powell (1668?–1714)', *Oxford Dictionary of National Biography*, www.oxforddnb.com.
Bacon, Francis (1929), *Nyu Atorantisu*, trans. Tessei Ohto (Tokyo: Shunju-Sha).

Baczko, Michel Porret, et al. (2016) (eds), *Dictionnaire critique de l'Utopie au temps des Lumières* (Chêne-Bourg: Georg).

Bahlcke, Joachim (2016), 'Calvinism and Estate Liberation Movements in Bohemia and Hungary', in Karin Maag (ed.), *The Reformation in Eastern and Central Europe* (London: Routledge), 72–91.

Bailyn, Bernard (2005), *Atlantic History: Concepts and Contours* (Cambridge, MA: Harvard University Press).

Baker, J. H. (1999), 'The Books of the Common Law', in L. Hellinga and J. B. Trapp (eds), *The Cambridge History of the Book in Britain*, vol. 3 (Cambridge: Cambridge University Press), 411–432.

Baker House, Seymour (2008), 'More, Sir Thomas', in *Oxford Dictionary of National Biography*, www.oxforddnb.com.

Baker-Smith, Dominic (1991), *More's Utopia* (London: HarperCollins Academic).

Baker-Smith, Dominic (1994), 'Uses of Plato by Erasmus and More', in A. Baldwin and S. Hutton (eds), *Platonism and the English Imagination* (Cambridge: Cambridge University Press), 86–99.

Baker-Smith, Dominic (2000), *More's Utopia* (Toronto: University of Toronto Press).

Baker-Smith, Dominic (2006a), 'Antonio Buonvisi and Florens Wilson: A European Friendship', *Moreana*, 43: 82–108.

Baker-Smith, Dominic (2006b), 'Antonio Buonvisi and Florens Wilson: Corrigenda and a Note', *Moreana*, 43: 253–254.

Baker-Smith, Dominic (2011), 'Reading *Utopia*', in George M. Logan (ed.), *The Cambridge Companion to Thomas More* (Cambridge: Cambridge University Press), 141–167.

Baker-Smith, Dominic (2014a), 'On Translating More's *Utopia*', *Canadian Review of Comparative Literature (CRCL)* (Dec.): 492–504.

Baker-Smith, Dominic (2014b), 'Thomas More', in *Stanford Encylopedia of Philosophy*, plato.standford.edu.

Balázs, Mihály (2009), 'Thomas Morus és Jacobus Paleologus', in Gábor Boros (ed.), *Reneszánsz filozófia* (Budapest: NMFT), 113–134.

Balázs, Mihály (2016), *Hitújítás és egyházalapítás között* (Kolozsvár: Unitárius Egyház).

Baldacchino, Godfrey (2007a), 'Introducing a World of Islands', in Godfrey Baldacchino (ed.), *A World of Islands: An Island Studies Reader* (Charlottetown, PE: Institute of Island Studies), 1–29.

Baldacchino, Godfrey (2007b), 'Islands as Novelty Sites', *Geographical Review*, 97: 165–174.

Baldry, H. C (1952), 'Who Invented the Golden Age?', *Classical Quarterly*, NS 2: 83–92.

Baldwin, A., and Hutton, S. (1994) (eds), *Platonism and the English Imagination* (Cambridge: Cambridge University Press).

Balestracci, Duccio (1999), *The Renaissance in the Fields: Family Memoirs of a Fifteenth-Century Tuscan Peasant*, trans. Betsy Merideth and Paolo Squatriti (University Park, PA: Pennsylvania State University Press).

Ballas, Shimon (1985), ' "La Nouvelle Jérusalem" ou la république utopique de Farah Antun', *Arabica*, 32: 1–24.

Bantman, Constance (2013), *The French Anarchists in London, 1880–1914: Exile and Transnationalism in the First Globalisation* (Liverpool: Liverpool University Press).

Barbaro, Ada (2013), *La fantascienza nella letteratura araba* (Rome: Carocci editore).

Barbier, Antoine-Alexandre (1882), *Dictionnaire des anonymes*, vol. 1 (Paris: P. Daffis).

Barend-van Haeften, Marijke (1990), 'Van scheepsjournaal tot reisverhaal: Een kennismaking met zeventiende-eeuwse reisteksten', *Literatuur*, 7: 222–228.
Barker, Francis, Hulme, Peter, and Iversen, Margaret (1998) (eds), *Cannibalism and the Colonial World* (Cambridge: Cambridge University Press).
Barker, Gerard A. (1975), *Henry Mackenzie* (Boston: Twayne Publishers).
Barker, Nicholas (1992), *Aldus Manutius and the Development of Greek Script and Type in the Fifteenth Century* (New York: Fordham University Press).
Barlow, William (1601), *A defence of the articles of the Protestants religion in aunsweare to a libell lately cast abroad, intituled Certaine articles, or forcible reasons, discouering the palpable absurdities, and most intricate errours of the Protestantes religion* (London: [John Windet] for John Wolfe).
Barnes, J. (1987), *Early Greek Philosophy* (Harmondsworth: Penguin).
Barney, R. (2001), 'Platonism, Moral Nostalgia and the "City of Pigs" ', *Proceedings of the Boston Area Colloquium in Ancient Philosophy*, 17: 207–227.
Baron, H. (1966), *The Crisis of the Early Italian Renaissance: Civic Humanism and Republican Liberty in an Age of Classicism and Tyranny* (Princeton: Princeton University Press).
Barron, Caroline (2004), *London in the Later Middle Ages: Government and People 1200–1500* (Oxford: Oxford University Press).
Barron, Caroline (2011), 'The Making of a London Citizen', in George M. Logan (ed.), *The Cambridge Companion to Thomas More* (Cambridge: Cambridge University Press), 1–21.
Barron, Nathaniel (2021), 'Ernst Bloch's Ontology of Not-Yet Being: Intuiting the Possibility of Anticipation's Fulfilment', in Jamie Brasset and John O'Reilly (eds), *A Creative Philosophy of Anticipation: Futures in the Gaps of the Present* (London: Routledge), 79–97.
Barry, J. (2000), 'Civility and Civic Culture in Early Modern England: The Meanings of Urban Freedom', in Peter Burke, Brian Harrison, and Paul Slack (eds), *Civil Histories: Essays Presented to Sir Keith Thomas* (Oxford: Oxford University Press), 181–196.
Barry, Jonathan, and Brooks, Christopher (1994) (eds), *The Middling Sort of People: Culture, Society and Politics in England 1550–1800* (Basingstoke: Palgrave Macmillan).
Bartolomeo, Joseph F. (2007), 'A Fragile Utopia of Sensibility: *David Simple*', in Nicole Pohl and Brenda Tooley (eds), *Gender and Utopia in the Eighteenth Century* (Aldershot: Ashgate), 39–52.
Basnage de Beauval, Henri (1704), Review of *Atlas historique*, in *Histoire des ouvrages des savants* (Amsterdam: Reinier Leers), 483–499.
Bataille, George (1994), *Visions of Excess: Selected Writings 1927–1939*, trans. A. Stoekl (Minneapolis: University of Minnesota Press).
Battalion, Marcel (1937), *Érasme et l'Espagne; recherches sur l'histoire spirituelle du XVIe siècle* (Paris: E. Droz).
Bataillon, Marcel (1950), *Erasmo y España*, vol. 1, trans. Antonio Alatorre (Mexico: Fondo de Cultura Económica).
Bataillon, Marcel (1972), 'L'Ostension prenuptiale utopienne et "l'antique habit des Espagnes" ', *Moreana*, 35: 57–58.
Batatu, Hanna (1984), *The Egyptian, Syrian, and Iraqi Revolutions: Some Observations on Their Underlying Causes and Social Character* (Washington DC: Georgetown University, Center for Contemporary Arab Studies).
Baudaurtius, Willem (1605), *Apophtegmata Christiana* (Deventer: Jans Evertsz Cloppenburch).
Baumann, Uwe (1985), 'Thomas More and the Classical Tyrant', *Moreana*, 22/2: 108–127.
Baumann, Uwe (2015), 'The Humanistic and Religious Controversies and Rivalries of Sir Thomas More: A Typology of Literary Forms and Genres', in Jill Kraye, David A. Lines, and

Marc Laureys (eds), *Forms of Conflict and Rivalries in Renaissance Europe* (Bonn: Bonn University Press), 79–108.

Bayle, Pierre (1692), *Projet et fragmens d'un Dictionaire critique* (Rotterdam: Reinier Leers).

Bayle, Pierre (1992–2016), *Correspondance*, ed. Élisabeth Labrousse et al., 15 vols (Oxford: Oxford University Press).

Beaumont, Matthew (2012), *The Spectre of Utopia: Utopian and Science Fictions at the Fin de Siècle* (Oxford: Peter Lang).

Bebel, August (1892), *Die Frau und der Sozialismus* (Stuttgart: Dietz).

Beckert, Jens (2006), 'The Moral Embeddedness of Markets', in Betsy J. Clary, Wilfred Dolfsma, and Deborah M. Figart (eds), *Ethics and the Market: Insights from Social Economics* (London: Routledge), 11–25.

Beckman, Jonathan (2014), *How to Ruin a Queen: Marie Antoinette, the Stolen Diamonds and the Scandal that Shook the French Throne* (London: John Murray).

Begheyn, Paul S. J. (2014), *Jesuit Books in the Dutch Republic and Its Generality Lands* (Leiden: Brill).

Behn, Aphra (1688), *Oroonoko* (London: for Will. Canning).

Beidelman, Thomas (1971) (ed.), *The Translation of Cultures: Essays to E. E. Evans-Pritchard* (London: Tavistock Publications).

Bell, Susan Groag (1969), 'Johan Eberlin von Günzburg's "Wolfaria": The First Protestant Utopia', *Church History*, 36: 122–139.

Bellamy, Edward (1888), *Looking Backward* (Boston: Ticknor and Co.).

Bellamy, Edward (1929), *Kaiko-Roku*, trans. Toshihiko Sakai, in *Shakai-Shugi Kenkyu*, 7 (Tokyo: Heibon-Sha).

Bellamy, Edward (1986), *Looking Backward*, ed. C. Tichi (London: Penguin).

Bembo, Pietro (1525), *Prose della volgar lingua* (Venice: [n.pub.]).

Bendemann, Oswald (1929), *Studie zur Staats und Sozialauffassung des Thomas Morus* (Stuttgart: Gebrüder Hoffmann).

Bender, Harold S. (1957), 'The Anabaptist Vision', in Guy F. Hershberger (ed.), *The Recovery of the Anabaptist Vision* (Scottdale, PA: Herald Press), 29–55.

Benjamin, Walter (1975), 'Eduard Fuchs: Collector and Historian', trans. Kurt Tarnowski, *New German Critique*, 5: 27–58 (first published in German in 1937).

Benjamin, Walter (1996), 'The Task of the Translator', in Walter Benjamin, *Selected Writings*, vol. 1: *1913–1926*, ed. Michael Bullock and Marcus W. Jennings (Cambridge, MA: Belknap), 253–263.

Benjamin, Walter (2004), *Selected Writings*, vol. 1: 1913–1926, ed. Michael Bullock and Marcus W. Jennings (Cambridge MA: Belknap Press).

Bennell, John (2004), 'Robinson, Ralph (1520–1577)', in *Oxford Dictionary of National Biography*, www.oxforddnb.com.

Bennett, John W. (1967), *Hutterian Brethren: The Agricultural Economy and Social Organization of a Communal People* (Stanford, CA: Stanford University Press).

Benson, C. D. (2006), 'Civic Lydgate: The Poet and London', in Larry Scanlon and James Simpson (eds), *John Lydgate: Poetry, Culture, and Lancastrian England* (Notre Dame, IN: University of Notre Dame Press), 147–168.

Bentham, Jeremy (1996), *An Introduction to the Principles of Morals and Legislation* (1789), in *The Collected Works of Jeremy Bentham*, ed. J. H. Burns and H. L. A. Hart (Oxford: Clarendon Press).

Berardi, Franco (2011), *After the Future*, ed. Gary Genosko and Nicholas Thoburn, trans. Arianna Bove et al. (Edinburgh: AK Press).
Berger, Lina (1879a), *Thomas Morus und Plato: Ein Beitrag zur Geschichte des Humanismus* (Tübingen: Druck H. Laupp).
Berger, Lina (1879b), 'Thomas Morus und Plato', *Zeitschrift für die gesamte Staatswissenschaft*, 35: 187–216, 405–483.
Bergerac, Cyranno de (1657), *L'Autre Monde ou L'Histoire comique des États et Empires de la Lune* (Paris: Charles de Sercy).
Berlin, Isaiah (1996), 'Two Concepts of Liberty', in Isaiah Berlin, *Four Essays on Liberty* (Oxford: Oxford University Press), 118–172.
Berman, Carolyn V. (2006), *Creole Crossings: Domestic Fiction and the Reform of Colonial Slavery* (Ithaca, NY: Cornell University Press).
Bernardin de Saint-Pierre, Jacques-Henri (2005), *Paul and Virginia*, trans. John Donovan (London: Peter Owen) (first published in French in 1788 as *Paul et Virginie*).
Berns, Jörg Jochen (1982), 'Utopie und Polizei: Zur Funktionsgeschichte der frühen Utopistik in Deutschland', in Hiltrud Gnüg (ed.), *Literarische Utopie-Entwürfe* (Frankfurt am Main: Suhrkamp), 101–116.
Berns, Jörg Jochen (1995), 'Der Weg von Amaurotum nach Laleburg: Unvorgreifliche Gedanken zur Bedeutung der Utopia-Allusionen des Lalebuchs', in Wilhelm Kühlmann (ed.), *Literatur und Kultur im deutschen Südwesten zwischen Renaissance und Aufklärung* (Amsterdam: Rodopi), 149–172.
Berschin, Walter (2005), 'Neulateinische Utopien im Alten Reich (1555–1741)', in Walter Berschin (ed.), *Mittellateinische Studien* (Heidelberg: Mattes Verlag), 377–387.
Bessenyei, György (1953), *Válogatott művei* (Budapest: Szépirodalmi Könyvkiadó).
Bevan Zlatar, Antoinina (2012), *Reformation Fictions: Polemical Dialogues in Elizabethan England* (Oxford: Oxford University Press).
Bevington, Louisa Sarah (1894), 'Why I Am an Expropriationist', in *The Why I Ams*, 2nd ser. (London: James Tochatti Liberty Press), 10–16.
Anon. (1837), 'Tomas Morus i ego Utopiya', *Biblioteka dlya chteniya*, 24/3: 45–96.
Bidermann, Jakob (1644), *Utopia Didaci Bemardini* (Dillingen: Formis academicis).
Bidermann, Jakob (1677), *Bacchusia Oder Faßnacht-Land: Allwo Es drey Teutschen jungen Herren auff ihrer Raiß sehr übel ergangen, darbey allerhand kurtzweilige Geschichten eingemischt warden*, trans. Christoph Andreas Hoerl von Wattersdorf (Munich: Straub).
Bidermann, Jakob (1984), *Jakob Bidermanns 'Utopia'* [1640], ed. and trans. Margit Schuster (Bern: Lang).
Bietenholz, Peter G. (1971), 'Grendler, "Critics of the Italian World, 1530–1560" ', *Canadian Journal of History*, 6: 100–101.
Bietenholz, Peter, and Deutscher, Thomas Brian (1985–7) (eds), *Contemporaries of Erasmus: A Biographical Register of the Renaissance and Reformation* (Toronto: University of Toronto Press).
Biot, Brigitte (1995a), 'Barthélemy Aneau, lecteur de *l'Utopie*', *Moreana*, 121: 11–28.
Biot, Brigitte (1995b), *Barthélemy Aneau, régent de la Renaissance lyonnaise* (Paris: Champion).
Bíró, Zoltán (1989) (ed), *Fejezetek a társadalomfilozófiai gondolkodás történetéből.* (Budapest: Aula-Marx Károly Közgazdaságtudományi Egyetem).
Bishop, Jennifer (2011), '*Utopia* and Civic Politics in Mid-Sixteenth-Century London', *Historical Journal*, 54: 935–953.
Bishop, Jennifer (2016), 'Currency, Conversation, and Control: Political Discourse and the Coinage in Mid-Tudor England', *English Historical Review*, 131: 763–792.

Bishop, M. (2005), 'Ambrosius Holbein's Memento Mori Map for Sir Thomas More's *Utopia*: The Meanings of a Masterpiece of Early Sixteenth Century Graphic Art', *British Dental Journal*, 199: 107–112.
Black, Robert (2013), *Machiavelli* (London: Routledge).
Blaim, Artur (2013), *Gazing in Useless Wonder: English Utopian Fictions, 1516-1800* (Oxford: Peter Lang).
Blaim, Artur (2016), *Robinson Crusoe and His Doubles: The English Robinsonade of the Eighteenth Century* (Oxford: Peter Lang).
Blanqui, August (2013), *Eternity by the Stars*, trans. F. Chouraqui (New York: Contra Mundum Press).
Blatchford, Montagu [as 'Mont Blong'] (1895), 'A Free Country', *The Clarion*, April–May.
Blatchford, Robert [as 'Nunquam'] (1891), Editorial, *The Clarion*, 12 Dec.
Blatchford, Robert (1892), 'Answers to Correspondents', *The Clarion*, 13 Feb.
Blatchford, Robert [as 'Nunquam'] (1893), 'Merrie England', *The Clarion*, 4 Mar.
Blatchford, Robert (1895a), *The Nunquam Papers* (London: Clarion Press).
Blatchford, Robert [as 'Nunquam'] (1895b), 'An Unpractical Paper', *The Clarion*, 20 July.
Blatchford, Robert [as 'R. B.'] (1896), Obituary for William Morris, The Clarion, 10 Oct.
Blatchford, Robert [as 'Nunquam'] (1898), 'As I Lay A Thynkynge', *The Clarion*, 15 Jan.
Blatchford, Robert (1900), *My Favourite Books* (London: Clarion Press).
Blatchford, Robert (1907), *The Sorcery Shop* (London: Clarion Press).
Blatchford, Robert (1908), *Merrie England* (London: Clarion Press).
Bloch, Ernst (1959), *Das Prinzip Hoffnung in fünf Teilen* (Frankfurt: Suhrkamp Verlag).
Bloch, Ernst (1962), *Subjekt-Objekt: Erläuterungen zu Hegel* (Frankfurt: Suhrkamp Verlag).
Bloch, Ernst (1968), 'Der scheidende Odysseus', *Gesamtausgabe*, 10 (Frankfurt: Suhrkamp Verlag): 72-73.
Bloch, Ernst (1975), *Experimentum Mundi* (Frankfurt: Suhrkamp Verlag).
Bloch, Ernst (1978), *Tendenz-Latenz-Utopia* (Frankfurt: Suhrkamp Verlag).
Bloch, Ernst (1986), *The Principle of Hope*, trans. Neville Plaice, Stephen Plaice, and Paul Knight, 3 vols (Cambridge, MA: Harvard University Press).
Bloch, Ernst (1995), *The Principle of Hope*, vol. 2, trans. Neville Plaice, Stephen Plaice, and Paul Knight (Cambridge, MA: MIT Press).
Bloch, Ernst (2000), *Spirit of Utopia*, trans. A. Nasser (Stanford, CA: Stanford University Press).
Bloch, Ernst (2006), *Traces*, trans. A. Nasser (Stanford, CA: Stanford University Press).
Blockmans, W. P. (1978), 'A Typology of Representative Institutions in Late Medieval Europe', *Journal of Medieval History*, 4: 189–215.
Bodor, Ádám (1952) (trans.), *Morus Bacon Hobbes Locke* (Budapest: Művelt Nép).
Boer, Josephine de (1955), '*La familia de los Garriga* by José Pin y Soler', *Books Abroad*, 29: 458.
Boesky, Amy (1996), *Founding Fictions: Utopias in Early Modern England* (Athens, GA: University of Georgia Press).
Bolt, Robert (1969), *Kinek se nap, se szél*, trans. István Vas (Budapest: Europa).
Bolton, J. L. (2011), 'The Howard Linecar Lecture: Was There a "Crisis of Credit" in Fifteenth-Century England?', *British Numismatic Journal*, 81: 144–164.
Bona, Giovanni (1670), *De Leidsman ten Hemel* (Rotterdam: Frans van Hoogstraten).
Bona, Giovanni (1675), *Beginselen en Leerstucken van het Christelijck Leven* (Rotterdam: Frans van Hoogstraten).
Bony, Alain (1977), 'Fabula, Tabula: L'Utopie de More et l'image du monde', *Études anglaises*, 30: 1–19.

Booth, Marilyn (2001), *May Her Likes Be Multiplied: Biography and Gender Politics in Egypt* (Berkeley and Los Angeles: University of California Press).

Borsi, Franco (1997), *Architecture and Utopia* (Paris: Éditions Hazan).

Botley, Paul (2010), *Learning Greek in Western Europe, 1396–1529: Grammars, Lexica, and Classroom Texts*, Transactions of the American Philosophical Society 100/2 (Philadelphia: American Philosophical Society).

Bougainville, Louis-Antoine de (1771), *Le Voyage autour du monde, par la frégate La Boudeuse, et la flûte L'Étoile* (Paris: Saillant et Nyon).

Bradbury, Jonathan David (2009), 'Anton Francesco Doni and His *Librarie*: Bibliographical Friend or Fiend?', *Forum for Modern Language Studies*, 45: 90–107.

Bradshaw, Brendan (1981), 'More on *Utopia*', *Historical Journal*, 21: 1–27.

Bradshaw, Brendan (1991), 'Transalpine Humanism', in J. H. Burns and Mark Goldie (eds), *The Cambridge History of Political Thought 1450–1700* (Cambridge: Cambridge University Press), 95–131.

Bradshaw, Brendan, and Morrill, John (1996) (eds), *The British Problem: State Formation in the Atlantic Archipelago, c 1534–1707* (Basingstoke: Palgrave).

Bradshaw, Brendan, and Roberts, Peter (1998) (eds), *British Consciousness and Identity: The Making of Britain, 1533–1707* (Cambridge: Cambridge University Press).

Branham, R. Bracht (1985), 'Utopian Laughter: Lucian and Thomas More', *Moreana* 22: 23–43.

Brathwait, Richard (1641), 'To the Pious Memory of Sir Richard Hutton Knight', in *Astraea's Teares: An Elegie Vpon the death of that Reverend, Learned and Honest Judge, Sir Richard Hutton, Knight* (London: T. H. for Philip Nevil), B1r–sD5r.

Bregman, Rutger (2018), *Utopia for Realists* (paperback edn, London: Bloomsbury).

Brewer, J. S., Gairdner, James, and Brodie, R. H. (1862–1932) (eds), *Letters and Papers, Foreign and Domestic, of the Reign of Henry VIII*, 28 vols (London: HMSO).

Bridgett, T. (1891), *Life and Writings of Sir Thomas More* (London: Burns & Oates).

Brie, Friedrich (1924), 'Deismus und Atheismus in der englischen Renaissance', *Anglia*, 48: 54–98.

Brie, Friedrich (1928), *Imperialistische Strömungen in der englischen Literatur* (Halle: Niemeyer Verlag).

Brie, Germain de [aka Brixius] (1519), *Germani Brixii Antissiodorensis Antimorus* (Paris: Pierre Vidoué for Konrad Resch).

Brigden, Susan (1989), *London and the Reformation* (Oxford: Clarendon Press).

Brigden, Susan (2009), *London and the Reformation* (Oxford: Clarendon Press).

Briggs, John, Harrison, Christopher, McInnes, Angus, and Vincent, David (1996), *Crime and Punishment in England: An Introductory History* (London: UCL Press).

Brink, Bernhard ten (1877–93), *Geschichte der Englischen Litteratur* (Berlin: R. Oppenheim).

Brisson, L. (1970), 'De la philosophie politique à l'épopée, le Critias de Platon', *Revue de métaphysique et de morale*, 4: 402–438.

Brissot, J. P. de Warville (1782), *Bibliothèque philosophique, du législateur, du politique, du jurisconsulte, ou Choix des meilleurs discours, dissertations, essais [...] sur la législation criminelle*, vol. 8 (Berlin: chez Desauges).

Britnell, R. H. (1998), 'The English Economy and the Government, 1450–1550', in Jon Watts (ed.) *The End of the Middle Ages? England in the Fifteenth and Sixteenth Centuries* (Stroud: Sutton), 89–116.

Britnell, R. H. (2004), *Britain and Ireland 1050–1530: Economy and Society* (Oxford: Oxford University Press).

Brotton, Jerry (2012), *A History of the World in Twelve Maps* (London: Penguin).

Browne, Thomas (1646), *Pseudodoxia epidemica, or, Enquiries into very many received tenets and commonly presumed truths* (London: Thomas Harper for Edward Dodd).
Bruce, Susan (1996) (ed.), *Three Early Modern Utopias* (Oxford: Oxford University Press).
Bruch, Rüdiger vom, Friedrich Wilhelm Graf, and Gangolf Hübinger (1989), (eds), *Kultur und Kulturwissenschaften um 1900: Krise der Moderne und die Glaube an die Wissenschaft* (Wiesbaden and Stuttgart: Franz Steiner).
Bruni, L. (1978), 'Panegyric to the City of Florence', trans. B. G. Kohl, in B. G. Kohl, R. G. Witt, and E. B. Wells (eds), *The Earthly Republic: Italian Humanists on Government and Society* (Manchester: Manchester University Press), 135–175.
Bruno, Hendrik (1660), *Treur-spel Thomas Morus, ofte verwinninge van Geloof en Stand-vastigheydt* (Hoorn: van der Beeck).
Buber, Martin (1965), 'Distance and Relation', in Martin Buber, *The Knowledge of Man* (London: Allen & Unwin), 59–71.
Buchanan, I. (1998), 'Metacommentary on *Utopia*, or Jameson's dialectic of hope', *Utopian Studies*, 9: 18–30.
Budé, Guillaume [aka Budaeus] (1520), *Epistolae Gulielmi Budaei Regii Secretarii* (Paris: Josse Badius).
Buijnsters, P. J. (1969), *Imaginaire reisverhalen in Nederland gedurende de 18de eeuw* (Groningen: Wolters-Noordhoff).
Burgess, Glenn (1999) (ed.), *The New British History: Founding a Modern State, 1603–1715* (London: IB Tauris).
Burgh, J. (1994), 'An Account of the First Settlement, Laws, Form of Government, and Police, of the Cessares, A People of South America' [1764], in Gregory Claeys (ed.), *Utopias of the British Enlightenment* (Cambridge: Cambridge University Press), 71–136.
Burke, Peter (1991), 'Heu Domine, Turcae Adsunt', in Peter Burke and Ray Porter (eds.), *Language, Self and Society: A Social History of Language* (Cambridge: Polity), 23–50.
Burke, Peter (1999), 'Erasmus and the Republic of Letters', *European Review*, 7: 5–17.
Burke, Peter (2004), *Language and Communities in Early Modern Europe* (Cambridge: Cambridge University Press).
Burke, Peter (2009), 'Cultures of Translation in Early Modern Europe', in Peter Burke and R. Po-chai Hsia (eds), *Cultural Translation in Early Modern Europe* (Cambridge: Cambridge University Press), 7–38.
Burmeister, Karl Heinz (2011), 'Cantiuncula (Cantziuncula, Chansonetus, Chanson[n]et[te]; selten Liedel), Claudius (Claude)', in Wilhelm Kühlmann et al. (eds), *Frühe Neuzeit in Deutschland 1520–1620: Literaturwissenschaftliches Verfasserlexikon*, vol. 1: *Aal, Johannes-Chytraeus, Nathan* (Berlin: De Gruyter), 458–465.
Burnet, Gilbert (1679), *The History of the Reformation of the Church of England: Of the Progress Made in it During the Reign of K. Henry the VIII* (London: Thomas Hodgkin for Richard Chiswell).
Burnet, Gilbert (1681), *The History of the Reformation of the Church of England: The second part, of the Progress Made in it Till the Settlement of it in the Beginning of Q. Elizabeth's Reign* (London: Thomas Hodgkin for Richard Chiswell).
Burnet, Gilbert (1682), *The Abridgment of the History of the Reformation of the Church of England* (London: J. Darby for Richard Chiswell).
Burnet, Gilbert (1683), *Dr Burnet's Letter to his Friend in London* (London: G. C. for A. Gad).
Burnet, Gilbert (1684), *A sermon Preached at the Chapel of the Rolls, on the 5th of November 1684. Being Gunpowder-Treason Day* (London: printed for the author; to be sold by R. Baldwin).

Burnet, Gilbert (1685a), *A Collection of Several Tracts and Discourses* (London: for Richard Chiswell).

Burnet, Gilbert (1685b), *The Life of William Bedell, D.D. Bishop of Kilmore in Ireland* (London: for John Southby).

Burnett, Amy Nelson (2016), 'The Reformation in Basel', in Amy Nelson Burnett and Emidio Campi (eds), *A Companion to the Swiss Reformation* (Leiden: Brill), 170–215.

Burnyeat, M. F. (1999), 'Culture and Society in Plato's *Republic*', *The Tanner Lectures on Human Values*, 20: 215–324.

Burton, Robert (1621), *The Anatomy of Melancholy* (Oxford: John Lichfield and James Short for Henry Cripps).

Burton, Robert (1989), *The Anatomy of Melancholy*, ed. Thomas C. Faulkner, Nicolas K. Kiessling, and Rhonda L. Blair, 6 vols (Oxford: Clarendon Press).

Bustani, Fu'ad Ifram al- (1928), 'Al-Farabi wa-Tumus Murus, aw, al-Madina al-fadila wa-jazirat "al-tuba"', *al-Mashriq* 26: 26–34.

[Bustani, Salim al-?] (1898), 'Susiyalism (al-ishtirakiyya)', in Butrus al-Bustani and Salim al-Bustani (eds), *Kitab Da' irat al-ma'arif wa-huwa qamus 'amm li-kull fann wa-matlab*, vol. 10 (Beirut: Matba'at al-Ma'arif), 227–232.

Butterfield, Ardis (2006) (ed.), *Chaucer and the City* (Cambridge: D. S. Brewer).

Butterworth, Charles (1992), 'Interpretive Essay', in Jean-Jacques Rousseau, *The Reveries of the Solitary Walker*, trans. Charles Butterworth (Indianapolis: Hackett Publishing), 145–240.

Byers, Thomas (1987), 'Commodity Futures: Corporate State and Personal Style in Three Recent Science Fiction Movies', *Science Fiction Studies*, 14: 326–339.

Caballeria i Ferré, Sílvia, and Codina i Cantijoch, Carme (1994), 'El món editorial de les lletres catalanes (des de finals del segle XIX fins al final de la Guerra Civil)', *Ausa*, 16: 81–112.

Cachey, Theodore J. Jr (2003), 'Petrarchan Cartographic Writing', in Stephen Gersh and Bert Roest (eds), *Medieval and Renaissance Humanism: Rhetoric, Representation and Reform* (Leiden: Brill, 2003), 73–92.

Calepino, Ambrogio (1565), *Dictionarium* (Lyon: Antoine Gryphius).

Calmann, Gerta (1960), 'The Picture of a Nobody: An Iconographical Study', *Journal of the Warburg and Courtauld Institutes*, 23: 60–104.

Cameron, Alan (1993), *The Greek Anthology from Meleager to Planudes* (Oxford: Clarendon Press).

Campanella, Tommaso (1623), *Civitas Solis: Idea Reipublicae Philosophicae*, in *Realis Philosophiae Epilogisticae Partes Quatuor, Hoc est De Rervm Natvra, Hominvm Moribvs, Politica, (cui Civitas Solis iuncta est) & Oeconomica* (Frankfurt am Main: Gottfried Tampach), 415–464.

Campanella, Tommaso (1900), *Der Sonnenstaat*, trans. Ignaz Emanuel Wessely, ed. Eduard Fuchs (Munich: Max Ernst) [= vols 14–15 *Sammlung Gesellschaftswissenschaftlicher Aufsätze*].

Campanella, Tommaso (1929a), *Taiyo no Miyako*, trans. Atori Kato (Tokyo: Shunju-Sha).

Campanella, Tommaso (1929b), *Taiyo no Miyako*, trans. Yushu Morita (Tokyo: Heibon-Sha).

Campbell, Charles S. (2019), 'Variations on Simplicity: Callimachus and Leonidas of Tarentum in Philip's *Garland*', in Maria Kanellou, Ivana Petrovic, and Chris Carey (eds), *Greek Epigram from the Hellenistic to the Early Byzantine Era* (Oxford: Oxford University Press), 102–118.

Canny, Nicholas (1976), *The Elizabethan Conquest of Ireland: A Pattern Established, 1565-1576* (New York: Barnes and Noble Books).

Canny, Nicholas (1988), *Kingdom and Colony: Ireland in the Atlantic World, 1560–1800* (Baltimore: Johns Hopkins University Press).
Canny, Nicholas (1998) (ed.), *The Origins of Empire: British Overseas Enterprise to the Close of the Seventeenth Century* (Oxford: Oxford University Press).
Cantiuncula, Claudius [aka Claude Chansonnette] (1522), *Clarissimi Iurisconsulti Claudii Cantiunculae, in Academia Basiliensi ciuileis leges profitentis, Oratio Apologetica in patrocinium Iuris Ciuilis […] Eiusdem de ratione stuii legalis Paraenesis* (Basel: Andreas Cratander).
Čapkova, Dagmar (1970), 'Recommendations of Comenius regarding the Education of Young Children', in C. H. Dobinson (ed.), *Comenius and Contemporary Education* (Hamburg: Unesco), 17–33.
Carey, Daniel (199), 'Henry Neville's *Isle of Pines*: Travel, Forgery, and the Problem of Genre', *Angelaki*, 1: 23–29.
Carey, Daniel (2010), 'Henry Neville's *The Isle of Pines*: From Sexual Utopia to Political Dystopia', in Chloë Houston (ed.), *New Worlds Reflected: Travel and Utopia in the Early Modern Period* (Farnham: Ashgate), 203–218.
Carey, John (1999) (ed.), *The Faber Book of Utopias* (London: Faber).
Carley, James P. (2008), 'Blount, William, fourth Baron Mountjoy (c.1478–1534)', in *Oxford Dictionary of National Biography*, www.oxforddnb.com
Carrier, James G. (2012) (ed.), *A Handbook of Economic Anthropology* (Cheltenham: Edward Elgar).
Carus-Wilson, E. M. (1963), *The Expansion of Exeter at the Close of the Middle Ages* (Exeter: Exeter University Press).
Carus-Wilson, E., and Coleman, O. (1963), *England's Export Trade 1275–1547* (Oxford: Oxford University Press).
Cassany, Enric (1992), *El constumisme en la prosa catalana del segle XIX* (Barcelona: Curial).
Cassany, Enric (2004), 'L'edició en curs de les obres de Josep Pin i Soler', *Anuari Verdaguer*, 12: 250–256.
Cassirer, Ernst (1953), *The Platonic Renaissance in England* (New York: Thomas Nelson and Sons).
Castor, Grahame (1964), *Pléiade Poetics: A Study in Sixteenth-Century Thought and Terminology* (Cambridge: Cambridge University Press).
Castor, Grahame, and Cave, Terence (1984) (eds), *Neo-Latin and the Vernacular in Renaissance France* (Oxford: Oxford University Press).
Cats, Jacob (1637), *t'Samen-sprake op 't ongelijck houwelick van Crates en Hipparchia*, in *s'Weerelts Begin, Midden, Eynde besloten in den Trou-ringh, met den proef-steen* (Dordrecht: Hendrick van Esch, voor Matthias Havius).
Catto, J. I., and Evans, T. A. R. (1992), *Late Medieval Oxford: The History of the University of Oxford* (Oxford: Clarendon Press).
Cavallé, Joan (1994), 'Pin i Soler: Amor als llibres i a la llengua', in Francesc Roig i Queralt and Josep M. Domingo (eds), *Actes del Simposi Pin i Soler* (Tarragona: Institut d'Estudis Tarraconenses), 405–412.
Cavallé, Joan, and Mallafrè, Joaquim (1994), 'Pin i Soler, editor i traductor dels humanistes', in Francesc Roig i Queralt and Josep M. Domingo (eds), *Actes del Simposi Pin i Soler* (Tarragona: Institut d'Estudis Tarraconenses), 167–191.
Cave, Alfred A. (1991), 'Thomas More and the New World', *Albion*, 23: 209–229.

Cave, Terence (2008a), 'Introduction', in Terence Cave (ed.), *Utopia in Early Modern Europe* (Manchester: Manchester University Press), 3–13.
Cave, Terence (2008b), 'The English Translation: Thinking about the Commonwealth', in Terence Cave (ed.), *Utopia in Early Modern Europe* (Manchester: Manchester University Press), 87–103.
Cave, Terence (2008d) (ed.), *Thomas More's* Utopia *in Early Modern Europe: Paratexts and Contexts* (Manchester: Manchester University Press).
Cavill, P. R. (2009), *The English Parliaments of Henry VII 1485–1504* (Oxford: Oxford University Press).
Caygill, H. (1995). *A Kant Dictionary* (Oxford: Blackwell).
Céard, Jean (1996), 'La Fortune de l'*Utopie* de Thomas More en France au XVIe siècle', in *La fortuna dell'*Utopia *di Thomas More nel dibattito politico del '500* (Florence: Olschki), 43–74.
Cell, Gillian T. (1969), *English Enterprise in Newfoundland, 1577–1660* (Toronto: University of Toronto Press).
Chambers, R. W. (1935), *Thomas More* (London: Jonathan Cape).
Chambers, R. W. (1963), *Thomas More* (Harmondsworth: Penguin).
Chanca, Diego Alvarez (1988), 'The Letter Written by Dr Chanca to the City of Seville', in Christopher Columbus, *The Four Voyages*, trans. J. M. Cohen (London: Hutchison) 129–157.
Chappey, Jean-Luc (2004), 'Le Portique républicain et les enjeux de la mobilisation des arts autour de brumaire an VIII', in Philippe Bourdin and Gérard Loubinoux (eds), *Les Arts de la scène et la Révolution française* (Clermont Ferrand: Presses universitaires Blaise-Pascal), 487–507.
Chappey, Jean-Luc (2013), 'Utopies en contexte: Questions sur le statut du pédagogue sous le Directoire', *La Française* [online], 4, <http://lrf.revues.org/874>.
Chappey, Jean-Luc (2015), 'Michel de Cubières et la question du statut d'auteur en révolution', in Quentin Deluermoz and Anthony Glinoer (eds.), *L'Insurrection entre histoire et littérature (1789–1914)* (Paris: Publications de la Sorbonne), 19–33.
Chappey, Jean-Luc, and Lilti, Antoine (2010), 'L'Écrivain face à l'État: Les Demandes de pensions et de secours des hommes de lettres et savants (1780–1820)', *Revue d'histoire moderne et contemporaine*, 57: 156–184.
Chappuys, Gabriel (1583) (trans.), *Les Mondes célestes, terrestres et infernaux* [1578] (Lyons: Barthelemy Honorati).
Chartist Circular (1840 [13 June]), 'Thoughts for the Thoughts for the Thoughtful. No. II'.
Châtelain, Zacharias (1719), *Atlas Historique ou Nouvelle Introduction à l'Histoire, à la Chronologie & à la Géographie Ancienne & Moderne*, vol. 6 (Amsterdam: Chez François L'Honoré & Compagnie).
Chaucer, Geoffrey (1896), *The Works of Geoffrey Chaucer Now Newly Imprinted*, ed. F. S. Ellis, ornamented with pictures designed by Edward Burne-Jones (Hammersmith: Kelmscott Press).
Chicherin, B. N. (1890), *Istoriya politicheskikh uchenii*, pt 1 (Moscow: Gracheva i komp), 309–317.
Chinard, Gilbert (1913), *L'Amérique et le rêve exotique au XVIIe et au XVIIIe siècles* (Paris: Hachette).
Chordas, Nina (2010), *Forms in Early Modern Utopia: The Ethnography of Perfection* (Farnham: Ashgate).
Cicero, Marcus Tullius (1909), *Ad Pisonem*, in *Orationes*, ed. Albert Clark (Oxford: Clarendon Press), 275–327.

Cicero, Marcus Tullius (1928), *De Re Publica* in *Cicero in Twenty-Eight Volumes*, vol. 16: *De Re Publica, De Legibus*, trans. C. W. Keyes (Cambridge, MA: Harvard University Press), 1–285.

Cicero, Marcus Tullius (1991), *Cicero: On Duties*, ed. M. T. Griffin, trans. E. M. Atkins (Cambridge University Press).

Claeys, Gregory (2016), 'Utopia at Five Hundred: Some Reflections', *Utopian Studies*, 27: 402–411.

Claeys, Gregory (2017), *Dystopia: A Natural History* (Oxford: Oxford University Press).

Clapperton, Jane Hulme (1888), *Margaret Dunmore, or, The Socialist Home* (London: Swan Sonnenschein, Lowrey, & Co.).

Clarke, John P. (2009), 'Anarchy and the Dialectic of Utopia', in Laurence Davis and Ruth Kinna (eds), *Anarchism and Utopianism* (Manchester: Manchester University Press), 9–29.

Clough, Cecil H. (2004), 'Rastell, John (c.1475-1536)', in *Oxford Dictionary of National Biography*, www.oxforddnb.com.

Cohen, J. M. (1988), (ed.), *The Four Voyages of Christopher Columbus* (London: Hutchinson).

Cohn, Norman (1970), *The Pursuit of the Millennium: Revolutionary Millenarians and Mystical Anarchists of the Middle Ages* (rev. and expanded edn, Oxford: Oxford University Press).

Coleman, Nathaniel (2011) (ed.), *Imagining and Making the World: Reconsidering Architecture and Utopia* (Bern: Peter Lang).

Coleman, Nathaniel (2013), ' "Building in Empty Spaces": Is Architecture a "Degenerate Utopia"?', *Journal of Architecture*, 18: 135–166.

Colie, Rosalie (1974), '*Mel* and *Sal*: Some Problems in Sonnet-Theory', in Rosalie Colie, *Shakespeare's Living Art* (Princeton: Princeton University Press), 68–134.

Collinson, Patrick (1994), *Elizabethan Essays* (London: Hambledon Press).

Columbus, Christopher (1988), *The Four Voyages*, trans. J. M. Cohen (London: Hutchison).

Connell, William J. (2020), 'Minding Gaps: Connecting the Worlds of Erasmus and Machiavelli', in Paula Findlen and Suzanne Sutherland (eds), *The Renaissance of Letters: Knowledge and Community in Italy, 1300–1650* (London: Routledge), 146–163.

Connolly, S. J. (2007), *Contested Island: Ireland 1460–1630* (Oxford: Oxford University Press).

Conrad, Sebastian (2010), *The Question for the Lost Nation: Writing History in Germany and Japan in the American Century* (Berkeley and Los Angeles: University of California Press).

Constantinidou, N. (2015), 'Printers of the Greek Classics and Market Distribution in the 16th Century: The Case of France and the Low Countries', in Richard Kirwan and Sophie Mullins (eds), *Specialist Markets in the Early Modern Book World* (Leiden: Brill), 273–293.

Constitution of the United States of America, https://constitutioncenter.org/interactive-constitution/full-text

Cook, A. M. (1935), 'The King's School, Grantham', *Lincolnshire Magazine*, 2.

Cooper, Ashley, Locke, John, et al. (1669), *The Fundamental Constitutions of Carolina: March 1, 1669*, https://avalon.law.yale.edu/17th_century/nc05.asp.

Cooper, John M. (2012), *Pursuits of Wisdom: Six Ways of Life in Ancient Philosophy from Socrates to Plotinus* (Princeton: Princeton University Press).

Copenhaver, Brian P. (2019), *Magic and the Dignity of Man: Pico della Mirandola and His Oration in Modern Memory* (Cambridge, MA: Harvard University Press).

Coroleu, Alejandro (2014), *Printing and Reading Italian Latin Humanism in Renaissance Europe (ca 1470–ca 1540)* (Newcastle: Cambridge Scholars).

Cosgrove, Denis (2005), 'Maps, Mapping, Modernity: Art and Cartography in the Twentieth Century', *Imago Mundi*, 57: 35–54.

Covarrubias Orozco, Sebastián de (1611), *Tesoro de la lengua castellana, o Española* (Madrid: Luis Sánchez).
CPR = *Calendar of the Patent Rolls preserved in the Public Record Office, Edward VI* (London: HMSO, 1925).
Crane, Walter (1911), 'William Morris and His Work', in Walter Crane, *William Morris to Whistler: Papers and Addresses on Art and Craft and the Commonweal* (London: G. Bell & Sons), 3–46.
Crary, Jonathan (2014), *24/7: Late Capitalism and the Ends of Sleep* (London: Verso).
Crawforth, Hannah, Dustagheer, Sarah, and Young, Jennifer (2014) (eds), *Shakespeare in London* (London: Bloomsbury).
Croft, Pauline (2003), *King James* (London: Palgrave).
Cruickshank, C. G. (1971), *The English Occupation of Tournai* (Oxford: Oxford University Press).
Csillag, Éva (2008), *Boldog Lelkek* (Budapest: Kairosz).
Cummings, Robert (2017), 'Epigram', in Victoria Moul (ed.), *A Guide to Neo-Latin Literature* (Cambridge: Cambridge University Press), 83–97.
Curtis, Cathy (2006), '"The Best State of the Commonwealth": Thomas More and Quentin Skinner', in James Tully, Annabel Brett, and Holly Hamilton-Bleakley (eds), *Rethinking the Foundations of Modern Political Thought* (Cambridge: Cambridge University Press), 93–112.
Curtis, Catherine (2008), 'The Social and Political Thought of Juan Luis Vives: Concord and Counsel in the Christian Commonwealth', in Charles Fantazzi (ed.), *A Companion to Juan Luis Vives* (Boston: Brill), 113–176.
Curtright, Travis (2013), *The One Thomas More* (Washington DC: The Catholic University of America Press).
Czigány, Lóránt (1984), *The Oxford History of Hungarian Literature* (Oxford: Oxford University Press).
Cziányik, Zsolt (2015), 'From the Bright Future of the Nation to the Dark Future of Mankind: Jókai and Karinthy in Hungarian Utopian Tradition', *Hungarian Cultural Studies*, 8 [online].
Cziányik, Zsolt (2016), 'The Hungarian Translations of Thomas More's *Utopia*', *Utopian Studies*, 27: 323–332.
Cziányik, Zsolt (2017), 'Negative Utopia in Central Europe: *Kazohinia* and the Dystopian Political Climate of the 1930s', in Zsolt Cziányik (ed.), *Utopian Horizons* (Budapest: CEU Press), 161–180.
Cziányik, Zsolt (2023), *Utopia Between East and West in Hungarian Literature* (London: Palgrave Macmillan).
d'Anghiera, Peter Martyr (1587), *De Orbe Novo Petri Martyris Anglerii Merioleaneris*, ed. Richard Hakluyt (Paris: Guillemum Auuray).
d'Anghiera, Peter Martyr (1912), *De Orbe Novo: The Eight Decades of Peter Martyr d'Anghiera*, trans. Frank M. MacNutt, 2 vols (New York: G. P. Putnam Sons).
da Gama, Vasco (1947), 'The Route to India, 1497–1498', trans. E. V. Ravenstein, in Charles David Ley (ed.), *Portuguese Voyages* (London: Dent), 1–38.
Dai, Liuling (1955), Pipan Hu Shi de suowei 'wenxue gailiang', *Zhongshan daxue xuebao*, (Jan.), 19–28.
Dainard, A., J. Orsini, D. Smith, and P. Allan, *Electronic Enlightenment*, www.e-enlightenment.com.
Damrosch, David (2007), 'Global Regionalism', *European Review*, 15: 135–143.
Darnton, Robert (1991), 'The Brissot Dossier', *French Historical Studies*, 17: 191–205.

Das, Nandini (2019) (ed.), *The Cambridge History of Travel Writing* (Cambridge: Cambridge University Press).

Davenport, Randi Lise, and Cabanillas Cárdenas, Carlos (2008), 'The Spanish Translations: Humanism and Politics', in Terence Cave (ed.), *Thomas More's* Utopia *in Early Modern Europe: Paratexts and Contexts* (Manchester: Manchester University Press), 110–127.

Davies, C. S. L. (1966), 'Slavery and Protector Somerset: The Vagrancy Act of 1547', *Economic History Review*, 19: 533–549.

Davies, C. S. L. (1998), 'Tournai and the English Crown', *Historical Journal*, 41: 1–26.

Davis, J. C. (1981), *Utopia and the Ideal Society: A Study of English Utopian Writing, 1516–1700* (Cambridge: Cambridge University Press).

Davis, J. C. (1991), 'Utopianism', in J. H. Burns (ed.), *The Cambridge History of Political Thought 1450–1700* (Cambridge: Cambridge University Press), 329–344.

Davis, J. C. (1992), 'Religion and the Struggle for Freedom in the English Revolution', *Historical Journal*, 35: 507–530.

Davis, J. C. (1993), 'Formal Utopia/Informal Millennium: The Struggle between Form and Substance as a Context for Seventeenth-Century Utopianism', in K. Kumar and S. Bann (eds), *Utopias and the Millennium* (London: Reaktion Books), 17–32.

Davis, J. C. (2000), 'Utopia and the New World, 1500–1700', in Roland Schaer, Gregory Claeys, and Lyman Tower Sargent (eds), *Utopia: The Search for the Ideal Society in the Western World* (Oxford: Oxford University Press), 95–118.

Davis, J. C. (2010), 'El pensamiento utópico y el discurso de los derechos humanos: ¿Una connexion útil?', in M. A. Ramiro Avilés and P. Cuenca Gómez (eds), *Los derechos humanos: La utopía de los excluidos* (Madrid: Dykinson), 39–62.

Davis, Lennard J. (1983), *Factual Fictions: The Origins of the English Novel* (New York: Columbia University Press).

Dawson, Jane E. A. (2002), *The Politics of Religion in the Age of Mary, Queen of Scots: The Earl of Argyll and the Struggle for Britain and Ireland* (Cambridge: Cambridge University Press).

de Armas, Frederick A. (2002), 'Cervantes and the Italian Renaissance', in Anthony J. Cascardi (ed.), *The Cambridge Companion to Cervantes* (Cambridge: Cambridge University Press), 32–57.

de Benavente Motolinia, Toribio (2014), *Historia de los indios de Nueva España*, ed. Mercedes Serna Arnaiz and Bernat Castany Prado (Madrid: RAE).

de Bom, Erik (2017), 'Realism vs Utopianism', in Han van Ruler and Giulia Sissa (eds), *Utopia 1516–2016: More's Eccentric Essay and Its Activist Aftermath* (Amsterdam: Amsterdam University Press), 109–142.

de Breen, Daniel (1677), *Compendium theologiae Erasmicae* (Rotterdam: Frans van Hoogstraten).

de Estella, Diego (1659), *De versmading der wereltsche ydelheden*, trans. Frans van Hoogstraten (Rotterdam: Frans van Hoogstraten).

de Juvigny, Jean Antoine Rigoley, et al. (1772) (eds), *Les Bibliothéques françoises de La Croix du Maine et de Du Verdier sieur de Vauprivas*, 6 vols (Paris: Saillant et Nyon).

de la Serre, Jean Puget (c.1641), *Thomas Morus, ou, Le triomphe de la foy, et de la constance* (Paris: Augustin Courbé).

de Mey, Johannes (1704), *Alle de Godgeleerde en Natuurkundige Wercken*, 2 vols (Delft: Hendrik van Krooneveld).

de Vet, J. J. V. M. (1980), *Pieter Rabus (1660–1702): Een wegbereider van de Noordnederlandse Verlichting* (Amsterdam: APA).

DeCoursey, Matthew (2010), 'The Thomas More/William Tyndale Polemic: A Selection', *Early Modern Studies*, Text Series, 3: 1–236.
Defoe, Daniel (1719), *Robinson Crusoe* (London: W. Taylor).
Defoe, Daniel (1994), *Robinson Crusoe: An Authoritative Text, Contexts, Criticism*, ed. Michael Shinagel (New York: Norton).
Deheuvels, Luc-Willy (1999), 'Le Livre des trois cités de Farah Antūn: Une utopie au cœur de la littérature arabe moderne', *Arabica*, 46: 402–434.
Deheuvels, Luc-Willy (2007), 'Fiction romanesque et utopie', in Boutros Hallaq and Heidi Toelle (eds), *Histoire de la littérature arabe moderne*, vol. 1: *1800–1945* (Paris: Sindbad), 220–230.
Deleuze, Gilles (2004), 'Desert Islands', in Gilles Deleuze, *Desert Islands and Other Texts, 1953–1974* (Los Angeles: Semiotext(e) Foreign Agents Series), 9–14.
Deleuze, Gilles, with Parnet, Claire (1991), *Dialogues* (Paris: Flammarion).
Démeunieur, Jean-Nicolas (1784), *Encyclopédie méthodique*, vol. 1 (Paris: A. Padoue).
Démeunier, Jean-Nicolas (1788), *Encyclopédie méthodique: Économie politique et diplomatique*, vol. 4 (Paris: Panckoucke; Liège: Plomteux).
Demos, T. J. (2012), 'Gardens Beyond Eden: Bio-aesthetics, Eco-Futurism and Dystopia at Documenta 13', *Brooklyn Rail* online (Oct.), https://brooklynrail.org/2012/10/art/gardens-beyond-eden-bio-aesthetics-eco-futurism-and-dystopia-at-documenta-13.
Denbo, Seth (2007), 'Generating Regenerated Generations: Race, Kinship and Sexuality on Henry Neville's *Isle of Pines* (1668)', in Brenda Tooley and Nicole Pohl (eds), *Gender and Utopia in the Eighteenth Century: Essays in English and French Utopian Writing* (Aldershot: Ashgate), 147–161.
Deneire, Tom (2014) (ed.), *Dynamics of Neo-Latin and the Vernacular* (Leiden: Brill).
Deneire, Tom (2017), 'Neo-Latin Literature and the Vernacular', in Victoria Moul (ed.), *A Guide to Neo-Latin Literature* (Cambridge: Cambridge University Press), 35–51.
Depuydt, Joost (2019), 'The Utopia Map by Abraham Ortelius: New Home—New Research', *De gulden passer: Journal for Book History*, 97: 242–246.
Derham, William (1713), *Physico-Theology* (London: for W. Innys).
Derham, William (1714), *Astro-theology: or, A demonstration of the being and attributes of God, from a survey of the heavens* (London: for W. Innys).
Derrida, Jacques (2001), *Cosmopolitanism and Forgiveness*, trans. M. Dooley and M. Hughes (London: Routledge).
Derrida, Jacques, with Anne Dufourmantelle (1997), *De l'hospitalité* (Paris: Calman-Lévy).
Dery, Mark (2016), 'Afrofuturism Reloaded: 15 Theses in 15 Minutes', *Afrofuturism* (1 Feb.), https://www.fabrikzeitung.ch/afrofuturism-reloaded-15-theses-in-15-minutes.
Devereux, E. J. (1976), 'John Rastell's Utopian Voyage', *Moreana*, 13: 119–123.
Dicke, Gerd (2011), 'Morus und Moros—*Utopia* und *Lalebuch*: Episteme auf dem Prüfstand lalischer Logik', in Beate Kellner, Jan-Dirk Müller, and Peter Strohschneider (eds), *Erzählen und Episteme: Literatur im 16. Jahrhundert* (Berlin: De Gruyter), 197–224.
Diderot, Denis (1796), *Supplément au voyage de Bougainville* [written 1772] (Paris: de Chevet).
Diderot, Denis and d'Alembert (1751–80) (eds), *Encyclopédie, ou Dictionnaire raisonné des sciences, des arts et des métiers, par un société de gens de lettres* (Paris: Briasson).
Dietrich, Ottmar (1926), *Geschichte der Ethik* (Leipzig: F. Meiner).
Dietrick, Linda (2014), ' "Swim across with me to the huts of our neighbors": Colonial Islands in Sophie von La Roche's *Erscheinungen am See Oneida* (1798) and Jacques Henri Bernardin de Saint-Pierre's *Paul et Virginie* (1788)', in Rob McFarland and Michelle Stott James (eds),

Sophie Discovers Amerika: German-Speaking Women Write the New World (Rochester, NY: Camden House/Boydell & Brewer), 16–29.

Dikeç, Mustafa, Clark, Nigel, and Barnett, Clive (2009) (eds), 'Extending Hospitality, Giving Space and Taking Time', *Paragraph: A Journal of Modern Critical Theory*, 32: 1–14.

Dillon, Anne (2002), *The Construction of Martyrdom in the English Catholic Community, 1535–1603* (Aldershot: Ashgate).

Dillon, J. M. (1992), 'Plato and the Golden Age', *Hermathena*, 153: 21–36.

Dinneen, Mark (2003), 'Vespucci, Amerigo', in Jennifer Speake (ed.), *Literature of Travel and Exploration*, 2 vols (London: Fitzroy Dearborn), 2.1245–1247.

Dionisotti, Carlo (1980), *Machiavellerie* (Turin: Einaudi).

Dioscorides Pedanius (1499), *De materia medica* (Venice: Aldus Manutius).

Dirlik, Arlif (1975), 'The Ideological Foundation of the New Life Movement: A Study in Counterrevolution', *Journal of Asian Studies*, 34: 945–980.

Dobson, R. B. (1977), 'Urban Decline in Late Medieval England', *Transactions of the Royal Historical Society*, 5th ser., 27: 1–22.

Dodds, Gregory D. (2017), 'Politicizing Thomas More's Utopia in Restoration England', *Moreana*, 54: 172–186.

Dollinger, P. (1970), *The German Hansa*, trans. D. S. Ault and S. H. Steinberg (London: Macmillan).

Domingo i Clua, Josep M. (1981), 'Sobre la relació entre Josep Pin i Soler i Josep Yxart: Tres cartes de Pin a Yxart', in Institut d'Estudis Tarraconenses Ramon Berenguer IV, *Treballs de la Secció de Filologia i Història Literària, II* (Tarragona: Diputació de Tarragona), 109–123.

Domingo, Josep M. (1996), *Josep Pin i Soler i la novel·la, 1869–1892: El cicle dels Garriga* (Barcelona: Curial Edicions Catalanes, Publicacions de l'Abadia de Montserrat, Institut d'Estudis Tarraconenses Ramon Berenguer IV).

Domingo, Josep M. (2004), 'Llibres i comentaris: En el gabinet de Josep Pin i Soler', in Josep Pin i Soler, *Comentaris sobre llibres i autors [Obres, 7]*, ed. Sandra Sarlé (Tarragona: Arola), 9–14.

'Don Emilio Castelar' (1879), *Leisure Hour*, 1434 (21 June), 392–396.

Doni, Anton Francesco (1552a), *I Marmi* (Venice: Marcolini).

Doni, Anton Francesco (1552b), *I Mondi* (Venice: Marcolini).

Doni, Anton Francesco (1555), *La seconda libraria* (Venice: [Marcolini]).

Donne, John (1953), *The Sermons of John Donne*, ed. George R. Potter and Evelyn M. Simpson, vol. 1 (Berkeley and Los Angeles: University of California Press).

Donner, H. W. (1945), *Introduction to Utopia* (London: Sidgwick & Jackson).

Dornau, Caspar (1619), *Amphitheatrum Sapientiae Socraticae Joco-Seriae* (Hanau: David und Daniel Aubry / Clemens Schleich).

Dostálová, Ruzena (1971) (ed.), *Catechesis christiana dierum duodecim* (Warsaw: Panstwowe Wydawnictwo Naukowe).

Du Bellay, Joachim (2001), *La Deffence et illustration de la langue françoyse [1549]*, ed. Jean-Charles Monferran (Geneva: Droz).

Duff, E. G. (1905), *A Century of the English Book Trade* (Cambridge: Cambridge University Press).

Duffy, Eamon (2009), *Fires of Faith: Catholic England under Mary Tudor* (New Haven: Yale University Press).

Dumolyn, J. (2008), 'Privileges and Novelties: The Political Discourse of the Flemish Cities and Rural Districts in Their Negotiations with the Dukes of Burgundy (1384–1506)', *Urban History*, 35/1: 5–23.

Duncan, H. H. (1892), 'The General Strike', *The Commonweal*, 4 June.
Dyer, A. (2000), ' "Urban Decline" in England, 1377–1525', in T. R. Slater (ed.), *Towns in Decline AD 100–1600* (Aldershot: Ashgate), 266–288.
Eaton, Ruth (2001), *Cités idéales: L'Utopisme et l'environnement (non) bati* (Anvers: Les Fonds mercator).
Eberlin von Günzburg, Johann (1521a), *Ein newe ordnung weltlichs standts das Psitacus anzeigt hat in Wolfaria beschriben, Der. XI. Bundtgnosz* (Basel: Pamphilus Gengenbach).
Eberlin von Günzburg, Johann (1521b), *New statuten die Psitacus gebracht hat vß dem land Wolfaria welche beträffendt reformierung geystlichen stand, Der. X. bundtgnosz* (Basel: Pamphilus Gengenbach).
Eden, Kathy (2001), *Friends Hold All Things in Common: Tradition, Intellectual Property, and the Adages of Erasmus* (New Haven: Yale University Press).
Eden, Kathy (2012), *The Renaissance Rediscovery of Intimacy* (Chicago: University of Chicago Press).
Eden, Richard (1555), *The Decades of the Newe Worlde or West India.* (London: William Powell for Richard Toy).
Egger, Vernon (1986), *A Fabian in Egypt: Salāmah Mūsá and the Rise of the Professional Classes in Egypt, 1909–1939* (Lanham, MD: University Press of America).
Eggertsdóttir, Margrét (2006), 'From Reformation to Enlightenment', in Daisy L. Neijmann (ed.), *Histories of Scandinavian Literature*, vol. 5 (Lincoln, NE: University of Nebraska Press in cooperation with the American–Scandinavian Foundation), 174–250.
Ehrlich, Max (1967), 'The Apple', *Star Trek*, season 2, episode 5, CBS, 13 Oct.
Eisenstein, Elizabeth (1979), *The Printing Press as an Agent of Change*, vol. 1 (Cambridge: Cambridge University Press).
Eliav-Feldon, M. (1982), *Realistic Utopias: The Ideal Imaginary Societies of the Renaissance 1516–1630* (Oxford: Clarendon Press).
Elliott, J. H. (2006), *Empires of the Atlantic World: Britain and Spain in America* (New Haven: Yale University Press).
Ellis, Steven G. (1985), *Tudor Ireland: Crown, Community and the Conflict of Cultures, 1470–1603* (Harlow: Longman).
Ellis, Steven G., and Barber, Sarah (1995) (eds), *Conquest and Union: Fashioning A British State, 1485–1725* (London: Routledge).
Ellis, Steven G., with Maginn, Christopher (2007), *The Making of the British Isles: The State of Britain and Ireland, 1450–1660* (Harlow: Pearson).
Elshakry, Marwa (2013), *Reading Darwin in Arabic, 1860–1950* (Chicago: University of Chicago Press).
Elsky, Stephanie (2013), 'Common Law and the Commonplace in Thomas More's *Utopia*', *English Literary Renaissance*, 43: 181–210.
Elton, G. R. (1955), *England Under the Tudors* (London: Methuen).
Elton, G. R. (1977), *Reform and Reformation* (Cambridge, MA: Harvard University Press).
Elton, G. R. (2003), *Studies in Tudor and Stuart Politics and Government: Volume 4, Papers and Reviews 1982-1990* (Cambridge: Cambridge University Press).
Elyot, Thomas (1538), *The Dictionary of Sir Thomas Eliot* (London: Thomas Berthelet).
Emig, Brigitte (1980), *Die Veredelung des Arbeiters: Sozialdemokratie als Kulturbewegung* (Frankfurt: Campus).
Engels, Friedrich (1907), *Kagaku-Teki Shakai-Shugi*, trans. Toshihiko Sakai (Tokyo: Shakai-Shugi Hakko-Sho).

Euripides (1503), *Euripidou tragōdiai heptakaideka* (Venice: Aldus Manutius).
Evans, Robert J. W. (1973), *Rudolf II and His World: A Study in Intellectual History 1576–1612* (Oxford: Clarendon Press).
Evans, Robert J. W. (1975), *The Wechel Presses: Humanism and Calvinism in Central Europe 1572–1627* (Oxford: Past & Present Society).
Fabricius, Hieronymus, Cabrolius, Bartolomeus, and Fernel, Jean (1661), *Hieronymi Fabritii ab Aquapendente Heelkonstige Handwerkingen, Bartolomaei Cabrolii A, B, C, Der Ontledinge: En Joannes Fernelii Boek der Natuurkunde vervattende een korte en bondige Beschrijvinge des Menschelijken Lichaams*, trans. Jacob Ostens (Rotterdam: Johannes Naeranus).
Fahy, Conor (1975), 'The Composition of Ortensio Lando's Dialogue *Cicero relegatus et Cicero revocatus*', *Italian Studies*, 30: 30–41.
Fairfull-Smith, George (2001), *The Foulis Press and Academy* (Glasgow: Glasgow Art Index).
Fáj, Attila (2004), 'Előszó', in Thomas More, *Erősítő párbeszéd balsors idején*, trans. Zsuzsa Gergely (Budapest: Szent István Társulat; Kolozsvár: A Dunánál), 7–34.
Fang, Fan, and Xue, Qian (2016), 'Utopian Landscapes: From Thomas More's *Utopia* to Tao Yuanming's *Peach Blossom Spring*' [unpublished item], http://bksy.zju.edu.cn/attachments/tlxjxj/2016-11/99999-1478221984-1098039.pdf
Fara, Patricia (2007), 'Hayley, Hell and Other People', *Studies in History and Philosophy of Science*, 38: 570–583.
Farkas, Ákos (1922), 'Tamás Morus, *Utópia*: Translated by Tibor Kardos', *Utopian Studies*, 3: 169–171.
Fassel, Horst (2005), *Hugo Meltzl und die Anfänge der Komparatistik* (Stuttgart: Franz Steiner).
Fassel, Horst (2006), 'Hugo Meltzl von Lomnitz: Der erste Ordinarius für Germanistik in Klausenburg', in Marta Fata et al. (eds), *Peregrinatio Hungarica: Studenten aus Ungarn an deutschen und österreichischen Hochschulen vom 16. bis zum 20. Jahrhundert* (Stuttgart: Franz Steiner), 437–458.
Fassin, Didier (2005), 'Compassion and Repression: The Moral Economy of Immigration Policies in France', *Cultural Anthropology*, 20: 362–387.
Fausett, David (1993), *Writing the New World: Imaginary Voyages and Utopias of the Great Southern Land* (Syracuse, NY: Syracuse University Press).
Fay, E. F. [as 'Quinbus Flestrin'] (1892), 'Tailoring Up to Date', *The Clarion* (14 May).
Febvre, Lucien, and Martin, Henri-Jean (1997), *The Coming of the Book: The Impact of Printing, 1450–1800*, trans. David Gerard (London: Verso).
Feinberg, Walter (2006), 'Philosophical Ethnography: Or, How Philosophy and Ethnography Can Live Together in the World of Educational Research', *Educational Studies in Japan: International Yearbook*, 1: 5–14.
Fénelon, François de Salignac de La Mothe (1699), *Les Aventures de Télémaque* (The Hague: Adrien Moetjens).
Feng, Zhi, Yang, Qisheng, Dai, Liuling, Cankun, Gui, Jueliang, Zhou, Shuzhen, Fang, et al. (1958), 'Yiding yao ba shehuizhuyi de hongqi caizai xiyu jiaoxue he yaojiu de zhendi shang', *Xifang yuwen* (Mar.): 250–260.
Fenlon, Dermot (1975), 'England and Europe: Utopia and Its Aftermath', *Transactions of the Royal Historical Society*, 25: 115–136.
Fenlon, Dermot (1981), 'Thomas More and Tyranny', *Journal of Ecclesiastical History*, 32: 453–476.
Ferguson, A. B. (1965), *The Articulate Citizen and the English Renaissance* (Durham, NC: Duke University Press).

Ferguson, Adam (1767), *An Essay on the History of Civil Society*, vol. 1 (Edinburgh: A. Millar and T. Caddel).

Fermon, Paul 2013), 'Cartes et plans à grande échelle', in Patrick Gautier Dalché (ed.), *La Terre: Connaissance, représentations, mesure au Moyen Âge* (Turnhout: Brepols), 581–624.

Fernández Rodríguez, Pedro (1994), *Los dominicos en el contexto de la primera evangelización de México, 1526–1550* (San Esteban: Editorial San Esteban).

Feyerabend, Sigmund (1584), *Reyßbuch deß heyligen Lands, Das ist Ein grundtliche beschreibung aller vnd jeder Meer vnd Bilgerfahrten zum heyligen Lande* (Frankfurt: Sigmund Feyerabend).

Ficino, Marsilio (1474), *Della christiana religione* (Florence: Nicolò di Lorenzo).

Ficino, Marsilio (1482), *Theologia Platonica* (Florence: Antonio Miscomini).

Fielding, Sarah (1753), *The Adventures of David Simple, Volume the Last* (London: for A. Millar).

Finamore, John, and Nejeschleba, T. (2019) (eds), *Platonism and Its Legacy: Selected Papers from the Fifteenth Annual Conference of the International Society for Neoplatonic Studies* (Lydney: The Prometheus Trust).

Finger, Jürgen (2019), 'Bankruptcy and Morality in a Capitalist Market Economy: The Case of Mid-Nineteenth-Century France', in Stefan Berger and Alexandra Przyrembel (eds), *Moralizing Capitalism: Agents, Discourses and Practices of Capitalism and Anti-Capitalism in the Modern Age* (Cham: Palgrave Macmillan), 205–229.

Fischart, Johann (1575), *Affenteurliche und Ungeheurliche Geschichtschrift vom Leben, rhaten und Thaten der for langen weilen Vollenwolbeschraiten Helden und Herrn Grandgusier, Gargantoa, und Pantagruel, Königen inn Vtopien und Ninenreich* (Strasbourg: Bernhard Jobin).

Fitting, Peter (1996), 'Buried Treasures: Reconsidering Holberg's *Niels Klim* in the World Underground', *Utopian Studies*, 7: 93–112.

Fitting, Peter (2010), 'Stories of a Hollow Earth', *Public Domain Review*, http://publicdomainreview.org/2011/10/10/stories-of-a-hollow-earth/.

Fitzmaurice, Andrew (2003), *Humanism and America: An Intellectual History of English Colonisation, 1500–1625* (Cambridge: Cambridge University Press).

Fix, Andrew C. (1991), *Prophecy and Reason: The Dutch Collegiants in the Early Enlightenment* (Princeton: Princeton University Press).

Fletcher, Anthony (1983), *Tudor Rebellions* (3rd edn, Harlow: Longman).

Fletcher, Christopher (2014), 'What Makes a Political Language? Key Terms, Profit and Damage in the Common Petition of the English Parliament, 1343–1422', in J. Dumolyn, J. Haemers, H. R. Oliva Herrer, and V. Challet (eds), *The Voices of the People in Late Medieval Europe: Communication and Popular Politics* (Turnhout: Brepols), 91–106.

Florio, John (1598), *A worlde of wordes, or Most copious, and exact dictionarie in Italian and English* (London: Arnold Hatfield for Edward Blount).

Foigny, Gabriel de (1676), *La Terre austral connue* (Geneva: Jacques Vernevil).

Foigny, Gabriel de (1993), *The Southern Land, Known*, trans. David Fausset (Syracuse, NY: Syracuse University Press).

Fokkema, Douwe (2011), *Perfect Worlds: Utopian Fiction in China and the West* (Amsterdam: Amsterdam University Press).

Fontaine, Laurence (2014), *The Moral Economy: Poverty, Credit, and Trust in Early Modern Europe* (New York: Cambridge University Press).

Ford, C. D. (1947), 'Good Master Bonvisi', *Clergy Review*, NS 27: 228–235.

Forsström, Rikka (2002), *Possible Worlds: The Idea of Happiness in the Utopian Vision of Louis-Sébastien Mercier* (Helsinki: Suomalaisen kirjallisuuden seura).

Forsyth, Katherine (2018), ' "Worthy to be hadde and redde of everye Englishe man": The Private, Public and Political Contexts of Thomas More's English *Workes*', *British Catholic History*, 34: 247–272.

Fortunati, Vita (2000), 'Utopia as a Literary Genre', in Vita Fortunati and Raymond Trousson (eds), *Dictionary of Literary Utopias* (Paris: Champion), 634–643.

Foucault, Michel (1978), *History of Sexuality*, trans. Robert Hurley and Frédéric Gros (New York: Pantheon Books).

Foucault, Michel (2006), 'Utopian Body', in Caroline A. Jones (ed.), *Sensorium: Embodied Experience, Technology and Contemporary Art* (Cambridge, MA: MIT Press), 229–234.

Fox, Alistair (1982), *Thomas More: History and Providence* (Oxford: Blackwell).

Fox, Alistair (1983), *Thomas More: History and Providence* (New Haven: Yale University Press).

Fox, Alistair (1993), *Utopia: An Elusive Vision* (Boston: Twayne).

Foxcroft, H. C. (1902) (ed.), *A Supplement to Burnet's History of My Own Time* (Oxford: Oxford University Press).

Foxe, John (1583), *Actes and monuments of matters most speciall and memorable, happenyng in the Church with an universall history of the same* (London: John Foxe).

Frank, Joseph (1990), 'Nikolai Chernyshevsky: A Russian Utopia', in Frank Joseph, *Through the Russian Prism: Essays on Literature and Culture* (Princeton: Princeton University Press), 187–200.

Franke, Paul (2022), *Feeling Lucky: The Production of Gambling Experiences in Monte Carlo and Las Vegas* (London: Palgrave Macmillan).

Fränkel, Ludwig (1906), 'Minckwitz, Johannes', *Allgemeine Deutsche Biographie*, 52: 411–416.

Fraser, Stewart E. (1970) (ed.), *Ludvig Holberg's Memoirs: An Eighteenth-Century Danish Contribution to International Understanding* (Leiden: Brill).

Freeman, John (2007), 'Utopia, Incorporated: Reassessing Intellectual Property Rights to "the Island" ', *English Literary Renaissance*, 37: 3–33.

Freud, Sigmund (1959), *The Standard Edition of the Complete Psychological Works of Sigmund Freud*, vol. 9, ed. James Strachey et al. (London: Hogarth Press).

Freund, Michael (1930), 'Zur Deutung der Utopia des Thomas Morus: Ein Beitrag zur Geschichte der Staatsräson in England', *Historische Zeitschrift*, 142: 254–278.

Frevert, Ute (2019a), 'Introduction', in Ute Frevert (ed.), *Geschichte und Gesellschaft*, special issue 26: *Moral Economies*, 7–12.

Frevert, Ute (2019b), 'Moral Economies, Present and Past: Social Practices and Intellectual Controversies', in Ute Frevert (ed.), *Geschichte und Gesellschaft*, special issue 26: *Moral Economies*, 13–43.

Friedmann, Robert (1956), 'Economic Aspects of Early Hutterite Life', *Mennonite Quarterly Review*, 30: 259–266.

Frijhoff, Willem, and Spies, Marijke (1999), *1650: Bevochten eendracht* (The Hague: Sdu).

Frye, Northrop (1957), *Anatomy of Criticism: Four Essays* (Princeton: Princeton University Press).

Fuchs, Eduard (1892), 'Der Prometheus unserer Zeit', *Süddeutscher Postillon*, 11: 9.

Fuchs, Eduard (1894), 'Programm des Herausgebers', in Johannes Huber, *Der Sozialismus. Rückblick auf das Altertum* (Munich: Max Ernst) [= *Sammlung Gesellschaftswissenschaftlicher Aufsätze*, issue 8], 3–6.

Fuchs, Eduard (1896), 'Vorwort des Herausgebers', in Thomas More, *Utopia*, trans. Ignaz Emanuel Wessely, ed. Eduard Fuchs (Munich: Verlag der Gesellschaftswissenschaft [= *Sammlung gesellschaftswissenschaftlicher Aufsätze*, issues 11–13], iii–xxii, xvii–xix.

Fuchs, Eduard (1902), mit Hans Kraemer, *Die Karikatur der europäischen Völker vom Altertum bis zur Neuzeit* (Berlin: A. Hoffman).

Fuchs, Eduard (1903), *Die Karikatur der europäischen Völker vom Jahre 1848 bis zur Gegenwart* (Berlin: A. Hoffman).

Fuchs, Eduard, Kaiser, Karl, and Klaar, Ernst (1894) (eds), *Aus dem Klassenkampf* (Munich: Max Ernst).

Fuller, Mary C. (1995), *Voyages in Print: English Travel to America, 1576–1624* (Cambridge: Cambridge University Press).

Fuller, Richard Buckminster (1972), *The Buckminster Fuller Reader*, ed. J. Meller (Harmondsworth: Penguin).

Fuller, Richard Buckminster (1999), *Your Private Sky*, ed. J. Krause and C. Lichtenstein (Baden: Lars Müller Publications).

Fulton, Valerie (1994), 'An Other Frontier: Voyaging West with Mark Twain and *Star Trek*'s Imperial Subject', *Postmodern Culture*, 4: 1–24.

Furey, Constance (2006), *Erasmus, Contarini, and the Religious Republic of Letters* (Cambridge: Cambridge University Press).

Gabriel, Elun (2012), 'Utopia, Science and the Nature of Civilisation in Theodor Hertzka's *Freiland*', *Seminar*, 48: 9–29.

Gadd, Ian, Eliot, Simon, and Louis, W. Roger (2013) (eds), *The History of Oxford University Press*, 3 vols (Oxford: Oxford University Press).

Gagliardi, Achille (1674), *Lichte Practyke voor alle chistene zielen om te geraken tot opperste volmaecktheid en haar eenig einde* (Rotterdam: Frans van Hoogstraten).

Gailus, Manfred, and Lindenberger, Thomas (1994), 'Zwanzig Jahre *Moralische Ökonomie*: Ein Sozialhistorisches Konzept Ist Volljährig Geworden', *Geschichte und Gesellschaft*, 20: 469–477.

Galen (1517), *Galeni de sanitate tuenda Libri sex*, trans. Thomas Linacre (Paris: Guillaume Le Rouge).

Galen (1519), *Galeni methodus medendi vel de morbis curandis*, trans. Thomas Linacre (Paris: Didier Maheu).

Galloway, J. A. (2001), 'Town and Country in England, 1300–1570', in S. R. Epstein (ed.) *Town and Country in Europe, 1300–1800* (Cambridge: Cambridge University Press), 106–131.

Games, Alison (2006a), 'Atlantic History: Definitions, Challenges, and Opportunities', *American Historical Review*, 111: 741–757.

Games, Alison (2006b), 'Beyond the Atlantic', *William and Mary Quarterly*, 63: 675–776.

Gamsa, Mark (2011), 'Cultural Translation and the Transnational Circulation of Books', *Journal of World History*, 22: 553–575.

Garanderie, Marie-Madeleine de La (1989), 'Guillaume Budé, lecteur de *l'Utopie*', in Clare M. Murphy, Henri Gibaud, and Mario A. di Cesare (eds), *Miscellanea Moreana: Essays for Germain Marc'hadour* (Binghamton, NY: Medieval and Renaissance Texts and Studies), 331–338.

García Hernán, Enrique (2016), *Vives y Moro: La amistad en tiempos difíciles* (Madrid: Cátedra).

Gaskell, Philip (1986) (ed.), *A Bibliography of the Foulis Press* (Charlottesville, VA: University of Virginia Press).

Gautier Dalché, Patrick (2003), 'Les Diagrammes topographiques dans les manuscrits des classiques latins (Lucain, Solin, Salluste)', in Pierre Lardet (ed.), *La Tradition vive: Mélanges d'histoire des textes en l'honneur de Louis Holtz* (Turnhout: Brepols), 291–306.

Gavin, Masako, and Middleton, Ben (2013) (eds), *Japan and the High Treason Incident* (London: Routledge).

Geddes, Patrick (1915/2012), *Cities in Evolution* (repr. Marston Gate: Forgotten Books).

Génette, Gerard (1997), *Paratexts; Thresholds of Interpretation*, trans. Jane E. Lewin (Cambridge: Cambridge University Press) (first published in French in 1981).

Geng, Chuanming (2010), 'Old State and New Mission: A Survey of Utopian Literature during the Late Qing Dynasty and the Early Period of the Republic of China', *Frontiers of Literary Studies in China*, 4: 402–424.

Genkel', Aleksandr Germanovich (1906), *Narodnoe obrazovanie na zapade i u nas* (St Petersburg: Brokgauz-Efron).

George, Henry (1884), *Progress & Poverty: An Inquiry into the Cause of Industrial Depressions, and of Increase of Want with Increase of Wealth* (London: William Reeves).

Geraghty, Lincoln (2004), 'Neutralizing the Indian: Native American Stereotypes in *Star Trek: Voyager*', *U.S. Studies Online: The BAAS Postgraduate Journal*. https://baas.ac.uk/baas-archive/2010/04/issue-4-autumn-2004-article-1/.

Gerard, W. B., and Sterling, Eric (2005), 'Sir Thomas More's *Utopia* and the Transformation of England from Absolute Monarchy to Egalitarian Socie.ty', *Contemporary Justice Review*, 8: 75–89.

Gershoni, Israel, and Jankowsi, James (2009), *Confronting Fascism in Egypt: Dictatorship versus Democracy in the 1930s* (Stanford, CA: Stanford University Press).

Gilbert, F. (1968), 'The Venetian Constitution in Florentine Political Thought', in Nicolai Rubenstein (ed.), *Florentine Studies: Politics and Society in Renaissance Florence* (London: Faber & Faber), 463–500.

Gilbert, Humphrey (1576), *A Discourse of a Discoverie for a new Passage to Cataia* (London: Henry Middleton for Richard Jones).

Gilmont, Jean-François (2013), 'I funerali di Erasmo da Rotterdam: In Des. Erasmi Roterdami funus dialogus lepidissimus', *Bibliothèque d'Humanisme et Renaissance*, 75: 389–390.

Given-Wilson, C. (2005) (ed.), *The Parliament Rolls of Medieval England* (Leicester: Scholarly Digital Editions).

Gjerpe, Kristin (2008), 'The Italian *Utopia* of Lando, Doni and Sansovino: Paradox and Politics', in Terence Cave (ed.), *Thomas More's* Utopia *in Early Modern Europe: Paratexts and Contexts* (Manchester: Manchester University Press), 47–66.

Gjerpe, Kristin, and Klem, Lone (2008) (ed. and trans.), 'The Italian Paratexts', in Terence Cave (ed.), *Thomas More's* Utopia *in Early Modern Europe: Paratexts and Contexts* (Manchester: Manchester University Press), 171–179.

Gladstone, William (1858), *Studies on Homer and the Homeric Age*, 3 vols (Oxford: Oxford University Press).

Glasse, John [as 'J.G.'] (1887), 'Edinburgh', *The Commonweal*, 12 Feb.

Glazemaker, J. H. (1668), *Thomas Morus of de Zegepraal des geloofs en stantvastigheit* (Amsterdam: Gerrit van Goedesberg).

Glomski, Jacqueline (2017), 'Epistolary Writing', in Victoria Moul (ed.), *A Guide to Neo-Latin Literature* (Cambridge: Cambridge University Press), 255–271.

Gnavi, Alessandro (1997), 'Ferrero, Pier Francesco', in *Dizionario Biografico degli Italiani*, 47, https://www.treccani.it/biografico/.

Goddard, R. (2016), *Credit and Trade in Later Medieval England, 1353–1532* (Basingstoke: Palgrave Macmillan).

Godwin, Francis (1638), *The Man in the Moone* (London: John Norton for Joshua Kirton and Thomas Warren).

Godwin, W. (1998), *Caleb Williams* [1794], ed. D. McCracken (Oxford: Oxford University Press).

Goerlitz, Uta (2002), 'Die "Utopia" des Thomas Morus im Spiegel ihrer ersten deutschen Übersetzung (Basel 1524): Tendenzen der Funktionalisierung der Volkssprache im Umbruch vom Mittelalter zur Neuzeit', in *Vorträge und Referate des Erlanger Germanistentags*, vol. 1, ed. Hartmut Kugler et al. (Bielefeld: Aisthesis), 399–413.

Gogotski, S. (1857–73), *Filosofskii Leksikon*, 3: 518–522.

Goldhill, Simon (2002), *Who Needs Greek? Contests in the Cultural History of Hellenism* (Cambridge: Cambridge University Press).

Goldie, Mark (1991), 'Ideology', in Terence Ball, James Farr, and Russell Hanson (eds.), *Political Innovation and Conceptual Change* (Cambridge: Cambridge University Press), 266–291.

Goldie, Mark, Harris, Tim, and Seaward, Paul (1990) (eds), *The Politics of Religion in Restoration England* (Oxford: Oxford University Press).

Goldman, M. (1987), 'The Party and the Intellectual: Phase Two', in R. MacFarquhar and J. K. Fairbank (eds), *The Cambridge History of China*, vol. 14 (Cambridge: Cambridge University Press), 432–477.

Golec, L. Z. (2017), 'The Slovenian Reception of Thomas More and His *Utopia*', *Moreana*, 5/4: 187–203.

Goodey, Brian R. (1970), 'Mapping "Utopia": A Comment on the Geography of Sir Thomas More', *Geographical Review*, 60: 15–30.

Goodwin, B. (1980), 'Utopia Defended Against the Liberals', *Political Studies*, 28: 384–400.

Gorev, B. I. (1922), *Ot Tomasa Mora do Lenina, 1516–1917* (Moscow: L. D. Frekel').

Gosling, William Gilbert (1911), *The Life of Sir Humphrey Gilbert: England's First Empire Builder* (London: Constable).

Gott, Samuel (1648), *Novae Solymae libri sex* (London: John Legat).

Gottlieb, Erika (2001), *Dystopian Fiction East and West* (Montreal: McGill-Queen's University Press).

Götz, Norbert (2015), '*Moral Economy*: Its Conceptual History and Analytical Prospects', *Journal of Global Ethics*, 11: 147–162.

Gould, Eliga H. (2007), 'Entangled Histories, Entangled Worlds', *American Historical Review*, 112: 764–786.

Grądziel, Olga (2013), 'Early Modern Travel Writing and Thomas More's *Utopia*: An Attempt at Literary Interpretation', in Jacek Fabiszak, Ewa Urbaniak-Rybicka, and Bartosz Wolski (eds), *Crossroads in Literature and Culture* (Berlin: Springer, 2013), 399–410.

Graf, Georg (1944), *Geschichte der christlichen arabischen Literatur*, vol. 3 (Vatican City: Biblioteca apostolica vaticana).

Graffigny, Françoise de (1747), *Lettres d'une Péruvienne* (Paris?: Pissot?).

Grafton, Anthony (1991), 'Humanism and Political Theory', in J. H. Burns and Mark Goldie (eds.), *The Cambridge History of Political Thought 1450–1700* (Cambridge: Cambridge University Press), 7–29.

Grafton, Anthony (2001), *Bring Out Your Dead: The Past as Revelation* (Cambridge, MA: Harvard University Press).

Grafton, Anthony (2009a), 'A Sketch Map of a Lost Continent: The Republic of Letters', *Republics of Letters: A Journal for the Study of Knowledge, Politics, and the Arts*, 1 http://rofl.stanford.edu/node/34.

Grafton, Anthony (2009b), *Worlds Made by Words: Scholarship and Community in the Modern West* (Cambridge, MA: Harvard University Press).

Graheli, Shanti (2013), 'Reading the History of the Academia Venetiana through Its Book Lists', in Malcolm Walsby and Natasha Constantinidou (eds), *Documenting the Early Modern Book World: Inventories and Catalogues in Manuscript and Print* (Leiden: Brill), 283–319.

Granovetter, Mark (2017), *Society and Economy: Framework and Principles* (Cambridge, MA: Harvard University Press).

Greek Anthology, The (1916–27), ed. and trans. W. R. Paton, 5 vols (London: William Heinemann).

Greenblatt, Stephen (1980), *Renaissance Self-Fashioning: More to Shakespeare* (Chicago: University of Chicago Press).

Greenblatt, Stephen (2005), *Renaissance Self-Fashioning: From More to Shakespeare* (Chicago: University of Chicago Press).

Greene, Jack P., and Morgan, Philip D. (2009) (eds), *Atlantic History: A Critical Appraisal* (Oxford: Oxford University Press).

Greene, Roland (2013), *Five Words: Critical Semantics in the Age of Shakespeare and Cervantes* (Stanford, CA: Stanford University Press).

Greengrass, Mark (2007), *Governing Passions: Peace and Reform in the French Kingdom, 1576–1585* (Oxford: Oxford University Press).

Greening, A. (2009), 'Tottell, Richard (b. in or before 1528, d. (1593)', in *Oxford Dictionary of National Biography*, www.oxforddnb.com.

Greig, Martin (2004), 'Burnet, Gilbert (1643–1715)', in *Oxford Dictionary of National Biography*, www.oxforddnb.com.

Grendler, Paul F. (1965), 'Utopia in Renaissance Italy: Doni's "New World" ', *Journal of the History of Ideas* 26: 479–494.

Grendler, Paul F. (1969), 'Francesco Sansovino and Popular History', *Studies in the Renaissance* 16: 139–180.

Grendler, Paul F. (1977), *The Roman Inquisition and the Venetian Press, 1540–1605* (Princeton: Princeton University Press).

Greschonig, Steffen (2006), 'Lüge und Utopie', in Helga Lutz, Jan-Friedrich Missfelder, and Tilo Renz (eds), *Äpfel und Birnen: Illegitimes Vergleichen in den Kulturwissenschaften* (Bielefeld: Transcript), 117–129.

Gresham, Stephen (1986), 'William Baldwin: Literary Voice of the Reign of Edward VI', *Huntington Library Quarterly*, 44: 101–116.

Griffin, Martin I. J. Jr (1992), *Latitudinarianism in the Seventeenth-Century Church of England*, annotated by Richard H. Popkin, ed. Lila Freedman (Leiden: Brill).

Griffiths, Jane (2014), *Diverting Authorities: Experimental Glossing Practices in Manuscript and Print* (Oxford: Oxford University Press).

Grimm, Jacob, and Grimm, Wilhelm, *Deutsches Wörterbuch*, online edn. University of Trier <http://dwb.uni-trier.de/de>.

Grimmelhausen, Hans Jakob Christoffel von (1668), *Der abenteuerliche Simplicissimus Teutsch* (Frankfurt: Müller).

Grummitt, David (2002) (ed.), *The English Experience in France c 1450–1558: War, Diplomacy, and Cultural Exchange* (Aldershot: Ashgate).
Gueudeville, Nicolas (1689), *Motifs de la conversion* (Rotterdam: [n.pub.]).
Gueudeville, Nicolas (1700), *Critique générale des Avantures de Télémaque* (Cologne: heirs of Pierre Marteau).
Guggisberg, Hans R. (1982), *Basel in the Sixteenth Century: Aspects of the City Before, During, and After the Reformation* (St Louis: Center for Reformation Research).
Guicciardini, Francesco (1932), *Dialogo e discorsi del reggimento di Firenze*, ed. Roberto Palmarocchi (Bari: G. Laterza).
Guicciardini, Francesco (1994), *Dialogue on the Government of Florence*, ed. and trans. Alison Brown (Cambridge: Cambridge University Press).
Guillén, Juan (2006), *Historia de las Biblitecas Capitular y Colombina* (Seville: Fundación José Manuel Lara).
Guitton, Edouard (1999), 'Gabriel Meusnier de Querlon', in *Dictionnaire des journalistes (1600–1789)*, ed. Jean Sgard (Oxford: Voltaire Foundation, no. 574), http://dictionnaire-journalistes.gazettes18e.fr/journaliste/574-gabriel-meusnier-de-querlon.
Guldi, Jo, and Armitage, David (2017), *The History Manifesto* (Cambridge: Cambridge University Press).
Gury, Jacques (1974), 'About the Maps of Utopia', *Moreana*, 11: 99–101.
Gury, Jacques (1976), 'Thomas More traduit par Thomas Rousseau ou une *Utopie* pour le Club des Jacobins', *Moreana*, 49: 79–86.
Guthrie, W. K. C. (1957), *In the Beginning: Some Greek Views on the Origin of Life and the Early State of Man* (Ithaca, NY: Cornell University Press).
Gutzwiller, Kathryn J. (1998), *Poetic Garlands: Hellenistic Epigrams in Context* (Berkeley and Los Angeles: University of California Press).
Guy, John (1980), *The Public Career of Thomas More* (New Haven: Yale University Press).
Guy, John (2000), *Thomas More* (London: Oxford University Press).
Hadfield, Andrew (1998), *Literature, Travel and Colonial Writing in the English Renaissance, 1545–1625* (Oxford: Clarendon Press).
Hadfield, Andrew (1999), 'Rethinking Early Modern Colonialism: The Anomalous State of Ireland', *Irish Studies Review*, 7: 13–27.
Hadfield, Andrew (2013) (ed.), *The Oxford Handbook of English Prose, 1500–1640* (Oxford: Oxford University Press).
Hadfield, Andrew (2017a), 'Edmund Spenser's Dublin', in Crawford Gribben, Kathleen Miller, and Theresa O'Byrne (eds.), *Dublin: Renaissance City of Literature* (Manchester: Manchester University Press), 55–72.
Hadfield, Andrew (2017b), *Lying in Early Modern English Culture from the Oath of Supremacy to the Oath of Allegiance* (Oxford: Oxford University Press).
Hake, Sabine (2017), *The Proletarian Dream: Socialism, Culture and Emotion in Germany, 1863–1933* (Berlin: Walter de Gruyter).
Hakluyt, Richard (1589), *The Principall Navigations, Voiages and Discoveries of the English Nation* (London: George Bishop and Ralph Newbery).
Hakluyt, Richard (1598–1600), *The Principal Navigations, Voiages, Traffiques and Discoveries of the English Nation*, 3 vols (London: George Bishop, Ralph Newbery, and Robert Barker).
Hale, Edward Everett (1869–70), *The Brick Moon*, serialized in *Atlantic Monthly* (Oct. 1869–Feb. 1870).
Halévy, Élie (1962?), *Tarikh al-ishtirakiyya al-Urubiyya*, trans. Jamal al-Atasi (Damascus: Atlas).

Hall, Edward (1548), *The union of the two noble and illustre famelies of Lancastre & Yorke* (London: Richard Grafton).
Hall, Edward, and Grafton, Richard (1809), *Chronicle, or History of England*, ed. H. Ellis, 2 vols (London: J. Johnson et al.).
Hall, Joseph (1605), *Mundus Alter et Idem Sive Terra Australis ante hac semper incognita longis itineribus peregrini Academici nuperrime lustrata* (Frankfurt: heirs of Ascanius de Rinialme).
Hall, Joseph (1613), *Utopiae Pars II: Mundus alter et Idem. Die heutige newe alte Welt*, trans. Gregor Wintermonat (Leipzig: Henning Grosse d. J.).
Hall, Joseph (1643), *Mundus Alter Et Idem Sive Terra Australis antehac semper incognita longis itineribus peregrini Academici nuperrime lustrata: Authore Mercvrio Britannico; Accessit propter affinitatem materiae Thomae Campanellae, Civitas Solis, Et Nova Atlantis, Franc. Baconis, Bar. de Verulamio* (Utrecht: Johannes van Waesberg).
Hall, Joseph (1981), *Another World and Yet the Same: Bishop Joseph Hall's* Mundus Alter et Idem, ed. and trans. John Millar Wands (New Haven: Yale University Press).
Hall, Martin (2002), 'Gender and Reading in the Late Eighteenth Century: The *Bibliothèque Universelle des Romans*', *Eighteenth-Century Fiction*, 14: 771–790.
Hallowell, Robert H. (1960), 'Jean Le Blond's Defense of the French Language (1549)', *Romanic Review*, 51: 86–92.
Halpern, Richard (1991), *The Poetics of Primitive Accumulation: English Renaissance Culture and the Genealogy of Capital* (Ithaca, NY: Cornell University Press).
Hammer, Espen (2011), *Philosophy and Temporality from Kant to Critical Theory* (Cambridge: Cambridge University Press).
Hanna, R. (2005), *London Literature, 1300–1380* (Cambridge: Cambridge University Press).
Hanou, André (2002), *Nederlandse literatuur van de Verlichting (1670–1830)* (Nijmegen: Vantilt).
Hanson, Ingrid (2013), 'Socialist Identity and the Poetry of European Revolution in *Commonweal*, 1885–1890', in Ingrid Hanson, W. Jack Rhoden, and Erin Snyder (eds), *Poetry, Politics and Pictures: Culture and Identity in Europe 1840–1914* (Oxford: Peter Lang), 225–246.
Haraway, Donna (1988), 'Situated Knowledges: The Science Question in Feminism and the Privilege of Partial Perspective', *Feminist Studies*, 14: 575–599.
Hardt, Michael, and Negri, Antonio (2000), *Empire* (Cambridge, MA: Harvard University Press).
Hardy, Dennis (2000), *Utopian England: Community Experiments 1900–1945* (London: E. and F. N. Spon).
Hardy, Karl (2012), 'Unsettling Hope: Settler-Colonialism and Utopianism', *Spaces of Utopia: An Electronic Journal*, 2nd ser., 1: 123–136.
Harison, Casey (2015) (ed.), *A New Social Question: Capitalism, Socialism and Utopia* (Cambridge: Cambridge Scholars Publishing).
Harmon, Katharine (2009), *The Map as Art: Contemporary Artists Explore Cartography* (New York: Princeton Architectural Press).
Harms, Roeland (2011), *Pamfletten en publieke opinie: Massamedia in de zeventiende eeuw* (Amsterdam: Amsterdam University Press).
Harpsfield, Nicholas (1932), *The life and death of Sir Thomas Moore, knight, sometimes Lorde high Chancellor of England* [written 1558–9], ed. E. V. Hitchcock, *Early English Texts Society*, os 186.
Harraway, Donna (1988), 'Situated Knowledges: The Science Question in Feminism and the Privilege of Partial Perspective', *Feminist Studies*, 14: 575–599.

Harrington, James (1656), *The Common-wealth of Oceana* (London: printed by J. Streater for Livewell Chapman).

Harrington, James (1977), 'The Commonwealth of Oceana' [1656], in *The Political Works of James Harrington*, ed. J. G. A. Pocock (Cambridge: Cambridge University Press), 155–359.

Harrington, John (1879), *A Short View of the State of Ireland*, ed. W. D. Macray (Oxford: J. Parker).

Harris, Kirsten (2016), *Walt Whitman and British Socialism: 'The Love of Comrades'* (London: Routledge).

Harris, Mary Dormer (1907–13) (ed.), *The Coventry Leet Book: Or Mayor's Register* (London: Kegan Paul, Tench, Trübner & Co.).

Harris, Roy (1981), *The Language Myth in Western Culture* (London: Duckworth).

Harrison, Albert A. (2014), 'Astrotheology and Spaceflight: Prophecy, Transcendence and Salvation on the High Frontier', *Theology and Science*, 12: 30–48.

Hartig, Irmgard, and Soboul, Albert (1976), 'Notes pour une histoire de *l'Utopie* en France au XVIIIe siècle', *Annales historiques de la Révolution française*, 48: 161–179.

Hartlib, Samuel (1647), *Considerations Tending to the Happy Accomplishment of Englands Reformation in Church and State* (London: [n.pub.]).

Hartlib, Samuel (1648), *A Further Discoverie of the Office of Publike Addresse for Accommodations* (London: [n.pub.]).

Hartrich, Eliza (2019), *Politics and the Urban Sector in Fifteenth-Century England, 1413–1471* (Oxford: Oxford University Press).

Hartvig, Gabriella (2013), *The Critical and Creative Reception of Eighteenth-Century British and Anglo-Irish Authors in Hungary* (Pécs: University of Pécs).

Harvey, David (2000), *Spaces of Hope* (Edinburgh: Edinburgh University Press).

Haselbach, Dietmar (1985), *Franz Oppenheimer: Soziologie, Geschichtsphilosophie und Politik des 'Liberalen Sozialismus'* (Wiesbaden: Springer, 1985).

Hatzenberger, Antoine (2012), *Rousseau et l'utopie: De l'état insulaire aux cosmotopies* (Paris: Champion).

Havas, László (2011), 'Egy II. József korabeli latin nyelvű fejedelemtükör Magyarországról', in Kecskeméti Gábor and Tasi Réka (eds), *Bibliotheca et Universitas: Tanulmányok a hatvanéves Heltai János tiszteletére* (Miskolc: University of Miskolc BTK Institute of Hungarian Language and Literature), 333–340.

Hawkins, Howie (2021), 'The Paris Commune and Grassroots Democracy', *Socialism and Democracy*, 35: 182–192.

Hay, C. J. (1979), 'The Making of a Radical: The Case of James Burgh', *Journal of British Studies*, 18: 90–117.

Hay, Pete (2006), 'A Phenomenology of Islands', *Island Studies Journal*, 1: 19–42.

He, Donghui (2011), 'Coming of Age in the Brave New World: The Changing Reception of *How the Steel was Tempered* in the People's Republic of China', in Thomas Bernstein and Hua-yi Li (eds), *China Learns from the Soviet Union, 1949–Present* (Lanham, MD: Lexington Books), 394–421.

Herodian (1503), *Historiae a Marci principatu* (Venice: Aldus Manutius).

Herodotus (1502), *Heroditi libri novem* (Venice: Aldus Manutius).

Herodotus (1972), *The Histories*, trans. Aubrey De Sélincourt, rev. A. R. Burn (Harmondsworth: Penguin).

Herrera, Fernando de (1617), *Vida de Thomas Moro* (Madrid: Luis Sanchez).

Hertzka, Theodor (1889), *Freiland: ein sociales Zukunftsbild* (Dresden: E. Pierson).

Herzl, Theodor (1902), *Altneuland* (Leipzig: Seemann).

Hesiod (2007), *Theogony; Works and Days; Testimonia*, ed. and trans. Glen W. Most (Cambridge, MA: Harvard University Press).

Hessels, J. H. (1887) (ed.), *Abrahami Ortelii et virorum eruditorum ad eundem et ad Jacobum Colium Ortelianum epistulae* (Cambridge: Cambridge University Press).

Hester, Natalie (1996), 'Textes volés? *L'Estat, description et gouvernement des royaumes et républiques du monde* de Gabriel Chappuys', *Bibliothèque d'Humanisme et Renaissance*, 58: 651–659.

Hester, Natalie (1998), 'Stolen Texts?', in Paolo Cherchi (ed.), *Sondaggi sulla riscrittura del Cinquecento* (Ravenna: Longo), 133–148.

Hesychius (1514), *Hesychii Dictionarium* (Venice: Aldus Manutius).

Hexter, J. H. (1952), *More's* Utopia: *The Biography of an Idea* (Princeton: Princeton University Press).

Hexter, J. H. (1963), 'The Composition of *Utopia*' in *Utopia*, ed. Edward Surtz and J. H. Hexter, *The Yale Edition of the Complete Works of St. Thomas More*, vol. 4 (New Haven: Yale University Press), xv–xxiii.

Hexter, J. H. (1973), *The Vision of Politics on the Eve of the Reformation: More, Machiavelli, and Seyssel* (London: Allen Lane).

Heyberger, Bernard (1994), *Les Chrétiens du Proche-Orient au temps de la Réforme catholique, Syrie, Liban, Palestine, XVIIe–XVIIIe siècles* (Rome: École française de Rome).

Heyberger, Bernard (1999), 'Livres et pratique de la lecture chez les chrétiens (Syrie, Liban) XVIIe–XVIIIe siècles', *Revue des mondes musulmans et de la Méditerranée*, 87–8: 209–223.

Heyer, Andreas (2009), *Sozialutopien der Neuzeit: Bibliographisches Handbuch*, vol. 2: *Bibliographie der Quellen des utopischen Diskurses von der Antike bis zur Gegenwart* (Berlin: LIT).

Hiatt, Alfred (2008), *Terra Incognita: Mapping the Antipodes before 1600* (London: British Library).

Hiatt, Alfred (2011), '*Terra Australis* and the Idea of the Antipodes', in Anne Scott, Alfred Hiatt, Claire McIlroy, and Chris Wortham (eds), *Perceptions of Terra Australis* (Farnham: Ashgate), 9–44.

Hill, Christopher (1964), *Society and Puritanism in Pre-Revolutionary England* (London: Secker & Warburg).

Hill, Peter (2015a), 'Early Arabic Translations of English Fiction: *The Pilgrim's Progress* and *Robinson Crusoe*', *Journal of Semitic Studies*, 60: 177–212.

Hill, Peter (2015b), 'The First Arabic Translations of Enlightenment Literature: The Damietta Circle of the 1800s and 1810s', *Intellectual History Review*, 24: 209–233.

Hill, Peter (2018), 'The Arabic Adventures of *Télémaque*: Trajectory of a Global Enlightenment Text in the Nahḍa', *Journal of Arabic Literature*, 49: 171–203.

Hill, Peter (2019), 'Translation and the Globalisation of the Novel: Relevance and Limits of a Diffusionist Model', in Marilyn Booth (ed.), *Migrating Texts: Translation around the Late Ottoman Mediterranean* (Edinburgh: Edinburgh University Press), 95–121.

Hill, Peter (2020), *Utopia and Civilisation in the Arab Nahda* (Cambridge: Cambridge University Press).

Hill, Tracey (2011), *Pageantry and Power: A Cultural History of the Early Modern Lord Mayor's Show, 1585–1639* (Manchester: Manchester University Press).

Hinds, A. B. (1912) (ed.), *Calendar of State Papers, Milan* (London: HMSO).

Hinsch, Moritz (2021), *Ökonomik und Hauswirtschaft im klassischen Griechenland* (Stuttgart: Franz Steiner Verlag).
Hirsch, Felix E. (1946), 'Hermann Oncken and the End of an Era', *Journal of Modern History*, 18: 148–159.
Hixson, Walter (2013), *American Settler Colonialism: A History* (New York: Palgrave).
Ho, Koon-Ki (1983–6), 'Several Thousand Years in Search of Happiness: The Utopian Tradition in China', *Oriens Extremus*, 30: 19–35.
Ho, Koon-Ki (1991), 'Japanese in Search of Happiness: A Survey of the Utopian Tradition in Japan', *Oriens Extremus*, 34: 201–214.
Hobbes, Thomas (1629), *Eight Books of the Peloponnesian War* (London: for Henry Seile).
Hobbes, Thomas (1651), *Leviathan* (London: for Andrew Crooke).
Hobbes, Thomas (1968), *Leviathan*, ed. Crawford B. Macpherson (New York: Penguin Books).
Hobbs, A. (2007), 'Plato on War', in D. Scott (ed.), *Maieusis: Essays in Honour of Myles Burnyeat* (Oxford: Oxford University Press), 176–194.
Hobbs, A. (2019), 'The Erotic Magus: Ficino's *De Amore* as a Guide to Plato's *Symposium*', in John Finamore and T. Nejeschleba (eds), *Platonism and Its Legacy: Selected Papers from the Fifteenth Annual Conference of the International Society for Neoplatonic Studies* (Lydney: The Prometheus Trust), 243–258.
Hocquet, Adolphe (1900), 'Tournai et l'occupation anglaise (1513–1519)', *Annales de la Société historique et archéologique de Tournai*, 5: 302–465.
Hodgson, Geoffrey M. (1995), 'The Political Economy of Utopia', *Review of Social Economy* 53: 195–213.
Hodgson, William (1994), 'The Commonwealth of Reason' [1795], in Gregory Claeys (ed.), *Utopias of the British Enlightenment* (Cambridge: Cambridge University Press), 199–247.
Höfener, Heiner (1980), 'Nachwort', in Heiner Höfener (ed.), *Thomas Morus: Von der wunderbaren Insel Utopia* (Hildesheim: Gerstenberg), i–vi.
Hoftijzer, P. G. (1999), *Pieter van der Aa (1659–1733), Leids drukker en boekverkoper* (Hilversum: Verloren).
Holberg, Ludvig (1741), *Nicolai Klimii Iter Subterraneum* (Copenhagen: [n.pub.]).
Holberg, Ludvig (1744), *Moralische Abhandlungen* (Copenhagen: [n.pub.]).
Holberg, Ludvig (1926), *Nachrichten von meinem Leben: In drei Briefen an einen vornehmen Herren. Mit einem Essay von Georg Brandes* (Frankfurt: Frankfurter Verlagsanstalt).
Holberg, Ludvig (1960), *The Journey of Niels Klim to the World Underground*, ed. James I. McNelis, Jr. (Lincoln, NE: University of Nebraska Press).
Holinshed, Raphael (1807–8), *Holinshed's Chronicles of England, Scotland and Ireland*, ed. H. Ellis, 6 vols. (London: J. Johnson et al.).
Holland, Anna, and Scholar, Richard (2009) (eds), *Pre-Histories and Afterlives: Studies in Critical Method* (Oxford: Legenda).
Holland, Owen (2017), *William Morris's Utopianism: Propaganda, Politics and Prefiguration* (Basingstoke: Palgrave Macmillan).
Hollstein, F. W. H (1954), *German Engravings, Etchings, and Woodcuts, ca 1400–1700* (Amsterdam: M. Hertzberger).
Hollstein, F. W. H (1977), *German Engravings, Etchings, and Woodcuts, Vol. XI, Urs Graf*, compiled by John K. Rowlands, ed. Fedja Anzelewsky and Robert Zijlma (Amsterdam: Van Gendt & Co).
Holmes, Colin (2016), *Anti-Semitism in British Society, 1876–1939* (new edn, London: Routledge).

Holt, Elizabeth M. (2009), 'Narrative and the Reading Public in 1870s Beirut', *Journal of Arabic Literature*, 40: 37–70.

Holtrop, J. W. (1867), *Thierry Martens d'Alost: Étude Bibliographque* (The Hague: Martinus Nijhoff).

Homann, Johann Baptist (1694/2000), *Accurata Utopiae Tabula: Das ist Der Neu entdeckten Schalck-Welt, oder des so offtbenanten, und doch nie erkanten Schlarraffenlandes Neu erfundene lacherliche Land-tabell* (repr. Bad Langensalza: Rockstuhl).

Homans, George C. (1942), *English Villagers of the Thirteenth Century* (Cambridge, MA: Harvard University Press).

Homer (1504), *Homerou Ilias* (Venice: Aldus Manutius).

Homer (2003), *Odyssey*, trans. E. V. Rieu (rev. edn, London: Penguin).

Hook, A., and Sher, R. B. (1995) (eds.), *The Glasgow Enlightenment* (East Linton: Tuckwell Press).

Hopfener, Birgit (2018), 'Transculturally Entangled—Qiu Zhijie's concept of *Total Art*', in Sarah Dornhof et al. (eds), *Situating Global Art: Topologies—Temporalities—Trajectories* (Bielefeld: Transcript), 275–287.

Hoppe, H. R. (1948), 'The Birthplace of Stephen Mierdman, Flemish Printer in London, c.1549–c.1552', *The Library*, ser. 5: 213–214.

Horace (1926), *Satires; Epistles; The Art of Poetry*, trans. H. Rushton Fairclough (Cambridge, MA: Harvard University Press).

Horn, Walter, and Born, Ernest (1979), *The Plan of St Gall: A Study of the Architecture and Economy of, and Life in, a Paradigmatic Carolingian Monastery*, 3 vols (Berkeley and Los Angeles: University of California Press).

Horváth, Iván (2007), 'A magyar vers a reneszánsz és a reformáció korában', in Mihály Szegedy-Maszák et al. (eds), *A magyar irodalom történetei* (Budapest: Gondolat), 177–187.

Hosington, Brenda (1984), 'Early French Translations of Thomas More's *Utopia*: 1550–1730', *Humanistica Lovaniensia: Journal of Neo-Latin Studies*, 33: 116–134.

Houston, Chloë (2009), 'Travelling Nowhere: Global Utopias in the Early Modern Period', in Jyotsna G. Singh (ed.), *A Companion to the Global Renaissance: English Literature and Culture in the Era of Expansion* (Oxford: Wiley-Blackwell), 82–98.

Houston, Chloë (2010) (ed.), *New Worlds Reflected: Travel and Utopia in the Early Modern Period* (Farnham: Ashgate).

Houston, Chloë (2014), *The Renaissance Utopia: Dialogue, Travel and the Ideal Society* (Farnham: Ashgate).

Houston, Garmaine A. (1986), *Marxism and the Crisis of Development in Pre-War Japan* (Princeton: Princeton University Press).

Howard, Donald R. (1971), 'The World of Mandeville's Travels', *Yearbook of English Studies*, 19: 1–17.

Howard, Ebenezer (1902), *Garden Cities of To-morrow* (London: Swan Sonnenschein & Co.).

Howe, Stephen (2009) (ed.), *The New Imperial Histories Reader* (London: Routledge).

Howells, Robin (2007), *Regressive Fictions* (Leeds: Taylor and Francis).

Hsia, R. Po-chia (1981), 'The Utopia in Chinese', *Moreana*, 18: 107–109.

Huang, Ko-wu (2003), 'The Reception of Yan Fu in Twentieth-Century China', in Cindy Yik-yi Chu and Ricardo K. S. Mak (eds), *China Reconstructs* (Lanham, MD: University Press of America), 25–44.

Hudson, W. S. (1980), *The Cambridge Connection and the Elizabethan Settlement of 1559* (Durham, NC: Duke University Press).

Hughes, Paul L., and Larkin, James F. (1964) (eds.), *Tudor Royal Proclamations*, vol. 1: *The Early Tudors (1485–1553)* (New Haven: Yale University Press).

Hughes, Robert (1980), *The Shock of the New* (London: BBC).

Hull, F. (1966) (ed.), *A Calendar of the White and Black Books of the Cinque Ports 1432–1955* (London: HMSO).

Hulme, Peter (1986), *Colonial Encounters: Europe and the Native Caribbean, 1492–1797* (London: Methuen).

Hume, David (1983), *The History of England: From the Invasion of Julius Caesar to the Revolution in 1688* (Indianapolis: Liberty Classics).

Hunt, Lynn (2007), *Inventing Human Rights: A History* (New York: Norton).

Hunt, Lydia (1991), 'The First Spanish Translation of *Utopia*', *Moreana*, 28: 21–41.

Huonker, Thomas (1985), *Revolution, Moral und Kunst: Eduard Fuchs, Leben und Werk* (Zurich: Limmat).

Hutten, Ulrich von (1518a), *Ulrichi de Hutten equitis Germani. Aula. Dialogus* (Augsburg: Sigismund Grimm and Marcus Wirsung).

Hutten, Ulrich von (1518b), *Ulrichi de Hutten, equitis Germani, Aula Dialogus* (Basel: Froben).

Hutton, Arthur Wollaston (1885), *Sir Thomas More & His Utopia: The 'New Learning' of the 16th Century in Relation to Social Reform: A Lecture Delivered Before the Sunday Lecture Society on Sunday Afternoon, 22nd November 1885* (London: Sunday Lecture Society).

Hutton, William Holden (1895), *Sir Thomas More* (London: Methuen & Co.).

Hylkema, C. B. (1900–2/1978), *Reformateurs: Geschiedkundige studiën over de godsdienstige bewegingen uit de nadagen onzer Gouden eeuw*, 2 vols. (repr. Groningen: Bouma).

I. D. M. G. T. (1616), *Histoire du grand et admirable royaume d'Antangil incogneu jusques a present à tous historiens et cosmographes: compose de six vingts provinces tres belles et tres fertiles, avec la description d'icelui et de sa police nompareille, tant civile que militaire* (Saumur: T. Portau).

Iggers, Georg G. (1988), 'The Crisis of the Rankean Paradigm in the Nineteenth Century', *Syracuse Scholar*, 9: 1–50.

IJsewijn, Jozef (2017), 'Latin and the Low Countries', in Theo Hermans and Reinier Salverda (eds), *From Revolt to Riches: Culture and History of the Low Countries, 1500–1700* (London: UCL Press), 2–18.

Ingram, Kevin (2009) (ed.). *The Conversos and Moriscos in Late Medieval Spain and Beyond*, vol. 1 (Boston: Brill).

'Institute of Things to Come', http://theinstituteofthingstocome.com/oldsite.

Ishay, M. R. (2008), *The History of Human Rights: From Ancient Time to the Globalization Era* (Berkeley and Los Angeles: University of California Press).

Israel, Jonathan I. (1995), *The Dutch Republic: Its Rise, Greatness, and Fall, 1477–1806* (Oxford: Oxford University Press).

Israel, Jonathan I. (2001), *Radical Enlightenment: Philosophy and the Making of Modernity, 1650–1750* (Oxford: Oxford University Press).

Jackson, Paul (1980), 'Freiland: Theodor Hertzka's Liberal-Socialist Utopia', *German Life and Letters*, 33: 269–275.

Jakovenko, V. I. (1891), *Tomas Mor: Ego zhizn' i obshchestvennaya deyatel'nost'* (St Petersburg: Erlich).

James, Susan (2012), *Spinoza on Philosophy, Religion and Politics*: The Theologico-Political Treatise (Oxford: Oxford University Press).

Jameson, Fredric (1977), 'Of Islands and Trenches: Naturalization and the Production of Utopian Discourse', *Diacritics*, 7: 2–21.
Jameson, Fredric (1991), *Postmodernism, or the Cultural Logic of Late Capitalism* (Durham, NC: Duke University Press).
Jameson, Fredric (1994), *The Seeds of Time* (New York: Columbia University Press).
Jameson, Fredric (2004), 'The Politics of Utopia', *New Left Review*, 25 (Jan.–Feb.), online: https://newleftreview.org/issues/ii25/articles/fredric-jameson-the-politics-of-utopia.
Jameson, Fredric (2005), *Archaeologies of the Future: The Desire called Utopia and Other Science Fictions* (London: Verso).
Jameson, Fredric (2015), 'The Aesthetics of Singularity', *New Left Review*, 92: 101–132.
Jankovics, Marcell (dir.) (2011), *As ember tragédiája*.
Janzen, Rod A., and Stanton, Max Edward (2010), *The Hutterites in North America* (Baltimore, MD: Johns Hopkins University Press).
Jardine, Lisa (1993), *Erasmus, Man of Letters: The Construction of Charisma in Print* (Princeton: Princeton University Press).
Jardine, Lisa (2015), *Erasmus, Man of Letters: The Construction of Charisma in Print* (updated edn, Princeton: Princeton University Press).
Jauss, Hans Robert (1982), *Toward an Aesthetic of Reception*, trans. Timothy Balti (Brighton: Harvester Press).
Jayne, Sears (1963), *John Colet and Marsilio Ficino* (Oxford: Oxford University Press).
Jayne, Sears, and Johnson, Francis R. (1956), *The Lumley Library: The Catalogue of 1609* (London: British Museum).
Jeanneret, Michel (1970), 'Introduction', in Thomas More, *La Description de l'isle d'Utopie*, trans. Jean Le Blond, ed. Michel Jeanneret (The Hague: S. R. Publishers), vii–xxii.
Jefferson, Thomas, et al. (1776), *The Declaration of Independence*, https://www.archives.gov/founding-docs/declaration-transcript.
Jiang, Qian (2013), 'Translation and the Development of Science Fiction in Twentieth-Century China', *Science Fiction Studies*, 40: 116–132.
Jillings, Lewis (1993), 'Ulrich von Hutten's Self-Stylization as Odysseus: The Conservative Use of Myth', *Colloquia Germanica*, 26: 93–107.
Johns, Alessa (2003), *Women's Utopias of the Eighteenth Century* (Chicago: University of Illinois Press).
Johnson, G. D. (1988), 'The Stationers versus the Drapers: Control of the Press in the Late Sixteenth Century', *The Library*, 6th ser., 10: 1–17.
Johnson, Samuel (2009), *The History of Rasselas, Prince of Abissinia*, ed. Thomas Keymer (Oxford: Oxford University Press).
Jones, Evan T. (2010), 'Henry VII and the Bristol Expeditions to North America: The Condon Documents', *Historical Research*, 83: 444–454.
Jones, Royston O. (1950), 'Some Notes on More's *Utopia* in Spain', *Modern Language Review*, 45: 478–482.
Jonktys, Daniel (1651), *De Pyn-Bank Wedersproken, en bematigt* (Rotterdam: Johannes Naeranus).
Jörgensen, K. E. Jordt (1968), *Stanislaw Lubieniecki: Zum Weg des Unitarismus von Ost nach West im 17. Jahrhundert* (Göttingen: Vandenhoeck & Ruprecht).
Jørgensen, Sven Aage (1983), 'Skandinavische Utopien', in Klaus Berghahn and Hans Ulrich Seeber (eds), *Literarische Utopien von Morus bis zur Gegenwart* (Königstein: Athenäum), 265–274.

Juvenal (1918), *Juvenal and Persius: With an English Translation*, ed. and trans. G. G. Ramsay (London: William Heinemann).

Kaganovich, B. (2014), *Evgenii Viktorovich Tarle: Istorik i vremya* (St Petersburg: Izdatel'stvo Evropeĭskogo universiteta v Sankt-Peterburge).

Kahn, James, Belanoff, Adam, and Piller, Michael (1992), 'The Masterpiece Society', *Star Trek: The Next Generation*, season 5, episode 13, CBS (10 Feb.).

Kahneman, Daniel (2003), 'A Psychological Perspective on Economics', *American Economic Review*, 93: 162–168.

Kahneman, Daniel (2011), *Thinking, Fast and Slow* (New York: Farrar, Straus and Giroux).

Kant, Immanuel (1977a), *Logik*, in *Schriften zur Metaphysik und Logik II* (Frankfurt am Main: Suhrkamp).

Kant, Immanuel (1977b), 'Versuch, den Begriff der negativen Grössen in die Weltweisheit einzuführen', in Immanuel Kant, *Vorkritische Schriften bis 1768* (Frankfurt am Main: Suhrkamp), 775–819.

Kant, Immanuel (1987), *Critique of Judgement*, trans. W. Pluhar (Indianapolis: Hackett).

Kant, Immanuel (1994), *Political Writings*, ed. H. Reiss, trans. H. B. Nisbet (Cambridge: Cambridge University Press).

Kant, Immanuel (1998), *The Critique of Pure Reason*, ed. and trans. P. Guyer and A. Wood (Cambridge: Cambridge University Press).

Kant, Immanuel (2002), *Theoretical Philosophy 1755–1770*, ed. and trans. D. Walford (Cambridge: Cambridge University Press).

Kapor, Vladimir (2008), 'Shifting Edenic Codes: On Two Exotic Visions of the Golden Age in the Late Eighteenth Century', *Eighteenth-Century Studies*, 41: 217–230.

Kaposi, Krisztina (2012), 'Zrínyi-paratextusok', *Első Század*, 11: 413–446.

Kapust, Daniel (2011), 'Cicero on Decorum and the Morality of Rhetoric', *European Journal of Political Theory*, 10: 92–112.

Karamzin, N. (1791), *Moskovskii zhurnal*, vol. 1, pp. 358–265, Review of More, Thomas (1789), *Kartina vsevozmozhnogo luchshego pravleniya ili Utopii. Sochinenie Tomasa Moritsa Kantslera Anglinskogo, v dvukh knigakh*, trans. Anon. (St Petersburg: Johan Karlovich Shnor).

Karp, S. Ya (1987), 'Brissot ob "*Utopii*" Tomasa Mora (80-e gody XVIII v)', in L. S. Chikolini (ed.), *Istoriya sotsialisticheskikh uchenii: sbornik statei* (Moscow: Academy of Sciences), 76–85.

Karrow, Robert W. (1993), *Mapmakers of the Sixteenth Century and Their Maps: Bio-Bibliographies of the Cartographers of Abraham Ortelius, 1570* (Chicago: Speculum Orbis Press).

Kastan, David Scott (2001), *Shakespeare and the Book* (Cambridge: Cambridge University Press).

Kautsky, Karl (1888), *Thomas More und seine Utopie* (Stuttgart: Dietz).

Kautsky, Karl (1889), 'Der jüngste Zukunftsroman', *Die Neue Zeit: Revue des geistigen und öffentlichen Lebens*: 268–276.

Kautsky, Karl [as 'K.K.'] (1895–6), 'Thomas Morus, Utopia: Herausgegeben von V. Michels und Th. Ziegler, Lateinische Literaturdenkmäler des 15. und 16. Jahrhunderts, 11 (Berlin, Weidmannsche Buchhandlung, LXX und 115 S. 3,60 Mark', *Die Neue Zeit: Revue des geistigen und öffentlichen Lebens*, 14/25: 794.

Kautsky, Karl [as 'K.K.'] (1896–7), 'Thomas Morus, Utopia, Uebersetzt und mit sachlichen Anmerkungen versehen von Dr I. E. Wessely, Nebst einem Vorwort des Herausgebers, Mit fünf phototypischen Nachbildungen und dem Bildniß des Thomas Morus. München, M. Ernst. XXII und 170S', *Die Neue Zeit*, 15/6: 826–827.

Kawato, Michiaki, and Nakabayashi, Yoshio (2001), *Meiji Hon-yaku Bungaku Zenshu Shimbun Zasshi Hen, Bekkan 1, Meijiki Hon-yaku Bungaku Sogo Nenpyo* (Tokyo: Ohzora-Sha).

Kearney, Hugh (1995), *The British Isles: The History of Four Nations* (Cambridge: Cambridge University Press).

Keene, Derek (1989), 'Medieval London and Its Region', *London Journal*, 14: 99–111.

Keiper, Hugo (1994). 'Introductory Essay', in *Nominalism and Literary Discourse: New Perspectives*, ed. Hugo Keiper, Christoph Bode, Richard J. Utz (Amsterdam: Rodopi).

Kempshall, M. S. (1999), *The Common Good in Late Medieval Political Thought* (Oxford: Oxford University Press).

Kennedy, John F. (1962), Speech at Rice Stadium, Houston, TX, USA (Sept (12), https://www.jfk library.org/learn/about-jfk/historic-speeches/address-at-rice-university-on-the-nations-space-effort.

Kermode, J. (1987), 'Merchants, Overseas Trade, and Urban Decline: York, Beverley, and Hull c 1380–1500', *Northern History*, 23: 51–73.

Kermode, J. (1991), 'Money and Credit in the Fifteenth Century: Some Lessons from Yorkshire', *Business History Review*, 65: 475–501.

Kermode, J. (1994), 'Medieval Indebtedness: The Regions vs London', in N. Rogers (ed.), *England in the Fifteenth Century: Proceedings of the 1992 Harlaxton Symposium* (Stamford: Paul Watkins), 72–88.

Kermode, J. (1998), *Medieval Merchants: York, Beverley and Hull in the Later Middle Ages* (Cambridge: Cambridge University Press).

Kerr, Anne, and Wright, Edmund (2015) (eds), *A Dictionary of World History* (Oxford: Oxford University Press).

Kessler, Sanford (2002), 'Religious Freedom in Thomas More's *Utopia*', *Review of Politics*, 64: 209–229.

Keymis, Lawrence (1596), *A Relation of the Second Voyage to Guiana* (London: Thomas Dawson).

Keynes, John Maynard (1936), *The General Theory of Employment, Interest and Money* (New York: Harcourt Brace and Co.).

Khuri-Makdisi, Ilham (2010), *The Eastern Mediterranean and the Making of Global Radicalism, 1860–1914* (Berkeley and Los Angeles: University of California Press).

Kidd, Colin (1999) (ed.), *British Identities Before Nationalism: Ethnicity and Nationhood in the Atlantic World, 1600–1800* (Cambridge: Cambridge University Press).

Kiesel, Helmuth (1979), *'Bei Hof, Bei Höll': Untersuchung zur Literarischen Hof kritik von Sebastian Brant bis Friedrich Schiller* (Tübingen: Niemeyer).

Kindermann, Eberhard (1744), *Die Geschwinde Reise auf dem Lufft-Schiff* (Berlin: Radetski).

King, John N. (1982), *English Reformation Literature: The Tudor Origins of the Protestant Tradition* (Princeton: Princeton University Press).

Kingsford, C. L. (1934) (ed.), *Historical Manuscripts Commission, Report on the Manuscripts of Lord de L'Isle and Dudley preserved at Penhurst Palace*, vol. 2 (London: HMSO).

Kinna, Ruth (1999), 'Morris, Anti-Statism and Anarchy', in Peter Faulkner (ed), *William Morris: Centenary Essays* (Exeter: University of Exeter Press), 215–228.

Kinna, Ruth (2009), 'Anarchism and the Politics of Utopia', in Laurence Davis and Ruth Kinna (eds), *Anarchism and Utopianism* (Manchester: Manchester University Press), 221–240.

Kinney, Arthur F. (1979), *Rhetoric and Poetic in Thomas More's* Utopia (Los Angeles: Undena Publications).
Kipling, Rudyard (1899), 'White Man's Burden', *McClure's Magazine*, 12/4 (Feb.).
Kirk, R. E. G., and Kirk, Ernest F. (1900) (eds), *Returns of Aliens Dwelling in the City and Suburbs of London from the Reign of Henry VIII to that of James I* (Aberdeen: Aberdeen University Press for the Huguenot Society of London).
Kirwan, Richard, and Mullins, Sophie (2015) (eds), *Specialist Markets in the Early Modern Book World* (Leiden: Brill).
Kisch, Guido (1970), *Claudius Cantiuncula: Ein Basler Jurist und Humanist des 16. Jahrhunderts* (Basel: Helbing & Lichtenhahn).
Kitzbichler, Josefine, Lubitz, Katja, and Mindt, Nina (2009), *Theorie der Übersetzung antiker Literatur in Deutschland seit 1800* (Berlin: Walter de Gruyter).
Kivistö, Sari (2009), *Medical Analogy in Latin Satire* (London: Palgrave Macmillan).
Klassen, Peter James (1964), *The Economics of Anabaptism: 1525–1560* (The Hague: Mouton & Co.).
Kleinwächter, Friedrich (1891), *Die Staatsromane: ein Beitrag zur Lehre vom Communismus und Socialismus* (Vienna. M. Breitenstein).
Knäble, Philip (2019), 'Moralische Ökonomie?—Zur Wirtschaftsethik Der Schule von Salamanca am Beispiel von Martín De Azpilcueta und Leonardus Lessius', *Saeculum*, 69: 55–78.
Knapp, Jeffrey (1992), *An Empire Nowhere: England, America, and Literature from* Utopia *to* The Tempest (Berkeley and Los Angeles: University of California Press).
Knight, Sarah, and Tilg, Stephan (2015) (eds), *The Oxford Handbook of Neo-Latin* (Oxford: Oxford University Press).
Knights, Mark (1994), *Politics and Opinion in Crisis, 1678–1681* (Cambridge: Cambridge University Press).
Kohli, Martin (1987), 'Retirement and the Moral Economy: An Historical Interpretation of the German Case', *Journal of Aging Studies* 1: 125–144.
Kolakowski, Leszek (1969), *Chrétiens sans Église: La Conscience religieuse et le lien confessionnel au XVIIe siècle* (Paris: Gallimard).
Komlósi, Sándor (1978) (ed.), *Neveléstörténeti olvasóköny* (Budapest: Tankönyvkiadó).
Konecsni, Johnemery (1976), 'Sir Humphrey Gilbert, *Utopia*, and America', *Moreana*, 13: 124–125.
Königliche Polizei-Direktion (1890), (ed.), *Adreßbuch für München für das Jahr 1890. Hierzu das Handels- und Gewerbeadreßbuch herausgegeben von der Handels- und Gewerbekammer für Oberbayern* (Munich: Mühlthaler, Huber, Knorr & Birth).
Koning, Paula (2011), 'De twee levens van Erasmus in Leiden: Petrus Scriverius en Paulus Merula als biografische beeldvormers', *De zeventiende eeuw*, 27: 37–48.
Kooi, Christine (2007), 'Conversion in a Multiconfessional Society: The Dutch Republic', in Ute Lotz-Heumann, Jan-Friedrich Missfelder, and Matthias Pohlig (eds), *Konversion und Konfession in der frühen Neuzeit* (Heidelberg: Gütersloher Verlaghaus), 271–286.
Kooi, Christine (2012), *Calvinists and Catholics during Holland's Golden Age* (Cambridge: Cambridge University Press).
Koselleck, Reinhart (2002), 'The Temporalization of Utopia', in Reinhart Kosselleck, *The Practice of Conceptual History: Timing History, Spacing Concepts*, trans. Todd Samuel Presner et al. (Stanford, CA: Stanford University Press), 84–99.

Kossmann, E. H. (1960/2000), *Political Thought in the Dutch Republic* (repr. Amsterdam: Royal Netherlands Academy of Arts and Sciences).

Kosznai, Ágnes (1994), *Az utópia gondolata a magyar irodalomban* (Budapest: Magyar Scifitörténeti Társaság).

Kovács, Márton (2005) (ed.), *Filozófiatörténeti áttekintés érettségizőknek* (Budapest: FISZ).

Kowaleski, M. (1990), 'The Commercial Dominance of a Medieval Provincial Oligarchy: Exeter in the Late Fourteenth Century', in R. Holt and G. Rosser (eds), *The English Medieval Town: A Reader in English Urban History* (London: Longman), 184–215.

Kraye, Jill (1988), 'Moral Philosophy', in Charles B. Schmitt, Eckhard Kessler, and Quentin Skinner with Jill Kraye (eds), *The Cambridge History of Renaissance Philosophy* (Cambridge: Cambridge University Press), 303–386.

Kristeller, Paul Oscar (1980), 'Thomas More as a Renaissance Humanist', *Moreana*, 65–6: 5–22.

Kruyfhooft, Cécile (1981), 'A Recent Discovery: Utopia by Abraham Ortelius', *Map Collector*, 16: 10–14.

Kruyfhooft, Cécile (2016), 'Abraham Ortelius. Map of the Island of Utopia', in Jan Van der Stock (ed.), *In Search of Utopia: Art and Science in the Era of Thomas More* (Amsterdam: Amsterdam University Press), 122–123.

Kucherenko, G. S. (1977), 'Problemy zapadnoevropeiskogo utopicheskogo sotsializma v tvorchestve E. V. Tarle', in G. S. Kucherenko (ed.), *Istoriya sotsialisticheskikh uchenii. Voprosy isoriografii. Sbk.st.* (Moscow: Nauka), 60–86.

Kühler, W. J. (1912/1980), *Het socinianisme in Nederland* (repr. Leeuwarden: De Tille BV).

Kukkonen, Karin (2017), *Cognition and Poetics: Neoclassicism and the Novel* (Oxford: Oxford University Press).

Kumar, Krishan (1991), *Utopianism* (Buckingham: Open University Press).

Kumar, Krishan (2003), *The Making of English National Identity* (Cambridge: Cambridge University Press, 2003.

Kumar, Krishan (2010), 'The Ends of Utopia', *New Literary History*, 41: 549–569.

Kuon, Peter (1986), *Utopischer Entwurf und Fiktionale Vermittlung: Studien zum Gattungswandel der Literarischen Utopie zwischen Humanismus und Frühaufklärung* (Heidelberg: C. Winter).

Kupperman, Karen Ordahl (2007), *The Jamestown Project* (Cambridge, MA: Harvard University Press).

L'Esprit des Cours de l'Europe (1699–1710) (The Hague and Amsterdam), 19 vols.

La Roche, Sophie von (1798), *Erscheinungen am See Oneida* (Leipzig: Heinr. Graff).

Labarge, Margaret Wade (1982), *Medieval Travellers: The Rich and Restless* (London: Hamish Hamilton).

Lacan, Jacques (2007), *Écrits*, trans. Bruce Fink (New York: Norton).

Lacan, Jacques (2008), *The Ethics of Psychoanalysis*, ed. Jacques-Alain Miller, trans. Dennis Potter (London: Routledge).

Ladani, Zahra Jannessari (2014), 'Henry Neville's *The Isle of Pines* and the Emergence of Racial and Colonial Discourses in the Genre of Utopia in Britain', *International Letters of Social and Humanistic Sciences*, 34: 33–44.

Laeven, A. H. (1992), 'The Frankfurt and Leipzig Book Fairs and the History of the Dutch Book Trade in the Seventeenth and Eighteenth Centuries', in C. Berkvens-Stevelinck et al. (eds), *Le Magasin de l'univers: The Dutch Republic as the Centre of the European Book Trade* (Leiden: Brill), 185–197.

Lahontan, Louis-Armand de Lom d'Arce, baron de (1705), *Nouveaux voyages de M. le baron de La Hontan dans l'Amérique septentrionale* (Amsterdam: L'Honoré).

Lahontan, Louis-Armand de Lom d'Arce, baron de (1931), *Dialogues curieux entre l'auteur et un sauvage de bons sens et Mémoires de l'Amérique Septentrionale*, ed. Gilbert Chinard (Baltimore: Johns Hopkins Press).

Lando, Ortensio (1535), *Forcianae Quaestiones* (Naples: Marinus de Ragusia).

Lando, Ortensio (1540), *In Des. Erasmi Roterodami funus: Dialogus lepidissimus* (Basel: Balthasar Lasius).

Lando, Ortensio (1543), *Paradossi* (Lyons: Giovanni Pullon).

Lando, Ortensio (1548), *Commentario delle piu notabili et mostruose cose d'Italia e altri luoghi* (Venice).

Lando, Ortensio (1550), *Miscellanae Quaestiones* (Venice?: [n.pub.]).

Lange, Victor (1948), 'Visitors to Lake Oneida: An Account of the Background of Sophie von La Roche's novel *Erscheinungen am See Oneida*', *Symposium*, 2: 48–78.

Langer, Ullrich (1999), 'Invention', in Glyn P. Norton (ed.), *The Cambridge History of Literary Criticism*, vol. 1: *The Renaissance* (Cambridge: Cambridge University Press), 136–144.

Langereis, Sandra (2001), *Geschiedenis als ambacht: Oudheidkunde in de Gouden eeuw. Arnoldus Buchelius en Petrus Scriverius* (Hilversum: Verloren).

Lankhorst, Otto (1983), *Reinier Leers. Uitgever en boekverkoper te Rotterdam (1654-1714)* (Amsterdam: APA-Holland University Press).

Lascaris, Constantine (1495), *Erotemata* (Venice: Aldus Manutius).

Lavater, J. C. (1783), *Essai sur la physiognomonie: Destiné a faire connoître l'homme & à le faire aimer*, vol. 2 (The Hague: Karnebeek).

Laxdal, Eiríkur (2006), *Ólandssaga*, ed. Þorsteinn Antonsson and María Anna Þorsteinsdóttir (Reykjavik: Háskólaprent).

Lazarus, Micha (2015), 'Greek Literacy in Sixteenth-Century England', *Renaissance Studies*, 29: 433–458.

Le Clerc, Jean (1717), *Bibliothèque ancienne et moderne*, vol. 7 (Amsterdam: Chez David Mortier).

Le Clerc, Jean (1724), *Bibliothèque ancienne et moderne*, vol. 22 (Amsterdam: Chez David Mortier).

Lederach, Jean Paul (2005), *The Moral Imagination: The Art and Soul of Building Peace* (Oxford: Oxford University Press).

Lefebvre, Henri (1991), *The Production of Space*, trans. Donald Nicholson-Smith (Oxford: Blackwell).

Lehnert, Gertrud (1982), '*Acta Comparationis Litterarum Universarum*—Eine komparatistische Zeitschrift des XIX. Jahrhunderts', *Arcadia*, 17: 16–36.

Lemos, William (1998), 'Voyages of Columbus', in Silvio A. Bedini (ed.), *Christopher Columbus and the Age of Exploration: An Encyclopaedia* (New York: Da Capo), 693–728.

Lenglet Du Fresnoy, Nicolas (1734), *De l'usage des romans*, vol. 1 (Amsterdam: Chez la Veuve de Poilras).

Leslie, Marina (1998), *Renaissance Utopias and the Problem of History* (Ithaca, NY: Cornell University Press).

Lesser, Zacharay (2006), 'Typographic Nostalgia: Play-Reading, Popularity, and the Meanings of Black Letter', in Marta Straznicky (ed.), *The Book of the Play: Playwrights, Stationers, and Readers in Early Modern England* (Amherst, MA: University of Massachusetts Press), 99–126.

Leucht, Robert (2016), *Dynamiken politischer Imagination: Die deutschsprachige Utopie von Stifter bis Döblin in ihren internationalen Kontexten, 1848–1930* (Berlin: De Gruyter).
Levitas, Ruth (1990), *The Concept of Utopia* (London: Phillip Allen).
Levitas, Ruth (2005), 'The Imaginary Reconstitution of Society, or why sociologists and others should take utopia more seriously', Inaugural Lecture, University of Bristol, 24 Oct. http://www.bristol.ac.uk/media-library/sites/spais/migrated/documents/inaugural.pdf.
Levitas, Ruth (2013), *Utopia as Method: The Imaginary Reconstitution of Society* (Basingstoke: Palgrave).
Levitskii, V. (1925), *Tomas Mor* (Moscow: Gos. izd-vo).
Lewes, Darby (2000), *Nudes from Nowhere: Utopian Sexual Landscapes* (Lanham, Maryland: Rowman and Littlefield).
Lewine, J. (1898), *Bibliography of Eighteenth-Century Art and Illustrated Books* (London: S. Low, Marston & Co.).
Lewis, Charlton T., and Short, Charles (1879), *A Latin Dictionary* (Oxford: Clarendon Press).
Li, Jiaju [Lee Ka Kui] (2007), *Shangwu yinshuguan yu jindai zhishi wenhua de chuanbo* (Hong Kong: Chinese University of Hong Kong Press).
Li, Zhun (2010), 'A Brief History of Li Shuangshuang' [1959], in Richard King (ed.), *Heroes of China's Great Leap: Two Stories*, trans. Richard King (Honolulu: University of Hawaii Press), 15–61.
Liao, Mingde (2009), '20 Shiji "xin tuoshuguan yundong" yanjiu shuping', *Tushu qingbao gongzuo*, 53: 128–131.
Libby, Lester J. (1973), 'Venetian History and Political Thought after 1509', *Studies in the Renaissance*, 20: 7–25.
Liddy, C. D. (2001), 'The Estates of Merchants in the Parliament of 1381', *Historical Research*, 74: 331–345.
Liddy, C. D. (2017), *Contesting the City: The Politics of Citizenship in English Towns, 1250–1530* (Oxford: Oxford University Press).
Lilley, Kate (1992), 'Seventeenth-Century Women's Utopian Writing', in Clare Brant and Diane Purkiss (eds), *Women, Texts and Histories 1575–1760* (London: Routledge), 102–133.
Lindner, Theodor (1868), 'Johann Matthäus Wacker von Wackenfels', *Zeitschrift des Vereins für Geschichte und Altert(h)um Schlsiens*, 8: 319–351.
Lipari, Lisbeth (2014), *Listening, Thinking, Being: Towards an Ethics of Attunement* (University Park, PA: Penn State University Press).
Lips, Joost [Lipsius, Justus] (1674), *Van de stantvastigheid* (Rotterdam: Frans van Hoogstraten).
Liss, Peggy K. (1975), *Mexico Under Spain, 1521–1556: Society and the Origins of Nationality* (Chicago: University of Chicago Press).
Litvak de Pérez de la Dehesa, Lily (1968), 'Naturalismo y teatro social en Cataluña', *Comparative Literature Studies*, 5: 279–302.
Liu, Jianhui, and Wang, Hongxu (2006), 'The Origins of the General Line for the Transition Period and of the Acceleration of the Chinese Socialist Transformation in Summer 1955', *China Quarterly*, 187: 724–731.
Liu, Yi-Chun (2016), 'Translating and Transforming *Utopia* into the Mandarin Context: Case Studies from China and Taiwan', *Utopian Studies*, 27: 333–345.
Liu, Yi-Chun (2017), 'The Textual Afterlives of *Utopia*: Titles Published in China and Taiwan since 2016', *Utopian Studies*, 28: 656–663.
Livingstone, E. A. (2013) (ed.), *The Concise Oxford Dictionary of the Christian Church* (3rd edn, Oxford: Oxford University Press).

Loach, Jennifer (1986), 'The Marian Establishment and the Printing Press', *English Historical Review*, 10: 135–148.

Loach, Jennifer (1991), *Parliament under the Tudors* (Oxford: Clarendon Press).

Lobscheid, W. (1869), *English and Chinese Dictionary with the Punti and Mandarin Pronunciation*, vol. 4 (Hong Kong: The Daily Press).

Lochrie, Karma (2016), *Nowhere in the Middle Ages* (Philadelphia: University of Pennsylvania Press).

Locke, Charley (2016), 'Trekkie—OK, and President—Barack Obama on Why Star Trek Is So Important', *Wired* (10 Dec.).

Locke, John (1690), *Essay concerning the true original, extent, and end of civil government* (London: for Awnsham Churchill).

Locke, John (1988), *Two Treatises of Government*, ed. Peter Laslett (Cambridge: Cambridge University Press).

Locke, John (1997), *Political Essays*, ed. Mark Goldie (Cambridge: Cambridge University Press).

Loft, Leonore (2002), *Passion, Politics, and Philosophie: Rediscovering J.-P. Brissot* (Westport, CT: Greenwood Publishing Group).

Logan, George M. (1983), *The Meaning of More's* Utopia (Princeton: Princeton University Press).

Logan, George M. (1994), '*Utopia* and Deliberative Rhetoric', *Moreana*, 31: 103–120.

Logan, George M. (2011) (ed.), *The Cambridge Companion to Thomas More* (Cambridge: Cambridge University Press).

Logan, George M. (2014), *The Meaning of More's* Utopia (Princeton: Princeton University Press).

Longhofer, Jeff (1993), 'All Things in Common? The Contingent Nature of Communalism among the Hutterites', *Journal of Mennonite Studies*, 11: 174–193.

López Estrada, Francisco (1965), 'La primera versión española de la *Utopía* de Moro, por Jerónimo Antonio de Medinilla (Córdoba, 1637)', in M. P. Hornik (ed.), *Collected Studies in Honour of Américo Castro's 80th Year* (Oxford: Lincombe Lodge Research Library), 291–309.

López Estrada, Francisco (1980), *Tomás Moro y España: Sus Relaciones hasta el Siglo XVIII* (Madrid: Editorial de la Universidad Complutense).

López Estrada, Francisco (1992), 'Une traduction espagnole précoce de l'*Utopie* de Thomas More', *Moreana*, 29: 15–18.

López Estrada, Francisco (1996), 'La fortuna de Tomás Moro y su "Utopia" en la España del Siglo de Oro', in *La Fortuna dell'*Utopia *di Thomas More nel dibattito politico europeo del Cinquecento* (Florence: Olschki), 75–93.

López Estrada, Francisco (2001), 'Tomás Moro y Sevilla', in Rogelio Reyes Cano et al. (eds), *Sevilla y la literature* (Seville: Universidad de Sevilla), 161–173.

Loveman, Kate (2008), *Reading Fictions, 1660–1740: Deception in English Literary and Political Culture* (London: Routledge).

Lowry, Martin (1976), 'The "New Academy" of Aldus Manutius: A Renaissance Dream', *Bulletin of the John Rylands Library*, 58: 378–420.

Lowry, Martin (1979), *The World of Aldus Manutius: Business and Scholarship in Renaissance Venice* (Oxford: Blackwell).

Lowry, Stanley Todd (1987), *The Archaeology of Economic Ideas: The Classical Greek Tradition* (Durham, NC: Duke University Press).

Lucan, M. Annaeus (1997), *De bello civili*, ed. D. R. Shackleton Bailey (2nd edn, Stuttgart: Teubner).
Lucian (1503), *Tade enestin en toide toi biblioi* (Venice: Aldus Manutius).
Lucian (1921), *Lucian*, vol. 3, trans. A. M. Harmon (London: Heinemann).
Lucian (1990), *The True History*, in Lucian, *Satirical Sketches*, trans. Paul Turner (Bloomington: Indiana University Press).
Lucian (2005), *Selected Dialogues*, trans. C. D. N. Costa (Oxford: Oxford University Press).
Lunn-Rockliffe, Sophie (2013), 'The Diabolical Problem of Satan's First Sin', *Studia Patristica*, 53: 121–140.
Lupić, Ivan (2019), *Subjects of Advice: Drama and Counsel from More to Shakespeare* (Philadelphia: University of Pennsylvania Press).
Lupton, Thomas (1580), *Sivqila, or Too Good to be True* (London: Henry Binneman).
Lutter, Tibor (1960) (ed.), *Angol irodalom* (Budapest: Tankönyvkiadó).
Luzzati, Michele (1972), 'Buonvisi, Vincenzo', in *Dizionario Biografico degli Italiani*, 15, https://www.treccani.it/biografico/.
Lyell, L., and Watney, F. D. (1936) (eds), *Acts of Court of the Mercers' Company 1453–1527* (Cambridge: Cambridge University Press).
Lytton, Edward Bulwer (1899), *Riwayat al-rawda al-nadira fi ayyam Bumbay al-akhira*, trans. Farida 'Atiyya (Cairo: [Matba'at al-Hilal]).
M. M* (1774), *Les Deux Sœurs* (Bordeaux: Chappuius et Phillippot).
Ma, Teyhun (2014), ' "The Common Aim of the Allied Powers": Social Policy and International Legitimacy in Wartime China, 1940–1947', *Journal of Global History*, 9: 254–75.
Macaulay, Thomas Babington (1932), 'Milton' [1825], in *Literary and Historical Essays Contributed to the Edinburgh Review*, ed. H. Milford (London: Oxford University Press), 1–50.
McCabe, Richard A. (1980), 'Elizabethan Satire and the Bishops' Ban of 1599', *Yearbook of English Studies*, 11: 188–193.
McCabe, Richard A. (1988), ' "Ut Publica Est Opinio": An Utopian Irony', *Neophilologus*, 72: 633–639.
McCarraher, Eugene (2019), *The Enchantments of Mammon: How Capitalism Became the Religion of Modernity* (Cambridge, MA: Belknap Press of Harvard University Press).
McClung, William A. (1994), 'Designing Utopia', *Moreana*, 31: 9–28.
McCollim, G. B. (2012), *Louis XIV's Assault on Privilege: Nicolas Desmaretz and the Taxs on Wealth* (Rochester, NY: University of Rochester Press).
McConica, James (1964), 'The Recusant Reputation of Thomas More', *Canadian Catholic Historical Association Report*, 30: 47–61.
McConica, James (2011), 'Thomas More as Humanist', in George M. Logan (ed.), *The Cambridge Companion to Thomas More* (Cambridge: Cambridge University Press), 22–45.
McCorristine, Laurence (1987), *The Revolt of Silken Thomas: A Challenge to Henry VIII* (Dublin: Wolfhound).
McCutcheon, Elizabeth (1971), 'Denying the Contrary: More's Use of Litotes in *Utopia*', *Moreana*, 31/
McCutcheon, Elizabeth (1977), 'Denying the Contrary: More's Use of Litotes in the *Utopia*', in R. S. Sylvester and G. P. Marc'hadour (eds), *Essential Articles for the Study of Thomas More* (Hamden, CT: Archon Books), 263–274.
McCutcheon, Elizabeth (1981), '<thin>"The apple of my eye": Thomas More to Antonio Bonvisi; A Reading and a Translation', *Moreana*, 18: 37–56.

McCutcheon, Elizabeth (1983), *My Dear Peter: The 'Ars Poetica' and Hermeneutics for More's 'Utopia'* (Angers: Moreanum).

McCutcheon, Elizabeth (1992), 'Review: Ten English Translations/Editions of Thomas More's *Utopia*', *Utopian Studies*, 3: 102–120.

McCutcheon, Elizabeth (2015a), 'Laughter and Humanism: Unity and Diversity in Thomas More's *Epigrammata*', *Moreana* 52: 221–233.

McCutcheon, Elizabeth (2015b), 'More's *Utopia* and Its Parerga (1516–1518)', *Moreana*, 52: 133–148.

McDiarmid, John F. (2007), 'Common Consent, Latinitas and the Monarchical Republic', in John F. McDiarmid (ed.), *The Monarchical Republic of Early Modern England* (Aldershot: Ashgate), 55–74.

McDonald, Alexander (2013), *The Long Space Age: An Economic Perspective on the History of American Space Exploration* (New Haven: Yale University Press).

McDonald, Grantley (2013), 'Thomas More, John Clement and the Palatine Anthology', *Bibliothèque d'Humanisme et Renaissance*, 75: 259–270.

Machiavelli, Niccolò (1920), *Lo prince*, trans. Josep Pin i Soler (Barcelona: Llibr. S. Babra).

Machiavelli, Niccolò (1921), *Traduccions*, trans. Josep Pin i Soler (Barcelona: LLibr. S. Babra).

Machiavelli, Niccolò (2019), *The Prince*, ed. Quentin Skinner and Russell Price (Cambridge: Cambridge University Press).

Mackenzie, Henry (1771), *The Man of Feeling* (London: T. Cadell).

Mackenzie, Henry (1976), *The Man of the World*, 2 vols (New York: AMS Press).

McKinnon, Dana (1970), 'The Marginal Glosses in More's *Utopia*: The Character of the Commentator', in D. G. Donovan (ed.), *Renaissance Papers, 1970* (Columbus, SC: Southeastern Renaissance Conference), 11–19.

MacLachlan, Colin (1988), *Spain's Empire in the New World: The Role of Ideas in Institutional and Social Change* (Berkeley and Los Angeles: University of California Press).

McNelis, James (1960), 'Introduction', in Ludvig Holberg, *The Journey of Niels Klim to the World Underground*, ed. James I. McNelis, Jr. (Lincoln, NE: University of Nebraska Press), xxiii–xlvii.

Macrobius, Ambrosius Theodosius (2001–3), *Commentarii in Somnium Scipionis*, ed. and trans. M. Armisen-Marchetti, 2 vols (Paris: Les Belles Lettres).

Maczelka, Csaba (2013), 'The Uses of Paratextuality and Dialogicity in Early Modern English Utopias', PhD thesis, Szegedi Tudományegyetem.

Maczelka, Csaba (2017), 'Dialógus, paratextus, polifónia', *Erdélyi Múzeum*, 79: 51–61.

Maczelka, Csaba (2019), *A kora újkori angol utópiák magyar története* (Kolozsvár: Erdélyi Múzeum Egyesület).

Madách, Imre (1998), *The Tragedy of Man*, trans. George Szirtes (3rd edn, Budapest: Corvina).

Madden, Samuel (1733), *Memoirs of the Twentieth Century: Being Original Letters of State, under George the Sixth: Relating to the most Important Events in Great Britain and Europe* (London: Osborn and Longman).

Magid, Annette (2016), 'Thomas More in America', *Utopian Studies*, 27: 521–528.

Mahfouz, Naguib (1994), *Sugar Street*, trans. William M. Hutchins and Angèle Butrus Sam'an (London: Black Swan).

Mahlberg, Gaby (2006a), 'The Critical Reception of *The Isle of Pines*', *Utopian Studies*, 17: 133–142.

Mahlberg, Gaby (2006b), 'Historical and Political Contexts of *The Isle of Pines*', *Utopian Studies*, 17: 111–129.

Mahlberg, Gaby (2008), 'Republicanism as Anti-patriarchalism in Henry Neville's *The Isle of Pines* (1668)', in John Morrow and Jonathan Scott (eds), *Liberty, Authority, Formality: Political Ideas and Culture 1600-1900: Essays in Honour of Colin Davis* (Exeter: Imprint Academic), 131–152.

Mahlberg, Gaby (2012a), 'Authors Losing Control: The European Transformations of Henry Neville's *The Isle of Pines* (1668)', *Book History*, 15: 1–25.

Mahlberg, Gaby (2012b), 'An Island with Potential: Henry Neville's *Isle of Pines*', in Miguel A. Ramiro Avilès and J. C. Davis (eds), *Utopian Moments: Reading Utopian Texts* (London: Bloomsbury), 60–66.

Mahmud, Zaki Najib (1977), *Ard al-ahlam* [1939] (Cairo: Dar al-Hilal).

Maillard Álvarez, Natalia, and Pérez García, Rafael M. (2013), 'Printing Presses in Antequera in the Sixteenth Century', in Benito Rial Costas (ed.), *Print Culture and Peripheries in Early Modern Europe* (Boston: Brill), 269–302.

Majeske, Andrew J. (2006), *Equity in English Renaissance Literature: Thomas More and Edmund Spenser* (London: Routledge).

Malcolm, Noel (2019), *Useful Enemies: Islam and the Ottoman Empire in Western Political Thought, 1450-1750* (Oxford: Oxford University Press).

Malinowski, Bronislaw (1922), *Argonauts of the Western Pacific*, trans. James George Frazer (London: Routledge & Kegan Paul).

Mallett, Michael (2003), 'Condottieri and Captains in Renaissance Italy', in David B. Trim (ed.), *The Chivalric Ethos and the Development of Military Professionalism* (Leiden: Brill), 67–88.

Malm, Andreas (2015), *Fossil Capital: The Rise of Steam-Power and the Roots of Global Warming* (London: Verso Books).

Malthus, T. R. (1992), *An Essay on the Principle of Population*, ed. Donald Winch (Cambridge: Cambridge University Press).

Manchester Times and Manchester and Salford Advertiser and Chronicle (1848), 'Pauperism & its Proposed Remedies: Communism; Competition; Organisation of Labour', 14 Oct.

Mancke, Elizabeth, and Shammas, Carole (2005), *The Creation of the British Atlantic World* (Baltimore: Johns Hopkins University Press).

Mandeville, John (1487), *Johannis de Mandeville Itinerarus a terre Angloe in partes Jerosolimitanas* (Antwerp: Thierry Martens).

Mandeville, John (1983), *The Travels of Sir John Mandeville*, ed. C. W. R. D. Moseley (Harmondsworth: Penguin).

Manfield, Bruce (1979), *Phoenix of His Age: Interpretations of Erasmus, c 1550-1750* (Toronto: Toronto University Press).

Mangeloja, Esa, and Ovaska, Tomi (2019), 'Sir Thomas More's Utopia: An Overlooked Economic Classic', *Economic Affairs*, 39: 65–80.

Manley, Lawrence (1995), *Literature and Culture in Early Modern London* (Cambridge: Cambridge University Press).

Mannheim, Karl (1997), 'Utopian Mentality', in Karl Mannheim, *Ideology and Utopia: An Introduction to Sociology*, with a preface by Louis Worth and new introduction by Bryan S. Turner (London: Routledge), 173–236.

Manning, Annie (1851), *The Household of Sir Thomas More* (London: Arthur Hall, Virtue & Co.).

Manuel, Frank E., and Manuel, Fritzie P. (1979), *Utopian Thought in the Western World* (Cambridge, MA: Harvard University Press).

Manutius, Aldus (1975), *Aldo Manuzio Editore: Dediche, prefazioni, note ai testi*, 2 vols, ed. Giovanni Orlandi (Milan: Edizioni il Polifilo).
Manutius, Aldus (2016), *Aldus Manutius: The Greek Classics*, ed. and trans. N. G. Wilson (Cambridge, MA: Harvard University Press).
Marcuse, Herbert (1964), *One Dimensional Man* (Pacifica, CA: Beacon Press).
Mardock, J. D. (2008), *Our Scene is London: Ben Jonson's City and the Space of the Author* (London: Routledge).
Marin, Louis (1973), *Utopiques: Jeux d'espaces* (Paris: Éditions de Minuit).
Marin, Louis (1984), *Utopics: Spatial Play*, trans. R. Vollrath (Atlantic Highlands, NJ: Humanities Press).
Marin, Louis (1993), 'The Frontiers of Utopia', in K. Kumar and S. Bann (eds), *Utopias and the Millenium* (London: Reaktion Books).
Marius, Richard (1984), *Thomas More: A Biography* (Cambridge, MA: Harvard University Press).
Marius, Richard (1999), *Thomas More: A Biography* (Cambridge, MA: Harvard University Press).
Markham, Clements R. (1894) (ed.), *The Letters of Amerigo Vespucci, and Other Documents Illustrative of his Career* (London: Hakluyt Society).
Markham, Clements R. (2010) (ed.), *The Letters of Amerigo Vespucci* (repr. Cambridge: Cambridge University Press).
Marr, Alexander, and Keller, Vera (2014) (ed.), *Intellectual History Review*, 24/3; special issue on invention in early modern Europe.
Marrash, Fransis (1865), *Kitab Ghabat al-Ḥaqq* (Aleppo: [Maronite Press]).
Marsh, David (1998), *Lucian and the Latins: Humor and Humanism in the Early Renaissance* (Ann Arbor: University of Michigan Press).
Marsh, David (2008), 'Dialogue and Discussion in the Renaissance', in Glyn Norton (ed.), *The Cambridge History of Literary Criticism*, vol. 3: *The Renaissance* (Cambridge: Cambridge University Press), 265–270.
Marshall, John (2006), *John Locke, Toleration and Early Enlightenment Culture: Religious Intolerance and Arguments for Religious Toleration in Early Modern and Early Enlightenment Europe* (Cambridge: Cambridge University Press).
Marshall, Peter (2017), *Heretics and Believers: A History of the English Reformation* (New Haven: Yale University Press).
Marsilius of Padua (2005), *The Defender of the Peace*, ed. and trans. Annabel Brett (Cambridge: Cambridge University Press).
Martí i Castell, Joan (2017), *Josep Pin i Soler: El personatge i la competència lingüística*, Discurs llegit el dia 20 d'abril de 2017 en l'acte de recepció pública de Joan Martí i Castell a la Reial Acadèmia de Bones Lletres de Barcelona i contestació de l'Acadèmic numerari Manuel Jorba (Barcelona: Reial Acadèmia de Bones Lletres de Barcelona).
Martial (1993), *Epigrams*, ed. and trans. D. R. Shackleton Bailey, 3 vols (Cambridge, MA: Harvard University Press).
Martin, Angus (1985), *La Bibliothèque universelle des romans* (Oxford: Oxford University Press).
Martin, C. T., rev. Morgan, Basil (2019), 'Buonvisi, Antonio [Antony] (1487–1558)', in *Oxford Dictionary of National Biography*, www.oxforddnb.com.
Martin, John Jeffries, and Romano, Dennis (2000) (eds), *Venice Reconsidered: The History and Civilization of an Italian City-State, 1297–1797* (Baltimore: Johns Hopkins University Press).

Marx, Karl (1996), *Capital*, vol. 1, Afterword to the Second German Edition, in Karl Marx and Friedrich Engels, *Collected Works*, vol. 35 (London: Lawrence and Wishart, 1996), 22–32.

Marx, Karl, and Engels, Friedrich (1969), 'Manifesto of the Communist Party', in Marx/Engels, *Selected Works*, vol. 1 (Moscow: Progress Publisher), 98–137.

Marx, Karl, and Engels, Friedrich (2012), *The Communist Manifesto: A Modern Edition*, ed. Eric Hobsbawn (London: Verso).

Mason, Laura (1996), *Singing the French Revolution: Popular Culture and Politics, 1787–1799* (Ithaca, NY: Cornell University Press).

Maurer, Shawn Lisa (1998), *Proposing Men: Dialectics of Gender and Class in the Eighteenth-Century English periodical* (Stanford, CA: Stanford University Press).

May, Steven W. (2009), 'Popularizing Courtly Poetry: Tottel's Miscellany and Its Progeny', in Mike Pincombe and Cathy Shrank (eds), *The Oxford Handbook of Tudor Literature, 1485–1603* (Oxford: Oxford University Press), 418–433.

Mayer, Thomas F. (1991), 'Tournai and Tyranny: Imperial Kingship and Critical Humanism', *Historical Journal*, 34: 257–277.

Mayer, Thomas F. (1995), 'On the Road to 1534: The Occupation of Tournai and Henry VIII's Theory of Sovereignty', in Dale Hoak (ed.), *Tudor Political Culture* (Cambridge: Cambridge University Press), 11–30.

Mayer, Thomas (2004), 'Thomas Starkey (c 1498–1538), in *Oxford Dictionary of National Biography*, www.oxforddnb.com.

Mazard, Eisel (2015), 'Thomas More's Utopia in Chinese and Japanese Translation], *à bas le ciel* [online], http://a-bas-le-ciel.blogspot.com/2015/05/thomas-mores-utopia-in-chinese-japanese.html.

Meadows, Donella H., Meadows, Dennis L., Randers, Jorgen, and Behrens, William W. (1972), *The Limits to Growth: A Report for the Club of Rome's Project on the Predicament of Mankind* (Washington DC: Potomac Associates).

Meale, Carol M. (1996), '*The Libelle of Englyshe Polycye* and Mercantile Literary Culture in Late Medieval London', in Julia Boffey and Pamela M. King (eds), *London and Europe in the Later Middle Ages* (London: Westfield Publications in Medieval Studies), 181–227.

Meikle, Scott (1995), *Aristotle's Economic Thought* (Oxford: Oxford University Press).

Meinecke, Friedrich (1925), *Die Idee der Staatsräson in der neueren Geschichte* (Berlin: R. Oldenbourg).

Meiner, Annemarie (1955), 'Brockhaus, Friedrich Arnold', *Neue Deutsche Biographie*, 2: 623–624.

Melles, J. (1958), *Joachim Oudaan: Heraut der verdraagzaamheid, 1628–1692* (Utrecht: Kemink).

'Meltzl von Lomnitz, Hugo von', *Kulturportal Ost–West*, https://kulturportal-west-ost.eu/biographien/meltzl-von-lomnitz-hugo-von-2, accessed on 17 Sept 2018.

Mendelsohn, Daniel (2017), *An Odyssey: A Father, a Son and an Epic* (Croydon: Collins).

Menke, Christoph (2010), 'Jenseits von Geistes- und Biowissenschaften; Vier kurze Bemerkungen zu Ottmar Ette: "Literaturwissenschaft als Lebenswissenschaft"', in Wolfgang Asholt and Ottmar Ette (eds), *Literaturwissenschaft als Lebenswissenschaft: Programm—Projekte—Perspektiven* (Tübingen: Narr Francke Attempto Verlag), 39–44.

Mercier, Louis-Sébastien (1770), *L'An deu mille quatre cent quarant: Rêve s'il en fut jamais* (London: [n.pub.]).

'Merlin' [pseud.] (1895), 'Laughter', *Labour Leader*, 16 Mar., 3.

Mertens, Frank (2012), *Van den Enden en Spinoza* (Voorschoten: Spinozahuis).

Meurer, Peter (1998), 'Ortelius as the Father of Historical Cartography', in Marcel van den Broecke, Peter van der Krogt, and Peter Meurer (eds), *Abraham Ortelius and the First*

Atlas: Essays Commemorating the Quadricentennial of his Death, 1598–1998 (Houten: HES), 133–159.
Michel, Louise (1889), 'To Battle', *The Commonweal*, 15 June.
Michel, Louise (1891-2), *The Strike*, serialized in *The Commonweal* (19 Sept. 1891–20 Feb. 1892).
Miéville, China (2018), 'The Limits of Utopia', *Salvage*, http://www.salvage.zone/mieville.html.
Mill, John Stuart (1870), 'Speech on Mr Macguire's Motion on the State of Ireland', in John Stuart Mill, *Chapters and Speeches on the Irish Land Question* (London: Longmans, Green, Reader, and Dyer), 108–125.
Miller, Clarence H., and Harp, Jerry (2011), *Humanism and Style: Essays on Erasmus and More* (Bethlehem, PA: LeHigh University Press).
Miller, Elizabeth Carolyn (2013), *Slow Print: Literary Radicalism and Late Victorian Print Culture* (Stanford, CA: Stanford University Press).
Millett, Paul (1991), *Lending and Borrowing in Ancient Athens* (Cambridge: Cambridge University Press).
Minckwitz, Johannes, and Wessely, Ignaz (1855–c.1875), *Aristophanes' Lustspiele deutsch von Johannes Minckwitz*, 10 vols (Berlin: Langenscheidt; Stuttart: Krais & Hoffmann).
Minerva, Nadia (1992), 'D'une définition à l'autre: Sur quelques préfaciers français d'*Utopia* de Thomas More', in Nadia Minerva (ed.), *Per una definizione dell'utopia: Metodologie e discipline a confronto* (Ravenna: Longo Editore).
Mitsi, Evi (2005), ' "Nowhere is a Place": Travel Writing in Sixteenth-Century England', *Literature Compass*, 2: 1–13.
Mohl, Robert (1855–8), *Die Geschichte und Literatur der Staatswissenschaften* (Erlangen: Enke).
Moichi, Yoriko (1999), 'Japanese Utopian Literature from the 1870s to the Present and the Influence of Western Utopianism', *Utopian Studies*, 10: 89–97.
Moir, Cat (2019), *Ernst Bloch's Speculative Materialism: Ontology, Epistemology, Politics* (Leiden: Brill).
Mols, Roger, SJ (1974), 'Population in Europe, 1500–1700', in Carlo M. Cipolla (ed.), *The Fontana Economic History of Europe: The Sixteenth and Seventeenth Centuries* (London: Fontana), 15–82.
Monsuez, R. (1966), 'Le Latin de Thomas More dans Utopia', *Annales publiées par la Faculté des lettres et sciences humaines de Toulouse*, 3: 35–78.
Montaigne, Michel de (2014), *Shakespeare's Montaigne: The Florio Translation of the Essays, A Selection*, ed. Stephen Greenblatt and Peter G. Platt (New York: New York Review of Books).
Montaigne, Michel de (2019), *Essais*, ed. Bernard Combeaud (Paris: Robert Laffont).
Montaño, John Patrick (2011), *The Roots of English Colonialism in Ireland* (Cambridge: Cambridge University Press).
Montesquieu, Charles de Secondat (1724), *Réflexions sur la Monarchie universelle en Europe* ([n.p.: n.pub.]).
Montesquieu, Charles de Secondat (1748), *De l'ésprit des lois* (Geneva: Barillot & Fils).
Montoliu, Manuel de (1947), *Pin y Soler: escritor humanista e independiente*, Seguida del discurso pronunciado en la misma sesión por José Macián alcalde de Tarragona y de las palabras de agradecimiento del hijo de aquél Armando Pin de Latour, con otras notas del mismo y unos datos biobibliográficos (Tarragona: Publicaciones del Excmo. Ayuntamiento de Tarragona).
Morales, Francisco (2001), 'Dos Figuras en la Utopía Franciscana de Nueva España: Fray Juan de Zumárraga y Fray Martín de Valencí', *Caravelle*, 76–7: 333–344.
More, Cresacre (1631?), *D.O.M.S. The life and death of Sir Thomas Moore* (Douai: B. Bellière).

Morera, Antonio Segura, et al. (1999) (eds), *Catálogo de Incunables de la Biblioteca Capitular y Colombina de Sevilla* (Seville: Cabildo de la Catedral).

Morgan, Diane (2015), 'Bunker Conversion and the Overcoming of Siege Mentality', *Textual Practice*, 31: 1333–1360.

Morgan, Hiram (1985), 'The Colonial Ventures of Sir Thomas Smith in Ulster, 1571–1575', *Historical Journal*, 28: 261–278.

Morgan, Hiram (1993), 'Hugh O'Neill and the Nine Years War in Tudor Ireland', *Historical Journal* 36: 21–37.

Morgan, Hiram (2004), ' "Never Any Realm Worse Governed": Queen Elizabeth and Ireland', *Transactions of the Royal Historical Society*, 14: 295–308.

Morgan, Nicole S. (1994), 'Le Petit Singe cercopithèque mangeur de bibliothèque', *Moreana*, 31: 141–153.

Morison, Samuel Eliot (1971), *The European Discovery of America: The Northern Voyages A. D. 500–1600* (New York: Oxford University Press).

Morison, Stanley (1963), *The Likeness of Thomas More: An Iconographical Survey of Three Centuries*, ed. Nicolas Barker (London: Burns and Oates).

Morris, William (1858), *The Defence of Guenevere, and Other Poems* (London: Bell & Daldy).

Morris, William (1868–70), *The Earthly Paradise* (London: F. S. Ellis).

Morris, William (1886), *A Dream of John Ball* (London: Reeves & Turner).

Morris, William, Mr. (1886 [2 Feb.]), *Pall Mall Gazette*, 'The Best Hundred Books – V'.

Morris, William (1888), *Signs of Change* (London: Reeves & Turner).

Morris, William (1892), *News from Nowhere* (Hammersmith: Kelmscott Press).

Morris, William (1894), 'Why I Am a Commumist', in *The Why I Ams*, 2nd ser. (London: James Tochatti Liberty Press), 2–10.

Morris, William (1904), *Riso-kyo*, trans. Toshihiko Sakai (Tokyo: Heimin-Sha).

Morris, William (1910–15), *The Collected Works of William Morris*, ed. May Morris, 24 vols. (London: Longmans, Green & Co.).

Morris, William (1912), *News from Nowhere; A Dream of John Ball; A King's Lesson*, in William Morris, *The Collected Works of William Morris*, ed. May Morris, vol. 16 (London: Longmans Green and Company).

Morris, William (1929a), *Mukayu-kyo Tsushin-ki*, trans. Yuzo Murayama (Tokyo: Shunju-Sha).

Morris, William (1929b), *Mukayu-kyo Tsushin-ki*, trans. Nubuo Fuse (Tokyo: Heibon-Sha).

Morris, William (1936), 'Preface to The Nature of Gothic by John Ruskin' [1892], in *William Morris: Artist, Writer, Socialist* (Oxford: Basil Blackwell), 292–295.

Morris, William (2004), *News from Nowhere and Other Writings*, ed. Clive Wilmer (London: Penguin).

Morrish, Jennifer (2001), 'A Note on the Neo-Latin Sources for the Word "Utopia" ', *Humanistica Lovaniensia*, 50: 119–130.

Morton, A. L. (1978), *The English Utopia* (London: Lawrence and Wishart).

Morus, P. (1700?), *P. Mori Beatior Utopia, Oder Entwurff Einer Paradigmatischen Policey: Wodurch Die Hohe Obrigkeit recht mächtig, die Spaltungen, Gerichts-Zänckereyen, böse Artzeneyen, ungleicher Vortheil im Handel […] gestillet, Gold und Silber fast unnöthig gemacht, der Staat starck, reich vergnügt […] und […] fast ein güldenes Seculum wiedergebracht wird* (Cologne: Pierre Marteau).

Moscati, Ivan (2019), *Measuring Utility: From the Marginal Revolution to Behavioral Economics* (New York: Oxford University Press).

Most, Johann (1892), 'Why I Am a Communist', *The Commonweal*, 20 Feb.

Mowbray, Charles [as 'CWM'] (1891), 'Notes', *The Commonweal*, 20 June.

Moylan, Tom (1998) (ed.), *Utopian Studies*, 9/2: special issue on Jameson and Utopia.
Moylan, Tom (2000), *Demand the Impossible: Science Fiction, Utopia and Dystopia* (Boulder, CO: Westview).
Moyn, S. (2010), *The Last Utopia: Human Rights in History* (Cambridge, MA: Harvard University Press).
Muldrew, Craig (1998), *The Economy of Obligation: The Culture of Credit and Social Relations in Early Modern England* (Basingstoke: Palgrave).
Mulier, Eco O. G. Haitsma (1980), *The Myth of Venice and Dutch Republican Thought in the Seventeenth Century* (Assen: Van Gorcum).
Mullan, John (1996), 'Sentimental Novels', in John J. Richetti (ed.), *The Cambridge Companion to the Eighteenth-Century Novel* (Cambridge: Cambridge University Press), 236–254.
Mulsow, Martin (2007), 'Das Planetensystem als *Civitas Dei*: Jenseits Lohn- und Strafinstanzen im Wolffianismus', in Lucian Hölscher (ed.), *Das Jenseits: Facetten eines religiösen Begriffs in der Neuzeit* (Göttingen: Wallstein), 40–62.
Muñoz, José (2009), *Cruising Utopia: The Then and There of Queer Futurity* (New York: New York University Press).
Murphy, Orville Theodore (1982), *Charles Gravier, Comte de Vergennes: French Diplomacy in the Age of Revolution, 1719–1787* (Albany, NY: SUNY Press).
Murray, David (1913), *Robert and Andrew Foulis and the Glasgow Press* (Glasgow: James Maclehose & Sons).
Murray, K. M. E. (1935), *The Constitutional History of the Cinque Ports* (Manchester: Manchester University Press).
Musa, Salama (1910), 'Kutub Wals wa-riwayatuhu', *al-Muqtataf* (Feb.), 119–122.
Musa, Salama (1926), *Ahlam al-Falasifa* (Cairo: Matba'at al-Hilal).
Musa, Salama (1936), 'al-Dunya ba'd 30 sana', special issue of *al-Majalla al-Jadida*.
Musa, Salama (1961), *The Education of Salāma Mūsā*, trans. L. O. Schuman (Leiden: Brill).
Mutch, Deborah, and Kelvin, Norman (2009), 'Commonweal', in Laurel Brake and Marysa Demoor (eds), *Dictionary of Nineteenth-Century Journalism in Great Britain and Ireland* (Ghent: Academia Press), 136.
N.N. (1896), 'Die Utopia von Thomas Morus', *Vorwärts*, 205: 2–3.
N.N. (1889), 'Ein "Regierungsvertreter" ', *Arbeiterzeitung*, 1/10 (1 Nov.).
Nancy, Jean-Luc (1986), *La communauté désoeuvrée* (Paris: C. Bourgois).
Nancy, Jean-Luc (1991), *The Inoperative Community*, trans. Peter Conner et al. (Minneapolis: University of Minnesota Press).
Nash, Gary, et al. (2000), *The American People: Creating a Nation and a Society*, vol. 2: *From 1865* (New York: Longman).
Nee, Victor, and Swedberg, Richard (2007), 'Introduction', in Victor Nee and Richard Swedberg (eds), *On Capitalism* (Stanford, CA: Stanford University Press), 1–18.
Nellen, Henk (2007), *Hugo de Groot: Een leven in strijd om de vrede, 1583–1645* (Amsterdam: Balans).
Nelson, Eric (2001), 'Greek Nonsense in More's *Utopia*', *Historical Journal*, 44: 889–917.
Nelson, Eric (2004), *The Greek Tradition in Republican Thought* (Cambridge: Cambridge University Press).
Nelson, Eric (2006), 'Utopia through Italian Eyes: Thomas More and the Critics of Civic Humanism'. *Renaissance Quarterly*, 59: 1029–1057.
Nelson, William E. (2005), 'The Utopian Legal Order of the Massachusetts Bay Colony, 1630–1686', *American Journal of Legal History*, 47: 183–230.

Neue Zeit, Die (1921), [Review of Tony Noah's translation of *Utopia*], 39: 216.

Neville, Henry (1668), *The Isle of Pines, or, A late Discovery of a fourth ISLAND near Terra Australis, Incognita BY Henry Cornelius Van Sloetten* (London: Sarah Griffin for Allen Banks and Charles Harper).

Neville, Henry (1668/W), *The Isle of Pines, or, A late Discovery of a fourth ISLAND near Terra Australis, Incognita BY Henry Cornelius Van Sloetten* (London: Sarah Griffin for Allen Banks and Charles Harper); Copy owned and annotated by Anthony à Wood, Bodleian Library, shelfmark: Bodleian Wood 386.

Neville, Henry (1999), 'The Isle of Pines' [1668], in Susan Bruce (ed.), *Three Early Modern Utopias: Utopia, New Atlantis, The Isle of Pines* (Oxford: Oxford University Press), 187–212.

Nevola, Fabrizio (2019), 'Ideal Cities', in Anthony M. Orum (ed.), *The Wiley Blackwell Encyclopedia of Urban and Regional Studies* (Oxford: John Wiley & Sons), 187–212.

Nevolin, K. A. (1857), *Entsiklopedia zakonovedeniia* [Kiev 1839], in K. A. Nevolin, *Polnoe sobranie sochinenii K. A. Nevolina*, vol. 1 (St Petersburg: Eduarda Pratsa).

Ní Chuanacháin, Deirdre (2016), *Utopianism in Eighteenth-Century Ireland* (Cork: Cork University Press).

Ní Dhúill, Caitríona (2010), *Sex in Imagined Spaces: Gender and Utopia from More to Bloch* (London: Routledge).

Nicholls, Thomas (1550), *The hystory writtone by Thucidides the Athenyan of the warre, whiche was between the Peloponesians and the Athenyans, translated oute of Frenche* (London: William Tylle).

Nicholls, Thomas? (1579), *A pleasant Dialogue between a Lady called Listra, and a Pilgrim. Concerning the governement and common weale of the great province of Crangalor* (London: John Charlewood).

Nicoll, D. J. (1891), 'The Glorious Reformation', *The Commonweal* (Jan.).

Nigg, Walter (1993), *A lelkiismeret szentje* (Budapest: EFO).

Nightingale, P. (1990), 'Monetary Contraction and Mercantile Credit in Later Medieval England', *Economic History Review*, 2nd ser., 43: 560–575.

Nightingale, P. (1996), 'The Growth of London in the Medieval English Economy', in R. Britnell and J. Hatcher (eds), *Progress and Problems in Medieval England: Essays in Honour of Edward Miller* (Cambridge: Cambridge University Press), 89–106.

Nightingale, P. (1997), 'England and the European Depression of the Mid-Fifteenth Century', *Journal of European Economic History*, 26: 631–656.

Nightingale, P. (2010), 'The Rise and Decline of Medieval York: A Reassessment', *Past & Present*, 206: 3–42.

Nisard, D. (1855), *Études sur la Renaissance: Erasme, Thomas Morus, Melanchton* (Paris: Michel-Lévy frères).

Norbrook, David (2002), *Poetry and Politics in the English Renaissance* (Oxford: Oxford University Press, 2002).

Norman, Philip, and Caroe, W. D. (1908), 'The History of Crosby Place', *British History Online*, http://www.british-history.ac.uk/survey-london/bk9/pp15-32.

North China Herald (1895 [19 Apr.]), 'Nanking Missionary Association', 587.

North China Herald (1900 [12 Dec.]), 'The Society for the Diffusion of Christian and General Knowledge: Annual Meeting', 1246–1247.

North China Herald (1919 [27 Dec.]), 'Hell or Utopia', 816.

Northmore, Thomas (1994), 'Memoirs of Planetes, Or a Sketch of the Laws and Manners of Makar' [1795], in Gregory Claeys (ed.), *Utopias of the British Enlightenment* (Cambridge: Cambridge University Press), 137–197.

Nussbaum, Martha C. (2009), *The Therapy of Desire: Theory and Practice in Hellenistic Ethics* (2nd edn, Princeton: Princeton University Press).
Oakeshott, Michael (1991), *Rationalism in Politics and Other Essays* (2nd edn, Indianapolis: Liberty Fund).
Obrist, Hans Ulrich (2012), 'Le 21ème siècle est Glissant', in Eduard Glissant and Hans Ulrich Obrist, *100 Notes—100 Thoughts/100 Notizen—100 Gedanken*, 38: 2–6.
Obrist, Hans Ulrich (2015), *Ways of Curating* (London: Penguin).
Ohler, Norbert (1989), *The Medieval Traveller*, trans. Caroline Hillier (Woodbridge: Boydell).
Ohlmeyer, Jane, and Macinnes, Allan (2002) (eds), *The Stuart Kingdoms in the Seventeenth Century* (Dublin: Four Courts Press).
Okino, Iwasaburo (1929), *Yuutopia Monogatari* (Tokyo: Shufu-No-Tomo-Sha).
Oldland, John (2014), 'The Expansion of London's Overseas Trade from 1475 to 1520', in Caroline Barron and Anne Sutton (eds), *The Medieval Merchant: Proceedings of the 2012 Harlaxton Symposium* (Donington: Shaun Tyas), 55–92.
Oldland, John (2018), 'The Clothiers' Century', *Rural History*, 29: 1–22.
Olin, John C. (1989), 'Erasmus's *Adagia* and More's *Utopia*', in Claire M. Murphy, Henri Gibaud, and Mario A. Di Cesare (eds), *Miscellanea Moreana: Essays for Germain Marc'hadour, Moreana* 100, vol. 26 (Binghamton, NY: Medieval & Renaissance Texts and Studies), 127–136.
Oncken, Hermann (1904), *Lassalle* (Stuttgart: Frommann).
Oncken, Hermann (1914), 'Politik, Geschichtsschreibung und öffentliche Meinung', in Hermann Onken, *Historisch-Politische Aufsätze und Reden,* vol. 1 (Munich: Oldenbourg), 203–244.
Oncken, Hermann (1916 [9 Apr.]), 'England's Militarism', *New York Times*, 1.
Oncken, Hermann (1922), *Die Utopia des Thomas Morus und das Machtproblem in der Staatslehre,* Vortrag, geh. in d. Gesamtsitzung d. Akademie am 4. Febr 1922. Sitzungsberichte der Heidelberger Akademie der Wissenschaften, Philosophisch-Historische Klasse (Heidelberg: Carl Winter Verlag).
Oncken, Hermann (1935), *Nation und Geschichte: Reden und Aufsätze, 1919–1935* (Berlin: Grote Verlag).
Oncken, Hermann (1966), *Lassalle. Zwischen Bismarck und Marx: Eine Biographie* (Stuttgart: Kohlhammer Verlag).
Ong, Walter (1967), *The Presence of the Word* (New Haven: Yale University Press).
Opisso, Alfred (1912 [9 Oct.]), 'Erasmo y Tomás Moro: Traducción catalana de don J. Pin y Soler', *La Vanguardia*, 6.
Oppenheimer, Franz (1895), *Freiland in Deutschland* (Berlin: W. F. Fontane & Co.).
Orlandi, Giovanni (1975) (ed.), *Aldo Manuzio Editore: Dediche, prefazioni, note ai testi,* 2 vols (Milan: Edizioni il Polifilo).
Osborne, Bernal (1852), Militia Bill, House of Commons debate, *Hansard*, 7 June <http://hansard.millbanksystems.com/commons/1852/jun/07/militia-bill>, accessed 21 Dec. 2017.
Osinovskii, I. N. (1978), *Tomas Mor: Utopicheskii kommunizm, gumanizm, Reformatsiya* (Moscow: Nauka).
Osinovskii, I. N. (1985), *Tomas Mor* (Moscow: Mysl).
Osorio, Jéronimo (1569), *In Gualterum Haddanum Anglum, de religione libri tres* (Dillingen: ex officina Sebald Mayer).
Ostens, Jacob (1651), *Liefde-Son, Omstralende de Hoedanigheyt der tegenwoordige genaamde Christenheyt* (Utrecht: J. Brouwer).
Ostens, Jacob (1662), *De Aanteikeningen van C. Gentman* (Amsterdam: Klaas Franssen).

Ostens, Jacob (1665), *De Aan-Teikeningen [...] krachteloos en ongelukkigh verdedight* (Utrecht: [n.pub.]).
Ostrom, Elinor (1995), *Governing the Commons: The Evolution of Institutions for Collective Action* (Cambridge: Cambridge University Press).
Oudaen, Joachim (1664), *Roomsche Mogentheid in gezag en staatbekleding der Oude Keyzeren* (Amsterdam: Frans Kuyper).
Oudaen, Joachim (1677), *Den Grooten Rotterdammer In zyn Geboorte-stad herstelt* (Rotterdam: [n.pub.]).
Ovid (1955), *Metamorphoses*, trans. Mary M. Innes (Harmondsworth: Penguin).
P.K. (1935), *Morus Szent Tamás élete* (Budapest: Élet Irodalmi Nyomda).
Pace, Richard (1517), *Richardi Pacei, invictissimi Regis Angliae primarii secretarii, eiusque apud Elvetios oratoris, De fructu qui ex doctrina percipitur, liber* (Basel: Johann Froben).
Pacquot, Thierry (2007), *Utopies et Utopistes* (Paris: La Découverte).
Padrón, Ricardo (2007), 'Mapping Imaginary Worlds', in James R. Akerman and Robert W. Karrow (eds), *Maps: Finding Our Place in the World* (Chicago: University of Chicago Press), 255–287.
Pagden, Anthony (1986), *The Fall of Natural Man: The American Indian and the Origins of Comparative Ethnology* (Cambridge: Cambridge University Press).
Pagden, Anthony (1998), 'The Struggle for Legitimacy and the Image of Empire in the Atlantic to c.1700', in Nicholas Canny (ed.), *The Oxford History of the British Empire*, vol. 1: *The Origins of Empire* (Oxford: Oxford University Press), 34–54.
Page, William (1893) (ed.), *Letters of Denization and Acts of Naturalization for Aliens in England, 1509–1603* (Lymington: C. T. King).
Palabiyik, Nil (2021), *Turkish Books in Early Modern Europe* (London: Routledge).
Palliser, David (1979), *Tudor York* (Oxford: Oxford University Press).
Palmer, J. H. S. (2016), 'Politics, Corporation and Commonwealth: The Early Reformation in Canterbury, c.1450–1559', PhD dissertation, University of Kent.
Paltock, Robert (1751), *The Life and Adventures of Peter Wilkins* (London: for J. Robinson and R. Dodsley).
Pantin, Isabelle (2010), 'Poetic Fiction and Natural Philosophy in Humanist Italy: Fracastoro's Use of Myth in *Syphilis*', in Richard Scholar and Alexis Tadié (eds), *Fiction and the Frontiers of Knowledge in Europe, 1500–1800* (Aldershot: Ashgate), 17–30.
Parent, Claude (2004), *Vivre à l'oblique* (Paris: Jean-Michel Place éditions).
Parker, Charles H. (2008), *Faith on the Margins: Catholics and Catholicism in the Dutch Golden Age* (Cambridge, MA: Harvard University Press).
Parks, George B. (1938), 'More's *Utopia* and Geography', *Journal of English and Germanic Philology*, 37: 224–236.
Parrish, John M. (2010), 'Education, Erasmian Humanism and More's *Utopia*', *Oxford Review of Education* 36: 589–605.
Parsons, Talcott (1968), *Structure of Social Action* (2nd edn, New York: Free Press).
Patricius, Franciscus (1549), *Le Livre de police humaine, contenant briefve description de plusieurs choses dignes de mémoire [...] traduict de latin en françois par maistre Jehan Le Blond [...] reveu et corrigé par ledict translateur* (Paris: Charles L'Angelier).
Patrick, J. Max (1948), 'Robert Burton's Utopianism', *Philological Quarterly*, 27: 345–358.
Paul, Joanne (2017), *Thomas More* (Cambridge: Polity).
Pérez Vidal, José (1951), 'Pérez Galdós y la noche de San Daniel', *Revista Hispánica Moderna*, 17: 94–110.

Pestre, Jean (2003), 'Happiness', in *The Encyclopedia of Diderot & d'Almbert Collaborative Translation Project*, trans. Nelly S. Hoyt and Thomas Cassirer (Ann Arbor: Michigan Publishing), http://hdl.handle.net/2027/spo.did2222.0000.153.

Peter, Karl A. (1987), *The Dynamics of Hutterite Society: An Analytical Approach* (Edmonton: University of Alberta Press).

Peters, Victor (1965), *All Things Common: The Hutterian Way of Life* (Minneapolis: University of Minnesota Press).

Peterson, William (1991), *The Kelmscott Press* (Oxford: Oxford University Press).

Peterson, William, and Peterson, Sylvia Holton (2014), 'The Library of William Morris: A Catalogue', <https://williammorrislibrary.wordpress.com/2014/03/21/¶-more-utopia-1556/>.

Pettas, William A. (2013), *The Giunti of Florence: A Renaissance Printing and Publishing Family; A History of the Florentine Firm and a Catalogue of Editions* (New Castle, DE: Oak Knoll Press).

Pettegree, Andrew (1992), *Emden and the Dutch Revolt* (Oxford: Clarendon Press).

Pettegree, Andrew (2002), 'Printing and the Reformation: The English Exception', in Peter Marshall and Alec Ryrie (eds.), *The Beginnings of English Protestantism* (Cambridge: Cambridge University Press), 157–179.

Petzler, John (1890), *Life in Utopia* (London: Authors' Co-operative Publishing Co.).

Phélippeau, Marie-Claire (2016a), 'The French Translations of Thomas More's Utopia', *Utopian Studies*, 27: 300–307.

Phélippeau, Marie-Claire (2016b), *Thomas More* (Paris: Éditions Gallimard, 2016).

Phillips, Joshua (2001), 'Staking Claims to *Utopia*: Thomas More, Fiction and Intellectual Property', in Curtis Perry (ed.), *Material Culture and Cultural Materialisms in the Middle Ages and Renaissance* (Turnhout: Brepols), 111–138.

Phythian-Adams, C. (1979), *Desolation of a City: Coventry and the Urban Crisis of the Late Middle Ages* (Cambridge: Cambridge University Press).

Piano, R. (1985), *Chantier ouvert au public* (Paris: Arthaud).

Pico della Mirandola, Giovanni (1998), *Oration on the Dignity of Man*, trans. Charles Glenn Wallis et al. (London: Hackett Classics).

Pietschmann, Horst (2002) (ed.), *Atlantic History: History of the Atlantic System, 1580–1830* (Göttingen: Vandenhoeck and Ruprecht).

Pin i Soler, Josep (1887), *La família dels Garrigas* (Barcelona: La Renaixença).

Pin i Soler, Josep (1888), *Jaume: novela cathalana* (Barcelona: [n.pub.]).

Pin i Soler, Josep (1889), *Níobe* (Barcelona: La Renaixença).

Pin i Soler, Josep (1905), 'El temple de la Sagrada Familia: L'arquitecte Gaudí', *La Veu de Catalunya*, 'Articles periodístics / fragments literaris de Josep Pin i Soler', Biblioteca de Catalunya (BC) MS 4504.

Pin i Soler, Josep (1912), 'Nota preliminar: Sobre llibres moderns d'educació pueril', in Desiderius Erasmus, *Llibre de civilitat pueril*, trans. J. Pin i Soler (Barcelona: L'Avenç), i–xvi.

Pin i Soler, Josep (1915), 'Breu comentari sobre la vida i obres de Joan Lluís Vives', in Joan Lluís Vives, *Diàlechs*, trans. J. Pin i Soler (Barcelona: Llibreria antiga y moderna de S. Babra), v–lxi.

Pin i Soler, Josep (1947), *Comentaris sobre llibres i autors* (Tarragona: Agrupació de Bibliòfils de Tarragona).

Pin i Soler, Josep (2004), *Comentaris sobre llibres i autors* [*Obres*, 7], ed. Sandra Sarlé (Tarragona: Arola).

Pin i Soler, Josep (2007), *Article, prolegs i estudis*, ed. Elisabet Velázquez (Tarragona: Arola).

Pipes, R. (2000), 'Private Property Comes to Russia: The Reign of Catherine II', in Zvi Gitelman (ed.), *Cultures and Nations of Central and Eastern Europe. Essays in Honor of Roman Szporluk* (Cambridge, MA: Harvard University Press), 431–442.

Pitzer, Donald E. (1997) (ed.), *America's Communal Utopias* (Chapel Hill: University of North Carolina Press).

Platform (2015), 'Energy beyond Neoliberalism', in Stuart Hall, Doreen Massey, and Michael Rustin (eds), *After Neoliberalism? The Kilburn Manifesto* (Chadwell Heath: Lawrence Wishart), 1–22.

Plato (1513), *Hapanta ta tu Platonos* (Venice: Aldus Manutius).

Plato (1925a), *Lysis; Symposium; Gorgias*, trans. W. R. M. Lamb (Cambridge, MA: Harvard University Press).

Plato (1925b), *Statesman; Philebus; Ion*, trans. Harold North Fowler and W. R. M. Lamb (Cambridge, MA: Harvard University Press).

Plato (1926), *Laws*, 2 vols, trans. R. G. Bury (Cambridge, MA: Harvard University Press).

Plato (1929), *Timeaus; Critias; Cleitophon; Menexenus; Epistles*, trans. R. G. Bury (Cambridge, MA: Harvard University Press).

Plato (1934–5), 'Muhawarat Aflatun', trans. Zaki Najib Mahmud, serialized in *al-Risala*, 73–106 (26 Nov. 1934–15 June 1935).

Plato (2007), *Republic*, trans. D. Lee; introd. M. Lane (Harmondsworth: Penguin.

Plato (2013), *Republic*, trans. C. Emlyn-Jones and W. Preddy, 2 vols (Cambridge, MA: Harvard University Press).

Plattes, Gabriel (1641), *A Description of the Famous Kingdome of Macaria: Shewing its Excellent Government* (London: Francis Constable).

Pliny the Younger (1969), *Letters. Panegyricus*, 2 vols, ed. and trans. Betty Radice (Cambridge, MA: Harvard University Press).

Plockhoy van Zierikzee, Pieter Cornelis (1662), *Kort en klaer ontwerp […] om den arbeyd*

[...] *van alderley-hand-wercxluyden te verlichten door een onderlinge compagnie ofte volck-planting* [...] *aen de Zuyt-revier in Nieu-neder-land op te rechten* (Amsterdam: O. B. Smient).

Plutarch (1509), *Plutarchi opuscula* (Venice: Aldus Manutius).

Plutarch (1914), *Lives*, vol. 1: *Theseus and Romulus; Lycurgus and Numa; Solon and Publicola*, trans. Bernadotte Perrin (Cambridge, MA: Harvard University Press).

Pocock, J. G. A. (1975a), 'British History: A Plea for a New Subject', *Journal of Modern History*, 47: 601–621.

Pocock, J. G. A (1975b), *The Machiavellian Moment: Florentine Political Thought and the Atlantic Republican Tradition* (Princeton: Princeton University Press).

Poeschel, Johannes (1878), 'Das Märchen vom Schlaraffenlande', *Beiträge zur Geschichte des Deutschen Sprache und Literatur*, 5: 389–427.

Pohl, Nicole (2007). '"The Emperess of the World": Gender and the Voyage Utopia', in *Gender and Utopia in the Eighteenth Century*, ed. Nicole Pohl and Brenda Tooley (London: Routledge): 121–132.

Pohl, Nicole (2010), 'Utopianism after More: The Renaissance and Enlightenment', in *The Cambridge Companion to Utopian Literature*, ed. Gregory Claeys (Cambridge: Cambridge University Press): 51–78.

Pohl, Nicole (2016), ' "The World Begins in Man": A Brief and Selected History of Translations of *Utopia* into German', *Utopian Studies*, 27: 493–504.

Polanyi, Karl (1944/2001), *The Great Transformation: The Political and Economic Origins of Our Time* (repr. Boston: Beacon Press).

Poliziano, Angelo (1553), *Angeli Politiani opera, quae quidem extitere hactenus, omnia, longe emendatus quam usquam antehac expressa* (Basel: Nicolaus Episcopius).

Pollmann, Judith (2012), 'Vondel's Religion', in Jan Bloemendal and Jan-Willem Korsten (eds.), *Joost van den Vondel (1587–1679): Dutch Playwright in the Golden Age* (Leiden: Brill), 85–100.

Polo, Marco (1958), *The Travels*, trans. R. E. Latham (Harmondsworth: Penguin).

Popper, Karl (1947), 'Utopia and Violence', *Hibbert Journal*, 46: 109–116.

Poza, Andrés de (1587), *De la antigua lengua, poblaciones, y comarcas de las Españas* (Bilbao: Mathias Mares).

Prasad, Pratima (2009), *Colonialism, Race, and the French Romantic Imagination* (London: Routledge).

Pratt, Julius W. (1927), 'The Origin of "Manifest Destiny', *American Historical Review*, 32: 795–798.

Pravilova, E. (2014), *A Public Empire: Property and the Quest for the Common Good in Imperial Russia* (Princeton: Princeton University Press).

Prescott, Anne Lake (2003), 'The Ambivalent Heart: Thomas More's Merry Tales', *Criticism*, 45: 417–433.

Preston Guardian (1891 [5 Dec.]), 'Sir Thomas More's "Utopia," Lecture by Mr. Phythian'.

Prévost, Antoine François (1733), *Le Philosophe anglois, ou histoire de Monsieur Cleveland* (Amsterdam: Arkstée & Merkus).

Price, Munro (2009), *Preserving the Monarchy: The Comte de Vergennes 1774–1787* (Cambridge: Cambridge University Press).

Prud'homme van Reine, Ronald (2013), *Moordenaars van Jan de Witt: De zwartste bladzijde van de Gouden Eeuw* (Amsterdam: De Arbeiderspers).

Prunč, Erich (1997), 'Translationskultur (Versuch einer konstruktiven Kritik des translatorischen Handelns)', *TEXTconTEXT*, 11: 99–127.

Prunč, Erich (2000), 'Vom Translationsbiedermeier zur Cyber-translation', *TEXTconTEXT*, 14: 3–74.
Pucci, Mario (1984), *Tommaso Moro* (Padua: Edizione Messagero).
Pucci, Mario (1992), *Morus Tamás* (Újvidék: Agapé).
Purchas, Samuel (1613), *Purchas his Pilgrimage: or Relations of the World and the Religions observed in all Ages and Places discovered, from the Creation unto this Present* (London: William Stansby for Henry Fetherstone).
Puttenham, George (1589), *The Arte of English Poesie* (London: William Ponsonby).
Quinn, David Beers (1940) (ed.), *The Voyages and Colonising Enterprises of Sir Humphrey Gilbert*, 2 vols (London: Hakluyt Society).
Quinn, David Beers (1945), 'Sir Thomas Smith (1513–1577) and the Beginnings of English Colonial Theory', *Proceedings of the American Philosophical Society*, 89: 542–560.
Quinn, David Beers (1966), 'The First Pilgrims', *William and Mary Quarterly*, 23: 359–390.
Quinn, David Beers (1976), 'Renaissance Influences in English Colonization', *Transactions of the Royal Historical Society*, 26: 73–99.
Quintilian (1922), *Institutio Oratoria*, ed. and trans. H. E. Butler, 4 vols (Cambridge, MA: Harvard University Press).
Quiroga, Gaspar de (1583), *Index et Catalogus Librorum prohibitorum* (Madrid: Alphonso Gómez).
Quiroga, Gaspar de (1584), *Index librorum expurgatorum* (Madrid: Alphonso Gómez).
Quiroga, Vasco de (1939), 'Información en Derecho del Lic: Quiroga sobre algunas provisiones del Real Consejo de Indias', in Rafael Aguayo Spencer (ed.), *Documentos* (Mexico: Editorial Polis), 289–406.
Raab, Felix (1965), *The English Face of Machiavelli: A Changing Interpretation 1500–1700* (London: Routledge & Kegan Paul.
Racault, Jean-Michel (1991), *L'Utopie narrative en France et en Angleterre 1675–1761* (Oxford: Voltaire Foundation).
Ra'if, Ahmad (1987), *al-Bu'd al-khamis* (Cairo: Al-Zahra' li-l-I'lam al-'Arabi).
Raisch, Jane (2016), 'Humanism and Hellenism: Lucian and the Afterlives of Greek in More's *Utopia*', *English Literary History*, 4: 927–958.
Ramiro Avilés, M. A. (2001), 'The Law Based Utopia', in B. Goodwin (ed.), *The Philosophy of Utopía* (London: Frank Cass), 225–248.
Ramiro Avilés, M. A. (2002), *Utopía y Derecho: El sistema jurídico en las sociedades ideales* (Madrid: Marcial Pons).
Ramsay, G. D. (1982), 'A Saint in the City: Thomas More at Mercers' Hall, London', *English Historical Review*, 97: 269–288.
Rankin, Mary (2008), 'Alarming Crises/Enticing Possibilities: Political and Cultural Changes in Late Nineteenth-Century China', *Late Imperial China*, 29: 40–63.
Rappaport, Steve (1989), *Worlds Within Worlds: Structures of Life in Sixteenth-Century London* (Cambridge: Cambridge University Press).
Rastell, John (1848), *The Interlude of the Four Elements*, ed. James Orchard Halliwell (London: for the Percy Society).
Raucault, Jean-Michel (1986), 'Virginie entre la nature et la vertu: Cohesion narrative et contradictions idéologiques dans *Paul et Virginie*', *Dix-huitieme siècle*, 18: 389–404.
Ray, Meredith K. (2009), 'Textual Collaboration and Spiritual Partnership in Sixteenth-Century Italy: The Case of Ortensio Lando and Lucrezia Gonzaga', *Renaissance Quarterly*, 62: 694–747.

Reed, Christopher (2004), *Gutenberg in Shanghai: Chinese Print Capitalism, 1876–1937* (Vancouver: University of British Columbia Press).

Rees Jones, Sarah (2001), 'Thomas More's "Utopia" and Medieval London', in Rosemary Horrox and Sarah Rees Jones (eds.), *Pragmatic Utopias: Ideals and Communities, 1200–1630* (Cambridge: Cambridge University Press), 117–135.

Regnard, Jean-François (1706), *Le Légataire universel* (Paris: J. Quillau).

Reinders, Michel (2013), *Printed Pandemonium: Popular Print and Politics in the Netherlands, 1650–1672* (Leiden: Brill).

Reitinger, Franz (2007), 'Literary Mapping in German-Speaking Europe', in David Woodward (ed.), *The History of Cartography*, vol. 3/1: *Cartography in the European Renaissance* (Chicago: Univsersity of Chicago Press), 438–449.

Reitz, Carolyn, and Mutch, Deborah (2009), '*Clarion*', in Laurel Brake and Marysa Demoor (eds), *Dictionary of Nineteenth-Century Journalism in Great Britain and Ireland* (Ghent: Academia Press), 122–123.

Remer, Gary (2009), 'Rhetoric as a Balancing of Ends: Cicero and Machiavelli', *Philosophy and Rhetoric*, 42: 1–28.

Reynolds, Anna (2017), 'Privy Tokens: Wastepaper in Early Modern England, 1536–1670', PhD thesis, University of York.

Rex, Richard (2011), 'Thomas More and the heretics: statesman or fanatic' in *The Cambridge Companion to Thomas More*, ed. George Logan (Cambridge: Cambridge University Press): 93–115.

Rhenanus, Beatus [aka Beatus Bild] (1886), *Briefwechsel des Beatus Rhenanus*, ed. Adelbert Horawitz and Karl Hartfelder (Leipzig: B. G. Teubner).

Rhodes, Neil (2018), *Common: The Development of Literary Culture in Sixteenth-Century England* (Oxford: Oxford University Press).

Ribeiro, Ana Claudia Romano (2014), 'Intertextual Connections between Thomas More's *Utopia* and Cicero's *De finibus bonorum et malorum*', *Moreana* 50: 63–84.

Richardson, Brian (1997), 'Prose', in Peter Brand and Lino Pertile (eds), *The Cambridge History of Italian Literature* (Cambridge: Cambridge University Press), 179–232.

Richardson, Laurel (2016), 'Evaluating Ethnography', *Qualitative Inquiry*, 6: 253–255.

Rider, John (2008), *Colonialism and the Emergence of Science Fiction* (Middletown, CT: Wesleyan University Press).

Rifkin, Mark (2014), *Settler Common Sense: Queerness and Everyday Colonialism in the American Renaissance* (Minneapolis: University of Minnesota Press).

Rîos Castaño, Victoria (2012), 'Not a Man of Contradiction: Zumárraga as Protector and Inquisitor of the Indigenous People of Central Mexico', *Hispanic Research Journal*, 13: 26–40.

Rist, J. M. (1969), *Stoic Philosophy* (Cambridge: Cambridge University Press).

Ritter, Gerhard (1941), *Machtstaat und Utopie: Vom Streit um die Dämonie der Macht seit Machiavelli und Morus* (2nd edn, Munich: R. Oldenbourg).

Roberts, R. Julian (2004), 'Renialme, Ascanius de [known as Ascanius] (c 1550–1600), bookseller', *Oxford Dictionary of National Biography*, www.oxforddnb.com.

Rogan, Tim (2018), *The Moral Economists: R. H. Tawney, Karl Polanyi, E. P. Thompson, and the Critique of Capitalism* (Princeton: Princeton University Press).

Roggen, Vibeke (2008), 'A Protean Text: *Utopia* in Latin, 1561–1631', in Terence Cave (ed.), *Utopia in Early Modern Europe* (Manchester: Manchester University Press), 14–31.

Roig, Francesc, and Domingo, Josep M. (1994) (eds), *Actes del Simposi Pin i Soler: Tarragona, 26–28 de novembre de 1992* (Tarragona: Diputació de Tarragona, Institut d'Estudis Tarraconenses Ramon Berenguer IV. Secció de Filologia i Història Literària).

Roldanus, C. W. (1935), 'Een republikein uit de nadagen', *Tijdschrift voor Geschiedenis*, 50: 134–166.
Romm, James (1992), *The Edges of the Earth in Ancient Thought: Geography, Exploration, and Fiction* (Princeton: Princeton University Press).
Roodenburg, Herman (1990), *Onder censuur: De kerkelijke tucht in de gereformeerde gemeente van Amsterdam, 1578–1700* (Hilversum: Verloren).
Roper, William (1935), *The lyfe of Sir Thomas Moore, knighte* [c.1557], ed. E. V. Hitchcock, *Early English Text Society*, 197.
Roper, William (1962), *The Life of Sir Thomas More* [c.1557], in R. S. Sylvester and D. P. Harding (eds), *Two Early Tudor Lives* (repr. New Haven: Yale University Press).
Rose, Gillian (1981), *Hegel Contra Sociology* (London: Verso).
Rose, Henry (1891), *The New Political Economy: The Social Teachings of Thomas Carlyle, John Ruskin, and Henry George* (London: James Speirs).
Rose, Jonathan (2010), *The Intellectual Life of the British Working Classes* (2nd edn, New Haven: Yale University Press).
Rose, Susan (2008), *Calais: An English Town in France* (Woodbridge: Boydell and Brewer).
Rosen, F. (1996), 'Introduction', in Jeremy Bentham, *An Introduction to the Principles of Morals and Legislations* (1789), in *The Collected Works of Jeremy Bentham*, ed. J. H. Burns and H. L. A. Hart (Oxford: Clarendon Press), xxxi–lxxviii.
Rosenberg, Aubrey (1982), *Nicolas Gueudeville and His Work (1652–172?)* (The Hague: Springer).
Rosner, Peter (2006), 'Theodor Hertzka and the Utopia of "Freiland" ', *History of Economic Ideas*, 14: 113–137.
Rouillard, Dominique (2006), 'Architecture', in M. Riot-Sarcey, T. Bouchet, and A. Picon (eds), *Dictionnaires des utopies* (Paris: Larousse), 10–14.
Rousseau, Jean-Jacques (1755), *Sur l'origine et les fondements de l'inégalité* (Amsterdam: Marc Michel Rey).
Rousseau, Jean-Jacques (1761), *Julie ou La Nouvelle Héloïse* (Amsterdam: Marc Michel Rey).
Rousseau, Jean-Jacques (1762a), *Du Contrat Social* (Amsterdam: Marc Michel Rey).
Rousseau, Jean-Jacques (1762b), *Émile, ou De l'éducation* (Amsterdam: Marc Michel Rey).
Rousseau, Jean-Jacques (1979), *Reveries of the Solitary Walker*, trans. Peter France (London: Penguin).
Rousseau, Thomas (An II), *Le livre utile et agréable pour la jeunesse* ([n.p.: n.pub.]).
Rousseau, Thomas (An VII), *Adresse, Thomas Rousseau, membre et archiviste de la société des Jacobins de Paris, à ses frères et amis, membres des sociétés populaires, patriotiques, républicaines, montagnardes et régénérées de tous les départements 14 prairial An II* ([n.p.: n.pub.]).
Rousseau, Thomas (1781), *Lettre à M* sur le spectacle des boulevards* (Brussels: chez les libraires qui vendent les nouveautés).
Rousseau, Thomas (1788), *Précis historique sur l'édit de Nantes* (Paris: [n.pub.]).
Rousseau, Thomas (1789), *La Liberté française, ode national* (Paris: Chez Blanchon).
Rousseau, Thomas (1796), 'Epitre au général Bonaparte' (Paris: Chez Johanneau).
Rowbotham, Sheila (2008), *Edward Carpenter: A Life of Liberty and Love* (London: Verso).
Rowe, Christopher, and Schofield, Malcolm (2000), *The Cambridge History of Greek and Roman Political Thought* (Cambridge: Cambridge University Press).
Rugemer, Edward B. (2013), 'The Development of Mastery and Race in the Comprehensive Slave Codes of the Greater Caribbean during the Seventeenth Century', *William and Mary Quarterly*, 70: 429–458.

Ruiz, Teofilo F. (1998), 'Chanca, Diego Alvarez', in Silvio A. Bedini (ed.), *Christopher Columbus and the Age of Exploration: An Encyclopaedia* (New York: Da Capo), 115–116.

Rummel, Erika (1998), *The Humanist–Scholastic Debate in the Renaissance and Reformation* (Cambridge, MA: Harvard University Press).

Ruskin, John (1903–12), *The Works of John Ruskin*, ed. E. T. Cook and Alexander Wedderburn, 39 vols (London: Allen).

Ruskin, John (1907), *Fors Clavigera: Letters to the Workmen and Labourers of Great Britain*, in *The Works of John Ruskin*, ed. E. T. Cook and Alexander Wedderburn, vols 27–8 (London: Allen).

Ruskin, John (1908), *Praeterita*, in *The Works of John Ruskin*, ed. E. T. Cook and Alexander Wedderburn, vol. 35 (London: Allen), 13–566.

Russell, William (1683), *The Speech of the Late Lord Russel, to the sheriffs: together with the paper deliver'd by him to them, at the place of his execution* (London: for John Darby, by the direction of the Lady Russel).

Russen, David (1703), *Iter lunare* (London: for J. Nutt).

Saage, Richard (2001–4), *Utopische Profile: Industrielle Revolution und technischer Staat im neunzehnten Jahrhundert*, 4 vols (Münster: Lit Verlag).

Saage, Richard (2001), *Utopische Profile*, vol. 1: *Renaissance und Reformation* (Münster: LIT).

Saage, Richard (2006), 'Morus' "Utopia" und die Macht: Zu Hermann Oncken und Gerhard Ritters Utopia-Interpretationen', *UTOPIE kreativ*, 183: 37–47.

Sacks, David Harris (1991), *The Widening Gate: Bristol and the Atlantic Economy, 1450–1700* (Berkeley and Los Angeles: University of California Press).

Sacks, David Harris (1999), 'Introduction: Thomas More's *Utopia* in Historical Perspective', in David Harris Sacks (ed.), *Thomas More: Utopia* (Bedford: St Martin's Press), 1–79.

Sacks, David Harris (2017), 'Utopia as a Gift: More and Erasmus on the Horns of a Dilemma', *Moreana*, 54: 157–171.

Saʻd, Faruq (1982), *Maʻa al-Farabi wa-l-mudun al-fadila* (Beirut: Dar al-Shuruq).

Saga Ólafs Þórhallasona (1987), ed. María Anna Þorsteinsdóttir (Reykjavík: Þjóðsaga).

Said, Edward (1993), *Culture and Imperialism* (New York: Vintage Books).

Saʻid, Rifʻat (1974), *Al-Sihafa al-yasariyya fi Misr*, vol. 1: *1925–1948* (Beirut: Dar al-Taliʻa).

Sako, Teruhito (2018), 'The Early English Formation of the Term "Society" ', *Jinbun Gakuho*, 514: 1–30.

Salberg, Trond Kruke (2008), 'The German Translations: Humanist Politics and Literary Journalism', in Terence Cave (ed.), *Thomas More's Utopia in Early Modern Europe: Paratext and Contexts* (Manchester: Manchester University Press), 32–46.

Salkeld, Duncan (2018), *Shakespeare and London* (Oxford: Oxford University Press).

Samʻan, Angèle Butrus (1965a), 'al-Riwaya al-yutubiyya fi al-adab al-injlizi al-hadith', *al-Majalla*, 97: 36–49.

Samʻan, Angèle Butrus (1965b), 'al-Riwaya al-yutubiyya fi al-adab al-hadith', *al-Majalla*, 100: 65–69.

Samʻan, Angèle Butrus (1966), 'al-Fikr al-ishtiraki fi al-riwayat al-yutubiyya', *al-Majalla*, 119: 34–45.

Sánchez de la Ballesta, Alonso (1587), *Dictionario de vocablos castellanos, aplicados a la propiedad latina* (Salamanca: Juan and Andrés Renaut).

Sánchez Herrero, José (1992), 'Sevilla del Renacimiento', in Carlos Ros (ed.), *Historia de la Iglesia de Sevilla* (Seville: Castillejo), 301–406.

Sandel, Michael J. (1998), 'What Money Can't Buy: The Moral Limits of Markets', the Tanner Lectures on Human Values, 11 and 12 May 1998, https://tannerlectures.utah.edu/_resources/documents/a-to-z/s/sandel00.pdf.

Sandgathe, Mechtild (1992), 'Tracing the Connection between Goethe and Thomas More', *Moreana*, 29: 53–57.

Sandoval y Rojas, Bernardo de (1620), *Index librorum prohibitorum et expurgatorum* (Geneva: Jacob Crispin).

Sansovino, Francesco (1561), *Del governo de i regni e delle republiche cosi antiche come moderne* (Venice: Francesco Sansovino).

Sansovino, Francesco (1562), *Le osservationi della lingua volgare di diversi huomini illustre* (Venice: Francesco Sansovino).

Sansovino, Francesco (1566), *Del governo de regni et delle repubbliche antiche et moderne [...] libri XXI* (Venice: Giovan Battista and Marchiò Sessa and brothers).

Sansovino, Francesco (1567), *Del governo de regni et delle repubbliche antiche et moderne [...] libri XXI* (Venice: Giovan Battista and Marchiò Sessa and brothers).

Sansovino, Francesco (1578), *Del governo et amministratione di diversi regni et republiche, cosi antiche come moderne [...] libri XXI* (Venice: Giovanni Antonio Bertano).

Sansovino, Francesco (1583), *Del governo et amministratione di diversi regni, et republiche, cosi antiche come moderne [...] libri XXII* (Venice: Altobello Salicato).

Sansovino, Francesco (1607), *Del governo et amministratione di diversi regni, et repubbliche, cosi antiche come moderne [...] libri XXII* (Venice: Altobello Salicato).

Santinello, Giovanni (1977), 'Thomas More's *Expositio Passionis*', in R. S. Sylvester and G. P. Marc'hadour (eds), *Essential Articles for the Study of Thomas More* (Hamden, CT: Archon Books), 455–461.

Saqqal, Mikha'ilal- (1907), *Lata'if al-samar fi sukkan al-Zuhara wa-l-Qamar, aw, al-ghaya fi bida'at al-nihaya* (Cairo: [n.pub.]).

Satz, Debra (2010), *Why Some Things Should Not Be for Sale: The Moral Limits of Markets* (New York: Oxford University Press).

Saulnier, V.-L. (1963), 'L'Utopie en France: Morus et Rabelais', in *Les Utopies à la Renaissance* (Brussels: Presses universitaires de Bruxelles; Paris: Presses universitaires de France), 137–163.

Sawada, Paul Akio (1967), 'The Praise of Realpolitik? H. Oncken and More's Utopia', *Moreana*, 4: 145–164.

Sawada, Paul Akio (1974), 'More's Utopia in Chinese', *Moreana*, 11: 25–28.

Sawada, Paul Akio (1980), 'Thomas More in Japan', *Moreana*, 16: 3–27.

Sayer, Andrew (2010), 'Approaching Moral Economy', in Nico Stehr, Christoph Henning, and Bernd Weiler (eds), *The Moralization of the Markets* (New Brunswick, NJ: Transaction Publishers), 77–97.

Sayers, Nicola (2020), *The Promise of Nostalgia: Reminiscence, Longing and Hope in Contemporary American Culture* (London: Routledge).

Scafi, Alessandro (2006), *Mapping Paradise: A History of Heaven on Earth* (London: British Library).

Scaliger, Julius Caesar (1561), *Poetices libri septem* (Geneva: Johann Crispin).

Scarisbrick, J. J. (1968), *Henry VIII* (Berkeley and Los Angeles: University of California Press).

Schaer, Roland (2001), 'Utopia: Space, Time, History', in Roland Schaer et al. (eds), *Utopia: The Search for the Ideal Society in the Western World* (Oxford: Oxford University Press), 3–7.

Schaer, Roland, Claeys, Gregory, and Tower Sargent, Lyman (2000) (eds), *Utopia: The Search for the Ideal Society in the Western World* (New York: Oxford University Press).
Scheckter, John (2011), *The Isle of Pines, 1668: Henry Neville's Uncertain Utopia* (Farnham: Ashgate).
Schérer, René (2004), *Hospitalités* (Paris: Anthropos, éditions Economica).
Schérer, René (1993), *Zeus hospitalier* (Paris: La table Ronde).
Schipper, Jan Jacobsz (1659), *Morus den grooten kanselier van Engelant met 'et verstooten der Koningin Katryne* (Amsterdam: Jacob Lescaille).
Schmelzer, Matthias (2016), *The Hegemony of Growth: The OECD and the Making of the Economic Growth Paradigm* (Cambridge: Cambridge University Press).
Schmidt, Gabriela (2018), 'Marketing *Utopia*: The Protean Paratexts in Ralph Robinson's English Translation', in Marie-Alice Belle and Brenda Hosington (eds), *Thresholds of Translation: Paratexts, Print, and Cultural Exchange in Early Modern Britain, 1473–1660* (Cham: Palgrave Macmillan), 183–206.
Schmidt, Peer, Weber, Gregor, Böswald-Rid, Elisabeth, Brenner, Tobias, and Paulus, Stefan 2008) (eds), *Traum und Res Publica: Traumkulturen und Deutungen sozialer Wirklichkeiten im Europa von Renaissance und Barock* (Berlin: Akademie Verlag).
Schnebelin, Johann Andreas (1650?), *Erklärung der wunder-seltzamen Land-Charten Utopiae, so da ist das neu-entdeckte Schlarraffen-Land* (Arbeitshausen [i.e. Nürnberg?]: [n.pub.]).
Schoeck, R. J. (1956), 'More, Plutarch, and King Agis: Spartan History and the Meaning of *Utopia*', *Philological Quarterly*, 35: 366–375.
Schoeck, R. J. (1977), 'More, Plutarch, and King Agis: Spartan History and the Meaning of *Utopia*', in R. S. Sylvester and G. P. Marc'hadour (eds), *Essential Articles for the Study of Thomas More* (Hamden, CT: Archon Books), 275–280.
Schofield, Malcolm (2000), 'Approaching the *Republic*', in Christopher Rowe and Malcolm Schofield (eds), *The Cambridge History of Greek and Roman Political Thought* (Cambridge: Cambridge University Press), 190–232.
Schofield, Malcolm (2006), *Plato: Political Philosophy* (Oxford: Oxford University Press).
Schofield, R. S. (1965), 'The Geographical Distribution of Wealth in England, 1334–1649', *Economic History Review*, 18: 483–510.
Schölderle, Thomas (2017), 'Thomas Morus und die Herausgeber-Werschuf den Utopiebegriff', in Alexander Amberger and Thomas Möbius (eds), *Auf Utopias Spuren: Utopie und Utopieforschung; Festschrift für Richard Saage zum 75. Geburtstag* (Wiesbaden: Springer), 17–44.
Schönhärl, Korinna (2019), 'Steuermoral in Westdeutschland Nach Dem Zweiten Weltkrieg. Eine Diskursanalytische Rekonstruktion', *Leviathan*, 47: 169–191.
Schüpbach-Guggenbühl, Samuel (2010), 'Adelberg Meyer (zum Pfeil)', *Historisches Lexikon der Schweiz*, online ed. <https://hls-dhs-dss.ch/de/articles/019316/2010-09-23>.
Schütz, Antal (1938) (ed.), *Korunk szentjei* (Budapest: Révai).
Schwabe, Klaus (1994), 'Change and Continuity in German Historiography from 1933 into the Early 1950s: Gerhard Ritter (1888–1967)', in Hartmut Lehmann (ed.), *Paths of Continuity: Central European Historiography from the 1930s to the 1950s* (Washington DC: German Historical Institute), 83–108.
Schwartz, Peter (1989), 'Imagining Socialism: Karl Kautsky and Thomas More', in John H. Kautsky (ed.), *Karl Kautsky and the Social Science of Classical Marxism* (Leiden: Brill), 44–56.
Schwenkbeck, Rahima (2021), *The Business of Marketing, Entrepreneurship and Architecture of Communal Societies in the 1960s and 1970s* (London: Palgrave Macmillan).

Scot, Thomas (1615), *Philomythie* (London: for Francis Constable).
Scott, D. (2007) (ed.), *Maieusis: Essays in Honour of Myles Burnyeat* (Oxford: Oxford University Press).
Scott, James C. (1976), *The Moral Economy of the Peasant: Rebellion and Subsistence in Southeast Asia* (New Haven: Yale University Press).
Scott, John (2015), 'Falangism', in John Scott (ed.), *A Dictionary of Sociology* (4th edn, Oxford: Oxford University Press).
Scott Baker, Nicholas (2013), *The Fruit of Liberty: Political Culture in the Florentine Renaissance, 1480–1550* (Cambridge, MA: Harvard University Press).
Scrivano, Riccardo (1980), *La norma e le scarto* (Rome: Bonnaci).
Sebastiani, Valentina (2018), *Johann Froben, Printer of Basel: A Biographical Profile and Catalogue of His Editions* (Leiden: Brill).
Seeber, Hans Ulrich (2017), *Globalisierung, Utopie und Literatur: Von Thomas Morus (1516) bis Darcy Ribeiro (1982)* (Berlin: LIT Verlag).
Seebohm, Frederick (1869), *The Oxford Reformers of 1498* (London: Longmans Green).
Séguy, Jean (1968), *Utopie coopérative et œcuménisme: Pieter Cornelisz Plockhoy van Zurik-Zee, 1620–1700* (Paris: Mouton).
Seidel Menchi, Silvana (1974), 'Sulla fortuna di Erasmo in Italia: Ortensio Lando e altri eterodossi della prima metà del Cinquento', *Schweizerische Zeitschrift für Geschicht*, 24: 537–634.
Seidel Menchi, Silvana (1987), *Erasmo in Italia, 1520–1580* (Turin: Bollati Boringheri).
Seidel Menchi, Silvana (1994), 'Chi fu Ortensio Lando?', *Rivista storica italiana*, 106: 501–562.
Seidel Menchi, Silvana (1996), 'Ortensio Lando cittadino di Utopia: Un esercizio di lettura', in *La fortuna dell'Utopia di Thomas More nel dibattito politico europeo del '500* (Florence: Luigi Firpo): 95-118.
Seidel, Robert (1994), *Späthumanismus in Schlesien: Caspar Dornau (1577–1631); Leben und Werk* (Berlin: Walter de Gruyter).
Selden, M. (1993), *Political Economy of Chinese Development* (Armonk: ME Sharpe).
Sellars, John (2006), *Stoicism* (Kinsealy: Acumen).
Sellers, Maud (1918) (ed.), *The York Mercers and Merchant Adventurers 1356–1917* (Durham: Surtees Society).
Sellevold, Kirsti (2008a), 'The French Versions of *Utopia*: Christian and Cosmopolitan Models', in Terence Cave (ed.), *Thomas More's* Utopia *in Early Modern Europe: Paratexts and Contexts* (Manchester: Manchester University Press), 67–86.
Sellevold, Kristi (2008b), 'Some "Hardis Repreneurs" in Sixteenth-Century France: Du Bellay, Aneau, Chappuys', in Hall Bjørnstad (ed.), *Borrowed Feathers: Plagiarism and the Limits of Imitation in Early Modern Europe* (Oslo: Unipub), 53–65.
Seneca, Lucius Annaeus (1529), *Opera L. Annaei Senecae*, ed. Desiderius Erasmus and Matthaeus Fortunatus (Basel: Officina Froben).
Seneca, Lucius Annaeus (1989), *Epistulae Morales* ed. and trans. Richard M. Gummere, 3 vols (Cambridge, MA: Harvard University Press).
Senocak, Neslihan (2012), 'The Franciscan *studium generale*: A New Interpretation', in K. Emery, W. J. Courteney, and S. M. Metzger (eds), *Philosophy and Theology in the 'Studia' of the Religious Orders and at Papal and Royal Courts* (Turnhout: Brepols), 221–236.
Shakespeare, William (1883), *Jin-niku Shichi-ire Saiban: Seiyo Chinsetsu*, trans. Tsutomu Inoue (Tokyo: Kokin-Do).

Shakespeare, William (1999), *The Tempest*, ed. Virginia Mason Vaughan and Alden T. Vaughan (London: Nelson).

Shalev, Zur (2012), *Sacred Words and Worlds: Geography, Religion, and Scholarship, 1550–1700* (Leiden: Brill).

Shannon, Laurie (2009), 'Minerva's Men: Horizontal Nationhood and the Literary Production of Googe, Turberville, and Gascoigne', in Cathy Shrank and Mike Pincombe (eds), *The Oxford Handbook of Tudor Literature: 1485–1603* (Oxford: Oxford University Press), 437–454.

Sharpe, R. R. (1899–1912), *Calendar of Letter-books Preserved among the Archives of the Corporation of London at the Guildhall*, 11 vols [A–L] (London: John Edward Francis).

Shephard, Robert (1995), 'Utopia, Utopia's Neighbors, *Utopia*, and Europe', *Sixteenth Century Journal*, 26: 843–856.

Shibl, Fu'ad Muhammad [n.d.], *al-Madina al-fadila: bahth fi al-nizam al-iqtisadi wa-l-ijtima'i 'inda al-kuttab al-mithaliyyin* (Cairo: Maktabat al-Nahda al-Misriyya).

Shrank, Cathy (2004), *Writing the Nation in Reformation England, 1530–1580* (Oxford: Oxford University Press).

Shrank, Cathy (2013), 'All Talk and No Action? Early Modern Political Dialogue', in Andrew Hadfield (ed.), *The Oxford Handbook of English Prose, 1500–1640* (Oxford: Oxford University Press), 27–42.

Shtein, L. (1899), *Sotsial'nyo vopros s filosofskoi tochki zreniya* (Moscow: Guttenberg).

Sidney, Philip (1973), 'A Defence of Poetry', in *Miscellaneous Prose of Sir Philip Sidney*, ed. Katherine Duncan-Jones and Jan van Dorsten (Oxford: Clarendon Press), 59–122, 185–208.

Siebenpfeiffer, Hania (2008), 'Die literarische Eroberung des Alls—Eberhard Christian Kindermanns *Die Geschwinde Reise auf dem Lufft = Schiff nach der Obern Welt*', in Christian Heitzmann (ed.), *Die Sterne lügen nicht: Astrologie und Astronomie im Mittelalter und in der Frühen Neuzeit* (Wolfenbüttel: Harrasowitz), 234–250.

Siebenpfeiffer, Hania (2013), '(Imagining) First Contact—Literary Encounters of the Extraterrestrial Other in 17th and 18th Century Novels', in Sabine Blackmore and Ralf Haekel (eds), *Discovering the Human: Life Science and the Arts in the Eighteenth and Early Nineteenth Centuries* (Göttingen: Vandenhoeck & Ruprecht), 139–157.

Siebers, Johan (2012), 'Front', 'Novum', 'Ultimum', in *Bloch Wörterbuch* (Berlin: De Gruyter), 161–165, 412–416, 582–589.

Siebers, Johan (2013), 'The Utopian Horizon of Communication: Ernst Bloch's *Traces* and Johann-Peter Hebel's *Treasure Chest*', in Roger D. Sell, Adam Borch, and Inna Lindgren (eds), *The Ethics of Literary Communication* (Amsterdam: John Benjamins), 189–212.

Siebers, Johan (2016), 'Die Welt gut im Gang: Der Friedenstopos in Ernst Bloch's Philosophie', in Francesca Vidal and Werner Wilds (eds), *Die Utopie des Friedens* (Würzburg: Königshausen & Neumann), 129–144.

Siebers, Johan (2019a), 'Being as Communication: An Explanatory Model', in Mats Bergman, Kęstas Kirtilis, and Johan Siebers (eds), *Models of Communication: Theoretical and Philosophical Approaches*, 59–148.

Siebers, Johan (2019b), 'Philosophy as Rhetoric', *Revue internationale de philosophie*, 3: 361–374.

Siebers, Johan (2021), 'Creativity and the Ontology of Not-Yet Being', in Sandra Kemp and Jenny Andersson (eds), *Futures* (Oxford: Oxford University Press), 160–173.

Sieveke, Franz Günter (2011), 'Bidermann (Biderman(n)us), Jakob, S. J.', in Wilhelm Kühlmann et al. (eds), *Frühe Neuzeit in Deutschland 1520–1620: Literaturwissenschaftliches Verfasserlexikon*, vol. 1: *Aal, Johannes—Chytraeus, Nathan* (Berlin: De Gruyter), 244–262.

Sissa, Giulia (2017), 'A Praise of Pain: Thomas More's Anti-Utopianism', in Han van Ruler and Giulia Sissa (eds), *Utopia 1516-2016: More's Eccentric Essay and Its Activist Aftermath* (Amsterdam: Amsterdam University Press), 25–70.

Skambraks, Tanja (2023), *Karitativer Kredit: Monti Di Pietà, Franziskanische Wirtschaftsethik und Städtische Sozialpolitik in Italien* (Stuttgart. Franz Steiner Verlag).

Skelton, R. A., and Harvey, P. D. A. (1986) (eds), *Local Maps and Plans from Medieval England* (Oxford: Clarendon Press).

Skinner, Quentin (1967), 'More's *Utopia*', *Past and Present*, 38: 153–168.

Skinner, Quentin (1978), *The Foundations of Modern Political Thought*, 2 vols (Cambridge: Cambridge University Press).

Skinner, Quentin (1987), 'Sir Thomas More's *Utopia* and the Language of Renaissance Humanism', in Anthony Pagden (ed.), *The Languages of Political Theory in Early-Modern Europe* (Cambridge: Cambridge University Press), 123–158.

Skinner, Quentin (1998), *Liberty before Liberalism* (Cambridge: Cambridge University Press).

Skinner, Quentin (2002a), 'Sir Thomas More's *Utopia* and the Language of Renaissance Humanism', in Anthony Pagden (ed.), *The Languages of Political Theory in Early-Modern Europe* (repr. Cambridge: Cambridge University Press), 123–158.

Skinner, Quentin (2002b), *Visions of Politics*, 3 vols (Cambridge: Cambridge University Press).

Skinner, Quentin and Russell Price (2019), (eds), *Machiavelli: The Prince* (Cambridge: Cambridge University Press).

Slack, Paul (1980), 'Social Policy and the Constraints of Government, 1547–1558', in Jennifer Loach and Robert Tittler (eds), *The Mid-Tudor Polity, c 1540–1560* (London: Palgrave), 94–115.

Slack, Paul (1998), *Poverty and Policy in Tudor and Stuart England* (London: Longman).

Smeeks, Hendrik (1708), *Beschryvinge van het magtig Koningryk Krinke Kesmes* (Amsterdam [=Zwolle]: Nicolaas ten Hoorn).

Smeeks, Hendrik (1995), *The Mighty Kingdom of Krinke Kesmes*, trans. Robert H. Leek, ed. David Fausset (Amsterdam: Rodopi).

Smith, Adam (1776), *An inquiry into the nature and causes of the Wealth of Nations* (London: for W. Strahan and T. Cadell).

Smith, David R. (2005), 'Portrait and Counter-Portrait in Holbein's *The Family of Sir Thomas More*', *Art Bulletin*, 87: 484–506.

Smith, Thomas (1571), *A Letter sent by I.B. Gentleman* (London: Henry Binneman).

Smith, Thomas (1583), *De Republica Anglorum* (London: Henry Middleton for Gregory Seton).

Smith, Thomas (1906), *De Republica Anglorum*, ed. Lucy Alston (Cambridge: Cambridge University Press).

Smith, Thomas (1929), *A Discourse of the Common Weal of This Realm of England*, ed. Elizabeth Lamond (Cambridge: Cambridge University Press).

Smits-Veldt, Mieke B. (1994), *Maria Tesselschade: Leven met talent en vriendschap* (Zutphen: Walburg).

Smyth, Jim (2001), *The Making of the United Kingdom, 1660–1800: State, Religion, and Identity in Britain and Ireland* (London: Longman).

Soleinne, Martineau de (1844), *Bibliothèque dramatique*, vol. 2 (Paris: Administration des Alliances des Arts).

Solomin, V. (1901), Review, *Narodnoe Khozyaistvo*, 6: 179–180.

Sombart, Werner (1915), *Händler und Helden: Patriotische Besinnungen* (Munich: Duncker & Humblot).

Song, Jiaqing (1956), 'Mo'er de "Wutuoban"', *Dushu yuebao* (Dec.), 16–17.
Sonni, A. I. (1905), 'Kritika i bibliografiya', *Zhurnal Ministerstva Narodnogo Prosveshcheniya*, 4: 393.
Sophocles (1502), *Tragaediae septem* (Venice: Aldus Manutius).
Sorel, Georges (1999), *Reflections on Violence*, ed. Jeremy Jennings (Cambridge: Cambridge University Press).
Söveges, Dávid (1993), *Fejezetek a lelkiség történetéből* (Pannonhalma: Szent Gellért Hittudományi Főiskola).
Spaans, Ronny, and Cave, Terence (2008a), 'The Dutch Translation: Austerity and Pragmatism', in Terence Cave (ed.), *Thomas More's Utopia in Early Modern Europe* (Manchester: Manchester University Press), 104–109.
Spaans, Ronny, and Cave, Terence (2008b), 'The Dutch Paratexts', in Terence Cave (ed.), *Thomas More's Utopia in Early Modern Europe* (Manchester: Manchester University Press), 219–231.
Spakowski, Nicola (2019), 'Dreaming a Future for China: Visions of Socialism among Chinese Intellectuals in the Early 1930s', *Modern Chinas*, 45: 91–122.
Spencer, Herbert (1893), *The Principles of Sociology* (London: Williams and Norgate).
Spierenburg, Pieter (1978), 'Judicial Violence in the Dutch Republic: Corporal Punishment, Executions, and Torture in Amsterdam, 1650–1750', PhD thesis, University of Amsterdam.
Spinoza, Benedictus de (1985–2016), *Collected Works*, 2 vols, ed. Edwin Curley (Princeton: Princeton University Press).
Spinozzi, Paola (2016), 'Italian Translations and Editions of Thomas More's *Libellus ver aureus*', *Utopian Studies*, 27: 505–520.
Sponde, Henri de (1671), *Continuationis annalium ecclesiasticorum emenentis Card. Baronii Ab Anno 1198. vsque ad Annum 1646. [...] Arabica Epitome*, trans. Joachim Brice de Rennes, vol. 3 (Rome: Sacra Congregazione de Propaganda Fide).
Springer, Else (1956) (ed.), *Handbuch zur Kinder und Jugendliteratur 1850–1900* (Mannheim: Buddeberg).
Sreenivasan, Jyotsna (2008), *Utopias in American History* (Santa Barbara: ABC-CLIO).
Stammler, Rudolf (1892), 'Utopien', *Deutsche Rundschau*, 70: 281–296.
Standish, David (2006), *Hollow Earth: The Long and Curious History of Imagining Strange Lands, Fantastical Creatures, Advanced Civilizations, and Marvelous Machines below the Earth's Surface* (Cambridge, MA: Da Capo Press).
Stapleton, Thomas (1588), 'Vita et obitus Thomae Mori', in Thomas Stapleton, *Tres Thomae* (Douai: Jean Bogard).
Stapleton, Thomas (2020), *The Life and Illustrious Martyrdom of Sir Thomas More*, trans. Philip E. Hallett, ed. Katherine Stearns and Emma Curtis (Dallas: CTMS Publishers).
Steenson, Gary (1978), *Karl Kautsky, 1854–1939: Marxism in the Classical Years* (Pittsburgh: University of Pittsburgh Press).
Steffen, Lisa (2001), *Defining a British State: Treason and National Identity, 1608–1820* (Basingstoke: Palgrave).
Stevenson, W. H., et al. (1883–1956) (eds), *Records of the Borough of Nottingham*, 9 vols (London: Quaritch).
Stiblin, Kaspar (1994), *Commentariolus de Eudaemonensium Republica (Basel 1555)*, ed. and trans. Isabel-Dorothea Jahn (Regensburg: Roderer).
Stoffers, Johannes (2001), 'Die Republik Utopia: Erläuterungen und Gedanken zu einer alten Karte', *Auswärtiger Dienst*, 62: 35–84.

Stowlow, Jeremy (1997), 'Utopia and Geopolitics in Theodor Herzl's *Altneuland*', *Utopian Studies*, 8: 55–76.
Stratford, Elaine (2013), 'The Idea of the Archipelago: Contemplating Island Relations', *Island Studies Journal*, 8: 3–8.
Streng, J. C. (1990), 'The Leiden Engraver Frans van Bleyswyck (1671–1746)', *Quaerendo*, 20: 111–136.
Strengholt, L. (1989), 'Epigrammen over en van Thomas More in Nederland', *De Nieuwe Taalgids*, 82: 211–225.
Studt, Christoph (1999), 'Oncken, Hermann', *Neue Deutsche Biographie*, 19: 538 f., [online version] URL: https://www.deutsche-biographie.de/pnd118589997.html#ndbcontent.
Sullivan, Ellen (2011), 'Drawing Blood: Patrick Geddes and Sectional Thinking', in Nathaniel Coleman (ed.), *Imagining and Making the World: Reconsidering Architecture and Utopia* (Bern: Peter Lang), 165–182.
Sumiya, Mikio (1974), *Dai-nippon-teikoku no Shiren* (Tokyo: Chuo-Koron).
Summit, Jennifer (2008), *Memory's Library: Medieval Books in Early Modern England* (Chicago: University of Chicago Press).
Surtz, Edward (1949a), 'The Defense of Pleasure in More's *Utopia*', *Studies in Philology*, 46/2: 99–112.
Surtz, Edward (1949b), 'Epicurus in Utopia', *English Literary History*, 16: 89–103.
Surtz, Edward (1952), 'Interpretations of *Utopia*', *Catholic Historical Review*, 38: 156–174.
Surtz, Edward (1953), 'St. Thomas More and His Utopian Embassy of 1515', *Catholic Historical Review*, 39: 272–297.
Surtz, Edward (1957), *The Praise of Wisdom: A Commentary of the Religious and Moral Problems and Backgrounds of St Thomas More's 'Utopia'* (Chicago: Loyola University Press).
Surtz, Edward (1967), 'Aspects of More's Latin Style in *Utopia*', *Studies in the Renaissance*, 14: 93–109.
Sutton, Anne F. (2002), 'The Merchant Adventurers of England: Their Origins and the Mercers' Company of London', *Historical Research*, 75: 25–46.
Sutton, Anne F. (2005), *The Mercery of London: Trade, Goods and People, 1130–1578* (Aldershot: Ashgate).
Sutton, Anne F. (2009), 'The Merchant Adventurers of England: The Place of the Adventurers of York and the North in the Late Middle Ages', *Northern History*, 46: 219–229.
Sutton, Robert B. (2003), *Communal Utopias and the American Experience*, 2 vols (Westport, CN: Praeger).
Suvin, Darko (1979), *Metamorphoses of Science Fiction: On the Poetics and History of a Literary Genre* (New Haven: Yale University Press).
Suvin, Darko (2014), 'Estrangment and Cognition', *Strange Horizons*, 24 Nov., strangehorizons.com/non-fiction/articles/estrangement-and-cognition.
Svyatlovskii, V. V. (1923), *Katalog utopii* (Moscow: Gos. izd-vo).
Swanson, Heather (1989), *Medieval Artisans: An Urban Class in Late Medieval England* (Oxford: Blackwell).
Swartz, Wendy (2008), *Reading Tao Yuanming: Shifting Paradigms of Historical Reception (427–1990)* (Cambridge, MA: Harvard University Press).
Swenson, Peter (1989), *Fair Shares: Unions, Pay, and Politics in Sweden and West Germany* (Ithaca, NY: Cornell University Press).
Swift, Jonathan [as Lemuel Gulliver] (1726), *Travels into Several Remote Nations of the World*, 2 vols (London: Benjamin Motte).

Swift, Jonathan (2008), *Gulliver's Travels*, ed. Claude Rawson and Ian Higgs (Oxford: Oxford University Press).

Sylvester, R. S., and Harding, D. P. (1962) (eds), *Two Early Tudor Lives* (New Haven: Yale University Press).

Sylvester, R. S., and Marc'hadour, G. P. (1977) (eds), *Essential Articles for the Study of Thomas More* (Hamden, CT: Archon Books).

Szakolczai, Árpád (2000), *Reflexive Historical Sociology* (London: Routledge).

Szakolczai, Árpád (2009), 'Liminality and Experience: Structuring Transitory Situations and Transformative Events', *International Political Anthropology*, 2: 141–172.

Szathmári, Sándor (2012), *Kazohinia*, trans. Inez Kemenes (North Adams, MA: New Europe Books).

Szőcs, Géza (2004), 'Morus Tamás végrendelete' in Thomas More, *Erősítő párbeszéd balsors idején*, trans. Zsuzsa Gergely (Budapest: Szent István Társulat; Kolozsvár: A Dunánál), 429–448.

Szűcs, Jenő (1983), 'The Three Historical Regions of Europe: An Outline', *Acta Historica Academiae Scientiarum Hungaricae*, 29: 131–184.

Szyska, Christian (1995), 'On Utopian Writing in Nasserist Prison and Laicist Turkey', *Die Welt des Islams*, 35: 95–125.

Tadema, Judith (2004), 'Een ambachtsman met beschaafde hobby's: De dichter en verzamelaar Joachim Oudaan (1628–1692)', *De zeventiende eeuw*, 20: 209–219.

Tadmor, Naomi (2010), *The Social Universe of the English Bible: Scripture, Society and Culture in Early Modern England* (Cambridge: Cambridge University Press).

Taine, H. (1864), *Histoire de la littérature anglaise* (Paris: Hachette & Cie).

Tankha, Brij (2006), *Kita Ikki and the Making of Modern Japan: A Vision of Empire* (Folkestone: Global Oriental).

Tantawi Jawhari (1912), *Kitab ayna al-insan* (Cairo: Matba'at al-Ma'arif).

Tantawi Jawhari (1935), *Ahlam fi al-siyasa wa-kayfa yatahaqqaq al-salam al-'alami* (Cairo: Matba'at Mustafa al-Babi al-Halabi).

Tarello, G. (1976), *Storia della cultura giuridica moderna*, vol. 1 (Bologna: Il Mulino).

Tarle, Evgenii (1901), *Obshchestvennie vozzreniya Tomasa Mora v svyazi s ekonomicheskom sostoyaniem ego vremeni. Prilozheniya. Perevod 'Utopii' s latinskogo, rukopis' sovremennika o Tomase More*, Masters thesis, St Petersburg: Mir bozhii.

Tarle, Evgenii (1957), *Akademik Evgenii Viktorovich Tarle, Sochineniya v dvenadtsati tomakh*, vol. 1 (Moscow: Academy of Sciences).

Tasso, M. L. (1999), 'Il deviante nella città perfetta: Modelli repressivi nelle utopie di Campanella e More', *Materiali per una storia della cultura giuridica*, 29: 299–330.

Tavárez, David Eduardo (2011), *The Invisible War: Indigenous Devotions, Discipline, and Dissent in Colonial Mexico* (Palo Alto, CA: Stanford University Press).

Tawfiq, Ahmad Khalid (2008), *Yutubiya* (Cairo: Daar Miiriit).

Tawney, Richard (1926/1936), *Religion and the Rise of Capitalism* (repr. London: John Murray).

Taylor, A. E. (1926/2013), *Plato: The Man and His Work* (repr. London: Routledge).

Taylor, Andrew (2014), 'Thomas More', in Philip Ford, Jan Bloemendal, and Charles Fantazzi (eds), *Brill's Encyclopaedia of the Neo-Latin World*, 2 vols (Leiden: Brill), 2.1047–2.1051.

Taylor, John (1630), *All the workes of John Taylor the Water-Poet* (London: John Beale, Elizabeth Allde, Bernard Alsop, and Thomas Fawcet for James Boler).

Temmer, M. J. (1982), '*Candide* and *Rasselas* Revisited', *Revue de littérature comparée*, 2: 177–193.

Terrahe, Tina (2010), 'Frankfurts Aufstieg zu Druckmetropole des 16. Jahrhunderts: Christian Egenolff, Sigmund Feyerabend und die Frankfurter Buchmesse', in Regina Töpfer and Robert Seidel (eds), *Frankfurt im Schnittpunkt der Diskurse: Strategien und Institutionen literarischer Kommunikation im späten Mittelalter und in der Frühen Neuzeit* (Frankfurt am Main: Klostermann), 177–194.

Testa, Simone (2015), *Italian Academies and Their Networks, 1525–1700: From Local to Global* (London: Palgrave Macmillan).

Theophrastus (1497), *Historia Plantarum* (Venice: Aldus Manutius).

Thieme, Hans, and Rowan, Steven (1985), 'Claudius Cantiuncula of Metz, d. October 1549', in P. G. Bietenholz and Thomas B. Deutscher (eds), *Contemporaries of Erasmus: A Biographical Register of the Renaissance and Reformation*, vol. 1: *A–E* (Toronto: University of Toronto Press), 259–261.

Thissen, Peter (1994), *Werk, netwerk en letterwerk van de familie Van Hoogstraten in de zeventiende eeuw: Sociaal-economische en en sociaalculturele achtergronden van geletterden in de Republiek* (Amsterdam: APA-Holland University Press).

Thomas, Chantal (2001), *The Wicked Queen: The Origins of the Myth of Marie-Antoinette*, trans. Julie Rose (Princeton: Princeton University Press).

Thomas, William (1550), *Principal rules of the Italian grammer* (London: Thomas Berthelet).

Thompson, E. P. (1963), *The Making of the English Working Class* (New York: Vintage Books).

Thompson, E. P. (1971), 'The Moral Economy of the English Crowd in the Eighteenth Century', *Past and Present*, 50: 76–136.

Thompson, E. P. (1994), *Customs in Common: Studies in Traditional Popular Culture* (New York: The New Press).

Thompson, E. P. (1996), *William Morris: Romantic to Revolutionary* (rev. edn, London: Merlin Press).

Thompson, Laurence (1951), *Robert Blatchford: Portrait of an Englishman* (London: Victor Gollancz.

Thompson, Noel (2006), *Political Economy and the Labour Party: The Economics of Democratic Socialism 1884–2005* (2nd edn, London: Routledge).

Thomson, James (2007), 'Modern Britain and the New Imperial History', *History Compass*, 5: 455–462.

Thucydides (1502), *Thukydidēs* (Venice: Aldus Manutius).

Tilley, Arthur (1938), 'Greek Studies in England in the Early Sixteenth Century', *English Historical Review*, 53: 221–239.

Tocqueville, Alexis de (1960), *Journey to America*, trans. George Lawrence, ed. J. P. Mayer (New Haven: Yale University Press).

To-Day (1888 [Mar.]), 'Books of To-Day'.

Took, P. M. (1978), 'Government and the Printing Trade, 1540–1560'. Unpublished PhD thesis, University of London.

Tóta, Péter Benedek (2002), 'Morus magyaros országmagyarázata', *Vigilia*, 67: 322–330.

Tower Sargent, Lyman (1975), 'A Note on the Other Side of Human Nature in the Utopian Novel', *Political Theory*, 3: 88–97.

Tower Sargent, Lyman (1982), 'Authority & Utopia: Utopianism in Political Thought', *Polity*, 14: 565–584.

Tower Sargent, Lyman (1984), 'More's *Utopia*: An Interpretation of Its Social Theory', *History of Political Thought*, 5: 195–210.

Tower Sargent, Lyman (2010a), 'Colonial and Postcolonial Utopias', in Gregory Claeys (ed.), *The Cambridge Companion to Utopian Literature* (Cambridge: Cambridge University Press), 200–222.

Tower Sargent, Lyman (2010b), *Utopianism: A Very Short Introduction* (Oxford: Oxford University Press).

Trapman, J. (1993), 'Erasmus Seen by a Dutch Collegiant: Daniel de Breen (1594–1664) and His Posthumous *Compendium Theologiae Erasmicae* (1677)', *Dutch Review of Church History*, 73: 156–177.

Trapman, J. (1999), *Het land van Erasmus* (Amsterdam: Balans).

Trapp, J. B. (2002), 'Dioscorides in Utopia', *Journal of the Warburg and Courtauld Institutes*, 65: 259–261.

Trencsényi, Balázs (2010), 'Patriotism and Elect Nationhood', in Balázs Trencsényi and Márton Zászkaliczky (eds), *Whose Love of Which Country?* (Leiden: Brill), 497–544.

Trencsényi, Balázs, Janowski, Maciej, Baar, Monika, Falina, Maria, and Kopecek, Michal (2016) (eds), *A History of Modern Political Thought in East Central Europe* (Oxford: Oxford University Press).

Trencsényi, Borbála (1992) (ed.), *A reneszánsz irodalmából* (Budapest: Holnap).

Trentmann, Frank (2007), 'Before *Fair Trade*: Empire, Free Trade, and the Moral Economies of Food in the Modern World', *Environment and Planning* D: Society and Space, 25: 1079–1102.

Trentmann, Frank (2012) (ed.), *The Oxford Handbook of the History of Consumption* (Oxford: Oxford University Press).

Trentmann, Frank (2016), *Empire of Things: How We Became a World of Consumers, from the Fifteenth Century to the Twenty-First* (London: Allen Lane).

Trevor Davies, R. (1967), *The Golden Century of Spain, 1501–1621* (London: Macmillan).

Trevor-Roper, Hugh (1996), 'The Image of Thomas More in England, 1535–1635', in *La Fortuna dell'Utopia di Thomas More nel dibattito politico europeo del Cinquecento* (Florence: Olschki), 5–23.

Trousson, Raymond (1993), 'L'Utopie est-elle un genre littéraire?', *Lettres actuelles*, 3: 91–94.

Trousson, Raymond (1995), *Historia de la literatura utópica: Viajes a países inexistentes*, trans. C. Manzano (Barcelona: Península).

Trunz, Erich (1992), *Wissenschaft und Kunst im Kreise Kaiser Rudolfs II (1576–1612)* (Neumünster: Wachhotlz Verlag).

Truskolaski, Sebastian (2011), *Adorno and the Ban on Images* (London: Bloomsbury).

Tryon, Thomas (1684), *Friendly Advice to the Gentlemen-Planters of the East and West Indies, In Three Parts* (London: Andrew Sowle).

Tschackert, P. (1896), 'Weigel, Rudolf', in *Allgemeine Deutsche Biographie*, vol. 41 (Leipzig: Duncker & Humblot).

Tsui, Brian (2018), *China's Conservative Revolution: The Quest for a New Order, 1927–1949* (Cambridge: Cambridge University Press).

Tsz, Wong (2017), 'Decoding the Translations of Political Terms in the Nineteenth-Century Chinese–English Dictionaries: Lobscheid and His Chinese–English Dictionary', *Comparative Literature: East & West*, 1: 204–215.

Tunberg, Terence (2017), 'Approaching Neo-Latin Prose as Literature', in Victoria Moul (ed.), *A Guide to Neo-Latin Literature* (Cambridge: Cambridge University Press), 237–254.

Turley, Steven E. (2014), *Franciscan Spirituality and Mission in New Spain, 1524–1599* (London: Routledge).

Tusser, Thomas (1984), *Five Hundred Points of Good Husbandry* (Oxford: Oxford University Press).

Ulibarri, Sarena (2018) (ed.), *Glass and Gardens: Solarpunk Summers* (Albuquerque, NM: World Weaver Press).

Underdown, David (1985), *Revel, Riot and Rebellion: Popular Politics and Culture in England 1603–1660* (Oxford: Oxford University Press).

Unwin, G. (1918), 'The Estate of Merchants, 1336–1365', in G. Unwin (ed.), *Finance and Trade under Edward III* (Manchester: Manchester University Press), 179–255.

Urbánek, Vladimír (2005), 'The Idea of State and Nation in the Writings of Bohemian Exiles after 1620', in Linas Eriksonas and Leos Müller (eds), *Statehood before and beyond Ethnicity* (Brussels: PIE-Peter Lang), 67–84.

Vajda, György (1916), 'Morus Tamás a magyar tudományos irodalomban', *Történelmi Szemle*, 21: 379–381.

Vallance, Aymer (1897), *The Art of William Morris* (London: George Bell & Sons).

Vallich, E. I. (1977), 'N. M. Karamzin—pervyi russkii retsenzent "Utopia" Tomasa Mora', in G. S. Kucherenko (ed.), *Istoriya sotsialisticheskikh uchenii. Voprosy isoriografii. Sbk.st* (Moscow: Nauka), 243–256.

van Berkel, Klaas (2013), *Isaac Beeckman on Matter and Motion: Mechanical Philosophy in the Making* (Baltimore: Johns Hopkins University Press).

van Bunge, Wiep (1990a), 'De Rotterdamse collegiant Jacob Ostens (1630–1678)', *De zeventiende eeuw*, 6: 65–81.

van Bunge, Wiep (1990b), 'Johannes Bredenburg (1643–1691): Een Rotterdamse collegiant in de van van Spinoza', PhD thesis, Erasmus Universiteit Rotterdam.

van Bunge, Wiep (2004), 'De bibliotheek van Jacob Ostens: *Spinozana* en *Sociniana*', *Doopsgezinde Bijdragen*, 30: 125–140.

van Bunge, Wiep (2012), *Spinoza Past and Present: Essays on Spinoza, Spinozism, and Spinoza Scholarship* (Leiden: Brill).

van Bunge, Wiep (2013), 'The Politics of Appropriation: Erasmus and Bayle', *Erasmus of Rotterdam Society Yearbook*, 22: 3–21.

van Bunge, Wiep (2020), ' "Qui toujours servant d'instruction": Socinian Manuscripts in the Dutch Republic', in Gianni Paganini, Margaret C. Jacob, and John Christian Laursen (eds), *Clandestine Philosophy: New Studies on Subversive Manuscripts in Early Modern Europe, 1620–1823* (Toronto: Toronto University Press), 123–142.

van den Broecke, Marcel (2004), 'De Utopia kaart van Ortelius', *Caert-Thresoor*, 23: 89–93.

van den Broecke, Marcel (2011), *Ortelius Atlas Maps: An illustrated Guide* (2nd rev. edn, Houten: HES and De Graaf).

van den Enden, Franciscus (1662), Kort Verhael van Nieuw-Nederlants Gelegentheden, Deughden, Natuerlijcke Voorrechten en bijzondere bequaemheidt ter bevolkingh (Amsterdam: [n.pub.]).

van der Blom, N. (1982), 'De beelden van Erasmus', in J. Smit and J. Spoelder (eds), *Florislegium: Bloemlezing uit de Erasmiaanse, Rotterdamse en andere opstellen* (Leiden: Brill), 29–54.

van der Lugt, Mara (2016), *Bayle, Jurieu, and the Dictionnaire historique et critique* (Oxford: Oxford University Press).

van Eijnatten, Joris (2003), *Liberty and Concord in the United Provinces: Religious Toleration and the Public in the Eighteenth-Century Netherlands* (Leiden: Brill).

van Gennip, Jeroen (2014), *Controversen in context: Een comparatief onderzoek naar de Nederlandstalige controversepublicaties van de jezuieten in de zeventiende-eeuwse Republiek* (Hilversum: Verloren).

van Hoogstraten, Frans (1668), *Het Voorhof der Ziele, Behangen met Leerzaeme Prenten en Zinnebeelden* (Rotterdam: Frans van Hoogstraten).

van Hoogstraten, Frans (1682), *Mengeldichten*, in Joseph Hall, *De Schoole der Wereld*, trans. Frans van Hoogstraten (Dordrecht: Frans van Hoogstraten).

van Hoogstraten, Samuel (1678), *Inleyding to de Hooge Schoole der Schilderkonst* (Rotterdam: Frans van Hoogstraten).

van Kempen, Thomas [Thomas à Kempis] (1674), *De navolging Christi* (Rotterdam: Frans van Hoogstraten.

van Nierop, Henk (2002), 'Sewing the Bailiff in a Blanket: Catholics and the Law in Holland', in R. Po-Chia Hsia and Henk van Nierop (eds), *Calvinism and Religious Toleration in the Dutch Golden Age* (Cambridge: Cambridge University Press), 102–111.

van Nierop, Henk, et al. (2008) (eds), *Romeyn de Hooghe: De verbeelding van de late Gouden Eeuw* (Zwolle: Waanders).

van Ruler, Han, and Sissa, Giulia (2017a), 'Introduction', in Han van Ruler and Giulia Sissa (eds), *Utopia 1516–2016: More's Eccentric Essay and Its Activist Aftermath* (Amsterdam: Amsterdam University Press), 7–22.

van Ruler, Han and Sissa, Giulia (2017b) (eds), *Utopia 1516–2016: More's Eccentric Essay and Its Activist Aftermath* (Amsterdam: Amsterdam University Press).

van Slee, J. C (1895/1980), *De Rijnsburger collegianten* (repr. Utrecht: HES).

Varaisse, Denis de (1675), *The History of the Sevarites* (London: for Henry Brome).

Vaughan, William (1600), *The Golden-Grove* (London: Simon Stafford).

Vaughan, William (1626), *The Golden Fleece* (London: for Francis Williams).

Venuti, Lawrence (1995), *The Invisibility of the Translator: A History of Translation* (London: Routledge).

Venuti, Lawrence (2008), *The Translator's Invisibility: A History of Translation* (2nd edn, London: Routledge).

Vereeniging Het Spinozahuis (1914), *Catalogus van de Boekerij der Vereeniging Het Spinozahuis* (The Hague: Belinfante).

Vergil, Polydore (1499), *De inventoribus rerum libri tres* (Venice: C. de Pensis).

Vergil, Polydore (2010), *Anglica Historia*, ed. Dana F. Sutton (Birmingham: Philological Museum).

Verne, Jules (1864), *Voyage au centre de la Terre* (Paris: J. Hetzel).

Vespucci, Amerigo (1907), *Four Voyages*, in Martin Waldseemüller, *The Cosmographiae Introductio of Martin Waldseemüller in Facsimile, followed by the Four Voyages of Amerigo Vespucci with their English translations, to which are added two World Maps of 1507*, ed. Charles George Herbermann (New York: United States Catholic Historical Society).

Vespucci, Amerigo (1916), *Mundus Novus: Letter to Lorenzo Pietro di Medici*, trans. George Tyler Northrup (Princeton: Princeton University Press).

Vidal Alcover, Jaume (1980 [27 Apr.]), 'Pin i Soler, en antologia', *Avui*, 25.

Vidal-Naquet, P. (1986), *The Black Hunter* (Baltimore: John Hopkins University Press).

Vieira, Fatima (2010), 'The Concept of Utopia', in Gregory Claeys (ed.), *The Cambridge Companion to Utopia* (Cambridge: Cambridge University Press), 3–27.

Villarroel, Diego de Torres (1723), *Viaje fantástico del Gran Piscátor de Salamanca* (Salamanca: [n.pub.]).

Vipper, R (1896), 'Utopia' Tomasa Mora', *Mir Bozhii*, 3.

Virgil (1990), *The Aeneid*, trans. David West (Harmondsworth: Penguin).
Visscher, Roemer (2013), *Brabbeling (1614): Een bloemlezing*, ed. Anneke C. G. Fleurkens (Hilversum: Koninklijke Bibliotheek).
Visser, Sibbe Jan (2011), *Samuel Naeranus (1582–1641) en Johannes Naeranus (1608–1679): Twee remonstrantse theologen op de bres voor godsdienstige verdraagzaamheid* (Hilversum: Verloren).
Vives, Júan Luís (1543), *De veritate fidei* (Basel: Oporinus).
Vives, Juan Luis (1964), *Opera Omnia*, 8 vols (London: Gregg Press).
Vives, Juan Luis (1970), *Tudor School-Boy Life: The Dialogues of Juan Luis Vives*, trans. Foster Watson (London: Frank Cass).
Vodovozov, V. V. (1901), 'Novoe Izsledovanie po sotsial'noi istorii Anglii', *Narodnoe Khozyaistvo*, 10: 1–16.
Voeglin, Eric (2002), *The Collected Works of Eric Voeglin*, vol. 10: *Published Essays, 1940–1952* (Columbia: University of Missouri Press).
Volgin, V. P. (1928), *Istoryia sotsialisticheskikh idei*, pt.1 (Moscow: Gos. Izd).
Volland, Nicolai (2008), 'Translating the Socialist World: Cultural Exchange, National Identity, and the Socialist World in the Early PRC', *Twentieth-Century China*, 33: 51–72.
Volland, N. (2009), 'A Linguistic Enclave: Translation and Language Policies in the Early People's Republic of China', *Modern China*, 35: 467–494.
Volland, Nicolai (2014), 'The Birth of a Profession: Translators and Translation of Modern China', in Hsiao-yen Peng (ed.), *Modern China and the West: Translation and Cultural Mediation* (Leiden: Brill), 126–150.
Voltaire [François-Marie Arouet] (1752), *Micromegas* (London: for J. Robinson and W. Meyer.
Voltaire [François-Marie Arouet] (1756), *Essai sur les mœurs* (Paris: Cramer).
Voltaire [François-Marie Arouet] (1994), *Letters Concerning the English Nation*, ed. Nicholas Cronk (Oxford: Oxford University Press).
Voltaire [François-Marie Arouet] (2003), *Candide, ou l'optimisme*, ed. Frédéric Deloffre (Paris: Gallimard).
Voltaire [François-Marie Arouet] (2005), *Candide, or Optimism*, trans. Burton Raffel (New Haven: Yale University Press).
von Kirchenhim, Arthur (1892), *Schlaraffia Politica: Geschichte der Dichtungen vom besten Staate* (Leipzig: Fr. Wilh. Grunow).
Von Reden, Sitta (1995), *Exchange in Ancient Greece* (London: Duckworth).
von Rudhart, Georg Thomas (1852), *Thomas Morus aus den Quellen* (Augsburg: [n.pub.]).
Von Schlachta, Astrid (2003), *Hutterische Konfession Und Tradition 1578–1619: Etabliertes Leben Zwischen Ordnung Und Ambivalenz* (Mainz: Philipp von Zabern).
Vorländer, Karl (1926), *Von Macchiavelli bis Lenin: Neuzeitliche Staats- und Gesellschaftstheorien* (Leipzig: Quelle & Meyer).
Vtopia, Thomæ Mori, *à mendis vindicata, et juxta Indicem libror. expurgat. Card. et Archiep. Toletani correcta*. (Coloniæ Agrippinæ: Apud Corn. ab Egmond & socios, 1629).
Wafi, Ali ('Abd al-Wahid) (1964), ''Ara' ahl al-madina al-fadila', *Turath al-insaniyya*, 7: 569–582.
Wagner, Phoebe, and Wieland, Brontë Christopher (2017) (eds), *Sunvault: Stories of Solarpunk and Eco-Speculation* (Nashville, TN: Upper Rubber Boot Books).
Waithe, Marcus (2006), *William Morris's Utopia of Strangers: Victorian Medievalism and the Ideal of Hospitality* (Cambridge: Boydell & Brewer).

Waithe, Marcus (2016), 'Medievalism and Modernity', in Laura Marcus, Michèle Mendelssohn, and Kirsten E. Shepherd-Barr (eds), *Oxford Twenty-First Century Approaches to Literature: Late Victorian to Modern* (Oxford: Oxford University Press), 21–37.

Wakeman, Frederick, Jr (1997), 'A Revisionist View of the Nanjing Decade: Confucian Fascism', *China Quarterly*, 150: 395–432.

Walder, A. (2015), *China under Mao: A Revolution Derailed* (Cambridge, MA: Harvard University Press).

Walker, Greg (2010), 'Folly', in Brian Cummings and James Simpson (eds), *Cultural Reformations: Medieval and Renaissance in Literary History* (Oxford: Oxford University Press), 321–341.

Waller, Philip (2006), *Writers, Readers, and Reputations: Literary Life in Britain 1870–1918* (Oxford: Oxford University Press).

Wallerstein, Immanuel (1986), 'Marxisms as Utopias: Evolving Ideologies', *American Journal of Sociology*, 91: 1295–1308.

Walter, William Joseph (1859), *Morus Tamás és korszaka* (Pest: Szent István Társulat).

Wands, John Millar (1980), 'The Early Printing History of Joseph Hall's *Mundus Alter et Idem*', *Papers of the Bibliographical Society of America*, 74: 1–12.

Wands, John Millar (1981), 'Antipodal Imperfection: Hall's *Mundus Alter et Idem* and Its Debt to More's *Utopia*', *Moreana* 18: 85–100.

Wang, David (1998), 'Translating Modernity', in David Pollard (ed.), *Translation and Creation: Readings of Western Literature in Early Modern China, 1840–1918* (Amsterdam: John Benjamin Publishing Company), 303–330.

Waquet, Françoise (2001), *Latin or the Empire of the Sign from the Sixteenth to the Twentieth Centuries*, trans. John Howe (London: Verso).

Warburg, Aby (2012), *L'Atlas mnémosyne* with an essay by Roland Recht (Paris: Lécarquillé–INHA) [written 1924–9].

Warhurst, Christopher (1994), 'The End of Another Utopia? The Israeli Kibbutz and Its Industry in a Period of Transition', *Utopian Studies*, 5: 103–121.

Wark, McKensie (2014), 'Utopian Realism', https://publicseminar.org/2014/10/utopian-realism/.

Warner, J. Christopher (1996), 'Sir Thomas More, "Utopia", and the Representation of Henry VIII, 1529–1533', *Renaissance and Reformation*, 20: 59–72.

Warren, Fintan B. (1963), *Vasco de Quiroga and His Pueblo-Hospitals of Santa Fe* (Washington DC: Academy of American Franciscan History).

Washton Long, Rose-Carol (2013) (ed.), *German Expressionism: Documents from the End of the Wilhelmine Empire to the Rise of National Socialism* (Berkeley and Los Angeles: University of California Press).

Watenpaugh, Keith David (2006), *Being Modern in the Middle East: Revolution, Nationalism, Colonialism, and the Arab Middle Class* (Princeton: Princeton University Press).

Waters, Chris (1982), 'William Morris and the Socialism of Robert Blatchford', *Journal of William Morris Studies*, 5: 20–31.

Watt, Ian (1957), *The Rise of the Novel* (London: Chatto & Windus).

Watts, Laura (2014), 'Liminal Futures: A Poem for Islands at the Edge', in James Leech and Lee Wilson (eds), *Subversion, Conversion, Development: Cross-Cultural Knowledge Exchange and the Politics of Design* (Cambridge, MA: MIT Press), 19–38.

Watts, Laura (2018a), 'Energy Future Islands as Living Labs', talk for the 'Exploratory Workshop: Energy Sustainability in the Transition to Renewables—Framings from Social Practices and Complex Systems Theories', Ispra, Italy (Mar.).
Watts, Laura (2018b), 'Making Energy Futures at the Island Edge: Diary of the Installation of the Newton Machine on the Island of Eday', https://lab.cccb.org/en/making-energy-futures-at-the-island-edge/.
Weaver-Hightower, Rebecca (2007), *Empire Islands: Castaways, Cannibals and Fantasies of Conquest* (Minneapolis, University of Minnesota Press).
Webster, Charles (1979), *Utopian Planning and the Puritan Revolution: Gabriel Plattes, Samuel Hartlib, and Macaria* (Oxford: Wellcome Unit for the History of Medicine).
Weeks, Gregory (1999), 'Gerhard Ritter' in *The Encyclopedia of Historians and Historical Writing*, ed. Kelly Boyd (Chicago: Fitzroy and Dearbor).
Wegemer, Gerard B. (1990), 'The Rhetoric of Opposition in Thomas More's *Utopia*: Giving Form to Competing Philosophies', *Philosophy & Rhetoric*, 23: 288–306.
Wegemer, Gerard B. (2011), *Young Thomas More and the Arts of Liberty* (Cambridge: Cambridge University Press).
Wegner, Philip (2002), *Imaginary Communities: Utopia, the Nation and the Spatial Histories of Modernity* (Berkeley and Los Angeles: University of California Press).
Weidhass, Peter (2007), *History of the Frankfurt Book Fair*, trans. and ed. C. M. Gossage and W. A. Wright (Toronto: Dundurn).
Weil Baker, David (1999), *Divulging Utopia: Radical Humanism in Sixteenth-Century England* (Amherst: University of Massachusetts Press).
Weil Baker, David (2003), 'Ruin and Utopia', *Moreana*, 40: 49–66.
Weinstein, Donald (1970), *Savonarola and Florence: Prophecy and Patriotism in the Renaissance* (Princeton: Princeton University Press).
Weinstein, Donald (2011), *Savonarola: The Rise and Fall of a Renaissance Prophet* (New Haven: Yale University Press).
Weiss, R. (1957), *Humanism in England During the Fifteenth Century* (Oxford: Blackwell).
Wells, H. G. (2005), *A Modern Utopia*, ed. Francis Wheen (London: Penguin).
Wernham, R. B. (1966), *Before the Armada: The Growth of English Foreign Policy, 1485–1588* (London: Cape).
Wessely, Ignaz Emanuel (1878), 'Kritische Bemerkungen zur deutschen Uebersetzungskunst: Nebst zwölf horazischen Oden in deutscher Nachdichtung', *Összehasonlító Irodalomtörténelmi Lapok / Acta comparationis litterarum universarum*, 22: 458–464; 25: 508–527; 26: 522–533; 28: 556–564; 29: 570–578; 30: 632–639.
Wessely, Ignaz (1883), *Grammatisch-Stilistisches Wörterbuch der Deutschen Sprache* (Leipzig: Fues).
Weststeijn, Arthur (2012), *Commercial Republicanism in the Dutch Republic: The Political Thought of Johan and Pieter de la Court* (Leiden: Brill).
Weststeijn, Thijs (2008), *The Visible World: Samuel van Hoogstraten's Art Theory and the Legitimation of Painting in the Dutch Golden Age* (Amsterdam: Amsterdam University Press).
Wheeler, Thomas (1970), 'Thomas More in Italy: 1535–1700', *Moreana*, 7: 15–23.
White, Paul (2014), 'Humanist Printers', in Philip Ford, Jan Bloemendal, and Charles Fantazzi (eds), *Brill's Encyclopaedia of the Neo-Latin World*, vol. 1 (Leiden: Brill), 173–184.
White, Thomas I. (1978), 'Festivitas, Utilitas, et Opes: The Concluding Irony and Philosophical Purpose of Thomas More's *Utopia*', *Albion*, 10: 135–150.

White, Thomas I. (1982), 'Pride and the Public Good: Thomas More's Use of Plato in *Utopia*', *Journal of the History of Philosophy*, 20: 329-354.
Whitehead, Alfred North (1938), *Modes of Thought* (Cambridge: Cambridge University Press).
Whittle, Jane (2010), 'Lords and Tenants in Kett's Rebellion 1549', *Past & Present*, 207: 3-52.
Whitton, Christopher (2019), *The Arts of Imitation in Latin Prose: Pliny's Epistles / Quintilian in Brief* (Cambridge: Cambridge University Press).
Wilde, Lawrence (2017), *Thomas More's Utopia. Arguing for Social Justice* (London: Routledge).
Wilde, Oscar (1986), 'The Soul of Man under Socialism' [1891], in Oscar Wilde, *De Profundis and other Writings*, ed. Hesketh Pearson (London: Penguin), 19-53.
Wilde, Oscar (2003), 'The Soul of Man Under Socialism', in *The Complete Works of Oscar Wilde*, ed. Merlin Holland (London: Collins), 1174-1197.
Wilkins, John (1638), *The Discovery of a World in the Moone* (London: E.G.).
Wilkins, John (1668), *An Essay Towards a Real Character and a Philosophical Language* (London: for Samuel Gellibrand and John Martyn).
Wilkinson, Alexander (2012), 'The Printed Book on the Iberian Peninsula, 1500-1540', in Malcolm Walsby and Graeme Kemp (eds), *The Book Triumphant: Print in Transition in the Sixteenth and Seventeenth Centuries* (Boston: Brill), 78-96.
Williams, Rhys (2016), 'Radical Politics, Recent Exhibitions, and Utopianism Now', *Science Fiction Studies*, 43: 183-187.
Williams, Rhys (2019a), 'Fieldnotes' (unpublished).
Williams, Rhys (2019b), 'Inventing New Worlds: The Age of Manifestos and Utopias', in Gerry Canavan and Eric Carl Link (eds), *The Cambridge History of Science Fiction* (Cambridge: Cambridge University Press), 69-85.
Williamson, James A. (1929) (ed.), *The Voyages of the Cabots and the English Discovery of North America under Henry VII and Henry VIII* (London: Argonaut Press).
Wilson, Kathleen (2004) (ed.), *A New Imperial History: Culture, Identity, and Modernity in Britain and the Empire, 1660-1840* (Cambridge: Cambridge University Press).
Wilson, N. G. (1992), 'The Name Hythlodaeus', *Moreana*, 29: 33-34.
Wilson, Thomas (1553), *The Arte of Rhetorique, for the use of all suche as are studious of Eloquence* (London: Richard Grafton).
Wilson, Thomas (1909), *Wilson's Arte of Rhetorique, 1560*, ed. G. H. Mair (Oxford: Clarendon Press).
Wilss, Wolfram (1982), *The Science of Translation: Problems and Methods* (Tübingen: Gunter Narr Verlag).
Winstanley, Gerrard (1965), 'The Law of Freedom in a Platform' [1652], in *The Works of Gerrard Winstanley*, ed. G. H. Sabine (New York: Russell & Russell), 499-602.
Winston, Jessica (2016), *Lawyers at Play: Literature, Law, and Politics at the Early Modern Inns of Court, 1558-1581* (Oxford: Oxford University Press).
Withington, Phil (2005), *The Politics of Commonwealth: Citizens and Freemen in Early Modern England* (Cambridge: Cambridge University Press).
Withington, Phil (2009a), ' "For This is True or Els I do Lye": Thomas Smith, William Bullein, and Mid-Tudor Dialogue', in Mike Pincombe and Cathy Shrank (eds), *The Oxford Handbook of Tudor Literature: 1485-1603* (Oxford: Oxford University Press), 456-470.
Withington, Phil (2009b), 'Putting the City into Shakespeare's City Comedy', in David Armitage, Conal Condren, and Andrew Fitzmaurice (eds), *Shakespeare and Early Modern Political Thought* (Cambridge: Cambridge University Press), 197-216.

Withington, Phil (2010a), 'Andrew Marvell's Citizenship', in Derek Hirst and Steven N. Zwicker (eds), *The Cambridge Companion to Andrew Marvell* (Cambridge: Cambridge University Press), 102–121.

Withington, Phil (2010b), *Society in Early Modern England: The Vernacular Origins of Some Powerful Ideas* (Cambridge: Polity).

Withington, Phil (2017), 'The Invention of Happiness', in Joanna Innes and Michael Braddick (eds), *Happiness and Suffering in Early Modern England* (Oxford: Oxford University Press), 23–45.

Wittgenstein, Ludwig (1953), *Philosophical Investigations*, trans. Elizabeth Anscombe (Oxford: Blackwell).

Wittkower, Rudolf (1942), 'Marvels of the East: A Study in the History of Monsters', *Journal of the Warburg and Courtauld Institutes*, 5: 159–197.

Wolff, Larry (1994), *Inventing Eastern Europe* (Palo Alto, CA: Stanford University Press).

Wood, Andy (2007), *The 1549 Rebellions and the Making of Early Modern England* (Cambridge: Cambridge University Press).

Wood, Anthony A. (1813), *Athenae Oxoniensis* (London: F. C. and J. Rivington).

Wood, William D. (2013), *Blaise Pascal on Duplicity, Sin, and the Fall: The Secret Instinct* (Oxford: Oxford University Press).

Woodward, Carolyn (1992), 'Sarah Fielding's Self-Destructing Utopia: The Adventures of David Simple', in Dale Spender (ed.), *Living bv the Pen: Early British Women Writers* (New York: Teachers College Press), 65–81.

Wootton, David (1998), 'Friendship Portrayed: A New Account of *Utopia*', *History Workshop Journal*, 45: 29–47.

Wootton, David (1999), 'Utopia: An Introduction', in Thomas More, *Utopia with Erasmus's The Sileni of Alcibiades*, trans. and ed. David Wootton (Cambridge: Hackett), 1–34.

Worms, Laurence (2004), 'Kip, William (fl. c.1585–1618)', in *Oxford Dictionary of National Biography*, www.oxforddnb.com.

Worth-Stylianou, Valerie (1999), '*Translatio* and Translation in the Renaissance: From Italy to France', in Glyn P. Norton (ed.), *The Cambridge History of Literary Criticism*, vol. 1: *The Renaissance* (Cambridge: Cambridge University Press), 127–135.

Wrightson, Keith (2000), *Earthly Necessities: Economic Lives in Early Modern Britain* (New Haven: Yale University Press).

Wriothesley, Charles (1877), *A Chronicle of England during the reigns of the Tudors, from A.D 1485 to 1559*, ed. William Douglas Hamilton (London: Camden Society).

Wu you zi xiang, http://www.wyzxwk.com/.

Wu, Liping (1930), *Shehui zhuyi shi* (Shanghai: Shenghuo shudian).

Wu, Qingyun (1995), *Female Rule in Chinese and English Literary Utopias* (Syracuse, NY: Syracuse University Press).

Yan, Jianfu (2014), *Cong 'shengti' dao 'shijie': Wan Qing xiaoshuo de xin gainian ditue* (Taipei: Guoli Taiwan daxue chuban zhongxin).

Yang, D. (1996), *Calamity and Reform in China: State, Rural Society, and Institutional Change Since the Great Leap Famine* (Stanford, CA: Stanford University Press).

Yanzhul, I. I. (1890), 'Novaya fantaziya na staryuyu temu', *Vestnik Evropy*, & 5.

Yardeni, M. (1972), 'Gueudeville et Louis XIV: Un précurseur du socialisme, critique des structures sociales louis-quatorziennes', *Revue d'histoire moderne et contemporaine*, 19: 598–620.

Yokoyama, Shun-yo (1961), 'Inoue Tsutomu no Yokogao', *Kyodo Kenkyu Happyo-kai Kiyo*, 6–8: 92.
Yoran, Hanan (2010). *Between Utopia and Dystopia: Erasmus, Thomas More, and the Humanist Republic of Letters* (Lanham, MD: Lexington Books).
Zak, Paul J. (2008), *Moral Markets: The Critical Role of Values in the Economy* (Princeton: Princeton University Press).
Zantop, Susanne (1997), *Colonial Fantasies: Conquest, Family, and Nation in Precolonial Germany, 1770–1870* (Durham, NC: Duke University Press).
Zapata, Antonio (1632), *Novus index librorum prohibitorum et expurgatorum* (Seville: Franciscus de Lyra).
Zarrow, P. (2012), *After Empire: The Conceptual Transformation of the Chinese State, 1885–1924* (Stanford, CA: Stanford University Press).
Zavala, Silvio (1955), *Sir Thomas More in New Spain: A Utopian Adventure of the Renaissance* (London: Hispanic and Luso-Brazilian Councils).
Zavala, Vicente (1985), *Fray Juan de Zumárraga*, vol. 1 (Durango: Vizcaya).
Zeller, Eduard (1875), 'Der Platonische Staat in seiner Bedeutung fur die Folgezeit', in Eduard Zeller, *Vortrage und Abhandlungen* (Leipzig: Fues), 68–88.
Zhang, Zaijun (2013), *Caiqing yu fengfan: Kangzhan shiqi de wuda jiaoshou xubian* (Taipei: Duli zuojia).
Zhongguo jingji lunwen xuanbian bianji weiyuanhui (1951), *Yi jiu wu ling nian Zhongguo jingji lunwen xuan*, 6 vols. (Shanghai: Sanlian shudian).
Zhongguo zhongyang bangongting (1956), *Zhongguo nongcun shehui zhuyi gaochao* (Beijing: Renmin shuju).
Zhongguo zhongyang bangongting (1957), *Socialist Upsurge in China's Countryside* (Beijing: Foreign Language Press).
Zhongyang xiju xueyuan yanjiu yanyueshi chuangzuo shi (1951), *Xin ge xuanji* (Beijing: Sanlian shudian).
Zhukovskii, Yu (1866), *Politicheskie i obshchesvtvennye teorii XVIv* (St Petersburg: A. Golovacheva).
Zijlmans, Jori (1999), *Vriendenkringen in de zeventiende eeuw. Verenigingvormen van het informele culturele leven te Rotterdam* (The Hague: Sdu).
Zingarelli, Luciana (1976). 'Vom militanten Journalismus zur Kulturgeschichte', *Ästhetik und Kommunikation*, 7/25: 32–53.
Zsuppán András (2017), 'A kőszívű ember ükunokái', *Heti Válasz*, 17: 110–115.
Zucchini, G. (1986), 'Critica del diritto, difetti della giurisprudenza e problemi di legislazione in utopie del Cinque e Seicento', *Rivista internazionale di filosofia del diritto*, 63: 409–423.
Zuidervaart, Huib (2001), 'Het natuurbeeld van Johannes de Mey (1617–1678), hoogleraar filosofie aan de Illustre School te Middelburg', *Archief* (Mededelingen van het Koninklijk Zeeuwsch Genootschap der Wetenschappen), 1–40.
Zumárraga, Juan de (1951), *Regla cristiana breve para ordenar la vida y tiempo del cristiano que se quiere salvar y tener su alma dispuesta*, ed. José Almoina (Mexico: Jus).

Index

For the benefit of digital users, indexed terms that span two pages (e.g., 52–53) may, on occasion, appear on only one of those pages.

Tables and figures are indicated by *t* and *f* following the page number

absolutism, 91–92, 326, 327, 335, 402, 523
Academia Veneziana, 242–43
Academic Affair (1929-31), 405–6
Accarisio, Alberto, 244–45
Act of Supremacy (1534), 468
Adams, John, 583–84, 588
Adams, Maurice, 468
Adams, Robert, 391–92
Adas, Michael, 557–58
Addams, Jane, 559
Addison, Joseph, 364–65
Adeimantus, 28, 30–31, 32–33
Adorno, Theodor, 572–73, 625n.12
Aegidius, Peter, 186–87, 451. *See also* Giles, Peter
Affair of the Diamond Necklace (1785), 355
Afrofuturism, 656–57
Afrogalactica (film series), 657
Agamben, Giorgio, 572–73
Albanell, Antoni Agusti í, 430–31
Albareda, Anselm Maria, 430–31
Alberti, Battista, 231–32
Albert the Great, 424–25
Alcott, Louisa M., 387–88
Aldine Press, 22–23, 29, 36, 40–41, 43, 44, 47–48, 49–50, 155–56, 168–69, 170, 185–86. *See also* Manutius, Aldus
Alexander I (Tsar of Russia), 396
Alexander II (Tsar of Russia), 395, 399, 467
Allen, Peter, 36–37
Alomar, Gabriel, 433
Alunno, Francesco, 244–45, 434–35
American Declaration of Independence (1776), 307, 345–46, 557, 586–87
American exceptionalism, 557–58
American Revolutionary War (1775-63), aka American War of Independence or American Revolution, 342–43, 345–46, 586–87
Amersin, Ferdinand, 379
Ames, Russell, 136–37
Amyot, Jacques, 193–94
André, Bernard, 125–26
Andreae, Johann Valentin, 204–5
Andriesz, Abraham, 298–99
Aneau, Barthélémy, 211, 248–50, 252–53, 256–61, 339
Anglo-Chinese Wars (1840-2, 1856-60), 463
Anguera, Pere, 432
anti-Catholicism, 328
anti-Semitism, 382–83, 543n.7
Antonius, Wilhelm, 206
Antun, Farah, 496
Antwerp, 75, 106–7, 117, 128, 129–30, 143–44, 145–46, 151, 153–54, 156–57, 211, 218–19, 236, 271, 295–96, 298, 301, 362, 638, 640–41, 651
   location in *Utopia*, 46, 47, 105, 145–46, 385, 617, 621–22, 625–27, 636–37
Aquinas, Thomas, 81–82, 601–2
Arab nationalism, 14, 495–96
Arab socialism, 503–4
Arabic writing, 492–506
   utopian writing in, 493–96
Arahata, Kanson, 466
Arber, Edward, 366–68
architecture, 428–29, 614–16, 617, 618–20, 621, 626, 629, 630–31

Arendt, Hannah, 538–39
Arese, Giulio, 189–90
Aristides, Aelius, 135–36
Aristophanes, 22–23, 30n.11, 37–39, 388–89
Aristotelianism, 123
Aristotle, 21–23, 27, 30n.11, 37–39, 87, 136, 141, 148, 176–77, 198–99, 204–5, 274, 399, 601–2, 620–21
  Politics, 31, 135–36, 138–39, 231–32, 242, 259
Armand, Louis, 330
Armitage, David, 128–29, 612–13
Arnold, Eberhard, 608, 610–11
Arnold, Matthew, 541–42
Arthur, Prince of Wales, 144–45
Ashcroft, Bill, 554–55, 557
Ashley-Cooper, Anthony, 311–12, 323, 525
Asquith, H. H., 457
Association of Bookbinders, 381
Astbury, Katherine, 8–9
Augustine, 13–14, 27, 85–87, 90, 94–95, 100–2, 403–4
  City of God, 23, 87, 215, 401–2, 484
Augustinianism, 123
Augustus (Emperor of Rome), 125–26
Aungerville, Richard, 430–31
Austin, J. L., 251
Austrian School of Economics, 604–5
Avilés, Miguel Angel Ramiro, 11–12
Avs'enko, V. G., 397, 398–99

Babeuf, Gracchus, 482, 496–97
Babits, Mihály, 411–12, 421–22
Bacon, Francis, 211–12, 364–65, 401, 423–24, 468–69, 498–99, 501, 503, 511, 521, 571–72, 644–45
Badoer, Andrea, 125
Bajaber, Musab, 11
Baker-Smith, Dominic, 128, 234, 241–42, 372–73, 539–40, 625–26, 627, 629, 630
Balázs, Mihály, 414–15
Baldwin, William, 293–94
Bale, John, 270–71
Ball, John, 375–76
Bammer, Angelika, 540
Barbier, Antoine-Alexandre, 341–42
Barcelona, 428–29, 431, 434–35
Barcelona Athenaeum, 443
Barcelona Conciliary Seminary, 428–29

Barcelona Episcopal Library, 437
Barker, Nicholas, 40–41
Barlow, William, 509
Barney, R., 29
Barry, Jonathan, 141
Bartók, Béla, 412
Bartolini, Lorenzo, 170
Bartolomeo de Félice, Fortunato, 603–4
Basel, 6–7, 15, 43, 153–54, 156–57, 161–62, 180–81, 185–86, 196–97, 199, 200–1, 204–5, 210–11, 217, 231, 302, 361–62, 449
Basnage de Beauval, Henri, 331
Bataille, George, 618–19
Bataillon, Marcel, 215–16
Ba'th Party, 503–4
Baudaurtius, Willem, 306
Bayle, Pierre, 299, 303–4, 325–26, 329, 338
Bebel, August, 380–81, 382–83
Beccaria, Cesare, 593
Beckert, Sven, 606
Bedell, William, 316–17
Behn, Aphra, 525
Belgium, 428–29, 455
Bellamy, Edward, 420, 484–85, 498–99, 549–50, 551, 630
  Looking Backward, 379, 468–69, 480–81, 538–39, 543–44, 545, 550–51, 617
Bellarmine, Robert, 191–92, 424–25
Belloni, Girolamo, 351–52
Bembo, Pietro, 244–45
Bendemann, Oswald, 459
Benjamin, Walter, 378–79, 386, 387
Bentham, Jeremy, 371, 464–65
Berardi, Branco, 652
Berger, Lina, 403–4
Bernardin de Saint-Pierre, Jacques-Henri, 353, 494, 529
  Paul et Virginie, 527–28
Berneri, Marie Louise, 504
Berns, Jörg Jochen, 195–96, 201
Bessenyei, György, 417–18, 420
Beveridge Plan, 486
Beza, Theodore, 192–93
Bible, 271, 300–1, 319–20, 601–2. *See also* Scripture
  Bible reading, 220, 316–17, 517–18
  Complutense Polyglot Bible, 216–17
  English Bible, 270–71

Latin Vulgate, 191–92
Old Testament, 68–69
Proverbs, 68, 332–33
Biblioteca de Catalunya, 436–37
Biblioteca d'Humanistes, 430–32
Bibliothèque universelle des romans (periodical), 339
Bidelli, Giovan Battista, 189–90
Bidermann, Jakob, 212–13
Birckmann, Arnold, 180–81, 557
Birckmann family, 204
Bíró, Zoltán, 423–24
Bischoff, Nicholas. *See* Episcopius, Nicolaus
Bishop, Jennifer, 8, 15, 278, 279, 318–19
Bishops' Ban (1599), 206
Bismarck, Otto von, 449
Blaeu, Jan, 333
Blaeu, Willem, 191–92
Blanchon, J., 353
Blanqui, August, 621–22
Blatchford, Robert, 538–39, 542–43, 545–46
Bloch, Ernst, 11–12, 13–14, 379, 527, 532, 551–52, 567–78, 615, 617, 626, 631–32
Blosius, Ludovicus, 425–26
Blount, William, 22, 128, 154
Boccaccio, Giovanni, 244–45, 397, 424, 531–32
Bodin, Jean, 207–10, 590
Bodleian Library (Oxford), 43
Bodor, András, 423–24
Boer War (1899-1902), 541–42
Bolshevik, seizure of power, 14
Bolshevik Russia, 395–96
Bolsheviks, 9, 14–15, 395
Bolshevik Third International, 497–98
Bolshevism, 399–400
Bona, Giovanni, 299
Bonvisi/Buonvisi, Antonio, 150–51, 234–36
Bonvisi, Francesco (Cardinal), 235–36
Bonvisi/Buonvisi brothers, 246–47
Bonvisi/Buonvisi family, 233–35, 236–37
Bonvisi/Buonvisi, Vincenzo, 233–34
Borsi, Franco, 614–15
Bowes, Martin, 267, 271–72, 278–79
Boxer revolt (1900), 477–78
Bradbury, Jonathan, 232–33
Bradford Mechanics' Institution, 369
Brand, Russell, 655–56
Brandt, Geerard, 296, 304–5
Brassai, Samuel, 388–89
Brathwait, Richard, 510
Bridges, Nathaniel, 180–81
Brie, Friedrich, 456–57
Brigden, Susan, 235–36
Brissot de Warville, Jacques-Pierre, 352–53
Brixius (Germaine de Brie), 170–71, 178–79
Bronchrost, Gerhard, 390
Browne, Thomas, 509
Bruni, Leonardo, 251–52
Bruno, Hendrik, 296
Buchanan, Ian, 625
Büchner, Georg, 382–83
Büchner, Ludwig, 495–96
Budé, Guillaume, 45, 74, 76–77, 97, 155–61, 176, 198–99, 220–21, 253–56, 384, 513–14
Bullein, William, 293–94
Buonvisi. *See* Bonvisi
Burgh, James, 582, 583–85
Burke, Peter, 36–37, 44, 361–62
Burnet, Gilbert, 5–6, 8–9, 188–89, 307–23, 375, 405, 416–17, 557
Burton, Robert, 510–11, 591–92
Bury, Richard de, 430–31
Busleyden, Jerome, 1–2, 32n.12, 42–43, 45, 73, 74, 76–77, 151, 152, 176, 215, 226, 288–89, 384, 445–46, 513, 626–27
Bustani, Salim al-, 505–6
Bustani, Fu'ad al-, 500–1
Butler, Samuel, 501

Cabanillas Cárdenas, Carlos, 215–16, 217–18, 229–30
Cabet, Étienne, 401, 503–4
Cabot, John, 114–15, 129–30, 133–34
Cachey, Theodore, 42–43
Calatrava, Santiago, 630
Calderini, Domizio, 328–29
Calderón de la Barca, Pedro, 441
Calepino, Ambrogio, 228–29
Callimachus, 62
Cambridge, 42, 206–7, 268–69
Camden, William, 638
Camerarius, Joachim, 192–93
Campanella, Tommaso, 204–5, 211–12, 246–47, 364–65, 382–83, 386, 401, 420, 468–69, 498–99, 511
Campbell, James, 549–50

Campeggi, Lorenzo, 167
Cantijoch, Codina i, 431
Cantiuncula, Claudius, 7, 196–98, 199–204, 203f, 210–11, 231, 449. *See also* Chansonette, Claude
Čapek, Karel, 421
Capel, Arthur, 312
capitalism, 11, 14–15, 380, 395, 402, 480–81, 482–83, 490, 495–96, 504, 505–6, 523, 538–39, 540–41, 544–46, 559–60, 565, 596–98, 604, 607, 608, 610–12, 617, 630
Čapkova, Dagmar, 415
Carey, Daniel, 519–20
Carey, John, 363
Carlyle, Thomas, 364–66, 369–71, 542–43
Carnegie, Andrew, 559
Caron, Johann, 256
Carpenter, Edward, 369–70
Casanova, Giacomo, 530
Cassell's National Library, 363–65
Cassirer, Ernst, 25
Castelar, Emilio, 428–29
Castilian Comuneros (1520-1 uprising), 136–37
Castor, Grahame, 251
Catalonia/Catalunya, 432–33, 434, 440–41, 443
Catherine of Aragon (Queen of England), 219
Catherine the Great (Empress of Russia), 396–97
Cats, Jacob, 296
Cavalcanti, Bartolomeo, 170
Cavanagh, Dermot, 8
Cave, Terence, 5, 123, 130–31, 189, 249–50, 266, 288–89, 374–75
Cayley, Arthur, 361
Cecil, Robert, 132–33
Cecil, William, 120–21, 130–32, 267–70, 271–72, 274, 275, 276–77, 279–80, 288–89
Cell, Gillian T., 130–31
Cervantes, Miguel de, 577
Chaloner, Thomas, 279–80
Chambers, R. W., 92
Chanca, Diego Alvarez, 110, 118
Chansonette, Claude, 7, 196–97. *See also* Cantiuncula, Claudius
Chappey, Jean-Luc, 357
Chappuys, Gabriel, 248–49, 261–64, 335
Charles, Duke of Burgundy; later Prince of Castile, Charles I (King of Spain), and Charles V (Holy Roman Emperor), 105, 120, 145–46, 153–54, 215–16, 239–40, 308, 441, 625–26
Charles II (King of England and Scotland), 308, 312–13, 315, 317–18
Chartists, 369–70, 373, 375, 376–77
Chayanov, Alexander, 408
Cheikho, Louis, 500–1
Chelpanov, Georgii, 404
Chen Tianhua, 480–81
Chernyshevskii, Nikolai, 399
Chiang Kai-shek, 483–84
China, 10–11, 119, 211, 456, 476–91
    Chinese Nationalist Party, 483–84
    Chinese Writers' Union, 488–89
    National Compilation and Translation Bureau of the General Publication Administration (NCTBA), 10–11, 13, 487
    People's Republic of China (PRC), 486
Chiswell, Richard, 313–14
Christians, life of, 100–1
Church, Charlotte, 655–56
Church of England, 127, 133–34
Church of Rome. *See* religion: Catholic Church
Cicero, 37–38, 54–55, 58–59, 78–79, 90, 95, 102–4, 133–34, 135–36, 176–77, 215, 233–34, 252, 256–57, 259, 331–32, 399, 573–74, 634–35
Cisneros, Francisco Jiménez de (Cardinal), 216–17
citizenship, 97, 140–41, 148, 159–60, 268–69, 277, 323, 584
    urban, 140–41, 147
Claeys, Gregory, 580, 600–1
Claparéde, Edouard, 424
Clapperton, Jane Hulme, 551
Clarendon Press, 436–37
Clarion, The (newspaper), 11, 538–46
Clarke, John P., 548–49
Clausewitz, Carl von, 482–83
Clava, Antonius, 156
Clement, John, 155, 235–36, 636–37
Clement XI (Pope), 328
Cleveland, Grover, 559
Cohn, Norman, 462
Coleman, Nathaniel, 621
Colet, John, 21–22, 39, 186

Collège de la Trinité (Lyon), 256–57
College of Bachelors of Both Laws (Louvain), 196–97
College of Santa Catalina (Córdoba), 223–24
Collegium Trium Linguarum (Louvain), 180–81
Collins, John Churton, 470–71
Collinson, Patrick, 277
Colón, Christóbal. *See* Columbus, Christopher
Colón, Hernando, 218
Colt, Jane, 1–2
Columbus, Christopher, 109–10, 113, 118, 119, 218, 219–20
Comenius, Johannes, 415
commercialism, 527, 617
commonality, 92, 93–104, 549–50, 565–66, 618
Commonweal, The (newspaper), 11, 537–40, 541–43, 546–48, 550–52
communal property, principle of, 599
communism, 12–13, 27, 394–95, 407, 462, 486, 496–97, 549–50, 559–60, 597, 610, 652, 653
    and More's *Utopia*, 13–14, 23, 26, 73, 74, 198–99, 200, 201, 363–64, 365–66, 368, 370–71, 374–75, 381, 392, 395–96, 402–3, 409, 451–52, 491, 498–99, 502–3
Communist Party, British, 597, 605
Communist Party, Chinese, 482, 486
Communist Party, Iraq, 503–4
Complutense University (Madrid), 216–17, 428–29
Confucianism, 467–68, 474, 480, 483–84
Confucian fascism, 468
Confucian scholars, 482
Confucian tradition, 479–80, 484
Confucian vocabulary, 476–77
Confucius, 476, 477–78
conscience, 60, 77–78, 79–81, 84, 325–26, 328, 338, 603. *See also* freedom: of conscience; liberty: of conscience; More, Thomas: conscience of
consensus, 68–69, 95, 98–99, 305, 551–52, 661
Cool, Jacob, 638
Cooper, James Fenimore, 387–88
Coornhert, Dirck Volckertszoon, 303
Cop, Guillaume, 156
Córdoba, Francisco Roco Campofrío y, 223–24

Cornish Rebellion (1497), aka Cornish Revolt, 115, 240–41
Corpus Christi College (Oxford), 267, 268–69, 275, 278–79, 288, 374–75
Corso, Rinaldo, 244–45
Cortés, Hernán, 221–22
Corvinus, Matthias (King of Hungary and Croatia), 413–14
cosmopolitanism, 123–24
Council of Trent (1545-63), 246, 492–93
    post-Tridentine Church, 190–91
Counter-Reformation, 190–91, 192, 246. *See also* Reformation
Covarrubias Orozco, Sebastián de, 229
Crane, Walter, 375–76
Croke, Richard, 160–61
Crom, Mattheus, 271
Cromwell, Oliver, 458
Cromwell, Thomas, 120–21, 235–36
Cronos, 29, 31
Csíkszentmihályi, Mihály, 412
Cultural Revolution, Mao, 476
Cuniculus (pseud.), 364–65
Curtright, Travis, 90
Czigány, Lóránt, 417–18
Czigányik, Zsolt, 10

D'Ablancourt, Nicolas, 361–62
da Chio, Giacomo, 414–15
Dadich, Scott, 565–66
da Gama, Vasco, 107
Dai Liuling, 10–11, 13, 489–90, 491
D'Alembert, Jean le Rond, 345–46
D'Anghiera, Peter Martyr, 74–75, 76, 79, 130–31
Dante, 244–45
Darwin, Charles, 482–83, 495–96
Dashkevich, N. P., 404
Davenport, Randi Lise, 215–16, 217–18, 229–30
Davis, J. C., 580
Davis, Lennard, 520
Day, John, 271
Déry, Tibor, 421–22
de Bergerac, Cyrano, 529, 530
de Bois, Lois, 425–26
de Breen, Daniel, 297
de Brie, Germaine. *See* Brixius
de Estella, Diego, 298–99
de Gama, Vasco, 74–75

de Keyser, Hendrick, 302
de La Court, Pieter, 296–97
de Laet, Hans, 295–96
de la Serre, Jean Puget, 296
De Fieux Mouhy, Charles, 530
de Lom d'Arce, Louis-Armand, 326
de Lyra, Nicolas, 150
de Mesmes, Jean-Antoine, 328
de Mey, Johannes, 296–97
de Querlon, Anne-Gabriel Meusnier, 184–85, 189–90, 342–43
de Rennes, Brice, 493, 496–97
de Saint-Simon, Henri, 379
de Schrijver. *See* Grapheus
de Witt, Johan, 301
Decembrio, Pier Candido, 21
Declaration of the Rights of Man and the Citizen (1789), 345–46, 586–87
decorum, 57, 102–4, 198, 285
DeCoursey, Matthew, 91–92
Defoe, Daniel, 364–65, 441–42, 465–66, 494, 526–27, 554
del Pozo, Joan Manuel, 442
Delcourt, Marie, 176, 187
Deleuze, Gilles, 652
Deloynes, Francis, 156
Demetrius, 187–88
Démeunier, Jean-Nicolas, 338–39
Demos, T. D., 617–18
Demosthenes, 38–39
Deneire, Tom, 189
Dent, J. M., 363–64
Dery, Mark, 656–57
Derham, William, 530, 531–32
Desmarez, Jean (aka Paludanus), 45, 74–75, 76–77, 152, 255
despotism, 353, 354–55, 498–99
Dewey, John, 482–83, 501
Dhúill, Caitríona Ní, 570–71
dialogue, 3–4, 6, 14, 15, 20–21, 22, 26, 29, 30, 31–32, 33, 43, 45–47, 53–54, 55, 59, 60, 66, 67–69, 71, 72, 79–80, 89, 96, 101, 105–6, 131–32, 167, 171, 176–77, 186, 190–91, 233–34, 236–37, 245, 246–47, 262, 278–94, 300–1, 330–31, 372–73, 413–15, 416–17, 447, 460, 494–95, 511–12, 515–16, 524, 527, 538–39, 540, 564, 573–74, 593, 594, 596, 599, 642–43, 655

Dibdin, T. F., 362, 371, 376
Dickens, Charles, 364–65, 387–88
Diderot, Denis, 345–46, 527
Die Schiltbürger, 205–6, 212–13
Dietrich, Ottmar, 456–57
Dietrick, Linda, 529
diglossia, 176
Dillon, J. M., 29
Diogenes, 269
Dionisotti, Carlo, 170
Dioscorides, 37–39
Dirlik, Arlif, 485–86
Disraeli, Benjamin, 9, 369–70
Doctors' Commons, 1–2
Dolet, Étienne, 233–34, 236–37, 251–52
Doni, Anton Francesco, 8, 205, 232–33, 236–37, 238–39, 241–42, 246–47, 263–64, 437–39
Donner, H. W., 447, 459
Dornau, Caspar, 183, 192–93, 211–12
Dorp, Maarten van, 149–50, 185–86, 196–98
D'Ors, Eugeni, 434
Drake, Francis, 120–21
Drapers' Company, 267, 270–71, 270n.3
dream, 95–96, 134, 246–47, 351, 371–72, 379, 419, 443, 446, 477–78, 500, 504–5, 509–10, 525, 529, 530–31, 532, 533, 541, 543, 549–50, 556, 562, 615–16, 622, 648, 653, 654–55
Drexel, Jeremias, 191–92
Du Bellay, Joachim, 251–52, 256, 263–64
Du Fresnoy, Nicolas Lenglet, 325
Duncan, H. H., 546, 547
Dunmore, Margaret, 551
Dury, John, 511
Dutch East India Company, 299
Dutch Golden Age, 189, 193, 304–5
Dutch Republic, 296–97, 301, 303, 304, 305, 324–25, 326, 332–33, 339–40. *See also* United Provinces
Dutch Revolt (c.1566/8-1648), 189
dystopia (literary genre), 411–12, 421–22, 525n.4, 544–45
dystopia (type of place), 363, 476, 504–6, 517–18, 561–62, 577, 580, 594–95, 645–46

Eaton, Ruth, 614–15
Eberlin, Johann, 201

Ebert, Friedrich, 448-49
Economic Miracle (1954-72), 474-75
Eden, Kathy, 60-61, 100-1
Eden, Richard, 130-32
Edict of Fontainebleau (1685), 327
Edict of Nantes (1598), 351-52
education, 36, 39-40, 179, 181-82, 197, 216-17, 238, 242-43, 268-70, 322, 345-46, 364-65, 376-77, 385-87, 392-93, 395, 406, 415, 424, 428-29, 471-72, 477-78, 482, 483, 489, 494, 495, 510-12, 527, 543-44, 579-80, 585, 597, 599-600, 604-5, 644-45. *See also* Utopia: education in
Edward VI (King of England), 235-36, 265, 267-68, 269-70, 279-80
Egger, Vernon, 498, 499
Egmond, Cornelius, 191-92
Elizabeth I (Queen of England), 120-21, 223-24, 295-96
Ellis, F. S., 365-66, 367
Elsky, Stephanie, 67, 94-95
Elton, G. R., 92
Elyot, Thomas, 319-20
Elzevier, Abraham, 333
Emancipation Act (1861), 399
embeddedness, Polanyi's concept of, 607
Emmeri, Jacques, 333
Empedocles, 29
enclosure, 99-100, 116, 144, 240-41, 276, 292, 344-45, 369-70, 596, 597-98, 601, 604. *See also* sheep/sheep-farming
Engels, Friedrich, 380-81, 392, 447-48, 462, 466-67, 496-97, 544-45, 604
England, 22, 24, 36, 39, 41-42, 44, 82-83, 90-91, 105-7, 125, 126, 127, 130-31, 186, 216-17, 218, 219, 223-24, 234-35, 265-66, 271, 273, 277, 280, 288, 322, 344, 369-70, 399-400, 417-18, 419, 446-47, 477-78, 482, 490, 502, 511, 520-21, 530, 554
   colonial settlements and settlers, 115, 132
   colonization, 116-17, 131-32, 554n.3
   colonialism and colonists, 6-7, 10, 49-50, 111-12, 114-15, 329
   economic problems, 3, 115, 116
   economy, 131-32, 137-38, 139-41, 143-44, 147, 401, 405-6
   urban ('corporate') system, 15, 135-48, 276-77

   and *Utopia*, 28, 42-43, 46-47, 67-68, 114-15, 128-29, 176, 195-96, 211, 220, 222-23, 224-25, 240-41, 285-86, 319-20, 321-22, 345-46, 369, 398, 415, 424-25, 441-42, 514-15, 523, 569, 607, 632. *See also* London: and Amaurot
Enlightenment, 8-9, 187-88, 309, 322, 341, 343, 347, 350, 356, 492-93, 580, 581, 582
Epicureanism, 75, 79-80, 87-88, 246, 371
Epicureans, 27, 79-80, 87-88
Epicurus, 25, 27, 31
epikeia (reasonableness), 198
epiphonema(ta), 54-55, 57
Episcopius (aka Bishcoff), Nicolaus, 180-81, 185-86, 204
equality, 92, 93, 94-95, 97, 99, 100-2, 119, 138-39, 143, 145-46, 147, 198-99, 200, 254-55, 290, 348, 394-95, 399, 408, 497, 523, 529, 531-32, 538-39, 557, 581, 586, 587-88, 593, 601-2, 607, 614
equity, 7, 11-12, 142, 198-200, 584, 592, 602
Erasmianism, 91-92, 215-16, 236-37, 298
Erasmus, Desiderius, 1-2, 8-9, 20, 27, 38-39, 44, 47-48, 60-61, 69, 74-75, 76, 78-80, 97, 128, 159, 170-71, 176, 185-86, 189, 196-97, 216-17, 220, 236-37, 253-54, 256-57, 268-69, 289, 298, 302-4, 305-6, 324-25, 390, 397, 425-26, 435-36, 440-41, 471-72
   Adages/Adagia, 27, 40-41, 44, 64, 67-68, 67n.6, 74, 78, 153-54, 155-56, 163, 177-78, 198-99, 523
   Annotationes in Novum Testamentum, 170-71
   Antibarbari, 44
   Budé and, 155-58, 160
   Cantiuncula (Chansonette) and, 196-97, 449
   Ciceronianus, 236-37
   Colloquies, 79-80, 324-25, 326, 430
   Declamatio de morte, 161, 163-65
   De Copia, 39, 163-65, 177-78
   De ratione studii, 38-39, 163-65
   Disticha catonis, 149-50
   Education of a Christian Prince, 75, 93, 153-54, 170
   Enarratio allegorica in primum psalmum, 149-50
   Enchiridion militis christiani, 297

Erasmus, Desiderius (*cont.*)
   Epigrammata, 156–57, 161–62, 217
   Epistola ad Dorpium, 154, 163–65
   Exomologesis sive modus confitendi, 201
   Institutio principis christiani. *See* Erasmus: Education of a Christian Prince
   Llibre de Civilitat pueril, 431, 432
   Lucubrationes, 156–57, 185–86
   ludic dimensions and, 183–85
   More and, 1–2, 22, 42, 75, 90, 91–92, 128, 154–56, 160, 169–70, 176, 183–85, 234, 305, 315, 430–31, 489–90. *See also* Erasmus: *Praise of Folly*
   Moria/Moriae Encomium. *See* Erasmus: *Praise of Folly*
   Opera Omnia, 331–32
   Praise of Folly, 33, 58–59, 93, 130, 149–50, 153–54, 160–61, 163–65, 167, 168, 177–78, 183, 184–85, 234–35, 279–80, 297, 324–25, 326, 332–33, 338–39, 430, 433–34, 436–37, 439–40, 523
   quarrel with Dorp, 149–50, 196–98
   Querela pacis, 161
   translations of Euripides, 42
   translations of Lucian, 1–2, 26, 156–57, 161, 168–70, 183–85, 205
   Utopia and, 6–7, 13–14, 20, 31–32, 41–42, 45, 73, 97, 149, 150–52, 153–54, 155, 156–57, 160–63, 165, 167, 169, 177–78, 186, 190–91, 207–10, 217, 226, 253–54, 268–69, 270–71, 297, 384, 385–86, 450–51, 513
Ernst, Max, 9, 378–79, 382
Erzberger, Matthias, 448–49
Espinal, Alonso de, 219–20
euchronia (good era), 524–25, 533–36, 538n.3, *See also* ouchronos
eudaimonia (flourishing), 25
eugenics, principles of, 499
Euripides, 37–39, 40–41, 42
eutopia/Eutopia (good place), 72–73, 87, 122–23, 131–33, 134, 238, 523, 533, 572–73, 579–80, 622–23. *See also* outopia/Outopia (no place)

Fabian Society, 497–98
Fabra, Pompeu, 431, 434–35
Fabyan's Chronicle, 269–70
Fahy, Conor, 237
Fáj, Attila, 413–14
fantasy, 27, 31, 42–43, 89–90, 94–95, 113, 303, 397, 399, 433, 554–56, 557–58, 559–60, 565–66, 570, 615
fantasy (genre), 33, 519–20, 524
Farabi, al- 492, 494–95, 500–1
Farkas, Ákos, 423
Fassmann, David, 416–17
Fénelon, François, 326, 399, 417–18, 494, 496–97, 526–27
Febvre, Lucien, 50
Feinberg, Walter, 576
felicific calculus, 371
Fell, John, 180–81
Ferdinand II (King of Aragon and Castile), 219–20
Ferguson, Adam, 532
Ferguson, J. C., 477–78
Ferré, Caballeria i, 431
Ferrero, Bonificio, 243
Ferrero, Filiberto, 243
Ferrero, Pier Francesco, 243
Fetscher, Iring, 570
Ficino, Marsilio, 21–22, 25, 27
Fielding, Henry, 213
First World War (1914-1918), 455–56
Fischart, Johann, 205–6
Fitzgerald, earl of Kildare, 115
Fitzwilliam, William, 132–33
Flanders, 67, 72, 106–7, 128, 142–43, 154, 195–96, 215, 298, 301
Florence, 2, 3, 4, 6–7, 39, 84–85, 135–36, 168–71, 231–33
Foigny, Gabriel de, 525
Fokkema, Douwe, 480
Foner, Philip, 487–88
Forster, W. E., 369
Forsyth, Katherine, 235–36
Fortunati, Vita, 524
Fortunio, Giovan Francesco, 244–45
Foulis, Andrew, 180–81, 187–88
Foulis, Robert, 187–89, 307, 557
Foulis brothers, 180–81, 187–89
Fourier, Charles, 401, 419, 482, 496–97

Fourier, Jean-Baptiste Joseph, 379
Fox, Richard, 268–69
Foxe, John, 270, 509
France, 125–26, 129–30, 143–44, 229–30, 241–42, 248–49, 251–54, 255, 256–57, 262–63, 297, 303, 318–19, 325–26, 327–28, 332–33, 338, 341, 342–43, 344, 345–46, 349, 350, 351, 352–53, 390–91, 396–97, 417–18, 455, 527–28, 529, 530, 533–34, 581
Francini, Antonio, 168
Frankfurt am Main, 182, 183, 192–93, 641–42
Frankfurt Book Fair, 182, 195–96, 204, 206, 206n.9, 207–10
Frankfurt Council, 182
Frankfurt School, 572–73
Franklin, Benjamin, 583–84
Frederick the Great (King of Prussia), 482–83
Free, John, 163–65
freedom, 227, 228–29, 305, 322, 323, 346, 347, 370–71, 398, 418, 446–47, 448–49, 457–58, 502, 544–46, 548, 573–74, 575, 589. *See also* liberty *and* rights and freedoms
  artistic/creative freedom, 430, 657
  of conscience, 338, 591–92. *See also* liberty: of conscience
  of the press, 586
  religious freedom, 81–82, 192–93, 351–52, 411, 412–13, 414–15, 425–27, 437–39, 470, 485, 582, 586, 587–88
  of speech, 468, 470, 531, 582
  of thought, 462–63, 468, 470, 504–5, 621
  of a town or city, 140–41
French Revolution, 9, 341, 353–57, 395, 419, 446, 496–97
Freund, Michael, 456–57
Frevert, Ute, 602–3, 605–6, 607, 612–13
Froben, Johann, 14–15, 43, 45, 53–54, 149–50, 151, 153–54, 156–57, 161–65, 167, 168–69, 176, 180–81, 182, 185–86, 190–91, 201, 204, 217, 378–79, 384, 385, 627–28
Frobisher, Martin, 120–21
Frye, Northrop, 524
Fuchs, Eduard, 9, 378–79, 381–87, 392–93, 450
Fukuyama, Francis, 612

Fuller, Buckminster, 619, 621
Fuller, Mary C., 133–34
Fundamental Constitutions of Carolina, 323
futurism, 9, 372, 433

Gabriele, Jacopo (aka Giocomo), 244–45
Gagliari, Achille, 299
Galarça, Agustin de, 225–26
Galen, 156–58, 159, 160–61, 176–77, 389–90
Galton, Francis, 497–98
garden cities, 371–72, 622–23, 626
gardens, 27, 28n.8, 46, 66, 369–70, 371–72, 614, 616, 617–18, 620–25, 626–27, 628–29, 631–32, 636–37, 654
Garden of Eden, 31, 419, 532, 546, 580, 634–36, 644–45
Garden of Epicurus, 27, 31
Gaza, Theodorus, 38–39
Geddes, Patrick, 616, 622–23
Geldenhauer (or Geldenhouwer), Gerard (or Gerhard), 45, 152, 178–79, 288–89, 295–96, 390, 513. *See also* Noviomagus, Gerardus
Gellius, Aulus, 155
Genkel, Aleksandr G., 12–13, 395–96, 409–10
Gentili, Alberico, 207–10, 209f
George, Henry, 369–70
Geréb, László, 422, 423
German Peasants' War (1524-25), aka Great Peasants' War/Revolt, 201, 497, 601
German People's Party, Weimar Republic, 449–50
German Philosophical Society, 456
German Social Democratic Party, 380, 385–86
Germany, 10, 444, 448, 449–50, 455, 456, 457, 458–59, 497, 526–27, 530, 537–38, 608–9, 610–11, 638
  trends in seventeenth- and eighteenth-century fiction, 212–14
Gershoni, Israel, 497–98
Giddens, Anthony, 461
Gilbert, Sir Humphrey, 107n.2, 114–15, 122, 133–34
Giles, Peter, 13–14, 45–46, 60–61, 75, 78, 97, 128, 145–46, 149–50, 151, 152, 153–54, 155–56, 160, 161, 162, 176, 202

Giles, Peter (*cont.*)
    character in *Utopia*, 20, 42–43, 46, 105, 106–7, 108, 156–57, 165, 201, 211, 345–46, 385, 515, 523, 598–99, 623–24, 625, 627–29, 631, 636–37
    letters to/from in *Utopia*, 42–43, 45–46, 48–49, 56, 59, 60–61, 62, 68, 73, 77, 106–7, 150, 151, 152, 155, 158, 160–61, 162, 163–65, 168–69, 178–79, 188, 202–4, 226, 232–33, 241–42, 255, 281–82, 288–89, 291, 384, 422, 437, 440, 451, 483, 489–90, 513, 515, 516–17, 518–19, 626–27, 631, 634–35
Giunta, Bernardo, 168
Giunta, Filippo, 168
Giuntine Press, 168–69
Gjerpe, Kristin, 233–34, 238–39
Gladstone, William, 374
Glasgow University, 180–81
    Glasgow University Press, 180–81, 187–88
Glasse, John, 537
Glaucon, 29–31, 33
Glazemaker, H., 296
Glissant, Eduard, 653–54
Glorious Revolution (1688), 308
God's World (*Mir Bozhii*) (journal), 400
Godwin, Francis, 511–12, 529
Godwin, William, 582
Goethe, Johann Wolfgang von, 389, 532–33
Goethe, J. W., 465–66
Golden Age, 29, 31, 112–13
Goldsmith, Oliver, 441–42
Goldsmiths' Company, 265, 267–68, 271–72, 275, 278–79, 318–20, 374–75
Gompers, Samuel, 559
Gondomar Manuscript, 217–18, 226–28, 437–39
Goodwin, Barbara, 581
Gordon, Andrew, 277
Gordon, Lady Duff, 364–65
Gorev, Boris, 408–9
Gott, Samuel, 511–12
Gottlieb, Erika, 419
Götz, Norbert, 602–3
Gourmont, Gilles de, 43, 45, 160–61, 217, 218, 253–54
Graf, Urs, 385

Grafton, Anthony, 36–37
Grafton, Richard, 271
Granada, 441
Granovetter, Mark, 606
Grapheus (aka Graphey or de Schrijver), Cornelius, 45, 152, 160–61, 168–69, 180–81, 288–89
Grapheus, Johannes, 180–81
Graphic, The (magazine), 363–64
Graunger, Agnes, 1–2
Gravier, Charles (comte de Vergenes), 342–43
Great Depression (1929-33), 470, 608
Great Encyclopedia of Utopias, 658
Great Kanto Earthquake (1923), 469
Great Leap Forward (1958-62), 476, 488, 490–91
Greek (language), 25, 26–28, 31, 33, 39–40, 42, 54–55, 62, 66, 72–73, 132, 156–58, 176–77, 179, 180–81, 186, 187–89, 193, 205–6, 256–57, 310–11, 317–18, 363, 403–4, 471, 501, 569, 638, 640–41, 648, 649, 654. *See also* More: and Greek; translations from Greek
    books, 6, 36–38, 41–42, 51–52, 168, 169, 314. *See also* Hythloday: books
    printing of, 40–41, 43, 160–61
    in *Utopia*, 20, 26–27, 31–32, 37–39, 40, 47–48, 49–52, 87, 105, 106–7, 128, 152, 155, 158–59, 161–62, 176–78, 185–86, 245, 250–51, 254–55, 290, 291, 363–64, 391
Greek Anthology, 21–22, 56
Greek Gnosticism, 81
Greenblatt, Stephen, 62, 115, 460
Greene, Roland, 251
Gregory I (Pope), 228–29
Grendler, Paul F., 231–32
Grey, Edward, 457
Griffin, Martin, 310–11
Griffo, Francesco, 40–41
Grocyn, William, 21–22, 39
Grosse, Henning the Younger, 207–10
Grotius, Hugo, 303, 581
Gryphe, Sébastien, 236–37
Gueudeville, Nicolas, 8–9, 324–40, 437
Guicciardini, Francesco, 170
Guldi, Jo, 612–13

gulliveriads, 417–18, 421
Guthkelch, A. C., 186
Gutiérrez, Cypriano, 223–24, 225–26
Gutzwiller, Kathryn, 54–55
Guy, John, 33
György Rákóczi II (ruler of Transylvania), 415

Haberdashers' Company, 269–70
Haddon, Walter, 295–96
Hadfield, Andrew, 6–7, 130–31
Hake, Sabine, 386
Hakluyt, Richard, 107–8
Haldane, Richard, 457
Halévy, Élie, 503–4
Hale, Edward Everett, 559–60
Hall, Edward, 125–26, 280
Hall, Joseph, 206–10, 209f, 212–13, 364–65, 511–12, 642–43, 646–47
Hall, William, 180–81
Halley, Edmond, 530
Hanseatic League, 136–37, 142–43
Hanson, Ingrid, 11
happiness, 25, 56, 78–80, 85, 99, 227, 258, 312–13, 316, 317, 322–23, 334, 345–46, 347, 352, 353, 354, 357, 370–71, 394–95, 415, 416–17, 418, 419–20, 472–74, 473t, 479–80, 504, 505, 532, 562, 583–84, 585, 586, 588, 593, 601, 610
Harp, Jerry, 601–2
Harpsfield, Nicholas, 21, 235–36
Harrington, James, 484, 511–12, 583, 584–85
Harrington, John, 134
Hartig, Irmgard, 356
Hartlib, Samuel, 511
Hartrich, Eliza, 6–7
Hatzenberger, Antoine, 343
Hawkins, John, 120–21
Hayes, Edward, 133–34
health, 19, 20, 27–28, 29, 60, 403–4, 446–47, 464, 495, 505, 572, 599–600
Hedonius, 79–80
Hegel, G. W. F., 487–88, 570
Heinsius, Anthonie, 328
Heinsius, Nicolaas, the Elder, 302
Hellenism, 6
Hélvetius, Claude Adrien, 343
Henri III (King of France), 261, 262–63

Henry VII (King of England), 114–15, 134, 144–45. *See also* Tudor, Henry
Henry VIII (King of England), 2, 83–84, 105, 113–14, 120–21, 125, 127, 129–30, 167, 179, 215, 219, 223–24, 236, 239–40, 268, 271, 334, 335, 344, 413–14, 425, 441, 453–54, 493, 625–26
Hentenius, Johannes, 190–91
Herodian, 37–39, 41
Herodotus, 37–39, 176–77
Herrera, Fernando de, 223–24
Hertzka, Theodor, 379, 380
Herzl, Theodor, 379, 380
Herzogin Anna Amalia Library (Weimar), 387–88
Hesiod, 20, 22–23, 29, 31, 40
Hesychius, 37–39, 41
Hexter, J. H., 471, 513
Heyer, Andreas, 211–12
Heywood, Ellis, 70–71
Hiatt, Alfred, 12
Hill, Peter, 10–11
Hilton, Rodney, 487–88
Hirai, Masao, 470–71
Hirsch, Felix, 458
Hitler, Adolf, 458, 614–15
Hobbes, Thomas, 320, 423–24, 461, 525, 532
Hobbing, Reimar, 454–55
Hobbs, Angela, 6
Hodgson, William, 582, 586–88
Höfener, Heiner, 204n.8
Hogarth Press, 419
Holbein, Ambrosius, 102–4, 103f, 163–65, 384–85, 513, 628f, 636–37
Holbein, Hans the Younger, 14, 47–48, 102–4, 163–65, 166f, 207–10, 385, 407, 437
Holberg, Ludvig, 530–32
Holland, Owen, 540
Holt, John, 21, 39
Holy Trinity, 414–15
Homann, Johann Baptist, 212–13, 642–43
Homer, 20, 22–23, 37–39, 40–41, 49, 108, 482–83, 569
homo economicus, 599, 608
Honda, Kensho, 470
Hooghe, Romeyn de, 298–99

hope, 16, 69–70, 77, 86, 134, 196, 222–23, 254, 256, 355, 371–72, 376–77, 408, 419, 468, 496–97, 505, 509–10, 519–20, 527, 545, 548–49, 565–66, 568, 569, 570, 571, 574, 575–76, 577–78, 617, 621–22, 640–41, 644–45, 657, 661
Horace, 22, 58–59, 177–78, 183
Horváth, Iván, 414–15
Hosei University, 470
Hosington, Brenda, 256, 257, 335
House of Orange, 296
Houston, Chloë, 11, 46–47, 524, 538–39
Howard, Ebenezer, 371–72
Howard, Thomas, 3rd Duke of Norfolk, 115
Hower, Jessica S., 6–7
Huber, Ernst Rudolf, 456–57
Hudson, W. H., 498–99, 500
Hu Feng, 488–89
Hughes, Robert, 615
humanism, 89–90, 179, 180, 270–71, 276, 395–96, 560, 634
   Christian, 4, 425–26, 447
   civic, 265–66, 268–69, 276
   Erasmian, 48, 193, 196–204, 223
   Italian, 168
   Northern, 237
   Renaissance, 3, 136, 331, 339, 579
   renewal of classical, 185–90
   Scottish, 308–9
   Spanish, 219–23
humanist
   circles/networks, 1–2, 4, 6–7, 13–14, 45, 46, 50, 131–32, 156–57, 196, 201, 232–33, 273
   curriculum/education, 47, 197, 205–6, 268–69
   readers, 43, 150
   reform, 170–71, 269–70
   scholarship, 43, 135–36
   writings, 270, 273–74, 324–25, 328–29
humanists, 43, 45–46, 91–92, 95–98, 216–17, 227, 235–36, 265–66, 268, 269, 275, 449, 637–39, 640–42
   civic, 276
   Dutch, 45
   English, 156–57
   Erasmian, 217–18
   European, 51–52, 176

   French, 156, 178–79, 182
   Italian, 229–30, 236–37
   Latin and, 176, 228–29
   Northern, 44, 45, 93, 128, 152, 590
human rights
   freedom of conscience. *See* freedom: of conscience; liberty: of conscience
   humanization of criminal law, 592–93
   invention of, 579
   phrase, 579
   in Utopia, 588–90
   Utopia and, 581–88
Humboldt, Wilhelm, 389
Hume, David, 91–92, 464–65
Humphrey, Duke of Gloucester, 21
Hundred Years War (1337-1453), 127
Hungarian Academy of Sciences, 422–23
Hungarian Socialist Workers' Party, 425–26
Hungary, 10, 411–27, 596–97
Hunne, Richard, 83–84
Hunt, Lydia, 437–39
Hunt, Lynn, 582, 587
Huonker, Thomas, 381–82
Hurtado de Mendoza, Domingo, 219–20
Hu Shi, 482–83
Hutcheson, Frances, 187–88
Hutten, Ulrich von, 150–51, 167
Hutterite Church, moral economy, 608–11
Hutton, Arthur Wollaston, 373
Huxley, Thomas, 481
Huygens, Christiaan, 331–32
Huygens, Constantijn, 296
Hyndman, Henry, 541–42
Hythloday, Raphael (character in *Utopia*), 14, 20, 26–27, 31–32, 33, 36, 37–38, 42–43, 45–47, 48, 66, 68, 69, 72, 73, 74–75, 95–96, 100, 101, 105, 111–12, 128–30, 135–36, 152, 165, 175, 178–79, 204–5, 215, 235–36, 239–40, 248–49, 254–55, 256, 262, 286–87, 293, 321–22, 363–64, 368–70, 371, 372–73, 460, 465–66, 498–99, 513–14, 515, 518–19, 554, 579–80, 582–83, 588–89, 592, 594, 596, 597–99, 601–2, 619–20, 621–22, 623–24, 625, 628–29, 631–32
   Book One, 23, 53–54, 63, 64–65, 78–79, 133–34, 138, 152, 159–60, 201, 211, 236, 548

Book Two, 64–66, 68–69, 138–39, 159–60, 245, 248–49, 290–91, 336
books, 22–23, 36–52, 163, 168
debate with Morus, 96–97, 320–21, 344–46, 523, 594, 629
on England and English affairs, 67–68, 94–95, 116–17, 220, 222–23, 370–71
on Europe, 25–26, 95–96, 98–100, 240–41, 290, 601
at Morton's house, 115, 413–14, 593
Morus as his amanuensis/transcriber, 61–62, 158, 281–82, 451, 515, 516–17, 623–24, 626–27
speaker of nonsense, 419, 523–24
style and tone, 63–64, 282–83, 284–86, 291–92
travels, 23, 42–43, 47–48, 105–7, 108, 109, 113, 225–26, 238–39, 396, 514–15
on war and standing armies, 128–29, 241

Ibn Tufayl, 492
iconoclasm, 201
idealism, 16, 50, 363, 399–400, 459, 555, 568–69, 570, 577, 629
I.D.M.G.T., 252–53
imagination, 11, 36–37, 51, 99, 107, 108, 132, 133–34, 160, 170, 171, 278–79, 285, 291, 296–97, 409, 414–15, 423, 445, 495, 500, 502, 530, 537, 545, 548–49, 551–52, 568, 572–73, 578, 618–19, 623, 629, 632, 635, 652, 662
imperialism, 15–16, 123–24, 128–29
imperial settler ideology, 11
imperial settler utopia, 556–60
Index of Prohibited Books, 184, 191–92, 224–25, 233
individualism, 485, 495–96, 525, 545–46, 547, 614–15
inequality, 89–90, 94–95, 101, 145, 200, 284–85, 348, 596–99, 611, 612–13. *See also* equality
injustice, 99, 198–99, 200, 331, 545, 546. *See also* justice
  social injustice, 285–86, 350, 357, 623–24
Inoue, Tsutomu, 10–11, 464–65, 466–67, 478–79, 481
internationalism, 176, 180–82, 364–65
invention, 250–54

Ireland, 6–7, 111–12, 114–15, 121–22, 123–24, 126–27, 130, 131–33, 134, 307
Irish Rebellion (1641), 316–17
Isabel II (Queen of Spain), 428–29
Isabella of Portugal (Holy Roman Empress), 217
Ishay, Micheline, 581
Islamism, 504–5
Italy, 2, 4, 21–22, 39, 41–42, 168, 205, 212–13, 231, 232–34, 241–42, 246–47, 318, 455–56, 498, 523, 635, 651

Jacobsz, Jan, 296
Jamaican Servant Act (1681), 322
James, William, 559
Jameson, Fredric, 538–39, 561–62, 616–17, 655
Jankowski, James, 497–98
Japan, 10–11, 463, 463*t*, 464*t*, 467, 469–70, 474–75, 477, 478–79, 481, 483–84, 485–86, 526–27, 643
Jardine, Lisa, 197–98
Jefferson, Thomas, 307, 323, 557, 583
Jinlin Women's College (Nanjing), 483
John Paul II (Pope), 425–26
Johnson, P. Louise, 10
Johnson, Samuel, 532–33
Johnston, Rachel, 309–10
Jókai, Mór, 411–12, 419–20
Jombert, Alexandre, 342–43
Jones, Owen, 655–56
Jones, Royston, 217
Jonktys, Daniel, 296–97
Julius Caesar, 125–26
Jurieu, Pierre, 325–26, 338
justice, 25, 28–29, 84–85, 86, 97, 99, 119, 132–33, 169–70, 198–99, 200, 231–32, 243–44, 257, 315, 316, 328, 330, 344–45, 351, 353, 399–400, 401, 557, 576, 584, 591, 593, 640. *See also* injustice
  social justice, 405–6, 447, 591, 593. *See also* social injustice
Juvenal, 42, 58–59, 328–29

Kagan, Judith, 395–96
Kaganovich, B., 405
Kahneman, Daniel, 611–12
Kaiser, Karl, 382
Kang Youwei, 479–80

Kant, Immanuel, 482–83, 571–72, 603–4, 614, 618, 620–21
Kapor, Vladimir, 527
Kaposi, Krisztina, 415–16
Karamzin, Nikolai, 395–96, 398–99
Kardos, Tibor, 422, 423
Kareev, Nikolai, 399–400
Karinthy, Frigyes, 411–12, 421
Kastan, David Scott, 36–37
Kato, Asatori, 469
Kautsky, Karl, 13–15, 379, 380–81, 383, 389–91, 392–93, 399–400, 401, 402, 403–4, 405–6, 409, 425–26, 450, 490, 597–98
Keek, Abraham, 518–19
Keene, Derek, 139–40
Kelen, Ferenc, 10, 422–23
Kelmscott Press, 365–68, 369f. *See also Utopia*, English translations: Robinson (Kelmscott edn)
Kempis, Thomas à, 299
Kennedy, John F., 559–60
Kepler, Johannes, 641–42
Kern, Darcy, 7–8
Keymis, Lawrence, 134, 509–10
Keynes, John Maynard, 603
Kiesel, Helmuth, 449
Kiev University, 400
Kildare Ascendancy, 115
Kindermann, Eberhard, 530
Kinna, Ruth, 551–52
Kip, William, 206–7
Kipling, Rudyard, 559
Kiwanga, Kapwani, 657–58
Klaar, Ernst, 382
Klassiker der Politik (book series), 454–55
Kleinwächter, Friedrich, 380
Kopff, Peter, 182
Korea, 480
Koselleck, Reinhart, 446, 597
Kothe, Hermann, 403–4, 405, 407
Krafft, Johann, the Elder, 182, 192
Krantz, Albert, 306
Kumar, Krishan, 446

Lacan, Jacques, 569–70, 577–78
Lachner, Wolfgang, 161
Lalebuch, 205–10, 212–13

Lamprecht, Karl, 453
Lando, Ortensio, 8, 231, 233–34, 236–38, 239–42, 244–47, 261
Lansburgen, Samuel, 299–301
La Prensa (newspaper), 428–29
Lascaris, Constantine, 37–39
Lascaris, Janus, 40
las Casas, Bartolomé de, 221–22
Lassalle, Ferdinand, 452
Latimer, William, 21–22
Latin, 4, 6, 13–14, 20–22, 23, 26, 37–38, 39, 40, 42, 43, 54, 55, 61, 78–79, 106–7, 122–23, 125–26, 202–4, 220–21, 225–26, 229–30, 231–32, 236–37, 244–45, 248–49, 250–51, 256–57, 269–71, 310–11, 313–14, 317–18, 319–20, 324–26, 328–29, 331–32, 342–43, 364–65, 382–83, 389, 390–91, 395–96, 403–4, 405, 407, 411, 428–29, 432, 434, 436, 437–39, 442, 449, 471, 483, 493, 494, 530, 538, 546, 575–76, 638, 640–41, 649, 654. *See also* Bible: Latin Vulgate; More, Thomas: More's Latin; *Utopia*, Latin editions
Latour, Alice de, 428–29
Latour, Armand Pin de, 434
Laudatio Florentinae Urbis, 135–36
Lavater, Johann Casper, 385
Laxdal, Eiríkur, 531–32
League of Nations, 458
Lebanese Civil War (1975-1990), 505
Lebenswissenschaft (living), 11, 14–15, 522, 525–26
Le Blond, Jean, 8, 211, 248–50, 254–56, 335, 339
Le Clerc, Jean, 326
Lee, Edward, 170–71
Lefevre, Henri, 539–40
Leighton, Robert, 310
Leipzig Disputation (1519), 170–71
le Mort, Jacobus, 331–32
Lenz, Max, 452, 453
Leopold II (King of Hungary), 416–17
Leo X (Pope), 169–70, 221–22
Leo XIII (Pope), 604
Le Sauvage, Jean, 151
Leslie, Marina, 391
L'Esprit des Cours de l'Europe (periodical), 326
Leunclavius, Johannes, 640–41
Leuven. *See* Louvain

Levitas, Ruth, 11–12, 571–73
Levitskii, V., 407–8
Leyes Pomplementarios de Valladolid (1513), 219–20
Leyes de Burgos (1512), 219–20
Leyni, Andrea Provana di, 243
L'Honoré, François, 338
Liang Qichao, 479–81
Libanius, 66
liberalism, 369–70, 375–76, 481–82, 504, 580–81, 589, 597, 645–46
liberty, 227, 318–19, 321–22, 323, 334–35, 337, 346, 353, 370–71, 456, 479, 540–41, 545, 557, 580–81, 583, 584–85, 586, 587–88, 589, 593–94, 618–19
  of conscience, 589–90, 591–92. *See also* freedom: of conscience
Libeskind, Daniel, 630
Liddy, Christian, 141
Liebknecht, Wilhelm, 386
Liguori, Alfonso de, 493
Lilley, Kate, 516–17
Lily, William, 21–22, 39, 95–96, 162
Linacre, Thomas, 21–22, 39, 154, 156, 157–61, 176–77
Lipari, Lisbeth, 574–75
Lips, Johann Heinrich, 385
Listrius, Gerard, 163–65
Liszt, Ferenc, 412
Literae Humaniores, 180–81. *See also* humanism
Litvak de Pérez de la Dehesa, Lily, 429
Liu, Yi-Chun, 477
Liu Lingsheng, 10–11, 483, 484–86
Lloyd, William, 311
Lobscheid, Wilhelm, 479
Locke, Charley, 565–66
Locke, John, 323, 399, 423–24, 583, 589
Logan, George M., 447, 590
London, 1–2, 3, 4, 8–9, 15, 21–22, 39, 83–84, 90–91, 114, 115, 120–21, 129–30, 136–38, 139–40, 141, 142–44, 145, 146–47, 148, 150–51, 154, 157–58, 182, 206, 231, 233–36, 265–67, 268, 269–73, 275, 276–77, 278–79, 288–89, 298–99, 307, 308–10, 311–12, 319–20, 371–72, 374–75, 453–54, 497–98, 511, 541–43, 586, 604–5, 638–39, 656
  and Amaurot, 136–37, 250–51, 266, 441–42
  Bridge, 70–71
  Common Council, 147
  Royal Hospitals of, 269–70, 271–72
  Tower of, 101, 102
López Estrada, Francisco, 215–16, 217–18
Louis XII (King of France), 125–26, 157–58
Louis XIV (King of France), 8–9, 326, 327–28, 329, 334, 336
Louis XVI (King of France), 189–90, 350, 353
Louvain (Leuven), 2, 6–7, 43, 45, 74, 129–30, 156–57, 161, 162, 168, 180–81, 196–98, 223, 233–34, 235–36, 362, 513
Low Countries, 2, 83–84, 145–46, 149–50, 179–80, 189, 216–17, 218, 229–30, 309–10, 311, 513. *See also* Flanders; Netherlands
Lucan, 635
Lucca, 15, 233–34, 235–36, 242
Luchitskii, Ivan V., 400
Lucian, 13–14, 22–23, 24, 29, 37–39, 49, 57, 93, 94, 102–4, 155, 161, 167, 169–70, 176–78, 183–84, 205, 220–21, 249–50, 269, 513, 515
Luhmann, Niklas, 461
Lumley, John, 181–82
Lunacharskii, Anatolii, 404–5
Lupset, Thomas, 45, 74, 97, 157–61, 176, 198–99, 217, 253–54, 384, 513–14
Lupton, J. H., 186, 362, 403, 470–71
Luther, Martin, 2, 81–82, 83–84, 87–88, 90–91, 170–71, 190–91, 192–93, 233, 255, 306
Lutz, Martin, 11–12
Lyons, 8, 233–34, 236–37, 248–49, 256–57
Lytton, Bulwer, 494

Ma, Tehyun, 10–11
Macaulay, Thomas Babington, 370–71
McCabe, Richard, 99–100
McCullough, Peter, 183–84
McCutcheon, Elizabeth, 62, 67, 177–78, 368, 450–51, 625–26
McDonald, Alexander, 559–60
Machiavelli, Giampiero, 169
Machiavelli, Niccolò, 2–7, 15–16, 397, 423–24, 430–31, 432, 442, 455–56, 457
Machiavellianism, 4–5
Mackenzie, Henry, 525, 527
McNelis, James, 530

McShane, Harry, 541–42
Maczelka, Csaba, 396–97, 411–12
Madách, Imre, 411–12, 419
Madagascar, 330
Madden, Samuel, 533–34
Madrid, 217–18, 299, 301, 428–29, 430
Magdalen College (Oxford), 180–81
Magdalen College School (Oxford), 21
Magid, Annette, 554–55
Mahmud, Zaki Najib, 501–3
Maister, Peter (of Winchelsea), 142–43
Maitland, John, 309–10
Maksheeva, N. A., 13
Malein, A. I., 395–96
Ma Lieying, 490–91
Malinowski, Bronislaw, 606
Mallafrè, Joaquim, 430–31, 436–37, 439–40
Malthus, Thomas, 371–72
Mandeville, John, 107–8, 109
Mangeloja, Esa, 612
Manley, Lawrence, 136
Mannheim, Karl, 461–62
Manrique de Lara, Alonso, 216–18
Manutius, Aldus, 22–23, 36, 40–42, 163, 168. See also Aldine Press
Mao, 476, 483–84, 486, 488, 490
Maoist collectivization, 14
Marie Antoinette (Queen of France), 355
Marin, Louis, 47–48, 524, 615, 616–17
Marischal College (Aberdeen), 309–10
Marius, Richard, 371
Marliano, Luigi, 153–54
Marlowe, Christopher, 489
Marmontel, Jean-François, 494
Marrash, Fransis, 495–96
Marriage Law, 490
Marsilius of Padua, 135–36, 141
Martens, Thierry (aka Dirk), 43, 45, 75, 149–50, 152, 154, 156, 180–81, 196–97, 217, 218, 513
Martin, Henri, 551
Martin, Henri-Jean, 50
Martinus, Thedoricus, 186–87. See also Martens, Thierry
Martorell, Joan, 432–33
Marx, Karl, 380–81, 392, 395, 399, 446, 447–48, 462, 466–67, 476, 496–97, 544–45, 570, 604

Marxism, 395, 503–4
Mary I (Queen of England), 265, 272, 274
Mason, Laura, 356
Massys, Quentin, 161
materialism, 495–96, 568–69
    dialectical, 570
    historical, 382–83
    speculative, 570–71
Matoba, Satomi, 643–44
Maupassant, Guy de, 422–23
Maurice (Landgrave of Hesse), 192
Maximilian (Duke of Milan), 125–26
Maximilian I (Holy Roman Emperor), 125–26
Maximus, Valerius, 256
May Fourth Movement, 481–82
Mazard, Eisel, 477, 483
Medici, Lorenzo II de', 169–70
Medinilla i Porres, Jerónimo Antonio de, 224–26, 229–30, 428–29
Mehring, Franz, 386
Meiji Westernization, 14
Meinecke, Friedrich, 453
Meinhold, Wilhelm, 364–65
Melanchthon, Philip, 192–93
Meldolesi, Luca, 380–81
Meltzl, Hugo, 388–89
Menchi, Silvana Seidel, 170
Mendelsohn, Daniel, 621–22
Menke, Christoph, 522
Mercers' Company, 1–2, 145, 146, 147, 278–79
Merchant Adventurers, 128, 142–43, 145–47
Mercier, Louis-Sébastien, 533
Mercure de France (journal), 343–44
'Mercurius Britannicus', 206
Merton College (Oxford), 180–81
Metge, Bernat, 432–33
Michelangelo, 419
Michels, Victor, 379, 381, 422, 450
Middleton, John, 1–2
Mierde, Hooge, 271
Mierdman, Stephen, 271, 272–73
Mikami, Masatake, 467–68
Miles, Peter, 149–50
Mill, John Stuart, 363, 464–65, 481, 597
Miller, Clarence, 177–78, 601
Miller, Elizabeth Carolyn, 538–39, 542–43
Miller, Johann, 167

Minckwitz, Johannes, 388–89
Mir Bozhii. See *God's World*
Mirandola, Giovanni Pico della, 84–85, 227
Moir, Cat, 10, 570–71
Molnár, Albert Szenczi, 414–15
Molnár, Pál C., 425
Monau, Jacob, 637–38, 641–42, 650–51
Montaigne, Michel de, 60–61, 111–12, 113
Montalbán, Juan Manuel, 428–29
Montaño, John Patrick, 111–12
Montesquieu, 481
Montessori, Maria, 424
Montoliu, Manuel de, 428–29, 435–36
moral economy, 11–12, 596–613
moral education, 26
More, Cresacre, 234–35, 422–23
More, John, 1–2
More, Thomas
   al-Farabi and, 500–1
   'Ad Quendam Poetam Extemporalem', 61–62
   Apologye, 82–84, 100–1
   in Arabic encyclopedia, 496–97
   career, 1–2, 13–14, 91, 278–79, 401
   citizen of London, 1–2, 15, 136, 141, 243–44, 253n.10, 278–79
   conscience of, 171, 303–4, 413–14, 425–26
   Confutacyon of Tyndales Answere, 48–49, 83–84, 90, 94–95, 234
   Debellacyon of Salem and Bizance, 82–84
   'Declamatio Lucianicae respondens', 185–86
   Dialogue of Comfort, 101, 273, 413–14, 425–26
   Dialogue Concerning Heresies, 82–83, 84
   embassy, 2, 45, 83–84, 128, 145–46, 149–50, 197–98, 215
   English Works, 274, 280
   Epigrammata, 53–55, 57, 59, 71, 156–57, 161, 163–65, 185–86, 217
   and Erasmus. *See* Erasmus: More and
   Expositio Passionis Domini/Treatise upon the Passion, 102, 190–91
   Fortune Verses, 94–95
   Four Last Things, 94
   and Greek, 13–14, 20–23, 28–29, 39, 40, 58–59, 186, 538
   Greek, translations from, 1–2, 22, 56, 57, 223–24. *See also* More, Thomas: translations of Lucian
   and heresy, 2, 81–85, 90–92, 94–95
   History of King Richard the Third, 95, 127
   images of (visual), 12–13, 14, 47–48, 207–10, 385, 407
   'In Efflatum Ventris e Graeco', 56, 58–59
   'In Fatuum', 59
   Letter to Bugenhagen, 90–91
   Letter to a Monk, 101
   Life of Pico, 84–85, 95
   as Lord Chancellor, 2, 82–84, 263–64, 416–17, 592
   as martyr, 6, 8, 171, 184, 190–91, 219, 223–26, 234, 235–36, 243–44, 262, 288–89, 315, 334, 383, 425–26, 440–41, 468, 492–93, 496–97, 500–1, 640–41
   Omnia latina opera, 190–91, 204, 223
   Plato and, 31–33
   undersheriff of London, 1–2, 83–84, 136, 145, 266–67, 278–79
   Progymnasmata, 162, 185–86
   Responsio ad Lutherum, 83–84, 90–91, 94–95, 170–71, 190–91
   Supplicacyon of Soulys, 84
   translations of Lucian, 1–2, 22, 49, 57–58, 93, 102–4, 152, 161, 168–70, 183–84, 185–86, 205, 220–21
   Utopia. *See Utopia* (the book); Utopia (fictional place)
Moréri, Louis, 331–32
Morgan, Nicole, 48
Morison, Stanley, 385
Morita, Yushu, 466
Morley, Henry, 363–64, 504
Morris, William, 9, 13–14, 365–69, 401–2, 420, 466–67, 498–99, 501, 504, 531–32, 537–38, 540–41, 571–72, 597–98, 626
   John Ball, 541, 545
   News from Nowhere, 466–67, 468–69, 501, 537–39, 540, 541
Morton, John (Cardinal), 21, 413–14
   character in *Utopia*, 42–43, 46, 67–68, 105–6, 115, 117, 150, 198–99, 225–26, 285–86, 349, 579–80
Most, Johann, 549–50
Moylan, Tom, 532
Mullan, John, 525

Muñoz, José, 570–71
Münster, Sebastian, 196–97
Müntzer, Thomas, 201
Murayama, Yuzo, 468–69
Musa, Salama, 497–500, 505–6
Muslim Brotherhood, 504–5

Naeranus, Isaac, 299, 301, 302
Naeranus, Johannes, 299–301
Nairn, James, 310
Nancy, Jean-Luc, 572–73
Nanking Missionary Association, 477–78
Nanterre University, 616–17
Napoleonic Wars, 405–6
Narodnaya Volya (terrorist organization), 467
Narodnoe Khozyaistvo. *See National Economy*
Nash, Gary, 558–59
Nasser, Gamal Abdel, 503–4
National Economy (*Narodnoe Khozyaistvo*) (journal), 402–3
nationalism, 456
National Liberation Front, 503–4
National Socialism, 10, 444, 456, 457. *See also* Nazism
Nazi ideology, 457
Nazism, 449–50, 458. *See also* National Socialism
Nee, Victor, 606
Nelson, Eric, 177–78, 236–37
Neoplatonism, 227
Nepos, Jacobus, 161
Nero, Barnardo del, 170
Nesbit, Molly, 655
Nethercott, Frances, 9, 12–13
Netherlands, 45, 46, 189, 192, 296, 298, 302, 453–54, 513. *See also* Low Countries
Neville, Henry, 512, 517–21, 526–27, 583
Nevola, Fabrizio, 231–32
Nevolin, K. A., 397
New Deal, 486
New Library Movement, 482
New Life Movement, 485–86
New Spain, 217, 218, 220, 221–22, 224–25
New World, 7–8, 24, 109, 113, 118, 120, 124–25, 128–29, 130, 133–34, 206–7, 223, 250–51, 254–55, 259–60, 445, 509–10, 525, 555, 556, 635, 643

New York Times (newspaper), 455, 459–60
Nicarchus, 56, 57
Nicholas, Lucy, 7
Nicholls, Thomas, 270, 319–20
Nicoll, D. J., 551–52
Nigg, Walter, 425–26
Nikolsky, Viktor, 408
Nisard, Jean Marie Napoléon, 401
Norbrook, David, 43
Northern Song Dynasty, 462
Northmore, Thomas, 582, 585–87, 588
Noviomagus, Gerardus, 390. *See also* Geldenhauer, Gerard
Nussbaum, Martha, 87–88

Oakeshott, Michael, 540
Oates, Titus, 311–12
Oath of Allegiance, 70
Oath of Supremacy, 234–35
Obama, Barack, 565–66
O'Brien, James Bronterre, 604
Obrist, Hans Ulrich, 655
Occupy Wallstreet movement, 612–13
October Revolution (1917), 394–95, 399–400
Oecolampadius, Johannes, 200–1
Ogiwara, Tamikichi, 466–67, 478–79
Okino, Iwasaburo, 469
Okunev, Yakov, 408
Oncken, Hermann, 10, 444, 448, 449–60
Ong, Walter, 574
Opisso, Alfred, 432–33
Opium Wars, 463, 482
Oppenheimer, Franz, 380
optimism, 12–13, 86–87, 229–30, 408–9, 421–22, 443, 511
Ortelius, Abraham, 650–51. *See also* Utopia, maps of: Ortelius
Orwell, George, 421–22
Osborne, Bernal, 363
Osinovskii, I. N., 395–96
Osorio, Jéronimo, 295–96
Ostens, Jacob, 299–301
Ostrom, Elinor, 612
Ottoman Empire, 413–15, 492–94, 497, 505–6, 533–34, 640–41
Ottoman language, 640–41
Ottoman state, 493–94, 495

ouchronos (no time), 60. *See also* euchronia
Oudaen, Joachim, 299–300, 301–2
outopia/Outopia (no place), 4, 60, 250–51, 523, 572–73, 622–23. *See also* eutopia/Eutopia
Ovaska, Tomi, 612
Ovid, 31, 58–59, 112–13, 256–57
Owen, John, 184–85
Owen, Robert, 379, 496–97, 604
Oxford University, 186, 272. *See also* University of Oxford
   Oxford University Press, 180–81

Pace, Richard, 39, 154
Pacquot, Thierry, 343–44
Paets, Adriaan, 299–300
Paget, Harold, 361
Paget, Zoe, 361
Palabiyik, Nil, 640–41
Palencia, Alfonso de, 228–29
Paleologus, Jacobus, 414–15
Palinurus, 105
Pall Mall Gazette (newspaper), 541–42
Paltock, Robert, 529
Paludanus. *See* Desmarez, Jean
Pan-German League, 449–50
Parent, Claude, 630
Paris, 4, 6–7, 8, 23, 43, 73, 156–58, 160–61, 162, 168–69, 176, 179–80, 233–34, 248–50, 253–54, 256–57, 261, 342–43, 344, 349, 547
Paris Commune (1871), 370–71, 496–97
Parsons, Talcott, 461
Paton, Bartolomé Ximénez, 224–26
Paul, Joanne, 6
Paul II (Pope), 328–29
Paul IV (Pope), 246
Peasants' Revolt (1381), 487–88, 541, 545
Pellikan, Konrad, 200–1
Penn, William, 556
pessimism, 15–16, 171, 241–42, 525
Peters, Victor, 610
Peterson, William, 365–66
Petrarca, Francesco (aka Petrarch), 60–62, 244–45, 397
Petronius, 212–13
Petrushevskii, D. M., 399–400

Petty, William, 364–65, 511
Petzler, John, 550–51
Pfeil, Adelberg Meyer zum, 201
Phélypeaux, Jean-Frédéric, 189–90
Philip of Habsburg (later Philip II, King of Spain), 302
Philip of Macedonia, 269
Phillips, Carl, 445
Phillips, Joshua, 276
Phillips, Rowland, 291
Philodemus, 54–55
philosophy, 11–12, 28–29, 30–31, 37–39, 65, 78, 80, 96–97, 106–7, 121, 183, 197, 199, 202, 221, 259–60, 293, 296–97, 311, 345–46, 354, 357, 381, 404, 453, 464–65, 501, 567–78, 581, 582, 583, 586, 607, 619, 624–25, 629
   Aristotelian, 310–11
   Chinese, 484
   Eastern, 371
   moral, 78–79, 464, 464*t*, 512
   natural, 48, 296–97
   political, 3, 8–9, 137, 148, 176–77, 249–50, 259, 376, 416–17, 454, 457, 466, 511–12, 607
   social, 422–24, 573–74
Pickering, John, 146
Pierson, Richard, 445
Pine, George, 517–18
Pine, William, 517–18
Pin i Soler, Josep, 10, 428–43
Pirckheimer, Willibald, 45, 161–62, 176
Pius XI (Pope), 2
Plantin, Christophe, 218–19
Plantin Press, 218–19
Plato, 13–14, 22–23, 27, 31, 33, 37–39, 41, 90, 105, 106–7, 109, 135–36, 176–77, 186, 215, 221, 249–50, 252, 256–57, 259–60, 274, 310, 397, 399, 401–2, 422–23, 500, 501
   Republic, 20–21, 23, 25, 26–29, 31–33, 106–7, 108, 135–36, 170, 215, 364–65, 401–2, 422–23, 447, 484, 501, 622
Platonism, 123
Plattes, Gabriel, 511
Pliny, 158–59, 176–77
Plockhoy, Pieter Corneliszoon, 296
Plutarch, 22–23, 27–28, 37–39, 41, 176–77, 193–94, 364–65

Pocock, J. G. A., 123–24
Pococke, Edward, 494
Poeschel, Johannes, 638–39
Pohl, Nicole, 11, 449
Poland, 411, 533–34, 648
　Minor Reformed Church of, 299–300
Polanyi, Karl, 596–98, 604–5, 607, 610
political economy, 323, 343–44, 350–51, 402–3, 488
Poliziano, Angelo, 185–86, 328–29
Pollmann, Judith, 304–5
Pollux, 169
Polo, Marco, 107–8, 119
Polylerites (people in *Utopia*, Book One), 105–6, 292, 349
Popish Plot (1678-81), 311–12, 315–16
Portinari, Pierfrancesco, 170
possibility, 3–4, 15, 38, 66, 72, 87–88, 151, 290, 321–22, 364–65, 375–77, 383, 386–87, 476, 480–81, 484–85, 509–10, 519–20, 523–24, 529, 530, 531–32, 538–39, 544–46, 568–69, 577–78, 594, 615, 619, 621–22, 643, 652, 653, 656
Pott, F. L. Hawks, 477–78
Powell, George, 313–14
Poynings, Edward, 126–27, 128
Poza, Andrés de, 223
Prescott, Anne Lake, 48
Preston Guardian (newspaper), 363–65
Prévost, Abbé, 532–33
Prévost, André, 167
Price, Munro, 342–43
property, 64, 69, 84, 86, 97, 101–2, 322, 348, 364–65, 373, 394–95, 496, 497, 502–3, 588, 589–90, 592, 593, 619–20, 623–24
　common (collective/public/shared), 74–75, 82, 97, 100–1, 249–50, 301–2, 334, 352–53, 383, 423, 447, 488, 513–14, 598, 599, 601, 608, 612–13
　intellectual, 100–1
　literary, 158
　private (individual/personal), 65, 66, 95–96, 97, 136, 170, 171, 269–70, 275–76, 293, 296–97, 396–97, 402–3, 409, 423, 447–48, 488, 490, 498–99, 582, 596, 597, 599, 601, 604–5, 608–9
Prussian Academy of Sciences, 452, 458
Pucci, Mario V., 425–26

Pugachev Rebellion (1773-5), 396–97
Purchas, Samuel, 509–10
Puskás, Ferenc, 412
Puttenham, George, 62–63
Pyham, John (of Sandwich), 142–43

Qiu Zhijie, 644–45, 644f, 646–47
Quevedo, Francisco de, 224–25
Quinn, David Beers, 133–34
Quintilian, 55–56, 60–61, 63, 95, 158–59
Quiroga, Gaspar de, 224
Quiroga, Vasco de, 217, 218, 220–21, 223, 224–26

Rabelais, François, 205–6, 212–13, 252–53
Ra'if, Ahmad, 504–5
Raisch, Jane, 40
Ralegh, Walter, 122
Ranke, Leopold von, 452
Rastell, John, 129–30
Rastell, William, 234–36, 273, 274, 280
Rathenau, Walter, 448–49
Rational Choice Theory, 611–12
Rational Press Association, 497–98
Reader's Digest (magazine), 339
Reading Books Monthly (magazine), 490
Reagan, Ronald, 565
Rebhorn, Wayne A., 89
Recht, Roland, 621
recycling, 616, 617
Red Terror, 395–96
Red Tsar, 405–6
Rees Jones, Sarah, 135–36, 137–38, 148, 266–67
Reformation (religious), 4, 7, 82–83, 90–91, 92, 127, 179, 180, 184, 190–93, 200–1, 233, 235–36, 265, 274, 280, 302, 303, 306, 307–8, 383, 396, 401, 403–4, 426–27, 449, 604, 609. *See also* Counter-Reformation
Regnard, Jean-François, 349
Reitinger, Franz, 213
Reixac, Baldiri, 432
religion. *See also* freedom: religious freedom
　Anabaptist Christianity, 134, 233, 299n.6, 598, 608–11
　Arminians, 299–300, 299n.6, 301, 302, 303
　Buddhism, 473t, 474, 479–80, 644–45
　Calvinism, 192, 400

Catholic Church, 14, 77, 79, 191–92, 220–21, 222–23, 224–25, 224n.13, 228–29, 295–96, 304–5, 424–26, 492–93, 494, 505–6
Catholicism, 91–92, 170–71, 216–17, 219–20, 229, 268, 272–73, 304, 305, 306, 308, 311–12, 316–17, 325, 335, 337, 400, 414–15, 493, 641–42. *See also* anti-Catholicism
Catholics, 190–91, 192–93, 235–36, 263, 304, 316–17, 424–25, 426–27
Christianity, 74–75, 76–77, 82–84, 86–88, 110, 118, 130, 178–79, 262, 302, 305–6, 311–12, 316, 330, 347, 464, 502–3, 513–14, 592
Christian Church, 81–82
Church of Rome, 123–24, 234, 235–36, 295–96, 304, 316–17, 505–6
evangelicalism, 91–92
evangelicals, 90–92, 94–95, 255
Hinduism, 644–45
Huguenots, 8–9, 192, 299, 324–25, 327, 337, 338
Islam, 503–4
Lutheranism, 94–95, 192
Lutherans, 201, 217–18, 641–42
Lutheran writings, 200–1
Protestantism/Protestant faith, 119, 133–34, 192, 270–71, 325, 424–25, 492–93, 604
Protestant ideas/writings, 213, 271, 272–73, 274, 280, 325, 497
Protestants, 82–84, 192–93, 235–36, 256–57, 263, 268, 270–71, 272–74, 301, 302, 304, 305, 307–8, 311–12, 316–17, 326, 338, 414–15, 416–17, 426–27, 494, 509, 641–42
religious orders
  Augustinians, 233
  Benedictines, 325, 425–26, 430–31
  Carthusians, 1–2, 21–22, 425–26
  Dominicans, 191–92, 219–20, 414–15
  Franciscans, 7–8, 200–1, 216–17, 218, 219–20, 221–22, 225–26, 298–99, 425–26, 601–2
  Jesuits, 70–71, 191–92, 204, 223–24, 226, 299, 304, 330, 338–39, 416–17, 483, 500–1, 533–34
Rembrandt, 298–99
Renialme, Ancanius de, 206
republicanism, 91–92
Republic of Letters, 4, 36–37, 43, 44–47, 49–50, 51, 265–66
  respublica litterarum, term, 44, 176

Revius, Jacobus, 296
Revocation of the Edict of Nantes (1685), 337
Revolt of Silken Thomas (1534), 115
Rhenanus, Beatus, 45, 54–55, 74–75, 76–77, 149–50, 154, 155–56, 161–62, 167, 176, 178, 196–97
rhetoric, 40, 42, 46–47, 60–61, 69, 89–90, 148, 155–56, 160, 176–78, 179, 189–90, 201, 251–52, 254–55, 276, 292, 317–18, 447–48, 458–59, 564, 573–74
rhetorical figures
  litotes, 62–63, 67, 71, 171, 177–78, 239–40, 523, 625–26
  metaphor, 48, 93, 94, 102–4, 177–78, 327, 372, 440, 547, 557–58, 565, 640–41
rhetorical techniques/strategies, 67, 73, 280–81, 287, 523–24
rhetoricians, 63, 221–22
Ribadeneira, Pedro de, 223–24
Ricardo, David, 597
Rice Price Crash (1930-1), 469
Rice University, 559–60
Richardson, Samuel, 582
rights and freedoms, 579–80, 581, 588, 589–90
Ritter, Gerhard, 10, 444, 457
Rivers, Ben, 657, 658–59
Robertson, John, 497–98
Robinson (aka Robynson), Ralph, 5–6, 8, 64, 65, 73, 130–32, 193–94, 201, 265, 281f, 307, 369f, 375, 502
Robinsonades, 519–20, 526–27, 532
Roddenberry, Gene, 560, 561
Roggen, Vibeke, 180–81, 204
romance, 11, 188–89, 252–53, 260–61, 487, 522–23, 524, 531–32, 544–45
romanticism, 369–70, 386, 429, 645–46
Rome, 2, 54–55, 127, 169–70, 185–86, 189, 202–4, 231–32, 233–34, 236, 242, 305, 329, 364–66, 419, 493, 494, 510, 526–27
Roosevelt, Teddy, 559
Roper, Margaret (née More), 70–71, 235–36
Roper, William, 234–36, 273, 422–23
Rose, Gillian, 572–73
Rose, Jonathan, 541–42
Rosenberg, Aubrey, 324–25
Rosetta Stone, 124–25
Rossi, Giacomo, 235–36
Rotterdam, 8–9, 15, 295–303, 305–6, 325–26, 440–41

Rouillard, Dominique, 614–15
Rousseau, Jean-Jacques, 347, 348, 351, 482–83, 525, 527, 581, 582, 603–4
Rousseau, Pierre, 351
Rousseau, Thomas, 8–9, 339–40, 341–57, 396, 399
Royal Library of Sweden, 406–7
Royal Palace Library (Madrid), 217–18
Royal Society, 308–9, 311, 318
Rugemer, Edward, 322
Ruskin, John, 365–66, 370–71, 373, 542–43
Russkoe Slovo. See Russian World
Russell, Bertrand, 482–83, 501
Russell, Lady Rachel, 312–13
Russell, William, Lord, 312–13
Russen, David, 529
Russia, 4–5, 10–11, 14–15, 42–43, 394–409, 559. *See also* Soviet Union
Russian Revolution, 497
Russian Word (*Russkoe Slovo*) (magazine), 397
Ruthall, Thomas, 154
Rye House Plot (1683), 8–9, 312–13

Saage, Richard, 444, 457, 458, 459
Sacks, David Harris, 6, 275–76
Sa'd, Faruq, 505
St. Paul's School (London), 39, 186
Saint-Simon, Henri de, 482, 496–97
Sakai, Toshihiko, 466–67
Sako, Teruhito, 10–11
Sampson, Richard, 126–27, 128
Sánchez de la Ballesta, Alonso, 228–29
Sandel, Michael, 607
Sander, Nicholas, 223–24
Sanlian Shudian, 487–89
Sansovino, Francesco, 8, 231–32, 233, 242–45, 246–47, 248–50, 261, 262, 263–64, 361–62, 437–39
satire, 8–9, 11, 29, 58–59, 135–36, 150, 163–65, 171, 183–84, 204–12, 213, 220–21, 275, 417–18, 421, 424–25, 450, 459, 484, 510, 515, 519–20, 522–25, 526–27, 529, 533–34, 545–46, 570, 642–48
Satz, Debra, 607
Saugrain, Jean, 256–58
Savin, A. N., 399–400
Savonarola, Giralamo, 84–85
Sawada, Akio, 471–72

Sayer, Andrew, 597
Sayers, Nicola, 571
Scaliger, Julius Caesar, 54
Schaer, Roland, 419
Scheckter, John, 517, 518–19
Schiller, Friedrich, 389
Schmidt, Gabriela, 7, 280
Schnebelin, Johann Andreas, 212–13
Schnor, Johan Karlovich, 396
Schofield, Malcolm, 29
Scholar, Richard, 8
Schütz, Antal, 424–25
Schwartz, Peter, 380–81
Schwegel, A. W., 362–63
science fiction, 421, 445, 478–79, 480–81, 487, 493–94, 495–96, 504–5, 511–12, 524, 530, 553–66, 624–25, 658, 662
Scot, Thomas, 134
Scott, James, 606
Scott, Walter, 363–64, 387–88
Scripture, 40, 68, 78, 94–95, 150, 190–91, 200–1, 223–24, 251–52, 310, 328. *See also* Bible
scriptural interpretation, 91
Scriverius, Petrus, 301–2
Sebillet, Thomas, 251–52
Second World War (1939-45), 435–36, 617
Seeber, Hans Ulrich, 522
Seebohm, Frederick, 186
Sellevold, Kirsti, 250, 253–54
Seneca, 37–38, 58–59, 95, 163–65, 176–77
sensus communis, concept of, 95
separatists, 14
Serbopoulos, John, 21
Seville, 110, 216–17, 218–20, 441
Seward, William, 559
Seymour, Thomas, 269–70
Shakespeare, William, 10–11, 111–12, 364–65, 388–89, 424, 464, 465–66
Shaw, Bernard, 497–98
sheep/sheep-farming, 115–16, 144, 240–41, 369–70, 373, 523, 593, 632
Shephard, Robert, 123
Shinto, 474
Showa Financial Crisis (1927-30), 469
Shrank, Cathy, 8, 46–47, 46n.17, 132
Sidney, Philip, 72–73, 424
Siebers, Johan, 11–12
Sino-Japanese War, 482

Sissa, Giulia, 89
Sisters Uncut, 655–56
Sixtus IV (Pope), 328–29
Skinner, Quentin, 90–91, 251, 593–94, 597–98
Slave Act (1684), 322
slavery, 15–16, 56, 228–29, 317–23, 373–74, 495, 496, 527–28, 532, 540, 546, 556, 601. *See also* unfreedom; Utopia: slavery in
Slavery Act (1547), 319–20, 321–22
Smeeks, Hendrik, 296–97, 526–27
Smith, Adam, 10–11, 464, 481, 525, 597, 602–3
Smith, Thomas, 120–21, 130–32, 276–77
Soboul, Albert, 356
socialism, 10, 15–16, 375–76, 380–81, 382–83, 394–95, 399–400, 408–9, 449–50, 452, 456, 474, 481–82, 484, 485, 489, 495–98, 499, 500, 501, 503–6, 537–39, 540–42, 543–44, 546, 548–49, 551, 604–5, 611, 644–45
    and *Utopia*, 380–81, 399–400, 406, 408, 409, 466–67, 468–70, 472, 482, 486, 487–88, 490, 491, 497, 502–3
Socialist League, 537–38
Socialist Party, Egyptian, 497–98
social utilitarianism, 402–3
Société des Jacobins, 356–57
Society for Utopian Studies, 607–8
Socrates, 20–21, 23–24, 25, 26, 28–29, 30–31, 33, 106–7
Solarpunk, 662
Soleinne, Martineau de, 341–42
Solomin, Vasily, 402–3
Sombart, Werner, 459
Sonni, Adol'f, 404, 407
Sophocles, 22–23, 37–38, 40–41
Sorbière, Samuel, 248–49, 253–54, 333, 339
Sorel, Georges, 548–49
Soubirous, Bernadette, 424–25
Soviet Academy of Sciences, 477
Soviet Union, 487, 564
Spaans, Ronny, 189
Spain, 7–8, 110, 215–30, 241–42, 403, 428–29, 434–35, 440–42, 443, 526–27, 559, 625
    colonies and colonialization, 7–8, 114–15, 117–18, 215–16, 219–23
Spakowski, Nicola, 485
Spanish-American War (1898), 559
Spanish Civil War (1936-39), 435–36

Spencer, Herbert, 461, 464–65
Spenser, Edmund, 364–65, 424
Spiegel, Jakob, 167
Spinoza, Baruch/Benedictus de, 296, 299, 301
Spinozism, 296–97
Spinozzi, Paola, 231–32
Sponde, Henri de, 493
Stalinism, 405–6, 504
Stammhaus (ancestral home), 568
Stammler, Rudolf, 380
Stapleton, Thomas, 70, 397, 416–17, 422–23
Starkey, Thomas, 235–36
Star Trek (television series), 11, 555–56, 560–66
Star Wars (film series), 560
Stationers' Company, 273
Stead, W. T., 541–42
Stewart, Janet, 9
Stiblin, Caspar, 204–5
St John, J. A., 364–65
Stoic doctrine, 79–80, 87–88
Stoicism, 75, 78–79, 87–88
Stoics, 27
Stowlow, Jeremy, 380
Strabo, 42
Strasbourg, 153–54, 204–6, 381
Strengholt, Leendert, 296
Stromer, Heinrich, 167
Suárez, Francisco, 581
Suez Canal Zone, 502
Summit, Jennifer, 43
Sun King, 327–28
Sun Ra, 656–57
Sun Yat-Sen, 483–84
Surtz, Edward, 471
Suthren, Carla, 6, 22–23
Swabian League, 136–37
Swedberg, Richard, 606
Swift, Jonathan, 196, 484, 524, 576
Swiss Confederation, 136–37
Synesius, 163–65
Szakolczai, Árpád, 412–13
Szapolyai, János (King of Hungary), 413–14
Szathmári, Sándor, 411–12, 421
Szent-Györgyi, Albert, 412
Szuhányi, Ferenc, 416–17

Tacitism, Spanish, 215–16
Tacitus, 27, 176–77, 215–16, 216n.3

Tadlowe, George, 267, 269–70, 271–72, 278, 279
Tadmor, Naomi, 319–20
Taisho Comprehensivism, 467–69
Tang Dynasty, 462
Tantawi Jawhari, 495–96, 504–5
Taoism, 644–45
Tao Yuanming, 462, 479–80, 491
Tarle, Evgenii, 9, 395–96, 399–400, 406–9
Tarragona, Municipal Corporation of, 435–36
Taut, Bruno, 626
Tawfiq, Ahmad Khalid, 504–5
Tawney, R. H., 596–97, 604–5, 610
Taylor, Andrew, 6–7
Taylor, John, 125–26, 510
Terence, 58–59
Terle, Evgeny, 9
Testa, Simone, 238–39
Themsecke, Georges de, 344, 625
Theocritus, 40
Theognis, 40
Theophrastus, 36, 37–39, 47–48
Thérèse of Lisieux, 424–25
Thirty Years' War (1618-48), 182, 526–27
Thom, Robert, 659–60
Thompson, E. P., 596–97, 604–6, 610
Thompson, Laurence, 543–44
Thompson, Noel, 540–41
Thrasymachus, 30
Thucydides, 37–39, 270, 319–20
Thule, 42–43
Tiberius (Emperor of Rome), 315
Tilley, Arthur, 39–40
Tiravanija, Rirkrit, 655
Tory, Geoffroy, 205
totalitarianism, 580–81
Tottel, Richard, 272–73, 275
Tower Sargent, Lyman, 582–83, 587–88, 594
Transylvania, 414–15
Trapp, J. B., 41
travel writing, 6–7, 75, 89–90, 105–19, 515, 522–23
Treaty of Capitulation (1513), 126–27
Treaty of Versailles (1919), 448
Treitschke, Heinrich von, 452
Trencsényi, Balázs, 412–13, 415
Trentmann, Frank, 607
Trevor-Roper, Hugh, 192

Trollope, Anthony, 363–64
Trousson, Raymond, 534–35, 591–92
Tryon, Thomas, 322
Tsui, Brian, 485–86
Tudor, Edmund, 125–26
Tudor, Henry, 125. *See also* Henry VII
Tugan-Baranovskii, Mikhail, 399–400
Tuke, Brian, 125–26
Tunstall, Cuthbert, 2, 67, 90–91, 105, 128, 149–50, 151, 152, 154, 157–58
Turley, Steven, 221–22
Turner, Paul, 27n.7, 445–46
Tusser, Thomas, 111–12
Twain, Mark, 559
Twersky, Amon, 611–12
Tyndale, William, 90–91, 119, 319–20
tyranny, 53–54, 97–98, 128–29, 169–70, 290–91, 315, 317, 321–22, 546, 581, 583–85, 589, 590, 593–94
  resistance to, 593–94
Tyrone's Rebellion, aka Nine Years' War (1593-1603), 132–33

Überlebenswissen (human survival), 522, 534–35
Undset, Sigrid, 424–25
unfreedom, 315–20, 321, 323. *See also* slavery
United Provinces, 325–26, 327–28, 337. *See also* Dutch Republic
United States of America, 123–24, 556–60
Universal Declaration of Human Rights, 581
Universidad Hispalense, 223
University College London, 363–64
University of Glasgow, 188–89. *See also* Glasgow University
University of Heidelberg, 449
University of Leiden, 333
University of Louvain, 45, 74
University of Oxford, 40, 371. *See also* Oxford University
University of Paris, 233
University of Seville, 223
University of Tokyo, 470–71
University of Tsukuba, 471
urbanism, 15
Ure, Andrew, 604
US Constitution, 557

US Geological Survey, 643–44
Utopia (the book). *See also* Utopia (fictional place)
   alphabet, 34f, 74–75, 128, 152, 160–61, 169, 187n.17, 201, 203f, 204, 205, 207–10, 226, 237, 275, 384, 385, 437, 451
   hexastichon, 34f, 152, 160–61, 203f, 226, 252
   marginal glosses, 8–9, 31–32, 45–46, 71, 78, 79–80, 85, 97, 152, 155, 160–61, 162, 168–69, 178, 190–91, 196, 197–98, 211, 217, 224, 237, 255, 260–61, 262, 263, 264, 275, 280–81, 282, 288–94, 354, 355, 365–68, 384, 385–86, 513
   monkey in, 47–49, 51–52
   Nusquama (alternative name for) 151, 152, 538
   paratext (aka parerga), 2, 4, 5–7, 13, 43, 45–46, 47, 59, 71, 128, 152, 160–61, 162–65, 169, 170–71, 180–81, 183, 185, 186–87, 190–91, 196, 198–99, 200, 202–4, 233, 237, 240–41, 243–44, 249–50, 252, 254, 255, 256–58, 262, 275, 280–81, 288–89, 293–94, 333–35, 354, 362, 384, 389–90, 391–93, 415–16, 422, 437, 445–46, 450–51, 472, 477, 483, 513–14, 515, 516–17, 518–19, 520, 619–20, 621, 627, 636–37, 643. *See also Utopia*: alphabet; hexastichon; marginal glosses; prefatory letters, title page, woodcuts
   prefatory letters, 41–42, 45–46, 48–49, 59, 73, 77, 97, 152, 155, 156–57, 163–65, 176–77, 178–79, 185–86, 198–99, 200–1, 215, 232–33, 243–44, 268, 269, 291, 472, 513, 514–15, 518, 626–27, 634–35
   reception of, 2–3, 8, 9, 195–96, 204–12, 215–17, 219–20, 248–50, 253–54, 264, 268, 288, 338–40, 342–44, 376–77, 378–79, 383, 399–400, 411–17, 425–27, 437, 441–42, 444, 448, 456–60, 492, 494–95
   title page, 24, 33, 51, 160–61, 162, 163–65, 164f, 167, 168–69, 183–84, 186–87, 191–92, 207–10, 208f, 238–39, 242, 243–44, 250, 252–53, 254, 257–58, 262, 267, 268, 272, 275, 278–79, 288, 289, 295–96, 313–14, 323, 333, 374–75, 384, 437
   woodcuts, 59, 162–65, 202, 226, 240–41, 254, 385, 627–28, 628f, *See also* Utopia, maps of: 1516; 1518

Utopia, Arabic translations
   al-Bustani (1928), 500–1
   Mahmud (1939), 501–4
   Musa (1926), 497–99, 500, 501
   Sam'an (1965), 503–4
Utopia, Catalan translations
   Pin (1912), 10, 428–29, 430, 431, 432–34, 436–43
Utopia, Chinese translations
   Dai (1956), 11, 13, 476–77, 486–91
   Liu (1935), 476–77, 481–86, 489–90
Utopia, Dutch translations
   Anon. (Amsterdam, 1553), 217, 295–96
   van Hoogstraten (1677), 8–9, 295–306
Utopia, English translations
   Burnet (1684), 5–6, 8–9, 307–23, 361, 363–65, 373–74, 375, 376, 405
   Burnet (Glasgow, 1743), 188–89, 557
   Cayley (1808), 361
   Lupton (1895), 193–94, 403
   Paget (1909), 361
   Robinson, 73, 193–94, 217, 278, 307, 308–9, 313–14, 317, 319–22, 323, 372, 373–74, 375, 376–77, 466, 467, 470–71, 600n.4
   Robinson (1551), 5–6, 8, 64, 65, 130–31, 265–72, 275–77, 278–80, 281–89, 316, 319t, 362, 376, 464–65
   Robinson (1556), 5–6, 8, 9, 265–66, 272–77, 280–81, 281f, 282, 288–94, 319t, 361, 363–64, 365–69, 376
   Robinson (Everyman edn, 1910), 483
   Robinson (Kelmscott edn, 1893), 369f, 376–77
Utopia, French translations
   Chappuys (1585), 248–50, 252, 261–64, 335
   F.N.D. (1611), 248–50
   Gueudeville (1715), 8–9, 324–25, 331–40, 342–44
   Gueudeville (1730), 338–39, 437–39
   Le Blond (1550), 8, 217, 248–50, 252, 253–56, 262, 335, 339, 438–39n.21
   Le Blond, rev. Aneau (1559), 211, 248–50, 253–54, 256–61
   Rousseau (1780), 8–9, 339–40, 341–52, 396
   Rousseau (1789), 8–9, 341, 343–44, 352–57, 396
   Sorbière (1643), 248–50, 253–54, 333, 338–39, 437–39, 438–39n.21, 441–42

Utopia, German translations
  Cantiuncula/Chansonette (1524), 7, 196–204, 203f, 205, 207–12, 217, 231, 361–62, 445, 449
  Fuchs-Wessely (1896), 9, 378–79, 381–93, 403–4, 450–52
  Kothe (1846), 389–90, 391–92, 403–4, 405, 407
  Noah (1920), 450n.5
  Oncken-Ritter (1922), 10, 444, 448–60
  Wintermonat (1612), 207–12, 207f, 208f, 637
Utopia, Hungarian translations
  Bodor (1952), 423–24
  Geréb (1941), 422, 423
  Kardos (1943), 422, 423
  Kelen (1910), 10, 422–23
Utopia, Italian translations
  Lando (1548), 8, 217, 231, 232–42, 243–47, 437–39
  Lando, rev. Sansovino (1561), 8, 231–32, 242–47, 248–50, 361–62, 437–39
  Lando, rev. Sansovino (1583), 8, 261, 262, 263–64
Utopia, Japanese translations
  Hirai (1948), 470–72
  Honda (1934), 470, 471
  Inoue (1882, 1883), 10–11, 464–302, 466–67, 478–79
  Mikami (1914), 467, 468, 469, 478–79
  Morita (1929), 466, 468–70, 471–72
  Murayama (1929), 468–70, 471–72
  Ogiwara (1894), 466–67, 478–79
  Sawada (1969, 1993), 471–72
Utopia, Latin editions, 149, 150–71, 175–94, 195–96
  1516 (Louvain), 2, 43, 45, 149, 150–55, 153f, 163–65, 186–87, 195–96, 217, 437–39, 450–51, 510
  1517 (Paris), 20, 43, 45, 73, 149, 157–61, 195–96, 217, 253–54, 384, 513–14
  1518, both editions (Basel), 7, 14–15, 43, 45, 57, 76–77, 102–4, 149, 156–57, 161–65, 169–70, 176, 195–97, 217, 218, 220, 226, 278–79, 395–96, 422, 437–39, 439n.22, 450–51, 513–14, 518, 627–28, 638–39
  1518, March (Basel), 53–54, 149, 156–57, 161–63, 165, 167, 168–69, 436–37, 513
  1518, Nov/Dec (Basel), 34f, 103f, 149, 162–63, 164f, 166f, 167, 186–87, 378–79, 384–85, 436–37
  1519 (Florence), 149, 168–71, 176, 183–84, 195–96, 205, 217, 231, 384n.3, 513
  1548 (Louvain), 170–71, 180–81, 182, 188n.19, 204, 224–25
  1555 (Cologne), 180–81, 182, 204, 307, 557
  1563 (Basel), 180–82, 185–86, 190–91, 204, 224
  1565-6 (Louvain), 180–81, 190–92, 204, 223
  1591 (Wittenberg), 182, 186–87, 192
  1601 (Frankfurt), 182, 192, 204, 206, 414–15
  1610 (Frankfurt), 182
  1613 (Hanover), 182
  1619 (Frankfurt), 192–93
  1619 (Hanover), 183
  1620 (Milan), 182, 189–90
  1629 (Amsterdam), 186, 189, 191–92
  1629 (Cologne?), 183–84, 186, 191–92
  1631 (Amsterdam), 183–84, 186, 189
  1663 (Oxford), 180–81, 183–85
  1670 (Frankfurt), 182, 183
  1689 (Frankfurt), 182
  1750 (Glasgow), 180–81, 182, 187–89
  1752 (Hamburg), 186
  1777 (Paris-London), 183–85, 187, 188, 189–90
  1895 (Berlin, ed. Michels, Ziegler), 186–87, 379, 381, 383, 384, 385–86, 390, 392–93, 422, 450–51
  1895 (Oxford, ed. Lupton; English-Latin), 186, 193–94
  1910 (London; English-Latin), 186–87, 193–94
  1936 (Paris, ed. Delcourt), 176, 187, 193–94
Utopia, Russian translations
  Anon. (1789), 395–97
  Genkel' (1903), 12–15, 395–96, 409–10
  Malein (1935), 395–96, 407
  Tarle (1901), 395–96, 406–9
Utopia, Spanish translations, 216–19, 229–30
  Gondomar MS (1519-35), 217–18, 226–29, 437–39
  Medinilla (1637), 224–29, 428–29, 437–39
  Quiroga (before 1535), 217, 218
Utopia (fictional place)
  Abraxa (former name), 81, 227, 553, 635–36
  Achorians (neighbours of Utopians), 158, 292, 309, 635–36, 640
  Ademus (title of ruler), 158, 581, 589–90, 593
  Amaurot (capital), 65, 135–36, 138–39, 141, 152, 158, 245, 254–55, 258, 371–72, 437,

600, 614n.2, 635–37, 638, 646, 649, 651. *See also* London: and Amaurot
Anemolius (Utopian poet), 19, 72–73, 152, 252, 328, 384, 580
Anyder/Anydros (river), 152, 155–56, 158, 165, 636–37, 653
beliefs and customs, 23–24, 25–26, 64, 68–69, 76–80, 81–82, 84–87, 99, 110–11, 118–19, 138–39, 144–45, 210–11, 290, 309–10, 316, 336, 350–51, 373–74, 446–48, 470–71, 515–16, 549–50, 579, 581, 591–92, 598, 599–601, 631–32
as colony, 128, 553–54
colonies of, 113–14, 115, 116, 117–18, 128–29, 138–39, 223, 227–28, 553–54, 600–1, 635–36
description of, 6–7, 75, 138–39, 155, 238–39, 413–14, 498–99, 537, 580, 608, 614–15, 631–32, 634–37, 639–40, 646–47, 651
economy of, 14–15, 86, 138–41, 170, 197, 364–65, 398, 408, 598–601
education in, 24, 25–26, 36, 39, 111–12, 117, 205–6, 238, 240, 348–49, 357, 390, 415, 446–47, 599–600
Macaria/Macarians (neighbours of Utopians), 31–32, 46, 204–5, 221, 258, 635–36
slavery in, 15–16, 23, 81, 84, 99, 139–40, 197–98, 228–29, 309, 317–23, 352–53, 392–93, 437, 470–71, 556, 600–1, 613
suicide (or euthanasia) in, 86, 87–88, 119, 239–40
Udepotia (alternative name for), 87, 158, 160, 171, 198–99, 254–55, 258, 513–14
Utopus (founder), 70, 75, 81–82, 128–30, 226–27, 303–4, 316, 337, 370–71, 413–14, 437–39, 553–54, 562–63, 565, 579–80, 588, 589, 591–92, 635–36, 640, 651, 652, 654
Utopia, maps of, 12, 51–52, 74–75, 204, 237, 240–41, 250, 634–37
Anon. (1516), 153*f*, 366–68, 636–37
Anon. (1612), 207–10, 207*f*, 653–54
Holbein (1518), 102–4, 103*f*, 187n.17, 204, 226, 385, 437, 513, 637
Matoba (1998), 643–44
Ortelius (1595), 15, 213, 637–43, 639*f*, 645–46, 648–49
Qiu Zhijie (2012), 644–45, 644*f*
Walter (2013), 12, 644–47, 646*f*, 647*f*
utopian fiction/literary utopias, 155, 183, 195–96, 204–5, 212–14, 241–42, 247n.18, 263–64, 379–81, 399, 419–20, 421, 426–27, 445–48, 471–72, 478–81, 486, 509–21, 522–35, 581
utopianism, 4–6, 7, 10–11, 12, 13–15, 16, 364–65, 379, 392, 411–12, 413–14, 417–18, 474–75, 484–85, 501, 504, 532, 554–55, 566, 582–83, 588, 607–8, 615, 621, 622–23, 630–31, 635, 644–45, 652–62

Vairasse, Denis, 525
Vajda, György, 416–17
Valdés, Alfonso de, 216–17
Valencia, Martín de, 221–22
Valla, Lorenzo, 177–78
Vallance, Aymer, 368
Vallich, E. I., 396–97
van Bleyswyck, Frans, 332
van Bracht, Tieleman, 298–99
van Bunge, Wiep, 8–9
van den Enden, Franciscus, 296
van den Vondel, Joost, 301–2
van der Aa, Pieter, 331–33, 338
van Hoogstraten, David, 301–2
van Hoogstraten, Dirk, 298
van Hoogstraten, Frans, 8–9, 295–96, 297–300, 302, 303–6
van Hoogstraten, Jan, 301–2
van Hoogstraten, Samuel, 298–99
van Koppenol, Wilhelm Linning, 295–96
van Nijevelt, Jacob van Zuijlen, 303–4
van Ruler, Hans, 89
Van Sloetten, Henry Cornelius, 517–19, 520–21
Vaughan, William, 120–23, 134
Veale, Abraham, 267, 270–71, 272–74, 280, 281*f*
Venice, 8, 36, 40, 44, 49, 163, 168, 231–32, 233, 236–37, 241, 242–43, 248–49, 655
Venuti, Lawrence, 374–75, 387
Vergennes, Charles Gravier, comte de, 342–43
Vergil, Polydore, 125
Verhaart, Floris, 8–9
Verne, Jules, 420, 465–66, 494
Vesey, Will, 180–81, 183–84
Vespucci, Amerigo, 23, 42–43, 74–75, 78–80, 106, 109, 110–11, 113, 119, 211, 215

Vidal Alcover, Jaume, 429
Vietnam, 480
Villarroel, Diego de Torres, 529
Vinogradov, P. G., 399–400
Virgil, 42–43, 108
Virilio, Paul, 630
Visscher, Maria Tesselschade Roemers, 304–5
Visscher, Roemer, 296
Vives, Juan Luis (or Joan Lluís), 38–39, 216–17, 270–71, 430–31
Vodovozov, Vasily, 403–5
Voeglin, Eric, 444
Volgin, V. P., 395–96
Vollmar, Georg von, 381–82
Voltaire, 343, 364–65, 529, 532–33, 579–80, 593
von Grimmelshausen, Hans Jakob Christoffel, 526–27
von Hochwart, Ludwig August Frankl, 387–88
von Humboldt, Alexander, 388–89
von Humboldt, Wilhelm, 362–63
von Hutten. *See* Hutten
von Kirchenheim, Arthur, 380
von La Roche, Sophie, 525
von Mechel, Christian, 385
von Schlegell, Mark, 658
von Weyhe, Eberard, 206
von Weyhe, Eberhard, 192

Wacker, Johannes, 637–38, 641–42, 650–51
Waithe, Marcus, 9
Walker, Frederick, 186
Walker, Greg, 539–40
Wallerstein, Immanuel, 380–81
Walsingham, Francis, 120–21
Walter, Stephen, 12, 644–47
Walter, William Joseph, 424–25
Wands, John Millar, 206–7
Wang, David D. W., 480–81
Wang Anshi, 462
Wang Yunwu, 482–83
Warburg, Aby, 621
Warham, William, 42, 154
Wark, McKensie, 660–61
War of the Spanish Succession (1701-15), 327–28
War of Urbino (1516-17), 169–70

waste
  discussion of, 116
  notion of, 111–12
Watanabe, Chifuyu, 467, 468
Waterlander Mennonites, 300–1
Waters, Chris, 541
Watts, Laura, 661
Weaver-Hightower, Rebecca, 11
Weber, Max, 453, 461–62, 604, 606
Weiditz, Hans, 167
Weigel, Rudolf, 387
Weil Baker, David, 274, 276
Weimar Classicism, 386
Weimar Republic, 448–50
Weitling, Wilhelm, 382–83
Wells, H. G., 371–73, 375, 445–46, 497, 498–99, 500, 501, 502, 503, 504–5, 571–72
Wessely, Ignaz, 9, 378–79, 384, 387–91, 392–93, 450
Wessely, Joseph Eduard, 387–88
Whitchurch, Edward, 271
White, T. I., 98–99
Whitehead, Alfred North, 576
Wilde, Lawrence, 447
Wilde, Oscar, 10, 373–74, 422–23
Wilkins, John, 310–11, 318–20, 321, 529
William of Orange, 308
Williams, Rhys, 12
Wilson, Thomas, 72–73
Windelband, Wilhelm, 453
Winstanley, Gerrard, 583
Winston, Jessica, 273
Wintermonat, Gregor, 200n.6, 207–12, 637
Winthrop, John, 557–58
Withington, Phil, 8–9, 141
Wittenberg Press, 182
Wittgenstein, Ludwig, 574, 576
Wolsey, Thomas, 2, 83–84, 154, 334
Woman Question, 379, 392–93
Wood, Andy, 276
Wood, Anthony à, 70, 71, 519–20
Woolcock, Penny, 655–56
Woolf, Leonard, 419
Wright, L., 364–65
Wriothesley, Charles, 235–36
Wu Luping, 482

Xenophon, 364–65

INDEX   785

Yale University Press, 471
Yamakawa, Hitoshi, 466
Yan Fu, 481
Yi-Chun Liu, 491
Yomiuri Shimbun (newspaper), 474
Yoneda, Minoru, 468
Yoran, Hanan, 36–37, 48
York Merchant Adventurers, 144–45

Zak, Paul, 607
Zeller, Eduard, 403–4

Zhukov, Innokenty, 408
Ziegler, Theobald, 379, 381, 422, 450
Zijlmans, Jori, 301–2
Zinnemann, Fred, 425
Zola, Émile, 429
Zrínyi, Miklós, 415–16
Zucchini, Giampaolo, 591
Zumárraga, Juan de, 218, 220–23
Zurcher, Andrew, 6
Zusammenlebenswissen (living together), 522, 534–35